BARRON'S

Accounting Handbook

Sixth Edition

Jae K. Shim, Ph.D.
Former Professor of Accounting
College of Business Administration
California State University, Long Beach

Joel G. Siegel, Ph.D., CPA
Former Professor of Accounting
Queens College of the City University of New York

Nick Dauber, MS, CPA
Lecturer in Accounting
Queens College of the City University of New York

Anique A. Qureshi, Ph.D., CPA
Professor of Accounting and Information Systems
Queens College of the City University of New York

CHUNG SHIM
Dedicated Wife

TO ROBERTA AND JACQUES SIEGEL
Loving Family

KAREN, KATHERINE, AND MICHAEL DAUBER
Loving Wife and Children

SHAHEEN, AQSA, AND YASEEN
Loving Wife and Children

All inquiries should be addressed to:
Barron's Educational Series, Inc.
250 Wireless Boulevard
Hauppauge, New York 11788
www.barronseduc.com

Library of Congress Catalog Card No.: 2014009657

ISBN: 978-0-7641-6657-0

Library of Congress Cataloging-in-Publication Data

Siegel, Joel G., author.
  Accounting handbook — Sixth edition / Jae K. Shim, Ph.D. (Former Professor of
Accounting, College of Business Administration, California State University, Long
Beach), Joel G. Siegel, Ph.D., CPA (Professor of Accounting, Queens College of
the City University of New York), Nick Dauber, MS, CPA (Lecturer in Accounting,
Queens College of the City University of New York), Anique A. Qureshi, Ph.D.,
CPA (Professor of Accounting and Information Systems, Queens College of the City
University of New York).
    pages cm
  Revised edition of: Accounting handbook / Joel G. Siegel, Jae K. Shim. 6th ed.
  Includes bibliographical references and index.
  ISBN: 978-0-7641-6657-0
  1. Accounting—Handbooks, manuals, etc. I. Shim, Jae K., author. II. Dauber,
Nicky A., author. III. Qureshi, Anique A., author. IV. Title.
  HF5636.S56 2015
  657—dc23   2014009657

PRINTED IN CHINA

9 8 7 6 5 4 3 2

Contents

Preface

This desk reference will prove invaluable to anyone involved in accounting. It can be used as a ready source of information about any area of accounting, and will be of value not only to practicing accountants but also to part-time bookkeepers, managers who deal with accountants, and others who need to understand the principles and practices of modern accounting. Whatever an accountant, creditor, investor, or business manager needs to know about accounting is covered in this book. The text is relevant to large, medium-size, and small organizations. This book will also prove useful to accounting students on both undergraduate and graduate levels, because it presents a sound overview of the most important areas in the field.

Whatever your particular interest and background, this handbook provides accounting rules, guidelines, measures, ratios, formulas, techniques, procedures, examples, illustrations, practical applications, charts, and graphs you need to know. Whether you are a bookkeeper, staff accountant, financial accountant, managerial accountant, financial analyst, personal financial planner, tax practitioner, auditor, computer analyst, or governmental accountant, you will obtain immediate and effective answers to specific problems. This reference guide shows you what to do and how to do it when dealing with an accounting situation. Keeping a copy of this desk book handy will provide explanations and demonstrations that will enable you to handle virtually any financial situation.

Accounting is a dynamic area that is constantly changing. This fourth edition covers the latest developments in financial accounting, managerial and cost accounting, auditing, financial statement analysis, international accounting, and quantitative applications to accounting, among others. For example, recent pronouncements of the Financial Accounting Standards Board and American Institute of CPAs are incorporated throughout. The new tax laws are also incorporated and the Sarbanes-Oxley Act is summarized. In addition, FASB's Accounting Codification (ASC) is referenced throughout the book. Reporting implications of International Financial Reporting Standards (IFRS) are discussed at great length.

Barron's Accounting Handbook is practical and comprehensive; it is written in a clear, straightforward manner. Using the index, you will easily find all the information needed on a specific area of interest.

We are grateful to our graduate assistant, Allison Shim, for her enormous research assistance.

Jae K. Shim
Joel Siegel
Nick Dauber
Anique A. Qureshi

Chapter 1
Financial Accounting:
The Financial Statements

*This chapter deals with financial statements: the income state-
ment, balance sheet, and statement of cash flows. The format of
the income statement and its major elements are presented, along
with methods of revenue recognition. The computation of earnings
per share is illustrated. In analyzing the balance sheet, the major
assets, liabilities, and stockholders' equity accounts are presented.
The statement of cash flows distinguishes between operating,
investing, and financing activities.*

INCOME STATEMENT REPORTING

The accountant is concerned with the format of the income statement and with extraordinary items, nonrecurring items, discontinued operations, revenue-recognition methods, accounting for
research and development, and presentation of earnings per share.

Format of the Income Statement

The entries in an income statement are usually classified into four
major functions—revenue, cost of goods sold, operating expenses,
and other revenue or expenses.

Revenue comprises the gross income generated by selling goods
(sales) or by performing services (professional fees, commission
income). To determine net sales, gross sales are reduced by sales
returns and allowances as well as sales discounts.

Cost of goods sold is the cost of the merchandise or services sold.
In a retail store, it is the cost of buying goods from the manufacturer.

Operating expenses consist of all expenses incurred or resources
used in generating revenue. Two types of operating expenses
exist—selling expenses and general and administrative expenses.

1

Selling expenses are those incurred in obtaining the sale of goods or services (e.g., advertising, salespeople's salaries) and in distributing the merchandise to the customer (e.g., freight paid on a shipment). They relate solely to the selling function. *General and administrative expenses* apply to the cost of running the business as a whole and do not relate to the selling function. Examples here are the wages of the general office clerical staff, salaries and other expenses of administrative executives, and depreciation on office equipment.

Other revenue (or expense) applies to incidental sources of revenue and expense that are of a *nonoperating* nature. These revenue (or expense) sources do not relate to the major purpose of the business. Examples are dividend income and interest expense. Such revenue and expenses are *netted* to arrive at the total for this category.

The format for a classified income statement follows:

Revenue		
Gross Sales		$10,000
Less: Sales Returns and		
Allowances	$ 1,000	
Sales Discounts	500	1,500
Net Sales		$ 8,500
Cost of Goods Sold		
Inventory—1/1	$ 2,000	
Add: Purchases	11,000	
Cost of Goods Available	$13,000	
Less: Inventory—12/31	8,000	
Cost of Goods Sold		5,000
Gross Margin		$ 3,500
Operating Expenses		
Selling Expenses	$ 1,000	
General and		
Administrative Expenses	500	
Total Operating Expenses		$ 1,500
Operating Income		$ 2,000
Other Expenses (net)		
Interest Expense	$ 200	
Less: Dividend Income	100	
Other Expenses (net)		100
Income from continuing		
operations before tax		$ 1,900
Less: Taxes (34%)		646
Income from continuing		
operations after tax		$ 1,254

After income from continuing operations, Accounting Principles Board (APB) Opinion No. 30 requires the presentation of additional income-statement categories to show unusual activities affecting the company's profitability. These items are separately shown because they do not apply to the typical activities of the business. A brief word about these income statement categories is in order before showing their exact placement in the income statement.

Discontinued operations are identifiable segments of the business that have been or will be disposed of. They are shown separately because the income or loss from them will not occur on an ongoing basis.

Extraordinary items are unusual and infrequent revenues or expenses.

Each of these items will be discussed in greater detail later in this chapter.

Starting with income from continuing operations after tax, the income statement format follows:

Income from continuing operations after tax
Discontinued operations:
    Income from discontinued operations (net of tax)
    Loss or gain on disposal of a division (net of tax)
Income before extraordinary items
Extraordinary items (net of tax)
Net income

Extraordinary Items

Extraordinary items are both unusual in nature and infrequent in occurrence, given the environment of the business. Unusual means the event is abnormal and of a character materially different from typical business activity. Infrequent means the event is not reasonably expected to recur in the foreseeable future. Extraordinary items include casualty loss, loss or gain on the early extinguishment of debt, loss on expropriation of property by a foreign government, gain on life insurance proceeds, and loss from prohibition under a newly enacted law. It should be noted that losses on receivables and inventory occur in the normal course of business and thus are not extraordinary. However, losses on receivables and inventory would be extraordinary when they apply to a casualty loss (e.g., earthquake) or governmental expropriation (e.g., taking a hazardous product off the market).

Nonrecurring Items

Nonrecurring items are *either* unusual or infrequent. They are presented as a separate line item before tax in computing income from continuing operations. An example of a nonrecurring item is the gain or loss on the disposal of a fixed asset.

Discontinued Operations

A discontinued operation is one that has been discontinued during the year or will be discontinued shortly after the year's end. The three possible elements of discontinued operations are:

- Income or loss from discontinued operations.
- Loss or gain on disposal of a division.
- Impairment loss of the component and subsequent increases in fair value.

In an annual report, the income of a component classified as held-for-sale are presented in discontinued operations in the year(s) in which they *occur*. Phase-out losses are *not* accrued.

The income of a component of a business that either has been disposed of or is held-for-sale are reported in discontinued operations only when *both* of the following criteria have been satisfied:

- The profit and cash flows of the component have been (or will be) eliminated from the ongoing operations of the company due to the disposal decision.
- The company will not have any major ongoing involvement in the activities of the component subsequent to the disposal decision.

In general, gain or loss from operations of the discontinued component should include operating gain or loss incurred and the gain or loss on disposal of a component taking place in the current period. Gains should not be recognized until the year actually realized.

EXAMPLE 1.1

ABC Company produces and sells consumer products. It has a number of product groups, each with different product lines and brands. For this company, a product group is the lowest level at which the operations and cash flows can be distinguished, operationally and for financial reporting purposes, from the rest of the company. ABC has suffered losses related to specific brands in its beauty product group. It has opted to get out of this group.

ABC commits to a plan to sell the product group, and as such classified it as held-for-sale at that date. The operations and cash flows of the group will be eliminated from the ongoing operations of ABC because of the sale transaction, and the company will not have any continuing involvement in the activities of the component, Therefore, ABC should report in discontinued operations the activities of the product group while it is classified as held-for-sale.

Assume ABC decided to continue in the beauty care business but discontinued the brands with which the losses are associated. Because the brands are part of a larger cash-flow-generating product group, and in the aggregate do not constitute a group that on its own is a component of ABC, the conditions for reporting in discontinued operations the losses associated with the brands that are discontinued would not be satisfied.

Comprehensive Income

Financial Accounting Standards Board (FASB) Statement No. 130 (Reporting Comprehensive Income) (ASC 220-10-45) mandates that businesses present comprehensive income and its elements. According to the pronouncement, net income is considered a major component of comprehensive income. If comparative financial statements are prepared, a restatement is needed. The two components of comprehensive income are:

Net Income
Add or Less: Other Comprehensive Income
Comprehensive Income

Other comprehensive income includes the following:
• Unrealized loss or gain on available-for-sale securities.
• Foreign currency translation gain or loss.
• Changes in market value of a futures contract that is a hedge on an asset presented at fair value.

There are three options in presenting "other comprehensive income" as follows:

1. After net income in the income statement.
2. A separate statement of comprehensive income beginning with net income.

Revenue Recognition

The important points of revenue recognition are point of sale, completion of production, during production, and when cash is collected.

Realization. Revenue is generally recognized at the time goods are sold or services performed. Revenue is recognized when it is realized. Revenue is recognized when earned (accrued), rather than when cash is received. Revenue is recognized at the point of sale when the selling price is determinable and future costs can be estimated.

Three other methods of revenue recognition are used in exceptional situations, as follows:

At the Completion of Production. Revenue can be recognized upon the completion of production where there is a stable selling price, absence of significant marketing costs, and interchangeable units. Examples of this are agricultural products and precious metals.

During Production. A construction company can use the percentage-of-completion method in accounting for construction projects. Thus, revenue is recognized gradually as work is performed. There must be an assured price for the project and a reliable measure of the degree of completion at various stages of the production process. This method is preferred over the completed contract method, under which revenue on the contract is recognized only when the project is completed. The percentage-of-completion method should be used when reliable estimates of the extent of completion during each period are possible. The formula to determine the revenue to be recognized for the year follows:

$$\frac{\text{Actual costs to date}}{\text{Total estimated costs}} \times \text{Contract price} = \text{Cumulative revenue}$$

Revenue recognized in previous years is subtracted from the cumulative revenue to compute the revenue in the current year.

EXAMPLE 1.2

In year 4 of a contract, the actual costs to date are $50,000. Total estimated costs are $200,000. The contract price is $1,000,000. Revenue recognized in the prior years (years 1–3) amounted to $185,000.

$$\frac{\$50,000}{\$200,000} \times \$1,000,000 = \$250,000 \text{ Cumulative revenue}$$

Cumulative revenue	$250,000
Prior year's revenue	185,000
Current year revenue	$ 65,000

Journal entries under the construction methods using assumed figures are as follows:

	Percentage of Completion		Completed Contract	
Construction-in-Progress	100,000		100,000	
Cash		100,000		100,000
Construction Costs				
Progress Billings Receivable	80,000		80,000	
Progress Billings on				
Construction-in-Progress		80,000		80,000
Periodic Billings				
Construction-in-Progress	25,000		No Entry	
Profit		25,000		
Yearly profit recognition based on percentage of completion during the year				

In the last year, when the construction project is completed, the following additional entry is made to record the profit in the final year:

Progress Billings on	Total		Total	
Construction-in-Progress	Billings		Billings	
Construction-in-Progress		Cost + profit		Cost Total
Profit		Incremental profit for last year		profit for all the years

Construction-in-Progress minus Progress Billings gives us the Carrying Value. If a debit results (which is usually the case), it is reported as a current asset. If a credit balance exists, the net amount is reported as a current liability.

Irrespective of whether the percentage-of-completion method or the completed-contract method is employed, a loss on the contract will immediately be reported in accordance with the conservatism principle.

Cash Is Collected. Under the cash basis, revenue is recognized when cash is received. It is used rather than accrual if one or more of the following is true: (1) there is collection risk; (2) there is an uncertain collection period; (3) there is an inability to estimate expenses at the time of sale; or (4) there is no objective selling price at the time of sale.

A service business not dealing in inventory (e.g., doctor, lawyer) has the option of using either the accrual basis or the cash basis.

This completes our discussion of the points of revenue recognition. Let us turn now to several pronouncements of the Financial Accounting Standards Board (FASB) relating to revenue recognition.

Right of Return. As per FASB Statement No. 48 (ASC 605-15-25), if the buyer has the privilege of returning goods, the seller may only recognize revenue at the time of sale if *all* of the following criteria are met: (1) selling price is known; (2) buyer must pay for the merchandise even if he finds no customer or loses it; (3) buyer's acquisition of the item makes sense in his business; (4) no requirement exists for the seller to perform future services; and (5) there is reasonable estimation of returns.

If any of the above criteria are not satisfied, revenue has to be deferred until the criteria are met or the right of return no longer exists. When revenue is deferred, expenses related to that revenue also have to be deferred.

Financing Arrangement. FASB Statement No. 49 (ASC 470-40-25) deals with product financing arrangements that usually provide for one entity to obtain inventory or product for another entity (the sponsor), who agrees to buy the inventory or product at given prices over a stated period. There are two types of product financing arrangements:

- Sponsor sells a product to another business and agrees to buy it back.
- Sponsor has another company purchase the product and agrees to repurchase the item from that company.

When the sponsor sells the good to the other company and in a related transaction agrees to repurchase it, the sponsor records a liability when the proceeds are received. *Caution:* A sale is *not* recorded, and the product should be kept as inventory on the sponsor's books.

In the situation where another business purchases the product for the sponsor, inventory is debited and a payable is credited at the time of acquisition on the sponsor's books.

Financing and holding costs paid by the sponsor to the other company are generally expensed.

EXAMPLE 1.3

On 1/1/2014, a sponsor borrows $100,000 from another company and gives the inventory as collateral for the loan. The entry is

Cash	100,000	
Loans Payable		100,000

A sale is *not* recorded here, and the inventory remains on the books of the sponsor.

On 12/31/2014, the sponsor pays back the other company. The inventory item is returned. The interest rate on the loan was 8%; storage costs were $2,000. The entry is

Loans Payable	100,000	
Interest Expense	8,000	
Storage Expense	2,000	
Cash		110,000

Franchise Fee Revenue. According to FASB Statement No. 45 (ASC 952-B05), the franchisor can record revenue from the initial sale of the franchise only when there has been *substantial performance* as indicated by:

- Absence of intent to provide refunds or forgive part of the account receivable. The franchisor has no material services still to perform.
- Initial services have been performed.

The earliest time of substantial performance is generally the franchisee's commencing of operations. If it is probable that the franchisor will eventually repurchase the franchise, the initial fee must be deferred.

If revenue recognition is deferred, the related expenses must be deferred for later matching in the year in which the revenue is recognized. Deferred revenue is revenue received in advance before being earned. It is a liability because future services must be provided. Deferred expenses are expenses paid for in advance before being incurred. It is an asset because you obtain later revenue from their incurrence. The entries follow:

Year of initial fee:	
Cash	
Deferred Revenue	
Deferred Expenses	
Cash	

Year substantial performance occurs:
Deferred Revenue
  Revenue
Expenses
  Deferred Expenses

Recurring franchise fees are recognized as earned and as they become receivable from the franchise. Related costs are expensed. If the franchisor sells equipment and inventory to the franchisee at cost, a receivable and a payable is recorded, but there is no revenue or expense recognition.

Costs relating to continuing franchise fees are expensed as incurred. Outstanding obligations under the agreement and the segregation of initial and continuing franchise fees received should be footnoted.

Research and Development (R&D)

According to FASB Statement No. 2 (Accounting for Research and Development Costs) (ASC 730-10-05), research and development costs are expensed as incurred. However, R&D costs incurred under contract for which reimbursement will be received are charged to a receivable account instead of being expensed. In addition, materials, equipment, and intangibles purchased from others that have alternative *future benefit* in R&D activities are capitalized. The depreciation or amortization on such assets are classified as an R&D expense.

According to FASB Statement No. 86 (Accounting for the Costs of Computer Software to be Sold, Leased, or Otherwise Marketed) (ASC 985-20-25), costs incurred for computer software to be sold or leased are expensed as R&D costs until there is *technological feasibility* (as evidenced by a detailed program or working model). After technological feasibility exists, software production costs should be deferred and recorded at the lower of book value or net realizable value. Amortization starts when the product is available for customer release. The amortization is the higher of (1) the straight-line amount or (2) the percent of current revenue to total revenue from the product.

According to American Institute of Certified Public Accountants (AICPA) Statement of Position No. 98-1 (Accounting for the Costs of Computer Software Developed or Obtained for Internal Use), a business must capitalize and amortize the costs to develop or obtain software for sole use within the company. However, data conversion costs must be immediately expensed.

Earnings Per Share (EPS)

FASB Statement No. 128 (Earnings Per Share) (ASC 260-10-50) mandates that a public company must present its earnings per share. The dual presentation of EPS is:

$$\text{Basic EPS} = \frac{\text{Net income} - \text{preferred dividends}}{\text{Weighted-average common stock outstanding}}$$

$$\text{Diluted EPS} = \frac{\text{Net income} - \text{preferred dividends}}{\substack{\text{Weighted-average common stock outstanding} \\ + \text{ other diluted securities}}}$$

The weighted-average common stock shares are computed based on the time period the shares are outstanding.

EXAMPLE 1.4

On 1/1/2014, 10,000 shares were issued. On 4/1/2014, 2,000 of those shares were bought back by the company. The weighted-average common stock outstanding is

$$(10,000 \times 3/12) + (8,000 \times 9/12) = \underline{8,500} \text{ shares}$$

Note: In the case of a stock split or stock dividend, the computation of weighted-average common stock shares outstanding requires retroactive adjustment as if the shares were outstanding at the beginning of the year.

Other diluted securities are securities that can become common stock at a subsequent date. These include stock options, stock warrants, and convertible securities.

In computing EPS, diluted convertible securities are included if they have a dilutive effect. Dilutive effect means that inclusion of a common stock equivalent reduces EPS. Antidilutive securities that increase EPS are not shown in the EPS computation because they will increase EPS, thus violating the principle of conservatism. (Conservatism means understating rather than overstating a financial statistic or financial position.)

The common stock equivalency of options and warrants is determined using the treasury stock method. Options and warrants are assumed to be exercised at the beginning of the year (or at time of issuance, if later). The proceeds received are assumed to be used to (1) reacquire common stock at the average market price for the year, as long as the total does not exceed 20% of shares outstanding at year-end; (2) with the balance remaining, reduce long or short-term debt; and (3) with any balance still remaining, invest in U.S. government securities and commercial paper.

We assume the exercise of options only when the market price of stock exceeds the exercise price for three consecutive months ending with the year-end month.

We now illustrate the computation of the common stock equivalency of options under the treasury stock method.

EXAMPLE 1.5

100 shares are under option at an option price of $10. The average market price of stock is $25. The common stock equivalent is 60 shares, as calculated below:

Issued shares from option	100 shares × $10 = $1,000
Less: Treasury shares	40 shares × $25 = $1,000
Common stock equivalent	60 shares

In the numerator of the EPS fraction, net income minus preferred dividends is the earnings available to common stockholders. With cumulative preferred stock, preferred dividends for the *current year* are deducted whether or not paid. However, if the preferred stock is a common stock equivalent, the preferred dividend would *not* be deducted since the preferred shares are included in the denominator.

As for the denominator of EPS, if convertible bonds are included, they are deemed equivalent to common shares. Therefore, interest expense (net of tax) must be added to the numerator.

EXAMPLE 1.6

The stockholders' equity section of ABC Company's balance sheet as of 12/31/2014 appears below:

$1.20 cumulative preferred stock (par value of $10 per share, issued 1,200,000 shares, of which 500,000 were converted to common stock and 700,000 shares are outstanding)	$ 7,000,000
Common stock (par value of $2.50, issued and outstanding 6,000,000 shares)	15,000,000
Paid-in capital	20,000,000
Retained earnings	32,000,000
Total stockholders' equity	$74,000,000

On 5/1/2014, ABC Company acquired XYZ Company in a pooling-of-interest. For each of XYZ Company's 800,000 shares ABC issued one of its own shares in the exchange.

On 4/1/2014, ABC Company issued 500,000 shares of convertible preferred stock at $38 per share. The preferred stock is convertible to common stock at the rate of two shares of common for each share of preferred. On 9/1/2014, 300,000 shares and on 11/1/2014 200,000 shares of preferred stock were converted into common stock. The market price of the convertible preferred stock is $38 per share.

In August, ABC Company granted stock options to executives to buy 100,000 shares of common stock at an option price of $15 per share. The market price of stock at year-end was $20.

ABC Company has $10,000,000 in 8% convertible bonds payable issued at fair value in 2014. The conversion rate is four shares of common stock for each $100 bond. No conversions have occurred yet. The tax rate is 34%. Net income for the year is $12,000,000.

Note: Stock options are always considered dilutive securities.

Shares outstanding from 1/1/2014 (including 800,000 shares issued upon acquisition of XYZ Company):		
6,000,000 − 1,000,000		5,000,000
Shares issued upon conversion of 500,000 shares of preferred stock to common stock:		
Issued 9/1/2014 600,000 × $\frac{4}{12}$	200,000	
Issued 11/1/2014 400,000 × $\frac{2}{12}$	66,667	266,667
Weighted-average shares of common stock		5,266,667
Dilutive securities:		
Convertible preferred stock:		
500,000 shares of convertible preferred issued on 4/1/2014		
500,000 × 2 × $\frac{9}{12}$	750,000	
Less: Common shares applicable to 500,000 preferred shares converted during the year	266,667	
Common stock equivalents of convertible preferred stock		483,333
Common stock equivalents of stock options:		
Option 100,000 × $15 = $1,500,000		
Less:		
Treasury stock 75,000 × $20 = 1,500,000		
Common stock equivalent of stock options	25,000	25,000
Total		5,775,000

Convertible bonds payable assumed converted at
  1/1/2014 ($10,000,000/$100) = 100,000 bonds
  100,000 bonds × 4 shares per bond   400,000
Weighted-average common stock outstanding plus
  diluted securities for diluted EPS   6,175,000
Basic EPS equals:

$$\frac{\$12,000,000}{5,266,667} = \$2.28$$

Diluted-EPS equals:

$$\frac{\$12,000,000 + \$528,000^*}{6,175,000 \text{ shares}} = \$2.03$$

* $10,000,000 × 8% = $800,000 × 66% = $528,000.

BALANCE SHEET

On the balance sheet, the accountant is concerned with reporting of assets, liabilities, and stockholders' equity.

Assets

The value of an asset is recorded at the price paid plus related costs of placing the asset in service (e.g., freight, insurance, installation). If an asset is bought in exchange for a liability, the asset is recorded at the present value of the payments.

EXAMPLE 1.7

A machine was acquired by taking out a loan requiring ten $10,000 payments. Each payment includes principal and interest. The interest rate is 10%. While the total payments (principal and interest) are $100,000, the present value will be less since the machine is recorded at the present value of the payments. The asset would be recorded at $61,450 ($10,000 × 6.145). The factor is obtained from the present value of annuity table for $n = 10$, $i = 10\%$.

   If an asset is acquired for stock, it is recorded at the fair market value of the stock issued.

   The four major assets are accounts receivable, inventory, fixed assets, and intangibles.

Accounts Receivable. It is expected that some customers will not pay their balances. Therefore, provision must be made in the accounting records to reflect this fact. Accounts Receivable less Allowance for Uncollectible Accounts is shown in the balance sheet. The *net* amount of accounts receivable represents the amount expected to be collected. Uncollectible Accounts Expense is shown in the income statement. This account represents the *anticipated* uncollectible accounts on sales made for the current year.

The direct write-off method and the allowance method are two ways of accounting for uncollectible accounts. Since only the allowance method is permissible for financial reporting purposes, we will only discuss that method.

Under the allowance method, the uncollectible accounts expense is deducted in the year of sale. Unless uncollectible accounts are *estimated* and shown in the balance sheet and income statement, the financial statements will be misstated.

The following journal entry is made at year's end to record the anticipated uncollectibles of accounts receivable:

> Uncollectible Accounts Expense
> Allowance for Uncollectible Accounts

The allowance account is shown as an offset (contra) to gross accounts receivable in order to arrive at net accounts receivable. The net figure is the *realizable value* of the receivables.

The uncollectible accounts expense may be computed based upon a percentage of current year *net credit* sales, a percentage of gross accounts receivable, or an *aging* of the year-end gross accounts receivable balance.

The percent-of-sales method is an income-statement approach to estimating bad debts. The bad-debts expense provision is computed by multiplying the current year's net credit sales by a flat rate for uncollectibles. The rate is based upon past experience and modified in light of the current environment.

EXAMPLE 1.8

Charge sales for 2014 are $220,000. The anticipated bad-debt rate is 1% of sales. The allowance account currently has a balance of $1,200. The journal entry is

> Uncollectible Accounts Expense   2,200
> Allowance for Uncollectible Accounts   2,200

Under this method, the balance in the allowance account of $1,200 is irrelevant in making the year-end journal entry. We must add to the allowance account for the anticipated uncollectibility of *current* year credit sales. The relationship stressed here is between the current year's uncollectible accounts and the current year's net credit sales. However, if the balance in the allowance account is significant, a change in the percentage for uncollectibles may be required. For example, an excessively high credit balance would warrant a reduction in the bad-debt percentage.

The aging method is balance-sheet oriented in that each customer's account balance is *aged* based upon the date of sale. The longer an account is past due, the greater is the probability of it being uncollectible.

EXAMPLE 1.9

Age of Account	Year-end Gross Accounts Receivable Balance	Uncollectible Percentage	Amount Needed in Allowance Account at Year's End
1–30 days	$12,000	1	$ 120
31–60 days	28,000	3	840
61–90 days	8,000	5	400
Over 90 days	2,000	12	240
	$50,000		$1,600

Since the amount needed in the allowance account is $1,600 based upon an analysis of year-end receivables, an adjusting entry is needed to bring the current-allowance account balance up to that amount. The amount of the adjusting entry is therefore equal to the difference between the current amount and the amount needed according to the aging schedule. If the allowance account has a credit balance of $1,200, the year-end journal entry is as follows:

Uncollectible Accounts Expense	400	
Allowance for Uncollectible Accounts		400

When it is obvious that a customer is no longer able to pay the amount due (if, for example, the customer has declared bankruptcy), the account should be written off. The journal entry is

Allowance for Uncollectible Accounts	1,000	
Accounts Receivable		1,000

The allowance account is debited because part of the allowance provision established for future uncollectibles has now been used up.

EXAMPLE 1.10

Joy Butler owes XYZ Company $1,000. Her account is deemed worthless. The entry is

Allowance for Uncollectible Accounts	1,000	
Accounts Receivable		1,000

The *net* amount of the accounts receivable is *not* affected by the write-off, because the gross receivables and the allowance account are reduced by the same amount.

A full or partial recovery of a previously written-off customer account balance may occur. For example, the customer may unexpectedly receive funds from another source and wish to reinstate his or her business activities. The journal entry to restore the account is

Accounts Receivable
    Allowance for Uncollectible Accounts

The receipt of funds to settle the account in full or in part would be recorded in the usual fashion by debiting cash and crediting accounts receivable.

EXAMPLE 1.11

Referring to Example 1.10, assume that Butler agrees to pay back only $600. The journal entries are

Accounts Receivable	600	
Allowance for Uncollectible Accounts		600
Cash	600	
Accounts Receivable		600

Loans Receivable

FASB Statement Nos. 114 (Accounting by Creditors for Impairment of a Loan) (ASC 310-10-350-13) and 118 (Accounting by Creditors for Impairment of a Loan—Income Recognition and Disclosures) (ASC 310-10-350-40) apply to how a creditor must account for an impaired loan. The impaired value equals the excess of the carrying value of the loan less the present value of expected net cash flows from it. Disclosure should include credit losses incurred and collateral value.

Inventory. The value of inventory is stated at the lower of cost or market value, in conformity with conservatism applied on a total basis, category basis, or individual basis. If cost is less than market value (replacement cost), cost is used. If market value is less than cost, we start with market value. Market value cannot be greater than the ceiling (net realizable value = selling price – costs to complete and dispose). If market value is greater than the ceiling, the ceiling is chosen as the valuation. Market value cannot be less than the floor (net realizable value – normal profit margin). If market value is less than the floor, the floor is used as the valuation. Of course, market value is employed when it is between the ceiling and the floor.

EXAMPLE 1.12

The lower-of-cost-or-market-value method is being applied on an item-by-item basis. The underlined figures are the appropriate valuation in each product category.

Product	Cost	Market	Ceiling	Floor
A	$5	$7	$9	$6
B	14	12	11	7
C	18	15	16	12
D	20	12	18	16
E	6	5	12	7

In case E, a market value of $5 was originally selected. The market value of $5 exceeded the floor of $7, so the floor value would be used. However, if, after applying the lower-of-cost-or-market-value rule, the valuation derived ($7) exceeds the cost ($6), the cost figure is more conservative and thus is used.

Losses on purchase commitments can occur if you contract to buy goods at a later date for a price that is above their current market value.

Material net losses on purchase commitments should be recognized at the end of the reporting period by debiting loss and crediting a liability.

FASB Statement No. 151 (Inventory Costs) (ASC 330-10) requires the immediate expensing of abnormal amounts of idle facility expense, freight handling, and wasted material (spoilage).

Fixed Assets. A fixed asset is recorded at its fair market value or the fair market value of the consideration given, whichever is more clearly evident.

Additions to an existing building (such as a new garage) are capitalized and depreciated over the shorter of the life of the addition or the life of the building. Rearrangement and reinstallation costs are capitalized when future benefit is created. If not, they should be expensed. Obsolete fixed assets should be reclassified from property, plant, and equipment to other assets and shown at salvage value reflecting a loss.

If an old building is demolished to make way for the construction of a new building, the demolition costs are debited to the land account.

A fixed asset donated to the company is recorded at its fair market value.

According to FASB Statement No. 34 (Capitalization of Interest Cost) (ASC 835-20-30), interest incurred on borrowed funds for the self-construction of an asset is deferred and amortized over the life of the asset. Interest capitalized is based on the average accumulated expenditures for that asset. To compute the average accumulated expenditures, each expenditure must be "weighted" for the time it was outstanding during the particular accounting period. The interest rate used is either the weighted-average interest rate on corporate debt or the interest rate on the specific borrowing.

EXAMPLE 1.13

In the purchase of a qualifying asset, a company expends $100,000 on January 1, 2014 and $150,000 on March 1, 2014. The average accumulated expenditures for 2014 are computed as follows:

Expenditure	Number of Months	Average Expenditure
$100,000	12	$100,000
150,000	10	125,000
$250,000		$225,000

FASB Statement No. 153 (Exchanges of Nonmonetary Assets) (ASC 845-10-05) states that usually an exchange of nonmonetary assets should be based on the fair market value of the asset given or that received, whichever is more clearly evident. As a result, a gain or loss from the exchange should be recorded. The reasoning is that there is *commercial substance* to the transaction. Thus, fair market value is the measurement basis for the asset received in a nonmonetary exchange when *commercial substance* exists. There is commercial substance when future cash flows change because of the transaction arising from a change in the economic positions of the two parties. However, if the exchange does *not* have commercial substance, we record at book value the asset given up with *no* recognition of gain or loss.

EXAMPLE 1.14

DEF Company exchanged autos plus cash for land. The fair value of the autos is $100,000. They cost $130,000 with accumulated depreciation of $50,000, so the book value is $80,000. Cash paid is $35,000.

The journal entry for the exchange is

Land (100,000 + 35,000)	135,000	
Accumulated Depreciation	50,000	
Autos		130,000
Cash		35,000
Gain		20,000

If instead we assumed that the autos had a fair market value of $78,000 (not $100,000), a loss would have been recorded for $2,000, computed as follows:

Book Value	$80,000
Fair Value	78,000
Loss	$ 2,000

According to FASB Statement No. 116 (Accounting for Contributions Received and Contributions Made) (ASC 985-605-05), a donated fixed asset is recorded at its appraised value. The entry is to debit the fixed asset and credit contribution revenue.

The company donating the fixed asset records an expense for its appraised value. A gain or loss is recognized for the difference between the asset's fair value and book value.

FASB Statement No. 144 (Accounting for the Impairment or Disposal of Long-Lived Assets) (ASC 205-20-45) states that an asset is impaired if its book value exceeds the total (undiscounted) predicted future cash flows from it. Assuming this recoverability test for asset impairment is present, an impairment loss must be recorded for the excess of book value over fair market value. The reduced carrying value becomes the new cost basis for the fixed asset. Hence, the fixed asset cannot later be written up for a recovery in market value.

The cost to treat property with asbestos is deferred to the asset. Disclosure should be made of the problem and associated costs.

A deposit on a fixed asset is presented as a long-term asset.

Intangible Assets. Intangibles are assets that have a life of one year or more, that lack physical substance (e.g., goodwill), or that represent a right granted by the government (e.g., patent) or by another company (e.g., franchise fee). FASB Statement No. 142 (Goodwill and other Intangible Assets) (ASC 350-20-55) is the authoritative pronouncement dealing with intangibles. All limited-life intangible assets are amortized using the straight-line method over the period benefited. Footnote disclosure should be made of the amortization period and method. Unlimited-life intangibles are subject to an annual impairment test. An impairment loss is recognized for the excess of the carrying (book) value over fair market value.

Internally developed goodwill is not recorded. Goodwill is only recorded in a business combination accounted for under the purchase method, when the cost to the acquirer is in excess of the fair market value of the net assets acquired. If the cost to the acquirer is less than the fair market value of the net assets acquired, there is a credit to goodwill. This credit reduces on a proportionate basis the acquired assets except for certain deferred assets (e.g., deferred tax charges, deferred pension assets), financial assets, and current assets. If a credit still remains, it is accounted for as an extraordinary gain.

According to FASB Statement No. 141 (Business Combinations) (ASC 805-10), intangible assets (except for goodwill) are recorded separately, if applicable, to contractual or other legal rights. If no such rights exist, these assets are recognized only if separable from the acquired company and disposed of. Footnote disclosure must be made of the major reasons for the business combination, total goodwill, and amount of goodwill by reportable segment.

Theoretically, goodwill equals the present value of future excess earnings of a company over other companies in the industry.

In acquiring a business, a determination must often be made as to the estimated value of goodwill. Two methods that can be used are (1) capitalization of earnings and (2) capitalization of excess earnings.

EXAMPLE 1.15

The following information is available for a business that we are considering acquiring:

Expected average annual earnings	$10,000
Expected future value of net assets exclusive of goodwill	$45,000
Normal rate of return	20%

Using the capitalization-of-earnings approach, goodwill is estimated as follows:

Total asset value implied ($10,000/20%)	$50,000
Estimated fair value of assets	45,000
Estimated goodwill	$ 5,000

Assuming the same facts as above, but with a capitalization rate of excess earnings of 22%, and using the capitalization-of-excess-earnings method, goodwill is estimated as follows:

Expected average annual earnings	$10,000
Return on expected average assets	
($45,000 × 20%)	9,000
Excess earnings	$ 1,000
Goodwill ($1,000/.22) = $4,545	

Internally generated research and development (R&D) costs to develop a patented product are expensed. The cost of the patent includes the registration fees to secure it, legal fees in a successful defense, and any cost of buying competing patents. Patents are amortized over the period benefited, not exceeding the 20-year, nonrenewable, legal life of a patent. Trademarks and tradenames have a 10-year, indefinitely renewable, legal life. Copyrights have a legal life of the life of the author plus 70 years. Franchises and licenses are amortized over their useful lives. If an intangible asset becomes worthless, it may be written off as an extraordinary loss.

Organization costs are the costs incurred to incorporate a business (e.g., legal fees). They are expensed as incurred. Startup costs are also expensed.

Leaseholds are rent paid in advance and are amortized over the life of the lease.

Liabilities

In accounting for liabilities, the accountant has many reporting and disclosure responsibilities. There may be an asset retirement obligation. Debt may be extinguished before the maturity date when the firm can issue new debt at a lower interest rate. There may also be an inducement offer in which the original conversion terms are changed by the debt or to induce the holder of the convertible debt to convert to equity securities of the debtor. Estimated liabilities may be recognized for probable losses, such as for lawsuits and warranties. An accrued liability may be established for future employee absences, such as for sick leave and vacations. The purpose is to record the expense when benefits are accumulating based on services rendered. Special termination benefits may also exist, such as for early retirement. Short-term debt may be refinanced to long-term debt, especially when the company is experiencing financial difficulties. There may be a callable obligation by the creditor because of the debtor's violation of the debt agreement. Finally, a liability may exist for exit or disposal activities. These topics are now discussed in detail.

Asset Retirement Obligations. As per FASB Statement No. 143 (Accounting for Asset Retirement Obligations) (ASC 410-20-15), a company must record a liability when a retirement obligation exists, even though it is years prior to the asset's planned retirement. The long-term asset is charged with the asset retirement costs. The asset retirement obligation is measured and recorded along with its related asset retirement cost. Asset retirements may occur from sale, abandonment, or disposal. The company must record the fair market value of a liability for an asset retirement obligation as incurred. When the initial obligation arises, the company records a liability and defers the cost to the fixed asset for the same amount. Subsequent to initial recognition, the liability will change over time, so the obligation must be accreted to its present value each year. The fixed asset's capitalized cost is depreciated over its useful life. When the liability is settled, the entity either settles the obligation for the amount recorded or it will have a settlement gain or loss.

Any additional liability incurred in a later year is an incremental layer of the original obligation. Each layer is initially measured at fair market value.

The interest method of allocation is used to reflect changes in the asset retirement obligation. The interest rate is multiplied by the liability balance at the beginning of the year. The interest rate used is the one existing when the liability was initially measured. The resulting accretion expense increases the book value of the liability each period. Accretion expense is presented in the income statement as an operating item.

The difference between the actual retirement costs and the asset retirement obligation is a gain or loss on retirement presented in the income statement.

Extinguishment of Debt. According to FASB Statement No. 140 (ASC 860-10-05), the gain or loss on the early extinguishment of debt is an ordinary item.

EXAMPLE 1.16

A $100,000 bond payable with an unamortized premium of $10,000 is called at 105. The entry is:

Bonds Payable	100,000	
Premium on Bonds Payable	10,000	
Cash (105% × $100,000)		105,000
Ordinary Gain		5,000

There should be a footnote describing the extinguishment transaction, including the source of funds used.

Inducement Offer. According to FASB Statement No. 84 (Induced Conversions of Convertible Debt) (ASC 470-20-05), if convertible debt is converted to stock in connection with an "inducement offer" in which the debtor changes conversion privileges, the debtor recognizes an expense rather than an extraordinary item. The amount is the fair value of the securities transferred in excess of the fair value of securities issuable under the original conversion terms. The fair market value is measured at the earlier of the conversion date or date of the agreement. An inducement offer may be made by giving debtholders a higher conversion ratio, by paying additional consideration, or by making other favorable changes in terms.

Estimated Liabilities. FASB Statement No. 5 (Accounting for Contingencies) (ASC 450-20-25) states that an estimated liability may be accrued if *both* of the following conditions exist:

- At year-end, it is *probable* (likely to occur) that an asset has been impaired or a liability incurred.
- The amount of loss is subject to reasonable estimation.

An example of a *probable loss* is the likelihood of foreign government expropriation of property in a very hostile environment.

For conservatism purposes, the following entry may be made of a probable loss:

> Expense (Loss)
> Estimated Liability (or Asset Impaired)

EXAMPLE 1.17

On 12/31/2014, warranty expenses are estimated at $20,000. On 3/15/2015, actual warranty costs paid were $16,000. The entries are:

12/31/2014 Warranty Expense	20,000	
Estimated Liability		20,000
3/15/2015 Estimated Liability	16,000	
Cash		16,000

If a probable loss cannot be estimated, it should be footnoted. Also, a probable loss occurring *after* year-end but before the audit report date requires subsequent event disclosure.

If the amount of estimated loss is within a range (similar to a minimum-maximum), the accrual is based on the best estimate within that range. If no amount within the range is better than another amount, the *minimum* amount of the range is recorded. Disclosure should also be made of the exposure to additional loss.

A loss that is *reasonably possible* (more than remote but less than likely) requires only footnote disclosure but not accrual. Examples may be notes receivable discounted or cosigning a loan. The disclosure includes the nature of the contingency and the estimate of probable loss or range of loss. If an estimate is not possible, that should be stated.

A *remote* contingency (slight chance of occurring) does not require disclosure. An example of a remote contingency may be an earthquake loss in New York.

There is no accrual for general contingencies (e.g., self-insurance). Only disclosure and/or an appropriation of retained earnings can be made.

To be recorded as an estimated liability, the future loss must be specific and measurable (e.g., warranties).

Compensated Absences. According to FASB Statement No. 43 (Accounting for Compensated Absences) (ASC 710-10-15), compensated absences include sick leave, holidays, and vacation time. An estimated liability may be accrued for future absences when *all* of the following criteria are satisfied: (1) employee rights have been vested; (2) employee services have already been performed; (3) there is probability of payment; and (4) the amount of estimated liability is reasonably ascertainable. If the criteria are met but the amount is not determinable, only a footnote is needed.

EXAMPLE 1.18

Estimated compensation for future absences is $30,000. The entry is:

Expense	30,000	
Estimated Liability		30,000

If at a later date a payment of $28,000 is made, the entry is:

Estimated Liability	28,000	
Cash		28,000

Special Termination Benefits. According to FASB Statement No. 74 (Accounting for Special Termination Benefits Paid to Employees) (ASC 71X-715-10), an expense for special termination benefits should be accrued when an employer offers early retirement to an employee, the employee accepts the offer, and the amount can be reasonably estimated. The amount of the accrual equals the current payment plus the discounted value of future payments.

EXAMPLE 1.19

On 1/1/2014, as an incentive for early retirement, the employee receives a lump sum payment of $50,000 today, plus payments of $10,000 in each of the next 10 years. The discount rate is 10%. The journal entry is:

Expense	111,450	
Estimated Liability		111,450

Present value $10,000 \times 6.145^* =$	$ 61,450
Current payment	50,000
Total	$ 111,450

* Present value factor for $n = 10$, $i = 10\%$ is 6.145

Refinancing Short-term Debt to Long-term Debt. According to FASB Statement No. 6 (Classification of Short-Term Obligations Expected to Be Refinanced) (ASC 470-10-45-12A), a short-term obligation is reclassified as long-term when either of the following conditions exist:

- Subsequent to year-end of the financial statements but before the audit report is issued, the short-term debt is rolled over into a long-term obligation, or an equity security is issued in substitution.
- Subsequent to year-end of the financial statements but before the audit report is issued, the firm enters into a contract to refinance current debt on a long-term basis and all of the following are satisfed: (1) the agreement does not expire within one year; (2) there is no violation of the agreement; and (3) the parties to the agreement are financially sound.

The refinanced item must be classified under long-term debt and *not* stockholders' equity, even in the case when equity securities are issued in exchange for the debt. When short-term debt is excluded from current liabilities, there should be a footnote describing the financing agreement and the terms of any new obligation to be incurred.

Where the amounts under the refinancing agreement vary, the amount of short-term debt excluded from current liabilities is the *minimum* amount expected to be refinanced based on conservatism.

If cash is paid for the short-term obligation, even if long-term debt of a similar amount is issued the next day, the short-term debt is presented under current liabilities because cash was disbursed.

Callable Obligations by the Creditor. According to FASB Statement No. 78 (Classification of Obligations That Are Callable by the Creditor) (ASC 470-10-45-11), if the debtor is in violation of a debt agreement and long-term debt thus becomes callable, the debt is shown as a current liability, except if either or both of the following conditions exist:

- The creditor forgives the violation or loses the right to require repayment for a period in excess of one year from the balance sheet date.
- There exists a grace period for the long-term debt during which the debtor may probably cure the violation.

Exit or Disposal Activities. FASB Statement No. 146 (Accounting for Costs Associated with Exit or Disposal Activities) (ASC 420-10-05) applies to costs (e.g., costs to consolidate facilities or relocate workers, operating lease termination costs, one-time termination benefits to current employees) associated with a restructuring, discontinued operation, plant closing, or other exit or disposal activity. These costs are recognized as incurred (not at the commitment date to an exit plan) based on fair market value along with the related liability. Thus, the company must actually incur the liability before recognition may be made. The best indicator of fair value is quoted market prices in active markets. In years after the initial measurement, changes to the liability should be measured based on the credit-adjusted risk-free rate that was used to initially measure the liability.

If there is an event that discharges the company's obligation to settle a liability for a cost associated with an exit or disposal activity recognized in a previous year, the liability associated with the related costs is reversed.

Footnote disclosure is required of the following:

- Description of the exit or disposal activity and the anticipated completion date.
- Where exit or disposal costs are shown in the income statement.

Stockholders' Equity

The stockholders' equity section of the balance sheet includes major categories for capital stock (stock issued and stock to be issued), paid-in-capital, retained earnings, unrealized loss on long-term investments, gains or losses on foreign-currency translation, and treasury stock.

In accounting for stockholders' equity, consideration is given to preferred stock characteristics, stock retirement, appropriation of retained earnings, treasury stock, quasi-reorganization, dividends, stock splits, stock options, and stock warrants.

Preferred Stock Characteristics. Participating preferred stock has the right to share in dividend distributions in excess of the preferred stock dividend rate and some basic common stock dividend rate on a proportionate basis using the total par value of the preferred stock and common stock. With cumulative preferred stock, if no dividends are paid in a given year, the preferred stock dividends accumulate and must be paid before any dividends can be paid to noncumulative stock.

If preferred stock is converted to common stock through the exchange of shares, the entry is to debit both preferred stock and paid-in-capital (preferred stock) and to credit common stock and paid-in-capital (common stock). If there is a debit difference in the entry, retained earnings would be charged.

Stock Retirement. If common stock is retired at a price less than par value, the entry is:

> Common Stock
> Cash
> Paid-in Capital

If common stock is retired for more than the original issue price, the entry is:

> Common Stock
> Paid-in Capital (original premium per share)
> Retained Earnings (excess over original premium per share)
> Cash

In retirement of stock, retained earnings can only be debited, not credited.

Appropriation of Retained Earnings (Reserve). Appropriation of retained earnings means restricting retained earnings and making them unavailable for dividends. Examples of appropriations are for general contingencies and plant expansion. The entry to record an appropriation for a general contingency is:

> Retained Earnings
> Appropriation of Retained Earnings

At the time a contingency occurs there is a reversal of the above entry.

Treasury Stock. Treasury stock represents shares that have been reacquired by the company and *not* canceled or retired. Treasury stock is recorded at the purchase cost or at par value. We will explain here the commonly used *cost method* rather than the par value method.

The purchase of treasury stock is recorded in the accounts at cost with the following entry:

> Treasury Stock
> Cash

If treasury stock is subsequently sold above cost, the entry is:

> Cash
> Treasury Stock
> Paid-in Capital

If treasury stock is sold for less than cost, the entry is:

> Cash
> Paid-in Capital—Treasury Stock (up to amount available)
> Retained Earnings (if paid-in capital is not available)
>   Treasury Stock

If treasury stock is donated, there is only a memo entry. When treasury shares are later sold, the entry based on market price at that time is:

> Cash
> Paid-in Capital—Donation

There must be an appropriation of retained earnings equal to the cost of treasury stock on hand.

Treasury stock is shown as a reduction from total stockholders' equity.

Quasi-reorganization. A financially troubled company with a deficit in retained earnings can gain an opportunity for a "fresh start" through a quasi-reorganization. Assets are written down to fair market value, and the deficit in retained earnings is eliminated by reducing paid-in capital. If paid-in capital is insufficient, then capital stock is charged. Retained earnings will show the date of quasi-reorganization for 10 years subsequent to the reorganization.

Dividends. A cash dividend is based on the outstanding shares (issued shares less treasury shares).

EXAMPLE 1.20

There are 5,000 issued shares and 1,000 treasury shares, thus a total of 4,000 outstanding shares. The par value of the stock is $10 per share. If a $.30 dividend per share is declared, the dividend is:

$$4,000 \times \$.30 = \underline{\$1,200}$$

If the dividend rate is 6%, the dividend is:

$$4,000 \times \$10 \text{ par value} = \$40,000$$
$$\frac{\times .06}{\$ 2,400}$$

Assuming a cash dividend of $2,400 is declared, the entry is:

Retained Earnings	2,400	
Cash Dividend Payable		2,400
No entry is made at the record date.		
The entry at the payment date is:		
Cash Dividend Payable	2,400	
Cash		2,400

A property dividend is a dividend payable in assets of the company other than cash. When the property dividend is declared, the company restates the distributed asset to fair market value, recognizing any gain or loss as the difference between the fair market value and carrying value of the property at the declaration date.

EXAMPLE 1.21

A company transfers investments in marketable securities costing $10,000 to stockholders by declaring a property dividend on December 16, 2014, to be distributed on 1/15/2015. At the declaration date, the securities have a market value of $14,000. The entries are:

Declaration:		
12/16/2014 Investment in Securities	4,000	
Gain on Appreciation of Securities		4,000
Retained Earnings	14,000	
Property Dividend Payable		14,000

Note that the net reduction is still the $10,000 cost of the asset.

Distribution:
1/15/2015 Property Dividend Payable   14,000
      Investment in Securities   14,000

A stock dividend is in the form of stock. If the stock dividend is less than 20–25% of outstanding shares at the declaration date, the retained earnings account is charged at the market price of the shares. If the stock dividend exceeds 20–25% of outstanding shares, retained earnings are debited at par value.

EXAMPLE 1.22

A stock dividend of 10% is declared on 5,000 shares of common stock having a par value of $10 and a market price of $12. The entries at the declaration and issuance dates follow:

Declaration:
Retained Earnings (500 shares × $12)   6,000
      Stock Dividend Distributable
           (500 shares × $10)   5,000
           Paid-in-Capital   1,000

Issuance:
Stock Dividend Distributable   5,000
      Common Stock   5,000

Assume instead that the stock dividend was 30%. The entries would be:

Declaration:
Retained Earnings (500 × $10)   5,000
      Stock Dividend Distributable   5,000

Issuance:
Stock Dividend Distributable   5,000
      Common Stock   5,000

A liability dividend is payable in the form of a liability (e.g., notes payable). Interest expense is often paid on the liability between the declaration and payment dates.

Stock Split. In a stock split, the number of shares is increased and the par value per share is decreased. But the total par value is the same. A memo entry is needed.

EXAMPLE 1.23

A company has 1,000 shares of $20 par value common stock. The total par value is thus $20,000. A two-for-one stock split is issued. There will now be 2,000 shares at a $10 par value. The total par value remains at $20,000.

Stock Options. FASB Statement No. 123 (Share-Based Payment), revised 2004 (ASC 718-10), sets standards to account for transactions in which a company issues its equity instruments for goods or services. A company must measure the cost of employee services obtained in exchange for an award of equity instruments based on the grant-date fair value of the award, based on an option pricing model. That cost is recognized over the period employees render services in exchange for the award (typically the vesting period).

A company will initially measure the cost of employee services received in exchange for an award of liability instruments based on current fair value. The fair value of that award will be remeasured subsequently at each reporting date through the settlement date. Changes in fair value during the service period will be recognized as compensation cost over that period.

Incremental compensation cost for modified terms of an award is measured by comparing the fair value of the modified award with the fair value of the award immediately before the modification.

EXAMPLE 1.24

On 1/1/2014, 1,000 shares are granted under a stock option plan. At the measurement date, the market price of the stock is $10 and the option price is $6. The amount of deferred compensation is:

Market price	$10
Option price	6
Deferred compensation	$ 4

Thus, total deferred compensation is $4,000 (1,000 × $4).

Assume the employees must perform services for four years before they can exercise the option.

On 1/1/2014, the entry to record total deferred compensation cost is:

Deferred Compensation Cost	4,000	
Paid-in Capital—Stock Options		4,000

On 12/31/2014, the entry to record the expense is:

Compensation Expense	1,000	
Deferred Compensation		1,000
$4,000/4 years = $1,000		

The capital stock section on 12/31/2014 would show stock options as follows:

Stock Options	$4,000
Less: Deferred Compensation	1,000
Balance	$3,000

Compensation expense of $1,000 would be reflected for each of the next three years as well.

If the market price of the stock at the time the options are exercised exceeds the option price, an entry must be made for stock issuance.

Assuming a par value of $5 and a market price of $22, the journal entry for the exercise is:

Cash ($6 × 1,000)	6,000	
Paid-in Capital—Stock Options	4,000	
Common Stock ($5 × 1,000)		5,000
Paid-in Capital		5,000

If the market price of the stock was below the option price, the options would lapse, requiring the following entry:

Paid-in Capital—Stock Options	4,000	
Paid-in Capital		4,000

If the grant date is before the measurement date, estimate the deferred-compensation costs until the measurement date, so that compensation expense is recognized when services are performed. The difference between the actual figures and the estimates is accounted for as a change in estimate in the year in which the actual cost is determined.

Footnote disclosure for a stock-option plan includes the option price, the number of shares under option, the number of shares exercisable, and the number of shares issued under the option during the year.

Stock Warrants. According to APB 14 (Accounting for Convertible Debt and Inserted Title Debt Issued With Stock Purchase Warrants) (ASC 470-20-25-2), when bonds are issued with *detachable*

stock warrants, the proceeds applicable to the warrants are credited
to paid-in capital. If the warrants are *not detachable,* premium on
bonds payable is credited for any excess over face value.

EXAMPLE 1.25

A $20,000 convertible bond is issued at $21,000 with $1,000 appli-
cable to stock warrants. If the warrants are not detachable, the entry
is:

Cash	21,000	
Bonds Payable		20,000
Premium on Bonds Payable		1,000

If the warrants are detachable, the entry is:

Cash	21,000	
Bonds Payable		20,000
Paid-in Capital — Stock Warrants		1,000

In the event that the proceeds of the bond issue were only
$20,000 instead of $21,000, with $1,000 attributable to detachable
warrants, the entry is:

Cash	20,000	
Discount	1,000	
Bonds Payable		20,000
Paid-in Capital — Stock Warrants		1,000

Disclosure. Footnote disclosure is required for stockholders' equity
including capital structure financing mix, call provisions, contingent
issuances, voting rights, conversion terms, dividend rights, dividend
in arrears, sinking fund provisions, and liquidation preferences.

STATEMENT OF CASH FLOWS

In accordance with FASB Statement No. 95 (Statement of Cash
Flows) (ASC 230-10-45-25), a statement of cash flows is required
in the annual report. Further, separate reporting is needed for
certain information related to noncash investments and financing
transactions.

This statement shows a company's cash receipts and cash payments during a period. There is also a reconciliation between net income and cash flow from operations. The change in cash and cash equivalents is shown. (A cash equivalent is a short-term, highly liquid investment that has an initial maturity of no more than three months. Examples are commercial paper and Treasury bills.)

The statement of cash flows classifies cash receipts and cash payments resulting from operating, investing, and financing activities.

Operating activities are the production and sale of merchandise or the performance of services, both as related to the company's business activities. Cash flow from operating activities measures the cash impact of transactions affecting the profit computation. Examples of operating cash inflows are cash sales, collections on accounts receivable, cash received from interest and dividend revenue, any awards received from a lawsuit, and insurance reimbursements. Examples of cash outflows for operating activities are cash paid to buy raw materials and merchandise, payments to other suppliers, payments of: employee wages, tax payments, and payments of: penalties and fines; interest; lawsuit damages; charitable contributions; and cash refunds to customers for defective goods.

Investing activities are making and collecting loans, buying and selling debt and equity securities of other companies, and acquiring and disposing of property, plant, and equipment. Examples of investing cash inflows are from collections of principal or loans to other entities, from sale of debt or equity securities of other entities, and from sale of property, plant, and equipment. Examples of cash outflows for investing activities include making loans to other entities, buying debt and equity securities of other businesses, and purchase of property, plant, and equipment.

Financing activities apply to receiving equity funds and providing owners with a return on their investment, issuing corporate debt, and paying off such debt. Examples of cash inflows from financing activities are funds obtained from issuing debt and equity securities. Examples of cash outflows for financing activities are payment of dividends, paying principal payments to long-term creditors, and purchase of treasury stock.

In the event a cash receipt or cash payment relates to more than one activity (operating, investing, financing), classification is given to the main activity for that cash flow. For example, the acquisition and sale of machinery is usually considered an investing activity.

The *direct method* is preferred in that companies will report cash flows from operating activities by major classes of receipts and payments and the resulting net amount.

Less preferable, but acceptable, is the *indirect method*. Here, the business reports net cash flow from operating activities indirectly, by adjusting net income to net cash flow from operating activities.

Regardless of which method is used, there should be a reconciliation of net income to net cash flow from operating activities. The reconciliation should highlight the major reconciling items. For instance, the major classes of deferrals and accruals affecting cash flows should be reported, including changes in receivables, inventory, and payables applicable to operating activities.

When the direct method of reporting cash flows from operating activities is used, the reconciliation of net income to cash flow from operations should be disclosed in a separate schedule. When the indirect method is followed, the reconciliation may appear within the body of the statement of cash flows or in a separate schedule.

There must be a *separate presentation* within the statement of cash flows of the cash inflows and the cash outflows from investing and financing activities. For instance, the acquisition of a fixed asset is a use of cash, while the sale of a fixed asset is a source of cash. Issuing debt is a source of cash, while debt payment is an application of cash.

There should be separate disclosure of investing and financing activities that affect assets or liabilities but do *not* impact cash flow. This disclosure may be in a footnote or schedule. Examples of noncash activities are bond conversions and the purchase of land through the incurrence of a mortgage payable.

A transaction having cash and noncash portions should be disclosed, but only the cash aspect is presented in the statement of cash flows.

EXAMPLE 1.26

Summarized below is financial information for the current year for Company M, which provides the basis for the statements of cash flows (dollar amounts are unrealistically low to enhance clarity and understanding of the example):

COMPANY M
CONSOLIDATED STATEMENT OF FINANCIAL POSITION

	1/1/2014	12/31/2014	Change
Assets:			
Cash and cash equivalents	$ 600	$ 1,665	$1,065
Accounts receivable (net of allowance for losses of $600 and $450)	1,770	1,940	170
Notes receivable	400	150	(250)
Inventory	1,230	1,375	145
Prepaid expenses	110	135	25
Investments	250	275	25
Property, plant, and equipment, at cost	6,460	8,460	2,000
Accumulated depreciation	(2,100)	(2,300)	(200)
Property, plant, and equipment, net	4,360	6,160	1,800
Intangible assets	40	175	135
Total Assets	$ 8,760	$11,875	$3,115
Liabilities:			
Accounts payable and accrued expenses	$ 1,085	$ 1,090	$ 5
Interest payable	30	45	15
Income taxes payable	50	85	35
Short-term debt	450	750	300
Lease obligation	———	725	725
Long-term debt	2,150	2,425	275
Deferred taxes	375	525	150
Other liabilities	225	275	50
Total Liabilities	4,365	5,920	1,555
Stockholders' Equity:			
Capital stock	2,000	3,000	1,000
Retained earnings	2,395	2,955	560
Total Stockholders' Equity	4,395	5,955	1,560
Total Liabilities and Stockholders' Equity	$ 8,760	$11,875	$3,115

Source: Statement of Financial Accounting Standards No. 95, *Statement of Cash Flows*, 1987, Appendix C, Example 1, pp. 44–51. Reprinted with permission of the Financial Accounting Standards Board.

COMPANY M
CONSOLIDATED STATEMENT OF INCOME
FOR THE YEAR ENDED DECEMBER 31, 2014

Sales	$13,965
Cost of sales	(10,290)
Depreciation and amortization	(445)
Selling, general, and administrative expenses	(1,890)
Interest expense	(235)
Equity in earnings of affiliate	45
Gain on sale of facility	80
Interest income	55
Insurance proceeds	15
Loss from patent infringement lawsuit	(30)
Income before income taxes	1,270
Provision for income taxes	(510)
Net income	$760

The following transactions were entered into by Company M during 2014 and are reflected in the above financial statements:

a. Company M wrote off $350 of accounts receivable when a customer filed for bankruptcy. A provision for losses on accounts receivable of $200 was included in Company M's selling, general, and administrative expenses.

b. Company M collected the third and final annual installment payment of $100 on a note receivable for the sale of inventory and collected the third of four annual installment payments of $150 each on a note receivable for the sale of a plant. Interest on these notes through December 31 totaling $55 was also collected.

c. Company M received a dividend of $20 from an affiliate accounted for under the equity method of accounting.

d. Company M sold a facility with a book value of $520 and an original cost of $750 for $600 cash.

e. Company M constructed a new facility for its own use and placed it in service. Accumulated expenditures during the year of $1,000 included capitalized interest of $10.

f. Company M entered into a capital lease for new equipment with a fair value of $850. Principal payments under the lease obligation totaled $125.

g. Company M purchased all of the capital stock of Company S for $950. The acquisition was recorded under the purchase method of accounting. The fair values of Company S's assets and liabilities at the date of acquisition are:

Cash	$ 25
Accounts receivable	155
Inventory	350
Property, plant, and equipment	900
Patents	80
Goodwill	70
Accounts payable and accrued expenses	(255)
Long-term note payable	(375)
Net assets acquired	$950

COMPANY M
CONSOLIDATED STATEMENT OF INCOME
FOR THE YEAR ENDED DECEMBER 31, 2014 *(continued)*

h. Company M borrowed and repaid various amounts under a line-of-credit agreement in which borrowings are payable 30 days after demand. The net increase during the year in the amount borrowed against the line-of-credit totaled $300.

i. Company M issued $400 of long-term debt securities.

j. Company M's provision for income taxes included a deferred provision of $150.

k. Company M's depreciation totaled $430, and amortization of intangible assets totaled $15.

l. Company M's selling, general, and administrative expenses included an accrual for incentive compensation of $50 that has been deferred by executives until their retirement. The related obligation was included in other liabilities.

m. Company M collected insurance proceeds of $15 from a business interruption claim that resulted when a storm precluded shipment of inventory for one week.

n. Company M paid $30 to settle a lawsuit for patent infringement.

o. Company M issued $1,000 of additional common stock of which $500 was issued for cash and $500 was issued upon conversion of long-term debt.

p. Company M paid dividends of $200.

Based on the financial data from the preceding example, the following computations illustrate a method of indirectly determining cash received from customers and cash paid to suppliers and employees for use in a statement of cash flows under the direct method:

Cash received from customers during the year:		
Customer sales		$13,965
Collection of installment payment for sale		
of inventory		100
Gross accounts receivable at beginning of year	$ 2,370	
Accounts receivable acquired in purchase of		
Company S	155	
Accounts receivable written off	(350)	
Gross accounts receivable at end of year	(2,390)	
Excess of new accounts receivable over		
collections from customers		(215)
Cash received from customers during the year		$13,850
Cash paid to suppliers and employees during		
the year:		
Cost of sales		$10,290
General and administrative expenses	$1,890	
Expenses not requiring cash outlay (provision		
for uncollectible accounts receivable)	(200)	
Net expenses requiring cash payments		1,690
Inventory at beginning of year	(1,230)	
Inventory acquired in purchase of Company S	(350)	
Inventory at year-end	1,375	
Net decrease in inventory from Company		
M's operations		(205)
Adjustments for changes in related accruals:		

Account balances at beginning of year			
Accounts payable and			
accrued expenses	$1,085		
Other liabilities	225		
Prepaid expenses	(100)		
Total		1,200	
Accounts payable and accrued			
expenses acquired in purchase			
of Company S		255	
Account balances at year-end			
Accounts payable and accrued			
expenses	1,090		
Other liabilities	275		
Prepaid expenses	(135)		
Total		(1,230)	

Additional cash payments not included in expense		225
Cash paid to suppliers and employees during the year		$12,000

Presented below is a statement of cash flows for the year ended December 31, 2014, for Company M. This statement of cash flows illustrates the *direct method* of presenting cash flows from operating activities.

COMPANY M
CONSOLIDATED STATEMENT OF CASH FLOWS
FOR THE YEAR ENDED DECEMBER 31, 2014
Increase (Decrease) in Cash and Cash Equivalents

Cash flows from operating activities:		
Cash received from customers	$13,850	
Cash paid to suppliers and employees	(12,000)	
Dividend received from affiliate	20	
Interest received	55	
Interest paid (net of amount capitalized)	(220)	
Income taxes paid	(325)	
Insurance proceeds received	15	
Cash paid to settle lawsuit for patent infringement	(30)	
Net cash provided by operating activities		$1,365
Cash flows from investing activities:		
Proceeds from sale of facility	600	
Payment received on note for sale of plant	150	
Capital expenditures	(1,000)	
Payment for purchase of Company S, net of cash acquired	(925)	
Net cash used in investing activities		(1,175)
Cash flows from financing activities:		
Net borrowings under line-of-credit agreement	300	
Principal payments under capital lease obligation	(125)	
Proceeds from issuance of long-term debt	400	
Proceeds from issuance of common stock	500	
Dividends paid	(200)	
Net cash provided by financing activities		875
Net increase in cash and cash equivalents		1,065
Cash and cash equivalents at beginning of year		600
Cash and cash equivalents at end of year		$1,665

Reconciliation of net income to net cash
 provided by operating activities:

Net income	$ 760

COMPANY M
CONSOLIDATED STATEMENT OF CASH FLOWS
FOR THE YEAR ENDED DECEMBER 31, 2014
Increase (Decrease) in Cash and Cash Equivalents *(continued)*

Adjustments to reconcile net income to net cash provided by operating activities:		
Depreciation and amortization	$ 445	
Provision for losses on accounts receivable	200	
Gain on sale of facility	(80)	
Undistributed earnings of affiliate	(25)	
Payment received on installment note receivable for sale of inventory	100	
Change in assets and liabilities net of effects from		
purchase of Company S:		
Increase in accounts receivable	(215)	
Decrease in inventory	205	
Increase in prepaid expenses	(25)	
Decrease in accounts payable and accrued expenses	(250)	
Increase in interest and income taxes payable	50	
Increase in deferred taxes	150	
Increase in other liabilities	50	
Total adjustments		605
Net cash provided by operating activities		$1,365

Supplemental schedule of noncash investing and financing activities:

The Company purchased all of the capital stock of Company S for $950. In conjunction with the acquisition, liabilities were assumed as follows:

Fair value of assets acquired	$1,580
Cash paid for the capital stock	(950)
Liabilities assumed	$ 630

A capital lease obligation of $850 was incurred when the Company entered into a lease for new equipment.

Additional common stock was issued upon the conversion of $500 of long-term debt.

Disclosure of accounting policy:

For purposes of the statement of cash flows, the Company considers all highly liquid debt instruments purchased with a maturity of three months or less to be cash equivalents.

Presented below is Company M's statement of cash flows for the year ended December 31, 2014, prepared using the *indirect method*.

COMPANY M
CONSOLIDATED STATEMENT OF CASH FLOWS
FOR THE YEAR ENDED DECEMBER 31, 2014
Increase (Decrease) in Cash and Cash Equivalents

Cash flows from operating activities:			
Net income			$ 760
Adjustments to reconcile net income to net cash			
provided by operating activities:			
Depreciation and amortization		$ 445	
Provision for losses on accounts receivable		200	
Gain on sale of facility		(80)	
Undistributed earnings of affiliate		(25)	
Payment received on installment note			
receivable for sale of inventory		100	
Change in assets and liabilities net of effects			
from purchase of Company S:			
Increase in accounts receivable		(215)	
Decrease in inventory		205	
Increase in prepaid expenses		(25)	
Decrease in accounts payable and			
accrued expenses		(250)	
Increase in interest and income taxes payable		50	
Increase in deferred taxes		150	
Increase in other liabilities		50	
Total adjustments			605
Net cash provided by operating activities			1,365
Cash flows from investing activities:			
Proceeds from sale of facility		600	
Payment received on note for sale of plant		150	
Capital expenditures		(1,000)	
Payment for purchase of Company S, net of			
cash acquired		(925)	
Net cash used in investing activities			(1,175)
Cash flows from financing activities:			
Net borrowings under line-of-credit agreement		300	
Principal payments under capital lease obligation		(125)	
Proceeds from issuance of long-term debt		400	
Proceeds from issuance of common stock		500	
Dividends paid		(200)	
Net cash provided by financing activities			875

COMPANY M
CONSOLIDATED STATEMENT OF CASH FLOWS
FOR THE YEAR ENDED DECEMBER 31, 2014
Increase (Decrease) in Cash and Cash Equivalents (*continued*)

Net increase in cash and cash equivalents	1,065
Cash and cash equivalents at beginning of year	600
Cash and cash equivalents at end of year	$1,665

Supplemental disclosures of cash flow information:

Cash paid during the year for:

Interest (net of amount capitalized)	$220
Income taxes	325

Supplemental schedule of noncash investing and financing activities:

The Company purchased all of the capital stock of Company S for $950. In conjunction with the acquisition, liabilities were assumed as follows:

Fair value of assets acquired	$1,580
Cash paid for the capital stock	(950)
Liabilities assumed	$ 630

A capital lease obligation of $850 was incurred when the Company entered into a lease for new equipment.

Additional common stock was issued upon the conversion of $500 of long-term debt.

Disclosure of accounting policy:

For purposes of the statement of cash flows, the Company considers all highly liquid debt instruments purchased with a maturity of three months or less to be cash equivalents.

Brief Summary

The accountant prepares the income statement, balance sheet, and statement of cash flows in accordance with generally accepted accounting principles (GAAP). Income statement components must be appropriately recorded. Revenue must be recognized based upon the particular circumstances. Assets, liabilities, and stockholders' equity are reported on the balance sheet in accordance with accounting requirements. The statement of cash flows presents the cash inflows and cash outflows from operating, investing, and financing activities.

Chapter 2
Financial Accounting: Financial Reporting Requirements

co-authored by Frank Grippo, C.P.A.

This chapter discusses the major financial reporting requirements. Accounting in interim reports is presented. The accountant's handling of accounting changes and prior period adjustments is covered. Rules of disclosure in segmented reports are provided. Noninterest-bearing notes are discussed. The criteria, accounting, and disclosures for purchase business combinations are presented. The accounting treatment for investments in stock is discussed. The accounting for leases by lessors and lessees is presented. Pension plan provisions and postretirement benefits are also taken up. The requirements in income tax allocation are covered. Foreign currency translation and transactions are discussed. Related party disclosures are presented.

INTERIM REPORTING

Interim reports may be prepared for an appropriate accounting period, such as monthly or quarterly; generally, these statements do not need auditor certification (ASC 270-10). Typically, interim reports include results of the period and the cumulative year-to-date figures. Usually, comparisons are made to comparable interim periods for the previous year.

Interim results should be based on the accounting principles employed in the previous year's annual report, unless of course a change has been made in the current year.

A gain or loss should not be deferred to a subsequent interim period unless the deferral would be permitted for annual reporting.

Revenue from the sale of goods or rendering of services should be recorded as earned in the appropriate interim period. If an advance is received in the first quarter that benefits the whole year, it should be allocated pro rata to the periods affected.

Costs and expenses should be matched to the related revenue in the interim period. If a cost cannot be associated with revenue in a later interim period, it should be expensed in the current quarter. Yearly expenses (e.g., pension plan, insurance) should be allocated to each quarter.

The gross-profit method may be used to estimate interim inventory and cost of goods sold. Disclosure should be made of the assumptions and method.

If there is a *permanent* inventory loss in the quarter, it should be recognized. A later recovery is considered a gain in the subsequent interim period. But *no* recognition is given to temporary inventory losses in a quarter. If a temporary liquidation of the LIFO base occurs but replacement is anticipated by year-end, cost of goods sold should be based on replacement cost.

EXAMPLE 2.1

The historical cost of an inventory item is $10,000, with replacement cost expected at $15,000. The entry is:

Cost of Sales	15,000	
Inventory		10,000
Reserve for Liquidation of LIFO Base		5,000

Note: The Reserve for Liquidation of LIFO Base account is shown as a current liability.

When replenishment is made at year-end, the entry is:

Reserve for Liquidation of LIFO Base	5,000	
Inventory	10,000	
Cash		15,000

When a standard cost system is used, variances expected to be reversed by year-end may be deferred to an asset or liability account.

Estimated income tax expense includes current and deferred taxes, both federal and local. The tax provision for an interim period should be cumulative. For instance, total tax expense for a six-month period is shown at the end of the second quarter based on six months' income.

The tax expense for the three-month period based on three months' income may also be presented. For instance, the second quarter's tax expense would be based on only the second quarter's income.

In determining tax expense, we use the estimated annual effective tax rate. The estimated rate should take into account all available tax credits (e.g., foreign tax credit) and alternative tax methods.

Tax expense relates only to the income from continuing operations. Income statement items after income from continuing operations (e.g., extraordinary items) are shown net of tax. The tax effect on these unusual items is reflected only in the interim period when they actually occur. Further, prior-period adjustments are shown net of tax in the interim period when they take place.

A change in accounting method made in an interim period shall be reported by retrospective application. If retrospective application to prechange interim periods is not practical, the desired change may only be made as of the beginning of a subsequent fiscal period.

Disclosure should be made of the effect of the change in accounting principle on net income and related per-share amounts for postchange interim periods. Disclosure should be provided of the nature and justification of the change in principle.

Disclosure should be made of the seasonality factors affecting interim results.

In case a fourth quarter is not presented, any material adjustments to that quarter must be commented upon in the footnotes to the annual report.

FASB ACCOUNTING STANDARDS CODIFICATION

The Accounting Standards Codification (ASC) integrates existing accounting standards by multiple standard-setters. The Codification is now the single official source of authoritative, nongovernmental U.S. GAAP, superseding existing FASB, AICPA, EITF, and related literature. Accounting guidance is classified as either "authoritative" or "nonauthoritative" based on its inclusion or exclusion from the Codification.

The Codification content is arranged within (a) Topics, (b) Subtopics, (c) Sections, and (d) Subsections, as follows:

- Topics. Topics represent a collection of related guidance and reside in four main areas: (1) presentation (e.g., income statement, balance sheet), (2) financial statement accounts (e.g., assets, liabilities, equity), (3) broad transactions (e.g., business combinations, derivatives), and (4) industries (e.g., airlines, real estate).
- Subtopics. Subtopics represent subsets of a "Topic" and are generally distinguished by type or by scope. For example,

"Operating Leases" and "Capital Leases" are two subtopics of the "Leases" topic.
- Sections. Sections represent the nature of the content in a "Subtopic" (e.g., recognition, measurement, disclosure).
- Subsections. Sections are further broken down into subsections, paragraphs, and subparagraphs.

The following is the structure of the classification system: XXX-YY-ZZ-PP, where:

XXX = Topic
YY   = Subtopic
ZZ   = Section
PP   = Paragraph

ACCOUNTING CHANGES

Change in Principle

A change in accounting principle requires retrospective application to prior years' financial statements, unless it is impractical to ascertain either the period-specific impact or the cumulative effect of the change. *Retrospective application* means the application of a different accounting method to previous years as if that new method had always been used. If it is impractical to determine the period-specific effect of a change in method on a prior period(s), the adjustment is made to the beginning balance of retained earnings. In this case, the new accounting principle is applied prospectively as of the earliest date it is practical to do so.

A change in depreciation or amortization must be accounted for as a change in estimate effected by a change in estimate.

The Retained Earnings Statement after a retroactive change for a change in accounting principle appears below:

> Retained Earnings – 1/1, as previously reported
> Add: Adjustment for the cumulative effect on previous years of applying retrospectively the new accounting method for long-term construction contracts
> Retained Earnings – 1/1, as adjusted

Footnote disclosure should be made of the nature of and justification for a change in principle, including an explanation of why the new principle is preferred. Disclosure should also be made of the new method. Further, there should be a description of prior year data that were retrospectively adjusted.

Change in Estimate

A change in estimate (e.g., life or salvage value of a fixed asset) is accounted for *only* over current and future years. A footnote should describe the nature of the change.

If a change in estimate is coupled with a change in principle and the effects cannot be distinguished, it is accounted for as a change in estimate.

EXAMPLE 2.2

Equipment was bought for $40,000 on 1/1/2010, at which time it had an original estimated life of 10 years with a salvage value of $4,000. On 1/1/2014, the estimated life was revised to eight more years remaining with a new salvage value of $3,200. The journal entry on 12/31/2014 for depreciation expense is:

Depreciation	2,800	
Accumulated Depreciation		2,800

Computations follow:

Book value on 1/1/2014:

Original cost	$40,000
Less: Accumulated depreciation	
$\dfrac{\$40,000 - \$4,000}{10} = \$3,600 \times 4$	14,400
Book value	$25,600

Depreciation for 2014:

Book value	$25,600
Less: New salvage value	3,200
Depreciable cost	$22,400

$$\frac{\text{Depreciable cost}}{\text{New life}} = \frac{\$22,400}{8} = \$2,800$$

Change in Reporting Entity

A change in reporting entity (e.g., after two previously separate companies combine) is accounted for by restating the prior year's financial statements as if both companies had always been combined. The restatement does not have to go back more than five years. Footnote disclosure should be made of the nature of and justification for the change in reporting entity only in the year of change.

PRIOR PERIOD ADJUSTMENTS

ASC 250-10-45 specifies two types of prior period adjustments:

- Recognition of a tax-loss carryforward benefit arising from a purchased subsidiary.
- Correction of an error made in a previous year.

Prior period adjustments adjust the beginning balance of retained earnings as follows:

>   Retained Earnings — 1/1 Unadjusted
>   Prior Period Adjustments (net of tax)
>   Retained Earnings — 1/1 Adjusted

Disclosure should be made of the nature of the error and of the effect of correction on earnings.

EXAMPLE 2.3

On 1/1/2011, a company paid $32,000 for a machine with a five-year life and a $2,000 salvage value. Repairs expense was charged in error. The mistake was discovered on 12/31/2014, before closing the books. The correcting entry is:

Depreciation Expense	6,000	
Machine	32,000	
Accumulated Depreciation		24,000
Retained Earnings (32,000 – 18,000)		14,000

Accumulated depreciation of $24,000 is calculated below:

$$\frac{\$32,000 - \$2,000}{5} = \$6,000 \text{ per year} \times 4 \text{ years} = \$24,000$$

EXAMPLE 2.4

At the end of 2014, a company failed to accrue telephone expense, which was paid at the beginning of 2015. The correcting entry on 12/31/2015 is:

Retained Earnings	16,000	
Telephone Expense		16,000

DISCLOSURE OF ACCOUNTING POLICIES

According to ASC 235-10, the first footnote or section preceding the notes to the financial statements should describe the accounting policies employed. Examples of accounting policies are depreciation and inventory methods followed.

SEGMENTAL REPORTING

According to ASC 280-10-50, segmental reporting may be by industry, foreign geographic area, export sales, major customers, and governmental contracts. The financial statement presentation of segments may be in the body, footnotes, or in a separate schedule to the financial statements.

Segmental reporting assists in appraising the earning power, risk, growth prospects, and financial difficulties of a business. According to the pronouncement, the amount reported for each financial statement item must be based on what the *chief operating decision maker* uses in making a decision on how resources are assigned to a segment. The term may apply to a function and not necessarily a particular person(s). This is a management approach in identifying segments. The segments are based on the entity's nature of activities, organizational structure, and revenue base.

A segment must be reported if any of the following criteria exist:

- Revenue of the segment is 10% or more of total revenue.
- Operating income of the segment is 10% or more of combined operating profit.
- Identifiable assets of the segment are 10% or more of the total identifiable assets.

If a segment does not meet the 10% test in the current year, but was significant in the past and is expected to be significant in the future, it should still be reported in the current year.

A segment satisfying the 10% test may not be reported in the current year if it was not reported before and is expected not to be reported in the future. The segment's profit in the current year is abnormal and not reasonable.

The segments that are reported must together constitute a substantial portion (75% or more) of the company's total revenue to outside customers. In order to derive 75%, smaller segments may have to be included. However, for practical purposes, no more than 10 segments should be presented.

Even though intersegment transfers are eliminated in preparing consolidated financial statements, they are includable for segmental disclosure in determining the 10% and 75% rules.

Note: Operating profit excludes general corporate revenue and expenses that are not allocatable, interest expense, and income taxes.

Identifiable assets are assets of a segment that are directly in it and general corporate assets that can rationally be allocated to it.

Disclosures are not needed for 90% enterprises (i.e., a firm that obtains 90% or more of its revenue, operating profit, and total assets from one segment). In essence, that segment *is* the business. The dominant industry segment should be identified.

The source of the segmental revenue should be disclosed along with the percent so derived, when:

- 10% or more of revenue or assets is derived from a foreign area.
- 10% or more of sales is to one customer.
- 10% or more of revenue is obtained from either domestic or foreign government contracts.

Disclosures include measurement basis used and how segmental financial data differs from that shown in the full set of financial statements.

Disclosure for each segment includes tax effects, geographic areas of operations, nature of products or services, cost allocation method, capital expenditures, aggregate depreciation and amortization, contribution margin, and transfer pricing method.

IMPUTING INTEREST ON NOTES

When the face value of a note does not represent the present value of the consideration given or received in the exchange, imputation of interest is required. Interest must be imputed on noninterest-bearing notes and notes that have unrealistically low interest rates. According to ASC 835-30, the imputed interest rate is the one that would have resulted if an independent borrower or lender had negotiated a similar transaction.

The difference between the face value of the note and the present value of the note represents a discount or premium. This is accounted for as a contra account and amortized as an element of interest over the life of the note. Present value of the payments of the note is based on an imputed interest rate.

The interest method is used to amortize the discount or premium on the note. Amortization equals interest rate multiplied by the present value of the liability or receivable at the beginning of the year.

Interest expense is recorded for the borrower, while interest revenue is recorded for the lender. Issuance costs are accounted for as a deferred charge.

The note payable is presented in the balance sheet as follows:

> Note Payable (Principal and Interest)
> Less: Discount (Interest)
> Present Value (Principal)

EXAMPLE 2.5

On 1/1/2015, a machine is bought for $10,000 cash and a $30,000, five-year, noninterest-bearing note is signed. The imputed interest rate is 10%. The present value factor for $n = 5$, $i = 10\%$ is 0.62. Appropriate journal entries are:

```
1/1/2014
Machine (10,000 + 18,600)        28,600
Discount                         11,400
     Note Payable                                    30,000
     Cash                                             10,000
Present value of note equals $30,000 × .62 = $18,600
```

On 1/1/2014, the balance sheet shows:

Notes Payable	$30,000
Less: Discount	11,400
Present Value	$18,600
12/31/2X09	
Interest Expense	1,860
Discount	1,860
10% × $18,600 = $1,860	

On 1/1/2014, the balance sheet shows:

Notes Payable	$30,000
Less: Discount (11,400 – 1,860)	9,540
Present Value	$20,460
12/31/2014	
Interest Expense	2,046
Discount	2,046
10% × $20,460 = $2,046	

BUSINESS COMBINATIONS

Business combinations in the form of mergers and acquisitions occur when companies choose to combine (rather than grow internally) to take advantage of cost efficiencies or transform their businesses to the next level. The result of a business combination is that the combined company may have additional product offerings, greater geographic presence, and increased market share, as well as control over all sources of production and product distribution (vertical integration). The accountant is frequently called upon to advise management of the impact of proposed combinations, as well as to prepare consolidated financial statements for completed transactions. Knowledge of the emerging accounting rules in this area is critical in supporting both functions.

ASC 805-10-25-1 requires that business combinations be accounted for using the "acquisition method." The acquisition method requires identifying the acquirer, determining the date of acquisition, recognizing and measuring identifiable assets that were acquired or liabilities that were assumed, and determining any noncontrolling interest in the acquire. Goodwill or gain from a bargain purchase should also be measured and recognized.

Disclosures

The acquirer is required to disclose the following for the reporting period (ASC 805-10-50-1): the name and description of the acquire, date of acquisition, the percentage of voting equity interests acquired, reasons for the business combination, and a description of how the control was obtained. A description of the transaction, how it was accounted, amount recognized, and how the settlement amount was determined should be disclosed for transactions that were separately recognized from the acquisition of assets and assumptions of liabilities.

CONSOLIDATION

Consolidation occurs when the parent owns in excess of 50% of the voting common stock of the subsidiary. The major objective of consolidation is to present as one economic unit the financial position and operating results of a parent and subsidiaries. It shows the group as a single company with one or more branches or divisions rather than as separate companies. It is an example of theoretical substance over legal form. The companies making up the consolidated group keep their individual legal identity. Adjustments and eliminations are for the sole purpose of financial statement reporting. Consolidation is still appropriate even if the subsidiary has a material amount of debt. Disclosure should be made of the firm's consolidation policy in footnotes or by explanatory headings.

A consolidation is negated, even if more than 50% of voting common stock is owned by the parent, in the following cases:

- The parent is not in actual control of a subsidiary—for example, the subsidiary is in receivership, or it is in a politically unstable foreign country.
- The parent has sold or contracted to sell a subsidiary shortly after year-end. The subsidiary is a temporary investment.
- Minority interest is very large in comparison to the parent's interest; thus individual financial statements are more meaningful.

Intercompany elimination includes those for intercompany payables and receivables, advances, and profits. However, for certain regulated companies, intercompany profit does not have to be eliminated to the extent the profit represents a reasonable return on investment. Subsidiary investment in the parent's shares is not consolidated outstanding stock in the consolidated balance sheet. Consolidated statements do not reflect capitalized earnings in the form of stock dividends by subsidiaries subsequent to acquisition.

Minority interest in a subsidiary is the stockholders' equity of those outside compared to the parent's controlling interest in the partially owned subsidiaries. Minority interest should be shown as a separate component of stockholders' equity. When losses applicable to the minority interest in a subsidiary exceed the minority interest's equity capital, the excess and any subsequent losses related to the minority interest are charged to the parent. If profit subsequently occurs, the parent's interest is credited to the degree of prior losses absorbed.

If a parent acquires a subsidiary in more than one block of stock, each purchase is on a step-by-step basis and consolidation does not occur until control exists.

When the subsidiary is acquired within the year, the subsidiary should be included in consolidation as if it had been bought at the beginning of the year, with a subtraction for the preacquisition part of earnings applicable to each block of stock. An alternative, but less preferable, approach is to include in consolidation the subsidiary's earnings subsequent to the acquisition date.

The retained earnings of a subsidiary at the acquisition date are not included in the consolidation financial statements.

When the subsidiary is disposed of during the year, the parent should always be consolidated.

Consolidation is still permissible without adjustments when the fiscal year-ends of the parent and subsidiary are three months or less apart. Footnote disclosure is needed of material events occurring during the intervening period.

The equity method of accounting is used for unconsolidated subsidiaries unless there is a foreign investment or a temporary investment. In a case where the equity method is not used, the cost method is followed. The cost method recognizes the difference between the cost of the subsidiary and the equity in net assets at the acquisition date. Depreciation is adjusted for the difference as if consolidation of the subsidiary were made. There is an elimination of intercompany gain or loss for unconsolidated subsidiaries to the extent the gain or loss exceeds the unrecorded equity in undistributed earnings. Unconsolidated subsidiaries accounted for with the cost method should have adequate disclosure of assets, liabilities, and earnings. Such disclosure may be in footnote or supplementary schedule form.

There may be instances when combined rather than consolidated financial statements are more meaningful, such as where a person owns a controlling interest in several related operating companies (brother–sister corporation).

There are cases in which parent company statements are required to properly provide information to creditors and preferred stockholders. In this event, dual columns are needed—one column for the parent and other columns for subsidiaries.

ASC 810-10 requires variable interest entities to be consolidated by the primary beneficiary. The primary beneficiary is the entity that holds the majority of the beneficial interests in the variable interest entity.

Although significant guidance is available on how consolidated financial statements are prepared under the acquisition method, little attention has been given to how an acquired subsidiary should present its assets and liabilities on the books. One perspective is that the subsidiary should retain its prior recording basis (e.g., historical cost, market value). Under that view, fair value adjustments to prepare consolidated financial statements would be shown only on the worksheet and not posted to the subsidiary's general ledger.

Under another perspective, the change in ownership arising from buying the subsidiary results in a new measurement basis, fair value, for that company. The balances on the subsidiary's general ledger are adjusted to fair value. Thus, there is no need for consolidated worksheet adjustments, as these are made directly to the accounts of the subsidiary on its books. This process is called "push-down accounting."

The difference in the two approaches is important only when the subsidiary issues separate GAAP financial statements, which could be mandated when the subsidiary issues stock or must borrow funds. Push-down accounting should be used in separately issued financial statements of a subsidiary when that subsidiary is substantially wholly owned (95% or more). The reasoning is that if the acquiree is merged into the parent (e.g., statutory merger), the accounting basis for the acquiree's net assets would be fair value and thus the accounting basis should not be different when the parent decides to maintain the existence of the subsidiary.

Noncontrolling Interests in Consolidated Financial Statements

ASC 810-10-65 states that a noncontrolling (minority) interest is the part of equity in a subsidiary not attributable to the parent. Ownership interests in subsidiaries held by parties other than the parent should be identified and presented in the consolidated balance sheet within equity, but separate from the parent's equity. The consolidated net income attributable to the parent and the noncontrolling interest should be identified and presented in the consolidated income statement. The computation of earnings-per-share amounts in consolidated financial statements is based on amounts attributable to the parent.

Changes in a parent's ownership interest in a subsidiary, such as when the parent buys additional equity interest or sells ownership interest, represents an equity transaction if the parent keeps the controlling financial interest in the subsidiary. An equity transaction is also when a subsidiary reacquires or issues additional ownership interests.

If a subsidiary is deconsolidated, any retained noncontrolling equity investment in the former subsidiary should initially be recorded at fair value. The gain or loss on the deconsolidation of the subsidiary is measured based on the fair value of any noncontrolling equity investment instead of the carrying amount of the retained investment. A parent deconsolidates a subsidiary at the date the parent no longer has a controlling financial interest in the subsidiary.

A subsidiary may incur losses with its ensuing negative financial impact on noncontrolling interests. If the noncontrolling interest in the subsidiary's net assets has been reduced to zero due to losses, the noncontrolling interest will continue to be charged for its share of additional losses, even if that causes a deficit balance in the non-controlling interest account.

Disclosures are made to identify and distinguish between the interests of the parent and the noncontrolling owners of the subsidiary. There should be reconciliation at the beginning and ending balances of the equity associated with the parent and the noncontrolling owners, as well as a schedule that presents the impact of changes in a parent's ownership interest in a subsidiary on the equity related to the parent.

INVESTMENTS IN SECURITIES

Market Value Adjusted

Securities are classified as either held-to-maturity, trading, or available-for-sale.

Held-to-maturity classification applies only to debt securities, because equity securities do not have a maturity date. Held-to-maturity debt securities are accounted for at amortized cost. Amortized cost equals the purchase price adjusted for the amortization of discount or premium. Held-to-maturity securities are not adjusted to market value. Held-to-maturity categorization only relates to debt securities if the company has the intent and ability to hold the securities to the maturity date.

Trading securities can be either equity or debt. The intent is to sell them in a short time period. Trading securities are frequently bought and sold to earn short-term profit. Trading securities are recorded at market value with the unrealized (holding) loss or gain shown as a separate item in the income statement. Trading securities should be reported as current assets in the balance sheet.

EXAMPLE 2.6

On 12/31/2014, the trading securities portfolio had a cost and market value of $400,000 and $410,000, respectively. The journal entry to reflect the portfolio at market value is:

Market Adjustment	10,000	
Unrealized Gain		10,000

The Market Adjustment account has a debit balance and is added to the cost of the portfolio in the current asset section of the balance sheet as follows:

Trading securities (cost)	400,000
Add: Market adjustment	10,000
Trading securities (market value)	410,000

The unrealized gain is presented in the income statement under "other income."

Available-for-sale securities may be either debt or equity. These securities are not held for trading purposes, nor is the intent to hold them to maturity. They are reported at market value with the unrealized loss or gain presented as a separate item in the stockholders' equity section of the balance sheet. The portfolio of available-for-sale securities may be presented in the current asset or noncurrent asset sections of the balance sheet depending on the circumstances.

EXAMPLE 2.7

On 12/31/2014, the available-for-sale securities portfolio had a cost and market value of $250,000 and $230,000, respectively. The journal entry to recognize the portfolio at market value is:

Unrealized Loss	20,000	
Market Adjustment		20,000

The portfolio is shown in the balance sheet at $230,000 net of the Market Adjustment account of $20,000. The unrealized loss is presented separately in the stockholders's equity section of the balance sheet.

When securities are sold, regardless of the type, the realized gain or loss is reported in the income statement. If the decline in market value of either available-for-sale or held-to-maturity securities is considered permanent, a realized loss is recognized in the income statement. When the security is written down, market value at that date becomes the new cost basis.

EXAMPLE 2.8

On 12/31/2014, a company presented the following accounts before adjustment:

Available-for-Sale Securities	600,000	
Market Adjustment		50,000

It was determined on 12/31/2014 that the portfolio's market value was $585,000. The journal entry required to bring the portfolio up-to-date is:

Market Adjustment	35,000	
Unrealized Gain		35,000

When one stock is exchanged for another, the new security received is valued at its fair market value.

EXAMPLE 2.9

Preferred stock that cost $10,000 is exchanged for 1,000 shares of common stock having a market value of $15,000. The entry:

Investment in Common Stock	15,000	
Investment in Preferred Stock		10,000
Gain		5,000

The receipt of a cash dividend requires a debit to cash and a credit to dividend revenue.

A stock dividend requires a memo entry indicating that additional shares were received at no extra cost. The cost per share will drop.

EXAMPLE 2.10

XYZ Company owns 50 shares purchased at $12 per share for a total cost of $600. A 20% stock dividend is declared, amounting to 10 shares. A memo entry is made reflecting the additional shares as follows:

		Investment	
50	$12	$600	
10		0	
60	$10	600	

If 10 shares are later sold at $15, the entry is:

Cash	150	
Long-term Investment		100
Gain		50

A stock split increases the shares held and reduces the cost basis proportionately. A memo entry is necessary.

EXAMPLE 2.11

ABC Company owns 100 shares of stock that cost $20 per share. A two-for-one split results in 200 shares at a cost per share of $10. Total par value remains at $2,000.

Equity Method

The equity method is used with the investor who owns between 20% and 50% of the voting common stock of a corporation. The equity method would also be used if the ownership was less than 20% but the investor still had effective control. Further, the equity method would be used even when more than 50% of the voting common stock was owned but at least one of the negating factors for consolidation existed. These negating factors include:

- The parent is not in actual control of the subsidiary (e.g., subsidiary is in receivership).
- The parent has sold or contracted to sell the subsidiary shortly after year-end.

The accounting under the equity method is illustrated by these "T-accounts":

Investment in Investee

Cost	Dividends
Ordinary Profit	Depreciation on Excess of Fair
Extraordinary Gain	Market Value Less Book Value
	of Specific Assets
	Permanent Decline in Market Price

Equity in Earnings of Investee

Depreciation	Ordinary Profit

Loss

Permanent Decline	

Extraordinary Gain

	Extraordinary Gain

The investor recognizes percentage ownership interest in the ordinary profit of the investee by debiting investment in investee and crediting equity in earnings of investee.

Extraordinary gain or loss and prior period adjustments are also recognized as shown on the investee's books.

Dividends reduce the investment account.

The excess paid by the investor for the investee's net assets is initially assigned to the specific assets and liabilities and is depreciated. Any remaining portion of the excess is considered goodwill and is subject to a yearly impairment test. Depreciation on the excess value of assets reduces the investment account and is charged to equity in earnings.

A temporary reduction in price of the investment in the investee is *not* recognized. However, a permanent decline in price is recognized by debiting loss and crediting investment in the investee.

Upon sale of the investee's stock, a realized gain or loss is recognized for the difference between the selling price and the cost of the investment.

Interperiod income-tax allocation will take place, because the investor recognizes the investee's profits for book purposes but only dividends for tax reporting. This results in the establishment of an account for deferred income tax liability.

The effect of using the equity method instead of the market value method on previous years at the old percentage of ownership should be recognized as an adjustment to retained earnings and other accounts so affected (e.g., investment in investee).

Footnote disclosures include name of investee, percent owned, investor's accounting policies, and quoted market price.

EXAMPLE 2.12

On 1/1/2014, X Company bought 30,000 shares of AB Company, amounting to a 40% interest in AB's common stock, at $25 per share. Brokerage commissions were $10,000. During 2014, AB's net income was $140,000 and dividends received were $30,000. On 1/1/2015, X Company received 15,000 shares of common stock as a result of a stock split by AB Company. On 1/4/2015, X Company sold 2,000 shares of AB stock at $16 per share. The journal entries follow:

1/1/2014		
Investment in Investee	760,000	
Cash		760,000
12/31/2014		
Investment in Investee	56,000	
Equity in Earnings of Investee		56,000
40% × $140,000 = $56,000		
Cash	30,000	
Investment in Investee		30,000
1/1/2015 Memo entry for stock split		
1/4/2015		
Cash (2,000 × $16)	32,000	
Loss on Sale of Investment	2,940	
Investment in Investee (2,000 × $17.47)		34,940

Balance in Investment in Investee account ($760,000 + $56,000 – $30,000).

$$\frac{\$786,000}{45,000} = \$17.47 \text{ per share}$$

EXAMPLE 2.13

On 1/1/2014, an investor purchased 100,000 shares of XY's 400,000 shares outstanding for $3,000,000. The book value of net assets acquired was $2,500,000. Of the $500,000 excess paid over book value, $300,000 is attributable to undervalued tangible assets and the remainder is attributable to goodwill. The depreciation period is 20 years. In 2014, XY's net income was $800,000, including an extraordinary loss of $200,000. Dividends of $75,000 were paid on June 1, 2014. The following journal entries are necessary for the acquisition of XY stock by the investor, as accounted for under the equity method.

1/1/2014		
Investment in Investee	3,000,000	
Cash		3,000,000
6/1/2014		
Cash	18,750	
Investment in Investee		18,750
25% × $75,000 = $18,750		
12/31/2014		
Investment in Investee	250,000	
Equity in Earnings of Investee		250,000
$1,000,000 × 25% = $250,000		
Extraordinary Loss from Investment	50,000	
Investment in Investee		50,000
$200,000 × 25% = $50,000		
Equity in Earnings of Investee	15,000	
Investment in Investee		15,000
Undervalued depreciable assets $300,000/20		
years		$15,000

FAIR VALUE MEASUREMENTS

ASC 820-10-05 states that a fair value measurement reflects current market participant assumptions about future inflows of the asset and future outflows of the liability. A fair value measurement incorporates the attributes of the particular asset or liability (e.g., location, condition). In formulating fair value, consideration is given to the *exchange price,* which refers to the market price at the measurement date in an *orderly transaction* between the parties to sell the asset or transfer the liability. The focus is on the price that would be received to sell the asset or paid to transfer the liability (exit price), *not* the price that would be paid to buy the asset or received to assume the liability (entry price).

The asset or liability may be by itself (e.g., financial security, operating asset) or a group of assets or liabilities (e.g., asset group, reporting unit).

The Fair Value Hierarchy

A hierarchy list of fair value measurements distinguishes between (1) assumptions based on market data from independent outside sources (observable inputs), and (2) assumptions by the company itself (unobservable inputs). The use of unobservable inputs allows for situations in which there is minimal or no market activity for the asset or liability at the measurement date. Valuation methods used to measure fair value shall maximize the use of observable inputs and minimize the use of unobservable ones.

Risk and Restrictions

An adjustment for risk should be made in a fair value measurement when market participants would include risk in the pricing of the asset or liability. Nonperformance risk of the obligation and the entity's credit risk should be noted. Further, consideration should be given to the effect of a restriction on the sale or use of an asset that impacts its price.

The Difference between the Principal Market and the Most Advantageous Market

In a fair value measurement, we assume that the transaction occurs in the principal (main) market for the asset or liability. This is the market in which the company would sell the asset or transfer the liability with the greatest volume. If a principal market is nonexistent, then the most advantageous market should be used. This is the market in which the business would sell the asset or transfer the liability with the price that maximizes the amount that would be received for the asset or minimizes the amount that would be paid to transfer the liability after taking into account any transaction costs. The fair value measurement should incorporate transportation costs for the asset or liability.

Valuation Approaches

In fair value measurement, valuation techniques based on the market, income, and cost approaches may be used. The *market approach* uses prices for market transactions for identical or comparable assets or liabilities. The *income approach* uses valuation techniques to discount future cash flows to a present value amount. The *cost approach* is based on the current replacement cost such as the cost to buy or build a substitute comparable asset after adjusting for obsolescence. Input availability and reliability related to the asset or liability may impact the choice of the most suitable valuation method.

A single or multiple valuation technique may be needed, depending on the situation. For example, a single valuation method would be used for an asset having quoted market prices in an active market for identical assets. A multiple valuation method would be used to value a reporting unit.

The Three Levels of Fair Value Hierarchy

The fair value hierarchy prioritizes the *inputs* to valuation techniques used to measure fair value into three broad levels. Level 1, the highest priority, assigns quoted prices (unadjusted) in active markets for identical assets or liabilities. Level 3, the lowest priority, is assigned for unobservable inputs for the assets or liabilities.

Level 2 inputs are those except quoted prices included within Level 1 that are observable for the asset or liability, either directly or indirectly. Level 2 inputs include:

- Quoted prices for similar assets or liabilities in active markets
- Quoted prices for similar or identical assets or liabilities in markets that are not active, such as markets with few transactions, noncurrent prices, limited public information, and where price quotations show substantial fluctuation

- Inputs excluding quoted prices that are observable for the asset or liability, such as interest rates observable at often-quoted intervals and credit risks
- Inputs obtained primarily from observable market information by correlation or other means

In the case of Level 3, unobservable inputs are used to measure fair value to the degree that observable inputs are not available. Unobservable inputs reflect the reporting company's own assumptions about what market participants consider (e.g., risk) in pricing the asset or liability.

Disclosures

Quantitative disclosures in a tabular format should be used for fair value measurements in addition to qualitative (narrative) disclosures about the valuation methods. Emphasis should be placed on the inputs used to measure fair value, and the effect of fair value measurements on profit or change in net assets. Any change in valuation techniques should be noted.

FAIR VALUE OPTION FOR FINANCIAL ASSETS AND FINANCIAL LIABILITIES

ASC 825-10 permits business entities to choose to measure most financial instruments and some other items at fair value. The eligible items for the fair value measurement option are:

1. Recognized financial assets and financial liabilities excluding (a) investment in a subsidiary or variable interest entity that must be consolidated, (b) employers' plan obligations or assets for pension and postretirement benefits, (c) financial assets and financial liabilities recognized under leases, (d) financial instruments classified by the issuer as a component of stockholders' equity (e.g., convertible bond with a noncontingent beneficial conversion feature), and (e) deposit liabilities that can be withdrawn on demand of banks
2. Written loan commitment
3. Nonfinancial insurance contracts and warranties that can be settled by the insurer by paying a third party for goods or services

4. Firm commitments applying to financial instruments, such as a forward purchase contract for a loan not readily convertible to cash
5. Host financial instruments arising from separating an embedded nonfinancial derivative instrument from a nonfinancial hybrid instrument

A business may measure eligible items at fair value at specified election dates. Included in earnings at each reporting date are the unrealized (holding) gains and losses on items for which the fair value option has been elected.

The fair value option is irrevocable (except if a new election date occurs) and is applied solely to *entire* instruments (*not* parts of those instruments or specified risks or specific cash flows). The fair value option may be applied in most cases instrument by instrument, including investments otherwise accounted for under the equity method.

Up-front costs and fees associated to items for which the fair value option is chosen are expensed as incurred.

Electing the Fair Value Option

A business entity may select the fair value option for all eligible items only on the date that *one* of these events occurs:

- The company first recognizes the eligible item.
- The company engages in an eligible firm commitment.
- There is a change in the accounting treatment for an investment in another company because the investment becomes subject to the equity method or the investor no longer consolidates a subsidiary because a majority voting interest no longer exists but still retains some ownership interest.
- Specialized accounting treatment no longer applies for the financial assets that have been reported at fair value, such as under an AICPA Audit and Accounting Guide.
- An event that mandates an eligible item to be measured at fair value on the event date but does not require fair value measurement at each later reporting date.

Events

Some events that require remeasurement of eligible items at fair value, initial recognition of eligible items, or both, and thus create an election date for the fair value option, are:

- Business combination
- Consolidation or deconsolidation of a subsidiary or variable interest entity.
- Major debt modification

Instrument Application

The fair value option can be chosen for a single eligible item without electing it for other identical items except in these four cases:

1. If the fair value option is selected for an investment under the equity method, it must be applied to all of the investor's financial interests in the same entity that are eligible items.
2. If the fair value option is selected to an eligible insurance contract, it must be applied to all claims and obligations under the contract.
3. If the fair value option is chosen for an insurance contract for which integrated or nonintegrated contract features or riders are issued at the same time or subsequently, the fair value option must be applied as well to those features or coverage.
4. If multiple advances are made to one borrower under a single contract, such as a construction loan, and the individual advances lose their identity and become part of the larger loan, the fair value option must be applied to the larger loan balance but *not* to the individual advances.

The fair value option typically does not have to be applied to all financial instruments issued or bought in a single transaction. An investor in stocks or bonds, for example, may apply the fair value option to only some of the stock shares or bonds issued or acquired in a single transaction. In this situation, an individual bond is considered the minimum denomination of that debt security. A financial instrument that is a single contract cannot be broken down into parts when using the fair value option. However, a loan syndication may be in multiple loans to the same debtor by different creditors. Each of the loans is a separate instrument, and the fair value option may be selected for some of the loans but not others.

An investor in an equity security can select the fair value option for its entire investment in that security including any fractional shares.

Balance Sheet

Companies must present assets and liabilities measured at the fair value option in a manner that separates those reported fair values from the book (carrying) values of similar assets and liabilities measured with a different measurement attribute. To accomplish this, a company must either:

- Report the aggregate fair value and nonfinancial fair value amounts in the same line items in the balance sheet and in parentheses disclose the amount measured at fair value included in the aggregate amount.
- Report two separate line items to display the fair value and non-fair value carrying amounts.

Statement of Cash Flows

Companies must classify cash receipts and cash payments for items measured at fair value based on their nature and purpose.

Disclosures

Disclosures of fair value are mandated in annual and interim financial statements.

When a balance sheet is presented, these six items must be disclosed:

1. The reasons why the company selected the fair value option for each allowable item or group of similar items.
2. For every line item on the balance sheet that includes an item or items for which the fair value option has been chosen, management must provide information on how each line item relates to major asset and liability categories. Further, management must provide the aggregate carrying amount of items included in each line item that are *not* eligible for the fair value option.
3. When the fair value option is selected for some but not all eligible items within a group of similar items, management must describe those similar items and the reasons for partial election. Further, information must be provided so that financial statement users can understand how the group of similar items applies to individual line items on the balance sheet.
4. Disclosure should be made of investments that would have been reported under the equity method if the company did not elect the fair value option.
5. The difference between the aggregate fair value and the aggregate unpaid principal balance of loans, long-term receivables, and long-term debt instruments with contractual principal amounts for which the fair value option has been chosen must be disclosed.

6. In the case of loans held as assets for which the fair value option has been selected, management should disclose the aggregate fair value of loans past due by ninety days or more. If the company recognizes interest revenue separately from other changes in fair value, disclosure should be made of the aggregate fair value of loans in the nonaccrual status. Disclosure should also be made of the difference between the aggregate fair value and aggregate unpaid principal balance for loans that are ninety days or more past due and/or in nonaccrual status.

When an income statement is presented, four items must be disclosed:

1. How dividends and interest are measured and where they are reported in the income statement
2. Gains and losses from changes in fair value included in profit and where they are shown
3. For loans and other receivables, the estimated amount of gains and losses (including how they were calculated) included in earnings applicable to changes in instrument-specific credit risk
4. For liabilities with fair values that have been significantly impacted by changes in the instrument-specific credit risk, the estimated amount of gains and losses from fair value changes (including how they were calculated) related to changes in such credit risk, and the reasons for those changes

Other disclosures include the methods and assumptions used in fair value estimation. Qualitative information concerning the nature of the event as well as quantitative information, including the impact on earnings of initially electing the fair value option for an item, should also be disclosed.

Eligible Items at Effective Date

A company may elect the fair value option for eligible items at the effective date. The difference between the book (carrying) value and the fair value of eligible items related for the fair value option at the effective date must be removed from the balance sheet and included in the cumulative-effect adjustment. These differences include (1) valuation allowances (e.g., loan loss reserves); (2) unamortized deferred costs, fees, discounts, and premiums; and (3) accrued interest associated with the fair value of the eligible item.

A company that selects the fair value option for items at the effective date must provide in financial statements these five points, including their effective dates:

1. Reasons for choosing the fair value option for each existing *eligible* item or group of similar items.
2. Amount of valuation allowances removed from the balance sheet because they applied to items for which the fair value option was selected.
3. Impact on deferred tax assets and liabilities of selecting the fair value option.
4. If the fair value option is chosen for some but not all eligible items within a group of similar eligible items, there should be a description of similar items and the reasons for the partial election. Further, information should be provided so financial statement users can understand how the group of similar items applies to individual items on the balance sheet.
5. Schedule presenting by line items in the balance sheet:
   (a) Before-tax portion of the cumulative-effect adjustment to retained earnings for the items on that line
   (b) Fair value at the effective date of eligible items for which the fair value option is selected and the book (carrying) amounts of those same items immediately before opting for the fair value option

Available-for-Sale and Held-to-Maturity Securities

Available-for-sale and held-to-maturity securities held at the effective date are eligible for the fair value option at that date. In the event that the fair value option is selected for any of those securities at the effective date, cumulative holding (unrealized) gains and losses must be included in the cumulative-effect adjustment. Separate disclosure must be made of the holding gains and losses reclassified from accumulated other comprehensive income (for available-for-sale securities) and holding gains and losses previously unrecognized (for held-to-maturity securities).

LEASES

According to ASC 840-10, the lessee obtains the right to use property owned by the lessor. Even though there is no legal transfer of title, many leases transfer substantially all the risks and benefits of ownership. These leases are called capital leases. Since substance governs over legal form in accounting, the lessee records an asset and a liability for a capital lease.

Lessee

The lessee may account for a lease using either the operating method or the capital method, depending on the nature of the agreement.

An *operating lease* is a regular rental of property. When rent payments are made, rent expense is debited and cash is credited. Nothing is reported on the lessee's balance sheet.

A *capital lease* occurs if any *one* of the following four criteria is satisfied:

1. The lessee obtains ownership of the property at the end of the lease term.
2. A bargain purchase option exists.
3. The life of the lease is 75% or more of the life of the property.
4. The present value of minimum lease payments at the start of the lease equals or exceeds 90% of the fair market value of the property. Minimum lease payments exclude executory costs to be paid by the lessor such as maintenance, insurance, and property taxes.

If criterion 1 or 2 is met, the depreciation period is the life of the property. If criterion 3 or 4 is satisfied, the depreciation period is the life of the lease.

The asset and liability are recorded at the discounted value of the minimum lease payments plus the present value of any bargain purchase option. If the total present value of the payments and bargain purchase option exceeds the fair value of the leased property, the asset must be shown at its fair market value.

The discount rate used by the lessee is the *lower* of the lessee's incremental borrowing rate or the lessor's implicit rate.

The liability is classified as either current or noncurrent.

Each minimum lease payment is allocated as a reduction of principal (debiting the liability) and as interest (debiting interest expense). Interest expense equals the discount (interest) rate times the book value of the liability at the beginning of the year.

A capital lease is shown in the balance sheet in the account "asset under lease" less accumulated depreciation. The income statement presents interest expense and depreciation expense.

EXAMPLE 2.14

On 1/1/2014, the lessee enters into a capital lease for property. The minimum rental payment is $20,000 a year for six years to be made at year-end. The interest rate is 5%. The present value of an ordinary annuity factor for $n = 6$, $i = 5\%$ is 5.0757. The journal entries for the first two years are:

1/1/2014		
Asset	101,514	
Liability		101,514
12/31/2014		
Interest Expense	5,076	
Liability	14,924	
Cash		20,000
$5\% \times \$101,514 = \$5,076$		
Depreciation	16,919	
Accumulated Depreciation		16,919

$$\frac{\$101,514}{6} = \$16,919$$

The liability as of 12/31/2014 is:

Liability			
12/31/2014	14,924	1/1/2014	101,514
		12/31/2014	86,590

12/31/2014		
Interest Expense	4,330	
Liability	15,670	
Cash		20,000
$5\% \times \$86,590 = \$4,330$		
Depreciation	16,919	
Accumulated Depreciation		16,919

Footnote disclosures under a capital lease include:

- Assets leased by category.
- Future minimum lease payments in total and for each of the next five years.
- Contingent rentals [rentals based on factors other than time (e.g., sales)].
- Sublease rentals.
- Description of the leasing agreement.

Lessor

The three methods that may be used by the lessor, depending on the terms of the agreement, are operating, direct financing, and sales-type.

Operating Method. This involves a regular rental by the lessor. The lessor records rental revenue less related expenses (e.g., depreciation, maintenance). *Initial direct costs* are deferred and amortized over the lease term on a proportionate basis, depending on rental income recognized. The lessor *retains* the asset under lease less accumulated depreciation in the balance sheet.

Direct Financing Method. In order for this method to be used, one of the four criteria for a capital lease by the lessee must be met, plus *both* of the following two criteria for the lessor:

- Collectibility of lease payments is assured.
- No material uncertainties surround the future costs to be incurred.

The lessor is not a manufacturer or dealer. The lessor *buys* the property to lease it out for a return (e.g., a bank leasing computers). The lessor uses as the discount rate the interest rate implicit in the lease considering the rate of return the lessor earns.

Interest income is recognized in the financial statements over the life of the lease. Interest income equals the interest rate times the present value of the receivable at the beginning of the year. Contingent rentals are accrued as earned. Initial direct costs (e.g., legal fees, commissions) of the lease are charged to the gross receivable. The following is presented on the balance sheet of the lessor:

> Lease Payments Receivable (Principal + Interest)
> Less: Unearned Interest Revenue (Interest)
> Net Receivable Balance (Principal)
> The presentation on the income statement is:
> Interest Revenue
> Less: Initial Direct Costs
> Net Income from leasing activity

Footnote disclosure includes:

- Assets leased by category.
- Future lease payments in total and for each of the next five years.
- Contingent rentals.
- Lease provisions.

Sales-Type Method

The same criteria identify leases that must use either the sales-type method or the direct financing method. The difference is that the sales-type method involves a lessor that is a manufacturer of or a dealer in the leased item. Hence, a manufacturer or dealer profit arises. Although legally there is no sale, substance once again dominates over legal form, and a sale is recognized. *Note:* The distinction between a sales-type lease and a direct financing lease affects only the lessor; for the lessee either type would be a capital lease.

In a sales-type lease, profit on the assumed sale of the item is recognized in the year of lease. Further, interest income is recognized over the life of the lease. The cost of the leased property is matched against the sales price in determining the profit in the year the lease is initiated. Initial direct costs of the lease are expensed.

Except for the initial entry to record the lease, the entries are the same for both the direct financing and the sales-type methods.

EXAMPLE 2.15

Assume the same facts as in the capital lease example on page 73. The accounting by the lessor assuming a direct financing lease and a sales-type lease is as follows:

	Direct Financing		*Sales-Type*		
1/1/2014					
Receivable	120,000		Receivable	120,000	
Asset		101,514	Cost of Sales	85,000	
Unearned					
Interest					
Revenue		18,486	Inventory		85,000
			Sales		101,514
			Unearned		
			Interest		
			Revenue		18,486

	Direct Financing		Sales-Type
12/31/2014			
Cash	20,000		
Receivable		20,000	
Unearned			
Interest			
Revenue	5,076		
Interest			
Revenue		5,076	
12/31/2015			
Cash	20,000		
Receivable		20,000	
Unearned			
Interest			
Revenue	4,330		
Interest			
Revenue		4,330	

The income statement for 2014 presents:

Interest Revenue $101,514	$5,076	Sales	
		Less: Cost of Sales	85,000
		Gross Profit	$
16,514			
		Interest Revenue	5,076

EXAMPLE 2.16

Jones leased equipment to Tape Company on October 1, 2014. It is a capital lease to the lessee and a sales-type lease to the lessor. The lease is for eight years with equal annual payments of $500,000 due on October 1 of each year. The first payment was made on October 1, 2014. The cost of the equipment to Tape Company is $2,500,000. The equipment has a life of 10 years with no salvage value. The appropriate interest rate is 10%.

Tape reports the following in its income statement for 2014:

Asset Cost ($500,000 × 5.868 = $2,934,000)

Depreciation	$\dfrac{\$2,934,000}{10} \times \dfrac{3}{12}$		$ 73,350

Interest Expense:

Present value of lease payments	$2,934,000
Less: Initial payment	500,000
Balance	$2,434,000

Interest Expense $2,434,000 × 10% × $\dfrac{3}{12}$	$ 60,850
Total Expenses	$134,200

Jones's income before tax is:

Interest revenue		$ 60,850
Gross profit on assumed sale of property:		
Selling price	$2,934,000	
Less: Cost	2,500,000	
Gross Profit		434,000
Income before tax		$494,850

The profit on the sale is deferred and amortized as an adjustment in proportion to depreciation expense in a capital lease, or in proportion to rental expense in an operating lease. But in the event the fair value of the property at the time of the sale-leaseback is less than book value, a loss is immediately recognized for the difference between book value and fair value.

Sale-Leaseback Arrangement

In a sale-leaseback, the lessor sells the property and then leases it back. Lessors may decide to do this when they need funds.

EXAMPLE 2.17

The deferred profit on a sale-leaseback is $50,000. An operating lease is involved. Rental expense in the current year is $10,000, and total rental expense is $150,000. Rental expense is adjusted as follows:

Rental Expense before adjustment	$10,000
Less: Amortization of deferred gross profit	
$50,000 \times \dfrac{\$10,000}{\$150,000}$	3,333
Rental Expense as adjusted	$ 6,667

PENSION PLANS

A company is not required to have a pension plan. If it does, the firm must conform to rules regarding the accounting and reporting for the pension plan. Accounting for pension costs must be done on the accrual basis. Pension expense is reflected in the service periods using a method that considers the benefit formula of the plan. On the income statement, pension expense is presented as a single amount. The pension plan relationship between the employer, trustee, and employee is depicted in Figure 2-1.

Figure 2-1.
Pension Plan Relationship

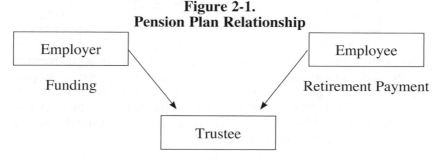

Pension Plan Assets on Books of Trustee

Pension accounting is divided and treated separately between the employer's accounting and the accounting for the pension fund. The employer incurs the cost and makes contributions to the pension fund. The fund (plan) is the entity that receives the contributions, administers pension assets, and makes benefit payments to retirees. The assets and liabilities of a pension plan are not included in the employer's financial statements. The pension fund is a separate legal and accounting entity.

The two types of pension plans are:

1. *Defined contribution.* In a defined contribution plan, the employer's annual contribution amount is specified, not the benefits to be paid.

2. *Defined benefit.* In a defined benefit plan, the determinable pension benefit to be received by participants upon retirement is specified. The employer has to provide plan contributions so that sufficient assets are accumulated to pay for the benefits when due. Typically, an annuity of payments is made.

The following pension plan terminology should be understood:

- *Actuarial assumptions.* Actuaries make assumptions as to variables in determining pension expense and related funding. Examples are mortality rate, employee turnover, compensation levels, and rate of return.
- *Actuarial cost (funding) method.* This method is used by actuaries in determining the employer contribution to ensure that sufficient funds will be available at employee retirement. The method used determines the pension expense and related liability.
- *Actuarial present value of accumulated plan benefits.* This is the discounted amount of money that would be required to satisfy retirement obligations for active and retired employees.
- *Benefit information date.* This is the date the actuarial present value of accumulated benefits is presented.
- *Vested benefits.* An employee vests when he or she has accumulated pension rights to receive benefits upon retirement. The employee no longer has to remain in the company to receive pension benefits.
- *Projected benefit obligation.* This is the year-end pension obligation based on future salaries. It is the actuarial present value of vested and nonvested benefits for services performed before a particular actuarial valuation date based on expected future salaries. It measures the deferred compensation amount.
- *Accumulated benefit obligation.* This is the year-end obligation based on current salaries. It is the actuarial present value of benefits (vested and nonvested) attributable to the pension plan based on services performed before a specified date, based on current salary levels.
- *Net assets available for pension benefits.* This represents plan assets less plan liabilities. The plan's liabilities exclude participants' accumulated benefits.

Defined Contribution Pension Plan

- Pension expense equals the employer's cash contribution for the year. There is no deferred charge or deferred credit arising.
- If the defined contribution plan stipulates that contributions are to be made for years subsequent to an employee's rendering of

services (e.g., after retirement), there should be an accrual of costs during the employee's service period.

Footnote disclosure includes:

- Description of plan including employee groups covered
- Basis of determining contributions
- Nature and effect of items affecting interperiod comparability
- Cost recognized for the period

Defined Benefit Pension Plan

Pension accounting is segregated between the employer's accounting and the accounting for the pension fund. The employer incurs the cost and makes contributions to the pension fund. The fund (plan) is the entity that receives the contributions, administers plan assets, and makes benefit payments to retirees. The assets and liabilities of a pension plan are *not* included in the employer's financial statements. The pension fund is a distinct legal and accounting entity.

Elements of Pension Expense

The components of pension expense in a defined benefit pension plan are:

- Service cost
- Amortization of prior service cost
- Return on plan assets (reduces pension expense)
- Interest on projected benefit obligation
- Amortization of actuarial gain or loss (gain reduces pension expense but loss increases pension expense)

Service cost is based on the present value of future payments under the benefit formula for employee services of the current period. It is recognized in full in the current year. The calculation involves actuarial assumptions.

The company must incorporate future salary levels in measuring pension expense and the present obligation if the plan benefit includes them. The benefits/years-of-service actuarial method, which computes pension expense based on future compensation levels, should be used. The employer must fund at a minimum the annual service cost.

Prior service cost is the pension expense applicable to services rendered before the adoption or amendment date of a pension plan. The cost of the retroactive benefits is the increase in the projected benefit obligation at the date of amendment. It involves the allocation of amounts of cost to future service years. Prior service cost determination involves actuarial considerations.

Amortization is accomplished by assigning an equal amount to each service year of active employees as of the amendment date who are expected to receive plan benefits. The amortization of prior service takes into account:

- Future service years
- Change in the projected benefit obligation
- Period employees will receive benefits
- Decrement in employees receiving benefits each year

"Other comprehensive income" is adjusted when amortizing prior service cost. Amortization of prior service cost typically increases pension expense.

The employer recognizes prior service cost as a component of pension expense over the remaining service lives of employees. A three-step years-of-service amortization method is preferred:

1. The total number of service years to be worked by eligible participants is calculated.
2. Prior service cost is divided by the total number of service years to compute a cost per service year (unit cost).
3. The number of service years each year is multiplied by the cost per service year to compute the annual amortization charge.

Companies can also use the straight-line method of amortization in which prior service cost is amortized over the average remaining service life of employees.

Prior service cost is reported as a component of "accumulated other comprehensive income" in the stockholders' equity section of the balance sheet.

EXAMPLE 2.18

On 1/1/2014, a company modifies its pension plan and grants $200,000 of prior service cost to employees. The workers are expected to provide 5,000 service years in the future with 250 service years in 2014. The amortization of prior service cost for the year 2014 is:

Cost per service year = $200,000/5,000 = $40
2014 amortization = 250 × $40 = $10,000

The return on plan assets (e.g., stocks, bonds) reduces pension expense. Plan assets are valued at the moving average of asset values for the accounting period.

The annual pension expense is adjusted for dividends and interest earned by the pension fund in addition to the appreciation or decline in the market value of plan assets.

Pension assets are increased from employer contributions and actual returns, but pension assets are decreased from benefit payments to retirees. Actual return on plan assets increases the fund balance and reduces the net cost to provide workers' pension benefits. Using assumed numbers, actual return on plan assets is calculated as:

Fair market value of plan assets – beginning of year	$600,000
Add: Contributions	80,000
Less: Benefit payments	(30,000)
Add: Actual return	?
Fair market value of plan assets—end of year	$725,000

Actual return must be $75,000 (the missing number).

Interest is on the projected benefit obligation at the beginning of the year. The settlement rate, representing the rate that pension benefits could be settled for, is employed.

Interest = Interest Rate × Projected Benefit
Obligation at the beginning of the year

In determining the settlement rate, consideration is given to the return rate on high-quality fixed-income investments whose cash flows match the amount and timing of the expected benefit obligations.

Actuarial gain and loss represents the difference between estimates and actual experience. For example, if the assumed interest rate is 10% and the actual interest rate is 12%, an actuarial gain results.

There may also be a change in actuarial assumptions regarding the future. Actuarial gains and losses are deferred and amortized as an adjustment to pension expense over future years. Actuarial gains and losses related to a single event not related to the pension plan and not in the ordinary course of business are immediately recognized in the current year's income statement. Examples are plant closing and segment disposal.

Gains and losses are changes in the amount of either the projected benefit obligation (PBO) or pension plan assets because of experience different from that assumed from changes in assumptions. Gains and losses that are not recognized immediately as a component of pension expense shall be recognized as increases or decreases, respectively, in "other comprehensive income" as they arise.

An Asset or Liability Gain or Loss

An asset gain or loss occurs on plan assets when the expected return is different from the actual return.

> Asset gain = Actual return > Expected return
> Asset loss = Actual return < Expected return

A liability gain or loss occurs when actuarial assumptions differ from actual experiences related to the computation of the projected benefit obligation.

> Liability gain = unexpected decrease in the PBO
> Liability loss = unexpected increase in the PBO

Asset gains and losses are combined with liability gains and losses to derive a net gain or loss, respectively. Net gain or loss is the change in the fair market value of plan assets and the amount of change in the projected benefit obligation.

The Corridor Method

Asset gains and losses and liability gains and losses offset each other. The corridor method is used to amortize the "accumulated other comprehensive income" account balance when it becomes excessive. There is a limit of 10% of the greater of the beginning balances of the market-related value of plan assets or the projected benefit obligation. Above the 10% limit, the "accumulated other comprehensive income" account related to gain and loss is too large and must be amortized. For example, if the projected benefit obligation and market-related asset value are $800,000 and $650,000, respectively, the corridor equals $80,000 (10% × $800,000). Any amount exceeding $80,000 would be amortized; if the "accumulated other comprehensive income" account balance was $120,000, the amount to be amortized would be $40,000 ($120,000 − $80,000). However, if the "accumulated other comprehensive income" account had a balance of $80,000 or less, *no* amortization is required.

If amortization is required, the minimum amortization is the excess ($40,000) divided by the average remaining service years of active employees to receive benefits. Assuming a 40-year service life, the amortization for the year would be $1,000 ($40,000/40 years).

The amortization of a loss increases pension expense while the amortization of a gain reduces it.

Pension Expense Differs from the Amount Funded

If Pension Expense > Cash Paid = Pension Liability
If Pension Expense < Cash Paid = Pension Asset

The Financial Statement Presentation

The change in the fair market value of pension plan assets equals:

Fair market value of plan assets — beginning of year
Plus: Actual return on plan assets
Plus: Contributions
Minus: Benefit payments
Fair market value of plan assets — end of year

The change in the projected benefit obligation equals:

Projected benefit obligation — beginning of year
Plus: Service cost
Plus: Interest cost
Plus: Amendments (prior service cost)
Plus: Actuarial loss
Minus: Benefit payments
Projected benefit obligation — end of year

The employer must measure the funded status (assets and liabilities) of a plan at its fiscal year-end date used for financial reporting.

The net funded status must be recognized on the balance sheet. If the projected benefit obligation exceeds the fair market value of plan assets, the plan is underfunded and there will be a pension liability. If the fair market value of plan assets exceeds the projected benefit obligation, the plan is overfunded and there will be a pension asset.

There should be an aggregation of the statuses of all overfunded plans, and the amount should be presented as a noncurrent asset. (*Note:* No part of a pension asset is reported as a current asset because the pension plan assets are restricted.) There should be an aggregation of the statuses of all underfunded plans, and the amount should be presented as a liability. The liability for an underfunded plan can be classified as a current liability, noncurrent liability, or a combination of both. The current portion is the amount by which the actuarial present value of benefits included in the benefit obligation payable within the year exceeds the fair market value of plan assets.

All overfunded plans should be combined and presented as a pension plan asset. Similarly, all underfunded plans should be combined and presented as a pension plan liability. It is *not* allowed to combine all plans and show a net amount as a single net asset or net liability.

Footnote Disclosure

Footnote disclosure for a pension plan includes:

- Description of plan including benefit formula, funding policy, employee groups covered, and retirement age
- Components of pension expense
- Pension assumptions (e.g., interest rate, mortality rate, employee turnover)
- Present value of vested and nonvested benefits
- Weighted-average assumed discount rate involved in measuring the projected benefit obligation
- Weighted-average return rate on pension plan assets
- Amounts and types of securities included in pension plan assets
- Amount of approximate annuity benefits to employees
- Investment policy, strategies, and objectives
- Measurement dates
- Risk management practices
- Unallowable investments in the pension plan such as certain derivatives
- Benefits expected to be paid
- Expected contributions
- Rates of compensation increase
- Nature and amount of changes in pension plan assets and benefit obligations recognized in net income and in "other comprehensive income"
- Amortization method used for the excess of the "accumulated other comprehensive income" balance over the corridor amount
- Reconciliation of how the fair market value of plan assets and the projected benefit obligation changed from the beginning to end of year

Settlement in a Pension Plan

A settlement is discharging some or all of the employer's pension benefit obligation. A settlement must satisfy all of the following criteria:

- It is irrevocable.
- It relieves pension benefit responsibility.
- It materially curtails risk related to the pension obligation.

Excess plan assets may revert back to the employer. The amount of gain or loss recognized in the income statement when a pension obligation is settled is limited to the unrecognized net gain or loss from realized or unrealized changes in either the pension benefit obligation or plan assets. Changes arise when actual experiences deviate from the original assumptions. All or a pro rata share of the unrecognized gain or loss is recognized when a plan is settled.

If full settlement occurs, all unrecognized gains or losses are recognized.

If only a part of the plan is settled, a pro rata share of the unrecognized net gain or loss is recognized.

EXAMPLE: When the employer furnishes employees with a lump-sum amount to give up pension rights, the gain or loss resulting is included in the current year's income statement.

A curtailment occurs when an event significantly reduces the future service years of present employees or eliminates for most employees the accumulation of defined benefits for future services. EXAMPLE: A plant closing ends employee services prior to pension plan expectations.

The gain or loss is recognized in the current year's income statement and contains these elements:

- Prior service cost attributable to employee services no longer needed
- Change in pension benefit obligation due to the curtailment

The projected benefit obligation may be decreased (a gain) or increased (a loss) by a curtailment. To the extent that such a gain (loss) exceeds any net loss (gain) included in "accumulated other comprehensive income," it is a curtailment gain.

The amount of net periodic benefit cost should include the gain or loss recognized because of settlements or curtailments.

Termination in a Pension Plan

When termination benefits are offered by the employer, accepted by employees, and the amount can reasonably be determined:

- An expense and liability are recognized.
- The amount of the accrual equals the down payment plus the present value of future payments to be made by the employer.
- The entry is to debit loss and credit cash (down payment) and liability (future payments).
- Footnote disclosure of the arrangement should be made.

Trustee Reporting for a Defined Benefit Pension Plan

We discuss the reporting and disclosures by the trustee of a defined benefit pension plan. Generally accepted accounting principles (GAAP) must be followed. Financial statements are not required to be issued by the plan. If they are issued, reporting guidelines have to be followed. The prime objective is to assess the plan's capability to meet retirement benefits.

Balance Sheet

Present *pension assets and liabilities* as an offset. Operating assets are at book value. In determining net assets available, accrual accounting is followed. EXAMPLE: Accruing for interest earned but not received. *Investments* are shown at fair market value. An asset shown is "contributions receivable due from employer." In computing pension plan liability, the participants' accumulated benefits are *excluded*. In effect, plan participants are equity holders rather than creditors of the plan.

Disclosure is required of:

- Net assets available for benefits
- Changes in net assets available for benefits, including net appreciation in fair value of each major class of investments
- Actuarial present value of accumulated plan benefits (i.e., benefits anticipated to be paid to retired employees, beneficiaries, and present employees)
- Changes in actuarial present value of accumulated plan benefits
- Description of the plan including amendments
- Accounting and funding policies

OTHER POSTRETIREMENT BENEFITS

The major differences between pension benefits versus postretirement benefits are:

- Pension benefits are typically funded while postretirement benefits are not.
- Pension benefits are well-defined within a level dollar amount while postretirement benefits are usually uncapped and show significant fluctuation.

ASC 715-60 applies to the employer's accounting and reporting for postretirement benefits other than pensions: (1) health care and welfare, and (2) life insurance. These benefits are accrued as employee services are rendered. Under the defined contribution plan, the amount contributed yearly is presented as a postretirement benefits expense. However, under the defined benefit plan, the amount contributed for the year will probably differ from the expense.

The postretirement benefit cost is based on actuarial determinations, and the benefits are allocated over the service periods of employees who will obtain them. Such benefits must be fully accrued by the date that the employee attains full eligibility, even if the employee is expected to continue working beyond that date.

Postretirement benefits for current and future retirees constitute deferred compensation. The time period the postretirement benefits accrue is called the *attribution period.*

The *accumulated postretirement benefit obligation (APBO)* is the actuarial present value of future benefits assigned to employees' services performed to a particular date. The *expected postretirement benefit obligation (EPBO)* is the actuarial present value as of a specified date of all benefits the employer expects to pay after retirement to workers, their beneficiaries, or covered dependents. The APBO equals the EPBO for retirees and active employees fully eligible for benefits at the end of the attribution period. Before full eligibility is reached, the APBO is a part of the EPBO. Therefore, the difference between the APBO and the EPBO is the future service costs of active employees who are not yet fully eligible.

Footnote disclosures include a description of the plan, types of benefits provided, components of postretirement expense, cost trend factors in health care, trend in compensation, fair market value of plan assets, accumulated postretirement benefit obligations, funding policy, return on plan assets, and the impact of a one-percentage-point increase in trend rates.

INCOME TAX ACCOUNTING

ASC 740-10 deals with income tax allocation. Temporary differences occur between book income and taxable income. The deferred tax liability or asset is measured at the tax rate under *current* law that will exist in the future year(s) when the temporary difference reverses. Further, the deferred tax liability or asset has to be adjusted for changes in tax law or in tax rate. Consequently, the *liability method* must be used to account for deferred income taxes. Comprehensive deferred tax accounting is followed. Tax expense equals taxes payable plus the tax effects of all temporary differences.

Interperiod tax allocation is used to account for temporary differences affecting the current year's results. Tax effects of *future* events should be reflected in the year they take place. It is improper to anticipate them and recognize a deferred tax liability or asset in the current year.

Temporary Differences

Temporary differences result from four types of transactions, as described below.

1. Revenue includable on the tax return after being reported on the financial records (e.g., installment sales).
2. Expenses deductible on the tax return after being deducted on the financial records (e.g., warranty provision).
3. Revenue includable on the tax return before being recorded in the financial records (e.g., subscriptions received in advance.)
4. Expenses deductible on the tax return before being deducted on the financial records (e.g., accelerated depreciation).

Disclosure should be made of the various type of temporary differences.

In the event that the tax rates are graduated based on taxable income, aggregate calculations may be made using an estimated average rate.

Permanent Differences

Permanent differences do not reverse and therefore do not require tax allocation. Examples are penalties and fines, which are not tax deductible, and interest on municipal bonds, which is not taxable.

Financial Statement Presentation

Deferred charges and deferred credits must be offset and presented (a) net current and (b) net noncurrent. Deferred tax assets or liabilities are classified according to the related asset or liability they apply to. For example, a deferred tax liability arising from depreciation on a fixed asset would be noncurrent. Deferred taxes not related to specific assets or liabilities are classified as current or noncurrent depending on the anticipated reversal dates of the temporary differences. Temporary differences reversing within one year are current, while those reversing after one year are noncurrent.

Intraperiod Tax Allocation

Intraperiod tax allocation occurs when tax expense is presented in different parts of the financial statements for the current year. The income statement shows the tax effect of income from continuing operations, of income from discontinued operations, of extraordinary items, and of the cumulative effect of a change in accounting principle. In the statement of retained earnings, prior-period adjustments are presented net of tax.

Net Operations Loss Carrybacks and Carryforwards

Tax effects of net operating *loss carrybacks* are allocated to the loss period. A company may carry back a net operating loss for two years and obtain a refund for taxes paid in those years. The loss is first applied to the earliest year; any remaining loss is carried forward up to 20 years.

A loss carryforward may be recognized to the extent that there exist net taxable amounts in the carryforward period (deferred tax liabilities) to absorb them. A loss carryforward benefit may also be recognized if there is more than a 50% probability of future realization.

Disclosure should be made of the amounts and expiration dates of operating-loss carryforwards.

Deferred Tax Liability vs. Deferred Tax Asset

If book income exceeds taxable income, then tax expense exceeds tax payable, resulting in a deferred tax credit. If book income is less than taxable income, then tax expense is less than tax payable, resulting in a deferred tax charge.

EXAMPLE 2.19

Assume that book income and taxable income are both $1,000. Depreciation for book purposes is $50, based on the straight-line method, and $100 for tax purposes, based on the accelerated cost recovery system. Assuming a tax rate of 34%, the entry is:

Income Tax Expense ($950 × 34%)	323	
Income Tax Payable ($900 × 34%)		306
Deferred Tax Liability		17

At the end of the asset's life, the deferred tax liability of $17 will be fully reversed.

A deferred tax asset may be recognized when it is more likely than not that the tax benefit will be realized in the future. The phrase "more likely than not" means at least slightly more than a 50% likelihood of occurring. The deferred tax asset must be reduced by a valuation allowance if it is more likely than not that some or all of the deferred tax asset will not be realized. The net amount is the amount likely to be realized. The deferred tax asset would be presented in the balance sheet as shown below, assuming a temporary difference of $100,000, tax rate of 40%, and $70,000 of the tax benefit has a probability in excess of 50% of being realized.

Deferred Tax Asset (gross) $100,000 × 40%	40,000
Less: Valuation Allowance $30,000 × 40%	12,000
Deferred Tax Asset (net) $70,000 × 40%	28,000

EXAMPLE 2.20

In 2014, a company sold a fixed asset and reported a gain of $70,000 for book purposes, which was deferred for tax purposes (installment method) until 2015. In addition, in 2014, $40,000 of subscription income was received in advance. The income was recognized for tax purposes in 2014 but was deferred for book purposes until 2015.

The deferred tax asset may be recorded, since the deductible amount in the future ($40,000) offsets the taxable amount ($70,000). Assuming a 34% tax rate and income taxes payable of $100,000, the entry in 2014 is:

Income Tax Expense	110,200	
Deferred Tax Asset ($40,000 × 34%)	13,600	
Deferred Tax Liability ($70,000 × 34%)		23,800
Income Taxes Payable		100,000

A deferred tax asset can also be recognized for the tax benefit of deductible amounts realizable by carrying back a loss from future years to reduce taxes paid in the current or a prior year.

Tax Rates

Deferred taxes are reported at the amounts of settlement when the temporary differences reverse.

EXAMPLE 2.21

Assume in 2012 a cumulative temporary difference of $200,000 that will reverse in the future, generating the following taxable amounts and tax rate:

	2013	2014	2015	Total
Reversals	$60,000	$90,000	$50,000	$200,000
Tax rate	× .34	× .30	× .25	
Deferred tax liability	$20,400	$27,000	$12,500	$ 59,900

On December 31, 2012, the deferred tax liability is recorded at $59,900.

A change in tax rate must immediately be accounted for by adjusting tax expense and deferred tax.

EXAMPLE 2.22

Assume that at the end of 2011, a law is passed reducing the tax rate from 34% to 30% starting in 2013. In 2011, Company XY made a deferred profit of $100,000 and showed a deferred tax liability of $34,000. The gross profit is to be reflected equally in 2012, 2013, 2014, and 2015. Thus, the deferred tax liability at the end of 2011 is $31,000, as shown below:

	2012	2013	2014	2015	Total
Reversals	$25,000	$25,000	$25,000	$25,000	
Tax rate	× .34	× .30	× .30	× .30	
Deferred tax liability	$ 8,500	$ 7,500	$ 7,500	$ 7,500	$ 31,000

The appropriate entry in 2011 is:

Deferred Tax Liability	3,000	
Income Tax Expense		3,000

Indefinite Reversal

No interperiod tax allocation is required in the case of indefinite reversal. Indefinite reversal is when undistributed earnings of a foreign subsidiary will indefinitely be postponed as to remission back to the United States or when earnings will be remitted in a tax-free liquidation. If a change in circumstances occurs and the assumption of indefinite reversal is no longer valid, tax expense should be adjusted. Disclosure should be made not only of the declaration to reinvest indefinitely or to remit tax free, but also of the cumulative amount of undistributed earnings.

FOREIGN CURRENCY TRANSLATION AND TRANSACTIONS

ASC 830-20 covers the translation of foreign currency statements and the gain and loss on foreign currency transactions. Generally, foreign currency statements should be translated based on the exchange rate at the end of the reporting year. Translation gains and losses are presented as a separate item in the stockholders' equity section.

Also important is the accounting treatment of gains and losses resulting from transactions denominated in a foreign currency. These are presented separately in the current year's income statement.

There are four key terms in this area:

- *Exchange Rate.* The ratio between a unit of one currency and that of another at a particular time.
- *Foreign Currency.* A currency other than the U.S. dollar.
- *Foreign Currency Transaction.* A transaction whose terms are denominated in a foreign currency. For example, a foreign currency transaction may occur when a business buys or sells on credit goods or services that are priced in foreign currency. Another example is when a company borrows or lends funds, and the amounts payable or receivable are denominated in foreign currency.
- *Foreign Currency Translation.* Expressing in the reporting currency (U.S. dollars) of the company those amounts that are denominated in a foreign currency. An example is the translation of the financial statements of a U.S. company's foreign subsidiary from the foreign currency to U.S. dollars.

In the translation of the balance sheet, assets and liabilities are translated at the *current exchange rate* (rate at the balance sheet date). Income statement items are translated at the *weighted-average exchange rate* for the year.

A material change in the exchange rate occurring between the date of the financial statements and the audit report date should be disclosed as a subsequent event.

There are two steps in translating the foreign country's financial statements into U.S. reporting requirements:

- Conform the foreign country's financial statements to U.S. GAAP.
- Convert the foreign currency into U.S. dollars (reporting currency).

EXAMPLE 2.23

An exchange gain or loss occurs when the exchange rate changes between the purchase date and sale date.

Merchandise is bought for 100,000 euros. The exchange rate is 0.77 euros to one dollar. The journal entry is:

Purchases	$129,870	
Accounts Payable		$129,870
100,000/0.77 = $129,870		

When the merchandise is paid for, the exchange rate is 0.8 to one. The journal entry is:

Accounts Payable	$129,870	
Cash		$125,000
Foreign Exchange Gain		$ 4,870

Thus, $125,000, using an exchange rate of 0.8 to one, can buy 100,000 euros. The transaction gain is the difference between the cash required of $125,000 and the initial liability of $129,870.

Note: A foreign transaction gain or loss has to be determined at each balance sheet date on all recorded foreign transactions that have not been settled.

EXAMPLE 2.24

A U.S. company sells goods to a customer in England on 11/15/2014 for £10,000 (British pounds sterling). The exchange rate is £1 to US $.75. Thus, the transaction is worth $7,500 (10,000 pounds × .75). Payment is due two months later. The entry on 11/15/2014 is:

Accounts Receivable—England	$7,500	
Sales		$7,500

Accounts receivable and sales are measured in U.S. dollars employing the spot rate on the transaction date. Even though the accounts receivable amount is measured and reported in U.S. dollars, the receivable is fixed in pounds. Thus, a transaction gain or loss can occur if the exchange rate changes between the transaction date (11/15/2014) and the settlement date (1/15/2015).

Since the financial statements are prepared between the transaction date and settlement date, receivables denominated in a currency other than the functional currency (U.S. dollar) must be restated to reflect the spot rate on the balance sheet date. On December 31, 2014, the exchange rate is one pound equals $.80. Hence, the £10,000 is now valued at $8,000 (10,000 × $.80). Therefore, the accounts receivable denominated in pounds should be adjusted upward by $500. The required journal entry on 12/31/2014 is:

Accounts Receivable—England	$500	
Foreign Exchange Gain		$500

The income statement for the year ended 12/31/2014 shows an exchange gain of $500. Note that sales totals are not affected by the exchange gain since sales are an operational activity.

On 1/15/2015, the spot rate is £1 = $.78. The journal entry is as follows:

Cash	$7,800	
Foreign Exchange Loss	200	
Accounts Receivable—England		$8,000

The 2015 income statement shows an exchange loss of $200.

FINANCIAL INSTRUMENTS

There are many different types of financial instruments. We discuss, for the major ones, their characteristics, accounting, and financial aspects.

1. *Floating rate note (FRN).* Debt having a variable interest rate. Interest expense is recorded based on the rate applicable for that period.
2. *Zero coupon bond.* A bond with no interest rate that is issued at a deep discount. Interest is accrued as incurred yearly even though payment will not be made until the maturity date.
3. *Collateralized mortgage obligations (CMOs).* Debt of a separate entity (e.g., trust) secured by a pool of mortgages or mortgage-backed securities. The separate entity is established by a sponsor that owns the loans, such as a commercial bank. The special-purpose entity buys the mortgage pool from the offering proceeds of the securities secured by the mortgages (CMOs). The issuer (e.g., trust) uses the cash flows of the collateralized funds for debt service on the CMOs. The prices of the CMOs are tied to their own maturity and return rate instead of the underlying mortgages. The issuer reports the CMOs as debt in its balance sheet. The investor records the bond at amortized cost.
4. *Interest rate swap.* A stipulation between two parties to exchange interest payments on a certain principal amount over a stated time period. The swap may apply to the exchange of both variable and fixed interest payments. Interest expense should incorporate the adjusted interest rate. Fees associated with swaps should be amortized over the life of the swap. There should be immediate recognition of unrealized losses on speculative swaps. However, unrealized gains should only be disclosed.
5. *Repurchase agreements (REPOs).* Stipulation among seller and buyer of securities (typically U.S. government securities) in which the seller contracts to reacquire the securities at a specified price and predetermined time period. In effect, there is a collateralized debt and loan based on the sales value of the collateral. In terms of accounting, REPOs constitute borrowings collateralized by the related securities. The proceeds amount represents a liability. Interest expense is also recognized on the REPOs.

6. *Debt with equity swaps.* The issuer of debt securities gives holders the right to convert those debt securities for common or preferred stock at a predetermined conversion price. The gain or loss on the early retirement of the debt is an extraordinary gain or loss. Such gain or loss is figured on the difference between the carrying value of the debt and the call price.

7. *Pay-in-kind (PIK) preferred stock.* The issuing company delays paying cash dividends to holders but instead issues more preferred stock. When dividends are paid in kind the entity debits retained earnings and credits preferred stock.

8. *Mortgage-backed (pass-through) securities.* There is participation in a pool of residential mortgages. Principal and interest are passed from mortgage originators via intermediaries that combine and repackage pass-through securities representing sales of the underlying mortgage loans with a gain or loss recognized on sale.

9. *Variable coupon redeemable notes (VCRs).* Notes that are periodically repriced. The initial maturity period is one year, with the interest rate changing each week. Interest expense is charged based on the actual interest rate for the period.

10. *Shared appreciation mortgage (SAM).* A mortgage allowing the lender to phase in appreciation in property value when the property is sold. For this privilege, the lender accepts a lower interest rate. In terms of accounting, the proceeds arising from appreciated value occurring at sale are treated as additional interest over the loan period.

11. *Increasing rate obligation.* A debt maturing in the short term but that may be extended periodically. Interest expense should be based on the average interest rate for the expected time period of the obligation. Issue costs should be deferred and amortized into expense over the expected maturity period.

12. *Dual currency bonds.* Debt paying interest in one currency but the maturity value in a different currency. The interest is typically payable in a currency having a low interest rate. Hedging may be used to minimize the foreign exchange risk.

13. *Adjustable rate preferred stock (ARPS).* Preferred stock having a changing dividend rate tied to some other security such as the interest rate on U.S. Treasury bills. Typically, there is a maximum interest rate allowed. The issuer records the dividend at the actual amount applicable for that specific year.

14. *Commercial paper.* Unsecured short-term debt of high quality companies having a maturity typically within one year.

It is issued on a discount basis. Interest expense is debited by the issuer and interest income is credited by the holder.

15. *European currency bonds (ECUs)*. A form of Eurobond stated in the 10 currencies of the nations belonging to the European Economic Community. Typically, interest and principal is payable in ECUs or another currency preferred by the investor. The effect of the change in exchange rates is reflected yearly in net income.

16. *Bunny bond*. A bond in which holders reinvest the interest into similar bonds. The issuing company debits interest expense and credits debt payable for the reinvested amount. The interest is tax-deductible to the issuer and treated as ordinary income to the investor.

17. *Covered option securities (COPs)*. Short-term dollar-denominated debt in which the issuing company may pay it at maturity in either dollars or a stipulated foreign currency. A higher yield rate exists because of the flexibility afforded the issuing company. Holding gains and losses on the foreign currency is reported in the income statement.

18. *Dutch auction notes*. Notes issued in which the coupon rate is adjusted periodically based on new, low bids for the notes (Dutch auction). Interest expense is recognized depending on the interest rate established at the Dutch auction.

Disclosures for Derivatives

A company must provide enhanced disclosures about (1) how and why a company uses derivative instruments; (2) how derivative instruments and related hedged items are accounted for; and (3) how derivative instruments and related hedged items impact a company's financial position, financial performance, and cash flows. Disclosure is required of the objective for using derivative instruments with respect to underlying risk and accounting designation. Further, disclosure is made of the fair value of derivative instruments and their gains or losses in tabular format. Finally, there should be disclosure of credit-risk-related contingent features to assess the company's liquidity from using derivatives. Disclosures for every reporting period for which a statement of financial position is issued are made for derivatives (and hedging nonderivatives) with contingent features that are related to credit risk:

- Nature of the features, how they may be activated in derivatives that are in a net liability position, and the aggregate fair values of such instruments

- An aggregate fair value of posted collateral, potentially required collateral, and immediate settlement amounts

Insurance Contracts

ASC 944-20-15-66 requires that an insurance company record a claim liability before a default (insured event) when evidence exists of credit deterioration occurring in an insured financial obligation. This is limited to financial guarantee insurance and reinsurance contracts. The Statement is effective for financial statements issued for fiscal years beginning after December 15, 2008.

The premium revenue recognition approach for a financial guarantee insurance contract links premium revenue recognition to the amount of insurance protection and the period it applies to. The amount of insurance protection provided is a function of the insured principal amount outstanding.

The recognition approach for a claim liability applying to a financial guarantee insurance contract mandates that an insurance company record a claim liability when the insurance company anticipates that a claim loss will be more than unearned premium revenue. The claim loss is based on the present value of anticipated net cash outflows to be paid discounted using a risk-free rate.

RELATED PARTIES

Related party transactions occur when a transacting party has the ability to materially influence or exercise control over another transacting party. Examples are a joint venture or activities between affiliates of the same parent company. Related party disclosures include terms and settlements, nature and type of control relationship, balances due from or owed to related parties at year-end (including payment terms), and description of transactions (whether or not dollar amounts are involved).

WEBSITES

1. Financial Accounting Standards Board – *www.fasb.org*
2. American Institute of CPAs – *www.aicpa.org*
3. Securities and Exchange Commission – *www.sec.gov*
4. New York State Society of CPAs – *www.nysscpa.org*
5. CPA examination – *www.cpa-exam.org*

6. Financial Executive Institute – *www.financialexecutives. org*
7. National Association of State Boards of Accountancy – *www.nasba.org*
8. Canadian Institute of Chartered Accountants – *www.cica. ca/*
9. International Accounting Standards Board – *www.iasb. org.uk*
10. International Federation of Accountants – *www.ifac.org*
11. Accounting Standards Codification – *www.fasb.org*

Brief Summary

Interim reports require special reporting. The accountant also has to be concerned with the appropriate treatment and disclosures of accounting changes, segmental information, business combinations, accounting for investments, leases, pensions, tax allocation, and foreign currency translation and transactions.

Chapter 3
Management Accounting/
Cost Management I

INTRODUCTION: THE ROLE OF MANAGEMENT ACCOUNTING

Management accounting, as defined by the Institute of Management Accountants (IMA), is the process of identification, measurement, accumulation, analysis, preparation, interpretation, and communication of financial information, which is used by management to plan, evaluate, and control operations within an organization. It ensures the appropriate use of, and accountability for, an organization's resources. Management accounting also includes the responsibility for the preparation of financial reports for nonmanagement groups, such as regulatory agencies and tax authorities. Simply stated, management accounting is the accounting system for the planning, control, and decision-making activities of an organization.

Financial Accounting vs. Management Accounting

Financial accounting is mainly concerned with the historical aspects of external reporting, that is, providing financial information to outside parties such as investors, creditors, and governments. To keep financial statements uniform and to protect those outside parties from being misled, financial accounting is governed by generally accepted accounting principles (GAAP). Management accounting, on the other hand, is concerned primarily with providing information to internal managers who are charged with planning and controlling the operations of the firm and making a variety of other management decisions. Owing to its internal use, management accounting is not subject to GAAP. More specifically, the differences between financial and management accounting are summarized in the chart at the top of the next page.

Financial Accounting	Management Accounting
1. provides data for external users	1. provides data for internal users
2. is required by FASB	2. is not required by FASB
3. is subject to GAAP	3. is not subject to GAAP
4. must generate accurate and timely data	4. emphasizes relevance and flexibility of data
5. emphasizes the past	5. has more emphasis on the future
6. looks at the business as a whole	6. focuses on the parts as well as on the whole of a business
7. primarily stands by itself	7. draws heavily from other disciplines such as finance, economics, and quantitative methods
8. is an end in itself	8. is a means to an end

COST ACCOUNTING VS. COST MANAGEMENT

For accountants, the difference between cost accounting and management accounting is a subtle one. The IMA defines cost accounting as "a systematic set of procedures for recording and reporting measurements of the cost of manufacturing goods and performing services in the aggregate and in detail. It includes methods for recognizing, classifying, allocating, aggregating, and reporting such costs and comparing them with standard costs." One thing is clear from this definition of cost accounting and the IMA's definition of management accounting: the major function of cost accounting is cost accumulation for inventory valuation and income determination. Management accounting, however, emphasizes the use of the cost data for planning, control, and decision-making purposes.

Cost management, especially in the new global production/service environment, encompasses both the cost accounting and the management accounting information systems. It processes cost data and provides cost information for internal users. Specifically, cost management reports cost information and other relevant objects for planning, controlling, making continuous improvements (CI), and decision making. In a nutshell, cost management is cost accounting plus management accounting plus continuous improvements.

Cost Accounting Standards Board

The Cost Accounting Standards Board (CASB), an agency of the U.S. Congress, was established in 1970 to promulgate cost accounting standards covering negotiated defense contracts. "Negotiated" means that the price is tied to costs rather than to competitive bidding.

The standards are mainly concerned with definitions, uniformity, and consistency in cost accounting practices. The standards begin with Number 400. Until the CASB's activities ceased in 1980, the Board had issued nineteen standards. The Government Accounting Office (GAO) is now responsible for interpreting CASB standards. The list of CASB standards is presented below.

The standards are classified into the following three categories:

1. Standards addressing overall cost accounting matters
   400 Definitions
   401 Cost accounting standard—consistency in estimating, accumulating, and reporting costs
   402 Cost accounting standard—consistency in allocating costs incurred for the same purpose
   405 Accounting for unallowable costs
   406 Cost accounting standard—cost accounting period
2. Standards addressing classes, categories, or elements of cost
   404 Capitalization of tangible assets
   407 Use of standard costs for direct material and direct labor
   408 Accounting for costs of compensated personal absence
   409 Depreciation of tangible capital assets
   411 Accounting for acquisition costs of material
   412 Composition and measurement of pension cost
   413 Adjustment and allocation of pension cost
   414 Cost of money as an element of the cost of facilities capital
   415 Accounting for the cost of deferred compensation
   416 Accounting for insurance costs
   417 Cost of money as an element of the cost of capital assets under construction
3. Standards addressing allocation of costs
   403 Allocation of home office expenses to segments
   410 Allocation of business unit general and administrative expenses to final objectives
   418 Allocation of direct and indirect costs
   (Proposed Standard 419 was combined with this standard)
   420 Accounting for independent research and development and bid and proposal costs

Copies of CASB standards, rules, and regulations are available from:

Superintendent of Documents
U.S. Government Printing Office
Washington, DC 20402

Cost Management in the New Production Environment

Over the past two decades, new technologies and management philosophies have changed the face of cost/managerial accounting. Following are the key developments that have reshaped the discipline. We will discuss these at length in future chapters. For example, where automation and computer-assisted manufacturing methods have reduced the human workforce, labor costs have shrunk from 30–50% of product and service costs to around 5%. Cost accounting in traditional settings required more work to keep track of labor costs than do present systems. On the other hand, in highly automated environments, cost accountants have had to become more sophisticated in finding causes of costs, because labor no longer drives many cost transactions.

Total Quality Management and Quality Costs. In order to be globally competitive in today's world-class manufacturing environment, firms place an increased emphasis on quality and productivity. Total quality management (TQM) is an effort in this direction. Simply put, it is a system for creating competitive advantage by focusing the organization on what is important to the customer.

Total quality management can be broken down as follows: *Total*—the whole organization is involved and understands that customer satisfaction is everyone's job. *Quality*—the extent to which products and services satisfy the requirements of internal and external customers. *Management*—the leadership, infrastructure, and resources that support employees as they meet the needs of those customers. Market shares of many U.S. firms have eroded because foreign firms have been able to sell higher-quality products at lower prices. Under TQM, performance measures are likely to include product reliability and service delivery, as well as such traditional measures as profitability.

In order to be competitive, U.S. firms have placed an increased emphasis on quality and productivity in order to:

1. produce savings such as reducing rework costs, and
2. improve product quality.

Quality costs are classified into three broad categories: prevention, appraisal, and failure costs. Quality cost reports can be used to point out the strengths and weaknesses of a quality system. Improvement teams can use them to describe the monetary benefits and ramifications of proposed changes.

Continuous Improvement (CI) and Benchmarking. Continuous improvement (CI), based on a Japanese concept called *Kaizen*, is a management philosophy that seeks endless pursuit of improvement of machinery, materials, labor utilization, and production methods through application of suggestions and ideas of team members. CI utilizes many different approaches, including *statistical process control (SPC)*, using traditional statistical control charts, and *benchmarking*, which examines excellent performers outside the industry and analyzing how observers can use their best practices. Benchmarking typically involves the following steps:

(a) Identify practices needing improvement.
(b) Identify a company that is a world leader in performing a similar process.
(c) Interview the managers of the company and analyze data obtained.

Continuous improvement and benchmarking are often called "the race with no finish" because managers and employees are never permanently satisfied with a particular performance level, but continue to seek ongoing improvement.

Business Process Reengineering (BPR). TQM seeks evolutionary changes in the processes, while the practice called *business process reengineering (BPR)* seeks to make revolutionary changes. BPR does this by taking a fresh look at what the firm is trying to do in all its processes, and then eliminating nonvalue-added steps and streamlining the remaining ones to achieve the desired outcome.

Just-in-Time and Lean Production. The inventory control problem occurs in almost every type of organization. It exists whenever products are held to meet some expected future demand. In most industries, cost of inventory represents the largest liquid asset under the control of management. Therefore, it is very important to develop a production and inventory planning system that will minimize both purchasing and carrying costs. Material cost, as a proportion of total product cost, has continued to rise significantly during the last few years and hence is a primary concern of top management.

Just-in-Time (JIT) is a demand-pull system. Demand for customer output (not plans for using input resources) triggers production. Production activities are "pulled," not "pushed," into action.

JIT production, in its purest sense, is buying and producing in very small quantities just in time for use. JIT production is part of a "lean production" philosophy that has been credited for the success of many Japanese companies. Lean production eliminates inventory between production departments, making the quality and efficiency of production the highest priority. Lean production requires the flexibility to change quickly from one product to another. It emphasizes employee training and participation in decision-making. The development of just-in-time production and purchasing methods also affects cost-accounting systems. Firms using just-in-time methods keep inventories to a minimum. If inventories are low, accountants can spend less time on inventory valuation for external reporting. Chapter 8 covers the JIT inventory system.

Theory of Constraints (TOC) and Bottlenecks Management. The theory of constraints (TOC) views a business as a linked sequence of processes that transforms inputs into salable outputs, like a chain. To improve the strength of the chain, a TOC company identifies the weakest link, which is the constraint. TOC exploits constraints so that throughput is maximized and inventories and operating costs are minimized. It then develops a specific approach to manage constraints to support the objective of *continuous improvement.*

Bottlenecks occur whenever demand (at least temporarily) exceeds capacity. For example, although a legal secretary has enough total time to do all her word processing, she may be given several jobs in quick succession, so that a queue (waiting line) builds up. This is a bottleneck, which delays the other activities waiting for the word processing to be finished. TOC seeks to maximize "throughput" by

1. larger lot sizes at bottleneck work stations, to avoid time lost on changeovers;
2. small transfer batches—forwarding a small batch of work to the next work station, so that the next operation can begin before the entire lot is finished at the preceding work station; and
3. rules for inserting buffer stock before or after certain bottlenecks.

Corporate Balanced Scorecard. A problem with merely assessing performance with financial measures like profit, ROI, and Economic Value Added (EVA) is that the financial measures are "backward looking." In other words, today's financial measures tell you about the accomplishments and failures of the past. An approach to performance measurement that also focuses on what managers are doing today to create future shareholder value is the Balanced Scorecard. The Balanced Scorecard is a set of performance measures constructed for four dimensions of performance—financial, customer, internal processes, and learning and growth.

Life-Cycle Costs and Target Costing. Life-cycle costing tracks and accumulates all product costs in the value chain from research and development and design of products and processes through production, marketing, distribution, and customer service. The value chain is the set of activities required to design, develop, produce, market, and service a product or service. The terms "cradle-to-grave costing" and "womb-to-tomb costing" convey the sense of fully capturing all costs associated with the product. Life-cycle cost concepts are associated with target costing and target pricing. A firm may determine that market conditions require that a product sell at a given target price. Hence, target cost can be determined by subtracting the desired unit profit margin from the target price. The cost reduction objectives of life-cycle cost management can therefore be determined using target costing.

Six-Sigma. An approach to reducing costs related to business processes is Six-Sigma. Six-Sigma is a structured and disciplined data-driven process for improving business performance. The Six-Sigma methodology concentrates on reducing variability in processes. "Sigma" is a statistical term that measures how far a given process deviates from customer requirements and a measure of process capability. The term "Six-Sigma" refers to the ability of highly capable processes to produce output within specification.

The Certified Management Accountant (CMA)

Management accounting has expanded in scope to cover a wide variety of business disciplines such as finance, economics, organization behavior, and quantitative methods. In line with this development, the Institute of Management Accountants (IMA) created the Institute of Certified Management Accountants, which offers a program leading to the *Certified Management Accountant (CMA)* examination.

The objectives of the CMA program are fourfold: (1) to establish management accounting as a recognized profession by identifying the role of the management accountant and financial manager, the underlying body of knowledge, and a course of study by which such knowledge is acquired; (2) to encourage higher educational standards in the management accounting field; (3) to establish an objective measure of an individual's knowledge and competence in the field of management accounting; and (4) to encourage continued professional development by management accountants.

The CMA program requires candidates to pass a series of uniform examinations covering a wide range of subjects. The examination consists of the following four parts:

> Part 1: Business Analysis (3 hours—110 multiple-choice questions)
>
> Part 2: Management Accounting and Reporting (4 hours—140 multiple-choice questions)
>
> Part 3: Strategic Management (3 hours—110 multiple-choice questions)
>
> Part 4: Business Applications (3 hours—4 to 7 essays/problems—Available February, May, August, November)

The exam is given twice yearly, in June and December.

Note: For more information, call IMA at (800) 638-4427, ext. 141 or (201) 573-6300, or visit its Website: *www.imanet.org.*

The Certified Internal Auditor (CIA)

This certification was created in 1974 by the Institute of Internal Auditors (IIA). The CIA exam is also broader than the CPA exam because it covers a broad range of areas, among them management, economics, finance, and quantitative methods. The CIA exam lasts 14 hours (four 3½-hour parts) and covers the following areas:

> Part 1—The Internal Audit Activity's Role in Governance, Risk, and Control
>
> Part 2—Conducting the Internal Audit Engagement
>
> Part 3—Business Analysis and Information Technology
>
> Part 4—Business Management Skills

Note: For more information, call IIA at (407) 830-7600 or visit its Website: *www.theiia.org.*

The Certified Fraud Examiner (CFE)

To become a qualified forensic accountant, there are several degrees, certifications, and positions that qualify the accountant as an expert in this field. Forensic accountants, who are usually involved in litigation support or investigative accounting, must have some form of credentials to deem them capable of the work or career they are pursuing. The major one is Certified Fraud Examiner (CFE), offered by the Association of Certified Fraud Examiners (*www.acfe.org*), established in 1988, and based in Austin, Texas. The 25,000-member professional organization is dedicated to educating qualified individuals (Certified Fraud Examiners), who are trained in highly specialized aspects of detecting, investigating, and deterring a wide variety of fraud and white-collar crime. In order to gain the CFE designation, you must pass the CFE Exam. The 500-question exam is designed to measure your academic as well as practical knowledge in four main areas: Criminology and Ethics, Financial Transactions, Legal Elements of Fraud, and Fraud Examination and Investigation. You may contact them at (800) 245-3321 or (512) 478-9070, or visit their Website at *customerservice@ cfenet.com*.

Part I: Processing Cost Data for Cost Accumulation

COST CONCEPTS, TERMS, AND CLASSIFICATIONS

In financial accounting, the term *cost* is defined as a measurement in monetary terms of the amount of resources used for some purpose. In managerial accounting, the term *cost* is used in many different ways. That is, there are different types of costs, and they are used for different purposes. Some costs are useful and required for inventory valuation and income determination. Some costs are useful for planning, budgeting, and cost control. Still others are useful for making short-term and long-term decisions.

Cost Classifications

Costs can be classified into various categories, according to:

1. Their management function
   a. manufacturing costs
   b. nonmanufacturing costs
2. Their ease of traceability
   a. direct costs
   b. indirect costs
3. Their timing of charges against sales revenue
   a. product costs
   b. period costs
4. Their behavior in accordance with changes in activity
   a. variable costs
   b. fixed costs
   c. mixed costs
5. Their relevance to control and decision-making
   a. controllable and noncontrollable costs
   b. incremental costs
   c. sunk costs
   d. opportunity costs
   e. relevant costs

We will discuss each of the cost categories in the remainder of this section.

Costs by Management Function

In a manufacturing firm, costs are divided into two major categories, according to the functional activities they are associated with: (1) manufacturing costs and (2) nonmanufacturing costs, also called operating expenses.

Manufacturing Costs. Manufacturing costs are those costs associated with the production activities of the company. Manufacturing costs are subdivided into three categories: direct materials, direct labor, and factory overhead.

Direct materials are all materials that become an integral part of the finished product. Examples are the steel used to make an automobile and the wood to make furniture. Glues, nails, and other minor items are called indirect materials (or supplies) and are treated as part of factory overhead, which is explained below. The reason for this treatment is that, although these items can be traced to individual units produced, the cost of doing so is greater than the benefit obtained.

Direct labor is the labor directly involved in making the product. Examples of direct labor costs are the wages of assembly workers on an assembly line and the wages of machine tool operators in a machine shop. Indirect labor, such as the wages of supervisory personnel and janitors, is classified as part of factory overhead.

Factory overhead comprises all costs of manufacturing except direct materials and direct labor. Some of the many examples include depreciation of factory building and machinery, indirect materials, indirect labor, factory utilities cost, quality costs, engineering, waste control costs, and factory insurance.

One important subcategory of factory overhead is that of *quality costs*. Quality costs are costs that occur because poor quality may exist or actually does exist. These costs are significant in amount, often totaling 20 to 25% of sales. The subcategories of quality costs are prevention, appraisal, and failure costs.

Prevention costs are those incurred to prevent defects. Amounts spent on quality training programs, researching customer needs, implementing quality circles, and improved production equipment are considered in prevention costs. Expenditures made for prevention will minimize the costs that will be incurred for appraisal and failure.

Detection costs are those incurred to identify problems, such as testing.

Appraisal costs are costs incurred for monitoring or inspection; these costs compensate for mistakes not eliminated through prevention. *Failure costs* may be internal (such as scrap and rework costs and reinspection) or external (such as product returns due to quality problems, warranty costs, lost sales due to poor product performance, and complaint department costs). Factory overhead may also be called manufacturing overhead, indirect manufacturing expenses, or factory burden. Many costs overlap within their categories. For example, direct materials and direct labor, when combined, are called *prime costs*. Direct labor and factory overhead, when combined, are termed *conversion costs* (or processing costs).

Nonmanufacturing Costs. Nonmanufacturing costs (or operating expenses) are divided into *selling expenses* and *general and administrative expenses*. Selling expenses are all the expenses associated with obtaining sales and the delivery of the product. Examples are advertising and sales commissions. General and administrative expenses include all the expenses that are incurred performing managerial and support services. Examples are executives' salaries and legal expenses.

Direct Costs and Indirect Costs

Costs may be viewed as either direct or indirect in terms of the extent they are traceable to a particular object of costing, such as particular products, jobs, departments, or sales territories. Direct costs are those costs that can be directly traced to the costing object. Factory overhead items are all indirect costs, as are costs shared by different departments, products, or jobs, which are called common costs or joint costs. National advertising that benefits more than one product or sales territory is an example of an indirect cost to each product or sales territory, though it is a direct cost to the company as a whole.

Product Costs and Period Costs

By their timing of charges against revenue or by whether they are inventoriable, costs are classified into (1) product costs and (2) period costs.

Product costs are inventoriable costs, identified as part of inventory on hand. They are therefore assets until the inventory is sold. Once the inventory is sold, product costs become expenses, i.e., cost of goods sold. All manufacturing costs are product costs.

Period costs are not inventoriable and hence are charged against sales revenue in the period in which the revenue is earned. Selling, general, and administrative expenses are period costs.

Variable Costs, Fixed Costs, and Mixed Costs

From a planning and control standpoint, perhaps the most important way to classify costs is by how they behave in accordance with changes in volume or some measure of activity. Costs can be classified into three basic categories, by behavior:

Variable costs vary in direct proportion to changes in activity. Examples are direct materials in a factory and gasoline expense based on mileage driven. *Fixed costs* remain relatively constant regardless of changes in activity. Examples are rent, insurance, and taxes. *Mixed* (or *semivariable*) *costs* vary with changes in volume but, unlike variable costs, do not vary in direct proportion. In other words, these costs contain both a variable component and a fixed component. Examples are the rental of a delivery truck, where a fixed rental fee plus a variable charge based on mileage is made, and power costs, where the expense consists of a fixed amount plus a variable charge based on consumption.

The breakdown of costs into their variable components and their fixed components is very important in many areas of management accounting, such as flexible budgeting, break-even analysis, and short-term decision-making.

Costs for Planning, Control, and Decision Making

Controllable and Noncontrollable Costs. A cost is said to be controllable when the level of the cost is significantly under the manager's influence. Noncontrollable costs are those costs not subject to influence at a given level of managerial supervision. A cost controllable at one level of management may be noncontrollable at another.

All variable costs such as direct materials, direct labor, and variable overhead are usually controllable by the department head. Further, a certain portion of fixed costs can also be controllable. For example, depreciation on the equipment used specifically for a given department would be an expense controllable by the manager of the department if the manager also makes replacement decisions.

Incremental (or Differential) Costs. The incremental cost is the difference in costs between two or more alternatives. Incremental costs are increases or decreases in total costs or changes in specific elements of cost (e.g., direct labor cost) that result from any variation in operations. Incremental costs will be incurred (or saved) if a decision is made to go ahead (or to stop) some activity, but not otherwise.

Consider the two alternatives A and B whose costs are as follows:

	A	B	Incremental Costs (B – A)
Direct materials	$10,000	$10,000	$ 0
Direct labor	10,000	15,000	5,000

The incremental costs are simply B – A (or A – B), as shown in the last column.

Decision-making is based on incremental cost or revenue.

Sunk Costs. Sunk costs are costs that have already been incurred and thus will not be affected by any decision made now or in the future. They represent past or historical costs.

Suppose that an asset you acquired for $50,000 three years ago is now listed at a book value of $20,000. The $20,000 is a sunk cost that does not affect a future decision.

Opportunity Costs. An opportunity cost consists of the benefits forgone by rejecting an alternative.

Suppose a company has a choice of using its capacity to produce an extra 10,000 units or renting out the capacity for $20,000. The opportunity cost of using the capacity is $20,000, because of the $20,000 *not* realized from renting out the capacity. Likewise, the opportunity cost of renting out the capacity would be the net profit realized from producing an extra 10,000 units.

Relevant Costs. Relevant costs are expected future costs that will differ between alternatives.

The incremental cost is relevant to the future decision. The sunk cost is irrelevant.

COST-ACCUMULATION SYSTEMS

A cost-accumulation system is a method of collecting costs and assigning them to the cost object. We will discuss the essentials of the system that is used to measure the manufacturing costs of products. This is essentially a two-step process: (1) the measurement of costs that are applicable to manufacturing operations during a given accounting period, and (2) the assignment of these costs to products.

There are two basic approaches to cost accounting and accumulation: job-order costing and process costing.

Job-Order Costing

Job-order cost accounting is the cost-accumulation system under which costs are accumulated by specific jobs, contracts, or orders. This costing method is appropriate when the products are manufactured in identifiable lots or batches or when the products are manufactured to customer specifications. Job-order costing is widely used by custom manufacturers such as printing plants, construction companies, auto repair shops, and professional services. Job-order costing keeps track of costs by tracing direct material and direct labor to a particular job; costs not directly traceable—factory overhead—are applied to individual jobs using a *predetermined overhead (application) rate*. The overhead rate is determined as follows:

$$\text{Overhead rate} = \frac{\text{Budgeted annual overhead}}{\begin{array}{c}\text{Budgeted annual activity units}\\\text{(direct labor hours, machine hours, etc.)}\end{array}}$$

At the end of the year, the difference between actual overhead and overhead applied is closed to cost of goods sold as either overapplied or underapplied. If a material difference exists, work-in-process, finished goods, and cost of goods sold are adjusted on a proportionate basis based on units or dollars at year-end for the deviation between actual and applied overhead.

A job cost sheet is used to record various production costs for work-in-process inventory. A separate cost sheet is kept for each identifiable job, accumulating the direct materials, direct labor, and factory overhead assigned to that job as it moves through production. The form varies according to the needs of the company. A sample job cost sheet is shown in Figure 3-1; a system flow chart for job costing is in Figure 3-2.

Typical journal entries required to account for job-order-costing transactions are as follows:

1. To apply direct material and direct
   labor to Job A.

Work-in-process (WIP) — Job A	XX	
Stores control		XX
Accrued payroll		XX

2. To *apply* overhead to the job in process.

WIP, Job A	XX	
Overhead applied		XX

3. To record *actual* overhead.

Overhead control	XX	
Stores control, accrued payroll,		
other sundries		XX

4. To transfer completed goods.

Finished goods, Job A	XX	
WIP, Job A		XX

5. To record sale of finished goods.

Cost of goods sold	XX	
Finished goods		XX
Accounts receivable	XX	
Sales		XX

Product _____   Job No. _____
Date Started _____
Date Completed _____

	Direct Material			Direct Labor			Overhead
Date	Reference	Amount	Date	Reference	Amount	Date	Amount
	(Store Requisition No.)			(Work Ticket No.)			(Based on predetermined overhead rate)

Figure 3-1. Sample job cost sheet

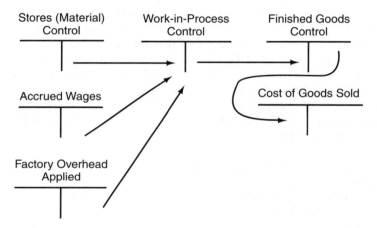

Figure 3-2. Job cost system. Flow chart of ledger relationships

More on Application of Factory Overhead

Regardless of what cost-accumulation system is used (i.e., job order, process, or standard costing), factory overhead is applied to a job or process using a *predetermined overhead rate,* which is based on budgeted factory overhead cost and budgeted activity. The rate is calculated as indicated on the previous page.

Budgeted activity units (capacity) used in the denominator of the formula, more often called the *denominator level,* are measured in direct labor hours, machine hours, direct labor costs, production units, or some other measure of production activity.

EXAMPLE 3.1

Assume that two companies have prepared the following budgeted data for the year 2014.

	Company X	Company Y
Predetermined rate based on	machine hours	direct labor cost
Budgeted overhead	$200,000 (1)	$240,000 (1)
Budgeted machine hours	100,000 (2)	
Budgeted direct labor cost		$160,000 (2)
Predetermined overhead rate (1) (2)	$2 per machine hour	150% of direct labor cost

Now assume that actual overhead costs and the actual level of activity for 2014 for each firm are shown as follows:

	Company X	Company Y
Actual overhead costs	$198,000	$256,000
Actual machine hours	96,000	
Actual direct labor cost		$176,000

Note that for each company the actual cost and activity data differ from the budgeted figures used in calculating the predetermined overhead rate. The computation of the resulting *underapplied* and *overapplied* overhead for each company is provided below:

	Company X	Company Y
Actual overhead costs	$198,000	$256,000
Factory overhead applied to work-in-process during 2014:		
96,000 actual machine-hours × $2	192,000	
$176,000 actual direct labor cost × 150%		264,000
Underapplied (overapplied) factory overhead	$ 6,000	($ 8,000)

Plantwide Versus Departmental Overhead Rates

As the degree of aggregation increases from simply combining related cost pools to combining all factory overhead, information may become more distorted. The following information is used to provide a simple example of the differing results obtained between using a departmental and plantwide overhead rate.

EXAMPLE 3.2

Allison Company has two departments: assembly and finishing. Assembly work is performed by robots, and a large portion of this department's overhead cost consists of depreciation and electricity charges. Finishing work is performed manually by skilled laborers, and most charges in this department are for labor, fringe benefits, indirect materials, and supplies.

The company makes two products: A and B. Product A requires five machine hours in assembly and one direct labor hour in finishing; Product B requires two machine hours in Assembly and three direct labor hours in finishing.

Table 3.1 provides information about estimated overhead costs and activity measures and shows the computations of departmental and plantwide overhead rates. Product overhead application amounts for A and B are also given.

Note the significant difference in the overhead applied to each product using departmental versus plantwide rates. If departmental rates are used, product cost more clearly reflects the different amounts and types of machine/labor work performed on the two products. If a plantwide rate is used, essentially, each product only absorbs overhead from a single department—from assembly if machine hours are used and from finishing if direct labor hours are used. Use of a plantwide rate ignores the dissimilarity of work performed in the departments.

Table 3.1
PLANTWIDE VERSUS DEPARTMENTAL
OVERHEAD RATES

	Assembly	*Finishing*	*Total*
Estimated annual overhead	$300,200	$99,800	$400,000
Estimated annual direct labor hours (DLH)	5,000	20,000	25,000
Estimated annual machine hours (MH)	38,000	2,000	40,000

(1) Total plantwide overhead = $300,200 + $99,800 = $400,000
    Plantwide overhead rate using DLH) ($400,000/25,000 = $16.00)

(2) Departmental overhead rates:
    Assembly (automated) $300,200/38,000 = $7.90 per MH
    Finishing (manual) $99,800/20,000 = $4.99 per DLH

	To Product A	*To Product B*
(1) Overhead assigned using plantwide rate: based on DLH	1($16.00) = $16.00	3($16.00) = $48.00
(2) Overhead assigned using departmental rates:		
Assembly	5($7.90) = $39.50	2($7.90) = $15.80
Finishing	1($4.99) = 4.99	3($4.99) = 14.97
Total	$44.49	$30.77

Use of plantwide overhead rates rather than departmental rates may also contribute to problems in product pricing. While selling prices must be reflective of market conditions, management typically uses cost as a starting point for setting prices. If plantwide rates distort the true cost of a product, selling prices might be set too low or too high, causing management to make incorrect decisions.

EXAMPLE 3.3

Assume in the case of Allison Company that direct materials and direct labor costs for product A are $5 and $35, respectively. Adding the various overhead amounts to these prime costs gives the total product cost under each method. Table 3.2 shows these product costs and the profit or loss that would be indicated if Product A has a normal market selling price of $105.

Use of the product costs developed from plantwide rates could cause Allison management to make erroneous decisions about Product A. If the cost figure developed from a plantwide direct labor hour basis is used, management may think that Product A is significantly more successful than it actually is. Such a decision could cause resources to be diverted from other products. If the cost-containing overhead based on the plantwide machine-hour allocation is used, management may believe that Product A should not be produced, because it appears not to be generating a very substantial gross profit.

In either instance, assuming that machine hours and direct labor hours are the best possible allocation bases for assembly and finishing, respectively, the only cost that gives management the necessary information upon which to make resource allocation and product development/elimination decisions is the one produced by using the departmental overhead rates.

Table 3.2
TOTAL PRODUCT COSTS AND PROFITS

	Departmental Rates	Plantwide Rate (DLH)
Direct materials	$ 5.00	$ 5.00
Direct labor	35.00	35.00
Overhead	44.49	16.00
Total Cost	$ 84.49	$ 56.00
Selling Price	$105.00	$105.00
Gross profit (margin)	$ 20.51	$ 49.00
Profit margin	19.5%	46.7%

Selecting the Denominator (Capacity) Measures

It is important to define different denominator (capacity) measures since they affect under- and overapplied factory overhead. *Capacity* is the ability to produce during a given time period, with an upper limit imposed by the availability of space, machinery, labor, materials, or capital. It may be expressed in units, weight, size, dollars, worker-hours, labor cost, etc. There are typically four concepts of capacity.

Theoretical Capacity. The volume of activity that could be attained under ideal operating conditions, with minimum allowance for inefficiency, is the theoretical capacity. It is the largest volume of output possible. It also is called *ideal capacity, engineered capacity,* or *maximum capacity.*

Practical Capacity. The highest activity level at which the factory can operate with an acceptable degree of efficiency, taking into consideration unavoidable losses of productive time (i.e., vacations, holidays, repairs to equipment), is also called *maximum practical capacity.*

Two variations of the practical capacity concept are widely used as the denominator volume. They are normal capacity and expected annual activity.

Normal Capacity. The average level of operating activity that is sufficient to fill the demand for the company's products or services for a span of several years, taking into consideration seasonal and cyclical demands and increasing or decreasing trends in demand, is the normal capacity.

Expected Annual Activity. Similar to normal capacity except that it is projected for a particular year, this measure is also called *planned capacity.*

The choice of activity level used in determining the overhead application rate potentially will have a large effect on over- or underapplied overhead. The four capacity measures above may be 100,000, 95,000, 70,000, and 80,000 units of activity, respectively. If the actual level of activity were 85,000 units, over- or overapplication would result.

Process Costing

Process costing is a cost-accumulation system that aggregates manufacturing costs by departments or by production process. Total manufacturing costs are accumulated in two major categories—direct materials and conversion costs (the sum of direct labor and factory overhead applied). Unit cost is determined by dividing the total costs charged to a cost center by the output of that cost center. Process costing is appropriate for companies that produce a continuous mass of similar units through a series of operations or processes. Process costing is generally used in such industries as petroleum, chemicals, oil refinery, textiles, and food processing.

Four major steps usually used in accounting for process costs are summarized below.

Summarize the Flow of Physical Units. The first step of the accounting provides a summary of all units on which some work was done in the department during the period. The basic relationship is expressed in the following equation:

Beginning inventory + Units started for the period
$\qquad$ = Units completed and transferred out + ending inventory

Compute Output in Equivalent Units. Equivalent units are a measure of how many whole units of production are represented by the units completed plus the units partially completed. For example, 100 units that are 60% completed are the equivalent of 60 completed units in terms of processing costs.

Summarize Total Costs. Total up all the costs to be accounted for, and compute the unit costs per equivalent unit. This step summarizes the total costs assigned to the department during the period. Then the unit cost per equivalent is computed as follows:

$$\text{Unit cost} = \frac{\text{Total costs incurred during the period}}{\text{Equivalent units of production during the period}}$$

Apply Total Costs. Apply the total costs to units completed and transferred out and to units in ending work-in-process.

Cost-of-Production Report. The process-costing method uses this report to summarize both total and unit costs charged to a department and to show the allocation of total costs between work-in-process inventory and the units completed and transferred out to the next department or the finished-goods inventory. The cost-of-production report covers all four steps described above. It is also the source for monthly journal entries and is a convenient compilation from which cost data may be presented to management. In computing the unit cost for a processing center, two specific assumptions about the flow of cost may be used—weighted-average costing or first-in-first out (FIFO).

Weighted-average costing is a procedure for computing the unit cost of a process by which the beginning work-in-process inventory costs are added to the costs of the current period and a weighted average is obtained by dividing the combined costs by equivalent units. In this method, there is no distinction between beginning inventory units worked on during the period and units started during the period. Thus, there is only one average cost for goods completed.

Equivalent units under weighted-average costing may be computed as follows:

$$\text{Units completed} + [\text{Ending work-in-process} \times \text{degree of completion (\%)}]$$

On the other hand, under FIFO, beginning work-in-process inventory costs are separated from added costs applied in the current period. Thus, there are two unit costs for the period: (1) beginning work-in-process units completed and (2) units started and completed in the same period. Under FIFO, the beginning work-in-process is assumed to be completed and transferred first. Equivalent units under FIFO costing may be computed as follows:

$$\text{Units completed} + [\text{Ending work-in-process} \times \text{degree of completion (\%)}] - \text{Beginning work-in-process} \times \text{degree of completion (\%)}]$$

EXAMPLE 3.4

To illustrate, the following data relate to the activities of Department A during the month of January:

	Units
Beginning work-in-process (100% complete as to materials; 2/3 complete as to conversion)	1,500
Started this period	5,000
Completed and transferred	5,500
Ending work-in-process (100% complete as to materials; 60% complete as to conversion)	1,000

Equivalent production in Department A for the month is computed, using weighted-average costing, as follows:

	Materials	Conversion Costs
Units completed and transferred	5,500	5,500
Ending work-in-process		
Materials (100%)	1,000	
Conversion costs (60%)		600
Equivalent production	6,500	6,100

Equivalent production in Department A for the month is computed, using FIFO costing, as follows:

	Materials	Conversion Costs
Units completed and transferred	5,500	5,500
Ending work-in-process		
Materials (100%)	1,000	
Conversion costs (60%)		600
Eqivalent production	6,500	6,100
Minus: Beginning work-in-process		
Materials (100%)	1,500	
Conversion costs (2/3)		1,000
	5,000	5,100

The following example offers a step-by-step illustration of process cost calculations by the weighted-average and FIFO methods.

EXAMPLE 3.5

The Tucker Cement Manufacturing Company, Inc., manufactures cement. Its processing operations involve quarrying, grinding, blending, packing, and sacking. For cost-accounting and control purposes, there are four processing centers: Raw Material No. 1, Raw Material No. 2, Clinker, and Cement. Separate cost-of-production reports are prepared in detail with respect to the foregoing cost centers. The following information pertains to the operation of Raw Material No. 2 Department for July 2014:

	Materials	Conversion
Units in process July 1		
800 bags	complete	60% complete
Costs	$12,000	$56,000
Units transferred out		
40,000 bags		
Current costs	$41,500	$521,500
Units in process July 31		
5,000 bags	complete	30% complete

Using weighted average-costing and FIFO costing, we will compute the following:

(1) Equivalent production units and unit costs by elements.
(2) Cost of work-in-process (WIP) for July.
(3) Cost of units completed and transferred.

Computation of Output in Equivalent Units

	Physical Flow	Materials	Conversion
WIP, beginning	800 (60%)		
Units transferred in	44,200		
Units to account for	45,000		
Units completed and transferred out	40,000	40,000	40,000
WIP, end	5,000 (30%)	5,000	1,500
Units accounted for	45,000		
Equivalent units used for *weighted average*		45,000	41,500
Less: old equivalent units for work done on beginning inventory in prior period		800	480
Equivalent units used for *FIFO*		44,200	41,020

Cost of Production Report: Weighted Average
Raw Material No. 2 Department
For the Month Ended July 31, 2014

	WIP Beginning	Current Costs	Total Costs	Equivalent Units	Average Unit Cost
Materials	$12,000	$ 41,500	$ 53,500	45,000	$ 1.1889
Conversion costs	56,000	521,500	577,500	41,500	13.9156
	$68,000	563,000	631,000		$15.1045

Cost of goods completed 40,000 × $15.1045 = $604,180

WIP, end:
Materials 5,000 × $1.1889	$ 5,944.50	
Conversion 1,500 × 13.9156	20,873.40	$ 26,817.90
Total costs accounted for		$631,000 (rounded)

Cost of Production Report: FIFO
Raw Material No. 2 Department
For the Month Ended July 31, 2014

	Total Costs	Equivalent Units	Unit Costs
WIP, beginning	$ 68,000		
Current costs:			
Materials	41,500	44,200	$ .9389
Conversion costs	521,500	41,020	12.7133
Total costs to account for	$631,000		$13.6522

WIP, end:
| Materials 5,000 × $.9389 | $ 4,694.50 | |
| Conversion 1.500 × $12.7133 | 19,069.95 | $ 23,764.45 |

Cost of goods completed, 40,000 units:
WIP, beginning to be		
transferred out first	68,000	
Additional costs to complete		
800 × (1 − .6) × $12.7133	4,068.26	
Cost of goods started and		
completed this month		
39,200 × $13.6522	535,166.24	$607,234.50
Total costs accounted for		$631,000 (rounded)

Answers are summarized as follows:

	Weighted Average		FIFO	
	Materials	Conversion	Materials	Conversion
a. Equivalent units	45,000	41,500	44,200	41,020
Unit costs	$1.1889	$13.9156	$.9389	$12.7133
b. Cost of WIP	$ 26,817.90		$ 23,764.45	
c. Cost of units completed and transferred		$604,180		$607,234.50

COSTING JOINT PRODUCTS AND BY-PRODUCTS

Joint products are two or more products produced simultaneously by a common manufacturing process. The common manufacturing costs are called *joint costs*. For example, gasoline, heating oil, and kerosene are joint products in oil refining. Each of the joint products has a significant market value. By-products, on the other hand, have a relatively low sales value in relation to the firm's other products. Examples include sawdust in lumber mills and bone in meat-packing plants. Generally speaking, if a product's value is too small to affect the decision to produce, it is a by-product. On the other hand, if it does affect the decision to produce, it is a joint product.

Joint Product Cost Allocation

Joint cost allocation is necessary for the valuation of inventory and determination of cost of goods sold. Two popular methods of allocating joint costs to individual products are the physical-unit method and relative-sales-value method. The *physical-unit method* allocates joint costs based on a physical measure of units such as gallons, pounds, or cubic feet. A major limitation of this method is that the method bears no relationship to the revenue-producing ability of the products. Also, there is a distortion in the gross profit computation any time the sales price per unit of quantity is not the same for the joint products.

The *relative-sales-value method* allocates joint costs on the basis of the products' relative sales value at the split-off point. This method is considered the best allocation method, since the costs are allocated in proportion to the relative revenue-generating power of the individual products.

Frequently, joint products have no sales value at the split-off point, Then, the costs are allocated on the basis of each product's *net realizable value,* which is the difference between sales value and separable cost needed to complete and sell.

Accounting for By-products

By-products result from a joint process and have a sales value that is relatively minor in comparison with the value of the joint products. There is no special accounting method for dealing with by-product costs. If by-products can be sold, net revenue, which is gross revenue from by-products sold less separable costs incurred, is used to reduce the cost of the main product in one of the following ways:

1. Net revenue is deducted from the cost of main products sold.
2. Net revenue is deducted from the cost of main products produced.
3. Net revenue is treated as "other sales."
4. Net revenue is treated as "other income."

ALLOCATION OF SERVICE DEPARTMENT COSTS TO PRODUCTION DEPARTMENTS

There are two basic types of departments in a manufacturing company: production departments and service departments. A production department (such as assembly or machining) is where the production or conversion occurs. A service department (such as engineering or maintenance) provides support to production departments. Before departmental factory overhead rates are developed for product costing, the costs of service departments should be allocated among the appropriate production departments (as part of factory overhead).

Basis of Assigning Service Department Costs

Some service department costs are *direct*. Examples are the wages or salaries of the workers in the department. Other service department costs are *indirect*—that is, they are incurred jointly with some other department. An example is building depreciation. These indirect costs must be allocated on some arbitrary basis.

The problem is that of selecting appropriate bases for assigning the indirect costs of service departments to other departments. Costs should be allocated on a basis that reflects the type of activity in which each service department is engaged. The ideal basis should be logical, have a high *cause-and-effect* relationship between the service provided and the costs of providing it, and be easy to implement. The basis selected may be supported by physical observation, by correlation analysis, or by logical analysis of the relationship between the departments. A list of some service departments and a possible basis for allocation is given below:

Service Department	Allocation Basis
Supplies	Number of requisitions
Power	Kilowatt hours used
Buildings and grounds	Number of square or cubic feet
Maintenance and repairs	Machine hours or number of calls
Personnel	Number of employees
Cafeteria	Number of employees
Purchasing	Number of orders

Procedure for Service Department Cost Allocation

Once the service department costs are known, the next step is to allocate the service department costs to the production departments. This may be accomplished by one of the following procedures:

- direct method
- step method
- reciprocal method

Direct Method. This method allocates the costs of each service department directly to production departments, with no intermediate allocation to other service departments. That is, no consideration is given to services performed by one service department for another. This is perhaps the most widely used method because of its simplicity and ease of use.

EXAMPLE 3.6

Assume the following data:

	Service Departments		Production Departments	
	General Plant (GP)	Engineering (E)	A Machining	B Assembly
Overhead costs before allocation	$20,000	$10,000	$30,000	$40,000
Direct labor hours by General Plant (GP)	15,000	20,000	60,000	40,000
Engineering hours by Engineering (E)	5,000	4,000	50,000	30,000

Using the direct method yields:

	Service Departments		Production Departments	
	GP	*E*	*A*	*B*
Overhead costs	$20,000	$10,000	$30,000	$40,000
Reallocation:				
GP (60%, 40%)*	($20,000)		12,000	8,000
E (5/8, 3/8)#		($10,000)	6,250	3,750
			$48,250	$51,750

* Base is (60,000 + 40,000 = 100,000); 60,000/100,000 = .6; 40,000/100,000 = .4
\# Base is (50,000 + 30,000 = 80,000); 50,000/80,000 = 5/8; 30,000/80,000 = 3/8

Step Method. This method allocates services rendered by service departments to other service departments using a sequence of allocation; this is also called the *step-down* method or the *sequential* method. The sequence normally begins with the department that renders service to the greatest number of other service departments, then continues in step-by-step fashion and ends with the allocation of costs of service departments that provide the least amount of service. After a given service department's costs have once been allocated, it will not receive any charges from the other service departments.

Using the same data, the step method yields:

	Service Departments		Production Departments	
	GP	*E*	*A*	*B*
Overhead costs	$20,000	$10,000	$30,000	$40,000
Reallocation:				
GP (1/6, 1/2, 1/3)*	($20,000)	3,333	10,000	6,667
E (5/8, 3/8)#		($13,333)	8,333	5,000
			$48,333	$51,667

*Base is (20,000 + 60,000 + 40,000 = 120,000); 20,000/120,000 = 1/6; 60,000/120,000 = 1/2; 40,000/120,000 = 1/3
\# Base is (50,000 + 30,000 = 80,000); 50,000/80,000 = 5/8; 30,000/80,000 = 3/8

Reciprocal Method. Also known as the *reciprocal service* method, the *matrix* method, or the *simultaneous allocation* method, the reciprocal method allocates service department costs to production departments, where *reciprocal* services are allowed between service departments. The method sets up simultaneous equations to determine the allocable cost of each service department.

Using the same data, we set up the following equations:

$$GP = \$20,000 + 50/85 \; E$$

$$E = \$10,000 + 1/6 \; GP$$

Substituting E from the second equation into the first:

$$GP = \$20,000 + 50/85 \; (\$10,000 + 1/6 \; GP)$$

Solving for GP gives GP = $28,695. Substituting GP = $28,695 into the second equation and solving for E gives E = $14,782. Using these solved values, the reciprocal method yields:

	Service Departments		Production Departments	
	GP	E	A	B
Overhead costs	$20,000	$10,000	$30,000	$40,000
Reallocation:	($28,695)	4,782	14,348	9,565
GP (0, 1/6, 1/2, 1/3)	8,695	($14,782)	5,217	870
E (50/85, 0, 30/85, 5/85)	0	0	$49,565	$50,435

ACTIVITY-BASED COSTING

Many companies use a traditional cost system such as job-order costing or process costing, or some hybrid of the two. This traditional system may provide distorted product cost information. In fact, companies selling multiple products are making critical decisions about product pricing, making bids, or product mix, based on inaccurate cost data. In all likelihood, the problem is not with assigning the costs of direct labor or direct materials. These prime costs are traceable to individual products, and most conventional cost systems are designed to ensure that this tracing takes place.

The assignment of overhead costs to individual products is another matter. Using the traditional methods of assigning overhead costs to products, using a single predetermined overhead rate based on any single activity measure can produce distorted product costs. Activity-based costing (ABC) gets around this problem.

Overhead Costing: A Single-Product Situation

The accuracy of overhead cost assignment becomes an issue only when multiple products are manufactured in a single facility. If only a single product is produced, all overhead costs are caused by it and traceable to it. The overhead cost per unit is the total overhead for the year divided by the number of hours or units produced. The cost calculation for a single-product setting is illustrated in Table 3.3. There is no question that the cost of manufacturing the product illustrated in Table 3.3 is $28.00 per unit. All manufacturing costs were incurred specifically to make this product. Thus, one way to ensure product-costing accuracy is to focus on producing one product. For this reason, some multiple product firms choose to dedicate entire plants to the manufacture of a single product.

By focusing on only one or two products, small manufacturers are able to calculate the cost of manufacturing the high-volume products more accurately and price them more effectively.

Overhead Costing: A Multiple-Product or -Job Situation

In a multiple-product or -job situation, manufacturing overhead costs are caused jointly by all products or jobs. The problem is one of identifying the amount of overhead caused or consumed by each. This is accomplished by searching for *cost drivers,* or activity measures that cause costs to be incurred.

Table 3.3
UNIT COST COMPUTATION: SINGLE PRODUCT

	Manufacturing Costs	Units Produced	Unit Cost
Direct materials	$ 800,000	50,000	$ 16.00
Direct labor	200,000	50,000	4.00
Factory overhead	400,000	50,000	8.00
Total	$1,400,000	50,000	$ 28.00

In a traditional setting, it is normally assumed that overhead consumption is highly correlated with the volume of production activity, measured in terms of direct labor hours, machine hours, or direct labor dollars. These volume-related cost drivers are used to assign overhead to products to develop *plant-wide* or *departmental* rates.

EXAMPLE 3.7

To illustrate the limitation of this traditional approach and ABC, assume that Global Metals, Inc. has established the following overhead cost pools and cost drivers for their product:

Overhead Cost Pool	Budgeted Cost	Overhead Cost Driver	Predicted Level for Cost Driver	Predetermined Overhead Rate
Machine set-ups	$100,000	Number of set-ups	100	$1,000 per set-up
Material handling	100,000	Weight of raw material	50,000 pounds	$2 per pound
Waste control	50,000	Weight of hazardous chemicals used	10,000 pounds	$5 per pound
Inspection	75,000	Number of inspections	1,000	$75 per inspection
Other overhead costs	$200,000	Machine hours	20,000	$10 per machine hour
Total	$525,000			

Job No. 107 consists of 2,000 special purpose machine tools with the following requirements:

Machine set-ups	2 set-ups
Raw material required	10,000 pounds
Waste materials required	2,000 pounds
Inspections	10 inspections
Machine hours	500 machine hours

The overhead assigned to Job No. 107 is computed below.

Overhead Cost Pool	Predetermined Overhead Rate	Level of Cost Driver	Assigned Overhead Cost
Machine set-ups	$1,000 per set-up	2 set-ups	$ 2,000
Material handling	$2 per pound	10,000 pounds	20,000
Waste control	$5 per pound	2,000 pounds	10,000
Inspection	$75 per inspection	10 inspections	750
Other overhead costs	$10 per machine hour	500 machine hours	5,000
Total			$37,750

The total overhead cost assigned to Job No. 107 is $37,750, or $18.88 per tool ($37,750/2,000). Compare this with the overhead cost that is assigned to the job if the firm uses a single predetermined overhead rate based on machine hours:

$$\frac{\text{Total budgeted overhead cost}}{\text{Total predicted machine hours}} = \frac{\$525,000}{20,000} = \$26.25 \text{ per machine hour}$$

With this approach, the total overhead cost assigned to Job No. 107 is \$13,125 (\$26.25 per machine hour × 500 machine hours). This is only \$6.56 per tool (\$13,125/2,000), which is about one-third of the overhead cost per tool computed when multiple cost drivers are used.

The reason for this wide discrepancy is that these special purpose tools require a relatively large number of machine set-ups, a sizable amount of waste materials, and several inspections. Thus, they are costly in terms of driving overhead costs. Use of a single predetermined overhead rate obscures that fact. Inaccurately calculating the overhead cost per unit to the extent illustrated above can have serious adverse consequences for the firm. For example, it can lead to poor decisions about pricing, product mix, or contract bidding.

The Choice of Cost Drivers

At least two major factors should be considered in selecting cost drivers: (1) the cost of measurement and (2) the degree of correlation between the cost driver and the actual consumption of overhead.

The Cost of Measurement. In an ABC system, a large number of cost drivers can be selected and used. However, it is preferable to select cost drivers that use information that is readily available. Information that is not available in the existing system must be produced, which will increase the cost of the firm's information system. A homogeneous cost pool could offer a number of possible cost drivers. For this situation, any cost driver that can be used with existing information should be chosen. This choice minimizes the costs of measurement.

Indirect Measures and the Degree of Correlation. The existing information structure can be exploited in another way to minimize the costs of obtaining cost driver quantities. It is sometimes possible to replace a cost driver that directly measures the consumption of an activity with a cost driver that indirectly measures that consumption. For example, inspection hours could be replaced by the actual number of inspections associated with each product; this number is more likely to be known. This replacement only works, of course, if hours used per inspection are reasonably stable for each product. *The least-squares method (regression analysis),* which will be covered later in this chapter, can be utilized to determine the degree of correlation.

A list of potential cost drivers is given in Table 3.4. Cost drivers that indirectly measure the consumption of an activity usually measure the number of transactions associated with that activity. It is possible to replace a cost driver that directly measures consumption with one that only indirectly measures it without loss of accuracy, provided that the quantities of activity consumed per transaction are stable for each product. In such a case, the indirect cost driver has a high correlation and can be used.

Table 3.4
COST DRIVERS

Manufacturing:

Number of setups	Direct labor hours
Weight of material	Number of vendors
Number of units reworked	Machine hours
Number of orders placed	Number of labor transactions
Number of orders received	Number of units scrapped
Number of inspections	Number of parts
Number of material handling operations	Square footage

Service:

Number of hospital beds occupied
Number of take-offs and landings for an airline
Number of rooms occupied in a hotel

ACTIVITY-BASED MANAGEMENT

Activity-based management (ABM) is now one of the most important ways to be competitive. It is a systemwide, integrated approach that focuses management's attention on activities with the goal of improving customer value, reducing costs, and the resulting profit. The basic premise of ABM is: *Products consume activities; activities consume resources.* To be competitive, you must know both (1) the activities that go into manufacturing the products or providing the services, and (2) the cost of those activities. To cut down a product's costs, you will likely have to change the activities the product consumes. An attitude such as "I want across-the-board-cuts—everyone reduce cost by 10%" rarely obtains the desired results.

In order to achieve desired cost reductions, you must first identify the activities that a product or service consumes. Then you must figure out how to rework those activities to improve productivity and efficiency. *Process value analysis* is used to try to determine why activities are performed and how well they are performed. *Activity-based costing*, discussed in this chapter, is a tool used in activity-based management.

Process Value Analysis

Process value analysis is the process of identifying, describing, and evaluating the activities a company performs. It produces the following four outcomes:

1. What activities are done.
2. How many people perform the activities.
3. The time and resources required to perform the activities.
4. An assessment of the value of the activities to the company, including a recommendation to select and keep only those that add value.

Understanding What Causes Costs

Effective cost control requires managers to understand how producing a product requires activities and how activities, in turn, generate costs. Consider the activities of a manufacturer facing a financial crisis. In a system of managing by the members, each department is told to reduce costs in an amount equal to its share of the budget cut. The usual response by department heads is to reduce the number of people and supplies, as these are the only cost items that they can control in the short run. Asking everyone to work harder produces only temporary gains, however, as the pace cannot be sustained in the long run.

Under ABM, the manufacturer reduces costs by studying what activities it conducts and develops plans to eliminate nonvalue-added activities and to improve the efficiency of value-added activities. Eliminating activities that do not create customer value is a very effective way to cut costs. For example, spending $100 to train all employees to avoid common mistakes will repay itself many times over by reducing customer ill will caused by those mistakes.

Value-Added and Nonvalue-Added Activities

A *value-added activity* is an activity that increases the product's service to the customer. For instance, purchasing the raw materials to make a product is a value-added activity. Without the purchase of raw materials, the organization would be unable to make the product. Sanding and varnishing a wooden chair are value-added activities because customers don't want splinters. Value-added activities are evaluated by how they contribute to the final product's service, quality, and cost.

Good management involves finding and, if possible, eliminating nonvalue-added activities. *Nonvalue-added activities* are activities that, when eliminated, reduce costs without reducing the product's potential to the customer. In many organizations poor facility layout may require the work in process to be moved around or temporarily stored during production. For example, a Midwest steel company that we studied had more than 100 miles of railroad track to move things back and forth in a poorly designed facility. Moving work around a factory, an office, or a store is unlikely to add value for the customer. Waiting, inspecting, and storing are other examples of nonvalue-added activities.

Organizations must change the process that makes nonvalue-added activities necessary. Elimination of nonvalue-added activities requires organizations to improve the process so that the activities are no longer required. Organizations strive to reduce or eliminate nonvalue-added activities because, by doing so, they permanently reduce the costs they must incur to produce goods or services without affecting the value to the customer.

Although managers should pay particular attention to nonvalue-added activities, they should also carefully evaluate the need for value-added activities. For example, in wine production, classifying storage as a value-added activity assumes the only way to make good-tasting wine is to allow it to age in storage. Think of the advantage that someone could have if he discovered a way to produce wine that tastes as good as conventionally aged wine but didn't require long storage periods.

Activity Drivers and Categories

Activity output is measured by activity drivers. An activity driver is a factor (activity) that causes (drives) costs. We can simply identify activity output measures by classifying activities into four general categories: (1) unit level, (2) batch level, (3) product level, and (4) facility level. Classifying activities into these general categories is useful because the costs of activities associated with the different levels respond to different types of activity drivers. Table 3.5 describes what they perform, examples, output measures, and examples of possible cost drivers.

The Value Chain of the Business Functions

The value chain concept of the business functions is used throughout the book to demonstrate how to use cost/managerial accounting to add value to organizations (see Figure 3.1). The *value chain* describes the linked set of activities that increase the usefulness (or value) of the products or services of an organization (value-added activities). Activities are evaluated by how they contribute to the final product's quality, service, and cost. In general, the business functions include the following:

- *Research and development:* the generation and development of ideas related to new products, services, or processes.
- *Design:* the detailed planning and engineering of products, services, or processes.
- *Production:* the aggregation and assembly of resources to produce a product or deliver a service.
- *Marketing:* the process that (a) informs potential customers about the attributes and benefits of products or services and (b) leads to the purchase of those products or services.
- *Distribution:* the mechanism established to deliver products or services to customers.
- *Customer service:* the product or service support activities provided to customers.

A **strategy and administration** function spans all the business activities described. Human resource management, tax planning, legal matters, and the like, for example, potentially affect every step of the value chain. Cost and managerial accounting are major means of helping managers (a) run each of the business functions and (b) coordinate their activities within the framework of the entire organization.

Table 3.5
ACTIVITY CATEGORIES AND DRIVERS

	Unit-Level Activities	*Batch-Level Activities*	*Product-Level (Product- and Customer-Sustaining) Activities*	*Facility-Level (Capacity-Sustaining) Activities*
Types of activities	Performed each time a unit is produced	Performed each time a batch is produced	Performed as needed to support a product	Sustain a factory's general manufacturing process

Table 3.5
ACTIVITY CATEGORIES AND DRIVERS (Continued)

	Unit-Level Activities	Batch-Level Activities	Product-Level (Product- and Customer-Sustaining) Activities	Facility-Level (Capacity-Sustaining) Activities
Examples:	Direct materials, direct labor, assembly, energy to run machines	Quality inspections, machine setups, production scheduling, material handling	Engineering changes, maintenance of equipment, customer records and files, marketing the product	Plant management, plant security, landscaping, maintaining grounds, heating and lighting, property taxes, rent, plant depreciation
Output measures:	Unit-level drivers	Batch-level drivers	Product-level drivers	Difficult to define
Examples:	Units of product, direct labor hours, machine hours	Number of batches, number of production orders, inspection hours	Number of products, number of changing orders	Plant size (square feet), number of security personnel

Strategic Cost Analysis

Companies can identify strategic advantages in the marketplace by analyzing the value chain and the information about the costs of activities. A company that eliminates nonvalue-added activities reduces costs without reducing the value of the product to customers. With reduced costs, the company can reduce the price it charges customers, thus giving the company a cost advantage over its competitors. Or the company can use the resources saved from eliminating nonvalue-added activities to provide greater service to customers. *Strategic cost analysis* is the use of cost data to develop and identify superior strategies that will produce a sustainable competitive advantage. The idea here is simple. Look for activities that are not on the value chain. If the company can safely eliminate nonvalue-added activities, then it should do so. By identifying and cutting them, you will save the company money and make it more competitive.

Global Strategies

Another approach to gaining a cost advantage is to identify where on the value chain your company has a strategic advantage. Many computer software companies, for example, are looking at foreign markets as a way to capitalize on their investment in research and development. The reservoir of intellectual capital gives these firms an advantage over local competitors who have not yet developed this expertise. These competitors would face research and development costs already incurred by established companies, making it difficult for the newcomers to charge competitive prices and still make a profit.

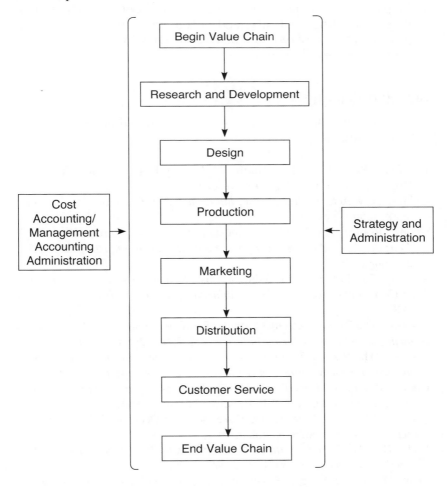

Figure 3-3. The value chain and cost/management accounting

Brief Summary

This part of the chapter discussed in detail how activity costing provides more accurate product cost figures for product costing and pricing, using multiple overhead cost pools and cost drivers. Conventional cost systems are not able to accurately assign the costs of nonvolume-related overhead activities. For this reason, assigning overhead using only volume-based drivers or a single driver can distort product costs. One case was provided to illustrate the use of the activity-based costing system versus the traditional system using a single driver such as machine hours. Activity-based costing may provide more accurate information about product costs. It helps managers make better decisions about product design, pricing, marketing, and mix, and encourages continual operating improvements. Activity-based management (ABM), of which ABC is a tool, was also discussed.

Selected Readings

For a more detailed discussion on activity-based costing, see the following articles:

Chaffman, Beth M., and Faye Borthick. "Activity-Based Costing in a Service Organization." *CMA Magazine,* December/January 1991.

Cokins, Gary. *Activity-Based Cost Management: An Executive's Guide.* New York: John Wiley, 2001.

Cooper, Robin, "The Two-Stage Procedure in Cost Accounting—Part One." *Journal of Cost Management for the Manufacturing Industry,* Vol. 1, No. 2, Summer 1987.

———. "The Two-Stage Procedure in Cost Accounting—Part Two." *Journal of Cost Management for the Manufacturing Industry,* Vol. 1, No. 3, Fall 1987.

———. "The Rise of Activity Costing—Part One." *Journal of Cost Management for the Manufacturing Industry,* Vol. 2, No. 2, Summer 1988.

———. "The Rise of Activity Costing—Part Three." *Journal of Cost Management for the Manufacturing Industry,* Vol. 2, No. 4, Winter 1989.

Cooper, Robin, and Robert S. Kaplan. *The Design of Cost Management Systems.* Englewood Cliffs, N.J.: Prentice-Hall, Inc., 1991.

———. "Measuring Costs Right: Make the Right Decisions." *Harvard Business Review,* September/October, 1988.

Hicks, Douglas T. *Activity-Based Costing: Making It Work for Small or Midsized Companies.* New York: John Wiley, 2002.

Jacobs, F., and A. Maiga. "Balanced Scorecard, Activity-Based Costing and Company Performance: An Empirical Analysis." *Journal of Managerial Issues.* Vol. 15, No. 3, 2003.

Musso, Francis, Jr. "Activity-Based Costing for Defense Contractors." *The CPA Journal,* May 1992.

Ness, J. and T. Cucuzza. "Tapping the Full Potential of ABC." *Harvard Business Review,* July/August 1995.

Raffish, Norm. "How Much Does That Product Really Cost?" *Management Accounting,* March 1991.

Reeve, James. "Projects, Models, and Systems—Where is ABM headed?" *Journal of Cost Management,* Summer 1996.

Sweeney, Robert B. and James W. Mays. "ABM Lifts Bank's Bottom Line." *Management Accounting,* March 1997.

JUST-IN-TIME (JIT) AND TOTAL QUALITY MANAGEMENT (TQM)

The inventory control problem occurs in almost every type of organization. It exists whenever products are held to meet some expected future demand. In most industries, cost of inventory represents the largest liquid asset under the control of management. Therefore, it is very important to develop a production and inventory planning system that will minimize both purchasing and carrying costs.

In recent years, the Japanese have demonstrated the ability to manage their production systems effectively. Much of their success has been attributed to what is known as the *Just-in-Time (JIT)* approach to production and inventory control, which has generated a great deal of interest among practitioners. The "Kanban" system—as they call it—has been a focal point of interest, with its dramatic impact on the inventory performance and productivity of the Japanese auto industry.

We provide an overview of the Just-in-Time (JIT) approach and its impact on quality improvement and cost management.

What Is Just-In-Time (JIT)?

JIT is a demand-pull system. Demand for customer output (not plans for using input resources) triggers production. Production activities are "pulled," not "pushed," into action. JIT production, in its purest sense, is buying and producing in very small quantities just in time for use. As a philosophy, JIT targets inventory as an evil presence that obscures problems that should be solved, and that by contributing significantly to costs, large inventories keep a company from being as competitive or profitable as it otherwise might be. Practically speaking, JIT has as its principal goal the elimination of waste, and the principal measure of success is how much or how little inventory there is. Virtually anything that achieves this end can be considered a JIT innovation.

Furthermore, the little inventory that exists in a JIT system must be of good quality. This requirement has led to JIT purchasing practices uniquely able to deliver high-quality materials. This ties very closely with the principle of *Total Quality Management (TQM)*.

JIT systems integrate five functions of the production process— sourcing, storage, transportation, operations, and quality control— into one controlled manufacturing process. In manufacturing, JIT means that a company produces only the quantity needed for delivery to dealers or customers. In purchasing, it means suppliers deliver subassemblies just in time to be assembled into finished goods. In delivery, it requires selecting a transportation mode that will deliver purchased components and materials in small-lot sizes at the loading dock of the manufacturing facilities just in time to support the manufacturing process.

JIT Compared with Traditional Manufacturing

JIT manufacturing is a demand-pull, rather than the traditional "push" approach. The philosophy underlying JIT manufacturing is to produce a product when it is needed and only in the quantities demanded by customers. Demand pulls products through the manufacturing process. Each operation produces only what is necessary to satisfy the demand of the succeeding operation. No production takes place until a signal from a succeeding process indicates a need to produce. Parts and materials arrive just in time to be used in production.

Reduced Inventories. The primary goal of JIT is to reduce inventories to insignificant or zero levels. In traditional manufacturing, inventories result whenever production exceeds demand. Inventories are needed as a buffer when production does not meet expected demand.

Manufacturing Cells and Multifunction Labor. In traditional manufacturing, products are moved from one group of identical machines to another. Typically, machines with identical functions are located together in an area referred to as a department or process. Workers who specialize in the operation of a specific machine are located in each department. JIT replaces this traditional pattern with a pattern of manufacturing cells or work centers. Robots supplement people to do many routine operations.

Manufacturing cells contain machines that are grouped in families, usually in a semicircle. The machines are arranged so that they can be used to perform a variety of operations in sequence. Each cell is set up to produce a particular product or product family. Products move from one machine to another from start to finish. Workers are assigned to cells and are trained to operate all machines within the cell. Thus, labor in a JIT environment is multi-function labor, not specialized labor. Each manufacturing cell is basically a minifactory or a factory within a factory.

Better Cost Management. Cost management differs from cost accounting in that it refers to the management of cost, whether or not the cost has direct impact on inventory or the financial statements. The JIT philosophy simplifies the cost accounting procedure and helps managers manage and control their costs.

JIT recognizes that with simplification comes better management, better quality, better service, and better cost. Traditional cost accounting systems have a tendency to be very complex, with many transactions and reporting of data. Simplification of this process will transform a cost "accounting" system into a cost "management" system that can be used to support management's needs for better decisions about product design, pricing, marketing, and mix, and to encourage continual operating improvements.

Total Quality Management, Zero Defects, and Quality Costs

JIT goes with a stronger emphasis on quality control. A defective part brings production to a grinding halt. Poor quality simply cannot be tolerated in a stockless manufacturing environment. In other words, JIT cannot be implemented without a commitment to *total quality management (TQM)*. TQM is essentially an endless quest for perfect quality. It is a *zero-defects* approach. It views the optimal level of quality costs as the level where zero defects are produced. This approach to quality is opposed to the traditional belief, called *acceptable quality level (AQL)*, which allows a predetermined level of defective units to be produced and sold. AQL is the level where the number of defects allowed minimizes total quality costs.

Quality costs are classified into four broad categories: prevention, detection, appraisal, and failure costs. *Prevention costs* are those incurred to prevent defects. Amounts spent on quality training programs, researching customer needs, quality circles, and improved production equipment are considered in prevention costs. Expenditures made for prevention will minimize the costs that will be incurred for appraisal and failure. *Detection costs* identify problems such as testing. *Appraisal costs* are costs incurred for monitoring or inspection; these costs compensate for mistakes not eliminated through prevention. *Correction costs* may be internal (such as scrap and rework costs and reinspection) or external (such as product returns due to quality problems, warranty costs, lost sales due to poor product performance, and complaint department costs).

Quality cost reports can be used to point out the strengths and weaknesses of a quality system. Improvement teams can use them to describe the monetary benefits and ramifications of proposed changes. Return-on-investment (ROI) models and other financial analyses can be constructed directly from quality cost data to justify proposals to management. In practice, quality costs can define activities of quality program and quality improvement efforts in a language that management can understand and act on—dollars.

The negative effect on profits resulting from products or services of less than acceptable quality or from ineffective quality management is almost always dynamic. Once started, it continues to mushroom until ultimately the company finds itself in serious financial difficulties due to the two-pronged impact of an unheeded increase in quality costs coupled with a declining performance image. Management that clearly understands this understands the economics of quality.

JIT Costing System

The cost accounting system of a company adopting JIT will be quite simple compared to job order or processing costing. Under JIT, raw materials and work-in-process (WIP) accounts are typically combined into one account called "resources in process (RIP)" or "raw and in-process." Under JIT, the materials arrive at the receiving area and are whisked immediately to the factory area. Thus, the Stores Control account vanishes. The journal entries that accompany JIT costing are remarkably simple as follows:

Raw and in-process (RIT) inventory	45,000	
Accounts payable or cash		45,000
To record purchases		
Finished goods	40,000	
RIP inventory		40,000
To record raw materials in completed units.		

As can be seen, there are no Stores Control or WIP accounts under JIT.

In summary, JIT costing can be characterized as follows:

1. There are fewer inventory accounts.
2. There are no work orders. Thus, there is no need for detailed tracking of actual raw materials.
3. With JIT, activities can be eliminated on the premise that they do not add value. Prime target for elimination are storage areas for WIP inventory and material handling facilities.
4. Direct labor costs and factory overhead costs are not tracked to specific orders. Direct labor is now regarded as just another part of factory overhead. Furthermore, factory overhead is accounted for as follows: virtually all of the factory overhead incurred each month, now including direct labor, flows through to cost of goods sold in the same month. Tracking overhead through WIP and finished goods inventory provides no useful information. Therefore, it makes sense to treat manufacturing overhead as an expense charged directly to cost of goods sold.

The major differences between JIT manufacturing and traditional manufacturing are summarized in Table 3.6.

Table 3.6
COMPARISON OF JIT AND TRADITIONAL MANUFACTURING

JIT	*Traditional*
1. Pull system	1. Push system
2. Insignificant or zero inventories	2. Significant inventories
3. Manufacturing cells	3. "Process" structure
4. Multifunction labor	4. Specialized labor
5. Total quality management (TQM)	5. Acceptable quality level (AQL)
6. Decentralized services	6. Centralized services
7. Simple cost accounting	7. Complex cost accounting

In a JIT system, an improved plant layout, through a manufacturing cell, can drastically increase *throughput*, which is the total volume of production through a facility during a period. It can significantly cut down *throughput time* (also known as *cycle time*), which is the time required to manufacture a product.

MEASURING QUALITY COSTS

Quality costs can also be classified as *observable* or *hidden*. *Observable quality costs* are those that are available from an organization's accounting records. *Hidden quality costs* are opportunity costs resulting from poor quality (opportunity costs are not usually recognized in accounting records). Consider, for example, all the examples of quality costs listed in the prior section. With the exception of lost sales, customer dissatisfaction, and lost market share, all the quality costs are observable and should be available from the accounting records. Note also that the hidden costs are all in the external failure category. These hidden quality costs can be significant and should be estimated. Although estimating hidden quality costs is not easy, three methods have been suggested: (1) the multiplier method, (2) the market research method, and (3) the Taguchi quality loss function.

The Multiplier Method

The multiplier method assumes that the total failure cost is simply some multiple of measured failure costs:

Total external failure cost = k (measured external failure costs)

where k is the multiplier effect. The value of k is based on experience. For example, Westinghouse Electric reports a value of k between 3 and 4. Thus, if the measured external failure costs are $2 million, the actual external failure costs are between $6 million and $8 million. Including hidden costs in assessing the amount of external failure costs allows management to more accurately determine the level of resource spending for prevention and appraisal activities. Specifically, with an increase in failure costs, we would expect management to increase its investment in control costs.

The Market Research Method

Formal market research methods are used to assess the effect of poor quality on sales and market share. Customer surveys and interviews with members of a company's sales force can provide significant insights into the magnitude of a company's hidden costs. Market research results can be used to project future profit losses attributable to poor quality.

The Taguchi Quality Loss Function

The traditional zero defects definition assumes that hidden quality costs exist only for units that fall outside of the upper and lower specification limits. The Taguchi loss function assumes any variation from the target value of a quality characteristic causes hidden quality costs. Furthermore, the hidden quality costs increase quadratically as the actual value deviates from the target value. The Taguchi quality loss function can be described by the following equation:

$$L(y) = k(y - T)^2$$

where

k = A proportionality constant dependent upon the organization's external failure cost structure
y = Actual value of quality characteristic
T = Target value of quality characteristic
L = Quality loss

The quality cost is zero at the target value and increases symmetrically at an increasing rate, as the actual value varies from the target value. Assume, for example, that $k = \$400$ and $T = 10$ inches in diameter. Table 3.7 illustrates the computation of the quality loss for four units. Notice that the cost quadruples when the deviation from the target doubles (from unit 2 to 3). Notice also the average deviation squared and the average loss per unit can be computed. These averages can be used to compute the total expected hidden quality costs for a product. If, for example, the total units produced is 2,000 and the average squared deviation is 0.025, then the expected cost per unit is $10 (0.025 × $400) and the total expected loss of the 2,000 units would be $20,000 ($10 × 2,000).

To apply the Taguchi loss function, k must be estimated. The value of k is computed by dividing the estimated cost at one of the specification limits by the squared deviation of the limit from the target value:

$$k = c/d^2$$

where

c = Loss at the lower or upper specification limit
d = Distance of limit from target value

This means that we still must estimate the loss for a given deviation from the target value. The first two methods, the multiplier method or the market research method, may be used to help in this estimation (a one-time assessment need). Once k is known, the hidden quality costs can be estimated for any level of variation from the target value.

Table 3.7
QUALITY-LOSS COMPUTATION ILLUSTRATED

Unit	(y)	Actual Diameter $y - T$	$(y - T)^2$	$K(y - T)^2$
1	9.9	−0.10	0.010	$4.00
2	10.1	0.10	0.010	4.00
3	10.2	0.20	0.040	16.00
4	9.8	−0.20	0.040	16.00
Total			0.100	$40.00
Average			0.025	$10.00

BACKFLUSH COSTING

Backflush costing is a streamlined cost accounting method that speeds up, simplifies, and reduces accounting efforts in an environment that minimizes inventory balances, requires few allocations, uses standard costs, and has minimal variances from the standard. During the period, this costing method records purchases of raw materials and accumulates actual conversion costs. Then, either at completion of production or upon the sale of goods, an entry is made to allocate the total costs incurred to Cost of Goods Sold and to Finished Goods Inventory, using standard production costs.

Implementation of a just-in-time system can result in significant cost reductions and productivity improvements. But even within a single company, not all inventories need to be managed according to a just-in-time philosophy. The costs and benefits of any inventory control system must be evaluated before management installs the system.

THROUGHPUT

One nonfinancial performance indicator that is becoming widely accepted is throughput, or the number of good units or quantity of services that are produced and sold or provided by an organization within a specified time. Because its primary goal is to earn income, a for-profit organization must sell inventory (not simply produced) for throughput to be achieved. Throughput can be analyzed as a set of component elements (in a manner similar to the way the DuPont model includes components of Rot). Throughput can be measured in either financial or nonfinancial terms (for example, cash flows generated from selling products or services to customers, units of products, batches produced, dollar turnover, or other meaningful measurements). Components of throughput include manufacturing cycle efficiency, process productivity, and process quality yield. Throughput can be calculated as follows:

Throughput = Manufacturing Cycle Efficiency $\times$ Process Productivity $\times$ Process Quality Yield

$$\text{Throughput} = \frac{\text{Value-Added Processing Time}}{\text{Total Time}} \times$$

$$\frac{\text{Total Units}}{\text{Value-Added Processing Time}} \times \frac{\text{Good Units}}{\text{Total Units}}$$

Manufacturing cycle efficiency is the proportion of value-added processing time to total processing time. Value-added processing time reflects activities that increase the product's worth to the customer. Total units produced during the period divided by the value-added processing time determines process productivity. Production activities can produce both good and defective units. The proportion of good units resulting from activities is the process quality yield. An example of these calculations is given in Example 3.8.

Management should strive to increase throughput by decreasing non-value-added costs, increasing total unit production and sales, decreasing the per-unit processing time, increasing process quality yield, or a combination of these. Some companies have increased throughput significantly by the use of flexible manufacturing systems (FMS) and, in some cases, by reorganizing production operations. At Intel, for example, throughput is enhanced by the technicians' ability to monitor automated operations from centralized locations, which allows for faster reaction time to production circumstances that might create downtime. Computer technologies such as bar coding, computer-integrated manufacturing (CIM), and electronic data interchange (EDI) have also enhanced throughput at many firms. Improved throughput means a greater ability to respond to customer needs and demands, to reduce production costs, and reduce inventory levels and, therefore, the non-value-added costs of moving and storing goods.

EXAMPLE 3.8

Given:

Total processing time	40,000 hours
Total value-added processing time	10,000 hours
Total quantity of product JKS#610 manufactured	50,000 tons
Total quantity of goods production manufactured and sold	44,000 tons

Manufacturing Cycle Efficiency = Value-Added Processing Time/Total Processing Time = 10,000/40,000 = 25% (means that 75% of processing time is non-value-added)

Process Productivity = Total Units/Value-Added Processing Time = 50,000/10,000 = 5 (means that 5 units can be produced per hour)

Process Quality Yield = Good Units/Total Units = 44,000/50,000 = 88% (means that 12% of the yield was defective)

	Manufacturing	Process	Process
Throughput = Yield	Cycle Efficiency ×	Productivity ×	Quality
	= 0.25	× 5	× 0.88
	= 1.1		

(means that 1.1 good units are produced per hour of total processing time, compared with the 5 units actually produced per value-added hour)

or

Throughput = Good Units/Total Time = 44,000 tons/40,000 hours = 1.1

Selected Readings

For more on JIT and TQM, see the following articles:

Bragg, Steven M. *Just in Time Cost Accounting: How to Decrease Costs and Increase Efficiency*, 2nd ed. New York: John Wiley and Sons, 2003.

Campanella, Jack. *Principles of Quality Costs*. Milwaukee: Quality Press, 2nd ed., 1990.

DeLuizio, M.C. "The Tools of Just-in-Time." *Journal of Cost Management,* 1993, vol. 7, No. 2, pp. 13–20.

Evans, James R., James W. Dean Jr., and James W. Dean. *Total Quality Management*. Ohio: South-Western, 2002.

Hirano, Hiroyuki and Makota, Furuya. *JIT Is Flow: Practice and Principles of Lean Manufacturing*. Washington, DC: PCS Press, Inc., 2006.

Hugos, Michael H. *Essentials of Supply Chain Management*. New York: John Wiley & Sons, 2002.

Jablonski, Joseph R. *Implementing TQM: Competing in the Nineties Through Total Quality Management.* San Diego, Ca.: Pfeiffer & Company, 1992.

Juran, J.M. *Juran on Planning for Quality.* New York: The Free Press, 1988.

Juran, J.M. and Frank M. Gryna. *Juran's Quality Control Handbook,* 4th ed. New York: McGraw-Hill Book Co., 1988.

Muller, Max. *Essentials of Inventory Management.* New York: Amacom, 2002.

Tenner, Arthur R. *Total Quality Management—Three Steps to Continuous Improvement.* Addison-Wesley Publishing Company, Inc., 1992.

ENVIRONMENTAL COSTS AND ECOEFFICIENCY

Measuring environmental costs has become an important issue for many companies. Two reasons stand out relating to the increased interest in this issue:

1. Many countries have increased their regulations. Enormous fines or penalties have become part of these new regulations.
2. Successful treatment of environmental concerns is becoming a significant competitive issue.

Ecoefficiency is an important concept in dealing with the second reason listed above. *Ecoefficiency* essentially maintains that organizations can produce more useful goods and services while simultaneously reducing negative environmental impacts, resource consumption, and costs. This means producing more goods and services using less materials, energy, water, and land, while minimizing air emissions, water discharges, waste disposal, and the dispersion of toxic substances. Ecoefficiency implies a positive relationship between environmental and economic performance.

Ecoefficiency is not the only environmental cost paradigm. A competing paradigm is that of *compliance management.* Compliance management is the practice of achieving the minimal environmental performance required by regulations with the least amount of cost. A second competing paradigm is that of *guided ecoefficiency.* Guided ecoefficiency maintains that pollution is a form of economic inefficiency and that properly designed environmental regulations will stimulate innovation such that environmental performance and economic efficiency will simultaneously improve.

There are at least five core objectives for the environmental perspective, including minimizing the use of raw or virgin materials, minimizing the use of hazardous materials, minimizing energy requirements for production and use of the product, minimizing the release of solid, liquid, and gaseous residues, and maximizing opportunities to recycle. Table 3.8 summarizes the objectives and measures for the environmental perspective:

Table 3.8
OBJECTIVES AND MEASURES
FOR THE ENVIRONMENTAL PERSPECTIVE

Objectives	*Measures*
Minimize hazardous materials	Types and quantities (total and per unit)
	Percentage of total materials cost
	Productivity measures (output/input)
Minimize raw or virgin materials	Types and quantities (total and per unit)
	Productivity measures (output/input)
Minimize energy requirements	Types and quantities (total and per unit)
	Productivity measures (output/input)
Minimize release of residues	Pounds of toxic waste produced
	Cubic meters of effluents
	Tons of greenhouse gases produced
	Percentage reduction of packaging materials
Maximize opportunities to recycle	Pounds of materials recycled
	Number of different components
	Percentage of units remanufactured
	Energy produced from incineration

Environmental costs are costs that are incurred because poor environmental quality exists or may exist. Environmental costs can be classified into four categories: prevention costs, detection costs, internal failure costs, and external failure costs.

Environmental prevention costs are the costs of activities carried out to prevent the production of contaminants and/or waste that could cause damage to the environment. Pollution prevention activities, often called "P2" activities, include...

- Evaluating and selecting suppliers
- Evaluating and selecting pollution-control equipment
- Designing processes

- Designing products
- Carrying out environmental studies
- Auditing environmental risks
- Developing environmental management systems
- Recycling products
- Obtaining ISO 14001 certification

Environmental detection costs are the costs of activities executed to determine whether products, processes, and other activities within the firm are in compliance with appropriate environmental standards. Environmental detection costs include...

- Auditing environmental activities
- Inspecting products and processes
- Developing environmental performance measures
- Testing for contamination
- Verifying supplier environmental performance
- Measuring contamination levels

Environmental internal failure costs are costs of activities performed because contaminants and waste have been produced but not discharged into the environment. They are incurred to eliminate and manage contaminants or waste once produced. Examples of environmental internal failure costs include...

- Operating pollution-control equipment
- Treating and disposing of toxic waste
- Maintaining pollution equipment
- Licensing facilities for producing contaminants
- Recycling scrap

Environmental external failure costs are the costs of activities performed after discharging contaminants and waste into the environment. These costs are realized if incurred and paid for by the firm. They are unrealized or societal if they are caused by the firm but incurred and paid for by parties outside the firm. Examples of environmental external failure costs include...

- Cleaning up a polluted lake
- Cleaning up oil spills
- Cleaning up contaminated soil
- Settling personal injury claims (environmentally related)
- Restoring land to natural state
- Losing sales due to poor environmental reputation
- Using materials and energy inefficiently

- Receiving medical care due to polluted air
- Losing employment because of contamination
- Losing a lake for recreational use
- Damaging ecosystems from solid waste disposal

An *environmental cost report* may be prepared to report the details of environmental costs. It is a good idea to report the costs by category. An example of an environmental cost report is presented in Table 3.9.

Table 3.9
A SAMPLE ENVIRONMENTAL COST REPORT

XYZ Chemicals
Environmental Cost Report
For the Year Ended December 31, 2014

		Environmental Costs	*Percentage**
Prevention costs:			
Evaluating suppliers	$120,000		
Recycling products	75,000	$195,000	0.33%
Detection costs:			
Inspecting products/processes	$600,000		
Developing perf. measures	60,000	660,000	1.10
Internal failure costs:			
Treating toxic waste	$4,800,000		
Operating equipment	840,000		
Licensing facilities	360,000	6,000,000	10.00
External failure costs:			
Settling claims	$1,200,000		
Cleanup of soil	1,800,000	3,000,000	5.00
Totals		$9,855,000	16.43%

*of operating costs: $60,000,000.

The distribution shown in Figure 3-4 reveals that the company is paying little attention to preventing and detecting environmental costs. To improve environmental performance, much more needs to be invested in the prevention and detection categories.

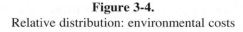

Figure 3-4.
Relative distribution: environmental costs

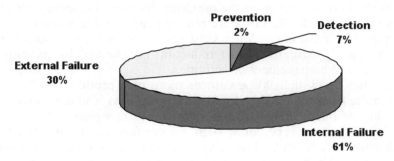

LIFE-CYCLE COSTS AND TARGET COSTING

Life-cycle costing tracks and accumulates all product costs in the value chain, from research and development and design of products and processes through production, marketing, distribution, and customer service. The value chain is the set of activities required to design, develop, produce, market, and service a product (or service). The terms "cradle-to-grave costing" and "womb-to-tomb costing" conveys the sense of fully capturing all costs associated with the product.

It focuses on minimizing locked-in costs, for example, by reducing the number of parts, promoting standardization of parts, and using equipment that can make more than one kind of product. Product life cycle is simply the time a product exists—from conception to abandonment. *Life-cycle costs* are all costs associated with the product for its entire life cycle. These costs include development (planning, design, and testing), manufacturing (conversion activities), and logistics support (advertising, distribution, warranty, and so on).

Can You Achieve Cost Reduction Through Life-Cycle Costing?

Because total customer satisfaction has become a vital issue in the new business setting, whole-life cost has emerged as the central focus of life-cycle cost management. *Whole-life cost* is the life-cycle cost of a product plus after-purchase (or post-purchase) costs that consumers incur, including operation, support, maintenance, and disposal. Since the costs a purchaser incurs after buying a product can be a significant percentage of whole-life costs and, thus, an important consideration in the purchase decision, managing activities so that whole-life costs are reduced can provide an important competitive advantage. *Note*: Cost reduction, not cost control, is the emphasis. Moreover, cost reduction is achieved by judicious analysis and management of activities.

Studies show that 90 percent or more of a product's costs are committed during the development stage. Thus, it makes sense to emphasize management of activities during this phase of a product's existence. Every dollar spent on premanufacturing activities is known to save $8-$10 on manufacturing and postmanufacturing activities. The real opportunities for cost reduction occur before manufacturing begins. Managers need to invest more in premanufacturing assets and dedicate more resources to activities in the early phases of the product life cycle so that overall whole-life costs can be reduced.

What Is the Role of Target Costing?
How Does It Differ from Cost-Plus Pricing?

Life-cycle and whole-life cost concepts are associated with target costing and target pricing. A firm may determine that market conditions require that a product sell at a given target price. Hence, target cost can be determined by subtracting the desired unit profit margin from the target price. The cost reduction objectives of life-cycle and whole-life cost management can therefore be determined using target costing.

Thus, *target costing* becomes a particularly useful tool for establishing cost reduction goals. Toyota, for example, calculates the lifetime target profit for a new car model by multiplying a target profit ratio times the target sales. They then calculate the estimated profit by subtracting the estimated costs from target sales. Usually, at this point, target profit is greater than estimated profit. The cost reduction goal is defined by the difference between the target profit and the estimated profit. Toyota then searches for cost reduction opportunities through better design of the new model. Toyota's management recognizes that more opportunities exist for cost reduction during product planning than in actual development and production.

The Japanese developed target costing to enhance their ability to compete in the global marketplace. This approach to product pricing differs significantly from the cost-based methods just described.

Instead of first determining the cost of a product or service and then adding a profit factor to arrive at its price, target costing reverses the procedure. Target costing is a pricing method that involves (1) identifying the price at which a product will be competitive in the marketplace, (2) defining the desired profit to be made on the product, and (3) computing the target cost for the product by subtracting the desired profit from the competitive market price.

Target Price – Desired Profit = Target Cost

Target cost is then given to the engineers and product designers, who use it as the maximum cost to be incurred for the materials and other resources needed to design and manufacture the product. It is their responsibility to create the product at or below its target cost.

Table 3.10 compares the cost-plus philosophy with the target costing philosophy.

Table 3.10
COST-PLUS PRICING VERSUS TARGET COSTING

	Formula	*Implications*
Cost-plus pricing	*Cost base + markup = selling price*	• Cost is the base (given) • Markup is added (given) • The firm puts the product on the market and hopes the selling price is accepted
Pricing based on target costing	Target selling price – desired profit = target cost	• Markets determine prices (given) • Desired profit must be sustained for survival (given) • Target cost is the residual, the variable to be managed

EXAMPLE 3.9

A salesperson at Cato Products Company has reported that a customer is seeking price quotations for two electronic components: a special-purpose battery charger (Product X101) and a small transistorized machine computer (Product Y101). Competing for the customer's order are one French company and two Japanese companies. The current market price ranges for the two products are as follows:

Product X101 $310–$370 per unit
Product Y101 $720–$820 per unit

The salesperson believes that if Cato could quote prices of $325 for Product X101 and $700 for Product Y101, the company would get the order and gain a significant share of the global market for those goods. Cato's usual profit markup is 25% of total unit cost. The company's design engineers and cost accountants put together the following specifications and costs for the new products:

Activity-based cost rates:
Materials handling activity $1.30 per dollar of raw materials
                                 and purchased parts cost
Production activity $3.50 per machine hour
Product delivery activity $24.00 per unit of X101
                                 $30.00 per unit of Y101

	Product X101	Product Y101
Projected unit demand	26,000	18,000
Per unit data:		
Raw materials cost	$30.00	$65.00
Purchased parts cost	$15.00	$45.00
Manufacturing labor		
Hours	2.6	4.8
Hourly labor rate	$12.00	$15.00
Assembly labor		
Hours	3.4	8.2
Hourly labor rate	$14.00	$16.00
Machine hours	12.8	28.4

The company wants to address the following three questions:

1. What is the target cost for each product?
2. What is the projected total unit cost of production and delivery?
3. Using the target costing approach, should the company produce the products?

1. Target cost for each product:

Product X101 = $325.00 ÷ 1.25 = $260.00*
Product Y101 = $700.00 ÷ 1.25 = $560.00

*Target Price – Desired Profit = Target Cost
$$\$325.00 - .25X = X$$
$$\$325.00 = 1.25X$$
$$X = \frac{\$325.00}{1.25} = \$260.00$$

2. Projected total unit cost of production and delivery:

	Product X101	Product Y101
Raw materials cost	$ 30.00	$ 65.00
Purchased parts cost	15.00	45.00
Total cost of raw materials and parts	$ 45.00	$110.00
Manufacturing labor		
X101 (2.6 hours × $12.00)	31.20	
Y101 (4.8 hours × $15.00)		72.00
Assembly labor		
X101 (3.4 hours × $14.00)	47.60	
Y101 (8.2 hours × $16.00)		131.20
Activity-based costs		
Materials handling activity		
X101 ($45.00 × $1.30)	58.50	
Y101 ($110.00 × $1.30)		143.00
Production activity		
X101 (12.8 machine hours × $3.50)	44.80	
Y101 (28.4 machine hours × $3.50)		99.40
Product delivery activity		
X101	24.00	
Y101		30.00
Projected total unit cost	$251.10	$585.60

3. Production decision:

	Product X101	Product Y101
Target unit cost	$260.00	$560.00
Less: projected unit cost	251.10	585.60
Difference	$ 8.90	($25.60)

Product X101 can be produced below its target cost, so it should be produced. As currently designed, Product Y101 cannot be produced at or below its target cost; either it needs to be redesigned or the company should drop plans to make it.

Part II: Using Cost Data for Planning

COST BEHAVIOR ANALYSIS–ANALYSIS OF MIXED COSTS

Depending on how a cost will react or respond to changes in the level of activity, costs may be viewed as variable, fixed, or mixed (semivariable). For planning, control, and decision-making purposes, mixed costs need to be separated into their variable and fixed components. Since mixed costs contain both fixed and variable components, the analysis takes the following functional form, which is called a *cost-volume formula:*

$$y = a + bx$$

where y = the mixed cost to be broken up
       x = any given measure of activity such as production volume,
             machine-hours, or direct labor-hours
       a = the fixed-cost component
       b = the variable rate per unit of x

Two popular methods are available to separate a mixed cost into its fixed and variable elements: the high-low method and the least-squares method (regression analysis). Engineering analysis and account analysis are often used for this purpose.

Engineering Analysis

Engineering analysis measures cost behavior according to what costs *should be,* not by what costs *have been.* It entails a systematic review of materials, labor, support services, and facilities needed for product and services. Engineers use time and motion studies and similar engineering methods to estimate what costs should be based on engineers' specifications of the inputs required to manufacture a unit of output or to perform a particular service. This can be used for existing products or for new products similar to what have been produced before. Disadvantages of this method are that it is prohibitively costly and often not timely. Further, it is difficult to estimate indirect costs. The engineering method is most useful when costs involved are variable costs, and where there is a clear input/output relation.

Account Analysis

Account analysis selects a volume-related cost driver, and classifies each account from the accounting records as a variable or fixed cost. The cost accountant then looks at each cost account balance and estimates either the variable cost per unit of cost driver activity or the periodic fixed cost. Account analysis requires a detailed examination of the data, presumably by cost accountants and managers who are familiar with the activities of the company and the way the company's activities affect costs. Because account analysis is judgmental, different analysts are likely to provide different estimates of cost behavior.

EXAMPLE 3.10

The cafeteria department of Los Al Health Center reported the following costs for October 2014:

Monthly Cost	October 2014 Amount
Food and beverages	$9,350
Hourly wages and benefits	18,900
Supervisor's salary	4,000
Equipment depreciation and rental	6,105
Supplies	2,760
Total cafeteria costs	$41,115

The cafeteria served 11,520 meals during the month. Using an account analysis to classify costs, we can determine the cost function. Note that in this example, the supervisor's salary ($4,000 per month) and the equipment depreciation and rental ($6,105 per month) are fixed, while the remainder ($31,010) varies with the cost driver, i.e., the number of meals served. Dividing the variable costs by the number of meals served yields $2.692; the department's cost-volume formula is $10,105 + $2.692 per meal.

The High-Low Method

As the name indicates, the high-low method uses two extreme data points to determine the values of a (the fixed-cost portion) and b (the variable rate) in the cost-volume formula

$$y = a + bx$$

The extreme data points are the highest cost-volume pair and the lowest cost-volume pair. The rule is that the activity level x, rather than the mixed cost item y, governs their selection.

The high-low method is explained, step by step, as follows:
Step 1: Select the highest pair and the lowest pair
Step 2: Compute the variable rate, b, using the formula

$$\text{Variable rate} = \frac{\text{Difference in cost } y}{\text{Difference in activity } x}$$

Step 3: Compute the fixed cost portion as

$$\text{Fixed cost portion} = \text{Total mixed cost} - \text{Variable cost}$$

EXAMPLE 3.11

Flexible Manufacturing Company decided to relate total factory overhead costs to direct labor hours (DLH) to develop a cost-volume formula in the form of $y = a + bx$. Twelve monthly observations were collected. They are given in the table and are plotted as shown in Figure 3-5.

Month	Direct Labor Hours (x) (thousands)	Factory Overhead (y) (thousands)
January	9 hours	$ 15
February	19	20
March	11	14
April	14	16
May	23	25
June	12	20
July	12	20
August	22	23
September	7	14
October	13	22
November	15	18
December	17	18
Total	174 hours	$225

The high-low points selected from the monthly observations are:

	x	y
High	23 hours	$25 (May pair)
Low	7	14 (September pair)
Difference	16 hours	$11

Thus

$$\text{Variable rate } b = \frac{\text{Difference in } y}{\text{Difference in } x}$$

$$= \frac{\$11}{16 \text{ hours}} = \$0.6875 \text{ per DLH}$$

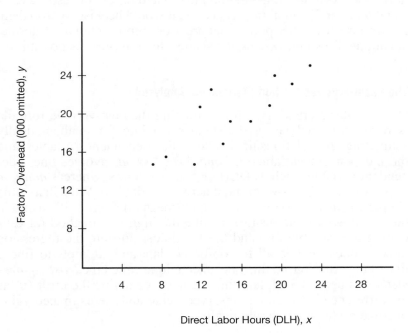

Figure 3-5. Scatter diagram

The fixed-cost portion is computed as:

	High	*Low*
Factory overhead (y)	$25	$14
Variable expense ($0.6875/DLH)	(15.8125)	(4.8125)
	$ 9.1875	$ 9.1875

Therefore, the cost-volume formula for factory overhead is:

$9.1875 fixed, plus $0.6875 per DLH

The high-low method is simple and easy to use. It has the disadvantage, however, of using two extreme data points, which may not be representative of normal conditions—for example, an unrepresentative, abnormally hight point could come from a large one-time order; an abnormally low data point could result from a strike, equipment failure, or a natural disaster such as an earthquake or hurricane. As a result, the method may yield unreliable estimates of *a* and *b* in our formula. In such a case, it would be wise to drop them and choose two other points that are more representative of normal situations. Be sure to check the scatter diagram for this possibility.

The Least-Squares Method (Regression Analysis)

One popular method used for estimating the cost-volume formula is regression analysis, a statistical procedure for mathematically estimating the relationship between the dependent variables and the independent variable(s). *Simple regression* involves one independent variable, such as DLH or machine hours, whereas *multiple regression* involves two or more activity variables. (We will assume simple linear regression here, which means that we will maintain the $y = a + bx$ relationship). Unlike the high-low method for estimating the variable rate and the fixed-cost portion, the regression method does include all the observed data and attempts to find a line of best fit. To find this line, a technique called the *least-squares method* is used. To explain this method, we define the error (u) as the difference between the observed value and the estimated value of some mixed cost. Symbolically,

$$u = y - y'$$

where y = observed value of a semivariable expense, and

y' (read "y prime") = estimated value based on $y' = a + bx$

The least-squares criterion requires that the line of best fit be such that the sum of the squares of the errors (or the vertical distance in Figure 3-6 from the observed data points to the line) is a minimum, i.e.,

$$\Sigma u^2 = \Sigma(y - y')^2$$

Using differential calculus, we obtain the following equations, called *normal equations:*

$$\Sigma y = na + b\Sigma x$$

$$\Sigma xy = a\Sigma x + b\Sigma x^2$$

Solving the equations for *b* and *a* yields:

$$b = \frac{n\Sigma xy - (\Sigma x)(\Sigma y)}{n\Sigma x^2 - (\Sigma x)^2}$$

$$a = \overline{y} - b\overline{x}$$

where $\overline{y} = \Sigma y/n$ and $\overline{x} = \Sigma x/n$.

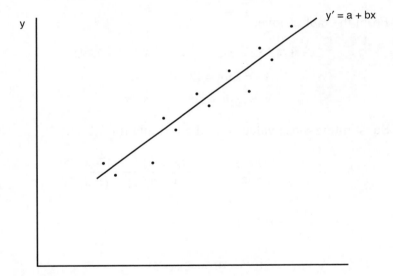

Figure 3-6. *Y* and *Y′*

EXAMPLE 3.12

To illustrate the computations of *b* and *a*, we will once again refer to the data in the table on page 162. All the required sums are computed and shown below.

DLH x	Factory Overhead y	xy	x^2	y^2
9 hours	$ 15	135	81	225
19	20	380	361	400
11	14	154	121	196
14	16	224	196	256
23	25	575	529	625
12	20	240	144	400
12	20	240	144	400
22	23	506	484	529
7	14	98	49	196
13	22	286	169	484
15	18	270	225	324
17	18	306	289	324
174 hours	$225	3,414	2,792	4,359

From the table above:

$$\Sigma x = 174 \quad \Sigma x = 225 \quad \Sigma xy = 3,414 \quad \Sigma x^2 = 2,792$$

$$\bar{x} = \Sigma x/n = 174/12 = 14.5$$

$$\bar{y} = \Sigma y/n = 225/12 = 18.75$$

Substituting these values into the formula for b first:

$$b = \frac{n\Sigma xy - (\Sigma x)(\Sigma y)}{n\Sigma x^2 - (\Sigma x)^2} = \frac{(12)(3,414) - (174)(225)}{(12)(2,792) - (174)^2}$$

$$= \frac{1,818}{3,228} = 0.5632$$

$$a = \bar{y} - b\bar{x} = 18.75 - (0.5632)(14.5)$$
$$= 18.75 - 8.1664 = 10.5836$$

Note that Σy^2 is not used here but, rather, is computed for future use.

Regression Statistics

Unlike the high-low method, regression analysis is a statistical method. It uses a variety of statistics to tell us about the accuracy and reliability of the regression results. They include:

1. correlation coefficient (r) and coefficient of determination (r^2).

2. standard error of the estimate (S_e).
3. standard error of the regression coefficient (S_b) and t-statistic.

The *correlation coefficient* r measures the degree of association between y and x. The values it takes on range between -1 and $+1$. The more widely used measure is the coefficient of determination, designated r^2 (read as "r-squared"). Simply put, r^2 tells us how good the estimated regression equation is. In other words, it is a measure of "goodness of fit" in the regression. Therefore, the higher the r^2, the more confidence we can have in our estimated cost-formula.

More specifically, the coefficient of determination represents the proportion of the total variation in y that is explained by the regression equation. It has a range of values between 0 and 1.

EXAMPLE 3.13

The statement "Factory overhead is a function of machine-hours with $r^2 = 70\%$," can be interpreted as "70% of the total variation of factory overhead is explained by the regression equation or the change in machine-hours and the remaining 30% is accounted for by something other than machine-hours."

The coefficient of determination is computed as

$$r^2 = 1 - \frac{\Sigma(y - y')^2}{\Sigma(y - \overline{y})^2}$$

In *simple* regression, however, there is a shortcut method available:

$$r^2 = \frac{[n\Sigma xy - (\Sigma x)(\Sigma y)]^2}{[n\Sigma x^2 - (\Sigma x)^2][n\Sigma y^2 - (\Sigma y)^2]}$$

Comparing this formula with the one for b in Example 3.12, we see that the only additional informatin we need to compute r^2 is Σy^2.

EXAMPLE 3.14

From the table prepared in Example 3.12, $\Sigma y^2 = 4,359$. Using the shortcut method for r^2,

$$r^2 = \frac{(1,818)^2}{(3,228)[(12)(4,359) - (225)^2]} = \frac{3,305,124}{(3,228)(52,308 - 50,625)}$$

$$= \frac{3,305,124}{(3,228)(1,683)} = \frac{3,305,124}{5,432,724} = 0.6084 = 60.84\%$$

This means that about 60.84% of the total variation in total factory overhead is explained by DLH and the remaining 39.16% is still unexplained. A relatively low r^2 indicates that there is a lot of room for improvement in our estimated cost-volume formula ($y' = \$10.5836 + \$0.5632x$). Using machine-hours or a combination of DLH and machine-hours might improve r^2.

The *standard error of the estimate,* designated S_e, is defined as the standard deviation of the regression. It is computed as

$$S_e = \sqrt{\frac{\Sigma(y - y')^2}{n - 2}} = \sqrt{\frac{\Sigma y^2 - a\Sigma y - b\Sigma xy}{n - 2}}$$

The statistic can be used to gain some idea of the accuracy of our predictions.

EXAMPLE 3.15

Going back to our example data, S_e is calculated as:

$$S_e = \sqrt{\frac{4,359 - (10.5836)(225) - (0.5632)(3,414)}{12 - 2}}$$

$$= \sqrt{\frac{54.9252}{10}} = 2.3436$$

If a manager wants the prediction to be 95% confident, the confidence interval would be the estimated cost $\pm 2(2.3436)$.

The *standard error of the regression coefficient,* designated S_b, and the *t*-statistic are closely related. S_b gives an estimate of the range where the true coefficient will "actually" fall. The *t*-statistic shows the statistical significance of an independent variable x in explaining the dependent variable y. It is determined by dividing the estimated regression coefficient b by its standard error S_b. Thus the *t*-statistic measures how many standard errors the coefficient is away from zero. Generally, any t value greater than $+2$ or less than -2 is acceptable. The higher the t value, the greater the confidence we have in the coefficient as the predictor.

Table 3.11
EXCEL REGRESSION OUTPUT

SUMMARY OUTPUT
Regression Statistics

Multiple R	0.779983
R *Square*	0.608373 (R^2)
Adjusted R Square	0.569211
Standard Error	2.343622 (S_e)
Observations	12

	Coefficients	Standard Error (S_b)	t Stat	P-value*
Intercept	10.58364	2.17960878	4.855754	0.0006656
Advertising	0.563197	0.142893168	3.941385	0.0027687

	Lower 95%	Upper 95%	Lower 95.0%	Upper 95.0%
Intercept	5.727171	15.44011	5.727171	15.44011
Advertising	0.244811	0.881583	0.244811	0.881583

*The P-value for X Variable (advertising here in this example) = .00277 indicates that we have a 0.277% chance that the true value of the X variable coefficient is equal to 0, implying a high level of accuracy about the estimated value of a coefficient for advertising.

The result shows:

$$Y' = 10.58364 + 0.563197 \times$$

with:

(1) R-squared (R^2) = .608373 = 60.84%
(2) Standard error of the estimate (S_e) = 2.343622
(3) Standard error of the coefficient (S_b) = 0.142893
(4) t-value = 3.94

The Contribution Income Statement

The traditional income statement required for external reporting shows the functional classification of costs, that is, manufacturing costs vs. nonmanufacturing expenses (or operating expenses). An alternative format of income statement, known as the *contribution income statement,* groups the costs by behavior rather than by function. It shows the relationship of variable costs and fixed costs, regardless of the function a given cost performs.

The contribution approach to income determination provides data that are useful for managerial planning and decision-making. For example, the contribution approach is useful:

1. for break-even and cost-volume-profit analysis
2. in evaluating the performance of the division and its manager
3. for short-term and nonroutine decisions

The contribution income statement is not acceptable, however, for income tax or external reporting purposes. A major reason why it is not acceptable is because it does not treat fixed overhead as a product cost.

The statement highlights the concept of *contribution margin,* which is the difference between sales and variable costs. The traditional format, on the other hand, emphasizes the concept of gross margin, which is the difference between sales and cost of goods sold. These two concepts are independent and have nothing to do with each other. Gross margin is available to cover nonmanufacturing expenses, whereas contribution margin is available to cover fixed costs. The concept of contribution margin has numerous applications for internal management, which will be taken up in later chapters.

The traditional format and the contribution format are compared below.

Traditional Format

Sales		$15,000
Less: Cost of Goods Sold		7,000
Gross Margin		$ 8,000
Less: Operating Expenses		
Selling	$2,100	
Administrative	1,500	3,600
Net Income		$ 4,400

Contribution Format

Sales		$15,000
Less: Variable Expenses		
Manufacturing	$4,000	
Selling	1,600	
Administrative	500	6,100
Contribution Margin		$ 8,900
Less: Fixed Expenses		
Manufacturing	$3,000	
Selling	500	
Administration	1,000	4,500
Net Income		$ 4,400

COST-VOLUME-PROFIT (CVP) AND BREAK-EVEN ANALYSIS

Cost-volume-profit (CVP) analysis using cost behavior information helps managers perform many useful analyses. CVP analysis deals with how profit and costs change with changes in volume. More specifically, it looks at the effects on profits of changes in such factors as variable costs, fixed costs, selling prices, volume, and mix of products sold. By studying the relationships of costs, sales, and net income, management is better able to cope with many planning decisions. Break-even analysis, a branch of CVP analysis, determines the break-even sales point, which is the level of sales where total costs equal total revenue.

Questions Answered by CVP Analysis

CVP analysis can be used to answer the following questions:

1. What sales volume is required to break even?
2. What sales volume is necessary to earn a desired profit?
3. What profit can be expected on a given sales volume?
4. How would changes in selling price, variable costs, fixed costs, and/or output affect profits?
5. How would a change in the mix of products sold affect the break-even and target income volume and profit potential?

Concepts of Contribution Margin (CM)

For accurate CVP analysis, a distribution must be made between variable and fixed costs. Mixed costs must be separated into their variable and fixed components, as discussed in the previous section.

In order to compute the break-even point and perform various CVP analyses, note the following important concepts.

Contribution Margin (CM). The contribution margin is the excess of sales (S) over the variable costs (VC) of the product. It is the amount available to cover fixed costs (FC) and generate profits. Symbolically, $CM = S - VC$.

Unit CM. The unit CM is the excess of the unit selling price (p) over the unit variable cost (v). Symbolically, unit $CM = p - v$.

CM Ratio. The CM ratio is the contribution margin as a percentage of sales, i.e.,

$$\frac{\$15,000 + \$15,000}{\$25 - \$10} = \frac{\$30,000}{\$15} = 2,000 \text{ units}$$

The CM ratio can also be computed using per-unit data as follows:

$$CM \text{ ratio} = \frac{Unit\ CM}{p} = \frac{p - v}{p} = 1 - \frac{v}{p}$$

Note that the CM ratio is 1 minus the variable-cost ratio. For example, if variable costs account for 70% of the price, the CM ratio is 30%.

EXAMPLE 3.16

To illustrate the various concepts of CM, consider the following data for Company Z:

	Total	*Per Unit*	*Percentage*
Sales (1,500 units)	$37,500	$25	100%
Less: Variable costs	15,000	10	40
Contribution margin	$22,500	$15	60%
Less: Fixed costs	15,000		
Net income	$ 7,500		

From the data listed above, CM, unit CM, and the CM ratio are computed as:

$$CM = S - VC = \$37,500 - \$15,000 = \$22,500$$

Unit $CM = p - v = \$25 - \$10 = \$15$

$$CM \text{ ratio} = \frac{CM}{S} = \frac{\$22,500}{\$37,500} = 60\% \text{ or } \frac{\text{Unit CM}}{P}$$

$$= \frac{\$15}{\$25} = 0.6 = 60\%$$

Break-Even Analysis

The break-even point, the point of no profit and no loss, provides managers with insights into profit planning. It can be computed using the following formulas:

$$\text{Break-even point in units} = \frac{\text{Fixed costs}}{\text{Unit CM}}$$

$$\text{Break-even point in dollars} = \frac{\text{Fixed costs}}{\text{CM ratio}}$$

EXAMPLE 3.17

Using the same data given in Example 3.16, where unit $CM = \$25 - \$10 = \$15$ and CM ratio = 60%, we get:

Break-even point in units = \$15,000/\$15 = 1,000 units
Break-even point in dollars = 1,000 units $\times$ \$25 = \$25,000

or, alternatively,

$$\$15,000/0.6 = \$25,000$$

Determination of Target Income Volume

Besides being able to determine the break-even point, CVP analysis determines the sales required to attain a particular income level. The formula is:

$$\text{Target income sales volume} = \frac{\text{Fixed costs plus target income}}{\text{Unit CM}}$$

EXAMPLE 3.18

Using the same data given in Example 3.16, assume that Company Z wishes to attain a target income of $15,000 on a particular product before tax.

Then, the target income volume required would be:

$$\frac{\$15,000+\$15,000}{\$25-\$10} = \frac{\$30,000}{\$15} = 2,000 \text{ units}$$

Impact of Income Taxes

If target income is given on an after-tax basis, the target income volume formula becomes:

Target income volume

$$= \frac{\text{Fixed costs} + [\text{Target after-tax income}/(1 - \text{tax rate})]}{\text{Unit CM}}$$

EXAMPLE 3.19

Assume in Example 3.16 that Company Z wants to achieve an after-tax income of $6,000. An income tax is levied at 40%. Then,

$$\text{Target income volume} = \frac{\$15,000+[\$6,000/(1-0.4)]}{\$15}$$

$$= \frac{\$15,000+\$10,000}{\$15} = 1,667 \text{ units}$$

Some Applications of CVP Analysis and What-If Analysis

The concepts of *contribution margin* and the *contribution income statement* have many applications in profit planning and short-term decision-making. Many "what-if" scenarios can be evaluated using them as planning tools. Some applications are illustrated in Examples 3.20–3.23 using the same data as in Example 3.16.

EXAMPLE 3.20

Recall from Example 3.16 that Company Z has a CM of 60% and fixed costs of $15,000 per period. Assume that the company expects sales to go up by $10,000 for the next period. How much will income increase?

Using the CM concepts, we can quickly compute the impact on profits of a change in sales. The formula for computing the impact is:

Change in net income = Dollar change in sales × CM ratio

Thus, in this question,

Increase in net income = $10,000 × 60% = $6,000

Therefore, the income will go up by $6,000, assuming there is no change in fixed costs.

If we are given the change in sales in units instead of dollars, then the formula becomes:

Change in net income = Change in unit sales × Unit CM

EXAMPLE 3.21

What net income is expected on sales of $47,500? The answer is the difference between the CM and the fixed costs:

CM: $47,500 × 60%	$28,500
Less: Fixed costs	15,000
Net income	$13,500

EXAMPLE 3.22

Company Z is considering increasing the advertising budget by $5,000, which should increase sales revenue by $8,000. Should the advertising budget be increased?

The answer is no, since the increase in the CM is less than the increased cost, as follows:

Increase in CM: $8,000 × 60%	$4,800
Increase in advertising	5,000
Decrease in net income	$ (200)

EXAMPLE 3.23

Consider the original data. Assume again that Company Z is currently selling 1,500 units per period. In an effort to increase sales, management is considering cutting its unit price by $5 and increasing the advertising budget by $1,000. If these two steps are taken, management feels that unit sales will go up by 60%. Should the two steps be taken?

A $5 reduction in the selling price will cause the unit CM to decrease from $15 to $10. Thus,

Proposed CM: 2,400 units $\times$ $10 $24,000
Present CM: 1,500 units $\times$ $15   22,500
Increase in CM $ 1,500
Increase in advertising outlay   1,000
Increase in net income $ 500

The answer, therefore, is yes. Alternatively, the same answer can be obtained by developing comparative income statements in a contribution format:

	Present (1,500 units)	Proposed (2,400 units)	Difference
Sales	$37,500 (@$25)	$48,000 (@$20)	$10,500
Less: Variable cost	15,000	24,000	9,000
CM	$22,500	$24,000	$ 1,500
Less: Fixed costs	15,000	16,000	1,000
Net income	$ 7,500	$ 8,000	$ 500

Sales Mix Analysis

Break-even and cost-volume-profit analysis require some additional computations and assumptions when a company produces and sells more than one product. Different selling prices and different variable costs result in different unit CM and CM ratios. As a result, break-even points vary with the relative proportions of the products sold, called the *sales mix*. In break-even and CVP analysis, it is necessary to assume that the sales mix does not change for a specified period. The break-even formula for the company as a whole is:

$$\text{Break-even sales (\$)} = \frac{\text{Fixed costs}}{\text{CM ratio}}$$

EXAMPLE 3.24

Assume that Company Y produces and sells three products with the following data:

	A	B	C	Total
Sales	$30,000	$60,000	$10,000	$100,000
Sales mix	30%	60%	10%	100%
Less: VC	24,000	40,000	5,000	69,000
CM	$ 6,000	$20,000	$ 5,000	$ 31,000
CM ratio	20%	33⅓%	50%	31%
Fixed costs				$ 18,600
Net income				$ 12,400

The CM ratio for Company Y is $31,000/$100,000 = 31%. Therefore, the break-even point in dollars is

$$\$18,600/0.31 = \$60,000$$

which will be split in the mix ratio of 3:6:1 to give us the following break-even points for the individual products A, B, and C:

$$
\begin{array}{ll}
\text{A: } \$60,000 \times 30\% = & \$18,000 \\
\text{B: } \$60,000 \times 60\% = & 36,000 \\
\text{C: } \$60,000 \times 10\% = & \underline{6,000} \\
& \underline{\$60,000}
\end{array}
$$

One of the most important assumptions underlying CVP analysis in a multiproduct firm is that the sales mix will not change during the planning period. But if the sales mix changes, the break-even point will also change.

EXAMPLE 3.25

Assume that total sales from Example 3.24 remain unchanged at $100,000 but that a shift is expected in mix from product B to product C, as follows:

	A	B	C	Total
Sales	$30,000	$30,000	$40,000	$100,000
Sales mix	30%	30%	40%	100%
Less: VC	24,000	20,000	20,000	64,000
CM	$ 6,000	$10,000	$20,000	$ 36,000
CM ratio	20%	33⅓%	50%	36%
Fixed costs				$ 18,600
Net income				$ 17,400

* $20,000 = $30,000 × 66⅔%

Note that the shift in sales mix toward the more profitable line C has caused the CM ratio for the company as a whole to go up from 31% to 36%. The new break-even point will be $18,600/0.36 = $51,667. The break-even dollar volume has decreased from $60,000 to $51,667. The improvement in the mix caused net income to go up.

Assumptions Underlying Break-even and CVP Analysis

The basic break-even and CVP models are subject to a number of limiting assumptions. They are:

1. The behavior of both sales revenue and expenses is linear throughout the entire relevant range of activity.
2. All costs are classified as fixed or variable.
3. There is only one product or a constant sales mix.
4. Inventories do not change significantly from period to period.
5. Volume is the only factor affecting variable costs.

ABSORPTION VERSUS VARIABLE COSTING

The most commonly accepted theory of product costing holds that the cost of producing a product includes direct materials, direct labor, and an apportioned share of the factory overhead costs. This method of assigning costs to products, called *absorption (full) costing*, is the method generally required for tax purposes.

Because all costs, including fixed overhead, are applied to production under absorption costing, variations in unit-product cost may result solely from variations in production volume. If fixed costs are $200,000 and 20,000 units are produced, unit fixed cost is $10; if volume is 40,000, unit fixed cost is $5. Because these variations are not controllable at the production manager level and may obscure other significant variations in cost, they can be excluded from product cost through the use of a costing technique referred to as *variable (direct or marginal) costing*.

Under variable costing, all variable manufacturing costs are charged to the product, and all fixed costs (including fixed manufacturing costs) are charged to expense. Thus, all manufacturing costs must first be classified as fixed or variable. Direct materials and direct labor costs are usually completely variable. But factory overhead costs must be separated into variable and fixed portions. All variable costs (direct materials, direct labor, and variable overhead) are assigned to production and become part of the unit costs of the products produced. All fixed costs are assumed to be costs of the period and are charged to expenses.

In summary, the only difference between absorption costing and variable costing is in the treatment of fixed manufacturing costs. Under absorption costing they are treated as product costs, and under variable costing they are treated as period costs.

Absorption and Direct Costing Compared

The differences between variable and absorption costing can be seen from an illustration comparing the income statement that would result from applying each technique to the same data. Assume the following information:

Beginning inventory	-0-	Variable costs (per unit)	
Production (units)	10,000	Direct materials	$2.00
Sales (units)	9,000	Direct labor	1.00
		Factory overhead	0.30
		Total	$3.30
Fixed factory overhead	$ 6,000		
Selling expenses	15,000	Variable selling expenses	
Administrative expenses	12,000	(per unit)	$0.20
Total	$33,000	Selling price (per unit)	$8.00

Income Statement Under Variable Costing

Under variable costing, the year's income statement would be as shown in Table 3.12.

Table 3.12
INCOME STATEMENT UNDER VARIABLE COSTING

Sales (9,000 units at $8)		$72,000
Cost of goods sold:		
Variable production costs incurred		
(10,000 units at $3.30)	$33,000	
Less: Inventory (1,000 units at $3.30)	3,300	29,700
Manufacturing margin		$42,300
Variable selling expenses		
(9,000 units at $0.20)		1,800
Contribution margin		$40,500
Period costs:		
Factory overhead	$ 6,000	
Selling expenses	15,000	
Administrative expenses	12,000	33,000
Net income.		$ 7,500

Note that all of the fixed manufacturing costs are considered costs of the period and are not included in inventories. The fixed factory overhead is treated as a period cost and is deducted, along with the selling and administrative expenses in the period incurred. That is,

Direct materials	xx
Direct labor	xx
Variable factory overhead	xx
Product cost	$xx

Income Statement Under Absorption Costing

Table 3.13 contains the income statement that would be prepared under absorption costing.

Table 3.13
INCOME STATEMENT UNDER ABSORPTION COSTING

Sales (9,000 units at $8)		$72,000
Cost of goods sold:		
Variable costs of production		
(10,000 units at $3.30)	$33,000	
Fixed overhead costs	6,000	
Total costs of producing 10,000 units	$39,000	
Less: Inventory (1,000 units at $3.90)	3,900	35,100
Gross margin		$36,900
Operating expenses:		
Selling ($15,000 fixed plus		
9,000 at $0.20 each)	$16,800	
Administrative	12,000	28,800
Net income		8,100

*$3.90 = $3.30 + ($6,000/10,000 units) = $3.30 + $.60

Note that the fixed manufacturing costs are included as part of the product cost and that some of these costs are included in the ending inventory. Under absorption costing, the cost to be inventoried includes all manufacturing costs, both variable and fixed. Non-manufacturing (operating) expenses—i.e., selling and administrative expenses—are treated as period expenses and thus are charged against current revenue:

Direct materials	$xx
Direct labor	xx
Variable factory overhead	xx
Fixed factory overhead	xx
Product cost	$xx

The ending inventory is priced at so-called full cost; that is, the cost of ending inventory includes fixed factory overhead.

Two important facts should be noted:

1. Effects of the two costing methods on net income:
   (a) When production exceeds sales, a larger net income will be reported under absorption costing.
   (b) When sales exceeds production, a larger net income will

be reported under direct costing.

(c) When sales and production are equal, net income will be the same under both methods.

2. Reconciliation of the variable and absorption costing net income figures:

(a) The difference in net income can be reconciled as follows:

$$\begin{array}{ccc} \text{Change in} \\ \text{inventory} \end{array} \times \begin{array}{c} \text{Fixed factory} \\ \text{overhead rate} \end{array} = \begin{array}{c} \text{Difference in} \\ \text{net income} \end{array}$$

(b) The above formula works only if the fixed overhead rate per unit does not change between the periods.

We can prove paragraphs 1 and 2 as follows:

1. Difference in net income: $8,100 − $7,500 = $600.
   Absorption costing shows a larger net income.
2. Reconciliation of difference in net income:

$$\begin{array}{ccc} \text{Change in} \\ \text{inventory} \end{array} \times \begin{array}{c} \text{Fixed factory} \\ \text{overhead rate} \end{array} = \begin{array}{c} \text{Difference in} \\ \text{net income} \end{array}$$

$$1,000 \ \times \ \$0.6 \ (\$6,000/10,000 \text{ units}) \ = \ \$600$$

Managerial Use of Variable Costing

Variable costing is used for internal purposes only. It highlights the concept of contribution margin and focuses on the costs by behavior rather than by function. Its managerial uses include: (1) relevant cost analysis; (2) break-even and cost-volume-profit CVP analyses; and (3) short-term decision making.

An understanding of cost behavior is extremely useful for managerial planning and decision-making purposes. It allows managerial accountants to perform short-term planning analysis, such as break-even analysis. Cost-volume-profit analysis is useful as a frame of reference, as a vehicle for expressing overall managerial performance, and as a planning device via break-even techniques and what-if scenarios. Breaking down the costs by behavior, which is reflected in a contribution (direct-costing) income statement, facilitates the use of various short-term profit-planning tools on the part of managerial accountants.

Variable costing is, however, not acceptable for external reporting or income tax reporting. Companies that use variable costing for internal reporting must convert to absorption costing for external reporting.

BUDGETING FOR PROFIT PLANNING

A comprehensive (master) budget is a formal statement of management's expectations regarding sales, expenses, volume, and other financial transactions of an organization for the coming period. Simply put, a budget is a set of *pro forma* (projected or planned) financial statements. It consists basically of a pro forma income statement, pro forma balance sheet, and cash budget.

A budget is a tool for both planning and control. At the beginning of the period, the budget is a plan or standard; at the end of the period, it serves as a control device to help management measure its performance against the plan so that future performance or planning may be improved.

The budget is classified broadly into two categories:

1. *Operating budget,* reflecting the results of operating decisions
2. *Financial budget,* reflecting the financial decisions of the firm

The operating budget consists of:

- Sales budget
- Production budget
- Direct materials budget
- Direct labor budget
- Factory overhead budget
- Selling and administrative expense budget
- *Pro forma* income statement

The financial budget consists of:

- Cash budget
- *Pro forma* balance sheet

The major steps in preparing the budget are:

1. Prepare a sales forecast.
2. Determine expected production volume.
3. Estimate manufacturing costs and operating expenses.
4. Determine cash flow and other financial effects.
5. Formulate projected financial statements.

Figure 3–7 shows a simplified diagram of the various parts of the comprehensive (master) budget, the master plan of the company.

To illustrate how all these budgets are put together, we will focus on a manufacturing company called the Johnson Company, which produces and markets a single product. We will assume that the company develops the master budget in *contribution* format for 20B on a quarterly basis. We will highlight the variable cost-fixed cost breakdown throughout the illustration.

The Sales Budget

The sales budget is the starting point in preparing the master budget, since estimated sales volume influences nearly all other items appearing throughout the master budget. The sales budget ordinarily indicates the quantity of each product expected to be sold, or the range of volumes expected to be sold.

After sales volume has been estimated, the sales budget is constructed by multiplying the expected sales in units by the expected unit sales price. Generally, the sales budget includes a computation of expected cash collections from credit sales, which will be used later for cash budgeting.

EXAMPLE 3.26

THE JOHNSON COMPANY
Sales Budget
For the Year Ending December 31, 20B

	Quarter				
	1	*2*	*3*	*4*	*Total*
Expected sales in units	800	700	900	800	3200
Unit sales price	× $80	× $80	× $80	× $80	× $80
Total sales	$64,000	$56,000	$72,000	$64,000	$256,000

Schedule of Expected Cash Collections

Accounts receivable, 12/31/20A	9,500*				$ 9,500
1st-quarter sales ($64,000)	44,800†	$17,920‡			62,720
2nd-quarter sales ($56,000)		39,200	$15,680		54,880
3rd-quarter sales ($72,000)			50,400	$20,160	70,560
4th-quarter sales ($64,000)				44,800	44,800
Total cash collections	$54,300	$57,120	$66,080	$64,960	$242,460

*All of the $9,500 accounts receivable balance (Example 3.34) is assumed to be collectible in the first quarter.
† 70% of a quarter's sales are collected in the quarter of sale.
‡ 28% of a quarter's sales are collected in the quarter following, and the remaining 2% are uncollectible.

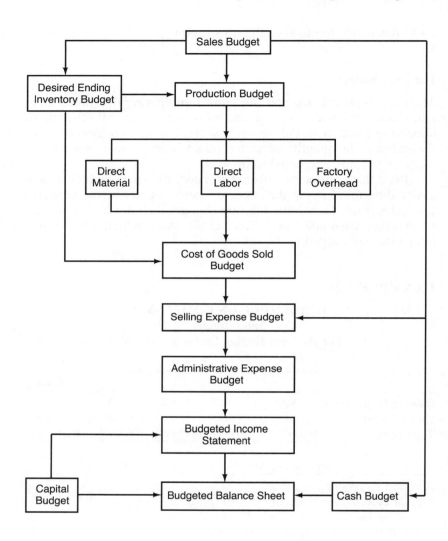

Figure 3-7. Comprehensive (master) budget

The Production Budget

After sales are budgeted, the production budget can be determined. The number of units expected to be manufactured to meet budgeted sales and inventory requirements is set forth in the production budget. The expected volume of production is determined by subtracting the estimated inventory at the beginning of the period from the sum of the units expected to be sold and the desired inventory at the end of the period. The production budget is illustrated as follows:

EXAMPLE 3.27

THE JOHNSON COMPANY
Production Budget
For the Year Ending December 31, 20B

		Quarter			
	1	2	3	4	Total
Planned sales (Example 3.26)	800	700	900	800	3200
Desired ending inventory*	70	90	80	100†	100
Total needs	870	790	980	900	3,300
Less: Beginning inventory‡	80	70	90	80	80
Units to be produced	790	720	890	820	3,220

* Ten percent of the next quarter's sales.
† Estimated.
‡ The same as the previous quarter's ending inventory.

The Direct-Material Budget

When the level of production has been computed, a direct-material budget should be constructed to show how much material will be required for production and how much material must be purchased to meet this production requirement. The purchase will depend on both expected usage of materials and inventory levels. The formula for computation of the purchase is as follows:

$$\text{Purchase in units} = \text{Usage}$$
$$+ \text{ Desired ending material inventory units}$$
$$- \text{ Beginning inventory units}$$

The direct-material budget is usually accompanied by a computation of expected cash payments for materials.

EXAMPLE 3.28

THE JOHNSON COMPANY
Direct-Material Budget
For the Year Ending December 31, 20B

		Quarter			
	1	2	3	4	Total
Units to be produced (Example 3.27)	790	720	890	820	3,220
Material needs per unit (lbs)	× 3	× 3	× 3	× 3	× 3

THE JOHNSON COMPANY
Direct-Material Budget
For the Year Ending December 31, 20B (continued)

	Quarter				
	1	*2*	*3*	*4*	*Total*
Material needs for production	2,370	2,160	2,670	2,460	9,660
Desired ending inventory of materials*	216	267	246	250†	250
Total needs	2,586	2,427	2,916	2,710	9,990
Less: Beginning inventory of materials‡	237	216	267	246	237
Materials to be purchased	2,349	2,211	2,649	2,464	9,673
Unit price	× $2	× $2	× $2	× $2	× $2
Purchase cost	$4,698	$4,422	$5,298	$4,928	$19,345

Schedule of Expected Cash Disbursements

Accounts payable, 12/31/20A	2,200				$ 2,200
1st-quarter purchases ($4,698)	2,349	2,349**			4,698
2nd-quarter purchases ($4,422)		2,211	$2,211		4,422
3rd-quarter purchases ($5,298)			2,649	$2,649	5,298
4th-quarter purchases ($4,928)				2,464	2,464
Total disbursements	$4,549	$4,560	$4,860	$5,113	$19,082

* 10% of the next quarter's units needed for production.
† Estimated.
‡ The same as the prior quarter's ending inventory.
** 50% of a quarter's purchases are paid for in the quarter of purchase; the remainder are paid for in the following quarter.

The Direct-Labor Budget

The production requirements as set forth in the production budget also provide the starting point for the preparation of the direct-labor budget. To compute direct-labor requirements, expected production volume for each period is multiplied by the number of direct-labor hours required to produce a single unit. This figure is then multiplied by the direct-labor cost per hour to obtain budgeted total direct-labor costs.

EXAMPLE 3.29

THE JOHNSON COMPANY
Direct-Labor Budget
For the Year Ending December 31, 20B

	Quarter				
	1	2	3	4	Total
Units to be produced					
(Example 3.27)	790	720	890	820	3,220
Direct labor hours per unit	× 5	× 5	× 5	× 5	× 5
Total hours	3,950	3,600	4,450	4,100	16,100
Direct labor cost per hour	× 5	× 5	× 5	× 5	× 5
Total direct labor cost	$19,750	$18,000	$22,250	$20,500	$80,500

The Factory-Overhead Budget

The factory-overhead budget should provide a schedule of all manufacturing costs other than direct materials and direct labor. Using the contribution approach to budgeting requires the development of a predetermined overhead rate for the variable portion of the factory overhead. In developing the cash budget, we must remember that depreciation does not entail a cash outlay and therefore must be deducted from the total factory overhead in computing cash disbursement for factory overhead.

EXAMPLE 3.30

To illustrate the factory overhead budget, we will assume that

- Total factory overhead budgeted = $6,000 fixed (per quarter), plus $2 per hour of direct labor.
- Depreciation expenses are $3,250 each quarter.
- All overhead costs involving cash outlays are paid for in the quarter incurred.

THE JOHNSON COMPANY
Factory-Overhead Budget
For the Year Ending December 31, 20B

	Quarter				
	1	2	3	4	Total
Budgeted direct-labor					
hours (Example 3.28)	3,950	3,600	4,450	4,100	16,000
Variable overhead rate	× $2	× $2	× $2	× $2	× $2

THE JOHNSON COMPANY
Factory-Overhead Budget
For the Year Ending December 31, 20B (continued)

	Quarter				
	1	*2*	*3*	*4*	*Total*
Variable overhead budgeted	7,900	7,200	8,900	8,200	32,300
Fixed overhead budget	6,000	6,000	6,000	6,000	24,000
Total budgeted overhead	13,900	13,200	14,900	14,200	56,200
Less: Depreciation	3,250	3,250	3,250	3,250	13,000
Cash disbursement for overhead	10,650	9,950	11,650	10,950	43,200

The Ending-Inventory Budget

The desired ending-inventory budget provides us with the information required for the construction of budgeted financial statements. Specifically, it will help compute the cost of goods sold on the budgeted income statement. Secondly, it will give the dollar value of the ending materials and finished-goods inventory to appear on the budgeted balance sheet.

EXAMPLE 3.31

THE JOHNSON COMPANY
Ending-Inventory Budget
For the Year Ending December 31, 20B
Ending Inventory

	Units	*Unit Cost*	*Total*
Direct materials	250 pounds (Example 3.28)	$ 2	$ 500
Finished goods	100 units (Example 3.27)	$41	$4,100

The unit variable cost of $41 is computed as follows:

	Unit Cost	*Units*	*Total*
Direct materials	$2	3 pounds	$ 6
Direct labor	5	5 hours	25
Variable overhead	2	5 hours	10
Total variable manufacturing cost			$41

The Selling and Administrative-Expense Budget

The selling and administrative-expense budget lists the operating expenses involved in selling the products and in managing the business. In order to complete the budgeted income statement in contribution format, variable selling and administrative expense per unit must be computed.

EXAMPLE 3.32

THE JOHNSON COMPANY
Selling and Administrative Expense Budget
For the Year Ending December 31, 20B

	Quarter				
	1	2	3	4	Total
Expected sales in units	800	700	900	800	3,200
Variable selling and admin. exp. per unit*	× $4	× $4	× $4	× $4	× $4
Budgeted variable expense	$ 3,200	$ 2,800	$ 3,200	$ 3,200	$12,800
Fixed selling and administrative expenses:					
Advertising	1,100	1,100	1,100	1,100	4,400
Insurance	2,800				2,800
Office salaries	8,500	8,500	8,500	8,500	34,000
Rent	350	350	350	350	1,400
Taxes			1,200		1,200
Total budgeted selling and administrative expenses†	$15,950	$12,750	$14,750	$13,150	$56,600

* Includes sales agents' commissions, shipping, and supplies.
† Paid for in the quarter incurred.

The Cash Budget

The cash budget is prepared for the purpose of cash planning and control. It presents the expected cash inflow and outflow for a designated time period. The cash budget helps management keep cash balances in reasonable relationship to its needs, thus helping to avoid keeping unnecessary idle cash and running into possible cash shortages. The cash budget consists typically of four major sections:

1. The receipts section, which is the beginning cash balance, cash collections from customers, and other receipts
2. The disbursements section, which is comprised of all cash payments made by purpose

3. The cash surplus or deficit section, which simply shows the difference between the cash-receipts section and the cash-disbursements section
4. The financing section, which provides a detailed account of the borrowings and repayments expected during the budgeting period

EXAMPLE 3.33

To illustrate, we will make the following assumptions:

- The company desires to maintain a $5,000 minimum cash balance at the end of each quarter.
- All borrowing and repayment must be in multiples of $500 at an interest rate of 10% per annum. Interest is computed and paid as the principal is repaid. Borrowing takes place at the beginning of each quarter and repayment at the end of each quarter.

THE JOHNSON COMPANY
Cash Budget
For the Year Ending December 31, 20B

		Quarter				
	Example	*1*	*2*	*3*	*4*	*Year a Whole*
Cash balance beginning	given	10,000	9,401	5,461	9,106	10,000
Add: Receipts						
Collection from customers	3.21	54,300	57,120	66,080	64,960	242,460
Total cash available		64,300	66,521	71,541	74,066	252,460
Less: Disbursements						
Direct materials	3.23	4,549	4,560	4,860	5,113	19,082
Direct labor	3.24	19,750	18,000	22,250	20,500	80,500
Factory overhead	3.25	10,650	9,950	11,650	10,950	43,200
Selling and admin.	3.27	15,950	12,750	14,750	13,150	56,600
Machinery purchase	given	—	24,300	—	—	24,300
Income tax	given	4,000	—	—	—	4,000
Total disbursements		54,899	69,560	53,510	49,713	227,682
Cash surplus (deficit)		9,401	(3,039)	18,031	24,353	24,778

THE JOHNSON COMPANY
Cash Budget
For the Year Ending December 31, 20B (continued)

			Quarter			Year
	Example	1	2	3	4	a Whole
Financing:						
Borrowing		—	8,500	—	—	8,500
Repayment		—	—	(8,500)	—	(8,500)
Interest		—	—	(425)*		(425)
Total financing		—	8,500	(8,925)	—	(425)
Cash balance, ending		9,401	5,461	9,106	24,353	24,353

* $8,500 × 10% × ½ = $425

The Budgeted Income Statement

The budgeted income statement summarizes the various component projections of revenue and expenses for the budgeting period. However, for control purposes the budget can be divided into quarters or even months, depending on need.

EXAMPLE 3.34

THE JOHNSON COMPANY
Budgeted Income Statement
For the Year Ending December 31, 20B

	Example		
Sales (3,200 units @ $80)	3.21		$256,000
Less: Variable expenses			
Variable cost of goods sold			
(3,200 units @ $41)	3.26	$131,200	
Variable selling & admin.	3.27	12,800	144,000
Contribution margin			112,000
Less: Fixed expenses			
Factory overhead	3.25	24,000	
Selling and admin.	3.27	43,800	67,800
Net operating income			44,200
Less: Interest expense	3.28		425
Net income before taxes			43,775
Less: Income taxes		20%*	8,755
Net income			35,020

* assumed

The Budgeted Balance Sheet

The budgeted balance sheet is developed by beginning with the balance sheet for the year just ended and adjusting it, using all the activities that are expected to take place during the budgeting period. Some of the reasons why the budgeted balance sheet must be prepared are:

- It could disclose some unfavorable financial conditions that management might want to avoid (such as poor liquidity and low return on investment).
- It serves as a final check on the mathematical accuracy of all the other schedules.
- It helps management perform a variety of ratio calculations.
- It highlights future resources and obligations.

EXAMPLE 3.35

To illustrate, we will use the following balance sheet for the year 20A.

THE JOHNSON COMPANY
Balance Sheet
December 31, 20A

Assets		*Liabilities and Stock Equity*	
Current Assets:		Current Liabilities:	
Cash	10,000	Accounts Payable	2,200
A/R	9,500	Income Tax Payable	4,000
Material Inventory	474	Total Current	
Finished Gd Inventory	3,280	Liabilities	6,200
	23,254		
Fixed Assets:		Stockholders' Equity:	
Land	50,000	Common Stock, No-Par	70,000
Buildings and		Retained Earnings	37,054
Equipment	100,000	Total Liabilities and	
Accumulated		Stockholders'	
Depreciation	(60,000)	Equity	113,254
	90,000		
Total Assets	113,254		

THE JOHNSON COMPANY
Budgeted Balance Sheet
December 31, 20B

Assets		*Liabilities and Stock Equity*	
Current Assets:		Current Liabilities:	
Cash	24,353 (a)	Accounts Payable	2,464 (h)
Accounts Receivable	23,040 (b)	Income Tax Payable	8,755 (i)
Material Inventory	500 (c)	Total Current Liabilities	11,219
Finished Goods			
Inventory	4,100 (d)	Stockholders' Equity:	
	$51,993	Common Stock, No-Par	70,000 (j)
Fixed Assets:		Retained Earnings	72,074 (k)
Land	50,000 (e)	Total Liabilities and	
Buildings and		Stockholders' Equity	153,293
Equipment	124,300 (f)		
Accumulated			
Depreciation	(73,000) (g)		
	101,300		
Total Assets	153,293		

Computations:
(a) From Example 3.33 (cash budget)
(b) $9,500 + $256,000 sales − $242,460 receipts = $23,040.
(c) and (d) From Example 3.31 (ending inventory budget).
(e) No change.
(f) $100,000 + $24,300 (from Example 3.33) = $124,300.
(g) $60,000 + $13,000 (from Example 3.31) = $73,000.
(h) $2,200 + $19,346 − $19,082 = $2,464 (all accounts payable relate to material purchases), or 50% of 4th-quarter purchase = 50% ($4,928) = 2,464.
(i) From Example 3.34 (budgeted income statement).
(j) No change.
(k) $37,054 + $35,020 net income = $72,074.

A SHORTCUT APPROACH TO FORMULATING THE BUDGET

In actual practice, a shortcut approach is very widely used in formulating a budget. The shortcut method assumes that all costs increase or decrease proportionately with sales. As a practical matter, of course, any cost that has a fixed component (any fixed or mixed cost) will not vary with sales. To this extent, the shortcut method sacrifices accuracy for speed. (In many cases, cost behavior is not known anyway.)

The shortcut approach can be summarized as follows:

First, a pro forma income statement is developed using past percentage relationships between certain expense and cost items and the firm's sales and applying these percentages to the firm's projected sales. The income statement can be set up in a *traditional* or *contribution* format. This can be done using a spreadsheet program such as Excel.

Second, a pro forma balance sheet is estimated, using the *percentage-of-sales method,* which involves the following steps:

1. Express balance sheet items that *vary directly with* sales as a percentage of sales. Any item that does not vary with sales (such as long-term debt) is designated *not applicable* (N/A). Multiply these percentages by the sales projected to obtain the amounts for the future period.
2. Where no percentage applies (such as long-term debt, common stock, and paid-in capital), simply insert the figures from the present balance sheet or their "desired" level in the column for the future period.
3. Compute the projected retained earnings as follows:

Projected retained earnings = Present retained earnings
+ Projected net income – Dividend to be declared

4. Sum the asset accounts and the liability and equity accounts to see if there is any difference. The difference, if any, is a *shortfall,* which is the amount of financing the firm has to raise externally.

Computer-Based Models and Spreadsheet Program Models for Budgeting

More and more companies are developing computer-based models for financial planning and budgeting, using powerful yet easy-to-use financial modeling languages such as Planet's Budget Maestro module. The models help not only to build a budget for profit planning but also to answer a variety of "what-if" scenarios. The resulting calculations provide a basis for choice among alternatives under conditions of *uncertainty*. Financial modeling can also be accomplished using spreadsheet programs such as Microsoft's Excel.

Chapter 4
Management Accounting/ Cost Management II

Part III: Using Cost Data for Control

RESPONSIBILITY ACCOUNTING: INTRODUCTION

Responsibility accounting is the system for collecting and reporting revenue and cost information by areas of responsibility. It operates on the premise that managers should be held responsible for their performance, the performance of their subordinates, and for all activities within their areas of responsibility. Responsibility accounting, also called *profitability accounting* and *activity accounting,* has the following advantages:

1. It facilitates delegation of decision-making.
2. It helps management promote the concept of *management by objective,* in which managers agree on a set of goals. A manager's performance is then evaluated based on his or her attainment of these goals.
3. It provides a guide to the evaluation of performance and helps to establish standards of performance, which are then used for comparison purposes.
4. It permits effective use of the concept of *management by exception,* which means that the manager's attention is concentrated on the important deviations (exceptions) from standards and budgets.

For an effective responsibility-accounting system, the following three basic conditions are necessary:

- The organizational structure must be well defined. Management responsibility and authority must go hand in hand at all levels and must be clearly established and understood.

- Standards of performance for costs, profits, and investments must be properly determined and well defined.
- The responsibility-accounting reports (or performance reports) should include only the items that are controllable by the manager of the responsibility center. Also, they should highlight items calling for managerial attention and remedial action.

Types of Responsibility Centers and Their Performance Evaluation

A well-designed responsibility-accounting system establishes responsibility centers within the organization. A *responsibility center* is defined as a unit in the organization that has control over costs, revenues, and/or investment funds. A responsibility center can be one of the following types:

Cost Center. A cost center is the unit within the organization that is responsible only for costs. Examples are production departments in a factory. Variance analysis based on standard costs and flexible budgets would be a typical tool for cost center control.

Profit Center. A profit center is the unit that is held responsible for the revenues earned and costs incurred in that center. Examples are various book divisions (such as a college book division) of a publishing company. The segmented reporting approach based on *contribution margin* is widely used to measure the performance of a profit center.

Investment Center. An investment center is the unit within the organization that is held responsible for the cost, revenues, and asset investment made in that center. Product line divisions in a large decentralized organization would be an example of an investment center. *Return on investment* and *residual income* are two key measures of investment center performance.

STANDARD COSTS AND VARIANCE ANALYSIS FOR COST CENTERS

One of the most important phases of responsibility accounting is establishing standard costs and evaluating performance by comparing actual costs with the standard costs. The difference between the actual costs and standard cost, called the *variance,* is calculated for individual cost centers. Variance analysis is a key tool for measuring performance of a cost center. The standard cost is based on physical and dollar measures; it is determined by multiplying the standard quantity of an input by its standard price. Two general types of variances can be calculated for most cost items: a price variance and a quantity variance. The *price variance* is calculated as follows:

$$\text{Price variance} = \text{Actual quantity} * (\text{Actual price}$$
$$- \text{Standard price})$$
$$= AQ \times (AP - SP)$$
$$= \underset{(1)}{(AQ \times AP)} - \underset{(2)}{(AQ \times SP)}$$

The *quantity variance* is calculated as follows:

$$\text{Quantity variance} \qquad = (\text{Actual quantity} - \text{Standard quantity})$$
$$* \text{Standard price}$$
$$= (AQ - SQ) \times SP$$
$$= \underset{(2)}{(AQ \times SP)} - \underset{(3)}{(SQ \times SP)}$$

Figure 4–1 shows a general model (three-column model) for variance analysis that incorporates items (1), (2), and (3) from the above equations. It is important to note four things:

First, a price variance and a quantity variance can be calculated for all three variable cost items—direct materials, direct labor, and variable portion of factory overhead. The variance is not called by the same name, however. For example, a price variance is called a materials-price variance in the case of direct materials, a labor-rate variance in the case of direct labor, and a variable-overhead-spending variance in the case of variable factory overhead.

Second, a cost variance is *unfavorable* (U) if the actual price (AP) or actual quantity (AQ) exceeds the standard price (SP) or standard quantity (SQ); a variance is *favorable* (F) if the actual price or actual quantity is less than the standard price or standard quantity.

Third, the standard quantity allowed for output—item (3)—is the key concept in variance analysis. This is the standard quantity that should have been used to produce actual output. It is computed by multiplying the *actual* output by the number of input units allowed.

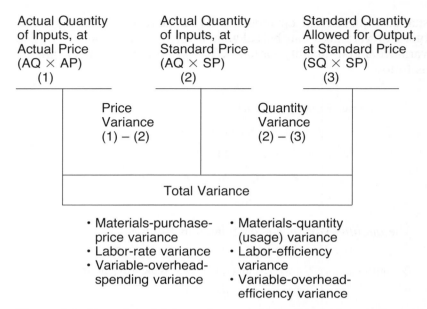

Figure 4–1. General model for variance analysis of variable manufacturing costs.

Fourth, variances for fixed overhead are of questionable usefulness for control purposes, since these variances are usually beyond the control of the production department. They are discussed later in this chapter. We will now illustrate variance analysis for each of the variable items in manufacturing costs.

Materials Variances

A materials-purchase-price variance is isolated at the time of purchase of the material. It is computed based on the actual quantity purchased. Unfavorable price variances may be caused by inaccurate standard prices, inflationary cost increases, scarcity in supplies of raw materials resulting in higher prices, and purchasing department inefficiencies. The purchasing department is responsible for any materials-price variance that might occur. In addition, the materials-quantity (usage) variance is computed based on the actual quantity used. Unfavorable materials-quantity variances may be explained by poorly trained workers, by improperly adjusted machines, or by outright waste on the production line. The production department is responsible for any materials quantity variance that might occur.

EXAMPLE 4.1

The Acme Corporation uses a standard cost system. The standard variable costs for product J are as follows:

> Materials: two pounds at $3 per pound
> Labor: one hour at $5 per hour
> Variable overhead: one hour at $3 per hour

During March, 25,000 pounds of material were purchased for $74,750, and 20,750 pounds of material were used in producing 10,000 units of finished product. Direct-labor costs incurred were $49,896 (10,080 direct-labor hours), and variable-overhead costs incurred were $34,776.

Using the general model (three-column model), the materials variances are shown in Figure 4–2.

It is important to note that the amount of materials purchased (25,000 pounds) differs from the amount of materials used in production (20,750 pounds). The materials-purchase-price variance was computed using 25,000 pounds purchased, whereas the materials-quantity (usage) variance was computed using the 20,750 pounds used in production. Because of this difference, a total variance cannot be computed.

Alternatively, we can compute the materials variances as follows:

Materials purchase price variance = AQ (AP – SP)

$\quad$ = (AQ × AP) – (AQ × SP)

$\quad$ = (25,000 pounds)($2.99 – $3.00)

$\quad$ = $74,750 – $75,000

$\quad$ = $250(F)

Materials-quantity (usage) variance = (AQ – SQ) SP

$\quad$ = (20,750 pounds – 20,000 pounds)($3.00)

$\quad$ = $62,250 – $60,000

$\quad$ = $2,250(U)

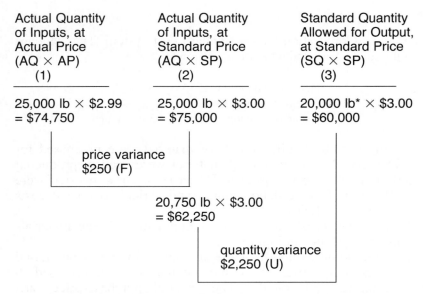

*10,000 units actually produced × 2 pounds allowed per unit = 20,000 pounds.

Figure 4–2. Materials variances

Labor Variances

Labor variances are isolated when labor is used for production. They are computed in a manner similar to the materials variances, except that in the three-column model, the terms *efficiency* and *rate* are used in place of the terms *quantity* and *price*. The production department is responsible for both the prices paid for labor services and the quantity of labor services used. Therefore, the production department must explain why any labor variances occur. Unfavorable rate variances may be explained by an increase in wages or by the use of labor commanding higher wage rates than contemplated. Unfavorable efficiency variances may be explained by poor supervision, poor quality of workers, poor quality of materials requiring more labor time, or machine breakdowns.

EXAMPLE 4.2

Using the same data given in Example 4.1, the labor variances can be calculated as shown in Figure 4–3.

Actual Hours of Inputs, at Actual Rate (AH × AR) (1)	Actual Hours of Inputs, at Standard Rate (AH × SR) (2)	Standard Hours Allowed for Output, at Standard Rate (SH × SR) (3)
10,080 h × $4.95 = $49,896	10,080 h × $5.00 = $50,400	10,000 h* × $5.00 = $50,000

Rate Variance (1) − (2) $504 (F)	Efficiency Variance (2) − (3) $400 (U)
Total Variance $104 (F)	

*10,000 units actually produced × 1 hour (h) allowed per unit = 10,000 hours.

Note: The symbols AQ, SQ, AP, and SP have been changed to AH, SH, AR, and SR to reflect the terms "hour" and "rate."

Figure 4–3. Labor variances

Alternatively, we can calculate the labor variances as follows:

Labor rate variance
$$= AH (AR − SR)$$
$$= (AH × AR) − (AH × SR)$$
$$= (10,080 \text{ hours})(\$4.95 − \$5.00)$$
$$= \$49,896 − \$50,400$$
$$= \$504 \text{ (F)}$$

Labor efficiency variance
$$= (AH − SH) SR$$
$$= (10,080 \text{ hours} − 10,000 \text{ hours}) * \$5.00$$
$$= \$50,400 − \$50,000$$
$$= \$400 \text{ (U)}$$

Variable-Overhead Variances

The variable-overhead variances are computed in a way very similar to the way the labor variances are figured. The production department is usually responsible for any variable-overhead variance that might occur. Unfavorable variable-overhead spending variances may be caused by a large number of factors: acquiring supplies for a price different from the standard, using more supplies than expected, waste, theft of supplies, and more. Unfavorable variable-overhead efficiency variances might be caused by such factors as poorly trained workers, poor-quality materials, faulty equipment, work interruptions, poor production scheduling, poor supervision, employee unrest, and more. When variable overhead is applied using direct-labor-hours, the efficiency variance will be the result of the same factors that cause the labor efficiency variance. However, when variable overhead is applied using machine-hours, inefficiency in machinery will cause a variable-overhead-efficiency variance.

EXAMPLE 4.3

Using the same data given in Example 4.1, the variable overhead variances can be computed as shown in Figure 4–4.

Actual Hours of Inputs, at Actual Rate (AH × AR) (1)	Actual Hours of Inputs, at Standard Rate (AH × SR) (2)	Standard Hours Allowed for Output, at Standard Rate (SH × SR) (3)
10,080 h × $3.45 = $34,776	10,080 h × $3.00 = $30,240	10,000 h* × $3.00 = $30,000

Spending Variance (1) – (2) $4,356 (U)	Efficiency Variance (2) – (3) $240 (U)
Total Variance $4,776 (U)	

*10,000 units actually produced × 1 hour (h) allowed per unit = 10,000 hours.

Figure 4–4. Variable-overhead variances

Alternatively, we can compute the variable overhead variances as follows:

Variance-overhead
  spending variance $= AH (AR - SR)$

$= (AH \times AR) - (AH \times SR)$

$= (10{,}080 \text{ hours}) (\$3.45 - \$3.00)$

$= \$34{,}776 - \$30{,}240$

$= \$4{,}536 \text{ (U)}$

Variable-overhead
  efficiency variance $= (AH - SH) SR$

$= (10{,}080 \text{ hours} - 10{,}000 \text{ hours}) \times \$3.00$

$= \$30{,}240 - \$30{,}000$

$= \$240 \text{ (U)}$

Flexible Budgets and Performance Reports

A flexible budget is a tool that is extremely useful in cost control. In contrast to a static budget, the flexible budget is characterized as follows:

1. It is geared toward a range of activity rather than a single level of activity.
2. It is dynamic in nature rather than static. By using the *cost volume formula* (or *flexible budget formula*), a series of budgets can be easily developed for various levels of activity.

The *static (fixed) budget* is geared for only one level of activity and is relatively ineffective in cost control. Flexible budgeting distinguishes between fixed and variable costs, thus allowing for a budget that can be automatically adjusted (through changes in variable-cost totals) to the particular level of activity *actually* attained. Thus, variances between actual costs and budgeted costs are adjusted for volume ups and downs before differences due to price and quantity factors are computed.

The primary use of the flexible budget is to give accurate measurements of performance by comparing actual costs for a given output with the budgeted costs for the *same level of output*.

EXAMPLE 4.4

To illustrate the difference between the static budget and the flexible budget, assume that the Assembly Department of Company Y is budgeted to produce 6,000 units during June. Assume further that the company was able to produce only 5,800 units. The budget for direct-labor and variable-overhead costs is as follows:

Company Y
Direct-Labor and Variable-Overhead Budget
Assembly Department
For the Month of June

Budgeted production	6,000 units
Actual production	5,800 units
Direct-labor cost	$39,000
Variable-overhead costs:	
Indirect labor	6,000
Supplies	900
Repairs	300
	$46,200

If a static budget is used, the performance report will appear as follows:

Company Y
Direct-Labor and Variable-Overhead Budget
Assembly Department
For the Month of June

	Budget	Actual	Variance (U or F)*
Production in units	6,000	5,800	200U
Direct-labor cost	$39,000	$38,500	$500F
Variable-overhead costs:			
Indirect labor	6,000	5,950	50F
Supplies	900	870	30F
Repairs	300	295	5F
	$46,200	$45,615	$585F

* A variance represents the deviation of actual cost from the standard or budgeted cost. U and F stand for unfavorable and favorable, respectively.

These cost variances are useless, in that they are comparing oranges with apples. The problem is that the budget costs are based on an activity level of 6,000 units, whereas the actual costs were incurred at an activity level below this (5,800 units). From a control standpoint, it makes no sense to try to compare costs at one activity level with costs at a different activity level. Such comparisons would make a production manager look good as long as the actual production is less than the budgeted production. Using the cost-volume formula and generating the budget based on the 5,800 actual units gives the following performance report:

Company Y
Performance Report
Assembly Department
For the Month of June

| Budgeted production | 6,000 units | | | |
| Actual production | 5,800 units | | | |

	Cost-volume formula*	*Budget* *5,800 units*	*Actual* *5,800 units*	*Variance* *(U or F)*
Direct-labor cost	$6.50 per unit	$37,700	$38,500	$800U
Variable-overhead costs:				
Indirect labor	1.00	5,800	5,950	150U
Supplies	.15	870	870	0
Repairs	.05	290	295	5U
	$7.70	$44,660	$45,615	$955U

*Assumed as given.

Notice that all cost variances are unfavorable (U), as compared to the favorable cost variances on the performance report based on the static budget.

Fixed-Overhead Variances

By definition, fixed overhead does not change over a relevant range of activity; the amount of fixed overhead *per unit* varies inversely with the level of production. In order to calculate variances for fixed overhead, it is necessary to determine a standard fixed-overhead rate, which requires the selection of a predetermined (denominator) level of activity. This activity should be measured on the basis of *standard inputs allowed*. The formula is as follows:

$$\text{Standard fixed overhead rate} = \frac{\text{Budgeted fixed overhead}}{\text{Budgeted level of activity}}$$

Total Fixed-Overhead Variance. This is simply *under-* or *over-applied* overhead. It is the difference between actual fixed overhead incurred and fixed overhead applied to production (generally on the basis of standard direct-labor hours allowed for actual production). Total fixed-overhead variance combines fixed-overhead *spending* *(flexible-budget)* variance and fixed-overhead *volume (capacity)* variance.

Fixed-overhead spending (flexible-budget) variance is the difference between actual fixed overhead incurred and budgeted fixed overhead. This variance is not affected by the level of production. Fixed overhead, by definition, does not change with the level of activity. The spending (flexible-budget) variance is caused solely by events such as unexpected changes in prices and unforeseen repairs.

Fixed-overhead volume (capacity) variance results when the actual level of activity differs from the denominator activity used in determining the standard fixed-overhead rate. Note that the denominator used in the formula is the expected annual activity level. Fixed-overhead volume variance is a measure of the cost of failure to operate at the denominator (budgeted) activity level, and may be caused by such factors as failure to meet sales targets, idleness due to poor scheduling, and machine breakdowns. The volume variance is calculated as follows:

$$\begin{aligned}
\text{Fixed overhead} \atop \text{volume variance} \; &= \; \text{(Budgeted fixed overhead)} \\
&\quad - \; \text{(fixed overhead applied)} \\
&\qquad\qquad\quad \text{or} \\
&= \; \text{(Denominator activity} \\
&\quad - \; \text{standard hours allowed)} \\
&\quad \times \; \text{standard fixed overhead rate}
\end{aligned}$$

When denominator activity exceeds standard hours allowed, the volume variance is unfavorable (U), because it is an index of less-than-denominator utilization of capacity.

It is important to note that there are *no* efficiency variances for fixed overhead. Fixed overhead does not change, regardless of whether productive resources are used efficiently or not. (For example, such costs as property taxes, insurance fees, and factory rents are not affected by whether production is being carried on efficiently or not.)

Figure 4–5 illustrates the relationship among the various elements of fixed overhead, together with the possible variances.

Incurred:	Flexible Budget	Flexible Budget	
Actual Hours × Actual Rate (1)	Based on Actual Hours (2)	Based on Standard Hours Allowed (3)	Applied (4)

3-way Analysis	Spending Variance (1) − (2)	Efficiency Variance (Not Applicable)	Volume Variance (3) − (4)
2-way Analysis	Flexible Budget Variance (1) − (3)		Volume Variance (3) − (4)
	(1) − (4) Under- or Overapplied		

Figure 4–5. Fixed-overhead variances

EXAMPLE 4.5

The Geige Manufacturing Company has the following standard cost of factory overhead at a normal monthly production (denominator) volume of 1,300 direct-labor hours:

Variable overhead (1 hour @ $2)

Fixed overhead (1 hour @ $5)

Fixed overhead budgeted is $6,500 per month. During the month of March, the following events occurred:

(a) Actual overhead costs incurred were:

Variable	$2,053
Fixed	$6,725

(b) Direct labor hours used, 1,350 hours @ $6.50

Note that:

(a) Flexible-budget formula:

Variable-overhead rate	$2 per direct labor hour
Fixed overhead budgeted	$6,500

(b) Standard overhead applied rates:

         Variable $2 per direct labor hour
         Fixed $5 per direct labor hour

Figure 4–6 shows all the variances for variable overhead as well as for fixed overhead.

Alternatively, fixed-overhead volume variance can be calculated as follows:

$$\text{Fixed overhead volume variance} = (\text{Denominator activity}$$

$$- \text{standard hours allowed})$$

$$\times \text{standard fixed overhead rate}$$

$$= (1{,}300 \text{ hours} - 1{,}250 \text{ hours}) \times \$5$$

$$= 50 \text{ hours} \times \$5 = \$250 \text{ U}$$

Methods of Variance Analysis

Variance analysis for factory overhead consists of a two-, three-, or four-way method of computation, depending on the significance of the variance amounts compared to the cost of analysis. These methods are indicated in Figures 4–5 and 4–6.

The *two-way* analysis computes two variances: budget variance (sometimes called the flexible-budget or controllable variance) and volume variances, which means:

(1) Budget variance = Variable-spending variance + Fixed-spending (budget) variance + Variable-efficiency variance
(2) Volume variance = Fixed-volume variance

The *three-way* analysis computes three variances: spending, efficiency, and volume variances. Therefore:

(1) Spending variance = Variable-spending variance + Fixed-spending (budget) variance
(2) Efficiency variance = Variable-efficiency variance
(3) Volume variance = Fixed-volume variance

The *four-way* analysis includes the following:

(1) Variable-spending variance
(2) Fixed-spending (budget) variance
(3) Variable-efficiency variance
(4) Fixed-volume variance

Incurred:	Flexible Budget	Flexible Budget	
Actual Hours × Actual Rate (1,350 hrs) (1)	Based on Actual Hours (1,350 hrs) (2)	Based on Standard Hours Allowed (1,250 hrs) (3)	Applied (1,250 hrs) (4)
V $2,853	$2,700 (1,350 × $2)	$2,500 (1,250 × $2)	$2,500
F 6,725	6,500	6,500	6,250
$9,578	$9,200	$9,000	$8,750

(3-way)	Spending Variance (1) – (2)	Efficiency Variance (Not Applicable)	Volume Variance (3) – (4)
V	$153 U	$200 U	Not Applicable
F	225 U	Not Applicable	$250 U
	$378 U	$200 U	$250 U

(2-way)	Flexible Budget Variance (1) – (3)	Volume Variance (3) – (4)
V	$353 U	Not Applicable
F	225 U	$250 U
	$578 U	$250 U

	Under- or Overapplied (1) – (4)	
V	$353 U	
F	475 U	
	$828 U	

Figure 4–6. Variance analysis for variable-overhead and fixed overhead

Production Mix and Yield Variances

The production mix variance is a cost variance that arises if the actual production mix deviates from the standard or budgeted mix. In a multi-product, multi-input situation, the mix variances explain the portion of the quantity (usage or efficiency) variance caused by using inputs (direct materials and direct labor) in ratios different from standard proportions, thus helping determine how efficiently mixing operations are performed.

The material mix variance indicates the impact on material costs of the deviation from the budgeted mix. The labor mix variance measures the impact of changes in the labor mix on labor costs.

• Material Mix Variance:

> (Actual Units used at standard–Actual Units used at actual mix) × Standard Unit Price

• Labor Mix Variance:

> (Actual Hours used at standard mix – Actual Hours used at actual mix) × Standard Hourly Rate

Probable causes of unfavorable production mix variances are as follows:

1. Capacity restraints force substitution.
2. Poor production scheduling.
3. Lack of certain types of labor.
4. Certain materials are in short supply.

EXAMPLE 4.6

J Company produces a compound composed of Materials Alpha and Beta that is marketed in 20-lb. bags. Material Alpha can be substituted for Material Beta. Standard cost and mix data have been determined as follows:

	Unit Price	Standard Mix Standard Unit	Proportions
Material Alpha	$3	5 lbs.	25%
Material Beta	4	15	75
		20 lbs.	100%

Processing each 20 lbs. of material requires 10 hrs. of labor. The company employs two types of labor, "skilled" and "unskilled," working on two processes, assembly and finishing. The following standard labor cost has been set for a 20-lb. bag.

	Standard Hours	Standard Wage Rate	Total	Standard Mix Proportions
Unskilled	4 hrs.	$2	$8	40%
Skilled	6	3	18	60
	10 hrs.	$2.60	26	100%

At standard cost, labor averages $2.60 per unit. During the month of December, 100 20-lb. bags were completed with the following labor costs:

	Actual Hrs.	*Actual Rate*	*Actual Wages*
Unskilled	380 hrs.	$2.50	$950
Skilled	600	3.25	1,950
	980 hrs.	$2.96	$2,900

We now want to determine the following variances from standard costs.

1. Material purchase price
2. Material quantity
   a. Material mix
   b. Material yield
3. Labor rate
4. Labor efficiency
   a. Labor mix
   b. Labor yield

Material records show:

	Beginning Inventory	Purchase	Ending Inventory
Material Alpha	100 lbs.	800 @ $3.10	200 lbs.
Material beta	225	1,350 @ $3.90	175

We will also prepare appropriate journal entries.
We will show how to compute these variances in a tabular form as follows:

(a) *Material Purchase Price Variance*

	Material Price per Unit			Actual Quantity Purchased	Variance
	Standard	*Actual*	*Difference*		
Material Alpha	$3	$3.10	$0.10 U	800 lbs.	$ 80 U
Material Beta	4	3.90	0.10 F	1,350	135 F
					$55 F

(b) *Material Mix Variance*

	Unit Which Should Have Been Used at Standard Mix*	Actual Unit at Actual Mix**	Diff.	Standard Unit Price	Variance
Material Alpha	525 lbs.	700 lbs.	175 U	$3	$525 U
Material Beta	1,575	1,400	175 F	4	700 F
	2,100 lbs.	2,100 lbs.			$175 F

The material mix variance measures the impact on material costs of the deviation from the standard mix. Therefore, it is computed holding the total quantity used constant at its actual amount and allowing the material mix to vary between actual and standard. As shown above, due to a favorable change in mix, we ended up with a favorable material mix variance of $175.

(c) *Material Quantity Variance*

	Unit Which Should Have Been Used at Standard Mix*	Standard Unit at Standard Mix**	Diff.	Standard Unit Price	Variance
Material Alpha	525 lbs.	500 lbs.	25 U	$3	$75 U
Material Beta	1,575	1,500	75 U	4	300 U
	2,100 lbs.	2,000 lbs.			$375 U

* This is the standard mix proportion of 25% and 75% applied to the actual material units used of 2,100 lbs.
**Actual units used = beginning inventory + purchases - ending inventory. Therefore,
     Material Alpha: 700 lbs. = 100 + 800 - 200
     Material Beta: 1,400 lbs. = 225 + 1,350 - 175

The total material variance is the sum of the three variances:

Purchase price variance	$55 F
Mix variance	175 F
Quantity Variance	375 U
	$145 U

The increase of $145 in material costs was due solely to an unfavorable quantity variance of 100 lbs. of material Alpha and Beta. The unfavorable quantity variance, however, was compensated largely by favorable mix and price variances. J Company must look for ways to cut down waste and spoilage.

The labor cost increase of $300 ($2,900 – $2,600) is attributable to three causes:

1. An increase of $.50 per hour in the rate paid to skilled labor and $.25 per hour in the rate paid to unskilled labor.
2. An unfavorable mix of skilled and unskilled labor.
3. A favorable labor efficiency variance of 20 hours.

Three labor variances are computed below.

(d) *Labor Rate Variance*

	Labor Rate per Hour Standard	Actual	Diff.	Actual Hours	Variance
Unskilled	$2	$2.50	$.5 U	380 U	$190 U
Skilled	3	3.25	$.25 U	600	150 U
					$340 U

e) *Labor Mix Variance*

	Actual Hours at Standard Mix*	Actual Hours at Actual Mix	Diff.	Standard	Variance
Unskilled	392 hrs.	380 hrs.	12 F	$2	$24 F
Skilled	588	600	12 U	3	36 U
	980 hrs.	980 hrs.			$12 U

*This is the standard proportions of 40% and 60% applied to the actual total labor hrs. used of 980.

(f) *Labor Efficiency Variance*

	Actual Hours at Standard Mix	Standard Hours at Standard Mix	Diff.	Standard Rate	Variance
Unskilled	392 hrs.	400 hrs.	8 F	$2	$16 F
Skilled	588	600	12 F	3	36 F
	980 hrs.	1,000 hrs.			$52 F

The total labor variance is the sum of these three variances:

Rate variance	$340 U
Mix variance	12 U
Efficiency variance	52 F
	$300 U

which is proved to be:

Total Labor Variance

	Actual Hrs. Used	Actual Rate	Total Actual Cost	Standard Hrs. Allowed	Standard Hrs. Rate	Total Cost	Variance
Unskille	380 hrs.	$2.50	$950	400	$2	$800	$150 U
Skilled	600	3.25	1,950	600	3	1,800	150 U
			$2,900			$2,600	$300 U

The unfavorable labor variance, as evidenced by the cost increase of $300, may be due to:

1. overtime necessary because of poor production scheduling resulting in a higher average labor cost per hour; and/or
2. unnecessary use of more expensive skilled labor. J Company should put more effort into better production scheduling.

Production Yield Variance

The production yield variance is the difference between the actual yield and the standard yield. Yield is a measure of productivity. In other words, it is a measure of output from a given amount of input. For example, in the production of potato chips, we might expect a certain yield such as 40% yield or 40 pounds of chips for 100 pounds of potatoes.

If the actual yield is less than the expected or standard yield for a given level of input, the yield variance is unfavorable. A yield variance is computed for labor as well as materials. A labor yield variance is considered the result of the quantity and/or the quality of labor used. The yield variance explains the remaining portion of the quantity variance and is caused by a yield of finished product that does not correspond with the quantity that actual inputs should have produced. When there is no mix variance, the yield variance equals the quantity variance.

- Material Yield Variance:

   (Actual Quantity used at standard mix – Actual Output Units at standard quantity at standard mix) × Standard Unit Price

- Labor Yield Variance:

   (Actual Hours used at standard mix – Actual Output Units at standard hours at standard mix) × Standard Hourly Rate

- Or, generically, simply:

   (Actual Input units at standard mix – Actual Output Units at standard input units at standard mix) × Standard Input Price or Rate

The probable causes of unfavorable production yield variances are: (1) use of low quality materials and/or labor; (2) existence of faulty equipment; (3) use of improper production methods; and (4) improper or costly mix of materials and/or labor.

EXAMPLE 4.7

The Giffen Manufacturing Company uses a standard cost system for its production of a chemical product. This chemical is produced by mixing three major raw materials, A, B, and C. The company has the following standards:

36 lbs. of Material A	@1.00	=	$36.00
48 lbs. of Material B	@2.00	=	$96.00
36 lbs. of Material C	@1.75	=	$63.00
120 lbs. of standard mix	@1.625	=	$195.00

The company should produce 100 lbs. of finished product at a standard cost of $1.625 per lb. ($195/120 lbs.) To convert 120 lbs. of materials into 100 lbs. of finished chemical requires 400 direct labor hours at $3.50 per hour, or $14 per lb. During the month of December, the company completed 4,250 lbs. of output with the following labor: direct labor 15,250 hours @$3.50. Material records show:

	Materials purchased during the month	Materials used during the month
Material A	1,200 @ $1.00	1,160 lbs.
Material B	1,800 @ 1.95	1,820
Material C	1,500 @ 1.80	1,480

The material *price variance is isolated at the time of purchase.* We want to compute the material purchase price, quantity, mix, and yield variances.

Also, we want to prepare appropriate journal entries. We will show the computations of variances in a tabular form as follows:

(a) *Material Variances*

Material Purchase Price Variance

	Material Price per unit			Actual Quantity	
	Standard	Actual	Diff.	Purchased	Variance
Material A	$1.00	$1.10	$.10 U	1,200 lbs.	$120 U
Material B	2.00	1.95	.05 F	1,800	90 F
Material C	1.75	1.80	.05 U	1,500	75 U
					$105 U

The material quantity variance computed below results from the change in the mix of materials as well as from changes in the total quantity of materials. The standard input allowed for actual production consists of 1,275 lbs. of Material A, 1,700 lbs. of Material B, and 1,275 lbs. of Material C, a total of 4,250 lbs. The actual input consisted of 1,160 lbs. of Material A, 1,820 lbs. of Material B, and 1,480 lbs. of Material C. The total variance is subdivided into a material mix variance and a material yield variance, as shown below.

Material Quantity Variance

	Actual Unit Used at Actual Mix	"Should have been" Inputs Based Upon Actual Output	Diff.	Standard Unit Price	Variance
Material A	1,160 lbs.	1,275 lbs.	115 F	$1.00	$115
Material B	1,820	1,700	120 U	2.00	240 F
Material C	1,480	1,275			358.75 U
	4,460 lbs.	4,250 lbs.			$483.75 U

The computation of the material mix variance and the material yield variance for the Giffen Manufacturing Company is given below.

Material Mix Variance

	"Should have been" Individual Input Based Upon Total Actual Throughput*	Actual Units Used at Actual Output*	Diff.	Standard Unit Price	Variance
Material A	1,338 lbs.	1,160 lbs.	178 F	$1.00	$178 F
Material B	1,784	1,820	36 U	2.00	72 U
Material C	1,338	1,480	142 U	1.79	248.5 U
	4,460 lbs.	4,460 lbs.			$142.5 U

*This is the standard mix proportions of 30%, 40%, and 30% applied to the actual material units used of 4,460 lbs.

Material Yield Variance

	Expected Input Units at Standard Mix	"Should have been" Inputs Based Upon Actual Output*	Diff.	Standard Unit Price	Variance
Material A	1,338 lbs.	1,275 lbs.	63 U	$1.00	$63 U
Material B	1,784	1,700	84 U	2.00	168 U
Material C	1,338	1,275	63 U	1.75	110.25 U
	4,460 lbs.	4,420 lbs.			$341.25 U**

* This is the standard mix proportions of 30%, 40%, and 30% applied to the actual throughput of 4,460 lbs. or *output* of 4,250 lbs.
**The material yield variance of $341.25 U can be computed alternatively as follows.

Actual input quantity at standard prices
Material A 1,338 lbs. @ $1.00 = $1,338
Material B 1,784 lbs. @ 2.00 =   3,568
Material C 1,338 lbs. @ 1.75 =   2,341.5 $7,247.50

Hence, $7,247.5 – $4,906.25 = $341.25 U

The material mix and material yield variances are unfavorable indicating that a shift was made to a more expensive (at standard) input mix and that an excessive quantity of material was used. Poor production scheduling requiring an unnecessarily excessive use of input material and an undesirable mix of Material A, B, and C was responsible for this result. To remedy the situation, the company must ensure that:

(a) the material mix is adhered to in terms of the least cost combination without affecting product quality;
(b) the proper production methods are being implemented; Inefficiencies, waste, and spoilage are within the standard allowance; and
(c) quality materials, consistent with established standards are being used.

Journal Entries

To record material purchases

Material and Supplies	7,425*	
Material Purchase Price Variance	105 U	
Cash (or Accounts Payable)		7,530**

* Actual quantities purchased at standard prices:

Material A (1,200 lbs. @ $1.00)	$1,200	
Material B (1,800 @ 2.00)	3,600	
Material C (1,500 @ 1.75)	2,625	7,425

**Actual quantities purchased at actual prices:

Material A (1,200 lbs. @ $1.10)	$1,320	
Material B (1,800 @ 1.95)	3,510	
Material C (1,500 @ 1.80)	2,700	7,530

To charge materials into production

Work-in-Process	$7,247.50*	
Material Mix Variance		142.50 U
Material and Supplies		7,390**

* Actual quantities used of standard mix at standard prices:

Material A (1,338 lbs. @ $1.00)	$1,338.00	
Material B (1,784 @ 2.00)	3,568.00	
Material C (1,480 @ 1.75)	2,341.50	7,247.50

**Actual quantities used at standard prices:

Material A (1,160 lbs. @ $1.00)	$1,160	
Material B (1,820 @ 2.00)	3,640	
Material C (1,480 @ 1.75)	2,590	7,390

To transfer material costs to finished goods

Finished Goods	$6,906.25†	
Material Yield Variance	341.25 U	
Work-in-Process		7,240.50†

†See the previous page for the numerical computations.

Employees seldom complete their operations according to standard times. Two factors should be brought out in computing labor variances if the analysis and computation will be used to fix responsibility:

1. The change in labor cost resulting from the efficiency of the workers, measured by a labor efficiency variance (in finding the change, allowed hours are determined through the material input).

2. The change in labor cost due to a difference in the yield, measured by a labor yield variance (in computing the change, actual output is converted to allowed input hours).

For the Giffen Manufacturing Company, more efficient workers resulted in a savings of 383.33 hours (15,250 hrs.–14,866.67 hrs.). Priced at the standard rate per hour, this produced an unfavorable labor efficiency variance of $1,341.66 as shown below:

Labor Efficiency Variance

Actual hrs. at standard rate	$53,375
Actual hrs. at expected output	
(4,460 hrs × 400/120 = 14,866.67 hrs @ $3.5	52,033.3
	$1,341.6

With a standard yield of 83⅓% (=100/120), 4,250 lbs. of finished material should have required 17,000 hrs. of direct labor (4,250 lbs. × 400 DLH/100). Comparing the hours allowed for the actual input 14,866.67 hrs. with the hours allowed for actual output, 17,000 hrs., we find a favorable labor yield variance of $7,466.66, as shown below:

Labor Yield Variance

Actual hrs. at expected output	$52,033.3
Actual output (4,250 lbs. × 400/100 =	
17,000 hrs. @ $3.5 or 4,250 lbs. @ $14.00)	59,500
	$7,466.6

The labor efficiency variance can be combined with the yield variance to give us the *traditional* labor efficiency variance, which turns out to be favorable as follows:

Labor efficiency variance	$1,341.66 U
Labor yield variance	7,466.66 F
	$6,125

This division is necessary when there is a difference between the actual yield and standard yield, if responsibility is to be fixed. The producing department cannot be rightfully credited with a favorable efficiency variance of $6,125. Note, however, that a favorable yield variance, which is a factor most likely outside the control of the producing department, more than offsets the *"unfavorable"* labor efficiency variance of $1,341.66, which the producing department rightfully should have been responsible for.

Journal Entries

To transfer labor costs to work-in-process

Work-in-Process	52,033.34	
Labor Efficiency Variance	1,341.66 U	
Payroll		53,375.00

To transfer labor costs to finished goods

Finished Goods	59,500	
Labor Yield Variance		7,466.66 F
Work-in-Process		52,033.34

SEGMENTAL REPORTING FOR PROFIT CENTERS

Segmental reporting is the process of reporting activities of profit centers such as divisions, product lines, or sales territories. The *contribution approach* is valuable for segmented reporting because it emphasizes the cost-behavior patterns and the controllability of costs that are generally useful for profitability analysis of various segments of an organization. The contribution approach is based on the thesis that:

1. Fixed costs are much less controllable than variable costs.
2. *Direct fixed costs* and *common fixed costs* must be clearly distinguished. Direct fixed costs can be identified directly with a particular segment of an organization, whereas common fixed costs cannot be identified directly with any one segment.
3. Common fixed costs should be clearly identified as *unallocated* in the contribution income statement by segments. Any attempt to allocate these types of costs, on some arbitrary basis, to the segments of the organization can destroy the value of responsibility accounting. It would lead to unfair evaluation of performance and misleading managerial decisions.

The following concepts are highlighted in the contribution approach:

1. *Contribution margin*—sales minus variable costs
2. *Contribution controllable by segment managers*—contribution margin less direct fixed costs controllable by segment managers. Direct fixed costs include discretionary fixed costs such as certain advertising, R&D, sales promotion, and engineering.
3. *Segment margin*—contribution controllable by segment managers less fixed costs controllable by others. Fixed costs controllable by others include such traceable and committed fixed costs as depreciation, property taxes, insurance and the segment managers' salaries.
4. *Net income*—segment margin less unallocated common fixed costs.

EXAMPLE 4.8

The following financial statement illustrates two levels of segmental reporting: by segments defined as divisions and by segments defined as product lines of a division.

SEGMENTAL INCOME STATEMENT

(1) *Segments Defined as Divisions*

	Total Company	Division 1	Division 2
Sales	$150,000	$90,000	$60,000
Less: Variable costs			
Manufacturing	40,000	30,000	10,000
Selling and admin.	20,000	14,000	6,000
Total variable costs	60,000	44,000	16,000
Contribution margin	$90,000	$46,000	$44,000
Less: Direct fixed costs controllable by division managers	55,000	33,000	22,000
Contribution controllable by division managers	$35,000	$13,000	$22,000
Less: Direct fixed costs controllable by others	15,000	10,000	5,000
Divisional segment margin	$20,000	$ 3,000	$17,000
Less: Unallocated common fixed costs	$10,000		
Net income	$10,000		

The column headers read: Total Company, then under *Segments:* — Division 1 and Division 2.

(2) Segments Defined as Product Lines of Division 2

	Division 2	Deluxe Model	Regular Model
		Segments:	
Sales	$60,000	$20,000	$40,000
Less: Variable costs			
Manufacturing	10,000	5,000	5,000
Selling and administrative	6,000	2,000	4,000
Total variable costs	16,000	7,000	9,000
Contribution margin	$44,000	$13,000	$31,000
Less: Direct fixed costs controllable			
by product line managers	22,000	8,000	14,000
Contribution controllable by product			
line managers	$22,000	$5,000	$17,000
Less: Direct fixed costs controllable			
by others	4,500	1,500	3,000
Product line margin	$17,500	$ 3,500	$14,000
Less: Unallocated common fixed costs	$ 500		
Divisional segment margin	$17,000		

The segment margin is the best measure of the profitability of a segment. Unallocated fixed costs are common to the segments being evaluated and should be left unallocated in order not to distort the performance results of segments.

Gross Profit Analysis

Gross profit analysis, often called profit variance analysis, deals with how to analyze the profit variance, which constitutes the departure between actual profit and the previous year's income or the budgeted figure. The primary goal of profit variance analysis is to improve performance and profitability.

Profit, whether it is gross profit in absorption costing or contribution margin in direct costing, is affected by at least three basic items: sales price, sales volume, and costs. In addition, in a multiproduct firm, if not all products are equally profitable, profit is affected by the mix of products sold.

The difference between budgeted and actual profits are due to one or more of the following:

1. Changes in unit sales price and cost, called sales price and cost price variances, respectively. The difference between the sales price variance and cost price variance is often called a

contribution-margin-per-unit variance or a gross-profit-per-unit variance, depending upon what type of costing system is being referred to, that is, absorption costing or direct costing. Contribution margin is, however, a better measure of product profitability because it deducts from sales revenue only the variable costs that are controllable in terms of fixing responsibility. Gross profit does not reflect cost-volume-profit relationships. Nor does it consider directly traceable marketing costs.

2. Changes in the volume of products sold summarized as the sales volume variance and the cost volume variance. The difference between the two is called the total volume variance.

3. Changes in the volume of the more profitable or less profitable items referred to as the sales mix variance.

Detailed analysis is critical to management when multiproducts exist. The volume variances may be used to measure a change in volume (while holding the mix constant), and the mix may be employed to evaluate the effect of a change in sales mix (while holding the quantity constant). This type of variance analysis is useful when the products are substituted for each other, or when products that are not necessarily substitutes for each other are marketed through the same channel.

Types of Standards in Profit Variance Analysis. To determine the various causes for a favorable variance (an increase) or an unfavorable variance (a decrease) in profit we need some kind of yardsticks to compare against the actual results. The yardsticks may be based on the prices and costs of the previous year, or any year selected as the base periods. Some companies are summarizing profit variance analysis data in their annual report by showing departures from the previous year's reported income. However, one can establish a more effective control and budgetary method rather than the previous year's data. Standard or budgeted mix can be determined using such sophisticated techniques as linear and goal programming.

Single Product Firms. Profit variance analysis is simplest in a single product firm, for there is only one sales price, one set of costs (or cost price), and a unitary sales volume. An unfavorable profit variance can be broken down into four components: a sales price variance, a cost price variance, a sales volume variance, and a cost volume variance.

The sales price variance measures the impact on the firm's contribution margin (or gross profit) of changes in the unit selling price. It is computed as:

Sales price variance = (actual price − budget price) × actual sales

If the actual price is lower than the budgeted price, for example, this variance is unfavorable; it tends to reduce profit. The cost price variance, on the other hand, is simply the summary of price variances for materials, labor, and overhead. (This is the sum of material price, labor rate, and factory overhead spending variances). It is computed as:

Cost price variance = (actual cost–budget cost) × actual sales

If the actual unit cost is lower than budgeted cost, for example, this variance is favorable; it tends to increase profit. We simplify the computation of price variances by taking the sales price variance less the cost price variance and call it the gross-profit-per-unit variance or contribution-margin-per-unit variance.

The sale volume variance indicates the impact on the firm's profit of changes in the unit sales volume. This is the amount by which sales would have varied from the budget if nothing but sales volume had changed. It is computed as:

Sales volume variance = (actual sales–budget sales) × budget price

If actual sales volume is greater than budgeted sales volume, this is favorable; it tends to increase profit. The cost volume variance has the same interpretation. It is:

(Actual sales–budget sales) × budget cost per unit.

The difference between the sales volume variance and the cost volume variance is called the total volume variance.

Multiproduct Firms. When a firm produces more than one product, there is a fourth component of the profit variance. This is the sales mix variance, the effect on profit of selling a different proportionate mix of products than that which has been budgeted. This variance arises when different products have different contribution margins. In a multiproduct firm, actual sales volume can differ from the budgeted amount in two ways. The total number of units sold could differ from the target aggregate sales. In addition, the mix of the products actually sold may not be proportionate to the target mix. Each of these two different types of changes in volume is reflected in a separate variance.

The total volume variance is divided into two: the sales mix variance and the sales quantity variance. These two variances should be used to evaluate the marketing department. The sales mix variance shows how well the department has done in terms of selling the more profitable products while the sales quantity variance measures how well the firm has done in terms of its overall sales volume.

They are computed as:

Sales Mix Variance
(Actual Sales at budget mix – Actual Sales at actual mix) ×
Budget CM (or gross profit / unit)

Sales Quantity Variance
(Actual Sales at budget mix – Budget Sales at budget mix) ×
Budget CM (or gross profit / unit)

Sales Volume Variance
(Actual Sales at actual mix – Budget Sales at budget mix) ×
Budget CM (or gross profit / unit)

EXAMPLE 4.9

The Lake Tahoe Ski Store sells two ski models—Model X and Model Y. For the years 2014 and 2015, the store realized a gross profit of $246,640 and $211,650, respectively. The owner of the store was astounded, because the total sales volume in dollars and in units was higher for 2015 than for 2014—yet the gross profit achieved actually declined. Given below are the store's unaudited operating results for 2014 and 2015. No fixed costs were included in the cost of goods sold per unit.

| | Model X | | | | Model Y | | | |
| | Selling Price | Cost of Goods Sold per unit | Sales in Units | Sales Revenue | Selling Price | Cost of Goods Sold per unit | Sales in Units | Sales Revenue |
Year								
1	$150	$110	2,800	$420,000	$172	$121	2,640	$454,080
2	160	125	2,650	424,000	176	135	2,900	510,400

Explain why the gross profit declined by $34,990. Include a detailed variance analysis of price changes and changes in volume both for sales and cost. Subdivide the total volume variance into change in price and change in quantity.

Sales price and sales volume variances measure the impact on the firm's CM (or GM) of changes in the unit selling price and sales volume. In computing these variances, all costs are held constant in order to stress changes in price and volume. Cost price and cost volume variances are computed in the same manner, holding price and volume constant. All these variances for the Lake Tahoe Ski Store are computed as follows:

Sales Price Variance
    Actual sales for 2015:
        Model X 2,650 × $160 = $424,000
        Model Y 2,900 × 176 = 510,400 $934,400
    Actual 2014 sales at 2014 prices:
        Model X 2,650 × $150 = $397,500
        Model Y 2,900 × 172 = 498,800   896,300
                                              $ 38,100 F

Sales Volume Variance
    Actual 2015 sales at 2014 prices: $896,300
    Actual 2014 sales (at 2014 prices):
        Model X 2,800 × $150 = $420,000
        Model Y 2,640 × 172 = 454,080   874,080
                                              $ 22,220 F

Cost Price Variance
    Actual cost of goods sold for 2015:
        Model X 2,650 × $125 = $331,250
        Model Y 2,900 × 135 = 391,500 $722,750
    Actual 2015 sales at 2014 costs:
        Model X 2,650 × $110 = $291,500
        Model Y 2,900 × 121 = 350,900   642,400
                                              $ 80,350 U

Cost Volume Variance
    Actual 2015 sales at 2014 costs: $642,400
    Actual 2014 sales (at 2014 costs):
        Model X 2,800 × $110 = $308,000
        Model Y 2,640 × 121 = 319,440   627,440
                                              $ 14,960 U

Total volume variance = sales volume variance - cost volume variance

= $22,220 F – $14,960 U = $7,260 F

The total volume variance is computed as the sum of a sales mix variance and a sales quantity variance as follows:

Sales Mix Variance

	2015 Actual Sale at 2014 Mix*	2015 Actual Sale at 2015 Mix	Diff.	2014 Gross Profit per Unit	Variance
Model X	2,857	2,650	207 U	$40	$ 8,280 U
Model Y	2,693	2,900	207 F	51	10,557 F
	5,500	5,550			$ 2,277 F

*This is the 2014 mix (used as standard or budget) proportions of 51.47% (or 2,800/5,440 = 51.47%) and 48.53% (or 2,640/5,440 = 48.53%) applied to the actual 2015 sales figure of 5,550 units.

Sales Quantity Variance

	2015 Actual Sale at 2014 Mix*	2015 Actual Sale at 2015 Mix	Diff.	2014 Gross Profit per Unit	Variance
Model X	2,857	2,800	57 F	$40	$2,280 F
Model Y	2,693	2,640	52 F	51	2,703 F
	5,550	5,440			$4,983 F

A favorable total volume variance is due to a favorable shift in the sales mix (that is from Model X to Model Y) and also to a favorable increase in sales volume (by 110 units), which is shown as follows:

Sale mix variance	$2,277 F
Sales quantity variance	4,983 F
	$7,260

However, there remains the decrease in gross profit. The decrease in gross profit of $34,990 can be explained as follows:

	Gains	Losses
Gain due to increased sales price	$38,100 F	
Loss due to increased cost		80,350
Gain due to increased in units sold	4,983 F	
Gain due to shift in sales mix	2,277 F	
	$45,360 F	$80,350

Hence, net decrease in gross profit equals $80,350 – $45,360 =	$34,990 U

Despite the increase in sales price and volume and the favorable shift in sales mix, the Lake Tahoe Ski Store ended up losing $34,990 compared to 2014. The major reason for this comparative loss was the tremendous increase in cost of goods sold, as costs for both Model X and Model Y went up quite significantly over 2014. The store has to take a close look at the cost picture; variable and fixed costs should be analyzed in an effort to cut down on controllable costs. In doing that, it is essential that responsibility be clearly assigned to given individuals. In a retail business like the Lake Tahoe Ski Store, operating expenses such as advertising and payroll of store employees must also be scrutinized.

EXAMPLE 4.10

Shim and Siegel, Inc., sells two products, C and D. Product C has a budgeted unit CM (contribution margin) of $3 and product D has a budgeted unit CM of $6. The budget for a recent month called for sales of 3,000 units of C and 9,000 units of D, for a total of 12,000 units. Actual sales totaled 12,200 units, 4,700 of C and 7,500 of D. Compute the sales volume variance and break this variance down into the sales quantity variance and sales mix variance.

Shim and Siegel's sales volume variance is computed below. As we can see, while total unit sales increased by 200 units, the shift in sales mix resulted in a $3,900 unfavorable sales volume variance.

Sales Volume Variance

	Actual Sales at Actual Mix	*Standard Sales at Budgeted Mix*	*Difference*	*Budgeted CM per Unit*	*Variance*
Product C	4,700	3,000	1,700 F	$3	$5,100 F
Product D	7,500	9,000	1,500 U	6	9,000 U
	12,200	12,000			$3,900 U

In multiproduct firms, the sales volume variance is further divided into a sales quantity variance and a sales mix variance. The computations of these variances are shown below:

Sales Quantity Variance

	Actual Sales at Actual Mix	*Standard Sales at Budgeted Mix*	*Difference*	*Budgeted CM per Unit*	*Variance*
Product C	3,050	3,000	50 F	$3	$150 F
Product D	9,150	9,000	150 F	6	900 F
	12,200	12,000			$1,050 F

Sales Mix Variance

	Actual Sales at Budgeted Mix	*Standard Sales at Actual Mix*	*Difference*	*Standard CM per Unit*	*Variance*
Product C	3,050	4,700	1,650 F	$3	$4,950 F
Product D	9,150	7,500	1,650 U	6	9,900 U
	12,200	12,200			$4,950 U

The sales quantity variance reflects the impact on the CM or GM (gross margin) of deviations from the standard sales volume, whereas the sales mix variance measures the impact on the CM of deviations from the budgeted mix. In the case of Shim and Siegel, Inc., the sales quantity variance came out to be favorable ($1,050 F), and the sales mix variance came out to be unfavorable ($4,950 U). These variances indicate that while there was a favorable increase in sales volume by 200 units, it was obtained by an unfavorable shift in the sales mix, that is, a shift from product D, with a high margin, to product C, with a low margin.

The sales volume variance of $3,900 U is the algebraic sum of the following two variances.

Sales quantity variance	$1,050 F
Sales mix variance	4,950 U
	$3,900 U

In conclusion, the product emphasis on high margin sales is often a key to success for multiproduct firms. Increasing sales volume is one side of the story; selling the more profitable products is another.

Managerial Planning and Decision Making. In view of the fact that Shim and Siegel, Inc., experienced an unfavorable sales volume variance of $3,900 due to an unfavorable (less profitable) mix in sales volume, the company is advised to put more emphasis on increasing the sale of product D.

In doing that the company might wish to:

1. increase the advertising budget for succeeding periods to boost product D sales;
2. set up a bonus plan in such a way that the commission is based on quantities sold rather than higher rates for higher margin items such as product D, or revise the bonus plan to consider the sale of product D;
3. offer more lenient credit terms for product D to encourage its sale;
4. reduce the price of product D enough to maintain the present profitable mix while increasing the sale of the product. This strategy must take into account the price elasticity of demand for product D.

Sales Mix Analysis. Many product lines include a lower-margin, price leader model and a high-margin deluxe model. For example, the automobile industry includes in its product line low-margin, energy-efficient small cars and higher-margin deluxe models. In an attempt to increase overall profitability, management would wish to emphasize the higher-margin expensive items, but salesmen might find it easier to sell lower-margin cheaper models. Thus, a salesman might meet his unit sales quota with each item at its budgeted price, but because of mix shifts he could be far short of contributing his share of budgeted profit.

Management should realize that greater proportions of more profitable products mean higher profits, and higher proportions of lower margin sales reduce overall profit despite the increase in overall sales volume. In other words, an unfavorable mix may easily offset a favorable increase in volume and vice versa.

Performance Reports. Profit variance analysis aids in fixing responsibility by separating the causes of the change in profit into price, volume, and mix factors. With responsibility resting in different places, the segregation of the total profit variance is essential. The performance reports based on the analysis of profit variances must be prepared for each responsibility center, indicating the following:

1. Is it controllable?
2. Is it favorable or unfavorable?
3. If it is unfavorable, is it significant enough for further investigation?
4. Who is responsible for what portion of the total profit variance?
5. What are the causes for an unfavorable variance?
6. What is the remedial action to take?

The performance report must address these types of questions. The report is useful in focusing attention on situations in need of management action and in increasing the precision of planning and control of sales and costs. The report should be produced as part of the overall standard costing and responsibility accounting system.

RESPONSIBILITY ACCOUNTING FOR INVESTMENT CENTERS

The ability to measure performance is essential in developing management incentives and controlling the operation toward the achievement of organizational goals. A typical decentralized subunit is an investment center that is responsible for an organization's invested capital (operating assets) and the related operating income. There are two widely used measurements of performance for the investment center: the rate of return on investment (ROI) and residual income (RI).

Rate of Return on Investment (ROI)

ROI relates net income to invested capital. Specifically,

$$\text{ROI} = \frac{\text{Operating income}}{\text{Operating assets}}$$

ROI can be expressed as a product of the following two important factors:

$$\text{ROI} = \text{Margin} \times \text{Capital turnover}$$

$$= \frac{\text{Operating income}}{\text{Sales}} \times \frac{\text{Sales}}{\text{Operating assets}}$$

$$= \frac{\text{Operating income}}{\text{Operating assets}}$$

Margin is a measure of profitability or operating efficiency, whereas turnover measures how well a division manages its assets.

EXAMPLE 4.11

Consider the following financial data for a division:

Operating assets	$100,000
Operating income	$ 18,000
Sales	$200,000

$$\text{ROI} = \frac{\text{Operating income}}{\text{Operating assets}} = \frac{\$18,000}{\$100,000} = 18\%$$

Alternatively,

$$\text{Margin} = \frac{\text{Operating income}}{\text{Sales}} = \frac{\$18,000}{\$200,000} = 9\%$$

$$\text{Turnover} = \frac{\text{Sales}}{\text{Operating assets}} = \frac{\$200,000}{\$100,000} = 2 \text{ times}$$

Therefore,

$$\text{ROI} = \text{margin} \times \text{turnover} = 9\% \times 2 \text{ times} = 18\%$$

The breakdown of ROI into margin and turnover (often called the *Du Pont* formula) has several advantages over the original formula in profit planning. They are:

- The importance of turnover as a key to overall return on investment is emphasized in the breakdown. In fact, turnover is just as important as profit margin.
- The importance of sales is explicitly recognized, which is not reflected in the regular formula.
- The breakdown stresses the possibility of trading one component for the other in an attempt to improve the overall performance of a division.

EXAMPLE 4.12

The breakdown of ROI into its two components shows that a number of combinations of margin and turnover can yield the same rate on return, as shown below.

Margin (%)	×	Turnover	=	ROI (%)
(1) 9	×	2 times	=	18
(2) 8	×	2.25	=	18
(3) 6	×	3	=	18
(4) 4	×	4.5	=	18
(5) 3	×	6	=	18
(6) 2	×	9	=	18

The turnover-margin relationship and its resulting ROI are depicted in Figure 4–7 which indicates that the turnover and margin factors complement each other. In other words, a weak margin can be complemented by a strong turnover, and vice versa. It also shows how important turnover is as a key to profit. In fact, these two factors are equally important in overall profit performance.

ROI and Profit Planning

The breakdown of ROI into turnover and margin gives management insight into planning for profit improvement. Generally speaking, management can:

1. improve margin
2. improve turnover
3. improve both

Alternative 1 demonstrates a popular way of improving performance. Margins may be increased by reducing expenses, raising selling prices, or increasing sales faster than expenses. Alternative 2 may be achieved by increasing sales while holding the investment in assets relatively constant, or by reducing assets while holding sales constant. Alternative 3 may be achieved by any combinations of alternatives 1 and 2.

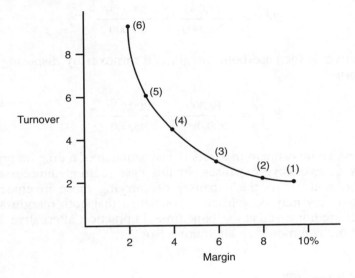

Figure 4–7. Turnover-margin relationship

EXAMPLE 4.13

Assume that management sets a 20% ROI as a profit target. It is currently making an 18% return on its investment.

$$\text{ROI} = \frac{\text{Operating income}}{\text{Sales}} \times \frac{\text{Sales}}{\text{Operating assets}}$$

Present:

$$18\% = \frac{18{,}000}{200{,}000} \times \frac{200{,}000}{100{,}000}$$

Alternative 1: Increase margin by reducing expenses.

$$20\% = \frac{20,000}{200,000} \times \frac{200,000}{100,000}$$

Alternative 2: Increase turnover by reducing investment in assets.

$$20\% = \frac{18,000}{200,000} \times \frac{200,000}{90,000}$$

Alternative 3: Increase both margin and turnover by disposing of inventories:

$$20\% = \frac{19,000}{200,000} \times \frac{200,000}{95,000}$$

Excessive investment in assets is just as much of a drag on profitability as excessive expenses. In this case, cutting unnecessary inventories also cuts the expenses of carrying those inventories (although they may be sold at discount), so that both margin and turnover are improved at the same time. In practice, alternative 3 is much more common than alternative 1 or 2.

Residual Income (RI)

Another approach to measuring performance in an investment center is residual income (RI)—the operating income that an investment center is able to earn above some minimum rate of return on its operating assets. RI, unlike ROI, is an absolute amount of income rather than a specific rate of return. When RI is used to evaluate divisional performance, the objective is to maximize the total amount of residual income, not to maximize the overall ROI figure.

RI = Operating income – (Minimum required rate of return × Operating assets)

EXAMPLE 4.14

In Example 4.11, assume the minimum required rate of return is 13%. Then the residual income of the division is:

$$\$18,000 – (13\% \times \$100,000) = \$18,000 – \$13,000 = \$5,000$$

RI is a better measure of performance than ROI because it encourages investment in projects that would be rejected under

ROI, as explained in the next section. A major disadvantage of RI, however, is that it can't be used to compare divisions of different sizes. RI tends to favor the larger divisions owing to the larger amounts of dollars involved.

Residual Income and Economic Value Added

Residual income is better known as *economic value added* (EVA*)*. Many firms are addressing the issue of aligning division managers' incentives with those of the firm by using EVA as a measure of performance. EVA encourages managers to focus on increasing the value of the company to shareholders because EVA is the value created by a company in excess of the cost of capital for the investment base. Improving EVA can be achieved in three ways:

- Invest capital in high-performing projects.
- Use less capital.
- Increase profit without using more capital.

Investment Decisions Under ROI and RI

The decision whether to use ROI or RI as a measure of divisional performance affects managers' investment decisions. Under the ROI method, division managers tend to accept only investments that offer returns equal to or above the division's ROI; otherwise, the division's overall ROI would decrease. Under the RI method, on the other hand, division managers would accept an investment as long as it earns a rate in excess of the minimum required rate of return. The addition of such an investment will increase the division's overall RI.

EXAMPLE 4.15

Consider the same data given in Examples 4.11 and 4.14:

Operating assets	$100,000
Operating income	$ 18,000
Minimum required rate of return	13%
ROI = 18% and RI = $5,000	

Assume that the division is presented with a project that would yield 15% on a $10,000 investment. The division manager would not accept this project under the ROI approach since the division is already earning 18%. Acquiring this project would bring down the present ROI to 17.73%, as shown here:

	Present	New Project	Overall
Operating assets (a)	$100,000	$10,000	$110,000
Operating income (b)	18,000	1,500*	19,500
ROI (b/a)	18%	15%	17.73%

* $10,000 × 15% = $1,500

Under the RI approach, the manager would accept the new project because it provides a higher rate than the minimum required rate of return (15% vs. 13%). Accepting the new project would increase the overall residual income to $5,200, as shown below:

	Present	New Project	Overall
Operating assets (a)	$100,000	$10,000	$110,000
Operating income (b)	18,000	1,500	19,500
Minimum required income at 13% (c)	13,000	1,300*	14,300
RI [(b) – (c)]	$ 5,000	$ 200	$ 5,200

* $10,000 × 13% = $1,300

BALANCED SCORECARD

A problem with just assessing performance with financial measures like profit, ROI, and Economic Value Added (EVA) is only that the financial measures are "backward looking." In other words, today's financial measures only tell you about the accomplishments and failures of the past. An approach to performance measurement that also focuses on what managers are doing today to create future shareholder value is the Balanced Scorecard.

Essentially, a balanced scorecard is a set of performance measures constructed for four dimensions of performance. As indicated in Table 4.1 (on page 237), the dimensions are financial, customer, internal processes, and learning and growth. Having financial measures is critical even if they are backward-looking. After all, they have a great effect on the evaluation of the company by shareholders and creditors. Customer measures examine the company's success in meeting customer expectations. Internal process measures examine the company's success in improving critical business processes. Learning and growth measures examine the company's success in improving its ability to adapt, innovate, and grow. The customer, internal processes, and learning and growth measures are generally thought to be predictive of *future* success (i.e., they are not backward-looking).

How Is Balance Achieved in a Balanced Scorecard?

A variety of potential measures for each dimension of a balanced scorecard are indicated in Table 4.1. After reviewing these measures, note how "balance" is achieved:

- Performance is assessed across a *balanced set of dimensions* (financial, customer, internal processes, and innovation).
- *Quantitative* measures (e.g., number of defects) are balanced with *qualitative* measures (e.g., ratings of customer satisfaction).
- There is a balance of *backward-looking* measures (e.g., financial measures like growth in sales) and *forward-looking* measures (e.g., number of new patents as an innovation measure).

Table 4.1
BALANCED SCORECARD

		Measures
Financial	Is the company achieving its financial goals?	Operating income Return on assets Sales growth Cash flow from operations Reduction of administrative expense
Customer	Is the company meeting customer expectations?	Customer satisfaction Customer retention New customer acquisition Market share On-time delivery Time to fill orders
Internal Processes	Is the company improving critical internal processes?	Defect rate Lead time Number of suppliers Material turnover Percent of practical capacity
Learning and Growth	Is the company improving its ability to innovate?	Amount spent on employee training Employee satisfaction Employee retention Number of new products New product sales as a percent of total sales Number of patents

Note: There are numerous Web resources that you can log onto to learn more about the balanced scorecard and performance evaluations. For example, managers frequently look to industry "best practices" or examples of successful implementations at other firms when developing measurement programs. The following Websites provide valuable resources for evaluating performance and business decision making across a wide range of industries: Balanced Scorecard Institute (*www.balancedscorecard.org*), American Productivity and Quality Center (*www.apqc.org*), Management Help (*www.managementhelp.org*), and Performance Measurement Association (*www.performanceportal.org*).

TRANSFER PRICING

Goods and services are often exchanged between various divisions
of a decentralized organization. A major goal of transfer pricing is to enable divisions that exchange goods or services to act
as independent businesses. The question then is: What monetary
values should be assigned to these exchanges or transfers? market
price? some kind of cost? some version of either? Unfortunately,
there is no single transfer price that will please everybody—that
is, top management, the selling division, and the buying division—
involved in the transfer.

The choice of a transfer pricing policy is normally made by top
management. The decision will typically include consideration of
the following:

- *Goal congruence.* Will the transfer price promote the goals of
  the company as a whole? Will it harmonize the divisional goals
  with organizational goals?
- *Performance evaluation.* Will the selling division receive
  enough credit for its transfer of goods and services to the buying division? Will the transfer price hurt the performance of
  the selling division?
- *Autonomy.* Will the transfer price preserve autonomy, the freedom of the selling and buying division managers to operate
  their divisions as decentralized entities?
- *Other factors,* such as minimization of tariffs and income taxes
  and observance of legal restrictions, are also important.

Transfer prices can be based on:

- market price
- cost-based price—variable or full cost
- negotiated price
- general formula, which is usually the sum of variable costs
  per unit and opportunity cost for the company as a whole (lost
  revenue per unit on outside sales)

Market Price

Market price is the best transfer price in the sense that it will maximize the profits of the company as a whole, if it meets the following
two conditions:

1. There exists a competitive market price.
2. Divisions are independent of each other.

If either of these conditions is violated, market price will not lead to an optimal economic decision for the company.

Cost-Based Price—Variable or Full Cost

Cost-based transfer price, another alternative transfer pricing scheme, is easy to understand and convenient to use. But there are some disadvantages, including:

- Inefficiencies of selling divisions are passed on to the buying divisions with little incentive to control costs. The use of standard costs is recommended to prevent this possibility.
- The cost-based method treats the divisions as cost centers rather than profit or investment centers. Therefore, measures such as ROI and RI cannot be used for evaluation purposes.

The variable-cost-based transfer price has an advantage over the full-cost method because in the short run it may tend to promote the best utilization of the overall company's resources. The reason for this is that, in the short run, fixed costs do not change. Any additional use of facilities without incurrence of additional fixed costs will increase the company's overall profits.

Negotiated Price

A negotiated price is generally used when there is no clear outside market. A negotiated price is agreed upon by the buying and selling divisions and reflects unusual or mitigating circumstance. This method is widely used when no intermediate market price exists for the product transferred and the selling division is assured of a normal profit. (Cost-based price can do the same thing.)

The following example illustrates alternative transfer prices that management might consider.

EXAMPLE 4.16

Company X just purchased a small company that specializes in the manufacture of part No. 123. Company X, a decentralized organization, will treat the newly acquired company as an autonomous unit called Division B with full profit responsibility. Division B's fixed costs total $30,000 per month, and variable costs per unit are $18. Division B's operating capacity is 5,000 units. The selling price per unit is $30. Division A of Company X is currently purchasing 2,500 units of part No. 123 per month from an outside supplier at $29 per unit, which represents the normal $30 price less a quantity discount. Top management of the company wishes to decide what transfer price should be used.

Top management may consider the following alternative prices:

1. $30 market price
2. $29, the price that Division A is currently paying to the outside supplier
3. $23.50 negotiated price, which is $18 variable cost plus half the benefits of an internal transfer [($29 – $18) × ½]
4. $24 full cost, which is $18 variable cost plus $6 ($30,000/ 5,000 units) fixed cost per unit
5. $18 variable cost

The first alternative, $30, would not be an appropriate transfer price. Division B cannot charge a price more than the price Division A is paying now ($29).

Second, $29 would be an appropriate transfer price if top management wishes to treat the divisions as autonomous investment centers. This price would cause all of the benefits of internal transfers to accrue to the selling division, with the buying division's position remaining unchanged.

Third, $23.50 would be an appropriate transfer price if top management wishes to treat the divisions as investment centers that share the benefits of an internal transfer equally between them, as follows:

Variable costs of Division B	$18.00
½ of the difference between the variable costs of Division B and the price Division A is paying ($29 – $18) × ½	5.50
Transfer price	$23.50

Note that $23.50 is just one example of a negotiated transfer price. The exact price depends on how the divisions divide the benefits and what bargaining power each division has.

Fourth, $24 [$24 = $18 + ($30,000/5,000 units)] would be an appropriate transfer price if top management treats the divisions like cost centers with no profit responsibility. All benefits from both divisions will accrue to the buying division. This will maximize the profits of the company as a whole but adversely affect the performance of the selling division. Another disadvantage of this cost-based approach is that any inefficiencies of the selling division are automatically passed on to the buying division.

The fifth and final alternative presented, $18, would be an appropriate transfer price for guiding top management in deciding whether transfers between the two divisions should take place. Since $18 is less than the outside purchase price of the buying division, and since the selling division has excess capacity, the transfer should take place because it will maximize the profits of the company as a whole. However, if $18 is used as a transfer price, then all of the benefits of the internal transfer would accrue to the buying division, hurting the performance of the division that is selling its product at cost.

General Formula

It is not easy to find a cure-all answer to the transfer pricing problem, since the three problems of goal congruence, performance evaluation, and autonomy must all be considered simultaneously. It is generally agreed, however, that some form of competitive market price is the best approach to the transfer pricing problem. The following formula would be helpful in this effort:

Transfer price = Variable costs per unit
             + Opportunity costs per unit for the company as a whole

Opportunity costs are defined here as net revenue foregone by the company as a whole if the goods and services are transferred internally. The reasoning behind this formula is that the selling division should be allowed to recover its variable costs plus opportunity cost (i.e., revenue that it could have made by selling to an outsider) of the transfer. The selling department should not have to suffer lost income by selling within the company.

EXAMPLE 4.17

Company X has more than 50 divisions, including A, B, and K. Division A, the buying division, wants to buy a component for its final product and has an option to buy from Division B or from an outside supplier at the market price of $200. If Division A buys from the outside supplier, it will in turn buy selected raw materials from Division K for $40. This will increase Division A's contribution to overall company profits by $30 ($40 revenue minus $10 variable costs). Division B, on the other hand, can sell its component to Division A or to an outside buyer at the same price. Division B, working at full capacity, incurs variable costs of $150. Will the use of $200 as a transfer price lead to optimal decisions for the company as a whole? Figure 4–8 depicts the situation.

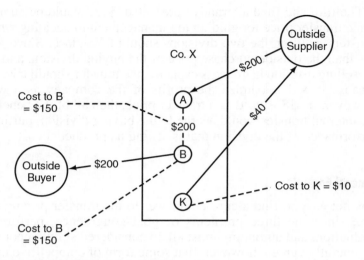

Figure 4–8. Transfer pricing situation

The optimal decision from the viewpoint of Company X as a whole can be looked at in terms of its net cash outflow, as follows:

	Division A's Action	
	Buy from B	*Buy from Outsider*
Outflow to the		
company as a whole	$(150)	$(200)
Cash inflows	——	to B: $50 ($200 – $150)
		to K: $30 ($40 – $10)
Net cash outflow to the		
company as a whole	($150)	$(120)

To maximize the profits of Company X, Division A should buy from an outside supplier. The transfer price that would force Division A to buy outside should be the sum of variable costs and opportunity costs, that is,

$$\$150 + \$50 + \$30 = \$230 \text{ per unit}$$

In other words, if Division B charges $230, Division A would definitely buy from the outside source for $200.

Part IV: Using Cost Data for Decision Making

SHORT-TERM AND NONROUTINE DECISIONS

When performing the manufacturing and selling functions, management is constantly faced with the problem of choosing among alternative courses of action. Typical questions to be answered include: What to make? How to make it? Where to sell the product? What price should be charged? In the short run, management is typically faced with the following nonroutine types of decisions:

1. Pricing a special order
2. Pricing standard products
3. Outsourcing: Make or buy
4. Sell or process further
5. Add or drop a certain product line
6. Utilization of scarce resources

Relevant Costs Defined

In each of the above situations, the ultimate management decision rests on cost-data analysis. Cost data are important in many decisions, since they are the basis for profit calculations. Cost data are classified by function, behavior patterns, and other criteria, as discussed previously. However, not all costs are of equal importance in decision-making, and managers must identify the costs that are important to a decision. Such costs are called *relevant costs*. Relevant costs are the expected future costs (and also revenues) and will differ depending on the decision alternative. Therefore, the sunk costs (past or historical costs) are not considered relevant in the decision at hand. The incremental (or differential) are relevant costs.

Under the concept of relevant costs, which may be appropriately titled the *incremental, differential,* or *relevant-cost approach,* the decision involves the following steps:

1. Gather all costs associated with each alternative.
2. Drop the sunk costs.
3. Drop those costs that do not differ between alternatives.
4. Select the best alternative based on the remaining cost data.

EXAMPLE 4.18

To illustrate the irrelevance of sunk costs and the relevance of incremental costs, let us consider a replacement decision. A company owns a milling machine that was purchased three years ago for $25,000. Its present book value is $17,500. The company is contemplating replacing this machine with a new one that will cost $50,000 and have a five-year useful life. The new machine will generate the same amount of revenue as the old one but will substantially cut down on variable operating costs. Annual sales and operating costs of the present machine and the proposed replacement are based on normal sales volume of 20,000 units and are estimated as follows:

	Present Machine	New Machine
Sales	$60,000	$60,000
Variable costs	35,000	20,000
Fixed costs:		
Depreciation (straight-line)	2,500	10,000
Insurance, taxes, etc.	4,000	4,000
Net income	$18,500	$26,000

At first glance, it appears that the new machine provides an increase in net income of $7,500 per year. The book value of the present machine, however, is a sunk cost and is irrelevant in this decision. Furthermore, sales and fixed costs such as insurance and taxes also are irrelevant, since they do not differ between the two alternatives being considered. Eliminating all the irrelevant costs leaves us with only the incremental costs, as follows:

Savings in variable costs	$15,000
Less: Increase in fixed costs	10,000*
Net annual cash savings arising from the new machine	$ 5,000

* exclusive of $2,500 sunk cost

Pricing a Special Order

A company often receives a short-term, special order for its products at lower prices than usual. In normal times, the company may refuse such an order since it will not yield a satisfactory profit. If times are bad, however, such an order should be accepted if the incremental revenue obtained exceeds the incremental costs involved. The company is better off receiving some revenue, above its incremental costs, than receiving nothing at all.

A price that is lower than the regular price is called a *contribution price*. This approach to pricing is often called the contribution approach to pricing or the *variable pricing model*. This approach is most appropriate under the following conditions:

1. When operating in a distress situation
2. When there is idle capacity
3. When faced with sharp competition or in a competitive bidding situation

EXAMPLE 4.19

Assume that a company with 100,000-unit capacity is currently producing and selling only 90,000 units of product each year at a regular price of $2.00. If the variable cost per unit is $1.00 and the annual fixed cost is $45,000, the income statement looks as follows:

Sales (90,000 units)	$180,000	$2.00
Less: Variable cost (90,000 units)	90,000	1.00
Contribution margin	$ 90,000	$1.00
Less: Fixed cost	45,000	0.50
Net income	$ 45,000	$0.50

The company has just received an order that calls for 10,000 units at a price of $1.20, for a total of $12,000. The acceptance of this order will not affect regular sales. The company's president is reluctant to accept the order, however, because the $1.20 price is below the $1.50 factory unit cost ($1.50 = $1.00 + $0.50). Should the company accept the order?

The answer is yes. The company can add to total profits by accepting this special order even though the price offered is below the unit factory cost. At a price of $1.20, the order will contribute $0.20 per unit (CM per unit = $1.20 − $1.00 = $0.20) toward fixed costs, and profit will increase by $2,000 (10,000 units × $0.20). Using the contribution approach to pricing, the variable cost of $1.00 will be a better guide than the full unit cost of $1.50. Note that the fixed costs do not change because of the presence of idle capacity.

The same result can be seen using the total project approach.

	Per Unit	Without Special Order (90,000 Units)	With Special Order (100,000 Units)	Difference
Sales	$2.00	$180,000	$192,000	$12,000
Less: Variable costs	1.00	90,000	100,000	10,000
CM	$1.00	$ 90,000	$ 92,000	$ 2,000
Less: Fixed cost	0.50	45,000	45,000	
Net income	$0.05	$ 45,000	$ 47,000	$ 2,000

Pricing Standard Products

Unlike pricing special orders, pricing standard products requires taking long-term considerations into account. Here, the key concept is to recognize that the established unit selling price must be sufficient in the long run to cover all manufacturing, selling, and administrative costs, both fixed and variable, as well as to provide for an adequate return and for future expansion. There are two primary approaches to pricing standard products that are sold on the regular market: the full-cost approach and the contribution approach. Both approaches use some kind of cost-plus pricing formula.

1. The *full (absorption) cost approach* defines the cost base as the full unit manufacturing cost at some set volume. Selling and administrative costs are provided for through the markup that is added to the cost base.
2. The *contribution approach* defines the cost base as the unit variable cost. Fixed costs are provided for through the markup that is added to this base.

EXAMPLE 4.20

The XYZ Company has accumulated the following cost data on its regular product:

	Per Unit	Total
Direct materials	$6	
Direct labor	4	
Variable overhead	4	
Fixed overhead (based on 20,000 units)	6	$120,000
Variable selling and admin. expenses	1	
Fixed selling and admin. expenses (based on 20,000 units)	2	40,000

Assume that in order to obtain its desired selling price, the firm has a general policy of adding a markup equal to 50% of the full unit cost or 100% of the unit variable cost.

Under the full-cost approach, the desired unit selling price is:

Direct materials	$ 6
Direct labor	4
Factory overhead	10 ($4 + $6)
Full unit cost	$20
Markup to cover selling and admin.	
expenses, and desired profit — 50%	
of full unit cost	10
Desired selling price	$30

Under the contribution approach, the desired selling price is determined as follows:

Direct materials	$ 6
Direct labor	4
Variable costs (overhead, selling, admin.)	5
Unit variable cost	$15
Markup to cover fixed costs and	
desired profit — 100% of unit variable cost	15
Desired selling price	$30

Companies use their desired rate of return as the basis for determining the percentage markup.

EXAMPLE 4.21

Assume that the XYZ Company has determined that a $500,000 investment is necessary to manufacture and market 20,000 units of its product every year. It will cost $20 to manufacture each unit at a 20,000-unit level of activity, and total selling and administrative expenses are estimated to be $100,000. If the company desires a 20% return on investment, what will be the required markup using the full-cost approach?

Desired rate of return	
(20% × $500,000)	$100,000
Selling and admin. expenses	100,000
Total	$200,000 (a)
Full unit cost	
(20,000 units × $20)	$400,000 (b)
Required markup — (a)/(b)	50%

Outsourcing: The Make-or-Buy Decision

Often companies purchase the subassembly components used to make their products instead of making them in their in-house manufacturing facilities. Buying services, products, or components of products from outside vendors instead of producing them is called **outsourcing**. The decision whether to produce a subcomponent in-house or to buy it externally from an outside vendor is called a "make-or-buy (outsource)" decision. Examples include:

(1) Process payroll in-house or outsource it to a service bureau
(2) Develop a training program in-house or send employees outside for training
(3) Provide data processing and network services internally or buy them (benefits: access to technology and cost savings)

Other strong candidates for outsourcing include: managing fleets of vehicles, sales and marketing, and custodial services.

This decision involves both qualitative and quantitative factors. The qualitative factors include ensuring product quality and the necessity for long-run business relationships with the supplier.

The quantitative factors deal with cost. The quantitative effects of the make-or-buy decision are best seen through the relevant cost approach.

EXAMPLE 4.22

Assume that a firm has prepared the following cost estimates for the manufacture of a subassembly component based on an annual production of 8,000 units:

	Per Unit	Total
Direct materials	$ 5	$ 40,000
Direct labor	4	32,000
Variable factory overhead applied	4	32,000
Fixed factory overhead applied		
(150% of direct labor cost)	6	48,000
Total cost	$19	$152,000

The supplier has offered to provide the subassemblies at a price of $16 each. Two-thirds of fixed factory overhead, which represents executive salaries, rent, depreciation, and taxes, continue regardless of the decision. Should the company buy or make the product?

The key to the decision lies in the investigation of those relevant costs that change between the make-or-buy alternatives. Assuming that part of the firm's productive capacity will be idle if not used to produce the subassembly, the analysis takes the following form:

	Per Unit		Total of 8,000 Units	
	Make	Buy	Make	Buy
Purchase price		$16		$128,000
Direct materials	$ 5		$ 40,000	
Direct labor	4		32,000	
Variable overhead	4		32,000	
Fixed overhead that can be avoided by not making (⅓ of $6)	2	—	16,000	—
Total relevant costs	$15	$16	$120,000	$128,000
Difference in favor of making	$ 1		$ 8,000	

The make-or-buy decision must be investigated, including consideration of how best to utilize available facilities. The alternatives involved in going outside for the parts are:

1. Buying the parts and leaving facilities idle
2. Buying the parts and renting out idle facilities
3. Buying the parts and using idle facilities for other products

The Sell-or-Process-Further Decision

When two or more products are produced simultaneously from the same input by a joint process, these products are called joint products. The term *joint costs* is used to describe all the manufacturing costs incurred prior to the point where the joint products are identified as individual products. At this point, which is referred to as the *split-off point,* some of the joint products may be in final form and salable to the consumer, whereas others may require additional processing. In many cases, however, the company has two options: It can sell the goods at the split-off point or process them further in the hope of obtaining additional revenue. In connection with this type of decision, called the "sell-or-process-further" decision, joint costs are irrelevant, since the joint costs have already been incurred at the time of the decision, and are therefore sunk costs. The decision will rely exclusively on additional revenue compared to the additional costs incurred for further processing.

EXAMPLE 4.23

The Jin Company produces three products, A, B, and C, from a joint process. Joint production costs for the year were $120,000. Product A may be sold at the split-off point or processed further. The additional processing requires no special facilities, and all additional processing costs are variable. Sales values and costs needed to evaluate the company's production policy regarding Product A follow:

| | | Additional Cost & Sales Value after Further Processing | |
Unit Produced	Sales Value at Split-off	Sales	Costs
3,000	$60,000	$90,000	$25,000

Should Product A be sold at the split-off point or processed further?

Incremental sales revenue	$30,000
Incremental costs, additional processing	25,000
Incremental gain	$ 5,000

In sum, Product A should be processed as shown above. Keep in mind that the joint production cost of $120,000 is not included in the analysis, since it is a sunk cost and, therefore, irrelevant to the decision.

Adding or Dropping a Product Line

The decision whether to drop an old product line or add a new one must take into account both qualitative and quantitative factors. However, any final decision should be based primarily on the impact the decision will have on contribution margin or net income.

EXAMPLE 4.24

The ABC grocery store has three major product lines: produce, meats, and canned food. The store management is considering whether or not to drop the meat line because the income statement shows it is being sold at a loss. Note the income statement for these product lines:

	Produce	Meats	Canned Food	Total
Sales	$10,000	$15,000	$25,000	$50,000
Less: Variable costs	6,000	8,000	12,000	26,000
CM	$ 4,000	$ 7,000	$13,000	$24,000
Less: Fixed costs				
Direct	$ 2,000	$ 6,500	$ 4,000	$12,500
Allocated	1,000	1,500	2,500	5,000
Total	$ 3,000	$ 8,000	$ 6,500	$17,500
Net income	$ 1,000	$(1,000)	$ 6,500	$ 6,500

In this example, direct fixed costs are those costs that are identified directly with each of the product lines, whereas allocated fixed costs are the amount of common fixed costs allocated to the product lines using some base such as space occupied. The amount of common fixed costs typically continues regardless of the decision and thus cannot be saved by dropping the product line to which it is distributed.

The comparative approach showing the effects on the company as a whole with and without the meat line is shown below:

	Keep Meats	Drop Meats	Difference
Sales	$50,000	$35,000	$(15,000)
Less: Variable cost	26,000	18,000	(8,000)
CM	$24,000	$17,000	$ (7,000)
Less: Fixed cost			
Direct	$12,500	$ 6,000	$ (6,500)
Allocated	5,000	5,000	—
Total	$17,500	$11,000	$ (6,500)
Net Income	$ 6,500	$ 6,000	$ (500)

Alternatively, the incremental approach would show the following:

IF MEATS DROPPED

Sales revenue lost		$15,000
Gains:		
Variable cost avoided	$8,000	
Direct fixed costs avoided	6,000	14,500
Increase (decrease) in net income		$ (500)

From either of the two methods, we see that by dropping meats the store will lose an additional $500. Therefore, the meat product line should be kept. One of the great dangers in allocating common fixed costs is that such allocations can make a product line look less profitable than it really is. With such an allocation, the meat business showed a loss of $1,000; looked at in another way, the meat line in effect contributes $500 ($7,000 – $6,500) to the recovery of the store's common fixed costs.

Utilization of Scarce Resources

In general, the emphasis on products with higher contribution margin maximizes a firm's total net income, even though total sales may decrease. This is not true, however, where there are constraining factors and scarce resources. Typical constraining factors include machine-hours, labor-hours, or cubic feet of warehouse space. In the presence of these constraining factors, maximizing total profits depends on getting the highest contribution margin per unit of the factor (rather than the highest contribution margin per unit of product output).

EXAMPLE 4.25

Assume that a company produces two products, A and B, with the following contribution margins per unit.

	A		B
Sales	$8.00		$24.00
Variable costs	6.00		20.00
CM	$2.00		$ 4.00
Annual fixed costs		$42,000	

As is indicated by CM per unit, B is more profitable than A since it contributes more to the company's total profits than A ($4.00 vs. $2.00). But let us assume that the firm has a limited capacity of 10,000 labor-hours. Further, assume that A requires two labor-hours to produce and B requires five labor-hours. One way to express this limited capacity is to determine the contribution margin per labor-hour.

	A	B
CM/unit	$2.00	$4.00
Labor hours required per unit	2	5
CM per labor hour	$1.00	$0.08

Since A returns the higher CM per labor hour, it should be produced and B should be dropped. However, there is another way to look at the problem, by calculating total CM for each product.

	A	*B*
Maximum possible production	5,000 units*	2,000 units†
CM per unit	$ 2.00	$ 4.00
Total CM	$10,000	$8,000

* (10,000 hours/2 hours)

† (10,000 hours/5 hours)

Again, product A should be produced since it contributes more than product B ($10,000 vs. $8,000).

CAPITAL BUDGETING DECISIONS

Capital budgeting is the process of deciding whether or not to commit resources to a project whose benefits will be spread over several time periods. There are typically the following two types of investment:

1. Selection decisions in terms of obtaining new facilities or expanding existing facilities. Examples include:
   a. Investments in long-term assets such as property, plant, and equipment
   b. Resource commitments in the form of new product development, market research, refunding of long-term debt, introduction of a computer, etc.
2. Replacement decisions involving existing facilities. Examples include replacing a manual bookkeeping system with a computerized system and replacing an inefficient lathe with one that is digitally controlled.

Capital budgeting decisions are a key factor in the long-term profitability of a firm. To make wise investment decisions, managers need tools at their disposal that will guide them in comparing the benefits and costs of various investment alternatives.

Capital Budgeting Techniques

Many techniques for evaluating investment proposals are widely available. They include:

1. Payback period
2. Accounting rate of return (ARR) (also called simple rate of return)

3. Net present value (NPV)
4. Internal rate of return (IRR) (also called time-adjusted rate of return)
5. Profitability index (also called the excess-present-value index)

The NPV method and the IRR method are called *discounted cash flow (DCF) methods,* since they both recognize the time value of money and thus discount future cash flows. Each of the methods presented above is discussed below.

Payback Period

Payback period measures the length of time required to recover the amount of initial investment. The payback period is determined by dividing the amount of initial investment by the cash inflow through increased revenues or cost savings.

EXAMPLE 4.26

Assume:

Cost of investment	$18,000
Annual cash savings	3,000

Then, the payback period is:

$$\frac{\$18,000}{\$3,000} = 6 \text{ years}$$

When cash inflows are not even, the payback period is determined by trial and error. When two or more projects are considered, the rule for making a selection decision is as follows:

Decision rule: Choose the project with the shorter payback period. The rationale behind this is, the shorter the payback period, the less risky the project and the greater the liquidity.

EXAMPLE 4.27

Consider two projects whose cash inflows are not even. (Assume each project costs $1,000.)

Year	A	B
1	$100	$500
2	200	400
3	300	300
4	400	100
5	500	——
6	600	——

Based on trial and error, the payback period of project A is four years ($100 + $200 + $300 + $400 = $1,000 in four years). The payback period of project B is:

$$2 \text{ years} + \frac{\$100}{\$300} = 2\frac{1}{3} \text{ years}$$

Therefore, according to this method, choose project B over project A.

Advantages of the payback-period method:

1. It is simple to compute and easy to understand.
2. It handles investment risk effectively.

Shortcomings of the payback-period method:

1. It does not recognize the time value of money.
2. It ignores the impact of cash inflows after the payback period—even though this cash flow determines the profitability of an investment.

Accounting (Simple) Rate of Return (ARR)

Accounting rate of return (ARR) measures profitability from the conventional accounting standpoint by relating the required investment to the future annual net income. Sometimes the former is the average investment.

Decision rule: Under the ARR method, choose the project with the higher rate of return.

EXAMPLE 4.28

Consider the investment:

Initial investment	$6,500
Estimated life	20 years
Cash inflows per year	$1,000
Depreciation by straight line	$325

then,

$$ARR = \frac{\$1,000 - \$325}{\$6,500} = 10.4\%$$

Using the average investment, which is usually assumed to be one-half of the original investment, the resulting rate of return will be doubled:

$$ARR = \frac{\$1,000 - \$325}{\frac{1}{2}\,(\$6,500)} = \frac{\$675}{\$3,250} = 20.8\%$$

The justification for using the average investment is that each year the investment amount is decreased by $325 through depreciation, and therefore the average is computed as one-half of the original cost.

Advantages of the AAR method:

1. It is easily understandable and simple to compute, and recognizes the profitability factor.

   Shortcomings of the AAR method:

1. It fails to recognize the time value of money.
2. It uses accounting data instead of cash flow data.
3. It does not recognize *total* project profitability. (The AAR would be the same for a project life of two years or 200 years.)

Net Present Value (NPV)

Net present value (NPV) is the excess of the present value (PV) of cash inflows generated by the project over the amount of the initial investment (I). Simply, NPV = PV − 1. The present value of future cash flows is computed using the cost of capital (or minimum required rate of return) as the discount rate. Decision rule: If NPV is positive, accept the project. Otherwise, reject.

EXAMPLE 4.29

Initial investment	$12,950
Estimated life	10 years
Annual cash inflows	$ 3,000
Cost of capital (minimum required rate of return)	12%
Present value of cash inflows (PV):	

$3,000 × PV of annuity of $1, 10 years and 12%
[= $3,000 (5.65)] $16,950
Initial investment (I)   12,950
Net present value (NPV = PV – I) $ 4,000

Since the investment's NPV is positive, the investment should be accepted.

Advantages: The NPV method obviously recognizes the time value of money and is easy to compute whether the cash flows form an annuity or vary from period to period. Furthermore, NPV recognizes total project profitability.

Disadvantage: It requires detailed long-term forecasts of incremental cash flow data.

Internal Rate of Return (or Time-Adjusted Rate of Return)

Internal rate of return (IRR) is defined as the rate of interest that equates I with the PV of future cash inflows. In other words, at IRR, I = PV, or NPV = 0. The internal rate is the true rate on the project.

Decision rule: Accept if IRR exceeds the cost of capital; otherwise, reject.

EXAMPLE 4.30

Assume the same data given in Example 4.29. We will set up the following equality (I = PV).

$$\$12,950 = \$3,000 \times PV \text{ Factor}$$

$$PV \text{ Factor } = \frac{\$12,950}{\$3,000} = 4.317$$

which stands somewhere between 18% and 20% in the 10-year line of the table. Using interpolation gives the exact rate:

	PV Factor	
18%	4.494	4.494
IRR		4.317
20%	4.192	
Difference	0.302	0.177

Therefore,

$$\text{IRR} = 18\% + \frac{0.177}{0.302} \ (20\% - 18\%) = 18\% + 0.586(2\%)$$

$$= 18\% + 1.17\% = 19.17\%$$

Since the investment's IRR is greater than the cost of capital (12%), the investment should be accepted.

Advantages: It does consider the time value of money and is therefore more exact and realistic than ARR.

Shortcomings:

1. It is difficult to compute, especially when the cash inflows are not even.
2. It fails to recognize the varying size of investment in competing projects and their respective dollar profitability.
3. It can give more than one IRR.

Can a Computer Help?

Spreadsheet programs can be used in making IRR calculations. For example, Excel has a function IRR *(values, guess)*. Excel considers negative numbers as cash outflows, such as the initial investment, and positive numbers as cash inflows. Many financial calculators have similar features. As in Example 4.29, suppose you want to calculate the IRR of a $12,950 investment (the value -12950 entered in year 0 that is followed by 10 monthly cash inflows of $3,000. Using a guess of 12% (the value of 0.12), which is in effect the cost of capital), your formula would be @IRR (values, 0.12) and Excel would return 19.15%, as shown below.

Year 0	1	2	3	4	5	6	7	8	9	10
$(12,950)	3,000	3,000	3,000	3,000	3,000	3,000	3,000	3,000	3,000	3,000

IRR = 19.15%
NPV = $4,000.67

Note: The Excel formula for NPV is NPV(discount rate, cash inflow values)+I, where I is given as a negative number.

Summary of Decision Rules Using Both NPV and IRR Methods

Net present value (NPV)

1. Calculate the NPV, using the cost of capital as the discount rate.

2. If the NPV is positive, accept the project; otherwise, reject the project.

Internal rate of return (IRR)

1. Using present-value tables, compute the IRR by trial-and-error interpolation. To obtain the exact IRR, use a financial calculator or Excel.
2. If this rate of return exceeds the cost of capital, accept the project; if not, reject the project.

Profitability Index (or Excess Present Value Index)

The profitability index is the ratio of the total PV of future cash inflows to the initial investment, that is, PV/I. This index is used as a means of *ranking* projects in descending order of attractiveness. If the profitability index is greater than 1, then accept.

EXAMPLE 4.31

Using the data in Example 4.29, the profitability index PV/I is $16,950/$12,950 = 1.31. Since this project generates $1.31 for each dollar invested (or its profitability index is greater than 1), you should accept the project.

Income-Tax Factors: Determining After-Tax Cash Flow

Income taxes make a difference in many capital budgeting decisions. In other words, the project which is attractive one a pre-tax basis may have to be rejected on an after-tax basis. Income taxes typically affect both the amount and the timing of cash flows. Since net income, not cash inflows, is subject to tax, after-tax cash inflows are not usually the same as after-tax net income.

Let us define: S = Sales
E = Cash operating expenses
d = Depreciation
t = Tax rate

Then, before-tax cash inflows = $S - E$ and net income = $S - E - d$. By definition,

After-tax cash inflow = Before-tax cash inflow – Taxes

After-tax cash inflow = $(S - E) - (S - E - d)(t)$

Rearranging gives the short-cut formula:

$$\text{After-tax cash inflow} = (S - E)(1 - t) + (d)(t)$$

$$[\text{or after-tax cash inflow} = (S - E - d)(1 - t) + d]$$

As can be seen, the deductibility of depreciation from sales in arriving at net income subject to taxes reduces income tax payments and thus serves as a tax shield.

$$\text{Tax shield} = \text{Tax savings of depreciation} = (d)(t).$$

EXAMPLE 4.32

Assume: $S = \$12,000$

$$E = \$10,000$$

$$d = \$500/\text{year by straight-line}$$

$$t = 40\%$$

Then,

$$\text{After-tax cash inflow} = (\$12,000 - \$10,000)(1 - 0.4)$$

$$+ (\$500)(0.4) = \$1,200 + \$200 = \$1,400$$

Note that

$$\text{Tax shield} = \text{Tax savings on depreciation}$$

$$= (d)(t) = (\$500)(0.4) = \$200.$$

After-tax cash outflow would be similarly computed by simply dropping S in the previous formula. Therefore,

$$\text{After-tax cash outflow} = (-E)(1 - t) + (d)(t)$$

EXAMPLE 4.33

Assume: $\qquad E = \$6,000$

$$d = \$800/\text{year by straight-line}$$

$$t = 40\%$$

Then,

After-tax cash outflow $= (-\$6,000)(1 - 0.4) + (\$800)(0.4)$

$\qquad\qquad\qquad\quad = -\$3,600 + \$320 = -\$3,280$

$\qquad\qquad\qquad\quad = \$3,280$

Because the tax shield is $(d)(t)$, the higher the depreciation deduction, the higher the tax savings on depreciation. Therefore, the Accelerated Cost Recovery System (ACRS) deduction method produces higher tax savings than the straight-line method during the early years. They will produce higher present values for the tax savings which greatly affect investment decisions.

EXAMPLE 4.34

XYZ Corporation has provided its revenues and cash operating costs (excluding depreciation) for the old and the new machine, as follows:

	Annual Revenue	Annual Cash Operating Costs	Net Profits before Depreciation and Taxes
Old machine	$150,000	$70,000	$ 80,000
New machine	$180,000	$60,000	$120,000

Assume that the annual depreciation of the old machine and the new machine will be $30,000 and $50,000, respectively.

To arrive at net profits after taxes, we first have to deduct depreciation expenses from the net profits before depreciation and taxes, as follows:

Net Profits after Taxes	Add Depreciation	After-Tax Cash Inflows
Old machine ($80,000 – 30,000)		
(1 – 0.46) = $27,000	$30,000	$57,000
New machine ($120,000 – $50,000)		
(1 – 0.46) = $37,800	$50,000	$87,800

Subtracting the after-tax cash inflows of the old machine from the cash inflows of the new machine results in the relevant, or incremental, cash inflows for each year.

Therefore, in this example, the relevant or incremental cash inflows for each year are $87,800 – $57,000 = $30,800.

Alternatively, the incremental cash inflows after taxes can be computed, using the following simple formula:

After-tax incremental cash inflows

= (increase in revenue)(1 – tax rate)

– (increase in cash charges)(1 – tax rate)

+ (increase in depreciation expenses)(tax rate)

EXAMPLE 4.35

Using the data in Example 4.34, after-tax incremental cash inflows for each year are:

Increase in revenue × (1 – tax rate):	
($180,000 – $150,000 (1 – 0.46)	$16,200
Increase in cash charges × (1 – tax rate):	
($60,000 – $70,000 (1 – 0.46) = – (– 5,400)	+5,400
+ Increase in depreciation expense ×	
tax rate: ($50,000 – $30,000)(0.46)	+9.200
	$30,800

HOW DOES MACRS AFFECT INVESTMENT DECISIONS?

Although the traditional depreciation methods still can be used for computing depreciation for book purposes, there is another way of computing depreciation deductions for tax purposes. It is called the *Modified Accelerated Cost Recovery System* (MACRS) rule. This rule is characterized as follows:

1. It abandons the concept of useful life and accelerates depreciation deductions by placing all depreciable assets into one of eight age property classes. It calculates deductions, based on an allowable percentage of the asset's original cost (see Tables 4.2 and 4.3).

   With a shorter asset life than useful life, the company is able to deduct depreciation more quickly and save more in income taxes in the earlier years, thereby making an investment more attractive. The rationale behind the system is that this way the government encourages the company to invest in facilities and increase its productive capacity and efficiency. [Remember that the higher d, the larger the tax shield (d)(t)].

2. Since the allowable percentages in Table 4.2 add up to 100%, there is no need to consider the salvage value of an asset in computing depreciation.

3. The company may elect the straight-line method. The straight-line convention must follow what is called the *half-year convention*. This means that the company can deduct only half of the regular straight-line depreciation amount in the first year.

4. If an asset is disposed of before the end of its class life, the half-year convention allows half the depreciation for that year (early disposal rule).

The reason for electing to use the MACRS optional straight-line method is that some firms may prefer to stretch out depreciation deductions using the straight-line method rather than to accelerate them. Those firms are the ones that are just starting out or have little or no income and wish to show more income on their income statements.

EXAMPLE 4.36

Assume that a machine falls under a three-year property class and costs $3,000 initially. The straight-line option under MACRS differs from the traditional straight-line method in that under this method the company would deduct only $500 depreciation in the first year and the fourth year ($3,000/3 years = $1,000; $1,000/2 = $500). The table below compares the straight line with half-year convention with the MACRS.

Year	Straight-Line (Half-Year) Depreciation	Cost		MACRS %	MACRS Deduction
1	$ 500	$3,000	×	33.3%	$ 999
2	1,000	3,000	×	44.5	1,335
3	1,000	3,000	×	14.8	444
4	500	3,000	×	7.4	222
	$3,000				$3,000

Table 4.2
MODIFIED ACCELERATED COST RECOVERY SYSTEM
CLASSIFICATION OF ASSETS

			Property Class			
Year	*3-Year*	*5-Year*	*7-Year*	*10-Year*	*15-Year*	*20-Year*
1	33.3%	20.0%	14.3%	10.0%	5.0%	3.8%
2	44.5	32.0	24.5	18.0	9.5	7.2
3	14.8a*	19.2	17.5	14.4	8.6	6.7
4	7.4	11.5a*	12.5	11.5	7.7	6.2
5		11.5	8.9a*	9.2	6.9	5.7
6		5.8	8.9	7.4	6.2	5.3
7			8.9	6.6a*	5.9a*	4.9
8			4.5	6.6	5.9	4.5a*
9				6.5	5.9	4.5
10				6.5	5.9	4.5
11				3.3	5.9	4.5
12					5.9	4.5
13					5.9	4.5
14					5.9	4.5
15					5.9	4.5
16					3.0	4.4
17						4.4
18						4.4
19						4.4
20						4.4
21						2.2
Total	100%	100%	100%	100%	100%	100%

*a Denotes the year of changeover to straight-line depreciation.

EXAMPLE 4.37

A machine costs $10,000. Annual cash inflows are expected to be $5,000. The machine will be depreciated using the MACRS rule and will fall under the 3-year property class. The cost of capital after taxes is 10%. The estimated life of the machine is 5 years. The salvage value of the machine at the end of the fifth year is expected to be $1,200. The tax rate is 30%. Should you buy the machine? The formula for computation of after-tax cash inflows $(S - E)(1 - t) + (d)(t)$ needs to be computed separately. The NPV analysis can be performed as follows:

		Present Value Factor @ 10%	Present Value

(S − E) (1 − t):

$5,000	$5,000 (1 − .3) = **$3,500**		
For 5 years	for 5 years	**$3.500** 3.791[a]	$13,268.50

(d)(t):

Year	Cost	MACRS %	d	(d)(t)		
1	$10,000 ×	33.3%	$3,330	**$999**	.909[b]	908.09
2	$10,000 ×	44.5	4,450	**1,335**	.826[b]	1,102.71
3	$10,000 ×	14.8	1,480	**444**	.751[b]	333.44
4	$10,000 ×	7.4	740	**222**	.683[b]	151.63

Salvage value:

$1,200 in	$1,200 (1 − .3) = **$840**[c] **$840**	.621[b]	521.64
year 5:	in year 5		
	Present value (PV)		$16,286.01

(a) T4 (10%, 4 years) = 3.170 (from Table 4.5).
(b) T3 values (year 1, 2, 3, 4, 5) obtained from Table 4.4.
(c) Any salvage value received under the MACRS rules is a taxable gain (the excess of the selling price over book value, $1,200 in this example), since the book value will be zero at the end of the life of the machine.

Since NPV = PV − I = $16,286.01 − $10,000 = $6,286.01 is positive, the machine should be bought.

Tax Effects of Disposal

In general, gains and losses on disposal of equipment are taxed in the same way as ordinary gains and losses. Immediate disposal of the old equipment results in a loss that is fully tax deductible from current income. The loss (the excess of the book value over the disposal value) must be computed to isolate its effect on current income tax, but the total cash inflow is the selling price *plus* the current income tax benefit.

Table 4.3
MACRS TABLES BY PROPERTY CLASS

MACRS Property Class and Depreciation Method	Useful Life (ADR Midpoint Life)[a]	Examples of Assets
3-year property 200% declining balance	4 years or less	Most small tools are included; the law specifically excludes autos and light trucks from this property class.
5-year property 200% declining balance	More than 4 years to less than 10 years	Autos and light trucks, computers, typewriters, copiers, duplicating equipment, heavy general-purpose trucks, and research and experimentation equipment are included.
7-year property 200% declining balance	10 years or more to less than 16 years	Office furniture and fixtures and most items of machinery and equipment used in production are included.
10-year property 200% declining balance	16 years or more to less than 20 years	Various machinery and equipment, such as that used in petroleum distilling and refining and in the milling of grain, are included.
15-year property 150% declining balance	20 years or more to less than 25 years	Sewage treatment plants, telephone, electrical distribution facilities, and land improvements are included.
20-year property 150% declining balance	25 years or more	Service stations and other real property with an ADR midpoint[a] life of less than 27.5 years are included.
27.5-year property Straight-line	Not applicable	All residential rental property is included.
31.5-year property Straight-line	Not applicable	All nonresidential real property is included.

[a] The term ADR midpoint life means the "useful life" of an asset in a business sense; the appropriate ADR midpoint lives for assets are designated in the tax regulations.

Table 4.4
PRESENT VALUE OF $1

Periods	4%	6%	8%	10%	12%	14%	20%
1	0.962	0.943	0.926	0.909	0.893	0.877	0.833
2	0.925	0.890	0.857	0.826	0.797	0.769	0.694
3	0.889	0.840	0.794	0.751	0.712	0.675	0.579
4	0.855	0.792	0.735	0.683	0.636	0.592	0.482
5	0.822	0.747	0.681	0.621	0.567	0.519	0.402
6	0.790	0.705	0.630	0.564	0.507	0.456	0.335
7	0.760	0.665	0.583	0.513	0.452	0.400	0.279
8	0.731	0.627	0.540	0.467	0.404	0.351	0.233
9	0.703	0.592	0.500	0.424	0.361	0.308	0.194
10	0.676	0.558	0.463	0.386	0.322	0.270	0.162

Table 4.5
PRESENT VALUE OF AN ANNUITY OF $1

Periods	4%	6%	8%	10%	12%	14%	20%
1	0.962	0.943	0.926	0.909	0.893	0.877	0.833
2	1.886	1.833	1.783	1.736	1.690	1.647	1.528
3	2.775	2.673	2.577	2.487	2.402	2.322	2.106
4	3.630	3.465	3.312	3.170	3.037	2.914	2.589
5	4.452	4.212	3.993	3.791	3.605	3.433	2.991
6	5.242	4.917	4.623	4.355	4.111	3.889	3.326
7	6.002	5.582	5.206	4.868	4.564	4.288	3.605
8	6.733	6.210	5.747	5.335	4.968	4.639	3.837
9	7.435	6.802	6.247	5.759	5.328	4.946	4.031
10	8.111	7.360	6.710	6.145	5.650	5.216	4.192

EXAMPLE 4.38

Assume that the equipment has a salvage value of $1,200, while its book (undepreciated) value is $2,000. *Two* cash inflows are connected with this sale. The tax rate is 30%.

(1) A $1,200 cash inflow in the form of the sale price, and
(2) A $240 cash inflow in the form of a reduction in income taxes, resulting from the tax shield provided by the loss sustained on the sale, and by the depreciation deduction, is computed as follows:

Book value	$2,000	
Selling price	1,200	
Loss	800	
Tax shield	× .3	$240

Thus, the total cash inflow from the disposal is $1,440 ($1,200 + $240).

Chapter 5
Financial Statement Analysis

The analysis of a company's financial statements is of interest to internal accountants, financial analysts, creditors, and investors. Financial statement analysis is an appraisal of a company's past financial performance and its potential for the future. It involves an analysis of the company's financial statements, including footnotes, contained in the annual report. Information also appears in Form 10-K, which is an annual filing by publicly traded companies with the Securities and Exchange Commission. The computation of various financial ratios is made to evaluate financial status and operating performance of the company for a given time period. The accountant is often involved in analyzing the financial statements of an existing company or a company targeted for a potential acquisition. Financial statement analysis aids the internal accountant in determining what areas to audit and in appraising the overall financial health of the business. After the internal accountant completes his financial statement analysis, he or she should consult with management to discuss their plans and prospects, identify problem areas, and offer possible solutions.

IMPORTANCE

The internal accountant analyzes the financial statements of the company for two very important reasons:

- To indicate areas requiring internal audit attention. The accountant looks at the percentage change in an account over the years or relative to some base year to identify inconsistencies. For example, if supplies' expense to sales was 2% of sales last year and shot up to 16% this year, the internal accountant would want to uncover the reasons. Supporting documentation for the charges would be requested and carefully reviewed.

- To indicate the financial health of the company, which is of interest to the internal accountant for the following reasons: (1) the accountant must ascertain if business failure may occur, and recommend appropriate corrective steps; (2) it provides vital information to be included in the management letter; (3) it aids the company in determining the appropriateness of mergers and acquisitions.

The company's financial health has a bearing upon its price-earnings ratio, bond rating, cost of financing, and availability of financing.

The financial statements of the company present the summarized data of its assets, liabilities, and equities in the balance sheet and its revenue and expenses in the income statement. If not analyzed, such data may lead one to draw incorrect conclusions about the company's financial condition. A number of measuring techniques may be employed to analyze the financial health of a business, including *horizontal, vertical,* and *ratio analyses.* An accountant uses the ratios to make two kinds of comparisons:

1. **Industry comparison.** A company's ratios are compared with those of similar companies or with industry norms to ascertain how the company is doing relative to its competitors. Industry average ratios can be found in a number of financial advisory services including Dun and Bradstreet, Standard and Poor's, Risk Management Association (RMA), and Value Line.
2. **Trend analysis.** A company's current year ratios are compared with its previous ratios to ascertain if the company's financial position is getting better or worse. An attempt is also made to uncover the reasons for the change.

    The optimum value for any given ratio usually varies across industry lines, through time, and within different companies in the same industry. In other words, a ratio deemed optimum for one company may be inadequate for another.

HORIZONTAL ANALYSIS

Horizontal analysis is employed to appraise the trend in the accounts over the years. A $5 million profit year is good after a $2 million profit year, but not after a $7 million profit year. Horizontal analysis is typically presented in comparative financial statements (see Examples 5.1 and 5.2). Companies usually report comparative financial data for five years in annual reports.

Because horizontal analysis concentrates on the trends of the various accounts, it is relatively easy to spot illogical trends that mandate additional attention. In the income statement shown in Example 5.2, the significant rise in sales returns and allowances coupled with the decrease in sales for the period 2014 to 2015 should raise a "red flag." The internal accountant might compare these results with those of competitors to see if the problem is industrywide or just within the firm.

Note that it is essential to present both the dollar amount of change and the percentage of change, since either one alone might be misleading. For instance, although the interest expense from 2013 to 2014 increased 100% (Example 5.2), it likely does not need further investigation because the dollar amount of increase is only $1,000. In a similar vein, a significant change in dollar amount might cause only a small percentage change and thus not be a reason for concern.

When an analysis covers numerous years, comparative financial statements may become cumbersome. To avoid this, the results of horizontal analysis may be presented by showing trends relative to a base year. In this case, a year typical of the company's operations is selected as the base. Each account of the base year is assigned an index of 100. The index for each respective account in later years is found by dividing the account's amount by the base-year amount and multiplying by 100. For example, if 2013 is the base year in the balance sheet of Example 5.1, Accounts Receivable would be assigned an index of 100. In 2014, the index would stand at 150 (15/10 × 100), and in 2015 it would be 200 (20/10 × 100). A condensed form of balance sheet using *trend analysis* appears in Example 5.3.

Vertical Analysis

In *vertical analysis,* the biggest item on a financial statement is used as a base value, and all other items on the financial statement are compared to it. In undertaking vertical analysis for the balance sheet, total assets are 100%. Each asset account is expressed as a percentage of total assets. Total liabilities and stockholders' equity is also assigned 100%. Each liability and equity account is then expressed as a percentage of total liabilities and stockholders' equity. In the income statement, net sales are assigned 100% and all other income statement items are compared to net sales. The resulting figures are then presented in a *common size statement.* The common size analysis of Ratio Company's income statement appears in Example 5.4.

EXAMPLE 5.1

The Ratio Company
Comparative Balance Sheet (In Thousands of Dollars)
December 31, 2015, 2014, and 2013

	2015	2014	2013	Increase or (Decrease)		Percentage of Increase or (Decrease)	
				2015–2014	2014–2013	2015–2014	2014–2013
ASSETS							
Current assets							
Cash	$ 30.0	$ 35	$ 35	$(5.0)	—	14.3	—
Accounts receivable	20.0	15	10	5.0	$ 5	33.3	50.0
Marketable securities	20.0	15	5	5.0	10	33.3	200.0
Inventory	50.0	45	50	5.0	(5)	11.1	(10.0)
Total current assets	$120.0	$110	$100	$10.0	$10	9.1	10.0
Plant assets	100.0	90	85	10.0	5	11.1	5.9
Total assets	$220.0	$200	$185	$20.0	$15	10.0	8.1
LIABILITIES							
Current liabilities	$ 55.4	$ 50	$ 52	$ 5.4	$(2)	10.8	(3.8)
Long-term liabilities	80.0	75	70	5.0	5	6.7	7.1
Total liabilities	$135.4	$125	$122	$10.4	$ 3	8.3	2.5
STOCKHOLDERS' EQUITY							
Common stock, $10 par value, 4,500 shares	$ 45	$ 45	$ 45	—	—	—	—
Retained earnings	39.6	30	18	$ 9.6	$12	32.0	66.7
Total stockholders' equity	$84.6	$ 75	$ 63	9.6	$12	12.8	19.0
Total liabilities and stockholders' equity	$220.0	$200	$185	$20.0	$15	10.0	8.1

EXAMPLE 5.2

The Ratio Company
Comparative Income Statement
(In Thousands of Dollars)
For the Years Ended December 31, 2015, 2014, and 2013

	2015	2014	2013	Increase or (Decrease)		Percentage of Increase or (Decrease)	
				2015–2014	2014–2013	2015–2014	2014–2013
Sales	$100	$110	$50	$(10.0)	$60	(9.1)	120.0
Sales returns and allowances	20	8	3	12.0	5	150	166.7
Net sales	$ 80	$102	$47	$(22.0)	$55	(21.6)	117.0
Cost of goods sold	50	60	25	(10.0)	35	(16.7)	140.0
Gross profit	$ 30	$ 42	$22	$(12.0)	$20	(28.6)	90.9
Operating expenses							
Selling expenses	$ 11.0	$ 13	$ 8	$ (2.0)	$ 5	(15.4)	62.5
General expenses	4.0	7	4	(3.0)	3	(42.9)	75.0
Total operating expenses	$ 15.0	$ 20	$12	$ (5.0)	$ 8	(25.0)	66.7
Income from operations	$ 15.0	$ 22	$10	$ (7.0)	$12	(31.8)	120.0
Nonoperating income	3.0	0	1	3.0	(1)	—	(100.0)
Income before interest & taxes	$ 18	$ 22	$11	$ (4.0)	$11	(18.2)	100.0
Interest expense	2.0	2	1	—	1	—	100.0
Income before taxes	$ 16.0	$ 20	$10	$ (4.0)	$10	(20.0)	100.0
Income taxes (40% rate)	6.4	8	4	(1.6)	4	(20.0)	100.0
Net income	$ 9.6	$ 12	$ 6	$ (2.4)	$ 6	(20.0)	100.0

EXAMPLE 5.3

The Ratio Company
Trend Analysis of the Balance Sheet
(Expressed as Percent)
Dec. 31, 2015, 2014, and 2013

	2015	2014	2013
ASSETS			
Current assets	120	110	100
Plant assets	117.6	105.9	100
Total assets	118.9	108.1	100
LIABILITIES AND STOCKHOLDERS' EQUITY			
Liabilities			
Current liabilities	106.5	96.2	100
Long-term liabilities	114.3	107.1	100
Total liabilities	111.0	102.5	100
Stockholders' equity			
Common stock	100	100	100
Retained earnings	220	166.7	100
Total stockholders' equity	134.3	119	100
Total liabilities and stockholders' equity	118.9	108.1	100

The accountant can use vertical analysis to understand the internal structure of the business. It shows the relationship between each income statement account and revenue. Vertical analysis indicates the mix of assets that produces the income and the mix of the sources of financing, whether by current or noncurrent debt or by equity issuance.

As is the case with horizontal analysis, vertical analysis is not the end of the process. The accountant has to examine the areas that either horizontal or vertical analysis, or both, indicate to be possible problem areas.

RATIO ANALYSIS

Vertical analysis compares one figure to the largest figure within the financial statement. It is also important to compare figures from different categories. This is achieved by *ratio analysis*. There are a number of ratios that the accountant can use, depending upon what he or she deems to represent important relationships for the company.

EXAMPLE 5.4

The Ratio Company
Income Statement and Common Size Analysis
(In Thousands of Dollars)
For the Years Ended December 31, 2015 and 2014

	2015		2014	
	Amount	Percent	Amount	Percent
Sales	$100.0	125.0%	$110	107.8%
Sales returns and allowances	20.0	25.0	8	7.8
Net sales	$ 80.0	100.0	$102	100.0
Cost of goods sold	50.0	62.5	60	58.8
Gross profit	$ 30.0	37.5	$ 42	41.2
Operating expenses				
Selling expenses	$ 11.0	13.8	$ 13	12.7
General expenses	4.0	5.0	7	6.9
Total operating expenses	$ 15.0	18.8	$ 20	19.6
Income from operations	$ 15.0	18.7	$ 22	21.6
Nonoperating income	3.0	3.8	—	—
Income before interest & taxes	$ 18.0	22.5	$ 22	21.6
Interest expense	2.0	2.5	2	2.0
Income before taxes	$ 16.0	20.0	$ 20	19.6
Income taxes	6.4	8.0	8	7.8
Net income	$ 9.6	12.0%	$ 12	11.8%

Financial ratios can be classified into five groups:

1. Liquidity ratios
2. Activity ratios
3. Leverage (solvency, long-term debt) ratios
4. Profitability ratios
5. Market value ratios

Some of the most important ones are now discussed.

Liquidity Ratios

Liquidity exists when the company can satisfy its maturing short-term debt. Liquidity is important in carrying out business activity, especially in times of adversity, such as is the case when a business is shut down by a strike or when operating losses result from a recession or a significant rise in the price of a raw material. If liquidity is inadequate to cushion such losses, serious financial problems may ensue. Poor liquidity is analogous to a person having a fever—it is a symptom of a fundamental problem.

Appraising corporate liquidity is particularly important to creditors. If a company has a poor liquidity position, it may represent a poor credit risk, perhaps be unable to make timely interest and principal payments.

Liquidity ratios are static as of year-end. Thus, it is essential for the internal accountant to also examine *future* cash flows.

Some important liquidity measures are discussed next.

Working Capital. Working capital equals current assets less current liabilities. Working capital is a safety cushion to creditors. A higher balance is needed when the company has a problem borrowing on short notice. However, an excessive working capital may be bad because funds could be invested in noncurrent assets for a greater return.

$$\text{Working capital} = \text{current assets} - \text{current liabilities}$$

The working capital for the Ratio Company for 2015 is:

$$\$120,000 - \$55,400 = \$64,600$$

In 2014, working capital was $60,000. The increase in working capital is a favorable sign.

Current Ratio. The current ratio equals current assets divided by current liabilities. Seasonal fluctuations will have an impact on this ratio. The current ratio is used to appraise the ability of the company to satisfy its current debt out of current assets. A high ratio is required if the company has a problem borrowing quickly, or if there are turbulent business conditions, among other reasons. A limitation of this ratio is that it may increase just prior to financial distress because of a company's attempt to improve its cash position by selling property and equipment. Such dispositions have a negative effect upon productive capacity. Another limitation of the ratio is that it will be higher when inventory is carried on a LIFO basis.

$$\text{Current ratio} = \frac{\text{Current assets}}{\text{Current liabilities}}$$

The Ratio Company's current ratio for 2015 is:

$$\frac{\$120,000}{55,400} = 2.17$$

In 2014, the current ratio stood at 2.2. The ratio had a minor decline over the year.

Quick (Acid-Test) Ratio. The quick ratio is a stringent test of liquidity. It is found by dividing the most liquid current assets (cash, marketable securities, and accounts receivable) by current liabilities. Inventory is not included since the length of time needed to convert to cash is long. Prepaid expenses are also not an element since they are not convertible into cash.

Quick Ratio

$$= \frac{\text{cash} + \text{marketable securities} + \text{accounts receivable}}{\text{current liabilities}}$$

The quick ratio for the Ratio Company in 2015 is:

$$\frac{\$30,000 + \$20,000 + \$20,000}{\$55,400} = 1.26$$

The ratio was 1.3 in 2014. The ratio dropped slightly over the year. Other useful liquidity ratios include:

- Working capital provided from operations to net income. Liquidity is deemed better when earnings are backed up by liquid funds.
- Working capital provided from operations to total liabilities. This indicates the degree to which internally generated working capital flow is available to satisfy obligations.
- Cash plus marketable securities to current liabilities. This indicates the immediate amount of cash flow to satisfy short-term debt.
- Cost of sales, operating expenses, and taxes to average total current assets. The internal accountant should look at the trend in this ratio in analyzing the adequacy of current assets to satisfy ongoing business-related expenses.
- Quick assets to year's cash expenses. This reveals the days of expenses that highly liquid assets could support.
- Accounts payable to average daily purchases. This reveals the number of days it takes for the entity to pay creditors.

Cash Flow Ratios. A company's cash flow from operations (cash earnings) equals:

Net income + Noncash expenses (e.g., depreciation) – Noncash revenue
(e.g., amortization of deferred revenue)

The ratio of cash flow from operations to net income may also be studied. Earnings are of higher quality if they are backed up by cash, because cash can be used to pay debt, buy fixed assets, etc. A company with a higher percentage of internally generated cash earnings has better liquidity.

The cash reinvestment ratio equals cash employed divided by cash obtained. Cash employed equals the increase in both gross fixed assets and net working capital. Cash obtained equals income after tax plus depreciation. The cash reinvestment ratio reveals the company's ability to grow. A high ratio indicates that more cash is being used in the business. The cash flow coverage ratio equals:

$$\frac{\text{Net operating income} + \text{lease expense} + \text{depreciation}}{\text{Interest} + \text{lease expense} + \text{preferred dividends}}$$

The ratio of cash plus cash equivalents divided by working capital indicates corporate liquidity. A high ratio provides protection to short-term creditors in receiving debt payments.

A variety of cash ratios show the entity's ability to use its fund balance to pay expenses and obligations. Sufficient cash flow is required for a company to stay afloat and grow. Some useful cash ratios are:

- Cash flow divided by total debt
- Cash flow divided by long-term debt
- (Cash + marketable securities + receivables) divided by year's cash expenses
- Cash + marketable securities divided by total current assets
- Cash + marketable securities divided by total current liabilities
- Cash flow to capital expenditures = cash flow from operations less dividends divided by capital expenditures for fixed assets

Activity Ratios

Activity ratios evaluate the utilization of assets in the business. In general, the greater the utilization of assets, the greater the rate of return earned. Various ratios measure the activity of receivables, inventory, and total assets.

Accounts Receivable Ratios. Accounts receivable ratios include the accounts receivable turnover and the average collection period. The *accounts receivable turnover ratio* reveals the number of times accounts receivable is collected during the period. It equals net sales divided by average accounts receivable. Average accounts receivable for the period is the beginning accounts receivable balance plus the ending accounts receivable balance divided by two. (However, if sales vary greatly during the year, this ratio can become distorted unless proper averaging takes place. In such a case, monthly or quarterly sales figures should be used). A higher turnover rate is generally desirable because it indicates faster collections. However, an excessively high ratio may point to too tight a credit policy, with the company not tapping the potential for profit through sales to customers in higher risk classes. But in changing its credit policy, the company must weigh the profit potential against the risk inherent in selling to more marginal customers.

$$\text{Accounts receivable turnover} = \frac{\text{Net credit sales}}{\text{Average accounts receivable}}$$

Ratio Company's average accounts receivable for 2015 is:

$$\frac{\$15,000 + \$20,000}{2} = \$17,500$$

The accounts receivable turnover for 2015 is:

$$\frac{\$80,000}{\$17,500} = 4.57 \text{ times}$$

In 2014, the accounts receivable turnover was 8.16. The decline in this ratio in 2015 is material and may be indicative of a serious collection problem. The company must reevaluate its credit policy, which may be too soft, or its billing and collection practices, or both. However, the company may have changed its policies deliberately.

The *average collection period* (days sales in receivables) is the number of days it takes to collect receivables.

$$\text{Average collection period} = \frac{365}{\text{Accounts receivable turnover}}$$

The Ratio Company's average collection period for 2015 is:

$$\frac{365}{4.57} = 79.9 \text{ days}$$

It takes almost 80 days to collect upon a sale. In 2014, the average collection period was 44.7 days. With the significant increase in collection days in 2015, there is a danger that customer balances may become uncollectible. However, reference should be made to the collection period common in the industry. One reason for the increase may be that the company is now selling to highly marginal customers. The internal accountant should compare the company's credit terms with the degree to which customer accounts are delinquent. An *aging schedule* may be quite helpful.

The quality of receivables may also be appraised by referring to customer ratings given by credit agencies.

Inventory Ratios. If the company is holding excess inventory, there is an opportunity cost of tying up money in inventory. Further, there is high carrying cost for storing merchandise and obsolescence risk. But if the inventory level is too low, the company may be out of stock, resulting in bad customer relations and lost sales. The two main inventory ratios are inventory turnover and average age of inventory.

$$\text{Inventory turnover} = \frac{\text{Cost of goods sold}}{\text{Average inventory}}$$

In 2015, the inventory turnover is:

$$\frac{\$50,000}{\$47,500} = 1.05 \text{ times}$$

In 2014, the inventory turnover was 1.26 times.

The reduction in the inventory turnover points to greater storage of goods. Are certain types of merchandise not selling well? If so, why not? Maybe there are obsolete goods not worth their carrying value. But a decline in the turnover rate would not be reason for alarm if it were mostly because of the introduction of a new product line for which the advertising effects have not yet been felt.

$$\text{Average age of inventory} = \frac{365}{\text{Inventory turnover}}$$

The average age in 2015 is:

$$\frac{365}{1.05} = 347.6 \text{ days}$$

In 2014, the average age was 289.7 days. The increased holding period indicates potentially great obsolescence risk.

Operating Cycle. The *operating cycle* of the company is the number of days it takes to convert inventory and receivables to cash. Thus, a short operating cycle is desirable.

Operating cycle = average collection period + average age of inventory

The operating cycle in 2015 is:

79.9 days + 347.6 days = 427.5 days

In 2014, the operating cycle was 334.4 days. This is an unfavorable trend since more funds are being tied up in noncash assets.

Total Asset Turnover. The total asset turnover ratio is useful in appraising the company's ability to use its asset base efficiently to obtain revenue. A low ratio may be caused from numerous factors; it is essential to correctly identify the causes. For instance, it must be determined if the investment in assets is excessive relative to the value of the output produced.

$$\text{Total asset turnover} = \frac{\text{Net sales}}{\text{Average total assets}}$$

In 2015 the total asset turnover is:

$$\frac{\$80,000}{\$210,000} = 0.381$$

In 2014, the ratio stood at 0.530 ($102,000/$192,500). The company's use of assets declined materially, and the reasons need to be pinpointed. For instance, perhaps inadequate repairs resulted in breakdowns. Or are the assets becoming older and need replacement?

Interrelationship of Liquidity and Activity to Earnings

There is a trade-off between liquidity risk and return. *Liquidity risk* is minimized by holding greater current assets than noncurrent assets. But the return rate will drop because the return on current assets (e.g., marketable securities) is usually less than the rate earned on productive fixed assets. Further, excessively high liquidity may mean that management has not aggressively searched for desirable capital investment opportunities. Having a proper balance between liquidity and return is essential to the overall financial health of the business.

It should be noted that high profitability does not necessarily imply a strong cash flow position. Income may be high but cash problems may occur due to maturing debt and the need to replace assets, among other reasons. For instance, it is possible that a growth company may experience a decline in liquidity because funds are tied up in noncurrent assets. The effect of earning activities on liquidity is highlighted by comparing *cash flow from operations* to net income.

If accounts receivable and inventory turn over quickly, the cash flow received from customers can be invested for a return, increasing profit.

Leverage (Solvency, Long-Term Debt) Ratios

Solvency is the company's ability to satisfy its long-term debt as it becomes due. An evaluation of solvency emphasizes the long-term financial and operating structure. Excessive long-term debt in the capital structure means greater risk. Additionally, solvency is dependent upon profitability since, in the long term, a company will not be able to satisfy its debts unless it is earning money.

When liabilities are excessive, additional financing should be obtained primarily from equity sources. The company might also contemplate lengthening the maturity of its debt and staggering the debt repayment dates.

Some leverage ratios are indicated below.

Debt Ratio. The debt ratio looks at total liabilities relative to total assets. It reveals the percentage of total funds obtained from creditors. Creditors would prefer to see a low debt ratio, since there is a better cushion for creditor losses if the company goes bankrupt.

$$\text{Debt Ratio} = \frac{\text{Total liabilities}}{\text{Total assets}}$$

In 2015, the debt ratio is:

$$\frac{\$135,400}{220,000} = 0.62$$

In 2014, the ratio was 0.63. There was a minor improvement in the ratio over the year as indicated by the lower degree of debt to total assets. However, it should be noted that an optimum debt/assets ratio may exist. At the optimum debt/assets ratio, the weighted average cost of capital is less than at any other debt to asset level. If, in this example, the optimum was 0.65, 2015 would not be an improvement.

Debt/Equity Ratio. The debt/equity ratio is a major solvency measure because a high degree of debt in the capital structure may make it difficult for the company to satisfy interest charges and principal payments at maturity. Further, with a high debt position comes the risk of running out of cash under adverse conditions. Further, excessive debt will cause less financial flexibility because the company will have more difficulty obtaining funds during a tight money market.

$$\text{Debt/equity ratio} = \frac{\text{Total liabilities}}{\text{Stockholders' equity}}$$

In 2015, the ratio was 1.60 ($135,400/$84,600) and 1.67 in 2014. The ratio remained fairly constant. A desirable debt/equity ratio depends on numerous factors, including the rates of other firms in the industry, the access to debt financing, and earnings stability.

Times-Interest-Earned (Interest-Coverage) Ratio. This ratio indicates the number of times before-tax profit covers interest expense. It represents a safety margin in the sense that it reveals how much of a drop in profits the company can tolerate. The ratio equals:

$$\text{Times-interest-earned ratio} = \frac{\text{Earnings before interest and taxes (EBIT)}}{\text{Interest expense}}$$

In 2015, interest was covered nine times ($18,000/$2,000), while in 2014 it was covered 11 times. The reduction in the coverage is a negative sign because less earnings are available to satisfy interest charges.

Other useful ratios to measure the long-term debt-paying ability of the company are:

- Net income before taxes and fixed charges in relation to fixed charges. This ratio is useful in gauging the company's ability to satisfy its fixed costs. A low ratio indicates risk because when business activity fails, the company may be unable to satisfy its fixed charges.

A better measure is the ratio of cash flow provided from operations plus fixed charges related to fixed charges since cash is what is used to meet fixed charges.

In looking at these ratios for a given company, it should be determined whether the company has stability in both operations and funds flow. Such stability affords more confidence in the firm's ability to meet its fixed charges.

- Noncurrent assets to noncurrent liabilities. Long-term debt will eventually be paid out of long-term assets; hence, a high ratio indicates protection for long-term creditors.

Profitability Ratios

A sign of good financial health and how effectively the firm is managed is its ability to generate a satisfactory profit and return on investment. Investors will refrain from investing in the business if it has poor earning potential because of the adverse effect on market price of stock and dividends. Creditors will be reluctant to get involved with a company having poor profitability because of collection risk. Absolute dollar profit by itself has minimal significance unless it is compared to its source.

Some key ratios of operating performance are now discussed.

Gross Profit Margin. The gross profit margin indicates the percentage of each dollar remaining after the business has paid for its goods. The higher the gross profit earned, the better.

$$\text{Gross profit margin} = \frac{\text{Gross profit}}{\text{Net sales}}$$

In 2015, the gross profit margin is:

$$\frac{\$30,000}{\$80,000} = 0.375$$

In 2014, the ratio stood at 0.41. The reduction in the ratio indicates the business is earning less gross profit on each sales dollar. The reasons for the decline should be determined. Perhaps there has been an increase in the cost of merchandise.

Profit Margin. Profit margin equals profit divided by net sales. It reveals the profitability obtained from revenue and thus is an essential indicator or operating activity. Further, it gives an indication of the entity's pricing, cost structure, and production efficiency.

$$\text{Profit Margin} = \frac{\text{Net income}}{\text{Net sales}}$$

In 2015 the ratio is:

$$\frac{\$9,600}{\$80,000} = 0.120$$

In 2014, the ratio stood at 0.120 as well. Thus, the earning power of the business has remained static.

Return on Investment. Return on investment (ROI) is an important indicator of performance. ROI points to the degree to which profit is achieved on the investment.

Two key ratios of return on investment are *return on total assets* and *return on owners' equity.*

The return on total assets (ROA) points to the efficiency with which management has employed its resources to obtain income.

$$\text{Return on total assets} = \frac{\text{Net income}}{\text{Average total assets}}$$

In 2015 the ratio is:

$$\frac{\$9,600}{(\$220,000 + \$200,000)/2} = 0.0457$$

The return in 2014 was 0.0623. A decline in asset productivity was evidenced over the year.

The Du Pont formula reveals an essential tie-in between the profit margin and the return on total assets. The relationship is:

$$\text{Return on total assets} = \text{profit margin} \times \text{total asset turnover}$$

Therefore,

$$\frac{\text{Net income}}{\text{Average total assets}} = \frac{\text{Net income}}{\text{Net sales}} \times \frac{\text{Net sales}}{\text{Average total assets}}$$

As is evident from this formula, the ROA can be raised by increasing either the profit margin or the asset turnover. The latter is to some degree dependent upon the industry, with retailers, for instance, having a greater potential for a better asset turnover than utilities. Even though the profit margin may change significantly within an industry because it is susceptible to sales, cost controls, and pricing, both profit margin and total asset turnover are dependent on the industry. For example, groceries have low margins but high turnover. The interrelationship shown in the Du Pont formula can thus be helpful to a firm attempting to increase its ROA since the area most sensitive to change can be targeted.

In 2015, the figures are:

$$\text{Return on total assets} = \text{Profit margin} \times \text{Total asset turnover}$$

$$0.0457 = 0.120 \times 0.381$$

Our previous analysis revealed that profit margin has been stable while asset turnover has declined, resulting in a lower ROI. Because asset turnover can be considerably higher, the company may want to try to enhance this ratio while at the same time reevaluating its pricing policy, cost controls, and sales practices. (However, the problem with ROA may be margin. We cannot tell without additional information.)

The *return on common equity* (ROE) measures the rate of return on the common stockholders' investment.

$$\text{Return on common equity} = \frac{\text{Earnings available to common stockholders}}{\text{Average stockholders' equity}}$$

In 2015, Ratio Company's return on equity is:

$$\frac{\$9,600}{(\$84,600 + \$75,000/2)} = 0.1203$$

In 2014, the ROE was 0.17. There has been a sizable decrease in the return earned by the owners of the business.

ROE and ROA are closely related through what is termed the *equity multiplier* (leverage, or debt ratio) as follows:

$$\text{ROE} = \text{ROA} \times \text{Equity multiplier}$$

$$= \text{ROA} \times \frac{\text{Total assets}}{\text{Common equity}}$$

or

$$= \frac{\text{ROA}}{1 - \text{Debt ratio}}$$

In 2015, the company's debt ratio was 0.62. Hence,

$$\text{ROE} = \frac{0.0457}{1 - 0.62} = 0.1203$$

Note that ROA = 0.0457 and ROE = 0.1203. This indicates that by using leverage favorably, the company's return to stockholders materially increased.

Market Value Ratios

Market value ratios compare the company's market price of stock per share to earnings (or book value) per share. Dividend-related ratios are also examined.

Earnings per Share (EPS). Earnings per share is the amount of profit per each share held. Net income is reduced by preferred dividends to arrive at the amount applicable to common shareholders. This statistic is a good indicator of operating performance and the dividend paying potential of the business.

$$\text{Earnings per share} = \frac{\text{Net income} - \text{Preferred dividends}}{\text{Common stock outstanding}}$$

In 2015 EPS is:

$$\frac{\$9,600}{4,500 \text{ shares}} = \$2.13$$

In 2014, EPS was $2.67. The decline in EPS should result in investor concern.

Please see Chapter 1 for a detailed explanation of the complexities surrounding EPS.

Almost all of the Ratio Company's profitability ratios went down over the year, pointing to a negative situation.

Price/Earnings Ratio (Multiple). The P/E ratio equals market price per share divided by earnings per share. A high P/E multiple is favorable, since it indicates that the investing public has confidence in the business.

$$\text{Price/Earnings Ratio} = \frac{\text{Market price per share}}{\text{Earnings per share}}$$

Assuming market price per share was $20 and $22 at year-end in 2015 and 2014, respectively, the P/E ratios are:

2015: $$\frac{\$20}{\$2.13} = 9.39$$

2014: $$\frac{\$22}{\$2.67} = 8.24$$

The rise in the P/E ratio over the period shows the stock is viewed favorably by the investors.

Book Value per Share. Book value per share equals net assets available to common stockholders divided by outstanding shares. Net assets for purposes of this calculation is stockholders' equity less preferred stock. Comparing book value per share with market price per share reveals how investors feel about the financial suitability of the firm.

$$\text{Book value per share} = \frac{\text{Total stockholders' equity} - \text{Preferred stock}}{\text{Outstanding shares}}$$

In 2015, the ratio is:

$$\frac{84,600 - 0}{4,500} = \$18.80$$

In 2014, the ratio was $16.67. Because investors look positively on the firm, the market price of its stock is greater than book value.

Market/Book Value Ratio. This ratio gives an indication of how the business is viewed by investors. Generally speaking, companies with high rates of return on equity (ROEs) sell at higher multiples of book value than those with low returns.

$$\text{Market/book value ratio} = \frac{\text{Market price per share}}{\text{Book value per share}}$$

In 2015, the ratio is:

$$\frac{\$20}{\$18.80} = 1.063$$

The ratio was 1.319 ($22/$16.67) in 2014.

It appears that investors are willing to pay less in 2015 than in 2014 for the company's book value.

Dividend Ratios. Most stockholders are quite interested in receiving dividends. Two useful ratios are *dividend yield* and *dividend payout*.

$$\text{Dividend yield} = \frac{\text{Dividends per share}}{\text{Market price per share}}$$

$$\text{Dividend payout} = \frac{\text{Dividends per share}}{\text{Earnings per share}}$$

EXAMPLE 5.5

Ratio	Formula	2014	2015	Trend
LIQUIDITY				
Working Capital	Current assets – current liabilities	60,000	64,600	I
Current Ratio	$\dfrac{\text{Current assets}}{\text{Current liabilities}}$	2.2	2.17	D
Quick Ratio	$\dfrac{\text{Cash + marketable securities + accounts receivable}}{\text{Current liabilities}}$	1.3	1.26	D
Cash equivalents to working capital	$\dfrac{\text{Cash equivalents}}{\text{Working capital}}$	0.83	0.77	D
Cash to total debt	$\dfrac{\text{Cash}}{\text{Total debt}}$	0.28	0.22	D
Cash to long-term debt	$\dfrac{\text{Cash}}{\text{Long-term debt}}$	0.47	0.38	D
Cash equivalents to current assets	$\dfrac{\text{Cash}}{\text{Current assets}}$	0.45	0.42	D
Cash equivalents to current liabilities	$\dfrac{\text{Cash}}{\text{Current liabilities}}$	1.0	0.90	D
ACTIVITY				
Accounts receivable turnover	$\dfrac{\text{Net credit sales}}{\text{Average accounts receivable}}$	8.16	4.57	D
Average collection period	$\dfrac{365}{\text{Accounts receivable turnover}}$	44.7 days	79.9 days	D
Inventory turnover	$\dfrac{\text{Cost of goods sold}}{\text{Average inventory}}$	1.26	1.05	D
Average age of inventory	$\dfrac{365}{\text{Inventory turnover}}$	289.7 days	347.6 days	D
Operating cycle	$\dfrac{\text{Average collection period}}{\text{+ average age of inventory}}$	334.4 days	427.5 days	D
Total asset turnover	$\dfrac{\text{Net sales}}{\text{Average total assets}}$	0.530	0.381	D
LEVERAGE				
Debt ratio	$\dfrac{\text{Total debt}}{\text{Total assets}}$	0.63	0.62	I
Debt/equity ratio	$\dfrac{\text{Total liabilities}}{\text{Stockholders' equity}}$	1.67	1.60	I
Times interest earned	$\dfrac{\text{Earnings before interest and taxes}}{\text{Interest expense}}$	11 times	9 times	D

EXAMPLE 5.5 (continued)

Ratio	Formula	2014	2015	Trend
PROFITABILITY				
Gross profit margin	$\dfrac{\text{Gross profit}}{\text{Net sales}}$	0.41	0.38	D
Profit margin	$\dfrac{\text{Net income}}{\text{Net sales}}$	0.12	0.12	C
Return on total assets	$\dfrac{\text{Net income}}{\text{Average total assets}}$	0.0623	0.0457	D
Return on common	$\dfrac{\text{Net income}}{\text{Common equity}}$	0.17	0.1203	D
MARKET VALUE				
Earnings per share	$\dfrac{\text{Net income} - \text{preferred dividends}}{\text{Common stock outstanding}}$	$2.67	$2.13	D
Price-earnings ratio	$\dfrac{\text{Market price per share}}{\text{Earnings per share}}$	8.24	9.39	I
Book value per share	$\dfrac{\text{Stockholders' equity} - \text{preferred stock}}{\text{Common stock outstanding}}$	$16.67	$18.80	I
Market/book value ratio	$\dfrac{\text{Market price per share}}{\text{Book value per share}}$	1.319	1.063	D
Dividend yield	$\dfrac{\text{Dividends per share}}{\text{Market price per share}}$			
Dividend payout	$\dfrac{\text{Dividends per share}}{\text{Earnings per share}}$			

D = Deteriorated
I = Improved
C = Constant

If the dividend ratios decline, stockholder concern will exist because the company may be decreasing dividends because of financial problems. Further, fixed income investors particularly rely on dividends.

Collective Inference of All the Ratios

By appraising the trend in the company's ratios from 2014 to 2015 as shown in Example 5.5, we see from the drop in the current and quick ratios that there has been a slight decline in liquidity, but working capital has improved. A material deterioration in the activity ratios has occurred, indicating that improved credit and inventory policies are required. Collection efforts have to be stepped up. The increased age of inventory may signal possible obsolescence. In a positive vein, leverage has improved, so the firm is generally better able to satisfy long-term obligations. However, there is less profit available to satisfy interest charges. Ratio Company's profitability has deteriorated over the year. As a consequence, the return on the owner's investment and the return on assets have gone down. The earnings decrease may be partly due to the company's higher cost of short-term financing. The higher costs may be due to receivable and inventory difficulties that caused a decline in the liquidity and activity ratios. Furthermore, as receivables and inventory turn over less, profit will fall off from a lack of sales and the cost of carrying more in current asset balances.

SUMMARY AND LIMITATIONS OF RATIO ANALYSIS

Financial statement analysis evaluates the financial strengths and weaknesses of a business.

When the company prepares ratios for a banker, liquidity is of prime concern, since the business must be liquid if the debt is to be repaid. If a long-term obligation is involved, earning power and operating efficiency of the borrower are emphasized. The long-term profitability of the firm is the basis for dividends and appreciation in market price of stock. Internal accountants are interested in all phases of financial analysis, since it is important that the firm look favorably to the investment and credit communities. Also, it is important that the company is a "going concern." Any financial problem should be recognized and corrective steps taken. Further, financial statement analysis is essential in planning and conducting the internal audit, since accounts having illogical relationships will be examined more closely. An example is when promotion and entertainment expense to sales changes significantly in the current year. The reasons why will be searched out to see if additional substantive procedures are necessary.

After a ratio is computed, it is compared with related ratios of the company, the same ratios from prior years, and the ratios of competing firms. The comparisons reveal trends over a period of time and hence the ability of the company to compete with others in the industry. Ratio comparisons do not mark the end of the analysis of the business, but rather point to areas requiring further investigation.

The internal accountant must be aware of the many limitations inherent in ratio analysis, including:

1. It is often difficult to identify the industry group to which the company belongs. This makes industry comparisons a problem.
2. Diversity among companies in applying GAAP may result in distorted ratios and comparisons. An example is a company using LIFO while another uses FIFO to value inventory.
3. Published industry norms are only approximations.
4. The historical cost of an asset may differ from its current value. An example is land.
5. A ratio does not reveal its components. For instance, the current ratio may be high but inventory may be composed of obsolete merchandise and receivables may include accounts owed from a politically unstable foreign country.
6. A company may "window dress," making its financial picture look better than it really is. An example is paying off current debt with cash just prior to year-end to artificially increase its current ratio.
7. Liabilities may be understated from an analytical sense. For example, an inadequate provision for lawsuits may exist.
8. Liabilities may be overstated from an analytical sense, such as a convertible bond having an attractive conversion privilege where the expectation is that it will be converted to stock and not paid.

The accountant has to adjust for these limitations in his or her analysis of the financial statements. This requires a more than sophisticated analytical knowledge of a company's financial statements. Consideration has to be given to uncovering certain relevant balance sheet and income statement items. We will now turn our attention to meeting this challenge.

Balance Sheet Analysis

Analyzing the balance sheet provides a check on the reliability of net income and furnishes the basis for evaluating the sources of profit. An overstatement in assets will result in an overstatement in net income, because profits will not include those charges necessary to reduce assets to their proper valuations.

Asset quality applies to the *cash realizability* of assets. Numerous factors bear upon asset quality, including changes in industry and economic conditions. A change in asset quality may point to a future change in earnings and in cash flow. For example, a reduction in the accounts receivable turnover may point to later write-offs of customer balances.

Earnings quality can be partly appraised by classifying assets according to risk category. The higher the percentage of dollars in the high-risk category, the lower the quality of earnings. Informative ratios are the percentage of high-risk assets to total assets and to sales. High asset realization risk is indicative of lower quality of earnings due to possible future charge-offs. For instance, the realizability of accounts receivable is superior to that of goodwill.

Multipurpose assets possess better quality than single-purpose assets due to greater available use.

Assets that lack separable value and cannot be sold easily have low realizability and high risk. Examples are intangibles and work-in-process. On the contrary, investments constitute solid realization in cash and are thus of higher quality.

Cash. In looking at cash, the internal accountant should ascertain if a portion is unavailable for use or restricted. A compensating balance, for instance, is not "free" cash. Cash held in a politically unstable foreign country, where remission restrictions exist, is not available for client use.

The ratio of sales to cash should be determined. A high turnover rate may indicate cash inadequacy and may result in financial problems if additional financing is not available at reasonable rates. A high turnover rate may also indicate stability of the company to such extent that more cash is not needed to support sales. A low turnover rate reveals excess cash, which involves an opportunity cost of the return foregone on the funds being tied up.

Receivables. The realization of receivables may be appraised through examination of the *nature* of the receivable balance. Examples of high-risk receivables are receivables from financially troubled companies or accounts receivable arising from uncollected note receivables.

A company dependent on one or two customers is in a somewhat more vulnerable position than one with a large number of approximately equally important accounts. In general, receivables from companies are safer than those from individuals; fair trade laws are more protective of consumers.

A significant increase in accounts receivable compared to the prior year may point to higher realization risk. The firm may be selling to marginal credit customers. The accountant should look at the trend in both accounts receivable to total assets and accounts receivable to sales.

The factoring of accounts receivable may mean the company has a liquidity problem because it must make use of a higher-cost financing source.

Inventory. An inventory buildup may mean that the amounts carried in inventory are of high realization risk. The buildup may be at the plant, wholesaler, or retailer. A buildup is indicated when inventory rises at a faster rate than the rate of increase in revenue.

When there is a decline in raw materials with an increase in work-in-process and finished goods, a future cut in production may occur.

Higher realization risk exists for goods vulnerable to wide price fluctuation or "fad" type, specialized, or perishable items. On the contrary, low realization risk applies to standardized, staple, and necessity goods because of easier salability.

Raw material is a safer inventory type than finished goods, since it has greater multipurpose use.

The inability to obtain sufficient insurance for inventory due to a high-crime location is another difficulty.

A determination should be made whether the company is properly managing its inventory. A favorable indicator is seen when the advance in sales materially exceeds the increase in inventory.

Sudden write-offs of inventory should make the accountant suspicious of the company's deferral policy. It may mean that prior years' earnings were overstated because of a failure to write down low quality inventory and that the current year's earnings are understated because they must absorb charges more properly belonging to previous years.

Liquidity Index. A liquidity index may be determined which represents the number of days current assets are removed from cash. It is determined as follows:

	Amount	×	Days Removed	Total
Cash	$ 20,000	×	—	—
Accounts receivable	60,000	×	20 days	$ 1,200,000
Inventory	70,000	×	40	$ 2,800,000
Total	$150,000			$ 4,000,000

$$\text{Index} = \frac{\$4,000,000}{\$150,000} = 26.67 \text{ days}$$

The more days current assets are away from cash, the less liquid is the company.

Investments. An investment portfolio of volatile securities has higher realization risk than one diversified by industry and economic sector. The accountant should appraise the extent of diversification and stability associated with the company's portfolio.

Securities with negative correlations to each other provide more market price stability to the portfolio than securities with positive correlations.

The investment portfolio's risk can be measured by computing the standard deviation of its return rate.

The internal accountant should be on the lookout for decreases in portfolio market values that are not entirely reflected in the accounts. A clue to the fair value of investments may be the revenue (dividend income, interest income) they generate. A declining trend in the percentage of earnings derived from such investments to their carrying value may indicate higher realization risk in assets.

Held-to-maturity securities that have a market value in excess of cost represents an undervalued asset.

Fixed Assets. Earnings quality depends on the degree to which sufficient provision has been made for the maintenance of productive assets and for the maintenance and enhancement of current and future earning power. Operational inefficiency will occur if obsolete assets are not replaced with new ones, or if needed repairs have not been made.

Accountants should determine the age and condition of each major asset category, as well as the replacement cost of the category's component parts. The rate of fixed-asset acquisitions to total gross assets should also be examined. This trend is particularly essential for technologically oriented companies. Inactive or unproductive assets should be noted. Asset efficiency can be determined by checking output levels, downtime, and discontinuances. Assets not being used for a long period must be written down if economic reality is to be reflected.

A company with specialized or risky fixed assets is more susceptible to asset obsolescence. Examples are machinery to manufacture specialized products and fad items.

Intangible Assets. A high ratio of intangible assets to total assets indicates an asset structure of high realization risk. The amounts recorded for intangibles may be overstated relative to their market value or to their future income-generating capacity. For example, during a business recession, the company's goodwill may be overstated and perhaps even worthless.

In some cases, however, intangible assets may contribute in an important way to the business, and may in fact be undervalued. For example, the carrying value of patents is almost always less than the present value of future cash flows to be derived from them, but patented products are less valuable when they may easily be infringed upon by minor alteration or when they relate to high-technology-oriented items. Furthermore, the accountant should carefully watch the expiration dates of the patents, as well as whether the firm has impending patented products coming on stream.

Off-Balance-Sheet Assets. The accountant should consider *unrecorded* assets representing resources of the company. They are positive attributes of financial position even though they are not presented on the balance sheet. Included are tax loss carryforward benefit, purchase commitment where the company has a contract to buy an item at a price materially less than the going rate, and expected rebates.

Off-Balance-Sheet Liabilities. Unrecorded liabilities are not reported on the balance sheet but may require future payment or services. They include litigation, noncapitalized lease commitment, excess of the projected benefit obligation over the accumulated benefit obligation of a pension plan, guarantees of future performance, and cosigning of a loan.

Income Statement Analysis

In evaluating the income statement, factors to consider in evaluating earnings quality are the nature of the accounting policies, degree of certainty of accounting estimates, discretionary costs, and the verifiability of earnings.

The Quality of Earnings. Quality of earnings is relative rather than absolute; it refers to comparing the attributes of reported earnings among companies. Earnings quality is lower if net income is overstated *or* understated. Poor earnings quality may be indicated when a company has not properly maintained assets or when its income statement elements are highly erratic. Quality of earnings affects the company's market price of stock, bond rating, and cost of capital. Consideration must be given to positive and negative attributes in earnings. Such attributes may exist in different proportions and intensities in the earnings profiles of various companies within an industry. Earnings quality depends on the use of realistic accounting policies, with the minimum use of assumptions and maximum use of projections based on historical data and trends.

Accounting Policies. Net income computed under conservative accounting is typically of higher quality than that determined using liberal accounting. Conservative earnings form a better base to predict future income projections. Diversity in GAAP allows accountants to choose from liberal or conservative accounting policies.

The accounting policies of the company can be compared to the standard accounting policies in the industry. If the company's policies are significantly more liberal than those prevalent in the industry, lower earnings quality exists.

The highest quality earnings are those reflecting the current economic reality for both the firm and the industry. The measurement standards used in determining earnings are considered realistic if they account for the economic substance of the company's transactions. For example, the depreciation method chosen should most closely approximate the reduction in service potential and usefulness of the asset. Examples of realistic accounting policies are cited in the American Institute of Certified Public Accountants' (AICPA) Industry Audit Guides and in accounting policy guides published by various CPA firms.

Accounting changes made to conform with new FASB Statements, AICPA Industry Audit Guides, and IRS Regulations are justifiable. However, an unjustified accounting change results in an earnings increment of low quality. Unwarranted changes may be made in accounting principles and estimates.

Discretionary Costs. Discretionary costs may be altered by management decision. They include advertising, repairs and maintenance, and research and development. The internal accountant should determine whether the current level of discretionary expenses is consistent with the company's previous trends and with its present and future requirements. Index numbers may be used to compare current discretionary expenditures with base year expenditures. A reduction in discretionary costs may result in a deterioration in earnings quality because management is starving the business of required expenses. Discretionary costs are often cut when a company is having financial difficulty or wants to overstate net income.

The accountant should determine the trend in discretionary costs as a percentage of net sales. A declining trend may indicate a deterioration in earnings quality. Also, discretionary costs should be compared to related assets. For example, a reduction in repairs and maintenance as a percent of fixed assets may indicate the firm's failure to maintain capital. A substantial increase in discretionary costs may have a favorable effect on the company's earning power and growth. A fluctuating trend in discretionary costs as a percent of revenue may indicate a company is smoothing net income by altering its discretionary costs. An example is a vacillating trend in advertising or research.

Cash Flow from Operations. Cash flow from operations equals net income plus noncash expenses (e.g., depreciation) less noncash revenue (e.g., amortization of unearned revenue). Net income backed up by cash is of higher quality. The accountant should evaluate the trend in the ratio of cash flow from operations to net income. High earnings quality is associated with recording transactions that are close to cash realization.

Degree of Certainty of Accounting Estimates. The greater the extent that subjective estimates are involved in determining net income, the more uncertain are reported earnings. This detracts from the quality of earnings.

The accountant may want to look at the difference between a company's estimated liabilities and its actual losses for previous years. An example is the ratio of warranty expense provision to actual warranty costs. A significant difference between the two may point to lower earnings quality. The greater the uncertainty in arriving at estimated liabilities, the more uncertain is net income.

The accountant should isolate revenue and expense items representing cash and near-cash transactions versus revenue and expense items that involve subjective estimates and interpretations. The accountant should attempt to segregate cash expenses versus estimated expenses. He or she may wish to determine trends in cash expenses to net sales and in estimated expenses to net sales.

Internal Control. A deficient system of internal control lowers earnings reliability. When the audit trail is weak, uncovering the errors may be difficult. Accounting errors place doubt on the company's financial reporting system and internal audit function. (See Chapter 10 for the different levels of assurance given by auditors.)

Bankruptcy Prediction

The internal accountant is interested in determining the potential for bankruptcy of the company for several reasons, including possible legal liability exposure and recommending ways to avoid failure. An excellent measure to use is Robert E. Altman's "Z-score," which is composed of selected financial ratios; it has proven to be effective in predicting bankruptcy within the short run (one or two years). See Robert E. Altman, "Financial Ratios, Discriminant Analysis and the Prediction of Corporate Bankruptcy," *The Journal of Finance,* September 1978, pp. 589–609. The "Z-score" equals:

$$\frac{\text{Working capital}}{\text{Total assets}} \times 1.2 + \frac{\text{Retained earnings}}{\text{Total assets}} \times 1.4$$

$$+ \frac{\text{Operating income}}{\text{Total assets}} \times 3.3$$

$$+ \frac{\text{Market value of common stock and preferred stock}}{\text{Total debt}} \times .6$$

$$+ \frac{\text{Sales}}{\text{Total assets}} \times .999$$

His scoring chart follows:

Score	Probability of Short-Term Failure
1.80 or less	Very high
1.81 to 2.7	High
2.8 to 2.99	Possible
3.0 or higher	Not likely

The score is also important for the company's managers to know, so that they may be in a better position to decide on possible cutbacks in capital expansion and dividends.

EXAMPLE 5.6

A company provides the following relevant information:

Working capital	$ 250,000
Total assets	900,000
Total liabilities	300,000
Retained earnings	200,000
Sales	1,000,000
Operating income	150,000
Common stock	
Book value	210,000
Market value	300,000
Preferred stock	
Book value	100,000
Market value	160,000

The Z-score is:

$$\frac{\$250,000}{\$900,000} \times 1.2 + \frac{\$200,000}{\$900,000} \times 1.4 + \frac{\$150,000}{\$900,000} \times 3.3$$

$$+ \frac{\$460,000}{\$300,000} \times 0.6 + \frac{\$1,000,000}{\$900,000} \times .999 = 0.332 + 0.310$$

$$+ 0.547 + 0.919 + 1.109 = 3.217$$

As indicated by the score, it is unlikely that the company will fail. The internal accountant should note the following quantitative factors in predicting corporate failure:

• Low cash flow to total liabilities
• High debt-to-equity ratio

- Low return on investment
- Low profit margin
- Low working capital to total assets
- Low fixed assets to noncurrent liabilities
- Inadequate interest coverage ratio
- Instability in earnings
- Significant decline in stock price
- Sharp increase in the cost of capital
- Reduction in dividend payments

The internal accountant should consider the following qualitative factors that may be indicative of future business failure:

- Declining industry
- Poor management quality
- High business risk
- Inadequate insurance coverage
- Fraudulent actions (e.g., intentionally misstating inventories)
- Inability to obtain further financing
- Inability to meet past-due obligations
- Failure to keep up to date
- Failure to control costs
- High degree of competition
- Inability to adjust production to meet consumption needs
- Movement into business areas unrelated to the basic business

The company may take the following steps to prevent failure:

- Maintain open lines of bank credit
- Dispose of losing divisions and product lines
- Stagger and extend debt maturity dates
- Vertically and horizontally diversify product line(s) and operations
- Diversify geographically
- Engage in cost-reduction programs
- Improve productivity
- Enhance the marketing effort
- Avoid fixed-fee contracts to customers

Extensible Business Reporting Language (XBRL): Financial Reporting on the Internet

There are many data formats on the Internet that prevent users from analyzing financial information without many labor–intensive conversions. Excessive time is devoted to extracting useful information from available accounting and financial data. Further, time is wasted re-keying the same information into a spreadsheet. For example, data in the Securities and Exchange Commission's (SEC) Electronic Data Gathering, Analysis, and Retrieval System (EDGAR) database cannot be imported directly into spreadsheets. EDGAR performs automated collection, validation, indexing, acceptance, and forwarding of submissions by companies and others who are required by law to file forms with the SEC. The comparison of numbers and ratios requires significant effort and very time-consuming re-keying.

XBRL makes financial information available in an easy-to-use format on the Internet. XBRL is an accounting and financial language for the Internet to show relationships such as associating the cash position and cash flow of a company in related financial statements like the balance sheet and statement of cash flows; a simple example is associating numbers with variables. Thus, XBRL is an *intelligent* Internet language that can be used in business by preparers and users of financial statements.

XBRL is a standard specifically designed for reporting accounting and finance information on the World Wide Web. XBRL is a cross-industry XML-based language that specifies a vocabulary specifically for the electronic interchange of financial information. XBRL "tags" specific information with a precise contextual description. This improves both the validity of reported data as per GAAP and investor access to that information.

❑ **Data Extraction**. Currently, extracting specific detailed information from a financial statement published on the Internet, even an electronic financial statement like an EDGAR filing, is a difficult and time-consuming task. For example, a user cannot obtain inventory turnover ratios of one or more corporations from the EDGAR website. On the other hand, if a financial statement is prepared with XBRL standards, numerous common computer programs can easily export every piece of information to that statement.

On May 30, 2008, the SEC issued a proposal that would require companies to provide XBRL financial statements, as well as posting such statements to company Websites. The SEC approved this proposal at their December 17, 2008, open meeting. The final rules will initially apply to domestic and foreign companies using U.S. GAAP and, eventually, to foreign private issuers using International Financial Reporting Standards (IFRS) as issued by the International Accounting Standards Board (IASB). The XBRL financial statements will be required, as an exhibit, with a company's traditionally filed (ASCII or HTML formatted) annual and quarterly reports, transition reports, and Securities Act registration statements. The information produced in an XBRL format will include companies' primary financial statements, footnote disclosures, and financial statement schedules.

Brief Summary

Financial statement analysis is vital to the accountant in appraising the financial position and operating performance of the company. This may be accomplished through trend analysis and ratio comparisons. The prediction of corporate failure is also essential to assure that proper steps are undertaken to avoid financial problems.

WEBSITES

1. Those of specific companies such as *www.ibm.com* or *www.ge.com.*
2. Securities and Exchange Commission – *www.sec.gov.*
3. Business Valuation Resources – *www.bvresources.com.*
4. U.S. Government statistics – *www.stat-usa.gov.*
5. New York Stock Exchange – *www.nyse.com.*
6. Chicago Board Options Exchange – *www.cboe.com.*
7. AICPA's XBRL site– (*www.aicpa.org/Professional+ Resources/Accounting+and+Auditing/BRAAS/XBRL.html*)
8. Stock quotes and financial data–*moneycentral.msn.com/ investor/home.asp, www.google.com/finance?client, finance.yahoo.com.*

Also refer to the COMPUSTAT database system on CD-ROM, which provides financial and market data on companies.

Chapter 6

Individual Income Taxation: Preparation and Planning

The taxpayer wants to pay the least tax possible. There are many legally allowable ways of reducing taxes. The taxpayer should shift income and expenses into tax years that will result in lower overall taxes. All tax-saving opportunities have to be used to pay minimum taxes.

All taxpayers should develop a long-term planning strategy that takes into account their age, income, liquidity needs, family status, estate planning preferences, and other individual factors. There are many comprehensive tax publications that may serve as references, such as those published by CCH and the Research Institute of America.

HOW TO POSTPONE TAXES

Reasons to Postpone Taxes

- Taxpayer will be in a lower tax bracket in a future year.
- Taxpayer lacks the funds to meet the present tax requirement.
- Taxpayer can earn a return on the funds that would be paid to the federal and local taxing authorities.
- Taxpayer, by deferring payment of taxes, will be paying in cheaper dollars because of the inflationary effect.
- Taxpayer may be able to avoid (legally) the tax payment.

Recommendation: Properly time the receipt of income and the payment of expenses to minimize the tax payment, particularly if income is borderline between two tax brackets. A good tax strategy is to receive income in a year it will be taxed at a lower rate. Try to convert income to less-taxed sources. Also, pay tax-deductible expenses in a year in which they will provide the most benefit. In other words, there should be a shifting of deductible expenses into years when the tax rates are higher. Further, there should be an acceleration of expenses that will no longer be deductible or will be restricted in the future. Finally, try to convert non-deductible expenses to deductible ones.

EXAMPLE 6.1

A taxpayer is in a high tax bracket this year but expects to be in a lower one next year. The taxpayer should increase tax-deductible expenses in the high-tax year (e.g., making a thirteenth mortgage payment). The taxpayer should delay receiving income in the high-tax year (e.g., have the employer pay a bonus next year for the services rendered in the prior year).

It may be advantageous to defer the receipt of salaries, bonuses, commissions, and professional fees to the following year so that the tax may be postponed until the filing of next year's tax return, but only if tax rates will be the same or decline the following year. Also, money has a time value, since it could be invested with the expectation of a return.

The taxpayer may take advantage of a deferred-compensation agreement, representing a contract for payments for current services to be made in the future. As a result, there are tax savings in the current year. The taxpayer may wish to postpone the receipt of income on the expectation that lower tax rates will exist, that later year gross income will be less, or that deductions will be higher.

SOURCES OF TAX-EXEMPT INCOME

The taxpayer should be aware of the types of income not subject to tax. Among the most important sources of tax-exempt income are the following:

- Child support.
- Payments received by matriculated students for fellowships and grants if the proceeds are used for educational purposes.
- Casualty insurance proceeds not exceeding the cost of the destroyed property.
- Personal injury proceeds.
- Life insurance proceeds.
- Certain relocation payments.

There is a tax-free buildup for certain types of life insurance and deferred annuity policies. Taxes may be postponed on the interest earned until the policy matures.

A single-premium whole life insurance policy (one lump-sum immediate payment) provides a good tax shelter. It offers tax-deferred income accumulations and tax-free cash potential. The minimum investment is $5,000, and the maximum amount is $1 million or more. These policies normally have borrowing privileges, allowing loans slightly in excess of 90% of the built-up cash value. Thus, almost all of the earnings may be borrowed without generating taxable income. Interest earned on the policy is not subject to tax unless the policy is surrendered during the insured's life. If the policy is in effect at the death of the insured, accumulated earnings go to the insured's beneficiaries free of tax. Single-premium policies are especially helpful to taxpayers who (1) want to fund a child's education (borrowed funds from the policy may be used to pay for college without incurring taxes) and (2) is near retirement age and already has a sizable portfolio of taxable fixed-income securities. The tax benefits of single-premium whole life insurance are:

• Tax-deferred accumulation of cash value
• Tax-free loans from principal
• Tax-free withdrawals of interest
• Tax-free benefits to named beneficiaries

Funds from a life insurance contract paid to beneficiaries when the insured dies are generally not taxable. Also, disability benefits and health insurance benefits are excludable when attributed to premiums paid by the holders.

The taxpayer who is in a high tax bracket may wish to obtain tax-exempt income. Tax-free income is worth much more than taxable income. One can determine the equivalent taxable return as follows:

$$\text{Equivalent taxable return} = \frac{\text{Tax-free return}}{1 - \text{Marginal tax rate}}$$

Interest earned on municipal bonds is not subject to federal tax and is exempt from tax of the state in which the bond was issued. Of course, the market value of the bonds changes with the prevailing interest rate. To reduce the risk of price fluctuation, the taxpayer can buy short-term bonds. However, short-term bonds will have lower interest rates than long-term bonds.

EXAMPLE 6.2

The taxpayer owns a municipal bond that pays an interest rate of 6%. The tax rate is 28%. The equivalent rate on a taxable instrument is:

$$\frac{0.06}{1 - 0.28} = \frac{0.06}{0.72} = 8.3\%$$

The table shows what return one would have to obtain in a taxable instrument to yield the same return in a nontaxable investment.

Tax-Free Return Equivalent
Taxable Return in Various
Income Tax Brackets

	15%	*28%*
6%	7.01%	8.3%
8	9.41	11.1
10	11.76	13.89

Interest on U.S. Government bonds is generally fully taxed by the federal government, but is exempt from state and local taxes.

The taxpayer must disclose on the tax return the amount of tax-exempt income received.

Some items such as sick pay are excludable in a limited amount. Prizes, awards, and gambling winnings are includable in full in gross income. Gambling losses may generally be deducted only to the extent of gambling winnings and, of course, only if the taxpayer itemizes his deductions. Also, unemployment compensation is includable in gross income. It is also possible that Social Security payments received may be tax free. At most, however, 85% of Social Security received may be taxable.

HOW TO DELAY PAYING TAX ON INTEREST

Taxpayers can defer reporting interest on U.S. savings bonds by holding onto the bonds after the maturity date or by making a tax-free exchange of the bonds for another nontransferable U.S. obligation.

Taxpayers can also postpone taxes by buying U.S. Series EE bonds. These bonds are issued on a discount basis with interest represented by yearly increases in the redemption value. Tax on the interest may be postponed until the maturity date of the bond or until the bond is redeemed. The difference between the maturity value and the purchase price is taxable interest in the year the obligation matures. Taxes may still be postponed by converting the Series EE bond to a Series HH bond at maturity.

It should be noted that an exclusion may be available for interest on Series EE U.S. Savings Bonds. In order to qualify for the exclusion (1) the bonds must have been issued after 1989 in the name of the taxpayer (and/or the taxpayer's spouse); (2) the owner of the bond must have attained the age of twenty-four at the time the bond was issued; and (3) the redemption proceeds (i.e., principal and interest) must be used for the qualified higher education expenses (i.e., tuition and fees for a college or a technical or vocational school) of the taxpayer, the taxpayer's spouse, or the dependents of the taxpayer. The exclusion, which is not available if the taxpayer's filing status is married filing separately, may be phased out (or completely disallowed) if adjusted gross income exceeds certain threshold amounts that change annually based on inflation.

Taxpayers may defer interest income by purchasing financial instruments (e.g., certificates of deposit, Treasury bills, U.S. savings bonds) that mature in a later year. Taxes are not due on the interest until the investment matures and the interest income is available.

Note: Interest on zero-coupon bonds is taxable each year when the interest is accrued even though not received.

GAINS OR LOSSES ON SECURITIES TRANSACTIONS

A long-term capital gain or loss occurs when a security is sold after being held for more than 12 months. A short-term gain or loss takes place if the security is held for less than 12 months. The gains and losses on the sale of stock have to be reported on the trade date rather than on the settlement date. The trade date is the date a security transaction actually takes place. The settlement date is the date when a security transaction must be paid by the buyer and the securities delivered by the seller. Stocks and bonds may have a settlement date of three business days after the trade date.

As of this time, several different capital gains tax rates apply, depending on the holding period before sale and the taxpayer's overall income level. Gains on securities held for 12 months or less are short-term capital gains subject to tax at the same rates as ordinary income. However, gains on securities held in excess of 12 months before sale are long-term capital gains subject to a maximum tax rate of 15%. Beginning in 2013, the maximum tax rate is increased to 20% if income is in excess of $400,000, if single, $450,000 if married filing jointly or a surviving spouse, $425,000 if a head of household, or $225,000 if married filing separately. The taxpayer can deduct net capital losses (losses less gains), whether the loss is long-term or short-term. The deduction, however, is limited to $3,000 per year. Any excess losses may be carried forward indefinitely, retaining their character.

EXAMPLE 6.3

The taxpayer sold shares of XYZ Company in 2013 netting $8,000. The initial cost (including brokerage fees) was $6,700. Assuming that the stock was held for less than one year and the taxpayer is in the 28% tax bracket, the tax is:

Gain ($8,000 – $6,700)	$1,300
Tax rate	× 0.28
Tax	$ 364

A technique for postponing the tax on the gain from a disposition of stock while simultaneously protecting that gain is to sell short. An investor who owns stock that has appreciated in value may sell short near the end of the year and then deliver the stock to the dealer and realize the gain after the new year. In selling short, one sells borrowed stock. If market price of the security declines, the investor can buy the shares back at a lower price, thus making a profit. Of course, if the price increases, there is a loss. For example, suppose that an investor sells short 100 shares of stock having a market price of $25 per share. Later on, the investor buys back the stock at $30 per share, taking a loss of $5 per share, or a total of $500, plus commissions. If the price of the stock declines by $5 per share, the $500 is profit.

TAX STRATEGIES WHEN CHILDREN ARE INVOLVED

Taxpayers can engage in several strategies to shift income to their children. With a tax-free gift from the parents, a child can buy U.S. savings bonds or purchase an annuity from an insurance company. A taxpayer can also give appreciating assets (e.g., growth stocks) to young children. Caution must be exercised, since there may be a gift tax consequence if the total value of gifts during the year is in excess of $14,000 ($28,000 where the taxpayer and spouse make a joint election). In any case, there may be no tax until the asset is sold or the annuity payments start. If the sale takes place after the child is 18, the capital gain is taxed at the child's tax rate, which is presumably lower than the parent's tax rate.

Net unearned income is taxed at the parent's rate if the child is under age 18. However, the child's lower tax rate is applied to the amount of investment income not in excess of the annual inflation-adjusted statutory amount. Beginning in 2013, a child whose unearned income is taxed at the parent's rate may be subject to the Net Investment Income Tax (NIIT). NIIT is equal to 3.8% of the lesser of net investment income or the excess of the child's modified adjusted gross income over a threshold amount.

Recommendation: The taxpayer should structure the child's investments so the child recognizes net unearned income in a particular year less than the annual inflation-adjusted statutory amount, with the excess deferred until the child is 18.

It pays to shift income to children over 18, such as through a savings account in the child's name, for a college education. The child may use the standard deduction to shelter income.

Series EE savings bonds provide an opportunity to maximize funds for the child's education. Bond interest is paid at maturity and is exempt from state and local taxation. The bonds guarantee a minimum yield established by the U.S. Treasury. If held for a minimum of five years, the bonds will pay the market-based average if higher than the minimum guaranteed rate. Taxpayers can give Series EE bonds to their child under age 18 and have the interest taxed at the child's lower rate. However, the bonds have to mature after the child has reached age 18.

Another approach is to use deferred annuity contracts issued by insurance companies. There is a deferment of payment of interest until withdrawals begin. Actual yield is based on market interest rates over the term of the annuity. To be taxed at the child's rate, withdrawals have to start after the child's 18th birthday.

ITEMIZED DEDUCTIONS

Itemized deductions are subtracted from adjusted gross income (AGI). Gross income includes wages, interest, dividends, state and city tax refunds, alimony received, gains on the sale of capital assets (including securities), royalties, rental income, all or part of pension income, and, under certain conditions, part of Social Security benefits. Adjustments to gross income to arrive at AGI include contributions to traditional individual retirement accounts (IRAs), contributions to self-employed (Keogh) retirement plans, alimony paid, forfeiture penalties paid to banks for premature withdrawals from certificates of deposit, moving expenses, and one-half of the self-employment tax.

Care must be taken to distinguish among adjustments, itemized deductions, and credits. Itemized deductions are subtracted from adjusted gross income to arrive at taxable income, which is then used to compute the tax. Credits are applied to the tax itself to determine the actual liability.

Itemized deductions include deductions for medical expenses, interest of certain types, state and local income taxes, real estate taxes, charitable contributions, casualty and theft losses, and miscellaneous expenses.

Itemized deductions (other than medical expenses, investment interest, and casualty and theft losses) must be reduced by 3% of adjusted gross income in excess of an applicable amount, as follows:

	2013	2014
Married filing jointly	$300,000	$305,050
Surviving spouse	300,000	305,050
Head of household	275,000	279,650
Single	250,000	254,200
Married filing separately	150,000	152,525

(For years after 2014, the applicable amount may be adjusted for inflation.)

In no event, however, may the reduction of itemized deductions exceed 80%.

The following items are the most important elements in an individual's tax picture:

Gross taxable income
Less: Adjustments (e.g., IRA, Keogh, alimony payments, moving
    expenses)
Adjusted gross income
Less: Itemized deductions (or the standard deduction) and
    exemptions
Net taxable income
Multiplied by tax rate
Tax
Less: Tax credits
Tax liability

Medical Expenses

Hospital costs, physician fees, and prescription drug expenses, net of insurance reimbursement, are deductible only if they exceed 10% (7½% through 2016 if the taxpayer or his or her spouse is age 65 before the end of the year) of adjusted gross income. Some less obvious medical items that should not be overlooked are listed below:

Cosmetic surgery (necessary to correct or improve a physical deformity caused by a congenital abnormality, an accident, or trauma-related personal injury or disfiguring disease)

Meals and lodging (generally limited to a set amount per day for the patient and an individual accompanying the patient) incurred en route to medical treatment

Medical portion of life insurance

Medicare Part B premiums

Medically prescribed items, such as hot tubs and escalators (to the extent that they do not increase the value of the taxpayer's residence)

Eyeglasses and hearing aids

Costs of smoking cessation programs

Prescribed drugs and insulin

Parking fees and tolls

Costs of weight-loss programs in connection with a specific disease, excluding the costs of diet foods

Transportation to and from the doctor's office

Prescribed vitamins

EXAMPLE 6.4

A 50-year-old taxpayer's 2014 adjusted gross income is $40,000. The medical fees incurred are $5,000. The allowable medical deduction may be calculated as follows:

Medical fees	$5,000
Nondeductible amount 10% × $40,000	$4,000
Deductible amount	$1,000

Interest Deductions

Mortgage interest is deductible only on a taxpayer's first and second homes (e.g., vacation home). Interest on up to $1,000,000 of acquisition indebtedness (i.e., debt relating to acquiring, constructing, or substantially improving a taxpayer's principal and/or second residence, which is secured by the residence) is deductible, as is interest on up to $100,000 of home equity indebtedness (regardless of the use of the proceeds). Points paid to obtain a *new* mortgage are tax deductible. However, points incurred on the refinancing of a mortgage are only deductible over the life of the loan, unless the proceeds of the refinanced mortgage are used for home improvements.

EXAMPLE 6.5

In a prior year Ms. Jones paid $100,000 for a home and in the current year made capital improvements of $10,000. She can borrow up to $110,000 and the interest will be entirely deductible, no matter what she does with the proceeds of the loan. She may use the available funds to meet payments on credit card balances and auto loans.

Interest on personal loans (e.g., auto loans, credit cards, education loans, and interest on tax deficiencies) is generally not deductible.

EXAMPLE 6.6

The taxpayer's interest on an auto loan is $1,800. The interest is not deductible unless the auto is used in the taxpayer's trade or business.

Tax Strategy: Take out a mortgage loan and use the proceeds to buy personal items (e.g., an auto) so that one may get a tax deduction for the interest.

A taxpayer who uses credit cards for expenses (e.g., medical expenses) just prior to year-end can still claim a current-year deduction even though the bill does not come due until the next year.

Interest on debt incurred for investment purposes may be partially or totally deductible. However, interest is disallowed on debt used to acquire securities that generate tax-free income.

Interest incurred on a loan prepayment penalty is deductible.

Deductions for Taxes

State and local income taxes paid are deductible. This includes amounts withheld, estimated payments, and deficiencies attributable to prior years. Real estate taxes are deductible, based on days of ownership. Personal property taxes are also deductible. The taxpayer may elect to deduct general sales taxes instead of state and local income taxes on Schedule A.

Charitable Contributions

Charitable contributions are deductible only by those who itemize their deductions. Such contributions are not deductible by those claiming the standard deduction. However, the itemized deduction is limited to 50% of adjusted gross income (with an additional limitation of 30% in the case of gifts of certain appreciated property). Political contributions, however, are not deductible.

You may deduct a gift of $250 or more only if you have a statement from the charity.

Theft and Casualty Losses

A personal theft or casualty loss is available as an itemized deduction only if such losses exceed 10% of adjusted gross income plus $100. Included are legal costs applicable to settling an insurance claim. Because of this low amount of tax deductibility, the taxpayer may wish to lower insurance deductibles on property and automobile insurance.

If property is used for both personal and business purposes, the loss must be allocated, since the 10% of AGI and $100 thresholds are not applicable to the business portion.

The amount of insurance reimbursement will reduce the deductible casualty loss, whether the loss is personal or business-related.

EXAMPLE 6.7

A taxpayer whose adjusted gross income is $50,000 can deduct a personal casualty loss if it exceeds

$$(\$50,000 \times 10\%) + \$100 = \$5,100$$

Miscellaneous Expenses

Total miscellaneous expenses are generally deductible only to the extent that they exceed 2% of adjusted gross income. Listed below are the most common miscellaneous deductions:

Financial counseling and investment newsletter magazine subscriptions
Safe deposit box rental used for investment or other income-producing property
Tax preparation fees
Subscriptions to professional journals
Unreimbursed employee expenses
Expenses incurred in seeking a new job in one's present field
Continuing education courses
Malpractice insurance premiums incurred as an employee
Professional and union dues, except for voluntary assessments
Specialized work clothes
Business use of personal residence
Appraisal fees applicable to casualty losses
Appraisal fees applicable to charitable contributions
Legal fees in connection with the generation, preservation, or conservation of taxable income (e.g., taxable alimony)

Pocket calculator and computer bought for business or invest-
   ment purposes
Videotape recorder to tape programs needed for business
Attaché case for business
Calls to the stockbroker

Taxpayers may deduct education expenses if the education is
necessary to maintain or improve skills required in their current
work or to meet employer or regulatory requirements for the job.

Gambling losses are generally allowed as an itemized deduction,
but are not subject to the 2% floor and may not be in excess of
gambling winnings.

Moving expenses are *not* allowable as an itemized deduction.
However, an employee or self-employed individual may claim a
limited deduction for moving expenses in arriving at adjusted gross
income if certain time and distance requirements are satisfied.

Business meals and entertainment are limited to 50% of the cost,
before the application of the 2% of adjusted gross income limitation. Club dues, however, are not deductible.

EXAMPLE 6.8

The taxpayer's adjusted gross income is $100,000 and miscel-
laneous expenses amount to $3,500. Thus, only $1,500 ($3,500 −
$2,000), representing the excess over 2% of adjusted gross income,
is deductible.

SELF-EMPLOYMENT

The taxpayer must make a profit in any business venture in three
out of the most recent five consecutive years. Otherwise, the losses
will be attributable to a hobby, and thus nondeductible. Hobby
expenses may be deducted only to the extent of hobby income.

A home office deduction is allowed to the extent attributable to
a portion of the taxpayer's residence, which is utilized exclusively
and on a regular basis as the principal place of business for the taxpayer's trade or business.

The deduction, however, is limited to the gross income derived
from the taxpayer's trade or business reduced by (1) all expenses
that are allowable regardless of qualified use (e.g., real estate taxes
and mortgage interest); and (2) deductible expenses that are not
attributable to the actual use of the home (e.g., postage, professional

fees, etc.). The home office expenses not deductible by virtue of this limitation may be carried forward to future years. As an alternative to the calculation of actual expenses, a deduction is allowed in the amount of $5 per square foot, limited to a maximum of 300 square feet.

In general, the taxpayer can immediately expense up to $500,000 of equipment acquired in 2013 ($25,000 in 2014). The amount that may be expensed must be reduced, dollar for dollar, to the extent that the cost of the equipment exceeds $2,000,000 in 2013 ($200,000 in 2014).

It should be noted that one-half of the taxpayer's self-employment tax is deductible in arriving at adjusted gross income (AGI).

PERSONAL EXEMPTIONS

Taxpayers can claim an exemption on their returns for each dependent. In general, subject to certain exceptions, to claim a dependency exemption, (1) one must provide more than 50% of the dependent's total support for the year; (2) the dependent's gross income subject to tax must be less than the appropriate exemption amount; (3) the dependent must live with the taxpayer, unless the dependent is a qualified relative; (4) the dependent must be a citizen, resident, or national of the United States, or a resident of Canada or Mexico for part of the year; and (5) the dependent may not file a joint return with another individual.

Be careful: If the taxpayer gives money to a multimember household (e.g., parents), and that aid, when divided equally among members of the household, does not satisfy the 50% support test for any one member, the taxpayer cannot claim the exemption. The best way to avoid this pitfall is to give the support directly to one person so that the support test can be met.

A taxpayer is also normally entitled to claim a "personal" exemption for himself or herself, unless the taxpayer is claimed as a dependent on another taxpayer's return.

In calculating taxable income, the number of exemptions multiplied by the exemption amount is subtracted from adjusted gross income (AGI). The exemption amount is $3,900 for 2013 and $3,950 for 2014.

STANDARD DEDUCTION

The standard deduction is available for taxpayers who do not itemize deductions. The standard deductions for 2013 and 2014 are:

	2013	2014
Married, joint return	$12,200	$12,400
Married, filing separately	6,100	6,200
Head of household	8,950	9,100
Single	6,100	6,200
Surviving spouse	12,200	12,400

Taxpayers who are age 65 or older or legally blind on the last day of the year are entitled to an additional standard deduction as follows:

	2013	2014
Married taxpayer	$1,200	$1,200
Head of household	1,500	1,550
Single taxpayer	1,500	1,550

TAX IMPLICATIONS OF PENSION PLANS

There are various types of pension plans. A qualified taxpayer may establish an Individual Retirement Account (IRA) and/or a Keogh plan. There are also employer-sponsored pension and profit-sharing plans. Taxpayers are not usually taxed on pension monies until they make withdrawals from their plans. A taxpayer who does withdraw money from a pension plan can avoid taxes by rolling it over into another qualified pension plan within 60 days. The funds will not be taxed until they are withdrawn.

Traditional Individual Retirement Account

Taxpayers who are working and who are not covered by (i.e., not an active participant in) another retirement plan may deduct an annual IRA contribution. For 2013 and 2014, the deductible contribution is generally equal to 100% of earned income (including taxable alimony) up to $5,500. If 50 years or older, the allowable IRA contribution is $6,500. Where a husband or wife are both employed, each qualifies for the maximum deduction. If only one spouse is working, a deduction for a spousal IRA may be claimed. The deduction is treated as an adjustment in arriving at adjusted gross income. A taxpayer who is working and who is an active participant in another retirement plan may deduct IRA contributions (up to the annual limit).

If a taxpayer (or spouse) is an active participant in another retirement plan, the IRA deduction is reduced ratably (in $10 increments) over the following ranges of adjusted gross income:

	2013	2014
Married filing jointly	$95,000–$115,000	$96,000–$116,000
Married filing separately	0–10,000	0–10,000
Single	59,000–69,000	60,000–70,000
Head of Household	59,000–69,000	60,000–70,000

In the case of a nonactive participant whose spouse is an active participant, the 2013 deduction is phased out when modified adjusted gross income is between $178,000–$188,000. The phase-out range for 2014 is between $181,000–$191,000.

Even if the IRA contribution is not deductible, the taxpayer does not have to pay tax now on the interest or other return earned from an IRA investment. The money earned on the account is tax-deferred until withdrawn. In most cases, the taxable income at retirement will be lower, resulting in less tax. Even if a lower retirement tax rate is not expected, the tax-deferred aspect is desirable so as to spread taxable income over several years or to lower taxable income in any one particular year. IRA distributions must commence at age 70½.

Warning. Early withdrawals (before age 59½) are subject to a 10% penalty in addition to the tax (unless there is reasonable cause such as disability). However, IRA withdrawals taken as a life annuity are not subject to the early withdrawal penalty.

Roth Individual Retirement Account

In lieu of making contributions to a traditional individual retirement account, contributions may be made to a Roth individual retirement account. Contributions to a Roth IRA, however, are nondeductible. The advantage of a Roth IRA is that qualified distributions are free of tax and penalty. Under certain circumstances, traditional IRAs may be rolled over to Roth IRAs without the imposition of tax or penalty.

The annual nondeductible contribution, which is generally the same as the amount for a traditional IRA, is phased out ratably (in $10 increments) over the following ranges of modified adjusted gross income:

	2013	2014
Married filing jointly	$178,000–$188,000	$181,000–$191,000
Married filing separately	0–10,000	0–10,000
Single	112,000–127,000	114,000–129,000
Head of Household	112,000–127,000	114,000–129,000

Keogh Plans

A self-employed individual may claim a deduction (in arriving at adjusted gross income) for contributions to Keogh (HR10) plans. The contribution is based on a percentage of the self-employed individual's earned income, which is defined as net earning from self-employment reduced by (1) the deductible Keogh contributions; and (2) one-half of the self-employment tax.

Keogh plans include defined-contribution plans as well as defined-benefit plans. The former may consist of a profit-sharing type plan and/or a money-purchase pension plan. Self-employed individuals can contribute to their Keogh plan(s) up to 25% of net earnings, or a maximum of $51,000 in 2013 ($52,000 in 2014). Contributions to defined-benefit Keogh plans must be determined by an actuary. Keogh funds earn interest without being currently taxed. Under certain conditions, the taxpayer can have both a Keogh and an IRA. In general, the taxpayer cannot withdraw Keogh funds without penalty until age 59½, and withdrawals must commence by age 70½.

401(k) Plans

A 401(k) plan is a salary-reduction plan permitting a taxpayer, through his or her employer, to deposit into a retirement account part of his or her wages. Such a plan enables the taxpayer to defer taxes on contributions and plan earnings. Money may be withdrawn with minimal or no penalty in the event of financial hardship. Loans are allowed from 401(k) plans but not from IRAs. Social Security and Medicare taxes must generally be withheld on contributions to salary-reduction plans.

REAL ESTATE TRANSACTIONS

While gain will normally result from the sale of a residence, if an individual sells his or her principal residence and buys and occupies another principal residence within twenty-four months before or twenty-four months after the sale, gain will be taxed only to the extent that the adjusted sales price (i.e., the selling price reduced by selling expenses, such as sales commissions, legal fees and advertising costs, and fixing-up expenses) of the old residence is in excess of the cost of the new residence. It should be observed that the gain is postponed, and not forgiven. The untaxed gain must be subtracted from the cost of the new residence in arriving at its basis. A loss resulting from the sale, however, is not deductible and would not adjust the basis of any replacement residence.

A taxpayer may exclude, on a one-time basis, gain on the sale of a principal residence of up to $250,000 ($500,000 if married filing jointly). It should be noted that the home must have been used as a principal residence for at least two of the five years preceding the sale.

A taxpayer who rents out part of his residence has to include the rental income in gross income but may deduct rental expenses against said income. If the taxpayer rents out a vacation home for less than 15 days during the year, the rental income is not taxable. But if the taxpayer rents the home for 15 days or more, all rental income is reportable.

Residential rental properties are depreciated over 27.5 years, while nonresidential rental properties are depreciated over 39 years (31.5 years if placed into service before May 13, 1993).

Individuals and closely held C corporations meeting certain statutory requirements may offset losses from rental real estate against all types of income.

An individual will qualify for this beneficial provision if (1) more than one-half of the personal services performed by the individual in trades or businesses is in connection with real property trades or businesses in which the individual owns more than a 5% interest and in which he or she materially participates; and (2) more than 750 hours of service are performed by the individual in real property trades or businesses in which he or she materially participates.

With respect to a C corporation, more than 50% of its gross receipts for the year must be from real property trades or businesses in which the corporation materially participates.

Child-Care Credit

A taxpayer may be entitled to claim a child-care credit. In general, to obtain the credit, the child must be a dependent and be under the age of 13. You may be able to take a credit on up to $3,000 for the expenses you paid for the care of a child and $6,000 for the care of two children. Further, the expenses must be incurred to enable the taxpayer to be gainfully employed.

GIFTS

Gifts are not includable in the recipient's taxable income. In order for them to be taxable, they must exceed an annual exclusion of $14,000 ($28,000 in the case of a joint gift) per donee (i.e., recipient). Gifts made for educational (tuition only) or medical purposes are allowed on an unlimited basis, and accordingly are not subject to the annual exclusion amounts, if the gifts are made directly to the provider of the educational or medical services.

DETERMINATION OF TAX

2013 Tax Rates

Below are the marginal tax brackets for 2013. Tax rates progressively increase as income increases. The tax rates apply only to the income in each tax bracket range. Also, the tax rates apply only to taxable income. Various adjustments and deductions, including the standard deduction and personal exemptions, all lower a person's taxable income. Taxable income is almost always less than your total income.

Single Filing Status

If taxable income is:		The tax is:	
Over—	But not over—		of the amount over—
$0	$8,925	— — 10%	$0
8,925	36,250	$892.50 + 15%	8,925
36,250	87,850	4,991.25 + 25%	36,250
87,850	183,250	17,891.25 + 28%	87,850
183,250	398,350	44,603.25 + 33%	183,250
398,350	400,000	115,586.25 + 35%	398,350
400,000	—	116,163.75 + 39.6%	400,000

Married Filing Jointly or Qualified Widow(er) Filing Status

| If taxable income is: | | The tax is: | |
Over—	But not over—		of the amount over—
$0	$17,850	— — 10%	$0
17,850	72,500	$1,785.00 + 15%	17,850
72,500	146,400	9,982.50 + 25%	72,500
146,400	223,050	28,457.50 + 28%	146,400
223,050	398,350	49,919.50 + 33%	223,050
398,350	450,000	107,768.50 + 35%	398,350
450,000	—	125,846.00 + 39.6%	450,000

Married Filing Separately Filing Status

| If taxable income is: | | The tax is: | |
Over—	But not over—		of the amount over—
$0	$8,925	— — 10%	$0
8,925	36,350	$892.50 + 15%	8,925
36,250	73,200	4,991.25 + 25%	36,250
73,200	111,525	14,228.75 + 28%	73,200
111,525	199,175	24,959.75 + 35%	111,525
199,175	225,000	53,884.25 + 35%	199,175
225,000	—	62,923.00 + 39.6%	225,000

Head of Household Filing Status

| If taxable income is: | | The tax is: | |
Over—	But not over—		of the amount over—
$0	$12,750	— — 10%	$0
12,750	48,600	$1,275.00 + 15%	12,750
48,600	125,450	6,652.50 + 25%	48,600
125,450	203,150	25,865.00 + 28%	125,450
203,150	398,350	47,621.00 + 33%	203,150
398,350	425,000	112,037.00 + 35%	398,350
425,000	—	121,364.50 + 39.6%	425,000

EXAMPLE 6.9

A single individual has taxable income of $40,000. The tax will be:

On the first $36,250	$4,991
Balance ($40,000 − $36,250) = $3,750 × .25	938
Total Tax	$5,929

The taxpayer is in the 25% marginal tax bracket, meaning that 25 cents of every dollar earned above $36,250 (up to $87,850) will be paid in tax. However, the average (effective) tax rate equals:

$$\frac{\text{Tax}}{\text{Taxable income}} = \frac{\$5,929}{\$40,000} = 14.82\%$$

The average (effective) tax rate is below the marginal tax rate because the first $36,250 of taxable income was taxed at a lower rate.

ESTATE PLANNING

The taxpayer should be familiar with some of the options available in deriving an estate-planning strategy. A will is usually adequate to settle a small estate. However, will substitutes and trusts may be needed for larger estates.

Good estate planning enables the smooth transfer of assets to designated heirs (prior to or after death), preserves assets during lifetime by lowering taxes, minimizes administrative confusion occurring at death, and reduces tax and legal expenses. A will is needed to minimize costs, disruptions, and other disadvantages of having a court decide to whom a decedent's estate will go.

Related parties should have separate, individual wills because joint wills (husband and wife) may cause problems (e.g., the husband or wife may change the will without the consent of the other).

A trust can shift the tax burden to beneficiaries in lower tax brackets in order to reduce the total tax assessment and/or assist the grantor in avoiding estate taxes altogether.

The taxpayer can give property to future heirs through judicious use of gift tax exemptions. Gifts to relatives are tax-free up to $14,000 per beneficiary per year. If a married couple files a joint election, $28,000 can be given tax-free.

Spouses enjoy tax-free spousal estate transfers. A spouse can pass his or her entire estate to the other without paying tax.

A lifetime charitable gift may result in an income-tax deduction. Also, the value of the gift plus any future appreciation is removed from the estate. A restriction exists on the amount of the tax deduction allowed to be taken, depending on the type of charity.

If an individual makes a testamentary charitable gift, the estate earns a deduction equal to the gift's fair market value. A remainder trust may also be established. Ownership of residence may be given to a charity with the donor having the right to continue living on the property. The charity receives the property upon the donor's death. The value of the property reduces the amount of the estate for tax purposes.

The taxpayer should calculate the estate's estimated net value as follows:

> Total assets
> Less: Funeral costs
>   Compensation to executors
>   Debt payments
> _____
> Estimated net value

EXAMPLE 6.10

Sam Johnson is single. When he dies, funeral costs are estimated at $1,000. His house is projected to have a fair market value of $300,000. There will be an outstanding mortgage of $50,000. Personal property is estimated at $100,000. Debts are estimated at $60,000. The IRA will be valued at $95,000. The taxpayer is entitled to a pension benefit from his employer projected at $150,000. There is also a life insurance policy of $200,000. In the will there is a provision for a $5,000 gift to a charity. Administration expenses will be $6,000. The taxpayer's net estate is estimated at:

Gross Estate		
Home	$300,000	
Personal property	100,000	
Pension plans	245,000	
Life insurance	200,000	
Total		$845,000
Less: Allowable deductions		
Funeral expense	$ 1,000	
Administration expense	6,000	
Mortgage and debts	110,000	
Charitable contribution	5,000	
Total deductions		122,000
Net Estate		$723,000

Estate tax is imposed on a graduated basis on the value of transferred property. *Warning:* Do not confuse estate taxes with inheritance taxes. Inheritance taxes are levied by the states and are payable by the heirs, not by the estate of the deceased.

The federal estate-tax exemption limit is $5,250,000 for 2013. *Recommendation:* To settle an estate of $5,250,000 or less, the taxpayer should have a joint ownership agreement with his or her spouse along with a will. Use a trust if minor children or other dependents are involved.

If the estate is above the federal estate tax exemption, make a combination of lifetime gifts to lower the estate value to the exemption limit. For example, by transferring real property and gifts 25 years prior to death, the donor transfers tax-free 25 years' worth of appreciating value.

The maximum estate tax rate for 2013 is 40% for estates exceeding $5,250,000. Inheritance tax rates vary among states.

Probate is the legal means of settling an estate's affairs. It involves the transfer of property and assets from the deceased to the survivors.

A trust is a special form of ownership that provides sound management of assets and insulates them from tax and creditors. Trusts transfer property ownership to a third party, the trust, while permitting the real owner to keep control by appointing himself, another person, or financial institution to act as trustee.

ADVANTAGES OF HAVING A TRUST

- Avoiding the costs applicable to outright ownership of property
- Improves administrative convenience
- Shelters owner from lawsuits and creditors
- Enables faster inheritance
- May reduce the tax burden
- Tailored to meet obligations
- Management may be done by a trusted third party
- Property is transferred to minors without the need for a guardian
- Protects inheritor's principal against unwise spending

Flexibility. One can give the trustee as much or as little power to make decisions as desired.

An irrevocable trust transfers trust assets outside the grantor's ownership and is immune from lawsuits and creditors' claims against the grantor. Irrevocable trusts established prior to death are not included in the deceased probatable estate, reducing access to the decedent's property by creditors' claims. Of course, a trust is not a total barrier to estate taxation.

Irrevocable and revocable living trusts are not includable in the probate of the decedent's estate and thus result in faster inheritance. Since trusts are not included in the probatable estate, probate costs, which depend on the estate's size, are lower.

To enable the trust's income to be taxed at the lower marginal tax rate of the beneficiary instead of the higher marginal tax rate of the grantor, the following conditions have to exist:

- The grantor relinquishes his or her reversionary interest in both the principal and income of the trust for more than 10 years or the beneficiary's lifetime.
- The grantor relinquishes control over the income payable to other persons during the trust period.
- The grantor gives up certain administrative powers (e.g., grantor cannot reacquire the trust capital).
- The grantor cannot revoke the trust.
- The trust's income cannot be distributed or accumulated for future disposition to the grantor or the grantor's spouse, nor can it be used to meet the grantor's support obligations (e.g., payment of college tuition for children).

Warning. Revocable trusts provide no tax advantages to the grantor and thus should be considered for nontax reasons.

Recommendation. Use an irrevocable trust when the grantor's main concern is to transfer some assets prior to death so as to lower estate taxes. The appreciation in value of the trust is not subject to gift or estate taxes.

ALTERNATIVE MINIMUM TAX

The alternative minimum tax is a special type of tax enacted to ensure that taxpayers who benefit from the special treatment of certain types of income and/or special deductions will pay at least a minimum amount of tax. The tax involves certain "tax preference items." The tentative alternative minimum tax is generally equal to 26% of alternative minimum taxable income (in excess of an applicable exemption amount) not in excess of $179,500 ($89,750 if married filing separately), plus 28% of the excess.

The actual alternative minimum tax is the excess of the tentative alternative minimum tax over the taxpayer's regular tax liability and alternative minimum tax foreign tax credit.

Other Key Features of 2013 Taxes

Filing Status
Same sex individuals who married in a state that recognizes same-sex marriages must file as married filing jointly or married filing separately.

Additional Medicare Tax
Beginning in 2013, an additional 0.9% Medicare tax is imposed on Medicare wages and self-employment income in excess of the following applicable amounts:

Married filing jointly	$250,000
Married filing separately	125,000
Single	200,000
Head of Household	200,000

Net Investment Income Tax
A 3.8% surcharge is imposed on the lesser of (1) net investment income or (2) the excess of modified adjusted gross income over a threshold amount. The threshold amounts are as follows:

Married filing jointly	$250,000
Surviving spouse	250,000
Married filing separately	125,000
Head of household	200,000
Single	200,000

Net investment income generally includes income from pass-through entities, income from passive activity, rental and royalty income, taxable interest income, and dividend income.

Brief Summary

Tax planning can be used before the year starts to minimize taxes. High-income people should make every effort to obtain tax-exempt income. Tax-deductible expenses should be sought out. Income should be deferred to the following taxable year to avoid tax in the current period. For example, service fees otherwise due before December 31 may be deferred by delaying the billing until late in the year, so that payment is received in January. Expenses should be accelerated to obtain a deduction in the current period rather than the next. For example, a taxpayer whose marginal tax rate is likely to be lower next year should *prepay* and deduct current-year state income taxes and property taxes. By lowering taxes in the current period, the savings can be invested for a return. Estate planning should be practiced to ensure that beneficiaries receive the most money possible. One possibility is to take advantage of the applicable annual gift tax exclusion.

Some Tax Planning Tips

- Use charge cards for deductible purchases. The taxpayer can deduct items charged in the current year even though they are paid for in the next year.
- Donate appreciated property instead of cash. A taxpayer who donates appreciated property to a charity can generally deduct the full market value and avoid paying tax on the gain.
- Put away the highest amount possible in a retirement plan. Even if the contribution is not deductible, interest earned is tax-deferred. Contribute at the beginning of the year to maximize the tax deferral on the interest.
- Offset gains with losses. The taxpayer can avoid paying taxes on gains by selling securities that have declined in value since purchase. The taxpayer can use tax swaps (selling an investment and replacing it immediately with a similar investment) to establish a gain or loss and still maintain the investment position.
- Transfer savings to members of the family in lower tax brackets (e.g., children over the age of 18).

Selected Readings

Federal Tax Course: A Guide for the Tax Practitioner (2013) (Commerce Clearing House)

Your Federal Income Tax - Publication 17 (Department of the Treasury, Internal Revenue Service)

WEBSITES

1. Internal Revenue Service – *www.irs.gov*
2. Tax and Accounting Sites Directory – *www.taxsites.com*
3. Tax Analysts – *www.tax.org/*
4. National Tax Association – *www.ntanet.org*
5. 1040.COM – *www.1040.com*
6. Tax Resources on the Web – *www.taxtopics.net*
7. H&R Block Tax Calculators – *www.hrblock.com*
8. Turbo Tax – *www.turbotax.com*
9. The Tax Technology Association – *www.taxact.org*

Chapter 7
Dictionary of Accounting Terms

Accounting is a dynamic area with a vocabulary that is constantly changing. To speak its language, you have to keep up to date with the latest terms that have just emerged and with the latest definitions of older terms. It is this chapter's purpose to present the working vocabulary of accounting today—defining new terminology as it affects the accounting profession, while updating the traditional language of accounting and its related disciplines.

Entries have been drawn from all areas within accounting, including financial accounting, managerial and cost accounting, auditing, financial statement analysis, and taxes. Definitions have also been provided for many terms from related business disciplines that accountants must know about in order to work efficiently in the business world. Included are essential words from finance, operations research and quantitative techniques, computers, and economics. In all, clear, concise definitions are provided for more than 2,500 terms, and further explanation of the term or a demonstration of its use is frequently given to amplify the definition.

Alphabetization: All entries are alphabetized by letter rather than by word, so that multiple-word terms are treated as single words. For example, **ACCOUNT FORM** follows **ACCOUNTANT,** and **AD VALOREM TAX** follows **ADMINISTRATIVE BUDGET.** In unusual cases (such as **BASIC**) abbreviations appear as entries in the main text, in addition to appearing in the back of the book in the separate listing of Abbreviations and Acronyms. This occurs when the short form or acronym, rather than the formal name, predominates in the common usage of the field. For example, **BASIC** is commonly used when speaking of the **"BEGINNER'S ALL-PURPOSE SYMBOLIC INSTRUCTION CODE";** thus, the entry is at **BASIC.** Numbers in entry titles are alphabetized as if they were spelled out. For example, **401(K) PLAN** follows **FORWARD RATE.**

Many words have distinctly different meanings, depending upon the context in which they are used. The various meanings of a term are listed by numerical or functional subheading. Readers must determine the context that is relevant to their purpose.

When terms are defined as different parts of speech, the grammatical forms are not labeled but the sequence is always nouns, followed by verbs, followed by qualifiers.

Abbreviations and Acronyms: A separate list of Abbreviations and Acronyms follows the Dictionary.

Cross-references: To add to your understanding of a term, related or contrasting terms are sometimes cross-referenced. The cross-referenced term will appear in SMALL CAPITALS either in the body of the entry (or subentry) or at the end. These terms will be printed in SMALL CAPITALS only the first time they appear in the text. Where an entry is fully defined by another term, a reference rather than a definition is provided—for example: **ALPHA RISK** *see* TYPE I ERROR.

Italics: Italic type is generally used to indicate that another term has a meaning identical or very closely related to that of the entry. Italic type is also used to highlight the fact that a word or phrase has a special meaning to the trade. Italics are also used for the titles of publications.

Parentheses: Parentheses are used in entry titles to indicate that an abbreviation is used with about the same frequency as the term itself; for example, **SECURITIES AND EXCHANGE COMMISSION (SEC).**

Special Definitions: Organizations and associations that play an active role in the field are included in the Dictionary, along with a brief statement of their mission.

A

ABACUS
1. instrument of ancient origin used to perform arithmetic calculations by sliding counters along rods or in grooves.
2. semiannual accounting research journal (founded in 1965) published by the Sydney University Press, edited by the University of Sydney, Department of Accounting. The subject matter covers all areas of accounting including international accounting.

ABANDONMENT voluntary surrender of property, owned or leased, without naming a successor as owner or tenant. The property will generally revert to a person holding a prior interest or, in cases where no owner is apparent, to the state.

ABATEMENT complete or partial cancellation of a levy imposed by a governmental unit. Abatements usually apply to tax levies, special assessments, and service charges.

ABC *see* ACTIVITY-BASED COSTING.

ABC METHOD inventory management method that categorizes items in terms of importance. Thus, more emphasis is placed on higher dollar value items ("A"s) than on lesser dollar value items ("B"s), while the least important items ("C"s) receive the least time and attention. Inventory should be analyzed frequently when using the ABC method. The procedure for ABC analysis follows: (1) Separate finished goods into types (chairs of different models, and so on); separate raw materials into types (screws, nuts, and so on). (2) Calculate the annual dollar usage for each type of inventory (multiply the unit cost by the expected future annual usage). (3) Rank each inventory type from highest to lowest, based on annual dollar usage. (4) Classify the inventory as A—the top 20%; B—the next 30%; and C—the last 50% of dollars usage, respectively. (5) Tag the inventory with its appropriate ABC classification and record those classifications in the item inventory master records.

ABNORMAL SPOILAGE spoilage that is recognized as a loss when discovered. NORMAL SPOILAGE is inherent in the manufacturing process and is unavoidable in the short run. Abnormal spoilage is spoilage beyond the normal spoilage rate. It is controllable because it is a result of inefficiency. It is not a cost of good production, but rather it is a loss for the period. Costs are assigned to the spoiled units and then credited to WORK-IN-PROCESS inventory and debited to a loss account.

ABSORB
1. to assimilate, transfer, or incorporate amounts in an account or a group of accounts in a manner in which the first entity loses its identity and is "absorbed" within the second entity. Examples include the sequential transfer of expenditure account amounts to WORK-IN-PROCESS, finished goods, and COST OF SALES.
2. to distribute or spread costs by the process of proration or allocation. *See also* ABSORPTION COSTING.

ABSORPTION COSTING method in which all manufacturing costs, variable and fixed, are treated as PRODUCT COSTS, while nonmanufacturing costs (e.g., selling and administrative expenses) are treated as PERIOD COSTS. Absorption costing for inventory valuation is required for external reporting. *See also* VARIABLE COSTING.

A comparison between absorption and variable costing follows:

Absorption Costing	Variable Costing
1. Required for outside reporting	1. Not accepted for outside reporting
2. Includes fixed overhead as an inventoriable cost	2. Does not include fixed overhead as an inventoriable cost
3. Stresses gross profit	3. Stresses contribution margin
4. Has a higher net income when production exceeds sales	4. Has a higher net income when sales exceed production

ABUSIVE TAX SHELTER limited partnership the IRS believes is claiming illegal tax deductions. This type of shelter usually inflates the value of purchased property, thus providing a basis for higher depreciation write-offs. When the IRS disallows the write-offs, back taxes as well as interest charges and high penalties must be paid. *See also* LIMITED PARTNER.

ACADEMY OF ACCOUNTING HISTORIANS voluntary organization dedicated to the study of accounting history. This organization (http://accounting. rutgers.edu/raw/aah) publishes the ACCOUNTING HISTORIANS JOURNAL in addition to monographs, working papers, and a newsletter.

ACCELERATED COST RECOVERY SYSTEM (ACRS) system of depreciation for tax purposes mandated by the Economic Recovery Act (ERA) of 1981 and modified by the Tax Reform Act of 1986. The type of property determines its class. Instead of providing statutory tables, prescribed methods of depreciation are assigned to each class of property. For 3, 5, 7, and 10 year classes, the relevant depreciation method is the 200% declining balance method. For 15 and 20 year property, the appropriate method is the 150% declining balance method switching to the STRAIGHT-LINE method when it will yield a larger allowance. For residential rental property (27.5 years) and nonresidential real property (31.5 years), the applicable method is the straight-line method. A taxpayer may make an irrevocable election to treat all property in one of the classes under the straight-line method. Property is statutorily placed in one of the classes. The purpose of ACRS is to encourage more capital investment by businesses. It permits a faster recovery of the asset's cost and thus provides larger tax benefits in the earlier years. *See also* MODIFIED ACCELERATED COST RECOVERY SYSTEM (MACRS).

ACCELERATED DEPRECIATION method recognizing higher amounts of depreciation in the earlier years and lower amounts in the later years of a fixed asset's life. Some machines, for example, are more efficient early on and generate greater service potential; matching dictates higher depreciation expense in those years. Over time, depreciation expense moves in a downward direction and maintenance costs tend to become higher; thus the effect of accelerated depreciation is fairly even charges to income. Greatest tax benefits from depreciation are enjoyed in the earlier years. *See also* ACCELERATED COST RECOVERY SYSTEM; DOUBLE DECLINING BALANCE; SUM-OF-THE-YEARS'-DIGITS (SYD) METHOD.

ACCELERATION CLAUSE provision contained in a BOND INDENTURE requiring that in an event of default any remaining interest and principal become immediately due and payable.

ACCEPTABLE QUALITY LEVEL (AQL) a quality standard that allows a prespecified number of defects.

ACCEPTANCE
1. drawee's promise to pay either a TIME DRAFT or SIGHT DRAFT. Typically, the acceptor signs his name after writing "accepted" on the bill along with the date. Instead of "accepted," similar wording indicating an intention to pay would also suffice to show a desire to honor the bill at maturity. An acceptance of a bill in effect makes it a PROMISSORY NOTE: the acceptor is the maker and the drawer is the endorser.
2. BANKER'S ACCEPTANCE.
3. binding contract effected when one party to a business arrangement accepts the offer of another. Acceptance may be in written or oral form.

ACCEPTANCE SAMPLING statistical procedure used in quality control. Acceptance sampling involves testing a batch of data to determine if the proportion of units having a particular attribute exceeds a given percentage. The sampling plan involves three determinations: (1) batch size; (2) sample size; and (3) maximum number of defects that can be uncovered before rejection of the entire batch. This technique permits acceptance or rejection of a batch of merchandise or documents under precisely specified circumstances, thereby ensuring that the auditor does not reject too many acceptable batches. Acceptance sampling is of particular value to the internal auditor who wants continuous control on the quality of clerical work. From acceptance sampling tables, one can select a sampling plan to assure that errors will not be greater than a specified percentage of the batch (tolerable error rate), provided a full check of rejected batches is made. Acceptance sampling can also be used by the internal auditor to inspect the documents flowing through information channels of the organization. Items that can be checked include pricing and mathematical calculations. Acceptance sampling is basically an internal audit tool. It would be very difficult for the external auditor to devise a sampling plan that, while rejecting, say, 90% of unsatisfactory batches, does not also reject a high number of satisfactory batches.

ACCESS CONTROLS used to ensure that only authorized individuals are able to access certain resources. In a computer system, access controls are used to limit the individuals who are allowed to log in. This is often done through the use of passwords or a combination of passwords with smart cards. Other forms of authentication, such as fingerprint or retinal scan, and other biometric systems are also becoming popular.

ACCESS DATABASE a relational database management system within Microsoft Office with a graphical user interface. A database like Access can store and track virtually any kind of data, including textual and audio/video. The data is stored in an SQL database; this provides for security and scalability. Newly introduced in 2013 are Access Web apps that can be hosted on SharePoint servers.

ACCESS POINT sends and receives signals from other local wireless devices and allows these devices to connect to a wired Local Area Network (LAN).

A router is similar to an access point device, but a router provides additional functionality, such as firewall and assignment of IP addresses. An access point may be used to extend coverage within a network to eliminate "dead spots." Also referred to as *wireless access point.*

ACCESS TIME length of time that a data storage device, associated with a computer, takes to process and return data from the time of the original request for the data.

ACCOMMODATION ENDORSEMENT written agreement to be liable made without consideration on a credit instrument (e.g., notes payable) to which another person or firm is a party, thus adding strength to the credit application. An example: a parent company *endorses* a note of a subsidiary payable to a bank or other lender.

ACCOUNT
1. systematic arrangement showing the effect of transactions and other events on a specific balance sheet or income statement item. An account is usually expressed in money. A separate account exists for each asset, liability, stockholders' equity, revenue, and expense. Accounts are the way in which differing effects on the basic business elements are categorized and collected. Accounts are in the ledger (ledger account). Examples are cash, accounts payable, and dividend revenue. *See also* CHART OF ACCOUNTS.
2. relationship between one party and another. Examples are a depositor or borrower with a bank or thrift institution or a credit relationship with a seller of goods or services.

ACCOUNTABILITY individual or departmental responsibility to perform a certain function. Accountability may be dictated or implied by law, regulation, or agreement. For example, an auditor will be held accountable to financial statement users relying on the audited financial statements for failure to uncover corporate FRAUD because of negligence in applying GENERALLY ACCEPTED AUDITING STANDARDS (GAAS).

ACCOUNT ANALYSIS way to measure cost behavior. It selects a volume-related cost driver and classifies each account from the accounting records as a variable or fixed cost. The cost accountant then looks at each cost account balance and estimates either the variable cost per unit of cost driver activity or the periodic fixed cost. Account analysis requires a detailed examination of the data, presumably by cost accountants and managers who are familiar with the activities of the company, and the way the company's activities affect costs. *See also* ENGINEERING ANALYSIS; HIGH-LOW METHOD; REGRESSION METHOD.

ACCOUNTANCY British term referring to the activities and theories comprising accounting including practice, research, and teaching. It includes the guidelines, principles, and procedures accountants are to follow in conducting their tasks. Accountants have legal and ethical responsibilities to their clients and public. *See also* ACCOUNTING.

ACCOUNTANT one who performs accounting services. Accountants prepare financial statements and tax returns, audit financial records, and develop financial plans. They work in private accounting (e.g., for a corporation), public accounting (e.g., for a CPA firm), not-for-profit accounting (e.g., for a governmental agency). Accountants often specialize in a particular area such as taxes, cost accounting, auditing, and management advisory services. A BOOKKEEPER is distinguished from an accountant as one who employs lesser professional skills. The bookkeeping function is primarily one of recording transactions in the journal and posting to the ledger. *See also* CERTIFIED PUBLIC ACCOUNTANT.

ACCOUNTANT IN CHARGE professional responsible for the field engagement associated with an audit. Duties include the general supervision of the engagement, distributing the workload to assistants, reviewing audit findings, and drafting required field reports.

ACCOUNTANTS FOR THE PUBLIC INTEREST (API) organization dedicated to serving the public welfare. API provides objective analysis of public policy questions in terms of their fiscal, accounting, or financial implications. Services include technical support to nonprofit organizations that do not have the resources to afford such services.

ACCOUNTANTS' INDEX bibliography of accounting books and articles of interest to accounting professionals. It is published quarterly and annually by the AMERICAN INSTITUTE OF CERTIFIED PUBLIC ACCOUNTANTS (AICPA). Included are publications on all phases of accounting, including auditing, tax, financial accounting, managerial accounting, and computer applications.

ACCOUNTANTS INTERNATIONAL STUDY GROUP (AISG) organization founded to examine and report on common interesting topics within the accounting discipline. This group consists of representatives from the AMERICAN INSTITUTE OF CERTIFIED PUBLIC ACCOUNTANTS (AICPA), CANADIAN INSTITUTE OF CHARTERED ACCOUNTANTS (CICA), and the INSTITUTE OF CHARTERED ACCOUNTANTS IN ENGLAND AND WALES.

ACCOUNTANT'S LIABILITY potential legal obligation of an accountant who commits fraud or is grossly negligent in the performance of professional duties. The term typically applies when an auditor conducting the ATTEST FUNCTION does not employ GENERALLY ACCEPTED AUDITING STANDARDS (GAAS) with sufficient care. To avoid liability, the accountant must be knowledgeable about the accounting profession's authoritative pronouncements such as FASB statements and AICPA STATEMENTS ON AUDITING PROCEDURE as well as SEC ACCOUNTING SERIES RELEASES. An accountant who violates the established rules and guidelines can be held legally liable to parties retaining him and those relying on work performed (e.g., investors, creditors). Most accounting practitioners carry malpractice insurance. *See also* NEGLIGENCE.

ACCOUNTANT'S MAGAZINE, THE journal founded in 1897, originally published monthly by the Aberdeen, Edinburgh, and Glasgow chartered accountants' societies. The INSTITUTE OF CHARTERED ACCOUNTANTS IN SCOTLAND, founded in 1951, later adopted this magazine as its monthly journal. Subject matter includes international accounting, accounting education, information systems, financial accounting, managerial accounting, and legal topics.

ACCOUNTANT'S RESPONSIBILITY ethical obligation to those relying upon the accountant's professional work. The accountant has a duty to management, investors, creditors, and regulatory bodies to exercise due care in performing the accounting and ATTEST FUNCTIONS. The accountant must follow with competence the promulgations of the ACCOUNTING PRINCIPLES

BOARD (APB) and FINANCIAL ACCOUNTING STANDARDS BOARD (FASB), among others.

ACCOUNT FORM balance sheet structure showing assets on the left, liabilities and stockholders' equity on the right. The alternative form, called the REPORT FORM, positions assets above liabilities and stockholders' equity.

ACCOUNTING

1. umbrella term encompassing the multitude of disciplines including auditing, taxation, financial statement analysis, and managerial accounting. Accounting-related functions include financial accounting, cost accounting, not-for-profit accounting, and financial planning.
2. process of recording, measuring, interpreting, and communicating financial data. The accountant prepares financial statements to reflect financial condition and operating performance. Also, the accounting practitioner renders personal accounting services to clients such as preparing personal financial statements and tax planning.

ACCOUNTING AND FINANCIAL WOMEN'S ALLIANCE (AFWA) organization of women accountants who are primarily CPAs and corporate accountants in middle management positions. AFWA publishes *The Woman CPA*, which covers all aspects of accounting including information systems, accounting education, financial accounting, and auditing. The organization attempts to promote women's interests in the profession.

ACCOUNTING CHANGE AND ERROR CORRECTIONS change in (1) accounting principles (such as a new depreciation method); (2) accounting estimates (such as a revised projection of doubtful accounts receivable); or (3) the reporting entity (such as a merger of companies). A change in principle requires retrospective application to previous years' financial statements, a change in estimate is accounted for prospectively over current and future years, and a change in reporting entities mandates the restatement of previous years' financial statements as if both companies were always combined. Corrections of errors adjust the beginning balance of retained earnings. *Note:* The correction of an error in previously issued financial statements is not an accounting change. However, the reporting of an error correction involves adjustments to previously issued financial statements similar to those generally applicable to reporting an accounting change retrospectively. FASB Statement No. 154, *Accounting Changes and Error Corrections* (ASC, 250-10-05) provides for accounting changes in principle, estimate, and reporting entity. Correction of an error in a prior year is also briefly mentioned. Proper disclosure of accounting changes is necessary. *See also* ERROR CORRECTION.

ACCOUNTING CONTROL procedures used to assure accuracy in the record keeping function. Controls exist to make certain source data placed in the system are proper and correct.

ACCOUNTING CONVENTION methods or procedures employed generally by accounting practitioners. They are based on custom and are subject to change as new developments arise. A new accounting or tax requirement, such as an SEC ACCOUNTING SERIES RELEASE (ASR), may make a convention inappropriate. The accountant in performing the reporting function should follow existing accounting conventions that apply to the given situation. *See also* ACCOUNTING PRINCIPLES.

ACCOUNTING CUSHION overstating an expense provision. This provides a larger balance in the estimated liability or allowance account so as to minimize the amount of an expense provision for a later period. It understates the current period's profit and in effect overstates the earnings in the period when the anticipated event occurs. For example, a company's allowance for bad debts from accounts receivable may substantially increase even though the company's bad debt write-off experience has become much better. In this case, the overstatement of bad debt expense unjustifiably understates the present year's net income. Because less of a bad debt expense provision will be needed next year due to the overstated allowance account, net income will be higher next period. The auditor should upwardly adjust net income for the charges creating the accounting cushion. It should be noted, however, that for tax purposes companies must use the direct write-off method for bad debts. *See also* INCOME SMOOTHING.

ACCOUNTING CYCLE series of steps in recording an accounting event from the time a transaction occurs to its reflection in the financial statements; also called *bookkeeping cycle*. The order of the steps in the accounting cycle are: recording in the journal, posting to the ledger, preparing a trial balance, and preparing the financial statements.

ACCOUNTING ENTITY business or other economic unit (including subdivisions) being accounted for separately. A system of accounts is kept for the entity. An accounting entity is isolated so that recording and reporting for it are possible. Examples of accounting entities are corporations, partnerships, trusts, and industry segments. A distinction should be made between an accounting entity and a legal entity. For example, a proprietor's accounting entity might be the business whereas the legal entity would include personal assets. Also, in the corporate environment, affiliated companies can be differently organized for legal and accounting purposes (e.g., industry segments). *See also* CONSOLIDATED FINANCIAL STATEMENT.

ACCOUNTING EQUATION double entry bookkeeping where there is an identity of debit and credit elements of a transaction. For each transaction, the total debits equal the total credits. For example, the payment of $100 to a creditor requires a debit to accounts payable and a credit to cash for $100. The accounting equation can also be expressed as:

$$\text{Assets} = \text{Liabilities} + \text{Equity}$$

An increase (or decrease) in total assets is accompanied by an equal increase (or decrease) in liabilities and capital.

ACCOUNTING ERROR inaccurate measurement or representation of an accounting-related item not caused by intentional FRAUD. An error may be due to NEGLIGENCE or may result from the misapplication of GENERALLY ACCEPTED ACCOUNTING PRINCIPLES (GAAP). Errors may take the form of dollar discrepancies or may be compliance errors in employing accounting policies and procedures. Errors can be minimized by diligently following accounting procedures and standards, and maintaining proper INTERNAL CONTROL.

ACCOUNTING EVENT transaction entered in the accounting records of a business. It can be an external transaction—that is, one with an outsider, such as recording a sale. It can also refer to an internal transaction such as making an adjusting entry (e.g., expense or revenue accrual).

ACCOUNTING HALL OF FAME organization honoring individuals who have made significant scholarly contributions to accounting since the beginning of the twentieth century. The Hall of Fame was founded at Ohio State University in 1950.

ACCOUNTING HISTORIANS JOURNAL publication of the ACADEMY OF ACCOUNTING HISTORIANS, which first appeared in 1977. All aspects relating to the history of accounting thought are covered in the journal.

ACCOUNTING INFORMATION SYSTEM (AIS) subsystem of a MANAGEMENT INFORMATION SYSTEM (MIS) that processes financial transactions to provide (1) internal reporting to managers for use in planning and controlling current and future operations and for nonroutine decision making; (2) external reporting to outside parties such as to stockholders, creditors, and government agencies.

ACCOUNTING INTERPRETATION prepared by the AMERICAN INSTITUTE OF CERTIFIED PUBLIC ACCOUNTANTS (AICPA) while the ACCOUNTING PRINCIPLES BOARD was in existence (1959 to 1973). Interpretations gave guidance to practitioners about accounting issues. Unlike APB Opinions, Interpretations are *not* requirements subject to the AICPA Code of Professional Ethics.

ACCOUNTING MANUAL handbook containing policy guidelines, procedures, and standards for accounts of a company or an individual. The chart (or classification) of accounts is part of the accounting manual.

ACCOUNTING MEASUREMENT quantification of accounting values in the form of money or other units. Transactions are recorded in the accounts in dollars based on historical cost. Some accounting measurements have to be expressed in volume such as direct labor hours used to apply overhead in a cost accounting system.

ACCOUNTING PERIOD time covered by financial statements, which can be for any length but is usually annual, quarterly, or monthly. The annual financial statements may be on a calendar or fiscal year basis. Quarterly (interim) financial statements are common and required of publicly owned companies.

ACCOUNTING POLICIES reporting methods, measurement systems, and disclosures used by a specific company. The accountant should evaluate the appropriateness of accounting policies employed by management. A description of the company's accounting policies should be presented in a separate section preceding the footnotes to the financial statements or as the first footnote. Disclosure of accounting policies should include ACCOUNTING PRINCIPLES and methods of application that involve: (1) a selection from generally accepted alternatives; (2) those peculiar to the industry or field of endeavor; and (3) unusual or different applications of GENERALLY ACCEPTED ACCOUNTING PRINCIPLES (GAAP). Examples of disclosures are basis of CONSOLIDATION, depreciation methods, and inventory pricing. Disclosure of accounting policies assists financial readers in better interpreting a company's financial statements. Thus it results in fair presentation of the financial statements.

ACCOUNTING POSTULATE basic assumption or fundamental proposition regarding the economic, political, or social environment that accounting operates in. Examples of postulates are accounting entity and continuity. A postulate is pertinent to developing an ACCOUNTING PRINCIPLE. Accounting postulates may relate to the environment of accounting, accounting entity, measurement process, and accounting objectives.

ACCOUNTING PRACTICE manner in which accountants and auditors carry out their daily work. It is the day-to-day implementation of accounting policies. Accounting practice relates to the practical application of accounting to the financial accumulation and reporting needs of clients. Practice may differ from accounting theory.

ACCOUNTING PRINCIPLES rules and guidelines of accounting. They determine such matters as the measurement of assets, the timing of revenue recognition, and the accrual of expenses. The "ground rules" for financial reporting are referred to as GENERALLY ACCEPTED ACCOUNTING PRINCIPLES (GAAP). To be "generally accepted," an accounting principle must have "substantial authoritative support" such as by promulgation of a FINANCIAL ACCOUNTING STANDARDS BOARD (FASB) pronouncement. Accounting principles are based on the important objectives of financial reporting. An example of an accounting principle is accrual.

ACCOUNTING PRINCIPLES BOARD (APB) former authoritative body of the AMERICAN INSTITUTE OF CERTIFIED PUBLIC ACCOUNTANTS (AICPA). It issued pronouncements on accounting principles until 1973. Of the 31 APB opinions, several were instrumental in improving the theory and practice of significant areas of accounting. The APB was replaced by the FINANCIAL ACCOUNTING STANDARDS BOARD (FASB).

ACCOUNTING PROCEDURE method or technique used to uncover, record, or summarize financial data in the preparation of financial statements.

ACCOUNTING RATE OF RETURN *see* SIMPLE RATE OF RETURN.

ACCOUNTING RECORDS the category of audit evidence that consists of the records of initial accounting entries and supporting records. Accounting records include checks, records of electronic fund transfers, sales and purchase invoices, contracts, the general ledger, subsidiary ledgers, journal entries, worksheets and spreadsheets, computations, and reconciliations.

ACCOUNTING RESEARCH BULLETINS (ARB) publications containing recommended accounting procedures. While the Bulletins were not binding on American Institute of CPAs members, the SECURITIES AND EXCHANGE COMMISSION (SEC) typically required their use by corporations under their jurisdiction. The Bulletins were issued by the COMMITTEE ON ACCOUNTING PROCEDURE of the AICPA. The Committee was replaced by the ACCOUNTING PRINCIPLES BOARD (APB) in 1959.

ACCOUNTING REVIEW, THE publication of the AMERICAN ACCOUNTING ASSOCIATION (AAA) covering all aspects of accounting of a scholarly nature. Many articles deal with hypothesis testing and empirical work. It is published four times a year.

ACCOUNTING RISK *see* TRANSLATION RISK.

ACCOUNTING SERIES RELEASES (ASRS) issued by the SECURITIES AND EXCHANGE COMMISSION (SEC) as official accounting pronouncements.

Releases include accounting requirements, disclosure mandates, auditing policies, and Commission activities regarding CPA firms filing financial statements with the SEC for publicly traded companies. The Accounting Series Releases are now codified as Financial Reporting Releases (FRRs).

ACCOUNTING SOFTWARE programs used to maintain books of account on computers. The software can be used to record transactions, maintain account balances, and prepare financial statements and reports. Many different accounting software packages exist, and the right package must be selected given the client's circumstances and needs. An accounting software package typically contains numerous integrated modules (for example, spreadsheet and word processing abilities). Some modules are used to account for the general ledger, accounts receivable, accounts payable, payroll, inventory, and fixed assets. Reviews of accounting software packages can be found in the *JOURNAL OF ACCOUNTANCY*, *PC Magazine*, and *Computers in Accounting*, among other journals.

ACCOUNTING STANDARD conduct to be followed by accountants as formulated by an authoritative body (e.g., AMERICAN INSTITUTE OF CERTIFIED PUBLIC ACCOUNTANTS (AICPA)) or law. *See also* ACCOUNTING PRINCIPLES.

ACCOUNTING STANDARDS COMMITTEE committee with members from six accounting bodies in the United Kingdom and Ireland who draft and approve Statements of Standard Accounting Practice.

ACCOUNTING STANDARDS EXECUTIVE COMMITTEE (AccSEC) committee whose members prepare Statements of Position on accounting issues not acted upon by the FASB. Since 1978, its promulgation functions have been integrated with those of the FASB.

ACCOUNTING SYSTEM methods, procedures, and standards followed in accumulating, classifying, recording, and reporting business events and transactions. The accounting system includes the formal records and original source data. Regulatory requirements may exist on how a particular accounting system is to be maintained (e.g., insurance company).

ACCOUNTING TRENDS AND TECHNIQUES annual publication of the AMERICAN INSTITUTE OF CERTIFIED PUBLIC ACCOUNTANTS (AICPA) containing a survey of the accounting and disclosure characteristics of corporate annual reports. It gives examples representative of financial reporting by 600 sampled companies (e.g., their treatment of leases and business combinations). Financial statistics are also given.

ACCOUNTING VALUATION valuation of assets in accounting. Correct valuation is important. If, for example, an asset is valued incorrectly, it is impossible to draw accurate conclusions about a firm's liquidity or its value in liquidation. Valuation is usually made in accordance with GENERALLY ACCEPTED ACCOUNTING PRINCIPLES (GAAP).

ACCOUNTS PAYABLE obligations to pay for goods or services that have been acquired on open account from suppliers. Accounts payable is a current liability in the balance sheet.

ACCOUNTS RECEIVABLE amounts due the company on account from customers who have bought merchandise or received services. Accounts receivable are presented as a current asset in the balance sheet. *See also* ACCOUNTS RECEIVABLE TURNOVER; AGING OF ACCOUNTS.

ACCOUNTS RECEIVABLE DISCOUNTED obligation assigned or sold with recourse. *See also* ASSIGNMENT OF ACCOUNTS RECEIVABLE; FACTORING.

ACCOUNTS RECEIVABLE TURNOVER degree of realization risk in accounts receivable. The lower the turnover rate, the longer receivables are being held—and the less likely they are to be collected. Also, there is an OPPORTUNITY COST of tying up funds in receivables for a longer period of time. The accounts receivable turnover equals:

$$\frac{\text{Annual Credit Sales}}{\text{Average Accounts Receivable}}$$

Assume annual credit sales are $100,000, beginning-of-year accounts receivable are $30,000, and end-of-year accounts receivable are $20,000. The turnover is:

$$\frac{\$100,000}{\left(\dfrac{\$30,000 + \$20,000}{2}\right)} = \frac{\$100,000}{\$25,000} = 4 \text{ times}$$

If sales vary greatly during the year, this ratio can become distorted unless proper averaging takes place. In such a case, quarterly or monthly sales figures should be used.

ACCRETION
1. growth in assets through mergers, acquisitions, and internal expansion. Examples are timber, livestock, nursery stock, and aging of wine.
2. adjustment of the difference between the face value of a bond and the price of the bond bought at an original discount.

ACCRUAL ACCOUNTING recognition of revenue when earned and expenses when incurred. They are recorded at the end of an accounting period even though cash has not been received or paid. The alternative is CASH BASIS ACCOUNTING. An example of accrued revenue is dividend income earned on stock owned even though it has not yet been received. Accrued salary expense due employees at period-end is an example of an accrued expense.

ACCRUED ASSETS *see* ACCRUED REVENUE.

ACCRUED EXPENSES incurred at the end of the reporting period but not yet paid; also called *accrued liabilities*. The accrued liability is shown under current liabilities in the balance sheet. For example, assume the last payroll date was January 28. The next payroll date is February 11. For the last few days of the month (January 29–January 31) the company owes its employees $500 in salaries. The appropriate journal entry on January 31 is to debit salaries expense and credit salaries payable for $500.

ACCRUED LIABILITIES *see* ACCRUED EXPENSES.

ACCRUED REVENUE money that has been earned but not received as of the end of the reporting period; also called *accrued assets*. To accrue means to accumulate. The accrued asset is shown under current assets in the balance sheet. For example, assume a landlord has not received January rent of $500 from a tenant. The adjusting entry at the end of January is to debit rent receivable and credit rental revenue for $500.

ACCUMULATED BENEFIT OBLIGATION (ABO) actuarial present value of benefits. Whether vested or nonvested, they are attributed by the pension benefit formula to employee services rendered before a specified date and based on employee service and compensation up to that date using *existing* salary levels. *See also* MINIMUM PENSION LIABILITY; PENSION PLAN; PROJECTED BENEFIT OBLIGATION (PBO); VESTED BENEFIT OBLIGATION (VBO).

ACCUMULATED DEPRECIATION sum of depreciation charges taken to date on a fixed asset. Accumulated depreciation is a CONTRA ACCOUNT to the fixed asset to arrive at BOOK VALUE. For example, on 1/1/2014 an auto is bought costing $10,000, with a salvage value of $1000 and a life of 10 years. Using STRAIGHT-LINE DEPRECIATION the accumulated depreciation on 12/31/2017 would be $3600 ($900 × 4).

ACCUMULATED EARNINGS TAX penalty tax levied upon the unreasonable accumulation of corporate earnings and profits. The intent is to tax earnings retained to avoid personal income tax on dividends.

ACCUMULATED INCOME
1. cumulative profit that has been retained and not distributed in the form of dividends.
2. income amount used as the base for the computation of the accumulated earnings tax. *See also* ACCUMULATED EARNINGS TAX.

ACCUMULATION
1. cumulative retained profit.
2. investment of a fixed dollar amount regularly and reinvestment of dividends and capital gains.
3. process of compounding.
4. periodic addition of interests to the principal amount.

ACCURACY correctness of an accounting item (e.g., account balance, invoice, financial statement); also called *accurate presentation*. The concept refers to an accounting objective that the item fully reflects and valuates the set of facts involved, including all economic implications of the underlying transactions and events.

ACCURACY-RELATED PENALTY a civil penalty imposed on the amount of underpayment (understatement) of tax. The penalty, which is equal to 20% of the underpayment, may be based on negligence or nonfraudulent lack of compliance with laws and regulations.

ACID TEST RATIO stringent test of LIQUIDITY; also called *quick ratio*. The ratio is found by dividing the most liquid current assets (cash, marketable securities, and accounts receivable) by current liabilities. (Notice that some current assets are not in the numerator: Inventory is not included because it usually takes a long time to convert into cash; prepaid expenses are left out because they cannot be turned into cash and thus are incapable of covering current liabilities.) In general, the ratio should at least be equal to 1. In other words, for every $1 in current debt there should be $1 in quick assets. Assume cash is $100, marketable securities are $400, accounts receivable are $800, inventory is $3,000, and current liabilities are $1,000. The acid test ratio equals:

$$\frac{\text{Quick Assets}}{\text{Current Liabilities}} = \frac{\$1,300}{\$1,000} = 1.3$$

The acid test ratio for the current year should be compared to prior years to evaluate the trend. It should also be compared to the acid test ratio of a competing company to get a relative comparison.

ACQUISITION COST price paid to buy goods, services, or assets. It equals the list price plus normal incidental costs to acquire the item including preparation, transportation, and installation.

ACQUISITION CYCLE the flow of transactions and related internal controls concerning the purchase of goods and services. Steps in the acquisition cycle are authorization, placing orders (including the preparation of purchase orders), receipt of goods (including preparation of receiving reports), inspection of goods, authorizing payments (including preparation of vouchers), as well as making and recording related cash disbursements.

ACQUISITION METHOD the method of accounting that must be used to record the acquisition of one entity by another. Under this method, the acquiring entity records all acquired assets, liabilities, and any noncontrolling interest at fair value.

ACTIVE PARTICIPATION a taxpayer is required to actively participate in an activity in order to qualify for the offset of rental real estate losses against nonpassive income. The maximum offset is $25,000 ($12,500 in cases of married couples filing separately), but is reduced by 50% of the amount of adjusted gross income in excess of $100,000 ($50,000 in cases of married couples filing separately). Active participation involves making significant and bona fide management decisions such as approving new tenants, repairs, capital improvements, and lease terms.

ACTIVITY in PROGRAM EVALUATION AND REVIEW TECHNIQUE (PERT), the action that consumes time or resources. Activities are represented by arrows in a PERT network.

ACTIVITY ACCOUNT name for a specific and distinguishable line of work performed by one or more organizational components of a governmental unit. For example, sewage treatment and disposal, garbage collection, and street cleaning are activities performed in carrying out the function of sanitation; and the segregation of the expenditures made for each of these activities constitutes an activity account.

ACTIVITY ACCOUNTING *see* RESPONSIBILITY ACCOUNTING.

ACTIVITY ANALYSIS evaluation involving the determination of the combination of production processes that maximizes output (or profits), subject to the restrictions on the required resources (inputs).

ACTIVITY ATTRIBUTES characteristics of activities. Attributes can be organized, sorted, or summarized according to the attribute categories. For example, a measure of the elapsed time required to complete an activity is an attribute. *See also* COST DRIVER; PERFORMANCE MEASUREMENT.

ACTIVITY BASE applicable to the production activity used to relate factory overhead to production (e.g., units produced, direct labor hours, direct labor cost, machine hours).

ACTIVITY-BASED BUDGETING (ABB) approach to budgeting that involves quantitative expression of the activities/business processes of the organization reflecting forecasts of workload (quantity of drivers) and other financial requirements to achieve strategic goals or planned changes to improve performance. Activity-based budgeting provides greater detail, especially regarding overhead, because it permits the identification of value-adding activities and their drivers. After operations, it is useful for comparing actual costing rates and driver usage with the amounts budgeted.

ACTIVITY-BASED COSTING (ABC) costing system that identifies the various activities performed in a firm and uses multiple cost drivers (volume and nonvolume based cost drivers) to assign overhead costs (or indirect costs) to products. ABC recognizes the causal relationship of cost drivers with activities.

ACTIVITY-BASED MANAGEMENT (ABM) approach to the management of activities within business processes as the route to continuously improve both the value received by customers and the profit earned by providing this value. Causes of activities are identified, measured, and used along with other activity information for performance evaluation; emphasis is on the reduction or elimination of nonvalue-adding activities. ABM draws on ABC data as a major source for information.

ACTIVITY-BASED SYSTEM information system that provides quantitative information about activities in an organization.

ACTIVITY CAPACITY demonstrated or expected capacity of an activity under normal operating conditions, assuming a specified set of resources and a long time period. An example is the rate of output for an activity expressed as 500 cycles per hour.

ACTIVITY CENTER pool of costs of two or more activities.

ACTIVITY COST ASSIGNMENT process in which the costs of activities are attached to cost objects using activity drivers. *See also* COST OBJECT; ACTIVITY COST DRIVER.

ACTIVITY COST DRIVER best single measure of the frequency and intensity of the demands placed on activities by intermediate and final cost objectives. It is used to reassign activity costs to cost objects. It represents a line item on the bill of activities for a product or customer. An example is the number of part numbers, which is used to measure the consumption of material-related activities by each product, material type, or component. The number of customer orders measures the consumption of order-entry activities by each customer. Sometimes an activity driver is used as an indicator of the output of an activity, such as the number of purchase orders prepared by the purchasing activity. *See also* INTENSITY; COST OBJECT; BILL OF ACTIVITIES.

ACTIVITY COST POOL grouping of all cost elements associated with an activity. *See also* COST ELEMENT.

ACTIVITY DICTIONARY listing and description of generic activities. It can include activity, activity description, business process, function source, whether value-added, inputs, outputs, supplier, customer, output measures, and cost drivers.

ACTIVITY DRIVER ANALYSIS identification and evaluation of the activity drivers used to trace the cost of activities to cost objects. Activity driver analysis may involve selecting activity drivers with a potential for cost reduction. *See also* PARETO ANALYSIS.

ACTIVITY LEVEL description of how an activity is used by a cost object or other activity. Some activity levels describe the cost object that uses the activity and the nature of this use. These levels include activities that are traceable to the product (i.e., unit-level, batch-level, and product-level costs), to the customer (customer-level costs), to a market (market-level costs), to a distribution channel (channel-level costs), and to a project, such as a research and development project (project-level costs).

ACTIVITY SEQUENCE-SENSITIVE calculation of time-based process costs taking into consideration the sequential relationships among activities.

ACTUAL COST expenditure required to buy or produce an item. The actual cost of a purchased item includes the list price (net of discounts) plus delivery and storage. The actual cost to manufacture a product is the total of direct material, direct labor, and factory overhead.

ACTUARIAL relating to analyses involving compound interest and/or statistics. It is usually associated with computations involved in insurance probability estimates. *See also* ACTUARY.

ACTUARIAL BASIS OF ACCOUNTING used in computing the amount of contributions to be made periodically to a pension fund. Total contributions plus the accumulated earnings on it must equal the required payments to be made out of the fund. Factors that must be considered are the length of time over which each contribution is to be held and the return on investment. A "Trust Fund" for a public employee retirement system is an example of a fund set up on an actuarial basis.

ACTUARIAL COST METHOD technique used by actuaries to determine the periodic employer contribution to the pension plan; also called *actuarial funding method*. It is used to measure pension expense and related funding. Two general approaches are usually considered when selecting an actuarial funding method, the *cost* approach and *benefit* approach. The cost approach projects an estimated total retirement benefit and then determines the level cost that will be adequate (including expected interest) to furnish total benefits at retirement. The benefit approach determines the amount of pension benefits attributable to service to date and then determines the present value of these benefits. *See also* ACTUARIAL GAINS, LOSSES.

ACTUARIAL FUNDING METHOD *see* ACTUARIAL COST METHOD.

ACTUARIAL GAINS, LOSSES difference between estimates and actual experience in a pension plan. For example, if the actual interest rate earned on pension assets exceeds the estimated rate, an actuarial gain results. Actuarial gains and losses are deferred and amortized to pension expense of future periods. The amortization of the actuarial gain will *reduce* pension expense. Actuarial gains and losses applicable to a single event not related to the pension plan and not in the ordinary course of business are recognized immediately in earnings. Examples are plant closing and segment disposal. *See also* ACTUARIAL COST METHOD.

ACTUARY practitioner involved in mathematical computations and analyses of insurance probability estimates.

ADDITIONAL PAID-IN CAPITAL excess received from stockholders over PAR VALUE or STATED VALUE of the stock issued; also called *contributed capital in excess of par*. For example, if 1000 shares of $10 par value common stock is issued at a price of $12 per share, the additional paid-in capital is $2000 (1000 shares × $2). Additional paid-in capital is shown in the STOCKHOLDERS' EQUITY section of the balance sheet.

ADEQUATE DISCLOSURE comprehensive and clear disclosure in the body of financial statements, FOOTNOTES, or supplemental schedules so that readers of a company's financial position and operating results can make proper investment and credit decisions.

AD HOC DSS is designed to handle a one-time or infrequently occurring problem. The purpose of a decision support system (DSS) is to assist decision makers in the various phases of unstructured or semi-structured business problem-solving.

ADJUNCT ACCOUNT one that accumulates either additions or subtractions to another account. Thus the original account may retain its identity. Examples include premiums on bonds payable, which is a contra account to bonds payable; and accumulated depreciation, which is an offset to the fixed asset.

ADJUSTABLE RATE LOAN *see* VARIABLE RATE LOAN.

ADJUSTED BASIS value used as a starting point to compute depreciation or gain on the disposition of fixed assets for tax purposes. The adjusted basis is similar to the concept of BOOK VALUE. It is the taxpayer's basis at the time of acquisition—usually cost—increased or decreased by certain required modifications such as capital improvements.

ADJUSTED GROSS INCOME (AGI) federal tax term applying to the difference between the gross income of the taxpayer and adjustments to income. Adjustments to income include deductions for IRA and Keogh pension plans. Adjusted gross income is the basis for determining the eligibility and limitations of other components in calculating the taxpayer's tax, such as for medical expenses (generally 10% of AGI) and miscellaneous expenses (2% of AGI).

ADJUSTING JOURNAL ENTRY
1. necessary entry at the end of the reporting period to record unrecognized revenue and expenses applicable to that period. It is required when a transaction is begun in one accounting period and concluded in a later one. An adjusting entry always involves an income statement account (revenue or expense) and a balance sheet account (asset or liability). The four basic types of adjusting entries relate to ACCRUED EXPENSES, ACCRUED REVENUE, PREPAID EXPENSES, and UNEARNED REVENUE.

2. correcting entry required at the end of the accounting period due to a mistake made in the accounting records; also called *correcting entry*. For example, if during the same year land was charged instead of travel expense, the correcting entry is to debit travel expense and credit land.

ADJUSTMENT
1. increase or decrease to an account resulting from an ADJUSTING JOURNAL ENTRY. For example, the accrual of wages at year-end will cause an increase in both salary expense and salary payable.
2. changing an account balance because of some happening or event. For example, a customer who returns merchandise will receive a credit adjustment to the account.

ADMINISTERED PRICE one determined by the pricing policy of a seller rather than by competitive forces of market supply and demand. It assumes the selling firm has sufficient control over the market of the item.

ADMINISTRATIVE ACCOUNTING
1. accounting that focuses upon management planning and control through a formal system of accumulating and reporting data to achieve administrative or management objectives.
2. accounting that involves internal decision-making with respect to prorations, valuations, and reporting. Controllership and internal auditor functions relate to administrative accounting.

ADMINISTRATIVE BUDGET formal and comprehensive financial plan through which management may control day-to-day business affairs and activities.

ADOBE SYSTEMS a computer software company headquartered in San Jose, California. Adobe is known for products such as Photoshop and Acrobat. Adobe also introduced the Portable Document Format (PDF), a technology that has been adopted worldwide for electronic documents.

AD VALOREM TAX levy imposed on the value of property. The most common ad valorem tax is that imposed by states, counties, and cities on real estate. Ad valorem taxes can, however, be imposed on personal property.

ADVANCE
1. prepayment received for goods or services to be rendered. Some contracts require an advance before completion (e.g., construction project). When the business receives an advance payment, it records it as a liability. For example, a utility receiving a deposit from a customer will record it as a liability. Assume a lawyer receives a retainer of $50,000 on 1/1/2014 for future services to be rendered for a four-year period. Thus, each year $12,500 will be recognized as revenue. The journal entries for 2014 follow:

```
1/1/2014
   Cash                      50,000
      Deferred revenue                  50,000

12/31/2014
   Deferred revenue          12,500
      Revenue                            12,500
```

See also DEFERRED CREDIT.

2. money given to an employee before it is earned (e.g., advance against salary). The advance appears on the company's books as a receivable from employee.

ADVANCED MANUFACTURING ENVIRONMENT an environment featured by intensive global competition, high-tech technology, TOTAL QUALITY MANAGEMENT (TQM), and continuous improvement.

ADVERSE OPINION 1. term used when an auditor reports that the company's financial statements do *not* present fairly the financial position, results of operations, or changes in financial position or are not in conformity with GAAP. The auditor must provide the reasons for the adverse opinion in the AUDIT REPORT. An adverse opinion is rare and usually results when the CPA has been unable to convince the client to amend the financial statements so that they reflect the auditor's estimate about the outcome of future events or so that they otherwise adhere to GAAP. **2.** under the Sarbanes-Oxley Act, an opinion that internal control over financial reporting is not effective, because of one or more material weaknesses. When one or more material weaknesses exist as of the assessment date, the auditor must express an adverse opinion on the effectiveness of the company's internal control over financial reporting. Auditing Standard No. 5 indicates that when expressing an adverse opinion on the effectiveness of internal control over financial reporting, the auditor should provide specific information about the nature of the material weakness and its actual and potential effect on the company's financial statements. The PCAOB has also stated that it expects disclosure sufficient to allow users to understand the weakness and its actual and potential implications on the financial statements.

ADVERTISING COSTS costs wherein advertising is expensed as incurred or when the advertising program first takes place. However, the cost of direct response advertising may be deferred if the prime objective of the promotion is to elicit sales to customers who respond specifically to the advertising and for which there is future benefit. The deferred advertising is amortized over the expected benefit period using the revenue method (current year revenue to total revenue). The cost of a billboard should also be deferred and amortized.

ADWARE programs installed on a user's computer without the user's permission. Adware differs from spyware in that most adware does not perform malicious acts or steal data. It does, however, watch user activity and produce pop-up ads.

AFFILIATED COMPANY entity holding less than a majority of the voting common stock of another related company, or in which both companies are subsidiaries of a third company. Often the same management oversees and operates both companies. Interrelationships exist between the activities of the entities.

AGENCY relationship between two individuals where one is a principal and the other is an agent representing the principal in transactions with other parties. For example, a trust officer in a bank can engage in activities on behalf of clients.

AGENCY COSTS reduction in the value of the organization when an agent (a subunit manager) pursues his interest to the detriment of the principal's (the organization's) interest.

AGENCY FUND assets held in a fund under an AGENCY relationship for another entity. In governmental accounting, the agency fund consists of resources retained by the governmental unit as an agent for another governmental unit. It is a FIDUCIARY relationship. An example: taxes retained by a municipality for a school district.

AGING OF ACCOUNTS classifying accounts by the time elapsed after the date of billing or the due date. The longer a customer's account remains uncollected or the longer inventory is held, the greater is its realization risk. If a customer's account is past due, the company also has an OPPORTUNITY COST of funds tied-up in the receivable that could be invested elsewhere for a return. An aging schedule of accounts receivable may break down receivables from 1–30 days, 31–60 days, 61–90 days, and over 90 days. With regard to inventory, if it is held too long, obsolescence, spoilage, and technological problems may result. Aging can be done for other accounts such as fixed assets and accounts payable. *See also* COLLECTION PERIOD; DAYS TO SELL INVENTORY.

AGREED-UPON PROCEDURES applies to engagements relating to agreed-upon procedures to specified elements or accounts. Agreed-upon procedures is when the accountant is hired to issue a report of findings based on specified financial statement items. The users of the report agree upon the procedures to be conducted by the accountant that the user believes are suitable. The user takes responsibility for the adequacy of the procedures. In this engagement, the accountant does not express an opinion or negative assurance. Instead, the report should be in the form of procedures and findings. A representation letter is prepared that depends on the nature of the engagement and the specified users.

AIS *see* ACCOUNTING INFORMATION SYSTEM (AIS).

ALGEBRAIC METHOD one of the methods used to solve linear programming problems, a trial-and-error technique. Pairs of constraints are solved algebraically to find their intersection. The values of the decision variables are then substituted into the objective function and compared to find the best combination. The basic rule is that the optimal solution will be at the intersection of two or more constraint equations. Thus, all intersections can be computed and each solution evaluated in the objective function to determine which solution is optimal.

ALIMONY PAYMENT term used in a divorce for payment from one spouse to another. For tax purposes, the party making the payments treats them as a deduction in arriving at ADJUSTED GROSS INCOME (AGI). Frontloading of payments (significantly higher payments in the earlier years) is not permitted. The recipient of the alimony payments treats them as income for tax reporting.

ALL INCLUSIVE INCOME CONCEPT change in equity for an accounting period from business transactions related to nonowner sources; also called *comprehensive income*. It excludes capital transactions and dividends. The income statement includes all items of profit and loss occurring during the period plus EXTRAORDINARY ITEMS. Inclusion of all items affecting earnings makes the profit and loss statement more informative and less subject to judgment. As per Financial Accounting Concept No. 5, comprehensive income items excluded from earnings include: (1) cumulative effect of a change in accounting principle; (2) foreign currency translation adjustments; and (3) unrealized losses on the write-down of a long-term investment portfolio from cost to market value.

ALLOCATE
1. spread a cost over two or more accounting periods usually based on time. An example is assigning the prepaid cost of a three-year insurance policy by one-third each year.
2. charge a cost or revenue to a number of departments, products, processes, or activities on some rational basis. For example, a cost may be assigned to divisions of a company based on sales.
3. distribute the cost associated with the acquisition of two or more items based on their relative fair market values. This relates to a LUMP-SUM PURCHASE.

ALLOCATED COMMON COSTS *see* CENTRAL ADMINISTRATION COSTS.

ALLOCATION process of partitioning a VALUATION ACCOUNT and assigning the resulting subsets to periods of time. Allocation includes the assignment of assets to expense as well as the assignment of liabilities to revenue over a time frame. Examples of the former are the depreciation of a fixed asset or the amortization of an intangible asset over the period benefitted. An example of the latter is reflecting unearned fee revenue (deferred revenue) into revenue over the period the services are performed. Allocations result from applying rules for the assignment of costs to products or period expenses and the assignment of the value of the product to specific periods as revenue.

ALLOTMENT part of an appropriation that may be encumbered or expended during an allotment period, which is usually less than one fiscal year. Bimonthly and quarterly allotment periods are most common.

ALLOWANCE
1. acceptable reduction in quantity or quality such as normal spoilage in a manufacturing operation.
2. reduction in the amount owed a supplier because of damaged goods received or delays encountered.
3. valuation account reducing the cost of an asset such as the allowance to reduce marketable securities from cost to market value.

ALLOWANCE FOR BAD DEBTS provision for possible uncollectibility associated with accounts receivable. In the balance sheet, accounts receivable, representing gross receivables, is reduced by the allowance account to obtain *net* receivables—the amount expected to be collected (realizable value). For example, if gross receivables are $100,000 and the allowance account balance is $5000, the current asset section of the balance sheet shows:

Accounts receivable	$100,000
Less: Allowance for bad debts	5,000
Net receivable	$ 95,000

The two ways of accounting for uncollectible accounts are the ALLOWANCE METHOD and the DIRECT WRITE-OFF METHOD.

ALLOWANCE FOR SAMPLING RISK (ASR) also known as *precision*, ASR is typically a concern in attribute sampling. ASR is the difference between the upper occurrence rate (i.e., projected population deviation rate) and the sample deviation rate.

ALLOWANCE METHOD accepted way to account for bad debts. Bad debt expense may be based on the percent of credit sales for the period, an aging of the accounts receivable balance at the end of the period, or some other method (e.g., percent of accounts receivable). The allowance method results in a good matching of bad debt expense against sales. The journal entry at year-end to record *anticipated* uncollectibility of accounts receivable is to debit bad debts and credit allowance for bad debts. When it is known that a customer will *actually* not pay the balance, because of bankruptcy, for example, the entry is to debit allowance for bad debts and credit accounts receivable. If for whatever reason the customer does pay at a later date, there is a recovery; reverse the last entry and make a second entry debiting cash and crediting accounts receivable. It should be noted that firms other than small financial institutions are required to use the DIRECT WRITE-OFF METHOD for tax purposes.

ALL-PURPOSE FINANCIAL STATEMENT one that satisfies the needs of all financial statement users. The financial statements included in the ANNUAL REPORT and in SEC Form 10-K are intended for diverse parties such as stockholders, potential investors, creditors, employees, and suppliers.

ALPHA RISK *see* TYPE I ERROR.

ALTERNATIVE COST
1. cost that would pertain if an alternative set of conditions or assumptions were to prevail (as compared to a cost assumed or experienced under current conditions).
2. choosing the next best or highest valued alternative, compared to the chosen alternative, will result in benefits forfeited, and thus an alternative cost. *See also* OPPORTUNITY COST.

ALTERNATIVE MINIMUM TAX (AMT) levy designed with the intent that everyone should pay a fair share of tax. The AMT is imposed on regular taxable income, adjusted for tax preference items, in excess of a statutory exemption. The AMT exemption is periodically adjusted for inflation. The AMT is applicable to individuals and corporations.

AMERICAN ACCOUNTING ASSOCIATION (AAA) organization primarily of accounting academicians emphasizing the development of a theoretical foundation for accounting. Its research with respect to education and theory is distributed through committee reports and a quarterly journal, THE ACCOUNTING REVIEW.

AMERICAN INSTITUTE OF CERTIFIED PUBLIC ACCOUNTANTS (AICPA) (www.aicpa.org) professional organization of practicing Certified Public Accountants. The "Institute" develops standards of practice for its members and provides technical guidance and advice to both governmental agencies (e.g., SEC) and AICPA membership. The AICPA publishes the

JOURNAL OF ACCOUNTANCY and *THE TAX ADVISER*. The AICPA puts out many publications in the areas of accounting, audit, tax, and management services. For example, the STATEMENTS ON AUDITING STANDARDS (SAS) are promulgated by the AICPA.

AMERICAN OPPORTUNITY CREDIT formerly known as the Hope Scholarship Credit, this may be claimed by individuals and is based on qualified college education expenses (i.e., tuition and fees). The credit is phased out ratably based on the taxpayer's modified adjusted gross income. The amount of qualified expenses and phase-out ranges are indexed annually based on inflation. The credit is applicable to the first four years of undergraduate education and is limited to $2,500 per eligible student.

AMERICAN WOMEN'S SOCIETY OF CERTIFIED PUBLIC ACCOUNTANTS (AWSCPA) professional organization of CPAs, consisting mostly of women, that aids women in their advancement within the accounting profession. Women are encouraged to take part in technical programs involving accounting, auditing, and tax. This organization in a joint effort with the AMERICAN SOCIETY OF WOMEN ACCOUNTANTS publishes *The Woman CPA*, a professional journal.

AMERICANS WITH DISABILITIES ACT (ADA) enacted in 1990 and later amended, the ADA is a group of laws prohibiting discrimination based on disability. The ADA includes provisions relating to employment, access to public entities and transportation, public accommodations, and telecommunications.

AMORTIZATION gradual reduction of an amount over time. Examples are amortized expenses on limited life intangible assets and deferred charges. Assets with limited life have to be written down over the period benefitted. The amortization entry is to debit amortization expense and credit the intangible asset. However, unlimited life intangibles are subject to an annual impairment test. *See also* ALLOCATION; DEPRECIATION.

AMORTIZE to write off a regular portion of an asset's cost over a fixed period of time. Examples are amortization expense on a limited life intangible asset and depletion expense on a natural resource. *See also* SALES RETURN.

AMOUNT OF $1 decimal ratio of the future value of an accumulation at compound interest to each dollar of the original sum. The FUTURE VALUE (compound amount) and PRESENT VALUE tables are available for the amount of $1. Also available are the future value and present value tables for an annuity of $1.

AMOUNT REALIZED tax term applied to money obtained or the fair market value of property or services *received* upon sale or exchange of property. The initial step in computing the realized gain or loss on a sale is to figure out the amount realized.

ANALYSIS OF VARIANCES seeking causes for variances between standard costs and actual costs; also called *variance analysis*. A VARIANCE is considered favorable if actual costs are less than standard costs; it is unfavorable if actual costs exceed standard costs. Unfavorable variances need further investigation. Analysis of variances reveals the causes of these deviations. This feedback aids in planning future goals, controlling costs, evaluating performance, and taking corrective action. MANAGEMENT BY EXCEPTION is based on the analysis of variances, and attention is given to only the variances that require remedial actions.

ANALYTICAL PROCEDURES auditing process that tests relationships among accounts and identifies material changes. It involves analyzing significant ratios and trends for unusual change and questionable items. Included in the analytical review process are: (1) reading important documents and analyzing their accounting and financial effects; (2) reviewing the activity in an account between interim and year-end, especially noting entries out of the ordinary; (3) comparing current period account balances to prior periods as well as to budgeted amounts, noting reasonableness of account balances by evaluating logical relationships among them (i.e., relating payables to expenses, accounts receivable to sales). In essence, therefore, analytical procedures involves reading the FINANCIAL STATEMENTS, scanning the figures, making comparisons to prior periods, appraising logical relationships among accounts, tracing financial statement items to the financial statements, and analyzing the overall process. The degree of analytical procedures required depends on the MATERIALITY of the item, available supporting data, and the quality of the internal control system. Analytical procedures assist in assuring the accuracy and reliability of the accounts.

ANALYTICAL TEST procedure evaluating data relationships to derive substantive audit evidence. It identifies areas requiring additional audit attention. For example, auditors would compare actual financial statement figures against their professional expectations and the firm's experience. Discrepancies are noted and investigated. A comparison may also be made between figures of competing firms and industry norms. Further, financial information can be compared to nonfinancial information, where appropriate. An example is the relationship between sales and number of employees. Analytical tests can be conducted in measures other than dollars, if desired, such as in physical quantities and ratio percentages. If the tests uncover illogical relationships, the CPA will perform more detailed audit testing. *See also* SUBSTANTIVE PROCEDURES.

ANALYZE to evaluate the condition of an accounting-related item and possible reasons for discrepancies. For example, an auditor will analyze the makeup of an expense account to determine whether it is properly stated; has it been charged for proper items that are verified by source documents? Another example: appraising the financial health of a company by analyzing its financial statements as a basis for making investment or credit decisions. *See also* EVIDENCE; EXAMINATION; VERIFICATION.

ANDROID OPERATING SYSTEM an open-source Linux-based operating system, primarily for smartphones and tablets, from Google Inc. Since it is "open source," a large number of companies and developers are making upgrades to the system. While this openness allows for innovation from many different sources, at times, this also creates compatibility problems for app developers.

ANNUAL BUDGET one prepared for a calendar or fiscal year. *See also* LONG-RANGE BUDGET.

ANNUALIZE to extend an item to an annual basis. It is a procedure specified by the INTERNAL REVENUE CODE whereby taxable income for part of a
year is multiplied by 12 and divided by the number of months involved. For
example, if taxable income for 3 months is $20,000, it will be annualized as
follows:

$$\$20,000 \times \frac{12}{3} = \$80,000$$

Annualizing is common in financial forecasting.

ANNUAL REPORT evaluation prepared by companies at the end of the
reporting year which might be either on a calendar or fiscal basis. Contained
in the annual report are the company's FINANCIAL STATEMENTS including
FOOTNOTES, supplementary schedules, MANAGEMENT'S DISCUSSION AND
ANALYSIS OF EARNINGS, president's letter, AUDIT REPORT, and other explanatory data (e.g., research and marketing efforts) helpful in evaluating the
entity's financial position and operating performance. The annual report is
read by stockholders, potential investors, creditors, employees, regulatory
bodies, and other interested financial statement users. *See also* COMPREHEN-
SIVE ANNUAL FINANCIAL REPORT (CAFR); 10-K.

ANNUITY series of equal periodic payments or receipts. Examples of an
annuity are semiannual interest receipts from a bond investment and cash
dividends from a preferred stock. There are two types of an annuity: (1)
Ordinary annuity, where payments or receipts occur at the end of the period;
(2) *Annuity due,* where payments or receipts are made at the beginning of the
period.

ANNUITY DUE *see* ANNUITY.

ANNUITY IN ARREARS *see* ANNUITY.

ANNUITY METHOD OF DEPRECIATION focusing upon cost recovery
and a constant rate of return on the investment in depreciable assets; also
called *compound interest method of depreciation.* This method entails first
obtaining the INTERNAL RATE OF RETURN (IRR) on the cash inflow and outflow of the asset. Then the asset's beginning book value is multiplied by
the IRR and this amount is subtracted from the cash flow for the period to
determine the periodic depreciation charge. If cash flow is constant over the
determined life of the asset, it is then called the annuity method. This method
is not used in practice and not recommended by GENERALLY ACCEPTED
ACCOUNTING PRINCIPLES (GAAP).

ANTEDATE assignment of a date that precedes the date on which a particular
contract or instrument was actually written or executed. For example, ante-
dated insurance coverage would be effective before the date the policy is
issued.

ANTIDILUTIVE practice of excluding a convertible security in the EARNINGS
PER SHARE (EPS) computation when the effect would be to *increase* EPS. This is
based on the CONSERVATISM principle. In the EPS, numerator interest expense
(net of tax) is added back to net income. The denominator is increased by the
number of shares the convertible bond would be converted into. If the impact of
including the convertible bond increased EPS, an antidilutive effect would exist.

ANTITRUST LAWS federal laws designed to improve market efficiency, encourage competition, and curtail unfair trade practices. This is accomplished by reducing barriers to entry, breaking up monopolies, and preventing conspiracies to restrict production or raise prices. There are three major antitrust laws: the SHERMAN ANTITRUST ACT of 1890, CLAYTON ANTITRUST ACT of 1914, and Federal Trade Commission Act of 1914.

ANTIVIRUS PROGRAM designed to protect against and destroy computer viruses. A computer virus is a malicious software program designed to interfere with a computer's normal operations, such as by corrupting or deleting data. Viruses are capable of spreading themselves to other computers, often through the Internet.

APB OPINION authoritative accounting pronouncement issued by the Accounting Principles Board before it was replaced in 1973 by the FINANCIAL ACCOUNTING STANDARDS BOARD (FASB). There were 31 Opinions issued. *See also* GENERALLY ACCEPTED ACCOUNTING PRINCIPLES (GAAP).

APPLICABLE FINANCIAL REPORTING FRAMEWORK represents the set of criteria used in the preparation of financial statements. Applicable financial reporting frameworks include general purpose financial reporting frameworks (e.g., U.S. generally accepted accounting principles and INTERNATIONAL ACCOUNTING STANDARDS) and special-purpose financial reporting frameworks (e.g., cash basis and income tax basis).

APPLICATION CONTROLS ensure accurate and automatic processing of transactional data, from input to output. Application controls, unlike general controls, are controls specific to a software application. Application controls perform a variety of functions, such as completeness check and validity check. Completeness check controls ensure that all data was processed, and validity check controls ensure that only valid data was inputted or processed.

APPLICATION PROGRAM in accounting, computer program written specifically to process data in an information system. It performs tasks or solves problems applicable to an accountant's work. Spreadsheet programs such as EXCEL and various software programs such as QUICKBOOKS and SPSS (Statistical Package for Social Scientists) are examples of application programs.

APPLICATION PROGRAM INTERFACE (API) a set of routines and protocols to support requests for services. APIs facilitate inter-organizational collaboration and information exchange. API protocols specify how information can be requested or exchanged online. One example of an API would be a Web service interface provided by Google for its mapping service.

APPLICATION SERVICE PROVIDER (ASP) an external entity that delivers software application or services across a wide area network to multiple clients based on either a flat rental fee or utilization pricing. Essentially, ASPs are utilized by an entity to outsource its information technology needs. An ASP generally owns the software and the servers on which the software is deployed. An ASP's employees maintain the software and the servers and make its services available through the Internet, generally through a standard browser or a "thin client."

APPLIED COST one that has been assigned to a product, department, or activity. An applied cost does not have to be based on actual costs incurred. Factory overhead applied to a product is an example of an applied cost. To apply overhead, a predetermined overhead rate is developed; it is based on budgeted overhead and budgeted volume of activity. *See also* PREDETERMINED OVERHEAD RATE.

APPLIED (ABSORBED) OVERHEAD is factory (manufacturing) overhead that has been allocated to products, usually on the basis of a predetermined rate. Overhead is over- or underapplied (absorbed) when overhead charged is greater or less than overhead incurred, respectively.

APPRAISAL
1. estimate of the value of an asset. An asset may be a piece of property, a collectible, or a precious metal. In the case of property, for example, an appraisal is made for the purposes of: (1) allocating the purchase price to the assets acquired (e.g., land, building, equipment); (2) determining the amount of hazard insurance to carry; (3) determining the value at death for estate tax purposes; and (4) determining a reasonable asking price in a sale.
2. activities such as inspection and testing of materials, in-process items, finished goods, and packaging.

APPRAISAL CAPITAL very rare practice in the U.S. (more common in other countries) of writing up an asset when appraised value exceeds book value. The entry would be to debit the asset for the increased value and credit appraisal capital, which is a stockholders' equity account.

APPRAISAL COSTS a category of QUALITY COSTS incurred to determine whether products and services are conforming to customer requirements, such as inspection and field testing costs.

APPRAISAL METHOD OF DEPRECIATION method in which depreciation expense charged to a period is the difference between the beginning and end-of-period appraised value of the asset if the appraised value has decreased. If not, there is no depreciation expense for that period. This method is not generally recognized as an acceptable method.

APPRAISAL VALUE *see* APPRAISAL.

APPRECIATION increase in the value of an asset. The asset may be real estate or a security. For example, an individual sold 100 shares of XYZ company's stock for $105 per share that he bought 10 years ago for $25 per share. The amount of appreciation was $8,000 = ($105 − $25) × 100 shares.

APPROPRIATED RETAINED EARNINGS term used when setting aside UNAPPROPRIATED RETAINED EARNINGS, thus making them unavailable for dividends. These appropriations might be used, for example, for plant expansion, sinking fund, and contingencies. When the appropriation is no longer needed, it is reversed.

APPROPRIATION
1. authorization of a governmental unit to spend money within specified restrictions such as amount, time period, and objective. There must be prior approval for such expenditure.
2. distribution of net income to various accounts.

3. allocation of retained earnings for a designated purpose such as for plant expansion. *See also* APPROPRIATED RETAINED EARNINGS.

APPROPRIATION ACCOUNT in GOVERNMENT ACCOUNTING, account of an agency that is credited when the appropriation has been authorized. It is reduced by expenditures during the period. When a budget is adopted by the governmental unit, the entry is to debit estimated revenues, credit appropriations, and debit or credit fund balance for the difference.

ARBITRAGE profiting from price differences when the same asset is traded in different markets. For example, an *arbitrageur* simultaneously buys one contract of silver in the Chicago market and sells one contract of silver at a different price in the New York market, locking in a profit if the selling price is higher than the buying price. It is also the process of selling overvalued and buying undervalued assets so as to bring about an equilibrium where all assets are properly valued.

ARITHMETIC MEAN *see* MEAN.

ARM'S LENGTH TRANSACTION one entered into by unrelated parties, each acting in their own best interest. It is assumed that in this type of transaction the prices used are the fair market values of the property or services being transferred in the transaction.

ARPANET founded in the late 1960s as a wide area network by the United States Defense Advanced Research Project Agency (ARPA). Its use of packet switching technology and the TCP/IP protocol makes it the father of our modern Internet. ARPANET is responsible for major innovations, including the development of e-mail, file transfer protocol (ftp), and remotely controlling a computer (telnet).

ARREARS past due payments or other liabilities. An example is cumulative preferred stock dividends that have been declared but have not been paid following their payment dates. (Common dividends cannot be paid as long as cumulative preferred dividends are in arrears.)

ARTICLES OF INCORPORATION formal documents prepared by individuals wishing to establish a corporation in the United States. They must file these documents with the authorities in the state in which the corporation wishes to reside. One copy is returned, after being reviewed, and, together with the Certificate of Incorporation, becomes the corporation's charter formally recognizing the corporation as a business entity entitled to begin business operations. Rules governing the company's internal management are set forth in its *bylaws*.

ARTICLES OF PARTNERSHIP formal document drawn up by partners indicating significant and important aspects of the partnership. Items included are capital contributions, profit and loss ratios, name of the enterprise, duration of relationship, and individual duties.

ARTICULATE to describe interrelationship between elements of any operating financial statements that have a common basis.

ARTIFICIAL INTELLIGENCE (AI) a branch of computer science in which human intelligence is simulated using computers. The aim is to create machines that can think like a human, yet are capable of doing computations like a computer. AI applications are used extensively today. These applications, however, do not recreate the human brain. Rather, modern AI applications rely on computer learning algorithms, massive amounts of data, and sensors to perform discrete tasks. For instance, Google uses AI to interpret human search engine queries. Netflix uses AI to recommend movies to its viewers.

ASC *see* FASB ACCOUNTING STANDARDS CODIFICATION.

ASCII (AMERICAN STANDARD CODE FOR INFORMATION INTERCHANGE) computer term. The code converts a character into a binary number used by most microcomputers and information services (online databases) so that different makes of microcomputers may be able to communicate with each other.

ASSEMBLY LANGUAGE intermediate-level computer language that is less complex to use than a machine language. Assembly languages use abbreviations or mnemonic codes to replace the 0s and 1s of machine language (A for "add," C for "compare," and MP for "multiply"). A translator is required to convert the assembly language program into machine language that can be executed by the computer. This translator is the assembly program. Every command in assembly language has a corresponding command in machine language. The assembly language differs among computers, and thus these programs are not easily transferable to machines of a different type from the one on which they were written.

ASSERTIONS statements or representations made by management that are explicitly or implicitly embodied in the financial statements. Assertions pertain to account balances, classes of transactions and events, and presentation and disclosure items. Assertions relevant to account balances involve existence, rights (ownership) and obligations, completeness, as well as valuation and allocation. Assertions relevant to classes of transactions and events involve occurrence, completeness, accuracy, cutoff, and classification. Assertions relevant to presentation and disclosure items involve occurrence, rights and obligations, completeness, accuracy and valuation, and classification and understandability.

ASSESSABLE CAPITAL STOCK
1. capital stock subject to calls and not fully paid.
2. capital stock of banks, subjecting stockholders to liabilities in excess of the amount originally paid in or subscribed. The assessment would occur only in cases in which the corporation was insolvent.

ASSESSED VALUE value established by a government for real estate or other property as a basis for levying taxes. For example, an individual receives a statement that, in the judgment of the local tax assessor, the individual's property is worth $50,000. If by law properties in this jurisdiction are assessed at 80% of market value, the individual's assessed value then is $40,000 (80% of $50,000), and property taxes will be based on this assessed value.

ASSESSMENT
1. process of making an official valuation of property for purposes of taxation.
2. valuation placed upon property as a result of this process. For example, an individual owns a parcel of land assessed on the tax roll for $50,000. The tax rate is $1.00 per $100 of value. The tax assessment for the land is $500.

ASSET economic resource that is expected to provide benefits to a business. An asset has three vital characteristics: (1) future probable economic benefit; (2) control by the entity; and (3) results from a prior event or transaction. Assets are expressed in money or are convertible into money and include certain deferred charges that are not resources (e.g., deferred moving costs). They can be recognized and measured in conformity with GENERALLY ACCEPTED ACCOUNTING PRINCIPLES (GAAP). Examples of ownership rights or service potentials are cash, automobiles, and land. An asset may be tangible or intangible. The former has physical substance such as a building. The latter lacks physical substance or results from a right granted by the government or another company such as goodwill and a patent. An asset may be current or noncurrent. A current asset has a life of one year or less (e.g., inventory) while a noncurrent asset has a life in excess of one year (e.g., machinery).

ASSET DEPRECIATION RANGE (ADR) range of depreciable lives allowed by the INTERNAL REVENUE SERVICE (IRS) for a specified asset. The ADR system was replaced by the ACCELERATED COST RECOVERY SYSTEM (ACRS) for properties placed into service after 1980. But it was revived under the 1986 Tax Reform Act as part of new ACRS rules to determine class lives.

ASSET RETIREMENT OBLIGATION FASB Statement No. 143 requires companies to record a liability at fair market value when a retirement obligation exists, provided fair value can be reasonably estimated even though it is years prior to the asset's planned retirement. The associated asset retirement cost is also recorded for the same amount when the initial obligation arises. After the initial recognition, the liability will change over time, so the obligation may be accrued to its present value each year. The long-term asset's capitalized cost is depreciated over its useful life.

ASSET TURNOVER ratio revealing the efficiency of corporate assets in generating revenue. A higher ratio is desired. What is considered a high ratio for one industry, however, may be considered a low ratio for another industry. If there is a low turnover, it may be an indication that the business should either utilize its assets in a more efficient manner or sell them. Asset turnover ratios can also be calculated for specific assets such as the ratios of sales to cash and sales to inventory. Higher ratios reflect favorably on the firm's ability to employ assets effectively.

ASSIGNMENT METHOD problem of determining how the assignments to machines or work centers should be made in order to minimize total costs. It is used to assign employees to jobs, jobs to machines, sales associates to territories, bidders to contracts, and so on.

ASSIGNMENT OF ACCOUNTS RECEIVABLE the process of writing a promissory note with accounts receivable as collateral. If the note is dishonored, the assignee can collect upon the accounts receivable. In a *general* assignment, all the receivables serve as collateral. New receivables can be substituted for those collected. In a *specific* assignment, the parties sign an agreement specifying who will receive collection (assignor or assignee), whether customers will be notified of the arrangement, specific accounts to be COLLATERALIZED, and the finance charges. *See also* FACTORING.

ASSOCIATED WITH designates the responsibility of an auditor for information in the footnotes to audited financial statements. Although the footnotes are not audited, the reasonableness of the disclosures should be reviewed by the auditor.

ASSOCIATION OF CERTIFIED FRAUD EXAMINERS an international, 25,000-member, professional organization (www.acfe.org) dedicated to fighting fraud and white-collar crime. With offices in North America and Europe—and chapters around the globe—the association is networked to respond to the needs of antifraud professionals everywhere.

ASSOCIATION OF GOVERNMENT ACCOUNTANTS (AGA) organization dedicated to the specific interests of accountants employed by a governmental entity. Its major publications include the GOVERNMENT ACCOUNTANTS JOURNAL. The association was originally founded in 1950 and was known as the Federal Government Accountants Association.

ASSUMPTIONS UNDERLYING COST-VOLUME-PROFIT (CVP) ANALYSIS assumptions that limit the usefulness of the basic BREAK-EVEN and COST-VOLUME PROFITS (CVP) models. They are: (1) The behavior of both sales revenue and expenses is *linear* throughout the entire relevant range of activity; (2) There is only one product or service or a constant SALES MIX; (3) Inventories do not change significantly from period to period; (4) Volume is the only factor affecting sales and expenses.

ASSURANCE SERVICES a CPA's examination of a contract, financial statement item (e.g., inventory), Web site, or loan terms being satisfied to provide assurance as to correctness or appropriateness. The engagement letter signed by the client must clearly specify what assurance is being provided.

AT PAR price that is the same as the FACE VALUE, or nominal amount, of a security. Bonds with a face value of $1000 that are bought or sold for $1000 are traded at par. If they sell for more than $1000 they would be traded at a PREMIUM; if less, at a DISCOUNT.

AT-RISK RULES tax term. A taxpayer can deduct losses for tax purposes only to the degree of risk. At-risk amounts are restricted to the cash investment and the debt for which the taxpayer is personally liable. Assume an individual incurs losses from real estate activities of $40,000. If the cash investment and personal debt incurred were $35,000, the most that could be deducted as losses is $35,000. Note there is an expansion of the at-risk amounts to real estate only to include certain nonrecourse loans from qualified lenders.

ATTACHMENT legally seizing property in order to satisfy a judgment.

ATTEST formal statement by an auditor after thorough examination and consideration, as to whether financial statements fairly present financial position and operating results. With an attest, the public accountant provides an objective evaluation to aid financial statement users.

ATTEST FUNCTION activity of the CERTIFIED PUBLIC ACCOUNTANT (CPA) in performing audit procedures. The accountant examines, tests, and verifies the accuracy of client accounting data as a basis for forming an audit opinion. In doing so, appropriate sampling of data is made. It is the process of an independent review of a company's financial statements including the rendering of an AUDIT REPORT.

ATTESTATION (ATTEST) ENGAGEMENT an assurance service provided by CPAs relative to subject matter or assertions about subject matter. Examples of subject matter include prospective financial information such as forecasts and projections, internal control, historical performance, and compliance with laws and regulations. In general, attestation engagements include examinations, reviews, and the application of agreed-upon procedures. Compilation of prospective financial information is also permissible.

ATTORNEY'S LETTER letter sent by the CERTIFIED PUBLIC ACCOUNTANT (CPA) to the client's lawyer to verify litigation information provided by management. The auditor is concerned that management has not revealed all lawsuits and claims. The auditor must assess the impact the contingencies may have on the client's financial position. This includes the possibility of the client losing the suit and suffering damages. The attorney's letter is a major audit procedure.

ATTRIBUTE SAMPLING statistical procedure used to study the characteristics of a population. Attribute is a qualitative characteristic that a unit of a population either possesses or does not possess. For example, an account receivable is either past due or not; proper authorization for a payment either exists or does not. Thus the population under consideration is composed of two mutually exclusive classes—units possessing the attribute and units not possessing it. The statistical procedure used to estimate the occurrence of a particular attribute in a population is referred to as *attribute sampling*. This technique can be used by the auditor to substantiate such accounting populations as cash receipts, cash payments, payrolls, sales, and entries posted to the wrong account. In this analysis, the auditor usually determines the expected *occurrence rate* and the upper *precision* limit. The occurrence rate equals the percentage of the population having the attribute. Precision is the magnitude of deviation of a sample value from the population parameter being estimated.

Attribute sampling is particularly valuable in estimating the extent of compliance, such as the effectiveness of accounting controls using tests of transactions. Tables are used to determine sample size based on the desired confidence level, upper precision limit, and the expected rate of occurrence. Note that when analyzing a sample, the auditor may test for several different attributes. The exact definitions of attributes and occurrences should be contained in the working papers. *See also* VARIABLES SAMPLING.

ATTRIBUTION used in situations where the tax law assigns to one taxpayer the ownership interest of another taxpayer; also called *constructive ownership*. For example, under the law a father is considered to own constructively all stock actually owned by his son.

AUDIT
1. *financial audit*—examination of a client's accounting records by an independent certified public accountant to formulate an AUDIT OPINION. The auditor must follow GENERALLY ACCEPTED AUDITING STANDARDS (GAAS). Source documents are examined to substantiate legitimacy of transactions. A careful evaluation of INTERNAL CONTROL is necessary.
2. INTERNAL AUDIT—investigation of the company's procedures and operations by the INTERNAL AUDITOR to assure that they conform to corporate policy.

3. MANAGEMENT AUDIT—evaluation of management's efficiency.

4. COMPLIANCE AUDIT—ascertainment of the firm's compliance with specified rules and regulations such as the Sarbanes-Oxley Act.

AUDITABILITY environment in which the auditor performs the ATTEST FUNCTION. Consideration is given to such factors as the condition of the records and the cooperation of the client's accounting staff. The accounting records must allow for sufficient evidence gathering. There must exist a good system of INTERNAL CONTROL. Management must also be honest and have no intention of perpetrating FRAUD.

AUDIT COMMITTEE body formed by a company's board of directors to oversee audit operations and circumstances. It selects and appraises the performance of the CPA firm. In accordance with SECURITIES AND EXCHANGE COMMISSION (SEC) regulation, the Committee must be composed of outside directors. Besides evaluating external audit reports, the Committee may evaluate internal audit reports as well. Management representations under the realm of the FOREIGN CORRUPT PRACTICES ACT are also reviewed. The Committee may also get involved with public disclosure of corporate activities.

AUDIT CYCLE period of time in which the accountant conducts audit procedures. Different parts of the audit may be carried out at different times. For example, inventory may be counted in November while accounts receivable confirmation may be conducted in December. The audit cycle also relates to when a particular business unit is examined. For instance, Production Department X may be examined once a year, while Production Department Y is audited biyearly.

AUDIT DOCUMENTATION *see* WORK PAPERS.

AUDIT GUIDE booklets from the AMERICAN INSTITUTE OF CERTIFIED PUBLIC ACCOUNTANTS (AICPA) that supplement STATEMENTS ON AUDITING STANDARDS (SAS) and STATEMENTS OF POSITION (SOP). Typically, an audit guide is directed toward the accounting practices in a particular industry, such as brokerages, finance companies, and insurance companies. Some guides apply to technical topics, such as personal financial statements. These guides are usually deemed authoritative in nature.

AUDITING EVIDENCE proof the auditor uses to substantiate a recorded item so that proper reliance may be placed on financial statement figures. *Proof* of accounting data includes examining source documents in support of a transaction. The degree to which evidence gathering is necessary partly depends on the quality of the client's internal control system. Also, the trend in an account should be looked at over time as a basis for determining the extent of testing required. For example, if travel expense went from 2% of sales last year to 25% of sales this year, this inconsistency requires close examination. Test checks of accounts and transactions are necessary. Evidence can be obtained through various means such as physical verification of inventory records or confirmation letters sent to verify recorded amounts of accounts receivable. *See also* ANALYTICAL PROCEDURES; AUDITING PROCEDURE.

AUDITING PROCEDURE auditor technique in gathering AUDITING EVIDENCE to substantiate the reliability of the accounting records. The auditor evaluates whether the information presented is logical and reasonable. Examples of auditing procedures are observing assets to verify existence and amount (e.g., fixed assets), collecting independent confirmations from external parties (e.g., bank confirmation), evaluating internal control, appraising management's activities, and obtaining management representations. The audit procedures to be followed on an engagement are indicated in the AUDIT PROGRAM. The WORK PAPERS indicate what has been done on the audit.

AUDITING PROCESS sequential order of steps followed by the auditor in the examination of client records. The audit process may vary depending upon the nature of the engagement, its objectives, and type of audit assurance desired. The process includes understanding the particular client's environment, conducting the auditing procedures and tests, appraising the audit results, and communicating the results to interested parties.

AUDITING STANDARDS guidelines that auditors follow when examining financial statements and other data. Auditing standards are promulgated by authoritative bodies, such as the AMERICAN INSTITUTE OF CERTIFIED PUBLIC ACCOUNTANTS (AICPA), which issues GENERALLY ACCEPTED AUDITING STANDARDS (GAAS) applicable to audits of nonissuers, and the Public Company Accounting Oversight Board (PCAOB), which issues GAAS applicable to audits of issuers. The INSTITUTE OF INTERNAL AUDITORS (IIA) also sets standards for internal auditors. Further, standards exist for auditors filing for companies with governmental regulatory bodies.

AUDITING STANDARDS BOARD (ASB) authoritative body of the AMERICAN INSTITUTE OF CERTIFIED PUBLIC ACCOUNTANTS (AICPA). The ASB formulates, revises, and interprets GENERALLY ACCEPTED AUDITING STANDARDS (GAAS). It issues authoritative auditing pronouncements called Statements on Auditing Standards, applicable to audits of nonissuers.

AUDIT OPINION report rendered by the independent CPA at the end of an audit investigation. The auditor reports on the nature of his or her work and on the degree of responsibility assumed. In the audit opinion, the auditor states that he or she has examined the client's financial statements for the year then ended in accordance with GENERALLY ACCEPTED AUDITING STANDARDS (GAAS) including tests of the accounting records and other necessary auditing procedures. The auditor then indicates whether in his or her opinion the client's financial statements present fairly the financial position, results of operations, and changes in financial position for the year-ended in conformity with GENERALLY ACCEPTED ACCOUNTING PRINCIPLES (GAAP) applied on a consistent basis. The four types of audit opinions are UNQUALIFIED (unmodified in the case of a nonissuer's financial statements) OPINION, QUALIFIED OPINION, ADVERSE OPINION, and DISCLAIMER.

AUDIT PLAN includes the nature, extent, and timing of the audit procedures to be performed by the auditor. The audit plan will vary from client to client and from year to year, due to the need to tailor the audit plan to meet the applicable circumstances. An audit plan should document the planned risk assessment procedures and planned further audit procedures, including relevant tests of controls and substantive procedures.

AUDIT PROGRAM a detailed list of the audit procedures to be performed. The audit program is the means by which an auditor documents the audit plan.

AUDIT REPORT

1. *short form* audit report expresses the CPA's *audit opinion* on whether the financial statements are presented fairly in all material respects in conformity with U.S. GAAP. There are instances when a modification to the standard format of the audit report is necessary. A QUALIFIED OPINION (or a disclaimer of opinion) must be given, for example, when audit scope limitations exist; an opinion partly based on the report of other auditors must be noted; the CPA wants to emphasize a key matter affecting financial position.

2. *long form* detailed audit report directed to the management or Board of Directors may supplement, include, or replace the short-form report. Typically, it includes audit scope particulars, makes explanatory comments on financial position and operating results, discusses trends in financial data along with reasons, and gives procedural suggestions.

AUDIT RISK possibility that the auditor will not uncover material misstatements in the financial records resulting from fraud, negligence, or other reasons. For example, the auditor's sampling techniques will not always uncover an improper item such as an overstated expense. Further, the evaluation of internal control and checks may not spot a deficiency. The auditor should try to protect against the adverse consequences of failing to uncover misstatements by obtaining REPRESENTATION LETTERS and adequate malpractice insurance.

AUDIT SOFTWARE computer programs designed to assist in examining and testing clients' accounting records. Different audit software packages accomplish varying objectives. Some packages assist in gathering evidence, conducting analytical tests, sampling data, evaluating internal control, documenting the audit, scheduling the audit, printing exception reports (e.g., employee salary exceeding a prescribed limit), preparing audit reports, sending out confirmations and management letters.

AUDIT TEST procedure applied to a sample within a population. For example, it might examine supporting evidence for half of promotion and entertainment expenses or send out confirmations for 75% of accounts receivable. The purpose of an audit test is to assure that no material exceptions are included in the sample. Audit tests are also applied in microcomputer applications to assure that the accounting software package is processing data correctly. A "dummy file" with predetermined manual results is processed by the computer to see if the computerized result is the same as the manually determined figure.

AUDIT TRAIL recorded flow of a transaction from initiation (e.g., source document) to finalization (e.g., financial statement), or vice versa. The auditor, assuring that data are processed correctly, appraises the material that forms the audit trail. An audit trail may be either visible or invisible (e.g., magnetic storage). Components of an audit trail include: (1) source records, (2) list of transactions processed, and (3) transaction identifiers so that reference can be made to the source of a transaction. An audit trail allows the tracing of transactions to control totals and from the control totals to supporting transactions. An audit trail is good when the tracing process is easy to accomplish.

AUTHORITY power to direct and exact performance from others. It includes the right to prescribe the means and methods by which work will be done. However, the authority to direct is only as good as one individual's willingness to accept direction from another. Moreover, with authority comes RESPONSIBILITY and ACCOUNTABILITY.

AUTHORIZED CAPITAL STOCK maximum number of shares of common stock that can be issued under a company's Articles of Incorporation. If a public issue of stock is involved, the SEC and the relevant state must approve it. Issued shares are usually less than the authorized shares.

AUTOCORRELATION term used in the statistical measurement of relationships within a series. It is one of the assumptions required in a regression in order to make it reliable, also called *serial correlation*. It means that the error terms are independent of each other [see (a) below]. That is, the deviation of one point about the line (i.e., the error $= \mu = y - y'$) is unrelated to the deviation of any other point. When autocorrelation exists [i.e., the error terms are *not* independent see (b) below], the standard errors of the regression coefficients are seriously underestimated. The problem of autocorrelation is usually detected by the DURBIN-WATSON STATISTIC. *See* illustration.

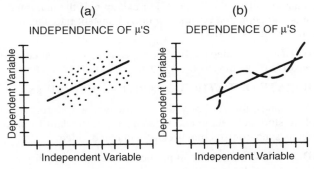

AUTOMATIC ERROR CORRECTION method to uncover computer transmission data errors and permit the retransmission or correction of information by employing an error-correcting code.

AUTONOMOUS one of 12 criteria that must be met to account for a BUSINESS COMBINATION as a POOLING-OF-INTERESTS. Autonomous means that a combining company must not have been a subsidiary or division of any other corporation within two years prior to the *initiation date* of the business combination. If a combining company is *not* autonomous, then the PURCHASE (ACCOUNTING) METHOD must be used. The initiation date is the date that stockholders are notified in writing of an exchange offer.

AVAILABLE FOR SALE SECURITIES represent securities and other financial investments that are not held (1) for trading, (2) to maturity, or (3) for strategic reasons, and that have a readily available market price. Under U.S. GENERALLY ACCEPTED ACCOUNTING PRINCIPLES (GAAP), available for sale securities are carried on an entity's balance sheet at fair value.

AVERAGE *see* MEAN.

AVERAGE AGE OF INVENTORY number of days an average inventory item takes to sell:

$$\text{Average Age of Inventory} = \frac{\text{Average Inventory}}{\text{Cost of Goods Sold}} \times 365 \text{ days}$$

For example, assume that average inventory is \$47,500 and cost of goods sold is \$500,000. The average age of inventory is (\$47,500/\$500,000) × 365 days = 34.7 days. *See also* DAYS TO SELL INVENTORY.

AVERAGE COST FLOW ASSUMPTION one of the two cost flow assumptions used under PROCESS COSTING, more often called WEIGHTED AVERAGE COST flow assumption. The other is the FIRST-IN, FIRST-OUT (FIFO) cost flow assumption. *See also* WEIGHTED AVERAGE COSTING.

AVERAGE COSTING *see* WEIGHTED AVERAGE COSTING.

AVERAGE COST OF CAPITAL minimum desired rate of return on invested capital that is computed by taking an average of the cost of debt, cost of preferred stock, cost of common stock, and the cost of retained earnings.

AVERAGE INVENTORY amount equaling about half maximum inventory when demand is relatively constant. For example, if the maximum inventory is 500 units and depletion occurs at a fairly constant rate, the average inventory equals 250 units (500/2).

AVERAGE LIFE estimated useful-life expectancy of a depreciable group of assets. *See also* DEPRECIATION; ECONOMIC LIFE; USEFUL LIFE.

AVERAGE RATE OF RETURN *see* SIMPLE RATE OF RETURN.

AVI FILES stands for Audio Video Interleave, a file format created by Microsoft to store both audio and video data in a standard form to allow for simultaneous/synchronized playback of audio and video.

AVOIDABLE COST cost that will not be incurred if an activity is suspended; also called escapable cost. For example, it is the cost that can be saved by dropping a particular product line or department (e.g., salaries paid to employees working in a particular product line or department). All costs are avoidable, except (1) SUNK COSTS and (2) costs that will continue regardless of the decision.

AZURE CLOUD Windows Azure by Microsoft is an open and flexible cloud platform that enables one to build, deploy, and manage applications using any language, tool, or framework. One can store data using relational SQL databases, NoSQL table stores, or unstructured blob (binary large object) stores.

B

BACK CHARGE item previously charged to an account but unpaid. The current invoice requests payment of the previous charge as well as of current charges.

BACKFLUSH COSTING product costing approach, used in a JUST-IN-TIME (JIT) operating environment, in which costing is delayed until goods are finished. Standard costs are then flushed backward through the system to assign costs to products. The result is that detailed tracking of costs is eliminated. The system is best suited to companies that maintain low inventories because costs then flow directly to cost of goods sold. Work-in-process is usually eliminated, journal entries to inventory accounts may be delayed until the time of product completion or even the time of sale, and standard costs are used to assign costs to units when journal entries are made, that is, to flush costs backward to the points at which inventories remain.

BACK ORDER customer's order that cannot be filled at the present time usually because the merchandise is not currently in stock. As soon as the product is available, it will be shipped to the customer. There usually exists a company policy of how long an unshipped order remains an order without some sort of confirmation or communication. An excessive amount of back orders may indicate to the accountant that poor inventory planning exists.

BACK UP to make a duplicate copy of original data or files usually stored on a separate data storage medium. Backup ensures the recoverability of files in the event of loss of the original data.

BACKUP WITHHOLDING procedure used to ensure that federal income tax is paid on earnings even though the recipient cannot be identified by a Social Security number. Banks, brokers, and other entities report nonwage earnings paid out on IRS Form 1099. When the form cannot be filed because it lacks the taxpayer's Social Security number, 20% of the interest, dividends, or fees is withheld by the payer and remitted to the federal government. For example, if interest earned on a bank account is $1,000 and there is no Social Security number on file for the account, the bank withholds $200. Financial institutions have account holders fill out a Federal W-9 form requiring the individual to certify that the Social Security numbers given are correct and that they are or are not subject to backup withholding. The information regarding interest payments is reported by the bank to the IRS for comparison with individual tax returns. Backup withholding is not an additional tax; the tax liability of persons subject to backup withholding will be reduced by the amount of tax withheld. The IRS Code Section 3406 (a)(1)(c) applies to backup withholding.

BAD DEBT account or note receivable that proves to be entirely or partially uncollectible despite collection efforts. If the allowance method of estimating bad debts is used, the entry at time of uncollectibility is to debit allowance for bad debts and credit accounts receivable. If the direct write-off method is employed, the entry is to debit bad debt expense and credit accounts receivable.

BAD DEBT EXPENSE account shown in the income statement representing estimated uncollectible credit sales for the current accounting period. *See also* ALLOWANCE METHOD; DIRECT WRITE-OFF METHOD.

BAD DEBT RECOVERY account receivable previously written off as uncollectible is now collected. The entry is to reverse the original write-off by debiting accounts receivable and crediting allowance for bad debts. A second entry is required for the collection by debiting cash and crediting accounts receivable. A high ratio of recoveries to write-offs may signify to the analyst that the firm writes off uncollected debts too quickly. *See also* ALLOWANCE METHOD.

BAIDU the market leader in paid online search engines in China with 62.1% market share in 2009, well ahead of Google China's 25.3% share.

BAILMENT contractual transfer of dollars or personal property for a specified objective. An example is the CONSIGNMENT of goods from the consignor to consignee. Another example is a bank holding an asset of a borrower as collateral. In a bailment, the deliverer is called the bailor and the receiver is termed the bailee.

BAILOUT PAYBACK METHOD PAYBACK PERIOD method incorporating the salvage value of the asset into the calculation. It measures the length of the payback period when the periodic cash inflows are combined with the salvage value.

"BAIT RECORDS" internal control device. Bait or dummy records may be in computer files so the auditor can see when these files are improperly used. Example: a nonexistent customer or inventory item with an assumed balance that should not be altered. Another example: a dummy record put into processing with an incorrect name and address file for an employee. When a mailing occurs, it will be returned.

BALANCE
1. difference between total debits and total credits in an account.
2. equality of total debits and total credits of all accounts in a GENERAL LEDGER in the preparation of a TRIAL BALANCE.
3. equality of a control account in the general ledger (e.g., accounts receivable) and the total balance of all accounts in the SUBSIDIARY LEDGER (e.g., customer accounts).
4. balance in a bank account.
5. balance of a loan.

BALANCED BUDGET one in which total expenditures equal total revenue. An entity has a budget surplus if expenditures are less than revenues. It has a budget deficit if expenditures are greater than revenues.

BALANCED SCORECARD a measurement and management system that suggests we view organization from four perspectives: financial, internal business processes, customer, and learning and growth.

BALANCE OF PAYMENTS record of the transactions of a country with the rest of the world. There are three main accounts in the balance of payments: (1) the current account, (2) the capital account, and (3) gold. The current account records trade in goods and services, as well as transfer payments.

Services include freight, royalty payments, and interest payments. Transfer payments consist of remittances, gifts, and grants. The *balance of trade* simply records trade in goods. The capital account records purchases and sales of investments, such as stocks, bonds and land.

BALANCE OF RETAINED EARNINGS accompanies the balance sheet and shows the beginning balance of retained earnings, adjustments to it during the year, and the final balance. An illustrative statement format follows:

> Retained Earnings—1/1 Unadjusted
> Plus or Minus: Prior Period Adjustments
>
> Retained Earnings—1/1 Adjusted
> Plus: Net Income
> Minus: Dividends Declared
> Retained Earnings—12/31

BALANCE OF TRADE *see* BALANCE OF PAYMENTS.

BALANCE SHEET statement showing a company's financial position at the end of an accounting period; also called *Statement of Financial Position*. It presents the entity's ASSETS, LIABILITIES, and STOCKHOLDERS' EQUITY. It is classified into major groupings of assets and liabilities in order to facilitate analysis. Examples are current assets, fixed assets, current liabilities, and noncurrent liabilities. The accounting equation for the balance sheet is:

Assets = Liabilities + Stockholders' Equity

The balance sheet is useful to financial statement users because it indicates the resources the entity has and what it owes. *See also* INCOME STATEMENT.

BALANCE SHEET ACCOUNT appears in the balance sheet. Unlike income statement accounts that are NOMINAL ACCOUNTS, balance sheet accounts are REAL ACCOUNTS. A real account is not closed out at the end of the year but continues to exist into the next year. Examples of balance sheet accounts are cash, accounts payable, and common stock.

BALLOON last loan payment when it is significantly more than the prior payments; also called *partially amortized loans*. For example, a debt agreement might provide for a balloon payment when future refinancing is anticipated.

BANDWIDTH the data transfer rate from one location to another in a given period of time, usually expressed in bits per second (bps) or kilo bits per second (kbps). Bandwidth is also used to refer to the width of the range of frequencies in electronic communication, often expressed in hertz (Hz).

BANK BALANCE amount in a bank deposit account, such as a checking or savings account, as of a certain specified time or date, indicated on a bank statement. Bank charges, deposits in transit, and outstanding checks usually are primary factors in reconciling an individual's or organization's books and the bank's statement, as of a particular date. *See also* BANK RECONCILIATION.

BANKER'S ACCEPTANCE time draft drawn by a business firm whose payment is guaranteed by the bank's "acceptance" of it. It is especially important in foreign trade, when the seller of goods can be certain that the buyer's draft will actually have funds behind it. Banker's acceptances are money market instruments actively traded in the secondary market.

BANK RECONCILIATION term used when settling differences contained in the BANK STATEMENT and the cash account in the books of the bank's customer. Rarely do the ending balances agree. To reflect the reconciling items, a bank reconciliation is required. Once completed, the adjusted bank balance must prove to the adjusted book balance. When it does, it indicates that both records are correct. Journal entries are then prepared to update the records and to arrive at an ending balance in the cash account that agrees with the ending balance in the bank statement.

The bank balance is adjusted for items reflected on the books that are not on the statement. They include OUTSTANDING CHECKS, DEPOSITS IN TRANSIT, and bank errors in charging or crediting the company's account.

The book balance is adjusted for items shown on the bank statement that are not reflected on the books. They include bank charges, not-sufficient funds checks, collections made by bank on the customer's behalf (e.g., collected notes receivable), interest earned, and errors on the books.

BANK STRESS TEST test that determines how much capital a bank needs to survive. For example, regulators may require that banks maintain a minimum 6% Tier 1 capital ratio, a common measure of financial health, and that at least half of that figure, or 3%, come from common stock. If a bank fails the test, its regulators will demand that it raise additional capital.

BANK TRANSFER SCHEDULE provides details of cash transfers between banks, including the dates and dollar amounts of transfers. Also known as an *interbank transfer schedule.*

BANKRUPTCY (BUSINESS) situation in which a business' debt exceeds the fair market value of its assets. It is also a court action under which a debtor may be discharged for unpaid debts, in whole or in part, and in which creditors receive distributions of assets from the debtor's property under the supervision of the court. CHAPTER 11 of the Bankruptcy Law provides for reorganization in which the debtor remains in possession of the business and in control of its operation, while the debtor and creditors are allowed to work together. *See also* BANKRUPTCY (PERSONAL).

BANKRUPTCY (PERSONAL) legal process that is available for an individual who is overextended financially and is unable to pay his debts. The individual can file for bankruptcy in order to seek to legally eliminate some or all of his debts. Under CHAPTER 7 of the Bankruptcy Law, often called straight bankruptcy, the intent is to liquidate assets to pay the debts. Should this method be elected, the bankrupt can claim certain property as "exempt" and this property can be retained to preserve the basic necessities of life (such as a certain amount of equity in the home, economical car, and personal clothing and effects). Once a person has declared bankruptcy, he cannot be discharged from debts again for six years. *Note:* The newest bankruptcy legislation, which came into effect in the fall of 2005, however, makes it difficult to file for Chapter 7 if their income is greater than the median for their state. As a result, more individuals are expected to file for Chapter 13.

Under CHAPTER 13, often called wage-earner plans, the assets are not liquidated. Instead, interest and late charges are eliminated and arrangements are made to pay off some or all of the debts over several years. Note that bankruptcy will not discharge all the debts. Debts that cannot be eliminated through bankruptcy proceedings include income taxes, child support, alimony, student loans, and debts incurred under false pretenses. Bankruptcy should not be taken lightly. One should be sure to consult an attorney on various decisions surrounding the issue and on how to get the greatest benefit from the new financial start. *See also* BANKRUPTCY (BUSINESS).

BANKRUPTCY PREDICTION ability of an auditor to project whether the client has a going-concern problem. If it does have a problem, this fact must be stated in the audit report and a QUALIFIED OPINION REPORT rendered. Failure to do so, if a client actually becomes bankrupt, will expose the CPA to lawsuits by financial statement users such as damaged investors and creditors. There are several ways to predict bankruptcy such as Altman's Z SCORE, trends in certain financial ratios (e.g., cash flow to total debt, net income to total assets), degree of FINANCIAL LEVERAGE, industry problems, poor economy, and low-quality management.

BANK STATEMENT form prepared by the bank and sent to the depositor to show transactions in the account. The bank statement reports the beginning balance, deposits made, checks cleared, charges to the account (e.g., bank service fees), credits to the account (e.g., interest earned on the account balance), and ending balance. Enclosed with the bank statement are the canceled checks, debit memoranda for charges, and credit memoranda for credits.

BARGAIN PURCHASE asset or goods acquired for materially less than fair market value. For example, a buyer may be able to get a bargain price on furniture from a seller in a liquidation situation.

BARGAIN PURCHASE OPTION one of the four criteria to be satisfied for a lessee to account for leased property under the CAPITAL LEASE method. A bargain purchase option exists if the lessee can buy the property at the end of the lease for a nominal (minimal) amount or renew at nominal rental payments. If this criterion exists, the leased asset is depreciated by the lessee over the life of the property. The PRESENT VALUE of the bargain purchase option payment is included in obtaining the present value of future payments as the capitalizable amount of the leased asset.

BARGAIN RENEWAL OPTION lessee's ability to renew a lease at subsequent minimal rental payments. Minimal rental payments are defined as those significantly below what typical rental payments on the property would be. This satisfies one of the criteria required for a CAPITAL LEASE. In effect, by doing so the lessee has acquired a property right.

BARTER exchange of products or services by two companies without cash involvement. The companies contract for a specified amount of the items and the proportions representing full payment. For financial reporting purposes, barter transactions should be reported at the estimated fair market value of the product or service received. This same requirement holds for tax purposes in that each party has to recognize as revenue the fair value of the exchange. For example, a barter takes place when an accountant renders services to a computer store in exchange for a personal computer.

BASEL II a new set of regulations designed by the Basel Committee on Banking Supervision to cover operational risk as well as financial risk for the global financial institutions. Set up in 1974, the Basel Committee on Banking Supervision is an international regulatory body for the world's financial institutions. In 1988, it introduced capital adequacy rules for banks in member countries, which required them to implement a financial risk measurement framework. The Committee is currently creating a new set of regulations to replace the original rules that would cover operational risk as well as financial risk. The new framework, usually called Basell II, is based around three "pillars": the first determines minimum capital requirements, the second stipulates an effective supervisory review process, and the third sets out to strengthen market discipline by greater disclosure of banks' financial status.

BASE PERIOD selected period of time that serves as a basis for a comparison, a standard, or a mathematical construct to aid in financial computations. The base period selected should be the one that is the most typical of the business. The term base period applies to economic statistics (e.g., Consumer Price Index) and certain stock indexes (e.g., the base period of the Standard & Poor's 500 is 1941–1943).

BASE STOCK minimum inventory level necessary to maintain effective and continuous operations. *See also* BASE STOCK METHOD.

BASE STOCK METHOD inventory valuation method in which the base amount of goods is valued at acquisition cost; also called *normal stock method*. The base amount should be continually maintained. Additional quantities above the base level are valued on a LIFO basis. The method is *not* accepted.

BASIC (BEGINNERS ALL-PURPOSE SYMBOLIC INSTRUCTION CODE) high-level computer programming language written in an easy-to-understand English format; the language was first used at Dartmouth in 1967. It is one of the easiest languages to learn and is undoubtedly the best known of any high-level computer language today. However, it runs more slowly than some other languages, such as C.

BASIC EARNINGS PER SHARE net income available to common stockholders divided by the weighted-average number of shares outstanding. Net income available to common stockholders is net income less declared preferred dividends for the year. If the preferred stock is noncumulative, preferred stock dividends are subtracted only if they are declared during the year. If the preferred stock is cumulative, the dividends are deducted even if they are not declared in the current year. The weighted-average number of common stock shares outstanding is determined by multiplying the number of shares issued and outstanding for any time period by a fraction, the numerator being the number of months the shares have been outstanding and the denominator being the number of months in the period (e.g., 12 months for annual reporting).

BASIC FEASIBLE SOLUTION term in LINEAR PROGRAMMING (LP) used to designate a solution that occurs at the *corner point* of the feasible region in a graph. According to a theorem in LP, one or a linear combination of the basic feasible solutions will turn out to be an optimal solution. *See also* GRAPHICAL METHOD.

BASING POINT specific geographical location that is associated with a given price of a commodity. This price will then serve as a base price for the same commodity in a different geographical location. Freight costs between locations will account for the difference with respect to the base price.

BASIS figure or value that is the starting point in computing gain or loss, depreciation, depletion, and amortization. For example, in an asset sale, gain is proceeds minus basis, where basis is the amount on which depreciation is calculated.

BASIS OF ACCOUNTING method of recognizing revenues and expenses. Under the *accrual basis* of accounting, revenues are recognized as goods are sold and services are rendered regardless of the time when cash is received. Expenses are recognized in the period when the related revenue is recognized and the difference is the net income figure for a particular period. Under the *cash basis* of accounting, revenues are recognized only when money is received and expenses are recognized only when money is paid. Cash basis financial statements, however, distort financial position and operating results of an organization.

BASKET PURCHASE *see* LUMP-SUM PURCHASE.

BATCH-LEVEL ACTIVITIES activities performed each time a batch of goods is produced; such activities vary with the number of batches prepared.

BATCH PROCESSING term for a processing mode in which the work to be accomplished is done sequentially. Input such as transaction records is processed through the system in a predetermined order. *See also* REAL-TIME SYSTEM.

BAYESIAN PROBABILITY revised prior estimates of probabilities, based on additional experience and information. An example of Bayesian probability applied to accounting is when the estimated bad debt percentage has to be revised because of recent uncollectibility experience of customer defaults, sales to more marginal customers, or poor economic conditions.

BEAR one who believes that prices in the security and commodity markets will decline. A bear can profit from a declining stock market by selling a stock *short* or buying a PUT option. A BULL, the opposite of a bear, thinks prices will rise.

BEARER BOND unregistered bond that entitles the holder to payments of both principal and interest; also called a *coupon bond*, because whoever presents the coupon is entitled to the interest. With respect to transfers, bond endorsement is not a requirement.

BEGINNING INVENTORY balance at the start of the accounting period. The three types of inventory are RAW MATERIALS INVENTORY, WORK-IN-PROCESS (WIP), and FINISHED GOODS INVENTORY. They are shown in the income statement in the analysis of cost of goods sold. *See also* ENDING INVENTORY.

BEHAVIORAL ACCOUNTING
1. approach to accounting that stresses psychological considerations in decision making; also called HUMAN RESOURCE ACCOUNTING. For example, a budget should be participative so departmental managers who are involved with it will internalize the goals. Also profit centers engage a manager's ego because the financial results of the entity are a direct reflection of the manager's performance. In human resource accounting, a valuation is placed on people and reflected as an asset in the balance sheet.
2. theory that the management accounting function is essentially behavioral. The theory states that the nature and scope of accounting systems is

materially influenced by the view of human behavior that is held by the accountants who design and operate these systems. PARTICIPATIVE BUDGETING is a simple application of behavioral accounting.

BELLWETHER SECURITY one that indicates the direction of the security market. General Electric is an example because much of it is owned by INSTITUTIONAL INVESTORS who influence supply and demand. In the bond market, the 20-year U.S. Treasury bond is a good indicator of the direction in which other bonds are moving.

BENCHMARK
1. a standard, norm, or yardstick to judge one's performance as an individual or company.
2. a standard measurement or metric used to evaluate the performance of a portfolio. For example, an appropriate stock or bond index can be used to gauge the performance of an investment such as a mutual fund. An example is the EUROPE, AUSTRALIA, AND FAR EAST (EAFE) INDEX, a value-weighted index of the equity performance of major foreign markets, which is often used to evaluate the performance of international mutual funds.

BENCHMARKING learning from others; also called COMPETITIVE.

BENCHMARKING (BEST PRACTICES) the process of searching for new and better procedures by comparing your own procedures to that of the very best. The objective is to measure the key outputs of a business process or function against the best and to analyze the reasons for the performance difference. Benchmarking applies to services and practices as well as to products and is an ongoing systematic process. It entails both quantitative and qualitative measurements that allow both an internal and an external assessment. *Process benchmarking* is the process of assessing the quality of key internal processes by comparing them with those of other firms. In *results benchmarking*, a firm examines the end product or service of another company, focusing on product/service specifications and performance results.

BENCHMARK RATES interest or loan rates that other rates are pegged to. An example is the U.S. prime rate on which other loan rates are based.

BENEFICIARY individual who will receive an inheritance upon the death of another. The proceeds of an insurance policy may be in the form of a lump-sum or annuity.

BENEFIT APPROACH TO PENSIONS term used when determining the amount of pension benefits applicable for services rendered to date and present value of these benefits. The two benefit approaches are the accumulated benefits approach and the benefits/years-of-service (projected unit credit) approach. With the former, pension expense and related liability are determined each year based on years of service to date using *existing salary levels*. With the latter, pension expense and liability are based on *final salary*. *See also* PENSION PLAN.

BEST PRACTICES *see* BENCHMARKING.

BETA measure of systematic or undiversifiable risk of a stock. A beta coefficient of more than 1 means that the company's stock price has shown more volatility than the market index (e.g., Standard & Poor's 500) to which it is being related; usually, that indicates it is a risky security. If the beta is less than 1, it is less volatile than the market average. If it equals 1, its risk is the same as the market index. High variability in stock price may indicate greater business risk, instability in operations, and low quality of earnings.

The following presents betas for some selected companies:

Betas for Some Selected Multinational Corporations

Company	March 23, 2009
Boeing (BA)	1.20
Google (GOOG)	1.26
Best Buy (BBY)	1.35
Nordstrom (JWN)	1.58
Intel (INTC)	1.25
Wal-Mart (WMT)	0.21

Source: MSN Money Central Investor (http://moneycentral.msn.com/investor/home.asp) and Google Finance (http://finance.google.com/finance)

BETA ALPHA PSI national accounting fraternity maintaining student chapters on more than 125 university campuses. Members discuss issues of interest to the accounting profession. Membership is gained by students demonstrating a high degree of scholastic achievement. It was founded in 1919.

BETA DISTRIBUTION probability distribution used to describe activity times.

BETA RISK *see* TYPE II ERROR.

BETTERMENT replacement of a major component of plant and equipment by another component that will result in *better* performance capability. The betterment increases overall efficiency of the asset. An example is a superior engine in an auto. Betterments represent CAPITAL EXPENDITURES.

BID AND ASKED term in the over-the-counter market for unlisted securities. Bid is the highest price an investor is willing to pay while asked is the lowest price a seller is willing to take. Together, the two prices represent a quotation in that stock. A spread is the difference between the bid and asked prices. Bid and offer are the more common terms in discussing listed securities.

BIG 4 ACCOUNTING FIRMS four major public accounting firms, from the original eight, with many regional and local firms as well. The four are: PricewaterhouseCoopers, Deloitte, Ernst & Young, and KPMG. The second-tier firms include BDO Seidman, Grant Thornton, and McGladrey & Pullen.

BILLINGS ON LONG-TERM CONTRACTS amount charged by a company (e.g., construction company, defense contractor) to the customer for work done or to be done on a long-term project. *See also* PROGRESS BILLINGS.

BILL OF ACTIVITIES listing of the activities and activity volumes and associated costs required by a product, service, process output, or other cost object.

BILL OF EXCHANGE *see* DRAFT.

BILL OF LADING written document issued by a carrier that specifies contractual conditions and terms (such as time, place, person named for receipt) for delivery of goods. It also evidences receipt of goods. Upon transfer of the bill, title is passed to the goods.

BILL OF MATERIALS (BOM) listing of all the assemblies, subassemblies, parts, and raw materials that are needed to produce one unit of a finished product. Thus, each finished product has its own bill of materials. The listing in the bill of materials file is hierarchical; it shows the quantity of each item needed to complete one unit of the next-highest level of assembly.

BILL OF SALE written document that transfers goods, title, or other interests from a seller to a buyer and specifies the terms and conditions of the transaction.

BINOMIAL MODEL the most commonly used LATTICE-BASED MODEL of option pricing. Unlike the BLACK-SCHOLES OPTION PRICING MODEL (OPM), the binomial method divides the time from the option's grant date to the expiration date into small increments. Because the share price may increase or decrease during any interval, the binomial model takes into account how changes in price over the term of the option would affect the employee's exercise practice during each interval. The binomial model can also consider an option grant's lack of transferability, its forfeiture restrictions, and its vesting restrictions—even for options with more complicated terms such as indexed and performance-based vesting restrictions.

BIOMETRIC IDENTIFICATION relies on specific information about an individual's biological characteristics, such as finger print, iris, retina, DNA, and voice print, to identify an individual.

BIT a contraction of binary digits. It refers to a basic unit in computing, which may be in a state of either "on" or "off." A bit can have only one of two values, and is commonly represented by a value of 0 or 1.

BLACK-SCHOLES OPTION PRICING MODEL (OPM) formula for valuing stock options designed in 1973 by Nobel laureates Fischer Black and Myron Scholes; also known as the Black-Scholes-Merton model. A model is used to determine the value of option securities prices based on the relationship between six variables—the current underlying asset price, the option strike price, the option time-to-expiration, the riskless return, the underlying asset payout return, and the underlying asset volatility.

BLANKET APPROPRIATION usually associated with governmental accounting, an expenditure that is authorized without specification of the individual project elements.

BLANKET INSURANCE policy covering several items of property. The insurance policy is allocated to the property items based on their fair market values.

BLIND ENTRY
1. entry that reveals only its classificatory identity, appropriate debit and credit amounts and does not include an explanatory description of the transaction. *See also* JOURNAL ENTRY.
2. posting to a ledger account not documented by a journal or other source record.

BLOCK DIAGRAM diagram using symbols to explain the interconnections and information flow between hardware and software.

BLOCK SAMPLING JUDGMENT SAMPLE in which accounts or items are chosen in a sequential order. After the initial item in the block is chosen, the balance of the block is automatically selected. *See also* CLUSTER SAMPLING; SYSTEMATIC SAMPLING.

BLOG a contraction for Web Log. A blog is a Web site where new content is added or updated on a continuous basis. Often, the content consists of an individual's opinion about a specialized topic. WordPress is a very popular blogging software.

BLUE CHIP common stock of high quality that has a long record of earnings and dividend payments. Blue chip stocks are often viewed as long-term investment instruments. They have low risk and provide modest but dependable return. Examples are International Telephone and Telegraph and Minnesota Mining and Manufacturing. Blue chip may also refer to a high-quality bond that is secure and stable in price and interest payments.

BLUE SKY LAW law providing for state regulation and supervision of the issuance of investment securities. The prevention of gross fraud is the primary purpose of these laws, which include procedures and regulations with respect to broker licensing, registration of new issues, and formal approvals by appropriate governing bodies.

BLUETOOTH the standard wireless Personal Area Network (PAN) for transmitting data over a 2.4 gigahertz (GHz) band frequency.

BOARD OF DIRECTORS group of persons elected by a company's stockholders to run the business according to the corporate charter. Senior management is appointed by the Board. Typically, the Board consists of top management executives (INSIDE DIRECTORS) and representatives external to the company (OUTSIDE DIRECTORS). The Board has significant influence over accounting and financial policies of the business entity.

BOILERPLATE standard legal language used in contracts, prospectuses, wills, and so on. Boilerplate typically appears in fine print. It contains important information rarely subject to modification between the parties.

BOND
1. written promise by a company, government, or other institution to pay the face amount at the maturity date. Periodic interest payments are usually required. Bonds are typically stated in $1,000 denominations. Bonds may be *secured* by collateral or *unsecured* (debenture). A *registered bond* has the name of the owner on the issuer's records, whereas the holder of a BEARER BOND presents coupons for interest payments. SINKING FUND bonds require the company to make annual deposits to a trustee. At maturity, the amount in the sinking fund (principal plus interest) is sufficient to pay the face of the bond. From the company's perspective, a bond issue has several advantages over a stock issue. Interest expense is tax deductible, whereas dividend payments are not. During inflation, debt is paid back in cheaper dollars. When bonds are issued at face value, the entry is to debit cash and credit bonds payable. When bonds are issued at a discount, such as with zero-coupon bonds, the entry is to debit cash and bond discount and credit bonds payable. The entry to record the interest each period is to

debit interest expense and credit cash. *See also* BOND CONVERSION; BOND DISCOUNT; BOND PREMIUM.

2. cash or property given to assure performance (i.e., contractor depositing a *performance bond* on a construction project to be completed by a specified date).

3. type of insurance compensating employer for employee dishonesty.

BOND CONVERSION exchange of a convertible bond for stock. While conversion is typically at the option of the investor, in some cases it may be at the option of the issuing company (e.g., forced conversion). The conversion may be accounted for under the BOOK VALUE METHOD or MARKET VALUE METHOD.

BOND DISCOUNT the amount below FACE VALUE at which a bond is issued. A bond may be issued at a discount when the interest rate on the bond is below the prevailing market interest rate, the company has financial problems, and the bond has a long maturity period. Bond discount is a CONTRA ACCOUNT to bonds payable to arrive at the CARRYING VALUE. Assume a $300,000 bond is issued at 93%. The bond discount is $21,000 ($300,000 × 7%). *See also* BOND PREMIUM.

BOND ELECTRONIC TRANSFER FUNDS (ETFs) fixed-income ETFs. Bond ETFs have several advantages: (1) They are well-diversified baskets of bonds with different maturities; (2) their expense ratio is low—15 basis points, compared with an average of 39 for bond mutual funds; and (3) their greater transparency over individual bonds further lowers costs. Also, with bonds, individual investors can't get good prices, but institutions can.

BOND FUND
1. IN GOVERNMENT ACCOUNTING, a fund established for the receipt and distribution of monies received from the issuance of a bond.

2. a MUTUAL FUND that invests in bonds. *See also* SINKING FUND.

BOND INDENTURE agreement between a bond issuer and holder covering the terms of issue; also called *deed of trust*. The bond terms include such conditions as dollar amount of issue; PLEDGED ASSETS; COVENANTS (e.g., working capital requirement); events of default; and call privileges. It also provides for the appointment of a trustee. *See also* INDENTURE.

BOND ISSUE COSTS expenditures incurred in preparing and selling a bond issue such as legal, underwriting, accounting, commission, printing, promotion, and registration fees. These costs represent a DEFERRED CHARGE that is amortized using the straight-line method over the period the bonds are outstanding (date of issue to the maturity date). Note that the amortization starts from the date the bonds are sold and *not* the date of the bonds (which may be before the issue date).

Assume a five-year bond dated 1/1/2014 is sold on 9/1/2014. Bond issue costs are $10,000. Since there are 52 months between 9/1/2014 and 1/1/2019, the amortization per month is $192.31 ($10,000/52 months). The amortization expense for 2014 is $769.24 ($192.31 per month × 4 months from 9/1/2014 to 12/31/2014). *See also* AMORTIZE.

BOND OUTSTANDING METHOD method of amortizing bond discount or premium. This is a variation of the straight-line method that spreads bond discount or premium over the life of a bond issue by periodic charges to expense.

The charges are determined by the ratio of the face value of bonds outstanding during the period to the total of such face values for all the periods during which the bonds are outstanding.

BOND PREMIUM the amount in excess of FACE VALUE (maturity value) at which a bond is issued. A BOND may be issued at a premium if the interest rate on the bond exceeds the market interest rate or it is from a financially strong company. For example, if a $100,000 bond was issued at 106, the bond premium is $6,000 ($100,000 × 6%). Bond premium is added to the bond payable account under noncurrent liabilities to arrive at the carrying value of the bond. The bond premium account is amortized each year so that at maturity the bond will equal its face value. The amortization entry each year is to debit bond premium and credit interest expense. When a bond is issued at a premium, the EFFECTIVE INTEREST RATE is less than the NOMINAL INTEREST RATE. *See also* BOND DISCOUNT; YIELD TO MATURITY.

BOND RATINGS calculations of the probability that a bond issue will go into default. They measure risk, and therefore have an impact on the interest rate. Bond investors tend to place more emphasis on independent analysis of quality than do common stock investors. Bond analysis and ratings are done by Standard & Poor and Moody's among other rating agencies.

BOND SINKING FUND represents cash that is set aside for the purpose of paying back bonds issued by an entity. The bond sinking fund, which may involve annual contributions, is typically administered by an independent trustee.

BONUS METHOD partnership accounting method in which a new partner contributing goodwill or intangible value is credited with capital in excess of the tangible assets contributed.

BOOK
1. used as a noun (usually plural), it refers to JOURNALS or LEDGERS.
2. used as a verb, it refers to the recording of an entry. *See also* BOOK VALUE.

BOOK BALANCE term used for the amount of an account balance at the end of an accounting period. For example, when preparing a BANK RECONCILIATION, the balance in the cash account at the end of the month is referred to as the book balance. In a similar vein, the auditor compares the book balance in ending inventory with the physical count to uncover any discrepancies.

BOOK INVENTORY inventory shown on the financial records. It is a book value as opposed to a physical count of inventory and is computed from the initial inventory plus purchases less requisitions or withdrawals. Book inventory typically differs from the physical inventory on hand due to SHRINKAGE (i.e., loss caused by such factors as evaporation and thefts).

BOOKKEEPER individual basically concerned with accounting support functions within the firm. Duties include recording journal entries in the various journals, posting and maintaining the ledger, preparing a trial balance, making up the payroll, and preparing a bank reconciliation. In a smaller firm, the bookkeeper often has a broader responsibility, such as accounts receivable collections.

BOOKKEEPING accounting support functions performed by the BOOK-KEEPER. Bookkeeping is the most basic of the accounting duties and requires less education and experience.

BOOKKEEPING CYCLE *see* ACCOUNTING CYCLE.

BOOK OF ORIGINAL ENTRY JOURNAL in which transactions are *first recorded.*

BOOK-TO-BILL RATIO a ratio comparing new orders against shipments of specific goods. As an example, the Semiconductor Industry Association's book-to-bill ratio monthly movements are an indication of strength or weakness in the computer business because it shows the current demand for computer chips.

BOOK VALUE
1. net amount shown for an asset on the balance sheet. It equals the gross cost less the related valuation account. For example, the book value of an auto is its initial cost less the accumulated depreciation. Since book value is based on HISTORICAL COST, it will differ from market value. Book value is a going-concern value.
2. carrying value of a liability equal to its face value less unamortized discount.
3. the difference between total tangible assets and total liabilities, less the value of the preferred stock. This gives the book value of the common stockholders' equity. Book value of the net assets of a company may have little or no significant relationship to their market value. It was once used as a proxy for a company's intrinsic value. Especially with the new economy, book value is a less relevant measure for a company's fair value for investors. For example, many new economy companies have assets that do not register significantly on their balance sheet, such as intellectual property, employees, strong brand, and market share. Book value per share of a stock is a company's books based on historical cost. It may differ significantly from current market price per share (as illustrated in the following table). Book value per share of common stock equals common stockholders' equity divided by outstanding common shares.

Book Value and Market Value for Selected Companies (In billions) (March 23, 2009)

Company	Book Value	Market Value
Microsoft (MSFT)	$34.53	$162.96
IBM (IBM)	13.08	132.44
Wal-Mart Stores (WMT)	64.90	201.93
General Electric (GE)	105.26	110.15

Source: moneycentral.msn.com/investor/home.asp

BOOK VALUE METHOD manner of accounting for a BOND CONVERSION into stock. The entry is to debit bonds payable and premium on bonds payable (or credit discount on bonds payable) and credit common stock and premium on common stock. Note that the total credit is based on the bond's book value. No gain or loss is recognized. Other entries may also be involved such as recording the interest payment prior to the bond conversion. *See also* MARKET VALUE METHOD.

BOOK VALUE PER SHARE worth of each share of stock per the books based on historical cost. It differs from market price per share. Book value per share can be computed for common stock and preferred stock as follows:

Book Value Per Share (Common Stock):

$$\frac{\text{Total Stockholders'}\ \text{Equity} - \left(\begin{array}{c}\text{Liquidation Value} \\ \text{of Preferred Stock}\end{array} + \begin{array}{c}\text{Preferred Dividends} \\ \text{in Arrears}\end{array}\right)}{\text{Total Common Shares Issued and Subscribed at Year-End}}$$

Book Value Per Share (Preferred Stock):

$$\frac{\text{Liquidation Value of Preferred Stock} + \text{Preferred Dividends in Arrears}}{\text{Total Preferred Shares at Year-End}}$$

BOOLEAN ALGEBRA the algebra of logic. It is sometimes called symbolic logic. Boolean algebra is a method of expressing logic in a mathematical context. It is primarily concerned with binary operations and based on the cumulative, associative, and distributive laws of binary operations. Boolean algebra provides the theoretical concepts for computer design. It is not used to solve managerial problems directly.

BOOT
1. in *computers*, process of starting up a computer. The term *boot* derives from the idea that the computer has to pull itself up by its bootstraps, that is, load into memory a small program that enables it to load larger programs. There are two types of booting operations. One is *cold boot*, which is the operation of booting a computer that has been completely shut down. The other is *warm boot*, which is a restarting operation in which some of the needed programs are already in memory. In the case of the PC, for example, the warm boot is done by pressing the *ctr*, *alt*, and *del* keys simultaneously. On Macs, this can be done by pressing the Restart button.
2. in taxation, cash or property of a type not included in the definition of a nontaxable exchange. The receipt of boot will cause an otherwise tax-free transfer to become taxable to the extent of the smaller of the fair market value of such boot or the realized gain on the transfer. Examples of those types include transfers to controlled corporations.

BOT a computer program used to perform structured and repetitive tasks across the Internet. Bots are sometimes referred to as "spyders" or "crawlers" that access Web sites and collect data. A common use of bots is to index Web sites for use by search engines. Bots may also be used for malicious purposes, such as harvesting e-mail addresses from Web sites, to use for spamming.

BOTTLENECK an activity for which the work equals or exceeds the capacity of the activity.

BOTTOM LINE
1. net income after taxes.
2. expression as to the result of something. An example is the sales generated from an advertising campaign.

BRAINSTORMING the exchange of ideas. Brainstorming among CPA firm personnel is mandatory in the planning stage of a financial statement audit and should address the risk of material misstatement due to fraud.

BRANCH ACCOUNTING maintenance of a separate accounting system for each branch of one legal entity. The home office opens an account in its general ledger entitled Branch, Branch Control, Investment in Branch, or some other similar name. Frequently, one account will be used to show the long-term investment in a branch while another account (such as Branch Current) will be used for more common accounts. In the home office ledger, this account or group of accounts is charged for everything sent to the branch or for services rendered to or for the branch, and it is credited for amounts received from the branch. In a similar manner, the branch ledger maintains an equity account entitled Home Office, Home Office Control, Home Office Current, or some other similar name. This account is credited for all assets received by the branch from the home office. It is also credited for all debts incurred for merchandise acquired or for services rendered by the home office for the branch. Such an account would also be credited as a result of expenses incurred by the home office for the benefit of the branch. It is debited for amounts sent by the branch to the home office. In operation, the branch account on the home office books will be debited when the home office account on the branch books is credited, and vice versa. Thus, the balances of such a pair of accounts should be equal in dollar amount, but the balances should be the opposite sides of the respective accounts. Two accounts that have such a relationship are often referred to as RECIPROCAL.

BREAK-EVEN ANALYSIS branch of COST-VOLUME-PROFIT (CVP) ANALYSIS that determines the break-even point, which is the level of sales where total costs equal total revenue. Thus, zero profit results. Breakeven sales is computed as follows:

Break-even sales in *units* = Fixed costs/Unit contribution margin.

Break-even sales in *dollars* = Fixed costs/Contribution margin ratio.

For example, assume:

Fixed costs = $15,000.

Unit contribution margin (selling price – unit variable cost) = $15, and

Contribution margin ratio (unit CM/selling price) = .6

Then, break-even sales in *units* = $15,000/$15 = 1,000 units *and* break-even sales in *dollars* = $15,000/.6 = $25,000.

A break-even chart is one in which sales revenue, variable costs, and fixed costs are plotted on the vertical axis while volume is plotted on the horizontal axis. The BREAK-EVEN POINT is the point at which the total sales revenue line intersects the total cost line. See the following sample chart.

BREAK-EVEN CHART chart where sales revenue, variable costs, and fixed costs are plotted on the vertical axis while volume is plotted on the horizontal axis. The break-even point is the point where the total sales revenue line intersects the total cost line.

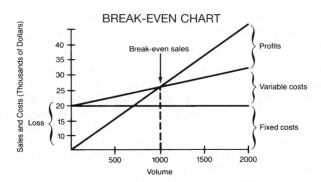

BREAK-EVEN EQUATION equation that helps determine BREAK-EVEN SALES.

Let: p = unit selling price
v = unit variable cost
FC = total fixed cost
x = sales in units

Then, the break-even equation can be set up as follows:

$$px = vx + FC$$

For example, assume that p = \$25, v = \$10, FC = \$15,000. The equation is:

$$\$25x = \$10x + \$15,000$$
$$\$25x - \$10x = \$15,000$$
$$\$15x = \$15,000$$
$$x = 1,000 \text{ units}$$

Therefore, break-even sales are 1000 units. Break-even sales expressed in dollars are \$25,000 (1,000 units $\times$ \$25).

BREAK-EVEN POINT *see* BREAK-EVEN SALES.

BREAK-EVEN SALES sales with no profit or loss, also called *break-even point*. It is the sales volume, in *units* or in *dollars*, where total sales revenue equals total costs. Thus, zero profit results. *See also* BREAK-EVEN ANALYSIS.

BREAK-EVEN TIME more sophisticated version of the payback method. It is the time required for the discounted expected future cash inflows on a project to equal the discounted cumulative cash outflows (usually the initial cost).

BRIDGE LOAN short-term loan that is made in expectation of intermediate- or long-term loans; also called a *swing loan*. The interest rate on the bridge loan is generally higher than on longer term loans. An example would be a temporary loan that is made to permit a closing on a building purchase prior to a closing on long-term mortgage financing.

BROKERAGE FEE commission paid to a broker who buys and sells securities. Fees vary depending on whether a full-service broker (e.g., one that provides recommendation reports) or a discount broker (e.g., one that just executes orders) is used. An example of a full-service broker is Prudential-Bache Securities. An example of a discount broker is Charles Schwab & Co. Fees also vary within each category so one full-service broker may charge you a different commission rate than another. Brokerage fees may depend on the market price per share and the number of shares traded.

BROKER CALL LOAN *see* CALL LOAN.

BUDGET quantitative plan of activities and programs expressed in terms of assets, liabilities, revenues, and expenses. Budget participants will be involved in carrying out the plan, or in other quantitative terms such as units of product or service. The budget expresses the organizational goals in terms of specific financial and operating objectives. Advantages of budget preparation are planning, communicating company-wide goals to subunits, fostering cooperation between departments, maintaining control by evaluating actual figures to budget figures, and revealing the interrelationship of one function to another. *See also* MASTER (COMPREHENSIVE) BUDGET.

BUDGETARY ACCOUNTABILITY in GOVERNMENT ACCOUNTING, process of recording budgetary amounts in the accounts of a fund. Recording the balances has a dual effect. (1) The control aspect of the budgetary function is stressed, and (2) recognition is given to the legal foundations of the budget. The need for such recording is consistent with the responsibility of fund accounting. It is concerned with performance in terms of authority to act and the action itself. Recording both the budget and actual transactions helps to fix responsibility. The journal entry at the adoption of a budget is:

Estimated revenue	x	
Fund balance	x or x	
Appropriations		x

The journal entry to close the budget at year-end is:

Appropriations	x	
Revenue	x	
Estimated revenue		x
Expenditures		x
Encumbrances		x
Fund balance	x or x	

BUDGETARY SLACK intentional underestimation of revenues and/or overestimation of expenses; also called *budget slack*. This must be avoided if a budget is to have its desired effects. Misstating projections of costs and revenues for this purpose is behavior that is both dysfunctional and unethical.

BUDGET COMMITTEE group, usually made up of top management and the chief financial officer, that reviews and approves, or makes appropriate adjustments to the budgets submitted from operational managers.

BUDGET CONTROL budgetary actions carried out according to a budget plan. Through the use of a budget as a standard, an organization ensures that managers are implementing its plans and objectives and that their activities are appraised by comparing their actual performance against budgeted performance. Budgets are used as a basis for rewarding or punishing managers, or perhaps for modifying future budgets and plans.

BUDGETED BALANCE SHEET schedule for expected assets, liabilities, and stockholders' equity. It projects a company's financial position as of the end of the budgeting year. Reasons for preparing a budgeted balance sheet follow:

(1) discloses unfavorable financial condition that management may want to avoid; (2) serves as a final check on the mathematical accuracy of all other budgets; and (3) highlights future resources and obligations.

BUDGETED INCOME STATEMENT summary of various component projections of revenues and expenses for the budget period. It indicates the expected net income for the period.

BUDGET INFORMATION quantifiable information about an entity's future activities and the revenues or expenses associated with those activities.

BUDGETING FUND annual budgets of estimated revenues and estimated expenditures prepared for most governmental funds. The approved budgets of such funds are recorded in "budgetary accounts" in the accounting system to provide control over governmental revenues and expenditures.

BUDGETING MODELS mathematical models that generate a profit planning budget. The models help managerial accountants and budget analysts answer a variety of what-if questions. The resultant calculations provide a basis for choice among alternatives under conditions of uncertainty. Budgeting models are usually quantitative and computer-based. There are primarily two approaches to modeling in the corporate budgeting process: SIMULATION and OPTIMIZATION MODEL. *See also* FINANCIAL MODEL; SIMULATION MODELS.

BUDGET MANUAL collection of procedures that describe how a budget is to be prepared. Items usually appearing in a budget manual include a budget planning calendar and distribution instructions for all budget schedules. Distribution instructions are important because, once a schedule is prepared, other departments in the organization use the schedule to prepare their own budgets. Without distribution instructions, someone who needs a particular schedule might be overlooked.

BUDGET PLANNING CALENDAR schedule of activities for the development and adoption of the budget. It should include a list of dates indicating when specific information is to be provided to others by each information source. The preparation of a master budget usually takes several months. For instance, many firms start the budget for the next calendar year in September, anticipating its completion by the first of December. Because all of the individual departmental budgets are based on forecasts prepared by others and the budgets of other departments, a planning calendar is essential to integrate the entire process.

BUDGET REPORT report that provides the basis for controlling (monitoring and revising) activities of an organization by comparing actual performance (actual sales or costs) with budgeted performance (budgeted sales or costs). A budget report has columns for budgeted and actual amounts. The difference between the two is the VARIANCE.

BUDGET VARIANCE
1. any difference between a budgeted figure and an actual figure.
2. any difference between actual factory overhead costs and standard (flexible budget) costs, multiplied by the standard units of activity allowed for actual production. The budget variance is used in the TWO-WAY ANALYSIS of factory overhead. It includes the fixed and variable spending variances

and the variable overhead efficiency variance that are used in the THREE-WAY ANALYSIS.

BUFFER area of a computer's memory set aside to hold information temporarily. The buffer compensates for the different rates that hardware devices process data. For instance, the buffer holds data waiting to be printed so that the central processing unit is free to perform other tasks. A buffer is also used to hold information received from a computer in a remote location when doing TELECOMMUNICATIONS. This is known as a *capture buffer*. A downloaded ASCII file may be loaded into a word processing program and edited. Further, the ASCII data file may then be loaded into a smart telecommunications software program's *transmit buffer* and uploaded to another remote computer over the telephone lines.

BUG
1. mistake in a software program. Two types of errors are logic and syntax. A *logic error* is when the program does not conduct the process it was supposed to. A *syntax error* is where the rules of the programming languages are not followed.
2. hardware malfunctioning in the computer system. *See also* DEBUG.

BULL stock market jargon for an individual or institution that believes a given stock or the stock market in general will experience a price rise. It is also an adjective to describe an upward price stock movement. *Compare with* BEAR.

BULLETIN BOARD (BB)
1. a collection of message boards and files devoted to a particular topic.
2. properly known as the *OTC Bulletin Board*, an electronic quotation service that lists the prices of stocks that don't meet the minimum requirements for listing on a stock exchange or the NASDAQ stock-listing system.

BUSINESS COMBINATION alliance of a company and one or more incorporated or unincorporated businesses into a single accounting entity that then carries on the activities of the separate entities. A business combination must be accounted for under the PURCHASE (ACCOUNTING) METHOD. It does *not* cover the transfer of a business to a substitute corporation. The business combination date comes before the CONSOLIDATION date when consolidated financial statements are prepared.

BUSINESS CONTINUITY PLAN (BCP) identifies an organzation's exposures to vulnerabilities and how to resume functioning after a major calamity, such as a fire, hurricane, or earthquake. Sometimes referred to as a *Disaster Recovery Plan (DSP)*.

BUSINESS CYCLE recurrence of periods of contracting and expanding economic conditions with effects on growth, employment, and inflation. The business cycle has an impact on corporate expansion, earnings, and cash flow.

BUSINESS EXPENSE DEDUCTION allowable reduction of business gross income, usually associated with expenses incurred that are reasonable and necessary for the production of business income. Examples include bad debts, depreciation, employee benefit programs, and insurance. Some business expenses are not deductible in the computation of taxable income (e.g., fines).

BUSINESS INTELLIGENCE (BI) software applications used to analyze an organization's raw data using techniques such as data mining, online analytical processing, and querying and reporting. BI is often used to identify inefficient processes that require dramatic reengineering.

BUSINESS PROCESS *see* PROCESS.

BUSINESS PROCESS REENGINEERING (BPR) the analysis and design of work flow within an organization. It is the key to transforming how people work in order to make an organization more efficient. BPR requires an organization to reexamine its core activity and implement a radical change.

BYLAWS self-imposed rules of a corporation. Unlike articles of incorporation, bylaws are not required to be filed with the Secretary of State. *See* ARTICLES OF INCORPORATION.

BY-PRODUCT item emerging from a single production process that has a relatively low sales value in comparison with the firm's main or JOINT PRODUCTS. Examples of by-products are sawdust or wood chips in lumber mill operations. Because the relative value of by-products is not very important, it is usually considered undesirable to use a refined accounting method in dealing with by-product costs. Generally, the sales value of by-products is used to reduce the cost of the main products. An alternative accounting approach is to treat the sales value of the by-products as "other revenue."

BYTE a basic unit of computing. A byte consists of 8 bits. Traditionally, an alphanumeric character has been represented by a byte. *See also* BITS.

C

CAFETERIA PLAN one permitting employees to choose from a variety of fringe benefits. The tax code provides that, with minor exceptions, no amount shall be included in the gross income of the participant in a cafeteria plan solely because the participant may choose among the benefits (including cash) of the plan.

CALL
1. option to buy (or call) an asset at a specified price within a specified period.
2. right to buy 100 shares of stock at a specified price within a specified period. *See also* OPTION.
3. process of redeeming a bond or preferred stock issue before its normal maturity. A security with a CALL PROVISION typically is issued at an interest rate higher than one without a call provision. This is because investors demand it—they look at yield-to-call rather than yield-to-maturity.

CALLABLE BOND bond issue with a call (buy back) provision. *See also* CALLABLE SECURITY.

CALLABLE SECURITY bond or preferred stock issue with a CALL PROVISION. The provision in the indenture or preferred stock agreement allows an issuing company to redeem the security early. When interest rates are expected to decline, a call provision in the bond issue is desirable from an issuer's standpoint. Such a provision enables the firm to buy back the high-interest security and issue a lower-interest one. *See also* CALL.

CALL LOAN one that brokers make from banks to cover the securities positions of their clients; also called *broker call loan*. The rate is quoted daily in newspapers as a money market indicator.

CALL PREMIUM
1. amount in excess of par value that a company must pay when it calls a security. It is the difference between the CALL PRICE and the maturity value. The issuer pays the premium to the security holder in order to acquire the outstanding security before the maturity date. The call premium is generally equal to one year's interest if the bond is called in the first year, and it declines at a constant rate each year thereafter.
2. OPTION.

CALL PRICE price that must be paid when a security is called. The call price is equal to the par value plus the CALL PREMIUM.

CALL PROVISION feature of some bond indentures allowing the issuing company to redeem bonds prior to maturity by paying holders a premium above face value. An issuing company typically wishes to retire a callable bond when interest rates decline.

CA MAGAZINE journal published monthly by the Canadian Institute of Chartered Accountants. It is read by accountants in public practice, industry, and government. The subject matter includes information systems, international accounting, professional ethics, estate planning, and taxation. E-mail: camagazine@cica.ca.

CANADIAN INSTITUTE OF CHARTERED ACCOUNTANTS (CICA) primary national organization of chartered accountants in Canada. The CICA handbook is the principal authoritative reference for policy on accepted accounting practices in Canada. CICA was originally founded in 1902 as the Dominion Association of Chartered Accountants.

CANCELED CHECK draft paid by the bank on which it is drawn and returned to the depositor. The canceled check is in effect the depositor's receipt that the payee has cashed it.

CAPACITY ability to produce during a given time period, with an upper limit imposed by the availability of space, machinery, labor, materials, or capital. Capacity may be expressed in units, weights, size, dollars, man-hours, labor cost, etc. Typically, there are five different concepts of capacity.
(1) *Ideal capacity*—volume of activity that could be attained under ideal operating conditions, with minimum allowance for inefficiency. It is the largest volume of output possible. Also called *theoretical capacity*, *engineered capacity*, or *maximum capacity*.
(2) *Practical capacity*—highest activity level at which the factory can operate with an acceptable degree of efficiency, taking into consideration unavoidable losses of productive time (i.e., vacations, holidays, repairs to equipment). Also called *maximum practical capacity*.
(3) *Normal capacity*—average level of operating activity that is sufficient to fill the demand for the company's products or services for a span of several years, taking into consideration seasonal and cyclical demands and increasing or decreasing trends in demand.
(4) *Expected actual capacity*—similar to normal capacity, except it is a short-run level based on demand, it minimizes under- or overapplied overhead but does not provide a consistent basis for assigning overhead cost. Per-unit overhead will fluctuate because of short-term changes in the expected level of output. Also called *planned capacity*.
(5) *Operating capacity*—similar to planned capacity except the time period is within a small slice of a single year (i.e., daily, monthly, quarterly).

CAPACITY COSTS fixed costs incurred to provide facilities that increase a firm's ability to produce such as those relating to space, equipment, and factory buildings. They include rents, depreciation, property taxes, and insurance. *See also* DISCRETIONARY (FIXED) COSTS; FIXED COST.

CAPACITY MANAGEMENT management of a company's costs of unused (excess) capacity. The unused capacity in production facilities, distribution channels, marketing organizations, and so on are ordinarily not assigned to products or services on a cause-and-effect basis, so their inclusion in overhead rates may distort pricing decisions. Including the fixed costs of unused capacity in a cost-based price results in higher prices and in what is known as the downward (black hole) demand spiral.

CAPACITY REQUIREMENTS PLANNING (CRP) system for determining if a planned production schedule can be accomplished with available capacity and, if not, making adjustments as necessary.

CAPITAL
1. equity interest of the owner in the business that is the difference between ASSETS and LIABILITIES, also called EQUITY or NET WORTH. In a corpora-

tion, capital represents the stockholders' equity. Capital stock consists of common stock and preferred stock. *See also* CAPITAL ACCOUNT; LEGAL CAPITAL: PAID-IN CAPITAL.

2. goods purchased for use in production.

3. WORKING CAPITAL, which is the difference between current assets and current liabilities.

4. long-term assets that are not bought and sold in the ordinary course of business. The term usually refers to FIXED ASSETS such as machinery, equipment, building, and land.

CAPITAL ACCOUNT general ledger account describing OWNERS' EQUITY in a business. CAPITAL is the *equity interest*, which is the difference between assets and liabilities. In a sole proprietorship, there is only one capital account since there is only one owner. In a partnership, a capital account exists for each owner. In a corporation, capital represents the STOCKHOLDERS' EQUITY, which equals the capital stock issued plus paid-in capital in excess of par (or stated) value plus retained earnings. DONATED CAPITAL is added to and TREASURY STOCK is deducted from total stockholders' equity in the balance sheet.

CAPITAL ADDITION
1. *new* (as opposed to replacement) part added to an existing noncurrent productive asset (e.g., equipment) used for business purposes that increases the useful life and service potential of the asset.
2. in taxation, cost of capital improvements and betterments made to the property by a taxpayer.
3. anything added to long-term productive assets.

CAPITAL ASSET
1. asset purchased for use in production over long periods of time rather than for resale. It includes (a) land, buildings, plant and equipment, mineral deposits, and timber reserves; (b) patents, goodwill, trademarks, and leaseholds; and (c) investments in affiliated companies.
2. in taxation, property held by a taxpayer, except cash, inventoriable assets, merchandise held for sale, receivables, and certain intangibles.
3. FIXED ASSET usually consisting of tangible assets such as plant and equipment and intangible assets such as a patent.

CAPITAL ASSET PRICING MODEL (CAPM) theory of asset pricing used to analyze the relationship between risk and rates of return in securities. The return of an asset or security is the risk-free return plus a risk premium based on the excess of the return on the market over the risk-free rate multiplied by the asset's systematic risk (which cannot be eliminated by diversification). The model is given as follows:

$$r = r_f + b \ (r_m - r_f)$$

where r = the expected (or required) return on a security, r_f = the risk-free rate (such as a T-bill), r_m = the expected return on the market portfolio (such as Standard & Poor's 500 Stock Composite Index or Dow Jones 30 Industrials), and b = beta, an index of systematic (nondiversifiable, uncontrollable) risk. For example, assume that the risk-free rate (r_f) is 8%, and the expected market return (r_m) is 12%. Then if $b = 0$, $r = 8\% + 0 \ (12\% - 8\%) = 8\%$. If $b = 2.0$, $r = 8\% + 2.0 \ (12\% - 8\%) = 16\%$. This shows that the higher the degree of systematic risk (*b*), the higher the return on a given security demanded by investors.

CAPITAL BUDGET plan of proposed acquisitions and replacements of long-term assets and their financing. A capital budget is developed using a variety of CAPITAL BUDGETING techniques such as the *payback* method, the NET PRESENT VALUE (NPV) method, or the INTERNAL RATE OF RETURN (IRR) method.

CAPITAL BUDGETING process of making long-term planning decisions for capital investments. There are typically two types of investment decisions: (1) Selecting new facilities or expanding existing facilities. Examples include: (a) investments in long-term assets such as property, plant, and equipment; and (b) resource commitments in the form of new product development, market research, refunding of long-term debt, introduction of a computer, etc. (2) Replacing existing facilities with new facilities. Examples include replacing a manual bookkeeping system with a computerized system and replacing an inefficient lathe with one that is numerically controlled. As such, capital budgeting decisions are a key factor in the long-term profitability of a firm. To make wise investment decisions, managers need tools at their disposal that will guide them in comparing the benefits and costs of various investment alternatives. Many techniques used for evaluating investment proposals are widely available. They include *payback*, ACCOUNTING RATE OF RETURN, INTERNAL RATE OF RETURN, and the NET PRESENT VALUE method.

CAPITAL DECAY
1. quantification of the lost revenues or reduction in net cash flows sustained by an entity due to obsolete technology.
2. measure of noncompetitiveness.

CAPITAL EXPENDITURE outlay charged to a long-term asset account. A capital expenditure either adds a fixed asset unit or increases the value of an existing fixed asset. An example is a new motor for a truck. *See also* REVENUE EXPENDITURE.

CAPITAL EXPENDITURE BUDGET plan prepared for individual capital expenditure projects. The time span of this budget depends upon the project. Capital expenditures to be budgeted include replacement, acquisition, or construction of plants and major equipment. *See also* CAPITAL BUDGETING.

CAPITAL GAIN tax term involved with selling or exchanging a CAPITAL ASSET.
Individual: Maximum tax rate on capital gains is substantially less than the maximum tax rate on ordinary income.
Corporation: Capital gains are taxed as ordinary income. *See also* CAPITAL LOSS.

CAPITAL INTENSIVE term that describes a company with significant CAPITAL ASSETS (e.g., machinery), such as those in the automobile and airline industries. Capital intensive companies run a higher risk; if there is a downturn in sales, profits will decrease sharply because FIXED COST cannot be reduced in the short-term to meet declining demand. A diagram illustrating the downside risk potential follows:

CAPITAL INTENSIVE DIAGRAM

Downside Risk

See also LABOR INTENSIVE.

CAPITAL INVESTMENT DECISIONS management decisions about when and how much to spend on capital facilities for the organization.

CAPITALIZATION
  1. total amount of the various securities issued by a corporation. Capitalization may include bonds, preferred and common stock.
  2. a technique used by real estate appraisers to convert the income of a property into a value estimate for that property.

CAPITALIZATION OF EARNINGS concept of valuing a business by determining the NET PRESENT VALUE (NPV) of expected future profits. In an economic sense, a company is worth the discounted amount of its net income. The concept can also be applied to valuing a particular asset (e.g., machine), which should theoretically be worth the present value of future earnings to be derived from it.

CAPITALIZATION OF INTEREST process of deferring interest as an asset rather than an expense. Interest charges can be deferred only for interest incurred on borrowed funds for the self-construction of an asset or for discrete projects (e.g., real estate). The amount of interest capitalized is based on the company's actual borrowings and interest payments. The interest rate to be used is the rate on the specific borrowing associated with that self-constructed asset. If this cannot be achieved, the weighted-average interest rate on corporate debt is used.

CAPITALIZATION RATE (CAP RATE) a tool used by real estate people to determine a value of an investment. It is calculated by dividing a property's net operating income by its purchase price.

CAPITALIZE to charge an expenditure to an asset account because it benefits a period in excess of one year. For example, a betterment to a machine would be capitalized to the machinery account.

CAPITAL LEASE one in which the LESSEE obtains significant property rights. Although *not* legally a purchase, THEORETICAL SUBSTANCE governs over legal form and requires that the leased property be recorded as an asset on the lessee's books. The asset equals the present value of MINIMUM LEASE PAYMENTS. A capital lease exists if any *one* of the following four criteria is met: (1) the lease transfers ownership of the property to the lessee at the end of the lease term; (2) a BARGAIN PURCHASE OPTION exists; (3) lease term is 75% or more of the life of the property; (4) the present value of minimum lease payments equals or exceeds 90% of the fair value of the property.

CAPITAL LEVERAGE see FINANCIAL LEVERAGE.

CAPITAL LOSS federal tax term for the loss on the sale or exchange of a CAPITAL ASSET.

Individual: Capital losses are fully deductible to offset CAPITAL GAINS and can offset $3,000 of ordinary income.

Corporation: Capital losses are deductible only to the extent of capital gains.

CAPITAL MAINTENANCE CONCEPT principle in accounting stating that earnings can be realized only after an organization's capital has been maintained at a predetermined level.

CAPITAL MARKET trading center for long-term debt and corporate stocks. The NEW YORK STOCK EXCHANGE (NYSE), which trades the stocks of many of the larger corporations, is a prime example of a capital market. The *American Stock Exchange* and the regional stock exchanges are also examples. In addition, securities are issued and traded through the thousands of brokers and dealers on the OVER-THE-COUNTER market.

CAPITAL PROJECTS FUND in governmental accounting, a fund that accounts for financial resources to be used for the acquisition or construction of capital facilities. The total cost of a capital project is accumulated in a single expenditures account, which accumulates until the project is completed, at which time the fund ceases to exist.

CAPITAL RATIONING selecting the mix of acceptable projects that provides the highest overall NET PRESENT VALUE (NPV) when a company has a limit on the budget for capital spending. The PROFITABILITY INDEX is used widely in ranking projects competing for limited funds.

CAPITAL RECOVERY ALLOWANCE in *taxation*, term describing a cost recovery of capital. An example is depreciation expense taken over the expected life of the capital asset, although an ACCELERATED COST RECOVERY SYSTEM (ACRS) ignores such time-honored concepts as useful life and salvage value. A recovery allowance may also take the form of depreciation with shorter useful lives and immediate expensing (e.g., research and development). *See also* DEPRECIATION.

CAPITAL STOCK equity shares in a corporation authorized by its Articles of Incorporation and issued to stockholders. The two basic types of capital stock are COMMON STOCK and PREFERRED STOCK.

CAPITAL STOCK SUBSCRIBED shares acquired under an installment plan; also termed *subscribed stock*. In this way by making a down payment, a potential stockholder reserves shares that may be issued only when full payment has been received. The entry at the time of subscription is to debit cash and/or subscriptions receivable and credit capital stock subscribed and premium on capital stock, if any. Capital stock subscribed is shown under capital stock in the stockholders' equity section of the balance sheet. If a subscriber defaults on the subscription, the company must account for it in accordance with the laws of the states of incorporation.

CAPITAL STRUCTURE composition of common stock, preferred stock and the various classes thereof, retained earnings, and long-term debt maintained by the business entity in financing its assets. However, not everybody agrees that long-term debt is part of the capital structure. Proponents say it finances long-term assets. Opponents say it is debt—due to creditors—which means it has significantly different characteristics compared to any form of owners' equity.

CAPITAL SURPLUS paid-in capital not assigned to common stock. An example is the amount received from stockholders in excess of the par value of shares issued. Capital surplus is an archaic term. *Premium on capital stock* is preferred.

CARRYING CHARGE *see* CARRYING COSTS.

CARRYING COSTS expenses incurred because a firm keeps inventories, also called *holding costs*. They include interest forgone on money invested in inventory, storage cost, taxes, and insurance. The greater the inventory level, the higher the carrying costs.

CARRYING VALUE amount shown on an entity's books for assets, liabilities, or owner's equity, net of reductions or offsets such as for accumulated depreciation, allowance for bad debts, and bond discount; also called BOOK VALUE. It may refer to the entire firm's excess of total assets over total liabilities.

CARRYOVER BASIS method used in the valuation of property acquired from a decedent for tax purposes. The unified transfer tax of 1976 provides for the valuation of property to be the adjusted basis immediately preceding death. This adjusted basis is then further adjusted with respect to such aspects of a transfer as appreciated property, election of fair market value for personal items, and exceptions for small estates.

CASH money deposited in a bank and items that a bank will accept for immediate deposit (e.g., paper money, coins, checks, money orders). Items not included in the definition of cash are postdated checks, IOUs, and notes receivable. The cash on hand and cash on deposit in the bank are shown in the balance sheet as one figure. Cash is the most liquid of the current assets and is listed first. Note that *restricted* cash in a bank account is not considered a current asset. An example is cash held in a foreign country where remission restrictions exist.

CASH BASIS ACCOUNTING method of recognizing revenue and expenses when cash is received or disbursed rather than when earned or incurred. A service business not dealing in inventory has the option of using the cash basis or *accrual* basis. Individual taxpayers preparing their tax returns are essentially on the cash basis.

CASH BUDGET budget for cash planning and control that presents expected cash inflow and outflow for a designated time period. The cash budget helps management keep cash balances in reasonable relationship to its needs. It aids in avoiding idle cash and possible cash shortages. The cash budget typically consists of four major sections: (1) *receipts section*, which is the beginning cash balance, cash collections from customers, and other receipts; (2) *disbursement section* comprised of all cash payments made by purpose; (3) *cash surplus or deficit section* showing the difference between cash receipts and cash payments; and (4) *financing section* providing a detailed account of the borrowings and repayments expected during the period.

CASH COW a business or the segment of the business that generates tons of money.

CASH DISBURSEMENT JOURNAL book used to record all payments made in cash such as for accounts payable, merchandise purchases, and operating expenses; also termed *cash payments journal*. There are usually separate columns for the date, check number, explanation, cash credit, purchase discount credit, other credit, accounts debited, accounts payable debit, purchases debit, and other debt. *See also* CASH RECEIPTS JOURNAL.

CASH DISCOUNT *see* SALES DISCOUNT.

CASH DIVIDEND usual type of dividend paid to stockholders. It is typically expressed on a dollar-and-cents-per-share basis. However, with preferred stock, the dividend is expressed as a percentage of par value. Dividends are paid on outstanding shares. Assume on 11/15/2014, a cash dividend of $1.50 per common share is declared. Issued shares are 12,000 and treasury shares are 2000. The record date is 12/20/2014. Payment is to be made on 1/15/2015. The entry on 11/15/2014 is to debit retained earnings and credit cash dividends payable for $15,000 (10,000 shares × $1.50). Cash dividends payable is a current liability. No entry is made on the record date. On 1/15/2015, cash dividends payable is debited and cash credited for $15,000. Assume there are 30,000 shares of $10 par value, 8% preferred stock.

The cash dividend is:

30,000	shares
× $10	par value
$300,000	total par value
× .08	dividend rate
$ 24,000	cash dividend

CASH EQUIVALENT
1. immediately realizable money that can be obtained in an exchange of goods or services.
2. financial instruments of high liquidity and safety. Examples are a TREASURY BILL and a MONEY MARKET fund.
3. in preparing the STATEMENT OF CASH FLOWS, a short-term, highly liquid investment having an original maturity of three months or less.

CASH EQUIVALENT VALUE funds that could be received upon the sale of an asset. It is the current realizable value for the item obtained in an exchange. *See also* FAIR MARKET VALUE; MARKET VALUE.

CASH FLOW
1. cash receipts minus cash disbursements from a given operation or asset for a given period. *Cash flow* and *cash inflow* are often used interchangeably.
2. in CAPITAL BUDGETING, monetary value of the expected benefits and costs of a project. It may be in the form of cash savings in operating costs or the difference between additional dollars received and additional dollars paid out for a given period.
3. *cash basis* net income. The procedures for converting an accrual basis net income amount to a cash basis net income figure are as follows:

	Accrual basis net income
+	Non-cash charges such as depreciation
+ or −	Changes in accounts receivable, inventory, prepaid expenses, accounts payable, and accrued liabilities
=	Cash basis net income

CASH FLOW FORECASTING future cash flow predictions including cash collections from customers, investment income, and cash disbursements.

CASH FLOW RATIOS ratios showing the cash position or change in cash of the business. Higher levels of cash flow indicate improved cash earnings and liquidity. Earnings are of higher quality if they are backed up by cash because cash can be used to pay debt, purchase fixed assets, and so on. Some cash flow ratios are (1) cash flow from operations/net income, (2) cash flow coverage equal to cash flow from operations/cash expenses, and (3) cash reinvestment ratio equal to cash used/cash obtained. A high cash reinvestment ratio indicates that more cash is being used in the business.

CASH FLOW STATEMENT statement showing from what sources cash has come into the business and on what the cash has been spent. The net result is reflected in the balance of the cash account as of a certain period of time. This is a valuable tool in FINANCIAL STATEMENT ANALYSIS. *See also* STATEMENT OF CASH FLOWS.

CASH FLOWS TO ASSETS ratio of net cash flows from operating activities to average total assets. Used to measure the ability of assets to generate operating cash flows.

CASH FLOWS TO SALES ratio of net cash flows from operating activities to sales. Used to measure the ability of sales to generate operating cash flows.

CASH-FLOW-TO-CAPITAL-EXPENDITURES RATIO computation indicating a company's ability to maintain plant and equipment from cash provided by operations, rather than by borrowing or issuing new stock. The ratio equals cash flow from operations less dividends divided by expenditures for plant and equipment.

CASH-FLOW-TO-TOTAL-DEBT RATIO rate indicating a company's ability to satisfy its debts. It is useful in predicting BANKRUPTCY. The ratio equals cash flow from operations divided by total liabilities.

CASH FLOW YIELD ratio of net cash flows from operating activities to net income. Used to measure the ability of a company to generate operating cash flows in relation to net income.

CASH-GENERATING EFFICIENCY ability of a company to generate cash from its current or continuing operations.

CASHIER'S CHECK check drawn by a bank on its own funds and signed by its cashier. It is thus a direct obligation of the bank. A cashier's check is distinguished from a MONEY ORDER, which is an order for the payment of money, as one issued by one bank or post office and payable at another.

CASH PAYMENTS JOURNAL *see* CASH DISBURSEMENT JOURNAL.

CASH RECEIPTS JOURNAL book used to record all transactions involving the receipt of cash. Examples are cash sales, receipt of interest and dividend revenue, collections from customer accounts, and cash sale of assets. Typically, there are separate columns for the date, explanation, cash debit, sales discount debit, other debit, account credit, accounts receivable credit, and other credit. *See also* CASH DISBURSEMENT JOURNAL.

CASH SHORTAGE AND OVERAGE situation in which the physical amount of cash on hand differs from the book recorded amount of cash. When a business is involved with over-the-counter cash receipts, occasional errors may occur in making change. The cash shortage or overage is revealed when the physical cash count at the end of the day does not agree with the cash register tape. Assuming that the count is $600 and the cash register reading shows $620, the cash shortage and overage account would be charged for $20. It is shown in the income statement.

CASH SURRENDER VALUE portion of life insurance premiums paid that can be received if the policy is canceled. The beneficiary has the option of canceling the policy. Cash surrender value is classified on the balance sheet under Investments. As the company pays premiums, part represents an expense and part applies to the cash surrender value. The difference between the premium paid and the increase in cash surrender value represents an expense.

Cash surrender value of life insurance applies to ordinary life and limited payment policies. Term insurance does not have a cash surrender value.

CASH-TO-CURRENT-LIABILITIES RATIO computation that measures a company's ability to satisfy short-term financial obligations immediately and is therefore a good *liquidity measure*. The ratio equals cash plus near-cash and marketable securities divided by current liabilities.

CASUALTY LOSS loss arising from the partial or complete destruction of property resulting from circumstances of a sudden, unexpected or unusual nature, such as storms, floods, fires, and auto accidents. These circumstances must be identifiable as the proximate cause of such a loss for classificatory purposes. Individuals may deduct a casualty loss as an itemized deduction to the extent of any amount not compensated for by insurance or otherwise if: (1) the loss is incurred in a trade or business; (2) the loss is incurred in a transaction entered into for profit; and (3) the loss is caused by fire, storm, shipwreck, or other casualty or by theft. In a business, casualty losses are typically shown as an extraordinary item net of tax in the income statement. For example, if the casualty loss is $10,000 and the company is in the 34% tax bracket, the after-tax loss presented in the income statement is $6,600 = $10,000 (1 − .34).

CDOs *see* CORPORATE DEVELOPMENT OFFICERS (CDOS).

CD-ROM (COMPACT DISK READ ONLY MEMORY) an optical-disk format that is used for prerecorded text, graphics, and sound.

CEILING amount equal to the NET REALIZABLE VALUE. The market cannot exceed the ceiling (upper limit) when employing the LOWER OF COST OR MARKET method of inventory valuation. If market is greater than the ceiling, the ceiling is chosen. For example, if market is $12 and ceiling is $9, the inventory value would be $9. However, if market was below the ceiling, the market value would be used.

CELL point of intersection between a row and column in an electronic spreadsheet. The spreadsheet's cells can be related to one another, through arithmetic and logical formulas, to create financial data. When data in one cell is changed such as in "what-if" analysis, the software instantly calculates the effects of the change on all cells displaying the results.

CELLULAR MANUFACTURING groups of machinery that are closely associated with each family of parts.

CENTRAL ADMINISTRATION COSTS allocated common costs.

CENTRAL BETA RISK *see* TYPE II ERROR.

CENTRALIZATION situation in which decision-making power is at the top of an organization and there is little delegation of authority. It is the opposite of DECENTRALIZATION. Centralization and decentralization are really a matter of degree. Full centralization means minimum autonomy and maximum restrictions on operations of subunits of the organization. As an organization grows in size and complexity, decentralization is generally considered to be effective and efficient.

CENTRAL LIMIT THEOREM one of the most important theorems in statistics. It says: If a large number of random samples of size μ are chosen from virtually any population (with mean μ and standard deviation σ), the means ($\bar{x}$'s) of these samples will themselves follow a NORMAL DISTRIBUTION with a mean

$$\mu_{\bar{x}} = \mu$$

and a standard deviation $\sigma_{\bar{x}}$, called the standard error of the mean, given by

$$\sigma_{\bar{x}} = \frac{\sigma}{\sqrt{n}}$$

Two important implications of this theorem follow:

(1) Random samples can be drawn from any population, normally distributed or not. Thus, even if it is known that the dollar value of a certain inventory item is not normally distributed, the theorem can be invoked and the assumption made that the sample mean inventory dollar value will be normally distributed.

(2) The theorem allows statements to be made about the value of the population mean without looking at the entire population. Thus, interval estimates can be made about the true value of an inventory item. Such interval estimates are called CONFIDENCE INTERVAL.

CENTRAL PROCESSING UNIT (CPU) component of a computer hardware system that combines control unit, storage unit, and arithmetic unit. The control unit interprets the instructions given to the computer. *Internal* storage is where the program of instructions is kept and where data from the input devices are sent. *External* storage can consist of disk and tapes. The arithmetic unit actually does the calculation required by the program.

CERTAINTY situation in which there is absolutely no doubt about which event will occur, and there is only one STATE OF NATURE with 100% probability attached. *See also* DECISION MAKING UNDER CERTAINTY.

CERTAINTY EQUIVALENT amount of cash (or rate of return) that a decision maker would require *with certainty* to make the recipient indifferent between this certain sum and a particular *uncertain, risky* sum. Multiplying the expected cash inflow by the certainty cash equivalent coefficient results in an *equivalent certain* cash inflow. For example, given the expected cash inflows and certainty cash equivalent coefficients, the equivalent certain cash inflows are obtained as follows:

Year	Cash Inflows	Certainty Equivalent Coefficients	Equivalent Certain Cash Inflows
1	$10,000	0.95	$ 9,500
2	15,000	0.80	12,000
3	20,000	0.70	14,000

CERTIFICATE AUTHORITY (CA) an independent trusted organization that issues digital certificates used for digital signatures and the creation of public and private keys. It is the CA's job to verify the identity of the individual or organization that is granted the certificate.

CERTIFICATE OF DEPOSIT (CD) special type of time deposit. A CD is an investment instrument available at financial institutions generally offering a fixed rate of return for a specified period (such as three months, six months, one year, or longer). The depositor agrees not to withdraw funds for the time period of the CD. If the funds are withdrawn, a significant penalty is charged. The fixed rate of return nominally increases with the amount or the term of the investment.

CERTIFIED ACCOUNTANT title given by the Association of Certified Accountants in the United Kingdom, Canada, Australia, India, and other British Commonwealth countries. They use the initials ACA (for member of the Association of Certified Accountants) or FCCA, which identifies a Fellow of the Association, one who has passed additional requirements. The accountant is authorized to provide an audit opinion on the propriety of a company's financial statements.

CERTIFIED CHECK depositor's check that a bank guarantees to pay. The funds are precommitted. When preparing a BANK RECONCILIATION, a certified check is *not* considered outstanding since both parties, the company and the bank, know about it.

CERTIFIED FINANCIAL PLANNER (CFP) professional designation requiring a high level of skill and competence in the analysis of client financial conditions and the development of client-oriented personal financial plans. Candidates must pass a series of national examinations administered by the College for Financial Planning, Denver, Colorado (www.fp.edu). The CFP program consists of six separate parts, each of which is a three-hour written examination. The program includes the following parts: (1) introduction to financial planning; (2) risk management; (3) investments; (4) tax planning and management; (5) retirement planning and employee benefits; and (6) estate planning. Candidates must also meet other educational and work experience requirements of the college in order to obtain the right to use the college's designation of Certified Financial Planner (CFP). *See also* FINANCIAL PLANNER.

CERTIFIED FINANCIAL STATEMENT one that is accompanied by the independent CPA's AUDIT REPORT. *See also* AUDIT OPINION.

CERTIFIED FRAUD EXAMINER (CFE) a new designation offered by the Association of Certified Fraud Examiners (www.acfe.org), established in 1988 and based in Austin, Texas. Each member of the association is designated a Certified Fraud Examiner (CFE) who has earned certification after an extensive application process and upon passing the uniform CFE examination is trained in the highly specialized aspects of detecting, investigating, and deterring fraud and white-collar crime.

CERTIFIED INFORMATION SYSTEMS AUDITOR (CISA) professional designation in the area of information systems audits. It is conferred by the EDP Auditor Association to candidates who successfully pass the examination. The examination covers the following topics: (1) application systems controls; (2) data integrity review; (3) systems development life; (4) application development review; (5) maintenance review; (6) general operational procedures; (7) security review; (8) systems software review; (9) acquisition review; (10) data processing resource management review; and (11) information systems audit.

CERTIFIED INSOLVENCY AND REORGANIZATION ACCOUNTANT (CIRA) another certification available to the forensic accountant. The CIRA's professional accounting experience includes insolvency and reorganizational accounting. There are three parts to the exam. The areas of concentration are financial reporting and taxes, managing turnaround and bankruptcy cases, and plan development and accounting.

CERTIFIED INTERNAL AUDITOR (CIA) recognition given by the Institute of Internal Auditors (www.theiaa.org) after a candidate has satisfied the organization's professional requirements. The INTERNAL AUDITOR verifies the accuracy of a company's record keeping and accounts as well as performing operational audits. The CIA must abide by a code of ethics.

CERTIFIED MANAGEMENT ACCOUNTANT (CMA) program requiring candidates to pass a series of uniform examinations covering a wide range of subjects. The examination consists of the following four parts: (1) Business Analysis, (2) Management Accounting and Reporting, (3) Strategic Management, and (4) Business Applications. The objectives of the CMA program are fourfold: (1) to establish management accounting as a recognized profession by identifying the role of the management accountant and financial manager, the underlying body of knowledge, and a course of study by which such knowledge is acquired; (2) to encourage higher educational standards in the management accounting field; (3) to establish an objective measure of an individual's knowledge and competence in the field of management accounting; and (4) to encourage continued professional development by management accountants. For more information, call IMA at (800) 638-4427, ext. 265 or (201) 573-6300 or visit its Web site: http://www.imanet.org/.

CERTIFIED PUBLIC ACCOUNTANT (CPA) title awarded in the United States to accountants who meet stringent professional qualifications. State authorities confer the title on those who pass the Uniform CPA Examination, administered by the AMERICAN INSTITUTE OF CERTIFIED PUBLIC ACCOUNTANTS (AICPA) (www.aicpa.org) and who satisfy the experience requirement of the particular state. The CPA is licensed to render an AUDIT OPINION on the fairness of a company's financial statements. A CPA in one state (e.g., New York) may be allowed to practice in another state (e.g., California) if reciprocal agreements exist.

CHAIN LINKS series of linked data items.

CHANCE VARIANCES *see* RANDOM VARIANCES.

CHANGE IN ACCOUNTING ESTIMATE restatement of an accounting assumption or forecast. Examples include changing the economic (useful) life or salvage value of a fixed asset. A change in accounting estimate is accounted for *prospectively* over current and future years. This will cause a change to the expense account in future years. Prior years are not restated. Note that a change in estimate coupled with a change in principle is accounted for as a change in estimate. Disclosure should be made of the particulars surrounding the estimate change.

CHANGE IN ACCOUNTING PRINCIPLE a change in principle justified by (1) a new FASB pronouncement, (2) a new tax law, (3) a new AICPA recommended practice, (4) a change in circumstances, or (5) the need to more readily conform to industry practice. A change in principle should be made only when necessary. Once an accounting principle is adopted, it is presumed that the principle should not be changed for events or transactions of a similar nature. A method used for a transaction that is being terminated or was a single, nonrecurring event in the past should not be changed. Retrospective application is required for all direct effects and the related income tax effects of a change in principle. Direct effects are changes in assets or liabilities necessary to effect a change in accounting principle. An example of a direct effect is an adjustment to an inventory balance to effect a change in inventory valuation method. Related changes, such as an effect on deferred income tax assets or liabilities or an impairment adjustment resulting from applying the lower-of-cost-or-market test to the adjusted inventory balance, also are examples of direct effects of a change in accounting principle. Footnote disclosure should be made of the nature of and justification for a change in principle, including an explanation of why the new principle is preferred. *See also* ACCOUNTING CHANGE AND ERROR CORRECTIONS.

CHANGE IN REPORTING ENTITY term used when two or more previously separate companies are combined into one. Changes in reporting entity are shown as the restatement of all comparative statements. The nature of the change in entity and the reasons for the change are described in the notes to the financial statements. In addition, the effects of changes on income before extraordinary items, net income, other comprehensive income, and related per-share amounts are disclosed for all periods presented.

CHAPTER 7 statute of the 1978 Bankruptcy Reform Act that covers LIQUIDA-TION proceedings. As a general rule, any debtor subject to Chapter 7 is also subject to CHAPTER 11. Liquidation proceedings are used to eliminate most of the debts of the debtor. Chapter 7 provides for a court-appointed trustee to make management changes, secure additional financing, and operate the debtor business so as to prevent further loss. The fundamental assumption of the proceedings is that honest debtors may sometimes not be able to discharge fully their debts and that fairness and public policy both dictate that the debtor be granted a "fresh start" in both personal and business lives. *See also* BANKRUPTCY; CHAPTER 11.

CHAPTER 11 statute of the 1978 Bankruptcy Reform Act. It covers the specific proceedings and provisions regarding REORGANIZATION and the execution of such a plan of an individual, partnership, corporation, or municipality. This statute provides possible solutions to insolvency and the difficulty of satisfying creditor claims. Under Chapter 11, unless the court rules otherwise, the debtor remains in control of the business and its operations. Debtor and creditors are allowed to work together, thus making possible the restructuring of debt, the rescheduling of payments, and even the granting of loans by the creditors to the debtor. *See also* BANKRUPTCY; CHAPTER 7.

CHAPTER 13 court approved and coordinated plan that pays off an individual's debts over a period of three years; also called *wage-earner plan*. It is a plan for the repayment of debts that allows a credit user in serious financial difficulty to pay off credit obligations without declaring bankruptcy. *See also* BANKRUPTCY (PERSONAL).

CHARGE
1. term used to describe a debit to an account.
2. to debit an account.
3. to buy on credit.

CHARGE AND DISCHARGE STATEMENT summary accounting of the principal and income associated with a fiduciary responsibility such as that of an administrator or trustee of an estate. The statement usually first describes the *charge* as to principal, namely assets or gains, and the credit or *discharge* of debts, expenses, or legacies distributed. Next the statement describes the charges and discharges as to income, for example, interest received and discharges such as income taxes, administrative expenses, and distributions to income beneficiaries. Finally the form of the statement clearly states and reconciles both the principal and income balances as properly administrated as of a given date.

CHARITABLE CONTRIBUTIONS DEDUCTION itemized deduction for amounts given to qualified *domestic* organizations. A charitable contribution may be deductible even though all or some portion of the funds of the donee organization may be used in foreign countries for charitable or educational purposes. Generally, contributions made to foreign organizations are not deductible. Taxpayers not itemizing deductions cannot deduct charitable contributions. To the extent that untaxed appreciation of charitable contribution property is allowed as a regular tax deduction, the appreciation is a preference item for the alternative minimum tax rules.

CHARTERED ACCOUNTANT (CA) (www.icaew.co.uk) recognition given by the chartered institutes in present and former British Commonwealth countries including Australia, Canada, India, New Zealand, Nigeria, Pakistan, South Africa, and the United Kingdom to individuals meeting examination and practical experience requirements. The chartered accountant is authorized to render an audit opinion on a company's financial statements.

CHARTERED FINANCIAL ANALYST (CFA) title given by the CFA Institute (www.cfainstitute.org) to an individual meeting examination and experience requirements. A CFA is recognized as a specialist in analyzing companies for investment or credit purposes.

CHARTERED FINANCIAL CONSULTANT (ChFC) professional designation given by the American College, Bryn Mawr, Pennsylvania (www.theamericancollege.edu). It is conferred upon candidates who will provide financial planning services for clients. To earn the ChFC designation the candidate must complete ten courses, six required and four electives. The six required courses are: (1) financial services, (2) income taxation, (3) financial statement analysis/individual insurance benefits, (4) investments, (5) estate and gift tax planning, and (6) financial and estate planning applications. *See also* CERTIFIED FINANCIAL PLANNER (CFP); FINANCIAL PLANNER.

CHARTERED MUTUAL FUND COUNSELOR (ChMFC) a new designation offered by the National Endowment for Financial Education, showing a financial advisor's enhanced ability to advise clients on their mutual fund questions and concerns.

CHARTING method used by a technical analyst to evaluate market trends and price behavior of individual securities. Standard & Poor's *Trendline* is one publication providing charting information on many securities. In order to interpret charts the analyst must be able to evaluate chart patterns (e.g., head and shoulders) and detect buy and sell indicators. Three basic types of charts are line, bar, and point-and-figure. Charts can reveal whether the market is in a major upturn or downturn and help analysts predict whether the trend will reverse. The analyst can see what price may occur on a given stock or market average. Further, charts help to predict the magnitude of a price swing.

CHART OF ACCOUNTS a list of ledger account names and numbers arranged in the order in which they customarily appear in the financial statements. The chart serves as a useful source for locating a given account within the ledger. The numbering system for the chart of accounts must leave room for new accounts. A range of numbers is assigned to each financial statement category. For example, asset accounts may be assigned the numbers 1–100 and liabilities assigned 101–200. For large businesses, a wider range of numbers would be required for each grouping. In fact, some companies employ a three-digit numbering system for each account. In such a case, the first digit identifies the financial statement category and the remaining digits apply to the position of that account within that category. For example, 1 may be the first digit for Assets, and Cash, being the first asset account, would be identified as 101.

CHATTEL MORTGAGE mortgage on personal (as opposed to real) property. *See also* MORTGAGES.

CHECK
  1. draft drawn upon a bank, payable upon demand to the person named upon the draft.
  2. to determine an item's accuracy such as by retotaling charges on an invoice or auditing source documents.

CHECK CLEARING FOR THE 21st CENTURY ACT a federal law that went into effect in October 2004 allowing banks to process checks faster by making electronic copies of checks. People who write checks can no longer count on several days of "float" time and getting back canceled checks.

CHECK DIGIT numeric digit added to a number, such as an employee identification number or account number, for the purpose of detecting data entry errors. A check digit serves as a redundancy check. For instance, if an organization uses a nine-digit account number, a tenth digit is added as the check digit. This tenth digit's value is calculated based upon the nine-digit account number.

CHIEF EXECUTIVE OFFICER (CEO) the highest-ranking executive in an organization. The CEO is responsible for developing corporate strategy and setting its vision. The CEO is also responsible for the organizational culture and setting tone at the top. The CEO conveys values through his or her actions. The CEO leads the senior management of an organization and is responsible for hiring and firing senior management, as well as resolving conflicts among senior management. The CEO reports to the BOARD OF DIRECTORS. Sometimes, the CEO is a member of the board of directors and may even chair the board.

CHIEF FINANCIAL OFFICER (CFO) executive who directs all financial aspects of the business. Examples of functions performed are keeping accounting records, designing accounting systems and procedures, financial forecasting, and using funds. Large companies have financial vice-presidents (or vice-presidents of finance) and controllers and treasurers. A smaller company may have one officer responsible for the accounting and treasury functions; frequently that official has the title of controller. INTERNAL AUDIT responsibilities are often assigned to the controller.

CHIEF INVESTMENT OFFICER (CIO) an executive who is responsible for managing and monitoring the company's investment portfolio. Responsibilities include managing the investment portfolio, investing surplus funds, managing pension monies, maintaining liaison with the investment community, and counseling with financial analysts.

CHIEF OPERATING OFFICER (COO) a corporate officer in charge of the daily running of the business. He or she may be the president or executive vice-president. The COO reports directly to the chief executive officer.

CIPHERTEXT encrypted text. Text before encryption is called plaintext. Ciphertext is generated by performing encryption on plaintext.

CIRCULATING CAPITAL that part of an entity's investment that is continually used up and renewed to enable ongoing operations, such as materials, labor, and overhead costs.

CIVIL PENALTY a fine imposed by a taxing authority for failure to comply with tax laws and regulations. Civil penalties may be imposed on taxpayers and tax return preparers. Civil penalties, which are less severe than criminal penalties, include penalties for late filing of tax returns and late payment of taxes.

CLASSICAL PROBABILITY number of outcomes favorable to the occurrence of an event divided by the total number of possible outcomes. In order for this ratio to be valid, each of the outcomes must be equally likely. Distributions are gained from actual occurrences in long-run experience and experimentation. An example is repeated trials under a constant-cause situation. It is useful in estimating dollar value, quantity, or other characteristics of a given universe. For example, the probability of rolling a 4 on one die is 1/6.

CLASSIFICATION AND UNDERSTANDABILITY an assertion in an entity's financial statements made by management that (1) financial information is appropriately presented and described, and (2) disclosures are expressed in a clear and comprehensible manner.

CLASSIFICATION OF ASSETS process of grouping economic resources under appropriate categories. Asset categories include CURRENT ASSETS,

FIXED ASSETS, INTANGIBLE ASSETS, INVESTMENTS, and DEFERRED COSTS. Assets are classified into major groupings to facilitate analysis of the entity's financial health. For instance, a company's liquidity can be appraised by concentrating on the current assets less prepaid expenses which are available to meet short-term debt.

CLASSIFICATION OF LIABILITIES process of grouping obligations by when they are due. The categories used are CURRENT LIABILITY and LONG-TERM LIABILITY. Liability classification assists financial statement users in evaluating the firm's financial position and ability to take on additional short-term or long-term debt.

CLASSIFICATION OF STOCKHOLDERS' EQUITY process of using group headings within the stockholders' equity section of the balance sheet. The headings include capital stock, paid-in capital, retained earnings, and treasury stock. Capital stock represents stock that has been issued (e.g., issued common or preferred stock) and stock to be issued at a later date (e.g., stock option). Paid-in capital consists of such items as contributed capital in excess of par and donations. Retained earnings are the accumulated earnings less cash dividends. Treasury stock is a deduction in determining stockholders' equity.

CLASSIFIED STOCK equity separated into different classes. For example, common stock may consist of Class A and Class B. Typically, Class A has greater voting rights. It may also contain dividend and liquidation privileges.

CLAYTON ANTITRUST ACT ANTITRUST LAW passed in 1914 as an amendment to the SHERMAN ANTITRUST ACT of 1890. The Act listed four illegal practices in restraint of competition. It outlawed price discrimination, tying contracts and exclusive dealerships, and horizontal mergers. It also outlawed interlocking directorates (the practice of having the same people serve as directors of two or more competing firms).

CLEAN OPINION *see* UNQUALIFIED (unmodified) OPINION.

CLEAN SURPLUS CONCEPT doctrine holding that entries to retained earnings are limited to record only periodic earnings and dividends.

CLEARING ACCOUNT usually a temporary account containing costs or amounts that are to be transferred to another account. An example is the income summary account containing revenue and expense amounts to be transferred to retained earnings at the close of a fiscal period.

CLEARING HOUSE STATEMENT report on a security or commodity broker's trading activity. This statement is submitted to the clearing house of the exchange by the broker, and through the reconciliation of other broker members' statements, amounts due or payable and net quantities of securities or commodities deliverable to or receivable by each broker are determined.

CLOSED CORPORATION *see* PRIVATELY HELD COMPANY.

CLOSED-END MUTUAL FUND one whose shares are limited and traded like the common stock of a corporation. Once shares are issued, the only way an investor can purchase or sell the fund shares is in the open market. An example of a closed-end mutual fund is Prudential-Bache Securities' Global Yield Fund. *See also* OPEN-END MUTUAL FUND.

CLOSED SYSTEM enterprise-wide scope of organization resource costs that are all reassigned through activities to final cost objects.

CLOSELY HELD CORPORATION firm that has only a few stockholders. It contrasts with a *privately held corporation* in that a closely held corporation is public although few of the shares are traded. The so-called "corporate pocketbooks" may become subject to the additional personal holding company tax on income not distributed. For example, deductions and losses in transactions between a major stockholder and the corporation may be disallowed under certain circumstances.

CLOSELY HELD STOCK *see* CLOSELY HELD CORPORATION.

CLOSING ENTRY journal entry at the end of a period to transfer the net effect of revenue and expense items from the income statements to owners' equity. Entries are for NOMINAL ACCOUNTS and not REAL ACCOUNTS. At the end of the year, expenses are credited so that zero balances are left in them, and the total is debited to the INCOME SUMMARY account. Revenue accounts are debited to arrive at zero balances, and the total is credited to the income summary account. The net income or loss that now exists in the income summary account is then transferred to retained earnings. After the closing entries, the new year will start fresh in that no income statement account balances will exist.

CLOUD COMPUTING a way for an organization to add computing capacity on the fly without directly investing in new long-term infrastructure. The "cloud" is often used as a metaphor for the Internet. Cloud computing is based upon a subscription or pay-per-use model, where the computer processing ability of an organization can be expanded or contracted, in real time, over the Internet.

CLUSTER SAMPLING method of selecting groups of units. The first unit of each group is selected with the use of a random number table. This allows selection of more than one item at a time. In cluster sampling, the population is broken into groups of items, and a RANDOM SAMPLE is selected from all the clusters. Each cluster becomes a sampling unit. After determining the adequate number of clusters, the auditor has a choice of either examining all items in a cluster (one-stage) or only a random number of items in the cluster (two-stage). Cluster sampling requires computing the mean for the individual sampling unit and multiplying this by the number of units in the population to determine the population's estimated value. The precision limit on this estimate must also be computed. Cluster sampling lowers sampling cost and the cost to replace the sample. Sample selection is made easier; however, less statistical efficiency exists. Applications of cluster sampling measure variables such as inventory value and the balance in accounts receivable. It can also be used to measure attributes.

CM *see* CONTRIBUTION MARGIN (CM).

CMA *see* CERTIFICATE IN MANAGEMENT ACCOUNTING (CMA).

CMA MAGAZINE journal published by the Society of Management Accountants of Canada (www.cma-canada.org) on a bimonthly basis. Subject matter concentrates on managerial accounting and information systems.

COBOL *see* COMMON BUSINESS ORIENTED LANGUAGE (COBOL).

COBRANDING the linking of a credit card with a business trade name offering "points" or premiums toward the purchase of a product or service. Examples are Ford Motor Company's Citibank Visa and MasterCard and Nordstrom's cobranded Visa. Bankers are realizing that cobranded credit cards help build customer loyalty.

CODE OF PROFESSIONAL ETHICS authoritative statement regarding the rules of conduct for certified public accountants in performing their functions. THE AMERICAN INSTITUTE OF CERTIFIED PUBLIC ACCOUNTANTS (AICPA) and each state society prepares these ethical guidelines. For example, a CPA may not divulge confidential client information to the public.

CODING OF ACCOUNTS assignment of an identification number to each account in the financial statements. A CHART OF ACCOUNTS lists the account titles and account numbers being used by a business. For example, the numbers 1 to 29 may be used exclusively for asset accounts; numbers from 30 to 49 may be reserved for liabilities; numbers in the 50s may signify OWNERS' EQUITY accounts; numbers in the 60s may represent revenue accounts; and numbers from 70 to 99 may designate expense accounts. In large or complex businesses with many more accounts, a more elaborate coding system would be needed. Some companies use a four-digit coding system. The coding system is especially necessary for computerized accounting.

COEFFICIENT OF DETERMINATION statistical measure of GOODNESS-OF-FIT. It measures how good the estimated regression equation is, designated as r^2 (*read as* r-squared). The higher the r-squared, the more confidence one can have in the equation. Statistically, the coefficient of determination represents the proportion of the total variation in the y variable that is explained by the regression equation. It has the range of values between 0 and 1. *See also* REGRESSION ANALYSIS.

Example: The statement "factory overhead is a function of machine-hours with $r^2 = .70$," can be interpreted as "70% of the total variation of factory overhead is explained by the machine hours and the remaining 30% is accounted for by something other than machine-hours." The 30% is referred to as the error term.

COEFFICIENT OF VARIATION measure of relative dispersion, or relative risk. It is computed by dividing the standard deviation (σ) by the expected value ($\bar{x}$). For example, consider two investment proposals, A and B, with the following data:

Proposal	Expected Value ($\bar{x}$)	Standard Deviation (σ)
A	$230	$107.07
B	250	208.57

The coefficient of variation for each proposal is:

For A: $107.70/$230 = .47
For B: $208.57/$250 = .83.

Therefore, because the coefficient is a relative measure of risk, B is considered more risky than A.

COINSURANCE CLAUSE provision in an insurance policy that limits the liability of the insurer. It specifies that the owner of property that has been damaged (e.g., by fire or water) must have another policy covering usually at least 80% of the *cash value* of the property at the time of damage in order to collect the full amount insured. This serves as an inducement for an individual to carry full coverage.

COLD SITE is an important aspect of disaster recovery planning, where the data center can operate for duration of the disaster from a backup location/site. An organization may have three types of backup locations: a cold site, a WARM SITE, or a HOT SITE. A cold backup site is least expensive. It generally consists of nothing more than an appropriately configured space in a building. All hardware and software must be acquired before the recovery process can begin. Often, there is a significant delay in resuming data center function to full operation from a cold backup site.

COLLATERALIZE to pledge assets to secure a debt. These assets will be given up if the borrower defaults on the terms and conditions specified in the debt agreement. An example is pledging inventory to collateralize a bank loan.

COLLECTIBLES art, stamps, coins, antiques, and other related items. They offer capital gains potential, inflation protection, and aesthetic enjoyment. Collectibles are acquired through dealers, at auctions, or directly from previous owners. Among the drawbacks are high security and insurance cost, poor liquidity, lack of income, and possible forgeries. Information about collectibles sometimes appears in magazines like *Money* and *Creditor/Investor*, and major categories of collectibles have magazines and newsletters devoted exclusively to them.

COLLECTION PERIOD number of days it takes to collect accounts receivable. The collection period should be or can be compared to the terms of sale. A long collection period may indicate higher risk in collecting the account; it ties up funds that could be invested elsewhere or used to make timely payments. It equals the number of days in a year divided by the ACCOUNTS RECEIVABLE TURNOVER. Assume a 360-day year and turnover rate of 10 times. The collection period is 36 days. *See also* AGING OF ACCOUNTS.

COLLEGE FUNDS term used in not-for-profit accounting. College funds consist of current funds, loan funds, endowment funds, annuity and life funds, agency funds, and plant funds.

COLLUSION exists when two or more people get together to perpetrate and conceal errors, fraud, or instances of noncompliance with laws or regulations. For example, collusion occurs when the TREASURER steals company funds and shares the stolen money with the CONTROLLER, who in turn covers up the theft by doctoring the company's books and records.

COMBINATION
1. agreement between two entities to undertake a mutually beneficial action. An example is an agreement related to pricing.
2. BUSINESS COMBINATION.

COMBINED APPROACH involves performing both tests of controls and substantive procedures in a financial statement audit. The objective of a combined approach is to determine that the entity's internal controls are operating effectively, which in turn will enable the reduction of substantive procedures to be performed by the auditor.

COMBINED FINANCIAL STATEMENT

1. presentation in which the balance sheet accounts or income statement accounts of a related group of entities have been added together so they are considered as one reporting entity. Intercompany transactions are eliminated in a combined statement.
2. in governmental accounting, statement in which the balance sheets of all fund and account groups are shown without interfund transfers being eliminated.

COMFORT LETTER term used when underwriters request "comfort" from an auditor about financial information in SEC registration statements not covered by the auditor's opinion and on subsequent events after the opinion date. Comfort letters are *not* filed with the SEC but are required by underwriters who have certain responsibilities under SEC regulations. Typically, comfort letters are mandated as part of the underwriting agreement. The adequacy of procedures conducted in the comfort review rests with the underwriter and not the auditor. Underwriting agreements typically provide for a closing date on which the agreement is to be consummated and a "cutoff date" shortly before the closing date. The comfort letter should specifically state that it does not cover the period between the cutoff date and the date of the letter. The contents of the comfort letter cover some or all of the following: compliance with SEC rules and regulations, audit procedures conducted, unaudited financial statements and schedules, statistics and tables, changes in certain financial statement items after the latest statement contained in the filing, auditor independence, and an understanding regarding the limited circulation of the letter. Note that comments on unaudited statements and subsequent changes should be restricted to NEGATIVE ASSURANCE since the auditor has not conducted an examination in accordance with GENERALLY ACCEPTED ACCOUNTING PRINCIPLES (GAAP). Any financial statement, schedule, or other information referenced in the letter should be clearly identified along with the auditor's responsibility regarding it. The auditor should not comment on matters involving management judgment (i.e., reasons for change in income statement items). Working papers should back up statements made in comfort letters and furnish evidence of procedures carried out.

COMMERCIAL PAPER short-term unsecured loan of a financially strong company having a maturity up to 270 days. It is typically issued on a discount basis meaning that the interest is subtracted immediately from the face of the debt to obtain the cash proceeds. Commercial paper interest rates are usually less than the prime interest rate (rate charged by banks to their best customers). Flexibility is another advantage; they can be issued at varying maturity dates when funds are needed.

COMMITMENT

1. expected expenditure backed by an agreement. A commitment may be disclosed in a *footnote* but generally is not given accounting recognition. Disclosure includes its nature and amount. However, a commitment can be recorded in the case of a loss commitment on a purchase contract where the market price has significantly declined below the agreed-upon delivery contract price. The entry for the difference is to debit loss on

purchase commitment and credit estimated liability. But a gain on a purchase contract is not recognized because it violates CONSERVATISM. *See also* CONTINGENT LIABILITY.

2. bank commitment to lend a company funds when needed.

COMMITTED COST *see* CAPACITY COSTS; DISCRETIONARY (FIXED) COSTS.

COMMITTEE OF SPONSORING ORGANIZATIONS (COSO) OF THE TREADWAY COMMISSION an organization that prepares audit related reports. COSO includes representatives from the American Institute of CPAs, American Accounting Association, Institute of Internal Auditors, Institute of Management Accountants, and the Financial Executives Institute. The Committee's purposes are to establish a common definition of internal control serving the needs for different parties and providing a standard against which companies can evaluate their control systems and how to improve them.

COMMITTEE ON ACCOUNTING PROCEDURE former senior technical committee of the American Institute of CPAs that promulgated Accounting Research Bulletins from 1938 up to 1959. It consisted of accounting practitioners and professors. It was replaced by the Accounting Principles Board, which was, in turn, replaced by the FASB.

COMMODITIES FUTURES contracts in which sellers promise to deliver a given commodity by a certain date at a predetermined price. Price is agreed to by open outcry on the floor of the commodity exchange. The contract specifies the item, the price, the expiration date, and a standardized unit to be traded (e.g., 50,000 pounds). Commodity contracts may run up to one year. Investors must continually evaluate the effect of market activity on the value of the contract. While the futures contract mandates that the buyer and seller exchange the commodity on the delivery date, the contract may be sold to another party prior to the settlement date. This may occur when the trader wants to realize a profit now or limit the loss. Investors engage in commodity trading in the hope of high return rates and inflation hedges.

COMMON BUSINESS ORIENTED LANGUAGE (COBOL) programming language for business data processing. As compared to FORTRAN and BASIC, *COBOL* statements resemble English sentences and thus are long and wordy, but easy to read.

COMMON COST expense shared by different departments, products, or jobs, also called JOINT COST or INDIRECT COST.

COMMON SIZE FINANCIAL STATEMENT form of financial statement analysis in which the relative percentages of financial statement items as well as their dollar amounts are shown. *See also* VERTICAL ANALYSIS.

ABC Company
Common Size Income Statement
For Year Ended December 31, 2014

Sales	$100,000	100%
Less: Cost of goods sold	20,000	20%
Gross profit	$80,000	80%
Operating expenses	30,000	30%
Net income	$50,000	50%

COMMON STOCK share in a public company or privately held firm. Common stockholders have voting and dividend rights. In the event of corporate bankruptcy, common stockholders are paid after bondholders and preferred stockholders. There is, however, a greater chance of capital appreciation by owning common stock.

The issuing company shows common stock at its total par value, or no-par value, or stated value in the capital stock section of stockholders' equity.

COMMON STOCK EQUIVALENT security that can be converted into common stock. It is *not* now in common stock form but has provisions enabling holders to become common stockholders. A common stock equivalent is included in PRIMARY EARNINGS PER SHARE if its effect is *dilutive*. Examples are stock options, warrants, two-class common stocks, and contingent shares (if related to the passage of time). Contingent shares are shares issuable upon the occurrence of a specified event. A convertible security is a common stock equivalent when its effective yield at the time of issuance is less than 66⅔% of the average Aa corporate bond yield. *See also* EARNINGS PER SHARE; FULLY DILUTED EARNINGS PER SHARE.

COMMUNICATION BETWEEN PREDECESSOR AND SUCCESSOR AUDITORS provides guidance on communications between predecessor and successor auditors. The successor auditor is responsible for initiating the oral or written confidential communication. In the communication, the successor auditor should inquire of matters relevant to accepting the engagement such as management honesty, internal control, and accounting policy disagreements.

COMPARABILITY ability to rank companies so as to facilitate financial decisions. Comparability is aided when companies employ similar accounting procedures, measurement concepts, classifications, basic financial statement formats, and methods of disclosure. *See also* UNIFORMITY.

COMPARATIVE STATEMENT statement on which balance sheets, income statements, or statements of changes in financial position are assembled side by side for review purposes. Changes that have occurred in individual categories from year to year and over the years are easily noted. The key factor revealed is the *trend* in an account or financial statement category over time. A comparison of financial statements over two to three years can be undertaken by computing the year-to-year change in absolute dollars and in terms of percentage change. Longer-term comparisons are best undertaken by means of INDEX-NUMBER TREND SERIES.

COMPARATIVE STATEMENT APPROACH *see* TOTAL PROJECT APPROACH.

COMPENSATED ABSENCE expected payments to employees who miss work because of illness, vacation, or holidays. A liability is accrued for compensation for future absences if *all* of the following criteria are satisfied: (1) employee services have already been performed; (2) rights have already been vested; (3) there is probable payment; and (4) the amount is subject to reasonable estimation. If the amount is not determinable, accrual is not possible, but footnote disclosure should be given.

COMPENSATING BALANCE deposit that a bank can use to offset an unpaid loan. No interest is earned on the compensating balance, which is stated as

a percentage of the loan. The compensating balance increases the EFFEC-
TIVE INTEREST RATE on the loan. The compensating balance is usually 10%.
Assume a company borrows $50,000 from the bank at a 10% interest rate
with a 5% compensating balance. The loan is on a discount basis meaning
interest is deducted immediately. The compensating balance is calculated at
$2500. The effective interest rate is:

$$\frac{\text{Nominal Interest}}{\text{Proceeds}} = \frac{\$5,000}{\$50,000 - \$5,000 - \$2,500} = \frac{\$5,000}{\$42,500} = 11.8\%$$

COMPENSATORY STOCK OPTION option offered to employees as partial
compensation for their services. Compensation for services is measured by
the quoted market price of the stock at the measurement date less the amount
the employee is required to pay (option price). The measurement date is the
earliest date on which both the number of shares to be issued and the option
price are known. Compensation involved in a compensatory stock option plan
should be expensed in the periods in which the related services are performed.
The entry is to debit compensation expense and credit deferred compensation.

COMPETITIVE BENCHMARKING *see* BENCHMARKING.

COMPILATION presentation of financial statement information by the
entity *without* the accountant's assurance as to conformity with GENERALLY
ACCEPTED ACCOUNTING PRINCIPLES (GAAP). In performing this accounting
service, the accountant must conform to the AMERICAN INSTITUTE OF CERTI-
FIED PUBLIC ACCOUNTANTS (AICPA) Statements on Standards for Accounting
and Review Services (SSARS). For guidance on issues not covered therein,
reference should be made to the STATEMENTS ON AUDITING STANDARDS (SAS).
The engagement letter should set forth the type of services to be rendered,
limitations of the service (such as nonreliance to disclose errors and irregularities), and nature of the compilation report. In undertaking a compilation
assignment, the CPA should be familiar with the client and industry accounting principles and practices. The accountant should understand the client's
accounting records, form and content of financial statements, and personnel
qualifications. The accountant is *not* gathering evidence and does *not* verify
client information provided. Rather, the CPA reads the compiled statements
to assure that they are in appropriate form and without obvious material
errors. Each page of the financial statement should refer to the compilation report. The accountant's report should indicate the completion of the
compilation, the fact that the compilation is restricted to financial statement
information presented by management, and that the statements have *not* been
audited or reviewed. The accountant does not express an opinion on the financial statements nor does he or she give any other form of assurance on them.
In the case where management omits needed disclosures, the CPA should
state so in the report. *See also* REVIEW.

COMPLETED CONTRACT METHOD profit is recognized only when a
long-term construction contract is completed. It should be used only when the
conditions of the PERCENTAGE OF COMPLETION METHOD cannot be applied.
However, if a loss on the contract is expected, it should be immediately
recognized consistent with the CONSERVATISM principle. *See also* CONSTRUC-
TION-IN-PROGRESS; PROGRESS BILLINGS.

COMPLEX CAPITAL STRUCTURE financial structure with stock outstanding that has potential for DILUTION. *Dual presentation* of earnings per share by showing BASIC EARNINGS PER SHARE and DILUTED EARNINGS PER SHARE is required.

COMPLIANCE AUDIT special auditor's report covering compliance with contractual agreements, such as bond indentures and loan agreements, and regulatory requirements. The lender or agency wishes to obtain the auditor's assurance as to compliance with the terms of the agreement. The data need not be audited for compliance; however, if the financial statements have been audited, the auditor may provide NEGATIVE ASSURANCE on compliance. The compliance report may be separately issued or addended to the auditor's report on the financial statements. In the latter case, usually an explanatory paragraph appears below the opinion paragraph. An example of a compliance audit is one conducted for the trustee of bondholders to determine whether provisions of the bond contract (such as the maintenance of required financial ratios) are being adhered to.

COMPLIANCE TEST manner of furnishing reasonable assurance that internal accounting control procedures are being applied as prescribed so that the auditor is assured of the validity of underlying evidence. Any exceptions to compliance must be noted. Underlying evidence comprises an examination of the accounts themselves including reviewing the journals, ledgers, and worksheets. If the compliance tests provide evidence that controls are functioning properly, the underlying evidence is deemed reliable, and the CPA can reduce the degree of validation and analytical review procedures. The following three audit procedures are typically used in conducting compliance tests: (1) inquiry of personnel regarding the performance of their duties; (2) observing personnel actions; and (3) inspecting documentation for evidence of performance in conducting employee functions. An example is examining invoices to assure that receiving documents and proof of delivery are attached when the invoices are presented for payment. Tests of compliance should be applied to transactions throughout the year under audit since the financial statements reflect transactions and events for the whole year. Compliance tests may be conducted on a subjective or statistical basis. *See also* SUBSTANTIVE TEST.

COMPONENT an entity or business activity that prepares financial statements to be included in group financial statements. Components include subsidiary corporations, divisions of a business, and investments accounted for under the equity method of accounting.

COMPONENT AUDITOR an auditor who audits the financial statements of a component included in group financial statements. A component auditor may be part of the group engagement partner's firm, a network firm, or another firm.

COMPONENTS OF INTERNAL CONTROL the interrelated elements of an entity's internal control used by management to provide reasonable assurance that their objectives will be achieved. Components of internal control consist of the control environment, risk assessment, information and communication systems, monitoring, and control activities.

COMPOSITE BREAK-EVEN POINT term used to designate break-even sales when a company sells more than one product or service. A break-even point for all the products or services combined can be determined, based on the expected SALES MIX and the composite or weighted average unit contribution margin. For example, assume that

	Baubles	Trinkets	Total
Sales	$1.00	$1.250	$2.250
Variable cost	0.60	0.375	0.975
Contribution margin	$0.40	$0.875	$1.275
Fixed costs			$7,600
Sales mix	60%	40%	

Then composite (or weighted average) unit contribution margin is ($0.40) (.6) + ($0.875)(.4) = $0.59. The break-even point for both products combined is $7600/$0.59 = 12,881 units. *See also* WEIGHTED AVERAGE CONTRIBUTION MARGIN.

COMPOSITE DEPRECIATION group depreciation of dissimilar assets with different service lives. Depreciation on all assets is determined by using the straight-line-depreciation method. Then, a composite depreciation rate is arrived at based on the ratio of depreciation per year to the original cost. Composite life equals the depreciable cost divided by the depreciation per year. In any given year, depreciation expense equals the composite depreciation rate times the gross cost balance in the asset account. The entry is to debit depreciation expense and credit accumulated depreciation. Under the method, when a particular asset is sold, the entry is to debit cash for the amount received and credit the asset for its original cost. The difference between the two is debited to accumulated depreciation. No gain or loss on the sale of a fixed asset is recognized under the composite method.

An illustrative schedule for composite depreciation is shown below:

Asset	Original Cost	Salvage Value	Depreciable Cost	Life	Depreciation Per Year
Autos	$100,000	$10,000	$ 90,000	10	$ 9,000
Trucks	55,000	5,000	50,000	4	12,500
	$155,000	$15,000	$140,000		$21,500
			$ 21,500		
Composite Rate =			$155,000	=	.139
Composite Life =			$140,000	=	6.512
			$ 21,500		

COMPOSITION agreement designed to allow a debtor to continue to operate. It includes a voluntary reduction of the amount the debtor owes the creditor. The creditor obtains from the debtor a stated percent of the obligation in *full* settlement of the debt regardless of how low the percentage is. The advantages of a composition are that court costs are eliminated as well as the stigma of a bankrupt company. *See also* BANKRUPTCY.

COMPOUNDING PERIOD time during which compound interest is computed. Compounding means interest on interest and the period can be on a daily, monthly, annual, or other basis.

COMPOUND INTEREST rate that is applicable when interest in subsequent periods is earned not only on the original principal but also on the accumulated interest of prior periods. For example, assume that the initial principal is $1000 and annual interest rate is 10%. At the end of first year, the amount is the principal and interest, which is $1,000 + .1($1,000) = $1,000 + $100 = $1,100. At the end of second year, the amount is accumulated: $1,100 + .1($1,100) = $1,100 + $110 = $1,210. *See also* FUTURE VALUE.

COMPOUND INTEREST METHOD OF DEPRECIATION *see* ANNUAL METHOD OF DEPRECIATION.

COMPOUND JOURNAL ENTRY more than one debit or credit in a journal entry.

COMPREHENSIVE ANNUAL FINANCIAL REPORT (CAFR) official annual report of a government. In addition to a combined, combining (assembling of data for all funds within a type), and individual balance sheet, the following are also presented as appropriate: (1) statement of revenues, expenditures, and changes in fund balance (all funds); (2) statement of revenues, expenditures, and changes in fund balance, budget and actual (for general and special revenue funds); (3) statement of revenues, expenses, and changes in retained earnings (for proprietary funds); and (4) statement of changes in financial position (for proprietary funds).

COMPREHENSIVE BUDGET *see* MASTER (COMPREHENSIVE) BUDGET.

COMPREHENSIVE INCOME change in equity (net assets) arising from either transactions or other occurrences with nonowners. It excludes investments and withdrawals by owners. Comprehensive income is comprised of two elements: net income and other comprehensive income. Other comprehensive income relates to all items of comprehensive income except for net income. Other comprehensive income includes foreign currency translation gain or loss; unrealized loss or gain on available-for-sale securities; and changes in market value of a futures contract that is a hedge of an asset reported at fair value.

COMPREHENSIVE TAX ALLOCATION method of measuring the tax effects of all transactions includable in book income for the period irrespective of the fact that they may be shown in taxable income in another year. It is an INTERPERIOD INCOME TAX ALLOCATION.

COMPTROLLER
1. misspelling of CONTROLLER, caused by confusion about the word's Latin and French roots.
2. chief auditor in the government sector. For example, the COMPTROLLER GENERAL heads the GENERAL ACCOUNTING OFFICE.

COMPTROLLER GENERAL chief of the GENERAL ACCOUNTING OFFICE (GAO). The GAO assists the Congress in overseeing the executive branch and serves as the independent legislative auditor of the federal government. The General Accounting Office reports directly to Congress on operating results, financial position, and accounting systems of government agencies. It conducts audits of all branches of the government, both here and abroad.

COMPUSTAT database published by Standard & Poor's Corporation (www.compustatresources.com). The Compustat tapes are comprehensive, containing over 50 years of annual financial data for more than 88,000 global securities. Each year's data for the industrial companies include more than 120 balance sheet and income statement items and market data. There is also a file on utilities and banks. The annual file is updated weekly.

COMPUTER-AIDED DESIGN (CAD) use of a computer to interact with a designer in developing and testing product ideas without actually building prototypes.

COMPUTER-AIDED DESIGN AND MANUFACTURING (CAD/CAM) computerized system to both integrate part design and to generate processing or manufacturing instructions.

COMPUTER-ASSISTED AUDIT TECHNIQUES (CAAT) used to simplify or automate the data analysis function in an audit. Auditors typically used specialized CAAT software, such as ACL's Data Analysis. However, CAAT may also be performed using a general purpose spreadsheet software like Excel or specialized statistical software such as SAS or SPSS.

COMPUTER-INTEGRATED MANUFACTURING (CIM) computer information systems utilizing a shared manufacturing data base for engineering design, factory production, and information management.

COMPUTER SECURITY method of protecting information, computer programs, and other computer system assets. *Hardware security*, which is the security of computer assets and capital equipment, refers to computer location, access control, fire protection, and storage procedures. Such measures as badges, electronic identification keys, alarm systems, and physical barriers at entries are used for this purpose. *Software security* entails the protection of software assets such as APPLICATION PROGRAMS, the OPERATING SYSTEM, and the DATA BASE MANAGEMENT SYSTEM and stored information. Special user numbers and passwords are typically used to prevent unauthorized access to software and data. In addition to security for hardware and software, good internal control also requires that measures be taken to prevent loss or accidental destruction of data.

COMPUTER VIRUS a program that replicates and spreads by attaching itself to other programs. When the infected program is run, the virus executes an event.

CONCENTRATION BANKING acceleration of cash collections from customers by having funds sent to several geographically situated regional banks and transferred to a main concentration account in another bank. The transfer of funds can be accomplished through the use of depository transfer checks and electronic transfers.

CONCEPTUAL FRAMEWORK study of the Financial Accounting Standards Board. It attempts to arrive at theoretical foundations for its Statements of Financial Accounting Standards. At this time, there are six Statements of Financial Accounting Concepts.

CONCURRENT AUDIT TECHNIQUES used to audit an entity on a continuous basis. Audit evidence is collected at the same time that an application system undertakes processing of its production. This is achieved by embedding the audit module into the application systems; the audit module is responsible for collecting and processing the audit evidenced.

CONFERENCE BOARD, THE not-for-profit group of business people that examines and studies economic and managerial issues to enhance business activities. The organization puts out such useful statistics as the help-wanted index. Recommendations are given to the business community regarding important business issues.

CONFERENCE CALL a valuable opportunity to hear senior management's take on the company's prospects of future earnings and new products in the pipeline. Institutional investors and financial analysts of brokerage firms call in to a special number to listen and ask questions. Yahoo Finance (http://finance.yahoo.com) maintains a calendar of upcoming conference calls. Enter a company's ticker to listen in on a current meeting or access an archive of a recent call.

CONFIDENCE INTERVAL estimated range of values with a given probability of including the population parameter of interest. The range of values is usually based on the results of a sample that estimated the mean and the sampling error or standard error. For example, for the population mean, the confidence intervals can be given by the interval whose lower (L) and upper (U) limits are as follows:

$$L = \mu - Z\sigma_{\bar{x}}$$
$$U = \mu + Z\sigma_{\bar{x}}$$

where μ is the *population mean, Z = standard normal variate, and* $\sigma_{\bar{x}}$ = *the standard error of the mean. See also* CENTRAL LIMIT THEOREM: NORMAL DISTRIBUTION.

CONFIDENCE LEVEL in statistical sampling, the degree of certainty that audit results are accurate. The sum of the confidence level (e.g., 95%) plus the risk of inaccurate results (e.g., 5%) totals 100%. Also known as *reliability*.

CONFIRMATION
1. verification of a condition or fact.
2. auditor's written or oral request to a third party to verify the existence or amount of a financial item related to the clients. A *positive* confirmation requests a reply in any event while a *negative* confirmation asks for a reply only in the event of disagreement. Examples are accounts receivable, accounts payable, and bank confirmations.

CONFORMANCE COSTS (CONTROL COSTS) category of QUALITY COSTS including costs of prevention and costs of appraisal, which are financial measures of internal performance.

CONGLOMERATE FINANCIAL STATEMENT *see* CONSOLIDATED FINANCIAL STATEMENT.

CONGLOMERATE MERGER combination of two or more firms with virtually unrelated activities. The key benefit claimed for conglomerates is the diversification of risk across various industries. *See also* MERGER.

CONSERVATISM accounting guideline that understates assets and revenues and overstates liabilities and expenses. Expenses should be recognized earlier than later, whereas revenue should be recognized later than sooner. Thus, net income will result in a lower figure. Conservatism holds that in financial reporting it is preferable to be pessimistic (understate) than optimistic (overstate) since there is less chance of financial readers being hurt by relying on prepared financial statements. One can argue that pessimism is needed to counteract the optimism of management. However, excess conservatism may result in misguided decisions.

CONSIGNMENT specialized way of marketing certain types of goods. The consignor delivers goods to the consignee who acts as the consignor's agent in selling the merchandise to a third party. The consignee accepts the goods without any liability except to reasonably protect them from damage. The consignee receives a commission when the merchandise is sold. Goods on consignment are included in the consignor's inventory and excluded from the consignee's inventory since the consignor has legal title.

CONSISTENCY
1. uniformity of accounting procedures used by an accounting entity from period to period.
2. uniformity of measurement concepts and procedures used for related items within the company's financial statements for one period.

It is difficult for financial statement users to make projections when data are not measured and classified in the same manner over time. A change in accounting principle should not be made unless it can be justified as being preferable. An example of a change is switching from the STRAIGHT-LINE DEPRECIATION method to the SUM-OF-THE-YEARS'-DIGITS method. A lack in consistency over time distorts the earnings trend and creates uncertainty in evaluating a company.

CONSOLIDATED BALANCE SHEET one that shows the financial position of an affiliated group of companies as though they constituted a single economic unit. The effect of intercompany relationships and the results of intercompany transactions will have been eliminated in the consolidation process. *See also* CONSOLIDATED FINANCIAL STATEMENT.

CONSOLIDATED (CONSOLIDATION) GOODWILL excess of cost over book value of the investment in a subsidiary. With consolidation, even when the assets and liabilities of the subsidiary are properly stated, and the net assets equal the values placed on them by the parent, an investor may still expect that the advantages of the combination will enable it to earn more than the two companies could earn separately. Therefore, the investor may be willing to pay an additional amount, which is, in effect, a bonus for control of the subsidiary. This bonus is an intangible asset, goodwill created as a result of consolidation. Consolidation has a special meaning in mergers because a new company is formed to own the stock of the companies being combined. In that type of reorganization, there is *no* goodwill. Goodwill arises from a PURCHASE METHOD merger and represents the difference between purchase price and book value of the acquired company. The meaning of the difference is theoretically the increased earning power of the companies as a result of their combination, but that value is not something superimposed on a balance sheet. It is what is actually paid less what is actually on the books.

CONSOLIDATED FINANCIAL STATEMENT statement that brings together all assets, liabilities, and operating accounts of a *parent* company and its subsidiaries. It presents the financial position and results of operations of the parent company and its subsidiaries as if the group were a single company with one or more branches. The technique for preparing consolidated financial statements is to take the individual statements to be consolidated and to combine them on a worksheet after eliminating all intercompany transactions and intercompany relationships. Most firms prepare consolidated statements when they hold more than 50% of the subsidiary's stock. *See also* COMBINED FINANCIAL STATEMENT; CONSOLIDATION.

CONSOLIDATION presentation as one economic entity of the financial statements of a parent and subsidiary (subsidiaries) subsequent to the date of acquisition. The parent company owns more than 50% of the voting common stock of the subsidiary, and is therefore in control. In consolidation, the reporting mechanism is the entire group and not the separate companies. Note that the entities that make up the consolidated group retain their separate legal entity; adjustments and eliminations are for CONSOLIDATED FINANCIAL STATEMENTS only.

CONSTANT DOLLAR ACCOUNTING method of measuring financial statement items in dollars of the same (constant) purchasing power. Historical cost is restated in units of constant purchasing power as follows:

$$\text{Historical Cost} \times \frac{\text{Average CPI for Current Year}}{\text{CPI at Time of Acquisition}}$$

Restating all accounts in constant dollars provides greater comparability among years because all assets appear in the same current year average dollars regardless of when the asset was bought. Constant dollar accounting also aids comparability among competing companies in the same industry because each company converts its accounts to the same CONSUMER PRICE INDEX (CPI) dollars.

CONSTANT VARIANCE *see* HOMOSCEDASTICITY.

CONSTRAINED OPTIMIZATION optimization with the restrictions imposed on the availability of resources and other requirements. Techniques such as linear programming (LP) and the Lagrangean multipliers are used for this purpose.

CONSTRAINING (LIMITING) FACTOR item that restricts or limits production or sale of a given product. Virtually all firms suffer from one or more constraining factors. Examples include limited machine-hours and labor-hours and shortage of materials and skilled labor. Other limiting factors may be cubic feet of display or warehouse space, or working capital.

CONSTRAINT-BASED COSTING method that assigns resource costs to products and services based on the existence and location of a capacity constraint. Often governed by revenue maximization, implying that pricing is combined with costing.

CONSTRAINT EQUATION *see* LINEAR PROGRAMMING (LP).

CONSTRAINTS explicit limitations that will be encountered in pursuing an objective. Examples of constraints are limitations in machine capacity, necessary materials, or skilled labor. In LINEAR PROGRAMMING (LP), constraints are typically expressed in terms of *inequalities*.

CONSTRUCTION-IN-PROGRESS inventory method used by construction companies. The inventory account reflects construction costs incurred using the COMPLETED CONTRACT METHOD and the PERCENTAGE OF COMPLETION METHOD. Under either method, when construction costs occur, the entry is to debit construction-in-progress and credit progress billings. Additionally, under the percentage of completion method, profit is recognized gradually each period when work is performed, requiring an additional entry to record the profit. The entry is to debit construction-in-progress and credit profit. Under either method, construction-in-progress is eliminated in the final year when the contract is completed. The entry is to debit PROGRESS BILLINGS and credit construction-in-progress and profit. Under the percentage method, the profit is for the last year only. Under the completed method, the profit is the cumulative profit for all the years.

CONSTRUCTIVE DIVIDEND tax concept in which a stockholder is considered to have constructively received a dividend although it was not actually paid by the company. For example, a shareholder who used company property for personal purposes rent-free might be considered to have received a constructive dividend equal to the fair market rental value of that property.

CONSTRUCTIVE OWNERSHIP *see* ATTRIBUTION.

CONSTRUCTIVE RECEIPT tax concept in which income not actually received is considered to be constructively received by a taxpayer and thus must be reported. An example is a bond interest coupon. The interest is taxable in the year the coupon matures, even though the holder delays cashing it until a later year.

CONSTRUCTIVE RETIREMENT assumption used in consolidation procedures that allows the treatment of debt or equity securities as if they had been retired, thus allowing a consolidated entity to be viewed as a single reporting entity.

CONSUMED COST measure of expired benefits. Examples include cost of goods sold and periodic depreciation expense of a fixed asset. Income statement expenses are consumed costs in the generation of revenue.

CONSUMER PRICE INDEX (CPI) measure of price level computed by the Bureau of Labor Statistics on a monthly basis. It is the ratio of the cost of specific consumer items in any one year to the cost of those items in the base period, 1982–1984 = 100. Because the CPI includes things consumers buy regularly, it is frequently called the *cost of living index*. The so-called market basket, covered by the index, includes items such as food, clothing, automobiles, homes, and fees to doctors.

CONSUMER'S RISK probability of accepting a bad lot.

CONSUMPTION TAX levy charged directly on a specified item or commodity. It may be viewed as an indirect form of taxation in that it is not contingent upon income but on consumption of an item. Examples include excise taxes on cigarettes and alcohol, and sales taxes.

CONTINGENCY PLANNING a strategy to minimize the effect of disturbances and to allow for timely resumption of activities. The aim of contingency planning is to minimize the effects of a disruption on an organization. A disruption is any security violation, man-made or natural, intentional or accidental, that affects normal operations.

CONTINGENT ASSET item that depends on some future happening that may or may not occur. Its existence or value is not assured. A contingent asset may emanate from a CONTINGENT LIABILITY. An example of a contingent asset may be a successful lawsuit claiming damages of another party. It *cannot* be shown as an asset on the balance sheet because it violates conservatism. However, footnote disclosure may be made.

CONTINGENT CONSIDERATION a payment that is contingent upon specified future events or transactions.

CONTINGENT LIABILITY potential liability that may exist in the future depending on the outcome of a past event. Examples are an adverse tax court decision, lawsuit, and notes receivable discounted. Footnote disclosure is required of the circumstances for possible losses. Note that an ESTIMATED LIABILITY can be booked only if there is a probable loss.

CONTINGENT RENTAL payment based on factors other than the passage of time. For example, a rental is contingent when the lessee must pay an extra amount based on sales or profitability. Footnote disclosure is made of the contingent rental payment and terms.

CONTINGENT RESERVE appropriation of retained earnings for general loss possibilities; also called RESERVE FOR CONTINGENCIES.

CONTINUING ACCOUNT balance sheet account that is carried over from the previous accounting period (i.e., asset, liabilities, and equity accounts).

CONTINUING INVESTMENT one maintained on a continuous basis, according to some plan, across one fiscal period to the next.

CONTINUING PROFESSIONAL EDUCATION (CPE) credits required in some states for a CPA to continue in practice. New York initiated a CPE requirement beginning September 1987. CPE credits may be earned by attending courses and seminars, teaching, and doing research.

CONTINUITY accounting assumption that expects a business to continue in life indefinitely; also called GOING CONCERN. It is the basis for using HISTORICAL COST to value accounts rather than liquidation value since the company will remain in existence. SAS Number 59 deals with the auditor's consideration of an entity's ability to continue as a going concern. The auditor must appraise if significant doubt exists of a client's ability to continue as a going concern for a period not exceeding one year after the date of the financial statements. If significant doubt exists, there should be a separate explanatory paragraph of a going concern problem after the unqualified opinion paragraph.

CONTINUOUS AUDIT examination conducted on a recurring basis throughout the accounting period to detect and correct mistakes and improper accounting practices prior to the reporting year-end. A continuous audit also *spreads* the CPA's work throughout the year.

CONTINUOUS BUDGET budget that rolls ahead each month or period without regard to the fiscal year so that a twelve-month or other periodic forecast is always available.

CONTINUOUS IMPROVEMENT (CI) never-ending effort for improvement in every part of the firm relative to all of its deliverables to its customers; also called *Kaizen* in Japanese.

CONTRA ACCOUNT
1. reduction to the gross cost of an asset to arrive at its net cost; also called *valuation allowance*. For example, accumulated depreciation is a contra account to the original cost of a fixed asset to arrive at BOOK VALUE.
2. reduction of a liability to arrive at its CARRYING VALUE. An example is bond discount, which is a reduction of bonds payable.

CONTRACT AUDITING examination of contracts to provide assurance that the terms are being carried out such as with regard to the time and quality of work performed, and appropriation of billing.

CONTRIBUTED CAPITAL *see* PAID-IN CAPITAL.

CONTRIBUTED CAPITAL IN EXCESS OF PAR *see* ADDITIONAL PAID-IN CAPITAL.

CONTRIBUTION APPROACH TO PRICING manner of pricing a special order. This situation occurs because a company often receives a non-routine, special order for its products at lower prices than usual. In normal times, the company may refuse such an order since it will not yield a satisfactory profit. If times are bad or there is idle capacity, an order should be accepted if the incremental revenue exceeds the incremental costs involved. Such a price, one lower than the regular price, is called a contribution price. This approach is called the contribution approach to pricing, or the VARIABLE PRICING MODEL. For example, assume that a company with 100,000-unit capacity is currently producing and selling only 90,000 units of product each year with a regular price of $2. If the variable cost per unit is $1 and the annual fixed cost is $45,000, the income statement looks as follows:

		Per Unit
Sales (90,000 units)	$180,000	$2.00
Less: Variable cost	90,000	1.00
Contribution margin	$ 90,000	$1.00
Less: Fixed cost	45,000	0.50
Net income	$ 45,000	$ 0.50

The company has just received an order that calls for 10,000 units at $1.20, for a total of $12,000. The acceptance of this special order will not affect regular sales. Management is reluctant to accept this order because the $1.20 price is below the $1.50 factory unit cost ($1.50 = $1.00 + $0.50). Is it advisable to refuse the order? The answer is no. The company can add to total profits by accepting this special order even though the price offered is below the unit factory cost. At a price of $1.20, the order will contribute $0.20 (CM per unit = $1.20 − $1.00 = $0.20) toward fixed cost, and profit will increase by $2000 (10,000 units × $0.20). Using the contribution approach to pricing, the variable cost of $1.00 will be a better guide than the full unit cost of $1.50. Note that the fixed costs will not increase because of the presence of idle capacity. *See also* INCREMENTAL ANALYSIS; RELEVANT COSTS.

CONTRIBUTION MARGIN (CM) difference between sales and the variable costs of the product or service, also called *marginal income*. It is the amount of money available to cover fixed costs and generate profits. For example, if sales are $15,000 and variable costs are $6,100, contribution margin is $8,900 ($15,000 less $6,100). Determining the contribution margin has many advantages. A company can sell an item below the normal selling price when idle capacity exists as long as there is a contribution margin since it will help to cover the fixed costs or add to profits. Also, the CM calculation requires the segregation of fixed and variable costs, which is needed in BREAK-EVEN ANALYSIS. Further, CM analysis is good in evaluating the performance of the department as a whole and its manager. However, the CONTRIBUTION (MARGIN) INCOME STATEMENT can only be used internally by management because it is not acceptable for external reporting in the annual report.

CONTRIBUTION MARGIN ANALYSIS *see* COST-VOLUME-PROFIT (CVP) ANALYSIS.

CONTRIBUTION (MARGIN) INCOME STATEMENT income statement that organizes cost by behavior. It shows the relationship of variable costs and fixed costs, regardless of the functions a given cost item is associated with. A contribution income statement highlights the concept of CONTRIBUTION MARGIN (CM). This format provides data that are useful for internal management. An illustrative format of the contribution margin income statement follows:

> Sales
> Less: Variable cost of sales
> > Variable selling and administrative expenses
> ___
> Contribution Margin (CM)
> Less: Fixed overhead
> > Fixed selling and administrative expenses
> ___
> Net income

CONTRIBUTION MARGIN METHOD variation of the EQUATION METHOD. It is used in COST-VOLUME-PROFIT (CVP) ANALYSIS or BREAK-EVEN ANALYSIS. The approach centers on the idea that each unit sold provides a certain amount of CONTRIBUTION MARGIN that goes toward the covering of fixed costs. Listed below are some formulas:
(1) Break-even Point *in units* = Fixed Costs/Unit Contribution Margin
(2) Break-even Point *in dollars* = Fixed Costs/Contribution Margin Ratio
(3) Target income volume *in units*:
   (Fixed Costs + Target Income)/Contribution Margin
(4) Target income volume *in dollars*:
   (Fixed Costs + Target Income)/Contribution Margin Ratio

CONTRIBUTION MARGIN (CM) RATIO computation showing CONTRIBUTION MARGIN (CM) as a percentage of sales.

CONTRIBUTION MARGIN (CM) VARIANCE difference between actual contribution margin per unit and the budgeted contribution margin per unit, multiplied by the actual number of units sold. If the actual CM is greater than the budgeted CM per unit, a variance is favorable; otherwise, it is unfavorable.

CM Variance = (Actual CM Per Unit − Budgeted CM Per Unit) ×
   Actual Sales

CONTRIBUTION PRICE *see* CONTRIBUTION APPROACH TO PRICING.

CONTROL ACTIVITIES collectively constitute a component of internal control. Control activities are an entity's policies and procedures designed to reasonably ensure that management directives (i.e., orders) are carried out. Examples of control activities are physical safeguards to restrict access to assets and records and proper segregation of duties.

CONTROL CHART graphical means of depicting sample characteristics, such as means, ranges, and attributes, over time used for process control.

CONTROL CONCEPT one ensuring that actions are carried out or implemented according to a plan or goal.

CONTROL (CONTROLLING) ACCOUNT general ledger account. Its balance reflects the aggregate balance of related subsidiary ledger accounts. Most firms maintain subsidiary records for credit customers and for creditors, Accounts Receivable being the control account. The balance in a control account should not be changed unless a corresponding change is made in the subsidiary accounts. Subsidiary ledgers are often used for Accounts Payable, Inventory, Buildings, and Equipment. *See also* SUBSIDIARY ACCOUNT; SUBSIDIARY LEDGER.

CONTROL ENVIRONMENT the component of internal control that sets the tone of an organization by influencing employee consciousness of controls. The control environment provides discipline and structure and is the foundation for all other components of internal control. The control environment includes an entity's ethical values, its commitment to competence, participation of those charged with governance, and management's philosophy and operating style in connection with taking business risks.

CONTROL PREMIUM an amount paid to buy control of a business to set policies, direct operations, and make decisions for the business. This is the amount that an acquirer is usually willing to pay over the current market price of a corporation. This premium is justified by the expected synergies, such as the expected increase in cash flow resulting from cost savings and revenue improvements from the merger. This premium is typically 20–30% of the market capitalization of a corporation calculated based on a 20 trading days average of its stock price. For example, ABC Corporation has 2,000,000 shares outstanding. The 20 day average price per share is $2. Assume that the acquirer wishes to obtain 70% of the stock to gain control. The market price will be 1,400,000 × $2.00 = $2,800,000. If the buyer expects to realize 20% synergy from the merger, then the maximum price he/she is willing to pay is $2,800,000 × 1.2 = $3,360,000. So the control premium is $560,000 ($3,360,000 − $2,800,000).

CONTROLLABILITY extent to which a manager can influence activities. Managerial performance theoretically should be evaluated only on the basis of those factors controlled by the manager. Thus, managers may control revenues, costs, or investment in resources. For example, a controllable cost is one that is directly regulated by a specific manager at a given level of production within a given time span. However, controllability and responsibility are rarely coextensive. One reason is that more than one manager may influence an activity.

CONTROLLABLE COSTS variable costs such as direct materials, direct labor, and variable overhead that are usually considered controllable by the department manager. Further, a certain portion of fixed costs can also be controllable. For example, certain advertising spent specifically for a given department would be an expense controllable by the manager of that department. Advertising expenses that benefit many departments or products are, however, NONCONTROLLABLE COSTS.

CONTROLLABLE MANUFACTURING OVERHEAD VARIANCE difference between actual manufacturing overhead costs incurred and the manufacturing overhead costs budgeted for the level of production reached.

CONTROLLABLE VARIANCE part of the total factory overhead variance not attributable to the volume variance in two-way analysis.

CONTROLLED COMPANY firm in which a majority of voting stock is held by an individual or corporation. The degree of control depends on the percentage of the voting stock owned.

CONTROLLED FOREIGN CORPORATION (CFC) foreign corporation in which more than 50% of the combined voting power of all classes of voting stock, or the total value of its stock, is owned by 10%-or-more U.S. shareholders on any day during its tax year.

CONTROLLER chief accounting executive of an organization. The controller is in charge of the Accounting Department. The principal functions of the controller are: (1) planning for control; (2) financial reporting and interpreting; (3) tax administration; (4) management audits and development of accounting systems; (5) internal audits.

In contrast with the controller, the TREASURER is concerned mainly with financial problems including planning the finances, managing working capital, formulating credit policy, and managing the investment portfolio. In a large firm, both the controller and treasurer report to Vice-President-Finance.

CONTROL LIMITS limits set for the purpose of effective quality control. Most commonly, *three-sigma* control limits are used. *See also* QUALITY CONTROL; THREE-SIGMA LIMITS.

CONTROLLING implementation of a decision method and the use of feedback so that the goals and specific strategic plans of the firm are optimally obtained. To do this, managers study accounting and other reports and compare them to the plans set earlier. These comparisons may show where operations are not proceeding as planned and who is responsible for what. The feedback that management receives may suggest the need to replan, to set new strategies, or to reshape the organizational structure.

CONTROLLING COMPANY (PARENT) ACCOUNTING method used in parent-subsidiary relationships. The holding of more than 50% of the voting stock of one corporation by another corporation generally creates a parent-subsidiary relationship. Control of a corporation may often be achieved with less than 50% of the subsidiary's voting stock, but this would not be regarded as a basis for preparing consolidated statements. In the latter situation, the investment would be accounted for under the EQUITY METHOD in an account called investment in investee. *See also* CONSOLIDATION; CONSOLIDATED FINANCIAL STATEMENT.

CONTROL RISK risk related to the effectiveness of a client's internal control structure policies and procedures. An ineffective internal control increases control risk.

CONTROL RISK ASSESSMENT risk that a material misstatement that could occur in an assertion will not be detected or prevented on a timely basis by an entity's internal controls.

CONTROL TOTALS in auditing, totals developed on "key" data fields in input records, and on the number of records processed to ensure that data have been properly transmitted, converted, and processed.

CONVENTION agreement or statement, expressed or implied, that is used to solve given types of problems. Conventions allow a standardized approach to problem solving and behavior in certain situations. An example of a convention is placing debits on the left side and credits on the right side of an account. The accountant performs daily functions by following conventions such as format guidelines in the preparation of financial statements.

CONVENTIONAL COSTING *see* ABSORPTION COSTING.

CONVENTIONAL COST SYSTEM a cost system that uses only unit- (or volume-) based COST DRIVERS to apply overhead costs to products and services.

CONVERGENCE the goal of establishing a uniform (worldwide) set of accounting standards in order to eliminate differences between U.S. GENERALLY ACCEPTED ACCOUNTING PRINCIPLES (GAAP) and the INTERNATIONAL FINANCIAL REPORTING STANDARDS (IFRS).

CONVERSION
1. act of exchanging one class of corporate security for another. An example is the conversion of convertible bonds into stock.
2. valuation substitution for another. An example is the restatement of historical cost for that of current cost. *See also* CONVERSION COST.
3. transfer of mutual fund shares from one fund to another in the same family.
4. switch from one currency to another using an exchange ratio.

CONVERSION COST sum of the costs of DIRECT LABOR and FACTORY OVERHEAD. *See also* PRIME COST.

CONVERSION PRICE effective price paid for common stock when the stock is obtained by converting either convertible preferred stock or convertible bonds. The face value of a convertible security divided by the CONVERSION RATIO gives the price of the underlying common stock at which the security is convertible. For example, if a $1,000 bond is convertible into 10 shares of stock, the conversion price is $100 ($1,000/10). An investor would usually not convert the security into common stock unless the market price was greater than the conversion price.

CONVERSION RATIO (RATE) number of shares of common stock that may be obtained by converting a convertible bond or share of convertible preferred stock:

Conversion Ratio (Rate) = Face Value/Conversion Price

For example, if the conversion price is $25 per share and the face value of a bond is $1,000, then an investor would receive 40 shares for each bond ($1,000/$25 per share).

CONVERSION VALUE value of the underlying common stock represented by convertible bonds or convertible preferred stock. This value is obtained by multiplying the conversion ratio (rate) by the per share market price of the common stock. For example, if the common stock is selling for $24 per share and the conversion ratio is 40 shares, the conversion value is $960 (40 shares × $24 per share).

CONVERTIBLE DEBT bond exchangeable for a specified number of common shares at a predetermined price, usually at the option of the holder. The investor in a convertible bond desires higher income than is available from common stock and the greater potential for capital appreciation than is possible with regular bonds. From the issuer's perspective the advantage of issuing a convertible bond is that its attractiveness results in greater marketability and a lower interest rate.

CONVERTIBLE SECURITY types of stocks and bonds that can be voluntarily converted into capital stock at a later date. Examples are convertible bonds and convertible preferred stock. The CONVERSION RATIO determines how many shares will be issued. For example, if a $100,000 convertible bond issue is convertible at 1 bond for 4 shares, 400 shares are involved calculated as follows:

$$\frac{\$100,000}{\$1,000} = 100 \text{ bonds} \times 4 \text{ shares} = 400 \text{ shares}$$

COOKIE a small file stored on a computer to facilitate interaction with a Web site. Generally, the information in a cookie is pretty innocuous. Web sites often use cookies to store personal preferences or track data.

COOKIE JAR ACCOUNTING accounting practice that inflates provisions for expected expenses and later reverses them to boost earnings—in many cases at very convenient times. This is traditionally abused when companies want to push reserves into future earnings. Reserves are set reserves to cover the estimated costs of taxes, litigation, bad debts, job cuts, and acquisitions. Company managers estimate reserves and the outside auditor judges whether the reserves are reasonable. Auditors rarely challenge company estimates because there are unclear guidelines for calculating reserves.

"COOK THE BOOKS" falsify financial records and statements to misrepresent the financial position and operating results of the entity.

COOPERATIVE
1. non-taxable entity that is formed to eliminate the middleman and gain profits or savings that would have been paid to it. Profit or savings is periodically distributed by the proportion of transactions and not in proportion to each member's investment.
2. an entity owned by members. For example, in terms of real estate, ownership shares in the apartment building are held by the occupants. They make decisions regarding the property.

COORDINATING process that involves a decision by management as to how best to put together the resources of the firm in order to carry out established plans. Coordinating also requires directing. In directing, managers oversee day-to-day activities and keep the organization functioning smoothly.

COPYRIGHT protection given by law to authors of literary, musical, artistic, and similar works. The copyright holder enjoys the following exclusive rights: (1) to print, reprint, and copy the work; (2) to sell, assign, or distribute copies; and (3) to perform the work. A copyright is recorded at its acquisition price. The legal life of a copyright is the life of the author plus 70 years. Rarely will the economic life of a copyright exceed its legal life. For example, some textbooks become obsolete in five years. As other limited life intangible assets, copyrights are amortized over the period benefited.

CORNER (LP) *see* GRAPHICAL METHOD.

CORNER POINT *see* BASIC FEASIBLE SOLUTION.

CORPORATE DEVELOPMENT OFFICERS (CDOs) the heads of in-house merger and acquisition (M&A) teams.

CORPORATE GOVERNANCE the system of checks and balances designed to ensure that corporate managers are just as vigilant on behalf of long-term shareholder value as they would be if it was their own money at risk. It is also the process whereby shareholders—the actual owners of any publicly traded firm—assert their ownership rights, through an elected board of directors and the CEO and other officers and managers they appoint and oversee. In the heels of corporate scandals including the Enron debacle in 2002, a series of sweeping changes are being sought, such as forcing boards to have a majority of independent directors, granting audit committees power to hire and fire accountants, banning sweetheart loans to officers and directors, and requiring shareholder's approval for stock option plans. More specifically, the following principles constitute good governance:

1. To avoid conflicts of interest, a company's board of directors should include a substantial majority of independent directors—*independent* meaning that directors don't have financial or close personal ties to the company or its executives.
2. A company's audit, nominating, and compensation committees should consist entirely of independent directors.
3. A board should obtain shareholder approval for any actions that could significantly affect the relationship between the board and shareholders, including the adoption of anti-takeover measures such as "poison pills."
4. Companies should base executive compensation plans on pay for performance and should provide full disclosure of these plans.
5. To avoid abuse in the use of stock options (and executive perquisites), all employee stock option plans should be submitted to shareholders for approval.

Institutional Shareholder Services, Inc. (http://www.issproxy.com/), an influential proxy advisor, started scoring companies on governance issues.

CORPORATE JOINT VENTURE cooperation between two or more corporations in which the purpose is to achieve jointly a specified business goal. Upon the attainment of the goal, the joint venture is terminated. An example is when two businesses agree to share in the development of a specific product. A joint venture, which is typically limited to one project, differs from a PARTNERSHIP that can work jointly on many projects. *See also* JOINT VENTURE.

CORPORATE PLANNING MODEL integrated business planning model in which marketing and production models are linked to the FINANCIAL MODEL.

More specifically, it is a description, explanation, and interrelation of the functional areas of a firm (accounting, finance, marketing, production, and others), expressed in terms of a set of mathematical and logical equations so as to produce a variety of reports including PRO FORMA financial statements. Corporate planning models are the basic tools for risk analysis and WHAT-IF experiments. The ultimate goals of the model are to improve quality of planning and decision-making, reduce the decision risk, and, more importantly, favorably influence or even shape the future environment.

CORPORATION business organized as a separate legal entity with ownership evidenced by shares of stock. The corporation is formed by filing the ARTICLES OF INCORPORATION with the state authority, who returns it with a certificate of incorporation; the two documents together become the *corporate charter*. Each founding stockholder receives from the company a specified number of shares of capital stock. A stockholder may sell owned shares to other investors. The corporation is a *legal entity* separate from its owners. Advantages of a corporation are the ability to obtain large amounts of financing through a public issuance, ease of transferring shares, limited liability of owners, unlimited life, and professional management.

CORRECTING ENTRY *see* ADJUSTING JOURNAL ENTRY.

CORRELATION degree of relationship between business and economic variables such as cost and volume. Correlation analysis evaluates cause/effect relationships. It looks consistently at how the value of one variable changes when the value of the other is changed. A prediction can be made based on the relationship uncovered. An example is the effect of advertising on sales. A degree of correlation is measured statistically by the COEFFICIENT OF DETERMINATION (r-squared).

CORRELATION COEFFICIENT (r) measure of the degree of correlation between two variables. The range of values it takes is between -1 and $+1$. A negative value of r indicates an inverse relationship; a positive value of r indicates a direct relationship; a zero value of r indicates that the two variables are independent of each other; the closer r is to $+1$ and -1, the stronger the relationship between the two variables. For example, we may expect a negative relationship between the demand for a product and its selling price, because the higher the selling price charged, the lower the demand.

COST
1. sacrifice, measured by the price paid, to acquire, produce, or maintain goods or services. Prices paid for materials, labor, and factory overhead in the manufacture of goods are costs.
2. an asset. The term cost is often used when referring to the valuation of a good or service acquired. When it is used in this sense, a cost is an ASSET.
   The concepts of cost and expense are often used interchangeably. When the benefits of the acquisition of the goods or services expire, the cost becomes an expense or loss. An EXPENSE is a cost with expired benefits. A LOSS is an expense (expired cost) with no related benefit.

COST ABSORPTION application of the costs to the physical units or other measures of output that pass through the process. First, costs must be accumulated by processing departments before applying the department costs to the units. An application of factory overhead costs to processing departments (or jobs), using a PREDETERMINED OVERHEAD RATE, is an example of cost absorption.

COST ACCOUNTING system for recording and reporting measurements of the cost of manufacturing goods and performing services in the aggregate and in detail. It includes methods for reorganizing, classifying, allocating, aggregating, and reporting actual costs and comparing them with standard costs. Determination of unit cost to make a product or render a service is needed to establish a selling price or fee to be charged. Also, costs for manufacturing a product for inventory valuation need to be known to prepare the balance sheet and income statement. Cost accounting systems include job order, process, standard, and direct costing.

COST ACCOUNTING STANDARDS BOARD (CASB) body established by Congress in August 1970 to promote consistency in cost accounting practices and to aid in the fair and accurate reporting of actual costs of governmental contracts. The board was authorized to promulgate standards and designed to achieve uniformity as to the application of cost accounting principles and concepts. The board ceased to exist in 1980, and its responsibilities are now handled by the Office of Federal Procurement Policy (OFPP).

COST ACCUMULATION collection of costs in an organized fashion by means of a cost accounting system. There are two primary approaches to cost accumulation: JOB ORDER and PROCESS COSTING. Under a job order system, the three basic elements of manufacturing costs—direct materials, direct labor, and factory overhead—are accumulated according to assigned job numbers. Under a process cost system, manufacturing costs are accumulated according to processing department or cost center.

COST ALLOCATION identification of costs with cost objectives, also called *cost apportionment*, *cost assignment*, *cost distribution*, and *cost reapportionment*. There are basically three aspects of cost allocation: (1) choosing the object of costing. Examples are products, processes, jobs, or departments; (2) choosing and accumulating the costs that relate to the object of costing. Examples are manufacturing expenses, selling and administrative expenses, joint costs, common costs, service department costs, and fixed costs; and (3) choosing a method of identifying (2) with (1). For example, a cost allocation base for allocating manufacturing costs would typically be labor-hours, machine-hours, or production units.

COST APPLICATION *see* COST ABSORPTION.

COST APPORTIONMENT *see* COST ALLOCATION.

COST ASSIGNMENT *see* COST ALLOCATION.

COST ASSIGNMENT PATH link between a cost and one of its two or more cost objects.

COST-BASED PRICE in a TRANSFER PRICING context, scheme in which the cost base can be either variable cost or full cost. It is easy to understand and convenient to use, but there are some disadvantages: (1) Inefficiencies of the selling divisions are passed on to the buying divisions with little incentive to control costs. The use of standard costs is recommended in such a case. (2) The cost-based method treats the divisions as COST CENTERS rather than PROFIT or INVESTMENT CENTERS. Therefore, measures such as RETURN

ON INVESTMENT (ROI) and RESIDUAL INCOME cannot be used for evaluation purposes.

The variable cost-based transfer price has an advantage over the full cost method because in the short run it may tend to ensure the best utilization of the company's overall resources. The reason is that, in the short run, fixed costs do not change. Any use of otherwise idle facilities, without incurrence of additional fixed costs, will increase the company's overall profits.

COST BEHAVIOR ANALYSIS separating MIXED COSTS into their variable and fixed elements. Mixed costs are common to a wide range of firms. Examples of mixed costs include sales compensation, repairs and maintenance, and factory overhead in general. Mixed costs must be separated into the variable and fixed elements in order to be included in a variety of business planning analyses such as COST-VOLUME-PROFIT (CVP) ANALYSIS. There are several methods available for this purpose including the LEAST-SQUARES METHOD. *See also* COST BEHAVIOR PATTERN.

COST BEHAVIOR PATTERN manner in which a cost will react to changes in the level of activity. Costs may be viewed as variable, fixed, or mixed (semi-variable). A mixed cost is one that contains both variable and fixed elements. For planning, control, and decision purposes, mixed costs need to be separated into their variable and fixed components, using such methods as the HIGH-LOW METHOD and the LEAST-SQUARES METHOD. An application of the variable-fixed breakdown is a BREAK-EVEN and COST-VOLUME-PROFIT (CVP) ANALYSIS.

COST-BENEFIT ANALYSIS manner of determining whether the favorable results of an alternative are sufficient to justify the cost of taking that alternative. This analysis is widely used in connection with capital expenditure projects. An example of cost-benefit analysis is where the cost incurred to uncover the reasons for a variance outweigh the benefit to be derived. *See also* PROFITABILITY INDEX.

COST CENTER unit within the organization in which the manager is responsible only for costs. A cost center has no control over sales or over the generating of revenue. An example is the production department of a manufacturing company. The performance of a cost center is measured by comparing actual costs with budgeted costs for a specified period of time.

COST CONTROL steps taken by management to assure that the cost objectives set down in the planning stage are attained and to assure that all segments of the organization function in a manner consistent with its policies. For effective cost control, most organizations use STANDARD COST SYSTEMS, in which the actual costs are compared against standard costs for performance evaluation and the deviations are investigated for remedial actions. Cost control is also concerned with feedback that might change any or all of the future plans, the production method, or both.

COST DEPLETION method by which the costs of natural resources are allocated to depletion over the accounting periods that make up the life of the asset. Cost depletion is computed by (1) estimating the total quantity of mineral or other resources acquired and (2) assigning a proportionate amount of the total resource cost to the quantity extracted in the period. For example, assume that a company invests $50,000 in an oil well that contains an estimated 120,000 barrels of oil. The residual value is estimated at \$6,000. In the first year, 12,000 barrels of oil are extracted and sold. The depletion for the first year is (\$50,000 − \$6,000) × (12,000/120,000) = \$4,400. *See also* PERCENTAGE DEPLETION.

COST DISTRIBUTION *see* COST ALLOCATION.

COST DRIVER factor that has a direct cause-effect relationship to a cost, such as direct labor hours, machine hours, beds occupied, computer time used, flight hours, miles driven, or contracts.

COST DRIVER ANALYSIS examination, quantification, and explanation of the effects of cost drivers. The results are often used for continuous improvement programs to reduce throughput times, improve quality, and reduce costs.

COST EFFECTIVE among decision alternatives, the one whose cost is lower than its benefit. The most cost effective program would be the one whose cost-benefit ratio is the lowest among various programs competing for a given amount of funds. *See also* COST-BENEFIT ANALYSIS.

COST ELEMENT most disaggregated level of resource cost. For example, power cost, engineering cost, and depreciation may be cost elements in the activity cost pool for a machine activity. *See also* ACTIVITY COST POOL; BILL OF ACTIVITIES; RESOURCE COSTS.

COST ESTIMATION measurement of past costs for the purpose of predicting future costs for decision-making purposes. For example, a COST VOLUME FORMULA (such as $y = \$300 + \$5x$) can be used to estimate a cost item y for any given value of volume x. *See also* COST PREDICTION.

COST FLOW *see* FLOW OF COSTS.

COST FUNCTION relationship between cost and activity. A cost function may be either linear or nonlinear. The general formula for a linear relationship is $y = a + bx$, where y is the estimated value of a cost item for any specified value of x (activity). The constant a, the intercept, is the fixed cost element; b, the slope, is the variable rate per unit of x. The possible measures of activity x include:

> units of product
> machine-hours
> dollar sales volume
> direct labor-hours
> mileage driven

The coefficients a and b are estimated using such methods as the HIGH-LOW METHOD and the LEAST-SQUARES METHOD.

COST HIERARCHY framework for classifying production-related activities according to the level at which their costs are incurred.

COST MANAGEMENT management and control of activities to help set enterprise strategies and to determine an accurate product and service cost, improve business processes, eliminate waste, identify cost drivers, and plan operations.

COST MANAGEMENT SYSTEM (CMS) cost and management accounting, control, and reporting system that identifies, monitors, and maintains continuous, detailed analyses of a company's activities and provides managers with timely measures of operating results.

COST MODULES convention that is used to classify cost by point where incurred (resource module), its use (activity module), and its ultimate user (final cost object module). Activities also feed a process module.

COST OBJECTS intermediate and final dispositions of cost pools. Intermediate cost objects receive temporary accumulations of costs as the cost pools move from their originating points to the final cost objects. Final cost objects, such as a job, product, or process, should be logically linked with the cost pool based on a cause-and-effect relationship.

COST OF CAPITAL rate of return that is necessary to maintain market value (or stock price) of a firm, also called a *hurdle rate, cutoff rate,* or *minimum required rate of return.* The firm's cost of capital is calculated as a weighted average of the costs of debt and equity funds. Equity funds include both capital stock (common stock and preferred stock) and retained earnings. These costs are expressed as annual percentage rates. For example, assume the following capital structure and the cost of each source of financing for the XYZ Company:

Source	Book Value	Percent of Total Weights	Cost
Debt	$20,000,000	40%	5.14%
Preferred stock	5,000,000	10	13.40
Common stock	20,000,000	40	17.11
Retained earnings	5,000,000	10	16.00
Totals	$50,000,000	100%	

The overall cost of capital is computed as follows:

$$5.14\%(.4) + 13.4\%(.1) + 17.11\%(.4) + 16.00\%(.1) = 11.84\%$$

The cost of capital is used for CAPITAL BUDGETING purposes. Under the NET PRESENT VALUE METHOD, the cost of capital is used as the DISCOUNT RATE to calculate the present value of future cash inflows. Under the INTERNAL RATE OF RETURN method, it is used to make an accept-or-reject decision by comparing the cost of capital with the internal rate of return on a given project. A project is accepted when the internal rate exceeds the cost of capital.

COST OF DEBT interest rate times 1 minus the marginal tax rate because interest is a tax deduction—symbolically, $i(1 - t)$. Hence, an increase in the tax rate decreases the cost of debt.

COST OF EQUITY CAPITAL minimum desired rate of return on invested capital that is determined by calculating net income as a percentage of invested capital.

COST OF GOODS MANUFACTURED BUDGET detailed schedule that summarizes the costs of production for a future period.

COST OF GOODS MANUFACTURED SCHEDULE form showing the cost of producing goods during the accounting period. The cost of goods manufactured is an element in preparing the income statement. It consists of the cost of producing goods: DIRECT MATERIAL, DIRECT LABOR, and FACTORY OVERHEAD. Also considered is the change in the work-in-process inventory.

Assume work-in-process inventory was $30,000 on 1/1/2014 and $35,000 on 12/31/2013. During the year, manufacturing costs were direct material $20,000, direct labor $23,000, and factory overhead $40,000. The cost of goods manufactured schedule follows:

Work-in-process – 1/1/2014		$30,000
Add: Manufacturing costs		
Direct material	$20,000	
Direct labor	23,000	
Factory overhead	40,000	
Total manufacturing cost		83,000
Total	$113,000	
Less: Work-in-process – 12/31/2013		35,000
Cost of goods manufactured		$ 78,000

COST OF GOODS SOLD *see* COST OF SALES.

COST-OF-LIVING ADJUSTMENT (COLA) upward change in an employee's compensation because of inflation. The adjustment is typically based on a price index such as the Consumer Price Index, Wholesale Price Index, and Gross National Product Index. COLA is sometimes built into labor contracts.

COST OF NEW EXTERNAL COMMON EQUITY cost of newly issued common stock. This is higher than the cost of retained earnings because of stock flotation costs. Providers of equity capital are exposed to more risk than lenders are because the firm is not obligated to pay them a return. Also, in case of liquidation, creditors are paid before equity investors. Thus, equity financing is more expensive than debt because equity investors require a higher return to compensate for the greater risk assumed.

COST OF PREDICTION ERROR cost of a failure to predict a certain variable (such as sales, earnings, and cash flow) accurately. For example, assume that a company has been selling a toy baby doll having a variable cost of $.50 for $.90 each (a contribution of $.40 per doll). The fixed cost is $200. The company has no privilege of returning any unsold dolls. It has predicted sales of 1,500 units. However, unforeseen competition has reduced sales to 1,000 units. What is the cost of its prediction error—that is, its failure to predict demand accurately?

(1) Initial predicted sales = 1,500 units.
    Optimal decision: purchase 1,500 units.
    Expected net income (1,500 × $.40) – $200 = $400
(2) Alternative parameter value = 1,000 units.
    Optimal decision: purchase 1,000 units.
    Expected net income (1,000 × $.40) – $200 = $200
(3) Results of original decision under alternative parameter value.
    Expected net income:

Revenue	Cost of Dolls	Fixed Costs	
(1,000 units × $.90) –	(1,500 units × $.50) –	$200	=
$900 –	$750 –	$200 = – $50	

(4) Cost of prediction error, (2) – (3) = $250.

COST OF PREFERRED STOCK minimum desired rate of return on invested capital that is the stated dividend rate of the individual preferred stock issue.

COST OF PRODUCTION REPORT summary of the total manufacturing cost of an item. It involves charges to a processing department and the allocation of the total cost between the ending work-in-process inventory and the units completed and transferred out to the next department or finished goods inventory. The cost of production report generally consists of four sections: (1) *Physical Flow* accounts for the physical flow of units in and out of a department. (2) *Equivalent Production* is the sum of: (a) units in process, restated in completed units, and (b) total units actually produced. The computation of equivalent units of production depends on the flow of cost method-weighted average or FIFO. (3) *Costs to Account For* accounts for the incurrence of costs that were: (a) in process at the beginning of the period, (b) transferred in from previous departments, and (c) added by the department during the current period. (4) *Costs Accounted For* accounts for the disposition of costs charged to the department that were: (a) transferred out to the next department or finished goods inventory, (b) completed and on hand, and (c) in process at the end of the period. The total of the *Costs to Account For* must equal the total of the *Costs Accounted For*. *See also* PROCESS COSTING.

COST OF RETAINED EARNINGS cost of internally generated funds. It is an imputed or opportunity cost or the dividends given up by the common stockholders. It is the rate that investors can earn elsewhere on investments of comparable risk.

COST OF SALES price of buying or making an item that is sold; also called *cost of goods sold*. The difference between sales and cost of sales is gross profit. For a retail business, the cost of sale is the purchase price of the item. For a manufactured good, the cost of sale includes DIRECT MATERIAL, DIRECT LABOR, and FACTORY OVERHEAD associated with producing it. An example would be the cost to General Motors of making a car. An illustrative example of a gross profit calculation for a retail business follows:

Sales		$100
Less: Cost of Sales		
Beginning inventory	$ 30	
Add: Purchases	80	
Cost of goods available	$110	
Less: Ending inventory	40	
Cost of sales		70
Gross profit		$ 30

COST-PLUS CONTRACT form of contract that requires the customer to pay for all costs incurred plus a predetermined amount of profit.

COST PLUS PRICING clear and convenient way to establish a selling price. This method may be used in determining a contract price by a supplier seeking to avoid the uncertainty associated with predicting costs. Cost plus pricing may be found in developmental contracts for new products. Federal agencies deal with cost plus fixed fee contracts. In cost plus pricing, an item is priced at its cost (including direct material, direct labor, and factory overhead) plus some fixed fee or profit markup. For example, if the total cost of a contract is

$325,000 and the fixed fee is $100,000, the contract price would be $425,000. If a profit markup is used, it should be based on the nature of the product and corporate considerations (e.g., marketing aspects). For example, if cost is $200,000 and a profit markup on cost of 30% is desired, the contract price is $260,000.

When cost plus pricing is used to determine a transfer price for an internal transfer of a product within the organization, it closely approximates an outside market price. Thus, the resulting synthetic market price is considered a good practical substitute.

COST-PLUS TRANSFER PRICE transfer price computed as the sum of the costs incurred by the producing division plus an agreed-on profit percentage.

COST POOL grouping of individual costs. Subsequent allocations are made of cost pools rather than of individual costs. Costs are often pooled by departments, by jobs, or by behavior pattern. For example, overhead costs are accumulated by service departments in a factory and then allocated to production departments before multiple departmental overhead rates are developed for product costing purposes.

COST PREDICTION forecast of costs for managerial decision-making purposes. The terms cost ESTIMATION and *cost prediction* are used interchangeably. To predict future costs, a COST FUNCTION is often specified and estimated statistically. The cost function may be either linear (i.e., $y = a + bx$) or nonlinear. The estimated cost function must pass some statistical tests, such as having a high R-SQUARED and a high T-VALUE, to provide sound cost prediction.

COST PRINCIPLE *see* HISTORICAL COST.

COST REAPPORTIONMENT *see* COST ALLOCATION.

COST-RECOVERY METHOD revenue recognition method under which no gross profit is recognized until all the cost of the merchandise has been recovered. That is, the first payments received from customers are treated as a recovery of the cost of goods sold. Once the cost has been recovered, the remaining collections are recognized as gross profit. Like the *installment* method, this method may be used because of the uncertainty of collections, and is not generally accepted. *See also* INSTALLMENT (SALES) METHOD.

COST REDUCTION PROGRAM policy of cutting costs to improve profitability. It may be implemented when a company is having financial problems and must "tighten its belt." In some cases, the firm is initiating a policy to eliminate waste and inefficiency. A cost reduction program may detract from the QUALITY OF EARNINGS when significant cuts are made in DISCRETIONARY COSTS.

COST REFERENCE source to determine the price of a good or service, such as a supplier's price list.

COST SHEET form prepared for each job or department. It serves as a means of accumulating the manufacturing costs—direct materials, direct labor, and overhead costs—chargeable to the job or department and as a means of determining unit costs. A JOB (ORDER) COST SHEET is used for job order costing; a COST OF PRODUCTION REPORT is used for process costing. Cost sheets may serve as a subsidiary ledger supporting a Work-in-Process Control.

COSTS OF CONFORMANCE costs incurred to produce a quality product or service.

COSTS OF NONCONFORMANCE costs incurred to correct defects in a product or service.

COSTS OF QUALITY costs incurred in association with quality conformance. It must be assessed in terms of relative costs and benefits. Thus, an organization should attempt to minimize its total cost of quality. *See also* CONFORMANCE COSTS; PREVENTION COSTS; APPRAISAL; NONCONFORMANCE COSTS; INTERNAL FAILURE COSTS; EXTERNAL FAILURE COSTS.

COST SUMMARY SCHEDULE PROCESS COSTING schedule that is used to determine the costs to be transferred to the finished goods inventory account of a department or production process and the ending balance of the work in process inventory account.

COST-TO-COST METHOD in construction contracts, an estimate of completion in which the state of completion is the ratio of costs incurred as of a given date divided by the estimated total project cost. *See also* PERCENTAGE OF COMPLETION METHOD.

COST-VOLUME FORMULA cost accounting formula used for COST PREDICTION and FLEXIBLE BUDGETING purposes. It is a cost function in the form of:

$$y = a + bx$$

where $y =$ the semi-variable (or mixed) costs to be broken up
    $x =$ any given measure of activity such as volume and labor-hours
    $a =$ the fixed cost component
    $b =$ the variable rate per unit of x

For example, the cost-volume formula for factory overhead is $y = \$200 + \$10x$ where $y =$ estimated factory overhead and $x =$ direct labor-hours, which means that the factory overhead is estimated to be \$200 fixed, plus \$10 per hour of direct labor.

COST-VOLUME-PROFIT (CVP) ANALYSIS analysis that deals with how profits and costs change with a change in volume. More specifically, it looks at the effects on profits of changes in such factors as variable costs, fixed costs, selling prices, volume, and mix of products sold. By studying the relationships of costs, sales, and net income, management is better able to cope with many planning decisions. For example, CVP analysis attempts to answer the following questions: (1) What sales volume is required to break even? (2) What sales volume is necessary in order to earn a desired (target) profit? (3) What profit can be expected on a given sales volume? (4) How would changes in selling price, variable costs, fixed costs, and output affect profits? (5) How would a change in the mix of products sold affect the break-even and target volume and profit potential? *See also* BREAK-EVEN ANALYSIS; TARGET INCOME SALES.

COUNTERBALANCING ERROR *see* OFFSETTING ERROR.

COUPON BOND *see* BEARER BOND.

COUPON RATE interest rate on the face amount of a debt security. For instance, the annual interest to be paid on a $1,000 bond with a nominal interest rate of 8% is $80. Typically, interest payments are made semiannually. The term derives from BEARER BONDS, once more common than now, which actually bore coupons to be detached and presented for payment as interest became due. Even with *registered bonds* the term survives and is distinguished from YIELD, which relates the coupon rate to the market price of the bond.

COVENANT promise, commonly found in the form of restrictions in a loan agreement imposed on the borrower to protect the lender's interest. Examples of typical restrictive provisions are a ceiling on dividends and the required maintenance of a minimum working capital. *See also* INDENTURE.

COVERDELL EDUCATION SAVINGS ACCOUNTS formerly known as education IRAs, these accounts permit nondeductible contributions for beneficiaries under the age of 18. Withdrawals made by beneficiaries for qualified education expenses are excluded from taxable income. The contribution limit is $2,000, but is phased out ratably based on modified adjusted gross income. Phaseout ranges are dependent on filing status and are periodically adjusted for inflation.

COVERED OPTION contract backed by owning the stock underlying the option. Assume the owner of 500 shares of XYZ writes (sells) 5 XYZ call options. The seller now has a covered option position. If the price of the stock rises and there is an exercise of the option, the seller has the stock to deliver to the purchaser. If the seller did not own the shares, he or she would be termed a naked writer.

CPM *see* CRITICAL PATH METHOD (CPM).

CRASHING process of reducing an activity time by adding resources and, hence, usually cost.

CREATIVE ACCOUNTING management's attempt to "fool around" with its accounting in order to overstate net income. Examples of income management include selling off low-cost basis assets to report gains, unjustifiably lengthening the expected life of an asset to reduce expense (e.g., depreciable life), and under-accruing expenses (e.g., bad debt provisions). To financial statement users, "creative accounting" has a negative connotation.

CREDIT
1. entry on the right side of an account. As a verb, to make an entry on the right side of an account. Under the DOUBLE ENTRY BOOKKEEPING system, credits increase liabilities, equity, and revenues and decrease assets and expenses.
2. to *enter* or *post* a credit.
3. the ability to buy an item or to borrow money in return for a promise to pay later.
4. in *taxation*, a dollar for dollar offset against a tax liability. *See also* TAX CREDITS.

CREDIT AGAINST TAX *see* TAX CREDIT.

CREDIT ANALYSIS process of determining, before a line of credit is extended, whether a credit applicant meets the firm's credit standards or those of a lender and what amount of credit the applicant should receive. It typically involves two steps: (1) obtaining credit information (such as financial statements, Dun & Bradstreet reports, etc.) and (2) analyzing the information in order to make the credit decision.

CREDIT BALANCE
1. balance in the right side of an account. According to DEBIT AND CREDIT CONVENTIONS, any asset and expense account will have a normal debit balance, while any liability, equity, and revenue account will have a normal credit balance.
2. overpaid customer account resulting in a credit amount in accounts receivable.

CREDIT LINE specified amount of money available to a borrower from a bank usually for one year. A credit line is a moral, not a contractual, commitment, and no commitment fee is charged. Compensating balances, though, are commonly required—10% of the line plus 10% of amounts borrowed under the line. There are confirmed lines of credit and guidance lines, the former being documented by a letter to the depositor, the latter being an internal limit observed by the bank. Credit lines contrast with revolving credits, which are contractual and involve a commitment fee.

CREDIT MEMORANDUM
1. form or document used by a seller to notify the buyer of merchandise that the buyer's accounts payable is being credited (decreased) due to errors or other factors requiring adjustments.
2. form given by a bank to a depositor to indicate that the depositor's balance is being increased due to some event other than a deposit, such as the collection by the bank of the depositor's note receivable.

CREDITOR business or individual that has extended credit and is owed money.

CREDITORS' EQUITY total amount of liabilities. The creditors' equity ratio equals total liabilities divided by total assets. This reflects the percentage of assets financed by creditors. In the event of corporate liquidation, creditors are paid before stockholders. *See also* STOCKHOLDERS' EQUITY.

CRIMINAL PENALTY fine or punishment imposed by a taxing authority for severe violations of tax laws and regulations. Criminal penalties, which may include imprisonment, include penalties for income tax evasion.

CRITICAL PATH longest path for a project. This is the minimum amount of time needed for the completion of the project. Thus, the activities along this path must be accelerated in order to speed up the project. On the other hand, delays in these activities would cause delays in the project. It is thus important to identify the critical path. *See also* PROGRAM EVALUATION AND REVIEW TECHNIQUE (PERT).

CRITICAL PATH ACCOUNTING method of accounting for costs and expenditures that must accompany the CRITICAL PATH METHOD (CPM) of project management. Costs for manpower, materials, and overhead must be accounted for by activities and paths of a given project. In many cases it is possible to shorten the project's total completion time by injecting additional money and labor. Critical path accounting should provide all the necessary cost data, including *indirect* costs such as facilities and equipment costs, supervision, and labor and personnel costs, and *direct* costs that are needed to speed up each activity or path. *See also* PROGRAM EVALUATION AND REVIEW TECHNIQUE (PERT).

CRITICAL PATH METHOD (CPM) technique in PROGRAM EVALUATION AND REVIEW TECHNIQUE (PERT) that uses a single time estimate for each activity, rather than three time estimates—*optimistic*, *most likely*, and *pessimistic*. The primary objective of CPM is to identify the CRITICAL PATH for a project.

CROSSFOOT procedure in which additions are made vertically as well as horizontally to assure the mathematical accuracy of totals. An example is verifying that the total debits equal the total credits in a journal (e.g., cash payments journal) at the end of the month.

CROSS-SITE SCRIPTING (XSS) a hacking technique that allows an attacker to embed malicious content into a dynamic Web page to fool the end user into executing that malicious code on his or her computer. Typically, a hacker attacks a legitimate Web site using XSS. When a user visits that legitimate Web site, the malicious code is downloaded and executed on the user's machine.

CROSS-SUBSIDY improper assignment of costs among objects such that certain objects are overcosted while other cost objects are undercosted relative to the activity costs assigned. For example, traditional cost accounting systems tend to overcost high-volume products and undercost low-volume products.

CRYPTOGRAPHY science of secret writing. It is a security safeguard to render information unintelligible if unauthorized individuals intercept the transmission. When the information is to be used, it can be decoded.

CULMINATION OF EARNINGS PROCESS method of recognizing revenue, usually at the time of sale or rendering of a service. A reasonable method for estimating collectibility must exist.

CUMULATIVE ACTIVITY COST cost of two or more activities added together. The buildup of activity cost so that each successive total includes activity costs that precede it.

CUMULATIVE EFFECT OF A CHANGE IN ACCOUNTING PRINCIPLE no longer allowed accounting treatment. Companies no longer will report a cumulative effect on the current year's income statement. Instead, they will report any necessary adjustment as an adjustment to the opening balance of retained earnings for the earliest period presented. FASB's retrospective approach eliminates all cumulative effect adjustments to current income and should greatly enhance the consistency and comparability of financial information over time and between companies. Because a change in principle is retrospectively applied to prior financial statements, there is a need to present pro forma information.

CUMULATIVE PREFERRED STOCK type of stock whose DIVIDENDS, if not paid in a given period, accumulate. All preferred dividends in arrears must be paid before common stockholders can receive distributions. Assume 10,000 shares of $10 par 8% cumulative preferred stock has not paid dividends from

1/1/2011 to 12/31/2014. At the end of 2014, the cumulative dividend not paid is $32,000 ($100,000 × 8% × 4 years). *See also* PREFERRED STOCK.

CUMULATIVE VOTING method of voting that enables a minority group of shareholders to obtain some voice in the control of a corporation. Normally, shareholders must apportion their votes equally among the candidates for the board of directors. Cumulative voting allows them to vote all their shares for a single candidate. The number of shares required to elect a desired number of directors (*NR*) is calculated by the formula:

$$NR = [(DN \times TN)/(N + 1)] + 1$$

where *DN* = number of directors stockholder desires to elect, *TN* = total number of shares of common stock outstanding and entitled to be voted, and *N* = total number of directors to be elected.

For example, a company will elect six directors. There are fifteen candidates and 100,000 shares entitled to be voted. If a group desires to elect two directors, the number of shares it must have is:

$$[(2 \times 100,000 \text{ shares})/(6 + 1)] + 1 = 28,572 \text{ shares}$$

Note that a minority group wishes to elect one-third (two out of six) of the board of directors. It can achieve its goal by owning less than one-third (28,572 shares out of 100,000 shares) the number of shares of stock.

CURRENT ACCOUNT
1. running account, typically involving related companies, showing the movement of an item (e.g., goods, cash) between them. In most cases, a periodic settlement is not required.
2. partner's account showing salary withdrawals and other transactions.

CURRENT ASSET item having a life of one year or less, or the normal OPERATING CYCLE of the business, whichever is greater. For example, if a construction company's operating cycle is three years because it is engaged in long-term construction activities, it would show as current assets items having up to a three-year life. However, in almost all cases, the one-year cutoff is used. Examples of current assets are cash, marketable securities, inventory, and prepaid expenses.

CURRENT COST price of replacing an asset identical to an existing one. It should be of the same condition and age as well as have the same service potential. *See also* REPLACEMENT COST.

CURRENT COST ACCOUNTING method of measuring assets in terms of REPLACEMENT COST. One of the following techniques is applied: (1) the use of *indexing* based on price movements applied to homogeneous asset groups; or (2) direct pricing applicable to assets for which prices are determined from either price lists, manufacturers' quotes, and other direct price sources. Replacement cost cannot exceed recoverable amounts referring to cash recoveries from the sale or use of an asset via either NET REALIZABLE VALUE or the PRESENT VALUE of future cash flows. Assume land is acquired at the beginning of the year for $100,000. At year-end, it is appraised at $130,000. Thus, there is a holding (unrealized) gain of $30,000.

CURRENT COST/CONSTANT DOLLAR historical cost is first stated in terms of current cost which in turn is adjusted to constant purchasing power using the average CONSUMER PRICE INDEX (CPI) for the current year. In effect replacement cost and CPI are combined. This is accomplished as follows:

$$\text{Replacement Cost} \times \frac{\text{Average CPI for Current Year}}{\text{CPI at Time of Transaction}}$$

CURRENT FILE includes documentation applicable only to the year being audited. Items to include in the current file include the engagement letter, the audit plan, results of audit procedures, and the management representation letter.

CURRENT LIABILITY obligation payable within one year or the normal operating cycle of the business. A current liability requires payment out of a current asset or the incurrence of another short-term obligation. Examples are accounts payable, short-term notes payable, accrued expenses payable (e.g., taxes payable, salaries payable). *See also* CURRENT ASSET.

CURRENT OPERATING CONCEPT method of measuring the efficiency of a company. Net income is based on recurring and usual income statement items. Concern is with the effective utilization of the entity's resources in operating the business and making a profit. In computing income, special attention is placed on current and operating items. Specifically, earnings consist of value changes and events controllable by management and resulting from decisions of the *current* period. Included, however, are factors acquired in a previous period but used in the present one. Note that relevant changes arise solely from normal operations. Those advocating the current operating concept argue that the resulting current operating performance net income enhances interperiod and interfirm comparisons and facilitates predictions.

CURRENT RATIO measure of liquidity. Current assets are divided by current liabilities. Assuming current assets are \$120,000 and current liabilities are \$40,000 the current ratio is

$$\frac{\$120,000}{\$40,000} = 3$$

The higher the current ratio, the more assurance that current liabilities can be paid. Thus, there is greater short-term creditor protection. (A company's ratio can be compared with the average in its industry to see whether it is high or low.) An excess of current assets over current liabilities is a buffer against losses that may occur in selling inventory, collecting accounts receivable, or liquidating current investment (e.g., marketable securities). A high current ratio provides a margin of safety against uncertainty and random fluctuations (e.g., strikes, extraordinary losses).

In general, a business with less inventory and more collectible accounts receivable can operate safely with a lower current ratio than a company having a high percentage of current assets in inventory.

Creditors looking at a company's current ratio must consider the quality of the current assets and the nature of the current liabilities. For example, work-in-process inventory has a higher realization risk than finished goods.

CURRENT VALUE term for an asset shown at its present worth. Some measures that can be used are CURRENT COST, current exit value, and PRESENT VALUE. *See also* CURRENT VALUE ACCOUNTING.

CURRENT VALUE ACCOUNTING periodical revaluation of the CURRENT VALUE of assets and liabilities. Unlike CONSTANT DOLLAR ACCOUNTING, it requires the recognition of holding gains or losses prior to realization through sales or exchanges.

CURTAILMENT IN PENSION PLAN materially *reducing* the expected years of future services of current employees or eliminating for a significant number of employees the accrual of defined benefits for some or all of their future services. Immediate recognition is given to the gain or loss upon curtailment. The components of the gain or loss include (1) unamortized PRIOR SERVICE PENSION COST applicable to employee service no longer needed and (2) change in PROJECTED BENEFIT OBLIGATION occurring from the curtailment. *See also* SETTLEMENT IN PENSION PLAN; TERMINATION IN PENSION PLANS.

CUSTOMER PROFITABILITY ANALYSIS analysis that assigns revenues and costs to major customers or groups of customers rather than to organizational units, products, or other objects. The results may direct organizational resources toward more profitable uses. It is an application of segmented reporting in which a customer group is treated as a segment. It is especially helpful when combined with an activity-based costing approach that determines which activities are performed for each group and assigns costs based on appropriate drivers. For example, activities, their drivers, and their costs may be classified as order level, customer level, channel level, market level, or enterprise level.

CUSTOMER RELATIONSHIP MANAGEMENT (CRM) SYSTEMS the modern version of the old-fashioned Rolodex. A CRM system allows an organization to store customer and prospective contact information, accounts, leads, and sales opportunities in a centralized location, often in the cloud. It is used to automate customer service and support. CRM systems often have advanced features to assist the sales force in collaborating with colleagues and customers. For instance, Amazon.com uses CRM technology to make suggestions to customers based on their personal purchase histories.

CUSTOMER RESPONSE TIME delay from placement of an order to delivery of the good or service; also called DELIVERY CYCLE TIME. Response time is a function of time drivers, e.g., uncertainty about arrivals of customers in the queue and BOTTLENECKS (points at which capacity is reached or exceeded). It is another crucial competitive factor. *See also* ORDER RECEIPT TIME; MANUFACTURING CYCLE TIME; MANUFACTURING CYCLE EFFICIENCY.

CUSTOMER RETENTION important measure of service quality because loyal customers spend more, refer new customers, and are less costly to service.

CUSTOMER VALUE difference between customer realization and sacrifice. Realization is what the customer receives, which includes product features, quality, and service. This takes into account the customer's cost to use, maintain, and dispose of the product or service. Sacrifice is what a customer gives up, which includes the amount the customer pays for the product plus the time and effort spent acquiring the product and learning how to use it. Maximizing customer value means maximizing the difference between realization and sacrifice.

CUTOFF DATE audit procedure for determining whether a transaction took place before or subsequent to the end of an accounting period. It assures that the transaction has been recorded in the proper period. It is the date chosen to stop the flow of transactions, merchandise, cash, and so on for audit purposes. For example, in taking a physical inventory, there must be a cutoff date applicable to sales and purchases. This may require closing receiving and shipping rooms while the inventory count takes place. Transactions of one period must be distinguished from those of another. Cutoff errors must be diligently avoided when recording transactions.

CUTOFF RATE *see* COST OF CAPITAL.

CUTOFF TEST involves examining transactions a few days before and after year-end in order to determine that accounting transactions have been recorded in the proper time period.

CVP ANALYSIS *see* COST-VOLUME-PROFIT (CVP) ANALYSIS.

CVP RELATIONSHIPS *see* COST-VOLUME-PROFIT (CVP) ANALYSIS.

CYBER INVESTING investing such as on-line trading on the Internet.

CYBERSPACE Originally used in *Neuromancer,* William Gibson's novel of direct brain-computer networking, refers to the collective realms of computer-aided communication.

CYCLE BILLING method of billing customers at different time intervals. For example, customers with last names starting with A may be billed on the first of the month while those with last names beginning with B are billed on the second day.

CYCLE TIME time required to produce and deliver a product or service. Thus, total cycle time is the sum of value-added processing time and total nonvalue-added time. *See also* DELIVERY CYCLE TIME; CUSTOMER RESPONSE TIME.

CYCLE TIME COMPRESSION reducing the time required to produce and deliver a product or service, in order to increase throughput and become more flexible and responsive to customers.

CYPHER solve secret writing in a transmission based on a key to the code.

D

DATABASE storehouse of related data records independently managed apart from any specific program or information system application. It is then made available to a wide variety of individuals and systems within the organization. In essence, it is an electronic filing cabinet providing a common core of information accessible by a program. An example is a database of inventory items.

DATA BASE MANAGEMENT SYSTEM (DBMS) software used to manage data in the database. It is a set of programs that provides for defining, controlling, and accessing the database. The database program allows accountants to enter, manipulate, retrieve, display, select, sort, edit, and index data. Advantages of a database management system include: (1) elimination of data redundancy, (2) improved efficiency in updating, (3) data sharing, (4) easy data access, and (5) reduced program maintenance cost. Major DBMs include Oracle, SQL Server, MySQL, and Access.

DATA FLOW DIAGRAM (DFD) graphically depicts the flow of data in an organization's information system. A DFD lets an organization visualize how its information system operates. The visual representation provided by DFD is generally preferable over narrative technical descriptions, making it easier to understand by technical and nontechnical users alike.

DATA INTERCHANGE FORMAT (DIF) FILE system to transfer computer files from one program to another. DIF files created on other systems (e.g., the client's) can be imported into the practitioner's spreadsheet or database. The DIF is produced as an output or export option by many of the existing spreadsheet programs and by some database programs. Various accounting packages can generate DIF files. An example of an application is extracting a spreadsheet from EXCEL and putting it into another spreadsheet program or a word processing program. It should be noted, however, a file written in DIF requires more storage space than the original it was built from.

DATA MINING the process of analyzing data, generally using specialized software, to increase revenue and cut costs. Essentially, data mining is the process of discovering correlations or patterns among muliple fields from a large database.

DATA PRIVACY security measures and devices employed by the accountant to assure that confidential information (e.g., client files) are not improperly accessed. For example, a password may be required to obtain access to electronic data files of clients.

DATA PROCESSING process that involves transformation of data into information through classifying, sorting, merging, recording, retrieving, transmitting, or reporting. Data processing can be manual or computer based.

DATAQUICK a national company that maintains a huge database that tracks 83 million properties. The firm provides information and analysis to clients such as newspapers, appraisers, mortgages and lending, and title insurance.

DATA REDUNDANCY
1. the storage of the same data in more than one field in a database. This repetition of data is generally discouraged since it can cause inconsisten-

cies in maintaining the data; the value may be updated in one field, but not the other.

2. the backing up of data on multiple servers.

DATA WAREHOUSES designed to help an organization analyze its data, a data warehouse is a database that focuses on query and analysis rather than on transaction processing. Historical data from transactions and other sources is generally included. Its purpose is to consolidate data from multiple sources and to separate the transaction processing workload from the data analysis workload.

DATE OF RECORD date on which HOLDERS OF RECORD in a company's stock ledger are entitled to receive DIVIDENDS or STOCK RIGHTS. Stock usually trades EX-DIVIDEND or EX-RIGHTS beginning the fourth business day before the date of record. It is different from the DECLARATION OF DATE; that is, the date that the board of directors announces its intention to pay a dividend. Once this is done, the company has created a LIABILITY; it owes the dividend to the stockholders of record. For example, on July 5, the board of directors of XYZ Corporation declared a 25 cent cash dividend on its common stock payable on August 15 to stockholders of record on July 17. This creates a liability by the company to stockholders of record. The common stockholders on the company's list on July 17 will receive the 25 cent dividend on August 15.

DAYBOOK rarely used BOOK OF ORIGINAL ENTRY. It is basically a descriptive, chronological record of day-to-day business transactions, like a diary. Details formerly kept in daybooks are now represented by original documents such as invoices and supporting documents. If daybooks are kept, their detail must subsequently be entered into journals in bookkeeping form to enable posting to ledgers.

DAYS PURCHASES IN ACCOUNTS PAYABLE ratio measuring the extent that accounts payable represent current rather than overdue obligations. A comparison should be made to the terms of purchase. Accounts payable are divided by the purchases per day. The latter is determined by dividing purchases by 360 days. Assume accounts payable is $50,000 and purchases are $800,000. The ratio is:

$$\frac{\$50,000}{\$800,000/360} = \frac{\$50,000}{\$2,222.22} = 22.50$$

DAYS TO SELL INVENTORY ratio measuring the number of days inventory is held. As a general rule, the longer inventory is held, the greater is its risk of not being sold at full value. This ratio is crucial in the case of inventory that is perishable or prone to obsolescence, such as high technology and fashion items. Inventory also involves an OPPORTUNITY COST of funds. Days to sell inventory is one of the components in determining a company's OPERATING CYCLE. Assume an INVENTORY TURNOVER of 10 times. This means that the number of days inventory is held equals:

$$\frac{360}{10} = 36 \text{ days}$$

See also AVERAGE AGE OF INVENTORY.

DEATH BENEFIT

1. in *taxation*, a payment or receipt of proceeds to a specified beneficiary or beneficiaries by an employer, by virtue of the death of the employee. Under certain conditions, the first $5,000 of such a payment may not be subject to federal income taxes.
2. portion (tax exempt) of the proceeds of a life insurance policy representing protection as distinguished from investment value. Policy loans reduce the death benefit by the amount of the outstanding loan balance.

DEATH TAX tax imposed on property upon the death of the owner, such as an inheritance or ESTATE TAX.

DEBENTURE long-term debt instrument that is not secured by a mortgage or other lien on specific property. Because it is unsecured debt, it is issued usually by large, financially strong companies with excellent BOND RATINGS. There are two kinds of debentures: a senior issue and a *subordinated* (junior) issue, which has a subordinate lien. The order of a prior claim is set forth in the bond INDENTURE. Typically, in the event of liquidation, subordinated debentures come after senior debt.

DEBENTURE CAPITAL CAPITAL obtained through the sale of unsecured bonds, called DEBENTURE.

DEBIT

1. an entry on the left side of an account. As a verb, to make an entry on the left side of an account. Under the DOUBLE ENTRY BOOKKEEPING system, debits increase assets and expenses and decrease liabilities, equity, and revenues.
2. to *enter* or POST a debit.

DEBIT AND CREDIT CONVENTIONS rules for debit and credit to be followed under DOUBLE ENTRY BOOKKEEPING. The rules or conventions using the T-account form for the balance sheet and income statement accounts are as follows:

Any Asset Account		Any Liability Account	
Dr.	Cr.	Dr.	Cr.
Increase	Decrease	Decrease	Increase
+	−	−	+
Ending			Ending
balance			balance

Any Equity Account		Revenues	
Dr.	Cr.	Dr.	Cr.
Decrease	Increase	−	+
	+		
−	Ending	**Expenses**	
	balance	Dr.	Cr.
		+	−

DEBIT MEMORANDUM

1. form or document used by a seller to notify a buyer that the seller is debiting (increasing) the amount of the buyer's accounts payable due to errors or other factors requiring adjustments.

2. form or document given by the bank to a depositor to notify that the depositor's balance is being decreased due to some event other than payment of a check, such as bank service charges.

DEBT money or services owed to an outside party. It is a legal obligation of the business arising either from written or oral agreement. Debt may either be short-term or long-term. *See also* CURRENT LIABILITY; LONG-TERM DEBT.

DEBT AND EQUITY SECURITIES ways of financing a business through credit obligations (e.g., bond issue) and CAPITAL STOCK. Usually, a company finances with both rather than just one. The CAPITAL STRUCTURE of a company is commonly referred to as consisting of debt and equity securities. *See also* WARRANT.

DEBT-EQUITY RATIO measure used in the analysis of financial statements to show the amount of protection available to creditors. The ratio equals total liabilities divided by total stockholders' equity; also called *debt to net worth ratio*. A high ratio usually indicates that the business has a lot of risk because it must meet principal and interest on its obligations. Potential creditors are reluctant to give financing to a company with a high debt position. However, the magnitude of debt depends on the type of business. For example, a bank has a high debt ratio but its assets are generally liquid. A utility can afford a higher ratio than a manufacturer because its earnings can be controlled by rate adjustments. Usually, book value is used to measure a firm's debt and equity securities in calculating the ratio. Market value may be a more realistic measure, however, because it takes into account current market conditions. *See also* CAPITAL STRUCTURE.

DEBT FINANCING raising money by selling bonds, notes, or mortgages or borrowing directly from financial institutions. The presence of debt financing in a firm's capital structure provides FINANCIAL LEVERAGE, which tends to magnify the effects of increased operating profits on the stockholder's returns. Since debt is normally the cheapest form of long-term financing, due to the tax deductibility of interest, it is a desirable component of the firm's capital structure as long as the borrowed funds produce a return in excess of their cost. Also, during inflation, the company will be paying back the debt in cheaper dollars. However, too much debt can result in higher levels of FINANCIAL RISK in meeting the principal and satisfying interest payments. Excessive debt will make it more difficult to raise funds and will increase the COST OF CAPITAL. *See also* EQUITY FINANCING.

DEBT LIMIT
  1. legal and maximum amount of debt that a governmental entity can undertake. This maximum debt amount minus the outstanding obligations is the legal debt margin.
  2. provision often found in a COVENANT in a corporate loan agreement.

DEBTOR individual who has a legal obligation to pay money to another.

DEBT RESTRUCTURING
  1. adjustment or realignment of debt structure reflecting concessions granted by creditors, to give the debtor a more practical arrangement for meeting financial obligations. Restructuring is needed when the debtor has severe financial problems. The agreement to restructure may result from legal

action or simply be an agreement to which parties consent. *See also* CHAPTER 11; CHAPTER 7; TROUBLED DEBT RESTRUCTURING.

2. realignment of debt structure based on a voluntary financial management decision—for example, to replace short-term debt with long-term debt.

DEBT SERVICE FUND in governmental accounting, fund used to account for the accumulation of resources for, and the payment of, general long-term debt principal and interest except that payable from proprietary, fiduciary, or special assessment funds.

DEBT TO NET WORTH RATIO *see* DEBT-EQUITY RATIO.

DEBUG process of tracing and correcting flaws in a software program or hardware device. In a complex program, it may take longer to correct the errors than originally to write the program. Debug aids are prewritten sets of computerized routines that assist in finding the BUGS.

DECENTRALIZATION delegation of decision-making to the subunits of an organization. It is a matter of degree. The lower the level where decisions are made, the greater is the decentralization. Decentralization is most effective in organizations where subunits are autonomous and costs and profits can be independently measured. The benefits of decentralization include: (1) decisions are made by those who have the most knowledge about local conditions; (2) greater managerial input in decision-making has a desirable motivational effect; and (3) managers have more control over results. The costs of decentralization include: (1) managers have a tendency to look at their division and lose sight of overall company goals; (2) there can be costly duplication of services; and (3) costs of obtaining sufficient information increase.

DECENTRALIZED ORGANIZATON organization that has several operating segments; operating control of each segment's activities is the responsibility of the segment's manager.

DECISION-MAKING purposeful selection from among a set of alternatives in light of a given objective. Decision-making is not a separate function of management. In fact, decision-making is intertwined with the other functions, such as PLANNING, COORDINATING, and CONTROLLING. These functions all require that decisions be made. For example, at the outset, management must make a critical decision as to which of several strategies would be followed. Such a decision is often called a *strategic* decision because of its long-term impact on the organization. Also, managers must make scores of lesser decisions, *tactical* and *operational*, all of which are important to the organization's well-being.

DECISION-MAKING UNDER CERTAINTY term used in a situation when for each decision alternative there is only one event and therefore only one outcome for each action. For example, there is only one possible event for the two possible actions: "Do nothing" at a future cost of $3.00 per unit for 10,000 units, or "rearrange" a facility at a future cost of $2.80 for the same number of units. A decision matrix (or payoff table) would look as follows:

Actions	State of Nature (with probability of 1.0)
Do nothing	$30,000 (10,000 units × $3.00)
Rearrange	28,000 (10,000 units × $2.80)

Note that there is only one STATE OF NATURE in the matrix because there is only one possible outcome for each action (with certainty). The decision is obviously to choose the action that will result in the most desirable outcome (least cost), that is to "rearrange." *See also* DECISION THEORY.

DECISION-MAKING UNDER UNCERTAINTY term used in a situation that involves several events for each action with its probability of occurrence. The decision problem can best be approached using a payoff table (or decision matrix). *See also* DECISION THEORY.

DECISION MATRIX *see* DECISION THEORY.

DECISION MODEL formal or informal conceptualization of the relationship of the various factors that are relevant in decision-making and planning. OPTIMIZATION MODELS, MATHEMATICAL MODELS, and DECISION MATRIX are examples of a decision model.

DECISION PACKAGE procedure used in ZERO-BASE BUDGETING when a manager specifies recommended and alternative ways to undertake a proposed project (e.g., product). Dollars and time involved with the recommended and alternative means of accomplishing the project are specified. Thus, upper management has three possible choices: (1) not funding the project at all; (2) accepting the project as recommended; or (3) accepting the project in an alternative form. Note that an alternative means of performing the project may be chosen because it is less expensive than the recommended way. A decision package looks as follows:

DECISION PACKAGE
for Product X

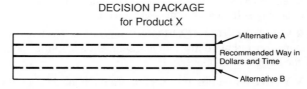

DECISION RULE designation of a specific condition or combination of conditions that may arise in the decision-making process and the appropriate action to take if the conditions exist. For example, in a CAPITAL BUDGETING decision, under the NET PRESENT VALUE (NPV) METHOD, a project should be accepted if its NPV is positive. Also, under the INTERNAL RATE OF RETURN (IRR) approach, a project should be accepted if the IRR of the project exceeds the cost of capital.

DECISION SUPPORT SYSTEM (DSS) branch of the broadly defined MANAGEMENT INFORMATION SYSTEM (MIS) that provides answers to problems and that integrates the decision maker into the system as a component. The system utilizes such quantitative techniques as *regression, linear programming,* and *financial planning modeling.* DSS software furnishes support to the accountant in the decision-making process. It analyzes a specific situation and can be modified as the practitioner wishes. Models are constructed and decisions analyzed. Planning and forecasting are facilitated.

DECISION THEORY systematic approach to making decisions especially under uncertainty. Although statistics such as EXPECTED VALUE and STANDARD DEVIATION are essential for choosing the best course of action, the decision problem can best be approached, using what is referred to as a *payoff table* (or *decision matrix*), which is characterized by: (1) the *row* representing a set of alternative COURSES OF ACTION available to the decision maker; (2) the *column* representing the STATE OF NATURE or conditions that are likely to occur and over which the decision maker has no control; and (3) the entries in the body of the table representing the outcome of the decision, known as *payoffs,* which may be in the form of costs, revenues, profits, or cash flows. By computing expected value of each action, we will be able to pick the best one.

Example 1: Assume the following probability distribution of daily demand for strawberries:

Daily Demand	0	1	2	3
Probability	.2	.3	.3	.2

Also assume that unit cost = \$3, selling price = \$5 (i.e., profit on sold unit = \$2), and salvage value on unsold units = \$2 (i.e., loss on unsold unit = \$1). We can stock either 0, 1, 2, or 3 units. The question is: How many units should be stocked each day? Assume that units from one day cannot be sold the next day. Then the payoff table can be constructed as follows:

	Demand	**State of Nature** 0	1	2	3	**Expected**
Stock\	**(probability)** (.2)	(.3)	(.3)	(.2)		**Value**
Actions 0	\$0	0	0	0		\$0
1	−1	2	2	2		1.40
2	−2	1*	4	4		1.90**
3	−3	0	3	6		1.50

*Profit for (stock 2, demand 1) equals (no. of units sold) (profit per unit) − (no. of units unsold)(loss per unit) = (1)(\$5 − 3) − (1)(\$3 − 2) = \$1

**Expected value for (stock 2) is: −2(.2) + 1(.3) + 4(.3) + 4(.2) = \$1.90. The optimal stock action is the one with the highest EXPECTED MONETARY VALUE, i.e., stock 2 units.

Suppose the decision maker can obtain a perfect prediction of which event (state of nature) will occur. The EXPECTED VALUE WITH PERFECT INFORMATION would be the total expected value of actions selected on the assumption of a perfect forecast. The EXPECTED VALUE OF PERFECT INFORMATION can then be computed as:

Expected value with perfect information *minus* the expected value with existing information.

Example 2: From the payoff table in Example 1, the following analysis yields the expected value *with* perfect information:

	Demand	**State of Nature** 0	1	2	3	**Expected**
Stock \		(.2)	(.3)	(.3)	(.2)	**Value**
0		\$0				\$0
Actions 1			2			.6
2				4		1.2
3					6	1.2
						\$3.00

With existing information, the best that the decision maker could obtain was select (stock 2) and obtain \$1.90. With perfect information (forecast), the decision maker could make as much as $3. Therefore, the expected value *of* perfect information is $3.00 − $1.90 = $1.10. This is the maximum price the decision maker is willing to pay for additional information.

DECISION TREE pictorial representation of a decision situation, normally found in discussions of decision-making under uncertainty or risk. It shows decision alternatives, states of nature, probabilities attached to the state of nature, and conditional benefits and losses. The tree approach is most useful in a sequential decision situation. For example, assume XYZ Corporation wishes to introduce one of two products to the market this year. The probabilities and present values (PV) of projected cash inflows follow:

Products	Initial Investment	PV of Cash Inflows	Probabilities
A	$225,000		1.00
		$ 450,000	0.40
		200,000	0.50
		−100,000	0.10
B	80,000		1.00
		320,000	0.20
		100,000	0.60
		−150,000	0.20

A decision tree analyzing the two products follows:

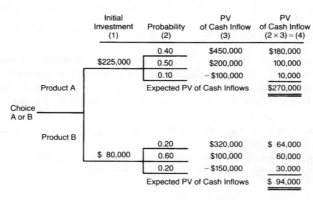

DECISION TREE

For Product A:

Expected NPV = expected PV − I = $270,000 − $225,000 = $45,000

For Product B:

Expected NPV = $94,000 − $80,000 = $14,000

Based on the expected net present value, the company should choose product A over product B.

DECISION VARIABLE *see* LINEAR PROGRAMMING.

DECLARATION DATE date on which the dividend is voted and announced (declared) by the board of directors. At the declaration date, the dividend is a legal liability of the company. *See also* DATE OF RECORD.

DECRYPTION process of converting encrypted data back into its original form, so it can be understood. *See also* ENCRYPTION.

DEDUCTIONS
1. itemized deductions, which are deductions *from* ADJUSTED GROSS INCOME (AGI). Certain personal expenditures are allowed by the Tax Code as deductions from adjusted gross income if they exceed the STANDARD DEDUCTION (formerly the ZERO BRACKET AMOUNT). Examples include medical expenses in excess of the applicable AGI threshhold, interest on home mortgages, real estate taxes, and charitable contributions. Itemized deductions are reported on Schedule A of Form 1040.
2. deductions *for* adjusted gross income, such as employee business expenses and contributions to an IRA pension plan.
3. adjustment to an invoice.

DEED OF TRUST *see* BOND INDENTURE; INDENTURE.

DEEP DISCOUNT BOND bond that has a coupon rate far below rates currently available on investments and that consequently can be traded only at a significant discount from par value—usually more than about 20%. It may offer an opportunity for capital appreciation.

DEFALCATION unlawful and fraudulent misappropriation of property or funds under one's (e.g., cashier, trustee, administrator) control by breach of trust (e.g., EMBEZZLEMENT).

DEFAULT failure of a debtor to meet principal or interest payment on a debt at the due date. In the event of default, creditors may make claims against the assets of the issuer in order to recover their principal.

DEFEASANCE
1. to render null or void, or to terminate the interest in a property according to strictly stipulated conditions as in a deed. It may refer to the physical instrument itself stipulating the above conditions.
2. to discharge old, low-rate debt (without repaying it before maturity) by adding new securities paying high interest or having a higher market value. The object is to have a more debt-free balance sheet and increased earnings by removing the old debt and adding high-yielding new securities.

DEFENSIVE INTERVAL RATIO liquidity ratio revealing the ability of the business to meet its current debts. It indicates the period of time the entity can operate on its current liquid assets without needing revenues from next period's sources. The ratio equals defensive assets (cash, marketable securities, and receivables) divided by projected daily operational expenditures less noncash charges. Projected daily operational expenditures are determined by dividing cost of goods sold plus operating expenses and other ordinary cash expenses by 360. Assume cash of $30,000, marketable securities of $38,000, receivables of $46,000, projected daily expenditures of $450,000, and noncash charges of $20,000. The ratio equals:

$$\frac{\$114,000}{\left(\dfrac{\$450,000 - \$20,000}{360}\right)} = \frac{\$114,000}{\$1,194.44} = 95 \text{ days (rounded)}$$

DEFERRED ANNUITY annuity whose first payment or receipt does not begin until some time after the first period; for example, an annuity of $1,000 is not paid for the first three years and then commences payments at the end of each year from the fourth and continues through the end of that annuity.

DEFERRED ANNUITY CONTRACT agreement in which payments to the annuitant are postponed until a specified number of periods have elapsed. An example is when annuity payments begin at the age of 60.

DEFERRED CHARGE cost already incurred that is deferred to the future. The deferral is made because of anticipated future benefit or because the charge constitutes an appropriate allocation of costs to future operations. The basic accounting convention applicable is the matching of costs and revenues. Deferred charges are classified as noncurrent assets because their life extends beyond one year. Deferred charges have no physical substance. Examples of deferred charges are: (1) start-up costs in putting into operation new, better, or more efficient facilities; (2) plant rearrangement and reinstallation costs; (3) moving costs from one location to another; and (4) deferred income tax charges resulting from INTERPERIOD INCOME TAX ALLOCATION. Note that a company sometimes has discretion of whether to defer a cost and amortize or immediately expense it. An example is advertising expense, which is capitalized when the benefits to be gained will affect future years' income. Since deferred charges lack cash realizability and cannot be used to meet creditor claims, they are (when material) subtracted from assets in most ratio calculations. *See also* PREPAID EXPENSE.

DEFERRED COMPENSATION *see* STOCK OPTION.

DEFERRED COST expenditure incurred having future benefit in excess of one year that is capitalized to an asset account. An example is interest incurred on borrowed funds for the self-construction of an asset that is capitalized.

DEFERRED CREDIT income items received by a business, but not yet reported as income; also called *deferred revenue* and *deferred income*. An example is a consulting fee received in *advance* before being earned. The term also applies to revenue normally includable in income but deferred until earned and matched with expenses. For example, a magazine publisher might defer a 3-year subscription to match revenue against later publication expenses. The deferred credit is classified under noncurrent liabilities. When a portion of the deferred credit is earned, the entry is to debit deferred credit and credit revenue. *See also* INTERPERIOD INCOME TAX ALLOCATION.

DEFERRED GROSS PROFIT method of installment sales. Any profit not collected is deferred on the balance sheet pending cash collection from the customer. When collections are subsequently made, realized gross profit is increased via a debit to the deferred gross profit account. The deferred gross profit account is a contra account to accounts receivable as follows:

Accounts Receivable (Cost + Profit)

Less: Deferred Gross Profit (Profit)

Net Accounts Receivable (Cost)

DEFERRED INCOME TAX CHARGE asset resulting when taxable income exceeds book income as a result of a temporary difference in the recognition of income and expense items. Thus, the tax payable will be greater than the tax expense. In INTERPERIOD INCOME TAX ALLOCATION, this difference is reported as a deferred income tax charge. For example, warranty expense is deducted for book purposes in the year of sale but taken off on the tax return only when paid. The Deferred Income Tax Charge account will be classified partly as current (for the warranty period for the next year) and partly as noncurrent (for the warranty period in excess of one year). Assume income for both books and tax is $5000, warranty expense for books is $500, warranty expense for tax is $200, and the tax rate is 34%. Relevant computations and journal entry follow:

	Book Income		Tax Income
Income	$5,000		$5,000
Warranty expense	500		200
Income before tax	$4,500		$4,800
Tax expense ($4,500 × 34%)		1,530	
Deferred income tax charge ($300 × 34%)		102	
Tax payable ($4,800 × 34%)			1,632

A deferred income tax charge results in a future deductible amount (for tax purposes), which can only be recognized as an asset in the current year if the entity is certain to have taxable income in the future. Thus, a deferred tax asset can only be booked for the amount of the certain future deductiblity of the item for tax purposes (e.g., resulting from temporary differences owing to DEFERRED INCOME TAX LIABILITIES already existing). A deferred income tax charge can also be recognized for the tax benefit of deductible amounts realizable by carrying back a loss from future years to reduce taxes paid in the current or a prior year.

DEFERRED INCOME TAX LIABILITY account showing estimated amount of future taxes on income earned and recognized for accounting purposes but not yet for federal income tax purposes. Thus, book income will exceed taxable income. In INTERPERIOD INCOME TAX ALLOCATION, this will result in tax expense being greater than tax payable. As a result, a deferred income tax liability will occur. It will eventually write itself off when the period for the temporary difference is fully reversed. Assume book income and taxable income are both $10,000. However, straight-line depreciation is used for book purposes amounting to a charge of $1,000 while an accelerated depreciation method is used for tax purposes amounting to $1,500. The corporate tax rate is 34%. Relevant computations and journal entry follow:

	Book Income		Tax Income
Income	$10,000		$10,000
Depreciation	1,000		1,500
Income before tax	$ 9,000		$ 8,500
Tax expense ($9,000 × 34%)	$ 3,060		
Tax payable ($8,500 × 34%)	$ 2,890		
Deferred income tax liability ($500 × 34%)		$170	

See also DEFERRED INCOME TAX CHARGE.

DEFERRED LIABILITY debt where the payment made is postponed beyond the present date. An example is deferred taxes. *See also* DEFERRED CREDIT.

DEFERRED MAINTENANCE

1. maintenance that has been postponed and that may result in physical damage, lack of efficiency, decline in production, and other negative effects. If a company does not have an adequate repair program, future earnings potential of the assets are diminished.
2. factor in real estate appraisal. For example, deferred maintenance may produce broken windows and discolored paint that adversely affect the value of a piece of property.

DEFERRED TAX ALLOCATION procedure by which deferred taxes are computed with the tax rates in effect when the temporary differences between book income and taxable income originate; they are not adjusted for rate changes. The method is not acceptable for INTERPERIOD INCOME TAX ALLOCATION. It is income statement-oriented in that the deferred income tax liability or charge awaits future adjustment to tax expense in later years when the temporary difference starts to reverse. *See also* LIABILITY TAX ALLOCATION METHOD; NET OF TAX METHOD.

DEFICIENCY additional tax liability that the IRS deems to be owed by a taxpayer. A taxpayer can argue the correctness of a deficiency with the IRS. If unsuccessful, the taxpayer can appeal to the Tax Court.

DEFICIENCY IN INTERNAL CONTROL a deficiency when the design or operation of a control does not allow management or employees, in the normal course of performing their assigned functions, to prevent or detect misstatements on a timely basis. *See also* SIGNIFICANT DEFICIENCY; MATERIAL WEAKNESS.

DEFICIENCY LETTER IRS communication to a taxpayer explaining why the correct amount of tax is greater than shown on the tax return. *See also* DEFICIENCY.

DEFICIT debit balance in the Retained Earnings account resulting from accumulated losses.

DEFINED BENEFIT PENSION PLAN program stipulating the pension benefits employees will obtain when they retire. The pension benefit formula usually is based on the worker's salary level nearing retirement age and considers the employment years. The calculation must take into account the current year employer contribution to satisfy expected pension benefit payments at retirement. There must be an appropriate funding pattern to assure adequate funds are available to meet promised benefits. Considered in the funding level are such factors as turnover rate, mortality rate, and return on investment. Since the pension expense each year will typically be different from the amount funded, a deferred pension liability or asset will result. *See also* DEFINED CONTRIBUTION PENSION PLAN.

DEFINED CONTRIBUTION PENSION PLAN program under which an employer agrees to make a specified contribution each year based on the pension benefit formula. The formula may consider such factors as years of service, salary levels, and age. Note that only the employer's contribution is defined and that there is no guarantee regarding the future benefits to be received by employees. The entry each year for the funding contribution is to debit pension expense and credit cash for the same amount. *See also* DEFINED BENEFIT PENSION PLAN.

DEFLATION the opposite of inflation. A decline in general price levels, often caused by a reduction in the supply of money or credit. Deflation can also be brought about by direct contractions in spending, either in the form of a reduction in government spending, personal spending, or investment spending. Deflation has often had the side effect of increasing unemployment, since the process often leads to a lower level of demand in the economy. Other downside effects include possible pay cuts and more expensive repayment of consumer debts. The upside of falling prices is that mild deflation would assure working people (at least those who fend off pay cuts) of steadily rising real wages.

DEGREE OF FINANCIAL LEVERAGE (DFL) percentage change in earnings available to common shareholders that is associated with a given percentage change in net operating income. The greater the DFL, the riskier the firm; however, if the return on assets exceeds the cost of debt, additional leverage is favorable.

DEGREE OF FREEDOM (DF) number of data items that are independent of one another. Given a sample of data and the computation of some statistic (e.g., the mean), the degrees of freedom are defined as (number of observations included in the formula) minus (number of parameters estimated using the data). For example, the mean statistic for N sample data points has n DF, but the variance formula has $(n - 1)$ DF because one parameter (the mean X) has to be estimated before the variance formula can be used.

DEGREE OF OPERATING LEVERAGE (DOL) change in operating income (earnings before interest and taxes) resulting from a percentage change in revenues. It measures the extent to which a firm incurs fixed rather than variable costs in operations. Thus, the greater the DOL, the greater the risk of loss when sales decline, and the greater the reward when sales increase.

DEGREE OF RELATIVE LIQUIDITY (DRL) percentage of a firm's cash expenditures that can be secured from (1) beginning fund and from (2) cash generated from its normal operation.

DEGREE OF TOTAL LEVERAGE (DTL) percentage change in net income that is associated with a given percentage change in sales. It is the product of DEGREE OF FINANCIAL LEVERAGE (DFL) and the DEGREE OF OPERATING LEVERAGE (DOL).

DELINQUENT TAX tax that is unpaid or remains unpaid as of or after the payment due date. Usually a penalty attaches to that sum. Any unpaid balance that may remain after a partial payment will still be considered delinquent. The penalty and the unpaid balance remain separately identifiable.

DELIVERY BASIS method of revenue recognition based on delivery instead of sale.

DELIVERY CYCLE TIME time period between acceptance of an order and final delivery of the product. *See also* CYCLE TIME.

DELIVERY TIME time period between product completion and customer receipt of the item.

DELPHI METHOD qualitative forecasting method that seeks to use the judgment of experts systematically to forecast what future events will be or when they may occur. It brings together a group of experts who have access to each other's opinions in an environment where no majority opinion is disclosed.

DEMAND DEPOSIT deposit from which funds may be drawn on demand and from which funds may be transferred to another party by means of a check. Demand deposits are the biggest component of the U.S. money supply. *See also* TIME DEPOSIT.

DEMILITARIZED ZONE (DMZ) in computer networking security, a computer inserted into a neutral zone between an organization's internal private network and outside public network. Its purpose is to prevent external users from accessing an organization's private network. When a request is received from the outside, only the computer in the DMZ is accessible. If a request is sent from the inside to access a public network, the computer in the DMZ will intercept that request and initiate a session with the public network on behalf on the internal user.

DE MINIMUS FRINGE BENEFITS fringe benefits provided to employees that are so minimal in value that they are impractical to account for and therefore are excludable from taxable income. Examples of de minimus fringe benefits include meal allowances, local transportation provided in connection with overtime work, and holiday gifts of property with a low fair market value.

DENIAL OF SERVICE ATTACK (DOS) an attack that essentially prevents a user from accessing some resource. Generally, a DoS attack does not result in a theft of data or other information, but rather a loss of availability of service. The attack is most commonly done by sending excessive data to a network address.

DENOMINATOR LEVEL *see* PREDETERMINED OVERHEAD RATE.

DENOMINATOR VARIANCE *see* FIXED OVERHEAD VOLUME (DENOMINATOR) VARIANCE.

DEPARTMENTAL RATE predetermined factory overhead rate for each production department. When products are heterogeneous, receiving different attention and effort as they move through various departments, departmental rates rather than a single plantwide rate are necessary to achieve more accurate overhead application to the products.

DEPENDENT person who derives primary support from another party. In order for a person to qualify as a dependent for federal income tax exemption purposes, five tests must be met: support test, gross income test, joint return test, citizenship or residency test, and relationship or member of household test.

DEPENDENT VARIABLE one whose value depends upon the values of other variables and constants in some relationship. For example, in the relationship $(y) = f(x)$, y is the dependent variable. For example, market price of stock is a dependent variable influenced by various independent variables, such as earnings per share, debt-equity ratio, and beta. *See also* INDEPENDENT VARIABLE.

DEPLETION physical exhaustion of a natural resource (e.g., oil, coal). The entry for recording annual depletion is to debit depletion expense and credit accumulated depletion. Accumulated depletion is a contra account to the natural resource.

DEPOSITS IN TRANSIT cash receipts that arrived at the bank too late to be credited to the depositor's bank statement for the current month. Such deposits are added to the bank balance when preparing the BANK RECONCILIATION.

DEPRECIABLE ASSET certain types of assets (e.g., plant and equipment) that gradually lose their value over time. The law permits depreciation charges except when such assets are held by individuals as personal property.

DEPRECIABLE COST fixed asset cost that is subject to depreciation. Depreciable cost equals acquisition cost less salvage value.

DEPRECIABLE LIFE economic or physical life of a fixed asset. All fixed assets except land are depreciated over the number of years of expected use.

DEPRECIATION
1. spreading out of the original cost over the estimated life of the fixed assets such as plant and equipment. Depreciation reduces taxable income. Among the most commonly used depreciation methods are STRAIGHT-LINE DEPRECIATION and ACCELERATED DEPRECIATION such as the SUM-OF-THE-YEARS'-DIGITS and DOUBLE DECLINING BALANCE METHODS.
2. decline in economic potential of limited life assets originating from wear and tear, natural deterioration through interaction of the elements, and technical obsolescence. To some extent, maintenance (lubrication, adjustments, parts replacement, and cleaning) may partially arrest or offset wear and deterioration. *See also* DEPRECIATION ACCOUNTING.

DEPRECIATION ACCOUNTING amortization of fixed assets, such as plant and equipment, in order to allocate the cost over its depreciable life. It is a process of cost allocation and not valuation. DEPRECIATION reduces taxable income but does not reduce cash. Depreciation is recorded by debiting depreciation expense and crediting accumulated depreciation. There are several methods of computing depreciation: STRAIGHT-LINE DEPRECIATION, UNITS-OF-PRODUCTION, and ACCELERATED DEPRECIATION methods (e.g., SUM-OF-YEARS'-DIGITS and DOUBLE DECLINING BALANCE). Depreciation expense is deducted by a business on its federal income tax return. The depreciation amount on the tax return, however, may differ from the amount reported in the firm's income statement. In fact, the method used on the tax return need not be the same method used in the financial statements. Typically, a firm uses an accelerated depreciation for tax purposes and the straight-line method in its financial statements. ACCELERATED COST RECOVERY SYSTEM (ACRS) is a system that allows a specific accelerated write-off pattern of the asset for tax purposes.

DEPRECIATION RECAPTURE *see* RECAPTURE OF DEPRECIATION.

DERIVATIVE transaction or contract whose value depends on or, as the name implies, derives from the value of underlying assets such as stocks, bonds, mortgages, market indexes, or foreign currencies. One party with exposure to unwanted risk can pass some or all of that risk to a second party. The first party can assume a different risk from the second party, pay the second party to assume the risk, or, as is often the case, create a combination. The objectives of users of derivatives may vary. A common reason to use derivatives is so that the risk of financial operations can be controlled. Derivatives can be used to manage foreign exchange exposure, especially unfavorable exchange rate movements. Speculators and arbitrageurs can seek profits from general price changes or simultaneous price differences in different markets, respectively. Others use derivatives to *hedge* their position; that is, to set up two financial assets so that any unfavorable price movement in one asset is offset by favorable price movement in the other asset.

DESK-TOP SOFTWARE auxiliary program that operates in WINDOWS overlaying the accountant's principal application. When such a desk accessory is called up, the practitioner is temporarily exiting the main program. Some accessories let the accountant transfer information to and from the main application. Features of desk-top software may include an appointment calendar, a clock that can measure and record time spent with particular files, a notepad, a directory for mail and telephone, telephone dialing, card filing, and calculator functions.

DETACHABLE STOCK WARRANT certificate conferring the right to buy stock that is issued along with a *detachable* bond. The warrant has a market life of its own. The portion of the proceeds received for the bond and warrant that are allocable to the warrant should be accounted for as PAID-IN-CAPITAL. The allocation should be based on the relative fair market values of the two securities at time of issuance. Assume a $1000 convertible bond is issued for $1,050, with $50 applicable to stock warrants. The entry is to debit cash $1,050 and credit bonds payable $1,000 and paid-in-capital (stock warrants) $50. *See also* UNDETACHABLE STOCK WARRANT.

DETAILED AUDIT procedure in which all or most of a company's transactions and related record keeping are examined and verified. This is much more comprehensive than audit testing through a sampling process. It should be undertaken when wrongdoing is expected such as EMBEZZLEMENT. A detailed audit is more readily associated with INTERNAL AUDIT activity rather than audits made by an EXTERNAL AUDITOR.

DETECTION RISK the risk that an auditor will fail to detect a material misstatement that exists in a financial statement assertion. Detection risk is a component of the audit risk and can be controlled by performing sufficient appropriate audit procedures at the proper times.

DEVELOPMENT STAGE ENTERPRISE business devoting substantially all of its efforts to establishing itself. Either of the following conditions exist: (1) planned principal operations have not started or (2) there has been no significant revenue although principal operations are underway. GENERALLY ACCEPTED ACCOUNTING PRINCIPLES (GAAP) applicable to established companies apply equally to development stage enterprises. In the BALANCE SHEET, cumulative net losses are reported as "deficit accumulated during the development stage." In the INCOME STATEMENT, cumulative amounts of revenue and expense from inception of the enterprise are reported. The STATEMENT OF CHANGES IN FINANCIAL POSITION shows the cumulative amounts of sources and uses of funds from inception. The financial statements are identified as those of a development stage enterprise and include a description of the development activities. In the first year in which a development stage enterprise is no longer considered such, it must disclose that in prior years it had been.

DEVIATION RATE in statistical sampling, the number of times, stated as a percentage, that a prescribed internal control is not properly applied in a sample of items.

DICTIONARY ATTACK a method for learning the credentials of a password-protected system. An attacker generally has two choices when trying to break into a password-protected computer system. The attacker can use "brute force" and try every possible combination; this approach can be very time consuming. In contrast, with a dictionary attack, the attacker will try every word in a dictionary to try to learn the credentials. This approach often works, because most people use ordinary words contained in the dictionary as their password.

DIF see DATA INTERCHANGE FORMAT (DIF) FILE.

DIFFERENCE ESTIMATION a type of variables sampling that utilizes the average difference between audit and book values of items to project population values. Difference estimation is useful when an auditor expects a disproportionate relationship between differences and book values.

DIFFERENTIAL
1. difference in revenues and costs that change between two or more alternative courses of action to be undertaken or considered. *See also* INCREMENTAL COST.
2. in INVESTMENTS, the typical extra commission charge of ⅛ of a point for an ODD-LOT stock transaction.

DIFFERENTIAL ANALYSIS *see* INCREMENTAL ANALYSIS.

DIFFERENTIAL BACKUP copies all the files that have changed since the last full backup. The main advantage of differential backup is that to restore, only two files are needed: the full backup file and the differential backup file. The main disadvantage of differential backup is that the size of the differential backup file tends to keep on increasing with each backup until a new full backup is made. Please note that a differential backup is not the same as incremental backup. In an incremental backup, only files that have changed from the last backup, whether full or incremental, are copied. The main disadvantage of incremental backup is that all incremental backup files plus the full backup file are needed to do a restore. Of course, its biggest advantage is that each time the incremental backup is performed, only the files that have changed are backed up, resulting in significant time savings.

DIFFERENTIAL COST *see* INCREMENTAL COST.

DIGITAL CERTIFICATE used to establish one's credentials when engaging in a transaction on the Web. It is used to verify the identity of the sender. Digital certificates are issued by a Certificate Authority (CA) and signed by the CA's private key.

DIGITAL SIGNATURE a message signed with a special key. It is used to authenticate the sender or message integrity to the receiver. A secure digital signature process consists of (1) a method of signing a document that prevents forgery and (2) validating that the signature is the one it purports to be.

DIGITAL VERSATILE DISK (DVD) an optical disc storage media format. Its main uses are video and data storage. Most DVDs are of the same dimensions as compact discs (CDs) but store more than six times as much data. Variations of the term DVD include DVD-ROM (Read Only Memory), DVD-R, DVD+R, DVD-RW, DVD+RW, DVD-Video, DVD-Audio, and Blu-ray Disc. Also known as *digital video disk.*

DILUTED EARNINGS PER SHARE smallest figure that can be obtained by computing a common stock earnings per share that reflects the possible exercise of all convertible securities. It is based on a broader denominator in the earnings per share fraction than BASIC EARNINGS PER SHARE. Not only does the denominator include the weighted average of common stock outstanding it also includes those shares that may result from convertible securities and stock options. Diluted earnings per share equals:

$$\frac{\text{Net Income} - \text{Preferred Dividends}}{\text{Weighted Average Common Stock Outstanding} + \text{Diluted Securities}}$$

DILUTION decrease, loss, or weakening of a financial statement-related item. For example, if more common shares are issued, the equity interest represented by each common share is reduced. Another example is the inclusion of a convertible security that reduces earnings per share.

DIRECT ACCESS method of processing data so that it can be stored and retrieved without consideration being given to data stored in preceding or subsequent locations; also called *random access.*

DIRECT ALLOCATION METHOD method allocating costs of each service department directly to production departments; also called *direct method.* Under this method, no consideration is given to services performed by one service department for another. Assume the following data:

	Production Departments		Service Departments	
	A Machining	B Assembly	General Plant (GP)	Engineering (E)
Overhead costs before allocation	$30,000	$40,000	$20,000	$10,000
Engineering hours by Engineering	50,000	30,000	5,000	4,000
Direct labor hours by General Plant	60,000	40,000	15,000	20,000

Using the direct method yields:

	Service Departments		Production Departments	
	GP	**E**	**A**	**B**
Overhead costs	$20,000	$10,000	$30,000	$40,000
Reallocation GP (60%, 40%)*	(20,000)		12,000	8,000
E (%, %) #		(10,000)	6,250	3,570
			$48,250	$51,750

* Base is (60,000 + 40,000 = 100,000); 60,000/100,000 = .6; 40,000/100,000 = .4.
\# Base is (50,000 + 30,000 = 80,000); 50,000/80,000 = ⅝; 30,000/80,000 = ⅜.

DIRECT COST expenses that can be directly identified with the costing object such as a product and department. Examples are direct materials, direct labor, and advertising outlays made directly to a particular sales territory. *See also* INDIRECT COST.

DIRECT FINANCING LEASE method used by lessors in capital leases when both of the following criteria for the lessor are satisfied: (1) collectibility of minimum lease payments is assured and (2) no important uncertainties surround the amount of unreimbursable costs yet to be incurred. In a direct financing lease, the lessor is *not* a manufacturer or dealer in the item; the lessor purchases the property only for the purpose of leasing it. The lessor uses the interest rate implicit in the lease to discount the future payments from the lessee. The difference between the gross investment in the lease and the cost of the leased property is reported as unearned interest income. Unearned interest income is then amortized using the interest method thus resulting in interest income over the life of the lease. Initial direct costs of the lease are expensed. *See also* SALES-TYPE LEASE.

DIRECT LABOR work directly involved in making the product. Examples of direct labor costs are the wages of assembly workers on an assembly line and the wages of a machine tool operator in a machine shop. Direct labor is an *inventoriable* cost.

DIRECT LABOR BUDGET schedule for expected labor cost. Expected labor cost is dependent upon expected production volume (production budget). Labor requirements are based on production volume multiplied by direct labor-hours per unit. Direct labor-hours needed for production are then multiplied by direct labor cost per hour to derive budgeted direct labor costs. For example, assume budgeted production of 790 units, direct labor-hours per unit of 5, and direct labor cost per hour of $5. The expected labor cost equals:

Expected production	790 units
Direct labor-hours per unit	× 5
Direct labor-hours	3,950
Direct labor cost per hour	× $5
Total direct labor cost	$19,750

DIRECT LABOR EFFICIENCY VARIANCE difference between standard direct labor hours allowed for the good units produced and actual direct labor hours worked, multiplied by the standard direct labor rate.

DIRECT LABOR RATE VARIANCE difference between the standard direct labor rate and the actual direct labor rate, multiplied by the actual direct labor hours worked.

DIRECT LABOR TIME STANDARDS expected time required for each department, machine, or process to complete production of one unit or one batch of output.

DIRECT LABOR VARIANCES difference between the standard direct cost and the actual direct labor cost. It is the sum of the DIRECT LABOR RATE VARIANCE and DIRECT LABOR EFFICIENCY VARIANCE.

DIRECT MATERIAL all the material that becomes an integral part of the finished product. Examples are the steel used to make an automobile and the wood to make furniture. Direct materials are charged to work-in-process as an *inventoriable* cost.

DIRECT MATERIALS BUDGET schedule showing how much material will be required for production and how much material must be bought to meet this production requirement. The purchase depends on both expected usage of materials and inventory levels. For example, assume expected production of 790 units, 3 lbs. of material needed per unit, desired ending inventory of material 216 lbs., beginning inventory of material 237 lbs., and unit cost per lb. of $2. Then lbs. of material to be purchased and purchase cost follow:

Material needed for production (790 units × 3)	2,370 lbs.
Add: Desired ending inventory	216
Total need	2,586
Less: Beginning inventory	237
Purchases of material	2,349
× Unit cost	× $2
Purchase cost	$4,698

DIRECT MATERIALS PRICE STANDARD careful estimate of the cost of a specific direct material in the next accounting period.

DIRECT MATERIALS PRICE VARIANCE actual price minus the standard price, times the actual quantity. The price variance may be isolated either at the time of purchase or at the time of transfer to WIP. The advantage of the former method is that the variance is identified earlier. Normal spoilage is considered in the calculation of standard direct materials cost per unit.

DIRECT MATERIALS QUANTITY STANDARD estimate of the amount of direct materials to be used, influenced by product engineering specifications, quality of direct materials, age and productivity of machinery, and quality and experience of the work force.

DIRECT MATERIALS QUANTITY (USAGE, EFFICIENCY) VARIANCE actual quantity minus standard quantity, times standard price. This variance is sometimes supplemented by the direct materials mix variance and the direct materials yield variance. These variances are calculated only when the production process involves combining several materials in varying proportions (when substitutions are allowable in combining materials).

DIRECT MATERIALS VARIANCES difference between the actual costs of materials and the standard costs of materials. They are usually divided into price and efficiency components. Part of a total materials variance may be attributed to using more raw materials than the standard and part to a cost that was higher than standard.

DIRECT MATERIALS YIELD VARIANCE weighted average unit standard cost of the budgeted mix multiplied by the difference between the actual quantity of materials used and the standard quantity. Certain relationships may exist among the various material variances. For instance, an unfavorable price variance may be offset by a favorable mix or yield variance because materials of better quality and higher price are used. Also, a favorable mix variance may result in an unfavorable yield variance or vice versa.

DIRECT METHOD
1. *see* DIRECT ALLOCATION METHOD.
2. procedure for converting the income statement from an accrual basis to a cash basis by separately adjusting each item in the income statement.

DIRECTOR
1. head of a governmental agency.
2. member on the board of directors of a corporation. The board of directors that is selected by the shareholders is the chief governing body of the corporation. It has the sole responsibility for the declaration of dividends. It also decides on major areas, including expansion, retraction, change of product, and selection of corporate officers.

DIRECTORS' REPORT financial report prepared for company directors. The report is typically prepared on a quarterly and annual basis. It includes detailed items such as the accountant's financial analyses and management recommendations. The report is usually unaudited.

DIRECT TEST OF FINANCIAL BALANCE substantive auditing procedure that is designed to validate or substantiate a recorded account balance, rather than the accounting treatment, errors, and irregularities associated with transactions.

DIRECT TRACING *see* TRACING.

DIRECT WRITE-OFF METHOD way of charging bad debt expense when an account receivable is actually deemed uncollectible. Thus, at the date it is certain that the customer will not be able to pay (in the most extreme instance, bankruptcy), the entry is to debit bad debt expense and credit accounts receivable. The advantage of this method is that it is based on *fact* rather than estimates. However, it is not accepted for financial reporting purposes because it fails to match bad debt expense against sales in the year of sale and does not show the realizable value of accounts receivable. It is the only method allowed for tax purposes (except for small banks and specified types of financial organizations).

DISASTER RECOVERY PLAN details the steps needed to recover an organization's IT system after a disaster. Recovery strategy should consider the loss of physical computer facilities, hardware, software, data restoration, and network connectivity.

DISBURSEMENT payment by cash or by check. *See also* EXPENDITURE.

DISC *see* DISK.

DISCLAIMER
1. rendered by the auditor when insufficient appropriate audit evidence exists to form an AUDIT OPINION. Examples are when audit SCOPE LIMITATIONS exist, or uncertainties (e.g., lawsuits) are such that the accountant cannot reasonably predict their ultimate outcome, which may have a devastating effect upon the firm. *See also* EVIDENCE.
2. under the Sarbanes-Oxley Act, a report stating that because of restrictions on the scope of the auditor's work, the auditor is unable to, and does not, express an opinion on the effectiveness of internal control over financial reporting.

DISCLOSURE information given as an attachment to the financial statements in footnote or supplementary form. It provides an elaboration or explanation of a company's financial position and operating results. Explanatory information concerning an entity's financial health can also be disclosed in the AUDIT REPORT. Anything that is material should be disclosed including quantitative (e.g., dollar components of inventory) and qualitative (e.g., lawsuit) information helpful to financial statement users. The SEC also requires special disclosures in filings with it. For example, any sudden significant happening affecting a company's financial position (e.g., Three Mile Island nuclear accident) must be disclosed in Form 8-K.

DISCONTINUED OPERATION sale, disposal, or planned sale in the near future of a business segment (i.e., product line, class of customer). The results of a discontinued operation are reported separately in the income statement as a separate line item after income from continuing operations and before extraordinary items. *See also* INCOME FROM DISCONTINUED OPERATIONS.

DISCOUNT
1. difference between the FACE VALUE (i.e., *future value*) and the PRESENT VALUE of a payment.
2. reduction in price given for prompt payment. *See also* SALES DISCOUNT; TRADE DISCOUNT.
3. excess of the *par value* (face value) of a financial instrument over the price paid for it. *See also* BOND DISCOUNT.

DISCOUNTED CASH FLOW (DCF) TECHNIQUES methods of selecting and ranking investment proposals such as the NET PRESENT VALUE (NPV) and INTERNAL RATE OF RETURN (IRR) methods where time value of money is taken into account.

DISCOUNTED PAYBACK PERIOD length of time required to recover the initial cash outflow from the *discounted* future cash inflows. This is the approach where the present values of cash inflows are cumulated until they equal the initial investment. For example, assume a machine purchased for $5,000 yields cash inflows of $5,000, $4,000, and $4,000. The cost of capital is 10%. Then we have

Year	Cash Flow	PV Factor at 10%	PV of Cash Flow
1	$5,000	.909	$4,545
2	4,000	.826	3,304
3	4,000	.751	3,004

The payback period (without discounting the future cash flows) is exactly 1 year. However, the discounted payback period is a little over 1 year because the first year discounted cash flow of $4,545 is not enough to cover the initial investment of $5,000. The discounted payback period is 1.14 years (1 year + ($5,000 − $4,545)/$3,304 = 1 year + .14 year).

DISCOUNTED PRESENT VALUE *see* PRESENT VALUE.

DISCOUNT LOST *cash discount* not taken because of the buyer's failure to pay within the specified time period. The discount lost occurs only when purchases are recorded *net* of the discount. If the discount is not taken advantage of, the gross amount will be paid. Assume a $1,000 purchase on terms of 2/10, net/60. The journal entry for the purchase is to debit purchases and credit accounts payable for $980. If payment is made after 10 days, the entry is to debit accounts payable $980 and purchase discount lost $20 and credit cash $1,000. Purchase discount lost is an expense account.

DISCOUNT RATE
1. interest rate charged by the Federal Reserve Bank to its member banks for loans; also called *rediscount rate*. The federal discount rate is less than the prime rate.
2. interest rate used to convert future receipts or payments to their present value. The COST OF CAPITAL (cutoff, hurdle, or minimum required rate) is used as the discount rate under the NET PRESENT VALUE METHOD.

DISCOVERY SAMPLING exploratory sampling to assure that the proportion of units with a particular attribute (i.e., error) is not in excess of a given percentage of the population. Three determinations needed to use discovery sampling are: (1) size of population; (2) minimum unacceptable error rate; and (3) confidence level. Sample size is provided by a sampling table. If none of the random samples has an error, the auditor can conclude that the actual error rate is below the minimum unacceptable error rate. Usually, discovery sampling is employed to identify batches of documents requiring detailed examination. Assume the auditor desires to determine the correctness of costing of documents from 20 branches. A discovery sample can uncover those batches having, for example, a 95% probability of an error rate below 1%. The auditor will accept those batches as satisfactory and examine in detail the remaining batches. It is a good procedure to follow in checking the quality of clerical work. When limited time exists, discovery sampling can reassure the auditor that the error rate is less then a certain percentage using a small sample size. Discovery sampling can also be used to test audit reliability ex post. Assume an error was not detected when the CPA used a random sample in examining the population. However, after the error is uncovered, the auditor can determine the probability of having found this error. The CPA may have checked random units giving him a 95% confidence level that the error rate in the population was below 1%. The incorrect units are, say .1% of the population, hence the method and assumptions used were appropriate. Assume the auditor looks at an inventory list comprising quantity, unit cost, and total cost. It would be impractical for auditors to examine each pricing and extension. They can utilize discovery sampling to derive a 90% confidence level that the error rate in pricing and extension is below 1%. The table indicates that for 2,000 inventory items, a random sample size of 220 is appropriate. If no errors are found, the accountant concludes the entire inventory list is correct. If one error is uncovered, the accountant ceases sampling and checks all of the extensions on the list. A problem with discovery sampling is the rejection of some acceptable batches. While discovery sampling may be used by the internal auditor as a final check, the external auditor should use it only as a *preliminary* scanning procedure to test the quality of data in a population.

DISCOVERY VALUE ACCOUNTING method of accounting for extractive enterprises (such as oil and gas). In this approach, the increase in value associated with the discovery of oil and gas reserves would be included in earnings. There are problems such as identifying the future market prices and the costs of production and making reliable estimates of the amount of resource (for example, number of barrels of oil that ultimately will be produced from the field). *See also* RESERVE RECOGNITION ACCOUNTING (RRA).

DISCRETIONARY COST cost changed easily by management decision such as advertising, repairs and maintenance, and research and development; also called *managed cost*. The analyst should note whether the current level of discretionary expense is consistent with previous trends and with the company's present and future requirements. Discretionary costs are often reduced when a firm is in difficulty or desires to show a stable earnings trend. A reduction in discretionary costs may cause a deterioration in the QUALITY OF EARNINGS since management is starving the firm by holding down necessary expenses (for example, a lack of repairs causing equipment breakdown). The trend in discretionary costs as a percent of net sales and related assets should be examined.

DISCRETIONARY (FIXED) COST fixed costs that change because of managerial decisions, also called *management (fixed) costs* or *programmed (fixed) costs*. Examples of this type of fixed costs are advertising outlays, training costs, and research and development costs. Management sometimes unjustly reduces these costs below normal levels in order to pad current net income, which may place the future net income of the company at risk.

DISCUSSION MEMORANDUM document published by the FASB to facilitate and encourage discussion of an issue or problem of current concern to the accounting profession and members of the interested public. It attempts to bring out all pertinent aspects of the subject under consideration both pro and con and provides a vehicle so that alternative solutions may be evaluated. It usually signifies that the FINANCIAL ACCOUNTING STANDARD BOARD (FASB) is considering the issuance of STATEMENTS OF FINANCIAL ACCOUNTING STANDARDS.

DISINVESTMENT opposite of capital budgeting decisions, because they concern whether to terminate rather than start an operation. In general, if the marginal cost of a project is greater than the marginal revenue, the firm should disinvest. Four steps should be taken in making a disinvestment decision. First, fixed expenses that would be curtailed by the disinvestment decision (e.g., depreciation and insurance on equipment used) should be identified.

Second, the revenue needed to justify continuing operations (variable cost of production) should be determined. Third, the opportunity cost of funds that will be received upon disinvestment (e.g., salvage value) should be established. Fourth, if the book value of the assets is not equal to the economic value of the capital, the decision should be reevaluated using current fair value rather than book value. When a firm disinvests, excess capacity may exist unless another project uses this capacity immediately. The cost of IDLE CAPACITY should be treated as a relevant cost.

DISK (or disc) a small round plate on which data can be stored. A *disk* refers to magnetic media, while a *disc* refers to optical media.

DISKETTE disk that is usually 3½" in diameter; also called a *floppy disk*. The disk is made of a flexible piece of Mylar. When magnetized, it is able to store BITS on tracks (circles) on one side if a single-sided floppy disk or on two sides if it is a double-sided disk. A floppy disk has sectors that divide each track into sections.

DISPOSABLE INCOME personal income minus personal income tax payments and other government deductions. It is the amount of personal income available for people to spend or save; also called *take-home pay*.

DISPOSAL DATE date on which an asset is sold or discarded. A higher selling price may be realized if the asset is sold in the ordinary course of business than in a forced liquidation.

DISPOSITION OF VARIANCES closing of variances to cost of goods sold or income summary if they are immaterial. Variances that are material may be prorated. A simple approach to prorating is to allocate the total net variance to work-in-process, finished goods, and the cost of goods sold based on the balances in those accounts.

DISTRESS PRICE markdown that a firm should accept rather than discontinue its operation under distress conditions. Under these conditions, any contribution that can be obtained to help cover fixed costs may be preferable to ceasing operations altogether. If operations are discontinued, the company will have no contribution available to cover fixed costs and will end up with a huge amount of shutdown costs. A distress price typically would be a variable-cost-plus price. *See also* CONTRIBUTION APPROACH TO PRICING.

DISTRIBUTED COMPUTER SYSTEM system in which linked computers are at various locations instead of being centralized at one particular place.

DISTRIBUTED PROCESSING technique in which physically separate computers share resources in their respective information processing functions. This means that a number of computers can use the same disk drives, printers, and other peripherals. This becomes an important advantage when a large database is required by two different computers. Instead of using separate disk drives, the system is set up so that both computers can access the same database. Distributed processing is often implemented by linking microcomputers and minicomputers to mainframes, or by linking mainframes together, with each computer having a number of users.

DISTRIBUTION COST any cost incurred to fill an order for a product or service. It includes all money spent on warehousing, delivering, and/or shipping products and services to customers.

DISTRIBUTION TO OWNERS payment of earnings to owners of a business organization in the form of a DIVIDEND. A dividend is a distribution to a corporation's stockholders usually in cash; sometimes in the corporation's stock, called a STOCK DIVIDEND; and much less frequently in property (usually other securities), called a *dividend in kind.*

DISTURBANCE TERM *see* ERROR TERM.

DIVERSIFIABLE RISK portion of an asset's risk that can be eliminated through diversification, also called UNSYSTEMATIC RISK or *controllable* risk. It results from the occurrence of random events such as labor strikes, lawsuits, or loss of key accounts. This type of risk is unique to a given asset. Business, liquidity, and default risks fall into this category. It is assumed that any investor can create a portfolio in which this type of risk is completely eliminated through diversification.

DIVERSITY conditions in which cost objects place different demands on activities, activities place different demands on resources, or processes place different demands on resources. This situation arises, for example, when there is a difference in mix or volume of products that causes an uneven assignment of costs. Different types of diversity include: batch size, customer, market, product mix, distribution channel, and volume.

DIVERSITY SEGMENTATION recognizing varying levels of demand by using cost drivers.

DIVIDEND distribution of earnings paid to stockholders based on the number of shares owned. The most typical type of dividend is a CASH DIVIDEND. Dividends may be issued in other forms such as stock and property. Dividend reinvestment plans also exist where stockholders can reinvest the proceeds of the dividend to buy more shares of stock. *See also* LIQUIDATING DIVIDEND; STOCK DIVIDEND.

DIVIDEND EXCLUSION applied to the amount of dividends received that are exempt from tax. Dividend exclusion is not applicable to individual investors. A corporation that owns less than 20% of the stock in another company can exclude 70% of the dividends received from taxable income. When between 20% and 79% of the stock of another company is owned, 75% of the dividends received from that firm can be excluded from taxation. When 80% or more of another company's stock is owned, all of the dividends received from that firm can be excluded from taxation.

DIVIDEND GROWTH MODEL cost of internal equity using the next expected dividend per share, the expected growth rate in dividends or earnings, and the market price, also called *Gordon's Dividend Model.*

DIVIDEND PAYOUT ratio that measures the percentage of net income paid out in dividends. It equals dividends per share divided by earnings per share. Stockholders generally favor companies that distribute a high percentage of their earnings in the form of dividends. Some industries, such as utilities, are known for their stable dividend records. Assume net income is $100,000, cash dividends are $60,000, and common shares outstanding are 10,000. The dividend payout ratio is:

$$\frac{\$6,000}{\$10,000} = \underline{\underline{.60}}$$

See also DIVIDEND YIELD.

DIVIDENDS IN ARREARS amount of dividends on CUMULATIVE PREFERRED STOCK from past periods that have not been paid.

DIVIDEND YIELD ratio providing an estimate of the return per share on a stock investment based on the market price at the end of the reporting period. The ratio equals dividends per share divided by market price per share. A disadvantage of this ratio is the timing mismatch between the numerator, which is based on the dividend declaration date, and the denominator, which is based on the year-end market price of the stock. Assume cash dividends are $80,000, market price per share is $10, and 80,000 shares are outstanding. The dividend yield is:

$$\frac{\$1}{\$10} = \underline{\underline{.10}}$$

See also DIVIDEND PAYOUT.

DIVORCE legal termination of a marriage. The tax benefits of the personal exemption claimed for a child are phased out as income increases. Thus only the lower income parent benefits from the personal exemption deduction. The party making an alimony payment can deduct it for tax purposes. The recipient reports it as taxable income. No gain or loss is recognized on a transfer of property incident to a divorce. Such transfers are treated as gifts, with the transferee taking the transferor's adjusted basis in the property. The gain on the property is taxed only when sold.

DNS (DOMAIN NAME SYSTEM) allows domain names, such as barronseduc.com, to be converted into its IP address. Using DNS allows users to substitute words (domain names) for numbers (IP address).

DNS HIJACKING redirecting Web traffic to a fraudulent Web site. With DNS hijacking, Web traffic is redirected to a different Web site, but no attempt is made to fool the user. In contrast, with DNS spoofing, the attacker is trying to fool the user into thinking that the user is connecting to the intended Web site. *See also* DNS (DOMAIN NAME SYSTEM), SPOOFING, DNS SPOOFING.

DNS SPOOFING making a DNS address resolve to a different IP address than the real one. DNS spoofing is often used to redirect Web traffic to a fraudulent Web site. In DNS spoofing, the attacker is trying to fool the user into thinking that the user is connecting to the intended Web site. In contrast, with DNS hijacking the Web traffic is simply redirected to a different Web site, but no attempt is made to fool the user. *See also* DNS (DOMAIN NAME SYSTEM), SPOOFING, DNS HIJACKING.

DODD-FRANK WALL STREET REFORM AND CONSUMER PROTECTION ACT more commonly referred to as Dodd-Frank, imposes major regulations on the financial industry. It is designed to (1) prevent the collapse of major financial institutions, and (2) protect consumers from abusive lending and mortgage practices.

DOLLAR ACCOUNTABILITY emphasis upon the flow of liquid assets in accounting for firms that have a not-for-profit purpose.

DOLLAR UNIT SAMPLING (DUS) procedure expressed in dollar amounts showing that a given attribute has been exceeded. The accountant combines a *probability proportionate to size sampling* of audit units, which have an upper level prediction of possible error based on dollar mistakes uncovered in the sample, with an attribute derived from a probability determination. For example, a supplier account with a book value of $100 constitutes 100 *dollar units*. The auditor undertakes a random sample of the dollar units with probabilities proportionate to size. Then the audit units applicable to the sampled dollars are audited. If a dollar mistake is uncovered in a sampled item, it is converted on a "per dollar" basis. Sample results are projected to the population.

DOLLAR VALUE LIFO inventory method computed in *dollars* (i.e., cost figures) rather than units. After dividing ending inventory into homogeneous "groupings" or "pools," each pool is converted to base year prices by means of appropriate price indices. The difference between beginning and ending balances, as converted, becomes a measure of change in inventory quantity for the year. An increase is recognized as an inventory layer to be added to the beginning inventory. It is converted at the current price index and added to the dollars identified with the beginning balance. Assume 12/31/2015 physical inventory is $130,000. The price index in 2015 is 1.30. The base inventory is $80,000 as of 12/31/2014 with a price index of 1.00. The dollar value inventory at 12/31/2015 is $106,000 as determined below:

12/31/2015 inventory in base dollars		
$130,000/1.30	$100,000	
12/31/2014 base inventory	80,000	$80,000
Increase in base dollars	$ 20,000	
2015 index	× 1.3	
Increase in current prices		26,000
12/31/2015 dollar value LIFO inventory		$106,000

The tax law allows a simplified dollar-value LIFO method for taxpayers having average annual gross receipts for the three preceding taxable years of $5,000,000 or less. Under this method, taxpayers keep a separate inventory pool for items in each major category in the applicable government price index. The adjustment for each separate pool is based on the change from the preceding taxable year in the component of that index for the major category. *See also* LAST-IN, FIRST-OUT (LIFO).

DOMESTIC CORPORATION company established under U.S. or state law. A FOREIGN CORPORATION, in one sense, is a domestic corporation organized in a state other than the one in which it does business.

DOMESTIC INTERNATIONAL SALES CORPORATION (DISC) in taxation, domestic corporations, usually subsidiaries, created by the Revenue Act (1971) to encourage exports and improve the balance of trade. A major benefit is the deferment of 50% of a DISC's income for a long period of time.

DONATION gift of assets to a company, usually by state or local governments, to induce a business to relocate. The item donated is recorded at its fair market value on the donation date. The donor does *not* have an owner's interest as a result of the donation. The recipient's entry is to debit the asset and credit contribution revenue. The donor debits contribution expense at fair value, credits the asset at cost, and the difference is a gain or loss.

DOUBLE DECLINING BALANCE METHOD ACCELERATED DEPRECIA-TION method in which a constant percentage factor of twice the straight-line rate is multiplied each year by the declining balance of the asset's book value.

The straight-line rate is simply the reciprocal of the useful life in years, multiplied by 100. If the useful life is five years, the straight-line rate is $1/5 \times 100$ = 20%. Therefore, the double declining rate is 40%.

To determine the annual depreciation expense, the asset's book value at the beginning of the period is multiplied by the double declining rate.

For example, assume that the asset costs $1,000 and has an estimated useful life of five years. The estimated salvage value at the end of the five-year period is $100. The calculations for this method follow:

Year	Original Cost	Beginning Book Value		Double Declining Rate		Annual Dep. Expense
1	$1,000	$1,000	×	40%	=	$400
2	1,000	600	×	40	=	240
3	1,000	360	×	40	=	144
4	1,000	216	×	40	=	86
5	1,000	130	×			30
					Total	$900

Note that in the fifth year depreciation expense is only $30, the amount needed to reduce the asset's book value to the estimated salvage value of $100. An asset is not depreciated below its salvage value. Thus, even though salvage value was ignored in the initial computation, the depreciation in the last year(s) cannot bring the asset's book value to less than the salvage value.

DOUBLE ENTRY BOOKKEEPING record of transactions that require entries in at least two accounts. Every transaction is reflected in offsetting debits and credits. For instance, when a telephone bill is accrued at year-end, (1) telephone expense must be recorded and (2) accrued expenses payable must be increased.

DOUBLE EXTENSION METHOD approach used to get a price index for DOLLAR VALUE LIFO when broad inventory pools of similar items are unavailable. The method uses a *representative portion* of items to obtain an index.

DOWNLOAD transmit a file or program from a central computer to the accountant's computer. The accountant can retrieve information to be used in an application package such as spreadsheet, file information from a subsidiary, or file data or program from an online database. A BUFFER is the temporary storage area holding information. *See also* TELECOMMUNICATIONS; UPLOAD.

DOWNSIDE RISK
1. an investment risk evaluation derived by estimating the total loss that could occur in a worst-case scenario. A variety of factors enter into such an evaluation including book value and net earnings as well as general market conditions.
2. a company's risk of loss in a downturn in business activity. For example, an auto manufacturer has downside risk in an economic downturn because it cannot slash its fixed costs, which results from the capital-intensive nature of the industry.

DRAFT instrument normally used in international commerce to effect payment; also called *bill of exchange*. It is simply an order written by an exporter (seller) requesting an importer (buyer) or its agent to pay a specified amount of money at a specified time. The person or business initiating the draft is known as the *maker, drawer,* or *originator*. The party to whom the draft is addressed is the *drawee*. *See also* ACCEPTANCE; SIGHT DRAFT, TIME DRAFT.

DRAWING ACCOUNT provision allowing a personal withdrawal of cash or other assets from a proprietorship by the owner. It is in effect a disinvestment in the firm and reduces owner's equity. The entry is to debit the owner's capital and credit cash. The drawing account of a proprietor or partner is equivalent to the dividend account used by a corporation.

DSS *see* DECISION SUPPORT SYSTEM.

DUAL PRICING TRANSFER PRICING scheme. For example, the seller could record the transfer to another segment at the usual market price that would be paid by an outsider. The buyer, however, would record a purchase at the variable cost of production. Each segment's performance would be improved by the use of a dual-pricing scheme, and the organization would benefit because variable costs would be used for decision-making purposes. In effect, the seller is given a corporate subsidy under the dual-pricing system.

DUAL PROBLEM one part of associated LINEAR PROGRAMMING (LP) problems called the *primal* and the *dual*. In other words, each maximizing problem in LP has its corresponding problem, called the dual, which is a minimizing problem; similarly, each minimizing problem has its corresponding dual, a maximization problem. For example, if the primal is concerned with maximizing the contribution from the three products A, B, and C and from the three departments X, Y, and Z, then the dual will be concerned with minimizing the costs associated with the time used in the three departments to produce those three products. An optimal solution to the dual problem provides a SHADOW PRICE of the time spent in each of the three departments.

DUAL PURPOSE TESTING involves performing tests of controls concurrently with substantive procedures (i.e., tests of details) on the same transaction. Dual purpose testing may be used by an auditor to increase audit efficiency.

DUE DATE promised delivery date.

DUE DILIGENCE a qualitative assessment of management's character and capability. Due diligence evaluation is like "kicking the tires" of the company by conducting plant tours, trade checks, and interviews with competitors, suppliers, customers, and employees. Comprehensive due diligence may also include an examination of the books and records, asset appraisals, reviews of the company's other debt obligations, legal and accounting affairs, internal controls, planned capital expenditures, and other matters that bear on the company's future success and profitability. Due diligence is a legal requirement before public offerings.

DUMMY ACTIVITY fictitious activity with zero activity time used to represent precedence or used whenever two or more activities have the same starting and ending nodes.

DUMPSTER DIVING in IT (information technology), refers to a technique where a hacker goes through someone else's trash to collect information that could be used to carry out an IT attack.

DU PONT FORMULA the breakdown of RETURN ON INVESTMENT (ROI) into margin and turnover.

$$\text{ROI} = \frac{\text{Net Profit After Taxes}}{\text{Total Assets}} = \frac{\text{Net Profit After Taxes}}{\text{Sales}} \times \frac{\text{Sales}}{\text{Total Assets}}$$

$$= \text{Net Profit Margin} \times \text{Total Asset Turnover}$$

For example, consider the following financial data:

Total assets $100,000
Net income $18,000
Sales $200,000

Then, ROI = $18,000/$100,000 = 18%

Margin = $18,000/$200,000 = 9%
Turnover = $200,000/$100,000 = 2 times

Therefore, ROI =18% = 9% × 2 = 18%

The breakdown provides a lot of insights to enable managers to improve profitability of the company and its investment center.

DURABLE GOODS costly manufactured products expected to last at least three years, including appliances and automobiles. The Census Bureau of the U.S. Commerce Department keeps track of them. The bureau tracks the dollar value of new orders. Separately, it also tracks shipments, unfilled orders, and inventories. Orders for durable goods can help forecast future manufacturing activity, although the overall number needs to be used with care because it can be strongly influenced by large orders in a particular sector, such as defense spending. For more information, two Web sites are helpful: www.census.gov/ftp/pub/ and www.haver.com.

DURBIN-WATSON STATISTIC summary measure of the amount of AUTO-CORRELATION in the error terms of the *regression*. Roughly speaking, if the statistic approaches a value of 2, there is no autocorrelation. If the error terms are highly positively correlated, the statistic would be less than 1 and could get near zero. If the error terms are highly negatively correlated, the statistic would be greater than 3 and could get near the upper limit of 4.

DVD *see* DIGITAL VERSATILE DISK (DVD).

DYNAMIC PROGRAMMING technique that divides the problem to be solved into a number of subproblems and then solves each subproblem in such a way that the overall solution is optimal to the original problem. For example, a company may wish to make a series of accounting and financial decisions over time that will provide it with the highest possible cash inflow.

E

EAFE *see* EUROPE, AUSTRALIA, FAR EAST (EAFE) INDEX.

EARLIEST FINISH TIME in PROGRAM EVALUATION AND REVIEW TECHNIQUE (PERT), earliest time at which an activity may be completed.

EARLIEST START TIME in PROGRAM EVALUATION AND REVIEW TECHNIQUE (PERT), earliest time at which an activity may begin.

EARLIEST TIME (ET) in PROGRAM EVALUATION AND REVIEW TECHNIQUE (PERT), the time an event will occur if all preceding activities are started as early as possible.

EARLY EXTINGUISHMENT OF DEBT long-term debt called back by a company before the maturity date. This may occur when the interest rate on the debt exceeds the current prevailing interest rate. The difference between the cash paid and the carrying value of the bond is treated as an ordinary loss or gain.

EARNED INCOME income from personal services. Earned income generally includes wages, salaries, tips, and other employee compensation. Compensation includes items that can be excluded from gross income, such as lodging, or meals furnished for the employer's convenience. Earned income also includes any net earnings from self-employment. Pension and annuity payments are not included.

EARNED INCOME CREDIT tax credit available to certain low-income taxpayers. This is an amount that eligible individuals can use to reduce their tax liability.

EARNED SURPLUS archaic term referring to retained earnings, the accumulated net income over the life of a corporation *less* all dividends.

EARNING POWER *discounted present value* of future profit of a business.

EARNINGS
1. NET INCOME of a business. *See also* EARNINGS PER SHARE (EPS).
2. revenues earned by an individual such as compensation and passive income (e.g., interest, dividends).

EARNINGS FORECAST projection of EARNINGS or EARNINGS PER SHARE (EPS) frequently made by management and independent security analysts. Examples of forecast sources include (1) Thomson First Call and (2) Reuters and Zacks Investment Research.

EARNINGS GROWTH a weighted average of the one-year earnings growth rates of the stocks in the fund. This calculation excludes stocks whose earnings changed from a loss to a gain and stocks whose earnings gains exceeded 999.99%.

EARNINGS MANAGEMENT see MANAGED EARNINGS.

EARNINGS MULTIPLE *see* PRICE-EARNINGS RATIO.

EARNINGS MULTIPLIER *see* PRICE-EARNINGS RATIO.

EARNINGS PER SHARE (EPS) profit accruing to stockholders for each share held. In a SIMPLE CAPITAL STRUCTURE, basic earnings per share equals:

$$\frac{\text{Net Income} - \text{Preferred Dividend}}{\text{Weighted Average Common Stock Outstanding}}$$

In a complex capital structure, BASIC EARNINGS PER SHARE and DILUTED EARNINGS PER SHARE are presented.

EARNINGS SURPRISES a company's announced net income for the reporting period that is above or below that expected by analysts (i.e., the consensus forecast). Stock price will typically increase if the earnings report is better than anticipated with the opposite effect if the earnings report is less than that expected. In fact, if earnings reported are much lower than those being forecasted by securities analysts, a drastic falloff in stock price may occur because of the disappointment. An example of a company that closely monitors earnings surprises is *First Call* (www.thomsonreuters.com).

EBIT earnings before interest expenses; also called *operating profit* or *operating income*. It is net sales minus operating expenses. It represents the amount of cash that a company will be able to use to pay off creditors.

EBITDA earnings before interest, taxes, depreciation, and amortization. It is EBIT + depreciation expenses + amortization expenses. EBITDA is essentially the income that a company has free for interest payments.

ECONOMIC GROWTH AND TAX RELIEF RECONCILIATION ACT OF 2001 tax legislation in the United States that made significant changes in several areas of the U.S. Internal Revenue Code, including income tax rates, estate and gift tax exclusions, and qualified and retirement plan rules. In general, the act lowered tax rates and simplified retirement and qualified plan rules such as those for Individual Retirement Accounts, 401(k) plans, 403(b) plans, and pension plans.

ECONOMIC LIFE estimated period that a fixed asset will provide benefits to the company. It is usually less than the physical life of an asset because an asset continues to have *physical life* despite inefficiency and obsolescence. Depreciation expense is typically based on the economic life. *See also* ACCELERATED COST RECOVERY SYSTEM (ACRS).

ECONOMIC ORDER QUANTITY (EOQ) size that minimizes the sum of carrying and ordering costs. At the EOQ amount, total ordering cost equals total carrying cost. *See also* ECONOMIC ORDER QUANTITY (EOQ) MODEL.

ECONOMIC ORDER QUANTITY (EOQ) MODEL mathematical model that determines the amount of goods to order to meet projected demand while minimizing inventory costs. In the original version of the model, demand is assumed to be known and constant throughout the year. Ordering cost is assumed to be a fixed amount per order, and carrying costs are assumed to be constant per unit. EOQ is computed as

$$\text{EOQ} = \sqrt{\frac{2\,(\text{Annual Demand})(\text{Ordering Cost})}{\text{Carrying Cost Per Unit}}}$$

If the carrying cost is expressed as a percentage of average inventory value (say, 12% per year to hold inventory), then the denominator value in the EOQ formula would be 12% times the price of an item. *See also* ECONOMIC PRODUCTION RUN SIZE.

ECONOMIC PRODUCTION RUN SIZE particular quantity of production that will minimize the total annual cost of setting up and carrying inventory, if produced in one production run. *See also* ECONOMIC PRODUCTION RUN SIZE MODEL.

ECONOMIC PRODUCTION RUN SIZE MODEL one that determines optimum production run quantity. The way it is computed is exactly the same as ECONOMIC ORDER QUANTITY (EOQ), except that the ordering cost in the EOQ formula is replaced by the setup cost. *See also* ECONOMIC ORDER QUANTITY (EOQ) MODEL.

ECONOMIC PROFITS difference between the total revenue and the total opportunity costs.

ECONOMIC VALUE ADDED (EVA) variation of RESIDUAL INCOME (RI) that defines the variable in specific ways. EVA = After-tax Income – (Cost of Capital × Capital Invested). The major difference between RI and EVA is that RI uses the market value or book value of assets for the capital invested in the division or firm while EVA uses the market value of total equity and interest-bearing debt.

EDGAR *see* ELECTRONIC DATA GATHERING, ANALYSIS, AND RETRIEVAL (EDGAR)

EDIT CONTROL in auditing, an input control used to identify incomplete, misleading, or invalid input data.

EDUCATIONAL TRAVEL DEDUCTION costs of transportation between a taxpayer's place of work and school that are deductible *for* adjusted gross income as ordinary and necessary employee business expenses. For these costs to qualify for deductibility, they have to meet the following conditions: (1) the education maintains or improves skills required by the taxpayer in employment or other trade or business; or (2) the education meets the expressed requirements imposed by either the individual's employer or applicable law, and such requirements must be satisfied to retain the taxpayer's job, position, or rate of compensation. Travel that itself is the educational activity is not deductible.

EFFECTIVE INTEREST METHOD manner of accounting for bond premiums or discounts. The interest expense equals the carrying value of a bond at the beginning of the accounting period times the EFFECTIVE INTEREST RATE (yield); also called *scientific amortization*. This method is *preferred* over the straight-line method of amortizing bond discount or bond premium. Amortization of a bond discount or premium is the difference between the interest expense and the nominal interest payment. The amortization entry is:

Interest Expense (effective interest rate × carrying value)

Cash (nominal interest rate × face value)

Bond Discount (for the difference)

EFFECTIVE INTEREST RATE
1. YIELD TO MATURITY.
2. real rate of interest on a loan equal to the nominal interest divided by the proceeds of the loan. Assume a company took out a $10,000, one-year, 10% discounted loan. Discounted loan refers to interest being deducted

immediately in arriving at proceeds. This effectively raises the cost of the loan. Further, assume a COMPENSATING BALANCE requirement of 5%. The effective interest rate equals:

$$\frac{\$1,000}{\$10,000 - \$1,000 - \$500} = \frac{\$1,000}{\$8,500} = 11.8\%$$

EFFECTIVENESS extent to which actual performance compares with targeted performance. For example, if a company has established a target sales plan of 10,000 units at the beginning of the year and the company's salespeople sell only 8,000 units during the year, the salespeople are appropriately considered "ineffective," as opposed to "inefficient." *See also* EFFICIENCY.

EFFECTIVE TAX RATE equals the tax divided by taxable income. For example, if the tax is $20,000 on taxable income of $80,000, the effective tax rate of the business is 25% ($20,000/$80,000). *See also* MARGINAL TAX RATE.

EFFICIENCY cost of inputs for each unit of output produced. For example, the assembly department spent 2,320 hours of direct labor in order to produce 2,000 actual units of output, while the budget allows only 2,000 direct laborhours for that level of output. Then the department was clearly *inefficient* (or wasteful) in the use of labor since it spent 320 hours more than allowed. *See also* ANALYSIS OF VARIANCES.

EFFICIENCY VARIANCE difference between inputs (materials and labor) that were actually used (i.e., actual quantity of inputs used) and inputs that should have been used (i.e., standard quantity of inputs allowed for actual production), multiplied by the standard price per unit. Efficiency (quantity, usage) variance = (actual quantity – standard quantity) × standard price per unit of input. The efficiency variance is unfavorable if the actual quantity exceeds the standard quantity: it is favorable if the actual quantity is less than the standard. *See also* MATERIAL QUANTITY VARIANCE; LABOR EFFICIENCY VARIANCE.

EFFICIENT MARKET HYPOTHESIS controversial theory holding that a stock's price is the same as its investment value. In an efficient market, all data are fully and immediately reflected in a stock price. Price changes in an efficient market are equally likely to be positive or negative. The hypothesis applies most directly to large companies trading on the major securities exchanges. The forms of the efficient stock market are weak, semi-strong, and strong.

In the weak form, no relationship exists between prior and future stock prices. The informational value of historical data is already included in current prices. Hence, studying previous stock prices is of no value.

In the semi-strong version, stock prices adjust immediately to new data; thus action after a known event results in randomness. All public information is reflected in a stock's value. Therefore, fundamental analysis is not usable in determining whether a stock is overvalued or undervalued.

In the strong form, stock prices reflect all information—public and private (insider). A perfect market exists. No group has access to information that would enable it to earn superior risk-adjusted returns.

8-K form a public company files with the Securities and Exchange Commission when an event deemed material requires public disclosure. Examples: a sudden and drastic lawsuit contingency or a change in auditors. *See also* 10-K.

ELECTRONIC COMMERCE (EC) the buying and selling of goods and services on the Internet. In practice, this term and a new term, "e-business," are often used interchangeably. For online retail selling, the term *e-tailing* is sometimes used. It is also called e-commerce for short, online commerce, Internet commerce, e-business, or CYBERSPACE commerce. E-commerce can be divided into: (1) e-tailing or "virtual storefronts" on Web sites with on-line catalogs, sometimes gathered into a "virtual mall." The gathering and use of demographic data through Web contacts; (2) Electronic Data Interchange (EDI), the business-to-business exchange of data; (3) e-mail and fax and their use as media for reaching prospects and established customers (for example, with newsletters); (4) business-to-business buying and selling; and (5) the security of business transactions.

ELECTRONIC DATA GATHERING, ANALYSIS, AND RETRIEVAL (EDGAR) service that the Securities and Exchange Commission uses to transmit company documents to investors. Those documents, which are available via Smart Edgar service, include 10-Qs (quarterly reports), 8-Ks (significant developments such as the sale of a company unit), and 13-Ds (disclosures by parties who own 5% or more of a company's shares).

ELECTRONIC DATA INTERCHANGE (EDI) transmission of business transactions from one company's computer to another company's computer. Transmission is achieved through an electronic communication network that uses translation software to convert transactions from a company's internal format to a standard EDI format. Companies that participate in EDI are referred to as trading partners. Trading partners may be involved in online banking, online retailing, and electronic funds transfer. There are paperless transactions in an electronic format. In the case of EDI, the auditor should be cognizant of the possible impact on the gathering of evidential matter.

ELECTRONIC FUND TRANSFER SYSTEM (EFTS) system for electronically transferring funds among sellers, buyers, and other parties without the need to write checks. The cost of processing a large number of checks has motivated financial institutions to develop a system of this kind. A typical example of EFTS is the payment of payroll. An employer deposits the payroll checks of its employees directly to their checking accounts. The company then sends to the bank a magnetic tape coded with the appropriate payroll data.

ELECTRONIC MAIL (e-mail) document transmitted electronically from the user's computer or terminal to an information service. Accountants and their clients can take advantage of electronic mail to transmit essential messages. With electronic mail, each user in the system has a "mailbox," which receives, holds, and sends information to others. The information sent may be spreadsheets, reports, memos, and so forth.

ELECTRONIC TRANSFER FUNDS (ETFs) equity indices that were introduced in 1993 as a way for investors to buy into a liquid, transparent, and diverse basket of stocks while paying less than for a mutual fund. The shares are priced in real time, tracking the value of their underlying index, and can be held as long-term investments, flipped for a quick profit or sold short to hedge equity risk.

ELEMENTS OF BALANCE SHEET items or accounts that appear on the balance sheet. They are various assets, liabilities, and equity accounts. A list of specific or detailed accounts is provided in the company's CHART OF ACCOUNTS. *See also* SETS OF ACCOUNTS.

ELIMINATIONS accounting entries used when preparing CONSOLIDATED FINANCIAL STATEMENTS between a PARENT COMPANY and a SUBSIDIARY COMPANY. Examples of eliminations are the elimination of intercompany profit, receivables, payables, sales, and purchases. Thus the consolidated entity reports financial statement figures applicable to outsider transactions. Where many eliminations are involved, an *eliminations ledger* may be used. Eliminations are also involved in preparing combining financial statements. *See also* CONSOLIDATION.

EMBEDDED AUDIT MODULE a program code that is added to a computer application that enables an auditor to collect data during processing of transactions.

EMBEZZLEMENT theft of money or property from a business by an individual in whose custody it has been placed. An example is a bookkeeper who steals from the petty cash fund. Proper INTERNAL CONTROLS can restrict or disclose such fraudulent activity.

EMPLOYEE EMPOWERMENT placing the authority to make critical decisions with those closest to the problem, for example, those in the work area directly affected. *See also* DECENTRALIZATION.

EMPLOYEE RETIREMENT INCOME SECURITY ACT OF 1974 (ERISA) federal legislation enacted to ensure that pension/retirement plans of employers are fair and secure. Provisions cover participation, vesting, funding, transferability, contributions, benefits, responsibilities, and termination procedures.

EMPLOYEE STOCK OWNERSHIP PLAN (ESOP) program that encourages employees to invest in the employer's stock. Employees may participate in the management of a company and even take control to save it from bankruptcy. The ESOP, however, is an inappropriate instrument for retirement savings. Because most of the funds are concentrated in the stock of one company, it does not provide any safety through diversification.

EMPLOYMENT COST INDEX (ECI) the most comprehensive and refined measure of underlying trends in employee compensation as a cost of production. Measures the cost of labor and includes changes in wages and salaries and employer costs for employee benefits. ECI tracks wages and bonuses, sick and vacation pay plus benefits such as insurance, pension and Social Security, and unemployment taxes from a survey of 18,300 occupations at 4,500 sample establishments in private industry and 4,200 occupations within about 800 state and local governments. This index can be obtained free from the Bureau of Labor Statistics' Internet site (www.stats.bls.gov). *See also* INFLATION.

ENCODING putting a message into a certain code, often as a control to assure confidentiality. *See also* CODING OF ACCOUNTS.

ENCRYPTION computer term relating to the process of concealing transmitted data from unauthorized users. For example, only the sender and receiver will be able to understand the transferred information because it is in a secret code. *See also* DECRYPTION.

ENCUMBRANCE
1. in government accounting, commitments related to unfilled contracts for goods and services including purchase orders. The purpose of encumbrance accounting is to prevent further expenditure of funds in light of commitments already made. At year-end, encumbrances still open are not accounted for as expenditures and liabilities but, rather, as reservations of fund balance. When an estimated or contractual liability is entered into, the entry is to debit encumbrances for the estimated amount and credit RESERVE FOR ENCUMBRANCES. When the actual expenditure of an amount previously encumbered is known, there are two entries. The first entry is to *reverse* the original encumbrance. The second entry is to record the expenditure by debiting expenditures and crediting VOUCHERS payable. At year-end, the encumbrance account is closed out against fund balance.
2. debt secured by a lien on assets.

ENDING INVENTORY goods on hand at the end of the accounting period. Ending inventory shows up in the income statement in the calculation of cost of goods sold and in the balance sheet. *See also* BEGINNING INVENTORY.

ENDORSEMENT signature on a draft or check by a payee before transfer to a third party. A payee provides such an endorsement when transferring this draft to the payee's bank. Checks can be endorsed in three different ways. In a *blank endorsement*, once signed, it becomes a negotiable instrument and can be used as such by anyone. A *restrictive endorsement* limits the use of the check to a single purpose. "For deposit only" is written on a check when it is deposited by mail. If the check is lost in the mail and subsequently found, it cannot be cashed. A *special endorsement* is used to pay someone else. All that is required is to indicate the payee and sign.

ENGAGEMENT LETTER letter written by the CPA or public accountant to the client citing the accounting functions to be performed, responsibilities assumed, the basis for billing, expense reimbursement, and so on. Typically, the CPA requests that the client sign the engagement letter showing agreement with the terms. The purpose of the engagement letter is to have a clear agreement among the parties regarding the accounting work to be done and related particulars.

ENGINEERED CAPACITY *see* IDEAL CAPACITY.

ENGINEERED COSTS costs having a clear relationship to output. Direct materials cost is an example.

ENGINEERING ANALYSIS way to measure cost behavior (or develop a COST-VOLUME FORMULA) according to what costs *should be*, not by what costs *have been*. It entails a systematic review of materials, labor, support services, and facilities needed for product and services. Engineers use time and motion studies and similar engineering methods to estimate what costs should be from engineers' specifications of the inputs required to manufacture a unit of output or to perform a particular service. *See also* ACCOUNT ANALYSIS; HIGH-LOW METHOD; REGRESSION METHOD.

ENROLLED AGENTS income tax specialists who have passed the IRS's comprehensive, two-day Special Enrollment Examination on all aspects of tax law or who have had five years of audit experience with the agency. Enrolled agents are authorized by the Treasury Department to represent the taxpayer, at all levels of audit, review, and appeal when dealing with the IRS. The examination includes true-false and multiple-choice questions and covers the following tax topics: (1) individuals; (2) sole proprietorships and partnerships; (3) corporations (including Subchapter S Corporations), fiduciaries, and estate and gift tax; and (4) ethics, recordkeeping procedures, appeal procedures, exempt organizations, retirement plans, practitioner penalty provisions, and research materials.

ENTERPRISE ACCOUNTING accounting for the *entire* business rather than its subdivisions (e.g., department).

ENTERPRISE FUND in governmental accounting, fund that provides goods or services to the public for a fee that makes the entity self-supporting. It basically follows GAAP as does a commercial enterprise. An example is a government-owned utility.

ENTERPRISE RESOURCE PLANNING (ERP) latest phase in the development of computerized systems for managing organizational resources. ERP is intended to integrate enterprise-wide information systems. ERP connects all organizational operations (personnel, the financial accounting system, production, marketing, distribution, etc.) and also connects the organization with its suppliers and customers.

ENTERPRISE RESOURCE PLANNING (ERP) SOFTWARE system that grew out of MATERIAL REQUIREMENTS PLANNING (MRP) systems, which have been used for more than 20 years. MRP systems computerized inventory control and production planning. Key features included an ability to prepare a master production schedule and a bill of materials and to generate purchase orders. ERP systems update MRP systems with better integration, relational databases, and graphical user interfaces. Features encompass supporting accounting and finance, human resources, and various e-commerce applications including supply chain management (SCM) and customer relationship management (CRM).

ENTERPRISE RISK MANAGEMENT (ERM) a broad term for risk management system that:
1. makes each area manager responsible for documenting and evaluating financial controls in his or her own area. People closest to each business unit manage the data, which improves accuracy and completeness;
2. identifies areas with inadequate control measures so action plans can be initiated to resolve problems;
3. tracks the progress of outstanding action plans, describes who is responsible for those actions, and sets the expected time for resolution;
4. protects against fraud with systematic data management that ensures multiple reviews and verification;
5. raises the level and precision of reporting to management;
6. puts "localized knowledge" to work. Area managers become empowered to understand the impact of their roles on corporate results.

See also RISK MANAGEMENT.

ENTERTAINMENT EXPENSE DEDUCTION tax deduction allowed only if the expenses are directly related or associated with the active conduct of a trade or business and are reasonable and necessary. This area of business expense deductions is scrutinized heavily by the IRS, and documentation requirements are usually quite stringent to prevent taxpayer abuse. A business may write off only 50% of the cost of business meals and entertainment costs.

ENTITY
Accounting: separate economic unit subject to financial measurement for accounting purposes. Examples are a corporation, partnership, sole-proprietor, and trust.
Legal: individual, partnership, corporation, and so on, permitted by law to own property and engage in business. Affiliated legal entities such as those consolidated for financial reporting may exist. Here, two or more companies operate under common control.

ENTITY ACCOUNTING accounting and measurement process for an entity that may not be the same as the legal entity. Usually, it involves measuring financial condition and operating performance.

ENTITY THEORY view in which a business or other organization has a separate accountability of its own. It is based on the equation:

$$\text{Assets} = \text{Liabilities} + \text{Stockholders' Equity}$$

The entity theory considers liabilities as equities with different rights and legal standing in the business. Under the theory, assets, obligations, revenues, and expenses and other financial aspects of the business entity are accounted for separately from its owners. In other words, the company has an identity distinct from its owners or managers. The firm is viewed as an economic and legal unit. *See also* PROPRIETARY THEORY.

ENTREPRENEUR individual who has the initiative to start an *enterprise* with its associated responsibilities, obligations, and risks. The entrepreneur usually hires people to work for him.

ENTRY recording of a transaction in the books of account, such as the receipt of cash in the cash receipts journal.

ENTRY VALUE replacement cost. It is the current estimated fair market price or cost of acquiring an asset already on the books or of service that has already been received and accounted for.

ENVIRONMENTAL COSTS expenditures incurred to prevent, contain, or remove environmental contamination. Such costs are generally expensed. However, in the following cases only, the company may elect to either expense or defer the costs: (1) the expenditures either extend the life or capacity of the asset or increase the property's safety; (2) the expenditures are made to get the property ready for sale; and (3) the expenditures prevent or lessen environmental contamination that may result from *future* activities of property owned.

EQUALIZATION adjustment of the tax valuation of property in a county relative to other counties in the same state. To assure that all property owners in the state pay a fair and uniform share of the state tax, an *equalization factor* is established by the state. For example, property in a county that assesses property at 60% of market value would be adjusted relative to other counties in the same state that assess their property at 50% of market value.

EQUALIZATION RESERVE allowance or reserve account credited periodically to offset charges to cover expenditures made during an accounting period. Its purpose is to allocate the expense uniformly over a period's operations. Maintenance expenses are sometimes handled in this manner. As the expenditures are actually paid, the allowance is debited, and the asset (e.g., cash) expended is credited.

EQUATION METHOD method used to find the break-even point or target income volume in COST-VOLUME-PROFIT (CVP) ANALYSIS or BREAK-EVEN ANALYSIS. The equation is:

$$\text{Sales} = \text{Variable Costs} + \text{Fixed Costs} + \text{Net Income}$$

Let p = unit selling price, x = volume, v = unit variable cost, and FC = total fixed costs; the equation becomes

$$px = vx + FC + \text{Net Income}$$

At the break-even volume, $px = vx + FC + 0$. To find the break-even point in units, simply solve the equation for x. Assume $p = \$250$, $v = \$150$, and $FC = \$35,000$. Then the equation is:

$$
\begin{aligned}
250x &= \$150x + \$35,000 + 0 \\
\$100x &= \$35,000 \\
x &= 350 \text{ units}
\end{aligned}
$$

EQUIPMENT TRUST CERTIFICATE debt instrument used to provide funds for the acquisition of equipment. The holder of the certificate has a secured interest in the asset in the event of corporate default. The trustee (usually a bank) has title to the equipment until the bond is paid. These certificates are sometimes issued by transportation companies (e.g., shipping company).

EQUITY
  1. assets minus liabilities, also called NET WORTH. In a sole proprietorship, it is the owner's equity. In a corporation, it is STOCKHOLDERS' EQUITY.
  2. any right to assets; property right; a liability. An equity holder may be a creditor, stockholder, or proprietor.

EQUITY FINANCING method of obtaining funds by issuing common or preferred stock. Receipts may be in the form of cash, services, or property. It is in the company's best interest to issue shares at a time when the market price of the stock is at its highest.

EQUITY METHOD means of accounting used by an investor who owns between 20% and 50% of the voting common stock of a company. It can also be used instead of the MARKET VALUE METHOD when the investor owns less than 20% of the company but has *significant influence* over the investee. Further, it is employed instead of CONSOLIDATION, even though more than 50% is owned, when one of the negating factors for consolidation exists (e.g., parent and subsidiary are not economically compatible, parent is not in actual control of subsidiary, parent has sold or contracted to sell subsidiary shortly after year-end). Under the equity method, the investor recognizes the percentage interest in the profit of the company by debiting investment in investee and crediting equity in earnings of investee. Dividends received by the investor are debited to cash and credited to the investment in investee account. *Permanent* declines in the market price of the investee are recognized by debiting loss and crediting investment in investee. However, temporary declines in market price are *not* reflected in the accounts. INTERPERIOD INCOME TAX ALLOCATION will arise because investee profits are recognized for book purposes but investee dividends are reflected for tax purposes. Assume investor company buys 10,000 shares of investee company for $10 per share acquiring a 30% interest. Investee's net income is $20,000 and dividends are $5000. The investment in investee account would look as follows:

Investment In Investee

Investment	100,000	Dividends	1,500
Profit	6,000		

EQUITY SPREAD calculation of equity value creation by multiplying beginning equity capital by the difference between the return on equity (net income/equity) and the percentage cost of equity.

EQUITY TRANSFER FUNDS (ETFs) equity indices that were introduced in 1993 as a way for investors to buy into a liquid, transparent, and diverse basket of stocks while paying less than they would for a mutual fund. The shares are priced in real time, tracking the value of their underlying index, and can be held as long-term investments, flipped for a quick profit or sold short to hedge equity risk.

EQUIVALENT PRODUCTION measure of the number of equivalent whole units produced in a period of time; also called EQUIVALENT UNITS.

EQUIVALENT TAXABLE YIELD method of comparing the taxable yield on a taxable bond such as a corporate bond to the tax-free yield on a municipal bond. The magnitude of difference, assuming equal credit quality, depends on the individual's tax rate. Of course, on an after-tax basis, the tax-free interest rate on a municipal bond can be less than the taxable interest rate on a corporate bond depending on the tax bracket of the taxpayer. Assume a taxpayer in 2000 is in the 28% tax bracket. A 6% municipal bond has the equivalent taxable yield of 8.3% (6%/.72) on a corporate bond. Thus the taxpayer would have the same after-tax return on a 6% municipal bond or an 8.3% corporate bond. To gain a higher after-tax return, the investor would therefore have to invest in a corporate bond paying in excess of 8.3%.

EQUIVALENT UNIFORM ANNUAL COST annualized sum of all relevant costs. It is like the amount of an installment loan payment.

EQUIVALENT UNITS number of fully completed units considered to be equivalent to a greater number of partially completed units. For example, if 1000 units are in WORK-IN-PROCESS at the end of the period and are considered 80% complete, the equivalent production is 800 units. The equivalent unit cost of manufacturing an item equals the total cost divided by the equivalent units. If the total cost of manufacturing the item was $2,400, the unit cost would be $3 ($2,400/800). Equivalent units are determined separately for DIRECT MATERIAL and CONVERSION COST. If 3,000 units in ending work-in-process are 70% complete as to direct material and 90% complete as to conversion, the equivalent units are 2,100 for direct material and 2,700 for conversion. *See also* PROCESS COSTING.

ERROR difference between a correct item or amount and an incorrect item or amount. Errors may be due to inaccurate measurement, representation, or mathematical mistake. An example of an error is charging to an expense account the wrong amount. Material errors can result in erroneous financial decisions. Proper safeguards such as a good system of internal checks can minimize the incidence of errors. An error may also occur in applying GAAP. *See also* PRIOR PERIOD ADJUSTMENT.

ERROR CORRECTION a change from an accounting principle that is not generally accepted to one that is generally accepted or a bookkeeping correction. This is shown as a restatement. Error corrections are distinguished from changes in accounting principles, which are considered retrospective applications. Thus, although error corrections, like changes in principles, are reflected by restating comparative financial statements along with a prior-period adjustment to the opening retained earnings balance, the term *restatement* is reserved for error changes. *See also* ACCOUNTING CHANGE AND ERROR CORRECTIONS.

ERROR TERM deviation of the actual value of an observation from the true regression line; also called *disturbance term* and *residual term*.

ESCAPABLE COST *see* AVOIDABLE COST.

ESTATE ACCOUNTING record keeping involved in and the preparation of reports by the one administering an estate of a deceased under the jurisdiction of a probate court.

ESTATE PLANNING manner of minimizing estate taxes at death. It involves deriving the most favorable tax treatment of wealth. Inheritance is passed on to beneficiaries with the smallest amount given over to taxes. Tax planning aspects for estates include: (1) determining what financial strategy could be developed taking into account the particular assets being considered; (2) the transfer of assets before the taxpayer's death (i.e., transfer title of property to those in low tax brackets); (3) drafting a will considering the tax and asset transfer ramifications (i.e., property can be transferred between spouses without any tax because of the unlimited marital deduction); and (4) having appropriate terms in life insurance policies.

ESTATE TAX levy paid to the federal government or state on a deceased person's assets that have been left to heirs. The estate pays the tax, not the recipients. No estate tax exists for property going from one spouse to another. *See also* INHERITANCE TAX.

ESTIMATED COST
1. cost that has been estimated or projected for a particular decision alternative or contract.
2. expenditures to be made after a sale. For example, expenditures for afterservice repairs under product warranty are *estimated costs*. Proper matching of revenue and expenses requires that the estimated costs of providing these warranties be recognized as an expense in the period of sale rather than of a later period when the warranty costs may actually be paid.

ESTIMATED LIABILITY obligation or service that actually exists but the amount requires estimation. Examples are estimated taxes payable and warranties payable. *See also* CONTINGENT LIABILITY.

ESTIMATED TAX quarterly payments for estimated tax liability on income that is not subject to employer withholding.

Individual: must pay 90% of the estimated tax liability for the year in quarterly installments. Further, estimated tax payments made under the SAFE-HARBOR RULE provision must be based on 90% of annualized taxable income. An underpayment penalty can be avoided by paying 100% or more of last year's tax liability.

Corporation: must remit 90% of the tax to be shown on the return for the taxable year in quarterly estimated tax payments to avoid a non-deductible underpayment penalty.

ETFs

1. mutual funds that change hands all day long on an exchange, just like stocks—which is very different from the once-a-day trading of ordinary mutual funds. *See also* EXCHANGE-TRADED FUNDS (ETFS).

2. *see* ELECTRONIC FUND TRANSFER SYSTEM (ETFS).

EUROPE, AUSTRALIA, AND FAR EAST (EAFE) INDEX compiled by Morgan Stanley Capital International (MSCI), the Morgan Stanley Europe, Asia, and Far East Index is a value-weighted index of the equity performance of major foreign markets. The EAFE index (it is pronounced EE-feh) is, in effect, a non-American world index of over 1000 stocks. It is considered the key "rest-of-the-world" index for U.S. investors, much as the Dow Jones Industrial Average is for the American market. The index is used as a guide to see how U.S. shares fare against other markets around the globe. It also serves as a performance benchmark for international mutual funds that hold non-U.S. assets. Morgan Stanley also compiles indexes for most of the world's major stock markets as well as for many smaller, so-called "emerging" markets. In addition, there are Morgan Stanley indexes for each continent and the entire globe. The index is quoted two ways: one in local currencies and two in the U.S. dollar.

EVALUATION OF INTERNAL CONTROL study and appraisal of the system of internal control within a company. The study aids in determining the extent of testing and other audit steps that must be performed. The auditor's evaluation concentrates on the nature of the internal controls, whether the controls are adequate in reducing to a minimum errors and irregularities, and whether the controls have been properly maintained and operated effectively. Evaluation steps include: (1) ascertaining the procedures and controls established by the client and their effectiveness; (2) determining which ones the auditor will rely on; (3) deciding which audit procedures must be expanded or curtailed; and (4) recommending to the client ways to improve internal controls. In evaluating the client's internal control, items to be considered are segregation of duties, internal checks and verifications, quality of personnel, duties and relationships of employees, quality and characteristics of the accounting system, and the effectiveness of the internal audit function. The Sarbanes-Oxley Act requires a company auditor to report on management's internal control assessment.

EVENT

1. in PROGRAM EVALUATION AND REVIEW TECHNIQUE (PERT), point in time that represents the start or completion of a set of activities.

2. in probability theory, one or more of the possible outcomes of doing something. For example, if a coin is tossed, getting a tail would be an *event*, and getting a head would be another event.

3. happening indicating a business transaction requiring a JOURNAL ENTRY has occurred.

EVIDENCE something that provides substantiation of the existence or amount of an item. The third standard of field work for a certified audit requires the auditor to obtain sufficient competent evidential matter as a basis for formulating an opinion on the financial statements. Evidence is more reliable when obtained from an independent source. Further, the stronger the internal control system, the more reliable the evidence. Finally, evidence obtained directly by the auditor through physical examination, observation, computation, and inspection is more persuasive than information obtained indirectly. For example, the accountant needs "backup" to support an entry made in the CASH DISBURSEMENTS JOURNAL. The cancelled check would serve as that evidence.

EXAMINATION
1. AUDIT of a company's financial records.
2. review of documents, procedures, and personnel to assure accuracy.
3. test administered by a professional organization to measure competence in an area, such as the CPA or CMA examinations.

EXCEL popular SPREADSHEET software by Microsoft.

EXCEPT FOR OPINION the only type of *qualified opinion* that an auditor can render. The auditor attests that the financial statements present the financial position fairly *except* for repercussions caused by conditions requiring disclosure. There may be a SCOPE LIMITATION in the auditor's work due to factors beyond the auditor's control or due to client restrictions that prevent the CPA from gathering objective and VERIFIABLE evidence in support of transactions and events. An example is the inability to confirm accounts receivable. There may exist a lack of conformity of the financial statements to GAAP.

EXCEPTION
1. EXCEPT FOR OPINION.
2. notification by a supervisor to a subordinate disagreeing with the subordinate's action. An example is where the supervisor questions an employee's expense reimbursement request. Such request may not be fully honored.
3. negative response to a confirmation request, such as when a customer disagrees with his or her account balance as per the confirmation request.
4. variance between actual and standard. *See also* EXCEPTION REPORT.

EXCEPTION REPORT material deviation between actual occurrence and expectation in a performance report, which warrants management investigation. Undesirable performance is identified, and corrective action is taken on a timely basis. If the variance is favorable, the reasons therefore are also searched out, so further advantage can be taken of the situation. An example is a variance between actual cost and standard cost for labor in a standard cost accounting system. In the area of data processing, an exception report may reflect those transactions not meeting the standards or requirements for the program being run. *See also* FLASH REPORTS.

EXCESS CAPACITY machinery and equipment kept on standby. *See also* IDLE CAPACITY.

EXCESS ITEMIZED DEDUCTION broad class of deductions for the computation of tax liability. They are deductions from ADJUSTED GROSS INCOME in excess of the STANDARD DEDUCTION (previously referred to as the ZERO-BRACKET AMOUNT or ZBA) and the personal and dependent exemption deductions.

EXCESS PRESENT VALUE INDEX *see* PROFITABILITY INDEX.

EXCHANGE
  1. reciprocal transfer of goods or services from one entity to another.
  2. market for securities or commodities, such as the NEW YORK STOCK EXCHANGE (NYSE) or the Chicago Mercantile Exchange.
  3. EXCHANGE RATE.

EXCHANGE GAIN (LOSS) a gain (loss) on the exchange of one currency for another due to appreciation (depreciation) in the home currency (for receivables).

EXCHANGE OF NONMONETARY ASSETS exchange based on the fair market value of the asset given or that received, whichever is more clearly evident. As a result, a gain or loss on the exchange is recorded because there is commercial substance to the transaction. The gain or loss equals the difference between the book value of the asset given up and the fair market value of the asset received. There is commerical substance when future cash flows change because of the transaction arising from a change in economic positions of the two companies. However, if the exchange lacks commercial substance, we record at book value the asset given up with *no* recognition or gain of loss.

EXCHANGE RATE *see* RATE OF EXCHANGE.

EXCHANGE-TRADED FUNDS (ETFs) index portfolios that you buy or sell just like stocks. The best of them are super-cheap—iShares S&P 500 Index (IVV) costs 0.09% a year, half the price of the Vanguard 500—and they can be traded instantly, sold short, or bought on margin. And ETFs track an astonishing variety of indexes, from biotech to Brazilian stocks.

Index Fund	Expense Ratio	Typical Commission
Vanguard 500 index	0.18%	None
iShares S&P 500 index	0.09%	$4 to $30 per trade*

*The commission on an automatic investment plan is $4; the top base rate for one national discount brokerage is $30.

EXCISE TAX one levied on specific products or services, for specific purposes. For example, an excise tax on gasoline might be used to fund road construction and repair. Excise taxes are levied at all levels of government, primarily federal and state. They are normally a percentage of the purchase price.

EX-DIVIDEND term used to indicate that a stock is selling without a recently declared dividend. The ex-dividend date is four business days prior to the date of record, according to rules applicable to NEW YORK STOCK EXCHANGE (NYSE)-listed companies and observed generally by other exchanges. *See also* DATE OF RECORD.

EXECUTIVE GAMES *see* MANAGEMENT GAME.

EXECUTORY COST cost excluded from MINIMUM LEASE PAYMENTS to be made by the lessee in a CAPITAL LEASE. The lessee reimburses the lessor for the lessor's expense payments. Examples are maintenance, insurance, and taxes.

EXEMPT INCOME income not subject to tax. Examples are interest on certain municipal bonds, employee achievement awards (length of service or safety achievement) up to a certain amount, scholarships and fellowship grants received from a college and used by degree candidates for qualified tuition and related expenses, and certain military benefits.

EXEMPTION deduction allowed in computing taxable income. There are basically two types: personal exemptions and dependency exemptions. There are three categories of exemptions, including personal and dependency types: (1) exemption for the taxpayer; (2) exemption for the taxpayer's spouse; and (3) exemption for dependent children and other dependents where more than one-half of the dependent's support is provided. *See also* DEPENDENT.

EXEMPTION ORGANIZATION one that is exempt from federal income taxes. An example is a not-for-profit corporation organized for religious, charitable, scientific, literary, educational, or certain other purposes.

EXERCISE PRICE price at which each share of stock underlying a call or put option can be bought or sold, also called *strike price*. It is standardized in trading at $5 intervals for stock between $50 and $100, $10 intervals for those between $100 and $200, and $20 for those over $200.

EXHIBIT formal statement prepared primarily for the dissemination of information. It may be of a financial or other nature. An example is a listing of product costs. Financial statements often make reference to accompanying exhibits.

EXISTENCE term used to refer to two audit objectives: (1) the verification that amounts in a company's financial statements do indeed exist and are proper; and (2) the verification that all events and amounts that do exist are duly recorded.

EXIT VALUE proceeds that would be received if an asset were sold or a liability terminated in an ARM'S LENGTH TRANSACTION. It may be expressed in terms of net realizable value, current selling price, or present value. *See also* ENTRY VALUE.

EXPECTED ACTUAL CAPACITY *see* CAPACITY.

EXPECTED ANNUAL ACTIVITY anticipated level of production for the coming year. If the total sales volume does not change from year to year, expected annual activity and NORMAL ACTIVITY would be the same, which is not usually the case. For example, normal activity, which reflects long-run average consumer demand is, say, 20,000 units of output or 100,000 direct labor-hours, while expected annual activity, which represents annual demand, fluctuates from year to year.

EXPECTED MONETARY VALUE expected value of PAYOFFS, measured in monetary terms. *See also* DECISION THEORY.

EXPECTED TIME FOR AN ACTIVITY in PROGRAM EVALUATION AND REVIEW TECHNIQUE (PERT), a weighted average time that is widely used in a real life application of PERT to a complex project, where the completion times for activities are not certain. First, estimate three possible duration times for each activity: an optimistic, a most likely, and a pessimistic time. A weighted average of these three time estimates is then calculated to establish the *expected time* for the activity. The formula applies to a weight of one to both the optimistic and the pessimistic estimates and a weight of four to the most likely estimate.

EXPECTED VALUE weighted average using the probabilities as weights. For decisions involving *uncertainty*, the concept of expected value provides a rational means for selecting the best course of action. The expected value ($E(x)$) is found by multiplying the probability of each outcome by its *payoff*.

$$E(x) = \Sigma x_i p_i$$

where x_i is the outcome for ith possible event and p_i is the probability of occurrence of that outcome. *See also* DECISION-MAKING UNDER UNCERTAINTY; DECISION THEORY.

EXPECTED VALUE OF PERFECT INFORMATION maximum amount a decision maker is willing to pay for perfect information. It is the difference between expected profit under conditions of UNCERTAINTY and EXPECTED VALUE WITH PERFECT INFORMATION. For example, assume that the expected value of perfect information is calculated as $2.50. There is no sense in paying more than $2.50 for the perfect forecast; to do so would lower the expected profit. *See also* DECISION THEORY.

EXPECTED VOLUME estimated volume of activity for a future period based on forecasts of sales of product or service, adjusted for planned changes in inventory levels. For example, assume on June 30 there are 10,000 finished units on hand. Sales for July are expected to be 50,000 units, and management wishes to have an inventory of 20,000 units on hand on July 31 in order to fill a growing demand. Then the expected production volume for July is 60,000 units (50,000 planned sales + 20,000 desired inventory − 10,000 beginning inventory). *See also* PRODUCTION BUDGET.

EXPENDITURE
1. payment of cash or property, or the incurrence of a liability to obtain an asset or service.
2. in GOVERNMENT ACCOUNTING, the incurrence of an actual liability in accordance with governmental authority.

EXPENSE results from or measures the using up of an asset (e.g., depreciation) or incurrence of a liability (e.g., warranty expense) to *obtain revenue* in the *current period*. An expense can apply to the cost of merchandise sold or services rendered. Expenses apply to the ordinary course of business (e.g., salary expense) rather than to incidental transactions (e.g., fire loss). Expenses are deducted from revenue to derive net income. An expense account is maintained for each type of expense for control purposes. *See also* COST; LOSS.

EXPERT SYSTEMS computer software involving stored reasoning schemes and containing decision making processes of human experts in an area. This is the area of ARTIFICIAL INTELLIGENCE (AI) that has received great attention from business decision makers. Recent advances have been made in this area of software systems that are designed to mimic the way human experts make decisions, providing computerized consultants. In effect, the expert system evaluates and solves problems requiring human imagination and intelligence that involve known and unknown information. The components of the systems include a knowledge base, inference engine, user interface, and knowledge acquisition facility.

EXPIRED COST a cost that will not provide any future benefit.

EXPONENTIAL SMOOTHING forecasting technique that uses a weighted moving average of past data as the basis for a forecast. The procedure gives heaviest weight to more recent information and smaller weight to observations in the more distant past. The reason for this is that the future may be more dependent upon the recent past than on the distant past. The method is effective when there is random demand and no seasonal fluctuations in the data. It is a popular technique for short-run forecasting by business forecasters. Each new forecast is based on the previous forecast *plus* a percentage of the difference between that forecast and the actual value of the time series at that point. That is:

$$\text{New Forecast} = \text{Old Forecast} + \alpha \, (\text{Actual} - \text{Old Forecast})$$

where α is a percentage, known as a smoothing constant and (Actual – Old Forecast) represents the prediction error. More concisely, we have

$$F(t + 1) = F(t) + \alpha \, (A(t) - F(t))$$

where F = forecast, A = actual, and $t + 1$ = forecast period. For example, assume that cash collections from credit sales are forecast by exponential smoothing using a smoothing constant of $\alpha = .30$. Suppose that the previous forecast for the latest period was \$20,000 and that actual cash collections were \$21,000. What is the forecast for the next period?

$$F \, (\text{next period}) = \$20,000 + (.30)(\$21,000 - \$20,000) = \$20,300$$

EXPOSURE DRAFT proposed Statement of Financial Accounting Standards or Concepts issued by the FINANCIAL ACCOUNTING STANDARDS BOARD (FASB). Exposure gives the public an opportunity to comment upon the draft before it is finalized and issued as an FASB pronouncement.

EX-RIGHTS term used to indicate that a stock is selling without a recently declared stock right. As with dividends, the ex-right date is generally four business days prior to the DATE OF RECORD.

EXTENDED NORMAL COSTING costing method that assigns direct costs to cost objects using budgeted rates and actual quantities of inputs. It assigns overhead based on budgeted rates and the actual quantity of the base used for cost assignment. This approach is prevalent in the service sector. Accordingly, overhead is assigned under normal costing to each job through a predetermined overhead rate equal to the budgeted overhead divided by the budgeted amount of the appropriate denominator measure. In a traditional system, a single overhead rate might be established for an entire department, e.g., \$3 of overhead for every direct labor-hour. If ABC is used, however, the multiple activities that use resources classified as overhead will be identified, a cost pool will be established for each activity, and the costs in each pool will be assigned based on the driver specific to the activity. If a driver cannot be easily identified, overhead is assigned to products or services using an allocation procedure; that is, it is determined using some indirect measure.

EXTENSIBLE BUSINESS REPORTING LANGUAGE (XBRL) formerly code named XFRML, a freely availabile electronic language for financial reporting. It is an XML-based framework that provides the financial community a standards-based method to prepare, publish in a variety of formats, reliably extract, and automatically exchange financial statements of publicly held companies and the information they contain. XBRL is not about establishing new accounting standards but enhancing the usability of the ones that we have through the digital language of business. XBRL will not require additional disclosure from companies to outside audiences. This new language allows the financial community to communicate in a universal language.

EXTENSIBLE BUSINESS REPORTING LANGUAGE On May 30, 2008, the SEC issued a proposal that would require companies to provide XBRL financial statements, as well as posting such statements to company Web sites. The SEC approved this proposal at their December 17, 2008, open meeting. The final rules will initially apply to domestic and foreign companies using U.S. GAAP and, eventually, to foreign private issuers using International Financial Reporting Standards (IFRS) as issued by the International Accounting Standards Board (IASB). The XBRL financial statements will be required, as an exhibit, with a company's traditionally filed (ASCII or HTML formatted) annual and quarterly reports, transition reports, and Securities Act registration statements. The information produced in an XBRL format will include companies' primary financial statements, footnote disclosures, and financial statement schedules.

EXTENSION OF TIME FOR FILING time period for filing a tax return that is extended beyond the due date. The typical extension granted to individuals and corporations is six months. Partnerships, estates, and trusts usually get a five-month extension. The taxpayer must file an application requesting the extension by the due date of the return. Interest will be charged for deficient estimated tax payments.

EXTERNAL AUDIT audit conducted by an *independent public accountant*. It refers to the type of audit and not the place of the audit. The entity's records may be subject to an audit by a CPA with an audit opinion rendered. *See also* INTERNAL AUDIT.

EXTERNAL AUDITOR independent public accountant who examines a business entity's books. The external auditor is not an employee of the company. *See also* INTERNAL AUDITOR.

EXTERNAL DOCUMENT term applies to documents needed for the company record keeping that has somehow been handled by outside individuals. Vendor invoices and cancelled checks are examples. The auditor can place much more reliance on external documents than INTERNAL DOCUMENTS because of the greater independence and verifiability associated with them.

EXTERNAL FAILURE COSTS a category of QUALITY COSTS incurred because products fail to conform to requirements after being sold to customers. They include warranty costs, returns, and lost sales.

EXTRANET private network that uses the Internet protocols and the public telecommunication system to securely share part of a business's information or operations with suppliers, vendors, partners, customers, or other businesses. An extranet can be viewed as part of a company's INTRANET that is extended to users outside the company.

EXTRAORDINARY ITEM one that is *both* unusual in nature and infrequent in occurrence. Extraordinary gains and losses are presented NET OF TAX separately in the income statement. They appear between INCOME FROM DISCONTINUED OPERATIONS and cumulative effect of a CHANGE IN ACCOUNTING PRINCIPLE. Examples of extraordinary items are casualty losses, losses from expropriation of assets by a foreign government, gain on life insurance, gain or loss on the early extinguishment of debt, gain on troubled debt restructuring, and write-off of an intangible asset.

Write-down and write-off of receivables and inventory are *not* extraordinary because they relate to normal business operational activities. They would be considered extraordinary, however, if they resulted from an Act of God (e.g., casualty loss arising from an earthquake) or governmental expropriation.

EXTRAORDINARY REPAIRS work that extends the life of a fixed asset more than one year and that is capitalized rather than expensed. An example is a new motor for a truck. Extraordinary repairs are charged to the accumulated depreciation account, thus increasing the book value of the asset. The asset is then depreciated over the new life. Assume on 1/1/2014 a truck costing $20,000 with a 10-year life is purchased. The book value on 12/31/2017 is $12,000 ($20,000 – $8,000). On 1/1/2018, an extraordinary repair of $6000 is made. The entry is to debit accumulated depreciation and credit cash for $6,000. The new book value on 1/1/2018 is thus $18,000 ($20,000 – $2,000). As a result of the expenditure, the *new* remaining life is 8 years rather than 6 years. The depreciation expense each year starting in 2018 is $2,250 ($18,000/8 years).

F

FACE VALUE nominal amount of a debt obligation (e.g., note, bond, mortgage) or equity security as stated in the instrument. It excludes interest and dividends. The face value of an instrument is often different from its issuance price; for example, a bond may be issued at a BOND DISCOUNT or BOND PREMIUM. Also, after issuance the going market price of an instrument will typically differ from its face value. At MATURITY, the debt instrument will be redeemed at its face amount. The nominal amount of a share of stock represents its PAR VALUE or stated value. *See also* MATURITY VALUE.

FACILITY LEVEL ACTIVITIES activities performed to support a facility's general manufacturing process.

FACTORING outright sale of a firm's accounts receivable to another party (the factor) *without recourse*, which means the factor must bear the risk of collection. Some banks and commercial finance companies factor (buy) accounts receivable. The purchase is made at a discount from the account's value. Customers either remit directly to the factor (notification basis) or indirectly through the seller (non-notification basis).

FACTORY BURDEN *see* FACTORY OVERHEAD.

FACTORY LEDGER group of accounts used to record factory-related transactions and to keep track of various manufacturing costs such as direct materials, direct labor, and factory overhead costs. It is a record kept by a factory.

FACTORY OVERHEAD total of all costs of manufacturing except direct materials and direct labor, also called *manufacturing overhead, indirect manufacturing expenses, factory expenses,* and *factory burden.* In addition to INDIRECT MATERIALS and INDIRECT LABOR, it includes such items as depreciation, setup costs, quality costs, cleanup costs, fringe benefits, payroll taxes, and insurance. It is an inventoriable cost charged by allocation to WORK-IN-PROCESS.

FACTORY OVERHEAD BUDGET schedule of all expected manufacturing costs except for direct material and direct labor. Factory overhead items include indirect material, indirect labor, factory rent, and factory insurance. Factory overhead may be variable, fixed, or a combination of both.

FAILURE COSTS quality control costs that are associated with products or services that have been found not to conform to requirements, as well as all related costs (such as that of the complaint department); they may be internal or external. *See also* EXTERNAL FAILURE COSTS; INTERNAL FAILURE COSTS.

FAILURE TO FILE PENALTY at the federal level is equal to 5% of the tax due for each month (or part thereof) that the tax return is not filed. The failure to file penalty is limited to 25%. The failure to file penalty is reduced by the FAILURE TO PAY PENALTY.

FAILURE TO PAY PENALTY at the federal level is equal to one-half of 1% of the unpaid tax for each month (or part thereof). The failure to pay penalty is limited to 25%.

FAIR AND ACCURATE CREDIT TRANSACTIONS (FACT) ACT OF 2003 a law that mandates the public's access to free copies of their reports, which track the amount of debt consumers have and whether they pay their bills on time. The law is better known as the FACT Act.

FAIR LABOR STANDARDS ACT (FLSA) act enacted in 1938 that applies to workers involved in interstate commerce. It sets standards with respect to working conditions, including such aspects as minimum wage and working hours. It has been periodically amended and adjusted to keep the standards relevant to the current working environment.

FAIR MARKET VALUE amount that could be received on the sale of an asset when willing and financially capable buyers and sellers exist and there are no unusual circumstances such as liquidation, shortages, and emergencies. *See also* LIQUIDATION VALUE.

FAIRNESS term indicating that an entity's financial condition and *operating results* are presented in a way that is understandable, appropriate, and comprehensive. Fairly presented financial statements are *not* slanted to favor one party over another and are not subject to management influence and limitations.

FAIR TRADE PRICE one that is mandated or fixed by a manufacturer for a specific product to decrease or remove any competition between wholesalers and retailers on the basis of price. In 1975 Congress repealed federal laws upholding the power of states to protect manufacturers through fair trade legislation.

FASB *see* FINANCIAL ACCOUNTING STANDARDS BOARD (FASB).

FASB ACCOUNTING STANDARDS CODIFICATION the FASB's Codification (http://asc.fasb.org/home) that is intended to simplify user access to all authoritative U.S. generally accepted accounting principles (GAAP) by providing all the authoritative literature related to a particular topic in one place. The Codification is organized into approximately 90 accounting topics. The Accounting Standards Codification (ASC) is not intended to change existing U.S. GAAP, but rather integrates existing accounting standards by multiple standard-setters within the current GAAP hierarchy. The Codification is the single official source of authoritative, nongovernmental U.S. GAAP, superseding existing FASB, AICPA, EITF, and related literature. Going forward, U.S. GAAP will no longer be issued in the form of an "accounting standard," but rather as an update to the applicable "topic" or "subtopic" within the Codification. As such, accounting guidance will be classified as either "authoritative" or "nonauthoritative" based on its inclusion or exclusion from the Codification.

The Codification content is arranged within (a) Topics, (b) Subtopics, (c) Sections, and (d) Subsections, as follows:

- Topics. Topics represent a collection of related guidance and reside in four main areas: (1) presentation (e.g., income statement, balance sheet); (2) financial statement accounts (e.g., assets, liabilities, equity); (3) broad transactions (e.g., business combinations, derivatives); and (4) industries (e.g., airlines, real estate).
- Subtopics. Subtopics represent subsets of a "Topic" and are generally distinguished by type or by scope. For example, "Operating Leases" and "Capital Leases" are two Subtopics of the "Leases" Topic.
- Sections. Sections represent the nature of the content in a "Subtopic" (e.g., recognition, measurement, disclosure).

- Subsections. Sections are further broken down into subsections, paragraphs, and subparagraphs.

The following is the structure of the classification system: XXX-YY-ZZ-PP, where:

XXX = Topic
YY = Subtopic
ZZ = Section
PP = Paragraph

For example, Statement of Financial Accounting Standards No. 141R (FAS-141R), *Business Combinations,* is now ASC 805-10, *Business Combinations-Overall.*

FAULT TOLERANCE a system that is able to continue in the event of a hardware failure. This is achieved by having multiples of all critical components, such as CPUs, memories, storage devices, and power supplies, into the same computer. If one component fails, another one automatically takes over. Hardware redundancy is the key to a fault tolerant system; of course, this redundancy in hardware results in a significant cost increase. Note that the processing capability of the computer system remains the same after hardware failure.

FAVORABLE VARIANCE excess of standard (or budgeted) costs over actual costs. *See also* STANDARD COST SYSTEM; VARIANCE.

FBAR the abbreviation for Report of Foreign Bank and Financial Accounts. An FBAR is required to be filed electronically (on or before June 30 of the year following the calendar year reported) with the Department of Treasury if (1) a U.S. taxpayer had a financial interest in or signature power over at least one financial account located outside of the U.S., and (2) the total value of all foreign financial accounts exceeded $10,000 at any time during the calendar year. Taxpayers subject to FBAR filing requirements include individuals, corporations, partnerships, and limited liability companies.

FEASIBILITY STUDY evaluation of a contemplated project or course of action, according to preestablished criteria (such as NET PRESENT VALUE, INTERNAL RATE OF RETURN, and *payback*) to determine if the proposal meets management requirements. An analysis is also made of alternative means of accomplishing the task. *See also* CAPITAL BUDGETING.

FEASIBLE SOLUTION values of decision variables that simultaneously satisfy all the restrictions of a LINEAR PROGRAMMING (LP) problem. Feasible solutions are found in the feasible region. The OPTIMAL SOLUTION is usually found at the corner of the region. *See also* GRAPHICAL METHOD.

FEDERAL INCOME TAXES levies by the federal government on personal and corporate income. Personal income taxes are government revenues collected from the earnings of individuals and unincorporated businesses, after allowance for certain exemptions and deductions. Corporate income taxes are revenues collected on a corporation's computed profits. Most federal tax revenues come from these sources.

FEDERAL INSURANCE CONTRIBUTION ACT (FICA) law dealing with SOCIAL SECURITY TAXES and benefits. The taxes withheld from the employee's wages for Social Security are called FICA taxes. The FICA taxes depend upon the tax rate and the base amount of the wages subject to the tax.

FEDERAL RESERVE BANK district bank of the Federal Reserve System. *See also* FEDERAL RESERVE BOARD (SYSTEM).

FEDERAL RESERVE BOARD (SYSTEM) organization created by an act of Congress in 1913. The System is made up of twelve *Federal Reserve District Banks*, their 24 branches, and many national and state banks throughout the nation. It is headed by a seven-member Board of Governors. The primary function of the Board is to establish and conduct the nation's monetary policy. The System manages the nation's monetary policy by exercising control over the money stock. It controls the money supply primarily in three ways: (1) by raising or lowering the reserve requirement; (2) by setting the DISCOUNT RATE for loans to commercial banks; and (3) through its open market operations by purchasing and selling government securities, mainly three-month bills and notes issued by the U.S. Treasury. The System also serves as the central bank of the United States, a banker's bank that offers banks many of the same services that banks provide their customers. It performs many other functions. It sets margin requirements, regulates member banks, and acts as Fiscal Agent in the issuance of U.S. Treasury and U.S. Government agency securities.

FEDERAL TRADE COMMISSION (FTC) organization created by the Federal Trade Commission Act in 1914. It is responsible for thwarting "unfair methods of competition" and preventing monopolies and activities in restraint of trade. It also investigates cases of industrial espionage, bribery for the purpose of obtaining trade secrets or gaining business, and boycotts.

FEDERAL UNEMPLOYMENT TAX ACT (FUTA) Social Security legislation affecting labor costs and payroll records. Unlike the FEDERAL INSURANCE CONTRIBUTION ACT (FICA), which is strictly a federal program, FUTA provides for cooperation between state and federal governments in the establishment and administration of unemployment insurance. Under FUTA, an employer must pay an unemployment insurance tax to the federal government. While the federal act requires no employee contribution, some states levy an unemployment tax on the employee.

FEEDBACK term used to refer to information concerning actual performance, particularly in comparison with the plan. The feedback process is a critical part of a management control system in order to test a given system or model to see if it is performing as planned. Timely feedback enables quick corrective action when things get out of hand.

FEES charges billed for services rendered. They are tied into the monetary value of those services. Professional fees apply to accounting, tax, and legal work. They may be on a flat basis or an hourly one. For example, the accountant may charge a client $5,000 per year for all services or $100 per hour times the hours worked.

FICO CREDIT SCORE an acronym for Fair, Isaac & Company. A computer-generated credit score that predicts a lender's risk in doing business with a borrower. Any company or individual that issues mortgage loans, home-equity loans, car loans, insurance policies, or health care services (even the IRS) bases much of its lending decisions and terms on the applicant's FICO score. FICO scores are determined by computers and released through the three credit bureaus to their subscribing members. At Experian, the scores are called Experian/Fair, Isaac; at Equifax, they are called Beacon scores; at

Trans Union, they are called Empirica scores. FICO scores five main kinds of credit information. Listed from most important to least important showing the percentage of the score based on the category, the categories are: (1) payment history (approximately 35% of score); (2) amount owed (approximately 30%); (3) length of credit history (approximately 15%); (4) new credit (approximately 10%); and (5) types of credit in use (approximately 10%). Credit scores range from 300 to 850. Scores provide an extremely valuable guide to future risk based solely on credit report data. The higher the consumer's score, the lower the risk to lenders when extending new credit to a consumer.

FIDELITY BOND insurance coverage against specified losses that occur from the dishonest acts or defalcations of employees. This bond may be applied to persons or positions.

FIDUCIARY individual or institution responsible for holding or administering property owned by another. An executor, guardian, trustee, and administrator are examples of a fiduciary. The PRUDENT MAN RULE is one way states ensure that fiduciaries invest responsibly.

FIDUCIARY ACCOUNTING proper accounting for property that is entrusted to the fiduciary acting under the conditions set forth in a deed. *See also* CHARGE AND DISCHARGE STATEMENTS.

FIDUCIARY FUND term used when a governmental unit acts in a fiduciary capacity such as a trustee or agent. The government unit is responsible for handling the assets placed under its control.

FIELD group of adjacent characters. For example, in a company's payroll system, separate fields can exist for an employee's name, employee's Social Security number, and hourly rate. *See also* RECORD.

FIELD AUDITOR individual who conducts audits at locations other than central headquarters such as in distant divisions and branches. *See also* TRAVELING AUDITOR.

FIFO *see* FIRST-IN, FIRST-OUT.

FILE collection of information stored as *records*. For example, the records for all charge customers at the local department store collectively form the *accounts receivable file*. Thus Mr. Smith's account is an *accounts receivable record*. A record that describes a single business activity is called a transaction record. Thus, when Mr. Smith buys a new suit on credit, the sales clerk writes up a credit sales ticket as a *transaction record*. The total set of credit sales tickets for that day would collectively comprise a *daily credit sales transaction file*.

FILE TRANSFER PROTOCOL (FTP) a standard TCP/IP for transmitting files between computers on the Internet. Using FTP, one can also copy, delete, rename, and move files on a server.

FILING STATUS one of four basic categories for taxpayer filing: (1) married, filing a joint return; (2) married, filing separately; (3) head of household; and (4) single. The filing status determines the tax rate schedules to be used to compute tax liability. Tax rates generally increase in each category with the respective order listed above.

FINANCIAL ACCOUNTING information developed in conformity with GENERALLY ACCEPTED ACCOUNTING PRINCIPLES (GAAP). It involves the recording and summarization of business transactions and events. Financial accounting relates to the preparation of financial statements for external users such as creditors, investors, and suppliers. The financial statements include the balance sheet, income statement, and statement of changes in financial position. These statements, including related footnotes, President's letter, management's discussion of operations, etc., appear in the annual report. *See also* MANAGEMENT ACCOUNTING.

FINANCIAL ACCOUNTING FOUNDATION (FAF) institution that funds the FINANCIAL ACCOUNTING STANDARDS BOARD (FASB) and appoints its members. Founded in 1972, the FAF is composed of nine trustees chosen by the board of directors of the AMERICAN INSTITUTE OF CERTIFIED PUBLIC ACCOUNTANTS (AICPA). They are the president of the AICPA, four CPAs who are accounting practitioners in public practice, two financial executives, one financial analyst, and one academician. Organizations that sponsor the FAF are AICPA, Financial Executives Institute, Financial Analysts Federation, National Association of Accountants, Securities Industry Association, and American Accounting Association.

FINANCIAL ACCOUNTING STANDARDS BOARD (FASB) (www.fasb. org) nongovernmental body with the authority to promulgate U.S. GENERALLY ACCEPTED ACCOUNTING PRINCIPLES (GAAP) and reporting practices. These are published in the form of FASB Statements. Practicing CPAs are required to follow the FASB pronouncements in their accounting and financial reporting functions. The FASB is *independent* of other companies and professional organizations. The AMERICAN INSTITUTE OF CERTIFIED PUBLIC ACCOUNTANTS (AICPA) and the SECURITIES AND EXCHANGE COMMISSION officially recognize the Statements issued by the Financial Accounting Standards Board. The FASB was established in 1973 to succeed the Accounting Principles Board (APB). *See also* FINANCIAL ACCOUNTING FOUNDATION.

FINANCIAL ANALYSIS use and transformation of financial data into a form that can be used to monitor and evaluate the firm's financial position, to plan future financing, and to designate the size of the firm and its rate of growth. Financial analysis includes the use of FINANCIAL STATEMENT ANALYSIS and FUNDS FLOW ANALYSIS.

FINANCIAL ANALYSIS SOFTWARE software capable of taking financial data from an online database to perform ratio and trend calculations. Investment and credit decisions are based on the analysis results.

FINANCIAL ANALYSTS JOURNAL bimonthly publication of the CFA Institute (www.cfapubs.org). Its readership includes financial analysts and executives. Subject matter covers security analysis, portfolio management, financial accounting theory, professional ethics, financial management, financial planning, and taxation.

FINANCIAL BUDGET one that embraces the impacts of the financial decisions of the firm. It is a plan including a BUDGETED BALANCE SHEET, which shows the effects of planned operations and capital investments on assets, liabilities, and equities. It also includes a CASH BUDGET, which forecasts the flow of cash and other funds in the business. Cash budgeting (cash planning) is a critical part of budgeting because it is essential to have the right sums of cash available at the right times.

FINANCIAL CRISIS

1. a situation in which the supply of money is outpaced by the demand for money. This means that liquidity evaporates quickly because available money is withdrawn from banks (called a run), forcing banks either to sell other investments to make up for the shortfall or to collapse.
2. the global financial crisis of 2008–2009 emerged in September 2008 with the failure, merger, or conservatorship of several large U.S.-based financial institutions, such as investment banks, insurance firms, and mortgage banks, consequent to the subprime mortgage crisis, and spread with the insolvency of additional companies, and of governments in Europe, recession, and declining stock market prices around the globe.

FINANCIAL DECISIONS decisions that involve: (1) determining the proper amount of funds to employ in a firm; (2) selecting projects and capital expenditure analysis; (3) raising funds on the most favorable terms possible; and (4) managing working capital such as inventory and accounts receivable.

FINANCIAL DERIVATIVE *see* DERIVATIVE.

FINANCIAL ENGINEERING application of economic principles to the dynamics of securities markets, especially for the purpose of structuring, pricing, and managing the risk of financial contracts.

FINANCIAL EXECUTIVES monthly publication of the FINANCIAL EXECUTIVES INSTITUTE (FEI) (www.financialexecutives.org). It is directed toward corporate financial executives and covers all aspects of financial management.

FINANCIAL EXECUTIVES INSTITUTE (FEI) (www.financial executives.org) organization primarily of controllers and treasurers as well as other executives involved in the accounting and financial functions. Its Corporate Reporting Committee represents the organization before authoritative accounting bodies. Research publications are supported and published by the Financial Executives Research Foundation.

FINANCIAL FORECAST *see* FINANCIAL PROJECTION.

FINANCIAL FUTURE contract to buy or sell a financial instrument at a specific price in a specified future month. There is a relationship between the price of the contract and the interest rate the underlying instrument bears; the contract's value decreases as market interest rates increase and vice versa. Some types of financial instruments used in financial futures contracts are Treasury bills, Treasury notes, Ginnie Maes, and certificates of deposit. Futures contracts are used to speculate on interest rate changes and to hedge investment portfolios against adverse movements in interest rates. Currency futures, a form of financial futures, are used to speculate on foreign exchange rates and to hedge currency values. These contracts are supervised by the Commodities Futures Trading Commission.

FINANCIAL HIGHLIGHT section of corporate annual reports that summarizes key financial data on a comparative basis. Sales, earnings per share (primary and after dilution), and dividends are always highlighted along with other information the company considers noteworthy.

FINANCIAL INDUSTRY REGULATORY AUTHORITY (FINRA) created in 1987 as a result of the merger of the National Association of Securities Dealers (NASD) and the regulation Committee of the New York Stock Exchange. The goal of FINRA, a not-for-profit organization, is to protect investors by establishing and enforcing ethical standards. *See also* NATIONAL ASSOCIATION OF SECURITIES DEALERS (NASD).

FINANCIAL INFORMATION SYSTEM term for a system that accumulates and analyzes financial data in order to make good financial management decisions in running the business. The basic objective of the financial information system is to meet the firm's financial obligations as they come due, using the minimal amount of financial resources consistent with an established margin of safety. Outputs generated by the system include accounting reports, operating and capital budgets, working capital reports, cash flow forecast, and various WHAT-IF ANALYSIS reports. The evaluation of financial data may be performed through ratio analysis, trend evaluation, and financial planning modeling. Financial planning and forecasting are facilitated if used in conjunction with a DECISION SUPPORT SYSTEM (DSS).

FINANCIAL LEVERAGE portion of a firm's assets financed with debt instead of equity. It involves contractual interest and principal obligations. Financial leverage benefits common stockholders as long as the borrowed funds generate a return in excess of the cost of borrowing, although the increased risk can offset the general cost of capital. For this reason, financial leverage is popularly called TRADING ON EQUITY. Financial leverage is measured by the DEBT-EQUITY RATIO.

FINANCIAL MODEL functional branch of a general CORPORATE PLANNING MODEL. It is used essentially to generate PRO FORMA financial statements and financial ratios. A financial model is a mathematical model describing the interrelationships among financial variables of the firm. It is the basic tool for budgeting and budget planning. Also, it is used for risk analysis and WHAT-IF experiments. Many financial models use spreadsheet programs such as EXCEL and LOTUS 1-2-3. *See also* CORPORATE PLANNING MODEL.

FINANCIAL PLANNER professional engaged in providing PERSONAL FINANCIAL PLANNING services to individuals. A financial planner assists a client in the following ways: (1) assesses a client's financial history, such as tax returns, investments, retirement plan, wills, and insurance policies; (2) helps decide on a financial plan, based on personal and financial goals, history, and preferences; (3) identifies financial areas where a client may need help, such as building up retirement income or improving investment return; (4) prepares a financial plan based on the individual situation and discusses it thoroughly; (5) helps implement the financial plan, including referring the client to specialists, such as lawyers or accountants, if necessary; and (6) reviews the situation and financial plan periodically and suggests changes when needed. Financial planners come from a variety of backgrounds and, therefore, may hold a variety of degrees and licenses. They include such credentials as Certified Financial Planner (CFP), Chartered Financial Consultant (ChFC), lawyer (JD), and Certified Public Accountant (CPA).

FINANCIAL PLANNING MODELS *see* FINANCIAL MODEL.

FINANCIAL PLANNING SOFTWARE personal finance computer programs that keep track of income and expenses by budget category, reconcile accounts, store tax records, figure net worth, track stocks and bonds, and print checks and financial reports. Some programs are sophisticated enough to generate a detailed, long-term personal financial plan covering planning for college education, investment, and retirement. Examples of financial planning software are *Quicken* and *Managing Your Money*.

FINANCIAL PROJECTION essential element of planning that is the basis for budgeting activities and estimating future financing needs of a firm. Financial projections (forecasts) begin with forecasting sales and their related expenses. The basic steps in financial forecasting are: (1) project the firm's sales; (2) project variables such as expenses and assets; (3) estimate the level of investment in current and fixed assets that is required to support the projected sales; and (4) calculate the firm's financing needs. The basic tools for financial forecasting include the percent-of-sales-method, REGRESSION ANALYSIS, and financial modeling.

FINANCIAL RATIO mathematical relationship between one quantity and another. There are many categories of ratios such as those that evaluate a business entity's liquidity, solvency, return on investment, operating performance, asset utilization, and market measures. An example of a ratio is the earnings yield that equals dividends per share divided by market price per share. Whereas the computation of a ratio is a basic arithmetical operation, its analytical interpretation is more complex. A financial ratio should be computed only if the relationship between accounts or categories has significance. The financial ratio may provide the accountant with clues and symptoms of underlying financial condition. To be meaningful, a given financial ratio of a company for a given year must be compared with (1) prior years to examine the trend, (2) industry norm, and (3) competing companies. *See also* FINANCIAL STATEMENT ANALYSIS.

FINANCIAL RATIO ANALYSIS *see* FINANCIAL STATEMENT ANALYSIS.

FINANCIAL REPORTING presenting financial data of a company's position, operating performance, and funds flow for an accounting period. Financial statements along with related information may be contained in various forms for external party use such as in the annual report, SEC Form 10-K, and prospectus.

FINANCIAL REPORTING FRAMEWORK FOR SMALL- AND MEDIUM-SIZED ENTITIES (FRF FOR SMEs) represents an accounting option for the preparation of financial statements for privately held, owner-managed businesses that are not required to follow U.S. GENERALLY ACCEPTED ACCOUNTING PRINCIPLES (GAAP). FRF FOR SMEs, which was developed by the American Institute of Certified Public Accountants, is not considered to be authoritative.

FINANCIAL RISK portion of total corporate risk, over and above basic BUSINESS RISK, that results from using debt. Business risk is caused by fluctuations of earnings before interest and taxes (operating income). Business risk depends on variability in demand, sales price, input prices, and amount of OPERATING LEVERAGE. Financial risk includes DEFAULT risk, which is the risk that the borrower will be unable to make interest payments or principal repayments on debt. The greater the firm's FINANCIAL LEVERAGE, the higher is its financial risk.

FINANCIAL STATEMENT report containing financial information about an organization. The required financial statements are balance sheet, income statement, and statement of changes in financial position. They may be combined with a supplementary statement to depict the financial status or performance of the organization. An example of a supplementary statement is an inflation-adjusted financial statement. Some supplementary material is required only for publicly held companies.

FINANCIAL STATEMENT ANALYSIS method used by interested parties such as investors, creditors, and management to evaluate the past, current, and projected conditions and performance of the firm. Ratio analysis is the most common form of financial analysis. It provides relative measures of the firm's conditions and performance. HORIZONTAL ANALYSIS and VERTICAL ANALYSIS are also popular forms. Horizontal analysis is used to evaluate the trend in the accounts over the years, while vertical analysis, also called a COMMON SIZE FINANCIAL STATEMENT, discloses the internal structure of the firm. It indicates the existing relationship between sales and each income statement account. It shows the mix of assets that produce income and the mix of the sources of capital, whether by current or long-term debt or by equity funding. When using the financial ratios, a financial analyst makes two types of comparisons:

(1) *Industry comparison.* The ratios of a firm are compared with those of similar firms or with industry averages or norms to determine how the company is faring relative to its competitors. Industry average ratios are available from a number of sources, including: (a) Dun & Bradstreet. Dun & Bradstreet computes 14 ratios for each of 125 lines of business. They are published in *Dun's Review* and *Key Business Ratios.* (b) Risk Management Association (RMA). This association of bank loan officers publishes *Annual Statement Studies.* Sixteen ratios are computed for more than 300 lines of business, as well as a percentage distribution of items on the balance sheet and income statement (*common size financial statements*).

(2) *Trend analysis.* A firm's present ratio is compared with its past and expected future ratios to determine whether the company's financial condition is improving or deteriorating over time.

After completing the financial statement analysis, the firm's financial analyst will consult with management to discuss plans and prospects, any problem areas identified in the analysis, and possible solutions. Given below is a list of widely used financial ratios.

Financial Statement Analysis: List of Ratios

Liquidity

Net Working Capital   Current Assets − Current Liabilities

Current Ratio $$\frac{\text{Current Assets}}{\text{Current Liabilities}}$$

Quick Ratio $$\frac{\text{Cash + Marketable Securities + Receivables}}{\text{Current Liabilities}}$$

Activity

Accounts Receivable

$$\frac{\text{Net Credit Sales}}{\text{Average Accounts Receivable}}$$

Average Collection Period

$$\frac{365}{\text{Accounts Receivable Turnover}}$$

Inventory Turnover

$$\frac{\text{Cost Of Goods Sold}}{\text{Average Inventory}}$$

Average Age of Inventory

$$\frac{365}{\text{Inventory Turnover}}$$

Total Asset Turnover

$$\frac{\text{Net Sales}}{\text{Average Total Assets}}$$

Leverage

Debt Ratio

$$\frac{\text{Total Debt}}{\text{Total Assets}}$$

Debt/Equity Ratio

$$\frac{\text{Total Liabilities}}{\text{Stockholders' Equity}}$$

Times Interest Earned

$$\frac{\text{Earnings Before Interest \& Taxes}}{\text{Interest Expense}}$$

Profitability

Gross Profit Margin

$$\frac{\text{Gross Profit}}{\text{Net Sales}}$$

Profit Margin

$$\frac{\text{Net Income}}{\text{Net Sales}}$$

Return On Total Assets

$$\frac{\text{Net Income}}{\text{Average Total Assets}}$$

Return On Common Equity

$$\frac{\text{Net Income}}{\text{Common Equity}}$$

Market Value

Earnings Per Share

$$\frac{\text{Net Income} - \text{Preferred Dividends}}{\text{Common Stock Outstanding}}$$

Price/Earnings Ratio

$$\frac{\text{Market Price Per Share}}{\text{Earnings Per Share}}$$

Book Value Per Share

$$\frac{\text{Stockholders' Equity} - \text{Preferred Stock}}{\text{Common Stock Outstanding}}$$

Dividend Yield	Dividends Per Share
	Market Price Per Share
Dividend Payout	Dividends Per Share
	Earnings Per Share

FINANCIAL STATEMENT AUDIT one performed by a CPA for the purpose of expressing an opinion as to the fairness of the information contained in the financial statements. The audit work is conducted in accordance with GENERALLY ACCEPTED AUDITING STANDARDS (GAAS) and includes those reviews of internal controls, tests, and verification of data and other activities deemed necessary by the auditor. Typically, annual financial statements are subject to audit while interim statements are not.

FINANCING ACTIVITIES transactions including the distribution, acquisition, movement, and management of money, in accordance with some overall objective, policy, or goal.

FINANCING LEASE *see* CAPITAL LEASE.

FINISHED GOODS INVENTORY amount of manufactured product on hand that awaits sale to customers. Finished goods inventory represents a current asset in the balance sheet. The income statement shows both beginning finished goods and ending finished goods only if cost of goods sold is calculated. When goods that were in process are completed, the entry is to debit finished goods and credit work-in-process. When merchandise is sold, the entry is to debit cost of goods sold and credit finished goods. The difference between the sales and cost of goods sold is the gross profit.

FIREWALL a program used to protect a private network from other networks. The firewall application analyzes data packets and determines whether they should be allowed through to the protected network.

FIRST-IN, FIRST-OUT (FIFO) method of inventory valuation that assumes merchandise is sold in the order of its receipt. The first-price in is the first-price out. Hence cost of sales is based on older dollars. Ending inventory is reflected at the most recent prices. Assume the following data regarding inventory during the year:

Jan. 1 Inventory	150 units @ $ 8	= $1,200
Feb. 20 Purchases	200 units @ $ 9	= 1,800
Apr. 12 Purchases	250 units @ $10	= 2,500
Sept. 20 Purchases	200 units @ $11	= 2,200
Goods Available	800	$7,700

Assume physical inventory on December 31 is 430 units. The year-end inventory valuation is:

Last purchase (Sept. 20)	200 units @ $11	= $2,200
Next most recent purchase (Apr. 12)	230 units @ $10	= 2,300
Total	430	$4,500

See also LAST-IN, FIRST-OUT (LIFO).

FIRST-IN, FIRST-OUT (FIFO) COSTING procedure for computing the unit costs of a process by which beginning work-in-process inventory costs are separated from added costs applied in the current period. Thus, there are two unit costs for the period: (1) beginning work-in-process units completed and (2) units started and completed in the same period. Under FIFO, the beginning WORK-IN-PROCESS is assumed to be completed and transferred first. Equivalent units under FIFO costing may be computed as follows:

Units completed + [Ending work-in-process × degree of completion (%)] − [Beginning work-in-process × degree of completion (%)]

To illustrate, the following data relate to the activities of Department A during the month of January:

	Units
Beginning work-in-process (100% complete as to materials; 2/3 complete as to conversion)	1,500
Started this period	5,000
Completed and transferred	5,500
Ending work-in-process (100% complete as to materials; 6/10 complete as to conversion)	1,000

Equivalent production in Department A for the month is computed, using FIFO costing, as follows:

	Materials	Conversion Costs
Units completed and transferred	$5,500	$5,500
Ending work-in-process		
Materials (100%)	1,000	
Conversion costs (60%)		600
Equivalent production	$6,500	$6,100
Minus: Beginning work-in-process		
Materials (100%)	1,500	
Conversion costs (2/3)		1,000
Equivalent production for FIFO	$5,000	$5,100

See also WEIGHTED AVERAGE COSTING.

FIRST-STAGE ALLOCATION *see* RESOURCE COST ASSIGNMENT.

FISCAL YEAR
1. Twelve consecutive months used by a business entity to account for and report on its business operations. Typically, businesses use a fiscal year ending December 31. However, many entities use the natural business year, referring to a year ending at the annual low point in business activity or at the end of a season. For example, governmental units often end their fiscal year on June 30.
2. in taxation, 12-month period ending other than December 31 (calendar year).

FISHBONE DIAGRAMS way of determining likely root causes of a problem, often called cause-and-effect diagrams; also called *an Ishikawa diagram*.

FIXED ASSET item that has physical substance and a life in excess of one year. It is bought for use in the operation of the business and *not* intended for resale to customers. Examples are building, machinery, auto, and land. Fixed assets with the exception of land are subject to DEPRECIATION. Fixed assets are usually referred to as property, plant, and equipment.

FIXED ASSET-TO-EQUITY CAPITAL RATIO computation that indicates the company's ability to satisfy long-term debt. The ratio equals fixed assets divided by equity capital. A ratio greater than 1 means that some of the fixed assets are financed by debt.

FIXED ASSET TURNOVER measurement that reflects the productivity and efficiency of property, plant, and equipment in generating revenue. A high turnover reflects positively on the company's ability to utilize its fixed assets in business operations properly. The turnover equals sales divided by fixed assets.

FIXED ASSET UNIT element making up the fixed asset account. An example is a specific machine within the machinery account.

FIXED BUDGET *see* STATIC (FIXED) BUDGET.

FIXED CHARGE *see* SETUP COST.

FIXED-CHARGE-COVERAGE RATIO equation that indicates whether the company is able to meet its fixed commitments (i.e., interest) from its profits. A high ratio reflects favorably upon the firm's ability to refinance obligations as they mature. The ratio equals earnings available to meet fixed charges divided by fixed charges. Fixed charges include rent and interest. The ratio is:

$$\frac{\text{Net Income Before Taxes and Fixed Charges}}{\text{Fixed Charges}}$$

FIXED COST expenses that remain constant in total regardless of changes in activity within a *relevant* range. Examples are rent, insurance, and taxes. Fixed cost *per unit* changes as volume changes. *See also* VARIABLE COSTS.

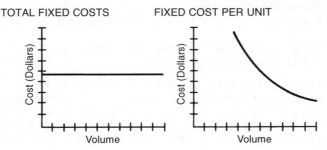

FIXED DISK *see* HARD DISK.

FIXED (FACTORY) OVERHEAD portion of total factory overhead that remains constant over a given time period without regard to changes in the volume of activity. Examples of fixed overhead are depreciation, rent, property taxes, insurance, and salaries of production supervisors.

FIXED OVERHEAD SPENDING (BUDGET) VARIANCE difference between actual fixed overhead incurred and fixed overhead budgeted. This variance is not affected by the level of production.

Fixed Overhead Spending Variance
     = Actual Fixed Overhead –
        Budgeted Fixed Overhead
  or = Actual Overhead –
        (Fixed Overhead Standard Rate
        × Budgeted Hours)

For example, assume actual fixed overhead costs were $31,000. Assume that the denominator activity in machine-hours was 5,000 and the fixed overhead applied rate is $6. The budgeted fixed overhead costs are then $30,000 (5,000 denominator hours × $6). The fixed overhead spending variance is $31,000 – $30,000 = $1,000, which is unfavorable possibly due to events such as unexpected changes in rents, insurance, and property taxes.

FIXED OVERHEAD VARIANCE difference between actual fixed overhead incurred and fixed overhead applied to production.

Fixed Overhead Variance = Fixed Overhead Incurred – Fixed Overhead
                      Applied
               = Fixed Overhead Incurred – (Fixed
                  Overhead Standard Rate × Standard
                  Inputs Allowed for Actual Production)

The total fixed overhead variance is divided into two specific variances: VOL-UME VARIANCE and FIXED OVERHEAD SPENDING (BUDGET) VARIANCE.

FIXED OVERHEAD VOLUME (DENOMINATOR) VARIANCE measure of utilization of plant facilities. It results when the actual activity level is measured in direct labor-hours, machine-hours, and so on. Differs from the budgeted (denominator) quantity used in determining the fixed overhead standard rate.

Fixed Overhead Volume Variance
     = Budgeted Fixed Overhead – Fixed Overhead Applied
or
     = (Denominator Hours – Standard Hours Allowed)
       × Fixed Overhead Standard Rate

The variance is unfavorable if the denominator hours exceed the standard hours allowed; it is favorable in the opposite case. For example, assume actual fixed overhead costs were $31,000. The denominator activity in machine-hours was 5,000 and the fixed overhead applied rate is $6. The budgeted fixed overhead costs are then $30,000 (5,000 denominator hours × $6). The standard machine-hours allowed was 4,000. The fixed overhead volume variance is (5,000 – 4,000) × $6 = $6,000, which is unfavorable because of the company's failure to operate at the budgeted (denominator) activity level. This may be caused by machine breakdowns, poor production scheduling, or failure to meet sales goals.

FIXED PRICE
  1. price that serves as a standard for the valuation of certain inventory accounts (i.e., raw materials, work-in-process, and finished goods) in STANDARD COSTing.

2. price that must be charged under a contract regardless of production costs.

3. economic concept utilized by governmental units establishing a fixed price for a price floor (below which the price is not legally allowed to fall) and price ceilings (above which the price is not legally allowed to rise) on certain regulated goods and services.

4. price at which INVESTMENT BANKERS agree to sell the issue to the investing public in a public offering of new security issues.

FIXTURE fixed asset whose utility is derived from its physical attachment to a property and that usually cannot be removed without causing loss of value or damage. An example is a lighting fixture. A fixture under the terms of a lease or other agreement can be detached. A fixture is classified as a FIXED ASSET.

FLASH REPORT one providing highlights of key information promptly to the responsible managerial accountant; also called EXCEPTION REPORT. An example is an exception report such as PERFORMANCE REPORTS that highlight favorable or unfavorable variances. A flash report allows managers to take a corrective action for an unfavorable variance. *See also* PERFORMANCE REPORT.

FLAT TAX one in which the income tax rate is the same for all income levels. It is a proportional tax. A pure flat tax would eliminate all deductions, exemptions, and loopholes, and tax all income at the same low tax rate. The tax would also make the tax system less complex and more equitable.

FLEXIBLE BUDGET FORMULA *see* COST-VOLUME FORMULA.

FLEXIBLE BUDGETING *see* FLEXIBLE (VARIABLE) BUDGET.

FLEXIBLE BUDGET VARIANCE *see* BUDGET VARIANCE.

FLEXIBLE FACTORY objective of a flexible factory is to provide a wide range of services across many product lines in a timely manner. An example is a fabrication plant with several integrated manufacturing cells that can perform many functions for unrelated product lines with relatively short lead times.

FLEXIBLE MANUFACTURING SYSTEM (FMS) computer-controlled process technology suitable for producing a moderate variety of products in moderate, flexible volumes. This system reduces setup or changeover times and facilitates the production of differentiated products in small numbers. The shift in emphasis is from mass production of a few products to a job-shop environment in which customized orders are manufactured. Automation allows for better quality and scheduling, rapid changes in product lines, and lower inventories and costs. *See also* COMPUTER INTEGRATED MANUFACTURING (CIM).

FLEXIBLE (VARIABLE) BUDGET one based on different levels of activity. It is an extremely useful tool for comparing the actual cost incurred to the cost allowable for the activity level achieved. It is dynamic in nature rather than static. By using the COST-VOLUME FORMULA (or FLEXIBLE BUDGET FORMULA), a series of budgets can be developed easily for various levels of activity. A STATIC (FIXED) BUDGET is geared for only one level of activity and has problems in cost control. Flexible budgeting distinguishes between fixed and variable costs, thus allowing for a budget that can be automatically adjusted (via changes in variable cost totals) to the particular level of activity *actually* attained. Thus variances between actual costs and budgeted costs are adjusted for volume ups and downs before differences due to price and quantity factors are computed. The primary use of the flexible budget is for accurate measure of performance by comparing actual costs for a given output with the budgeted costs for the *same level of output*.

FLEXTIME scheduling concept that allows for nontraditional work hours to be employed on a systematic basis. Hours can be arranged for different times or periods of time to accommodate such aspects as efficiency, traffic, motherhood, disabilities, continuous operations, etc.

FLIPPING buying an investment—such as real estate or stock in an initial public offering (IPO)—in anticipation of reselling it quickly as a profit. Analysts argue that a period of growing popularity of flipping in a rising housing or stock market can signal that a downturn is near.

FLOAT
1. amount of funds represented by checks that have been issued but not yet collected.
2. time between the deposit of checks in a bank and payment. Due to the time difference, many firms are able to "play the float," that is, to write checks against money not presently in the firm's bank account.
3. to issue new securities, usually through an underwriter.

FLOATING CAPITAL net working capital or that part of capital that is invested in current assets of the organization (net of current liabilities) as opposed to its fixed or other capital assets.

FLOATING (FLEXIBLE) EXCHANGE RATE international monetary exchange system in which the prices of currencies are determined by competitive market forces; after 1971 exchange rates between the dollar and other foreign currencies were allowed to float. Under this system, rates, which are determined by the supply and demand for foreign exchange, can change from moment to moment.

FLOPPY DISK *see* DISKETTE.

FLOTATION COST cost of issuing new securities in the market. It consists of (1) the INVESTMENT BANKER'S compensation representing the price the issuer receives versus the price the public pays (commonly referred to as the underwriting spread) and (2) expenses incurred by the issuer such as for legal, accounting, and printing fees. Flotation costs are usually higher for stocks than for bonds. Also, it is a higher percentage of gross proceeds for smaller issues than larger ones.

FLOWCHART traditional method of representing in schematic form the flow of data in a system. The flowchart shows the points of input and output, the logic or sequence of the various processing steps in the system, and the relationship of one element of the system to the other parts of the system or to other information systems.

FLOW OF COSTS cost passing through various classifications within an organization. See the following exhibit for a summary of *product* and *period* cost flows.

FLOW OF COSTS EXHIBIT

FLOW PROCESS CHART description of the sequence of operations in a production process. These generally are operation, inspection, movement, storage, and delay.

FLOW STATEMENT *see* CASH FLOW STATEMENT.

FOCUSED FACTORY objective of a focused factory is to organize around a specific set of resources to provide low cost and high throughput over a narrow range of products.

FOLIO NUMBER manner of referring in a journal or ledger to the origination or disposition of the item. For example, if in the CASH DISBURSEMENTS JOURNAL a debit was made to rent expense having the account number 523, then the number 523 would be put in the folio reference column of the journal.

FOOTING summary of the debits (left side of any account) and credits (right side of any account) to obtain a new balance. An example follows:

Cash

1,000	2,000
500	400
3,000	
4,500	2,400
2,100	

The side that has the largest amount of balance ($4,500) is not moved while the smaller side ($2,400) is brought over and subtracted. The new balance ($2,100) remains on the side that has the larger balance.

FOOTNOTE explanatory data that follows the financial statements and is integrally related to them. Footnotes help the user understand financial statement figures and any other matters essential in gauging a company's financial position. Examples of footnotes are disclosure of accounting policies, lawsuits, pension plan particulars, and tax considerations.

FORCING ALLOCATION costs of a sustaining activity to a cost object even though that cost object may not clearly consume or causally relate to that activity. Allocating a plant-level activity (such as heating) to product units using an activity driver such as direct labor-hours, for example, forces the cost of this activity to the product. *See also* SUSTAINING ACTIVITY COST.

FORECAST
1. projection or estimate of future sales, revenue, earnings, or costs. *See also* SALES FORECASTING.
2. projection of future financial position and operating results of an organization. *See also* FINANCIAL PROJECTION.

FORECLOSURE the forced sale of mortgaged property by the holder of a MORTGAGE to satisfy the indebtedness of the mortgagee. Foreclosure of residential property usually results when a mortgagee stops making payments on a mortgage because the principal balance of the mortgage exceeds the fair value of the property.

FOREIGN CORPORATION
1. corporation that is chartered under state law and resides in a particular state of the union or other country, which is considered a foreign corporation to the remaining states.
2. corporation formed under the laws of a foreign country.

FOREIGN CORRUPT PRACTICES ACT legislation enacted in 1977 to amend the SECURITIES EXCHANGE ACT OF 1934. It provides penalties for certain corrupt practices, such as bribes made to foreign officials, and defines standards relating to internal accounting controls. Management must submit to external audit procedures so the SEC can verify that such internal controls are in place.

FOREIGN CURRENCY FUTURES contracts representing a commitment to buy or sell a specific amount of foreign currency at a later date at a specified rate of exchange. They are used to speculate on currency movements and to hedge currency values.

FOREIGN CURRENCY TRANSACTION one that requires settlement in a currency other than the entity's FUNCTIONAL CURRENCY. A foreign currency transaction gain or loss is produced from redeeming receivables/payables that are fixed in terms of amounts of foreign currency received/paid. That is, a business (1) buys or sells on credit goods or services whose prices are denominated in a foreign currency or (2) borrows or lends funds whose amounts payable or receivable are denominated in a foreign currency. Gain or loss results from changes in exchange rates between the functional currency and the foreign currency in which the transaction is denominated. Foreign transaction gains or losses are typically included in the INCOME STATEMENT for the period in which the exchange rate changes. Gains or losses on foreign currency transactions deemed to be hedges and intercompany transactions of a long-term investment nature (settlement is not anticipated in the foreseeable future) are *not* included in net income but are considered as gain or loss on FOREIGN CURRENCY TRANSLATION shown in the stockholders' equity section.

Assume merchandise is bought by a company in Country X for 100,000 euros. Assume the exchange rate is 0.7 euros = $1. The journal entry is to debit purchases and credit accounts payable for $142,857 (100,000/.7). When the merchandise is paid for, the exchange rate is .8 euros = $1. The cash payment is therefore $125,000. The journal entry is to debit accounts payable for $142,857 and credit cash for $125,000 and foreign exchange gain for $17,857.

FOREIGN CURRENCY TRANSACTION GAIN OR LOSS *see* FOREIGN CURRENCY TRANSACTION.

FOREIGN CURRENCY TRANSLATION process of expressing amounts denominated in one currency in terms of a second currency, by using the exchange rate between the currencies. Assets and liabilities are translated at the current exchange rate at the balance sheet date. Income statement items are typically translated at the weighted-average exchange rate for the period. Cumulative (total) translation gains and losses are reported separately as a component of STOCKHOLDERS' EQUITY under "Accumulated Other Comprehensive Income." They are *not* included in net income unless there is a sale or liquidation of the investment in the foreign entity. *See also* FOREIGN CURRENCY TRANSACTION.

FOREIGN PERSONAL HOLDING COMPANY in taxation, foreign corporation in which more than 50% of the total combined voting power of all classes of voting stock or the total value of the stock is owned by or for no more than five U.S. citizens or residents.

FOREIGN SALES CORPORATION (FSC) tax term for a company incorporated in a foreign country that the United States qualifies as a host country. A country qualifies by entering into an exchange of information agreement of the type that allows tax benefits, such as the Caribbean Basin Initiative. Nonexempt income and certain foreign trade income, which would be taxable on a distribution, are subject to ordinary income treatment. There is a 100% dividends-received deduction for distributions from earnings attributable to foreign trade income of an FSC. There is also an 85% deductible for dividends from earnings attributable to qualified interest and carrying charges derived from a transaction resulting in foreign trade income. *See also* DOMESTIC INTERNATIONAL SALES CORPORATION (DISC).

FOREIGN TAX levy imposed by a foreign government on United States individuals or corporate taxpayers. The tax code generally allows a deduction for these taxes if they were incurred in a trade of business or for the production of income.

FOREIGN TAX CREDIT credit allowed against U.S. income taxes for foreign taxes paid. The credit can be used only to lower U.S. taxes on *income earned overseas*. A foreign tax credit limitation is computed by multiplying the U.S. tax liability prior to the credit by the ratio of foreign taxable income to total taxable income (U.S. and foreign). For example, a taxpayer earns $120,000, half in the U.S. and half in a foreign country. The U.S. tax prior to the tax credit is $40,800 ($120,000 × .34). The foreign tax credit limitation is $20,400 ($60,000/$120,000 × $40,800). Assume foreign taxes paid were $10,000 on the $60,000 income. Thus the foreign tax credit is $10,000. The U.S. tax on the foreign earnings is therefore $10,400 ($20,400 − $10,000).

FORENSIC ACCOUNTING a science (i.e., a department of systemized knowledge) dealing with the application of accounting facts gathered through auditing methods and procedures to resolve legal problems. Forensic accounting is much different from traditional auditing. Forensic accounting is a specialty requiring the integration of investigative, accounting, and auditing skills. The forensic accountant looks at documents and financial and other data in a critical manner in order to draw conclusions and calculate values and to identify irregular patterns and/or suspicious transactions. A forensic accountant does not merely look at the numbers but rather looks *behind* the numbers.

FORFEITURE
1. losing a right or deposit because of the nonoccurrence of an event or action. An example is where one party makes a deposit on property that is later not used, resulting in a loss of the deposit. The recipient of the forfeiture accounts for it as revenue.
2. as per tax law, reallocating a forfeiture in a money purchase plan to other participants under a nondiscriminatory formula or reducing future employer contributions.

FORGERY act of fabricating or producing something falsely. Signing someone else's name on a check and cashing it is a common example.

FORMAT
1. type or version of format used on the storage medium.
2. process of initializing or preparing a disk or form of computer data storage medium, by recording a special pattern of data over the medium's reactive surface, thereby allowing a computer operating system the ability to store and retrieve data.

FORM OF BALANCE SHEET presentation form of a balance sheet, which generally follows one of two formats: (1) the traditional form called the account form, which presents assets on the left and liabilities and owner's equity on the right; and (2) the report form, which presents assets above, liabilities and stockholders' equity below. Both types of format are widely used.

FORTRAN (*FORMULA TRANSLATION*) first high-level programming language, developed by IBM in the late 1950s. It allows programmers to describe calculations by means of mathematical formulas.

FORWARD ACCOUNTING type of accounting that reflects aspects of judgment, PRO FORMA numbers, projections, budgets, and standard costs, as they may affect the future operating environment. Forward costs are distinguished from *historical accounting,* which accounts for past, historical financial activities. MANAGERIAL ACCOUNTING, which involves the use of accounting data for forward planning, control, and decision making, is part of *forward accounting.*

FORWARD CONTRACT a contract similar to a futures contract. However, forward contracts are not uniform or standardized. They are not traded on exchanges. In such a contract, goods are actually delivered at a future date or settlement may be in cash. Forward contracts may be on commodities or instruments. The contract fixes the quantity, price, and date of purchase or sale.

FORWARD EXCHANGE CONTRACT agreement to exchange at a given future date currencies of different countries at a specified rate (forward rate). A forward contract is a FOREIGN CURRENCY TRANSACTION. The gain or loss on the contract is typically included in determining net income. The amount of gain or loss, except on a speculative forward contract (designed as a risky investment rather than as a hedge), is computed by multiplying the foreign currency amount of the forward contract by the difference between the spot rate at the balance sheet date and the spot rate at the date of inception of the contract.

FORWARD FINANCIAL STATEMENT projective and detailed estimate of an organization's financial position. An income statement, balance sheet, and funds flow may be prepared based upon the assumptions in FORWARD ACCOUNTING. These statements are primarily prepared for comparative analysis purposes to evaluate current and future courses of action.

FORWARD RATE price at which two currencies are to be exchanged at some future date.

401(K) PLAN employee investment plan; also called *salary reduction plan.* It allows employees to defer part of their gross salary and to invest the amount in stocks, bonds, or money market funds. The amount is indexed for inflation, using the CONSUMER PRICE INDEX (CPI). Employee contributions and all earnings arising from them go tax-free until withdrawn at the request of the employee or until the employee retires or leaves the company. Usually the employer provides a choice of investment vehicles into which the funds may be placed while earning tax-deferred returns. Furthermore, many employers offer matching contributions. The limitation of annual deferrals to 401(k) plans applies only to an employee's elective deferrals—not the employer's matching funds. These contributions, plus the current reduction in income taxes, make 401(k) salary reduction plans an excellent long-term investment.

FRACTIONAL SHARE unit of stock that is less than one full share. For example, under a dividend reinvestment program, the dividend amount is insufficient to purchase one full share at the present market price of stock. In this case, the stockholder is credited with the fractional share; when there has been an accumulation of sufficient dividends for one share, it will be issued.

FRAMEWORK integrated computer software developed by Ashton-Tate that combines a spreadsheet, a database manager, a word processor, a graphics program, and communications.

FRANCHISE
1. privilege granted by a franchisor to a franchisee permitting the latter to operate using the franchisor's name. The franchisee must pay a franchise fee for such right. In addition, the franchisee is typically required to use the franchisor's products. The franchisee usually receives other benefits from the franchisor, such as advertising.
2. government right granted to an entity giving it a monopolistic advantage (e.g., public utility). *See also* FRANCHISE FEE REVENUE.

FRANCHISE FEE REVENUE revenue obtained by a company that allows an *independent party* to operate a business using its name, merchandise, and supplies. Franchise fee revenue from the initial sale of a franchise is recognized by the franchisor *only* when all material services or conditions applicable to the sale have been *substantially performed.* Substantial performance is indicated by: (1) absence of intent to refund cash received or forgive any unpaid balance; (2) performance of substantially all initial services; and (3) nonexistence of other material conditions related to performance. Commencement of operations by the franchise is presumed to be the earliest possible time at which substantial performance occurs. If the initial fee is deferred, related expenses for later MATCHING against revenue must also be deferred. Continuing franchise fees are recognized as earned. An estimated uncollectible account expense provision should be made. *See also* DEFERRED CREDIT.

FRAUD

1. deliberate action by individual or entity to cheat another, causing damage. There is typically a *misrepresentation* to deceive, or purposeful withholding of material data needed for a proper decision. An example of fraud is when a BOOKKEEPER falsifies records in order to steal money. *See also* NEGLIGENCE.

2. falsification of a tax return by an individual. Examples of tax fraud are intentionally not reporting taxable income or overstating expenses. Tax fraud is a criminal act.

FRAUD RISK FACTORS conditions that typically exist when fraud occurs; namely, incentive/pressure (i.e., a reason to commit fraud), opportunity (i.e., ineffective internal controls), and rationalization/attitude (i.e., justification for committing fraud).

FREE CASH FLOW amount of cash that remains after deducting the funds a company must commit to continue operating at its planned level; net cash flows from operating activities, minus dividends, minus net capital expenditures.

FREE ON BOARD (FOB) term indicating delivery will be made on board or into a carrier by the shipper without charge. The abbreviation FOB is followed by a shipping point or destination. The invoice price includes delivery at seller's expense and seller's risk to the specified location. For example, "FOB our warehouse in Duluth, Minnesota," means to a buyer requesting New York City delivery that the seller who might have its headquarters and billing office in Chicago, will pay shipping costs from Duluth to New York. Title usually passes from seller to buyer at the FOB point.

FREIGHT-IN transportation charge the company pays when it receives goods from a supplier. It is a separate account that is added to purchases in determining the cost of goods and ending inventory. *See also* FREIGHT-OUT.

FREIGHT-OUT cost of transporting goods to a customer. It is a selling expense. When the freight is included in the selling price, it is deducted from sales. *See also* FREIGHT-IN.

FREQUENCY DISTRIBUTION schedule showing the number of times each observation in the data occurs. Data collected need to be organized in some fashion. One method of summarizing a population or sample is to organize the data in terms of their frequency.

For example, assume that a sales slip can have 0, 1, 2, or 3 errors after it is filled out. Fifty sales slips are randomly selected with the following results: 10 had no errors, 20 had only one error, 12 had two errors, and 8 had three errors. These results can be constructed in a tabular format as follows:

Number of Errors	Frequency
0	10
1	20
2	12
3	8
	50

FRINGE BENEFIT compensation or other benefit provided by the employer to the employee at no charge that is above and beyond salary or wages. Examples include health plans, CAFETERIA PLANS, and life insurance.

FRONT-END LOADING practice of investment houses and mutual funds in which administrative, selling, brokerage, and other fees are deducted from the initial deposit or installment.

F-TEST ratio of two mean squares (variances); often can be used to test the significance of some item of interest. For example, in regression, the ratio of the mean square due to the regression to the mean square due to error can be used to test the overall significance of the regression model. By looking up F-tables, the degree of significance of the computed F-value can be determined.

FULL COSTING *see* ABSORPTION COSTING.

FULL COST METHOD accounting method used by some extractive industries, particularly oil and gas companies, in which *all* exploration costs are capitalized whether the projects are successful or unsuccessful. The capitalized cost is then amortized into expense as the total reserves are produced. *See also* SUCCESSFUL EFFORTS ACCOUNTING.

FULL-COST-PLUS PRICING method in which the cost base is the full manufacturing cost per unit. Selling and administrative costs are provided for through the markup that is added to this base. *See also* COST PLUS PRICING.

FULL COST PROFIT MARGIN difference between total revenue and total costs traceable to a work cell or product.

FULL DISCLOSURE comprehensively and understandably presenting all material facts in the footnotes to the financial statements so that financial statement users are properly informed. Standards of disclosure are formulated by the FASB and SEC. *See also* DISCLOSURE.

FULL FAITH AND CREDIT backing of the debt of a government entity with all the resources of the entity, including its taxing and borrowing power. Bonds backed up by the full faith and credit of the issuer are called GENERAL OBLIGATION BONDS.

FULL PRODUCT COST cost that includes not only the costs of direct materials and direct labor, but also the costs of all production and nonproduction activities required to satisfy the customer.

FULLY VESTED term describing an employee who will be *completely* entitled to pension plan benefits at retirement. *See also* VESTED.

FUNCTIONAL ACCOUNTING accounting and reporting by activity. It aids in conforming organizational performance to plan so that proper budgetary and operational controls can be maintained.

FUNCTIONAL CLASSIFICATION system under which costs are classified according to the function they perform within the business; for example, manufacturing, selling, general and administrative, or financial costs. The *traditional approach* to the income statement, which is required for external reporting, uses this classification of costs. There are different ways of classifying costs. For example, costs are classified by behavior, as variable or fixed according to their response to changes in levels of activity.

FUNCTIONAL CURRENCY legal tender of the primary economic environment in which a company operates. Usually, it is the country where a company generates and expends most of its cash. For example, if a company in Italy (as an independent entity) generated its cash and incurred related expenses in Italy, the Italian currency would be the functional currency. However, if the Italian company was an extension of a Greek parent company, the functional currency would be the Greek currency. *See also* REPORTING CURRENCY.

FUNCTIONAL DECOMPOSITION identification of the activities performed in the organization. It yields a hierarchical representation of the organization and shows the relationship between the different levels of the organization and its activities. For example, a hierarchy may start with the division and move down through the plant, function, process, activity, and task levels.

FUNCTIONAL GAMES *see* MANAGEMENT GAME.

FUNCTIONAL REPORTING OF EXPENSES presenting expenses by major activity. Functional reporting is used by not-for-profit entities other than governmental units and hospitals. Under functional reporting, expenses are accumulated according to program purpose (e.g., research) rather than by object of expenditure. By contrast, under object reporting, items are accounted for according to their natural classification (e.g., salaries expense). Functional classification is also used for profit operations: manufacturing, selling, and administrative.

FUNCTION COST classification showing the nature of the output for which costs are incurred, such as product packaging, sales promotion, or other such specific activities.

FUNCTION KEY group of keys on the computer keyboard (i.e., F1-F12) whose function depends on the particular program being run at the time. For example, the F1 function key may mean Help for one software program and quite another thing in another software package. Programmable function keys may be used as the equivalent of a combination of other keys.

FUND
1. cash, securities, or other assets designated for a specified purpose such as in a SINKING FUND.
2. in GOVERNMENT ACCOUNTING, fiscal and accounting entity with a self-balancing set of accounts recording cash and other financial resources, together with related liabilities and residual equities or balances, and changes therein. Funds are segregated for the purpose of conducting specific activities or attaining certain objectives in accordance with special regulations, restrictions, or limitations. An example is the SPECIAL REVENUE FUND. *See also* FUND ACCOUNTING.
3. as a verb, to finance, using long-term debt, usually bonds.

FUND ACCOUNTING system used by nonprofit organizations, particularly governments. Because there is no profit motive, ACCOUNTABILITY is measured instead of profitability. The main purpose is stewardship of financial resources received and expended in compliance with legal requirements. Financial reporting is directed at the public rather than investors. The accounting equation is Assets = Restrictions on Assets. Funds are established to ensure accountability and expenditure for designated purposes. Revenues must be raised and expended in accordance with special regulations and restrictions. Budgets are adopted and recorded in the accounts of the related fund. Contractual obligations are given effect in some funds.

FUNDAMENTAL ANALYSIS evaluation of a company's stock based on an examination of the firm's financial statements. It is distinguished from TECHNICAL ANALYSIS, which attempts to predict the market price of a company's stock based on historical price performance and overall stock market trends. It considers overall financial health, economic and political conditions, industry factors, marketing aspects, management quality, and future outlook of the company. The analysis attempts to ascertain whether stock is overpriced, underpriced, or priced in proportion to its market value. Fundamental analysis provides much of the data needed to forecast earnings and dividends. Fundamental analysis tools include HORIZONTAL ANALYSIS, VERTICAL ANALYSIS, and RATIO ANALYSIS, which give a relative measure of the operating performance and financial condition of the company. The following figure summarizes various factors that will go into your investment decision-making process, ranging from economics and the external environment surrounding the investment vehicle to the company's performance measures.

Economic Analysis
(Assessing the Future Performance
of the Overall Economy)

Business Cycles: Monetary Fiscal Policy,
Economic Indicators, Government Policy,
World Events and Foreign Trade, Public
Attitudes of Optimism or Pessimism,
Domestic Legislation, Inflation, GNP
Growth, Unemployment, Productivity,
Capacity Utilization, Interest Rates, and More

Industry Analysis
(Based on the Economic and Market
Analysis, Determining the Business Cycle's
Impact on Specific Industries and
Evaluating Industry Characteristics)

Business Cycle Exposure, Industry Structure,
Growth of the Industry, Competition, Product
Quality, Cost Elements, Government Regulations,
Labor Position, Technological Development,
and Financial Norms and Standards

Company Analysis
(Analyzing How Specific Companies
Perform in Terms of Their Operating and
Financial Features Given Industry
Changes and the Economy)

Growth of Sales, Earnings, Dividends,
Quality of Earnings, Position in the Industry,
Discount Rates, Fundamental Analysis
(Balance Sheet Analysis, Income Statement
Analysis, Cash Flow Analysis), Analysis of
Accounting Policy and Footnotes, Management,
Research and Development, Return and Risk,
Brands, Patents, Goodwill, and Diversification

FUNDED DEBT long-term debt of a business. Long-term debt may consist of long-term notes of banks or other lending institutions, but the term funded usually connotes bonds.

FUNDED PENSION PLAN one in which the employer contributes pension funds to a trustee who manages the fund and pays employees from the fund when they retire. *See also* ACTUARIAL GAINS, LOSSES; DEFINED BENEFIT PENSION PLAN; DEFINED CONTRIBUTION PENSION PLAN; PENSION PLAN; VESTED.

FUNDS-FLOW-ADEQUACY RATIO computation showing the extent to which a company can generate sufficient funds from operations to meet budgeted capital expenditures, increase in inventories, and cash dividends. Typically, a five-year total is used to eliminate cyclical and other distortions. The ratio equals:

$$\frac{\text{Five-Year Sum of Sources of Funds From Operations}}{\text{Five-Year Sum of Capital Expenditures, Inventory Additions, and Cash Dividends}}$$

A ratio of 1 shows the business has covered its needs based on attained levels of growth without having to resort to external financing. If the ratio is less than 1, there may be inadequate internally generated funds to maintain dividends and current operating growth levels.

FUNDS-FLOW-FIXED-CHARGE COVERAGE ratio of funds provided by operations plus fixed charges to fixed charges. This ratio indicates whether a company can satisfy its annual fixed charges from funds flow. Fixed charges remain constant under varying rates of production and are often contractual. Examples of fixed charges are rent, lease payments, insurance, and interest. Funds flow can be expressed as working capital from operations or cash flow from operations. Assume funds provided by operations before tax is $2,000,000, which includes a deduction of fixed charges for $300,000. The ratio is thus $2,300,000 divided by $300,000, or 7.67.

FUND THEORY system applied to governmental and nonprofit entities (e.g., colleges, charities, hospitals). The fund includes a group of assets and liabilities and restrictions representing specific economic functions or activities. Each fund has its assets restricted for designated purposes. The equation is:

$$\text{Assets} = \text{Restrictions of Assets}$$

Assets are future services to the fund or operational unit. Liabilities are restrictions against those assets. *See also* FUND ACCOUNTING.

FURNITURE AND FIXTURES noncurrent depreciable asset consisting of office or store equipment (e.g., desks), lighting, and showroom items.

FUTURES CONTRACT agreement to buy or sell a given amount of a commodity or financial instrument at a specified price in a specified future month. The seller of a futures contract agrees to deliver the item to the buyer of the contract, who agrees to purchase the item. The contract specifies the amount, valuation, method, quality, month and means of delivery, and commodity exchange to be traded in. The month of delivery is the expiration date when the commodity or financial instrument must be delivered. *See also* COMMODITIES FUTURES; FINANCIAL FUTURE.

FUTURE VALUE amount to which an investment will grow at a future time if it earns a specified interest that is compounded annually. The process of calculating future values is called *compounding*. Let us define:

F_n = future value = the amount of money at the end of year n
P = principal
i = annual interest rate
n = number of years
Then F_1 = the amount of money at the end of year one
   = principal and interest = $P + iP = P(1 + i)$
F_2 = the amount of money at the end of year 2
   = $F_1 (1 + i) = P(1 + i)(1 + i) = P(1 + i)^2$

The future value of an investment compounded annually at rate 1 for n years is $F_n = P(1 + i)^n = P\, FVIF(i,n)$ where $FVIF(i,n)$ is the future value of \$1 and can be found in table 1 in the back of the book.

For example, assume that Mr. A placed \$1,000 in a savings account earning 8% interest compounded annually. How much will he have in the account at the end of four years? Then $F_4 = \$1,000\,(1 + 0.08)^4$.

From table 1 in the back of the book, the $FVIF(8\%$, four years$) = 1.361$. Therefore,

$$F_4 = \$1,000(1.3605) = \$1,361.$$

FUTURE VALUE OF AN ANNUITY compound annuity in which an equal sum of money is deposited at the end of each year for a certain number of years and allowed to grow.

Let S_n = the future value of an n-year annuity and A = the amount of an annuity. Then S_n can be found from using table 2 in the back of the book as follows:

$$S_n = A\, FVIFA\ (i,n)$$

where $FVIFA(i,n)$ is the future value of an annuity of \$1 and can be found in table 2 in the back of the book. For example, assume Mrs. A wishes to determine the sum of money she will have in her savings account at the end of six years by depositing \$1,000 at the end of each year for the next six years. The annual interest rate is 8%. The $FVIFA(8\%$, six years$)$ is given in table 2 as 7.336. Therefore, $S_6 = \$1,000(7.336) = \$7336$.

G

GAAP *see* GENERALLY ACCEPTED ACCOUNTING PRINCIPLES (GAAP).

GAAP CODIFICATION *see* FASB ACCOUNTING STANDARDS CODIFICATION™.

GAIN excess of money or fair value of property received on sale or exchange over the carrying value of the item. An example is the sale of a fixed asset when cash received exceeds book value. Gains also occur when the cash payment to eliminate a debt is less than the liability's carrying value. An example is retiring debt before maturity at a price below book value. Gains relate to *incidental* and nonrecurring transactions of the business. *See also* LOSS.

GAIN CONTINGENCY potential or pending development that may result in a future gain to the company, such as a successful lawsuit against another company. Conservative accounting practice dictates that gain contingencies should not be booked, although footnote disclosure of the particulars may be made. *See also* LOSS CONTINGENCY.

GAME THEORY analytical approach to competitive situations where two or more participants pursue conflicting objectives. The theory attempts to offer a solution that resolves the conflict among the participants. In games, the participants are competitors; the success of one is usually at the expense of the other. Each person selects and executes those strategies that he believes will result in "winning the game." Game theory attempts to provide a guideline for a variety of game situations.

GANTT CHART graphical representation of a project schedule used to plan or monitor progress.

GARNISHMENT the legal process that requires a third party in possession of a debtor's money or property to turn it over to a CREDITOR of the DEBTOR. A third party becomes liable for the value of the property if it fails to turn over the property.

GENERAL ACCOUNTING OFFICE (GAO) a legislative branch (www. gao.gov), headed by the Comptroller General, that was established to assist the Congress in its oversight of the executive branch and to serve as the independent legislative auditor of the federal government. Among the other roles of the GAO are: (1) prescribing principles and standards for federal agency accounting systems; (2) assisting agencies in accounting system design; and (3) reporting to Congress on the status of agency accounting systems.

GENERAL AGREEMENT ON TARIFFS AND TRADE (GATT) an agreement between noncommunist nations with economic interests in international trade relations. It is dedicated to encouraging mutually beneficial bilateral agreements that focus upon reducing tariffs, restrictions, and barriers. Established in 1948, GATT also acts as international arbitrator with respect to trade agreement abrogation.

GENERAL AND ADMINISTRATIVE EXPENSES all expenses incurred in connection with performing general and administrative activities. Examples are executives' salaries and legal expenses. General and administrative expenses are shown under OPERATING EXPENSES in the income statement.

GENERAL BALANCE SHEET presentation form of the balance sheet of institutions such as governmental, religious, charitable, educational, and social entities, prepared in the usual standard commercial form.

GENERAL BUSINESS CREDIT credit directly reducing tax applicable to low-income housing and targeted jobs.

GENERAL CONTINGENCY RESERVE appropriation of retained earnings for *general* purposes rather than for a specific item of future loss or expense. In effect, it is a reserve for unspecified possible events.

GENERAL FIXED ASSET ACCOUNT GROUP in GOVERNMENT ACCOUNTING, self-balancing set of accounts to account for the general fixed assets of a governmental unit. The account group is *not* a fund. It provides double-entry control in *memorandum* fashion of fixed assets that are not accounted for specifically in a fund (e.g., proprietary fund). *See also* GENERAL LONG-TERM DEBT ACCOUNT GROUP.

GENERAL FUND in GOVERNMENTAL ACCOUNT, fund used to account for all assets and liabilities of a nonprofit entity except those particularly assigned for other purposes in another more specialized fund. It is the primary operating fund of a governmental unit. Much of the usual activities of a municipality are supported by the general fund. Examples are the purchase of supplies and meeting operating expenditures. An example of a specialized fund, on the other hand, is the capital projects fund that accounts for financial resources used for the acquisition or construction of major capital facilities. *See also* FUND.

GENERAL JOURNAL simplest type of journal. It is used when *no special journal exists* to record a transaction, usually when a transaction occurs infrequently. Examples are the declaration of a dividend, correction of an accounting error, and an appropriation of retained earnings. It has only two money columns, one for debits, the other for credits.

GENERAL LEDGER record of a business entity's accounts. The general ledger contains the accounts that make up the entity's financial statements. Separate accounts exist for individual assets, liabilities, stockholders' equity, revenue, and expenses. In some cases, control accounts summarize detail appearing in a SUBSIDIARY LEDGER (e.g., individual customer accounts tying into the accounts receivable account). A trial balance is prepared of the general ledger accounts at the end of the accounting period to assure that total debits equal total credits. The general ledger may be in bound or loose-leaf form, magnetic tape, in computer memory, or other form. *See also* LEDGER.

GENERAL LONG-TERM DEBT ACCOUNT GROUP GOVERNMENT ACCOUNTING term. Grouping is used to account for the outstanding principal on all long-term debt except that payable from a special assessment, proprietary, or trust fund. At maturity, the funds are transferred to the debt service fund. *See also* GENERAL FIXED ASSET ACCOUNT GROUP.

GENERAL OBLIGATION BOND security whose payment is unconditionally promised by a governmental unit that has the power to levy taxes. Many state, county, city, town, and school district obligation bonds are of this type. General obligation bonds are backed by the FULL FAITH AND CREDIT (and taxing power) of the issuing government, whether it be the U.S. or a municipality.

GENERAL PARTNER

1. member of a partnership who is jointly and severally liable for all debts incurred by the PARTNERSHIP—that is, a partner who does not have LIMITED LIABILITY.

2. managing partner of a limited partnership who is in charge of its operations. A general partner has unlimited liability. *See also* LIMITED PARTNER.

GENERAL PRICE INDEX measure of change in the general level of prices of goods and services. The general indexes gauge the change in the purchasing power of the dollar. Widely used indexes of price change are calculated regularly by U.S. Government agencies. Examples are the Gross Domestic Product Implicit Price Deflator, Consumer Price Index (CPI) for Urban Consumers, and the Producer Price Index. For example, the Consumer Price Index reflects the average change in the retail prices of a broad but select "basket" of consumer goods. The Consumer Price Index is required by the accounting profession for use in CONSTANT DOLLAR ACCOUNTING. It is reported monthly by the U.S. Department of Labor.

GENERAL PRICE LEVEL ACCOUNTING restating financial statements in terms of general purchasing power by using a GENERAL PRICE INDEX. *See also* CONSTANT DOLLAR ACCOUNTING.

GENERAL-PURPOSE FINANCIAL STATEMENT statement prepared to meet the needs of *all* financial statement users as opposed to meeting the needs of only a particular group such as investors, creditors, management, or regulatory bodies. This is the purpose of financial statements based on GAAP. *See also* SPECIAL-PURPOSE FINANCIAL STATEMENT.

GENERAL REVENUE SHARING unrestricted funds provided by the federal government to the fifty states and to cities, towns, counties, etc., under the State and Local Fiscal Assistance Act of 1972, which expired in 1987. These funds could be used for any purpose by the recipient governments.

GENERAL USE REPORT any auditor's report that is not intended only for specified parties. Auditor's reports based on financial statement audits are considered general use reports because they are not restricted as to use.

GENERALIZED AUDIT SOFTWARE (GAS) used to select and apply audit routines to electronic data. GAS is the most commonly used COMPUTER ASSSISTED AUDIT TECHNIQUE (CAAT).

GENERALIZED AUDIT SOFTWARE PACKAGE (GASP) software used by an auditor to (1) access an entity's computerized accounting files, and (2) analyze and test data.

GENERALLY ACCEPTED ACCOUNTING PRINCIPLES (GAAP) standards, conventions, and rules accountants follow in recording and summarizing transactions, and in the preparation of financial statements. GAAP derive, in order of importance, from: (1) issuances from an authoritative body designated by the AICPA Council (for example, the FASB Statements, AICPA APB Opinions, and AICPA Accounting Research Bulletins); (2) other AICPA issuances such as AICPA Industry Guides; (3) industry practice; and

(4) accounting literature in the form of books and articles. Principles also derive from tradition, such as the concept of matching. In the audit report, the CPA must indicate that the client has followed GAAP on a consistent basis.

GENERALLY ACCEPTED AUDITING STANDARDS (GAAS) broad rules and guidelines promulgated by the AICPA's *Auditing Standards Board*. CPAs employ GAAS in preparing for and performing audits of a client's financial statements. The guidelines include references to the auditor's qualifications, audit field work, and reporting the audit results. The broad standards are backed by detailed interpretative literature. An auditor unable to express an opinion on the financial statements must give reasons. A CPA who does not conduct an examination in accordance with GAAS can be held in violation of the AICPA's Code of Professional Ethics and face legal action by affected parties. *See also* STATEMENTS ON AUDITING STANDARDS (SAS).

GENERATION SKIPPING TRANSFER TAX may result when an individual attempts to avoid gift and estate tax by transferring money or property to beneficiaries more than one generation below the transferor's generation. For example, the generation skipping transfer tax might apply to transfers directly to a decedent's grandchildren, rather than first making transfers to a decedent's children. If imposed, the rate of tax is equal to the maximum gift and estate tax rate.

GIFT TAX tax levied on the transfer of property or money made without adequate legal consideration. This tax is imposed on the donor of a gift and is based upon the fair market value of the property as of the date of transfer. Under the law, each parent may give each recipient $13,000 a year ($26,000 for parents electing *gift-splitting*) without gift tax consequences. Also, gifts between spouses are untaxed.

GOAL CONGRUENCE term used when the same goals are shared by top managers and their subordinates. This is one of the many criteria used to judge the performance of an accounting system. The system can achieve its goal more effectively and perform better when organizational goals can be well aligned with the personal and group goals of subordinates and superiors. The goals of the company should be the same as the goals of the individual business segments. Corporate goals can be communicated by budgets, organization charts, and job descriptions.

GOAL PROGRAMMING form of LINEAR PROGRAMMING that considers multiple goals that are often in conflict with each other. With multiple goals, all goals usually cannot be realized exactly. For example, the twin goals of an investor who desires investments with maximum return and with minimum risk are generally incompatible and therefore unachievable. Other examples of multiple conflicting objectives can be found in organizations that want to: (1) maximize profits and increase wages; (2) upgrade product quality and reduce product cost; (3) pay larger dividends to stockholders and retain earnings for growth; and (4) reduce credit losses and increase sales. Goal programming does not attempt to maximize or minimize a single objective function as does the linear programming model. Rather, it seeks to minimize the deviations among the desired goals and the actual results according to the priorities assigned. The objective function of a goal programming model is expressed in terms of the deviations from the target goals.

GOAL SEEKING situation in which a manager wishes to determine what change would have to take place in the value of a specified variable in a specified time period to achieve a specified value for another variable. For example, a manager can ask the following "goal seeking" question: "What would the unit sales price have to be for the project to achieve a target return on investment of 20%?" Software such as MYSTRATEGY and EXCEL can help answer this type of question.

GOING CONCERN *see* CONTINUITY.

GOING-CONCERN VALUE worth of a business to another company or person. Going-concern value less asset value (liquidating value) is the entity's value as differentiated from the value of its assets. In a business combination accounted for under the purchase method, going-concern value less liquidation value is referred to as GOODWILL. For example, if Company A pays $5 million cash for Company B, which has net assets worth $4 million, $1 million represents goodwill.

GOING PUBLIC process by which shares of common stock are first offered for sale in the public markets (through the organized exchanges or over-the-counter); also called an *initial public offering*. The advantages of going public must be weighed against the disadvantages. Going public may give the company and major stockholders greater access to funds, as well as additional prestige and wealth. It also means that shares assume a market value—a value placed on expected future earnings. On the other hand, the company must open its books to the public through SEC and state filings and put up with pressure for short-term performance by security analysts and large institutional investors.

GOLDEN HANDCUFFS contractual agreement almost virtually assuring that the stockbroker will stay with the brokerage firm for a specified time period. The incentive may be in the form of high commission rates, bonuses, participation in a forthcoming initial public offering (IPO) of the brokerage firm itself, or other attractive fringe benefits. The contract may specify a penalty the broker will incur such as forfeiting past commissions if he or she leaves the brokerage firm before a specified date.

GOLDEN HANDSHAKE a clause in executive employment contracts that provides the executives with lucrative severance packages in the event of their termination. May include a continuation of salary, bonus, and/or certain benefits and perquisites, as well as accelerated vesting of stock options.

GOLDEN PARACHUTE AGREEMENT highly lucrative contract giving a senior corporate executive monetary or other benefits if his or her job is lost in a merger or acquisition. Examples of benefits are severance pay, bonus, and stock option.

GOODNESS-OF-FIT degree to which a model fits the observed data. In a REGRESSION ANALYSIS, the goodness-of-fit is measured by the COEFFICIENT OF DETERMINATION (*r*-squared).

GOODS items of merchandise, finished products, supplies, or raw materials. Sometimes the term is extended to cover all inventoriable items or assets such as cash, supplies, and fixed assets.

GOODS AND SERVICES revenue sources of businesses. *See also* GOODS; SERVICES.

GOODS-IN-PROCESS INVENTORY *see* WORK-IN-PROCESS.

GOODWILL theoretically, the present value of future excess earnings of a company over other companies in the industry. In other words, it is the value of the company's name and reputation, its customer relations, and other factors that, although intangible, give a concern its competitive edge and produce better-than-typical future earnings. It can only be recorded in a business combination accounted for under the PURCHASE (ACCOUNTING) METHOD. Goodwill equals the purchase price less the book value of the acquired company's net assets less the amount by which the acquired company's depreciable assets are written up to their fair market value. The fair market value of the total going concern should be equal to the purchase price. For example, if XYZ Company paid $3,000,000 for the net assets of ABC Company having a fair value of $2,800,000, the excess of $200,000 represents goodwill. Goodwill is an intangible asset subject to an annual impairment test.

GOOGLE
1. The most widely used search engine on the Web. Its search engine is known for providing relevant search results using a simple and clean interface. Most of Google's services are free to the public. Google makes money through highly targeted, unobtrusive Internet advertisement.
2. The term "google" is also used as a verb to describe the process of doing a Web search.

GOVERNMENT ACCOUNTING principles and procedures in accounting for federal, state, and local governmental units. The National Council on Governmental Accounting establishes rules. There is also a governmental group in the FASB. Unlike commercial accounting for corporations, encumbrances and budgets are recorded in the accounts. Assets of a governmental unit are restricted for designated purposes. *See also* MODIFIED ACCRUAL.

GOVERNMENT ACCOUNTING STANDARDS BOARD (GASB) organization that formulates accounting standards for governmental units. It is under the auspices of the FINANCIAL ACCOUNTING FOUNDATION and replaced the National Council on Government Accounting.

GOVERNMENTAL BUDGETING financial plan and a basis for evaluating performance and an expression of public policy and a form of control having the force of law. Thus, a governmental budget is a legal document adopted in accordance with procedures specified by applicable laws. A governmental budget must be complied with by the administrators of the governmental unit for which the budget is prepared. By law, the administrators cannot exceed the budget without a formally approved budget amendment. Moreover, because the effectiveness and efficiency of governmental efforts are difficult to measure in the absence of the profit-centered activity that characterizes business operations, the use of budgets in the appropriation process is of major importance. Accordingly, budgetary accounts may be incorporated into the formal accounting systems of governments, and a budgetary comparison statement must be issued.

GOVERNMENT FUND term used in GOVERNMENT ACCOUNTING to apply to all funds except for the profit and loss funds (e.g., enterprise fund, internal service fund, and trust and agency fund). Examples of government funds are the general fund, special assessment fund, and capital projects fund. Governmental funds use the MODIFIED ACCRUAL accounting method.

GRANT-IN-AID contribution or donation by a superior governmental entity to a local government for a specified purpose. Grants for specified categories are termed *categorical grants*; grants for general purposes, *block grants*.

GRANULARITY decomposition of an activity or process.

GRAPHICAL METHOD technique used to find graphically the break-even point and highlight the cost-volume-profit relationships over a wide range of activity. The graphical method requires preparation of a BREAK-EVEN CHART. *See also* BREAK-EVEN ANALYSIS; COST-VOLUME-PROFIT (CVP) ANALYSIS; PROFIT-VOLUME (PV) CHART.

GRAPHICAL METHOD OF LP solution procedure used when a LINEAR PROGRAMMING (LP) problem has two (or at most three) decision variables. The graphical method follows these steps:
(1) Change inequalities to equalities.
(2) Graph the equalities.
(3) Identify the correct side for the original inequalities.
(4) Then identify the *feasible region*, the area of FEASIBLE SOLUTION.
(5) Determine the CONTRIBUTION MARGIN (CM) or cost at each of the *corner points* (*basic feasible solutions*) of the feasible region.
(6) Pick either the most profitable or least cost combination, which is an OPTIMAL SOLUTION.

For example, suppose that our LP model is:

$$\text{Maximize CM} = \$25A + \$40B$$
$$\text{Subject to:} \quad 2A + 4B \leqq 100 \text{ hours}$$
$$3A + 2B \leqq 90$$
$$A \geqq 0, B \geqq 0$$

After going through steps 1 through 4, the feasible region (shaded area) is obtained, as shown in the following exhibit. Then all the corner points in the feasible region are evaluated in terms of their CM as follows:

LINEAR PROGRAMMING GRAPH

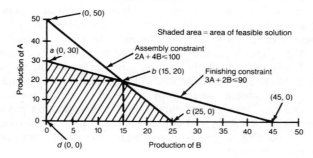

	Corner Points		CM
	A	B	$25A + $40B
(a)	30	0	$25(30) + $40(0) = $750
(b)	20	15	$25(20) + $40(15) = $1,100
(c)	0	25	$25(0) + $40(25) = $1,000
(d)	0	0	$25(0) + $40(0) = $0

The corner 20A, 15B produces the most profitable solution.

GRAPHICAL USER INTERFACE (GUI) relies on windows, menus, icons, and other graphics for interaction between a human and a computer. Interaction generally takes place using a touch screen, mouse, or keyboard. In contrast, a command line interface (CLI) relies exclusively on text, and interaction is only by a keyboard.

GRAPHIC SOFTWARE program for depicting accounting information in graphic form, including charts, diagrams, and signs. This enhances understanding of financial statement accounts, trends, and relationships.

GREENMAIL PAYMENT payoff given to a potential acquirer by a company targeted for a takeover. In most cases, the targeted company buys back its shares at a significantly higher price. In reciprocation for selling the shares back, the suitor agrees to end the attempted takeover.

GROSS DOMESTIC PRODUCT (GDP) an economic indicator that measures the value of all goods and services produced by the economy within its boundaries and is the nation's broadest gauge of economic health. GDP is divided among personal consumption, investment, net exports, and government spending. Consumption makes up roughly two-thirds of the total. GDP is normally stated in annual terms, though data are compiled and released quarterly. The U.S. Bureau of Economic Analysis releases an advance estimate of quarterly GDP, followed by a "preliminary" estimate and a "final" figure. It is reported as a "real" figure, that is, economic growth minus the impact of inflation. The figure is tabulated on a quarterly basis, coming out in the month after a quarter has ended. It is then revised at least twice, with those revisions being reported once in each of the months following the original release. Changes in the GDP of the United States are calculated quarterly and announced in annualized terms (what the annual change would be if the quarter's pace of growth or contraction continued for a year). GDP reports appear in most daily newspapers and online at services like America Online. Also visit the federal government statistics Web site on the Internet at www.bea.gov/bea/newsrel/gdpnewsrelease.htm, www.fedstats.gov/, or www.economicindicators.gov. GDP is often a measure of the state of the economy. For example, many economists speak of recession when there has been a decline in GDP for two consecutive quarters. The GDP in dollars and real terms is a useful economic indicator.

GROSS INCOME amount of money earned (which is collected or will be collected) from the sale of goods minus the cost of the goods sold; also called GROSS PROFIT or *gross margin*. For example, if sales total $4,000 and the cost of goods sold is $1,200, the gross income is $2,800 ($4,000 − $1,200). Gross profit less operating expenses equals net income.

GROSS MARGIN *see* GROSS PROFIT.

GROSS MARGIN PRICING cost-based pricing approach in which the price is computed using a markup percentage based on a product's total production costs.

GROSS MARGIN RATIO percentage of each sales dollar remaining after a firm has paid for its goods; also called *gross profit margin*. It is calculated by dividing gross income (profits) by net sales. For example, assume that net sales are $80,000 and gross profit is $30,000. The gross margin ratio is 0.38 ($30,000/$80,000).

GROSS PRICE METHOD accounting procedure in which the purchase of merchandise is recorded at the gross amount of the invoice, without regard for the cash discount being offered. *See also* NET PRICE METHOD.

GROSS PROFIT sales minus cost of sales; also called *gross margin*.

GROSS PROFIT ANALYSIS analysis of the profit variance that constitutes the departure between actual profit and the previous year's income or the budgeted figure; also called *profit variance analysis*. The primary goal of profit variance analysis is to improve performance and profitability.

GROSS PROFIT MARGIN *see* GROSS MARGIN RATIO.

GROSS PROFIT METHOD system used to estimate inventory at the end of an interim period (e.g., quarter) when preparing INTERIM FINANCIAL STATE-MENTS. However, estimating inventory for annual reporting is not acceptable. The method can be used to estimate what the inventory was at the date of a loss (e.g., fire, theft, other type of casualty loss) for insurance reimbursement. Under the method, the expected GROSS-PROFIT RATIO is used. The ending inventory can be computed by preparing a partial income statement starting with sales and ending with gross profit. Assume beginning inventory is $15,000, purchases are $90,000, sales are $200,000, and the gross profit rate is 60%.

Sales		$200,000
Less: Cost of goods sold		
Beginning inventory	$ 15,000	
Purchases	90,000	
Cost of goods available	$105,000	
Less: Ending inventory	?	
Cost of goods sold		80,000
Gross profit (60% × $200,000)		$120,000

The ending inventory must be $25,000 ($105,000 – 80,000).

GROSS-PROFIT RATIO gross profit divided by net sales. High ratios are favorable in that they indicate the business is earning a good return on the sale of its merchandise, although that may also invite competition. *See also* GROSS PROFIT.

GROSS SALES total sales *before* sales discounts and sales returns and allowances. It equals total unit sales times the selling price per unit. For example, if total units sold are 20,000 and the selling price is $5, gross sales are $100,000.

GROUP AUDIT the audit of group financial statements.

GROUP DEPRECIATION method for depreciating multiple-asset accounts using one rate. It is used to depreciate a collection of assets that are *similar* in nature and have approximately the same useful lives such as equipment. The method approximates a single unit cost procedure since the dispersion from the average is not significant. The method of computation and journal entries are basically the same as that of the COMPOSITE DEPRECIATION method.

GROUP FINANCIAL STATEMENTS financial statements that include financial information of two or more components. For example, consolidated financial statements of a parent corporation and its subsidiaries are considered to be group financial statements. *See also* COMPONENT.

GROWTH RATE amount of change in some financial characteristic of a company.
1. percentage change in earnings per share, dividends per share, revenue, market price of stock, or total assets compared to a base year amount.
For example, growth in earnings per share equals:

$$\frac{\text{EPS (end of period)} - \text{EPS (beginning of period)}}{\text{EPS (beginning of period)}}$$

2. percentage change in an item such as net income considering the time value of money. Here, a future value of $1 table must be used. Assume net income in 2010 is $300,000 and in 2014 is $500,000. The future value of $1 table factor is 1.667 ($500,000/$300,000). The future value of $1 table indicates that the intersection of n = four years and a factor of 1.667 is about 14%, as evidenced here:

Partial Future Value of $1 Table [FVIF (i, n)]

Periods	10%	12%	14%
4	1.464	1.574	1.689

3. change in retained earnings divided by beginning stockholders' equity.
4. net income less dividends divided by common stockholders' equity. A high ratio reflects a company's ability to generate internal funds, and thus it does not have to rely on external sources.

GROWTH STOCKS said of shares of young companies with little or no earnings history. They are valued on the basis of anticipated future earnings and thus have high price-earnings ratios. They generally grow faster than the economy as a whole and also faster than the industry of which they are a part. They are risky because capital gains are speculative, especially in the case of young companies in new industries. An example of a growth stock is a high-tech company.

G7 a group of the largest industrial nations, which includes all G6 nations and Canada.

G6 a group that includes the six countries with the largest industrial economies. G6 currently includes the United States, the United Kingdom, Japan, France, Italy, and Germany.

GUARANTEED BOND
1. debt issued by one party with payment guaranteed by another party. A considerable number of railroad bonds have been guaranteed by firms other

than the debtors. Some of the guaranties assure payment of both principal and interest; some assure interest only.

2. bonds issued by *subsidiaries* and guaranteed by *parent companies* or *affiliates*.

GUARANTEED PAYMENTS TO PARTNERS payments made to partners without regard to the partnership's income or loss. Guaranteed payments are deductible by a partnership, because they are typically considered wages paid to a partner who has performed services for the partnership.

H

HACKER very knowledgeable computer user who attempts to break into and corrupt a computer system.

HALF-YEAR CONVENTION a tax rule assuming that a newly acquired asset is in service for one-half of the taxable year regardless of when it is actually placed in service.

HARD COPY computer term for output printed directly on paper. The user types commands, instructions, or data on a keyboard. The computer's responses, as well as the information entered, are printed on paper, which gives the user a permanent copy of the input.

HARD DISK a device for storing computer data. Internally, it consists of a set of electromagnetic disks on which data is stored. A standard hard disk is capable of storing several terrabytes (TB) of data; it can also access its data in milliseconds.

HARDWARE the "computer name" given to all the electronic and mechanical devices that make up a computer, as opposed to software, which refers to programs.

HASHING technique used to find an accounting record within a computer file. The key field of the record is the input. A mathematical process leads to the approximate location of the desired accounting data within the file.

HASH TOTAL summation of numbers having no practical meaning as a control precaution; used by auditors primarily in a computer application. The purpose is to identify whether a record has been lost or omitted from processing. For example, check numbers may be summed to get a hash total. If the total of the check numbers processed does not agree with the hash total, a discrepancy exists, and investigation is required to uncover the error.

HEAD OF HOUSEHOLD FILING STATUS category of a taxpaying entity. The head of household is an unmarried individual who maintains a household for another and satisfies the following conditions: (1) the taxpayer maintains a home in which a dependent relative lives for the whole year; (2) the taxpayer pays more than 50% of the cost of maintaining the home; and (3) the taxpayer is either a U.S. citizen or a resident alien.

HEDGE
1. process of protecting oneself against unfavorable changes in prices. Thus one may enter into an offsetting purchase or sale agreement for the express purpose of balancing out any unfavorable changes in an already consummated agreement due to price fluctuations. Hedge transactions are commonly used to protect positions in (1) foreign currency, (2) commodities, and (3) securities.
2. financing an asset with a liability of similar maturity.

HEDGE FUND
1. a limited partnership of investors that invests in speculative stocks.
2. a mutual fund that seeks to make money betting on a particular bond market, currency movements, or directional movements based on certain events such as mergers and acquisitions. It attempts to hedge in order to minimize an exposure to currency risk. In general, international short-term

bond funds usually hedge most of the currency risk, while longer-term funds have substantial exposure. Funds use currency options, futures, convertible bond arbitrage, merger arbitrage, and elaborate cross currency hedges, but the most effective hedges are expensive. Among the most successful hedge fund strategies in recent years has been convertible bond arbitrage. Hedge funds buy convertible bonds, which carry a low coupon but can be exchanged for equity at a certain price. They then take short position against the company's stock, trading on the relationship between the company's stock and bond prices.

3. a mutual fund that hedges its risk by buying or selling options to protect its position against market risk. For example, a fund specializing in government debt securities may hedge its position by selling call options against its position to protect it against downside risk. Contrary to popular opinion, a hedge fund constructively uses options to protect investment positions and pursues an extremely conservative investment philosophy.

HELD-TO-MATURITY SECURITIES debt securities for which an investor has the positive intent and ability to hold until maturity. Held-to-maturity securities should be reported at amortized cost, which takes into account amortization of premium or discount.

HETEROGENEITY *see* DIVERSITY SEGMENTATION.

HETEROSCEDASTICITY condition in which the variance of the error term is not constant in REGRESSION (LEAST SQUARES) ANALYSIS.

HIDDEN RESERVE understatement of owners' equity or net worth. This understatement can arise either from the undervaluation of assets or from a complimentary overaccrual of liabilities. For purposes of published financial statements, full disclosure must be made with respect to this departure from standard reporting practices. The ultimate effect of putting up a hidden reserve is that in a future period net income will be inflated by the amount of hidden asset value converted to cash.

HIERARCHY OF COST approach to group activity costs as they vary with external end-unit volume, internal volumes, batch-related volumes, and cost object diversity-sensitivity.

HIERARCHY OF GAAP the sources of accounting principles and the framework for selecting them in preparing financial statements in conformity with GAAP, identified by FASB Statement No. 168, *The FASB Accounting Standards Codification,* and Accounting Standards Codification (ASC) 105, *Generally Accepted Accounting Principles.* The hierarchy consists of authoritative and nonauthoritative guidance:

- Authoritative Guidance includes FASB Statements, Interpretations, Technical Bulletins, Staff Positions, Staff Implementation Guides, EITF Abstracts, Accounting Principles Board (APB) Opinions, Accounting Research Bulletins, Accounting Interpretations, AICPA Statements of Positions, Audit and Accounting Guides, and Practice Bulletins.
- Nonauthoritative Guidance includes FASB Concepts Statements, AICPA Issues Papers, Technical Practice Aids, IFRS, and widely recognized industry accounting practices.

HIGHLIGHT *see* FINANCIAL HIGHLIGHT.

HIGH-LOW METHOD algebraic procedure used to separate a SEMIVARIABLE COST or MIXED COST into the fixed and the variable components. The high-low method, as the name indicates, uses two extreme data points to determine the values of a (the fixed cost portion) and b (the variable rate) in the COST-VOLUME FORMULA $y = a + bx$. The extreme data points are the highest and lowest $x - y$ pairs.

HISTORICAL COST acquisition of an asset less discounts plus all *normal* incidental costs necessary to bring the asset into existing use and location. Note that the list price is often higher than the acquisition price. Examples of incidental costs are taxes, transportation, installation, and insurance; also called *cost principle*. If an asset is acquired for the incurrence of a long-term liability rather than cash payment, it is recorded at the PRESENT VALUE of the future payments. An asset acquired in exchange for stock is recorded at the fair market value of the stock issued. If the fair value of the stock is not known, then the fair value of the asset received is used.

HISTORICAL COST ACCOUNTING financial accounting based on the original cost of an item *ignoring* inflationary increases. It is the only allowable method of preparing the primary financial statements that appear in the annual report. However, inventory and investments in securities are reflected at the lower of cost or market value. *See also* CONSTANT DOLLAR ACCOUNTING; CURRENT COST ACCOUNTING.

HISTORICAL SUMMARY supplemental section appearing in the corporate annual report to stockholders in which significant items such as income, revenues, expenses, assets, liabilities, equity, earnings per share, and dividends are presented, usually over a period of at least five years (legal requirement).

HOLDERS OF RECORD owners of a firm's shares on the DATE OF RECORD indicated on the firm's *stock ledger*. Holders of record receive STOCK RIGHTS or DIVIDENDS when they are announced. Because of the time needed to make bookkeeping entries when a stock is traded, the stock will sell EX-DIVIDEND for four business days prior to the date of record.

HOLDING COMPANY corporation owning enough voting stock in another company to control its policies and management. Advantages of holding companies include: (1) the ability to control sizable operations with fractional ownership; (2) the isolation and diversification of risks through subsidiaries; and (3) the fact that approval of stock purchases by the stockholders of the acquired company is not required. Disadvantages of holding companies include: (1) partial multiple taxation when less than 80% of a subsidiary is owned; (2) the ease of enforced dissolution by the U.S. Department of Justice; and (3) the risks of negative leverage effects in excessive pyramiding.

HOLDING COSTS *see* CARRYING COSTS.

HOLDING GAIN, LOSS increment or decrement in the value of an asset or liability for an accounting period. They may be realized or unrealized depending upon whether the asset or liability has been exchanged or is still held. Realized gains or losses are recognized in the financial statements. Only in a few cases are unrealized losses recognized, such as with marketable securities and inventory applying the lower of cost or market value rule. However, permanent declines in the value of assets such as obsolete machinery should be reflected in the accounts. It should be noted that if current cost financial statements are prepared, holding gains and losses would be reflected.

HOLDING PERIOD time interval that property has been owned by the entity.

HOME OFFICE DEDUCTION deduction allowed for income tax purposes if certain requirements are met for maintaining an office in the home. Requirements are that the portion of a home is exclusively used on a regular basis as a principal place of business, or as a place for meeting with clients or customers in the normal course of the taxpayer's business. An additional requirement for employees holds that the office must be maintained only for the convenience of the employer.

HOMOGENEITY cost of an activity that has a similar cause-and-effect relationship with a cost object. Occurs when all the cost elements in an activity's cost pool are consumed in the same proportion by all cost objects. *See also* COST ELEMENT; ACTIVITY COST POOL; ACTIVITY COST DRIVER.

HOMOGENEOUS COST POOL a group of overhead costs associated with activities that can use the same COST DRIVER.

HOMOSCEDASTICITY condition found in a type of scatter graph; also known as *constant variance*. It is one of the assumptions required in a REGRESSION ANALYSIS in order to make valid statistical inferences about population relationships. Homoscedasticity requires that the standard deviation and variance of the error terms (μ) are constant for all x (see graphs below), and that the error terms are drawn from the same population. This indicates that there is a uniform scatter or dispersion of data points about the regression line. If the assumption does not hold (see graphs below), the accuracy of the b coefficient is open to question.

HORIZONTAL ANALYSIS time series analysis of financial statements covering more than one accounting period; also called TREND ANALYSIS. It looks at the percentage change in an account over time. The percentage change equals the change over the prior year. For example, if sales in 20X0 are $100,000 and in 20X1 are $300,000, there is a 200% increase ($200,000/$100,000). By examining the magnitude of direction of a financial statement item over time, the analyst can evaluate its reasonableness. *See also* VERTICAL ANALYSIS.

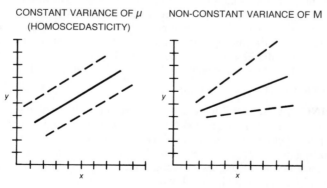

CONSTANT VARIANCE OF μ NON-CONSTANT VARIANCE OF M
(HOMOSCEDASTICITY)

HORIZONTAL AUDIT technique used by the CPA to observe the client's accounting procedures to assure that the system of internal controls is running smoothly. An example is testing whether goods received from a vendor have been properly ordered, are of suitable type and quality as per inspection, and have been properly accounted for in the records.

HORIZONTAL MERGER a merger of competing entities.

HOT SITE is a backup location/site, from where an organization's data center can operate for the duration of a disaster. An organization may have three types of backup locations: a COLD SITE, a WARM SITE, or a hot site. A hot backup site is generally the most expensive of the three options. Everything needed to restore operations is in place. All hardware and software has already been acquired; generally the only thing needed to begin the recovery process is a copy of the latest data backup. Data center function can be restored to full operation without any significant delay.

HOTSPOT a location where Wi-Fi network access is available. Hotspots work through wireless access point devices and provide access to the INTERNET and other devices, such as networked printers or networked storage devices. Users generally connect to a hotspot network by knowing network name. *See also* SSID.

H.R. 10 PLAN *see* KEOGH PLAN.

HUB connection point between the server and the workstation in a LAN.

HUMAN RESOURCE ACCOUNTING method that recognizes a variety of human resources and shows them on a company's balance sheet. Under human resource accounting, a value is placed on people based on such factors as experience, education, and psychological traits, and, most importantly, future earning power (benefit) to the company. The idea has been well received by human-resource-oriented firms, such as those engaged in accounting, law, and consulting. Practical application is limited, however, primarily because of difficulty and the lack of uniform, consistent methods of quantifying the values of human resources. *See also* BEHAVIORAL ACCOUNTING.

HURDLE RATE term used in capital budgeting. Hurdle rate is the *required rate of return* on a long-term investment opportunity. A proposal would be accepted when the expected rate of return exceeds the hurdle rate. The hurdle rate should equal the incremental cost of capital. *See also* COST OF CAPITAL.

HYPERLINK *see* HYPERTEXT.

HYPERTEXT database approach linking related data, programs, and pictures. A hypertext document has highlighted words, called hyperlinks, which when clicked on will direct one to more information about the word.

HYPERTEXT MARKUP LANGUAGE (HTML) consists of a set of tags or codes that are applied to text to create Web pages. The HTML tags tell the Web browsers how to display the text or images on a Web page. HTML is a formal recommendation by the World Wide Web Consortium (W3C), and major browsers generally, but not always, adhere to these standards. The current version of HTML is known as HTML 5. It is an extensible form of HTML called Extensible Hypertext Markup Language (XHTML).

HYPOTHESES TESTING use of a statistical test to discriminate between two hypotheses at two specific risk (or probability) levels. They are called the null (H_0) and the alternative (H_1) hypotheses. These two hypotheses are usually stated in terms of (anticipated) population parameters—for example:

$$H_0 : \mu = \$100$$
$$H_1 : \mu \neq \$100$$

Statistics (e.g., $\bar{x}$) from the random sample may serve as estimators of the population parameters. For example, in auditing, two commonly used alternative hypotheses are:

H_0: The financial statement amount (e.g., book value) is correct.
H_1: The financial statement amount is materially in error.

The risk levels, symbolized as α and β are specified for two types of errors— TYPE I and TYPE II, respectively—that can occur in the decision process. A Type I error occurs when the null hypothesis (H_0) is rejected when it is, in fact, true (i.e., the book value is correct, but the sample results lead you to believe otherwise). A Type II error occurs when the null hypothesis is accepted when it is, in fact, false (i.e., H_1 is true).

The decision to accept or reject the null hypothesis is based on (1) statistics computed from the random sample and (2) the probability of obtaining such values (determined from the underlying sampling distribution).

I

ICA *see* INTERNATIONAL CONGRESS OF ACCOUNTANTS (ICA).

IDEA *see* INTERACTIVE DATA ELECTRONIC APPLICATION (IDEA).

ICFA *see* INSTITUTE OF CHARTERED FINANCIAL ANALYSTS (ICFA).

IDEAL CAPACITY largest volume of output possible if a facility maintained continuous operation at optimum efficiency, allowing for no losses of any kind, even those deemed normal or unavoidable; also called *maximum capacity, theoretical capacity*, or *engineered capacity*. Since it is impossible to obtain ideal capacity, unfavorable variances will result if it is used to apply fixed cost. *See also* CAPACITY.

IDLE CAPACITY
1. presence of unused capacity together with insufficient raw materials or skilled labor. When idle capacity exists, a firm can take on an incremental order without increasing the fixed costs.
2. economic situation in which the market will not absorb all of the maximum possible output at a price exceeding the variable cost of production. *See also* CAPACITY.
3. capacity that is potentially available but not currently being used, perhaps due to market pressures from competition, distribution constraints, or management policy (such as union contract laws, holidays, overtime rules); also called *excess capacity*. On the other hand, increased idle capacity may represent the rewards and evidence of improved productivity and efficiencies by operations.

IDLE CAPACITY VARIANCE measure of utilization of plant facilities. The variance results when a plant is underutilized (idle), and actual production falls below the expected, budgeted, or normal activity, known as DENOMINATOR ACTIVITY.

$$\begin{pmatrix} \text{Fixed Overhead} \\ \text{Idle Capacity} \\ \text{Variance} \end{pmatrix} = \left[\begin{pmatrix} \text{Denominator} \\ \text{Hours} \end{pmatrix} - \begin{pmatrix} \text{Actual} \\ \text{Hours} \\ \text{Allowed} \end{pmatrix} \right] \times \begin{pmatrix} \text{Fixed Overhead} \\ \text{Standard} \\ \text{Rate} \end{pmatrix}$$

The variance is unfavorable if the denominator hours exceed the actual hours allowed; otherwise, it is favorable.

For example, assume that the denominator activity in machine-hours was 5,000 and the fixed overhead applied rate is $6. The actual hours used were 4,200. The idle capacity variance is $(5,000 - 4,200) \times \$6 = \$4,800$, an unfavorable variance because the company's plant was underutilized.

IDLE TIME cost of direct labor for employees unable to perform their assigned tasks because of machine breakdowns, shortage of materials, power failure, sloppy production scheduling, and the like. The cost of idle time is treated as part of factory overhead—that is, as part of indirect manufacturing costs that should be spread over all the production of a period.

IEEE 802.11 PROTOCOL a family of specifications developed by the U.S. Institute of Electrical and Electronics Engineers (IEEE). There are currently three specifications in the family (802.11a, 802.11b, and 802.11g), with more being developed. The 802.11b standard often referred to as Wi-Fi is currently more widespread. However, hardware manufacturers are increasingly offering multi-standard equipment that can work with various standards.

IF-CONVERTED METHOD method used to determine the dilution of convertible securities that are *not* common stock equivalents entering into the computation of fully diluted earnings per share. The method assumes convertible securities are converted at the beginning of the year or at issuance date, if later. The TREASURY STOCK METHOD is used to account for any cash received from convertible securities when the if-converted method is used. However, theoretical stock acquisitions are assumed only if the market price of the stock is greater than the exercise price.

ILLEGAL ACT violation of law or governmental regulations by an audited entity or its management or employees acting on behalf of the entity.

ILLIQUID
1. unable to convert an investment to cash in a short period of time with a minimum capital loss.
2. lacking cash (or working capital) or having a low current ratio. *See also* LIQUID.

IMPACT STATEMENT document that analyzes the projected effects of a contemplated project. A primary reference point within this statement concerns probable externalities (e.g., negative implications to the environment). An example would be the proposal of a large industrial corporation located on an upriver site to dump some level of pollutants into the air and streams. The proposal would lead to an environmental impact statement about the effects upon health.

IMPAIRMENT OF CAPITAL
1. amount by which stated capital has been decreased by distributions such as dividends or losses.
2. legal restriction enacted to protect creditors by limiting payments of dividends to retained earnings.
3. excess of liabilities over assets due to losses.

IMPAIRMENT OF VALUE permanent decline in the value of an asset. The entry is to debit the loss account and credit the asset for the reduction in utility. Recovery of the asset's cost or book value is not a realistic expectation.

IMPERFECT MARKET one where imperfect competition exists. Imperfect competition includes monopoly and oligopoly with one or more sellers controlling the market price. *See also* PERFECT MARKETS.

IMPLEMENTATION, BOTTOM UP APPROACH approach to implementing ABC with emphasis on achieving operational improvements. Activities and cost objects are disaggregated for high resolution; accuracy requirements are high.

IMPLICIT COST *see* IMPUTED COST.

IMPOUND
1. to take custody of and seize property or money by some legal action (e.g., court mandate).
2. in GOVERNMENT ACCOUNTING, to reduce authority to incur debt by withholding some portion or all of an APPROPRIATION.

IMPREST FUND *see* PETTY-CASH FUND.

IMPROVEMENT capitalized expenditure usually extending the useful life of an asset or improving it in some manner over and above the original asset. Thus if an expenditure adds years to an asset or improves its rate of output, it would be considered an improvement that is capitalized. In contrast, a maintenance or repair expense is not capitalized.

IMPUTED COST cost that is implied but not reflected in the financial reports of the firm; also called *implicit cost*. Imputed costs consist of the OPPORTUNITY COSTS of time and capital that the manager has invested in producing the given quantity of production and the opportunity costs of making a particular choice among the alternatives being considered.

IMPUTED INTEREST interest assumed on a noninterest-bearing note, including discounted or zero-coupon instruments, or on a note with an unrealistically low interest rate. It applies to both notes payable and notes receivable. The imputed interest rate is the one the borrower would normally incur in a similar transaction. Assume a $10,000 one-year noninterest-bearing note payable was issued on 1/1/2014. It would be unrealistic to believe that someone would take a one-year note without interest. Thus, interest must be imputed, to arrive at the present value of the note on 1/1/2015. If we use a 10% imputed interest rate, the present value of the note is $9,091 ($10,000/1.10). Hence, the note consists of a principal portion of $9,091 and an imputed interest portion of $909.

INADEQUACY loss or expense that is incurred by virtue of lost or reduced capacity, technological obsolescence, and/or abnormal wear and tear and that requires premature replacement or abandonment.

INCENTIVE STOCK OPTION (ISO) stock option granted employees under an option plan that provides a more favorable tax effect than QUALIFIED STOCK OPTIONS. With incentive stock options, employees receive the right to purchase a specified number of shares of company stock at a specified price during a specified period. ISOs are not taxable at the time of grant or at the time of exercise. Only when the stock is sold are the gains subject to federal taxation. Gains from incentive stock options will be taxed at an ordinary income tax rate. There is a cap on capital gain tax at 28%. Options may be exercised in any order. Also, an employer may not grant an employee more than $100,000 in stock options that first become exercisable in any one year.

IN-CHARGE ACCOUNTANT *see* ACCOUNTANT IN CHARGE.

INCOME
1. money earned during an accounting period that results in an increase in total assets.
2. items such as rents, interest, gifts, and commissions.
3. revenues arising from sales of goods and services.
4. excess of revenues over expenses and losses for an accounting period (i.e., net income).
See also GROSS INCOME; INCOME REALIZATION; NET INCOME; REVENUE.

INCOME ACCOUNT term used for revenue and expense accounts.

INCOME BOND bond on which the payment of interest is required only when earnings are available. Typically, interest that is bypassed does *not* accumulate. Income bonds are commonly used during the reorganization of a failing or failed business firm.

INCOME DEDUCTION nonoperating expenses of an organization that are listed in the final section of the income statement before arriving at net income. These costs, not usually subject to management control of day-to-day operations, are necessarily incurred in the operation of an ongoing enterprise and include interest expense, income taxes, and amortization of bond discount.

INCOME EXCLUSION RULE gross income not subject to tax, including: (1) interest on municipal securities; and (2) annuities and pensions that are returns of capital.

INCOME FROM CONTINUING OPERATIONS revenues and expenses after tax arising from the *ongoing* operations of the business for the accounting period. In arriving at income from continuing operations, NONRECURRING gains and losses are *included. After* income from continuing operations the following separate line items appear: INCOME FROM DISCONTINUED OPERATIONS, EXTRAORDINARY ITEMS, and cumulative effect of a CHANGE IN ACCOUNTING PRINCIPLE.

INCOME FROM DISCONTINUED OPERATIONS the results of operations of a component classified as held for sale are reported in the results of operations in the year(s) in which they *occur*. That is, phase-out losses are not accrued. In general, gain or loss from operations of the discontinued component should include operating gains or losses incurred and the gain or loss on disposal of a component incurred in the current period. Gains shall not be recognized until the year actually realized. The results of operations of a *component* of a company that either has been disposed of or is classified as being held for sale are reported in discontinued operations only if *both* of the following conditions are met: (1) the operations and cash flows of the component have been (or will be) eliminated from the ongoing operations as a result of the disposal decision, and (2) the company will not have any significant continuing involvement in the operations of the component after the disposal decision.

INCOME IN RESPECT OF A DECEDENT any income that a decedent earned or was entitled to receive prior to dying. Income in respect of a decedent is generally taxable to the survivor who receives the income, as in the case of pension income received by a decedent's widow.

INCOME REALIZATION recognition of income at the time of sale or the rendering of the service. The transfer of title in an ARM'S LENGTH TRANSACTION makes the process of earning income complete, as does the delivery of a service.

INCOME SMOOTHING form of income management that reflects economic results, not as they are, but rather as management wishes them to look. This results in lower earnings quality since net income does not representatively portray the economic performance of the business entity for the period. Income smoothing relies not on falsehoods and distortions but on the wide leeway existing in alternatively accepted accounting principles and their interpretations. It is conducted within the structure of GAAP. In effect, it redistributes income statement credits and charges among periods. The prime objective is to moderate income variability over the years by shifting income from good years to bad years. Future income may be shifted to the present year or vice versa. In a similar vein, income variability can be modified by shifting expenses or losses from period to period. An example is reducing a DISCRETIONARY COST (e.g., advertising expense, research and development expense) in the current year to improve current period earnings. In the next year, the discretionary cost will be increased.

For analytical purposes, the analyst should restate net income for profit increases or decreases due to income smoothing attempts.

INCOME SPLITTING shifting income from one member of a family to another. This, of course, is done to reduce the tax effects of a person in a higher marginal tax bracket, by diverting, allocating, or assigning income to a person in a lower tax bracket. A parent in a higher tax bracket could, for example, give money or property to a child. Income generated by that gift would be taxed at the child's lower rate.

INCOME STATEMENT form showing the elements used in arriving at a company's NET INCOME for the accounting period; also called *profit and loss statement*. It must be included in the annual report. An illustrative condensed income statement follows:

Sales
Less: Cost of sales
Gross Margin
Less: Operating expenses (including selling expenses and
      general & administrative expenses)
Income from operations
Add or Less: Other income and expenses
Income before tax
Less: Provision for income taxes
Income from continuing operations
Add or Less: Income from discontinued operations (net of tax)
Income before extraordinary items and cumulative effect
Add or Less: Extraordinary items (net of tax)
Add or Less: Cumulative effect of a change in accounting principle (net of
      tax)
Net income

INCOME SUMMARY temporary account in which revenues and expenses are closed at the end of the year. Income summary shows the net income or net loss for the year since total revenue and total expenses have been closed to it. The resulting profit or loss is then transferred to retained earnings. *See also* CLOSING ENTRY.

INCOME TAX government levy on the net earnings of an individual, corporation, or other taxable unit. The tax rate is usually a graduated one as earnings go from one tax bracket to another. Tax rates for individuals also depend on the status of the taxpayer (e.g., single, married). Income tax may include an addition to the regular tax such as a surtax. The income tax provision is shown as an expense in the income statement.

INCORPORATED legal state of existence signifying that a corporate entity has been recognized; that is, a legal entity has been authorized by a state or other political authority to operate according to the entity's approved articles of incorporation or charter. Incorporated entities share basic attributes: an exclusive name, continued and independent existence from shareholders or members, paid-in capital, and limited liability.

INCREMENTAL ANALYSIS decision-making method that utilizes the concept of RELEVANT COSTS; also known as *relevant cost approach* or *differential analysis*. Under this method, the decision involves the following steps: (1) gather all costs associated with each alternative; (2) drop the SUNK COSTS; (3) drop those costs that do not differ between alternatives; and (4) select the best alternative based on the remaining cost data.

For example, assume the ABC Company is planning to expand its productive capacity. The plan consists of purchasing a new machine for $50,000 and disposing of the old machine without receiving anything for it. The new machine has a five-year life. The old machine has a five-year remaining life and a book value of $12,500. The new machine will reduce variable operating costs from $35,000 per year to $20,000 per year. Annual sales and other operating costs are shown as follows:

	Present Machine	**New Machine**
Sales	$60,000	$60,000
Variable costs	35,000	20,000
Fixed costs:		
Depreciation		
(straight-line)	2,500	10,000
Insurance, taxes, etc.	4,000	4,000
Net income	$18,500	$26,000

At first glance, it appears that the new machine provides an increase in net income of $7,500 per year. The book value of the present machine, however, is a sunk cost and is irrelevant in this decision. Furthermore, sales and fixed costs such as insurance and taxes are also irrelevant since they do not differ between the two alternatives being considered. Eliminating all the irrelevant costs leaves us with only the incremental costs, as follows:

Savings in variable costs	$15,000	
Less: Increase in fixed costs	10,000	(a $2,500 sunk cost is irrelevant)
Net annual cash savings arising from the new machine	$ 5,000	

INCREMENTAL BACKUP *see* DIFFERENTIAL BACKUP.

INCREMENTAL COST-ALLOCATION METHOD variation of the stand-alone technique, establishes a priority among users and allocates common costs to the primary party up to the amount of that user's stand-alone costs. The remaining common costs are then allocated to the incremental party or parties.

INCREMENTAL (DIFFERENTIAL) COST
    1. difference in costs between two or more alternatives. This is equivalent to the marginal cost concept but involves multiple changes in output and discrete output choices, rather than a single-unit change. For example, consider the two alternatives A and B, whose costs are as follows:

	A	B	**Incremental Costs (B − A)**
Direct Materials	$10,000	$10,000	$ 0
Direct Labor	10,000	$15,000	5,000

The incremental costs are simply B − A (or A − B) as shown in the last column.

2. cost associated with increasing the output of an activity or project above some base level.

3. cost associated with increasing the quantity of a cost driver; also known as *differential cost*.

INCREMENTAL REVENUE ALLOCATION allocation method establishing priorities among the items in a bundle. The primary product is assigned 100% of its stand-alone revenue, with the remaining revenue from the bundle assigned sequentially to the other items.

INDEFINITE REVERSAL condition in which INTERPERIOD INCOME TAX ALLOCATION is not required for the undistributed earnings of a foreign subsidiary when there is sufficient evidence that those earnings will be undistributed *indefinitely*. A footnote is needed declaring the intention to reinvest the earnings indefinitely and the cumulative amount of the undistributed profits. When there is a change in circumstances and earnings will be remitted back to the U.S. parent, tax allocation is required.

INDEMNIFICATION reimbursement provided to a party to compensate for loss or damage.

INDENTURE legal document that specifically states the conditions under which a bond has been issued, the rights of the bondholders, and the duties of the issuing corporation; also called BOND INDENTURE; *deed of trust*. An indenture normally contains a number of standard and restrictive provisions (COVENANTS), including a sinking fund requirement, a minimum debt-equity ratio to be maintained, and an identification of the collateral if the bond is secured. It also covers redemption rights and call provisions. The indenture provides for the appointment of a trustee to act on behalf of bondholders.

INDEPENDENCE condition of accountant having no bias and being neutral regarding the client or another party in performing the audit function. Some independence guidelines for an auditor engaged in the attest function include: (1) no family relationship with the client's executives; (2) no financial interest in the company; and (3) no contingent fee based on the type of audit opinion rendered. The external auditor must furnish an impartial opinion on the client's financial position and operating performance. The audit opinion is based solely on the evidence found while conducting proper auditing procedures. Independence is created and maintained to enable the auditor to establish credibility for the audit opinion that financial statement users rely upon. *See also* INDEPENDENT ACCOUNTANT.

INDEPENDENT *see* INDEPENDENCE.

INDEPENDENT AUDITOR'S REPORT ON INTERNAL CONTROL OVER FINANCIAL REPORTING the auditor's opinion on the effectiveness of the company's internal control over financial reporting.

INDEPENDENT ACCOUNTANT CERTIFIED PUBLIC ACCOUNTANT (CPA) in public practice having no financial or other interest in the client whose financial statements are being examined. The CPA must be completely objective and impartial to conduct the attest function properly. Note that the term applies to an external auditor as distinguished from an internal auditor on the client's staff. An external auditor who has been involved with the client as an underwriter, promoter, trustee, or officer is *not* independent. *See also* INDEPENDENCE.

INDEPENDENT (OUTSIDE) DIRECTOR member of the Board of Directors of an entity who is an outsider, meaning he or she is not an employee of that entity. An example is a broker sitting on the Board of a client company. Such directors are important because they bring unbiased opinions regarding the company's decisions and diverse experience to the company's decision-making process. In order not to have a conflict of interest, independent directors should not participate on the boards of directly competing businesses. Directors are typically compensated based on a standard fee for each board meeting.

INDEPENDENT VARIABLE one that may take on any value in a relationship; for example, in $y = f(x)$, x is the independent variable. For example, independent variables that influence sales are advertising and price. *See also* DEPENDENT VARIABLE.

INDEXATION feature of a contract or agreement designed to adjust its value for general price-level changes. An example is a COST-OF-LIVING ADJUSTMENT (COLA) in a labor contract.

INDEXED BOND obligation with interest payments tied to an inflation index. If price levels rise, the rate of bond interest is adjusted accordingly. *See also* INDEXATION.

INDEX FUND a mutual fund that has as its primary objective the matching of the performance of a particular stock index such as the S&P 500 index. The beauty of index funds is twofold: (1) they minimize costs. All the fund company has to do is construct a portfolio out of the stocks in a chosen index. The fund is passively managed, with changes being made only to fine-tune the fund's performance to match more closely the index's results. The alternative is an actively managed fund, which even sounds more expensive. (2) The index funds eliminate your need to work so hard and worry too much. You can be fairly assured that your performance will be as good—or as bad—as the overall performance of the market or markets you select. A drawback to index funds is that since the index is made up of the stocks of large, well-known, and highly regarded companies, they can miss out on the opportunity of superior stock-price appreciation that some small companies often provide.

INDEXING *see* INDEXATION.

INDEX-NUMBER TREND SERIES method recommended when a comparison of financial statements covering more than two years is involved. In computing a series of index numbers, a base year must be selected and 100% assigned to it. The base year should be the one that is most typical or normal. Assume that the base year is 20X0. On 12/31/20X0 the cash balance of $8,000 is assigned 100%. The cash balances are $10,000 at 12/31/20X1 and $14,000 on 12/31/20X2. The index number for 20X1 is 125% ($10,000/$8,000) and for 20X2 is 175% ($14,000/$8,000).

INDEX OPTIONS calls and puts on indexes of stocks. There are "broad" indexes applying to a wide range of firms and industries. There are also "narrow-based" indexes relating to one industry or economic sector. An advantage of investing in an index option is that an interest in many companies is possible with a limited investment. It should be noted, however, that options have a limited life, are used to speculate or to hedge, and are settled in cash. In other words, if an index option is exercised (not normally done), the investor would not receive (or pay) the underlying stock, but would, rather, settle in cash.

INDIRECT COST expense that is difficult to trace directly to a specific costing object; also called COMMON COST. National advertising that benefits more than one product and sales territory is an example of an indirect cost. Fixed factory overhead is another example. *See also* DIRECT COST.

INDIRECT LABOR labor *not* directly involved in production but essential to the manufacturing process, such as supervisory personnel and janitors. It is classified as part of FACTORY OVERHEAD.

INDIRECT LIABILITY
1. situation in which responsibility for payment or satisfaction may arise in the future. An example is cosigning a loan for another party.
2. potential obligation, one that may eventually occur depending on some future event beyond the control of the company; also called CONTINGENT LIABILITY. Contingent liabilities may originate with such events as lawsuits, credit guarantee, and contested income tax assessments.

INDIRECT MANUFACTURING EXPENSES *see* FACTORY OVERHEAD.

INDIRECT MATERIAL primarily supplies, including glue, nails, and other minor items. They are classified as part of FACTORY OVERHEAD.

INDIRECT METHOD the method used in preparing an entity's statement of cash flows that involves reconciling NET INCOME to net cash flows from operating activities.

INDIRECT TAX one levied on a certain entity but not borne by that entity. For example, the retail sales tax is usually paid by the consumer in the form of an increase in price on goods or services—the retailer collects and passes on a tax actually borne by the consumer.

INDIVIDUAL RETIREMENT ACCOUNT (IRA) personal account that an employee can set up with a deposit that is tax deductible up to $5,000 a year (if 50 years or older, the contribution is $6,000). A working taxpayer *not* covered by another retirement plan may deduct IRA contributions. Also a taxpayer may deduct IRA contributions if ADJUSTED GROSS INCOME (AGI) is less than a certain amount. IRA funds are available to their depositors, penalty-free, at the age of 59½—or sooner in cases of death or disability. Early withdrawal of deductible contributions for any other reason will cost the taxpayer a penalty.

INDUSTRIAL DEVELOPMENT BOND (IDB) debt issued by a municipality to finance plants and facilities that are then leased to private industrial businesses; also called *industrial revenue bond*. The subsequent lease payments are used to service the bonds. The intent of IDBs is to attract private industry to promote local economic development. IDBs appealed to investors because they were exempt from federal income taxes. Exemption for IDBs is being phased out. A new category of tax-exempt bonds, called *qualified redevelopment bonds*, is to be used to finance land acquisition and redevelopment in blighted areas.

INDUSTRIAL ENGINEER professional who is engaged in the following activities: (1) product design and quality specification; (2) facilities design and layout; (3) design of production processes and machine systems; (4) work measurements; (5) quality control; and (6) scheduling and maintenance.

INDUSTRIAL REVENUE BOND *see* INDUSTRIAL DEVELOPMENT BOND (IDB).

INDUSTRY RATIOS mean or median financial ratios for a particular industry. The computed ratios for a company being analyzed should be compared to the industry average to form a basis of comparison. To what extent is the company better or worse than typical? Industry ratios are published by financial information services such as Dun & Bradstreet.

INDUSTRY STANDARDS in FINANCIAL RATIO ANALYSIS, industry average ratios used as standards to test whether ratios of a particular firm are normal. There are many widely used sources of industry standards. The Risk Management Association (RMA) (www.rmahq.org), the national association of banks and credit officers, computes a set of 16 key ratios for more than 300 lines of business. These ratios are published in *Annual Statement Studies*. *See also* FINANCIAL STATEMENT ANALYSIS.

INFLATION general rise in the price level. When inflation is present, a dollar today can buy more than a dollar in the future. In the presence of hyperinflation, with prices rising at 100% a year or more, there is a tendency for people to prefer hard assets (such as real estate and precious metals) to financial assets (stocks and bonds) in their investment choices.

INFLATION ACCOUNTING method of reporting that allows for the financial effects of changes in the price level. Two possible means of taking inflation into account are CONSTANT DOLLAR ACCOUNTING and CURRENT COST ACCOUNTING.

INFORMATION AND COMMUNICATION SYSTEMS the component of internal control concerned with (1) the methods and records used to identify and record business transactions, and (2) ensuring that employees understand their individual roles and responsibilities in connection with internal control over financial reporting.

INFORMATION PROCESSING transformation of data by classifying, sorting, merging, recording, retrieving, transmitting, or reporting. DATA PROCESSING is any operation or combination of operations that transforms data into useful information, whereas information processing goes one step further to include information generation and INFORMATION RETRIEVAL.

INFORMATION RETRIEVAL utilization of micrographics or computer storage for filing, storing, and retrieving information. Micrographics includes microfilm and microfiche that can be indexed for later retrieval on special orders.

INFORMATION RETURN return filed with the Internal Revenue Service for which no tax liability is imposed. Examples of such returns are Form 1065 (partnership return), Form W-2, and Form 1099. The law charges a penalty for each failure to file an information return with the IRS and for each failure on the part of businesses to supply a copy of the information return to the taxpayer. The law also adds a penalty for each information return submitted to the IRS, or the taxpayer, that contains incorrect information.

INFORMATION SYSTEM system of transforming raw data into useful information for a decision maker. *See* MANAGEMENT INFORMATION SYSTEM (MIS).

INHERENT LIMITATIONS OF INTERNAL CONTROL "built-in" limitations that result in limited assurance, rather than absolute assurance, that an entity's INTERNAL CONTROL objectives will be achieved. Inherent limitations include potential collusion, management override of controls, human error, and lack of segregation of duties.

INHERENT RISK the "built-in" susceptibility of an assertion to material misstatement presuming no related internal controls. Inherent risk is a component of the risk of material misstatement and exists independently of the audit. Neither management nor the auditor can limit inherent risk.

INHERITANCE TAX state tax levied upon the cash or fair market value of property received through inheritance. This tax is borne by the receiver of such property and not by the estate, as in federal ESTATE TAX.

INITIAL PUBLIC OFFERING *see* GOING PUBLIC.

INITIATION DATE *see* AUTONOMOUS.

INPUT COST cost of DIRECT MATERIAL, DIRECT LABOR, and other overhead items devoted to the production of a good or service.

INPUT-OUTPUT ANALYSIS study of linear production processes with fixed input coefficients. It attempts to develop a matrix relationship between the flow of goods and services from industries or branches of an economic system. The RECIPROCAL ALLOCATION METHOD that is used to allocate service department costs to production departments is an application of input-output analysis in accounting.

INQUIRY request for information; investigation. The auditor in conducting the examination seeks to obtain audit evidence by asking pertinent questions of client personnel or third parties. Answers obtained from such questions typically require corroboration. For example, the auditor may ask an employee why promotion expense is so high for the period, and the reply may be that some of it represents nonbusiness items. The propriety of the promotion expense account must then be evaluated by examining source documents. Another example is that of an auditor asking an employee where a given asset is located so that the asset can be visually corroborated. The question-asking aspect of the auditor with regard to third parties may be in such form as confirmations and legal letters.

INSIDE DIRECTOR individual on the board of directors who is an employee of the company. *See also* OUTSIDE DIRECTOR.

INSIDE INFORMATION privileged information obtained regarding material business results and pending security transactions that will not be made public until a certain date. Taking advantage of inside information for the purpose of making a profit is illegal.

INSIDER as defined by the *Securities Exchange Act of 1934*, corporate director, officer, or shareholder with more than 10% of a registered security, who through influence of position obtains knowledge that may be used primarily for unfair personal gain to the detriment of others. The definition has been extended to include relatives and others in a position to capitalize on inside information.

INSIDER TRADING
1. the buying and selling of the company's securities based on material information relating to the company that has not been made public. Insider trading according to this definition is against the law in most countries.
2. the buying and selling of shares of a public company by its officers, directors, and stockholders who own more than 10% of the company's stock. In the United States, such transactions must be reported monthly to the SEC under Section 16 of the Securities Exchange Act of 1934: reporting rules for similar trading may also exist in different countries or markets.

INSOLVENCY failure of a company to meet its obligations as they become due. An analysis of insolvency concentrates on the operating and capital structure of the business. The proportion of long-term debt in the capital structure must also be considered. *See also* BANKRUPTCY.

INSOURCING the opposite of OUTSOURCING.

INSPECTION TIME time spent either looking for product flaws or reworking defective units.

INSPECTOR GENERAL federal office that performs audit and investigative activities with a focus upon the independent review and appraisal of the activities of some federal agencies. The office is generally required to make periodic reports to Congress, and specifically to the secretary or undersecretary of certain federal agencies. The office was created by the Inspector General Act of 1978.

INSTABILITY INDEX OF EARNINGS deviation between actual income and trend income. The higher the index, the more instability associated with a firm's profitability. The index equals:

$$I = \frac{\sqrt{\Sigma(y^T - y)^2}}{n}$$

where y = reported net income

y^T = trend income

A simple TREND EQUATION solved by computer is used to determine trend income.

INSTALLMENT SALE
1. sale made on the installment basis. Many business firms—such as TV dealers, furniture stores, and appliance dealers—make installment sales. Typically, a customer purchases merchandise by signing an installment contract in which the customer agrees to a down payment plus install-

ment payments of a fixed amount over a specified period. The installment receivable so created by the contract is usually classified as a current asset.
2. transaction with a predetermined contract price in which payments are made on an installment basis over a period of time.

INSTALLMENT (SALES) METHOD manner of recognizing revenue when cash is collected. That is, when each payment is received from the customer, a portion of gross profit on the sale (and the gain) is recognized (based on the gross profit percentage in the year of the sale), so that by the final payment the entire gross profit is recorded. For example, ABC Company reports income on the installment basis, and the following information is available:

Year of Sale	Gross Profit %	Collected During 2014
2013	46%	$60,000
2014	40%	80,000

The realized gross profit on installment sales is computed as follows:

2013	46% × $60,000 =	$27,600
2014	40% × 80,000 =	32,000

Promulgated GAAP prohibit accounting for sales by any form of installment accounting except under exceptional circumstances where collectibility cannot be reasonably estimated or assured. The doubtfulness of collectibility can be caused by the length of an extended collection period or because no basis of estimation can be established. In such cases a company can use either the installment (sales) method or the COST-RECOVERY METHOD.

A taxpayer can elect *not* to use the installment method. The election is made by reporting on a timely filed tax return the gain computed by the taxpayer's usual method of accounting (cash or accrual).

INSTITUTE FOR SUPPLY MANAGEMENT'S INDEX the index, based on a survey of 375 companies in 17 industries, which measure new orders, inventories, exports, and employment in the service sector. Services account for five-sixths of the $10 trillion U.S. economy and include industries such as entertainment, utilities, health care, farming, insurance, retail, restaurants, and zoos.

INSTITUTE OF CHARTERED ACCOUNTANTS IN ENGLAND AND WALES large and influential accountancy association in the British Isles. It issues guidelines for practitioners, evaluates credentials of prospective members, and holds summer school every year. The institute puts out numerous publications, including two journals, *Accountancy* and *Accounting and Business Research*.

INSTITUTE OF CHARTERED ACCOUNTANTS IN SCOTLAND collective organization made up of the Edinburgh Society and similar societies in Glasgow and Aberdeen. It dates in its original form to 1854. This institute issues guidance to practitioners, evaluates candidates for membership, and holds annual summer schools. It publishes THE ACCOUNTANT'S MAGAZINE.

INSTITUTE OF INTERNAL AUDITORS (IIA) (www.theiia.org) professional organization that was established to develop the status of internal auditing. It administers and confers the CERTIFIED INTERNAL AUDITOR (CIA) designation.

INSTITUTE OF MANAGEMENT ACCOUNTING (IMA) *see* CERTIFICATE IN MANAGEMENT ACCOUNTING (CMA).

INSTITUTIONAL INVESTOR entity that trades large volumes of securities, such as banks, pension funds, insurance companies, mutual funds, labor unions, and corporate profit-sharing and pension plans. A very high percentage of daily trading on the stock exchange results from purchases and sales by institutional investors.

INSURANCE agreement through an insurance contract, termed a *policy*, that one party, for an agreed premium, will provide insurance or pay the insured a specified sum of money, contingent upon the specified conditions within the insurance contract, such as loss of life or property of the insured. Employers provide many types of insurance for employees, including health, disability, and life insurance.

INSURE to provide or obtain INSURANCE for reimbursement against loss to minimize risk.

INTANGIBLE ASSET item lacking physical substance (e.g., goodwill) or representing a right granted by the government (e.g., patent, trademark) or by another company (e.g., franchise). Intangibles have a life in excess of one year. Limited life intangible assets are amortized into expense over the period benefitted. Unlimited life intangibles are subject to a yearly impairment test.

INTANGIBLE DRILLING COST (IDC) all necessary intangible expenditures incurred in drilling from the surface to the natural resource deposit. An oil or gas deposit has the option of either capitalizing (and depleting) or immediately expensing certain intangible drilling costs. Among the qualifying intangible costs are labor, taxes, repairs, supplies, power, and equipment rentals.

INTANGIBLE VALUE total value of an organization as a going concern less the total value of its net tangible assets, leaving the residual intangible value. This residual value may represent PATENTS, TRADEMARKS, SECRETS, GOODWILL, and the like. In theoretical terms, intangible value is the present value of excess earning power of an entity over the normal rate of return.

INTEGRATED AUDIT involves auditing financial statements and internal control over financial reporting concurrently. All issuers (i.e., publicly traded entities) are required to undergo an annual integrated audit. The objective of an integrated audit is to enable an auditor to express opinions on the (1) fairness of the financial statement presentation, and (2) the effectiveness of internal control over financial reporting.

INTERACTIVE DATA ELECTRONIC APPLICATION (IDEA) a system that will replace Edgar. IDEA is a different approach from EDGAR. IDEA will initially supplement EDGAR but ultimately will replace it. IDEA provides investors with easier and quicker access to financial information about public companies. IDEA uses data-tagging software akin to bar codes for financial data. The technology is based on the extensible business reporting language (XBRL). It allows for fast comparisons of different business entities or different time periods. The information will be available at no cost on the Internet.

INTEGER PROGRAMMING mathematical approach maintaining that solutions to mathematical problems should appear in whole numbers (integers). For example, quantities like 12⅔ chairs, 34½ tables, 4.25 cars, or 2.75 persons may be unrealistic; yet simply rounding off the LINEAR PROGRAMMING solution to the nearest whole numbers may not produce a feasible solution. The integer programming method allows one to find the optimal *integer* solution to a problem without violating any of the constraints.

INTEGRATED SOFTWARE software package that combines many applications in one program. Previously, the accountant needed a utility program to load the data from one program into another program. Now there are integrated programs of two or more modules that interact. Integrated packages can move data among several programs utilizing common commands and file structures. In effect, there are multiple applications in memory simultaneously. An integrated package is recommended when identical source information is to be used for varying purposes and activities. For example, *MS Office* lets the accountant do word processing, outlining, telecommunications, graphics, data base, and spreadsheets and save each as a frame that can be integrated with the other frames.

INTEGRATED TEST FACILITY test using simulated transactions and dummy master records within a client's master file so that test data are processed simultaneously with actual input. The objective is to substantiate control reliability.

INTENSITY cost consumed by each unit of the activity driver. It is assumed that the intensity of each unit of the activity driver for a single activity is equal. Unequal intensity means that the activity should be broken into smaller activities or that a different activity driver should be chosen. *See also* DIVERSITY.

INTER-AMERICAN ACCOUNTING ASSOCIATION (IAAA) professional organization that meets every two to three years in different countries comprising the Americas. Technical aspects of the accounting profession are discussed at these meetings. Mexico City serves as the location for the secretariat of the organization.

INTERCEPT in a coordinate system, the distance from the origin to the point at which a line or curve intersects an axis. For example, the y-intercept is the value a of the dependent variable y in the formula $y = a + bx$ when x is zero. In a COST-VOLUME FORMULA, a is interpreted as the fixed cost portion of a mixed cost. *See also* COST FUNCTION.

INTERCOMPANY ACCOUNT general ledger account recording a transaction between related companies (e.g., affiliates). Typically, intercompany accounts are reciprocal records between the entities in their general ledgers. Examples are intercompany receivables and payables, and intercompany sales and purchases. In preparing combining or CONSOLIDATED FINANCIAL STATEMENTS, intercompany account balances must be eliminated.

INTERCOMPANY ELIMINATION deduction of intercompany items when preparing the combining or consolidated balance sheet and income statement. Examples are intercompany loans and intercompany investments between the parent and subsidiary. In the case of extensive eliminations, an eliminations ledger may be used.

INTERCOMPANY PROFIT excess of sales over cost of sales for merchandise or revenue minus related expenses for services to a related company when consolidated financial statements are being prepared. Intercompany profit is *fully* eliminated irrespective of the MINORITY INTEREST. Thus only earnings applicable to the outside are reflected as being realized.

INTEREST
1. amount charged by a lender to a borrower for the use of funds. The interest rate is typically expressed on an annual basis. Interest equals principal $\times$ interest rate $\times$ period of time. For example, the interest on a $10,000, 8% loan for 9 months is: $10,000 $\times$ 8% $\times$ 9/12 = $600.
2. equity ownership of an individual or other entity in a business or property expressed in percentage terms or in dollars. For example, if an investor company owns 50,000 shares of the investee company's 150,000 outstanding shares, the investor has a 33½% ownership *interest.*

INTEREST COVERAGE RATIO ratio that equals income before interest and taxes, divided by interest; also called *times-interest-earned ratio.* The ratio reveals the number of times interest is covered by earnings. A potential creditor would like to see a high ratio because it indicates that the company is able to meet its interest obligations with room to spare.

INTEREST DEDUCTION
Individual: itemized interest deduction on Schedule A of Form 1040. Interest can be only for the taxpayer's own debt and not for that of another individual. The taxpayer can deduct interest on a home mortgage for the principal residence and, within limits, for a second residence. Interest on a margin account with a broker is also deductible to the extent it offsets investment income.
Corporation: interest expense for business purposes that is tax deductible. Prepaid interest, however, is not deductible in the year of payment but has to be allocated over the period to which the interest amounts relate, irrespective of whether the cash basis or accrual basis is used.

INTEREST EXPENSE current period cost of borrowing funds that is shown as a financial expense in the income statement. Assume that on 11/1/2014 a $6000, one-year, 10% note is taken out. An accrual for interest expense is needed on 12/31/2014 for $100 ($6000 $\times$ 10% $\times$ 2/12).

INTEREST METHOD manner of determining interest expense or interest revenue. The effective interest rate is multiplied by the carrying value of the related debt or receivable at the beginning of the accounting period. The method results in a constant rate of interest but different dollar amounts each period. It is a preferred method over the straight-line method to amortize bond discount or premium. The amount of amortization equals the difference between the debit to interest expense (effective interest rate $\times$ carrying value of bond at beginning of year) and the cash payment (nominal interest rate $\times$ face value). Assume that on 1/1/2014 a $500,000, 10% bond is issued at 94%. The effective interest rate is 12%. The computation on 12/31/2014 for the bond discount is:

Interest expense (12% $\times$ $470,000)	$56,400
Cash (10% $\times$ $500,000)	$50,000
Bond discount (for difference)	$ 6,400

INTEREST ON INVESTMENT actual return earned or expected to be earned on a debt instrument. *See also* OPPORTUNITY COST.

INTEREST RATE rate, usually expressed as a percentage per annum charged on money borrowed or lent. The interest rate may be variable or fixed. *See also* VARIABLE RATE LOAN.

The various types of interest rates are:

(1) *prime (interest) rate*: rate charged on business loans to the most credit-worthy customers by the nation's leading banks. The prime rate fluctuates with changing supply and demand relationships for short-term funds.

(2) *nominal* or *stated interest rate*: predetermined loan rate. The stated interest rate often differs from the effective interest rate. If the interest is paid when a loan matures, the actual rate of interest paid is equal to the stated interest rate. However, if the interest is paid in advance, it is deducted from the loan, so that the borrower actually receives less money than requested, which will raise the interest rate above the stated rate. The actual rate thus paid is called the EFFECTIVE INTEREST RATE, or YIELD. It is computed by dividing the dollar interest paid by the amount of loan proceeds available to the borrower. For example, for a $1,000 loan with an annual interest of 10% with a provision of interest paid in advance, the effective rate is 11.11% [$100/($1,000 minus $100) = $100/$900]. In bonds the BOND YIELD usually differs from the nominal (coupon) interest rate.

(3) *discount rate*: rate the Federal Reserve charges member banks for loans. It is also the interest rate used in determining the present value of future cash flows. *See also* DISCOUNT RATE.

INTEREST RATE FUTURES contracts where the holder agrees to take delivery of a given amount of the related debt security at a later date (usually no more than three years). Futures may be in Treasury bills and notes, certificates of deposit, commercial paper, or GNMA certificates, etc. Interest rate futures are stated as a percentage of the par value of the applicable debt security. The value of interest rate futures contracts is directly tied to interest rates. For example, as interest rates decrease, the value of the contract increases. As the price or quote of the contract goes up, the purchaser of the contract has the gain, while the seller loses. A change of one basis point in interest rates causes a price change. Those who trade in interest rate futures do not usually take possession of the financial instrument. In essence, the contract is used either to hedge or to speculate on future interest rates and security prices. For example, a pension fund manager might use interest rate futures to hedge the bond portfolio position. Speculators find financial futures attractive because of their potentially large return on a small investment due to the low deposit requirement. However, significant risk exists.

INTEREST RATE RISK possibility that the value of an asset will change adversely as interest rates change. For example, when market interest rates rise, fixed-income bond prices fall.

INTERGOVERNMENTAL REVENUE revenue received from other governmental agencies and municipalities. An example is grants.

INTERIM AUDIT
1. part of an audit carried out while the accounting period of the full audit is still in process. During interim audit work periods, the work scheduled may

be confirmations, inventory observation, or other audit steps that will be concluded during the final phase of the annual audit.

2. audit of an interim period (e.g., of quarterly statements).

INTERIM FINANCIAL STATEMENT statement issued for an accounting period of less than one year, such as quarterly or monthly. Interim financial statements should be based on the accounting principles employed in the previous year's annual report unless a change has been adopted in the current year. Interim financial statements are typically unaudited. Footnote disclosure is given of seasonality effects. If a fourth quarter is not presented, any significant adjustments to it must be commented upon in the annual report.

INTERIM REPORT *see* INTERIM FINANCIAL STATEMENT.

INTERNAL AUDIT auditing procedures and techniques conducted by INTERNAL AUDITORS primarily concentrating on adherence to management policies, existence of proper internal controls, uncovering misappropriation of funds (i.e., fraud), existence of proper record keeping, and effective operations of the business.

INTERNAL AUDITOR employee of the organization who is conducting an internal audit. The internal auditor works independently of the accounting and other departments and is concerned with financial and/or operational activities of the organization. The internal auditor attempts to assure the accuracy of business records, uncover internal control problems, and identify operational difficulties. The internal auditor's opinion on the company's financial records does not have the same acceptance as that of a CPA doing the same work. *See also* EXTERNAL AUDITOR.

INTERNAL AUDITOR, THE bimonthly publication of the INSTITUTE OF INTERNAL AUDITORS (IIA). Readership includes internal auditors, controllers, treasurers, CPAs, EDP auditors, managers, and financial managers. Subject matter includes internal auditing, internal control, information systems auditing, professional ethics, and financial management.

INTERNAL CHECK accounting procedure or physical control to safeguard assets against loss due to fraud or other irregularities. Internal check is an element of INTERNAL CONTROL. Weak internal check mechanisms mandate a greater degree of auditing procedures. An example of internal control is segregating the record keeping for an asset and its physical custody, such as in the case with inventory and cash. No one individual should have complete control over a transaction from beginning to end. Internal checks make it difficult for an employee to steal cash or other assets and concurrently cover up by entering corresponding amounts in the accounts. An example of internal check is the establishment of input and output controls within a data processing department. A group or person has the responsibility of checking control totals provided by the user department with those generated during the processing of the data. Examples of physical controls are guards and gates to restrict access.

INTERNAL CONTROL plan of organization and all the methods and measures used by a business to monitor assets, prevent fraud, minimize errors, verify the correctness and reliability of accounting data, promote operational efficiency, and ensure that established managerial policies are followed.

Internal control extends to functions beyond the accounting and financial departments. Accounting controls encompass safeguarding assets and the accuracy of financial records. They are designed to give assurance that transactions are properly authorized and are recorded to allow for financial statement preparation in accordance with GAAP. Further, accounting controls deal with maintaining accountability for assets, proper authorization to access assets, and periodic reconciliations between recorded assets on the books and the physical assets that exist. Administrative or managerial controls deal with operational efficiency, adherence to managerial policies, and management's authorization of transactions. Examples are quality control and employee performance reports. Accounting and administrative controls are not mutually exclusive since some procedures and records falling under accounting control may also be used for administrative control. An essential ingredient in maintaining internal control is the internal audit function. The CPA reports on the adequacy of existing controls within the entity. The external auditor must carefully evaluate the internal control system as a basis to determine the degree of audit procedures necessary in the circumstances.

INTERNAL CONTROL OVER FINANCIAL REPORTING a process designed and maintained by management to provide reasonable assurance regarding the reliability of financial reporting and the preparation of the financial statements for external purposes in accordance with United States GAAP.

INTERNAL DOCUMENT record made up and kept *within* the entity in connection with its accounting records. It does not go to or come from external parties. Examples are employee time sheets, employee W-2s, inventory receiving reports, and duplicate purchase invoices. The auditor puts much more reliance on external documents than internal ones since they are derived from outside independent parties. Internal documents do not serve as very reliable evidence in the CPA's examination of a client's records. *See also* EXTERNAL DOCUMENT.

INTERNAL FAILURE COSTS category of QUALITY COSTS incurred because products and services fail to conform to requirements prior to external sale, such as scrap and rework; a cost of nonconformance.

INTERNAL RATE OF RETURN (IRR) rate earned on a proposal. It is the rate of interest that equates the initial investment (I) with the present value (PV) of future cash inflows. That is, at IRR, $I = PV$, or NPV (net present value) $= 0$. Under the internal rate of return method, the decision rule is: accept the project if IRR exceeds the cost of capital; otherwise, reject the proposal.

For example, consider the following data:

Initial investment	$16,200
Estimated life	10 years
Annual cash inflows	$ 3,000
Cost of capital (minimum required of return)	10%

Set up the following equality ($I = PV$):

$$\$16,200 = \$3,000 \times PV$$

Then $PV = \$16,200/\$3,000 = 5.400$, which stands somewhere between 12% and 14% in the 10-year line of table 4 in the back of the book. Because the investment's IRR (13.15%) is greater than the cost of capital (10%), the investment should be accepted.

The IRR method is easy to use as long as cash inflows are even from year to year. Where cash flows are uneven, the IRR can be determined by using Excel.

Excel has a function IRR(*values, guess*). Excel considers negative numbers as cash outflows such as the initial investment, and positive numbers as cash inflows. Many financial calculators have similar features. Suppose you want to calculate the IRR of a $12,950 investment (the value "−12,950" entered in year 0, followed by 10 monthly cash inflows of $3,000). Using a guess of 12% (the value of 0.12), which is in effect the cost of capital, your formula would be @IRR(values, 0.12) and Excel would return 19.15%, as shown below.

Year 0	1	2	3	4	5	6	7	8	9	10
−12,950	3,000	3,000	3,000	3,000	3,000	3,000	3,000	3,000	3,000	3,000

IRR = 19.15%

An advantage of the IRR method is that it considers the TIME VALUE OF MONEY and is therefore more exact and realistic than ACCOUNTING RATE OF RETURN (ARR). Disadvantages are: (1) it fails to recognize the varying size of investment in competing projects and their respective dollar profitabilities, and (2) in limited cases, where there are multiple reversals in the cash-flow streams, the project could yield more than one internal rate of return.

INTERNAL REPORTING financial data or other information accumulated by one individual to be communicated to another within the business entity. The information assists others in the managerial decision-making process. Examples are expense reports, capital budgeting analysis, and other reports designed to guide management rather than inform outsiders.

INTERNAL REVENUE CODE federal tax law of the United States that comprises the rules and regulations to be followed by taxpayers. The Internal Revenue Code of 1954 is being followed, including subsequent amendments and revisions.

INTERNAL REVENUE SERVICE (IRS) (www.irs.gov) branch of the federal government in charge of collecting most types of taxes, such as personal, corporate, gift, estate, and excise. Some taxes are collected by other agencies, such as custom duties, tobacco, and alcohol. The IRS administers tax rules and regulations, and investigates tax improprieties. Criminal prosecution may be made by the IRS for tax fraud through the U.S. Tax Court. Examinations of tax returns can involve: (1) simple matters that are resolved by mail; (2) IRS office examination concentrating on additional verification by the taxpayer of selected items; or (3) field examination at the taxpayer's office or representative's office. A field audit is typically broader in scope than an office audit, covering many items on a tax return, and often for more than one year.

INTERNAL SERVICE FUND in GOVERNMENT ACCOUNTING, fund used to account for goods or services given to one department by another on a cost reimbursement basis. The fund is profit and loss oriented and hence follows accrual accounting.

INTERNATIONAL ACCOUNTING STANDARDS (IAS) a set of international accounting and reporting standards that will help to harmonize company financial information, improve the transparency of accounting, and ensure that investors receive more accurate and consistent reports. Statements of International Accounting Standards issued by the Board of the INTERNATIONAL ACCOUNTING STANDARDS COMMITTEE (IASC) between 1973 and 2001 are designated International Accounting Standards. The INTERNATIONAL ACCOUNTING STANDARDS BOARD (IASB) announed in April 2001 that its accounting standards would be designated INTERNATIONAL FINANCIAL REPORTING STANDARDS (IFRS). Also in April 2001, the IASB announced that it would adopt all of the International Accounting Standards issued by the IASC.

INTERNATIONAL ACCOUNTING STANDARDS BOARD (IASB) (www. iasb.org) an independent regulatory body, based in the United Kingdom, that aims to develop a single set of global accounting standards. Board members come from nine countries and have a variety of functional backgrounds. The Board is committed to developing, in the public interest, a single set of high-quality, understandable, and enforceable global accounting standards that require transparent and comparable information in general-purpose financial statements. In addition, the Board cooperates with national accounting standard-setters to achieve convergence in accounting standards around the world.

INTERNATIONAL ACCOUNTING STANDARDS COMMITTEE (IASC) group consisting of members from influential accounting bodies in the U.S., England, West Germany, France, Canada, Japan, and other countries. The organization proposes internationally accepted accounting standards and issues discussion papers, drafts, and formal statements on important accounting issues. A major purpose of the committee is to aid comparability of financial reporting among countries.

INTERNATIONAL AUDITING PRACTICES COMMITTEE (IAPC) panel of the INTERNATIONAL FEDERATION OF ACCOUNTANTS (IFA) that gives guidance to auditors in various countries.

INTERNATIONAL BANK FOR RECONSTRUCTION AND DEVELOPMENT (IBRD) organization that assists less-developed countries in strengthening their economies; also called *World Bank*. The IBRD makes loans to countries or firms for such purposes as roads, irrigation projects, and electric-generating plants.

INTERNATIONAL CONGRESS OF ACCOUNTANTS (ICA) body whose aim is to present and resolve international accounting and auditing issues to encourage uniformity, congruity, and international cooperation. This congress meets every five years.

INTERNATIONAL FEDERATION OF ACCOUNTANTS (IFA) organization of international representatives whose purpose is to develop and enhance concordance with respect to standards and accounting practices on a worldwide basis. It was formed in 1977.

INTERNATIONAL FINANCIAL REPORTING STANDARDS (IFRS) standards and interpretations adopted by the International Accounting Standards Board (IASB). Many of the standards forming part of IFRS are known by the older name of International Accounting Standards (IAS). IFRS are sometimes confused with IAS, which are the older standards that IFRS replaced. IAS was issued from 1973 to 2000. The implementation in 2005 of IFRS as the reporting language for all listed companies in the European Union and for many others around the world has been one of the biggest revolutions in the accounting world for a generation. The Financial Accounting Standards Board (FASB) and International Accounting Standards Board (IASB) are committed to crafting one set of accounting standards. The goal of the convergence project is to unify accounting standards, which in turn should improve comparability of financial statements across national jurisdictions.

INTERNATIONAL MONETARY FUND (IMF) organization created at the close of World War II to supervise the international financial system, to lend official reserves to nations with temporary payments deficits, and to decide when exchange rate adjustments are needed to correct chronic payments deficits.

INTERNET a worldwide network of computers that utilizes TCP/IP technology for communication. The Internet is decentralized in design, and no one organization owns it. Most individuals get access to the Internet through a commercial Internet Service Provider (ISP).

INTERPERIOD INCOME TAX ALLOCATION temporary difference between years in which a transaction affects taxable income and accounting (book) income. Temporary differences originate in one period and subsequently reverse in another. The differences result from four types of transactions, as follows: (1) income included in taxable income after being included in book income (e.g., installment sale); (2) expenses deducted for taxable income subsequent to accounting income (e.g., warranty expense is deducted for book purposes in the year of sale but for tax purposes when paid); (3) income recognized for tax purposes prior to being included for accounting purposes (e.g., rental received in advance); and (4) expenses subtracted for taxable income before being deducted for accounting purposes (e.g., accelerated depreciation method for tax and straight-line depreciation for books). *See also* INTRAPERIOD TAX ALLOCATION; PERMANENT DIFFERENCE.

INTERPOLATION process used to estimate an unknown value between two known values by utilizing a common mathematical relation (e.g., proportion, function, linear, or logarithmic). Interpolation is commonly needed when consulting present value tables in which a present value interest factor is desired for a given period and unlisted interest rate. One would use the two closest listed interest rates, above and below the given interest rate, to estimate the present value factor needed for a given computation. Interpolation is more than likely used to find the INTERNAL RATE OF RETURN on an investment project.

INTERPRETATION opinion regarding a set of facts. A degree of subjectivity is involved on the part of the individual, based on his or her experience, personality, and biases. For example, after performing a detailed analysis of the financial statements of a company, two financial analysts may differ in their perceptions of what the market price of the company's stock should be.

INTRANET private network used within the company. An intranet serves the internal needs of the business entity. Intranet users are able to access the Internet, but firewalls keep outsiders from accessingconfidential data. It makes use of the infrastructure and standards of the Internet and the Web. Intranets use low-cost Internet tools, are easy to install, and offer flexibility. Intranets have already been established by virtually all Fortune 500 companies and many other organizations.

INTRAPERIOD TAX ALLOCATION distribution of tax for the *current year* in different parts of the financial statements. For example, tax expense is shown on income before tax, cumulative effect of a change in principle net of tax, extraordinary items net of tax, and prior period adjustments net of tax. *See also* INTERPERIOD INCOME TAX ALLOCATION.

INVENTORIABLE COST *see* PRODUCT COST.

INVENTORY merchandise or supplies on hand or in transit at a particular point in time. The three types of inventory for a manufacturing company are raw materials, work-in-process, and finished goods. Included in inventory are (1) goods in transit for which title has been received and (2) goods out on consignment. Inventory is recorded in the accounting records typically at the lower of cost or market value. An inventory count usually occurs at year-end to assure that the physical quantity equals the quantity per books. At the end of the accounting period, beginning and ending inventories are presented in the income statement in the cost-of-goods-sold calculation, and ending inventory is shown in the balance sheet under current assets.

INVENTORY CONTROL monitoring the supplies, raw materials, work-in-process, and finished goods by various accounting and reporting methods. Some controls are the maintenance of detailed stock records showing receipts and issuances; inventory ledger showing quantities and dollars; and written policies regarding purchasing, receiving, inspection, and handling. Periodic inventory counts should occur to verify that the inventory amounts per books physically exist. A good system of inventory control assists in reducing inventory ordering and carrying costs. *See also* ABC METHOD.

INVENTORY MODELS quantitative models designed to control inventory costs by determining the optimal time to place an order (or begin production) and the optimal order quantity (or production run). The timing of an order can be periodic (placing an order every X days) or perpetual (placing an order whenever the inventory declines to X units).

INVENTORY OBSERVATION observation by an auditor, as part of the examination, of the taking of a company's physical inventory by the client staff. The auditor also checks on a sample basis the count arrived at by the employees to assure it is being done accurately. A review is also made of the client's written policies regarding the inventory counting process.

INVENTORY PROFIT unrealized profit derived from holding inventory during a price rise. One measure of inventory profit is the difference between the original cost and the higher current replacement cost. Another measure is the increased value arising from the increase in the CONSUMER PRICE INDEX (CPI) since the acquisition date. Assume that on 1/1/2014, inventory was bought for $50,000. On 12/31/2014, the replacement cost is $54,000. The inventory profit is $4,000.

INVENTORY RESERVE
  1. appropriation of retained earnings to reflect *future* declines in price of inventory.

2. archaic term relating to the allowance account to reduce inventory from cost to market value in applying the lower of cost or market value rule. The reserve amount is usually calculated from inventory sheets for the specific items.

3. reserve for temporary liquidation of the LAST-IN, FIRST-OUT (LIFO) base, used in interim reporting; the LIFO base that is expected to be replenished by year end. Assume that the original cost of the liquidated LIFO base is $10,000 and its replacement cost is $12,000. The entry at the interim period is to debit cost of sales $12,000, credit inventory $10,000, and reserve for liquidation of LIFO base $2,000.

INVENTORY STATUS FILE file indicating how much inventory is on hand or on order.

INVENTORY TURNOVER equation that equals the cost of goods sold divided by the average inventory. Average inventory equals beginning inventory plus ending inventory divided by 2. A low turnover rate may point to overstocking, obsolescence, or deficiencies in the product line or marketing effort. However, in some instances a low rate may be appropriate, such as where higher inventory levels occur in anticipation of rapidly rising prices or shortages. A high turnover rate may indicate inadequate inventory levels, which may lead to a loss in business. Assume cost of sales is $70,000, beginning inventory is $10,000, and ending inventory is $9,000. The inventory turnover equals 7.37 times ($70,000/$9,500). It should be noted that some compilers of industry data (e.g., Dun & Bradstreet) use sales as the numerator instead of cost of sales. Cost of sales yields a more realistic turnover figure, but it is often necessary to use sales for purposes of comparative analysis.

INVENTORY VALUATION determination of the cost assigned to raw materials inventory, work-in-process, finished goods, and any other inventory item. Various methods are allowed in valuing inventory including LAST-IN, FIRST-OUT (LIFO), FIRST-IN, FIRST-OUT (FIFO), and WEIGHTED AVERAGE. Inventory is valued at the lower of cost or market value applied on either an item-by-item basis, a category basis, or a total basis.

INVESTING ACTIVITIES business activities that involve the acquiring and selling of long-term assets, the acquiring and selling of equity or debt securities other than trading, and the making and collecting of loans.

INVESTMENT

1. *see* CAPITAL ASSET.
2. expenditure to acquire property, equipment, and other capital assets that produce revenue.
3. securities of other companies held for the long term, called *long-term investments* and shown in the noncurrent asset section of the balance sheet.
4. securities of other companies held for a very short term (short-term investments). They are shown as a MARKETABLE SECURITY in the current asset section of the balance sheet.

INVESTMENT ADVISOR financial professional who specializes in making portfolio recommendations for clients. The advisor recommends a mix of investments (i.e., stocks, bonds, real estate) based on the particular needs of the client (i.e., tax rate, risk preferences, liquidity requirements). The investment advisor may also recommend specific companies in which to invest.

INVESTMENT BANKER intermediary between an issuer of new securities and the investor. The investment banker buys new securities and then sells them to the public at a higher price, earning a profit on the spread. Depending on the arrangement with the issuing company, the investment banker may perform the functions of underwriting, distribution of securities, and advice and counsel.

INVESTMENT CAPITAL *see* CAPITAL ASSET.

INVESTMENT CENTER responsibility center within an organization that has control over revenue, cost, and investment funds. It is a profit center whose performance is evaluated on the basis of the return earned on invested capital. The corporate headquarters or division in a large decentralized organization would be an example of an investment center. RETURN ON INVESTMENT and RESIDUAL INCOME are two key performance measures of an investment center.

INVESTMENT SOFTWARE computer program that tracks investments in shares, cost, and revenue. Some investment software includes price and dividend histories of securities. Comparisons can be made with major market indicators. Automatic valuation of securities, including current value, unrealized gain or loss, and daily price change, can be made. Tax ramifications of investment decisions can be analyzed by some packages.

INVESTMENT TURNOVER return earned on capital invested in a business. It equals:

$$\frac{\text{Sales}}{\text{Net Worth} + \text{Long-Term Liabilities}}$$

A higher ratio indicates good use of the funds placed into the business.

INVOICE bill prepared by a seller of goods or services and submitted to the buyer. The invoice describes such items as date, customer, vendor, quantities, prices, freight, and credit terms of a transaction.

INVOLUNTARY BANKRUPTCY financial failure that is legally and formally declared by petition of the debtor's creditors, and not by the debtor. *See also* CHAPTER 11; CHAPTER 7.

INVOLUNTARY CONVERSION sudden loss of an asset that does not occur in the ordinary course of business, such as destruction by fire or condemnation by a governmental agency. The difference between the cash received from the insurance company and the carrying value of the destroyed asset (or portion thereof) represents a loss or gain for financial reporting purposes. Under the INTERNAL REVENUE CODE, the loss on an involuntary conversion is recognized, but the gain is reflected only to the degree that the proceeds are *not* reinvested in similar property within two or three years subsequent to the conversion.

IP (INTERNET PROTOCOL) ADDRESS consists of a series of four numbers of up to three digits, separated by decimal points. All computers and devices connected to the Internet have an IP (Internet Protocol) address.

IRRELEVANT COSTS costs that may be either sunk costs or costs that do not differ among alternatives.

iSHARES index funds that trade like stocks on stock markets. Each share represents a proportion of ownership in each stock that makes up an index. iShares are a great way for smaller investors to get the diversification of 50 or more companies without having to buy each individual stock.

ISO 9000 certification standards developed by the International Organization for Standardization (ISO) that serve as a basis for quality standards for global manufacturers.

ISSUED CAPITAL STOCK authorized shares that have been issued for cash, services, or other property. Included in issued shares are TREASURY SHARES. *See also* OUTSTANDING CAPITAL STOCK.

ISSUERS publicly traded entities that are subject to the rules of the PUBLIC COMPANY ACCOUNTING OVERSIGHT BOARD (PCAOB).

ITEMIZED DEDUCTION subtraction from adjusted gross income for individual taxpayers. Examples of allowable deductions are mortgage interest, certain casualty losses, medical expenses, contributions, real estate taxes, and state and local government income taxes.

J

JAVA a highly popular, fast, secure, and reliable computer programming language that is used everywhere from computers to game consoles to cell phones to the INTERNET.

JOB ORDER customer order for a specific number of specially designed, made-to-order products.

JOB ORDER COSTING accumulation of costs by specific jobs, contracts, or orders. This costing method is appropriate when direct costs can be identified with specific units of production. Job order costing is widely used by custom manufacturers such as printing, aircraft, construction, auto repair, and professional services. Job order costing keeps track of costs as follows: (1) direct material and direct labor are traced to a particular job; (2) costs not directly traceable — factory overhead — are applied to individual jobs, using a *predetermined overhead rate*. The overhead rate is equal to the budgeted annual overhead divided by the budgeted annual activity units (direct labor-hours, machine-hours, etc.). At the end of the year, the difference between actual overhead and overhead applied is closed to cost of goods sold, if there is an immaterial difference. On the other hand, if a material difference exists, work-in-process, finished goods, and cost of goods sold are adjusted on a proportionate basis based on units or dollars at year-end for the deviation between actual and applied overhead.

JOB (ORDER) COST SHEET subsidiary record for work-in-process inventory under a job order production system. A separate cost sheet is kept for each identifiable job, accumulating the direct materials, direct labor, and factory overhead assigned to that job as it moves through production. The form varies according to the needs of the company. A sample job cost sheet follows:

JOB COST SHEET

Job No. _____

For Stock _____ Customer _____

Product _____ Date Started _____ Date Completed _____

Direct Material			Direct Labor			Overhead	
Date	Reference	Amount	Date	Reference	Amount	Date	Amount
	(Stores Requisition Number)			(Work Ticket Number)			(Based on Predetermined Overhead Rate)

Summary of Costs

Direct Materials	x x
Direct Labor	x x
Factory Overhead Applied _____	x x
Total	x x x

JOB PROJECT-PERFORMANCE COST VARIANCE used in controlling job projects, the difference between the actual cost of work performed (CWP) and the budgeted CWP. This variance may further be divided into price and efficiency variances. It measures cost overruns or underruns.

JOB PROJECT-SCHEDULE COST VARIANCE difference between the budgeted cost of work performed and the budgeted cost of work scheduled. It measures the extent to which the project is ahead of or behind schedule.

JOINT AND SEVERAL LIABILITY legal concept in which two or more persons have an obligation that can be enforced against them by joint action, against all members, and against themselves as individuals, hence several liability or responsibility.

JOINT COSTS common manufacturing costs incurred prior to the point, referred to as the SPLIT-OFF POINT, where JOINT PRODUCTS are identified as individual products. There are several methods of allocating joint costs to the joint products, including sales value and volume. *See also* COMMON COST; SELL-OR-PROCESS-FURTHER DECISION.

JOINT PRODUCTS items that have a relatively significant sales value when two or more types are produced simultaneously from the same input by a joint process. For example, gasoline, fuel oil, kerosene, and paraffin are the joint products produced from crude oil. *See also* SELL-OR-PROCESS FURTHER DECISION.

JOINT RETURN income tax return that effectively provides that income earned by a husband and wife will be treated as though it had been earned by both equally. This is allowed even though one spouse may not have income or deductions. A joint return usually provides a favorable tax effect compared to the filing of a non-joint return.

JOINT STOCK COMPANY assemblage of individuals formed to start and operate a business organization. A joint stock company generally shares the same characteristics as a corporation, but it does not provide limited liability, and in many states it lacks formal and official authorization. Once popular because of the ease of formation under the common law, joint stock companies are not seen as much today because it has become easier to form limited liability corporations under state authorization.

JOINT TENANCY two or more persons to whom real or personal property is deeded or who together own an undivided interest in such property as a whole. Upon the death of one of the joint tenants, the deceased's property goes to the survivor without becoming an element of the estate of the deceased; also called *joint tenancy with right of survivorship.*

JOINT TENANCY WITH RIGHT OF SURVIVORSHIP *see* JOINT TENANCY.

JOINT VENTURE joining together of two or more business entities or persons in order to undertake a specific business venture. A joint venture is not a continuing relationship such as a partnership but may be treated as a partnership for income tax purposes.

JOURNAL book or place where business transactions are first recorded in chronological order before being posted to the general ledger accounts. The general journal is used to record miscellaneous transactions that do not fit into SPECIAL JOURNALS (sales, purchases, cash receipts, cash disbursements, and payroll journals). A general journal will help link together debit and credit parts of transactions.

JOURNAL ENTRY record of the accounting information for a business transaction. The entry is made in a journal and then posted to the ledger. The journal entry has a date, account(s) debited, and account(s) credited. If there is more than one debit or credit, it is referred to as a compound entry. Total debits must equal total credits. The journal entry is accompanied by a short explanation.

JOURNAL OF GOVERNMENT FINANCIAL MANAGEMENT formerly, *Government Accountants Journal,* quarterly journal of the Association of Government Accountants (AGA). Subject matter includes all aspects of accounting and financial management relating to government.

JOURNALIZE to make an entry for a transaction in the JOURNAL (book of original entry). For example, if rent is paid with cash, this transaction would be entered in the journal. Rent Expense is debited and Cash is credited. Transactions are entered on a daily basis in chronological order. Debits and credits are listed along with their appropriate explanations. Thus the journal reflects in one place all information about a transaction.

JOURNAL OF ACCOUNTANCY monthly publication of the AMERICAN INSTITUTE OF CERTIFIED PUBLIC ACCOUNTANTS (AICPA) (www.aicpa.org). Its readership includes practicing CPAs, controllers, treasurers, private accountants, and academicians. All aspects of accounting appear in the *Journal of Accountancy* including auditing, management advisory services, financial accounting applications, international accounting, computer applications, professional ethics, and taxation.

JOURNAL OF ACCOUNTING RESEARCH semiannual publication of the Graduate School of Business of the University of Chicago. It is one of the leading academic journals. It includes an annual supplement containing papers presented at conferences held at the university. Subject matter concentrates on empirical, analytical, and experimental research in all areas of accounting.

JOURNAL VOUCHER one that documents and authorizes a business transaction. It will lead to a journal entry in a journal.

JUDGMENT
1. accountant's opinion regarding a set of facts or evidence. Besides interpreting the meaning of the situation, the accountant must also determine its perceived implications. For example, the degree of audit testing required in a given situation depends on the auditor's judgment of the quality of the internal control system.
2. court order to pay money.

JUDGMENT SAMPLE determination by an auditor, based on personal experience and familiarity with the client, of the number of items, as well as the particular items, to be examined in a population. This function allows the accountant to maintain objectivity and thoroughness in testing the sampled items for accuracy. A judgmental sample may be appropriate when only a specific area within the universe is under auditor scrutiny or timely information is required. The sampling is *not* done on a random basis. Furthermore, there is no determination of a sampling error, nor any statistical conclusions about precision or confidence levels. *See also* RANDOM SAMPLE.

JUNIOR ACCOUNTANT public accounting firm employee who has duties and responsibilities associated with the early years of professional practice and works under the close supervision of a senior accountant.

JUNIOR STOCK shares, issued to employees, that are usually subordinate to regular common stock. The subordination may apply to voting rights, dividends, or liquidation rights. Junior stock may be converted to common stock when the employees meet certain performance requirements.

JUST-IN-TIME (JIT) the idea that inventory is manufactured (or acquired) only as the need for it arises or in time to be sold (or used). A major goal is to cut down on inventory investment.

JUST-IN-TIME (JIT) MANUFACTURING a "demand-pull" approach that produces only what is necessary to satisfy the demand of the ensuing manufacturing process.

JUST-IN-TIME (JIT) PRODUCTION SYSTEMS demand pull system. Purchases of materials and output depend on actual customer demand. Inventories are reduced greatly or eliminated, a few suppliers must reliably deliver small amounts on a frequent basis, plant layouts must become more efficient, a zero defects policy is established, and workers must be able to perform multiple tasks, including continuous monitoring of quality.

K

KAIZEN Japanese term for CONTINUOUS IMPROVEMENT. Kaizen budgeting incorporates expectations for continuous improvement into budgetary estimates. Kaizen costing determines target cost reductions for a period, such as a month. Thus, variances are the differences between actual and targeted cost reduction. The objective is to reduce actual costs below standard costs. The cost-reduction activities associated with the Kaizen approach minimize costs throughout the entire product life cycle. Therefore, it has the advantage of being closely related to the entity's profit-planning procedures. *See* TARGET COST.

KANBAN Japanese word for *card* or *ticket*. It is essentially a Japanese information system for coordinating production orders and withdrawals from in-process inventory to realize just-in-time production. Originated from the use of cards to indicate a work station's need for additional parts. A basic kanban system includes a *withdrawal kanban* that states the quantity that a later process should withdraw from its predecessor, a *production kanban* that states the output of the preceding process, and a *vendor kanban* that tells a vendor what, how much, where, and when to deliver.

KEOGH PLAN tax-deferred retirement plan for self-employed individuals meeting certain requirements; also called *H.R. 10 plan*. Self- employed individuals can contribute to their Keogh plan up to 25% of earnings, subject to annual limitations that are periodically adjusted for inflation.

KEYLOGGER a software used for surveillance. It records every keystroke of a user to a log file. Keylogger may be used by an organization to ensure employees are performing only authorized tasks. Keyloggers can sometimes be embedded in spyware, allowing an organization's information to be compromised.

KIDDIE TAX a tax imposed on a child's unearned income (e.g., interest and dividends) in excess of an amount that is determined annually (based on inflation) by the Department of the Treasury. The Kiddie Tax is imposed at the parents' highest rate of tax. The Kiddie Tax is only applicable if a child (1) is under the age of 18, or (2) is age 18 or 19 to 23 and is a full-time student who has earned income not in excess of one-half of his or her support.

KITING illegal practice in which a cash shortage is concealed by exploiting the time required for a check to clear. Assume XYZ Company has its home office on Long Island and a branch office in Chicago. The company has accounts with Long Island and Chicago banks. There is a shortage of $50,000 in the Long Island bank. The corporate bookkeeper covers this shortage by drawing a check on December 30, 2014, on the Chicago bank and depositing it to the account in the Long Island bank on the same day. The check is not entered as a cash disbursement in the current year. Rather, the transaction is recorded on January 2, 2015, and the check clears the Chicago bank on January 3, 2015. Unless the discrepancy is found, the Long Island bank balance and book balance reconcile on December 31, 2014, but do not reconcile on January 2, 2015. The auditor can uncover this irregularity by examining bank transfers prior to and after year-end to ascertain that the entry on the books is recorded in the same accounting period as the check is dated and the deposit in the Long Island bank is made. A schedule of interbank transfers should be made showing transfers of funds between bank accounts for several days before and after year-end. Included in the schedule are the dates of withdrawal and deposit per books and per bank. The CPA should trace transfer checks in transit at the balance sheet date to outstanding checks and deposits in transit in the respective bank reconciliations. The accountant should verify the deposit date of all transfers by tracing the deposit to the cutoff bank statement for the receiving bank.

KNOWLEDGE MANAGEMENT (KM) the process of connecting people to people and people to information to create a competitive advantage.

L

LABOR EFFICIENCY VARIANCE difference between the amount of labor time that should have been used and the labor that was actually used, multiplied by the standard rate. For example, assume that the standard cost of direct labor per unit of product A is 2.5 hours × $14 = $35. Assume further that during the month of March the company recorded 4,500 hours of direct labor time. The actual cost of this labor time was $64,800, or an average of $14.40 per hour. The company produced 2,000 units of product A during the month. The labor efficiency variance is (4,500 − 5,000) × $14 = $7,000, where 5,000 hours = 2.5 hours × 2,000 units of output. This variance is favorable since the actual hours used are less than the standard hours allowed. This may be the result of efficient use of labor time due to automation or the use of improved production methods.

LABOR INTENSIVE industry or company where labor costs are more important than capital costs. Labor intensive companies generally have greater earnings stability than CAPITAL INTENSIVE ones, because the former have a higher percentage of variable costs, while the latter have a higher percentage of fixed costs. However, labor intensive firms may experience difficulty during inflation due to employee discontent resulting from the decline in real earnings. But higher wage rates would be passed on in higher prices.

LABOR LAW legislation enacted to protect workers' rights and the working environment. Significant labor laws were enacted with the *National Labor Relations Act of 1935 (Wagner Act)* and the *Taft Hartley Act of 1948*.

LABOR RATE (PRICE) VARIANCE any deviation from standard in the average hourly rate paid to workers:

$$\frac{\text{Labor Rate}}{\text{Variance}} = (\text{Actual Rate} - \text{Standard Rate}) \times \text{Actual Hours of Labor Used}$$

For example, assume that the standard cost of direct labor per unit of product A is 2.5 hours × $14 = $35. Assume further that during the month of March the company recorded 4,500 hours of direct labor time. The actual cost of this labor time was $64,800, or an average of $14.40 per hour. The company produced 2,000 units of product A during the month. The labor rate variance is ($14.40 − $14.00) × 4,500 hours = $1,800, which is unfavorable since the actual hourly rate exceeded the standard rate. This may be the result of unavoidable increases in labor rates, or it may reflect excessive labor costs due to use of higher skilled labor commanding higher wages.

LABOR STANDARD efficiency standard that is often set via time and motion studies and laboratory experiments regarding the various labor operations needed to produce the finished good. The standard time must incorporate allowances for normal loss of time due to rest periods, machine downtime, and fatigue. It may be computed as follows:

Basic labor time per unit (in hours)	2.0
Allowance for breaks, fatigue, and machine downtime	.4
Allowance for rejects	.3
Standard hours per unit	2.7

LABOR VARIANCE difference between the actual costs and the standard costs of direct labor. Labor variance is divided into two specific variances: LABOR RATE (PRICE) VARIANCE and LABOR EFFICIENCY VARIANCE. This breakdown is needed from a control standpoint.

LAGGARD INDUSTRY one that lags behind the rest of the economy in output, employment, and contributions to the gross national product (GNP). A laggard industry in one nation may not be one in another nation.

LAGGING INDICATORS series of indicators that follow or trail behind aggregate economic activity. Six lagging indicators are currently published by the government: unemployment rate, business expenditures, labor cost per unit, loans outstanding, bank interest rates, and book value of manufacturing and trade inventories. *See also* LEADING INDICATORS.

LAND real estate held for productive use or investment. Land is recorded at the acquisition price plus incidental costs including real estate commissions, attorney's fees, escrow fees, title and recording fees, delinquent taxes paid by the buyer, surveying costs, draining, and grading of the property.

The cost of knocking down an old building to clear the land to construct a new building is charged to the land account. Amounts received from selling materials salvaged from the old building reduces the cost of the land.

Land is usually presented under the property, plant, and equipment section of the balance sheet. However, land bought for investment purposes or as a future plant site is classified under investments. If land is held by a real estate business for resale, it is shown as inventory.

Land is *not* subject to depreciation because it is not a wasting asset.

LAND IMPROVEMENTS items having limited lives, such as walkways, driveways, fences, and parking lots. The land improvement account is subject to depreciation over the estimated lives of the improvements. It is a different account than land.

LAPPING concealing a shortage by delaying the recording of cash receipts. For example, cash received from customer X is withheld by the cashier, and a subsequent cash receipt from customer Y is entered as a credit to X's account. Customer Y's account will not be credited until a collection is received from customer Z. If the money taken by the cashier is not replaced, there is an overstatement in total accounts receivable. However, by carefully shifting the overstatement from one customer to another the bookkeeper averts customer complaints when the monthly statements are received. Cashiers with access to the general accounting records have been known to transfer shortages to inventory or other accounts for temporary concealment. Lapping is possible when the bookkeeper receiving customer collections also records transactions to customer accounts. To prevent lapping, the accountant should prepare a control listing of cash receipts by a department not having access to the accounting records. But even without the control listing, it is difficult for the bookkeeper to have agreement between the detail of daily entries in the books and daily bank deposits. It should be noted that duplicate deposit tickets may be altered. The CPA should compare the duplicate copy with the original retained at the bank. In conclusion, the auditor should compare entries in the cash receipts journal and postings to customers' accounts to mailroom listings and daily deposit slips.

LAPSE termination or forfeiture of an item—for example, when coverage under an insurance contract expires because of nonrenewal.

LAPSING SCHEDULE specific accounting data regarding fixed assets. Included in the Schedule are the original purchase cost of each asset, additions to the assets, sales of the assets, accumulated depreciation, and depreciation expense. This type of worksheet aids in control over fixed assets by keeping detailed track of each fixed asset.

LAST-IN, FIRST-OUT (LIFO) inventory method in which it is assumed that goods are sold in the reverse order of their acquisition. Thus cost of sales is based upon the most recent costs. Ending inventory is based upon the costs of the earliest purchase made. During a period of inflation, net income is lower under LIFO than under FIRST IN, FIRST-OUT (FIFO) because current costs are being matched against revenue. However, the ending inventory figure in the balance sheet will be lower under LIFO than FIFO, because inventory is being stated in older dollars. A company can increase or decrease its earnings through the timing of inventory acquisitions. *See also* DOLLAR VALUE LIFO.

LATEST FINISH TIME in PROGRAM EVALUATION AND REVIEW TECHNIQUE (PERT), latest time at which an activity must be completed without holding up the complete project.

LATEST START TIME in PROGRAM EVALUATION AND REVIEW TECHNIQUE (PERT), latest time at which an activity must begin without holding up the complete project.

LATEST TIME (LT) in PROGRAM EVALUATION AND REVIEW TECHNIQUE (PERT), latest time at which an activity can be completed without extending the completion time of the project.

LATTICE-BASED MODEL also called *lattice model,* an option pricing mode model that divides time between now and the option's expiration into N discrete periods. *See also* BINOMIAL MODEL.

LEADING INDICATORS series of indicators that tend to predict future changes in economic activity; officially called *Composite Index of 11 Leading Indicators.* This series is published monthly by the U.S. Department of Commerce and includes average work week, average weekly initial claims, index of net business formation, new orders, and stock prices. The index of leading indicators, the components of which are adjusted for inflation, has an excellent track record of forecasting ups and downs in the business cycle. *See also* LAGGING INDICATORS.

LEAD TIME interval between placing an order and receiving delivery. For example, if it will take two weeks to receive a new delivery, the lead time is two weeks. *See also* REORDER POINT.

LEARNING CURVE chart line representing the efficiencies gained from experience. Basically, it is a curve describing the relationship between the consecutive number of units produced (*x*-axis) and the time per unit produced (*y*-axis). More specifically, it is based on the statistical findings that as the cumulative output doubles, the cumulative average labor input time required per unit will be reduced by some constant percentage, ranging between 10% and 40%. The curve is usually designated by its complement. For example, if the rate of reduction is 20%, the curve is referred to as an *80% learning curve.*

Applications of the learning curve theory include (1) pricing decisions, based on the estimates of expected costs; (2) requirements for scheduling labor; (3) capital budgeting decisions; and (4) setting incentive wage rates.

The following data illustrate the 80% learning curve relationship:

Quantity (in Units)		Time (in Hours)	
Per Lot	Cumulative	Total (Cumulative)	Average Time per Unit
15	15	600	40.0
15	30	960	32.0 (40.0 × 0.8)
30	60	1,536	25.6 (32.0 × 0.8)
60	120	2,460	20.5 (25.6 × 0.8)
120	240	3,936	16.4 (20.5 × 0.8)

As can be seen, as production quantities double, the average time per unit decreases by 20% of its immediate previous time. It can be graphed as seen in the illustration below.

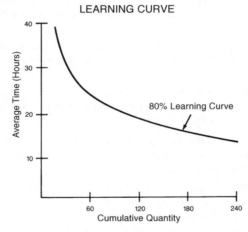

LEARNING CURVE

LEASE legal agreement whereby the lessee uses real or personal property of the lessor for a rental charge. The contract may provide for the time period of lease, designated purposes, and restrictions. *See also* CAPITAL LEASE; DIRECT FINANCING LEASE; OPERATING LEASE; SALES TYPE LEASE.

LEASEBACK *see* SALE AND LEASEBACK.

LEASEHOLD agreement between the lessee and lessor specifying the lessee's rights to use the leased property for a given time at a specified rental payment. As rental payments are made, rent expense is charged. When the rental is paid in advance, a prepaid rent account (prepaid expense) that has to be allocated into expense over the rental period is recorded. If the prepayment is for a long-term lease, however, it is recorded as a deferred charge and then amortized. The amortization entry for a long-term lease is to charge rent expense and credit leasehold. *See also* LEASEHOLD IMPROVEMENT.

LEASEHOLD IMPROVEMENT upgrading made by a lessee to leased property. Examples are paneling and wallpapering. These improvements revert to the lessor at the expiration of the lease term. As improvement costs are incurred under an operating lease, the leasehold improvement account is charged. The leasehold improvement is amortized to expense over the shorter of the life of the improvement or the remaining lease term. If there is a lease renewal option and the prospect of renewal cannot be predicted with certainty, the amortization period should be the original lease term rather than the longer possible term. However, the amortization expense on a leasehold improvement is not tax deductible. Leasehold improvement is usually considered an INTANGIBLE ASSET, because the lessee does not own the leased property. However, some companies show it under the property, plant, and equipment section of the balance sheet.

LEAST-SQUARES ANALYSIS *see* LEAST-SQUARES METHOD.

LEAST-SQUARES METHOD widely used statistical technique employed to study trends in revenue, costs, production, and other data and to investigate the relationships among accounting and financial variables. It fits a straight line through a set of points in such a way that the sum of the squared distances from the data points to the line is minimized. The least-squares method involves the following steps:

(1) Define the distance from the data point from the line, denoted by u, as follows:

$$u = (y - y')$$

where y = observed value and y' = estimated value base on the line $y' = a + bx$ (see the following figure).

(2) Minimize the sum of the squared distances:

$$\text{Min } u^2 = (y - y')^2 = (y - (a + bx))^2$$

Using differential calculus yields the following equations, called NORMAL EQUATIONS:

$$y = na + bx$$
$$xy = ax + bx^2$$

Solving the equation for b and a yields:

$$b = \frac{nxy - (x)(y)}{nx^2 - (x)^2}$$

$$a = \bar{y} - b\bar{x} \text{ where } \bar{y} = y/n \text{ and } \bar{x} = x/n$$

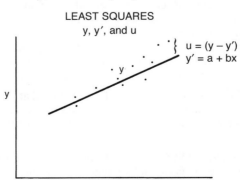

LEAST SQUARES
y, y', and u

$u = (y - y')$
$y' = a + bx$

To illustrate the computations of b and a, refer to the following data. All the sums required are computed and shown here:

Direct Labor-Hours (x)	Factory Overhead (y)	xy	x^2
9 hours	$ 15	135	81
19	20	380	361
11	14	154	121
14	16	224	196
23	25	575	529
12	20	240	144
12	20	240	144
22	23	506	484
7	14	98	49
13	22	286	169
15	18	270	225
17	18	306	289
174 hours	$225	3,414	2,792

From the table above:

$x = 174 \qquad y = 225 \qquad xy = 3,414 \qquad x^2 = 2,792$
$\bar{x} = x/n = 174/12 = 14.5 \qquad \bar{y} = y/n = 225/12 = 18.75$

Substituting these values into the formula for b first:

$$b = \frac{n\,xy - (x)(y)}{n\,x^2 - (x)^2}$$

$$= \frac{(12)(3,414) - (174)(225)}{(12)(2,792) - (174)^2} = \frac{1,818}{3,228} = \underline{0.5632}$$

$a = \bar{y} - b\bar{x}$

$\quad = (18.75) - (0.5632)(14.5) = 18.75 - 8.1664 = \underline{10.5836}$

Therefore, $y' = 10.5836 + 0.5632\,x$

LEDGER book in which all accounts of the business are kept. In effect, the ledger is a classification and summarization of financial transactions and the basis for the preparation of the balance sheet and income statement. The ledger also allows one to see the balance in a given account at a particular time. For example, the cash balance at the end of the month can be seen to determine whether the business has a cash problem. Also revealed in looking at the cash account are the cash receipts and cash disbursements for the period.

In a computerized environment, accounts may be stored on magnetic tape or disks instead of in a ledger binder. The accounting principles are, of course, still the same.

LEGAL CAPITAL amount of stockholders' equity that cannot be reduced by the payment of dividends. It is defined by the par value of par-value issued stock or the stated value of no-par issued stock. *See also* PAR VALUE; STATED VALUE.

LEGAL EXCHANGE INFORMATION SERVICE (LEXIS) online database containing laws, legal cases, and tax regulations of interest to practitioners.

LEGAL LIABILITY

1. obligation with specified terms and conditions by which a defined payment amount in money, goods, or services is to be paid within a defined time period in return for a current benefit.
2. responsibility of the accountant to the client and third parties relying on the accountant's work. Accountants can be sued for fraud and negligence in performance of duties.

LESSEE individual paying a rental fee to the LESSOR for the right to use real or personal property. The two methods used to account for leases by the lessee are the CAPITAL LEASE and the OPERATING LEASE.

LESSOR owner of real or personal property who gives another the right to use it in return for rental payments. The three types of leases for the lessor are the DIRECT FINANCING LEASE, the SALES-TYPE LEASE, and the OPERATING LEASE. *See also* LESSEE.

LETTER OF CREDIT (L/C) financial instrument normally issued by the buyer's bank in which the bank promises to pay money up to a stated amount for a specified period for merchandise when delivered. It substitutes the bank's credit for the buyer's and eliminates the seller's risk. It is used in international trade.

LETTER OF RECOMMENDATION auditor's letter addressed to the client. It contains the public accountant's conclusions regarding the company's accounting policies and procedures, internal controls, and operating policies. An evaluation is made of the present system, pointing out problem areas. Recommendations for improvement are cited.

LETTER OF REPRESENTATION client's letter addressed to the CPA on the audit engagement. It is usually signed by an officer of the company but may be signed by the corporate attorney. The letter states that the financial statements are the responsibility of management and that management's statements to the auditor during the audit process are true. Examples of representations include information regarding a subsequent event occurring after year-end and the existence of off-balance sheet contingencies. As per GENERALLY ACCEPTED AUDITING STANDARDS (GAAS), this letter is mandatory on an audit.

LEVERAGE term commonly used in finance and accounting to describe the ability of fixed costs to magnify returns to a firm's owners. OPERATING LEVERAGE, a measure of operating risk, refers to the fixed operating costs found in the firm's income statement. FINANCIAL LEVERAGE, a measure of financial risk, refers to financing a portion of the firm's assets, bearing fixed financing charges in hopes of increasing the return to its owners. *Total leverage* is a measure of total risk. The way to measure total leverage is to determine how EARNINGS PER SHARE (EPS) is affected by a change in sales.

LEVERAGED BUYOUT acquisition of one company by another, typically with borrowed funds. Usually, the acquired company's assets are used as collateral for the loans of the acquiring company. The loans are paid back from the acquired company's cash flow. Another possible form of leveraged buyout occurs when investors borrow from banks, using their own assets as collateral to acquire the other company. Typically, public stockholders receive an amount in excess of the current market value for their shares.

LEVERAGED LEASE

1. lease arrangement of property financed by someone other than the lessee or lessor. A long-term creditor finances the lease, and recourse in the event of default is generally not available to the creditor via the lessor.
2. special lease arrangement involving a creditor, lessor, and lessee. A creditor finances most of the cost to acquire an asset, while the lessor puts in a small amount of cash and acquires the asset, using it as security. The asset is then leased to the lessee on a noncancellable basis, and periodic payments to the lessor service the debt. The lessor, having borrowed most of the funds to acquire the asset, has "leveraged" himself, while having both the rewards and the risks of the lease.

LEVY imposition or collection, usually by legal or governmental authority, of an assessment of a specified amount. An example is a tax assessment.

LIABILITY amount payable in dollars (e.g., accounts payable) or future services to be rendered (e.g., warranties payable). The party having the liability is referred to as the debtor. There are various types of liabilities. An *actual liability* actually exists and has a stated amount (e.g., bonds payable). An ESTIMATED LIABILITY also actually exists, but the amount has to be predicted (e.g., estimated tax liability). These liabilities are booked and are shown in the balance sheet as credit balances under current or noncurrent liabilities, depending upon whether they will be paid in a period of more or less than one year. A CONTINGENT LIABILITY is one that may or may not become due (e.g., notes receivable discounted; a pending lawsuit). A contingent liability is usually footnoted in the financial statement.

LIABILITY DIVIDEND dividend in the form of notes payable when the company is short of cash but has adequate retained earnings; also called SCRIP DIVIDEND. The cash payment for the dividend will take place in the future. The recipient of the liability dividend may hold it until the due date to collect funds or may be able to discount it before the maturity date to obtain immediate cash. The entry at the declaration date is to debit retained earnings and credit the liability scrip dividend payable. When paid, scrip dividend payable is debited and cash credited. In the case where the liability involves interest, the interest part of the cash payment is charged to interest expense with the principal portion being debited to scrip dividend payable.

LIABILITY TAX ALLOCATION METHOD method of computing deferred taxes based on the estimated tax rates to be in effect when the temporary difference reverses itself. The tax rate is adjusted for rate changes. The method is the only one allowed for financial reporting purposes and is balance-sheet oriented. *See also* DEFERRED TAX ALLOCATION METHOD; NET OF TAX METHOD.

LIEN right of a party, typically a creditor, to hold, keep possession of, or control the property of another to satisfy a debt, duty, or liability. A mortgage would create such a security interest or lien upon property in the event of default.

LIFE CYCLE movement of a firm or its product through stages of development, growth, expansion, maturity, saturation, and decline. Not all products go through such a life cycle. For example, paper clips, nails, knives, drinking glasses, and wooden pencils do not seem to exhibit such a life cycle; most new products seem to, however. Some current examples include high-tech items such as computers, VCRs, CDs, and DVDs.

PRODUCT LIFE CYCLE

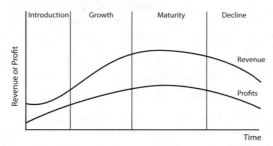

LIFE-CYCLE ANALYSIS forecasts of new product growth based on S-curves. Central to the analysis are the phases of product acceptance by the various groups such as innovators, early adapters, early majority, late majority, and laggards.

LIFE-CYCLE BUDGET estimates of a product's revenues and expenses over its entire life cycle beginning with research and development, proceeding through the introduction and growth stages, into the maturity stage, and finally into the harvest or decline stage. Life-cycle budgeting adopts a LIFE-CYCLE COST approach. It is intended to account for the costs at all stages of the VALUE CHAIN (R&D, design, production, marketing, distribution, and customer service). This information is important for pricing decisions because revenues must cover costs incurred in each stage of the value chain, not just production. Life-cycle budgeting emphasizes the relationships among costs incurred at different value-chain stages, for example, the effect of reduced design costs on future customer-service costs.

LIFE-CYCLE COSTING estimates of a product's revenues and expenses over its expected life cycle. The result is to highlight upstream and downstream costs in the cost planning process that often receive insufficient attention. Emphasis is on the need to price products to cover all costs, not just production costs.

LIFE INSURANCE policy taken out by the insured to pay the beneficiary a certain amount upon the insured's death. Proceeds on the death of the policyholder are includable in his or her gross estate under two sets of circumstances: (1) the insurance is payable to his or her estate and (2) the decedent possessed at least one incident of ownership in the policy. The latter means that the decedent either owned the policy until death, or transferred it but retained the right to change the beneficiary, borrow on the policy, and cancel it. To accomplish estate tax *exclusion*, transfer of the policy must occur more than three years prior to death.

LIFETIME LEARNING CREDIT may be claimed by individuals and is equal to 20% of up to $10,000 of qualified education expenses (i.e., tuition and fees). The maximum credit of $2,000 is phased out ratably based on the taxpayer's modified adjusted gross income. The phaseout ranges are indexed annually based on inflation. Unlike the AMERICAN OPPORTUNITY CREDIT, the

Lifetime Learning Credit is not limited to the first four years of undergraduate education.

LIKE-KIND EXCHANGE involves the swapping of property used for business or investment purposes (but not including securities) for property of a similar nature. The grade or quality of the properties exchanged do not have be the same. For example, an exchange of a building for undeveloped land qualifies for like-kind exchange treatment because both properties are real property. Realized gain on the exchange qualifies for tax-deferred treatment, but only to the extent that dissimilar property is not received.

LIMITED AUDIT audit of only *specific* accounts or transactions.

LIMITED LIABILITY one that does not go beyond the owner's investment in a business. A CORPORATION and LIMITED PARTNERS enjoy this particular feature. The stockholders of a corporation usually have limited liability; they risk only their investment in the business. Sole PROPRIETORS and *general partners* have unlimited liability. *See also* PARTNERSHIP; UNLIMITED LIABILITY.

LIMITED LIABILITY COMPANY (LLC) business form that provides limited personal liability, as a corporation does. Owners, who are called members, can be other corporations. The members run the company unless they hire an outside management group. The LLC can choose whether to be taxed as a regular corporation or as a pass through to members. Profits and losses can be split among members any way they choose. The LLC rules vary by state.

LIMITED LIABILITY PARTNERSHIP (LLP) a form of organization in which the individual partners are protected from the liabilities of the other partners. These entities are considered partnerships for both federal and state tax purposes.

LIMITED PARTNER member of a partnership whose liability for partnership obligations is limited to the investment in the partnership. A limited partner is not allowed to take active part in the management of the partnership. Limited partnerships have always been useful for tax shelters. However, limited partnerships are ruled *passive investments* and their tax benefits are severely limited. GENERAL PARTNERS have unlimited joint and several liability, and manage the partnership.

LIMITED REVIEW CPA engagement consisting of procedures and inquiries that provide a reasonable basis to express limited assurance that no material changes are needed to the financial statements to bring them into conformity with GAAP. *See also* AUDIT; COMPILATION.

LIMIT ORDER instruction to execute an order for a stock only at a specified price or better. The broker continues the order until a specified date or until the customer terminates it. Assume an investor places a limit order to buy at $10 or less a stock now selling at $11. If the stock goes up to $20, the broker will not execute a buy order; if it falls to $10, the broker will execute a buy order immediately. Note that the broker does *not* buy a stock for the broker's own account. The broker brings a buyer and seller together and executes a transaction for a commission. Only a dealer (or a broker-dealer acting in its capacity as a dealer) ever actually buys or sells—i.e., takes an inventory position.

LINE AND STAFF typical categorical classifications in which authority and personnel structure are organized in a company. Line personnel usually are defined as deriving from direct operational activities such as financing, distribution, leadership, and strategic decision making. A manager is a line person. Staff personnel are usually advisory and facilitative in nature for the line personnel. An accountant is a staff person to upper management because accounting advice is given. Thus line personnel contribute directly to the firm's objectives, while staff contribute indirectly to the accomplishment of these objectives by advising and facilitating the execution of such objectives.

LINEARITY

1. in LINEAR PROGRAMMING (LP), the requirement that the measure of effectiveness, such as contribution margin or cost and resource usage, must be proportional to the level of each activity conducted individually. For example, each unit of a resource must make the same contribution to the objective function that every other unit of that resource makes.
2. in LINEAR REGRESSION, the requirement that the relationship between a mixed cost and an activity variable such as machine-hours is straight line in the form of $y = a + bx$. This means that the variable portion changes by a *constant* amount per hour no matter how many hours are used.

LINEAR PROGRAMMING (LP) mathematical approach to the problem of allocating limited resources among competing activities in an optimal manner. Specifically, it is a technique used to maximize revenue, CONTRIBUTION MARGIN (CM), or profit function *or* to minimize a cost function, subject to constraints. Linear programming consists of two important ingredients: (1) objective function and (2) constraints, both of which are *linear*. In formulating the LP problem, the first step is to define the *decision variables* that one is trying to solve. The next step is to formulate the objective function and constraints in terms of these decision variables. For example, assume a firm produces two products, A and B. Both products require time in two processing departments, assembly and finishing. Data on the two products are as follows:

| | Products | | |
	A	**B**	**Available**
Assembly (hours)	2	4	100
Finishing (hours)	3	2	90
CM/unit	$25	$40	

The firm wants to find the most profitable mix of these products. First, define the decision variables as follows:

A = the number of units of product A to be produced
B = the number of units of product B to be produced

Then, express the objective function, which is to maximize total contribution margin (TCM), as:

$$\text{TCM} = \$25A + \$40B$$

Formulate the constraints as inequalities:

$$2A + 4B \leq 100$$
$$3A + 2B \leq 90$$

and do not forget to add the non-negative constraints:

$$A \geq 0, B \geq 0$$

LINEAR REGRESSION method dealing with a straight-line relationship between variables. It is in the form of $y = a + bx$, whereas nonlinear regression involves curvilinear relationships such as exponential and quadratic functions. *See also* LINEARITY; REGRESSION ANALYSIS.

LINE AUTHORITY power to give orders to subordinates. It contrasts with STAFF AUTHORITY, which is the authority to advise but not command others. Line managers are responsible for attaining the organization's goals as efficiently as possible. Production and sales managers typically exercise line authority.

LINE ITEM BUDGET budget typically used by governmental entities in which budgeted financial statement elements are grouped by administrative entities and object. These budget item groups are usually presented in an incremental fashion that is in comparison to previous periods. Line item budgets are used also in private industry for the comparison and budgeting of selected object groups and their previous and future estimated expenditure levels within an organization.

LINE OF BUSINESS REPORTING *see* SEGMENTED REPORTING.

LINE OF CREDIT bank's moral commitment to make loans to a company for a specified maximum amount for a given period of time, typically one year. There is usually *no* commitment fee charged on the unused line. However, a compensating balance requirement often exists.

LIQUID having cash or assets readily convertible into cash. A business entity is said to be liquid when it has cash or near-cash assets that are adequate to satisfy short-term liabilities when due.

LIQUID ASSET cash asset (e.g., cash or an unrestricted bank account) or readily marketable security. A liquid asset can be converted into cash in a short time period without a material concession in price. Excluded from this definition are accounts receivable and inventory.

LIQUIDATING DIVIDEND return of capital rather than a distribution of retained earnings. Such a dividend may occur with a natural resource company having wasting assets (e.g., oil, coal) or when a company in a state of liquidation desires to distribute cash or other assets on a pro rata basis to its owners. The journal entry is to debit paid-in capital and credit cash. Because the distribution to stockholders is from capital rather than earnings, no tax is paid on it.

LIQUIDATION process of closing a business entity, including selling or disposing of the assets, paying the liabilities, and having whatever is left over returned to the owners.

LIQUIDATION BASIS OF ACCOUNTING must be used when preparing an entity's financial statements when liquidation is imminent (i.e., a plan for liquidation is in effect and there is a remote likelihood that the entity will return from liquidation). Under the liquidation basis of accounting, assets should be valued at the estimated amount of cash or other consideration expected to be received upon disposition of the assets. Liabilities should be valued under the normal rules of GENERALLY ACCEPTED ACCOUNTING PRINCIPLES (GAAP).

LIQUIDATION VALUE cash price or other consideration that can be received in a forced-sale of assets, such as that occurring when a firm is in the process of going out of business. Typically, the liquidation value is less than what could be received from selling assets in the ordinary course of business.

LIQUIDITY
1. ability of current assets to meet current liabilities when due. The degree of liquidity of an asset is the period of time anticipated to elapse until the asset is realized or is otherwise converted into cash. A liquid company has less risk of being unable to meet debt than an illiquid one. Also, a liquid business generally has more financial flexibility to take on new investment opportunities.
2. immediate convertibility into cash without significant loss of value. For example, marketable securities are more liquid than fixed assets, because securities are actively traded in an organized market.

LIQUIDITY INDEX guideline showing the number of days in which current assets are removed from cash. The fewer the days removed, the better the entity's liquidity. An illustrative computation follows:

	Amount	×	Days Away from Cash	= Total
Cash	$ 20,000	×	–	
Accounts Receivable	50,000	×	30	$1,500,000
Inventory	80,000	×	50	4,000,000
	$150,000			$5,500,000

$$\text{Index} = \frac{\$5,500,000}{\$150,000} = 36.7 \text{ days}$$

LIQUIDITY RATIO measurement of a business entity's LIQUIDITY, such as the CURRENT RATIO, ACID-TEST RATIO, ACCOUNTS RECEIVABLE TURNOVER, and INVENTORY TURNOVER.

LISTED SECURITIES stocks and bonds traded on an organized security exchange such as the NEW YORK STOCK EXCHANGE (NYSE) and the American Stock Exchange (AMEX). They are distinguished from unlisted securities, which are traded in the OVER-THE-COUNTER (OTC) MARKET. The organized exchanges have certain requirements that firms must meet before their stock can be listed. Among the requirements are size of the company, number of years in business, earnings record, number of shares outstanding, and market value of shares.

LOAN agreement by which an owner of property (the lender) allows another party (the borrower) to use the property for a specified time period, and in return the borrower will pay the lender a payment (usually interest), and return the property (usually cash) at the end of the time period. A loan is usually evidenced by a PROMISSORY NOTE. Examples are commercial, consumer, mortgage, and auto loan.

LOAN CAPITAL short- and long-term liabilities that have a due date and provide for interest.

LOAN FUND available for loans. Such funds may be restricted in the sense that only the income generated from the fund may be used for making loans; in this case, the principal is placed in an endowment fund. In cases where both principal and income may be available, all funds are placed in the loan fund group.

LOAN MODIFICATION PROGRAM also called the *"Making Home Affordable" initiative,* a new program designed to help homeowners avoid foreclosure. Under this plan, borrowers will have to provide their most recent tax return and two pay stubs, as well as an "affidavit of financial hardship" to qualify for the $75 billion loan modification program, which runs through 2012. Borrowers are allowed to have their loans modified only once, and the program applies only to loans made on January 1, 2009, or earlier.

LOCAL AREA NETWORK (LAN) linking of microcomputers within a limited area or a common environment. An example is a network within a building. A LAN improves the client's efficiency and timeliness through the sharing of files, data, and messages. The system comprises hardware and software. A network operating system, network programs, and application programs for a shared environment are required.

LOCKBOX box in a U.S. Postal Service facility, used to facilitate collection of customer remittances. The use of a lockbox also reduces processing float. The recipient's local bank collects from these boxes periodically during the day and deposits the funds in the appropriate corporate account. The bank also furnishes the company with a computer listing of payments received by account, together with a daily total. Because the lockbox arrangement has significant per-item cost, it is most cost-effective with low-volume, high-dollar payments.

LODGING facility where one sleeps away from home (e.g., hotel, apartment). For tax years beginning in 1987, lodging expenses are deductible by individuals as employee business expenses only if the aggregate amount of miscellaneous deductions exceeds 2% of the taxpayer's adjusted gross income. Further, the tax law establishes rules for including in income qualified campus lodging provided by a school to an employee. In general, gross income does *not* include the value of qualified campus lodging. However, it is included to the extent the rent paid is less than the lesser of 5% of the appraised value of the lodging or the average rentals paid (by persons other than employees and students) to the school for comparable housing.

LOG record kept of the use of an item, often for internal control purposes. For example, in a computer application, a log may be kept of those using data files, programs, or hardware devices. The log may include information about data, time-in and time-out, the use of the item, and the reason for use.

LOGISTIC INFORMATION SYSTEM one that facilitates shipping, transportation, and warehousing activities. It aims to ensure customer service by getting adequate quantities of the finished product to the proper place in a cost- and time-efficient manner.

LONG-FORM REPORT detailed report by an external auditor about the examination of a client's financial statements. It may add to, replace, or include the SHORT-FORM REPORT. The long-form report may contain the audit scope, auditor opinions regarding the financial position and operating performance of the client, percentage change in accounts, evaluation of financial status, and recommendations for client improvement in its accounting system.

LONG-LIVED ASSET one whose future benefit is expected for a number of years; also called *long-term asset*. It includes such noncurrent assets as building, equipment, and intangibles.

LONG-RANGE BUDGET projections that cover more than one fiscal year; also called *strategic budgeting*. The five-year budget plan is most commonly used. *See also* ANNUAL BUDGET.

LONG-TERM ASSET *see* LONG-LIVED ASSET.

LONG-TERM DEBT monies owed for a period exceeding one year. Examples are bonds payable and long-term notes payable. The major features of the debt (i.e., interest rate, maturity date) are disclosed in the financial statements, usually in footnotes. Long-term liabilities are distinguished from long-term debt because the former include obligations requiring the rendering of future services (e.g., unearned revenue).

LONG-TERM LIABILITY obligation payable in money, goods, or services for a period in excess of one year. It is presented under noncurrent liabilities in the balance sheet. Examples are mortgage payable and the noncurrent portion of warranties payable.

LOSS
1. decrease in net assets for which no revenue is obtained and which arises from incidental transactions. Examples are the loss on the sale of a fixed asset, a catastrophe loss (e.g., fire loss, hurricane damage, flood loss), and a loss on the early extinguishment of debt. A loss is usually unanticipated and nonrecurring.
2. excess of expenses over revenue resulting in a net loss.

LOSS CARRYBACK offsetting the current year's net loss against net income of the previous years (currently three years) for tax purposes. For financial reporting purposes, the tax effects of a loss carryback should be allocated to the loss period and a refund in taxes should be obtained. *See also* LOSS CARRYFORWARD.

LOSS CARRYFORWARD offsetting the current year's net operating loss against future years' net income for tax purposes, assuming that a LOSS CARRYBACK is not possible in whole or in part. For financial reporting purposes, the tax effects of a loss carryforward should not be recognized until the year in which the tax liability is reduced unless earlier realization is assured beyond any reasonable doubt. This assurance is indicated when the entity has been profitable, future earnings are assured, and the loss results from a nonrecurring event.

LOSS CONTINGENCY posting of a future loss that may result from some event or happening (e.g., probable damages from a lawsuit). Loss contingencies that are probable should be booked by a charge to the loss account and a credit to the estimated liability. In addition, there should be footnote references to the nature of the contingency. *See also* CONTINGENT LIABILITY; GAIN CONTINGENCY.

LOSS OF UTILITY decline in usefulness and hence value of an asset. Loss of utility is the reason to write down the asset. An example is writing down an investment in securities for a permanent decline from cost to market value.

Theoretically, an asset should be written down when the present value of its future cash flows is less than its historical cost.

LOWER OF COST OR MARKET valuation rule based on CONSERVATISM. Certain accounts are shown at the *lower* of their historical cost or current replacement cost reflecting an unrealized loss in the financial statements. In the opposite case (unrealized gain), *no* accounting recognition is given. For example, inventory is reflected at the lower of cost or market on an item-by-item, category, or total basis. In applying the rule, however, market cannot exceed the ceiling (net realizable value = selling price less costs to complete and dispose) nor can market be less than the floor (net realizable value less normal profit margin).

LP *see* LINEAR PROGRAMMING (LP).

LUMP-SUM PURCHASE acquisition of a group of assets for a single price. The cost should be allocated to the assets based on their fair market values. Assume $75,000 is paid to acquire land, building, and equipment having the fair market values of $40,000, $25,000, and $35,000, respectively. The allocated cost is shown below:

	Fair Market Value	**Allocated Cost**
Land	$ 40,000	$30,000
Building	25,000	18,750
Equipment	35,000	26,250
Total	$100,000	$75,000

For example, the allocated cost assigned to the land account is arrived at as follows:

$$\frac{\$40,000}{\$100,000} \times \$75,000 = \$30,000$$

M

MAC (MEDIA ACCESS CONTROL) ADDRESS a unique identifier of each node of a network.

MACHINE-HOUR cost allocation base that provides a systematic and contemporaneous method of applying overhead costs to work-in-process inventory. An overhead rate of cost per hour of work expended by a machine is applied to the work-in-process. With respect to modern mechanized production, such machine-hour-based rates produce more accurate application of overhead than rates based on direct labor-hours.

MACRO ACCOUNTING *see* MICRO ACCOUNTING.

MACROS technique that allows the user to combine several keystrokes into one. Macros are simply miniprograms that allow the user to design a menu to include in a TEMPLATE.

MACRS *see* MODIFIED ACCELERATED COST RECOVERY SYSTEM.

MAINFRAME large computer that may support 100–500 users at one time. Typically, mainframes have a word length of 64 bits and are significantly faster and have greater capacity than the minicomputer and the microcomputer. Mainframes are recommended when vast amounts of data must be processed.

MAINTENANCE periodic expenditures undertaken to preserve or retain an asset's operational status for its originally intended use. These expenditures do not improve or extend the life of the asset. An example is the cost of a tune-up for an automobile. Maintenance is an expense and is distinguished from CAPITAL IMPROVEMENTS, which are capitalized.

MAKE-OR-BUY (OUTSOURCE) DECISION determination whether to produce a component part internally or to buy it from an outside supplier. This decision involves both qualitative and quantitative factors. Qualitative considerations include product quality and the necessity for long-run business relationships with subcontractors. Quantitative factors deal with cost. The quantitative effects of the make-or-buy decision are best seen through the RELEVANT COST APPROACH. For example, assume a firm has prepared the following cost estimates for the manufacture of a subassembly component based on an annual production of 8000 units:

	Per Unit	**Total**
Direct materials	$ 5	$ 40,000
Direct labor	4	32,000
Variable overhead applied	4	32,000
Fixed overhead applied (150% of direct labor cost)	6	48,000
Total cost	$19	$152,000

The supplier has offered the subassembly at a price of $16 each. Two-thirds of fixed factory overhead, which represents executive salaries, rent, depreciation, and taxes, continue regardless of the decision. Should the company buy or make the product? The key to the decision lies in the investigation of those relevant costs that change between the make or buy alternatives. Assuming that the productive capacity will be idle if not used to produce the subassembly, we can make the following analysis:

	Per Unit		Total of 8000 units	
	Make	**Buy**	**Make**	**Buy**
Purchase price		$16		$128,000
Direct materials	$ 5		$ 40,000	
Direct labor	4		32,000	
Variable overhead	4		32,000	
Fixed overhead that can be avoided by *not* making	2		16,000	
Total relevant costs	$15	$16	$120,000	$128,000
Difference in favor of making	$ 1		$8,000	

The make-or-buy decision must be investigated in the broader perspective of available facilities. The alternatives are: (1) leaving facilities idle; (2) buying the parts and renting out idle facilities; or (3) buying the parts and using unused facilities for other products.

MALWARE viruses, worms, Trojan horses, spyware, and adware.

MALPRACTICE INSURANCE liability insurance for the accountant against legal action in connection with professional services rendered. Insurance coverage varies but may include attorney fees and awarded damages. The accounting practitioner may be sued by clients and third parties (i.e., creditors, investors) relying on his or her work. The increasing cost of obtaining malpractice insurance is a problem of both accounting and other professions.

MANAGED COST *see* DISCRETIONARY COST.

MANAGED EARNINGS manipulating (pumping up or down) earnings to shed a more favorable light on companies. All companies have flexibility in how they account for some revenues and costs. For example, they can depreciate a capital cost (say, a fleet of cars) in one year or over several years. If they take it in one chunk, their earnings look lower that year and larger every year after that. If they report it in many smaller pieces, they avoid the big hit in the first year. Even though earnings are not perfect, investors' love affair with earnings is here to stay.

MANAGED (FIXED) COST *see* DISCRETIONARY (FIXED) COST.

MANAGEMENT ACCOUNTING *see* MANAGERIAL (MANAGEMENT) ACCOUNTING.

MANAGEMENT ADVISORY SERVICES (MAS) consulting services performed by CPA firms to improve client efficiency and effectiveness. Within the CPA firms, MAS departments are kept independent of other departments such as audit and tax. Examples of MAS services include IT installation and use, marketing, and financial planning.

MANAGEMENT AUDIT examination and appraisal of the efficiency and effectiveness of management in carrying out its activities. Areas of auditor interest include the nature and quality of management decisions, operating results achieved, and risks undertaken. *See also* OPERATIONAL AUDIT.

MANAGEMENT BY EXCEPTION concept or policy by which management devotes its time to investigating only those situations in which actual results differ significantly from planned results. The idea is that management should spend its valuable time concentrating on the more important items (such as shaping the company's future strategic course). Attention is given only to material deviations requiring investigation. The tools that facilitate use of this concept include DECISION SUPPORT SYSTEM (DSS); EXPERT SYSTEM; PERFORMANCE REPORT.

MANAGEMENT BY OBJECTIVE (MBO) system of performance appraisal having the following characteristics: (1) each manager is required to take certain prescribed actions and to complete certain written documents; and (2) the manager and subordinates discuss the subordinate's job description, agree to short-term performance targets, discuss the progress made towards meeting these targets, and periodically evaluate the performance and provide the feedback.

MANAGEMENT CONSULTING SERVICE broad service area covering aspects of organizational management, such as planning, finance, inventory, computers, and personnel. These services may include the design and implementation of MANAGEMENT INFORMATION SYSTEMS (MIS), strategic planning, DATA PROCESSING, hardware and software evaluation, data privacy and security, evaluation of management, and suggestions for improvement. Public accounting firms have expanded their services into management consulting. Some critics have expressed concerns that this may weaken auditor independence.

MANAGEMENT CONTROL SYSTEM plan assuring that resources are obtained and used effectively and efficiently in the accomplishment of the organization's goals. Major characteristics of a management control system are: (1) it focuses on programs and RESPONSIBILITY CENTERS; (2) it is a total system in that it encompasses all aspects of a firm's operation; (3) it is usually built around a financial and accounting structure; and (4) it uses two types of information for managerial control, *planned data* (such as budgets, standards, and projections) and *actual data*.

MANAGEMENT DECISION CYCLE five steps managers take in making decisions and following up on them. The five steps are: (1) the discovery of a problem or need; (2) alternative courses of action to solve the problem or meet the need are identified; (3) a complete analysis to determine the effects of each alternative on business operations is prepared; (4) with the supporting data, the decision maker chooses the best alternative; and (5) after the decision has been carried out, the accountant conducts a post decision review to see if the decision was correct or if other needs have arisen. Any data that relates to future costs, revenues, or uses of resources and that will differ among alternative courses of action are considered relevant decision information.

MANAGEMENT GAME form of simulation used in management training. Both SIMULATION and management games are mathematical models, but they differ in purpose and mode of use. Simulation models are designed to simulate a system and to generate a series of financial and operating results regarding system operations. Games do the same thing except that in games human beings play a significant part; that is, participants make decisions at various stages. The major goals of the management game are:

(1) To improve decision-making and analytical skills.

(2) To develop awareness of the need to make decisions lacking complete information.

(3) To develop an understanding of the interrelationships of the various functions of business (accounting, finance, marketing, production, etc.) within the firm and how these interactions affect overall performance.

(4) To develop the ability to function cooperatively and effectively in a small group situation.

Management games offer a unique means of training accountants and have been used successfully as an executive training device. These games generally fall into two categories: executive and functional. *Executive games* are general management games and cover all functional areas of business and their interactions and dynamics. Executive games are designed to train general executives. *Functional games*, on the other hand, focus on middle management decisions and emphasize particular functional areas of the firm. Examples of executive games in wide use include XGAME, COGITATE, and IMAGINIT. Examples of functional games include MARKSIM, FINSIM, and PERT-SIM.

MANAGEMENT INFORMATION SYSTEM (MIS) computer-based or manual system that transforms data into information useful in the support of decision making. MIS can be classified as performing three functions:

(1) To generate reports — for example, financial statements, inventory status reports, or performance reports needed for routine or non-routine purposes.

(2) To answer what-if questions asked by management. For example, questions such as "What would happen to cash flow if the company changes its credit term for its customers?" can be answered by MIS. This type of MIS can be called SIMULATION.

(3) To support decision making. This type of MIS is appropriately called DECISION SUPPORT SYSTEM (DSS). DSS attempts to integrate the decision maker, the database, and the quantitative models being used.

MANAGEMENT LETTER *see* LETTER OF RECOMMENDATION.

MANAGEMENT REPRESENTATION LETTER a letter written by management to an auditor at the end of an audit. The purpose of the letter is to confirm explicit and implicit management assertions (representations) made during the course of the audit. The letter is typically signed by the entity's CEO and CFO.

MANAGEMENT REVIEW analysis and evaluation by the external auditor of management's performance, including an analysis of the quality of decision making, efficiency of operations, profitability, corporate policies, internal controls, personnel relations, social responsibility, marketing factors, and ability to keep up-to-date technologically, as well as factoring economic and political considerations into decisions among other criteria.

MANAGEMENT SCIENCE *see* QUANTITATIVE METHODS (MODELS).

MANAGEMENT'S DISCUSSION AND ANALYSIS OF EARNINGS section in FORM 10-K and in the ANNUAL REPORT to stockholders that is required by SEC *Accounting Series Release* No. 159. Management must summarize the reasons for changes in results of operations, capital resources, and liquidity, among others. The section is designed to help investors understand the extent to which accounting changes, as well as changes in business activity, have affected the comparability of year-to-year data. Investors will then be in a better position to assess the source and probability of recurrence in earnings. Examples of subjects to be discussed by management include material changes in discretionary costs, material changes in assumptions underlying deferred costs, and significant changes in product mix or in the relative profitability of lines of business.

MANAGEMENT'S REPORT management's assessment of the effectiveness of the company's internal control over financial reporting.

MANAGER
1. executive whose function is to plan, organize, and control, and to make decisions in order to achieve organizational objectives.
2. in a public accounting firm, person in charge of an audit engagement. The manager is responsible for all aspects of the engagement, from initiation to closing and rendering an opinion.

MANAGERIAL EFFORT extent to which a manager attempts to accomplish a goal. Managerial effort may include psychological as well as physical commitment to accomplish a goal. Motivation is the desire of managers to attain a specific goal (GOAL CONGRUENCE) and the commitment to accomplish the goal (managerial effort).

MANAGERIAL (MANAGEMENT) ACCOUNTING process of identification, measurement, accumulation, analysis, preparation, interpretation, and communication of financial information that is used by management to plan, evaluate, and control within an organization. It is the accounting used for the planning, control, and decision-making activities of an organization. Managerial accounting is concerned with providing information to internal managers who are charged with directing, planning, and controlling operations and making a variety of management decisions. Managerial accounting can be contrasted with FINANCIAL ACCOUNTING, which is concerned with providing information, via financial statements, to stockholders, creditors, and others *outside* the organization. More specifically, the differences between financial and managerial accounting are summarized here:

Financial Accounting	**Managerial Accounting**
(1) Provides data for *external* users.	(1) Provides data for *internal* use.
(2) Is required by FASB.	(2) Is not mandated by FASB.
(3) Is subject to GAAP.	(3) Is not subject to GAAP.
(4) Must generate accurate and timely data.	(4) Emphasizes relevance and flexibility of data.
(5) Emphasizes the past.	(5) Has more emphasis on the future.
(6) Looks at the business as a whole.	(6) Focuses on parts as well.
(7) Primarily stands by itself.	(7) Draws heavily from other disciplines such as finance, economics, and operations research.
(8) Is an end in itself.	(8) Is a means to an end.

MANAGERIAL MOTIVATION a combination of managerial effort and goal congruence.

MANUFACTURING AND PRODUCTION SYSTEM plan that either creates goods or provides services (or both). Manufacturing and production systems produce output that ranges from highly standardized to highly customized. Depending on the type of system used, an appropriate cost accounting system can be designed. For example, a JOB ORDER costing system is used by custom manufacturers such as shipbuilders, aircraft manufacturers, and printers, whereas a process costing system is used by processing industries such as refineries and chemical manufacturers.

MANUFACTURING CELLS plant layout in a lean JIT production environment. Cells are sets of machines, often grouped in semicircles, that produce a given product or product type. Each worker in a cell must be able to operate all machines and, possibly, to perform support tasks, such as setup activities, preventive maintenance, movement of work-in-process within the cell, and quality inspection. In a pull system, workers might often be idle if they are not multi-skilled. Hence, central support departments are reduced or eliminated, space is saved, fewer and smaller factories may be required, and materials and tools are bought close to the point of use. Manufacturing cycle time and setup time are reduced. As a result, on-time delivery performance and response to changes in markets are enhanced, and production of customized goods in small lots becomes feasible.

MANUFACTURING COST FLOW flow of manufacturing costs (direct materials, direct labor, and manufacturing overhead) from when incurred through the direct materials inventory, work-in-process inventory, and finished goods inventory accounts to the cost of goods sold account.

MANUFACTURING COSTS expenses associated with the manufacturing activities of the company. They consist of three categories: direct materials, direct labor, and factory overhead.

MANUFACTURING CYCLE EFFICIENCY (MCE) quotient of the time required for value-added production divided by TOTAL CYCLE TIME. It is a measure of how well a company's manufacturing capabilities use time resources.

MANUFACTURING CYCLE TIME delay from the moment the order is ready for setup to its completion. Sometimes called manufacturing lead time or throughput time.

MANUFACTURING EXPENSE see MANUFACTURING COSTS.

MANUFACTURING LEAD TIME see MANUFACTURING CYCLE TIME.

MANUFACTURING OVERHEAD see FACTORY OVERHEAD.

MANUFACTURING OVERHEAD VOLUME VARIANCE difference between the manufacturing overhead costs budgeted for the level of production achieved and the manufacturing overhead cost applied to production using the standard variable and fixed manufacturing overhead rates.

MANUFACTURING RESOURCE PLANNING (MRP-II) integrated information system that steps beyond first-generation MRP to synchronize all aspects (not just manufacturing) of the business, including production, sales, inventories, schedules, and cash flows. MRP-II uses an MPS (master production schedule), which is a statement of the anticipated manufacturing schedule for selected items for selected periods. MRP also uses the MPS. Thus, MRP is a component of an MRP-II system.

MARGIN

1. *see* GROSS MARGIN; PROFIT MARGIN.
2. partial payment made by an investor to a broker for securities purchased, with the remainder on credit. The broker retains the securities as collateral and charges the investor interest on the money owed. The Federal Reserve Board determines margin requirements. The margin requirement for stocks is higher than that for convertible bonds because of greater risk. Assume that with a margin requirement of 50% (present requirement), 100 shares of XYZ stock are bought at $100 per share. The actual amount invested is $5000, with a margin of $5000 on credit.
3. in commodities trading, *deposits* required by commodities exchanges.
4. in accounting, a reference to revenue or profitability. Examples are gross profit margin (gross profit/sales) and profit margin (net income/sales).

MARGINAL ANALYSIS approach utilizing such concepts as marginal revenue, marginal cost, and marginal profit for economic decision making. For example, decisions for allocating scarce resources are typically expressed in terms of the marginal condition(s) that must be satisfied in order to attain an optimal solution. The familiar profit-maximizing rule of setting production or sales volume at the point where "marginal revenue equals marginal cost" is one such example.

MARGINAL COST calculation showing the change in total cost as a result of a change in volume. For example, if one more unit of output causes an increase in total cost of $40, the $40 is the marginal cost. It is useful to calculate marginal cost to determine whether the rate of production should be changed. In general, as activity increases, economies of scale (LEARNING CURVE principle) set in because of greater experience and manufacturing efficiency. Eventually, however, a point is reached where diseconomies of scale (e.g., increased management supervision) occur, causing marginal costs to rise. When a company is at an optimum output level, marginal cost coincides with average total unit cost. The marginal cost curve is usually shown as a U-shape on a graph.

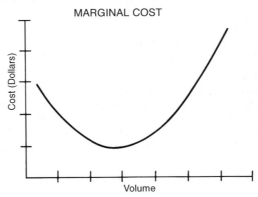

MARGINAL COST

MARGINAL COSTING *see* DIRECT COSTING.

MARGINAL INCOME *see* CONTRIBUTION MARGIN (CM).

MARGINAL INCOME RATIO *see* CONTRIBUTION MARGIN (CM) RATIO.

MARGINAL REVENUE change of the total revenue of a business resulting when an extra unit is sold.

MARGINAL TAX RATE rate paid on the last dollar of taxable income. For example, assume for married couples filing jointly that there are two tax brackets:

15% on taxable income equal to or below $29,750
28% on taxable income in excess of this amount

If income adds up to $50,000, total taxes paid will be $10,132.50:

First $29,750 of taxable income at 15%   = $ 4,462.50
Remaining $20,250 at 28%   = $ 5,670.00
                                                 $10,132.50

The 15% and 28% are marginal tax rates, while the average tax rate is a little over 20% ($10,132.50/$50,000).

MARGIN OF SAFETY difference between the actual level of sales and BREAK-EVEN SALES. It is the amount by which sales revenue may drop before losses begin and is often expressed as a percentage of budgeted sales:

$$\text{Margin of Safety} = \frac{\text{Budgeted Sales} - \text{Break-Even Sales}}{\text{Budgeted Sales}}$$

The margin of safety is often used as a measure of OPERATING RISK. The larger the ratio, the safer the situation is since there is less risk of reaching the break-even point.

MARITAL DEDUCTION tax deduction allowed upon the transfer of property from one spouse to another. This deduction is allowed under the federal gift tax for lifetime transfers or under the federal estate tax for testamentary transfers of a decedent.

MARK-TO-MARKET
1. the daily adjustment of margin accounts to reflect profits and losses. At the end of each day, the futures contracts are settled and the resulting profits or losses paid.
2. valuing a trading security or available-for-sale security at its market value at the end of the reporting period. The security is presented at its market value whether it is below or above cost. Also called *fair value*.

MARKDOWN
1. reduction of the original selling price. It may be due to any of several reasons, such as a decline in overall prices of goods, excessive competition, special sale, damaged merchandise, or excess supply. In *markdown cancellation*, the markdown is partially offset at a subsequent date by increases in the prices of goods that had been marked down below the original selling price. *See also* MARKUP.
2. dealer markdowns in securities trading.

MARKETABLE SECURITY readily tradable equity or debt security with quoted prices, including commercial paper and Treasury bills. It is a near-cash asset and is classified under current assets. Marketable securities are initially recorded at cost, which consists of the market price and incidental costs to acquire, including brokerage commissions and taxes. Some types of securities, such as restricted stock, are *not* marketable. At year-end, marketable securities are valued at market value.

MARKET CAP (MARKET CAPITALIZATION) value of a business entity equal to its outstanding shares multiplied by the current market price per share. For example, if 5,000,000 shares are issued and outstanding and the market price per share is $10, the company's market capitalization is $50,000,000. Institutional investors including insurance companies and pension plans will not invest in a company unless its market capitalization is a minimum amount (e.g., $100 million) predetermined by them. Higher market capitalization reflects a larger and higher quality company, which is probably more widely held and actively traded. *See also* BOOK VALUE.

MARKET INDEX OF STOCK PRICES aggregate of prices of stock of a certain type on one of the stock exchanges. Stock market indexes show how the market is doing and may assist the investor in picking the right type stocks at the proper time. For example, Standard & Poor's has several common stock indexes, such as the S&P 500.

MARKETING EXPENSE *see* SELLING EXPENSE.

MARKET PRICE
1. price at which the seller and the buyer agree to trade on the open market.
2. in TRANSFER PRICING, best transfer price (i.e., the price that will maximize the profits of the company as a whole), under the following conditions: (1) a competitive market price exists; and (2) divisions are independent of each other. If divisions are free to buy and sell outside the company, the use of market prices preserves divisional autonomy and leads divisions to act in a manner that maximizes the profits of the company as a whole.

MARKET RISK PREMIUM amount above the risk-free rate required to induce average investors to enter the market.

MARKET SHARE VARIANCE difference between the actual market share percentage and the budgeted market share percentage, times the actual market size in units, times the budgeted weighted average unit contribution margin.

MARKET SIZE VARIANCE budgeted market share percentage, times the difference between the actual market size in units, times the budgeted weighted average UCM. One of the two components of SALES QUANTITY VARIANCE.

MARKET TIMING
1. an abusive practice where big stock market traders move in or out of funds at the end of the trading day, exploiting stale price data. The practice is not illegal, but it can be damaging to the interests of other investors in the funds. Regulators are currently studying ways to thwart timing-related trades in mutual fund shares.
2. an ideal investing strategy of switching into stocks before they rise and switching out of them before they decline.

MARKET TRANSFER PRICE *see* MARKET PRICE.

MARKET VALUE
  1. typically, price at which an item could be sold.
  2. as used in the LOWER OF COST OR MARKET rule for inventory valuation, replacement cost subject to ceiling and floor limits.
  See also FAIR MARKET VALUE.

MARKET VALUE METHOD
  1. method used to account for a BOND CONVERSION. The credit to common stock and premium on common stock may be based either on the market value of the bond or the market value of the stock issued. The difference between the book value of the bond and the market value credited to equity represents a gain or loss. *See also* BOOK VALUE METHOD.
  2. valuation of inventory at its market value whether above or below cost recognizing an unrealized (holding) loss or gain. This method is not acceptable because to show inventory in *excess* of cost is not conservative.
  3. method to account for trading (shown under current assets) and available-for-sale (shown under noncurrent assets) equity and debt securities at their market value at the end of the reporting period. The difference between the cost and market value of the securities portfolio is presented as an unrealized loss or gain. For trading securities, the unrealized loss or gain is reported in the income statement. For available-for-sale securities, the unrealized loss or gain for the current year is reported under "other comprehensive income" in the income statement and the cumulative amount is reported under stockholders' equity in the balance sheet classified as "accumulated other comprehensive income."

MARKOV ANALYSIS method of analyzing the current behavior of some variable to predict its future behavior. One important application of this method in accounting is the estimation of that portion of the accounts receivable that will eventually become uncollectible.

MARKUP
  1. increase on the original selling price. It is associated primarily with the pricing of items for sale in a retail or wholesale environment. *Markup cancellation* is a reduction on the price of merchandise that has been marked up on the original retail price. *See also* MARKDOWN.
  2. amount added to the cost of an item to arrive at a selling price. Markup may be expressed as a percentage of cost or in dollars. For example, if an item costing $20 has a profit markup on cost of 30%, the selling price will be $26 ($20 + $6).
  3. dealer markups in securities trading.

MAS90, MAS200, MAS500 accounting, distribution, and light manufacturing software, developed by Sage Software, ideal for medium-sized companies that can benefit from an outstanding combination of high performance, breadth of application, complete modularity, and exceptional ease of use (www.sagemas.com).

MASQUERADING an attack that relies on a fake identity, such as stolen passwords, to gain unauthorized access to an IT system. Essentially, the attacker pretends to be an authorized user in a masquerading attack.

MASTER (COMPREHENSIVE) BUDGET plan of activities expressed in monetary terms of the assets, equities, revenues, and costs that will be involved in carrying out the plans. Simply put, a master budget is a set of projected or planned financial statements. It consists basically of a PRO FORMA INCOME STATEMENT, PRO FORMA BALANCE SHEET, and CASH BUDGET. A budget is a tool used for both planning and control. At the beginning of the period, the budget is a plan or standard; at the end of the period, it serves as a control device to help management measure its performance against the plan so that future performance may be improved.

MATCHING process of reporting expense on a cause-effect basis against the reported revenue it relates to. Net income is measured by the difference between revenue over associated expenses during the same period. Expenses are incurred in order to obtain that revenue. An example is the matching of sales commission expense to sales.

MATCHING GRANT contingent grant awarded only if the receiving entity is able to put up (or independently raise) a sum equal to the amount provided by the granting entity.

MATERIAL
1. raw material, direct or indirect. An example is steel to make a car. Usually accounted for separately by a debit to materials (stores control) and a credit to accounts payable or cash. When materials are transferred to work-in-process, inventory is credited.
2. relatively important and significant in dollar amounts. *See also* MATERIALITY.

MATERIALITY magnitude of an omission or misstatement of accounting data that misleads financial statement readers. Materiality is judged both by relative amount and by the nature of the item. For example, even a small theft by the president of a company is material. Unfortunately, the FINANCIAL ACCOUNTING STANDARDS BOARD (FASB) has no specific criteria as to what is or is not material. If an item is material, it should be disclosed in the body of the financial statements or footnotes. Some CPA firms use a 5% test for materiality. The SEC in *Accounting Series Release* No. 159 provides that an item is material if it changed by 10% or more relative to the prior year.

MATERIAL MIX relative combination (or proportion) of components when a manufacturing process requires several different types of materials. The combination is not necessarily the standard. In many industries, such as chemicals, petroleum products, steel, and food, it is quite possible to vary the material mix and end up with essentially the same product. For example, in the textile industry, different mixes of fibers can produce the same quality of yarn.

MATERIAL MIX VARIANCE effect on material costs of a deviation from the expected or standard mix of materials. *See also* PRODUCTION MIX VARIANCE.

MATERIAL PARTICIPATION participation in an activity that involves a taxpayer's regular, continuous, and substantial participation. One condition for material participation is performance of more than 500 hours of service during the year. A taxpayer who materially participates in an activity will not be subject to the passive activity rules and, accordingly, may fully deduct an activity's loss against ordinary income.

MATERIAL REQUIREMENT PLANNING (MRP) computer-based information system designed to handle ordering and scheduling of dependent-demand inventories (such as raw materials, component parts, and subassemblies that will be used in the production of a finished product). MRP is designed to answer three questions: *what* is needed, *how much* is needed, and *when* is it needed. The primary inputs of MRP are a *bill of materials*, which tells what goes into a finished product; a *master schedule*, which tells how much finished product is desired and when; and an *inventory-records file*, which tells how much inventory is on hand or on order. This information is processed, using various computer programs to determine the net requirements for each period of the planning horizon. Outputs from the process include planned-order schedules, order releases, changes, performance-control reports, planning reports, and exception reports.

MATERIAL REQUISITIONS *see* STORES REQUISITIONS.

MATERIAL WEAKNESS a deficiency in internal control or a combination of deficiencies in internal control that results in a reasonable possibility that a material misstatement of the annual or interim financial statements will not be prevented or detected (and corrected in the case of a nonissuer) on a timely basis. It does not mean that a material misstatement has occurred or that it will occur, but that it could occur. *See also* DEFICIENCY IN INTERNAL CONTROL; SIGNIFICANT DEFICIENCY.

MATERIALS PRICE VARIANCE difference between what is paid for a given quantity of materials and what should have been paid, multiplied by the actual quantity of materials used: Materials price variance = (actual price – standard price) × actual quantity. In reality, since material price variances are isolated at the time of purchase, it is customary to multiply the difference between the actual price and the standard price by the actual quantity *purchased* rather than used. It is more often called *materials purchase price variance*.

MATERIALS PURCHASE PRICE VARIANCE *see* MATERIALS PRICE VARIANCE.

MATERIALS QUANTITY (USAGE) VARIANCE difference between the actual quantity of materials used in production and the standard quantity of materials allowed for actual production, multiplied by the standard price per unit. Materials quantity variance = (actual quantity – standard quantity) × standard price per unit. The variance is unfavorable if the actual quantity exceeds the standard quantity; it is favorable if the actual quantity is less than the standard.

MATERIALS VARIANCE difference between the actual and standard costs of materials. Materials variance is divided into two specific variances: MATERIALS PRICE VARIANCE and MATERIALS QUANTITY (USAGE) VARIANCE. This breakdown is needed from a control standpoint.

MATHEMATICAL MODEL mathematical representation of reality that attempts to explain the behavior of some aspect of it. The mathematical model serves the following purposes: (1) to find an optimal solution to a planning or decision problem; (2) to answer a variety of what-if questions; (3) to establish understandings of the relationships among the input data items within a model; and (4) to attempt to extrapolate past data to derive meaning. Mathematical models include techniques such as LINEAR PROGRAMMING (LP), computer simulation, DECISION THEORY, REGRESSION ANALYSIS, ECONOMIC ORDER QUANTITY (EOQ), and BREAK-EVEN ANALYSIS. *See also* FINANCIAL MODEL; MODEL; QUANTITATIVE METHODS (MODELS); SIMULATION MODELS.

MATHEMATICAL PROGRAMMING *see* OPTIMIZATION MODEL.

MATURITY due date of a debt at which time the PRINCIPAL must be paid. *See also* MATURITY VALUE.

MATURITY VALUE amount to be paid on the maturity date of a financial instrument. It may be a greater amount (i.e., bond issued at a discount) or a lesser amount (i.e., bond issued at a premium) than the initial price. Maturity value is typically the *face value* of a bond or note. Assume that a five-year $20,000 bond is issued at 95—at a discount. The proceeds at issuance are $19,000, but at the due date of the five-year bond, the maturity value will be $20,000.

MAXIMIZATION behavior that attempts to maximize such performance measures as revenue, profits, contribution margin, or expected net present value. For example, a marketing manager wishes to maximize sales revenue or market share of the firm's product or service. Profit maximization has been the traditional goal of the firm in classical economic theory.

MAXIMUM CAPACITY *see* IDEAL CAPACITY.

MAXIMUM PRACTICAL CAPACITY *see* PRACTICAL CAPACITY.

MAXIMUM TAX rate that would apply to the various tiers of income subject to tax. As of 2014, the highest federal tax rate for individuals is 39.6%.

MEAL EXPENSE DEDUCTION income tax allowance for business meals. It is limited to 50% of the amount on the individual's tax return. Food and beverages are not deductible unless the taxpayer (1) shows the item *directly* applied to the active conduct of the taxpayer's trade or business and (2) sufficient substantiation exists. No deduction is permitted unless business is discussed during, just before, or just after the meal. Further, the meal cannot be *extravagant* as defined by the IRS.

MEAN measure of central tendency; also called *average*. Mean and STANDARD DEVIATION are the two most widely used statistical measures that summarize the characteristics of the data. Suppose a new car dealer sells 630 cars during a 30-day period. Then the mean (average) daily sales is obtained by dividing the total number of cars by the number of days as follows:

Mean daily sales per day = 630/30 = 21 per day

Symbolically,

$$\bar{x} = \Sigma x_i / n$$

where $\bar{x}$ = the mean, x_i = the values in the data, Σ (read as sigma) is the summation sign, and n = the number of observations in the data.

MEAN-PER-UNIT (MPU) ESTIMATION a technique used in statistical sampling that projects the average value of the items in the sample to estimate the value of the population.

MEDIAN value of the midpoint variable when the data are arranged in ascending or descending order. For example, in the following data set: 2, 3, 4, 8, 8, the median is the value of the third variable since there are two variables above it and two variables below it. Therefore, the median of the five variables is 4.

MEDICAL EXPENSE DEDUCTION itemized deduction allowed when total medical expenses, less reimbursements from medical insurance plans, exceed the applicable adjusted gross income threshold. The applicable threshold is generally 10% of adjusted gross income. For tax years 2013 through 2016, the threshold is reduced to 7.5% of adjusted gross income for individuals age 65 and older.

MEDICARE a health insurance program administered by the federal government covering individuals age 65 and older and those with certain disabilities.

MEMORY space within a computer where information and program are stored while being actively worked on; also called *core*. It is expressed in terms of the number of characters (BYTES) that can be retained. The memory of the computer is in the form of *read-only (ROM)* and RAM (RANDOM-ACCESS MEMORY) or read/write memory.

MERCHANDISE INVENTORY goods acquired for resale. Merchandise inventory is held by a merchandising concern including wholesalers and retailers. Contrast with FINISHED GOODS INVENTORY.

MERGER combination of two or more companies into one, with only one company retaining its identity. Typically, the larger of the two companies is the company whose identity is maintained. It often involves an exchange of stock, which avoids taxes; the *purchase (accounting) method*, where goodwill is recorded, must be used. The merger of two companies can be accomplished in one of two ways. The acquiring company can negotiate with management of the other company, or it can make a TENDER OFFER directly to the stockholders of the company it wants to take over.

METCALF REPORT critical report published in 1976 indicating, among other things, that the accounting profession's structure and independence were in need of realignment. It suggested that accounting and auditing standards should be established by the federal government rather than by the profession itself. The actual title of this report, which was prepared by the Subcommittee on Reports, Accounting and Management of the U.S. Senate, is "The Accounting Establishment." Presently, no legislation has resulted from the release of this report.

MICRO ACCOUNTING term connoting the accounting for a person, company, or government agency, as distinguished from *macro accounting*, which is the accounting for aggregate economic activities of a nation. Micro accounting also applies to the accounting and reporting of financial information of subunits of the entity.

MICROPROCESSOR general, all-purpose circuit, placed on a silicon chip. It is a power source of MICROCOMPUTERS. The microprocessor is at the heart of the micro-electronics revolution. This chip is used in calculators, watches, video games, microwave ovens, and, of course, computers. While a microprocessor is inexpensive, its power is equivalent to that of computers that cost several hundred thousand dollars in the 1960s.

MIDDLEWARE a type of software application that allows two or more existing disparate applications to communicate with each other using a messaging service.

MID-MONTH CONVENTION used when depreciating real property under the MODIFIED ACCELERATED COST RECOVERY SYSTEM (MACRS) for tax purposes and assumes that the property is placed into service (or disposed of) at the mid-point of the month.

MID-QUARTER CONVENTION used when depreciating personal property under the MODIFIED ACCELERATED COST RECOVERY SYSTEM (MACRS) for tax purposes, assumes that the property is placed into service (or disposed of) at the mid-point of the quarter. This convention is applicable to all MACRS property placed into service during the year when more than 40% of the total cost of all property placed into service during the year is placed into service in the last quarter of the year.

MINICOMPUTER computer that possesses the same components as large mainframes but has reduced memory and slower processing speeds. Before the advent of the minicomputer industry in the 1960s, companies wishing to automate were forced to use a large mainframe. With the evolution of minicomputers, managers could choose computers with substantially lower costs. During the 1980s, the use of minicomputers declined as microcomputers (also known as personal computers, or PCs) became more powerful and cheaper.

MINIMIZATION behavior that attempts to minimize such undesirable factors as cost, time, and inconvenience. Cost minimization is a usual goal of the production department of a firm. For example, a production department manager wishes to find the least cost combination of input materials in order to make a finished product. LINEAR PROGRAMMING (LP) models may be formulated in the format of either profit maximization or cost minimization.

MINIMUM CASH BALANCE safety cushion needed to avoid a possible cash shortage. In cash budgeting, projecting cash inflows (such as collections from customers) and cash disbursements (such as purchases and capital spending) is a difficult task. Even though the company attempts to forecast cash flows as accurately as possible, it is always a good idea to keep a certain minimum cash balance on hand.

MINIMUM LEASE PAYMENTS regular rental payments excluding EXECUTORY COSTS to be made by the lessee to the lessor in a CAPITAL LEASE. The lessee reports an asset and liability at the discounted value of the future minimum lease payments.

MINIMUM PENSION LIABILITY condition that is recognized when the ACCUMULATED BENEFIT OBLIGATION is greater than the fair value of plan assets. However, *no* recognition is given in the opposite case. When an accrued pension liability exists, only an additional liability for the difference between the minimum liability and the accrued pension liability can be recorded. When an additional liability is recorded, it is offset by recognizing an intangible asset not exceeding the amount of unamortized prior service cost. If it does exceed that amount, the excess is shown as a reduction of stockholders' equity in an account called net loss not recognized as pension expense. Assume an accumulated benefit obligation of $500,000, and a fair value of pension plan assets of $400,000, leaving a minimum pension liability of $100,000. If we assume that the accrued pension liability is $40,000, then the additional pension liability is $60,000. The unamortized prior service cost is assumed to be $50,000. The journal entry to record the additional liability is:

Intangible Asset – Pension Plan	50,000	
Minimum Pension Liability Adjustment	10,000	
Additional Pension Liability		60,000

MINIMUM REQUIRED RATE OF RETURN *see* COST OF CAPITAL.

MINIMUM TAX levy imposed on taxpayers with large income to assure that all pay a fair share of the total tax burden. The traditional minimum tax was replaced by the ALTERNATIVE MINIMUM TAX (AMT) under the Tax Reform Act of 1986. AMT not only replaced the minimum tax, but extended it to corporations. The tax base for minimum tax starts with regular taxable income. This base then is adjusted by recomputing certain deductions and deferrals—such as depreciation, long-term contracts, and installment sales gain—in a manner that offsets to a great extent the reduction that these items generate in regular taxable income. The base then is increased by certain TAX PREFERENCE ITEMS (such as excess of accelerated depreciation over straight line).

MINORITY INTEREST ownership interest of those *not* in the consolidated group of companies when consolidated financial statements are prepared. An example is an *outside* group that owns 5% of the shares of a subsidiary, with the parent owning 95%.

MIS *see* MANAGEMENT INFORMATION SYSTEM (MIS).

MISCELLANEOUS EXPENSE incidental expense of a business, not classified as manufacturing, selling, or general and administrative expenses. It is presented on an income statement after operating income. Miscellaneous expenses are immaterial. A more precise designation or separate accounting for them results in a cost greater than the benefit received.

MISERY INDEX an index that tracks economic conditions including inflation and unemployment. It was particularly referred to in the economically depressed period of 1977 through 1981 in the United States. The inflation rate was in the double digits at that time.

Misery Index = Inflation Rate + Unemployment Rate + Prime Rate

The index typically is negatively correlated to the current condition of the stock market. The misery index has little value as a predictor of future stock prices. The index may be found in the Bureau of Labor Statistics publications and *The Wall Street Journal.*

MISLEADING pointing to an interpretation that is not factual or is unrealistic. Facts or statements that may be misstated, distorted, augmented, omitted, and arranged in such a manner as to obscure and conceal material aspects of an item are misleading. The accountant carefully prepares, based on the reliance on accepted standards of auditing practice and statement presentation, financial information to avoid misleading inferences.

MIXED COST *see* SEMIVARIABLE COSTS.

MODEL abstraction of a real-life system used to facilitate understanding and to aid in decision making. It has become a popular device in business. The model can be classified into three popular types: (1) physical model; (2) graphical model; and (3) mathematical model. Examples of physical models are childhood toys such as dolls and toy airplanes. Graphical models are abstractions of lines, symbols, shapes, or charts—for example, a BREAK-EVEN CHART. Mathematical models are the ones that have stimulated most of the recent interest in models for decision making. Any mathematical formula or equation is a model. Mathematical models are used to solve planning and decision problems and to answer various *what-if* scenarios. Examples include the *break-even* model and LINEAR PROGRAMMING.

MODEM device that enables one computer to communicate with another over telephone lines. The word modem stands for *mo*dulator/*dem*odulator. To modulate is to change digital signals to analog, so data can be transmitted by audio tones over telephone lines to another computer whose modem can change the audio tones back to the needed digital (bits). To demodulate, the opposite of modulate, is to change analog to digital.

MODIFIED ACCELERATED COST RECOVERY SYSTEM (MACRS) a method of accelerated depreciation permitted by tax codes, as modified by recent changes. It classifies depreciable assets into one of several recovery periods, each of which has a designated pattern of allowable depreciation (double-declining balance, 150% declining balance, or straight-line with a half-year convention). *See also* ACCELERATED COST RECOVERY SYSTEM (ACRS).

MODIFIED ACCRUAL governmental accounting method. Revenue is recognized when it becomes available and measurable. Expenditures are typically recognized in the period in which the liability is incurred *except for*: (1) inventories of materials and supplies that may be considered expenditures either when bought or used; (2) interest on general and special assessment long-term debt that is recognized on the date due; and (3) use of encumbrances. Most governmental funds follow the modified accrual method. *See also* ACCRUAL ACCOUNTING.

MODULAR DESIGN design of components that can be assembled in a variety of ways to meet individual consumer needs.

MONETARY ITEM asset or liability whose amounts are fixed or determinable in dollars without reference to future prices of specific goods or services. Their economic significance depends heavily upon the general purchasing power of money. The two types of monetary items are *monetary assets* and *monetary liabilities*. Monetary assets are those stated in current dollars needing no adjustment in the price-level balance sheet, such as cash, accounts receivable, and marketable securities at market value. Monetary liabilities are obligations payable in dollars requiring no adjustment in the price-level balance sheet, such as accounts payable and bonds payable. However, holding monetary items during a period of inflation will result in a PURCHASING POWER LOSS, GAIN in the price-level income statement. *See also* NONMONETARY ITEM.

MONEY
1. cash.
2. term broadly used to refer to a medium of exchange and unit of value.

MONEY MARKET market for short-term (less than one year) debt securities. Examples of money market securities include U.S. Treasury bills, federal agency securities, bankers' acceptances, commercial paper, and negotiable certificates of deposit issued by government, business, and financial institutions.

MONEY ORDER check issued by a bank to a payee when an individual gives the bank funds in exchange. Payees sometimes require a money order since it is, in effect, guaranteed payment. An example is a person giving ABC Savings Bank $1000 and asking the bank to make out its own check payable to an auto dealer.

MONITORING a component of internal control that involves the process of assessing the quality of INTERNAL CONTROL performance over a period of time. An entity's use of internal auditors represents an effective means of monitoring internal controls.

MONOPOLY exists when an entity has the total control of specific goods or services in a specific area or market.

MONTE CARLO SIMULATION *see* MONTE CARLO TECHNIQUE (METHOD, OR ANALYSIS).

MONTE CARLO TECHNIQUE (METHOD, OR ANALYSIS) special type of SIMULATION, where the variables of a given system are subject to uncertainty. The technique gets its name from the famous Mediterranean resort often associated with games of chance. In fact, the chance element is an important aspect of Monte Carlo simulation: the approach can be used only when a system has a *random*, or chance, component. Under this approach, a probability distribution is developed that reflects the random component of the system under study. Random samples taken from this distribution are analogous to observations made on the system itself. As the number of observations increases, the results of the simulation will tend to more closely approximate the random behavior of the real system, provided an appropriate model has been developed. Sampling is accomplished by the use of random numbers. Simulation applications include testing alternative inventory policies and simulating a cash budget.

MORTGAGE lien securing a note payable that has as collateral real assets and that requires periodic payments. For personal property, such as machines or equipment, the lien is called a CHATTEL MORTGAGE. Mortgages can be issued to finance the acquisition of assets, construction of plants, and modernization of facilities. The bank will require that the value of the property exceed the mortgage on that property. Mortgages have a number of advantages over other debt instruments, including favorable interest rates, fewer financing restrictions, and extended maturity date for loan repayment.

MORTGAGE BOND debt secured by a real asset. There are two types of mortgage bonds: senior mortgages, which have first claim on assets and earnings and junior mortgages, which have a subordinate lien. A mortgage bond may have a closed-end provision that prevents the firm from issuing additional bonds of the same priority against the same property or may be an open-end mortgage that allows the issuance of additional bonds having equal status with the original issue.

MORTGAGE INTEREST DEDUCTION federal tax deduction allowed for interest paid or accrued within the taxable year with respect to mortgage indebtedness. Interest is deductible on mortgages secured by principal homes and second homes. A taxpayer may not write off interest on any part of the mortgage that exceeds the original purchase price plus improvements of property, unless the taxpayer uses the money for medical or educational purposes.

MOST LIKELY TIME in PROGRAM EVALUATION AND REVIEW TECHNIQUE (PERT), the time that the activity would most likely take if it were repeated time and time again; denoted by *m*. *See also* EXPECTED TIME FOR AN ACTIVITY.

MOVING AVERAGE average that is updated as new information is received. With the moving average, an accountant employs the most recent observations to calculate an average, using the result as the forecast for the next period. For example, assume that the accountant has the following cash inflow data:

Month	Cash Collections (000)
May	20
June	24
July	22
August	26
Sept.	25

Using a four-period moving average, the accountant computes the predicted cash collection for October as follows:

$$\frac{(24 + 22 + 26 + 25)}{4} = \frac{97}{4} = 24.25, \text{ or } \$24,250.$$

MOVING AVERAGE INVENTORY METHOD method used under a PERPETUAL INVENTORY SYSTEM, which requires that a new weighted average cost must be calculated after *each* purchase. The new weighted average is computed in the same way as in the WEIGHTED AVERAGE INVENTORY METHOD; that is, the average cost is the cost of the units available for sale after the purchase divided by the number of units available for sale at that time. This average cost is used to determine the cost of each sale made prior to the next purchase.

For example, assume the following inventory data for Company J:

Inventory, March 1	100 units @ $10 per unit	$1,000
Purchases, March 10	80 units @ $11 per unit	880
Purchases, March 20	70 units @ $12 per unit	840
Goods available for sale	250 units	$2,720
Sales, March 18	90 units	
Sales, March 27	50 units	
	140 units	
Inventory, March 31	110 units	

The moving average costs are computed as follows:

March 1, beginning inventory	100 units @ $10		$1,000
March 10, purchases	80	@ $11	880
March 10, balance	180	@ $10.44	$1,880
March 18, sales	90	@ $10.44	940
March 18, balance	90	@ $10.44	$ 940
March 20, purchases	70	@ $12	840
March 20, balance	160	@ $11.125	$1,780
March 27, sales	50	@ $11.125	556
March 30, balance	110	@ $11.125	$1,224

Cost of goods sold (140 units) $940 + $556 .... $1,496

Ending inventory (110 units @ $11.125) $1,224

MOVING EXPENSE DEDUCTION deduction allowed in computing adjusted gross income of employees and self-employed individuals who paid or incurred moving costs. Two major requirements must be satisfied before a deduction is allowed: minimum distance moved and minimum period of employment. Allowable expenses are transportation and storage of household goods and personal effects, as well as travel (including lodging) from the old residence to the new residence. The cost of meals, however, is not deductible.

MOVING TIME time spent moving a product from one operation or department to another.

MRP *see* MATERIAL REQUIREMENT PLANNING (MRP).

MULTICOLLINEARITY condition that exists when independent variables are highly correlated with each other. In the presence of multicollinearity, the estimated REGRESSION COEFFICIENTS may be unreliable. The presence of multicollinearity can be tested by investigating the correlation (r) between the independent variables.

MULTIPLE DISCRIMINANT ANALYSIS (MDA) statistical classificatory technique similar to regression analysis that can be used to evaluate financial ratios.

MULTIPLE OVERHEAD RATES manner of measuring product costs. A different predetermined overhead rate is set for each department of a factory, rather than having a single predetermined rate for the entire factory. When products are heterogeneous, receiving uneven attention and effort as they move through various departments, departmental rates are necessary to achieve more accurate and equitable product costs. For example, if department A is labor intensive, application of overhead costs could be done more equitably on a basis of direct labor-hours or labor cost. If department B is machine oriented, allocation should be based on machine hours. *See also* PLANTWIDE OVERHEAD RATE; PREDETERMINED OVERHEAD RATE.

MULTIPLE RECORDING OF TRANSACTIONS in GOVERNMENTAL ACCOUNTING, entries made in more then one fund, when two or more funds each have authority over the same transaction. For example, the general fund may expend money to acquire fixed assets; however, the fund does not capitalize fixed assets. Thus the entry in the general fund is to debit expenditures and credit vouchers payable, and a memo entry is made in the general fixed asset account group to show the fixed asset.

MULTIPLE REGRESSION *see* MULTIPLE REGRESSION ANALYSIS.

MULTIPLE REGRESSION ANALYSIS statistical procedure that attempts to assess the relationship between a dependent variable and *two* or more independent variables. Examples: Total factory overhead (the dependent variable) is related to both labor-hours and machine-hours (the independent variables). Sales of a popular soft drink (the dependent variable) is a function of various factors, such as its price, advertising, taste, and the prices of its major competitors (the independent variables). *See also* REGRESSION ANALYSIS.

MULTI-STEP COST REASSIGNMENT reassignment of resource costs requiring one or more intermediate activity cost reassignments prior to cost assignment into the final cost objects.

MULTIPLE-STEP INCOME STATEMENT one providing multiple classifications and multiple intermediate differences. The multiple-step format reports amounts for the following income captions: (1) gross margin, (2) income from continuing operations, (3) income before extraordinary items, and (4) net income. An illustrative multiple-step income statement follows:

Sales
Less: Sales returns and allowances
Net sales
Less: Cost of sales
Gross margin
Less: Operating expenses
Income from continuing operations
Add: Other revenue and expenses
Less: Other expenses and losses
Income before tax and extraordinary items
Less: Provision for taxes
Income before extraordinary items
Add or Less: Extraordinary items (net of tax)
Net income

MULTITASKING simultaneous execution of two or more computer functions.

MUNICIPAL BOND *see* TAX-EXEMPT BOND.

MUNICIPAL FINANCE OFFICERS ASSOCIATION (MFOA) organization of financial officers working for municipalities. The goal of MFOA is to bring together representatives of various groups concerned with municipal accounting and to put into effect sound principles of accounting, budgeting, and reporting.

MUTUAL FUND portfolio of securities professionally managed by the sponsoring *management company* or *investment company* that issues shares to investors. A no-load fund does not charge a sales commission to buy shares, whereas a load fund does charge one. Mutual funds also charge management fees. The major advantages of mutual funds are diversification, professional management, and ownership of a variety of securities with a minimal capital investment. Further, dividend reinvestment and check-writing options may exist. Mutual funds are also convenient because recordkeeping is done by the fund. There are several drawbacks, however. Mutual funds may be costly to acquire because of sizable commissions and professional management fees. Traditionally, mutual fund performance on average has not outperformed the market as a whole. Quotations for mutual funds are stated in dollars and cents. The sale price is known as the NAV or net asset value. An illustrative quote for XYZ Stock Growth Fund follows:

	NAV	Offer Price	NAV Change
XYZ Stock Growth Fund	11.22	12.26	+.02

The quotation tells us that a share in the fund on a particular day could be sold for $11.22—the NAV. On the same date, a share could be bought for $12.26. The difference between the sale price and the purchase price is due to the commission charged on the purchase transaction. The NAV change value of +.02 indicates that the sale price (NAV) increased by 2 cents a share from the preceding day.

Mutual funds may be classified into types, according to organization, fees charged, methods of trading funds, and investment objectives. In open-end funds, investors buy from and sell their shares back to the fund itself. Closed-end funds operate with a fixed number of shares outstanding. These shares are traded like common stocks among individuals in secondary markets. Closed-end funds, although a variation of the investment company, have quite different investment characteristics from open-end funds. For example, they may sell at discounts or premiums to NAV and have variations within the category (e.g., dual-purpose funds).

Many different types of mutual funds exist, including growth stock funds, bond funds, money market funds, and tax-free security funds. A mutual fund family, which offers many various types of funds, typically allows its investors switching privileges at no cost or at a nominal fee.

MUTUALLY EXCLUSIVE INVESTMENTS group of CAPITAL BUDGET projects that compete with one another in such a way that the acceptance of one automatically excludes all others from further consideration. Analysis of competing projects using the NET PRESENT VALUE (NPV) and INTERNAL RATE OF RETURN (IRR) methods may give decision results contradictory to each other. From a practical standpoint, the NPV method generally gives correct ranking to mutually exclusive projects.

MySQL the most popular open-source database. It is cost effective, high performance, highly reliable, and scalable.

N

NAA *see* NATIONAL ASSOCIATION OF ACCOUNTANTS (NAA).

NASDAQ *see* NATIONAL ASSOCIATION OF SECURITIES DEALERS (NASD).

NATIONAL ASSOCIATION OF ACCOUNTANTS (NAA) organization made up mostly of non-CPAs. It has made significant contributions over the years to the development of management accounting principles. It has created the Institute of Management Accounting, which offers a program leading to the CERTIFICATE IN MANAGEMENT ACCOUNTING (CMA).

NATIONAL ASSOCIATION OF SECURITIES DEALERS (NASD) self-policing organization of brokers and dealers who handle OVER-THE-COUNTER (OTC) MARKET securities. The NASD functions principally along five lines: (1) it has developed a written code of fair practices dealing with such matters as the appropriateness of prices quoted to customers; (2) it has promulgated standard procedures in transactions between members; (3) it has improved the quality of service that the OTC market gives the investing public; (4) it undertakes to investigate and arbitrate disputes between parties and to take disciplinary measures when justified; and (5) it undertakes to study and make recommendations on pending legislation in the security field. It also owns and operates a computerized system providing price quotations for OTC and some exchange-listed securities. The system is known as NASDAQ, an acronym for *National Association of Securities Dealers Automated Quotations* system. In 2007, NASD merged with the regulation committee of the New York Stock Exchange, effectively creating the Financial Industry Regulatory Authority (FINRA).

NATIONAL ASSOCIATION OF STATE BOARDS OF ACCOUNTANCY (NASBA) national organization representing the 54 state licensing boards/agencies that regulate the CPA profession in all states and four U.S. territories.

NATIONAL AUTOMATED ACCOUNTING RESEARCH SYSTEM (NAARS) AMERICAN INSTITUTE OF CERTIFIED PUBLIC ACCOUNTANTS' (AICPA) online database containing recommended accounting practices and footnote references. It answers practice questions and gives proper accounting for a transaction or event. In accessing NAARS, a key word or group of words is used to describe the question or problem, and relevant references are obtained.

NATIONAL COMMISSION ON FRAUDULENT FINANCIAL REPORTING (TREADWAY COMMISSION) has as its purpose to determine how fraudulent financial reporting practices can be constrained. This commission defined fraudulent financial reporting as "intentional or reckless conduct, whether act or omission, that results in materially misleading financial statements."

NATIONAL DO NOT CALL REGISTRY managed by the Federal Trade Commission (FTC), the government's consumer protection agency, the registry limits the telemarketing calls you receive. Telemarketers are required to remove the numbers on the registry from their call lists.

NATIONAL FEDERATION OF INDEPENDENT BUSINESS (NFIB) (www.nfib.com) the largest advocacy organization representing small and independent businesses in Washington, D.C., and all 50 state capitals. NFIB was ranked the most influential business organization (and third overall) in "Washington's Power 25" survey conducted by *Fortune* magazine. NFIB's purpose is to impact public policy at the state and federal level and be a key business resource for small and independent business in America. NFIB also gives its members a power in the marketplace. By pooling the purchasing power of its 600,000 members, the National Federation of Independent Business gives members access to many business products and services at discounted costs. NFIB also provides timely information designed to help small businesses succeed. The NFIB's well-known small-business optimism index is based on responses from 1,221 member firms.

NATIONAL INCOME ACCOUNTING necessary step in learning how macroeconomic variables—such as the economy's total output, the price level, the level of employment, interest rates, and other variables are determined. The national income accounts provide regular estimates of GROSS DOMESTIC PRODUCT (GDP), the basic measure of the performance of the economy in producing goods and services. They are also useful because they provide a conceptual framework for describing the relationships among three key macroeconomic variables: output, income, and spending.

NATURAL BUSINESS YEAR *see* FISCAL YEAR.

NEGATIVE ASSURANCE method used by the CERTIFIED PUBLIC ACCOUNTANT to assure various parties, such as bankers and stockbrokers, that financial data under review by them is correct. Negative assurance tells the data user that nothing has come to the CPA's attention of an adverse nature or character regarding the financial data reviewed. This type of assurance is normally given to investment bankers and the SEC when the financial data are being used for stock and bond issuance. In addition, this assurance is given whenever a CPA is asked to comment on financial statements upon which a previous AUDIT OPINION has been rendered. (This type of assurance is unacceptable for the basic financial statements on which a certifying audit has been performed.) Further, negative assurance comments are made on unaudited financial statements and subsequent changes, indicating that nothing came to the auditor's attention that suggests the statements do not comply with applicable accounting requirements; are not fairly presented in conformity with GAAP applied on a consistent basis; or do not fairly present information shown therein. Negative assurance is given because the auditor has not made an examination in conformity with GENERALLY ACCEPTED AUDITING STANDARDS (GAAS). Negative assurance is not appropriate unless the CPA has made an examination in accordance with GAAS for the accounting period before the current one. This is due to the fact that the auditor needs evidence that can be related to COMFORT LETTER procedures. For negative assurance to be permissible, the evidence must have been gathered directly by the CPA giving the assurance, and not by another CPA.

NEGATIVE CONFIRMATION written request by the external auditor sent to a party having a financial relationship with the client and asking for a reply only in the case of disagreement. For example, a company may mail a form on behalf of the CPA firm to sampled customers requesting them to notify the auditor only if a discrepancy in the account balance exists. *See also* POSITIVE CONFIRMATION.

NEGATIVE GOODWILL term used in a business combination. Negative goodwill is accounted for under the PURCHASE (ACCOUNTING) METHOD when the fair market value of the net assets of the acquired company exceeds the purchase price paid. The credit difference reduces certain assets acquired. If any remaining credit exists, it is accounted for as an extraordinary gain.

NEGLIGENCE accountant's failure to conduct an audit with "due care." *Ordinary negligence* applies to judgment errors resulting from a lack of experience, training, or oversight: it is unintentional. *Gross negligence* results when the accountant recklessly disregards established accounting, reporting, and auditing standards. *See also* GENERALLY ACCEPTED ACCOUNTING PRINCIPLES (GAAP).

NEGOTIATED PRICE *transfer* price that is established through meetings between the buying and supplying divisions. Negotiated transfer prices, like *market price*-based transfer prices, are believed to preserve divisional autonomy. In case divisions cannot agree on a transfer price, some companies establish arbitrary procedures to help settle disputes. However, intervention by an arbitrator reduces divisional autonomy.

NEGOTIATED TRANSFER PRICE *see* NEGOTIATED PRICE.

NET
1. gross amount reduced by applicable reductions. For example, net sales equals gross sales less sales returns and allowances and sales discounts. Another example is net purchases that equal gross purchases less purchase returns and allowances and purchase discounts.
2. (informal) net profit after taxes.

NET ASSETS total assets less total liabilities. *See also* NET WORTH.

NET CASH INFLOW balance of increases in cash receipts over increases in cash payments resulting from a proposed capital investment.

NET INCOME revenue less all expenses; also called *net profit*. Other elements involved in computing net income include extraordinary items (net of tax) and cumulative effect of a change in accounting principle (net of tax). *See also* INCOME STATEMENT.

NET LOSS amount by which total costs and expenses exceed total revenue for the accounting period. *See also* NET INCOME.

NET OF TAX term used when certain items presented in the financial statements have been adjusted for all income tax effects. Some examples of financial statement items shown net of tax in the income statement are *extraordinary gains and losses*, cumulative effect of a CHANGE IN ACCOUNTING PRINCIPLE, and INCOME FROM DISCONTINUED OPERATIONS. In the retained earnings section of the balance sheet, PRIOR PERIOD ADJUSTMENTS are presented net of tax.

NET OF TAX METHOD unacceptable method of handling the effects of deferred taxes when temporary differences exist. Deferred taxes caused by temporary differences adjust the specific assets and liabilities to which they apply as well as the related revenues and expenses. *See also* DEFERRED TAX ALLOCATION METHOD; LIABILITY TAX ALLOCATION METHOD.

NET OPERATING LOSS (NOL) excess of operating expenses over operating revenues. It excludes income statement items that do not relate to normal business activities, such as extraordinary gains or losses. It also excludes financial expenses and revenue (i.e., interest expense, dividend income). *See also* LOSS CARRYBACK; LOSS CARRYFORWARD.

NET PRESENT VALUE (NPV) difference between the PRESENT VALUE (PV) of cash inflows generated by the project and the amount of the initial investment (*I*). The present value of future cash flows is computed using the COST OF CAPITAL (*minimum desired rate of return*, or HURDLE RATE) as the discount rate. *See also* NET PRESENT VALUE METHOD.

NET PRESENT VALUE METHOD widely used approach for evaluating an investment project. Under the net present value method, the present value (*PV*) of all cash inflows from the project is compared against the initial investment (*I*). The NET PRESENT VALUE (NPV), which is the difference between the present value and the initial investment (i.e., $NPV = PV - I$), determines whether the project is an acceptable investment. To compute the present value of cash inflows, a rate called the COST OF CAPITAL is used for discounting. Under the method, if the net present value is positive ($NPV > 0$ or $PV > I$), the project should be accepted.

NET PRICE METHOD accounting procedure in which purchases are recorded at the net price after cash discounts rather than at the gross amount. When discounts are not taken, the amount paid in excess of the recorded purchase price is charged to a discounts lost account. *See also* GROSS PRICE METHOD.

NET PROCEEDS
1. amount received from the sale or disposal of property less all relevant deductions (direct costs associated with the sale or disposal).
2. amount received from the issuance of securities less FLOATATION COSTS.

NET PROFIT *see* NET INCOME.

NET PURCHASE net cost of purchases, which is purchases *minus* purchase returns and allowances and purchase discounts *plus* transportation. This calculation appears in the cost of goods sold section of the income statement.

NET REALIZABLE VALUE
1. expected selling price of an inventory item less expected costs to complete and dispose. This is the ceiling amount in applying the LOWER OF COST OR MARKET rule to inventory valuation.
2. gross accounts receivable less allowance for doubtful accounts, representing the expected collectibility of those receivables.

NET SALES gross sales less sales returns and allowances and sales discounts.

NETWORK
1. foundation for a PROGRAM EVALUATION AND REVIEW TECHNIQUE (PERT) or CRITICAL PATH METHOD (CPM) analysis. It (1) visualizes all of the individual tasks to complete a given job or program; (2) points out interrelationships; and (3) comprises arrows linking circles (nodes).
2. system used as a complement to multiprogramming, time sharing, and satellite transmission of computer data and programs. Accounting, auditing, and

tax practitioners may benefit from the linking of microcomputers through LOCAL AREA NETWORKS (LANS). LANs allow for data exchange, electronic mail, and pooling of data files.

NET WORKING CAPITAL *see* WORKING CAPITAL.

NETWORK INTERFACE CARD (NIC) a circuit board used to connect a computer to a network. A NIC is also referred to as an Ethernet card or a network adapter.

NET WORTH total assets less total liabilities. Net worth, for an individual, is equal to his or her personal equity. In a business, net worth represents the stockholders' equity. *See also* OWNERS' EQUITY.

NEURAL NETWORKS technology in which computers actually try to learn from the data base and operator what the right answer is to a question. The system gets positive or negative response to output from the operator and stores that data so that it will make a better decision the next time. While still in its infancy, this technology shows promise for use in accounting, fraud detection, economic forecasting, and risk appraisals. The idea behind this software is to convert the order-taking computer into a "thinking" problem solver.

NEUTRALITY absence of bias. For example, financial information should be neutral and is not intended to favor an investor over a creditor. Neutrality is one of the ingredients of RELIABILITY.

NEW ECONOMY the new, digital economy driven by industrial information technology, much of which is related to telecommunications such as the Internet—a technology that, many argue, has a huge potential to transform the engineering industry. In the new economy, production and distribution systems are automated, computer-based systems. The old economy, classical or traditional, is undergoing sweeping changes through the speed and efficiency brought by applications of information technology and the Internet.

NEW YORK STOCK EXCHANGE (NYSE) national stock exchange that is located at the corner of Broad and Wall Streets in New York City; often called the *Big Board*. It has a central trading location where securities are bought and sold in an auction market by brokers acting as agents for the buyer and seller. It is governed by a board of directors consisting of one-half exchange members and one-half public members. The NYSE is the largest exchange and generates the most dollar volume in large, well-known companies. Its listing requirements are the most restrictive. For a company to be listed on the NYSE for the first time, for example, the corporation must have at least 2000 stockholders owning 100 shares, and its aggregate market value must be $18 million or more.

NEXT-IN, FIRST-OUT (NIFO) inventory valuation method whereby the cost of sale of the item is based on the cost to replace it rather than on historical cost. For example, an item costing $10 with a replacement cost of $12 is sold for $20. Under NIFO, gross profit is $8 ($20 minus $12). This method is *not* GAAP. However, during inflationary periods a company may want to price ahead of inflation by establishing its selling price on a replacement-cost basis and would thus use NIFO as a basis for pricing.

NODAL COST FLOW NETWORK network view of ABC in which the sources of the cost reassignments and downstream cost objects are thought of as "sending" and "receiving" nodes in a closed-system network.

NODE in PROGRAM EVALUATION AND REVIEW TECHNIQUE (PERT), circle in a network representing the beginning and ending of activities. A node symbolizes an event.

NOMINAL ACCOUNT income statement account (revenue and expense) that is closed out at the end of the year. *See also* CLOSING ENTRY; REAL ACCOUNT.

NOMINAL CAPITAL par or stated value of a company's issued capital stock.

NOMINAL INTEREST RATE stated interest rate on the face of a debt security or loan. For example, if a bond having a face value of $100,000 has a coupon interest rate of 8%, the nominal interest is $8,000, which will be paid each year. The terms *nominal interest rate* and COUPON RATE are synonymous in discussing bonds; the latter term is still commonly used even though it is rare these days for bonds to be issued with physical coupons. *See also* EFFECTIVE INTEREST RATE.

NONBUSINESS EXPENSE DEDUCTION broad category of deductions, such as state and local sales taxes and certain miscellaneous deductions. Individuals cannot take an itemized deduction for state and local sales taxes. Also, no deduction is allowed for expenses related to attending a convention, seminar, or similar meeting unless such expenses are connected with a trade or business. Thus expenses for a convention, or for a meeting in connection with investments, financial planning, or other income-producing activity, will no longer be deductible. Certain miscellaneous itemized deductions, including unreimbursed employee business expenses, are deductible by individuals only if the aggregate amount of the deductions exceeds two percent of the taxpayer's ADJUSTED GROSS INCOME (AGI).

NONCASH EXPENSE expense that did not require a cash outlay during the period under review.

NONCASH INVESTING AND FINANCING TRANSACTIONS significant investing and financing transactions that do not involve an actual cash inflow or outflow. They involve only long-term assets, long-term liabilities, or stockholders' equity, such as the exchange of a long-term asset for a long-term liability or the settlement of a debt by issuing capital stock.

NONCONFORMANCE COSTS a category of QUALITY COSTS, including internal failure costs (a financial measure of internal performance) and external failure costs (a financial measure of customer satisfaction).

NONCONTROLLABLE COST cost not subject to influence at a given level of managerial supervision. For instance, a manager's salary is not within the control of the manager himself. Rent of the factory building is another example. *See also* CONTROLLABLE COST.

NONCONTROLLABLE INTEREST *see* MINORITY INTEREST.

NONCONTROLLABLE RISK *see* SYSTEMATIC RISK.

NONDEDUCTIBLE TAX tax paid but not allowed as a deduction. An example is for state and local sales taxes, making them examples of *nondeductible taxes*.

NONDIVERSIFIABLE RISK *see* SYSTEMATIC RISK.

NONINTEREST-BEARING NOTE note receivable or note payable that does not provide for interest. In this unrealistic case, IMPUTED INTEREST on the note is required. Until tax reform, such notes were commonly used in transactions between parents and children (e.g., crown loans) and are still permitted under limited circumstances. The term *interest-bearing* is also used in contradistinction to *discount* or *zero-coupon instruments*.

NONINVENTORIABLE COST *see* PERIOD COST.

NONISSUER an entity whose equity or debt securities are *not* publicly traded on a stock exchange or in the over-the-counter market; it is not required to file financial statements with the SEC. Nonissuers are *exempted* from numerous accounting requirements (i.e., SEGMENT REPORTING) and are sometimes referred to as nonpublic companies.

NONLINEARITY situation where the relationship between variables is not directly proportional. For example, a per unit cost may decrease as production increases, because of economies of scale. The following diagram shows a comparison between a linear and a nonlinear cost function. *See also* LINEARITY.

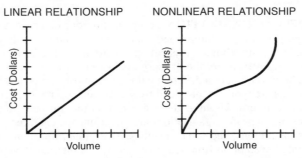

NONMANUFACTURING EXPENSES *see* OPERATING EXPENSES.

NONMONETARY EXCHANGE method of handling an exchange between one business entity and another that results in the acquisition of assets or services or the satisfaction of liabilities by surrendering cash assets (boot) or services or issuing other obligations. If the transaction has commercial substance, all gains and losses are recognized. If the nonmonetary transaction lacks commercial substance, then none of the gain is recognized but all of the loss is recognized. If boot is received and the amount of boot is less than 25% of the fair market value of the asset, then a partial gain is recognized. The gain recognized equals the total potential gain times the ratio of the boot to the total fair market value of the assets plus the boot. If the boot received is equal to or more than 25%, the boot is ignored and the full gain or loss is recognized.

NONMONETARY ITEM item stated in *older* dollars and therefore requiring direct adjustment in the price-level financial statements. It is any financial statement item that is not classified as a MONETARY ITEM. Examples of nonmonetary assets are land, buildings, and autos. Nonmonetary liabilities are obligations not payable in money, such as those payable in services (i.e., warranties payable) or those that will adjust an expense (i.e., deferred income tax credit). Stockholders' equity accounts are also considered nonmonetary. Examples of nonmonetary income statement accounts are depreciation and amortization.

NONPARAMETRIC STATISTICS type of statistics applied to problems for which rank order is known, but the specific distribution is not; also known as *distribution-free statistics*. Thus, various metals may be ranked in order of hardness without having any measure of hardness.

NONPRODUCTIVE CAPACITY capacity that is useable but is temporarily in a nonproductive state due to setups, scheduled downtime, unscheduled downtime or rework (repeating production because the first run came out wrong, or discarding materials rendered unusable after an unsuccessful run).

NONPROFIT ACCOUNTING accounting policies, procedures, and techniques employed by NONPROFIT ORGANIZATIONS. Nonprofit accounting is somewhat different for governmental units than for nongovernmental units (i.e., colleges, hospitals, voluntary health and welfare organizations, and charities). Governmental units employ *fund accounting*, which measures ACCOUNTABILITY rather than profitability. The MODIFIED ACCRUAL basis is typically employed by governmental funds. Nongovernmental units use the *accrual* basis.

NONPROFIT ORGANIZATION group, institution, or corporation formed for the purpose of providing goods and services under a policy where no individual (e.g., stockholder, trustee) will share in any profits or losses of the organization. Profit is *not* the primary goal of nonprofit entities. Profit may develop, however, under a different name (e.g., surplus, increase in fund balance). Assets are typically provided by sources that do not expect repayment or economic return. Usually, there are restrictions on resources obtained. Examples of nonprofit organizations are governments, charities, universities, religious institutions, and some hospitals. Most nonprofit organizations have been granted exemption from federal taxes by the Internal Revenue Service. Many of these organizations refer to themselves according to the IRS Code section under which they receive exempt status (i.e., 502(c)(3) organization). This identification lets donors know that their contributions to this organization may be deductible for income tax purposes.

NONRECIPROCAL TRANSFER
1. transfer of assets or services from a business to its owners or to another entity, or vice versa.
2. exchange of dissimilar assets in a nonmonetary transaction. *See also* NONMONETARY EXCHANGE.

NONRECURRING income statement item that is either unusual in nature or infrequent in occurrence. An example is the gain or loss on the sale of a fixed asset. Nonrecurring items are shown before arriving at income from continuing operations. They are *not* shown with a tax or earnings per share effect. *See also* EXTRAORDINARY ITEM.

NONROUTINE DECISION short-term, nonrecurring decision such as the following: (1) to accept or reject a special order; (2) to make or buy a certain part; (3) to sell or process further; or (4) to keep or drop a certain product line or division. In these types of decisions, a choice is typically made considering the RELEVANT COSTS and CONTRIBUTION MARGIN.

NONSAMPLING RISK any component of audit risk that is not associated with sampling. Nonsampling risk includes applying an audit procedure that does not fit an audit objective, misinterpretation of test results, and the outright failure to detect a material misstatement.

NONSTATISTICAL SAMPLING any sampling plan that is based on judgment rather than on probability theory. Nonstatistical and statistical sampling may result in the same sample size and evaluation of test results.

NONTAXABLE GROSS INCOME income received by the taxpayer that is not taxable, such as a gift.

NONTAXABLE INVESTMENT INCOME income such as interest on a tax-free municipal bond that is not included in taxable income when preparing the federal tax return.

NONVALUE-ADDED ACTIVITY activity that increases the time spent on a product or service but does not increase its worth to the customer. The designation "nonvalue-added" reflects a belief that the activity can be redesigned, reduced, or eliminated without reducing the quantity, responsiveness, or quality of the output required by the customer or the organization. *See also* CUSTOMER VALUE and VALUE ANALYSIS.

NONVALUE-ADDING COST cost of an operating activity that adds cost to a product or service, but, from a customer's perspective, does not increase its market value.

NO-PAR-VALUE CAPITAL STOCK shares designated in the charter that do not have a par or assigned value printed on the stock certificate. However, some states authorize the issuance of no-par stock with a stated value. When no-par stock is issued, the entry is to debit cash and credit capital stock for the total proceeds received. No premium is required on the capital stock account. An advantage of no-par stock is that it avoids a contingent liability to stockholders in the case of a stock discount. One of the original reasons for no-par stock was to avoid state taxes based on par value, but states will sometimes tax no-par stock as if it had par value. A disadvantage of no-par stock is that inept directors may lower the value of outstanding shares by accepting minimal prices on new issues.

NORMAL ABSORPTION COSTING method of product costing. It includes actual costs of direct material and direct labor plus factory overhead applied by using predetermined overhead rates times actual units of inputs (such as direct labor hours, machine hours, direct material dollars, or direct labor cost). This method smoothes fluctuations in overhead costs that occur during the year. It also provides timely costing information that would not be available if the firm waited until year-end to determine the actual rates. *See also* EXTENDED NORMAL COSTING.

NORMAL ACTIVITY level of production that will satisfy average demand by consumers over a time span (often five years) that includes trend, seasonal, and cyclical factors. It is a long-run average expected activity that is a basis for developing the factory overhead application rate.

NORMAL CAPACITY *see* CAPACITY.

NORMAL COSTING *see* NORMAL ABSORPTION COSTING.

NORMAL COSTS
   1. annual average of product costs, not actual product costs that are affected by month-to-month fluctuations in production volume and by erratic or

seasonal behavior of many overhead costs. Typical examples of erratic behavior include repairs and maintenance, fuel, air-conditioning costs, vacation and holiday pay, and the employer's share of Social Security taxes. All the costs that distort monthly overhead rates are collected in the annual overhead pool along with the kinds of overhead that do have uniform behavior patterns. In summary, normal costs are the sum of actual direct materials, actual direct labor, and applied factory overhead.
2. pension plan costs incurred during an accounting period for services performed during the period. *See also* NORMAL PENSION COST.

NORMAL DISTRIBUTION probability distribution. It has the following important characteristics: (1) the curve has a single peak; (2) it is bell-shaped; (3) the mean (average) lies at the center of the distribution, and the distribution is symmetrical around the mean; (4) the two tails of the distribution extend indefinitely and never touch the horizontal axis; (5) the shape of the distribution is determined by its MEAN (μ) and STANDARD DEVIATION (σ).

NORMAL DISTRIBUTION

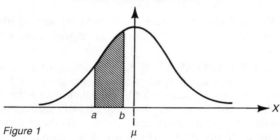

Figure 1

As with any continuous probability function, the area under the curve must equal 1, and the area between two values of X (say, a and b) represents the probability that X lies between a and b as illustrated on *Figure 1*. Further, since the normal is a symmetric distribution, it has the nice property that a known percentage of all possible values of X lie within ± a certain number of standard deviations of the mean, as illustrated by *Figure 2*. For example, 68.27% of the values of any normally distributed variable lie within the interval ($\mu - 1, \mu + 1$).

STANDARD DEVIATION OF THE MEAN

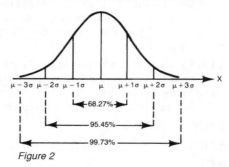

Figure 2

Percent	99.73%	99%	95.45%	95%	90%	80%	68.27%
No. of ± 's	3.00	2.58	2.00	1.96	1.645	1.28	1.00

The probability of the normal as given above is difficult to work with in determining areas under the curve, and each set of X values generates another curve as long as the means and standard deviations are translated to a new axis, a Z-axis, with the translation defined as

$$Z = \frac{X - \mu}{\sigma}$$

The resulting values, called Z-values, are the values of a new variable called the *standard normal variate*, Z. The translation process is depicted in *Figure 3*.

STANDARD NORMAL VARIATE

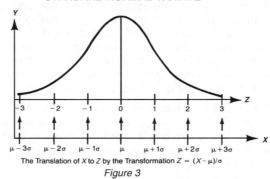

The Translation of X to Z by the Transformation $Z = (X - \mu)/\sigma$

Figure 3

The new variable Z is normally distributed with a mean of zero and a standard deviation of 1. Tables of areas under this standard normal distribution have been compiled and widely published so that areas under any normal distribution can be found by translating the X values to Z values and then using the tables for the standardized normal. For example, assume the total book value of an inventory is normally distributed with $\mu = \$8,000$ and $\sigma = \$1,000$. What percent of the population lies between $6,000 and $10,000? To answer, first translate these two X-values to Z-values using the Z formula:

$$Z_1 = (\$6,000 - \$8,000)/\$1,000 \qquad Z_2 = (\$10,000 - \$8,000)/\$1,000$$
$$= -2 \qquad\qquad\qquad\qquad\qquad = +2$$

Referring to *Figure 2*, note that 95.45% of the population lies between these two values. Interpreted as a probability, the statement can be made that total book value will lie between $6,000 and $10,000, with a probability of .9545.

NORMAL EQUATIONS ones obtained via the LEAST-SQUARES METHOD, which minimizes the sum of squares of the deviations of the actual points from the line $y = a + bx$. The idea is to obtain the line of best fit. The normal equations are:

$$\Sigma y = na + b \Sigma x$$
$$\Sigma xy = a \Sigma x + bx^2$$

where Σ denotes summation over all n observations. *See also* REGRESSION ANALYSIS.

NORMAL PENSION COST actuarial present value of benefits attributed by the pension formula to employee service performed during the current year;

also called *service cost*. Normal pension cost is funded dollar for dollar. *See also* PRIOR SERVICE PENSION COST.

NORMAL SPOILAGE product deterioration that is expected even under the best operating conditions. It is inherent and unavoidable in the short run. Costs of normal spoilage are allocated to the remaining good units in inventory. Management establishes a *normal spoilage rate* that is acceptable under a given combination of production factors. Normal spoilage is a cost of goods produced. *See also* ABNORMAL SPOILAGE.

NORMAL STOCK METHOD *see* BASE STOCK METHOD.

NOTE PAYABLE written promise to pay money at a future date. The payment consists of principal and usually interest. For example, a $10,000 three-month 6% note will require a payment at maturity of $10,150 ($10,000 principal plus $150 interest). The interest of $150 equals $10,000 $\times$ 6% $\times$ 3/12. A note payable may be classified as either a current or a noncurrent liability, depending on whether the note is due within one year or less. A note payable may be issued either to make a purchase, to refinance an open account payable, or to borrow from the bank. *See also* NOTE RECEIVABLE.

NOTE RECEIVABLE written promise to receive money at a future date, comprising principal and usually interest. Depending on whether the note is for one year or less, it can be classified as either a current or a noncurrent asset. Interest earned on the note is credited to the interest income account. *See also* NOTE PAYABLE.

NOTE RECEIVABLE DISCOUNTED discounted proceeds from a note, received by the holder of a customer's note, from a third party, usually a bank or finance company, prior to its maturity date. The proceeds received by the holder equal the maturity value less the bank discount (interest charge). The bank discount is based upon (1) the time period the bank will be holding the note and (2) the note's interest rate. The interest rate charged by the bank is usually higher than the interest rate on the note. The maturity value of the note equals the face value of the note plus interest. The bank discount equals the maturity value times the discount rate times the period the note is held by the bank. The net proceeds received by the payee at the time of discounting equals the maturity value less the bank discount. Note that notes receivable discounted represents a contingent liability to be footnoted.

NOT-FOR-PROFIT ORGANIZATION *see* NONPROFIT ORGANIZATION.

NOT-SUFFICIENT-FUNDS CHECK (NSF CHECK) check not covered by sufficient bank balance. In preparing its BANK RECONCILIATION, the depositing entity must deduct the NSF check from the cash book balance.

NUMBER OF DAYS INVENTORY IS HELD *see* DAYS TO SELL INVENTORY.

O

OBJECTIVE FUNCTION *see* LINEAR PROGRAMMING (LP).

OBJECTIVE PROBABILITY characteristic obtained as a result of repeated experiments or repeated trials rather than on the basis of subjective estimates. It is useful in estimating dollar value, quantity, or other characteristics of a given universe for purposes of making statistical decisions.

OBJECTIVES OF FINANCIAL REPORTING goal of presenting useful information to financial statement users so that proper decisions can be made. Data presented should be comprehensive so that a good understanding of the entity's activities is possible. Financial information should aid in the evaluation of the amounts, timing, and uncertainties of cash flows. Also, financial reporting should furnish information about the firm's economic resources, claims against those resources, owners' equity, and changes in resources and claims. Financial reporting should provide information about financial performance during a period and management's discharge of its stewardship responsibility to owners. It should likewise be useful to the managers and directors themselves in making decisions on behalf of the owners.

OBJECTIVES OF FINANCIAL STATEMENTS goals financial statements are supposed to accomplish. The intent of financial statements is to provide information useful in economic decision making. In particular, the data should be useful in making investment and credit decisions. Financial statements should provide a reliable indication of a company's financial position, operating results, and changes in financial position. Also, statement components and categories should aid in decisions. Financial statements may provide information in addition to that specified by authoritative requirements and regulatory groups. Inasmuch as management knows the most about the business, it is encouraged to identify certain circumstances and explain their financial effects on the enterprise. Note that the FINANCIAL ACCOUNTING STANDARDS BOARD (FASB) Statement of Financial Accounting Concepts No. 1, "Objectives of Financial Statements," provides reporting goals.

OBJECTIVITY freedom from subjective valuation and bias in making an accounting decision. Objectivity applies to a measurement having supporting evidence. Verifiability exists in that two accountants working independently of each other will come up with similar answers. An example of objectivity is recognizing revenue at time of sale because it emanates from an independent external transaction.

OBSERVATION TEST physical and visual verification by inspection of financial statement items or activities. The external auditor observes and evaluates how company employees conduct a variety of accounting related tasks such as documenting the existence and valuation of assets, safeguarding assets, approving expense accounts, and counting inventory. Observation tests may be conducted for *substantive* reasons, such as observing inventory, and for *compliance* purposes, such as the segregation of duties. However, an observation test does not require *detailed* physical inspection or examination of documentation. Depending on what is being tested and the method being used, the observation test may be performed by other than accounting personnel.

OBSOLESCENCE major factor in depreciation, resulting from technological or market changes. Wear and tear from use and natural deterioration through interaction of the elements are other factors that cause depreciation in assets. It is also a big factor in inventory risk.

OCCUPATIONAL SAFETY AND HEALTH ACT (OSHA) federal law concerned primarily with the regulation of working conditions in commerce and industry. It contains guidelines and regulations issued by the Department of Labor that mandate standards with respect to occupational safety and health of workers involved in interstate commerce.

OCR *see* OPTICAL CHARACTER RECOGNITION (OCR).

ODD-LOT any exception to the standard trading unit of a security. For example, with minor exceptions a standard or round-lot of stock is 100 shares, so any amount other than 100 shares or multiples thereof would be an odd-lot. The commission rate on an odd-lot transaction usually includes an *odd-lot differential*, typically 1/8th of a point. Thus the commission rate on an odd-lot transaction is relatively higher than on a round-lot transaction.

OFF-BALANCE SHEET ASSET item representing a resource of the entity or something expected to have future economic benefit. It is a positive sign of financial position even though it is not shown in the balance sheet. A going concern is assumed here, since in liquidation unrecorded assets would generally not be realizable. Unrecorded assets include a tax loss carryforward benefit, a purchase contract for an item at a price significantly less than the going rate, anticipated rebates, and a contingent asset (as when the entity may receive a payment if a certain event occurs).

OFF-BALANCE SHEET FINANCING manner of obtaining funds, often through a long-term, noncancelable lease accounted for as an operating lease. Since the lease does not meet any of the four criteria for a CAPITAL LEASE, the present value of the lease obligation is not presented on the lessee's balance sheet.

OFF-BALANCE SHEET LIABILITY item not reported in the body of the financial statements as a liability but possibly requiring future payment or services. These items include litigation, guarantees of future performance, and renegotiation of claims under a government contract.

OFFICE OF MANAGEMENT AND BUDGET (OMB) agency within the Executive Office of the President. The OMB has broad financial management power as well as the responsibility of preparing the executive budget. Among the other duties assigned OMB are: (1) to study and recommend to the president changes relative to the existing organizational structure of the agencies, their activities and methods of business, etc.; (2) to apportion appropriations among the agencies and establish reserves in anticipation of cost savings, contingencies, etc.; and (3) to develop programs and regulations for improved data gathering pertaining to the government and its agencies.

OFFSET ACCOUNT one that reduces the gross amount of another account to derive a net balance. Accumulated depreciation, which is a contra account to fixed assets to obtain book value, is an example of an offset account. Discount on note payable, which is a reduction of notes payable to derive the carrying value, is another example.

OFFSETTING ERROR error that cancels out another error; also called *counterbalancing error*. For example, if an accountant charged an expense to 20X1 when it should have been charged to 20X2, the effects of the two errors are cancelled out in 20X3. This occurs because in 20X1 the expense is overstated and the profit is understated whereas in 20X2 the expense is understated and profit overstated. Thus the beginning balance of retained earnings on 1/1/20X3 will be properly stated, since the effects of the errors offset each other. Thus over a period of two years, the effects of the errors in expense will counterbalance, and the total net income for the two years together will be the same as if the errors had not occurred. However, it should be noted that the yearly net income figures for 20X1 and 20X2 are still misstated, so the trend in earnings is distorted.

ON ACCOUNT
1. purchase or sale on credit. For example, the journal entry for a sale on account is to debit accounts receivable and credit sales.
2. partial payment on an obligation.

100% APPORTIONED COST DRIVER type of cost driver that relies entirely on an informed estimator's judgment of how much cost should be traced to each cost object and to which cost objects. Does not provide rates per unit of the cost driver (for predictive planning).

ONE-YEAR TREASURY CONSTANT MATURITY INDEX an index of rates on U.S. Treasury borrowings that determines the changes in many adjustable-rate mortgages. The index is released by the Federal Reserve Board, which recalculates yields on a variety of Treasury securities as if each would mature in one year.

ONLINE
1. computer equipment under the control of the central processing unit (CPU). Examples are disk drives and printers.
2. Linking up one computer to another computer in a remote location through the use of the INTERNET.

ONLINE PROCESSING term used to refer to equipment that operates under control of the central processing unit (CPU). Online processing equipment can be placed in the same location as the CPU or in a remote location. Generally, online processing refers to processing using a terminal (input) that is remote from the CPU.

ONLINE SEARCHING using a computer retrieval system to obtain information from a database such as on the Internet.

OPEN ACCOUNT
1. account that has a nonzero credit or debit balance.
2. credit or charge account—that is, an account initiated by a creditor on the basis of credit standing. It may also refer to a balance currently owing due to a credit sale, under mutually agreed-upon terms (such as method of payment, trade discounts, delivery date, and quantities).

OPEN BOOK MANAGEMENT management philosophy that gets all employees involved in increasing financial performance and ensures that all workers have access to operational and financial information necessary to accomplishing performance improvements.

OPEN-END MUTUAL FUND one that issues new shares and stands ready to buy shares back at net asset value. There is usually no restriction on the amount of money that can be invested in a fund although management companies may decide at some point that the fund has gotten too large and may stop issuing new shares. The fact that there are no fixed number of shares outstanding distinguishes open-end funds from CLOSED-END MUTUAL FUNDS. *See also* MUTUAL FUND.

OPENING ENTRY one or a series of entries usually undertaken upon forming a new enterprise, or new accounts, or a new accounting period. A new enterprise requires opening entries with respect to the owner's interests, assets, and liabilities on the books.

OPERATING ACTIVITIES business activities that involve the cash effects of transactions and other events that enter into the determination of net income.

OPERATING BUDGET *see* OPERATIONAL (OPERATING) BUDGET.

OPERATING BUDGET SEQUENCE part of the master budget process that begins with the sales budget and culminates in the pro forma income statement. Its emphasis is on obtaining and using resources.

OPERATING CAPACITY *see* CAPACITY.

OPERATING CYCLE average time period between buying inventory and receiving cash proceeds from its eventual sale. It is determined by adding the *number of days inventory is held* and the COLLECTION PERIOD for accounts receivable. Some industries, such as distillery and lumber, have a long operating cycle.

OPERATING DECISIONS decisions that involve routine tasks, such as planning production and sales, scheduling personnel and equipment, adjusting production rates, and controlling the quality of production.

OPERATING ENVIRONMENT shell program surrounding the *Disk Operating System* (DOS) of a personal computer. It turns the display into a desk-top that is basically a menu from which one selects and runs PC applications. A shell program is a software package with an integration capability. This is created when the resident operating system and application programs are surrounded with a superimposed "shell" of command structures and menus. Microsoft Windows, Linux, and IBM's OS/2, different examples of operating environments, do away with the DOS prompt. An alternative operating environment allows switching of programs, windowing, and cut-and-paste capabilities. Windowing is the capability to accommodate more than one program if the accountant wants the main memory partitioned to handle the programs. For each program in memory, a separate window is displayed on the screen.

OPERATING EXPENSES costs associated with the selling and administrative activities of the company; also called *nonmanufacturing expenses*. They represent a PERIOD COST related to time rather than to the product. They are subdivided into SELLING EXPENSES and GENERAL AND ADMINISTRATIVE EXPENSES.

OPERATING INCOME revenue less cost of goods sold and related operating expenses applying to the normal business activities of the entity. It excludes financial related items (i.e., interest income, dividend income, interest expense), extraordinary items, taxes, and other peripheral activities. *See also* OPERATING LOSS.

OPERATING LEASE rental of property between the lessee and lessor for a fee. An operating lease does *not* meet the criteria for a CAPITAL LEASE. An example is renting of an apartment or automobile. The lessee debits rental expense and credits cash. Rental expense should be recognized on a straight-line basis, unless another systematic and rational basis is more representative of the time pattern in which benefit use is derived. The lessee shows nothing about the lease on the balance sheet. Lessee footnote disclosure includes future minimum lease payments in aggregate and for each of the five succeeding fiscal years, contingent rentals, and sublease rentals. The lessor, upon receipt of rental payments, debits cash and credits rental revenue. The lessor also records depreciation expense on the leased item and any expenses related to the leased property, such as maintenance expense. Normal accrual basis accounting techniques are followed for the recognition of income and expense. The lessor reports on his balance sheet the leased asset less accumulated depreciation. Footnote disclosure by the lessor includes the cost of property on lease or held for leasing by major class, minimum future rentals in the aggregate and for each of the five succeeding years, and contingent rentals. *See also* DIRECT FINANCING LEASE; SALES TYPE LEASE.

OPERATING LEVERAGE measure of fixed costs in a company's operating structure. High operating leverage magnifies changes in earnings so that small changes in sales lead to earnings instability. Operating leverage can be measured through the following ratios: (1) fixed costs to total costs; (2) percentage change in operating income to the percentage change in sales volume; and (3) net income to fixed charges. An increase in (1) and (2) or a decrease in (3) shows higher fixed charges, resulting in greater instability.

OPERATING LOSS amount by which the cost of goods sold plus operating expenses exceeds operating revenues. The net loss from operations applies only to the normal business activities of the entity. Excluded are financial revenue and expense items and ancillary operations of the firm (i.e., extraordinary items). However, interest would be an includable expense in calculating NET OPERATING LOSS for carryforward purposes. *See also* OPERATING INCOME.

OPERATING PERFORMANCE RATIO measure of profitability to sales to determine the return earned on the revenue generated. Some operating performance ratios are the profit margin (net income to sales), gross margin ratio (gross margin to sales), and operating profit margin (operating income to sales). The higher these ratios, the better the profitability earned on the company's sales.

OPERATING REVENUE net sales plus other regular income sources related to the normal business operations of the entity (e.g., lease income if a major activity).

OPERATING RISK one caused by fluctuations of operating income. This type of risk depends on variability in demand, sales price, input prices, and amount of OPERATING LEVERAGE. A business with a high degree of risk in its operations will have greater instability, often resulting in lower market price of stock and increased cost of financing.

OPERATING SYSTEM computer program that allows users to enter and run their software packages. The operating system allows the machine to recognize and carry out the accountant's command. Further, there are built-in routines permitting the user's software to conduct input-output operations without specifying the exact hardware configuration. The operating system normally consists of the job control program, the input/output control system, and the processing program. If a computer operates under one system, it cannot use programs designated for a different operating system.

OPERATIONAL AUDIT evaluation made of management's performance and conformity with policies and budgets. The organization and its operations are analyzed, including appraisal of structure, controls, procedures, and processes. The objective is to appraise the effectiveness and efficiency of a division, activity, or operation of the entity in meeting organizational goals. Recommendations to improve performance are also made. The primary user of an operational audit is management. However, an operational audit is slightly different from a MANAGEMENT AUDIT since it concentrates on the organization. Many companies maintain internal audit staffs for the sole purpose of performing operational audits on a recurring basis. For each review, management receives a report from the audit team that will indicate how well the activities are performed, suggest improvements, and offer other conclusions drawn from the work.

OPERATIONAL COST DRIVER higher order of an activity cost driver. Usually thought of as the driver of a business process.

OPERATIONAL (OPERATING) BUDGET one that embraces the impacts of operating decisions. It contains forecasts of sales, net income, the cost of goods sold, selling and administrative expenses, and other expenses. The cornerstone of an operational budget is forecasted sales. Therefore, the SALES BUDGET is the basic building block for the operational budget. Once the sales budget is prepared, then the PRODUCTION BUDGET can be formulated. The operational budget also consists of the ending inventory budget, direct material budget, direct labor budget, factory overhead budget, selling and administrative budget, and budgeted income statement.

OPERATION COSTING hybrid of job-order and process cost systems. Companies that manufacture goods that undergo some similar and some dissimilar processes use this system. Operation costing accumulates total conversion costs and determines a unit conversion cost for each operation. However, direct material costs are charged specifically to products as in job-order systems.

OPERATIONS set of all activities associated with the production of goods and services.

OPERATIONS RESEARCH (OR) *see* QUANTITATIVE METHODS (MODELS).

OPERATIONS STRATEGY strategy specifying how the firm will employ its production capabilities to support its corporate strategy.

OPINION
  1. AUDIT OPINION.
  2. APB OPINION.

3. accountant's judgment regarding a set of facts. For example, the auditor must formulate an opinion on the adequacy of a client's internal control system to determine the degree of audit testing required.

OPPORTUNITY COST revenue forfeited by rejecting an alternative use of time or facilities. For example, assume a company has a choice of using its capacity to produce an extra 10,000 units or renting it out for $20,000. The opportunity cost of using that capacity is $20,000. A further example is the return lost by having money tied up in accounts receivable because of a collection problem. If the extra funds tied up in receivables for a three-month period were $400,000, on which the firm could earn 10% per annum, the opportunity cost is $10,000 ($400,000 $\times$ 3/12 $\times$ 10%).

OPPORTUNITY COST APPROACH method in which the concept of OPPORTUNITY COST is applied to solve a short-term, nonroutine decision problem. Opportunity cost represents the net benefit lost by rejecting some alternative course of action. Its significance in decision making is that the best decision is always sought, since it considers the cost of the best available alternative *not* taken. The opportunity cost does not appear on formal accounting statements. *See also* INCREMENTAL ANALYSIS.

OPTICAL CHARACTER RECOGNITION (OCR) computer tool that recognizes typed or printed characters (alphabetic and numeric) on paper so they can be recorded on disk or magnetic tape. Optical character recognition can also read foreign characters (e.g., Japanese).

OPTIMAL CAPITAL STRUCTURE capital structure with a minimum weighted-average cost of capital and thereby maximizes the value of the firm's stock, but it does not maximize earnings per share (EPS). Greater leverage maximizes EPS but also increases risk. Thus, the highest stock price is not reached by maximizing EPS. The optimal capital structure usually involves some debt, but not 100% debt. Ordinarily, some firms cannot identify this optimal point precisely, but they should attempt to find an optimal range for the capital structure. The required rate of return on equity capital (R) can be estimated in various ways, for example, by adding a percentage to the firm's long-term cost of debt. Another method is the CAPITAL ASSET PRICING MODEL (CAPM).

OPTIMAL (OPTIMUM) SOLUTION either the most profitable or the least costly solution that simultaneously satisfies all the constraints of a LINEAR PROGRAMMING (LP) problem. There are two important general properties of an optimal solution: (1) The optimal solution lies on the boundary of the feasible region; the implication of this property is that one can ignore the (infinitely many) interior points of the feasible solution region when searching for an optimal solution. (2) The optimal solution occurs at one of the corner points of the region; this property reduces even further the magnitude of the search procedure for an optimal solution. *See also* BASIC FEASIBLE SOLUTION; FEASIBLE SOLUTION; GRAPHICAL METHOD.

OPTIMAL PRICE typically profit maximizing price.

OPTIMISTIC TIME in PROGRAM EVALUATION AND REVIEW TECHNIQUE (PERT), the shortest possible time in which an activity is likely to be completed, symbolized as *a*. *See also* EXPECTED TIME FOR AN ACTIVITY.

OPTIMIZATION maximization or minimization of a special goal.

OPTIMIZATION MODEL type of mathematical model that attempts to optimize (maximize or minimize) an *objective function* without violating resource constraints; also known as *mathematical programming*. Optimization models include LINEAR PROGRAMMING (LP), INTEGER PROGRAMMING, and ZERO-ONE PROGRAMMING.

OPTION

1. ability or right to choose a certain alternative.
2. right to buy or sell something at a specified price within a specified period of time. If the right is not exercised within the specified time, the option expires.

A PUT option on a security (such as stock, commodity, or stock index) is an option to sell 100 shares of the underlying security at a specified price for a given period of time, for which the option buyer pays the seller (writer) a price, termed a *premium*. A CALL is the opposite of a put and allows the owner the right to buy 100 shares of the underlying security from the option writer at a specified price for a given period of time.

An *Employee Stock Option* is the option granted to key employees to buy company stock at a below-market price.

OPTIONS BACKDATING as an incentive for executives to improve their firms' performance and share price, companies routinely issue stock options, giving executives the right to buy shares later at the price of the stock on the date of the grant. Recently, many companies have sweetened the pot by "backdating" options to dates when share prices were especially low.

ORDER ENTRY

1. recording of an order placed or received.
2. initial input system of the order processing system. Marketing is responsible for taking orders. Accounting is responsible for billing the customer and collecting payments.

ORDERING COSTS all costs associated with preparing a purchase order. These include the cost of preparing a purchase invoice, telephone, salaries of purchasing clerks, and stationery.

ORDER RECEIPT TIME delay between the placement of an order and its readiness for setup.

ORDINARY ANNUITY *see* ANNUITY.

ORDINARY INCOME

1. earnings attributable to the nominal and recurring business operations of the entity.
2. in taxation, income on the sale of an investment held for 6 months or less.

ORGANIZATIONAL STRUCTURE *see* CENTRALIZATION; DECENTRALIZATION.

ORGANIZATION CHART visual diagram of an organization's structure that depicts formal lines of reporting, communication, and responsibility among managers. Below is a sample organization chart of the controllership.

ORGANIZATION CHART

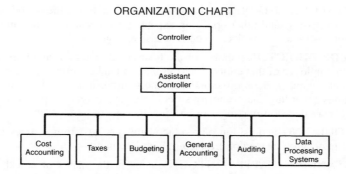

ORGANIZATION COSTS expenditures incurred in launching a business. They include attorney's fees, various registration fees paid to state governments, and other start-up costs. These costs are expensed as incurred.

ORGANIZATION FOR ECONOMIC COOPERATION AND DEVELOPMENT (OECD) (www.oecd.org) a forum set up to discuss, develop, and refine economic and social policies. It is an international organization that encourages economic growth, high employment, and financial stability among its members.

ORIGINAL COST initial amount recorded for an asset excluding any adjustments to the account subsequent to the initial acquisition date (e.g., betterments, additions). Original cost equals the price paid or present value of liability incurred or fair value of stock issued plus normal incidental costs necessary to put the asset into its initial use (i.e., installation, freight).

ORIGINAL ENTRY recording a business transaction in a journal. An explanation is given below the entry describing the particulars. The explanation may refer to supporting data (i.e., voucher) as the basis for the entry.

OTHER ASSETS balance sheet category for minor assets not classified under the typical headings (e.g., current assets, intangible assets, and long-term investments). This type of asset may be immaterial in amount relative to total assets. An example is obsolete machinery to be sold.

OTHER COMPREHENSIVE BASIS OF ACCOUNTING (OCBOA) a basis of accounting, other than GAAP, that an entity uses to report its assets, liabilities, equity, revenues, and expenses. Examples of OCBOA include income tax basis and cash basis of accounting.

OTHER COMPREHENSIVE INCOME any gains and losses that are included in comprehensive income but are not included in net income. Examples include unrealized gains and losses attributable to available-for-sale securities and adjustments pertaining to foreign currency translation.

OUTGO *see* OUTLAY.

OUTLAY *expenditure*; also called *outgo*. For example, in CAPITAL BUDGETING, initial cash outlay for a machine is the amount of the purchase price and the normal incidental costs to put it into operation, such as charges for delivery, taxes, installation, and flooring.

OUTLAY COST expenditure by cash. *See also* OUTLAY.

OUT-OF-POCKET COST actual cash outlays made during the period for payroll, advertising, and other operating expenses. Depreciation is not an out-of-pocket cost, since it involves no current cash expenditure.

OUTSIDE DIRECTOR member of the board of directors of an entity who is not an employee of that entity. An example is a banker sitting on the board of a client company. Such directors are important because they bring unbiased opinions regarding the company's decisions and diverse experience to the company's decision-making process. *See also* INSIDE DIRECTOR.

OUTSOURCING acquisition of products and services from sources outside the organization instead of producing them internally.

OUTSTANDING CAPITAL STOCK shares in the hands of stockholders. Outstanding shares are issued shares minus treasury shares. Dividends are based on outstanding shares. *See also* TREASURY STOCK.

OUTSTANDING CHECK one issued by the company but not yet cleared by the bank. It is listed in the cash payments journal for the month but is not included on the bank statement for that month. In preparing the bank reconciliation, it is deducted from the bank balance. The exception is an uncleared CERTIFIED CHECK, which is not considered outstanding since both parties, the company and the bank, know about it and have subtracted it.

OVERABSORPTION credit balance in the Factory Overhead account that arises when the overhead costs applied to WORK-IN-PROCESS exceed the overhead costs incurred during a period. *Underabsorption* results if there is a debit balance. *See also* OVERAPPLIED OVERHEAD.

OVERAPPLIED OVERHEAD amount by which the factory overhead added to work-in-process inventory at a predetermined overhead rate (and credited to factory overhead applied) exceeds the actual overhead shown in factory overhead control. *See also* PREDETERMINED OVERHEAD RATE; UNDERAPPLIED OVERHEAD.

OVERDRAFT
1. situation where a borrower draws money against a previously established line of credit. The basic cost to the borrower is the interest rate levied on the daily overdraft balance. The borrower typically pays interest only on funds used, since there is no compensating balance requirement, and only for the period in days for which the funds are taken. For this reason, the effective interest cost of an overdraft "loan" is the nominal or stated interest rate paid on the overdraft balance.
2. negative balance in a checking account caused by payment of checks drawn against insufficient funds.

OVERHEAD APPLICATION *see* PREDETERMINED OVERHEAD RATE.

OVERHEAD COST *see* FACTORY OVERHEAD.

OVERHEAD RATE *see* PREDETERMINED OVERHEAD RATE.

OVERHEAD VARIANCE *see* FACTORY OVERHEAD.

OVER-THE-COUNTER (OTC) MARKET market for buying and selling securities not listed on organized stock exchanges. The OTC is typically a telephone market, with most business conducted by phone or, now, electronic device. Dealers, called *market makers*, stand ready to buy or sell specific securities for their own accounts. These dealers will buy at a bid price and sell at an asked price that reflects the competitive market conditions. The OTC market is the largest of all markets in the United States in dollar terms.

OWNERS' EQUITY interest of the owners in the assets of the business represented by capital contributions and retained earnings. *See also* CREDITORS' EQUITY; NET WORTH.

P

PACIOLI, LUCA author of the first statement and commentary on double-entry bookkeeping. This treatise, published in Venice in 1494, was part of a work *Summa de Arithmetica, Geometria Proportioni et Proportionalita*. His treatise had great influence in Europe.

PAID-IN CAPITAL section of stockholders' equity that shows: (1) amount of stock a corporation has issued; (2) the premiums or discounts that have resulted from selling stock (paid-in capital in excess of par or stated value); (3) stock received from donations; and (4) the resale of TREASURY STOCK. Stockholders' equity consists of paid-in or contributed capital and retained earnings.

PAID-IN SURPLUS PAID-IN CAPITAL in excess of par or stated value. It is the result of selling capital stock (or issuing stock) at a price greater than par or stated value.

PAPER PROFIT *unrealized gain* from holding an item while its market value has increased. The amount equals the difference between the current market price and the initial cost. Examples are appreciation in value of inventory or securities. Paper profits are realized profits at the time of sale, at which point income statement recognition is given to them.

PARALLEL PROCESSING simultaneous performance of two or more tasks by a computer. For example, parallel processing takes place when one instruction is being run while another instruction is being read from memory.

PARAMETER
1. constant or coefficient of a variable in an equation or a system of equations. For example, in a COST-VOLUME FORMULA of the form $y = a + bx$, the constant a and the slope b are parameters. The total fixed costs, the unit variable cost, and the unit selling price are examples of parameters.
2. numerical characteristic of a population computed using every element in the population. For example, the mean and the mode are parameters of a population.

PARENT COMPANY
1. owner of a SUBSIDIARY COMPANY. *See also* CONSOLIDATION.
2. HOLDING COMPANY that is not engaged in a trade or business.

PARETO ANALYSIS analysis used to differentiate between *the vital few* and *the trial many*. It is based on the concept that about 80 percent of the problems come from 20 percent of the items. Pareto analysis can be used to identify cost drivers or activity drivers that are responsible for the majority of cost incurred by ranking the cost drivers in order of value. *See also* COST DRIVER ANALYSIS; ACTIVITY DRIVER ANALYSIS.

PARITY
Computers: number that is odd or even. Usually when bits (1's and 0's) are transferred or stored, there is an extra bit added so that the total number of 1's is always odd (alternatively, always even). This is referred to as the parity of the data. Since a transmission error has a one-half chance of altering the parity, frequent errors will warn the receiver of the data of possible errors.

Economics: term designating a constant spread between prices; for example, having a constant relationship between domestic and world sugar prices.

Labor law: salary equality among workers such as policemen and firemen.

PARITY CHECK test conducted by checking a unit of data (e.g., a word or a BYTE) for even or odd parity to ascertain whether a mistake has taken place in reading, writing, or transmitting information. For instance, if data is written, the computed parity bit is compared to the parity bit already appended to the data. If these match, it indicates the data are correct. If they do not agree, a parity error exists.

PARITY PRICE measuring device for price levels in terms of an index number of 100. The price of a commodity or service is linked to another price or a cumulative average of prices determined from a historical base period. Subsequent changes in both price levels are reflected in an index number on a scale of 100. Parity price devices are employed frequently by the federal government for social and economic objectives. Farm price support programs are examples of such uses.

PARTIALLY AMORTIZED LOANS *see* BALLOON.

PARTIAL PRODUCTIVITY output divided by a single input factor. Factors of production may include direct materials, direct labor, overhead, or capital (for example, use of machinery instead of direct labor). A partial productivity measure comparing results over time determines whether the actual relationship between inputs and outputs has improved or deteriorated. A disadvantage of a partial productivity measure is that it relates output to a single factor of production and, therefore, fails to consider tradeoffs among input factors.

PARTICIPATING PREFERRED STOCK rarely issued type of preferred stock. In addition to receiving the regular specified dividend, preferred stockholders will "participate" with common stockholders in any extra dividends paid. There are two types of participating preferred stock, partially participating and fully participating. If partially participating, preferred stockholders participate above the preferential rate on a pro rata basis with common stockholders, but only up to an additional rate specified on the stock certificate. For instance, on a 7% preferred stock issue, the allowed participation may be up to 10%. Thus the participating privilege is limited to an additional 3%. With fully participating preferred stock, preferred stockholders enjoy a preference for the current year at the preference rate (plus any cumulative preference) and they share on a pro rata basis in any dividends above the preference rate. For example, a 6% fully participating preferred stock receives its 6% preference rate plus a pro rata share based on the total par value of the common stock and preferred stock of excess dividends after common stockholders have received their matching 6% of par of the common stock.

PARTICIPATIVE BUDGETING system enabling key employees in a department to provide input into the budgetary process. Thus the accountant receives useful budgeting information from those affected by the budget. Participative budgeting is a good motivational tool because the people participating may work harder to accomplish the budgeting goals, cooperation is facilitated, and more realistic budgeting figures are obtained.

PARTNERSHIP form of business organization created by an agreement between two or more persons who contribute capital and/or their services to the organization. Advantages are: (1) it is easily established with minimal organizational effort and costs; and (2) it is free from special government regulation. Disadvantages are: (1) it carries unlimited liability for the individual partners (firms organized as co-partnerships do not dissolve with the death or withdrawal of a partner); (2) it is dissolved upon the withdrawal or death of any of the partners; and (3) its ability to raise large amounts of capital is limited. GENERAL PARTNERS are those who are responsible for the day-to-day operations of the partnership and who are responsible for the partnership's total liabilities, while LIMITED PARTNERS are those who contribute only money, who are not involved in management decisions, and whose liability is limited to their investment.

PAR VALUE amount arbitrarily assigned by the corporate charter to one share of stock and printed on the stock certificate. The par value represents the legal capital per share. There can be no dividend declared that would cause the stockholders' equity to go below the par value of the outstanding shares. Par value may be a minimum cushion of equity capital existing for creditor protection. The par value is the amount per share entered in the capital stock account. It is usually significantly lower than the market price per share.

PASSIVE ACTIVITY any activity in which the taxpayer does not materially participate. Passive activities include all limited partnership investments as well as rentals of REAL PROPERTY. In general, losses from passive activities may only be used to offset gains from passive activities.

PASSWORD secret character string that is required before one can log onto a computer system, thus preventing unauthorized persons from obtaining access to the computer. The primary reason for using a password is to protect confidential information from modification, destruction, misuse, and other security-related dangers by unauthorized persons.

PAST COSTS *see* SUNK COST.

PATENT exclusive right given by the government to the company to use, manufacture, and sell a product or process for a nonrenewable 20-year period without interference or infringement by other parties. Patent is classified as an intangible asset. Costs such as registration fees and attorney costs incurred in obtaining the patent are capitalized. Research and development costs applicable to developing the product, process, or idea are immediately expensed. Legal costs of a *successful* defense of a patent are capitalized and amortized over the remaining life. If the patent right is lost in court it should be written off and shown as an extraordinary charge. The cost of a patent purchased from an outsider is deferred and amortized. If the *sole* purpose of buying the outsider patent is to eliminate the competition, the amortization period is the *remaining* life of the company's patent that is being protected. The patent is amortized on a straight-line basis over its 20-year life, or its economic life, if less. As a practical matter, often the useful life is less than 20 years due to changes in the marketplace and new technology. If a patent is assigned to others, royalties obtained are accrued as revenue is earned.

PAYABLE amount owed to another party. It is presented as a liability in the balance sheet. A payable is an item that is unpaid, whether or not due. If a payable is due in one year or less (e.g., accounts payable), it is a current liability. If it is to be paid in more than one year, it is shown as a long-term liability.

One type of payable is accrued expenses payable (e.g., salaries payable). The failure to satisfy a payable on the due date may result in a penalty (interest) charge, creditor action against the firm (e.g., lawsuit), or in an extreme case, bankruptcy.

PAYBACK PERIOD length of time required to recover the initial amount of a capital investment. If the cash inflows occur at a uniform rate, it is the ratio of the amount of initial investment over expected annual cash inflows, or:

Payback Period = Initial Investment/Annual Cash Inflows

For example, assume projected annual cash inflows are expected to be $6,000 a year for five years from an investment of $18,000. The payback period on this proposal is three years, which is calculated as follows: Payback period = $18,000/$6,000 = 3 years. If annual cash inflows are not even, the payback period would have to be determined by trial and error. Assume instead that the cash inflows are $4,000 in the first year, $5,000 in the second year, $6,000 in the third year, $6,000 in the fourth year, and $8,000 in the fifth year. The payback period would be 3.5 years. In three years, all but $3,000 has been recovered. It takes one-half year ($3,000/ $6,000) to recover the balance. When two or more projects are considered, the rule for making a selection decision is as follows: Choose the project with the shorter payback period. The rationale behind this is that the shorter the payback period, the greater the liquidity, and the less risky the project. Advantages of the method include (1) it is simple to compute and easy to understand and (2) it handles investment risk effectively. Disadvantages of the method include (1) it does not recognize the TIME VALUE OF MONEY and (2) it ignores profitability of an investment.

PAYBACK RECIPROCAL 1 divided by the PAYBACK PERIOD (i.e., the reciprocal of the payback time). This often gives a quick, accurate estimate of the INTERNAL RATE OF RETURN (IRR) on an investment when the project life is *more* than twice the payback period and the cash inflows are uniform during every period. For example, XYZ Company is contemplating three projects, each of which would require an initial investment of $10,000, and each of which is expected to generate a cash inflow of $2,000 per year. The payback period is five years ($10,000/$2,000), and the payback reciprocal is 1/5, or 20%. The table of the present value of an annuity of $1 shows that the factor of 5.00 applies to the following useful lives and internal rates of return:

Useful Life (Years)	IRR (%)
10	15
15	18
20	19

It can be observed that the payback reciprocal is 20% as compared with the IRR of 18% when the life is 15 years, and 20% as compared with the IRR of 19% when the life is 20 years. This shows that the payback reciprocal gives a reasonable approximation of the IRR if the useful life of the project is at least twice the payback period.

PAYMENT IN KIND settlement of a charge for goods or services or satisfaction of liabilities with similar or identical mediums of exchange and value (e.g., money for money, goods for goods, and services for services). It also connotes a transaction where one medium of exchange is satisfied with another. For example, a carpenter fixes a lawyer's roof. The value of the work is $200, which is paid with one hour's worth of legal services.

PAYOFF *see* DECISION THEORY.

PAYOFF TABLE *see* DECISION THEORY.

PAYOUT RATIO ratio of cash dividends declared to earnings for the period. It equals dividends per share divided by earnings per share. Stockholders investing for income favor a higher ratio. Stockholders looking for capital gains tolerate low ratios when earnings are being reinvested to finance corporate growth. Assume cash dividends of $100,000, net income of $400,000, and outstanding shares of 200,000. The payout ratio equals 25% ($.50/$2.00).

PAYROLL COSTS employer costs incurred for employees' services. Payroll costs consist of the actual cash paid to the employees and the withheld amounts (liabilities) for employee's federal income taxes, FICA, and various voluntary health and benefit plans. Employer's payroll costs also consist of its matching share of employee's FICA taxes and contributions to the state and federal unemployment insurance programs.

PAYROLL REGISTER form with many columns that contains and summarizes payroll information (amount of money paid to employees less deductions). Information includes employee's name, regular hours, sick hours, overtime hours, federal income taxes withheld, medical insurance deductions, union dues, gross pay, and net pay. The payroll register may be used as a supplementary record or as a special journal.

PAYROLL TAX taxes levied on employee's salaries or net income of self-employed individuals. Social Security taxes are imposed upon employees; self-employed individuals and employers are responsible for a matching amount. Unemployment taxes are levied only upon the employer.

PDCA *see* PLAN-DO-CHECK ACT CYCLE.

PEACHTREE SOFTWARE accounting system programs developed by Peachtree Software of Norcross, Georgia (www.peachtree.com).

PEER REVIEW review of the work of one CPA or CPA firm by another CPA or CPA firm. The purpose of peer review is to assure that quality controls are being applied in conformity with AMERICAN INSTITUTE OF CERTIFIED PUBLIC ACCOUNTANTS (AICPA) Quality Control Standards. The review process includes looking at working papers and accounting procedures followed. Mandatory peer review applies to a CPA firm's accounting and auditing services but not to tax and management advisory services. The following is involved in the peer review process when appraising a CPA firm's quality control policies and procedures: (1) reviewing each organizational or functional level within the firm; (2) reviewing selected engagement working paper files and reports; and (3) reviewing documentation indicating the firm's compliance with membership requirements. At the completion of the peer review, the reviewer discusses the findings with the reviewee and issues a report. Sanctions may be imposed on deficient CPA firms including continuing professional education (CPE) training, censures and reprimands, fines, and suspension from membership.

PEER-TO-PEER NETWORKING networking that allows all computers to communicate and share resources as equals. Music-file sharing, instant messaging, and other applications rely on P2P technology.

PENETRATION PRICING method of pricing a standard product. It sets a low initial price for a product in order to gain quick acceptance in a broad portion of the market. It calls for a sacrifice of short-term profits in order to establish a certain amount of market share. One objective is to obtain a committed customer. *See also* SKIMMING PRICING.

PENNY STOCK low priced, highly speculative stock. A penny stock is usually traded on the OVER-THE-COUNTER (OTC) MARKET, but the New York and American stock exchanges also list penny stocks. Penny stock is issued by a company with a short life or with past instability in operations. These stocks typically experience volatility in price relative to the stock of established companies on the major stock exchanges.

PENSION FUND resources set aside on a periodic basis by the employee and/ or employer that will earn a return so that the accumulated principal and interest will be sufficient to meet employee retirement benefits. The pension fund money is retained by a trustee who directly pays the employees at retirement. Annuity payments to employees will be made from pension fund assets. The administration of the fund may be done by the employing company, a trustee, or an insurance company or other similar organization. *See also* DEFINED BENEFIT PENSION PLAN; DEFINED CONTRIBUTION PENSION PLAN; KEOGH PLAN.

PENSION PLAN contractual arrangement in which the employer provides benefits to employees upon retirement. Many plans include disability and death benefits. A pension plan involves recognizing the employer's cost and the funding of pension benefits. Pension expense is tax-deductible to the employer. The employee is taxed when the pension annuity is received from employer contributions or originally not-taxed employee contributions. The two most common types of plans are DEFINED CONTRIBUTION PENSION PLAN and DEFINED BENEFIT PENSION PLAN. Pension plan provisions vary from company to company. For example, the pension plan may be contributory or noncontributory, meaning the employee may or may not also make payments to the pension plan.

PENSION PLAN LIABILITY RESERVE obligation recognized by the employer for the future liability to make annuity payments to employees. The reserve is typically a liability when it results from charging pension expense. However, in a revocable plan, the reserve is considered an appropriation of retained earnings regardless of whether it effects specific assets.

PENSION-PLAN VESTING *see* VESTED.

PERCENTAGE DEPLETION method of computing depletion for income taxes. It is not allowed on financial statements; only COST DEPLETION is permitted. For tax purposes, the Internal Revenue Service Code allows businesses to deduct the larger of cost depletion or percentage depletion in computing taxable income. It is computed as a percentage of revenue. Rates allowed vary widely, from 22% for oil and certain minerals to 5% for sand and gravel. Percentage depletion is often greater than cost depletion.

PERCENTAGE-OF-COMPLETION METHOD method that recognizes profit on a long-term construction contract as it is earned gradually during the construction period. This approach is preferred over the COMPLETED CONTRACT METHOD because it does a better job of matching revenue and expense in the period of benefit. It should be used when *reliable estimates* of the degree of completion are possible. It is more realistic and levels out the earnings. Under the method, the measure of revenue to be recognized each year is equal to percentage completed × contract price. One approach to estimate the percentage completed is based on the following relationship:

$$\frac{\text{Cost Incurred to Date}}{\text{Total Estimated Costs}} \times \text{Contract Price} = \text{Cumulative Revenue}$$

Any revenue that had been recognized in a prior period is subtracted from the cumulative total in arriving at the current period's income.

See also CONSTRUCTION-IN-PROGRESS; PROGRESS BILLINGS.

PERCENTAGE STATEMENT approach by which items in the financial statements are shown as percentages of a total; in the income statement, each item is shown as a percentage of sales; in the balance sheet, each item is shown as a percentage of total assets or equities. *See also* COMMON SIZE FINANCIAL STATEMENTS.

PER DIEM on a daily basis. The term is used to designate payment on a daily basis; e.g., the daily rate that an accountant charges for services performed.

PERFECT MARKET market structure characterized by a very large number of buyers and sellers of a homogeneous (nondifferentiated) product. Entry and exit from the industry is costless, or nearly so. Information is freely available to all market participants, and there is no collusion among firms in the industry. It is difficult to identify a perfect market in reality; however, lumber and agriculture provide close approximations in the United States.

PERFORMANCE AUDIT appraisal of how a particular activity is carrying out the company's policies and procedures. Such review may cover any activity within a department, division, or local area. A performance audit can be a review of a program to assure that it is satisfying its objectives. The program may apply to management and accounting procedures, guidelines, or policies. The performance audit may take into account the anticipated benefits of a program relative to the actual performance. Also relevant may be the costs and time associated with the activity. A report of management's abilities is typically prepared to meet particular goals. Included in the report are measures of the effectiveness of internal controls and efficiency of procedures and processes. The performance audit may be initiated by the organization or by external interested parties. However, the performance audit is *not* performed as a means to attest to the financial records and statements of the company. An example of a performance audit is how certain work routines are being conducted.

PERFORMANCE BUDGET medium- to short-range budget used in governmental accounting. It is typical of the type incorporated by a PROGRAM PLANNING-BUDGETING SYSTEM (PPBS) but without references to long-range goals.

PERFORMANCE EVALUATION cumulative consideration of factors (that may be subjective or objective) to determine a representative indicator or appraisal of an individual or entity's activity, or performance in reference to some subjective (or standard) over some period of time. Factors to consider may include degree of goal attainment, how items are measured, and what standards are to be applied. *See also* COST CENTER; INVESTMENT CENTER; PROFIT CENTER.

PERFORMANCE MEASUREMENT quantification of a company's or segment's efficiency or effectiveness in conducting business operations for the accounting period. Some possible measures of performance are revenue center, cost center, profit center, and investment center. In the revenue center approach, a comparison is made between actual revenue and expected revenue. With the cost center method, actual cost is compared to budgeted cost. The profit center is accountable for costs and revenues in deriving net income. It is even better to use an investment center method of performance evaluation because responsibility is placed not only for revenue and costs but also for the investment employed. Two investment center measurements are RETURN ON INVESTMENT and RESIDUAL INCOME.

PERFORMANCE REPORT statement that displays measurements of actual results of some person or entity's activity over some time period. These results are ideally compared with budgeted or standard measurements obtained under some conditional assumptions over the same period. Variations from such budget or standards are known as VARIANCES and may be favorable or unfavorable depending upon lower or higher measurements relative to the standards. Corrective action is taken for unfavorable performance.

PERIOD COST expense that is *not* inventoriable; it is charged against sales revenue in the period in which the revenue is earned, also called *period expense*. Selling and general and administrative expenses are period costs. *See also* PRODUCT COST.

PERIOD EXPENSE *see* PERIOD COST.

PERIODIC AUDIT
1. audit for an intermediate period (e.g., one month, three months).
2. audit carried out at specified intervals within the year.

PERIODIC INCOME proportional accounting, over time periods, for income already accounted for but not received (deferred revenue), or income already received and accounted for but not earned (prepaid subscriptions), or income receivable in the future and not recorded (interest on fixed-income securities).

PERIODIC INVENTORY SYSTEM one that does not require a day-to-day record of inventory changes. Costs of materials used and costs of goods sold cannot be calculated until ending inventories, determined by physical count, are subtracted from the sum of opening inventories and purchases (or costs of goods manufactured in the case of a manufacturer).

For calculating the cost of ending inventory, there are several methods available: LIFO, FIFO, and WEIGHTED AVERAGE.

PERIODICITY CONCEPT concept under which each accounting period has an economic activity associated with it, and the activity can be accounted for, measured, and reported.

PERIODIC ORDER SYSTEMS places minimal emphasis on record keeping. However, a risk of substantial overstock or understock may arise unless inventories are checked for assurance that the model is still appropriate.

PERIOD OF BENEFIT accounting period in which revenue is matched against related expenses (e.g., cost allocation). If an expenditure benefits a future period, it is charged to an asset account. However, if an expenditure benefits the current accounting period or if there is an inability to ascertain the period of benefit, it should be expensed in the current period.

PERIPHERALS auxiliary equipment used in computer systems. They include printers, CDs, tape and disk drives, and other input-output and storage devices. Peripherals do not include the central processing unit (CPU).

PERMANENT DIFFERENCE difference between book income and taxable income caused by an item that affects one but not the other. The difference will *not* reverse. For example, interest on municipal bonds is included in book income but not in taxable income. Another example: premiums on officers' life insurance that are not deductible for tax purposes but are for financial reporting. Tax expense on the INCOME STATEMENT is based on book income less permanent differences. *See also* INTERPERIOD INCOME TAX ALLOCATION.

PERMANENT FILE items to include in the permanent file include copies of long-term contracts and leases, copies of an entity's ARTICLES OF INCORPORA- TION and bylaws, and copies of benefit plans. A permanent file is sometimes referred to as a continuing file because it includes documentation that is applicable to future audit engagements and not just the current audit engage- ment.

PERMANENTLY RESTRICTED ASSETS in not-for-profit accounting, assets that are restricted by outside agencies or persons, as contrasted with assets over which the entity has control and discretion. An example of a per- manently restricted asset is donated property on which the donor has placed a restriction on its use.

PERPETUAL INVENTORY SYSTEM one keeping continual track of addi- tions or deletions in materials, work-in-process, and cost of goods sold on a day-to-day basis. Physical inventory counts are usually taken at least once a year in order to check on the validity of the book records. Cost of goods sold therefore is kept on a day-to-day basis rather than being determined periodi- cally. *See also* PERIODIC INVENTORY SYSTEM.

PERPETUITY ANNUITY that goes on indefinitely. An example of a perpetuity is preferred stock that yields a constant dollar dividend indefinitely. The PRES- ENT VALUE of a perpetuity is A/i where A is the periodic payment (the amount of an annuity) and i is the DISCOUNT RATE per period. For example, assume that a perpetual bond has an $80-per-year interest payment and that the dis- count rate is 10%. The present value of this perpetuity is $800 ($80/0.10).

PERSONAL EXEMPTION amount an individual can exclude from taxable income. The tax law provides a $3,950 exemption for the 2014 tax year. If an individual has dependents and meets the specified definitional requirements, an additional exemption is allowed for each dependent. Personal exemptions are phased out based on adjusted gross income thresholds, which are adjusted annually based on inflation.

PERSONAL FINANCIAL PLANNING field of financial planning for indi- viduals. It involves (1) analyzing a client's personal finances; and (2) recommending how to improve the client's financial condition. Personal financial planning covers the following specific areas:

Analysis of current financial position	Long-term accumulation plans
	Life insurance
Investment strategies	Tax planning
Estate planning	Disability insurance
Cash flow analysis	
Retirement income	

See also FINANCIAL PLANNER.

PERSONAL FINANCIAL PLANNING SOFTWARE computer program assisting users in examining revenue and expenses, comparing actual to budget, monitoring assets and liabilities, goal analysis, investment portfolio analysis, tax planning, and retirement planning. Personal financial planning templates can be used in conjunction with a spreadsheet program. An example of personal planning software is Quicken.

PERSONAL FINANCIAL SPECIALIST (PFS) designation in personal financial planning awarded by AICPA to those who have met practice requirements and passed an examination.

PERSONAL FINANCIAL STATEMENT document prepared for an individual using the *accrual* basis of accounting rather than the CASH basis. A Statement of Financial Condition shows ASSETS at estimated current values listed by order of liquidity and maturity without classification as current and noncurrent. Business interests that constitute a large part of total assets should be shown separately from other investments. Only the person's interest (amount that person is entitled to) as beneficial owner should be included when assets are jointly owned. *Liabilities* are shown by order of maturity without classification as current or noncurrent. A Statement of Changes in Net Worth is *optional* showing the major sources and uses of net worth. Comparative financial statements are also *optional*. Footnote disclosures should be made of the following: (1) individuals covered by the financial statements; (2) major methods used in determining current value; (3) nature of joint ownership of assets; (4) face amount of life insurance owned; (5) NONFORFEITURE rights that do not qualify for asset inclusion (i.e., pensions based on life expectancy); (6) methods and assumptions used to compute estimated income taxes; (7) maturities and interest rates relating to RECEIVABLES and debt; and (8) noncancellable commitments not reflected under liabilities (i.e., OPERATING LEASE).

PERT *see* PROGRAM EVALUATION AND REVIEW TECHNIQUE (PERT).

PERT/COST project management system developed by the United States government that measures and controls costs by work packages. In this method, cost estimates must be made for each activity. Then the system monitors dollar expenditures for each activity as well as time expenditures. A variety of analyses can be performed, including the "crashing" of certain activities in the project. *Also see* PROGRAM EVALUATION AND REVIEW TECHNIQUE (PERT).

PESSIMISTIC TIME in PROGRAM EVALUATION AND REVIEW TECHNIQUE (PERT), the longest possible time in which an activity is likely to be completed, symbolized *b*. *See also* EXPECTED TIME FOR AN ACTIVITY.

PETTY-CASH FUND minimal amount of money kept on hand by a business
entity to meet small expenditures (e.g., postage, taxi fare). One individual
(custodian) should be responsible for the fund to maintain control. The fund
is available currency and is periodically reimbursed, usually monthly. At any
point, the fixed amount of the fund consists of the total currency left and the
vouchers (receipts) for the expenditures made. The vouchers should be per-
forated so they will not be used again.

PHISHING scams by e-mail.

PHP an acronym for "PHP Hypertext Preprocessor," a widely used, server-side
open-source scripting language.

PHYSICAL INVENTORY determining the quantity of inventory on hand
through an inventory count (i.e., quantity, weight). By multiplying the quantity times the unit cost, the total inventory cost is derived. There are three
types of physical inventories. One is a continuous inventory to supplement
the perpetual inventory records. Another is an inventory count of only specific merchandise on a periodic basis. The third is an annual year-end count.
The physical inventory is compared to the book inventory. Discrepancies are
noted and investigated. The financial statements must show inventory at the
perpetual amount. Assume book inventory is $10,000 and physical inventory
is $9,900. The entry for the inventory difference is to debit inventory shortage
and credit inventory for $100.

PHYSICAL VERIFICATION observation, listing, counting, and measuring
of the assets of a company, such as inventory, fixed assets, cash on hand,
stocks, or bonds. It also includes other items such as insurance policies and
contracts. The auditor typically substantiates the figure as per the financial
records by physically determining the existence of the item and examining it.
For example, the fixed asset account can be physically verified by inspecting the individual machines, buildings, or other fixed assets. The methods
used for verification will depend on the scope of work required and type of
asset being verified. With some types of items, the auditor will require the
assistance of other professionals familiar with the item—for example, with
precious metals, minerals, construction projects, and some manufacturing
activities. Standards of auditing require some form of physical verification
when inventory is present in the financial statements of a company. The timing of the verification depends upon such factors as method of accounting
used for the item, auditor's satisfaction with internal controls associated with
the item, size of the item in dollars and physical bulk (gold vs. widgets), and
other matters relating to the audit. *See also* INVENTORY CONTROL; INVENTORY
OBSERVATION; INVENTORY VALUATION.

PIECEMEAL OPINION external auditor's opinion regarding the fairness of
presentation of specific financial statement items. A piecemeal opinion is
not permitted anymore under GENERALLY ACCEPTED AUDITING STANDARDS
(GAAS). It was previously used in some cases where a disclaimer or adverse
opinion was involved on the financial statements as a whole.

PLAINTEXT ordinary readable text. This term is used in cryptography
to describe text that has not yet been encrypted, or text after it has been
decrypted. Once plaintext is encrypted, it is called CIPHERTEXT.

PLAN-DO-CHECK ACT CYCLE (PDCA) "management by fact" or scientific method approach to continuous improvement (the Deming Wheel). PDCA creates a process-centered environment, because it involves studying the current process, collecting and analyzing data to identify causes of problems, planning for improvement, and deciding how to measure improvement (Plan). The plan is then implemented on a small scale if possible (Do). The next step is to determine what happened (Check). If the experiment was successful, the plan is fully implemented (Act). The cycle is then repeated using what was learned from the preceding cycle.

PLANNED CAPACITY see CAPACITY.

PLANNING selection of short- and long-term objectives and the drawing up of tactical and strategic plans to achieve those objectives. In planning, managers outline the steps to be taken in moving the organization toward its objectives. After deciding on a set of strategies to be followed, the organization needs more specific plans, such as locations, methods of financing, hours of operations, and so on. As these plans are made, they will he communicated throughout the organization. When implemented, the plans will serve to coordinate, or meld together, the efforts of all parts of the organization toward the company's objectives.

PLANT AND EQUIPMENT fixed assets used in business operations, including land and buildings; sometimes termed PROPERTY, PLANT, AND EQUIPMENT.

PLANT ASSET noncurrent physical asset applicable to manufacturing activities. See also FIXED ASSET.

PLANT LEDGER SUBSIDIARY LEDGER that consists of supporting accounts to a company's general ledger fixed asset account. The ledger provides the detail of individual assets necessary for proper control, tracking, record keeping, and maintenance. Information concerning a particular asset such as those for acquisitions, additions, replacements, extraordinary repairs, and retirements, is recorded in this account.

PLANTWIDE OVERHEAD RATE single predetermined overhead rate used in all departments of a company, rather than having a separate rate for each department. If the company's departments are homogeneous, the use of a single plantwide rate may be adequate as a means of allocating overhead costs to production jobs. See also MULTIPLE OVERHEAD RATES; PREDETERMINED OVERHEAD RATE.

PLEDGED ASSET one used as collateral to secure a debt obligation or contract. A footnote reference is given of the circumstances surrounding the pledged asset; otherwise, the asset appears as it would ordinarily be classified on the balance sheet and is not presented as an offset under liabilities.

POINT-OF-SALE (POS)
1. system that uses a computer terminal located at the point of sales transaction so that the data can be captured immediately by the computer system.
2. general point for revenue recognition. GENERALLY ACCEPTED ACCOUNTING PRINCIPLES (GAAP) require the recognition of revenue in the accounting period in which the sale is deemed to have occurred. For services, the sale is deemed to occur when the service is performed. In the case of merchandise, the sale takes place when the title to the goods transfers from seller to

buyer. In many cases, this coincides with the delivery of the merchandise. As a result, accountants usually record revenue when goods are delivered.

POINTS a fee paid by a borrower to a lender. Typically, a point is equal to 1% of the amount borrowed. Points paid in connection with the purchase or improvement of a principle residence are fully deductible in the year paid. All other points must be amortized over the life of the loan.

POOL RATE the overhead costs for a HOMOGENEOUS COST POOL divided by the appropriate COST DRIVER associated with the pool.

PONZI SCHEMES a method of escalating values built on fabricated assets. The most famous of these schemes occurred during the 1920s, perpetrated by Charles Ponzi, in which dividends were paid to early investors out of the payments received from later investors. When no new investors joined the investment scheme, it collapsed. In 2009, two infamous Ponzi schemes surfaced: (1) According to civil charges filed by the SEC, R. Allen Stanford, the Stanford Financial Group and Stanford Capital Management defrauded investors worldwide, resulting in losses of more than $9 billion, using a Ponzi scheme. (2) Bernard Madoff, who served as a non-executive chairman of the NASDAQ stock exchange, pled guilty to an 11-count criminal complaint, admitting to defrauding thousands of investors of billions of dollars. He was convicted of operating a Ponzi scheme that has been called the largest investor fraud ever committed by a single person, resulting in client losses estimated at almost $65 billion. On June 29, 2009, he was sentenced to 150 years in prison, the maximum allowed.

POPULATION set of data consisting of all conceivable observations of a certain phenomenon. A SAMPLE contains only part of these observations. Examples of populations are: (1) number of defective and nondefective bolts produced in a factory on a given day; (2) heights and weights of students in a university; and (3) all possible outcomes (heads, tails) in successive tosses of a coin. Population can be finite or infinite. The first two examples are finite and the third example is infinite. Assume the auditor wants to verify promotion and entertainment expense of the company. The *population* is the total expense for the accounting period under examination. A sample can be derived on a random basis to check selected promotion and entertainment documentation so as to derive an inference about the population balance.

PORTFOLIO combining securities to reduce risk by diversification. An example of a portfolio is a mutual fund. This is a popular investment vehicle consisting of a variety of securities or assets that are professionally managed. A major advantage of investing in mutual funds is diversification. Investors can own a variety of securities with a minimal capital investment. Since mutual funds are professionally managed, they tend to involve less risk. To reduce risk, securities in a portfolio should have negative or no correlation to each other.

PORTFOLIO THEORY idea advanced by H. Markowitz about a well-diversified portfolio. The central theme of the theory, also referred to as modern portfolio theory, is that rational investors behave in a way that reflects their aversion to taking increased risk without being compensated by an adequate increase in expected return. Also, for any given expected return, most investors will prefer a lower risk, and for any given level of risk, they will prefer a higher return to a lower return. Markowitz showed how *quadratic programming* could be used to calculate a set of "efficient" portfolios. An investor then will choose among a set of efficient portfolios the best that is consistent with the risk profile of the investor.

POS *see* POINT-OF-SALE (POS).

POSITION the financial condition of an entity.

POSITIVE ASSURANCE an opinion or affirmative statement made by an auditor that usually results from the performance of an audit of financial statements or other high-level examination engagement.

POSITIVE CONFIRMATION written or oral request by the auditor of a party having financial dealings with the client about the accuracy of an item. A response is required whether the particular item is correct or incorrect. A positive confirmation can be sent to customers to verify account balances. *See also* NEGATIVE CONFIRMATION.

POST transfer from the journal to the ledger a debit or credit to the given account involved.

POSTAUDIT
1. examination of a transaction after its occurrence. A postaudit determines if a company's policies and procedures have been properly followed. The test may be to verify if paid invoices have necessary documentation and approvals. This test verifies internal control procedures and work performed by clerks.
2. in an audit performed by a public accountant, period that exists between the completion of the auditor's field work and the issuance of the report on the financial statements. During this period, the auditor is in constant contact with the client while the audit report is prepared and the final review of the drafted financial statements takes place. The auditor has a responsibility to disclose subsequent events so that the financial statements are not misleading. *See also* PREAUDIT.

POST BALANCE-SHEET REVIEW audit procedures applicable to the interval of time between the date of the financial statements and the completion date of the audit fieldwork. Attention is given to SUBSEQUENT EVENTS materially affecting the fair presentation of the financial statements.

POST-CLOSING TRIAL BALANCE one prepared from the general ledger for the end of the accounting period after preparing the *closing entries*. Since revenue and expense accounts have been closed out, the only accounts with balances are balance sheet accounts.

POST DATE placing on a document or a check a date that follows the date of initiation or execution. An example is buying something on January 10th and dating the check January 25th, so the check cannot be cashed until later. *See also* ANTEDATE.

POST-OPTIMALITY ANALYSIS *see* SENSITIVITY ANALYSIS.

POSTPONABLE COST cost being shifted to the future with little effect on the efficiency of current operations. Routine maintenance is an example.

PRACTICAL ACCOUNTANT, THE monthly journal published by Accountants Media Group (www.webcpa.com). The subject matter relates to all aspects of accounting, information systems, and estate planning. The readership is primarily accountants in general practice.

PRACTICAL CAPACITY highest activity level at which the factory can operate with an acceptable degree of efficiency, taking into consideration unavoidable losses of productive time (i.e., vacations, holidays, repairs to equipment); also called *maximum practical capacity. See also* CAPACITY.

PREAUDIT substantiation that proper authorization exists for an act, such as making up a purchase order or entering into a contract. There is also examination of documentation prior to payment of an item, such as an invoice or payroll request. The controller is responsible for conducting preaudits. The internal auditor tests to assure that appropriate preaudit procedures are being carried out.

PREACQUISITION CONTINGENCY a contingent asset, liability, or impairment of an asset of the acquired entity that existed before the business combination. It is normally included in the allocation of the purchase price.

PRECIOUS METALS valuable commodities (e.g., gold and silver) representing a private store of value. Precious metals are liquid, have international markets, and provide a hedge against inflation, currency risk, and unfavorable political and economic developments. However, they are a volatile investment. Their prices typically increase in difficult periods and decline in good times. Precious metals usually go in the opposite direction of common stock; as common stock returns move down, returns on gold move up. Tax must be paid on the gain when sold. Precious metal ownership has several disadvantages including high storage cost, high transaction cost, and no annual dividend revenue.

PREDECESSOR AUDITOR independent CPA who either leaves the client willingly or is terminated and replaced by a SUCCESSOR AUDITOR.

PREDETERMINED OVERHEAD RATE rate, based on budgeted factory overhead cost and budgeted activity, that is established before a period begins.

$$\frac{\text{Predetermined}}{\text{Overhead Rate}} = \frac{\text{Budgeted Yearly Total Factory Overhead Costs}}{\text{Budgeted Yearly Activity (direct labor-hours, etc.)}}$$

Budgeted activity units used in the denominator of the formula, more often called the *denominator level*, are measured in direct labor-hours, machine-hours, direct labor costs, or production units.

PREDICTION ERRORS *see* COST OF PREDICTION ERRORS.

PREEMPTIVE RIGHT right of a current stockholder to maintain the percentage ownership interest in the company by buying new shares on a pro rata basis before they are issued to the public. It prevents existing stockholders from dilution in value or control. The typical procedure is that each existing stockholder receives a *subscription warrant* indicating how many shares can be bought. Usually, the new shares are issued to the current stockholder at a lower price than the going market price. In addition, brokerage commissions do not have to be paid. For example, if an individual owns 2% of the shares of a company that is coming out with a new issue of 100,000 shares, the individual is entitled to buy 2,000 shares at a favorable price to maintain the proportionate interest.

PREFERRED CREDITOR one having priority over another creditor when the company becomes bankrupt. For example, a secured creditor (who has secured assets in support of his claim) has precedence over a general creditor (who has loaned money to the business without collateral).

PREFERRED STOCK class of capital stock that has preference over common stock in the event of corporate liquidation and in the distribution of earnings. It usually pays dividends at a fixed rate, but there is also adjustable rate preferred and "Dutch auction" preferred. For example, 6% preferred stock means that the dividend equals 6% of the total par value of the outstanding shares. Except in unusual instances, no voting rights exist. Types include CUMULATIVE PREFERRED STOCK and PARTICIPATING PREFERRED STOCK.

PRELIMINARY AUDIT
1. fieldwork done prior to the end of the accounting period under examination in order to quicken the issuance of the audit report. The preliminary audit includes evaluating internal controls, financial records, and transactions. An analysis of account balances is begun. The CPA determines what audit scope and steps will be required so that an opinion on the financial statements may be rendered. The preliminary audit is different from a periodic audit because it typically involves no audit report and is an element of a regular annual audit.
2. first engagement with a client, examining the overall business and its accounting system and operations before deciding on the extent of audit procedures that will be necessary.

PREMIUM
1. excess of the amount received over the par or face value of a security. For example, if a $1,000 bond is issued at 102, the premium on the bond is $20 ($1,000 × 2%).
2. price paid for a contract.
3. periodic payment made on an insurance policy.
4. promotion item given away in a marketing effort.
5. excess paid over a typical expense item, such as a bonus above employee's regular salary.
6. extra payment made for incentive purposes.
7. price a call or put buyer pays to the writer (seller) for an option contract.
8. amount in excess of market value paid in a TENDER OFFER.

PREMIUM ON CAPITAL STOCK excess received over the par value of stock issued. The premium account is shown under the paid-in capital section of stockholders' equity because it resulted from the issuance of stock. It is *not* an income statement account since the company earns profit by selling goods and services to outsiders, *not* by issuing shares of stock to owners.

PREPAID EXPENSE expenditures paid for in one accounting period but not completely used or consumed until the next accounting period. Examples of expenses paid in advance are insurance, advertising, and rent. Prepaid expenses are often of a recurring nature. They are shown under current assets.

PREREQUISITE event or action that has to be satisfied before the next event or action can occur. For example, an accounting student must take intermediate accounting before advanced accounting.

PRESENT FAIRLY term used in the *auditor's report* where there exists adequate disclosure, reasonable detail, and absence of bias. Adequate disclosure requires all management information necessary to interpret financial statements. Reasonable detail requires that certain particulars of broad statement classifications be presented, such as intangible assets that are broken down into types. Absence of bias means that the auditor is independent and impartial and does not favor one party over another (i.e., STOCKHOLDER over *investor*).

PRESENT VALUE current worth of future sums of money. The process of calculating present value, or *discounting*, is actually the opposite of finding the compounded future value. Recall from FUTURE VALUE that $F_n = P(1 + i)^n$. Therefore, $P = F_n/ [(1 + i)^n] = F_n[1/(1 + i)^n] = \text{PVIF}(i,n)$ where $\text{PVIF}(i,n)$ is the present value of $1 and is given in Table 3 in back of book.

For example, assume Mr. B has been given an opportunity to receive $20,000 six years from now. If he can earn 10% on his investment, what is the most he should pay for this opportunity? To answer this question we need to find the present worth of $20,000 to be received six years from now. The PVIF(10%, 6 years) is in table 3—0.564. Therefore,

$$P = \$20,000(0.564) = \$11,280$$

This means that Mr. B could be indifferent to the choice between receiving $11,280 now or $20,000 six years from now since the amounts are time equivalent at 10%.

PREVENTIVE COSTS a category of QUALITY COSTS incurred to prevent defects of products and services, such as quality training programs and quality circles.

PRICE DISCOUNT *see* TRADE DISCOUNT.

PRICE-EARNINGS RATIO (P/E RATIO) statistic that equals market price per share divided by earnings per share. It is a good ratio to use in evaluating the investment possibility of a company. A steady decrease in the P/E ratio reflects decreasing investor confidence in the growth potential of the entity. Some companies have high P/E multiples reflecting high earnings growth expectations. Young, fast-growing companies often have high P/E stocks with multiples over 20. A company's P/E ratio depends on many factors such as risk, earnings trend, quality of management, industry conditions, and economic factors.

PRICE LEVEL ACCOUNTING method of measuring the impact of changes in general purchasing power of the dollar. Inflation is measured and reported in the financial statements. Balance sheet and income statement accounts are restated to average current year dollars using the Consumer Price Index. *Purchasing power gains and losses* on MONETARY ITEMS are reflected in the price-level income statement. *See also* CONSTANT DOLLAR ACCOUNTING; CURRENT VALUE ACCOUNTING.

PRICE-TO-BOOK RATIO market price per share divided by book value (tangible assets less all liabilities) per share. It is a measure of stock valuation relative to net assets.

PRICE-TO-SALES RATIO the current price divided by the sales per share for the trailing twelve months. If there is a preliminary earnings announcement for a quarter that has recently ended, the revenue (sales) values from this announcement will be used in calculating the trailing twelve month revenue per share.

PRICE VARIANCE difference between actual unit price and standard unit price, multiplied by actual quantity of input used. It reflects a change between the expected price and actual price of input.

Price Variance = (Actual Price − Standard Price) × Actual Quantity

where a positive result indicates an increase in costs (i.e., an unfavorable variance), while a negative result means a reduction in costs (i.e., a favorable variance). *See also* LABOR RATE (PRICE) VARIANCE; MATERIALS PRICE VARIANCE; SALES PRICE VARIANCE.

PRICING DECISIONS decisions faced by top management and marketing managers. How much to charge for a product or service depends on a multitude of factors such as competition, cost, advertising, and sales promotion. Economic theory suggests that the best price for a product or service is the one that maximizes the difference between total revenue and total costs. However, in reality, the price charged is usually some form of cost-plus, which is later adjusted for market conditions and competition.

PRIME COST in manufacturing, DIRECT MATERIAL plus DIRECT LABOR. It excludes overhead. *See also* CONVERSION COST.

PRIME RATE interest rate charged by banks to their most financially sound customers. The prime rate is a reference point for other interest rates—some are lower than the published prime, most are higher. For example, the interest rate on commercial paper is less than the prime interest rate. Most companies have to borrow from financial institutions at a rate in excess of the prime rate. The rate is influenced by the cost of funds to the bank and the rates borrowers will accept.

PRINCIPAL
1. face amount of a financial instrument on which interest accrues. For example, a $25,000, 8%, one-year note has a principal portion of $25,000 and an interest portion of $2,000.
2. carrying value of an obligation (i.e., bonds payable).
3. amount invested, excluding return on investment.
4. high-level individual (i.e., partner) in a CPA firm having major authority and responsibilities.
5. owner, especially one with executive authority, of a business firm.

PRIOR PERIOD ADJUSTMENT revenue or expenses applicable to a previous period. The beginning balance of retained earnings is adjusted for the prior period adjustment (net of tax). An illustrative retained earnings section of the balance sheet follows:

Retained Earnings 1/1/2014 − Unadjusted
Add or Deduct: Prior Period Adjustment
Retained Earnings 1/1/2014 − Adjusted
Add: Net Income
Less: Dividends
Retained Earnings 12/31/2014

The *only* two examples of prior period adjustments are: (1) the correction of an error made in a prior year; and (2) the recognition of a tax LOSS CARRYFORWARD benefit arising from a purchased subsidiary.

PRIOR SERVICE PENSION COST retroactive benefits cost for services rendered in *periods prior* to the initiation of a pension plan or an amendment to a plan. The cost of these retroactive benefits is the resulting increase in the projected benefit obligation. It involves the allocation of equal amounts to future years of service for active employees. *See also* NORMAL PENSION COST.

PRIVATE ACCOUNTANT individual employed only by one organization as distinguished from an individual working for an independent accounting firm that serves many clients. The private accountant is an internal accountant reporting to the managers of the entity. A private accountant may be involved in preparing internal management reports for decision making such as capital budgeting, budgeting, and segmental performance analysis.

PRIVATE ACTIVITY BOND a bond issued by a state or local government, the proceeds of which are used to finance the facilities of an entity other than the government issuing the bond. Private activity bonds may be used, for example, to finance airports, docks and wharves, and qualified educational facilities. Interest received by the holder of qualified private activity bonds is tax-exempt for regular tax purposes, but is considered to be an adjustment when calculating the ALTERNATIVE MINIMUM TAX.

PRIVATE COMPANIES PRACTICE SECTION (PCPS) division of the AMERICAN INSTITUTE OF CERTIFIED PUBLIC ACCOUNTANTS (AICPA) for CPA firms serving nonpublic companies. Member CPA firms participate in PEER REVIEW. The other section is the SEC practice section.

PRIVATE COMPANY COUNCIL (PCC) created by the Financial Accounting Foundation to work with the FINANCIAL ACCOUNTING STANDARDS BOARD (FASB) in order to establish alternatives to GENERALLY ACCEPTED ACCOUNTING PRINCIPLES (GAAP) for private entities.

PRIVATE CORPORATION *see* PRIVATELY HELD COMPANY.

PRIVATE EQUITY money raised from big investors such as pension funds and college endowments. Private equity companies buy companies with the goal of eventually reselling the takeover targets for a profit.

PRIVATE OFFERING *see* PRIVATE PLACEMENT.

PRIVATELY HELD COMPANY firm owned by a few people. It is distinguished from a PUBLICLY HELD COMPANY, which is also a private company, but whose shares are traded in the public market; also called a *closed corporation* or *private corporation*. A publicly held company can either be closely held (meaning most of the public shares are owned or controlled by a few people) or widely held, as with a company whose shares are listed on a national stock exchange. A privately held company is typically referred to as a NONISSUER.

PRIVATE PLACEMENT sale of securities by the issuing company directly to an investor (generally a large institutional investor) rather than an offering through the public exchange markets. A private placement does not have to be registered with the SEC, as a PUBLIC OFFERING does, if the securities are not purchased for resale.

PRIVILEGED COMMUNICATION confidential communication, such as that between a client and his attorney. The receiver of the information (attorney) is not legally required to disclose it. Common-law privileged communication between the client and the CPA exists only in a few states where it is permitted by statute.

PRIZES AND AWARDS items received for winning a contest or in recognition of an activity. Cash prizes or awards generally must be included in taxable income. The prize or award can be excluded from taxable income *only* when the taxpayer assigns it to a charitable organization.

PROBABILITY degree of likelihood that something will happen. Probabilities are expressed as fractions ($\frac{1}{2}$, $\frac{1}{4}$, $\frac{3}{4}$), as decimals (.5, .25, .75), or as percentages (50%, 25%, 75%) between 0 and 1. For example, a probability of 0 means that something can never happen; a probability of 1 means that something will *always* happen. The probability of an event is calculated as follows:

$$p(a) = \frac{\text{Number of Outcomes Favorable to the Occurrence of the Event}}{\text{Total Number of Possible Outcomes}}$$

The probability of getting heads in one toss is: $p(\text{heads}) = 1/(1 + 1) = \frac{1}{2}$.

PROBABILITY DISTRIBUTION table or graph showing the *relative frequency* of each of various outcomes. Widely known probability distributions include the binomial distribution and the NORMAL DISTRIBUTION. A probability distribution of a possible number of tails from two tosses of a fair coin may look like this:

Number of Tails	Probability of This Outcome
0	.25
1	.50
2	.25

PROBABILITY SAMPLE *see* RANDOM SAMPLE.

PROCEDURAL AUDIT evaluation of internal controls, accounting policies, and other procedures of a business entity by an independent CPA. Recommendations for improvement in procedures or activities in the system are made. An overall appraisal may be made of the entire business, or the audit may be directed to a particular business segment. At the conclusion of the audit, management receives a report that will list the findings. These audits are normally performed by the internal audit staff in many companies and take place during the entire year. Where a company does not have an internal audit staff, it may hire the auditor that certifies its financial statements to perform a procedural review as part of the annual audit. When such an arrangement is made, management expects to receive a separate report on this review, offering its findings with recommendations.

PROCEEDS funds received from the sale of assets or issuance of securities such as capital stock or bonds.

PROCESS sequence or arterial network of logically related and time-based work activities to provide a specific output for an internal or external customer. For example, the assembly of a television set or the paying of a bill or claim entails several linked activities. *See also* BUSINESS PROCESS.

PROCESS-BASED MANAGEMENT managing business processes to achieve a desired result.

PROCESS BENCHMARKING *see* BENCHMARKING.

PROCESS COST cost assigned to a business process based on the cost of the activities that compose the process.

PROCESS COSTING method that aggregates manufacturing costs by departments or by production processes. Total manufacturing costs are accumulated by major categories—direct materials, direct labor, and factory overhead applied. Unit cost is determined by dividing the total costs charged to a cost center by the output of that cost center. Process costing is appropriate for companies that produce a continuous mass of like units through a series of operations or processes—generally used in such industries as petroleum, chemicals, oil refinery, textiles, and food processing. A COST OF PRODUCTION REPORT is a cost sheet used for process costing that summarizes the total cost charged to a department and the allocation between the ending work-in-process inventory and the units completed and transferred to the next department or finished goods inventory. The output of a processing department during a given period is measured in terms of *equivalent units* of production which is the expression of the physical units of output in terms of doses or amount of work applied thereto. In computing the unit cost for a processing center, when a beginning inventory of work-in-process exists, two specific assumptions about the flow of cost are used—WEIGHTED AVERAGE and FIFO. Under weighted average, the costs in the beginning inventory are averaged with the current period's costs to determine one average unit cost for all units passing through the cost center in a given month. Under FIFO, costs in the beginning inventory are not mingled with the current period's costs but transferred out as a separate batch of goods at a different unit cost than units started and completed during the period.

PROCESS COST REPORT set of three schedules that help managers track and analyze costs in a process costing system; it consists of the schedule of equivalent production, the unit cost analysis schedule, and the cost summary schedule.

PROCESSING COSTS *see* CONVERSION COST.

PROCESSING TIME actual amount of time spent working on a product.

PROCESSOR
1. device that can perform operations on data. Examples are the central processing unit (CPU) and a front-end processor. For instance, the CPU directs data and instructions to and from other devices in the computer system, like the computer's memory and input devices. It also interprets programs.
2. language processor, such as an assembler, compiler, or interpreter.

PROCESS REENGINEERING analysis of business processes resulting in radical change rather than incremental improvement. Redesign of processes is intended to result in the elimination of unnecessary steps, reduction of circumstances in which mistakes can occur, cost minimization, quicker response time, and better quality.

PROCESS VALUE ANALYSIS (PVA) analytical method of identifying all activities and relating them to the events that cause or drive the need for the activities and the resources consumed.

PRODUCER'S RISK probability of rejecting a good quality lot.

PRODUCT COST cost of inventory on hand, also called *inventoriable cost*. They are assets until the products are sold. Once they are sold, they become expenses, i.e., *cost of goods sold*. All manufacturing costs are product costs. Examples are DIRECT MATERIAL, DIRECT LABOR, and FACTORY OVERHEAD.

PRODUCT COSTING SYSTEM set of procedures that accounts for an organization's product costs and provides timely and accurate unit cost information for pricing, planning and control, inventory valuation, and financial statement preparation.

PRODUCT DEVELOPMENT TIME performance measure of competitive strategy. A company that is first in the market with a new product has obvious advantages. Reducing development time is also important because product life cycles are becoming shorter, and organizations need to respond quickly and flexibly to new technology, changes in consumer tastes, and other competitive challenges. One financial measure of product development is BREAK-EVEN TIME. CUSTOMER RESPONSE TIME is another crucial competitive factor.

PRODUCT FAMILY group of products or services that have a defined relationship because of physical and production similarities. The term PRODUCT LINE is used interchangeably.

PRODUCT FINANCING ARRANGEMENT agreement to finance the acquisition of a product through debt. Another entity may buy a product on behalf of the purchaser. At the time of acquisition, the purchaser debits inventory and credits a liability for the amount owed to the other entity. When payment of the obligation is made, the liability is debited for the principal, interest expense is debited for the interest, and cash is paid for the total amount.

PRODUCT LIFE CYCLE *see* LIFE CYCLE.

PRODUCTION BUDGET schedule for expected units to be produced. It sets forth the units expected to be manufactured to satisfy budgeted sales and inventory requirements. Expected production volume is determined by adding desired ending inventory to planned sales and then subtracting beginning inventory.

PRODUCTION COST *see* MANUFACTURING COST.

PRODUCTION CYCLE TIME time it takes for production personnel to make the product available for shipment to the customer.

PRODUCTION MIX VARIANCE cost variance that arises if the actual production mix deviates from the standard or budgeted mix. In a multi-product, multi-input situation, the mix variances explain the portion of the *quantity (usage, or efficiency) variance* caused by using inputs (direct materials and direct labor) in ratios different from standard proportions, thus helping to determine how efficiently mixing operations are performed. The MATERIAL MIX VARIANCE indicates the impact on material costs of the deviation from the budgeted mix. The *labor mix variance* measures the impact of changes in the labor mix on labor costs.

Material Mix Variance	=	(Actual Units Used at Standard Mix	−	Actual Units Used at Actual Mix)	×	Standard Unit Price
Labor Mix Variance	=	(Actual Hours Used at Standard Mix	−	Actual Hours Used at Actual Mix)	×	Standard Hourly Rate

Probable causes of unfavorable production mix variances are as follows: (1) substitution forced by capacity restraints; (2) poor production scheduling; (3) lack of certain types of labor; and (4) certain materials in short supply.

PRODUCTION RUN MODEL *see* ECONOMIC PRODUCTION RUN SIZE MODEL.

PRODUCTION VOLUME VARIANCE *see* VOLUME VARIANCE.

PRODUCTION YIELD VARIANCE difference between the actual yield and the standard yield. YIELD is a measure of productivity. In other words, it is a measure of output from a given amount of input. For example, in the production of potato chips, a certain yield such as 40% or 40 pounds of chips for 100 pounds of potatoes might be expected. If the actual yield is less than the expected or standard yield for a given level of input, the yield variance is unfavorable. A yield variance is computed for labor as well as materials. A *labor yield variance* is considered the result of the quantity and/or the quality of labor used. The yield variance explains the remaining portion of the QUANTITY VARIANCE and is caused by a yield of finished product that does not correspond with the quantity that actual inputs should have produced. When there is no mix variance, the yield variance equals the quantity variance.

Material Yield Variance	=	(Actual Units Used at Standard Mix	−	Actual Output Units Used at Standard Mix)	×	Standard Unit Price
Labor Yield Variance	=	(Actual Hours Used at Standard Mix	−	Actual Output Hours Used at Standard Mix)	×	Standard Hourly Rate

Probable causes of unfavorable production yield variances are: (1) use of low quality materials and/or labor; (2) existence of faulty equipment; (3) use of improper production methods; and (4) improper or costly mix of materials and/or labor.

PRODUCTIVITY ratio of outputs to inputs.

PRODUCTIVITY MEASURES related to the efficiency, mix, and yield variances. They can be developed for both manufacturing and service entities, although the latter may sometimes find that output is difficult to measure. Productivity is the relationship between outputs and inputs (including the mix of inputs). The higher this ratio, the greater the productivity. Improvements in productivity depend on technical efficiency and input trade-off efficiency. A process becomes more technically efficient when, for any set of inputs that will produce a given output, nonvalue-added activities are eliminated and value-added activities use the minimum resources needed to produce the given output.

PRODUCT LEVEL ACTIVITIES activities performed to support the diversity of products in a manufacturing plant.

PRODUCT LIFE CYCLE period that starts with the initial product specification and ends with the withdrawal of the product from the marketplace. A product life cycle is characterized by certain defined stages, including research, development, introduction, maturity, decline, and abandonment. *See* LIFE CYCLE.

PRODUCT LINE *see* PRODUCT FAMILY.

PRODUCT MIX *see* SALES MIX.

PRODUCT MIX DECISIONS decisions that concern the relative amounts of each type of product or service that, given demand and resource constraints, will maximize total profits. For example, if the firm can sell as much as it can produce and has a single resource constraint, the decision rule is to maximize the contribution margin per unit of the constrained resource. However, given multiple constraints, the decision is more difficult and more sophisticated techniques must be used, such as linear programming for example.

PRODUCT UNIT COST manufacturing cost of a single unit of product; total cost of direct materials, direct labor, and manufacturing overhead for the units produced divided by the total units produced.

PROFESSIONAL ETHICS moral principles and standards of conduct guiding CPAs in performing their functions. Codes of professional ethics are established by organizations of CPAs, such as the American Institute of CPAs and state societies. A violation of professional ethics will make the accountant subject to disciplinary action. The accountant's professional ethics affect the reputation of the profession and the confidence of the public. Some of the professional ethic requirements follow. The CPA should be *independent* of clients served so that objectivity and integrity are maintained. For example, independence is violated if the CPA has a financial interest in the client, or is connected with the enterprise as an underwriter or director. The CPA must be professionally *competent*, exercise *due professional care*, properly *plan and supervise* the engagement, and *obtain adequate data* to form a conclusion about an engagement. CPAs cannot have their names associated with forecasts in such a way as to have users believe they vouch for the achievability. The CPA must follow GAAS in the pursuance of the audit function and may not express an unqualified opinion on financial statements if they depart from GAAP. The CPA must keep confidential information obtained from the client in the course of a professional engagement. Further, professional services cannot be offered on a contingent fee based on findings or results of services. A CPA in public practice shall not engage in an incompatible occupation creating a conflict of interest.

PROFITABILITY ability of a business entity to generate net income. Potential investors closely analyze a firm's current and prospective profitability since they affect dividends and market price of stock. *See also* PRICE-EARNINGS RATIO (P/E RATIO).

PROFITABILITY ACCOUNTING *see* RESPONSIBILITY ACCOUNTING.

PROFITABILITY INDEX ratio of the total present value (PV) of future cash inflows to the initial investment (I). That is, PV/I. This index is primarily used as a means of ranking projects in descending order of attractiveness. In a single project case, if the index is greater than 1, the project should be accepted. For example, consider the following data:

Initial investment	$12,950
Estimated life	10 years
Annual cash inflows	$ 3,000
Cost of capital (minimum	
required of return)	12%

The profitability index is 1.31 (PV/I = $16,950/$12,950). Note PV = $3,000 $\times$ PV of an annuity of $1 for 10 years and 12% = $3,000 $\times$ 5.65 = $16,950. Since this project generates $1.31 for each dollar invested (or its index is greater than 1), it should be accepted.

PROFITABILITY OBJECT level cost accumulation at which revenues are matched to cost consumption to analyze profitability.

PROFIT AND LOSS STATEMENT *see* INCOME STATEMENT.

PROFIT CENTER responsibility unit that measures the performance of a division, product line, geographic area, or other measurable unit. Divisional profit figures are *best* obtained by subtracting from revenue only the costs the division manager can control (direct division costs) and eliminating allocated costs common to all divisions (e.g., an allocated share of company image advertising that benefits all divisions but is not controlled by division managers). Profit is a very often used method to evaluate a division's financial success as well as the performance of its manager. In determining divisional profit, a TRANSFER PRICE may have to be derived. The divisional profit center allows for decentralization. as each division is treated as a separate business entity with responsibility for making its own profit. *See also* RESPONSIBILITY ACCOUNTING; RESPONSIBILITY CENTER.

PROFIT MARGIN ratio of income to sales. (1) net profit margin equals net income divided by net sales. It indicates the entity's ability to generate earnings at a particular sales level. By examining a company's profit margin relative to previous years and to industry norms, one can evaluate the company's operating efficiency and pricing strategy as well as its competitive status with other companies in the industry. (2) gross profit margin equals gross profit divided by net sales. A high profit margin is desirable since it indicates the company is earning a good return over the cost of its merchandise sold.

PROFIT MAXIMIZATION hypothesis that the goal of a firm is to maximize its profit.

PROFIT PLANNING process of developing a profit plan that outlines the planned sales revenues and expenses and the net income or loss for a time period. Profit planning requires preparation of a MASTER BUDGET and various analyses for risk and *what-if* scenarios. Tools for profit planning include the COST-VOLUME-PROFIT (CVP) ANALYSIS and *budgeting*.

PROFIT-SHARING PLAN plan by which corporate executives and employees receive a share of the company's net income on some equitable basis. Such basis may relate to salary level and service years. The maximum amount that an employer can deduct in any one year for the profit-sharing plan is 15% of compensation. Two or more profit-sharing plans are treated as one plan for purposes of limiting employer deductions. Under the present tax law, employer contributions are *not* limited to the employer's current or accumulated earnings.

PROFIT VARIANCE difference between actual profit and budgeted profit. Profit, whether it is GROSS PROFIT in ABSORPTION COSTING or CONTRIBUTION MARGIN in DIRECT COSTING, is affected by three basic items: sales price, sales volume, and costs. In a multi-product firm, if all products are not equally profitable, profit is also affected by the mix of products sold. If actual profit is greater than budgeted profit, the total profit variance is favorable and credited; otherwise, it is unfavorable and debited. *See also* CONTRIBUTION MARGIN (CM) VARIANCE; SALES PRICE VARIANCE.

PROFIT VARIANCE ANALYSIS *see* GROSS PROFIT ANALYSIS.

PROFIT-VOLUME (PV) CHART one that determines how profits vary with changes in volume. Profits are plotted on the vertical axis and units of output are shown on the horizontal axis. See the sample chart below.

PROFIT-VOLUME

PRO FORMA financial statement with amounts or other information that are fully or partially assumed. The assumptions underlying these amounts are also typically given. For example, pro forma disclosure is required for a change in accounting principle in the current year of what earnings would have been in the prior year if the new principle had been used in the previous period. In this case, the pro forma disclosure is at the bottom of the income statement.

PRO FORMA BALANCE SHEET *see* BUDGETED BALANCE SHEET.

PRO FORMA INCOME STATEMENT *see* BUDGETED INCOME STATEMENT.

PRO FORMA STATEMENT *see* FINANCIAL MODEL; PRO FORMA.

PRO FORMA STATEMENT OF CASH FLOWS projected statement of cash flows. As with the regular statement, it classifies cash receipts and disbursements depending on whether they are from operating, investing, or financing activities. The direct presentation reports the major classes of gross cash operating receipts and payments and the difference between them. The indirect presentation reconciles net income with net operating cash flow. The reconciliation requires balance sheet data, such as the changes in accounts receivable, accounts payable, and inventory, as well as net income. Thus, all the pro forma statements are interrelated. For example, the pro forma cash flow statement will include anticipated borrowing. The interest on this borrowing will appear in the pro forma income statement.

PROGRAM set of instructions written in a computer language directing operations to be performed. A utility program is a standard program that conducts routine tasks like merging files and sorting.

PROGRAM EVALUATION AND REVIEW TECHNIQUE (PERT) useful management tool for planning, coordinating, and controlling large, complex projects such as formulation of a MASTER BUDGET, construction of buildings, installation of computers, and scheduling of the closing of books. The development and initial application of PERT dates to the construction of the Polaris submarine by the U.S. Navy in the late 1950s. The PERT technique involves the diagrammatical representation of the sequence of activities comprising a project by means of a network consisting of arrows and circles (nodes), as shown in *Figure 1*. *Arrows* represent "tasks" or "*activities*," which are distinct segments of the project requiring time and resources. *Nodes (circles)* symbolize "*events*," or milestone points in the project representing the completion of one or more activities and/or the initiation of one or more subsequent activities. An event is a point in time and does not consume any time in itself as does an activity. An important aspect of PERT is the CRITICAL PATH METHOD (CPM). A path is a sequence of connected activities. In *Figure 1*, 2-3-4-6 is an example of a path. The CRITICAL PATH for a project is the path that takes the greatest amount of time. This is the minimum amount of time needed for the completion of the project. Thus, activities along this path must be shortened in order to speed up the project. To compute this, calculate the *earliest time (ET)* and the *latest time (LT)* for each event.

CRITICAL PATH

Figure 1

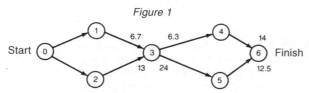

The earliest time is the time an event will occur if all preceding activities are started as early as possible. Thus, for event 4 in *Figure 2*, the earliest time is 19.3 (i.e., 13 + 6.3). The latest time is the time an event can occur without delaying the project beyond the deadline. The earliest time for the entire project is 49.5. Working backward from event 6 (finish) it is seen that the latest time for event 4 is 35.5. The SLACK for an event is the difference between the latest time and earliest time. For event 4 the slack is 35.5 − 19.3 = 16.2. This is the amount of time event 4 can be delayed without delaying the entire project beyond its due date. Finally, the *critical path* for the network is the path leading to the terminal event so that all events on the path have zero path. *Figure 2* shows the earliest and latest times for each event.

CRITICAL PATH

Figure 2

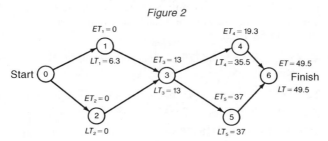

Event	Earliest Time	Latest Time	Slack
1	0	6.3	6.3
2	0	0	0
3	13	13	0
4	19.3	35.5	16.2
5	37	37	0
6	49.5	49.5	0

The path 2-3-5-6 is the critical path.

In a real-world application of PERT to a complex project, the estimates of completion time for activities will seldom be certain. To cope with the uncertainty in activity time estimates, proceed with three time estimates: an *optimistic time* (labeled *a*), a *most likely time* (*m*), and a *pessimistic time* (*b*). A weighted average of these three time estimates is then calculated to establish the *expected time* for the activity. The formula is: $(a + 4m + b)/6$. For example, given three time estimates, $a = 1$, $m = 3$, and $b = 5$, the expected time is $[1 + 4(3) + 5]/6 = 3$.

PROGRAMMED (FIXED) COSTS *see* DISCRETIONARY (FIXED) COST.

PROGRAMMING process of writing instructions for a computer. The program has to be turned into machine-readable form and put into the computer. The program must be tested to assure accuracy, and supporting documentation prepared.

PROGRAM-PLANNING-BUDGETING SYSTEM (PPBS) planning-oriented approach to developing a program budget. A program budget is a budget in which expenditures are based primarily on programs of work and secondarily on character and object. It is a transitional type of budget between the traditional character and object budget, on the one hand, and the performance budget on the other. The major contribution of PPBS lies in the planning process, i.e., the process of making program policy decisions that lead to a specific budget and specific multi-year plans.

PROGRESS BILLINGS interim billings for construction work or government contract work. The entry is to debit progress billings receivable and credit progress billings on construction in progress. Progress billings is a contra account to CONSTRUCTION-IN-PROGRESS. *See also* BILLINGS ON LONG-TERM CONTRACTS.

PROGRESSIVE TAX levy that requires a higher percentage payment on higher income. The personal income tax structure in the United States with its multiple brackets has been traditionally an example of a progressive tax. *See also* TAX RATE SCHEDULE.

PROJECT broad, complex, multidisciplinary approach to the production of a good or service.

PROJECT COSTING cost system that collects information on activities and costs associated with a specific activity, project, or program.

PROJECTED BALANCE SHEET *see* BUDGETED BALANCE SHEET.

PROJECTED BENEFIT OBLIGATION (PBO) actuarial present value as of a date of all benefits attributed by the pension benefit formula to employee service performed before that date. It is measured using assumptions as to *future* compensation levels if the pension benefit formula is based on those future salary levels (e.g., pay-related, final-pay). *See also* ACCUMULATED BENEFIT OBLIGATION (ABO); VESTED BENEFIT OBLIGATION (VBO).

PROJECTED INCOME STATEMENT *see* BUDGETED INCOME STATEMENT.

PROJECT PLANNING making planning decisions for capital investments, many of which may extend over long periods. For example, the decision to buy a particular piece of machinery and equipment is the result of project planning. Project planning has long-term effects on the company's future profitability. CAPITAL EXPENDITURE *analysis* or COST-BENEFIT ANALYSIS is a technique needed for project planning. *See also* CAPITAL BUDGETING.

PROJECT SELECTION choosing the best among alternative proposals on the basis of cost-benefit analysis. *See also* CAPITAL BUDGETING.

PROMISSORY NOTE formal unconditional promise in writing to pay on demand or at a future date a definite sum of money. The person who signs the note and promises to pay is called the maker of the note. The person to whom payment is to be made is called the payee of the note.

PROMOTION EXPENSE cost of samples or promotional items made available to the public at large. Promotion expense is fully tax deductible. Examples are distributed merchandise samples and tickets to a show offered as a customer prize.

PROPERTY DIVIDEND one paid in property. The dividend is recorded on the declaration date at the market value of the property.

PROPERTY, PLANT, AND EQUIPMENT long-lived *fixed productive assets* used in business activities. It is a noncurrent asset balance sheet classification. Property, plant, and equipment are shown at their book values. Examples are buildings and machinery. *See also* PLANT AND EQUIPMENT.

PROPRIETARY FUND in governmental accounting, one having profit and loss aspects; therefore it uses the *accrual* rather than modified accrual accounting method. The two types of proprietary funds are the ENTERPRISE FUND and the INTERNAL SERVICE FUND.

PROPRIETARY THEORY theory that assets are owned by the proprietor and liabilities are owed by him. The accounting equation is:

$$\text{Assets} - \text{Liabilities} = \text{Capital}$$

Capital is the net value of the business to the owner.

Under the proprietary theory, revenues increase capital, while expenses reduce it. Net income belongs to the owner, representing an increase in the proprietor's capital.

The proprietary theory best applies to single proprietorship entities because there exists a personal relationship between the management of the business and the owner. Often, in fact, they are the same person. It also applies to a partnership where net income is added each period to the partners' capital accounts.

PROPRIETORSHIP
1. assets minus liabilities of an organization. It equals contributed capital plus accumulated earnings.
2. form of business organization. *See also* SOLE PROPRIETOR.

PRO RATA basis for allocating an amount proportionately to the items involved. An amount may be proportionately distributed to assets, expenses, funds, and so forth. For example, at year end, underapplied overhead may be allocated to work-in-process, finished goods, and cost of sales based on the dollars or units applicable to those accounts. Assume underapplied overhead is $1,000, work-in-process is $4,000, finished goods is $5,000, and cost of sales is $1,000. The pro rata charge to work-in-process, for instance, would be $400 ($4,000/$10,000 × $1,000). The journal entry is:

Work-in-process	400	
Finished goods	500	
Cost of sales		100
Factory overhead		1,000

PRORATION allocating or assigning an amount in proportion to some base to an activity, department, or product. Service costs are frequently allocated to user departments based on the base allocation formula/procedure (e.g., number of employees, machine hours spent). *See also* ALLOCATION.

PROSPECTUS document that must accompany a new issue of securities. It contains the same information appearing in the registration statement, such as a list of directors and officers, financial reports certified by a CPA, underwriters, the purpose and use for the funds, and other reasonable information that prospective buyers of a security need to know. A preliminary prospectus, RED-HERRING (so named because of a red stamp indicating the tentative nature of the document during the period in which it is being reviewed for fraudulent or misleading statements by the SECURITIES AND EXCHANGE COMMISSION (SEC)), is issued prior to the *final, statutory* prospectus, which also contains offering instructions.

PROTOCOL guidelines and principles associated with the workings of a network. Rules surround data and electrical signals on the network, the manner of information transmissions, the way in which the network is accessed, and the processing of applications on the network.

PROVISION
1. amount of an expense that must be recognized currently when the exact amount of the expense is uncertain. An example is an expense such as provision for income taxes.
2. contra asset account such as allowance for bad debts and allowance to reduce securities from cost to market value.
3. making an appropriation of retained earnings for a specified purpose.

PROXY
1. power of attorney by which the holder of stock transfers the voting rights to another party. Sometimes PROXY FIGHTS erupt with outside groups competing in the solicitation of proxies that would give them voting control.
2. short for *proxy statement,* a written document that the SEC requires to be provided to shareholders before they vote by proxy on corporate matters. It typically contains proposed members of the BOARD OF DIRECTORS, INSIDE DIRECTORS' salaries, and any resolutions of minority stockholders and of management.

PROXY FIGHTS competition that erupts when outsiders attempt to gain control of a company's management. This requires soliciting a sufficient number of votes by proxy to unseat the existing management. The fights (battles) generally occur when the present management is performing poorly; however, the odds of outsiders winning a proxy fight are generally slim.

PROXY STATEMENT *see* PROXY.

PRUDENT INVESTMENT
1. investment made prudently and intelligently. A reasonable degree of safety and return are expected. *See also* FIDUCIARY.
2. rule that allows an uninstructed trustee considerable discretionary authority to purchase investments of any type that an ordinarily prudent person would find suitable in the case at hand.

P2P *see* PEER-TO-PEER NETWORKING.

PUBLIC ACCOUNTANT (PA) one performing professional accounting services for the public. The public accountant is licensed by a state to use the PA designation. Licensing requirements for a PA are significantly less than for a CERTIFIED PUBLIC ACCOUNTANT.

PUBLIC ACCOUNTING profession that public accountants are engaged in. Independent public accountants perform many functions, including auditing financial statements, designing financial accounting systems, assisting in the managerial accounting function, providing managerial advisory services, and tax preparation. The public accountant may perform services for corporations, partnerships, individuals, and other organizations. The certified public accountant is regulated by state law and must meet stringent technical and ethical requirements. These requirements include passing the CPA examination, satisfying experience requirements (e.g., two years in New York), and abiding by the American Institute of CPA's Code of Professional Ethics.

PUBLIC COMPANY ACCOUNTING OVERSIGHT BOARD (PCAOB)
(www.pcaobus.org) a private sector, nonprofit corporation, created by the Sarbanes-Oxley Act of 2002, to oversee the auditors of public companies in order to protect the interests of investors and further the public interest in the

preparation of informative, fair, and independent audit reports. All accounting firms auditing public companies must register with the PCAOB.

PUBLIC INTEREST ACCOUNTING *see* ACCOUNTANTS FOR THE PUBLIC INTEREST (API).

PUBLICLY HELD COMPANY enterprise whose ownership is held by the general public, including individuals, officers, employees, and institutional investors. A publicly held company has stock listed on an exchange and must file financial statements and reports with the SEC. *See also* PRIVATELY HELD COMPANY.

PUBLIC OFFERING presenting new securities to the investing public, after registration requirements have been filed with the SEC. The securities are usually made available to the public at large by a managing investment banker and its underwriting syndicate. In the public offering, unlike PRIVATE PLACEMENT, the corporation does not deal directly with the ultimate buyers of the securities. The public market is an impersonal one.

PUBLIC OVERSIGHT BOARD (POB) group consisting mostly of nonaccountants that oversees activities of CPA firms belonging to the AICPA's SEC practice section. The POB's objective is to assure quality professional services.

PULL-THROUGH PRODUCTION production system in which a customer's order triggers the purchase of materials and the scheduling of production for the required products.

PURCHASE (ACCOUNTING) METHOD manner of accounting for a business combination. Under the purchase method, the acquiring corporation records the net assets acquired at the fair market value of the consideration given. Any excess of the purchase price over the fair market value of the net identifiable assets is recorded as goodwill. The acquiring corporation then records periodic charges to income for the depreciation of the excess price over book value of net identifiable assets. Goodwill is subject to an annual impairment test. Note that goodwill already on the books of the acquired company is not brought forth. Net income of the acquired company is brought forth from the acquisition date to year-end. Direct costs of the purchase reduce the fair value of securities issued. Indirect costs are expensed.

PURCHASE DISCOUNT reduction given under the heading CASH DISCOUNT or TRADE DISCOUNT. A cash discount is intended for prompt payments by the purchaser, whereas a trade discount represents a reduction in list price in return for quantity purchases.

PURCHASE GROUP *see* SYNDICATE.

PURCHASE ORDER form used by the purchasing department to order goods or merchandise. Several copies are usually prepared, each on a different color paper. The original is sent to the supplier; this purchase order is an authorization to deliver the merchandise and to submit a bill based on the prices listed. Carbon copies of the purchase order are usually routed to the purchasing department, accounting department, receiving department, and finance department.

PURCHASE ORDER LEAD TIME time it takes for raw materials and parts to be ordered and received so that production can begin.

PURCHASE PRICE VARIANCE *see* MATERIAL PRICE VARIANCE.

PURCHASE REQUISITION a document used by a user department to request the acquisition of goods or services. An approved purchase requisition is sent to the purchasing department and serves as the basis for the preparation of a PURCHASE ORDER.

PURCHASING POWER LOSS (OR GAIN) event that occurs when holding MONETARY ITEMS during a period of inflation or deflation. A purchasing power loss occurs on holding monetary assets during inflation because of the decline in purchasing power of the dollar. A purchasing power gain arises, from a borrowing company's standpoint, on monetary liabilities in an inflationary environment, because the company will be paying back in *cheaper dollars*. Purchasing power gains or losses are shown in the price-level adjusted income statement. Assume that on 1/1/20X9 net monetary assets are $55,000, and during 20X9 the increase in net monetary assets is $6,000. The relevant Consumer Price Indices are: 1/1/20X9 212.9, average for 20X9 220.9, and 12/31/20X9 243.5. The computation of the purchasing power loss for 20X9 follows:

	Historical Cost		Conversion Factor	Average 20X9 Dollars
1/1/20X9	$55,000	×	220.9	$57,067
			212.9	
Increase in monetary items	6,000	×	220.9	6,000
			220.9	
				$63,067
12/31/20X9	$61,000	×	220.9	$55,338
			243.5	
Purchasing Power Loss				$ 7,729

See also CONSTANT-DOLLAR ACCOUNTING.

PURCHASING SYSTEM procedures, manual or computerized, followed by an organization to achieve the following basic objectives: (1) to determine the quality and quantity needed and the time when an item is needed; (2) to obtain the best possible price; and (3) to maintain information on sources of supply. The system should utilize such concepts as ECONOMIC ORDER QUANTITY (EOQ), *optimal reorder point*, QUANTITY DISCOUNTS, and MATERIAL REQUIREMENT PLANNING (MRP).

PUSH-DOWN ACCOUNTING method of accounting in which the financial statements of a subsidiary are presented to reflect the costs incurred by the parent company in buying the subsidiary instead of the subsidiary's historical costs. The purchase costs of the parent company are shown in the subsidiary's statements.

PUSH-THROUGH METHOD production system in which products are manufactured in long production runs and stored in anticipation of customers' orders.

PUT

1. option to sell a specific security at a specified price within a designated period for which the option buyer pays the seller (writer) a premium or option price. Contracts on listed puts (and CALLS) have been standardized at date of issue for periods of three, six, and nine months, although as these contracts approach expiration, they may be purchased with a much shorter life.

2. bondholder's right to redeem a bond prior to maturity.

PV CHART *see* PROFIT-VOLUME (PV) CHART.

Q

Q RATIO the market value of all securities (not just equity) divided by the replacement cost (not book value) of all assets. The Q ratio reflects the market's valuation of new investment. A ratio greater than one means that a firm is earning returns greater than the amount invested. For this reason, a company with a ratio exceeding one should attract new resources and competition; also called *Tobin's Q*. The higher the Q ratio, the greater the industry attractiveness and/or competitive advantage. The notion of this ratio holds that a firm's market value ultimately equals the replacement cost of its tangible assets. Some argue that calculating the replacement cost of assets is subject to enormous measurement errors; thus, the Q ratio is useless as a valuation tool.

QUALIFICATION
1. reference in the audit report to a material limitation placed on the auditor's examination or to uncertainty regarding a specific item in the financial statements. *See also* QUALIFIED OPINION.
2. reservation in a proposed agreement making the agreement unenforceable unless a specified condition is met.
3. technical competence to perform a particular job, such as passing the CPA examination and meeting experience requirements in order to be licensed as a certified public accountant.

QUALIFIED OPINION judgment by the CPA in the AUDIT REPORT that "except for" something, the financial statements fairly present the financial position and operating results of the firm. An "EXCEPT FOR" OPINION relates to a limitation placed on the scope of the audit. The result of the limitation is the failure of the CPA to obtain sufficient objective and verifiable evidence in support of business transactions of the company being audited.

QUALIFIED STOCK OPTION plan granting an employee the right to purchase company stock at a later date at a specified option price that will most always be lower than the market price; also called *incentive stock option*. If the stock price goes below the option price, the company can issue the executive a second incentive option with a lower exercise price. There is a $100,000 per employee ceiling on the value of stock covered by options that are exercisable in any one calendar year. Another advantage to the corporate executive of an incentive stock option is that no tax is paid until the stock bought with the option is sold.

QUALITATIVE FACTORS considerations in decision making, in addition to the quantitative or financial factors highlighted by INCREMENTAL ANALYSIS. They are the factors relevant to a decision that are difficult to measure in terms of money. Qualitative factors may include: (1) effect on employee morale, schedules, and other internal elements; (2) relationships with and commitments to suppliers; (3) effect on present and future customers; and (4) long-term future effect on profitability. In some decision-making situations, qualitative aspects are more important than immediate financial benefit from a decision.

QUALITY measure of conformance of a product or service to certain specifications or standards. *See also* TOTAL QUALITY MANAGEMENT; APPRAISAL COSTS; INTERNAL FAILURE COSTS; EXTERNAL FAILURE COSTS; PREVENTIVE COSTS.

QUALITY ASSURANCE all of the activities necessary to ensure that the customer receives satisfactory performance.

QUALITY AT THE SOURCE responsibility of every employee, work group, department, or supplier to inspect the work.

QUALITY CONTROL
1. procedures to establish an optimal level of audit performance by practitioners. Included are proper supervision over field work, evaluation of internal control, and employment of generally accepted auditing standards. The monitoring of a CPA firm's system of quality control by a peer reviewer involves consideration of the adequacy and relevance of the CPA firm's procedures, practices, and compliance thereto, effectiveness of professional development, and quality of the CPA firm's practice aids.
2. policies and techniques used to assure that some level of performance has been achieved. Included are controls in design and inspection. Variances from established norms are identified and rectified.
3. in manufacturing, procedures to achieve a desired level of satisfaction of the operation or product being produced. A number of tests and measurements may be required to determine that a part meets required specifications.

QUALITY CONTROL CHART graph sometimes used in analyzing deviations of actual results from standards, known as VARIANCES. Measurements of actual results are shown on the graph and compared with measurements of the expected mean and upper and lower control limits, which are established by using statistical procedures. In statistical quality control charts, the upper and lower control limits are set three STANDARD DEVIATIONS from the mean. *See also* THREE-SIGMA LIMITS.

QUALITY CONTROL CHART

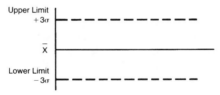

QUALITY COSTS costs incurred because poor quality cost may exist or actually does exist.

QUALITY OF EARNINGS extent that net income is realistic in portraying the operating performance of a business—that reported results have not intentionally been overstated or understated by management. In appraising net income, quantitative techniques, such as ratio analysis, can be employed.

QUALITY REVIEW evaluation by one accounting firm or accountant of the soundness of the practices of another accounting firm or accountant. A professional organization may also be engaged to examine the audit functions performed by a CPA firm. The quality review will include an appraisal of such areas as working paper preparation, audit programs, internal control, audit reports, staff functions, scheduling, supervision, client relations, and training. *See also* PEER REVIEW.

QUALITY TRAINING familiarizing all employees with the means for preventing, detecting, and eliminating nonquality. The educational processes are tailored to the appropriate groups.

QUANTIFICATION expression of economic activity in monetary units. Thus financial statement items are typically expressed in numbers comprising monetary units, such as dollars.

QUANTITATIVE FACTORS considerations relevant to a decision that can be measured in terms of money or quantitative units. Examples are incremental revenue, added cost, and initial outlay. *See also* QUALITATIVE FACTORS.

QUANTITATIVE METHODS (MODELS) collection of mathematical and statistical methods used in the solution of managerial and decision-making problems, also called *operations research* (OR) and *management science*. There are numerous tools available under these headings such as LINEAR PROGRAMMING (LP), ECONOMIC ORDER QUANTITY (EOQ), LEARNING CURVE THEORY, PERT, and REGRESSION ANALYSIS.

QUANTITY DISCOUNT *see* TRADE DISCOUNT.

QUANTITY DISCOUNT MODEL form of an economic order quantity (EOQ) model that takes into account quantity discounts. Quantity discounts are price reductions designed to induce large orders. If quantity discounts are offered, the buyer must weigh the potential benefits of reduced purchase price and fewer orders against the increase in carrying costs caused by higher average inventories. Hence, the buyer's goal in this case is to select the order quantity that will minimize total costs, where total cost is the sum of carrying cost, ordering cost, *and* purchase cost.

QUANTITY (USAGE) VARIANCE efficiency variance for direct materials. *See also* EFFICIENCY VARIANCE.

QUARTERLY REPORT financial report issued every three months between annual reports. It includes unaudited financial statements consisting of the balance sheet, income statement, and statement of changes in financial position along with related footnotes. Also, typically there is a narrative overview of business operations. *See also* INTERIM FINANCIAL STATEMENT.

QUASI CONTRACT legal duty or obligation to pay for a benefit received as though a contract had actually been made. This will be done in a limited number of situations in order to attain an equitable or just result. For example, when a homeowner permits repairs to be made with the knowledge that they are being made by a stranger who would expect to be paid for such repairs, there is *quasi-contractual duty* to pay for the reasonable value of the improvement, i.e., in order to avoid the homeowner's unjust enrichment at the expense of the person making the repair.

QUASI-REORGANIZATION procedure used to eliminate a retained earnings deficit by restating certain assets, liabilities, and capital accounts. It allows a company a fresh start when it appears that operations can be turned around. It permits the company to proceed on much the same basis as if it had been legally reorganized, without the difficulty and expense generally connected with such a legal reorganization. Stockholders and creditors must agree to it. The following steps are taken: (1) assets are written down to fair market value; (2) capital stock is restated, creating additional paid-in capital by reducing par value; and

(3) a zero balance in retained earnings is created by eliminating the deficit in retained earnings by transferring part of capital to the account. Retained earnings bear the date of the quasi-reorganization.

QUATTRO PRO spreadsheet software offered by Corel.

QUERY LANGUAGE used to request data from a database table. An example of a query language is SQL.

QUESTIONABLE PAYMENT improper and often illegal monies given to obtain favorable treatment by another party. An example is a bribe made to a government official or buyer of goods in another company.

QUEUE waiting line that forms wherever there is more than one user of a limited resource.

QUEUE DISCIPLINE rules that determine the order in which arrivals are serviced.

QUEUING THEORY (WAITING LINE THEORY) quantitative technique for balancing services available with services required. It evaluates the ability of service facilities to handle capacity and load at different times during the day. It is useful in problems of balancing cost and service level, such as determining the number of toll booths on a highway and the number of tellers in a bank.

QUICK ASSET current asset that can be converted into cash in a short period of time. Examples are cash, marketable securities, and accounts receivable. Certain current assets, such as inventory and prepaid expenses, are excluded.

QUICKBOOKS PRO leader in accounting software for small business, brings complete financial management capabilities to small business owners who do not want to deal with the hassle of trying to understand accounting jargon or debit/credit accounting. QuickBooks (www.quickbooks.com) users can easily set up their business with QuickBooks, making it easy to create custom invoices, enter sales, perform electronic banking and bill payment, track customer contracts, track time, perform job costing, manage inventory, handle payroll, and even prepare for tax time.

QUICKEN personal finance software by Intuit, Inc. (www.quicken.com).

QUICK RATIO see ACID TEST RATIO.

QUOTED PRICE price of the last transaction of a listed security or commodity. In over-the-counter trading, *quote* means bid and asked.

R

r *see* CORRELATION COEFFICIENT (*r*).

RAM (RANDOM-ACCESS MEMORY) computer's main memory where programs, application software, and data are stored. The size of the RAM (measured by kilobytes) is an important indicator of the capacity of the computer; also called *read/write memory*.

RANDOM ACCESS *see* DIRECT ACCESS.

RANDOM ACCESS FILE file constructed in a manner in which records may be placed in a random order; also called *direct access file*. Each record in a random access file has associated with it a relative index number. Whenever a record is read from a random access file, a computer program must produce a relative index number for this record in order to locate the record in the file. This type of file design offers the following advantages: (1) it provides rapid access to the desired information. In a decision-making environment where information is needed quickly, random access is a requisite to rapid retrieval; (2) it is efficient for retrieving a relatively few records at a time; and (3) it provides a method of keeping files up to date as transactions or events occur. *See also* DIRECT ACCESS.

RANDOM SAMPLE one allowing for the equal probability that each item will be chosen. To assure this, identification numbers are assigned to each item in a group and a table of random numbers is used to determine the sample members.

RANDOM VARIANCES differences that are due to chance, also called *chance variances*. The identification of random variances avoids unnecessary investigations of variances and eliminates frequent changes in a process or an operation. Statistical control charts are often used to distinguish random variances from variances that need investigation. *See also* STATISTICAL QUALITY CONTROL.

RANDOM WALK theory that stock prices behave in an unpredictable fashion because the stock market is efficient. The market price of a stock goes randomly around real (intrinsic) value. Current security prices are independent of prior prices. Thus historical prices are not a reliable predictor of future ones.

According to random walk, financial information significant enough to affect future value is available to knowledgable investors. Thus new data affecting stock prices are immediately reflected in market value. At any given time, the price of a stock is the optimum estimate of its value including all available information. *See also* EFFICIENT MARKET HYPOTHESIS.

RAPID APPLICATION DEVELOPMENT (RAD) a software development process that allows software to be developed in a short time, often with compromises. RAD is achieved by taking advantage of modern automated tools and techniques that significantly reduce development times.

RATE EARNED ON COMMON STOCKHOLDERS' EQUITY ratio indicating the earnings on the common stockholders' investment. It equals net income minus preferred dividends divided by average common stockholders' equity. Assume net income of $50,000, preferred dividends of $10,000, and average common stockholders' equity of $200,000. The ratio is 20% ($40,000/$200,000).

RATE EARNED ON STOCKHOLDERS' EQUITY statistic reflecting profit to the owners of the business. It equals net income divided by average owners' equity. Assume net income of $60,000, stockholders' equity at the beginning of the year of $700,000, and stockholders' equity at the end of the year of $500,000. The return rate is 10% ($60,000/$600,000).

RATE EARNED ON TOTAL ASSETS *see* RETURN ON INVESTMENT (ROI).

RATE OF EXCHANGE term used for the rate at which one currency (or commodity) can be exchanged for another. For example, one British pound may be equivalent to $1.80 in U.S. dollars. One Japanese Yen may equal $.0065 in American currency.

RATE OF RETURN ON INVESTMENT annual percentage return after taxes that actually occurs or is anticipated on an investment. For example, if $100,000 is invested in a stock and the after-tax return on it for the year is $8000, the rate of return is 8%. *See also* RETURN ON INVESTMENT (ROI).

RATE VARIANCE *see* LABOR RATE (PRICE) VARIANCE.

RATIO relationship of one amount to another. Ratios may compare balance sheet items, income statement items, or balance sheet items to income statement items. In effect, they relate financial statement components to each other. They are used to evaluate the company's financial health, operating results, and growth prospects. For example, ACCOUNTS RECEIVABLE TURNOVER will reveal collection problems with customers. *See also* RATIO ANALYSIS.

RATIO ANALYSIS study undertaken by financial statement preparers and users to evaluate the financial strength or weakness of a company and its operating trend. Various *ratios* are computed, depending upon the objective of the user analyzing the financial statements. Short-term creditors are primarily concerned with a company's ability to meet short-term debt from current assets, so they concentrate on the LIQUIDITY RATIOS emphasizing cash flow. Long-term creditors want to be paid back in the long term, so they look to solvency ratios such as total debt to total stockholders' equity. Potential investors are interested in dividends and appreciation in market price of stock, so they focus on profitability ratios (e.g., profit margin) and market measures (e.g., price-earnings ratio). Auditors zero in on the going concern of the client by determining its ability to meet debt (e.g., interest coverage ratio). Also, auditors wanting to know where to concentrate their audit attention look for illogical relationships in accounts over time such as the ratio of promotion and entertainment expense to sales. The limitations of financial ratios for analytical purposes must be considered, including: (1) a ratio is static in nature and does not reveal future flows; (2) a ratio does not reveal the amount of its components (e.g., a current ratio figure does not tell you how much is in cash or inventory); (3) a ratio does not reveal the quality of its components (e.g., a high current ratio that is made up of poor quality receivables and obsolete inventory); and (4) a ratio is based on historical cost not taking into account inflation. *See also* SOLVENT; TURNOVER.

RATIO ESTIMATION a technique used in statistical sampling that is used to estimate the dollar amount of a population using the ratio of the audit value of a sample to the book value (recorded amount) of a sample. Ratio estimation is an alternative to both DIFFERENCE ESTIMATION and MEAN-PER-UNIT (MPU) ESTIMATION.

RAW IN PROCESS INVENTORY ACCOUNT inventory account in the just-in-time operating environment that combines the materials inventory and the work-in-process inventory accounts.

RAW MATERIALS INVENTORY beginning or ending balance of raw materials on hand for an accounting period. It represents items that will be a component of a produced good. The beginning and ending balances of raw materials inventory are shown in the income statement when cost of goods sold is presented. The ending balance is reported in the balance sheet. *See also* RAW MATERIALS USED.

RAW MATERIALS USED items placed into the production process. They are a cost of making the product. An example is steel used in the manufacture of an automobile.

REACQUIRED STOCK *see* TREASURY STOCK.

READ/WRITE MEMORY *see* RAM (RANDOM-ACCESS MEMORY).

REAL ACCOUNT balance sheet account that is carried forward into the next year. It is a proprietary account. *See also* NOMINAL ACCOUNT.

REAL ESTATE
1. real property such as land, land improvements, and building held for business use in the production of income. It is contrasted with personal property.
2. real property held for investment purposes. Increased value in real estate has typically exceeded the rate of inflation. But real estate as an inflation hedge varies from locality to locality. Also, leverage exists with real estate since a high percentage of the investment may be made with debt funds. Down payments are often less than 25%. However, a large capital investment is usually required. Real estate provides capital appreciation or depreciation. Certain real estate investments, such as residential and commercial property, generate annual income. Directly managed real estate income property provides tax deductions in the form of depreciation expense, interest expense, and property taxes.

REAL ESTATE INVESTMENT TRUST (REIT) a type of investment company that invests money (obtained through the sale of its shares to investors) in mortgages and various types of investment in real estate, in order to earn profits for shareholders. Shareholders receive income from the rents received from the properties and receive capital gains as properties are sold at a profit. REITs have been formed by a number of large financial institutions such as banks and insurance companies. The stocks of many of them are traded on security exchanges, thereby providing investors with a marketable interest in a real estate investment portfolio. REITs that distribute all of their income generally pay no entity-level tax. However, in exchange for this special tax treatment, REITs are subject to numerous qualifications and limitations including: (1) Shareholder qualifications. Generally, REITs are not permitted to be closely held and must have a minimum of 100 shareholders. (2) Qualified asset and income tests. REITs are required to have at least 75% of their value represented by qualified real estate assets and to earn at least 75% of their income from real estate investments.

REALIZATION recognizing revenue at the time of sale of merchandise if a retail business, or at the time of rendering the service if a service business. At realization, the earnings process is complete because the transaction is consummated, selling price is determinable, cost of sale is known, and future costs can be accurately estimated. Realization also applies to recognizing a gain on the sale of a security.

REALIZED GAIN, LOSS difference between the amount received from the sale or disposal of an asset and its carrying value. Realized gains and losses are shown in the income statement. They are also typically included in arriving at taxable income. In some cases, a realized loss can occur even though no sale has taken place. Examples are the write-down of a long-term investment due to a permanent decline in value, and the transfer of a security from long-term to short-term when market value is below cost.

REAL ECONOMY economy made up of manufacturing and services sectors as compared with the financial sector.

REAL PROPERTY rights, interests, and benefits inherent in the ownership of real estate, as distinguished from *personal property*; frequently thought of as a bundle of rights. Real estate may be loosely defined as land (including air rights) and other properties that are permanently attached to land such as houses, fences, and landscaping. The terms real property and REAL ESTATE are often used interchangeably.

REAL-TIME SYSTEM computer term for a system that uses a nonsequential processing method. This differs from batch processing, which employs sequential processing. It provides access to any piece of information and finds that piece of data in the same amount of time as any other piece. Real-time processing systems are more expensive than batch processing but provide decision-making information on a current basis, that is, when the decision needs to be made, or while a customer waits for a response.

REASONABLENESS TEST procedure to examine the logic of accounting information. For example, the trend in promotion and entertainment expense for a company can be compared to that of prior years of the same company or to competitive companies, or to industry norms. If the promotion and entertainment expense is relatively high, it will require investigation because it does not appear reasonable.

REBATE
1. ABATEMENT.
2. amount paid back or credit allowed because of an overcollection or the return of an object sold, also called *refund*.
3. unearned interest refunded to borrower if the loan is paid off prior to maturity.
4. payment to a customer upon completion of a purchase as an inducement or sales promotion tactic.

RECAPITALIZATION process of changing a firm's capital structure by altering the mix of debt and equity financing without changing the total amount of capital. This process often occurs as part of REORGANIZATION under the bankruptcy laws. In DEFEASANCE, the total capital amount can change.

RECAPTURE OF DEPRECIATION portion of a capital gain (the amount of a gain on depreciable assets) representing tax benefits previously taken and taxed as ordinary income.

RECEIPTS

1. cash or other assets received.

2. evidence substantiating the occurrence of an event. Accounting documents showing receipt include a receiving report of merchandise or a bill for an expenditure incurred (e.g., hotel bill, restaurant check).

RECEIVABLES claims held against customers and others for money, goods, or services. If collection is expected in one year or less (or in the normal operating cycle of the business if longer), they are classified as current assets. If not, they are presented as noncurrent assets. Receivables are further classified in the balance sheet as trade or nontrade. Trade receivables are due from customers for merchandise sold or services performed in the ordinary course of business. Trade receivables may either be accounts receivable or notes receivable. Nontrade receivables come into being from other types of transactions and may he written promises to pay monies or deliver services. Examples are advances to employees, claims against other entities (i.e., tax refunds, insurance receipts), deposits, and financial receivables (i.e., interest receivable, dividend receivable).

RECEIVABLE TURNOVER *see* ACCOUNTS RECEIVABLE TURNOVER.

RECEIVING REPORT document used within a firm, upon receiving the shipment of merchandise to formally record quantities and description.

RECESSION downturn in the economy. Many economists speak of recession when there has been a decline in the gross national product for two consecutive quarters.

RECIPROCAL result derived from the division of 1 by a given quantity. For example, the reciprocal of 2 is ½.

RECIPROCAL ALLOCATION METHOD process of allocating service department costs to production departments, where RECIPROCAL services are allowed between service departments; also known as the *reciprocal* method, the *matrix* method, the *double-distribution* method, the *cross-allocation* method, and *simultaneous equation* method. The method sets up simultaneous equations to determine the allocatable cost of each service department. The data for an example follows:

	Production Departments		Service Departments	
	A **Machining**	**B** **Assembly**	**General** **Plant (GP)**	**Engineering** **(E)**
Overhead costs before allocation	$30,000	$40,000	$20,000	10,000
Engineering hours by Engineering	50,000	30,000	5,000	4,000
Direct labor hours by General Plant	60,000	40,000	15,000	20,000

Using the direct method yields:

	Service Departments		Production Departments	
	GP	**E**	**A**	**B**
Overhead costs	$ 20,000	$10,000	$30,000	$40,000
Reallocation:				
GP(1/2, 1/3, 1/6)	($20,791)*	3,465	10,396	6,930
E(50/85, 30/85,				
5/85)	791	($13,465)*	7,921	4,753
	0	0	$48,317	$51,683

The following equations are set up:

$$GP = \$20{,}000 + 5/85\ E$$
$$E = \$10{,}000 + 1/6\ GP$$

Substituting M from the second equation into the first:

$$GP = \$20{,}000 + 5/85\ (\$10{,}000 + 1/6\ GP)$$

Solving for GP gives GP = $20,791. Substituting GP = $20,791 into the second equation and solving for E gives E = $13,465.

RECIPROCAL ARRANGEMENT agreement in which one party will perform a certain act if the other performs a specified act as well. An example is where Company X agrees to buy certain goods from Company Y if Company Y orders merchandise from some division of Company X.

RECOGNITION
  1. recording a business occurrence in the accounting records. An example is recognizing an unrealized loss on an investment portfolio at year-end, when aggregate market value is below cost. In this case, the transaction is recognized even though realization (sale) has not occurred.
  2. ascertaining the particulars of an item (i.e., amount, timing) before accepting and recording it.

RECOGNIZED GAIN OR LOSS the amount of gain or loss on a transaction that is required to be reported for income tax purposes. Recognized gain or loss is not necessarily the amount of the realized gain or loss, which is the economic gain or loss.

RECONCILIATION adjusting the difference between two items (i.e., amounts, balances, accounts, or statements) so that the figures agree. The practitioner often has to analyze the deviation between two items, such as in preparing a BANK RECONCILIATION. For example, a reconciliation occurs when comparing the home office books account related to branch transactions with the corresponding account on the branch office books related to home office transactions. These two accounts are adjusted for the reconciling items causing the difference.

RECORD collection of related data items. For example, a company may store information regarding each employee in a single record consisting of a FIELD representing the name, a field representing the Social Security number, and so on. A collection of records is called a *file*.

RECORD DATE *see* DATE OF RECORD.

REDEMPTION
1. right to call or redeem a firm's outstanding preferred stock by paying the preferred stockholders the par value of the stock plus a premium.
2. repayment of bonds by a CALL before maturity, usually involving a call premium.
3. repayment of mutual funds at *net asset value* when a shareholder's holdings are liquidated.

RED FLAGS
1. signifying a warning and demanding attention, such as unfavorable cost variance.
2. internal controls within and outside the accounting information system software that indicate possible suspect transactions.

RED HERRING slang term for a preliminary PROSPECTUS that outlines the important features of a new issue. This prospectus contains no selling price information or offering date. It is so named because of the stamped red-ink statement on the first page telling the reader that the document is *not* an official offer to sell the securities. Once the REGISTRATION STATEMENT is approved by the SEC, the *offering circular*, the final, statutory prospectus, is printed and the security can be offered for sale.

REDISCOUNT RATE *see* DISCOUNT RATE.

REDISTRIBUTED COST reassignment of a cost. For example, rent of the computer department is first assigned to it. Then, the total service cost of the computer department is redistributed on some rational basis (such as space occupied) to other service departments and to production departments. *See also* PRORATION.

REDUNDANT ARRAYS OF INDEPENDENT DISKS (RAID) allows an organization to save the same data on multiple hard drives. This usually improves performance and reduces the possibility of data loss by incorporating redundancy in storage.

REENGINEERING *see* BUSINESS PROCESS REENGINEERING (BPR).

REFUND *see* REBATE.

REG FD *see* REGULATION FULL DISCLOSURE.

REGISTERED SECURITY
1. security whose owner is recorded by the issuing corporation or its registrar. In the case of a registered bond, principal of such a bond and interest, if registered as to interest, is paid to the owner of the bond listed on the record of the issuing company. It contrasts with BEARER (*coupon*) BONDS, where detachable coupons must be presented to the issuer for interest payment.
2. public issue registered with the SEC.

REGISTRATION
1. act or fact of making an entry of any class of transactions or statements for the purpose of documentation for future reference. Such documentation may be in the form of financial information noted in registers, such as a cash register.

2. process set up by the *Securities Exchange Acts of 1933 and 1934* that requires publicly issued securities to be reviewed by the SEC.

3. recording of stocks or bonds in the owner's name as opposed to bearer's name.

REGISTRATION STATEMENT document that must be submitted to the SEC disclosing all facts relevant to the new securities issue that will permit an investor to make an informed decision. It is a lengthy document containing (1) historical, (2) financial, and (3) administrative facts about the issuing corporation. *See also* PROSPECTUS.

REGRESSION ANALYSIS statistical procedure for estimating the average relationship between the dependent variable (sales, for example) and one or more independent variables (price and advertising, for example). It is a popularly used method for estimating the COST-VOLUME FORMULA ($y = a + bx$). SIMPLE REGRESSION involves one independent variable, e.g., direct labor-hours or machine-hours alone, whereas MULTIPLE REGRESSION involves two or more independent variables. Assuming a *linear* relationship, the simple regression model indicates that the relationship is $y = a + bx$, where a, and b are unknown constants, called regression coefficients. The multiple regression model is $y = a_0 + a_1x_1 + a_2x_2 + \cdots + a_kx_k$, where a's are coefficients and x's represent the number of independent variables.

In estimating the cost-volume formula, regression analysis attempts to find a line of best fit. To find the line of best fit, a technique called the LEAST-SQUARES METHOD is widely used.

REGRESSION COEFFICIENT parameter value in a regression equation. For example, in a LINEAR REGRESSION EQUATION $y = a + bx$, a and b are regression coefficients. Specifically, a is called *y-intercept* or *constant*, while b is called a SLOPE.

REGRESSION EQUATION (MODEL) statistical model that relates the dependent variable (sales, for example) to one or more independent variables (advertising and income, for example). *See also* REGRESSION ANALYSIS.

REGRESSIVE TAX system in which the percentage of income paid declines as income rises. Under a regressive system, as income rises from $15,000 to $100,000, the tax rate would fall from 20% to 10%, for example. In this sense, a regressive tax is the opposite of a PROGRESSIVE TAX. The term is also used generally to refer to any tax system that favors the rich at the expense of the poor. The general sales tax with its fixed rate is considered regressive, because lower income groups tend to spend a higher percentage of their incomes on goods and services than higher income groups.

REGULATION Q the Federal Reserve Bank's regulation that sets deposit interest rate ceilings and regulates advertising of interest on savings accounts. This regulation applies to all commercial banks. It is a rule, first instituted in the Banking Act of 1933.

REGULATION FULL DISCLOSURE a rule passed by the Securities and Exchange Commission in an effort to prevent selective disclosure by public companies to professionals and certain shareholders. This requires a company to fully disclose any information of a material nature simultaneously to everyone to ensure a level playing field for individual and institutional investors.

REGULATIONS authoritative body of rules specifying details of procedure and conduct to be followed in accordance with such criteria as uniformity, efficiency, control, ethics, and legal considerations.

REGULATION S-X SECURITIES AND EXCHANGE COMMISSION (SEC) regulation specifying the specific format and content of financial reports. It also requires companies that intend to offer securities to the public to provide adequate disclosure so that the investing community can evaluate the merits of the issue.

REGULATION T the Federal Reserve Bank's regulation governing the amount of credit that may be advanced by brokers and dealers to customers for the purchase of securities. *See also* INITIAL MARGIN; MARGIN BUYING.

REGULATION U the federal regulation governing the amount of credit that may be advanced by a bank to its customers for the purchase of securities.

REHABILITATION TAX CREDIT special tax incentive given for the continued use and rehabilitation of historical buildings and old structures in an effort to arrest urban decay. Developers receive a credit based upon a percentage of the cost they incur rehabilitating these structures.

REINSURANCE agreement in which one insurer indemnifies another insurer for all or part of the risk of a policy originally issued and assumed by that other insurer.

REIT *see* REAL ESTATE INVESTMENT TRUST (REIT).

RELATED PARTY TRANSACTION interaction between two parties, one of whom can exercise control or significant influence over the operating policies of the other. A *special relationship* may exist, for example, between a business enterprise and its principal owners. In related party situations, the following footnote disclosures are required: (1) nature of the relationship; (2) description of the transaction including amounts; (3) amounts due from, or to, related parties at year-end; (4) the effects of any change in terms; and (5) manner of settlement. Even though no transactions occurred between related parties in the current year, disclosure of the nature of the control relationship is still required.

RELATIONAL DATA BASE data base consisting of relationships between data items.

RELATIVE FREQUENCY OF OCCURRENCE proportion of times that an event occurs in the long run when the conditions are stable, or the observed relative frequency of an event in a very large number of trials. For example, suppose that an accounts receivable manager knows from past data that about 70 of 1,000 accounts usually become uncollectible after 120 days. The manager would estimate the probability of bad debts as 70/1000 = .07 or 7%.

RELATIVE SALES VALUE METHOD manner of allocating JOINT COSTS in proportion to relative sales values of joint products. For example, joint products X and Y have a joint cost of $1,200 and X sells for $70 while Y sells for $50. Then X would be allocated $1,200 × ($70/$120) = $700 of the joint cost while Y would be allocated $1,200 × ($50/$120) = $500 of the cost.

RELEVANCE item that is capable of making a difference in decision-making. Information is available in a *timely* fashion before it loses its value in decision-making. Data have *predictive value* about outcomes past, present, and future. Information has *feedback value* that provides information about earlier expectations.

RELEVANT COST APPROACH *see* INCREMENTAL ANALYSIS.

RELEVANT COSTS expected future costs that differ from the alternatives being considered. SUNK COSTS are *not* relevant to the decision at hand, because they are historical costs. *Incremental* or *differential* costs are *relevant* because they are the ones that differ from the alternatives. Since not all costs are of equal importance, managers must identify those that are relevant to a decision. For example, in a decision on whether to replace an existing business with a new one, the cost to be paid for the new venture is relevant. However, the initial cost of the old business is not relevant because it is a sunk cost. *See also* INCREMENTAL ANALYSIS.

RELEVANT RANGE span of activity over which a certain cost behavior holds true. It is risky to extrapolate beyond the relevant range because there are no observations outside the range. For example, fixed costs will not change only for a specified range of volume of activity, called the relevant range. Beyond this, fixed costs are not constant. BREAK-EVEN ANALYSIS and analysis of MIXED COSTS are most useful only in this range of activity—that is, the volume zone in which the behavior of variable costs, fixed costs, and selling prices can be predicted with reasonable accuracy.

RELIABILITY
1. in auditing, confidence that the financial records have been properly prepared and that accounting procedures and internal controls are correctly functioning.
2. in financial accounting theory, term describing information that is reasonably free from error and bias and accurately presents the facts. *Verifiability* exists when a reconstruction of financial data, following acceptable accounting practices, results in the same actual results previously attained; further, two accountants working independently will come up with similar results. *Representational faithfulness* exists when there is agreement between a portrayal (description) and the item it is supposed to represent (validity). Information is *neutral* when it does not favor one company over another. *See also* VERIFIABLE.
3. probability that a product or process will perform satisfactorily over a period of time under specified operating conditions.

REMOTE JOB ENTRY SYSTEM one commonly found in ONLINE PROCESSING. Online computer processing can be used for BATCH PROCESSING or can be *real time*. When it is used for batch processing, it is generally referred to as real batch processing, or remote job entry.

RENT EXPENSE cost to lease an item of property. The rental charge incurred by the lessee may be based on time and/or some other factor (e.g., sales). It is shown in the income statement as an operating expense.

REORDER POINT inventory level at which it is appropriate to replenish stock. The calculation is as follows:

Reorder Point =
    Average Usage Per Unit of Lead Time × Lead Time + SAFETY STOCK

First, multiply average daily (or weekly) usage by the lead time in days (or weeks) yielding the lead time demand. Then add safety stock to this to provide for the variation in lead time demand to determine the reorder point. If average usage and lead time are both certain, no safety stock is necessary and should be dropped from the formula.

See also ECONOMIC ORDER QUANTITY (EOQ) MODEL.

REORGANIZATION process of restating company assets to reflect current market value and restating the financial structure downward to reflect reductions on the asset side of the balance sheet. A financially troubled firm usually goes through reorganization. Under a reorganization, the firm continues in existence. Chapter 11 of the BANKRUPTCY law provides for reorganization. Chapter 7 provides for LIQUIDATION.

REPETITIVE MANUFACTURING manufacture of identical products (or a family of products) in a continuous flow.

REPLACEMENT COST
1. CURRENT COST to replace the service potential of an existing asset. Emphasis is placed on obtaining an asset with identical future service capabilities.
2. current cost to replace property in a particular geographic area.

REPLACEMENT COST ACCOUNTING valuing assets and liabilities, at their cost to replace. It is a departure from historical cost accounting. The effect of inflationary changes on items bought and sold is considered. Holding gains and losses arise from a change between the historical cost and the replacement cost. *See also* CURRENT VALUE ACCOUNTING; GENERAL PRICE LEVEL ACCOUNTING.

REPLACEMENT METHOD OF DEPRECIATION method in which the current depreciation expense amount, usually determined by the STRAIGHT-LINE DEPRECIATION method, is augmented by a percentage derived from a comparison of the anticipated replacement cost of a depreciable asset with its original cost. This method requires an estimate to be made of the anticipated replacement cost.

REPLICATION duplicating methods or processes to gather data to confirm or deny a standing assumption or set of circumstances. Results may be replicated if such methods are employed independently and these results are verified under similar conditions, thus providing two independent checks upon the data gathered and their implied assumptions. An example is when two accountants independently add the total of daily cash receipts and find agreement.

REPORT FORM
1. format of an income statement that reads from top to bottom. It begins with sales or revenues at the top leading to net income at the bottom, with significant totals in between. *See also* FORM OF BALANCE SHEET.
2. auditor's report format, either in short or long form.

REPORT FORM OF BALANCE SHEET *see* FORM OF BALANCE SHEET.

REPORTING periodically furnishing others with financial information to aid in control or decision making. In internal reporting, the internal auditor may provide management with an analysis of operations and internal controls within the company. In external reporting, the CPA may render an audit opinion on the financial statements of a client includable in the annual report and Securities and Exchange Commission filings.

REPORTING CURRENCY currency in which a company prepares its financial statements, i.e., U.S. dollars for a U.S. company. *See also* FUNCTIONAL CURRENCY.

REPORT RELEASE DATE the date on which an auditor gives permission to a client to use the auditor's report on the financial statements. The report release date typically follows the date of the audit report and serves as the starting point for retention of audit documentation. *See also* RETENTION PERIOD.

REPRESENTATION LETTER written confirmation from management to the auditor about the fairness of various financial statement elements. The purpose of the letter is to emphasize that the financial statements are management's representations, and thus management has the primary responsibility for their accuracy. Also, the letter provides supplementary audit evidence of an internal nature by giving formal management replies to auditor questions regarding matters that did not come to the auditor's attention in performing audit procedures. Some auditors request written representations of all financial statement items. All auditors require representations regarding receivables, inventories, plant and equipment, liabilities, and subsequent events. Frequently, all these representations are included in one letter. The letter is required at the completion of the audit fieldwork and prior to issuance of the financial statements with the auditor's opinion. Management acknowledges its responsibilities for running the company, the adequacy of financial policies employed, confirmation of practices observed during the audit, and confirmation to the auditor that management has made full disclosure of all material activities and transactions in its financial records and statements.

REPRESENTATIVE SAMPLE random sample that is a good indicator of the accuracy of the items in a population. The sample may or may not have a determinable error.

REPRODUCTION COST current cost to replace an asset with an *identical* asset. Typically, there is an allowance for depreciation.

REQUIRED MINIMUM DISTRIBUTION (RMD) the minimum amount that must be withdrawn annually from a retirement plan starting with the year in which the account owner reaches 70½ years of age or, if later, the year in which the account owner retires. RMDs must begin once the account holder is age 70½, regardless of whether he or she is retired, in the case of an IRA or a retirement plan in which the account owner is a 5% owner of the business sponsoring the plan. The RMD rules do not apply to Roth IRAs during the lifetime of the owner.

REQUISITION written request within an organization for a particular service or good. It typically is issued from one department to another. An example is a request form that must be filled out for office supplies to be released by the storeroom.

RESEARCH AND DEVELOPMENT (R&D) COSTS expenditures incurred to discover new knowledge and to develop that knowledge into a design for a new product. R&D costs are usually *expensed* as incurred. However, the following two classes of costs have future use in R&D activities and are capitalized: (1) materials and equipment and (2) intangibles purchased from others. The costs of such assets used or consumed (depreciated) are expensed as R&D costs. Note that R&D costs incurred for others under contract are capitalized.

Costs of computer software to be sold, leased, or otherwise marketed should be charged to expense as R&D costs until technological feasibility has been established through completion of either a detailed program or a working model. When technological feasibility has been established, all software production costs are capitalized and subsequently reported at the lower of unamortized cost or net realizable value. Amortization will start when the product is available for general release to customers. Periodic amortization should be the greater of: (1) the ratio of current revenue to the total current and anticipated future gross revenues from the product or (2) the straight-line method over the remaining economic life of the property.

RESEARCH AND DEVELOPMENT (R&D) TAX CREDIT provision of the tax law under which companies can deduct 20% of "increased" qualified expenditures for researching and developing new products. The tax credit reduces taxes due on a dollar-for-dollar basis. The "increased" amount equals the current year R&D expenditure less the average R&D expenditure over the last three years. Assume R&D in 2015 is $250,000. In the prior years, R&D costs were $150,000 in 2012, $225,000 in 2013, and $210,000 in 2014. The average is thus $195,000. Therefore, the credit equals:

Current year R&D	$250,000
Average 3-year R&D	195,000
"Increased" R&D	55,000
Tax credit percent	× .20
Tax credit	$ 11,000

The credit significantly aids research-oriented, high-technology businesses. *Excluded* from "qualified" R&D expenses as a basis for the tax credit are efficiency studies, trial production runs, market tests, and management studies. "Qualified" R&D have to be of a technological nature, involve experimentation, and aid in a new or improved product or process.

RESERVE
1. appropriation of retained earnings for a designated purpose, such as plant expansion or a bond sinking fund. The purpose of the reserve is to tell stockholders and creditors that part of retained earnings is unavailable for dividends.
2. accrued liability, such as reserve for taxes (outdated usage).
3. contra account to the gross cost of an asset to arrive at the net amount, such as reserve for depreciation or reserve for bad debts. In this use, the term *reserve* is outdated; *accumulated depreciation* and *allowance for bad debts* are used instead.

RESERVE FOR CONTINGENCIES appropriated retained earnings for general unspecified contingencies such as possible damage due to Acts of God.

RESERVE FOR ENCUMBRANCES in GOVERNMENT ACCOUNTING, account reflecting part of the fund balance that has been committed by a contract, purchase order, salary agreement, travel claim, etc. Therefore, reserve for encumbrances represents a reservation of the fund's equity. Entries for this account occur when an ENCUMBRANCE comes into being and when the actual expenditure is later made.

RESERVE FOR RETIREMENT OF PREFERRED STOCK appropriation of RETAINED EARNINGS that has the effect of restricting common dividend declarations. This provides for the gradual reacquisition and cancellation of an organization's PREFERRED STOCK. Upon complete retirement of the preferred stock, the account maintained for preferred stock will cease to exist. Any excess of retirement premium not fully absorbed by the PAID-IN CAPITAL accounts will necessitate a charge to retained earnings. The remaining amount of appropriated retained earnings, if any, constitutes the residual retirement reserve, which is closed to unrestricted retained earnings. The implementation of a reserve is not a necessary action to ensure that the reacquisition of preferred stock will take place. In fact, in a well-run organization this may well be unnecessary. Rather, it serves as a device to allay fears of security holders that liquid assets will be depleted through dividend distributions.

RESERVE RECOGNITION ACCOUNTING (RRA) procedural attempt by the SEC to improve the reporting practices of oil and gas companies' valuations of natural resource reserves. Supplemental income statements are required that must exhibit the discounted value of new proven reserves discovered during the year and previously discovered reserves. The SEC specifies the use of a 10% discount rate, which among other difficulties (such as the definition of "proven," estimations of reserve quantities, projected selling prices, and inclusion of foreign reserves with foreign co-ownership), provides a somewhat arbitrary method of accounting for reserves. *See also* DISCOVERY VALUE ACCOUNTING.

RESIDUAL synonym for error. It is calculated by subtracting the forecast value from the actual value to give a "residual" or error value for each forecast period.

RESIDUAL EQUITY THEORY theory that common stockholders are considered to be the real owners of the business. The residual equity theory is in part the basis for the EARNINGS PER SHARE (EPS) computation that applies only to common stockholders. The purpose of this approach is to furnish better information for common stockholders in making investment decisions and in predicting possible future dividends. The theory lies between the PROPRIETARY THEORY and the ENTITY THEORY. Under it, the accounting equation is:

$$\text{Assets} - \text{Liabilities} - \text{Preferred Stock} = \text{Common Stock}$$

RESIDUAL INCOME (RI) operating income that an INVESTMENT CENTER is able to earn above some minimum return on its assets. It is a popular alternative performance measure to RETURN ON INVESTMENT (ROI). RI is computed as:

$$\text{RI} = \text{Net Operating Income} - (\text{Minimum Rate of Return on Investment} \times \text{Operating Assets})$$

Residual income, unlike ROI, is an absolute amount of income rather than a rate of return. When RI is used to evaluate divisional performance, the objective is to maximize the total amount of residual income, not to maximize the overall ROI percentage figure. For example, assume that operating assets are $100,000, net operating income is $18,000, and the minimum return on assets is 13%. Residual income is $18,000 − (13% × $100,000) = $18,000 − $13,000 = $5,000. RI is sometimes preferred over ROI as a performance measure because it encourages managers to accept investment opportunities that have rates of return greater than the charge for invested capital. Managers being evaluated using ROI may be reluctant to accept new investments that lower their current ROI, although the investments would be desirable for the entire company. Advantages of using residual income in evaluating divisional performance include: (1) it takes into account the opportunity cost of tying up assets in the division; (2) the minimum rate of return can vary depending on the riskiness of the division; (3) different assets can be required to earn different returns depending on their risk: (4) the same asset may be required to earn the same return regardless of the division it is in; and (5) the effect of maximizing dollars rather than a percentage leads to GOAL CONGRUENCE.

RESIDUAL TERM *see* ERROR TERM.

RESIDUAL VALUE
  1. value of leased property at the end of the lease term.
  2. at any time, the actual or estimated value (that is, proceeds minus disposal costs) of an asset, also called SALVAGE VALUE or SCRAP VALUE.
  3. value of a depreciable asset after all allowable depreciation has been taken.

RESOURCE COST ASSIGNMENT process by which cost is attached to activities. The process requires the assignment of cost from general ledger accounts to activities using resource drivers. For example, the chart of accounts may list information services at a plant level. It then becomes necessary to trace (assuming that tracing is practical), or to allocate (when tracing is not practical), the cost of information services to the activities that benefit from the information services by means of appropriate resource drivers. It may be necessary to set up intermediate activity cost pools to accumulate related costs from various resources before the assignment can be made. *See also* ACTIVITY COST POOL; RESOURCE COST DRIVER.

RESOURCE COST DRIVER best single measure of the quantity of resources consumed by an activity. An example of a resource cost driver is the percentage of total square feet occupied by an activity. This factor is used to allocate a portion of the cost of operating the facilities to the activity.

RESOURCE COSTS costs of economic elements or inputs used to perform activities. They include people's salaries, as well as the cost of materials, supplies, equipment, technologies, and facilities. *See also* COST ELEMENT.

RESPONSIBILITY obligation to perform. In the classical view, this obligation formally comes down from a superior position and is inherent in any job (it has its origins in the rights of private property as defined by the appropriate laws). In the behavioral view, responsibility must and should be delegated; a successive dividing and passing down of obligation occurs. The appropriate amount of authority or power must be delegated with the responsibility. However, a higher position can never rid itself of ultimate responsibility.

RESPONSIBILITY ACCOUNTING collection, summarization, and reporting of financial information about various decision centers (*responsibility centers*) throughout an organization; also called *activity accounting* or *profitability accounting*. It traces costs, revenues, or profits to the individual managers who are primarily responsible for making decisions about the costs, revenues, or profits in question and taking action about them. Responsibility accounting is appropriate where top management has delegated authority to make decisions. The idea behind responsibility accounting is that each manager's performance should be judged by how well he or she manages those items under his or her control. *See also* RESPONSIBILITY CENTER.

RESPONSIBILITY CENTER unit in the organization that has control over costs, revenues, or investment funds. For accounting purposes, responsibility centers are classified as COST CENTERS, REVENUE CENTERS, PROFIT CENTERS, and INVESTMENT CENTERS. A well-designed responsibility accounting system should clearly define *responsibility centers* in order to collect and report revenue and cost information by areas of responsibility.

The following figure illustrates the manners in which responsibility accounting can be used within an organization and highlights profit and cost centers.

RESPONSIBILITY CENTERS

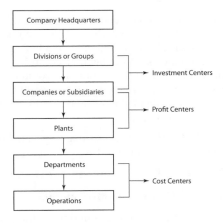

RESPONSIBILITY REPORTING *see* RESPONSIBILITY ACCOUNTING.

RESTATEMENT reiteration or republication of a financial statement or document, such as a balance sheet or income statement, in a manner that incorporates revisions and changes based on accounting principles or policies.

RESTATEMENT OF OVERHEAD RATES approach implemented at the end of the period to calculate the actual overhead rates and then restate every entry involving overhead. The effect is that job-cost records, the inventory accounts, and cost of sales are accurately stated with respect to actual overhead. This means the disposing of overhead variances is costly but has the advantage of improving the analysis of profitability. If a restatement approach is not taken, the treatment of the balance in the overhead account (over- or underapplied overhead) depends on the materiality of the amount. For example, a manufacturer may write off the amount to cost of goods sold if it is not material. If the amount is material, it should be prorated to work-in-process, finished goods, and costs of goods sold on the basis of the currently applied overhead in each of the accounts. An alternative is to prorate the variance based on the total balances in the accounts. The improvements in information technology and decreases in cost have made *restatement of overhead rates* more appealing.

RESTRICTED FUND in not-for-profit accounting, fund whose assets are limited to designated purposes as per donor or grantor request.

RESTRICTED STOCK OPTION offerings provided by employers to executives after 1950 and prior to 1964 that were restricted in the sense that the option price had to be a minimum of 85% of the fair market value of the stock on the grant date. Upon exercising and holding the stock for the required time period, long-term capital gain treatment was available. Income was not recognized on the stock options as of the grant date and was also not recognized at the purchase date by virtue of the lower purchase price. Restricted stock options were subsequently replaced by QUALIFIED STOCK OPTIONS with more rigorous requirements in 1964. However, qualified stock options were eliminated in The Economic Recovery Tax Act of 1981, whereupon the INCENTIVE STOCK OPTION was introduced.

RESTRICTED USE REPORT any auditor's report that is intended only for specified parties. Restricted use reports include reports on subject matter based on measurement criteria specified in contractual agreements or regulatory provisions, communications on internal control-related matters noted in a financial statement audit, and the auditor's communications with those charged with governance. A restricted use report would include a paragraph indicating the report is not intended to be, and should not be, used by anyone other than the specified parties.

RESTRUCTURING CHARGES costs to rearrange facilities and downsize, which are expensed as they are incurred.

RESTRUCTURING OF DEBT *see* DEBT RESTRUCTURING.

RESULT BENCHMARKING *see* BENCHMARKING.

RETAIL INVENTORY METHOD accounting method used for inventory control and formulation of purchasing policy by retail businesses. Both selling price and cost of the inventory are taken into account. A cost/retail ratio is determined that is multiplied by the retail value of the ending inventory to arrive at its cost. The *conventional retail* method approximates the lower of cost or market valuation by the *exclusion of markdowns* and other reductions below original selling price and the *inclusion of markups* in computing the cost/retail ratio. Assume the following: (1) inventory on 1/1/2014 at cost $14,200; (2) inventory on 1/1/2014 at selling price $20,100; (3) purchases at cost $32,600; (4) purchases at selling price $50,000; (5) markups $1,900; (6) markdowns $2,200; and (7) sales $60,000. The computation of conventional retail follows:

	Cost	Retail
Beginning inventory	$14,200	$20,100
Purchases	32,600	50,000
Markups		1,900
Available	$46,800	$72,000
Less: Sales		(60,000)
Markdowns		(2,200)
Inventory at retail		$ 9,800
Cost/retail ratio	46,800/$72,000 = 65%	
Inventory at cost under conventional retail:		
$9,800 × 65%		$ 6,370

Note again that the conventional retail method includes markups but not markdowns in calculating the cost to retail ratio that results in a lower inventory figure. If the retail method was used, markups and markdowns would both be included in calculating the cost/retail ratio, resulting in a higher inventory figure.

RETAINED EARNINGS accumulated earnings of a corporation since inception less dividends. Retained earnings is also net of PRIOR PERIOD ADJUSTMENTS and transfers to paid-in capital accounts. Retained earnings is shown as a separate category within the stockholders' equity section of the balance sheet. It typically has a credit balance; a deficit is unusual. Retained earnings is broken down into the following two types: UNAPPROPRIATED RETAINED EARNINGS and APPROPRIATED RETAINED EARNINGS.

RETAINED EARNINGS STATEMENT accounting form showing the beginning balance of retained earnings, adjustments to it during the year, and ending balance. The retained earnings statement may be presented separately or in a combined statement of income and retained earnings. An illustrative retained earnings statement follows:

Retained Earnings—Unadjusted beginning balance
Plus or Minus: Prior period adjustments
Retained Earnings—Adjusted beginning balance
Plus: Net income
Minus: Dividends
Retained Earnings—Ending balance

RETENTION PERIOD the period of time for which an auditor is required to keep audit documentation. In the case of an audit of a nonissuer, audit documentation should be retained for a period of five years from the report release date; the retention period is extended to seven years in the case of an audit of an issuer.

RETIREMENT
1. removal of a fixed asset from operative service with the appropriate adjustments to the fixed asset and accumulated depreciation accounts. Retirement may be due to a variety of reasons such as the asset having reached the end of its useful life or it having been disposed of by sale.
2. repayment of a debt.
3. cancellation of reacquired shares of stock or bonds by a corporation.
   See also REDEMPTION; TREASURY STOCK.
4. permanent withdrawal of an employee from employment.

RETIREMENT METHOD OF DEPRECIATION manner of fixed asset accounting under which no depreciation expense entry is recorded until the asset is retired from service. At retirement, depreciation expense is debited and the asset account for the retired asset is credited. If the asset has salvage value, the debit to depreciation expense is reduced by this amount and there is a corresponding debit to cash, receivables, or salvage. This method, once popular among public utilities, is now largely discarded.

RETIREMENT OF DEBT elimination of a debt obligation through repayment, conversion, or refunding. *See also* EARLY EXTINGUISHMENT OF DEBT.

RETROACTIVE ADJUSTMENT
1. restatement of prior years' financial statements to show financial data on a comparable basis, such as in the case of a CHANGE IN REPORTING ENTITY.
2. PRIOR PERIOD ADJUSTMENT. Retroactive pension benefits should not he recognized as pension expense in the year of adoption or amendment to a pension plan but should be recognized during the service periods of those employees who are expected to receive benefits under the plan. The cost of this retroactive adjustment benefit is the increase in the projected benefit obligation at the amendment date.

RETROACTIVE APPLICATION the application of a different accounting principle to prior accounting periods as if that principle had always been used or as the adjustment of previously issued financial statements to reflect a change in the reporting entity.

RETURN ON ASSETS net income divided by average total assets. Used to measure the amount earned on each dollar of assets invested. A measure of overall earning power or profitability.

RETURN ON ASSETS PRICING pricing method in which the objective of price determination is to earn a profit equal to a specific rate of return on assets employed in the operation.

RETURN ON EQUITY a measure of the returns earned on the owners' (both preferred and common stockholders') investment. The return on equity (ROE) is calculated as:

$$\text{ROE} = \frac{\text{Net profit after taxes}}{\text{Stockholders' equity}} = \frac{\text{Net profit after taxes}}{\text{Total assets}} \times \frac{\text{Total assets}}{\text{Stockholders' equity}}$$

$$= \text{ROI} \times \text{Equity multiplier}$$

ROE measures the returns earned on the owners' (both preferred and common stockholders') investment. The use of the equity multiplier to convert the ROI to the ROE reflects the impact of the leverage (use of debt) on the stockholders' return.

$$\text{The equity multiplier} = \frac{\text{Total assets}}{\text{Stockholders' equity}}$$

$$= \frac{\text{Total assets}}{\text{Total assets} - \text{Total liabilities}}$$

$$= \cfrac{1}{1 - \cfrac{\text{Total liabilities}}{\text{Total assets}}}$$

$$= \frac{1}{(1 - \text{debt ratio})}$$

For example, XYZ Company presents the following financial data:

Total assets	=	$100,000
Net profit after taxes	=	18,000
Stockholders' equity	=	$45,000

Then,

$$\text{ROI} = \frac{\text{Net profit after taxes}}{\text{Total assets}} = \frac{\$18,000}{\$100,000} = 18\%$$

Then,

$$\text{equity multiplier} = \frac{\text{Total assets}}{\text{Stockholders' equity}} = \frac{\$100,000}{\$45,000} = 2.22$$

$$= \frac{1}{(1 - \text{debt ratio})} = \frac{1}{(1 - 0.55)} = \frac{1}{0.45} = 2.22$$

$$\text{ROE} = \frac{\text{Net profit after taxes}}{\text{Stockholders' equity}} = \frac{\$18,000}{\$45,000} = 40\%$$

ROE = ROI × equity multiplier = 18% × 2.22 = 40%

If the company used only equity, the 18% ROI would equal ROE. However, 55% of the firm's capital is supplied by creditors ($45,000/$100,000 = 45% is the equity-to-asset ratio; $55,000/$100,000 = 55% is the debt ratio). Because the 18% ROI all goes to stockholders, who put up only 45% of the capital, the ROE is higher than 18%. This example indicates that the company was using leverage (debt) favorably.

The following figure shows the relationship among ROI, ROE, and financial leverage.

ROI, ROE, AND FINANCIAL LEVERAGE

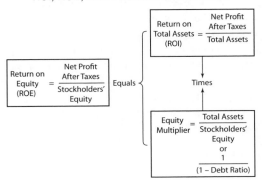

RETURN ON INVESTMENT (ROI) measure of the earning power of assets. The ratio reveals the firm's profitability on its business operations and thus serves to measure management's effectiveness. It equals NET INCOME divided by average total assets; also called *rate earned on total assets*. Other versions of ROI exist, such as net income before interest and taxes divided by average total assets. Return on investment is a commonly used measure to evaluate divisional performance. *See also* RESIDUAL INCOME.

RETURN ON PENSION PLAN ASSETS deduction in arriving at pension expense. Plan assets (i.e., STOCKS, BONDS, REAL ESTATE) are valued at the MOVING AVERAGE of asset values over a time period. Plan assets include employer and employee contributions. Pension assets have to be segregated in a TRUST or restricted to be deemed plan assets.

REVALUATION SURPLUS valuation equity account that is adjusted to a higher level, caused by an upward appraisal of capital assets and a resultant increase in the carrying value of such assets.

REVENUE
1. increase in the assets of an organization or the decrease in liabilities during an accounting period, primarily from the organization's operating activities. This may include sales of products (SALES), rendering of services (*revenues*), and earnings from interest, dividends, lease income, and royalties.
2. in GOVERNMENT ACCOUNTING, the gross receipts and receivables from taxes, customs, etc., without consideration of appropriations and allotments.

REVENUE ANTICIPATION NOTE term for note issued by a municipality in expectation of future revenues to be received from given sources such as sales taxes. Once funds are obtained from the particular sources, the note is paid off. *See also* TAX ANTICIPATION NOTE (TAN).

REVENUE BONDS debt whose principal and interest are payable exclusively from earnings of the project built with proceeds, such as a stadium, toll bridge, hospital or other enterprise. Revenue bonds are issued normally by municipalities. In addition to a pledge of revenues, such bonds sometimes contain a mortgage on the enterprise's property and then are known as mortgage revenue bonds.

REVENUE CENTER unit within an organization that is responsible for generating revenues. A revenue center is a PROFIT CENTER since for all practical purposes there is no revenue center that does not incur some costs during the course of generating revenues. A favorable variance occurs when actual revenue exceeds expected revenue.

REVENUE EXPENDITURE outlay benefitting *only* the current year. It is treated as an expense to be matched against revenue. An example is a tune-up of a car that has a period of benefit of one year or less. Repairs expense is charged. *See also* CAPITAL EXPENDITURE; MATCHING.

REVENUE RECOGNITION process of recording revenue, under one of the various methods, in the accounting period. In the period of revenue recognition, related expenses should be matched to revenue. The most often used method of recognizing revenue is at the time of sale or rendering of service. The cash basis of revenue recognition is also popular among service businesses. Other methods of revenue recognition include during production and at the completion of production. *See also* COMPLETED CONTRACT METHOD; INSTALLMENT (SALES) METHOD; PERCENTAGE-OF-COMPLETION METHOD; REALIZATION.

REVENUE RULING rule published by the INTERNAL REVENUE SERVICE (IRS) giving taxpayers guidance in the preparation of their tax returns. A revenue ruling provides an official interpretation of the tax law related to a particular type of transaction.

REVERSE STOCK SPLIT a stock split that reduces, rather than increases, the number of shares of stock outstanding, and effectively increases the par value of each share.

REVERSING ENTRY bookkeeping technique in which adjusting entries involving subsequent receipts or payments are literally reversed on the first day of the following accounting period. This procedure permits the routine recording of subsequent related receipts and payments without having to recognize the portions that were accrued at an earlier date.

REVIEW accounting service providing some assurance to the Board of Directors and interested parties as to the reliability of financial data without the CPA conducting an examination in accordance with generally accepted auditing standards. The AICPA Auditing Standards Board formulates review standards for public companies while the AICPA Accounting and Review Services Committee provides review standards for nonpublic businesses. A review consists primarily of inquiry and ANALYTICAL PROCEDURES. It is *not* an audit nor does it furnish a basis for an opinion since there is no gathering of audit evidence. The review program includes reading minutes of meetings, reading interim financial information to see whether it conforms to GAAP, and obtaining management's written representations as to its responsibility for the information provided. The accountant's report should include: (1) a statement that the review is conducted in accord with appropriate standards for reviews; (2) identification of the interim data reviewed; (3) description of the procedures followed; (4) a statement that a review is much less in scope than an audit in conformity with GENERALLY ACCEPTED AUDITING STANDARDS (GAAS); (5) a statement as to whether material modifications exist to make the information conform with GAAP; and (6) a statement that financial statement information is the representation of management. In a review of financial statements of nonpublic businesses, the objective is to give limited assurance that no significant modifications to the financial statements are needed to make them conform with GAAP. Procedures of a corroborative nature are not necessary. Work should be documented in the working papers indicating the disposition of unusual items. A report should not be issued if the accountant is unable to conduct an appropriate review. If the CPA finds a departure from GAAP in performing the review, the financial statements should be modified. If they are not modified, the CPA should state in the review report the departure and its financial statement effect. *See also* COMPILATION.

REVOLVING FUND account that is repeatedly expended, replenished, and then expended again. An *imprest petty-cash fund* is an example. Vouchers are paid daily and the petty-cash fund is usually replenished at the end of each month.

RIGHT

1. moral or legal claim. An example is the right of a common stockholder to vote in a corporate election.

2. privilege to subscribe to new stock issues. One right attached to existing shares may provide the opportunity to purchase a fractional share or particular number of shares of a new capital stock issue. A PREEMPTIVE RIGHT allows a shareholder the opportunity of maintaining a proportionate share of the enterprise by subscribing to an appropriate amount of newly issued shares. *See also* RIGHTS OFFERING.

RIGHT-HAND SIDE

1. amount of resources or capacities available to a firm for a given period, appearing on the right-hand side of a LINEAR PROGRAMMING (LP) problem.

2. right-hand side of the balance sheet that covers LIABILITIES and STOCK-HOLDERS' EQUITY.

RIGHT OF RETURN option of purchaser to give goods back to the seller for full credit. The buyer's right to return merchandise precludes revenue recognition by the seller at the time of sale unless all of the following conditions are met: (1) selling price is determinable; (2) buyer's obligation to pay is not contingent on resale of the product; (3) buyer must pay for item if lost; (4) acquisition by buyer has economic substance; (5) future performance by seller is not required for resale by buyer; and (6) future returns may be reasonably estimated. If these conditions are not satisfied, revenue and related expenses must be deferred until the conditions are met or the right of return has expired.

RIGHTS AND OBLIGATIONS an assertion in an entity's financial statements made by management that (1) the entity has legal title to recorded assets, and (2) recorded liabilities represent legal obligations to be paid.

RIGHTS OFFERING issue of rights to current stockholders to buy new common shares in the company at a specified subscription price that is less than what the offering price to the public will be. It enables existing stockholders to maintain their proportionate ownership in the company when the new issues are made, called PREEMPTIVE RIGHTS.

RISK

1. state in which each alternative leads to one of a set of specific outcomes, each outcome occurring with a probability that is known to a decision maker.

2. variation in earnings, sales, or other financial variable.

3. probability of a financial problem affecting the company's operational performance or financial position, such as economic risk, political uncertainties, and industry problems. *See also* UNCERTAINTY.

RISK ADJUSTED DISCOUNT RATE riskless rate plus a risk premium. It is a rate adjusted upward as the investment becomes riskier. By increasing the discount rate from 10% to 15%, for example, the expected flow from the investment must be relatively larger or the increased discount rate will generate a negative NPV, and the proposed acquisition/investment will be rejected. Although difficult to apply in extreme cases, this technique has much intuitive value.

RISK ANALYSIS process of measuring and analyzing the RISK associated with financial and investment decisions. Risk refers to the variability of expected returns (earnings or cash flows). Statistics such as STANDARD DEVIATION and COEFFICIENT OF VARIATION are used to measure various risks. BETA coefficient is used to measure a stock's relative volatility in relation to the market and to analyze a portfolio risk. *Risk analysis* is important in making capital investment decisions because of the large amount of capital involved and the long-term nature of the investments being considered. The higher the risk associated with a proposed project, the greater the return that must be earned to compensate for that risk. There are several methods for the analysis of risk, including: *risk-adjusted discount rate*, CERTAINTY EQUIVALENT, MONTE CARLO SIMULATION, SENSITIVITY ANALYSIS, and DECISION TREES.

RISK ASSESSMENT the component of INTERNAL CONTROL concerned with the identification and analysis of the risks that management may not achieve its objectives. Management is responsible for performing risk assessment.

RISK ASSESSMENT PROCEDURES the procedures performed during an audit to obtain an understanding of the entity and its environment, including its INTERNAL CONTROL. Risk assessment procedures, which include inquiries and analytical procedures (e.g., ratio analysis), enable an auditor to identify changes from the prior period that might represent the risk of material financial statement misstatement. The performance of risk assessment procedures is mandatory in a financial statement audit.

RISK MANAGEMENT
1. the analysis of and planning for potential risks and their subsequent losses. The objective of risk management is to try to minimize the financial consequence of random losses.
2. the business activity that assesses the risks a company is faced with and a plan for the potential coverage or payment of those risks.

RISK MEASURES quantitative measures of risk. They attempt to assess the degree of variation or uncertainty about earnings or return. There are several measures, including the standard deviation, coefficient of variation, and beta. The standard deviation is a statistical measure of dispersion of the probability distribution of possible returns. The smaller the deviation, the tighter the distribution and, thus, the lower the riskiness of the investment. One must be careful in using the standard deviation to compare risk since it is only an absolute measure of dispersion (risk) and does not consider the dispersion of outcomes in relationship to an expected return. In comparisons of securities with differing expected returns, we commonly use the *coefficient of variation*. The coefficient of variation (CV) is computed simply by dividing the standard deviation for a security by its expected value. The higher the coefficient, the more risky the security. Beta measures a stock's or mutual fund's volatility relative to the general market.

RISK OF ASSESSING CONTROL RISK TOO HIGH in audit sampling, the chance, when performing a test of controls, that a sample indicates a higher rate of deviation from a prescribed control than the true deviation rate in the population. Since this may result in the performance of unnecessary additional substantive procedures, risk of assessing control risk too high relates to the inefficiency of the audit.

RISK OF ASSESSING CONTROL RISK TOO LOW in audit sampling, the chance, when performing a test of controls, that a sample indicates a lower rate of deviation from a prescribed control than the true deviation rate in the population. Since this may result in a reduction of substantive procedures, the auditor might ultimately express an incorrect opinion on the financial statement presentation. Accordingly, risk of assessing control risk too low relates to ineffectiveness of the audit.

RISK OF INCORRECT ACCEPTANCE in audit sampling, the chance, when performing a substantive procedure, that a sample indicates no material misstatement in a recorded account balance when in fact it is materially misstated. Ultimately, this could cause an auditor to express an incorrect opinion on the financial statement presentation. Accordingly, risk of incorrect acceptance relates to ineffectiveness of the audit.

RISK OF INCORRECT REJECTION in audit sampling, the chance, when performing a substantive procedure, that a sample indicates material misstatement in a recorded account balance when in fact it is not materially misstated. Since this may result in the performance of unnecessary additional substantive procedures, risk of incorrect rejection relates to the inefficiency of the audit.

RISK OF MATERIAL MISSTATEMENT (RMM) the chance that financial statements may include material misstatement. The risk of material misstatement is a combination of inherent risk and control risk. An auditor is required to assess the risk of material misstatement in every audit. The product of RMM and detection risk is equal to audit risk.

RISK PREMIUM amount by which the required return on an asset or security exceeds the *risk-free rate*, r_f. In terms of the CAPITAL ASSET PRICING MODEL (CAPM), it can be expressed as $b(r_m - r_f)$, where b is the security's BETA coefficient, a measure of SYSTEMATIC RISK, and r_m is the required return on the market portfolio. The risk premium is the additional return required to compensate investors for assuming a given level of risk. The higher this premium, the more risky the security and vice versa.

RISK-RETURN TRADE-OFF the concept that the higher the return or yield, the larger the risk; or vice versa. All financial decisions involve some sort of risk-return trade-off. The greater the risk associated with any financial decision, the greater the return expected from it. Proper assessment and balance of the various risk-return trade-offs available is part of creating a sound financial and investment plan. For example, the less inventory a firm keeps, the higher the expected return (since less of the firm's current assets is tied up). But there is also a greater risk of running out of stock and thus losing potential revenue. In an investment arena, you must compare the expected return from a given investment with the risk associated with it. Generally speaking, the higher the risk undertaken, the more ample the return; conversely, the lower the risk, the more modest the return. In the case of investing in stock, you would demand higher return from a speculative stock to compensate for the higher level of risk. On the other hand, U.S. T-bills have minimal risk so a low return is appropriate. The proper assessment and balance of the various risk-return trade-offs is part of creating a sound investment plan.

The following figure illustrates a risk-return trade-off.

RISK-RETURN TRADE-OFF CHART

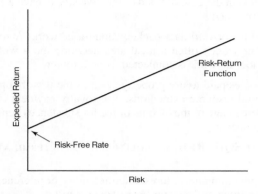

RISK TAKER a person who is not fearful of uncertainty and may even enjoy risky, speculative situations. He or she is a person who will take a chance or gamble in hopes of winning.

ROBINSON-PATMAN ACT legislation that forbids quoting different prices to competing customers unless such price discrimination is justified by differences in costs of manufacturing, sales, or delivery.

ROBUST QUALITY quality control concept, its goal is to reach the target value in every case for the reason that hidden quality costs occur when output varies from the target even though the units are within specifications.

ROLLING FORWARD BUDGET *see* CONTINUOUS BUDGET.

ROLLOVER
1. renewal of a short-term obligation by mutual agreement of debtor and creditor. This short-term debt appears under current liabilities. Footnote disclosure of the arrangement is made along with major provisions.
2. movement of funds from one investment to another. For example, when a certificate of deposit or bond matures, the funds may be rolled over into another certificate of deposit or bond.

ROM (READ-ONLY MEMORY) computer memory containing instructions that do not need to be altered; the permanent memory of the computer put in by the manufacturers. The computer can read instructions out of ROM, but no data can be stored there.

ROOT CAUSE ANALYSIS identification of the underlying cause(s) of specific areas of deficiency in business processes.

ROTH IRA an IRA to which nondeductible contributions may be made. Earnings on and distributions from a Roth IRA are not taxable. Contributions to a Roth IRA are subject to income limitations, which are adjusted periodically for inflation. The RMD rules do not apply to Roth IRAs during the lifetime of the owner. *See also* REQUIRED MINIMUM DISTRIBUTION (RMD).

ROUND-LOT unit of trading on a securities exchange. For example, a round-lot on the NEW YORK STOCK EXCHANGE (NYSE) is 100 shares of stock or one $1000-face-value bond (although brokers may have their own higher round-lot requirements in the case of bonds). Inactive stocks have a 10-share round-lot. *See also* ODD-LOT.

ROUTER used to forward data packets along a network. A router is used to connect two networks: often a local area network and a wide area/Internet Service Provider network is connected using a router.

ROYALTY monies paid to use property, such as the use of copyrighted materials and natural resource extractions. The royalty payment is usually based upon some percentage of the income or fee for substances generated from the use of such property.

R-**SQUARED (*r*-SQUARED)** *see* COEFFICIENT OF DETERMINATION.

RULE
1. statement governing procedures, interpretations, or inferences belonging to sets of operations or decisions. *See* DECISION RULE.
2. directive, instruction, or order detailing something to be done. Requiring the cash receipts to be counted at the end of the day to assure that the physical cash received agrees with the recorded book amount is an example of rule.

RULE OF 72 a rule of thumb method used to determine how many years it takes to double investment money at a given growth or interest rate. Under the method, dividing the number 72 by the fixed rate of return equals the number of years it takes for annual earnings from the investment to double. That is, $72/r$ (in percent). For example, if you bought a share of ADR yielding an annual return of 25%, the investment will double in less than three years: $72/25 = 2.88$ years. The rule can be reversed, too. For example, if you know that your money doubled in four years, you can divide 72 by 4. You will see that you earned roughly 18% per year.

Note: The Rule of 72 does not work, however, when dealing with extreme numbers. For example, dividing 72 by a 72% return indicates that you expect to double your money in one year. It is not true. It would rather take a 100% return. Furthermore, it is more accurate when dealing with somewhat higher returns to use 76, not 72.

RULE OF 69 very similar to the rule of 72, a rule stating that an amount of money invested at r percent per period will double in $69/r$ (in percent) + .35 periods. For example, if you bought a share of ADR yielding an annual return of 25%, the investment will double in a little over three years. $69/25 + .35 = 2.76 + .35 = 3.11$ years

RULE OFF physical underscoring of a total or amount in a ledger to indicate that it should not be disturbed or altered because it represents a cumulative significant figure. Bookkeepers frequently rule off to indicate the balancing or closing of accounts.

RULINGS official interpretation by the INTERNAL REVENUE SERVICE (IRS) of the tax law as applied to specific situations; also called REVENUE RULING. Unlike a Treasury Department regulation, the IRS interpretation does not have complete authoritative significance and, as such, is more limited in application. Letter rulings of interest to the general public have been published subsequent to 1976 and are available as references to taxpayers.

RUSSELL 2000/3000 two useful indexes of small cap stocks, calculated by Frank Russell Co. of Seattle (www.russell.com). The Russell 2000 consists of smaller capitalization stocks. The Russell 3000 consists of the largest 3,000 publicly traded stocks of U.S. domiciled corporations and includes large, medium, and small capitalization stocks. It represents about 98% of the total capitalization of the New York, American, and NASDAQ markets.

S

SAAS (SECURITY AS A SERVICE) outsourcing of security management to another entity that delivers e-mail, Web, and network protection through the cloud. Outsourcing security provides numerous benefits, including easier administration and automatic updates of the security system. SaaS product vendors include Cisco, McAfee, Symantec, Trend Micro, and VeriSign.

SAFARI Apple Inc.'s default Web browser that is available for Macintosh, iPhone, and iPad devices.

SAFEGUARDING OF ASSETS protecting the firm's assets through a good internal control system. The objective is to guard against loss of assets because of theft, accidental destruction, and errors. Assurance must exist that transactions related to assets have been properly processed and that appropriate physical handling and control over assets exist.

SAFE HARBOR RULE tax provision enacted as part of the Economic Tax Recovery Act of 1981 to guarantee *sale/leaseback* treatment to certain transactions if specific requirements are met. The purpose of this provision was to make it easier for loss companies to "sell" their tax benefits accruing on new asset purchases by entering into sale/leaseback transactions with profitable companies. The intent was to generate an immediate cash flow for such loss companies, rather than deferring the benefits through carryover provisions.

SAFETY MARGIN excess of actual sales over break-even sales. If the break-even point is 3,000 units and actual sales volume is 3,400 units, a safety margin of 400 units exists. Thus sales can decrease by 400 units before the company would incur a loss. *See also* BREAK-EVEN POINT.

SAFETY STOCK extra units of inventory carried as protection against possible stockouts. The safety stock must be carried when the firm is not sure about either the demand for the product or *lead time* or both. In the case where demand is uncertain, safety stock is the difference between the maximum usage and the average usage multiplied by the lead time. For example, assume that a store is faced with an uncertain usage for its baseballs. Lead time is constant at two weeks. Normal weekly usage is 700 dozen but it can go as high as 850 dozen. The store would compute the safety stock as follows:

Maximum weekly usage	850 dozen
Average weekly usage	700
Excess	150
Lead time	× 2 weeks
Safety stock	300 dozen

See also REORDER POINT.

SALARY REDUCTION PLAN *see* 401(K) PLAN.

SALE

1. revenue recognition from the delivery of merchandise or from rendering a service in exchange for consideration. Consideration may be in the form of cash, cash equivalent, or other property. Revenue can be recognized at the time of sale because an exchange has taken place, selling price is determinable, and expenses are known.

2. in retailing, temporary reduction of prices to move inventory and raise cash.

SALE AND LEASEBACK sale of property by the owner to a purchaser who then leases it to the former owner. The net effect of this transaction is similar to a loan to the former owner with the property serving as collateral. Any profit or loss on the sale is deferred and amortized in proportion to the amortization expense on the leased asset if a CAPITAL LEASE, or in proportion to the rental payments if this is an OPERATING LEASE. However, when the fair value of the property at the time of the transaction is less than its book value, a loss will be recognized immediately, up to the amount of the difference between undepreciated cost and fair value.

SALES ALLOWANCE reduction in the selling price of goods because of a particular problem (e.g., breakage, quality deficiency, incorrect quantity). Sales allowance is a deduction from gross sales to arrive at net sales. It is a contra revenue account.

SALES BUDGET operating plan for a period expressed in terms of sales volume and selling prices for each class of product or service. Preparation of a sales budget is the starting point in budgeting since sales volume influences nearly all other items.

SALES DISCOUNT cash given by the seller to the purchaser for early payment of the account due. For example, assume that the credit terms of a sale are 1/10, net/30. This means that if the customer pays in 10 days, 1% off the invoice price is granted. However, the customer must pay for the goods no later than 30 days after the date of sale. Note that if the customer remits after 10 days (but before 30 days), no cash discount is obtained.

Sales discount is subtracted from gross sales in arriving at net sales. It is a contra revenue account.

Another common term of sale is giving a percentage discount when the customer pays within a specified time period after the end of the month (EOM) of sale. An example is a discount of 2% if payment is received within 20 days after the month of sale.

SALES FORECASTING projection or prediction of future sales. It is the foundation for the quantification of the entire business plan and a MASTER (COMPREHENSIVE) BUDGET. Sales forecasts serve as a basis for planning. They are the basis for capacity planning, budgeting, production and inventory planning, manpower planning, and purchasing planning. There are two primary approaches to sales forecasting: qualitative and quantitative. Qualitative approaches include salespeople polls and consumer surveys. Quantitative methods include MOVING AVERAGE, EXPONENTIAL SMOOTHING, TREND ANALYSIS, and REGRESSION ANALYSIS.

SALES JOURNAL special book in which credit sales are recorded. The total columns of the sales journal are posted as a debit to accounts receivable and a credit to sales. Separate columns may exist to classify sales by category (e.g., product line).

SALES MIX relative proportions of the product sold. For example, a company has three products and their respective sales are as follows:

	A	B	C	TOTAL
Sales	$30,000	$60,000	$10,000	$100,000

Then the sales mix ratios for A, B, and C are 30%, 60%, and 10%, respectively.

SALES MIX VARIANCE effect on profit of selling a different proportionate mix of products than had been budgeted. This variance arises when different products have different CONTRIBUTION MARGINS. The sales mix variance shows how well the department has done in terms of selling the more profitable products while the SALES VOLUME VARIANCE measures how well the firm has done in terms of its sales volume.

$$
\begin{matrix} \text{Sales} \\ \text{Mix} \\ \text{Variance} \end{matrix} = \left(\begin{matrix} \text{Actual Sales} \\ \text{at Budgeted} \\ \text{Mix} \end{matrix} - \begin{matrix} \text{Actual Sales} \\ \text{at Actual Mix} \end{matrix} \right) \times \begin{matrix} \text{Budgeted} \\ \text{Contribution} \\ \text{Margin per Unit} \end{matrix}
$$

SALES ORDER a document, essential for effective internal control, that includes the details of an approved customer's order, formatted to meet the needs of the seller. A sales order typically includes the buyer's name and address, a description of the goods ordered, the quantity ordered, and any special terms of the sale.

SALES PRICE VARIANCE difference between actual selling price per unit and the budgeted selling price per unit, multiplied by the actual number of units sold.

Sales Price Variance = (Actual Price − Budgeted Price) × Actual Sales

If the actual price is greater than the budgeted price, a variance is favorable; otherwise, it is unfavorable.
See also SALES VOLUME VARIANCE.

SALES QUANTITY VARIANCE *see* SALES VOLUME VARIANCE.

SALES RETURN merchandise given back to the seller because of defects. Sales returns reduce the seller's gross sales. Sales return is a contra revenue account.

SALES TAX state or local tax based on a percentage of the selling price of the goods or service that the buyer must pay. It is not revenue to the seller, who simply collects it and passes it onto the state or local government. Assume credit sales of $30,000 are made with a sales tax rate of 8%. The entry to record the sale is:

Accounts receivable	32,400	
Sales		30,000
Sales tax payable		2,400

The purchaser cannot deduct sales tax as an itemized deduction.

SALES TYPE LEASE accounting by LESSOR in which one or more of the four criteria required for a CAPITAL LEASE are met and both of the following criteria are satisfied: (1) collectibility of minimum lease payments is predictable and (2) no important uncertainties surround the amount of unreimbursable costs yet to be incurred. A sales type lease gives rise to a manufacturer's or dealer's profit or loss on the assumed sale of the item in the year of lease as well as interest income over the life of the lease. Lease payments receivable is recorded representing the minimum lease payments (net of amounts, if any, including executory costs with any profit thereon) plus the unguaranteed residual value accruing to the benefit of the lessor. The difference between lease payments receivable and the discounted value of the payments is recorded as unearned interest income. The DISCOUNT RATE used to determine the present value of lease payments is the lessor's implicit rate. Assume a sales type lease is entered into on 1/1/2014. Six year-end annual lease payments of $20,000 are to be received. The discount rate is 5%. The present value of an ORDINARY ANNUITY for $n = 6$, $i = 5\%$ is 5.0757. The cost of the leased item is $85,000. Initial direct costs of the lease are $4,000. Appropriate journal entries for 2014 and 2015 follow:

```
1/1/2014
Receivable                        120,000
   Sales                                       101,514
   Unearned Interest Revenue                    18,486
   $20,000 × 5.0757 = 101,514
Cost of Sales                      85,000
   Inventory                                    85,000
Direct Expenses                     4,000
   Cash                                          4,000
12/31/2014
Cash                               20,000
   Receivable                                   20,000
Unearned Interest Revenue           5,076
   Interest Revenue                              5,076
   5% × 101,514 = 5076
12/31/2015
Cash                               20,000
   Receivable                                   20,000
Unearned Interest Revenue           4,330
   Interest Revenue                              4,330
   5% × 86,590 = 4330
```

See also DIRECT FINANCING LEASE.

SALES VOLUME VARIANCE difference between the actual number of units sold and the budgeted number, multiplied by the budgeted selling price per unit; also called *sales quantity variance*.

Sales Price Variance = (Actual Sales − Budgeted Sales) × Budgeted Price

If the actual sales are greater than the budgeted sales, a variance is favorable; otherwise, it is unfavorable. For example, ABC Shops sold 50,000 units of product A for $21 each, in comparison with the budgeted 60,000 units at $22. The sales volume variance is (60,000 − 50,000) × $22 = $220,000. Since the actual sales were lower than the budgeted sales, the sales volume variance is unfavorable. *See also* SALES PRICE VARIANCE.

SALVAGE VALUE expected price for a fixed asset no longer needed in business operations; also called SCRAP VALUE. In determining depreciation expense, salvage value is deducted from cost (except when the double-declining-balance method of accelerated depreciation is used).

SAMPLE selected items in a POPULATION. It is often impossible or impractical to observe a population if it is large. A decision maker relies on a sample of it, then tries to draw conclusions or make inferences about the population.

SAMPLING process of selecting items from a POPULATION to reach a conclusion about the population. For example, counting selected inventory items in performing an audit to verify the total inventory balance. *See also* STATISTICAL SAMPLING.

SAMPLING DISTRIBUTION giving the probability of each possible value of a statistic. It is computed from a sample of n items, for all possible samples of size n from a particular population. For example, compute a statistic such as the mean, standard deviation, and so on, which will vary from sample to sample. In this manner, a distribution is obtained of a statistic that is its sampling distribution.

SAMPLING ERROR difference between the value obtained by sampling and the value that would have been obtained if the entire population had been investigated. The auditor is concerned that sampling error is minimized.

SAMPLING RISK percentage likelihood that a sample result is not representative of the population. An allowance for sampling risk refers to the difference between the achieved upper precision limit (UPL) and the actual sample deviation rate.

SARBANES-OXLEY (SARBOX) ACT (www.sarbanes-oxley.com) wide-ranging U.S. corporate reform legislation, coauthored by the Democrat in charge of the Senate Banking Committee, Paul Sarbanes, and Republican Congressman Michael Oxley. The Act, which became law in July 2002, lays down stringent procedures regarding the accuracy and reliability of corporate disclosures, places restrictions on auditors providing non-audit services, and obliges top executives to verify their accounts personally. Each issuer's annual report must include an internal control report containing an assessment of the effectiveness of the internal control structure and procedures.

SAS *see* STATEMENT ON AUDITING STANDARDS (SAS); STATISTICAL ANALYSIS SYSTEM (SAS).

S_b *see* STANDARD ERROR OF THE REGRESSION COEFFICIENT.

SCALABILITY the ability of a system to expand or contract to meet business needs without modifying the application software. Scalability is achieved by adding or upgrading hardware.

SCAN to read through a document rather hastily. In a *desk-top publishing computer system*, a document can be quickly passed through a *scanner* and subsequently edited on-screen.

SCATTERGRAPH METHOD graphical procedure used to separate a SEMI-VARIABLE EXPENSE (or mixed cost) into the fixed and the variable cost portion. In this method, a semivariable expense is plotted on the vertical axis (or y-axis) and activity measure is plotted on the horizontal axis (or x-axis). Then a *regression* line is fitted by visual inspection of the plotted data, as shown in the following graph. The scattergraph method is relatively easy to use and simple to understand. However, it should be applied with extreme caution, because it does not provide an objective test for assuring that the regression line drawn is the most accurate fit for the underlying observations.

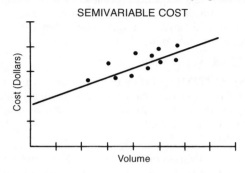

SCHEDULE
1. supporting set of calculations, data, information, or analysis that shows or amplifies how figures in primary statements are derived. An example is a schedule for an aging of accounts.
2. auditor's set of working papers for an audit.
3. to prioritize, arrange, or position with respect to a finite time period.
4. assignment of work to a facility and the specification of the sequence and timing of the work.

SCHEDULE OF EQUIVALENT PRODUCTION process costing schedule in which a period's equivalent units are computed for both material costs and conversion costs.

SCIENTER refers to knowledge or intent of malfeasance (wrongdoing). In order to be guilty of securities fraud under Section 10(b) of the Securities Exchange Act of 1934, a defendant must have acted with scienter.

SCIENTIFIC AMORTIZATION *see* EFFECTIVE INTEREST METHOD.

SCOPE aspects of an audit concerning the procedures employed, the extent of what was done, and the financial items examined.

SCOPE LIMITATION situation that may include client-imposed restrictions upon the audit, restrictions beyond the client's control, or the existence of other conditions precluding necessary auditing procedures. Client-imposed restrictions commonly limit the observation of inventories and the confirmation of accounts receivable. Time elements, geographical distances, and disappearances of evidence may prevent audit observation. All of these limitations in the scope of the audit may hamper the statement of an auditor's unqualified (unmodified) opinion as to the financial state of the enterprise.

SCRAP VALUE sales value of scrap. Scrap is residue from manufacturing operations that has relatively minor recovery value. In accounting for scrap, the sales value of scrap is treated as an offset to factory overhead. However, in some job order situations, the sales value of scrap is credited to the particular job that produced the scrap.

SCRIP DIVIDEND *see* LIABILITY DIVIDEND.

SCROLL movement of the WINDOW up or down relative to the contents of a computer file in order to reach parts not originally seen on the screen.

S_e *see* STANDARD ERROR OF THE ESTIMATE.

SEARCH to seek a particular sequence of characters by working through a file on the screen. It is a function of an *editor*, which is a computer program that enables the user to sit at a terminal or a keyboard, view the contents of a file, SCROLL, add material, or make other changes.

SEARCH ENGINE *see* WEB SEARCH ENGINE.

SEARCH ENGINE OPTIMIZATION (SEO) consists of a set of strategies and techniques to naturally or organically increase the number of visitors to a Web site by obtaining a top ranking in the results of a search engine. SEO techniques ensure that a Web site will be found and indexed by search engines.

SEASONALITY seasonal variation in business or economic activity that takes place on a recurring basis. Seasonality may be caused by various factors, such as weather, vacation, and holidays. In appraising a company's financial statements at a particular time, the accountant or analyst must consider the seasonal effects upon them and make appropriate seasonal adjustments.

SEC EDGAR DATABASE database that contains electronic copies of SEC filings by publicly traded companies (www.edgar-online.com and www. tenkwizard.com).

SECONDARY DISTRIBUTION "off the board" offering of a previously issued security from an investment institution, acting as underwriter or as selling investor, to other members of the exchange on which the security is listed. Sales of this nature are usually block sales. Allowing such a sale to take place on the exchange floor might severely lower the price of the stock. Certain block dispositions require SEC sanction.

SECRET RESERVE *see* HIDDEN RESERVE.

SECTION 404(a) OF SARBANES-OXLEY ACT applicable to all publicly traded entities and requires annual reports filed with the SEC to include a report prepared by management that includes its (1) acknowledgment of its responsibility for establishing and maintaining adequate INTERNAL CONTROL, and (2) assessment about the effectiveness of its internal control.

SECTION 404(b) OF SARBANES-OXLEY ACT applicable to publicly traded entities with a market capitalization in excess of $75,000,000. It requires the independent auditor to audit internal control and express an opinion as to its effectiveness.

SECTION 906 OF THE SARBANES-OXLEY ACT a section that requires the CEO and the CFO to certify each periodic report that includes financial statements. The certification, which is separate from the Section 302 certification, may state that the periodic report fully complies with the requirements of the Securities Exchange Act of 1934 and that "information contained in the periodic report fairly presents, in all material respects, the financial condition and results of operations of the issuer."

SECTION 179 EXPENSE ELECTION an election by a taxpayer to deduct the cost of tangible depreciable personal property used in a trade or business. The deduction under Section 179 is in lieu of depreciating the property. The

Section 179 expense deduction is claimed on Form 4562, and is subject to certain limitations that vary from year to year.

SECTION 302(A) OF THE SARBANES-OXLEY ACT a section that requires a company's CEO and CFO to certify each quarterly and annual report. They are required to certify that the financial statements and other financial information included in the report are fairly presented in all material respects.

SECTION 1250 ASSETS depreciable real property, subject to depreciation recapture upon disposition.

SECTION 1245 ASSETS depreciable personal property, subject to depreciation recapture upon disposition.

SECTION 1231 ASSETS assets used in a trade or business that are held for more than one year and include depreciable tangible and intangible personal property and depreciable and non-depreciable real property (e.g., land).

SECURE SOCKETS LAYER (SSL) a protocol to provide a secure communication channel between two devices operating over the Internet or Intranet. Data is encrypted/decrypted using two keys: a public key and a private key. It is a transparent protocol and does not require much from the end user when establishing a connection; the end user simply establishes a connection using https rather than http.

SECURED LIABILITY obligation secured by a pledge of assets that can be sold, if necessary, to ensure payment.

SECURITIES ACT OF 1933 landmark legislation that provided governmental regulation over the initial issuance of securities. It covered *registration* and disclosure. The Securities Exchange Act of 1934 dealt with the trading of already outstanding securities. It covered enforcement. The regulating body set up to enforce and promulgate regulations, as well as mandate policies and standards within the accounting and auditing disciplines is the SECURITIES AND EXCHANGE COMMISSION (SEC).

SECURITIES AND EXCHANGE COMMISSION (SEC) federal government agency monitoring and regulating corporate financial reporting and disclosure, use of accounting principles, auditing practices, and trading activities. Its ACCOUNTING SERIES RELEASES (ASRS) and STAFF ACCOUNTING BULLETIN (SAB) apply to publicly held companies. SEC requirements promote full disclosure to protect investor interests. For the most part, the SEC follows the accounting and auditing pronouncements of bodies organized by the public accounting profession. It therefore relies on the FINANCIAL ACCOUNTING STANDARDS BOARD (FASB), the *Committee on Auditing Procedure*, and the AUDITING STANDARDS BOARD (ASB).

SECURITIES EXCHANGE ACT OF 1934 *see* SECURITIES ACT OF 1933.

SECURITY
1. financial instrument that shows ownership, such as an equity item (e.g., stock), debt instrument (e.g., bond, note), or right (e.g., option).
2. collateral in support of debt. An example is real estate that serves as security for a bank loan.

SEED MONEY funds put up by venture capitalists to finance a *new* business. Often, seed money involves a loan or investment in preferred stock or convertible bonds. A major purpose of seed money is to form a basis for additional financing to aid in the firm's growth.

SEGMENT functional or responsibility area within a business that can be reported upon separately. The assets, revenue, and earnings of a segment are operationally distinguishable. Examples of business segments are division, department, product line, and geographic area. *See also* SEGMENT REPORTING.

SEGMENTED REPORTING process of reporting activities of various segments of an organization such as divisions, product lines, or sales territories; also called *line of business reporting.* The *contribution approach* is valuable for segmented reporting because it emphasizes cost behavior patterns and controllability of costs. The contribution approach is based on the theses that: (1) fixed costs are much less controllable than variable costs; (2) *direct fixed costs* and *common fixed costs* must be clearly distinguished. Direct fixed costs are those that can be identified directly with a particular segment of an organization, whereas common fixed costs are those that cannot be identified directly with the segment; and (3) common fixed costs should be clearly identified as *unallocated* in the contribution income statement by segments. Any attempt to allocate these types of costs, on some arbitrary basis, to the segments of the organization can destroy the value of responsibility accounting. It would lead to unfair evaluation of performance and misleading managerial decisions.

SEGMENT MARGIN profitability measure used to evaluate the financial performance of a business segment (i.e., division, territory, product line). It equals segmental revenue less related product costs and traceable operating expenses attributable to that segment. In preparing a contribution margin income statement, segment margin equals net revenues less variable manufacturing and selling costs less controllable fixed costs by the segment manager and others. Segment earnings do not include common costs—those costs not logically or practically assigned to the business segment (i.e., president's salary, interest expense).

SEGMENT REPORTING presentation required in the ANNUAL REPORT when a reportable segment meets one or more of the following tests: (1) revenue is 10% or more of combined revenue; (2) operating profit is 10% or more of combined operating profit (operating profit excludes unallocable general corporate revenue and expenses, interest expense, and income taxes); or (3) identifiable assets are 10% or more of the combined identifiable assets; also called *line of business reporting.* FASB Statement No. 131 requires that financial statements include information about operations in different industries, foreign operations, export sales, major customers, and government contracts. The disclosures provide data useful in evaluating a segment's profit potential and riskiness. A significant segment in the past that is expected to be so again should be reported even though it failed the 10% test in the current year. Segments shall represent a substantial portion (at least 75%) of the company's total revenue to unaffiliated customers. As a matter of practicality, however, no more than 10 segments should be shown. While intersegment sales or transfers are eliminated in consolidated financial statements, they are included for purposes of segment disclosure in determining the 10% and 75% rules. The DISCLOSURES are not required for an enterprise that derives 90% or more of its revenues from one industry. The segmental disclosures may be presented in the body of the financial statements, footnotes, or a separate schedule. The disclosure requirements are not applicable to nonpublic companies or in interim reports.

SEGREGATION OF DUTIES internal control concept in which individuals do not have responsibility for incompatible activities. For example, the record-keeping or authorization function should be divorced from the physical custody of the asset to guard against misuse. The person who approves invoices for payment should not be responsible for writing and signing checks. An auditor should note situations where one individual's responsibility extends improperly over related areas, i.e., the person maintaining inventory records has physical possession of the merchandise. Segregation of duties assists in detecting errors and deterring improper activities. The smaller the organization, the more difficult this practice becomes.

SELF-BALANCING term referring to an equality of debits and credits, such as in the case of the general ledger.

SELF-CONSTRUCTED ASSET entity that makes its own asset (e.g., manufactures the asset rather than buying it from outside). Such an asset is recorded at the incremental costs to build (material, labor, and overhead), assuming idle capacity. Fixed overhead is excluded unless it increases because of the construction effort. However, self-constructed assets should not be recorded at an amount exceeding the outside price.

Example: Incremental costs to self-construct equipment are $40,000. The equipment could be bought from outside at $37,000. The journal entry is:

Equipment	37,000	
Loss	3,000	
Cash		40,000

SELF-EMPLOYMENT INCOME net taxable income of a self-employed individual. The income is reported on Schedule C of Form 1040. If there is more than one business, self-employment income is the total earnings of all businesses. A loss in one business is deductible from the profits of another. A self-employed individual pays a higher social security tax than a regular employee.

SELF-EMPLOYMENT TAX paid by self-employed individuals and consists of social security and Medicare taxes. The self-employment tax is based on net earnings from self-employment, as opposed to TAXABLE INCOME.

SELF-INSURANCE coverage borne by the person or company itself against the risk of loss that may occur if property is destroyed or damaged from some cause (e.g., fire). A company that self-insures cannot establish an estimated liability. It can appropriate retained earnings and footnote the nature of the self-insurance.

SELF-LIQUIDATING LOAN seasonal loan that is used to pay for a temporary increase in accounts receivable or inventory. As soon as cash is realized from the assets, the loan is repaid. The borrowed money is used to acquire resources that are combined for later sale, and the proceeds from the sale are used to repay the loan. Most short-term unsecured loans are self-liquidating. This kind of loan is recommended for companies with excellent credit ratings for financing projects that have quick cash flows.

SELLING AND ADMINISTRATIVE EXPENSE BUDGET detailed plan of operating expenses, other than those of the production function, needed to support the sales and overall operations of the organization for a future period.

SELLING EXPENSE cost incurred to sell (e.g., advertising, salesperson commission) or distribute (e.g., FREIGHT-OUT) merchandise. It is one of the types of operating expenses and is a period cost. *See also* GENERAL AND ADMINISTRATIVE EXPENSES.

SELLING GROUP *see* SELLING SYNDICATE.

SELLING SHORT selling securities (or commodities futures contracts) not owned by the seller. The investor (seller) earns a profit when the market price of the security declines, and loses money when the purchase price is higher than the original selling price. To make a short sale, the broker borrows stock and loans it to the investor. Later on, hopefully when the market price is lower, the investor buys the shares to repay the lending broker. Assume an investor sells short 50 shares of stock having a market price of $25, for a total of $1250. The broker borrows the shares and holds onto the proceeds of the short sale to secure the loan and satisfy margin requirements. Later on, the investor buys the stock at $20 a share, repays the 50 shares, earning a per share profit of $5, or a total of $250.

Investors "sell short against the box" when they sell short shares they actually own (*not* borrowed shares). Short sales against the box may occur so that a loss is minimized or the tax consequences of a long sale may be postponed to a subsequent tax year.

SELLING SYNDICATE security dealers or brokers united for the purpose of distributing a new or secondary security issue to the public; also called *selling group*. The group is chosen by a syndicate manager (managing underwriter). This group usually has an established reputation for the disposition of the type of securities to be issued. If the disposition of securities comes under the supervision of the SEC, then the appointment of such a group does not occur until filing and SEC confirmation takes place. A member of the selling syndicate may have to take a position in securities that have not yet been resold to the public.

SELL-OR-PROCESS-FURTHER DECISION short-term, nonroutine decision about whether to sell a product at a particular stage of production or to process it further in the hope of obtaining additional revenue. When two or more products are produced simultaneously from the same input by a joint process, these products are called JOINT PRODUCTS. The term JOINT COSTS is used to describe all the manufacturing costs incurred prior to the point where the joint products are identified as individual products, referred to as the SPLIT-OFF POINT. At the split-off point some of the joint products are in final form and salable to the consumer, whereas others require additional processing. In many cases, the company might have the option to sell the products at the split-off point or process them further for increased revenue. In connection with this type of decision, joint costs are considered irrelevant, since the joint costs have already been incurred at the time of the decision, and therefore are SUNK COSTS. The decision will rely exclusively on additional revenue compared to the additional costs incurred due to further processing.

SEMI-FIXED COST *see* SEMIVARIABLE COST.

SEMIVARIABLE COST one that varies with changes in volume but, unlike a variable cost, does not vary in direct proportion; also called *mixed cost*. In other words, this cost contains both a variable and fixed component. Examples are the rental of a delivery truck, where a fixed rental fee plus a variable charge based on mileage is made; and power costs, where the expense consists of a fixed amount plus a variable charge based on consumption. A further example is a total factory overhead, which is a mixture of fixed overhead and variable overhead.

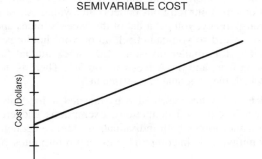

SEMIVARIABLE COST

SENIOR ACCOUNTANT staff accountant, employed by a CPA firm, who supervises a client engagement. Functions performed by the senior accountant include preparing an audit program and the audit of the client's financial statements. A senior accountant is below the manager level.

SENIOR DEBT debt that a company must repay first if it goes out of business. If a company goes out of business, senior debt holders are paid before junior debt holders. It is one of the safest forms of financing from the perspective of the debt holder.

SENIOR SECURITY one that in liquidation has preference over other securities in a company's capital structure. For example, bonds and preferred stock rank ahead of common stock in the distribution of earnings or in liquidation. Note that bonds are senior to preferred stock, which is senior to common stock.

SENSITIVITY ANALYSIS
1. in LINEAR PROGRAMMING (LP), a technique for determining how the optimal solution to a linear programming problem changes if the problem data such as objective function coefficients or right-hand side values change; also called *post-optimality analysis*. To an alert accountant, the optimal solution not only provides answers—given assumptions about resources, capacities, and prices in the problem formulation—but should raise questions about what would happen *if* conditions should change. Some of these changes might be imposed by the environment, such as changes in resource costs and market conditions. Some, however, represent changes that the manager can initiate, such as enlarging capacities or adding new activities.
2. form of SIMULATION that enables decision makers to experiment with decision alternatives using a what-if approach. The manager might wish to

evaluate alternative policies and assumptions about the external environment by asking a series of what-if questions.

SEPARABLE COSTS costs incurred beyond the split-off point and identifiable with specific products.

SEPARATELY MANAGED ACCOUNTS (SMAs) managed accounts with customized investment products in search of a performance edge or just the ability to brag about having a personal money manager. The allure of SMAs stems from their flexibility and transparency. Don't like semiconductor stocks? No problem. Your religious beliefs ban owning "sin stocks"? They're out. As for transparency, you get a list of this week's trades and the Web site address and password so you can check up on your holdings. SMAs can be pricey, especially for smaller investors. U.S. stock mutual funds charge an average 1.4% in fees, and SMA fees can top 3%. There is disagreement on the point at which they become "fee-efficient."

SEPARATE RETURN tax return filed by married individuals who chose to state their own income and deductions, exemptions and credits. A return filed in this manner forces both individuals to itemize deductions. Tax rates are generally unfavorable in comparison to joint return rates. *See also* FILING STATUS.

SEQUENTIAL ACCESS storing of records based upon some sequence determination, such as alphabetic or numeric order. Direct access file processing requires a direct access device such as magnetic disk unit, where retrieval time can be in milliseconds as compared with several seconds or even minutes in a sequential file utilizing a tape unit. A majority of today's computerized information systems that use the direct access method also use sequential processing for some portion of the processing activities in the same information system.

SEQUENTIALITY recognition that activity costs are governed by a logical order that mirrors how work is performed.

SEQUENTIAL METHOD *see* STEP ALLOCATION METHOD.

SERIAL BONDS bonds that mature in installments rather than at one maturity date. They are typically issued by a municipality. Each bond certificate has a given redemption date. *See also* BOND.

SERIAL CORRELATION *see* AUTOCORRELATION.

SERVER computer that houses the LAN operating system as well as shared files and programs.

SERVICE AUDITOR an independent auditor of a service organization's internal controls. A service auditor typically issues one of two types of reports: (1) a Type 1 report, which covers management's description of the service organization's internal controls as well as the suitability of the design of the controls, and (2) a Type 2 report, which covers matters covered in a Type 1 report and the operating effectiveness of the service organization's internal controls. In order to assess control risk at below the maximum level for the internal controls at the service organization, the service auditor should generally obtain a Type 2 report.

SERVICE CENTER *see* SERVICE DEPARTMENT.

SERVICE COST *see* NORMAL PENSION COST.

SERVICE DEPARTMENT responsibility center within a factory that performs a class of service distinct from operating departments of the factory. Examples are purchasing, building and ground personnel, and power departments. All of these activities are necessary parts of the manufacturing process and primarily supportive of production departments. SERVICE DEPARTMENT COSTS must be allocated to production departments before *factory overhead rates* are determined.

SERVICE DEPARTMENT COSTS costs incurred in rendering service to production departments and to other service departments. Service department costs are factory overhead costs. Since the production departments are directly benefitted by service departments, the costs of a service department should be allocated to the appropriate production departments (as part of factory overhead costs).

SERVICE LEVEL percentage of time in which a company can satisfy all orders arriving during the reorder period. It is computed as 1 minus the probability of being out of stock. For example, assume that a company establishes the acceptable probability of being out of stock as 5%. Then the service level is 95%.

SERVICE LIFE time an asset will provide benefit to the business. The depreciation expense calculation requires an estimate of years of usefulness. The service life of an asset may be less than its physical life due to obsolescence or future lack of need.

SERVICE ORGANIZATION an entity that provides processing services to other entities, commonly referred to as user entities. For example, a service organization may process payroll transactions for a user entity.

SERVICE-ORIENTED ARCHITECTURE (SOA) defined by the World Wide Web Consortium (W3C) as "a set of components which can be invoked, and whose interface descriptions can be published and discovered." SOA is an approach to developing software that has its origins in middleware. Middleware is software that allows two or more independent software systems to interact and exchange data. SOA utilizes modular software services to interact within a system, as well as between systems. SOA systems are flexible and capable of expanding or evolving over time.

SERVICE POTENTIAL anticipated future benefits to be obtained from an asset.

SERVICE RATE number of customers or units that can be serviced by one server in a given period of time.

SERVICES useful labor performed by an individual or organization on behalf of others. Doctors, lawyers, interior decorators, etc., provide services for which they are paid by their clients. *See also* GOODS.

SET OF ACCOUNTS group of ledger accounts that a particular firm adopts. Ledger accounts are customarily sequenced and numbered in the order in which they will appear in the financial statements. Listed first are the balance sheet accounts—assets, liabilities, and stockholders' equity, in that order. The income statement accounts—revenue and expenses—follow. Of course, the more complex the operation, the greater the number of ledger accounts required. Each specific account has its own number. A listing of account names and numbers is called the CHART OF ACCOUNTS.

SETTLEMENT DATE time at which a security transaction must be paid by the buyer and the securities delivered by the seller. Stocks and bonds have a settlement date of *three* business days subsequent to the TRADE DATE. Listed options and government securities must be settled by the next business day.

SETTLEMENT IN PENSION PLAN discharge of all or a portion of an employer's pension benefit obligation. Any excess plan assets revert to the company. A settlement must satisfy *all* of the following criteria: (1) it is irrevocable; (2) it relieves responsibility for a pension benefit obligation; and (3) it eliminates significant risk applicable to the obligation. An example is giving a lump-sum payment to employees in exchange for pension rights. There is immediate recognition of the gain or loss arising from the settlement. *See also* CURTAILMENT IN PENSION PLAN; TERMINATION IN PENSION PLANS.

SETUP COST expenses incurred each time a batch is produced. It consists of engineering cost of setting up the production runs or machines, paperwork cost of processing the work order, and ordering cost to provide raw materials for the batch.

SHADOW PRICE maximum price that management is willing to pay for an extra unit of a given limited resource. Management may wish to know whether it pays to add capacity in a particular department. It would be interested in the monetary value to the firm of adding, say, an hour per week of assembly time. This monetary value is usually the additional CONTRIBUTION MARGIN (CM) that could be earned. This amount is the shadow price. A shadow price is, in a way, an OPPORTUNITY COST—the CM that would be lost by not adding an additional hour of capacity. To justify a decision in favor of a short-term capacity decision, the decision maker must be sure that the shadow price exceeds the actual price of that expansion. For example, suppose that the shadow price of an hour of the assembly capacity is $8.75 while the actual market price is $9.50. That means it does not pay to obtain an additional hour of the assembly capacity.

SHARE one unit of ownership interest in a company, mutual fund, limited partnership, etc. For example, the owner of 1000 shares of a company's common stock that has 100,000 shares outstanding has a 1% equity interest.

SHAREHOLDER *see* STOCKHOLDER.

SHAREHOLDERS' EQUITY *see* STOCKHOLDERS' EQUITY.

SHAREPOINT a Microsoft product that allows an entity to create Web sites. SharePoint allows an organization to securely store, organize, share, and access information from any PC, tablet, or smartphone. SharePoint Online is available as a cloud-based service for organizations that do not want to install and deploy SharePoint servers on premises.

SHARPE RATIO *see* SHARPE'S RISK-ADJUSTED RETURN.

SHARPE'S RISK-ADJUSTED RETURN risk-adjusted grades that compare five-year, risk-adjusted return, developed by Nobel Laureate William Sharpe. The fund manager is thus able to view his excess returns per unit of risk. This measure combines standard deviation and mean total return to show a risk-adjusted measure of the fund's performance. The higher this number is, the better. *Note:* As a rule of thumb, a Sharpe ratio of more than 1.00 is pretty good.

SHERMAN ANTITRUST ACT legislation, passed in 1890, after a series of major corporate mergers. It outlaws any form of monopoly. It also outlaws acts or contracts to create monopoly and any attempt to acquire monopoly power. *See also* ANTITRUST LAWS.

SHIPPING DOCUMENT *See* BILL OF LADING.

SHORT ACCOUNT one used in short sales of securities or commodities. The short seller makes a profit if the price of the security or commodity declines because the securities or commodities purchased to repay the lender of the stock or contracts borrowed to cover the short sale have a lower price than that recorded in the sale. *See also* SELLING SHORT.

SHORT FORM MERGER the merger of companies by a simplified procedure in which one company owns 90% of the stock of another.

SHORTAGE COSTS costs incurred when an item is out of stock; also called *stockout costs*. These costs include the lost CONTRIBUTION MARGIN (CM) on sales plus lost customer goodwill.

SHORT-RUN PERFORMANCE MARGIN contribution margin minus controllable (discretionary) fixed costs. Discretionary costs are characterized by uncertainty about the relationship between input (the costs) and the value of the related output. Examples are advertising and research costs.

SHORT SELLING (SALE) a trading technique in which one sells a security he or she does not own (by borrowing it from a broker) and later buying a like amount of the same security. This technique is used to make a profit from a fall in stock price. The rationale behind short selling goes as follows: The simplest way to make money in the stock market is to buy a stock at a low price and sell it later at a higher one. In a short-selling situation, investors are reversing the sequence; they are selling high, promising to buy back the stock later at what they hope will be a lower price. If the stock price falls, they make money. If it rises and they have to buy back their stocks for more than they sold them for, they lose money.

SHORT-TERM DEBT money payable by the debtor to the creditor within one year. It is a current liability. Short-term debt includes the portion of a long-term liability payable within the year.

SHORT-TERM DEBT RATIO calculation of debt payable within one year to total debt. The ratio indicates whether a firm will be able to satisfy its immediate financial obligations. A high ratio points to a lack of liquidity since most of the corporate debt will have to be met in the current year.

SHORT-TERM INVESTMENT funds placed in securities that are expected to be held for one year or less. Examples include *marketable securities*, commodities, money market instruments, and options. The return on short-term investments may come in the form of financial income (i.e., dividend income, interest income) and/or capital appreciation.

SHORT-TERM (SHORT-RUN) DECISIONS decisions usually involving idle capacity, a time period of one year or less during which certain factors of production are fixed and cannot be changed. *See also* NONROUTINE DECI-SIONS; SPECIAL-ORDER DECISIONS.

SHRINKAGE excess of inventory shown on the books over actual quantities on hand. It can result from theft, evaporation, or general wear and tear. *See also* WASTE.

SIGHT DRAFT order signed by the drawer asking the drawee to pay the amount due the payee upon demand. In many cases the drawer and payee are the same. *See also* TIME DRAFT.

SIGNIFICANT important, essential, distinctive, or of sufficient nature to warrant special notice relative to a standard or norm. The deviation may be of such magnitude that its occurrence is probably not due to chance. Significant events often require disclosure in the body or footnote to the financial statements.

SIGNIFICANT DEFICIENCY a deficiency in internal control or a combination of deficiencies in internal control that is less severe than a material weakness, yet is important enough to warrant attention by those charged with governance (in the case of a nonissuer) or those individuals in the client organization having financial statement oversight responsibility (in the case of an issuer). It does not mean that a material misstatement has occurred or that it will occur, but that it could occur. *See also* DEFICIENCY IN INTERNAL CONTROL and MATERIAL WEAKNESS.

SIGNIFICANT TESTING methodology incorporating probability theory to investigate the possible outcomes of events or population parameters to determine whether or not their occurrence is associated with chance. A popular approach entails the use of the null hypothesis (i.e., there is no difference between groups or variables). At a chosen *level of significance* (ALPHA), a sample statistic is compared with the specified population. If there is found to be a difference, the null hypothesis is rejected and the finding is significant at the given alpha level. If the null hypothesis is retained, the relationship is referred to as nonsignificant. *See also* HYPOTHESIS TESTING; T-TEST.

SIMPLE CAPITAL STRUCTURE capital structure having no COMMON STOCK EQUIVALENTS. There are no securities outstanding that are potentially dilutive. *See also* COMPLEX CAPITAL STRUCTURE.

SIMPLE INTEREST computations based only on the original principal. COMPOUND INTEREST is applied to the original principal and accumulated interest. For example, $100 deposited in a savings account at 10% simple interest would yield the interest of $10 *per year* (10% of $100).

SIMPLE RATE OF RETURN measure of profitability obtained by dividing the expected future annual net income by the required investment; also called ACCOUNTING RATE OF RETURN or *unadjusted rate of return*. Sometimes the *average* investment rather than the original initial investment is used as the required investment, which is called *average rate of return*. For example, consider the following investment:

Initial investment	$6,500
Estimated life	20 years
Expected annual net income	$675

Then the simple rate of return is \$675/\$6,500 = 10.4%. Using the average investment, which is usually assumed to be one-half of the original investment, the average rate of return will be doubled as follows:

$$\frac{\$675}{\$6,500/2} = \frac{\$675}{\$3,250} = 20.8\%$$

SIMPLE REGRESSION regression analysis that involves *one* independent variable. For example, total factory overhead is related to one activity variable (either direct labor-hours or machine-hours). Also, the demand for automobiles is a function of its price only. *See also* MULTIPLE REGRESSION ANALYSIS; REGRESSION ANALYSIS.

SIMPLEX METHOD technique most commonly used to solve a LINEAR PROGRAMMING (LP) problem. It is an algorithm, a step-by-step procedure for moving from corner point to corner point of the feasible region in such a manner that successfully larger (smaller) values of the objective function in a maximization (minimization) problem are obtained at each step. The procedure is guaranteed to yield the optimal solution in a finite number of steps.

SIMPLE YIELD return equal to the nominal dollar interest divided by the MARKET VALUE (price) of the bond. It is an approximate, simplified rate reflecting the cost to the debtor and the return to the holder of a debt instrument. The *yield maturity* is a much more accurate measure. Assume a \$100,000, 8%, five-year bond is issued at 93%. The simple yield is:

$$\frac{\text{Nominal Interest}}{\text{Market Value}} = \frac{8\% \times \$10,000}{93\% \times \$10,000} = \frac{\$800}{\$9,300} = 8.6\%$$

See also YIELD TO MATURITY.

SIMPLIFIED EMPLOYEE PENSION (SEP) a type of retirement plan that enables an employer to make deductible contributions on behalf of its employees. Amounts deducted by the employer are excludible from the employee's gross income. Deductible contributions are generally limited to 25% of the employee's compensation and may not exceed the annual defined contribution plan limit. In essence, a SEP is an individual retirement account established by an employer.

SIMULATION attempt to represent a real-life system with a MODEL to determine how a change in one or more variables affects the rest of the system, also called *what-if analysis*. Simulation will not provide optimization except by trial and error. It will provide comparisons of alternative systems or how a particular system works under specified conditions. It is a technique used for what-if scenarios. The advantages of simulation are: (1) when a model has been constructed, it may be used over and over to analyze different kinds of situations; (2) it allows modeling of systems whose solutions are too complex to express by one or several mathematical relationships; (3) it requires a much lower level of mathematical skill than do OPTIMIZATION MODELS.

SIMULATION MODELS what-if models that attempt to simulate the effects of alternative management policies and assumptions about the firm's external environment. They are basically a tool for management's laboratory. It is a detailed representation of the real world. Most financial models are simulation models that are designed primarily for generating projected financial statements, budgets, and special reports, and for performing a variety of what-if analyses in an effort to find the best course of action for the company. Due to technological advances in computers (such as spreadsheets, financial modeling languages, graphics, data base management systems, and networking), more and more companies are building and using modeling for their planning and decision-making efforts. Another version of simulation is MONTE CARLO SIMULATION that is used when a system has a random, or chance, component.

SIMULTANEOUS EQUATION METHOD *see* RECIPROCAL ALLOCATION METHOD.

SINGLE AUDIT ACT OF 1984 consists of uniform audit requirements for state and local governments that are the recipients of federal financial assistance programs. Under the act, an entity is required to undergo a Single Audit (also known as an OMB A-133 audit) if it expends at least $500,000 of federal financial assistance. A single audit is concerned with both financial and compliance aspects.

SINGLE-CHANNEL LINE waiting line with only one server.

SINGLE ENTRY BOOKKEEPING simple bookkeeping system in which transactions are recorded in a single record. An example is a checkbook showing expenditures. For example, an accounts payable listing may represent purchases on account; no journal entries are made or ledgers kept. It is an incomplete form of DOUBLE ENTRY BOOKKEEPING because it does not rely on equal debits and credits. Although financial statements cannot readily be prepared in a single entry system, they are usually derived from inspection or count and comparison of beginning and ending totals. Plugging is usually necessary to derive owner's equity for the balance sheet.

SINGLE-STEP INCOME STATEMENT income statement format that eliminates most intermediate subtotals such as GROSS INCOME and OPERATING INCOME by accumulating and showing first all ordinary revenue and gain items and then all ordinary expense and loss items. Net income is then displayed as their difference plus considerations for discontinued operations and extraordinary gains and losses. *See also* MULTIPLE-STEP INCOME STATEMENT.

SINKING FUND fund set aside for periodic payments, aimed at reducing or amortizing a financial obligation. A bond with a sinking fund provision is an example. The issuer makes periodic payments to the trustee, who can retire part of the issue by purchasing the bonds in the open market. The trustee can invest the cash deposited periodically in the sinking fund in income-producing securities. The objective is to accumulate investments and investment income sufficient to retire the bonds at their maturity. A sinking fund may be established for other purposes such as for plant expansion.

SINKING FUND METHOD OF DEPRECIATION a method of depreciation under which the depreciation expense is an amount of an ANNUITY so that the amount of the annuity at the end of the useful life would equal the ACQUISITION COST of the asset. Theoretically, the depreciation charge should include interest on accumulated depreciation at the beginning of the period. This method is rarely used in practice.

SKIMMING PRICING strategy used when a new product is introduced. It involves setting a high initial price primarily to recoup research and development investments; the price is progressively lowered as time passes and competition sets in. The objective is to maximize short-term profits. *See also* PENETRATION PRICING.

SLACK in PROGRAM EVALUATION AND REVIEW TECHNIQUE (PERT), free time in a network. The slack for an event is the difference between the *latest time (LT)* and the *earliest time (ET)*. It is the length of time an activity can be delayed without interfering with the project completion.

SLACK PATH in PROGRAM EVALUATION AND REVIEW TECHNIQUE (PERT), a path representing a series of activities that require less time than the CRITICAL PATH.

SLIDE error caused by misplacing a decimal point. 35.9750 recorded incorrectly as 3597.50 is an example of a slide.

SLOPE tangent of the angle between a given straight line and the x-axis. It is equal to $(y_2 - y_1) / (x_2 - x_1)$ when (x_1, y_1) and (x_2, y_2) are two distinct points on a nonvertical line. The slope indicates generally the steepness and direction of the line. More specifically, the slope is the change in y for every unit change in x. Slope is a necessary parameter for utilization of LINEAR REGRESSION models. It is b in the COST-VOLUME FORMULA $y = a + bx$.

SMALL BUSINESS CORPORATION
1. under Internal Revenue Code section 1244, corporation that enables shareholders to claim an ordinary loss (rather than a capital loss).
2. SUBCHAPTER S CORPORATION. For legal purposes, an S corporation is no different than other corporations. For tax purposes, however, an S corporation is a PARTNERSHIP. That is, corporate income and losses pass through the shareholders' individual tax returns. To qualify as an S corporation, a company must meet the following requirements: (1) it cannot have more than 100 shareholders; (2) it cannot have more than one class of stock; (3) it cannot have any nonresident foreigners as shareholders; and (4) it must properly elect S corporation status.

SMART CARD small plastic card resembling a credit card with a unique embedment of an integrated circuit of electronic data. It provides security on who uses it, how it is used, and what data are contained or stored on it.

SMARTPHONE a mobile phone offering advanced computer capabilities, such as e-mail and Web access. Most smartphones run on Apple's iOS or Google's Android operating system. Smartphones allow one to install "apps," or application software, to do just about anything from staying organized to playing games.

SMISHING the sending of text messages that trick you into loading viruses onto your cell phone.

SOCIAL ACCOUNTING application of DOUBLE ENTRY BOOKKEEPING system to macro-economic analysis; also called NATIONAL INCOME ACCOUNTING. It is a tool used to measure economic performance of a nation. It is concerned with the determination, estimation, and analysis of such economic welfare factors as national income and GROSS DOMESTIC PRODUCT (GDP). Social accounting also involves such areas as health and education, and their measurement by a double entry system.

SOCIAL AUDIT review of the public-interest, nonprofit, and social activities of a business. These audits usually are performed primarily for internal benefit and typically are not released to the public. The social audit may be performed routinely by internal or external consulting groups, as part of regular internal audits. These evaluations consider social and environmental impacts of business activities.

SOCIAL IMPACT STATEMENT evaluative and detailed report to assess the effect and consequences of the public-interest, nonprofit activities of an entity (such as a corporation, region, or even society) upon an area of specified social concern.

SOCIAL SECURITY TAX levy on employers and employees on a stated percentage of salary charged by the federal government to fund the social security program and other benefits that permit payments to eligible retired persons or their survivors. The social security tax is withheld from the employee's pay, and with the employer's payroll tax share, is remitted to the government periodically. *See also* FEDERAL INSURANCE CONTRIBUTION ACT (FICA).

SOFT LANDING term used to describe the economy slowing enough to eliminate the need for the Fed to further raise interest rates to dampen activity—but not enough to threaten a recession, which is what results when the economy contracts instead of expands. Hard landing, on the hand, could mean a recession.

SOFTWARE computer instructions. A collection of instructions for a particular function is a program. A collection of programs to carry out a specific task is referred to as a package. The term *software* applies to applications programs, specialized system programs, or operating system utilities (which relates to operating the computer system). Software packages are available for many accounting-related applications, including bookkeeping, tax preparation and planning, management advisory services, audit, spreadsheets, database management, preparing formal reports and documents, and practice administration (i.e., time and billing).

SOFTWARE AS A SERVICE business model whereby companies (such as Google, eBay, and Amazon.com) provide services based on their software, rather than providing software as a product (such as Microsoft Office). *See also* WEB 2.0.

SOFTWARE THINKING PROGRAMS computer software used by accountants preparing written reports for clients, including management letters and specialized analyses of operations. Writing skills (e.g., clarity, organization) can be greatly enhanced through the use of thinking software. Idea (outline) programs enable CPAs to create a logical outline from a random set of ideas entered into the microcomputer in nonlogical order. The information is labeled, organized, and structured. A given information set can be a major category, while other pieces are identified as subordinates.

SOLE PROPRIETOR unincorporated business with one owner having all the net worth. In the event the business fails, the owner is *personally* liable for all debts incurred.

SOLID STATE STORAGE DEVICES devices that store data on flash memory. Unlike traditional hard drives, these devices have no moving parts. The data is stored in an array of semiconductor memory using integrated circuits, rather than on magnetic or optical media. Data access time is much faster on solid state storage devices.

SOLVENT condition of a company able to satisfy its debt obligations when due. Various financial ratios can be computed to measure a company's degree of solvency, such as the DEBT-EQUITY RATIO and the INTEREST COVERAGE RATIO. Solvency partly depends on corporate earning power because a company sustaining losses will sooner or later become insolvent. The going-concern assumption lies on the premise of a solvent business. *See also* INSOLVENCY.

SOURCE DOCUMENT basic evidence needed to record an accounting transaction. Journal entries, financial records, and accounting reports are eventually derived from source documents. Examples of source documents are purchase orders, sales invoices, and time cards.

SOURCES OF EVIDENCE supporting documentation, financial records, and written and oral statements from external and internal people to the organization, gathered by the auditor in order to formulate an audit opinion on a company's financial statements.

SPAM a computer term for unwanted e-mail. In a Monty Python television skit, a group of Vikings in a restaurant sing about the meat product, "Spam, spam, spam, spam, spam, spam, spam, spam, lovely spam! Wonderful spam!" until told to shut up. As a result, something that keeps being repeated to great annoyance was called spam, and computer programmers picked up on it.

SPECIAL ASSESSMENT FUND in GOVERNMENT ACCOUNTING, fund used to account for the financing of public improvements or services from the issuance of bonds or assessments levied against the properties benefitted.

SPECIAL AUDIT one with a restricted, narrow scope to conform with a governmental agency's regulatory requirements. *See also* LIMITED AUDIT.

SPECIALIST the work of a specialist may be used in the performance of an audit. A specialist has special knowledge in a field other than accounting, such as actuarial science, appraisal, or environment. The auditor will typically use the work of the specialist unless the auditor's procedures lead to the belief that the specialist's findings are unreasonable. The auditor should test any data provided to the specialist considering the auditor's assessment of control risk. In general, the auditor should not refer to the specialist's findings in an unqualified (unmodified) opinion.

SPECIALIZED INDUSTRY one having its own unique methods of accounting and reporting. An example is the uniform system of accounts mandated by the Interstate Commerce Commission for railroads.

SPECIAL JOURNAL records of original entry other than the general journal that are designed for recording specific types of transactions of similar nature. Advantages of special journals are threefold: (1) their use permits a division of labor; (2) they save time in posting from the journals to the general ledgers; and (3) they reduce recording time and errors. Most firms use at least the following special journals:

Special Journal	Special Transactions Recorded
Sales journal	Sales on credit terms
Purchase journal	Purchase on account
Cash receipts journal	Receipt of cash
Cash disbursements journal	Payment of cash
Payroll journal	Payroll

SPECIAL-ORDER DECISIONS short-term and nonroutine decisions such as whether to accept a production order at an offered price that is below the normal selling price, or what price to charge for a product that could be produced with otherwise idle facilities. *See also* CONTRIBUTION APPROACH TO PRICING.

SPECIAL-PURPOSE FINANCIAL REPORTING FRAMEWORKS include (1) cash basis, (2) income tax basis, (3) regulatory basis, and (4) compliance basis. The PUBLIC COMPANY ACCOUNTING OVERSIGHT BOARD (PCAOB) refers to the first three bases as "other comprehensive bases of accounting."

SPECIAL-PURPOSE FINANCIAL STATEMENT one having usefulness only to *limited* users. Some companies may accompany certified GENERAL PURPOSE FINANCIAL STATEMENTS with special-purpose statements. Further, these specialized statements are typically seen when companies file information to be used for governmental and trade statistics.

SPECIAL PURPOSE VEHICLE/ENTITY (SPV/SPE) a type of corporate entity or limited partnership created for a specific transaction or business, especially one unrelated to a company's main business. Their losses and risks generally are not recorded on a company's balance sheet. The SPV/SPE is usually a subsidiary company with an asset/liability structure and legal status that makes its obligations secure even if the parent company goes bankrupt. A company can use such an entity to finance a large project without placing the entire firm at risk. The problem is that, due to accounting loopholes, these vehicles became a way for companies to conceal debt. Essentially, it looks like the company has no liability when they really do. As the Enron bankruptcy showed, if things go wrong, the results can be devastating.

SPECIAL REPORT type of auditor's report that is prepared in accordance with GENERALLY ACCEPTED AUDITING STANDARDS (GAAS). It attempts to elaborate, explain, or exhibit in a prescribed fashion certain sections, accounts, or items of a financial statement. Examples of such reports are cash receipts/disbursements reports, proposed acquisitions, and tax basis financial statements. Financial statements may be prepared in accordance with rules other than GAAP, such as insurance regulatory requirements.

SPECIAL REVENUE FUND in GOVERNMENT ACCOUNTING, fund used to account for the proceeds of special revenue sources (other than special assessments, expendable trusts, or major capital projects) that are legally restricted to expenditure for specified purposes. Examples of special revenue funds are those established for the purpose of financing schools, parks, or libraries.

SPECIAL SITUATION unusual occurrence or event requiring special accounting or legal treatment because of its importance.

SPECIFIC IDENTIFICATION inventory valuation in which ending inventory items are identified in some manner, such as by serial number and purchase date. Assume the following items were purchased during the year:

Purchase invoice #102 (Feb. 20)	180 units @ $ 9	= $1,620
Purchase invoice #129 (Apr. 12)	130 units @ $10	= 1,300
Purchase invoice #165 (Sept. 20)	120 units @ $11	= 1,320
Total	430 units	$4,240

Assume the ending inventory is 145 units consisting of 85 units from the Feb. 20 purchase and 60 units from the Sept. 20 purchase. The ending inventory valuation is:

Feb. 20	85 units @ $ 9	$ 765
Sept. 20	60 units @ $11	660
Total	145 units	$1,425

See also AVERAGE COST FLOW ASSUMPTION; FIRST-IN, FIRST-OUT (FIFO); LAST-IN, FIRST-OUT (LIFO).

SPECIFIC PERFORMANCE when ordered by a court, requires the performance of a specific act, which is usually stated in a contract. Specific performance is normally not enforced if (1) the contract is unconscionable or terminable at will by either party, (2) severe hardship would result, or (3) personal services are involved.

SPECIFIC PRICE INDEX one reflecting the price change of a particular type item (i.e., goods, services) or of related groups of items. It is computed at a given date and compared to a base date. *See also* GENERAL PRICE INDEX.

SPECIFIC PRICE-LEVEL CHANGE difference in the replacement cost or market price of a particular good or service, or a related group of products or services. It differs from a general price-level change that applies to a broad base of goods and services. *See also* SPECIFIC PRICE INDEX.

SPECULATION placing funds in a high-risk investment, such as an option or futures contract. Risk is measured by variability of outcome and the probability distribution of those outcomes. A speculative investment has predictable results, but over a wide range of possible outcomes and with high probabilities of the extremes occurring. Speculation is basically short-term trading with the hope of obtaining a higher profit in the form of capital gain but with greater risk. The potential loss on a speculative investment can be limited by employing a HEDGE.

SPEECH RECOGNITION SOFTWARE program in which verbal commands activate the MICROCOMPUTER to perform functions such as WORD PROCESSING, SPREADSHEET, or DATA BASE MANAGEMENT SYSTEM (DBMS). For instance, hardware (boards) and software exist so the accountant can input data by talking to the computer, moving the cursor, and filling in the details of a spreadsheet.

SPEECH SYNTHESIS software program that allows a microcomputer with a speech chip to speak in an understandable voice.

SPENDING VARIANCE *see* FIXED OVERHEAD SPENDING (BUDGET) VARI-
ANCE; VARIABLE OVERHEAD SPENDING VARIANCE.

SPINOFF type of corporate reorganization in which the original corporation
transfers some of its assets to a newly formed corporation. In exchange for
the assets, the original corporation receives all of the new corporation's capital stock, which it then distributes to its shareholders as a property dividend.

SPLIT *see* STOCK SPLIT.

SPLIT-OFF POINT juncture of production where JOINT PRODUCTS become
individually identifiable. A diagram follows on the next page. *See also* SELL-
OR-PROCESS-FURTHER DECISION.

SPLIT-OFF POINT DIAGRAM

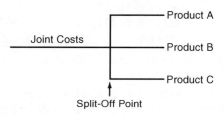

SPOILAGE production that does not result in good finished products. The
amount of spoilage can be considered either normal or abnormal. Spoilage
can be classified into the following categories: (1) Spoiled goods—goods that
do not meet production standards and are either sold for their salvage value
or discarded; (2) Defective units—goods that do not meet standards and are
sold at a reduced price or reworked and sold at the regular or a reduced price;
(3) Waste—material that is lost in the manufacturing process by shrinkage,
evaporation, etc.; and (4) Scrap—by-product of the manufacturing process
that has a minor market value.

SPOOFING a technique to mask one's identity. For example, e-mail spoofing (or "fooling") is used by spammers to modify the e-mail header so that
the message appears to have originated from someone other than the actual
source.

SPREADSHEET a computer program for displaying and analyzing data in a
tabular form. Computer spreadsheet programs evolved from manual paper-
based worksheets, where calculations could be tedious, time-consuming, and
error-prone. Spreadsheet programs are excellent for performing simulations,
financial projections, and various accounting applications. Microsoft Excel is
the most widely used spreadsheet program in the market today.

SPREADSHEET PROGRAMS *see* SPREADSHEET.

SPYDERS *see* STANDARD & POOR'S DEPOSITARY RECEIPT (SPDR).

SPYWARE any technology that aids in gathering information about a person or
organization without their knowledge. Spyware can get into a computer as a
software virus or as the result of installing a new program.

SSID (SERVICE SET IDENTIFIER) used to differentiate one WLAN (wireless local area network) from another. SSID is a 32 alphanumeric character

unique identifier that is attached to the header of each data packet that is sent over a WLAN.

***STAFF ACCOUNTING BULLETIN* (SAB)** detailed and technical publication from the Office of the Chief Accountant of the SEC that suggests how the various ACCOUNTING SERIES RELEASES (ASRS) should be applied in practice. A substantial amount of the SAB deals with the implementation of REPLACEMENT-COST ACCOUNTING, as required by ASR No. 190. The SABs were begun in 1975.

STAFF AUDITOR
1. external auditor employed by a public accounting firm that examines a client's financial records.
2. internal auditor working for the company to assure corporate accounting policies are being carried out, internal controls are adequate, and operating activities are running smoothly.

STAFF AUTHORITY power to give advice, support, and service to line departments. Staff managers do not command others. Examples of staff authority are found in personnel, purchasing, engineering, and finance. The management accounting function is usually "staff" with responsibility for providing line managers and also other staff people with a specialized service. The service includes budgeting, controlling, pricing, and special decisions. *See also* LINE AUTHORITY.

STAND-ALONE COST METHOD method that allocates a portion of common costs to each user by applying a ratio equal to the stand-alone cost of providing benefits to that user divided by the sum of the stand-alone costs for all users. A variation of the stand-alone technique is the INCREMENTAL COST-ALLOCATION METHOD.

STAND-ALONE REVENUE ALLOCATION weighting scheme based on unit selling prices, for example, average actual prices, which is the theoretically preferable method; unit costs; or physical units in the bundle. A variation of the stand-alone revenue allocation technique is the INCREMENTAL REVENUE ALLOCATION.

STANDARD quantitative expression of a performance objective, such as standard hours of labor allowed for actual production or a standard purchase price of materials per unit. Sometimes the terms *standard* and *budget* are used interchangeably. For example, budgeted sales revenue could be used as a standard in evaluating the performance of the marketing department. A standard is set for the following three reasons: (1) to measure performance of a responsibility center; (2) to simplify recordkeeping; and (3) to improve performance by taking appropriate remedial action on an unfavorable deviation from the standard.

STANDARD & POOR'S DEPOSITARY RECEIPT (SPDR) shares of a security designed to track the value of the S&P 500; also called *SPDRs* or *Spyders*. Spyders trade on the American Stock Exchange under the symbol SPY. One SPDR unit is valued at approximately one-tenth of the value of the S&P 500. Dividends are distributed quarterly and are based on the accumulated stock dividends held in trust, less any expenses of the trust.

STANDARD BILL OF MATERIALS listing of the standard quantity per unit of each item of material going into a unit of finished product. It should be adjusted for unavoidable waste, spoilage, and other normal inefficiencies.

STANDARD COST production or operating cost that is carefully predetermined. A standard cost is a target cost that *should be* attained. The standard cost is compared with the actual cost in order to measure the performance of a given costing department or operation. *Variances*, which are the differences between actual costs and standard costs, may indicate inefficiencies that have to be investigated. Corrective action may have to be taken.

STANDARD COST SYSTEM process by which production activities are recorded at standard costs and variances from actual costs are isolated. Standard costs are carefully predetermined target costs that should be attained under efficient operating conditions. A standard cost system is designed to aid management in judging performance of a responsibility center in an organization. The standard costing system is designed to facilitate: (1) planning and controlling costs; (2) judgment of performance; (3) budget preparation; (4) inventory valuation; and (5) employee motivation. The analysis of variances that are the differences between standard and actual costs is the key in a standard cost system. This reveals the causes of deviations between actual and standard costs. This feedback aids in planning future goals, controlling costs, and measuring performance.

STANDARD COST VARIANCE *see* VARIANCE.

STANDARD DEDUCTION amount allowed to an individual taxpayer who does not elect to itemize deductions. This standard deduction is incorporated into the tax rate and table schedules. A taxpayer who elects to itemize deductions may deduct only the excess over the standard deduction amount to determine taxable income.

STANDARD DEVIATION
1. statistic that measures the tendency of data to be spread out. Accountants can make important inferences from past data with this measure. The standard deviation, denoted with Σ and read as *sigma*, is defined as follows:

$$\sigma = \frac{\sqrt{\Sigma(x - \bar{x})^2}}{n - 1}$$

where $\bar{x}$ is the mean.

For example, one-and-one-half years of quarterly returns for XYZ stock follow:

Time Period	x	$(x - \bar{x})$	$(x - \bar{x})^2$
1	10%	0	0
2	15	5	25
3	20	10	100
4	5	−5	25
5	−10	−20	400
6	20	10	100
	60		650

From the preceding table, note that

$$\bar{x} = 60/6 = 10\%$$
$$= \sqrt{\Sigma(x-\bar{x})^2/n-1} = \sqrt{650/(6-1)} = \sqrt{130} = \underline{11.40\%}$$

The XYZ stock has returned on the average 10% over the last six quarters and the variability about its average return was 11.40%. The high standard deviation (11.40%) relative to the average return of 10% indicates that the stock is very risky,

2. measure of the dispersion of a probability distribution. It is the square root of the mean of the squared deviations from the EXPECTED VALUE $E(x)$.

$$\sigma = \sqrt{\Sigma(x_i - E(x))^2 \, p_i}$$

It is commonly used as an absolute measure of risk. The higher the standard deviation, the higher the risk.

For example, consider two investment proposals, A and B, with the following probability distribution of cash flows in each of the next five years:

	Cash Inflows			
Probability	**(.2)**	**(.3)**	**(.4)**	**(.1)**
A	$ 50	200	300	400
B	$100	150	250	850

The expected value of the cash inflow in proposal A is:

$$\$50(.2) + 200(.3) + 300(.4) + 400(.1) = \underline{\$230}$$

The expected value of the cash inflow in proposal B is:

$$\$100(.2) + 150(.3) + 250(.4) + 850(.1) = \underline{\$250}$$

The standard deviations of proposals A and B are computed as follows:

For A:

$$\sqrt{\begin{array}{l}(\$50-230)(.2)+(200-230)(.3)+(300-230)(.4)\\+(400-230)(.1)\end{array}} = \underline{\$107.70}$$

For B:

$$\sqrt{\begin{array}{l}(\$100-250)(.2)+(150-250)(.3)+(250-250)(.4)\\+(850-250)(.1)\end{array}} = \underline{\$208.57}$$

Proposal B is more risky than proposal A, since its standard deviation is greater.

STANDARD DIRECT LABOR COSTS standard hours of direct labor multiplied by the standard wage for direct labor.

STANDARD DIRECT MATERIALS COST standard price for direct materials multiplied by the standard quantity for direct materials.

STANDARD ERROR OF THE ESTIMATE measure of the scatter of the actual observations above the regression line; designated S_e. It is computed as

$$S_e = \sqrt{\Sigma(y - y')^2/(n - k - 1)}$$

where k is the number of independent variables in the regression equation. The statistic can be used to gain some idea of the accuracy of our predictions.

STANDARD ERROR OF THE REGRESSION COEFFICIENT measure of the amount of sampling error in a REGRESSION COEFFICIENT; designated S_b. It is computed as

$$S_b = \frac{S_e}{\sqrt{(x - \bar{x})^2}}$$

where S_e is the standard error of the estimate. *See also* STANDARD ERROR OF THE ESTIMATE.

STANDARD FIXED MANUFACTURING OVERHEAD RATE total budgeted fixed manufacturing overhead costs divided by an expression of capacity, usually normal capacity in terms of standard hours or units.

STANDARD HOURS ALLOWED time that should have been used to manufacture actual units of output during a period. It is obtained by multiplying actual units of production by the standard labor time. For example, a company actually produced 2000 units during the month of March. The standard labor time required to produce one unit of output was 3 hours. The standard hours allowed for actual production is 2000 units × 3 hours = 6000 hours.

STANDARD LABOR RATE direct labor rate that should be paid for each hour of labor time. It includes not only base wages earned but also an allowance for fringe benefits and other labor-related costs. For example, it can be determined as follows:

Wage rate per hour	$9.00
Payroll taxes at 10%	.90
Fringe benefits at 30%	2.70
Standard rate per hour	$12.60

STANDARD MANUFACTURING OVERHEAD COST sum of the estimates for variable and fixed manufacturing overhead costs in the next accounting period.

STANDARD MATERIAL PRICE per unit price for direct materials that should be paid for a single unit of materials. It reflects the final, delivered cost of the materials, net of any discounts taken. It may be determined as follows:

Purchase price per pound	$ 5.00
Freight by truck	.35
Receiving and handling	.10
Less: purchase discount	(.50)
Standard price per pound	$ 4.95

STANDARD OF COMPARISON standard used in relating a base or typical item to a current one. For example, budgeted sales may be compared to actual sales, with deviations noted. Corrective action can then be taken. Also, the trend in a financial statement item may be examined for a percentage change. If sales last year were $100,000 and this year are $150,000, the percentage increase is 50%. A comparison can also be made of a company's financial statement figures to those of other companies in the industry as well as to industry norms.

STANDARD OPINION judgment rendered by a CPA who is satisfied that the company's financial statements are fairly presented in conformity with U.S. GAAP. Further, it means that excessive uncertainty does not exist with regard to material transactions or events. Financial statements with standard opinions can normally be relied upon in making business judgments concerning the company.

STANDARD QUANTITY ALLOWED amount of materials that should have been used to manufacture units of output during a period. It is obtained by multiplying actual units of production by the standard material quantity per unit. For example, a company actually produced 2000 units during the month of March. The standard material quantity required to produce one unit of output was 5 pounds. The standard quantity allowed for actual production is 2000 units × 5 pounds = 10,000 pounds.

STANDARD VARIABLE MANUFACTURING OVERHEAD RATE total budgeted variable manufacturing overhead costs divided by an expression of capacity, such as the expected number of standard machine-hours or standard direct labor-hours.

STARTUP COSTS pre-opening one-time expenditures incurred to open a new facility, introduce a new product or service, conduct business in a new territory, start business with a new customer class, or begin some new operation. All startup costs are expensed as incurred.

STATED CAPITAL
1. amount of capital contributed by stockholders of a corporation. It may also refer to the method of valuing no-par-value stock where the portion of the amount contributed is credited to the capital stock account and the balance is credited to PAID-IN CAPITAL.
2. LEGAL CAPITAL of a company.

STATED LIABILITY amounts listed under liabilities in the various financial records and statements without audit or verification. They are subject to future adjustment or correction. It is basically a face value observation of liabilities.

STATED VALUE per share value sometimes assigned to no-par stock by the corporation. It defines the legal capital of the corporation. It is the amount credited to the no-par capital stock account. A typical journal entry made for the issuance of stated value stock is given below:

	Dr.	Cr.
Cash (or other assets)	XX	
Capital stock (at stated value)		XX
Paid-in capital in excess of stated value		XX

STATEMENT

1. formal document presenting the financial condition and operating performance of an enterprise. These include the income statement, balance sheet, and statement of changes in financial position. Also included may be documents for internal use such as performance appraisals, budgets, and so on.

2. summary statement documenting terms, conditions, or status of an account. An example is a statement of retail credit account status.

3. verbal utterance or proposition.

STATEMENT OF ACCOUNT report indicating the account status of an agreement between creditor and debtor. The statement is usually issued by the creditor indicating details such as the unpaid balance due and payment history. An example of such a statement is that of a department store credit account or MasterCard billing statement.

STATEMENT OF AFFAIRS financial report showing assets and liabilities at expected liquidation values and stockholders' equity. The statement is prepared primarily when an actual or pending BANKRUPTCY exists. Or a creditor may want to see pessimistic figures for a company facing severe financial problems. This is a worst-case scenario.

STATEMENT OF CASH FLOWS statement that provides information about an entity's cash receipts and cash disbursements for a period as they apply to operating, investing, and financing activities. The statement is required in the annual report. Cash flows from operating activities comprise the first section of the statement. These apply to transactions impacting net income. Examples of cash inflows from operating activities are cash sales, customer collections on account, interest income, and dividend income. Examples of cash outflows from operating activities are paying suppliers of merchandise, paying suppliers of operating expense items, employee wages, interest expense, and taxes. Investing activities relate to the purchase or sale of equity and debt securities of other entities and the acquisition or sale of property, plant, and equipment. The financing section appears last in the statement of cash flows. Financing activities relate to obtaining equity capital, dividend payments to stockholders, debt issuance, and repayment of bonds.

When a cash receipt or cash payment is for more than one activity, classification is based on the activity that is the prime reason for that cash flow. For instance, the purchase and sale of equipment to be used by the company is often deemed as an investing purpose.

Emphasis is placed on explaining the change in cash and cash equivalents for the year. In general, a cash equivalent is a very liquid short-term investment that has an initial maturity date of three months or less.

The statement cash flows for the company would be presented as follows:

Liverpool Sugar Corporation
Statement of Cash Flows
for the Year Ended December 31, 2009

Cash flows from operating activities:

Cash received from customers	$1,004,000
Cash payment for acquisition of materials	(469,000)
Cash payment for interest and dividends	(12,000)
Cash payment for taxes	(136,000)
Net cash provided by operating activities	$ 387,000

Cash flows from investing activities:

Cash paid to purchase plant and equipment	$(676,000)
Sale of long-term investment	100,000
Net cash provided by investing activities	(576,000)

Cash flows from financing activities:

Sale of bonds	$ 300,000
Cash paid for dividends	(36,000)
Net cash used in financing activities	264,000
Net decrease in cash and cash equivalents	$(75,000)
Cash and cash equivalents at the beginning of the year.	198,000
Cash and cash equivalents at the end of the year	$273,000

STATEMENT OF CASH RECEIPTS AND DISBURSEMENTS *see* CASH-FLOW STATEMENT.

STATEMENT OF CHANGES IN NET WORTH reflects the revenue and expenses of an individual as well as increases and decreases in estimated current values of an individual's assets and liabilities.

STATEMENT OF CHANGES IN STOCKHOLDERS' EQUITY details specific changes in an entity's main equity components, which include retained earnings, stock, additional paid-in-capital, and, if applicable, comprehensive income. In essence, this statement reconciles beginning and ending balances of accounts in the stockholder's equity section of an entity's balance sheet.

STATEMENT OF COSTS OF GOODS MANUFACTURED *see* COSTS OF GOODS MANUFACTURED SCHEDULE.

STATEMENT OF FINANCIAL POSITION *see* BALANCE SHEET.

STATEMENT OF REALIZATION AND LIQUIDATION presentation prepared by an enterprise going out of business. It is a summary type presentation of the realization (receipts from asset disposals) and the liquidation (retirement and settlement of liabilities) and operating statement of enumerated revenues, losses, and expenses of the liquidator.

STATEMENT OF RETAINED EARNINGS one that accompanies the balance sheet and shows the beginning balance of retained earnings, adjustments to it during the year, and the final balance. An illustrative statement format follows:

Retained Earnings—1/1 Unadjusted
Plus or Minus: Prior Period Adjustments
Retained Earnings—1/1 Adjusted
Plus: Net Income
Minus: Dividends Declared
Retained Earnings—12/31

STATEMENT OF STOCKHOLDERS' EQUITY statement included in the annual report presenting the individual components of STOCKHOLDERS' EQUITY and the changes therein during the last year. The major elements of stockholders' equity include capital stock, paid-in capital, retained earnings, treasury stock, unrealized loss on long-term investments, and foreign currency translation gains and losses.

STATEMENTS OF FINANCIAL ACCOUNTING CONCEPTS (SFAC) reports issued by the FINANCIAL ACCOUNTING STANDARDS BOARD (FASB) to indicate the fundamental concepts of financial accounting, reporting, and disclosure. They reflect the objectives of financial statements. Included in the Financial Accounting Concepts are fundamental theories and practices underlying financial accounting. The elements of financial statements of business enterprises are presented, as well as financial reporting objectives of nonbusiness organizations.

STATEMENTS OF FINANCIAL ACCOUNTING STANDARDS (SFAS) accounting, reporting, and disclosure requirements of the FINANCIAL ACCOUNTING STANDARDS BOARD (FASB). They are rules to be followed by accountants in accumulating financial data and preparing financial statements. The standards are, in effect, GENERALLY ACCEPTED ACCOUNTING PRINCIPLES (GAAP). They cover diverse subjects, such as leases, pensions, and income statement presentation.

STATEMENTS OF POSITION (SOPs) recommendations, rather than requirements, issued by the ACCOUNTING STANDARDS EXECUTIVE COMMITTEE of the AMERICAN INSTITUTE OF CERTIFIED PUBLIC ACCOUNTANTS (AICPA) concerning specialized accounting policies practiced in given industries. They are issued in the public interest. For instance, one Statement of Position covers the accounting and reporting for universities. The FASB is currently promulgating specialized accounting principles that were previously dealt with by the SOPs.

STATEMENTS OF REVENUES AND EXPENDITURES in GOVERNMENT ACCOUNTING, statements showing revenues obtained less expenditures incurred. The difference represents the change in fund balance.

STATEMENTS ON AUDITING PROCEDURE (SAP) name for auditing pronouncements before 1972. Since then, STATEMENTS ON AUDITING STANDARDS (SAS) have been issued.

STATEMENTS ON AUDITING STANDARDS (SAS) reports issued by the AICPA's AUDITING STANDARDS EXECUTIVE COMMITTEE that represent preferable auditing standards and practices. *See also* AUDITING STANDARDS BOARD (ASB).

STATEMENTS ON STANDARDS FOR ACCOUNTING AND REVIEW SERVICES (SSARS) name for pronouncements issued by the AMERICAN

INSTITUTE OF CERTIFIED PUBLIC ACCOUNTANTS (AICPA) applicable to compilations and reviews of financial statements of nonissuers (i.e., nonpublic entities).

STATEMENTS ON STANDARDS FOR ATTESTATION ENGAGEMENTS (SSAE) name for pronouncements issued by the AICPA applicable to attest engagements concerning subject matter or assertions about subject matter. *See also* ATTESTATION (ATTEST) ENGAGEMENT.

STATEMENTS ON STANDARDS FOR TAX SERVICES (SSTS) name for pronouncements issued by the AICPA that include enforceable standards of tax practice. While SSTS are applicable to AICPA members, they parallel the responsibilities specified by the INTERNAL REVENUE SERVICE. These standards are designed to protect the profession, the public, and the government.

STATES OF NATURE conditions that are likely to occur and over which the decision maker has no control. *See also* DECISION THEORY.

STATE UNEMPLOYMENT COMPENSATION money paid to eligible unemployed individuals. It is financed by a payroll tax levied on employers by the various states. Some variation exists as to the filing and payment requirements among different states.

STATIC (FIXED) BUDGET one based on a single level of activity (e.g., a particular volume of sales or production). It has two characteristics: (1) it is geared toward only one level of activity; (2) actual results are compared against budgeted (standard) costs only at the original budget activity level. A FLEXIBLE (VARIABLE) BUDGET differs from a static budget on both scores. First, it is not geared to only one activity level, but rather, toward a *range* of activity. Second, actual results are not compared against budgeted costs at the original budget activity level. Managers look at what activity level was attained during a period and then turn to the flexible budget to determine what costs should have been at that actual level of activity.

STATISTIC numerical characteristic of a sample (taken from a population) computed using only the elements of a sample of the population. For example, the mean and the mode are statistics of the sample.

STATISTICAL ANALYSIS SYSTEM (SAS) statistical software package, developed by the SAS Institute, Inc., Cary, North Carolina. The SAS package aids in extensive statistical analyses, including descriptive statistics, REGRESSION ANALYSIS, and data graphing of statistical information.

STATISTICAL COST CONTROL procedure for distinguishing between random and other types of cost variances. Decisions to investigate variances are frequently based on THREE-SIGMA LIMITS rather than on a formal analysis of expected costs. Statistical cost control utilizes the control chart that helps distinguish random (chance) variances from variances that need investigation. The analysis of the latter helps to obtain improvements in production and processes. The identification of chance variances avoids unnecessary investigations of variances and eliminates frequent changes. A process or production method is said to be in statistical control if the variances are within three-sigma limits of the control chart.

STATISTICAL CURVE FITTING methodology commonly used as a quantitative forecasting technique. Many different types of curves can be used in fitting historical data for predicting such variables as sales and costs—linear, exponential, and others. For example, some form of curve fitting is often done to approximate the basic *trend* component of a time series. The trend can be linear (straight line) or curvilinear. The problem is to determine which form of curve will best fit the available data and provide the basis for an accurate forecast of the future. Statistics such as *r-squared* (COEFFICIENT OF DETERMI-NATION) can be of tremendous help for this purpose.

STATISTICAL QUALITY CONTROL method of quality control that uses statistical sampling of units produced by a production process. These are checked for defectives (variances) to determine whether or not the process is in control. If not, corrective action is taken. In the field of statistical quality control, the statistical control chart is used as a basic tool to formally distinguish between normal and abnormal variances. Control charts help distinguish RANDOM VARIANCES from variances that need managerial investigation. The analysis of the latter helps to obtain improvements in products and processes. The identification of chance variances avoids unnecessary investigations of variances and eliminates frequent changes. *Three-sigma control limits* are most popularly used to decide whether a process (operation) is in a state of statistical control.

A process is said to be in a state of statistical control if the sample variations stay within the limits. If the process is out of control, it is important to locate specific causes for the variation and take a corrective action. *See also* THREE-SIGMA LIMITS.

STATISTICAL SAMPLING method based on the assumption that, within a given confidence level and allowance for sampling risk, a randomly selected sample of items from a population will reflect the same characteristics that occur in the population. For example, auditors may draw conclusions based on data derived from a relatively small sample of the total population.

STATISTICAL SOFTWARE computer programs that perform functions helpful to accountants, particularly managerial accountants, such as determining STANDARD DEVIATION, multiple regression analysis, CORRELATION, VARIANCE ANALYSIS, and FREQUENCY DISTRIBUTION. A model base management system produces mathematical models and can change and store components. Examples are SPSS, SAS, and Minitab.

STATISTICS field of study concerning information calculated from sample data. The field is divided into two categories: DESCRIPTIVE STATISTICS and INFERENTIAL STATISTICS. Both are widely used in business.

STATUTE OF FRAUDS requires certain types of contracts to be in the form of a signed document in order to be enforceable. In general, contracts subject to the statute of frauds include contracts that (1) cannot be performed within one year, (2) involve the transfer of interest in land, and (3) involve the sale of goods totaling at least $500.

STATUTORY AUDIT one conducted to meet the particular requirements of a governmental agency. Where such audits take place, the scope and audit programs are set by the governmental body. Banks, insurance companies, and brokerage firms have statutory audits. Since the auditor's report must conform to standards required by the governing agency, the statements and other financial data generated from these audits may not conform to GAAP.

STATUTORY CONSOLIDATION a merger in which a new corporate entity is created from the two merging companies, which cease to exist. *See also* STATUTORY MERGER.

STATUTORY MERGER a merger in which one of the merging companies continues to exist as a legal entity, rather than being replaced by the new entity. *See also* STATUTORY CONSOLIDATION.

STEP ALLOCATION METHOD manner of allocating services rendered by service departments to other service departments using a sequence of allocation; also called the *step-down method* and the *sequential method*. The sequence normally begins with the department that renders service to the greatest number of other service departments; the sequence continues in step-by-step fashion and ends with the allocation of costs of service departments that provide the least amount of service. But no *reciprocal* service is considered.

STEP COSTS costs that are approximately fixed over a small volume range, but are variable over a large volume range. For example, supervision costs are fixed for a given range of production volume, but increased production often requires additional work shifts leading to added supervisory costs in a lump-sum fashion. The figure below illustrates this.

STEP COSTS

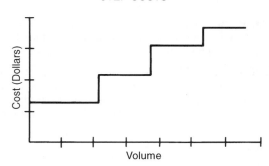

STEP-DOWN METHOD *see* STEP ALLOCATION METHOD.

STEP FUNCTION COSTS *see* STEP COSTS.

STOCK
1. evidence of ownership in a company and a claim against a company's assets and earnings. It is the legal capital of the entity divided into shares. Two types of stock are COMMON STOCK and PREFERRED STOCK. *See also* CAPITAL STOCK; CUMULATIVE PREFERRED STOCK; PARTICIPATING PREFERRED STOCK; STOCK CERTIFICATE.
2. inventory available for sale.

STOCK APPRECIATION RIGHTS awards entitling employees to receive cash or stock, in any combination thereof (determined at grant date or when exercised), in an amount equivalent to the excess of market price on a specified number of shares of the corporation's stock above an option price.

STOCK BONUS PLAN plan similar to a PROFIT-SHARING PLAN except that contributions do not necessarily depend on profitability, and benefits are distributable in the employer's stock. The maximum amount that an employer may deduct for tax purposes in any one year is 15% of compensation. The only exception is for limitation carryforwards accumulated for tax years beginning before 1987. Two or more stock bonus plans are treated as one plan for purposes of limiting employer deductions.

STOCK CERTIFICATE document showing stockholder's ownership in the company. The certificate shows the number of shares, par value, class of stock (e.g., common stock), and voting rights. When endorsed, stock certificates are negotiable.

STOCK COMPANY firm whose capital is in the form of shares with transferable ownership rights.

STOCK DIVIDEND pro rata distribution of additional shares of a corporation's own stock to its stockholders. A stock dividend may be declared when the cash position of the firm is inadequate and/or when the company wishes to prompt more trading by reducing the market price of stock. A *small* stock dividend (less than 20%–25% of the shares outstanding at the date of declaration) decreases retained earnings and increases the capital accounts (capital stock and paid-in capital) for an amount equal to the fair value of the shares issued. A *large* stock dividend (in excess of 20%–25% of shares outstanding) decreases retained earnings and increases capital stock at the par or stated value only. *See also* CASH DIVIDEND.

STOCKHOLDER individual or business that owns shares in a corporation. A STOCK CERTIFICATE is evidence of ownership. The stockholder's return comes from DIVIDENDS and appreciation of the stock in the MARKET PRICE.

STOCKHOLDERS' EQUITY ownership interest of stockholders in the corporation; also called *shareholders' equity*, OWNERS' EQUITY, and NET WORTH. Stockholders' equity is the difference between total assets less total liabilities. The components of the stockholders' equity section of the balance sheet are:

> Capital Stock
> Plus: Paid-in capital
> Plus: Retained earnings
>   Unappropriated
>   Appropriated
> Plus or Minus: Foreign currency translation gain or loss
> Minus: Unrealized loss on long-term investment portfolio
> Total
> Minus: Treasury stock
> Total Stockholders' Equity

STOCKHOLDERS OF RECORD holders of stock as of the DATE OF RECORD who are entitled to receive a cash dividend already declared. For example, on January 8, the board of directors of a company declared a $.30 per share cash dividend on its common stock payable on February 18 to *stockholders of record* on January 20. The common stockholders who are on the company's records on January 20 will receive the $.30 dividend per share on February 18 (*date of payment*). Stockholders of record are also entitled to rights, voting privileges, and dividends other than cash.

STOCK INDEX FUTURES contract to buy or sell a broad stock market index. Introduced in 1982, futures contracts at the present time are available on the S&P 500 Stock Index, the New York Stock Exchange Composite Stock Index, and the Value Line Composite Stock Index. Smaller investors can avail themselves of the S&P 100 futures contract, which involves a smaller margin deposit. Stock index futures allow the investor to buy and sell the "market as a whole" rather than a specific security. An investor anticipating a bull market but unsure which particular stock will rise might buy (long position) a stock-index future. Another investor, seeking to hedge the portfolio against loss of value in a bear market might, on the other hand, sell a stock-index future.

STOCK OPTION right given the holder to buy a specified number of shares of stock at a certain price by a particular date. Stock option plans are often used to compensate corporate officers and other employees for specific services. Under a compensatory stock option plan, compensation should be expensed in the periods in which the related services are actually performed. Compensation is measured by the quoted market price of the stock at the *measurement date* less the option price the employee is to pay. The measurement date is the earliest date on which both the number of shares to be issued and the option price are known. Assume 2,000 shares are under option, market price at measurement date of 1/1/2014 is $15, option price is $10, par value is $6, and there is a four-year benefit period. Deferred compensation equals $10,000 (2,000 shares × $5). The entry at the measurement date is:

1/1/2014	Deferred compensation 10,000	
	Stock options	10,000

On 12/31/2014, the entry is:

12/31/2014	Compensation expense 2,500	
	Deferred compensation	2,500

Deferred Compensation is a contra account to stock options in the capital stock section of stockholders' equity, shown as follows on 12/31/2014:

Stock options	$10,000
Less: Deferred compensation	7,500
Balance	$ 2,500

If the market price of stock on the exercise date exceeds the option price, the employee will exercise. Otherwise, the employee will not. Assume the market price is $23 a share upon exercise of the options. The entry is:

Cash ($10 × 2000)	20,000	
Stock options	10,000	
Common stock (2000 × 6)		12,000
Paid-in capital		18,000

Note the employee pays only $10 (option price), not the current market price of $23. Footnote disclosures in a stock option plan include the number of shares under option, option price, number of shares exercisable, and shares issued under the option during the year.

STOCK-OUT COSTS *see* SHORTAGE COSTS.

STOCK OUTSTANDING *see* OUTSTANDING CAPITAL STOCK.

STOCK REGISTER record of the particulars related to the issuance of stock certificates to stockholders. Included are the shares issued, par value, name and address of owner, date of issuance, shares returned, cancelled shares, and other pertinent information.

STOCK RIGHT privilege giving current stockholders the first right to buy shares in a new offering, thus maintaining their proportionate ownership interest; also called PREEMPTIVE RIGHT. Suppose the investor owns 3% of XYZ Company. If the company issues 5,000 additional shares, the investor may receive a stock rights offering—a chance to buy 3%, or 150 shares, of the new issue. This right enables the investor to purchase new common stock at a subscription price for a short time, usually no more than several weeks. The subscription price (exercise price) is lower than the public offering price of the stock. A single right is the privilege applicable to one old share of capital stock to purchase a certain number of shares of new capital stock. When the rights are exercised, the issuing company makes a journal entry to record the proceeds received, and the common shares are issued.

STOCK SPLIT issuance of a substantial amount of additional shares, thus reducing the par value of the stock on a proportionate basis. No journal entry need be made, because the company's accounts do not change. However, there should be a memorandum entry describing the stock split. A stock split is often prompted by a desire to reduce the market price per share in order to stimulate investor buying. Assume XYZ Company has 1000 shares of $20 par value common stock. The total par value is thus $20,000. A two-for-one stock split is issued. There will now be 2,000 shares at a $10 par value. The total par value remains at $20,000. Typically, the market price per share of the stock should also drop to one-half of what it was before the split.

STOCK SUBSCRIPTION agreement to purchase a given number of shares at a specified price at a later date. Often, a down payment is required, and typically the payments are on an installment basis. It is a legal contract that is reflected in a debit owner's equity contra account. Subscribed stock is credited as the capital is contributed. *See also* CAPITAL STOCK SUBSCRIBED.

STOCK WARRANT option to purchase a certain number of shares at a stated price for a specified time period at a subscription price that is higher than the current market price (properly called *subscription warrant*). A warrant may or may not come in a one-to-one ratio with the stock already owned. Unlike a put or call option, a warrant is usually good for several years; some, in fact, have no maturity date and are known as *perpetual warrants*. Warrants are often given as sweeteners for a bond issue (e.g., to lower the interest rate or enhance the marketability). Warrants included with a bond may also exist in a merger when the acquiring company offers cash plus warrants in exchange for voting common stock of the acquired business. Generally, warrants are detachable from the bond and have a market life of their own. Warrants pay no dividends nor do they have voting rights. The warrant enables the holder to take part indirectly in price appreciation. *See also* DETACHABLE STOCK WARRANT; UNDETACHABLE STOCK WARRANT.

STOP-LOSS ORDER direction given to a broker to buy or sell a stock when it rises to or drops below a certain price. Assume an investor owns XYZ Company stock, having a current market price of $50 per share. The investor gives the broker a stop-loss order to sell this stock if it slips down to $46 a share. By selling the shares at a predetermined price, the investor is protected from further stock price declines.

STOP-OR-GO SAMPLING also referred to as sequential sampling, a technique that may enable an auditor to form conclusions when testing less than the full sample size.

STOP PAYMENT instruction to the bank not to honor a check when presented. As long as the check has not been cashed, the maker has up to six months to present a stop payment notice. However, a stop payment right does not apply to electronic funds transfers.

STORAGE TIME time a product spends in materials storage, work-in-process inventory, or finished goods inventory.

STORE CARDS perpetual-inventory records that are subsidiary ledger accounts for Stores (Control). All purchases of materials and supplies are charged to Stores (Control) as purchased because the storekeeper is accountable for them. At a minimum, these cards contain quantity columns for receipts, issuances, and balance. A sample store card follows.

STORE CARD

STORES

1. raw materials, supplies, and parts.
2. control account for all purchases of materials and supplies. All purchases of materials, parts, and supplies are charged to Stores as purchased because the storekeeper is accountable for them. The Stores Control account is supported by an underlying subsidiary ledger, called STORE CARDS.
3. retail outlets.

STORES REQUISITIONS forms used to keep track of materials charged to a particular job or department. The form contains such items as job number, department, description of the material, quantity, unit cost, and dollar amount. A sample form follows.

STORES REQUISITION

STRADDLE to combine a CALL and PUT on the identical stock with the same expiration date and strike price. It is employed to take advantage of significant variability in stock price. High BETA (a measure of volatility) stocks might be most suited for this. A significant price movement on one side will cover the cost of obtaining the options.

STRAIGHT-LINE DEPRECIATION method providing equal depreciation charges for each period because it assumes *constant* benefit from the asset. It is the easiest and most popular method of computing depreciation expense. Straight-line depreciation expense equals cost less salvage value divided by life. Assume an auto having a five-year life was acquired for $13,000, with salvage value of $1,000. Depreciation expense per year is $2,400 [($13,000 − $1,000)/5].

STRATEGIC ALLIANCE agreement of two or more companies with complementary core competencies to jointly contribute to the VALUE CHAIN.

STRATEGIC BUDGETING *see* LONG-RANGE BUDGET.

STRATEGIC COST MANAGEMENT managerial use of cost information for the purpose(s) of establishing organizational strategy, controlling the success methods to achieve the strategies, and evaluating the level of success in meeting the proclaimed strategies.

STRATEGIC FINANCE a monthly publication (www.strategicfinancemag. com), published by the Institute of Management Accountants (IMA), dealing with leadership strategies in accounting, finance, and information management.

STRATEGIC PLANNING implementing an organization's objectives. In any organization, strategic planning occurs in two phases: (1) deciding on the products to produce and/or the services to render; (2) deciding on the marketing and/or manufacturing strategy to follow in getting the intended product or service to the proper audience. Strategic planning decisions will have long-term impacts on the organization while operational decisions are day-to-day in nature.

STRATIFIED SAMPLING method used to divide a population into homogeneous subgroups (strata). Each stratum is then sampled individually. The auditor may separately evaluate the sample results or may combine them to furnish an estimate of the characteristics of the total population. When very high- or low-value items are segregated into separate populations, each population is more homogeneous. A more representative sample can be derived from a relatively homogeneous population. Hence, fewer items need to be examined when several strata are examined separately than when the entire population is evaluated. Stratification improves the sampling process and enables auditors to relate sample selection to the materiality and turnover of items. Various audit procedures may be applied to each stratum, depending on the circumstances. An example of stratified sampling occurs when total accounts receivable (population) is divided into groups based on dollar balances for confirmation purposes. An illustration follows:

Stratum	Method of Selection Used	Type of Confirmation
1. All accounts of $100,000 or more	100% confirmed	Positive
2. All other accounts under $100,000	Random number table selection	Positive

Stratification may not be by dollar amount only but also by type of transaction and by transaction frequency. Stratification is suggested when the characteristic under audit examination varies materially within different portions of the population. This approach is employed typically in variables sampling and often in attributes sampling.

STREET NAME term used when securities are held in the name of a broker or other nominee rather than the investor. Because the broker is holding the securities, it is easier to make a transfer of them at the time of sale. If the stock were registered in the investor's name and physically held by him or her, transfer of shares would take longer.

STRIKE PRICE *see* EXERCISE PRICE.

STRUCTURED QUERY LANGUAGE (SQL) a programming language that is used for creating, updating, deleting, and reading data from a database. SQL is the standard database query language for virtually all databases, including Oracle, Microsoft SQL Server, Microsoft Access, and MySQL.

SUBCHAPTER S CORPORATION form of corporation whose stockholders may be taxed as partners. That is, income is taxed as direct income of the shareholders, regardless of whether it is actually distributed to them. To qualify as an S corporation, a company cannot have more than 100 shareholders; it cannot have more than one class of stock; it cannot have any nonresident foreigners as shareholders; and it must properly elect S corporation status. The key advantage of this form of organization is that the shareholders receive all the organizational benefit of a corporation while escaping the double taxation of a corporation.

SUBJECTIVE PROBABILITY estimate of the *relative frequency* of each of various future outcomes, based on the intuition or experience of the accountant making the estimate. Subjective probability is used in many business situations (i.e., estimating rates and/or dollar returns on investment decisions). Based on his or her experience, assume a treasurer is considering possible interest rates the company can expect to pay on bonds it intends to issue next week. The treasurer feels that interest rates can have only four possible values. The subjective assessment is as follows:

Interest Rate	Probability This Will Happen
9%	.2
9¼%	.3
9½%	.4
9¾%	.1

SUBJECT MATTER includes historical or prospective performance or condition (e.g., financial forecasts and projections), physical characteristics (e.g., square footage of a building), historical events (e.g., price of an item at a specified date), analyses (e.g., break-even analyses), systems or processes (e.g., internal control over financial reporting), and behavior (e.g., compliance with laws and regulations). *See also* ATTESTATION(ATTEST) ENGAGEMENTS.

SUBLEASE agreement in which the lessee contracts with a third party allowing the latter to use the lessee's right to the leased property. An example is the sublease of an apartment by the tenant to another party. If the lessee accounts under the operating lease method, the sublessee would also account under this method.

SUBOPTIMIZATION optimization of the goals of different departments of the entire organization. Suboptimization occurs when different subunits each attempt to reach a solution that is optimal for that unit, but that may not be optimum for the organization as a whole.

For example, the quality control department of a factory may want to introduce a program that will guarantee that every bulb that is produced is perfect. However, the higher cost and the resulting high price would lead to a disaster for the overall company in the form of lower sales.

SUBORDINATED DEBT securities that have a claim on the firm's assets only after the claims of holders of senior debt have been satisfied. The subordinated debt holder is in a much riskier position than the senior debt holders.

SUBORDINATED SECURITY *see* SUBORDINATED DEBT.

SUBPRIME MORTGAGES mortgages for people with credit scores that are under 620; also called *non-prime mortgages*. Many such homeowners found themselves unable to pay off their mortgages as interest rates rose and house values sank. *See also* TOXIC ASSETS.

SUBSCRIBED STOCK *see* CAPITAL STOCK SUBSCRIBED.

SUBSCRIPTION
1. agreement to purchase a security.
2. pledge to give a contribution to an organization for a cause (e.g., charity).

SUBSEQUENT ACTIVITY activity that receives service from another activity.

SUBSEQUENT DISCOVERY OF FACTS identification of matters after the issuance of an audit report. If the matters existed at the date of the audit report and are significant, the auditor should advise the client that the financial statements need to be recalled and modified. If the client refuses to do so, the auditor should take the appropriate legal action to recall the financial statements and advise actual and potential users of the financial statements that the audit report can no longer be relied upon.

SUBSEQUENT EVENT material happening occurring after the date of the financial statements but before the audit report is issued. Footnote disclosure is required so that financial statement users are properly informed. The subsequent event typically has a significant impact on financial position or earning capacity. Examples of subsequent events requiring disclosure are lawsuits, impairment of assets, and permanent decline in price of securities.

SUBSIDIARY ACCOUNT one of the accounts in a particular SUBSIDIARY LEDGER. The balance of all the subsidiary accounts should agree with the control account in the GENERAL LEDGER. An example is an individual customer's account (i.e., Mr. X) in the accounts receivable ledger of a department store. All the customer accounts should agree with the accounts receivable account in the general ledger.

SUBSIDIARY COMPANY firm in which a controlling interest is owned by another company, called the PARENT COMPANY. After acquisition, the parent company accounts for its investment in the subsidiary company including intercompany eliminations. *See also* CONSOLIDATION.

SUBSIDIARY COMPANY ACCOUNTING method undertaken by a subsidiary for the recording of its transactions with the parent. Subsidiary companies have separate books or accounting records. In theory, transactions between the subsidiary and parent should be accounted for in *arm's-length* terms. Even though each is a separate incorporated entity, consolidated financial statements are usually prepared for financial presentation purposes. Consequently, the subsidiary's assets and liabilities are combined with the parent. The common ownership aspect presents many difficulties in the fair and informative presentation of a consolidated entity's financial condition for reporting and tax purposes.

SUBSIDIARY LEDGER supporting ledger of related accounts that in total equals the control account appearing in the GENERAL LEDGER. Examples are individual creditor accounts agreeing with accounts payable (creditors' ledger) and individual factory overhead items such as factory rent and factory insurance agreeing with the factory overhead account (factory overhead ledger).

SUBSTANTIVE PROCEDURES performed by an auditor in order to identify material misstatements in financial statement amounts and disclosures. Substantive procedures enable an auditor to obtain the sufficient appropriate audit evidence needed to provide the auditor with a reasonable basis for his or her opinion about the fairness of the financial statement presentation. The two types of substantive procedures are (1) tests of details of account balances, classes of transactions, and disclosure items, and (2) substantive analytical procedures. The first type of substantive procedures is required in an audit, while the second type is discretionary. Tests of details of transactions may be performed continually throughout the year under audit or at or close to the balance sheet date. When the CPA traces a sales invoice from the sales journal to the ledger for correctness, it is considered a test of details of transactions. When the CPA compares the book balance (i.e., recorded amount) of cash to the bank reconciliation, it is considered a test of details of account balances. Comparing recorded interest expense to recorded corporate debt is an example of a substantive analytical procedure. *See also* TESTS OF DETAILS.

SUBSYSTEM component of a larger system. For example, the financial, marketing, accounting, and production systems are subsystems or components of a MANAGEMENT INFORMATION SYSTEM (MIS).

SUCCESSFUL EFFORTS ACCOUNTING method of accounting for exploration costs by companies in the extractive industries, especially oil and gas. Expenditures for successful projects are deferred while those for unsuccessful ones are immediately expensed. Capitalized costs applicable to producing properties are amortized based on the reserves produced. *See also* FULL COST METHOD.

SUCCESSOR AUDITOR external auditor of a company who displaces the PREDECESSOR AUDITOR.

SUMMARY FINANCIAL STATEMENTS derived from audited financial statements, but include less detail. An auditor may express an opinion on summary financial statements provided the auditor did not issue an adverse opinion or disclaimer of opinion on the audited financial statements. Also referred to as *condensed financial statements*.

SUMMARY OF SIGNIFICANT ACCOUNTING POLICIES a required description of all significant accounting policies used by the entity. The summary is typically the first or second note to the financial statements. Alternatively, the summary may be placed after the basic financial statements and before the notes to the financial statements.

SUM-OF-THE-YEARS'-DIGITS (SYD) METHOD accelerated depreciation method in which the amounts recognized in the early periods of an asset's useful life are greater than those recognized in the later periods. The SYD is found by estimating an asset's useful life in years, assigning consecutive numbers to each year, and totaling these numbers. For n years, the short-cut formula for summing these numbers is $SYD = n(n + 1)/2$. The yearly depreciation is then calculated by multiplying the total depreciable amount for the asset's useful life by a fraction whose numerator is the remaining useful life and whose denominator is the SYD. Thus annual depreciation equals

$$(\text{Original Cost} - \text{Salvage Value}) \times \frac{\text{Remaining Useful Life}}{\text{SYD}}$$

For example, assume that an asset costs $1000 and has an estimated useful life of five years. The estimated salvage value at the end of the five-year period is $100. The SYD is $5(5 + 1)/2 = 15$. The calculations for this example are shown below:

Year	Fraction			Depreciation
1	$5/15$	×	$900 =	$300
2	$4/15$	×	900 =	240
3	$3/15$	×	900 =	180
4	$2/15$	×	900 =	120
5	$1/15$	×	900 =	60
			Total	$900

SUNK COST costs incurred in the past whose total will not be affected by any decision made now or in the future. Sunk costs are usually past or historical costs. For example, suppose a machine acquired for $50,000 three years ago has a book value of $20,000. The $20,000 book value is a sunk cost that does not affect a future decision involving its replacement.

SUPERABSORPTION COSTING costing method treating costs from all links in the value chain as an inventory cost.

SUPERCOMPUTER data processing machine designed to be significantly larger and/or faster than the typical mainframe computer. It can process both scalar and vector quantities. It handles many thousands of operations simultaneously. Supercomputers can perform billions of additions per second. An example is the Cyberplus parallel processor.

SUPERVARIABLE COSTING treats only direct materials as the only variable cost.

SUPPLEMENTARY STATEMENT schedules or statements that amplify, elaborate on, or detail the income statement, balance sheet, and statement of changes in financial position. An example is inflation-adjusted statements.

SUPPLIERS' MANAGEMENT the careful selection of suppliers and the cultivation of long-term relationships based on the consistent ability to meet mutual expectations.

SUPPLY CHAIN interdependent collection of organizations that supply materials, products, or services to a customer.

SUPPLY CHAIN MANAGEMENT managing the "virtual" enterprise composed of suppliers and customers. Collaborative behavior will lead to streamlined business processes and mutual benefits.

SUPPLY CHAIN MANAGEMENT (SCM) SOFTWARE software that facilitates supply chain management function seamlessly. SCM is the organization of activities between a company and its suppliers in an effort to provide for the profitable development, production, and delivery of goods to customers. As a result of information sharing, production lead times and inventory holding costs have been reduced, and on-time deliveries to customers have been improved. SCM software systems support the planning of the best way to fill orders and help tracking of products and components among companies in the supply chain.

SUPPORT COSTS costs of activities not directly associated with production. Examples are the costs of process engineering and purchasing.

SURETY a promise by one party to assume responsibility for the debt of a borrower in the event of the borrower's default. The party that provides this promise is also known as a surety or guarantor.

SURPLUS
1. earned surplus or RETAINED EARNINGS reflecting the accumulated net income less dividend distributions.
2. CAPITAL SURPLUS, the stockholders' equity in a corporation in excess of par or stated value of capital stock.

SURROGATE ACTIVITY DRIVER activity driver that is not descriptive of an activity, but that is closely correlated to the performance of the activity. The use of a surrogate activity driver should reduce measurement costs without significantly increasing the costing bias. The number of production runs, for example, is not descriptive of the material-disbursing activity, but the number of production runs may be used as an activity driver if material disbursements coincide with production runs.

SURROGATE COST DRIVER acceptable substitute for a cost driver. It is used because the driver cannot be easily measured.

SURTAX additional tax applied to income above some specified figure resulting in a higher effective tax rate. *See also* MAXIMUM TAX.

SURVIVING COMPANY in a BUSINESS COMBINATION, the one that acquires the net assets and continues the operations of the predecessor company. The surviving company may be a newly organized entity or a previously existing business.

SURVIVING SPOUSE wife or husband who survives the other. A surviving spouse is entitled to the income-splitting advantages permitted on joint tax returns if the spouse died during either of the two taxable years before the current taxable year. Also, the surviving spouse must have a dependent child at home and not have remarried. All amounts paid to a beneficiary of a life insurance policy at a date after the insured's death (i.e., an annuity) are included in gross income to the degree the amount is greater than the amount payable as a death benefit.

SUSPENSE ACCOUNT temporary account (i.e., not included in the financial statements) for recording part of a transaction, such as those involving receipts or disbursements, prior to final analysis or identification of that transaction.

SUSTAINING ACTIVITY COST cost of an activity that benefits the organization but is not caused by any specific supplier, product, service, or customer cost object. Examples of such activities are preparation of financial statements, plant management, and support of community programs.

SWAP CONTRACT involves an agreement between two parties to exchange future cash payments. Swap contracts may involve interest rate swaps, currency swaps, commodity swaps, or equity swaps.

SWING LOAN *see* BRIDGE LOAN.

SYNDICATE temporary association of investment bankers brought together for the purpose of selling securities; also called *purchase group*. One investment banker in the group, usually the originating house, is selected to manage the syndicate. There are two types of underwriting syndicates, divided and undivided. In a *divided* account, the liability of each member investment banker is limited in terms of participation. Once a member sells the securities assigned, that investment banker has no additional liability regardless of whether the other members are able to sell their portion of the security or not. In an *undivided* account, each member is liable for unsold securities up to the amount of its percentage participation irrespective of the number of securities that investment banker has sold. Most syndicates are based on the undivided account arrangement.

SYSTEMATIC RANDOM SELECTION *see* SYSTEMATIC SAMPLING.

SYSTEMATIC SAMPLING sampling approach used in auditing. In a population of n units and a desired sample of s units, the auditor selects every rth unit (n/s) systematically beginning at a random point among the first r units in the population. In the case where a population is not in numerical sequence, it is easier to choose a systematic random sample instead of a pure random sample. If documents or transactions are unnumbered, no need exists with this approach to number them physically, as would be the case with random number table selection. Instead, with systematic sampling the auditor counts off the sampling interval to choose the documents. Some audit software packages have routines for systematic selection purposes. A problem with this sampling approach is that every *r*th unit may correspond to an existing sequence in the population, so sample items are continually selected from the same part of a recurring pattern. Assume the auditor is examining 500 paid checks from a total population of 15,000 checks. One random starting point is used. The auditor will select every 30th check (15,000/500). So that 500 checks may be chosen, the auditor goes upward or downward from their random starting point. Assume a random starting point of check number 80. Therefore, check numbers 50 (80 − 30) and 20 (80 − 60) are includable in the sample, as well as every 30th check number subsequent to number 80 (i.e., 110, 140, etc.). If the auditor chose 10 random starting points, 50 checks (500/10) would be chosen from each random start. Hence, the auditor would pick every 300th check number (15,000/50) prior to and subsequent to each of the random starting points.

SYSTEMIC RISK the risk that an entire financial system could collapse. Systemic risk might be based on an economic crisis that results in financial system instability.

SYSTEM PROGRAM product of the computer manufacturer to aid the user in easily and productively operating the system. *See also* OPERATING SYSTEM.

SYSTEMS ANALYST one who is engaged in systems analysis involving identification, measurement, and recommendation of system alternatives to management for final selection. After an intensive investigation of the information needs of the different levels of management, the systems analyst should identify the available system alternatives. These include: (1) acquisition of a new system; (2) modification of the old system; and (3) use of a third party's services, such as a timeshare outside service bureau, which could eliminate or continue the use of the old system. For each available alternative, feasibility studies should be conducted before a recommendation is made to management for final selection.

SYSTEM WEAKNESS inadequate internal controls in the client's accounting system resulting in a higher risk environment. The auditor must expand the audit procedures and techniques when internal control is weak.

SYSTRUST a type of trust service that addresses the risks and opportunities of an information technology system. Systrust engagements are governed by STATEMENTS ON STANDARDS FOR ATTESTATION ENGAGEMENTS (SSAE).

T

T-ACCOUNT common accounting form in the shape of the capital letter T. It has the following components: (1) a title describing the particular financial statement item (e.g., sales revenue), (2) a left side referred to as a DEBIT, and (3) a right side called a CREDIT. There is a separate T-account for each item in the ledger. A T-account looks as follows:

Account Name	
Debit	Credit

TAG in markup languages such as HTML and XML, notation used to define a data element for display or other purposes.

TAGUCHI METHOD OF QUALITY CONTROL a method of controlling quality, developed by Genich Taguchi, a past winner of the Deming Award, that emphasizes robust quality design and the *quality loss function* (QLF). Taguchi claims that quality is greatly determined at the design level. In addition to quality control in production, he emphasizes quality control in four other functions: (1) product planning, (2) product design, (3) process design, and (4) production service after purchase. Further, Taguchi's QLF quantitatively measures the success or failure of quality control. The traditional view is that any product that measures within the upper and lower specification limits is "good," and a product outside the limits is "bad." In contrast, the QLF presumes that *any* deviation from the target specification is important because it means economic losses for the customer. Furthermore, the economic losses increase quadratically as the actual value deviates from the target value.

TAKE-HOME PAY *see* DISPOSABLE INCOME.

TAKEOVER form of acquisition usually followed by a merger. Takeover can be hostile or friendly. The public TENDER OFFER is a means of acquiring a target firm against the wishes of management. In a friendly takeover the acquiring firm negotiates with the targeted company, and common agreement is reached in an amiable atmosphere for subsequent approval by shareholders. *See also* MERGER; PROXY FIGHTS (BATTLES).

TALF PROGRAM *see* TERM ASSET-BACKED LOAN FACILITY (TALF) PROGRAM.

TAKEOVER TAX TREATMENT implications based on the terms of a takeover by one company of another. The tax effects will differ depending on the method used to account for the business combination.

TANGIBLE ASSET one having physical substance and a life greater than one year. It is not held for resale in the ordinary course of business. Examples are machinery, furniture, and building.

TARGET COST *see* STANDARD COST.

TARGET COSTING method used in the analysis of product design that involves estimating a target cost, via a desired profit and sales price, and then designing the product/service to meet that cost. This method precedes KAIZEN costing. The Japanese concept of Kaizen is relevant to target costing. A policy of seeking continuous improvement in all phases of company activities facilitates cost reduction, often through numerous minor changes.

TARGET INCOME amount of income an organization is trying to achieve during a particular period. The specification of target income may be based upon a desired rate of return on invested money (for example, 20% return on investment) or a growth in earnings per share (EPS). The target income may be also specified as a percentage of sales (for example, 15% of sales).

TARGET INCOME SALES amount required to attain a particular income level or target net income. TARGET INCOME sales volume is computed as:

$$\text{Target Income Sales Volume} = \frac{\text{Fixed Costs} + \text{Target Income}}{\text{Unit Contribution Margin}}$$

For example, assume that unit contribution margin is $15, fixed costs are $15,000, and target income is $15,000. Target income sales volume = ($15,000 + $15,000)/$15 = 2,000 units. This means that 2,000 units need to be sold to make $15,000 profit.

TARGET PRICE expected market price for a product, given the company's knowledge of its customers and competitors.

TARGET PRICING a pricing method that involves (1) identifying the price at which a product will be competitive in the marketplace, (2) defining the desired profit to be made on the product, and (3) computing the target cost for the product by subtracting the desired profit from the competitive market price. The formula

$$\text{Target Price} - \text{Desired Profit} = \text{Target Cost}$$

Target cost is then given to the engineers and product designers, who use it as the maximum cost to be incurred for the materials and other resources needed to design and manufacture the product. It is their responsibility to create the product at or below its target cost.

TARIFF
1. tax on imports or exports, most often calculated as a percent of the price charged for the good by the foreign supplier. The money collected is *duty*. A tariff may be imposed as a source of revenue for the government. A more common purpose of tariffs is protection against foreign competition. By raising prices of imported goods relative to the prices of domestic goods, tariffs encourage consumers to buy domestic rather than foreign products.
2. schedule of rates or fares in the transportation industry.

TARP *see* TROUBLED ASSET RELIEF PROGRAM (TARP).

TAX charge imposed by a governmental body on personal income, corporate income, estates, gifts, or other sources to obtain revenue for the public good. Tax filing and payment are legally enforceable.

TAXABLE INCOME
Individual: ADJUSTED GROSS INCOME (AGI) less itemized deductions and PERSONAL EXEMPTIONS. After taxable income is derived, the tax to be paid can be determined by looking at the tax rate schedules.
Corporation: gross income less allowable business deductions.

TAX ADVISOR, THE monthly journal published by the AMERICAN INSTITUTE OF CERTIFIED PUBLIC ACCOUNTANTS (AICPA) designed primarily for CPAs, attorneys, and tax executives. All major areas of taxation of interest to practitioners are covered including their practical applications. Theoretical discussion of federal tax law sometimes appears.

TAX ALLOCATION *see* INTERPERIOD INCOME TAX ALLOCATION.

TAX ANTICIPATION BILL (TAB) short-term obligation issued by the U.S. Treasury to raise funds during a period when tax receipts are not large enough to cover current disbursements. TABs mature approximately one week after quarterly corporate tax payments are due. The attractiveness of TABs is that the government will accept them in payment for taxes at their face value.

TAX ANTICIPATION NOTE (TAN) short-term debt instrument issued by a municipality in order to raise funds to cover shortages prior to tax receipts. TAN debt is retired once individual and corporate tax revenues are received.

TAX AVOIDANCE payment of the least tax possible by using legal tax planning opportunities such as estate planning. Engaging in tax avoidance measures is not in any way construed as betraying or shirking a public or patriotic duty. In fact, a majority of court decisions have supported this assertion. TAX EVASION, in contrast, utilizes illegal methods to achieve this end.

TAX BENEFIT RULE Internal Revenue Service provision stating that amounts received in one period, representing a recovery of an amount deducted in a prior year, are to be included in income to the extent that the prior deduction resulted in a decrease in taxable income in that year.

TAX COURT U.S. administrative court where judges handle cases of dispute between the taxpayer and the Internal Revenue Service. No jury trials are available. Taxpayers must file a petition to the court within 90 days of receiving a statutory deficiency notice. Areas decided on by the court include estate, gift, and federal income taxes. The court findings are reported generally in writing and are open to public inspection.

TAX CREDIT reduction in taxes payable to the Internal Revenue Service or local government. A tax credit is more beneficial to the taxpayer than an itemized deduction because it reduces taxes on a dollar-for-dollar basis.

TAX DEED document evidencing the passage of title to a purchaser of property sold for taxes. The tax deed is issued upon foreclosure of the property lien. Typically, there is a grace time period permitting the owner to make good on the delinquent taxes in order to redeem the property.

TAX EFFECT
1. general term describing the consequences of a specific tax scenario with respect to a particular tax-paying entity. Many factors are considered such as time elements, projections and estimates of revenues, expenses, deductions, acquisitions, disposals, and the like and their relationship upon present and future tax liability.
2. impact on taxes of a taxable revenue or expense item. For instance, an interest expense itemized deduction of $2,000 will result in tax savings of $560 at the 28% tax bracket.

TAX ELECTION choice of an option or options with respect to tax treatments of specified situations, transactions, report form, and timing of reports. Some elections must have the Commissioner's approval, such as certain changes in accounting method, and some may be done without approval, on an annual basis, such as the filing of a joint tax return.

TAX EQUITY AND FISCAL RESPONSIBILITY ACT OF 1982 (TEFRA) legislation notably involving accelerating estimated tax payments by corporations, restricting the medical deduction, and establishing 10% withholding on interest and dividends. The Act repealed *safe-harbor* leasing.

TAX EVASION failure to pay taxes legally due a governmental agency. Examples are failure to report income received and claiming of fictitious deductions. There is a penalty for tax fraud based on the underpayment of tax. Criminal prosecution also may apply. *See also* TAX AVOIDANCE.

TAX-EXEMPT BOND security whose interest is not subject to federal or local tax in the state of the issuer. Though often called a *municipal bond*, it may also be issued by a county, state, or state agency. For example, a New York City resident does not pay federal, state, or city tax on the interest received from a New York City obligation. It is triple tax-free, though this is not necessarily true of other states. An investor in a mutual fund that invests solely in tax-exempt bonds often pays no tax on interest earned. However, some states tax fund dividends. The return on a tax-exempt bond is equivalent to a higher return on a taxable corporate bond because of the tax savings. The dollar advantage of a tax-exempt security increases as the tax rate rises. Assume a taxpayer in the 35% tax bracket receives 6% on a tax-exempt bond. The equivalent taxable yield on a corporate bond is 9.23% (6%/.65). It should be noted, however, that the holder of a tax-exempt security *does* have to pay tax on the gain at the time of sale representing the difference between the cost and the selling price. For example: An investor buys a $1,000, 5% tax-exempt bond for 90%. The cost is therefore $900. The taxpayer will be taxed on the gain of $100 in the year the bond is redeemed.

TAX-FREE EXCHANGE transfers of assets or property from one taxpayer to another that are specifically exempted from federal income tax consequences. Examples are exchanges of property or assets to certain corporate entities in which ownership of transferred assets are still maintained; a controlled corporation (Section 351) or like-kind exchanges under Section 1031. In the year of exchange, there is no recognized gain or loss. However, there is an adjustment to basis of the assets received in the transfer, in effect deferring the gain upon future disposition.

TAX HAVEN foreign country providing significant, permanent tax breaks to individuals and companies operating within it. In a tax haven country, foreigners may receive income or own assets and pay very low taxes. Many companies are situated or have subsidiaries in tax havens for TAX AVOIDANCE reasons. There are two objectives for establishing a subsidiary in a tax haven: (1) a subsidiary can operate as a legitimate operation and generate profits while simultaneously enjoying the tax advantages; and (2) a parent may establish a subsidiary in a tax haven for the purpose of tax avoidance only. The major purpose is to shift income from a country with high taxes to a tax haven country by using a subsidiary as an intermediary.

TAX INDEXING method using a form of INDEXATION to decrease the overall impact of the erosion of purchasing power in periods of inflation and subsequent "bracket creep."

TAX LIEN governmental agency claim to a taxpayer's property for delinquent or overdue taxes. Tax assessment, demand, and refusal to pay effectively create the lien. The tax lien may on occasion attach to property held by a third-party transferee. When full taxes are paid, the lien ceases.

TAX ON SCHOLARSHIPS OR FELLOWSHIPS charges levied on grants received by a degree candidate at a university. An exclusion is available only for amounts used for tuition, fees, and course-related costs. This exclusion does *not* apply to amounts paid for teaching, research, or other related services. Thus funds received for scholarships and fellowships are includable in gross income for tax purposes except for those directly related to pursuing a degree.

TAX PLANNING systematic analysis of differing tax options aimed at the minimization of tax liability in current and future tax periods. Whether to file jointly or separately, the timing of a sale of an asset, ascertaining over how many years to withdraw retirement funds, when to receive income, when to pay expenditures, the timing and amounts of gifts to be made, and ESTATE PLANNING are examples of tax planning. TAX SOFTWARE can be used for tax-planning purposes.

TAX PREFERENCE ITEM certain items defined under Section 57 of the Internal Revenue Code that may result in the imposition of the ALTERNATIVE MINIMUM TAX (AMT). These items of otherwise exempt income or deductions or of special tax benefit were targeted to ensure that taxpayers who benefit should pay at least a minimum amount of tax. Items include tax-exempt interest on nonessential municipal bonds and contributions of appreciated property.

TAX RATE amount of tax to be paid based on taxable income. The tax rate typically changes as the unit of the tax base changes.
Individual: tax rate depends on whether the tax return is for a single filer, joint filer, or head of household.
Corporation: the maximum tax rate is 35%.

TAX RATE SCHEDULE schedule used to determine the tax on a given taxable income. The marginal tax rate typically increases as the taxable income rises.

TAX REFORM federal law making changes to the tax provisions, including filing requirements, income reporting, allowable deductions, tax credits, and tax rates.

TAX RETURN general name of the form used to file taxes payable to a federal or local government. Included on the tax return are such items as gross income, allowable deductions, tax credits, and tax due. Individual taxpayers file on a calendar-year basis using Form 1040, which is due 3½ months after the tax year. Corporations can file Form 1120 on a calendar-year or fiscal-year basis. It is due 2½ months after the tax year. Tax returns are also prepared for partnerships (Form 1065), estates (Form 706), and gifts (Form 709).

TAX SHELTER investments, typically in limited partnerships, that can protect or defer (shelter) a portion of income from current taxes. Passive losses can be applied only to passive income. Usually, a significant amount of capital along with a very high amount of debt is necessary. Allowable deductions are generally permitted only to the amount *at-risk*. A tax shelter is desired by taxpayers in high tax brackets so they can take the losses from it to reduce their taxable income. Examples of tax shelters are real estate and oil and gas. Other permissible tax shelters are tax-exempt municipal obligations and single-premium life insurance policies. For failing to register a tax shelter there is a penalty of 1% of the aggregate amount invested, with no maximum. Failure to report a tax shelter identification number is $250. Penalties for shelters deemed abusive can be staggering. Tax shelters have been *greatly restricted. See also* AT-RISK RULES.

TAX SHIELD deductions that result in a reduction of income tax payments. The tax shield is computed by multiplying the deduction by the tax rate itself. For example, assume an annual depreciation deduction is $3,000 and the tax rate is 40%; the tax shield, or tax savings on depreciation is $3,000 $\times$ .4 = $1,200. The company saves $1,200 annually in taxes from the depreciation deduction. The higher the deduction, the larger the tax shield. Therefore, an accelerated depreciation method produces higher tax savings than the straight line method. Note that the term applies to other non-cash charges (e.g., amortization and depletion) as well.

TAX SOFTWARE tax modules that prepare federal and state returns and TAX PLANNING modules for corporations, partnerships, individuals, and estates and trusts. A microcomputer—with its ability to store large amounts of data that can be manipulated at tremendous rates of speed—performs many of the mechanical and repetitive tasks involved in income tax return preparation. For example, Turbo Tax prepares individual, corporate, partnership, fiduciary, and deferred compensation tax returns. Tax-planning software essentially performs spreadsheet *what-if* tax scenarios.

TAX YEAR period that a tax return covers. Taxpayers file on a calendar-year basis unless another accounting period has been chosen. A fiscal-year basis referring to any other one-year interval can also be selected. If a tax year is to be changed, approval must be received from the Internal Revenue Service. A new company or estate may employ any allowable tax year, but a new partnership has to use the same period employed by the major partners.

TCP/IP *see* TRANSFER CONTROL PROTOCOL/INTERNET PROTOCOL.

TECHNICAL ANALYSIS means of predicting stock prices based on historical price and trading patterns; it is not concerned with the financial statistics that are the focus of FUNDAMENTAL ANALYSIS. It uses charts (e.g., head and shoulders, rising bottoms) to identify trends in the market or individual securities. Technical analysts believe the market can be predicted in terms of direction and magnitude. Stock prices tend to move with the market because they react to various demand and supply forces. An attempt is made to uncover a consistent pattern in prices or a relationship between stock price changes and other market data. Technical analysts try to predict short-term price changes and then recommend the timing of a purchase or sale. A sample company stock chart follows:

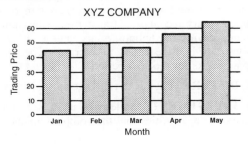

TECHNOLOGY COSTS category of cost associated with the development, acquisition, implementation, and maintenance of technology assets. It can include costs such as the depreciation of research equipment, tooling amortization, maintenance, and software development.

TEFRA *see* TAX EQUITY AND FISCAL RESPONSIBILITY ACT OF 1982 (TEFRA).

TELECOMMUNICATIONS transmission of data between computers at different locations. Data are typically sent over telephone lines, but radio waves and satellites are also used. A computer with a communications board (RS-232C Serial Port), telecommunications software, and modem are needed for communication; a terminal may also be used. Software is required to communicate between computers within the firm, for time-sharing situations, and for accessing commercial data-bases. Software also aids in the manipulation of information coming over the modem. Communications packages usually reserve some of the computer memory as a buffer. Information is placed in the capture buffer, awaiting future disposition (saving to disk or printing the information). Alternatively, one can load data from a disk into the buffer for uploading to another computer in ASCII if a synchronous communication is used. Information handling functions are the core of the telecommunications program. Some communications programs do error checking of information received (i.e., XModem Protocol). Communications software permits CPAs in different geographic areas to communicate with each other by electronic mail or to transfer data files and documents between offices. Bulletin boards can be established by CPAs to share up-to-date accounting and auditing information with their clients.

TEMPLATE
1. mechanical aid in drawing flowcharts and flowchart symbols.
2. worksheet that includes the relevant formulas for a particular application but not the data. It is a blank worksheet on which data are saved and filled in as needed for a future accounting application. Templates are guides for preparing the spreadsheet. They are predefined files, including cell formulas and row or column labels for specific applications. In effect, they are worksheet models designed to solve specific types of problems. Templates allow for the referencing of cells and formulations of interrelated formulas and functions. They are reused to analyze similar transactions.

TEMPORARILY RESTRICTED NET ASSETS funds whose use is restricted by outside parties until some event occurs. For example, a not-for-profit organization may have received donated assets that are restricted by the donor until some time period has elapsed.

TEMPORARY ACCOUNT account that does not appear on the balance sheet; also called NOMINAL ACCOUNT. Revenue and expense accounts, along with income distribution accounts (such as dividend) are temporary accounts. The balances in all temporary accounts are transferred to the capital or the retained earnings account, leaving the temporary accounts with zero balances. This procedure, called *closing*, is necessary to determine a periodic net income (or loss) and prepare books for the next period.

TEMPORARY DIFFERENCE *see* INTERPERIOD INCOME TAX ALLOCATION.

TEMPORARY INVESTMENTS strategy of using seasonal excess of cash to invest in marketable securities that the company intends to convert back into cash within one year. The investments produce dividend and/or interest income as well as possible capital appreciation for the company. Temporary investments are considered short-term investments and are classified as current assets under the MARKETABLE SECURITY heading on the balance sheet.

TENDER OFFER bid to buy the stock of a firm at a specified price (usually at a premium over the market price). The objective of a tender offer is to take control of the *target company*. Sometimes the offer is submitted for approval to the board of directors of the target company, or the offer may be made directly to the shareholders of the company. The SEC requires that any corporate suitor accumulating 5% or more of a target company make disclosures to the SEC, the target company, and the pertaining exchange. *See also* TAKEOVER.

10-K annual filing with the SECURITIES AND EXCHANGE COMMISSION (SEC) for publicly traded companies. Financial statements and supporting details are provided. Form 10-K typically contains more financial information than the annual report to stockholders. Audited basic financial statements are included. Examples of disclosures are sales, operating income, segmental sales by major line of business for the last five years, and general business information.

10-Q quarterly filing with the SECURITIES AND EXCHANGE COMMISSION (SEC) by publicly traded companies. It contains interim financial statements and related disclosures and may cover one particular quarter or be cumulative. It should present comparative figures for the same period of the prior year. The statements may or may not be audited. Form 10-Q is less comprehensive than Form 10-K.

TERM ASSET-BACKED LOAN FACILITY (TALF) PROGRAM a program created by the U.S. Federal Reserve Board, announced on November 25, 2008. The facility will support the issuance of asset-backed securities (ABS) collateralized by student loans, auto loans, credit card loans, and loans guaranteed by the Small Business Administration (SBA). Under the TALF, the Federal Reserve Bank of New York (FRBNY) will lend up to $1 trillion on a non-recourse basis to holders of certain AAA-rated ABS backed by newly and recently originated consumer and small business loans.

TERM BOND issue whose component bonds mature at the same time. *See also* SERIAL BONDS.

TERMINATION BENEFITS amounts due employees who cease to work for the employer. The amount of the termination benefit may be in the form of an ANNUITY or *lump-sum payment*. The termination benefit may arise from lay-off of TERMINATION IN PENSION PLANS.

TERMINATION IN PENSION PLAN termination benefits may either be special, offered only for a short time period, or contractual, required by the terms of the plan in a specific event such as a plant closing. Loss and liability should be recognized for special termination benefits when employees accept the offer and the amount can be reasonably estimated. The entry when "early retirement payoff" occurs is to debit loss and credit estimated liability equal to the current payment plus discounted value of termination benefits. *See also* CURTAILMENT IN PENSION PLAN; SETTLEMENT IN PENSION PLAN.

TERM LOANS intermediate- to long-term (typically, two- to ten-year) business loans with provisions for systematic repayments (amortization during the life of the loan). The repayment or amortization schedule is a particularly important feature of such loans. Amortization protects both the lender and borrower against the possibility that the borrower will not make adequate provisions for retirement of the loan during its life. The term loan sometimes ends with a *balloon* payment.

TESTCHECK substantiation of certain items in an account or financial record so the auditor can form an opinion as to the accuracy of the entire account or financial record. The items examined can be based on a representative sample. An example is testchecking every fifth entertainment expense voucher for supporting documentation and approval.

TESTDECK in computer applications, body of test data processed by a program that compares computerized results with predetermined manual results. If the two agree, computer processing of information is being performed properly. If not, the program has not been implemented in accordance with the documentation. The testdeck procedure is an audit control mechanism.

TEST OF TRANSACTION auditing procedure related to examining specified transactions and supporting documentation. It is part of the testing process used by the auditor to check internal-controls reliability. It is undertaken to gather evidence so that an audit opinion can be rendered as to the fairness of financial statement presentation. Included in such a test is verifying transaction amounts and tracing transactions to accounts in the financial statements. Transaction tests are of a much more limited scope than ANALYTICAL REVIEW. In transaction tests, a selected number of specific transactions are tested to see if controls are performing properly. A resulting error rate for complying with the procedures is established. Based on the rate of error, auditors determine if they can rely on the information developed from posting or recording transactions. The test helps auditors determine the scope of audit work. *See also* COMPLIANCE TEST; SUBSTANTIVE TEST.

TESTS OF CONTROLS procedures performed by an auditor to evaluate the effectiveness of the operation of an entity's internal controls. When performing tests of controls, an auditor is concerned with how controls were performed, when controls were performed, by whom controls were performed, and how consistently controls were performed. Tests of controls include inquiry, observation, inspection, and transaction walkthroughs. Tests of controls are required in (1) integrated audits of issuers, and (2) audits of nonissuers when the auditor wants to base the risk of material misstatement on effective internal controls.

TESTS OF CONTROLS THROUGH THE COMPUTER test of a client's controls over internal control may take the form of the test data (deck) method or the parallel simulation method. In the former, the auditor uses test data to examine the controls and procedures embodied in the client's program. Here, the auditor is not testing the client's data files. Under the parallel simulation method, the auditor uses parallel simulation as part of testing the controls related to internal control. Actual client data are reprocessed with the auditor's simulation of the client program. It creates a simulated client output. The major purpose of parallel simulation is to insure that unauthorized changes have not been made by the client's program.

TESTS OF DETAILS the type of substantive procedures applied to account balances, classes of transactions, and disclosure items to obtain audit evidence that the amounts and disclosures in the financial statements are fairly stated.

THEORETICAL CAPACITY *see* CAPACITY; IDEAL CAPACITY.

THEORETICAL SUBSTANCE theory in which substance rules over legal form in financial accounting; also called *substance over form*. Examples are the inclusion of common stock equivalents in the earnings-per-share calculation even though such securities are not legally common stock at the present time, and treating a CAPITAL LEASE as an asset even though the property is not legally owned by the lessee.

THEORY OF CONSTRAINTS approach to continuous improvement (reducing operating expenses and inventory and increasing throughput) based on a five-step procedure: (1) identifying constraints, (2) exploiting the binding constraints, (3) subordinating everything else to the decisions made in the second step, (4) increasing capacity of the binding constraints, and (5) repeating the process when new binding constraints are identified. It seeks to identify a company's constraints or bottlenecks and exploit them so that throughput is maximized and inventories and operating costs are minimized.

THOSE CHARGED WITH GOVERNANCE the individuals who are responsible for overseeing the strategic direction and obligations of an entity, including the financial reporting process. Those charged with governance include the audit committee and the board of directors.

THREE-SIGMA LIMITS three STANDARD DEVIATIONS from the mean, used as the upper and lower control limits, in STATISTICAL QUALITY CONTROL charts. There are about three chances in one thousand that a variation that falls outside the control limits will be only random in character.

THREE-WAY ANALYSIS computation of three variances for factory overhead: *spending, efficiency*, and *volume* variances. The budget variance in the TWO-WAY ANALYSIS is separated into spending and efficiency variances. When an analysis of historical costs permits the estimation of variable and fixed overhead, but the accounting records do not allow the separation of actual overhead costs into their variable and fixed elements, this three-way analysis of overhead variance is used. The three-way analysis provides the following reconciliation between actual and applied overhead:

Actual (1)	Flexible (2) budget	Flexible (3) budget	Applied (4) costs
Actual Factory Overhead Costs	(AH × SR) for Variable + Budgeted Fixed Overhead Costs	(SH × SR) for Variable + Budgeted Fixed Overhead Costs	(SH × SR) for Variable + Fixed Overhead Rate × Activity Allowed

Spending Variances (1–2)	Efficiency Variances (2–3)	Volume Variances (3–4)

Budget Variance (1–3)	Volume Variance (3–4)

where AH = actual hours used, SH = standard hours allowed, and SR = standard overhead rate.

THROUGHPUT rate of production of a defined process over a stated period of time. Throughput can be measured in either financial or nonfinancial terms (for example, cash flows generated from selling products or services to customers, units of products, batches produced, dollar turnover, or other meaningful measurements. Components of throughput include MANUFACTURING CYCLE EFFICIENCY, process productivity, and process quality yield.

$$\text{Throughput} = \frac{\text{Manufacturing}}{\text{Cycle Efficiency}} \times \frac{\text{Process}}{\text{Productivity}} \times \frac{\text{Process}}{\text{Quality Yield}}$$

$$\frac{\text{Good Units}}{\text{Total Time}} = \frac{\text{Value-Added Processing Time}}{\text{Total Time}} \times \frac{\text{Total Units}}{\text{Value-Added Processing Time}} \times \frac{\text{Good Units}}{\text{Total Units}}$$

TICK MARK symbol, usually a check mark or asterisk, that the auditor places next to work completed on items being audited. WORK PAPERS will have tick marks next to individual functions performed. Different tick marks can be used to signify different things. An explanation of the tick mark appears somewhere within the work papers. For instance, a certain mark may be placed beside the total of promotion and entertainment expense. The commentary to the mark may be something like "verified supporting documentation for promotion and entertainment expenditure."

TIME-ADJUSTED RATE OF RETURN (TARR) *see* INTERNAL RATE OF RETURN (IRR).

TIME AND BILLING SOFTWARE computer program that tracks hours spent by function and chargeable expenses of staff accountants for a given client. Sources are hourly rates, time sheets, practice and time management reports, and accounting reports. At the end of a period, a bill based on expenses, time spent, and hourly rates is sent. When billing on a flat-fee basis, hourly information is useful to the practitioner in evaluating staff accountants' proficiency. Hourly rates of staff accountants can be varied, depending on the client serviced. Time and billing programs also furnish projected fees to present and prospective clients. Client payment history—when payments were made, last time fees were increased—can be part of the report.

TIME AND MATERIALS PRICING approach to pricing used by service businesses in which the total billing is composed of actual direct materials and parts cost, actual direct labor cost, plus a percentage markup of each to cover overhead costs, and a profit factor.

TIME AND MOTION STUDY systematic study of the time and human motions used to perform an operation. The purpose is to eliminate unnecessary motions and to identify the best sequence of motions for maximum efficiency. Therefore, time and motion study can be an important source of productivity improvements. For example, a time and motion study analyzing the functioning of tellers in a bank might be conducted in an effort to effect savings in costs and processing time.

TIME-BASED MANAGEMENT using time as a strategic weapon by identifying market opportunities, responding to customers' needs, and eliminating waste.

TIME CARD *see* WORK TICKET.

TIME DEPOSIT savings account at a financial institution that earns interest but is not legally subject to withdrawal on demand or transfer by check. The depositor can withdraw only by giving notice. A CERTIFICATE OF DEPOSIT (CD) is a special type of time deposit. Should the CD depositor wish to withdraw funds prior to the date of maturity, the financial institution imposes a substantial penalty.

TIME DRAFT written order to be paid at a given future time after the drawee accepts it. It differs from a SIGHT DRAFT, which is payable on demand. *See also* ACCEPTANCE.

TIME SERIES ANALYSIS considers the fact that data points taken over time may have an internal structure, such as autocorrelation, trend, or seasonal variation, that should be accounted for when analyzing data.

TIME SHARING
1. information system that services many users from one computer; these users are served simultaneously until the volume of work to be processed forms a waiting line. Time sharing is a multiuser environment whereby many terminals are usually logged-on to a mainframe computer. All of the users are able to access the computer to upload information, to download information, obtain electronic mail, use programs on the computer, and so on.
2. in real estate, division of ownership or use of a resort unit or apartment on the basis of time periods.

TIMES-INTEREST-EARNED RATIO *see* INTEREST COVERAGE RATIO.

TIME SOFTWARE computer program that tracks hours worked by employees by function, operation, or activity. It prepares an analysis of the variance between budgeted and actual hours as well as prepares trends in actual hours over a stated time period (e.g., quarterly comparisons).

TIME STANDARD amount of time required to perform a task by a trained operator working at a normal pace and using a prescribed method.

TIME STUDY development of standards through stopwatch observation.

TIME VALUE OF MONEY concept that a dollar one has today is worth more than a dollar tomorrow. The reason: today's dollar can earn interest by putting it in a savings account or placing it in an investment. The longer it takes to get $1, the less it is worth today because interest is being lost. *See also* FUTURE VALUE; PRESENT VALUE.

TOLERABLE
1. In cost accounting, acceptable variance between actual and standard cost or revenue.
2. In auditing, degree of acceptable misstatement in substantive testing without materially misstating the financial statements. A tolerable rate is the maximum deviation rate in tests of controls that is acceptable by the auditor in his or her assessment of control risk.

TOLERABLE DEVIATION RATE in audit sampling, the maximum population deviation rate from a prescribed INTERNAL CONTROL that an auditor is willing to accept or tolerate without having to alter his or her planned reliance on the control.

TOLERABLE MISSTATEMENT in audit sampling, the maximum dollar amount of misstatement in an account balance or class of transactions that an auditor is willing to accept or tolerate and still be able to conclude that there is no material misstatement.

TOP-DOWN APPROACH in an integrated audit, the approach to be used in selecting internal controls to be tested. An auditor should first evaluate overall risks at the financial statement level and then risks at the entity level. Finally, an auditor should focus on account balances, disclosure items, and assertions for which material misstatement is a reasonable possibility.

TOTAL COST sum of the various costs incurred. For example, total manufacturing costs are the sum of direct materials, direct labor, and factory overhead. By management function, the total costs of a manufacturing business are the sum of manufacturing costs and selling and administrative expenses. By behavior in relation to fluctuations in activity, total costs are the sum of variable costs and fixed cost. *See also* UNIT COST.

TOTAL COST OWNERSHIP (TCO) tracing costs to a person or organization responsible for costs related to their designated products, services, and/or customers.

TOTAL DIRECT LABOR COST VARIANCE difference between standard direct labor cost for the good units produced and the actual direct labor costs incurred.

TOTAL DIRECT MATERIALS COST VARIANCE difference between standard cost for direct materials and the actual cost incurred for those items.

TOTAL FACTOR PRODUCTIVITY *see* TOTAL PRODUCTIVITY.

TOTAL FIXED COSTS costs that remain constant in total regardless of changes in activity.

TOTAL MANUFACTURING COSTS total costs of direct materials, direct labor, and manufacturing overhead incurred and charged to production during an accounting period.

TOTAL MANUFACTURING OVERHEAD VARIANCE difference between the actual manufacturing overhead costs incurred and the standard manufacturing overhead costs applied to production using the standard variable and fixed manufacturing overhead rates.

TOTAL PRODUCTIVITY (TOTAL FACTOR PRODUCTIVITY) quantity of output divided by the cost of all inputs.

TOTAL PROJECT APPROACH method that looks at all the items of revenue and cost data under two alternatives and compares the net income or contribution margin results; also called *comparative statement approach*. It differs from the INCREMENTAL ANALYSIS approach. For example, assume the ABC Company is planning to expand its productive capacity. The plans consist of purchasing a new machine for $50,000 and disposing of the old machine without receiving anything. The new machine has a five-year life. The old machine has a five-year remaining life and a book value of $12,500. The new machine will reduce variable operating costs from $35,000 per year to $20,000 per year. Annual sales and other operating costs follow:

	Present Machine	**New Machine**
Sales	$60,000	$60,000
Variable costs	35,000	20,000
Fixed costs:		
Depreciation (straight-line)	2,500*	10,000
Insurance, taxes, etc.	4,000	4,000

*Note that the depreciation expense of the old machine is irrelevant because it is a SUNK COST.

The total project approach results in the following:

	Present Machine	**New Machine**	**Increment (or Difference)**
Sales	$60,000	$60,000	—
Less: VC	35,000	20,000	($15,000)
CONTRIBUTION MARGIN	$25,000	$40,000	$15,000
Less: FC			
Depreciation	—	$10,000	$10,000
Other	4,000	4,000	—
Net income	$21,000	$26,000	$ 5,000

The schedule for the total project approach shows an increase in profit of $5,000 with the purchase of the new machine.

TOTAL QUALITY CONTROL (TQC) philosophy that aggressively strives for a defect-free manufacturing process.

TOTAL QUALITY MANAGEMENT (TQM) approach to quality that emphasizes continuous improvement, a philosophy of "doing it right the first time" and striving for zero defects and elimination of all waste. It is a concept of using quality methods and techniques to strategic advantage within firms.

A comparison between TQM and BUSINESS PROCESS REENGINEERING (BPR) is presented below.

	TQM	*BPR*
Goals	Small-scale improvements at all levels of management with cumulative effects	Outrageous
Case for action	Assumed to be necessary	Compelling
Scope and focus	Attention to tasks, steps, and processes across the board	Select but broad business processes
Degree of change	Incremental, evolutionary, and continual	Order of magnitude and periodic; revolutionary
Role of information technology (IT)	Incidental	Cornerstone
Senior management involvement	Important up front	Intensive throughout

TOTAL VARIABLE COSTS costs that vary in total in direct proportion to changes in activity.

TOXIC ASSETS worthless assets such as subprime mortgages, bad mortgages, or bad stocks, so-called because there is no market for them.

TQM *see* TOTAL QUALITY MANAGEMENT.

TRACE to determine if a financial statement item has been handled according to proper corporate or accounting policy. For example, if the auditor wants to trace the balance in the travel expense account, he will trace account postings from the ledger to the journal they came from. The auditor will then trace from the journal transaction to the source document to assure that proper backup exists.

TRACEABILITY ability to assign a cost directly to an activity or a cost object in an economically feasible way by means of a causal relationship. *See also* TRACING.

TRACEABLE COST one directly assigned to a given item or function. For example, costs may be identified to a given department, process, product-line, geographic area, industry segment, class of customer, etc. An example is advertising expense that is applicable to a particular product.

TRACING assignment of cost to an activity or a cost object using an observable measure of the consumption of resources by an activity. Tracing is generally preferred to allocation if the data exists or can be obtained at a reasonable cost. For example, if a company's cost accounting system captures the cost of supplies according to which activities use the supplies, the costs may be traced (as opposed to allocated) to the appropriate activities. Tracing is also called direct tracing. The 1998 draft also defines cost tracing broadly as the ability to assign a cost to a cost object. Thus, it treats assignment and tracing as synonymous.

TRACK
1. reference or supporting computation for a particular item, such as an account balance or entry. Tracking an item will reveal how it was obtained.
2. concentric circle on a computer disk where data are recorded.

TRACKING STOCK a stock created by a company to follow, or "track," the performance of one of its divisions—typically one that is in a line of business that is fast-growing and commands a higher industry price-to-earnings ratio than the parent's main business; also called letter stock or targeted stock. The objective is to increase value to shareholders, and thereby lower a company's cost of capital. Some companies distribute tracking stock to their existing shareholders. Others sell tracking stock to the investing public, raising additional cash for themselves. Some companies do both. Tracking stock, however, does not typically provide voting rights. Issuing tracking stock is an increasingly popular corporate-financing technique.

TRADE CREDIT type of credit extended by one business to another business, allowing the latter to buy goods from the former without making immediate full payment by check or with cash. It is credit obtained through open-account purchases represented by an ACCOUNTS PAYABLE by the buyer and an ACCOUNTS RECEIVABLE by the seller. Trade credit is an important external source of working capital for a business, although it can be very expensive. For example, a credit of 2/10 net 30 (2% cash discount if paid within 10 days, otherwise due in 30 days) translates into a 37% annual interest rate if the cash discount is foregone.

TRADE DATE date a security transaction actually occurs. Typically, the SETTLEMENT DATE is *five* business days after the trade date.

TRADE DEFICIT excess of imports of goods (raw materials, agricultural and manufactured products, and capital and consumer products) over the exports of goods, resulting in a negative *balance of trade*. Trade surplus is the reverse. The balance of trade is distinguished from the BALANCE OF PAYMENTS, which consists of the CURRENT ACCOUNT including services as well as merchandise trade and other *invisible items* such as interests and profits earned abroad. Factors that affect a country's balance of trade include the strength or weakness of its currency value in relation to those of the countries with which it trades and the comparative advantage in key manufacturing areas.

TRADE DISCOUNT reduction of the list or regular price in return for the purchase of large quantities, also called *quantity discount* or *price discount*.

TRADEMARK legal protection afforded names, symbols, and other specific identities assigned to a product. A trademark is generally considered to have no limited term of existence or natural limited life. U.S. Patent Office registration gives legal protection for an indefinite number of renewals for periods of 10 years each. A trademark is deferred and amortized to expense over the benefit period. The costs capitalized include design and registration, as well as the legal costs of successfully defending the trademark in court.

TRADING ON EQUITY FINANCIAL LEVERAGE, or the use of borrowed funds, particularly long-term debt, in the capital structure of a firm. Trading *profitably* on the equity, also known as *positive (favorable) financial* leverage, means that the borrowed funds generate a higher rate of return than the interest rate paid for the use of the funds. The excess accrues to the benefit of the owners because it magnifies, or increases, their earnings.

TRADITIONAL COST ALLOCATIONS allocating indirect costs without using cost drivers. A cause-and-effect relationship may not exist between the cost and the base used for the allocation.

TRADITIONAL COST SYSTEM *see* CONVENTIONAL COST SYSTEM.

TRANSACTION CYCLE repetitive flow of the activities of an ongoing enterprise described in terms of three major transaction cycles as follows: (1) *Revenue Cycle*, relating to sales, shipping, receivables, and collections; (2) *Buying Cycle*, referring to purchases, payables, and payments; and (3) *Production Cycle*, relating to manufacturing products and storage.

TRANSACTION RISK the risk that future cash transactions will be affected by changing exchange rates.

TRANSACTIONS events or happenings in a business that change its financial position and/or earnings. Transactions are recorded in a journal and then posted to a ledger. Examples of business transactions are investing in the business, buying supplies, paying bills, withdrawing money from the business, buying equipment, and paying rent.

TRANSACTION TEST *see* TEST OF TRANSACTION.

TRANSACTION-VOLUME COST DRIVER type of cost driver that draws on a measurement from a feeder subsystem that not only varies with cost magnitude but proportionately assigns the costs to its cost objects. It yields a per-unit cost.

TRANSCRIBE
1. act that serves to transfer an amount from one financial record to another. Transferring an original source document amount to a journal or posting to a ledger is an example of this act.
2. transforming audio representation manually into typed copy.

TRANSFER AGENT representative, usually a bank or trust company, designated by a corporation to make legal transfers of stocks and bonds and, in some cases, to distribute dividends. In this event the agent keeps the current stock-transfer books, ledger, and payment lists. Transfer agent and *registrar* duties may be performed by the same agent.

TRANSFER CONTROL PROTOCOL/INTERNET PROTOCOL (TCP/ IP) protocol explaining the subdivision of information into packets for transmission and the way in which applications involve transmitting e-mail and file transfer.

TRANSFER PRICE charge made when one division of a company provides goods or services to another division of the company. A good transfer price will help evaluate the performance of the divisions. *See also* TRANSFER PRICING.

TRANSFER PRICING deciding on the price of goods or services that are exchanged between various divisions of a decentralized organization. A major goal of transfer pricing is to enable divisions that exchange goods or services to act as independent businesses. Various transfer pricing schemes are available, such as MARKET PRICE, COST-BASED PRICE, or NEGOTIATED PRICE. Unfortunately, there is no single transfer price that will please everybody—that is, top management, the selling division, and the buying division. Usually the best transfer price is the outside market price less costs saved by dealing within the company (e.g., transportation costs, advertising, salesperson salaries). If the two division managers—buying division and selling division—cannot agree on a price, one will be arbitrated by upper management. When an outside market price is not available, *budgeted* cost plus profit markup may be used so that cost efficiencies at the selling division are still maintained.

TRANSFERRED-IN COSTS costs of processing a product or performing a service from a prior department to the current department. The costs usually occur under a PROCESS COSTING system. Consider two processing departments in a chain—Department A and Department B. Transferred-in costs would be the costs attached to partially completed units transferred in from Department A.

TRANSFER TAX
1. state tax levied upon the transfer or sale of a security or property. Some states base the tax on selling price (e.g., New York) while other states base the tax on the par value (e.g., Texas).
2. federal tax on the sale of stocks and bonds.
3. federal tax on gifts made and estate proceeds.

TRANSLATION RISK also called ACCOUNTING RISK, the degree to which a firm's finanicial statements are exposed to exchange rate fluctuations.

TRANSPARENT MARKET a market in which there is open communication between stockholders, investors, and company officials and current trade and quote information is readily available to the public.

TRANSPORTATION LP PROBLEM problem of determining how much to ship from each origin to each destination in order to minimize total shipping costs.

TRAVEL AND ENTERTAINMENT EXPENSE DEDUCTION tax allowance for a percentage of business expenses. The rules apply regardless of whether the expense was paid while the taxpayer was away from home overnight or not. A business meal is deductible only if it is *directly related* to the active conduct of the taxpayer's trade or business. *Unreimbursed* employee expenses for business travel and entertainment become miscellaneous itemized deductions subject to a 2% adjusted gross income "floor."

TRAVELING AUDITOR
1. company employee who visits branches or subsidiaries or other outlying locations from the home office.
2. CPA firm employee who is primarily involved in auditing clients at distant locations on a continuous basis.

TREADWAY COMMISSION popular name for the National Commission on Fraudulent Reporting that has issued a number of recommendations for the prevention of fraud in financial reports, ethics, and effective internal controls.

TREASURER person in a firm who deals with financial and money problems. The treasurer is engaged in (1) capital obtainment, (2) investor relations, (3) short-term financing, (4) banking and custody, (5) credits and collections, (6) investments, and (7) insurance and employee benefits. The treasurer's functions are distinguished from those of the CONTROLLER, who supervises the accounting activities of the firm.

TREASURY BILL short-term obligation of the federal government, commonly called T-bill. Treasury bills are auctioned weekly through competitive bidding by the Treasury with maturities of 91 days and 182 days. In addition, nine-month and one-year bills are sold periodically. Treasury bills carry no coupon but are sold on a discount basis. Denominations range from $10,000 to $1 million. The yields on T-bills are lower than those on any other marketable securities due to their virtually risk-free nature. The market is very active, and the transaction costs involved in the sale of Treasury bills in the secondary market are small.

TREASURY BOND
1. long-term debt instrument issued by the U.S. Treasury department with maturities of 10 years or longer issued in minimum denominations of $1,000.
2. bond issued by a corporation and then repurchased. Such a bond is considered as retired when repurchased.

TREASURY CERTIFICATE debt security of the United States government that pays coupon interest and whose maturity date is one year or less from the issuance date.

TREASURY NOTES intermediate government obligations with maturities of one to ten years. Denominations range from $1000 to $1 million or more. Due to the existence of a strong secondary market, they are attractive marketable security investments. Like Treasury bills, Treasury notes have a low yield because of their virtually risk-free nature.

TREASURY STOCK issued shares that have been reacquired by the company. Treasury shares may be resold or canceled. Dividends are *not* paid on treasury shares nor are voting fights associated with them. The two acceptable methods of accounting for treasury stock are the COST METHOD and PAR VALUE method. Under the cost method, treasury stock is shown at the *cost* to reacquire the shares. Under the par value method, treasury stock is recorded at the par value of the reacquired stock. Treasury stock is shown as a deduction in arriving at stockholders' equity. Under either method, there is an appropriation of retained earnings equal to the cost of the treasury stock held.

TREASURY STOCK METHOD procedure for determining the common stock equivalency of options and warrants when computing earnings per share. The treasury method assumes that options or warrants were exercised at the beginning of the period (or at time of issue, if later), and that the funds obtained were used to purchase and retire common stock at the average market price during the period. The number of shares required cannot exceed 20% of the common stock outstanding at year-end. If funds remain, it is assumed that they are used to reduce long-term or short-term debt. If there are any funds remaining after debt is reduced, they are assumed to be invested in U.S. government securities or commercial paper.

TREASURY WARRANT order on the U.S. Treasury that a certain dollar amount be paid with a bank check.

TREND ANALYSIS forecasting technique that relies primarily on historical time series data to predict the future. The analysis involves searching for a right TREND EQUATION that will suitably describe trend of the data series. The trend may be linear, or it may not. A linear trend can be obtained by using a LEAST SQUARES METHOD. The line has the equation $y = a + bt$ where $t = 1,2,3 . . .$, $b =$ slope of the line, and $a =$ value of y when $t = 0$. The coefficients of the equation, a and b, can be determined using these equations:

$$b = \frac{n\Sigma ty - (\Sigma t)(\Sigma y)}{n\Sigma t^2 - (\Sigma t)^2}$$

$$a = \frac{\Sigma y}{n} - b\,\frac{\Sigma t}{n}$$

TREND EQUATION special case of SIMPLE REGRESSION, where the x variable is a time variable. This equation is used to determine the trend in the variable y, which can be used for forecasting. For example, assume the following sales data are given for the last 16 months:

Time (*t*)	Sales (*y*)
1	$6.18
2	5.92
3	6.49
4	6.69
5	7.24
6	7.20
7	7.24
8	7.49
9	7.45
10	7.66
11	7.89
12	7.85
13	7.77
14	8.01
15	8.35
16	8.38

Using the NORMAL EQUATIONS of simple regression gives the following result:

$$y = 6.1135 + 0.147014t$$

where t is time (1,2,3 . . .) and y is sales. The forecasted sales for the next period ($t = 17$) can be computed as follows:

$$y = 6.1135 + 0.147014t = 6.1135 + 0.147014(17) = 8.6127$$

See also TREND ANALYSIS.

TRIAL BALANCE

1. listing of the account balances from the general ledger, prepared at the end of the accounting period. All accounts are listed in the order in which they appear in the ledger. Total debits must equal total credits; otherwise, an error has been made. Even though the trial balance furnishes arithmetical proof that debits equal credits, it does not detect all errors. For example, a posting to the wrong account may have occurred. The trial balance is a work sheet and *not* a formal financial statement. It serves as a convenient basis for the preparation of the balance sheet and income statement. *See also* POST-CLOSING TRIAL BALANCE.

2. listing of the account balances of a subsidiary ledger (i.e., customer accounts) that must agree with the total of the control account (i.e., accounts receivable) in the general ledger.

TROUBLED ASSET RELIEF PROGRAM (TARP) a program of the U.S government to purchase assets and equity from financial institutions to strengthen its financial sector. It is the largest component of the government's measures to curb the ongoing financial and subprime mortgage crisis of 2007–2008. *See also* SUBPRIME MORTGAGE.

TROUBLED DEBT RESTRUCTURING situation, defined in State-ment of Financial Accounting Standards No. 15, where the DEBTOR has financial difficulties and asks the CREDITOR for some relief from the obligation. The debtor will recognize an extraordinary gain on the restructuring of the payable equal to the difference between the fair value of assets exchanged and the book value of the debt, inclusive of accrued interest. The creditor recognizes a loss on the difference between the fair value of assets received and the book value of his investment. Appropriate footnote disclosure should also be given by the debtor and creditor related to the restructuring terms.

TRUST agreement in which the trustee takes title to property (called the *corpus*) owned by the grantor (donor) to protect or conserve it for either the grantor or the trust's beneficiary. The trust is established by the grantor. The trustee is typically given authority to invest the property for a return. Trusts may be revocable or irrevocable.

TRUSTEE
1. third party to a BOND indenture. The trustee's function is to make sure the issuer lives up to the numerous provisions in the indenture. A trustee is usually a trust department of a commercial bank. The trustee is paid a fee and acts to protect the interests of the bondholders.
2. third party to a BANKRUPTCY proceeding. The trustee's responsibility is to value and recapitalize the firm if it is to be reorganized.

TRUST FUND one used to account for a government's fiduciary responsibilities and activities in managing trusts. There are basically three types of trust funds: expendable trust funds, nonexpendable trust funds, and pension trust funds.

TRUST RECEIPT instrument acknowledging that the borrower holds specified property in trust for the lender. The lender retains title. This type of financing is used for equipment dealers, automobile dealers, and others involved in durable expensive goods. When the lender receives the sale proceeds, title is given up.

***T*-STATISTIC** *see* *T*-VALUE.

***T* TABLE** table that provides *T*-VALUES for various degrees of freedom and sample sizes. The *t* table is based on the *Student t* probability distribution. See the *t* table (Table 5).

***T*-TEST**
1. in REGRESSION ANALYSIS, test of the statistical significance of a regression coefficient. It involves basically two steps: (1) compute the *T*-VALUE of the regression coefficient as follows: *t*-value = coefficient/standard error of the coefficient; (2) compare the value with the *t* table value. High *t*-values enhance confidence in the value of the coefficient as a predictor. Low values (as a rule of thumb, under 2.0) are indications of low reliability of the coefficient as a predictor.
2. general statistical test for hypotheses, based on *t*-distribution, known as a small sample distribution. The *t*-test is used to estimate and test hypotheses about population means, the difference between two means, a population variance, and a comparison of two population variances. For example, an accounting instructor wishes to test to determine if the use of a new and old textbook had anything to do with the difference in performance of the two classes.

TURNOVER frequency with which an item (i.e., fixed asset, inventory, accounts receivable, personnel) is replaced during an accounting period. Assume credit sales of $360,000 and average receivables of $60,000. The number of times receivables turned over for the period is 6 ($360,000/$60,000). In Great Britain, turnover means sales.

TURNOVER RATIO measure of a particular asset's activity (e.g., sales, cost of sales). The average asset balance for the period is used equal to the beginning balance plus the ending balance divided by 2. A turnover ratio is an *activity* ratio. By looking at the turnover of an asset in terms of generating revenue, the accountant can properly appraise a company's ability to manage assets efficiently. Examples are the turnover in fixed assets (sales/fixed assets), accounts receivable (sales/accounts receivable), and inventory (cost of sales/inventory).

TURNOVER TAX indirect tax, typically on an ad valorem basis, applicable to a production process or stage. For example, when manufacturing activity is completed, a tax may be charged on some companies. Sales tax occurs when merchandise has been sold. *See also* AD VALOREM TAX.

***T*-VALUE** measure of the statistical significance of an independent variable b in explaining the dependent variable y. It is determined by dividing the estimated regression coefficient b by its standard error S_b. That is

$$t\text{-Value} = b/S_b$$

Thus, the t-statistic measures how many standard errors the coefficient is away from zero. Generally, any t-value greater than $+2$ or less than -2 is acceptable. The higher the t-value, the greater the confidence we have in the coefficient as a predictor. Low t-values are indications of low reliability of the predictive power of that coefficient.

TWITTER a public forum where a user can read, write, and share messages called Tweets. Each Tweet is limited to 140 characters.

TWO-BIN INVENTORY CONTROL involving the use of two containers for inventory. Items are withdrawn from the first bin. When its contents are exhausted, it is time to reorder. Sometimes an order card is placed at the bottom of the first bin. The second bin contains stock sufficient to satisfy expected demand during the lead time period and a safety stock that is needed to avoid a possible stockout.

TWO-WAY ANALYSIS computation of two variances—*price* and *quantity* variances for direct materials and direct labor and *budget* and *volume* variances for factory overhead. The budget variance is the difference between actual overhead costs and the budget overhead based on standard hours allowed. The volume variance (denominator variance) is the difference between denominator volume and actual volume, multiplied by a predetermined fixed overhead rate. The two-way analysis for factory overhead stops here; it does not break up the budget variance into *spending* and *efficiency* variances. *See also* THREE-WAY ANALYSIS.

TWO-WAY ANALYSIS OF OVERHEAD VARIANCE dividing the total overhead variance into two variances: volume and controllable (the latter is sometimes called the budget, total overhead spending, or flexible budget variance). The variable overhead spending and efficiency variances and the fixed overhead budget variance are combined.

TYPE I ERROR risk that the sample supports the conclusion that recorded book value (e.g., account balance) is materially misstated when it is, in fact, not; also called *alpha risk*. *See also* HYPOTHESIS TESTING.

TYPE II ERROR risk that the sample supports the conclusion that the recorded account balance is not materially misstated when it is, in fact, materially misstated; also known as *beta risk*. *See also* HYPOTHESIS TESTING.

U

ULTRA VIRES an action outside the proper authority or power of a corporation or corporate officer as established in the corporate charter (Latin for "beyond the power").

UNADJUSTED RATE OF RETURN *see* SIMPLE RATE OF RETURN.

UNADJUSTED TRIAL BALANCE one showing account balances in debit and credit columns prior to preparing an ADJUSTING JOURNAL ENTRY.

UNAMORTIZED BOND DISCOUNT balance of the BOND DISCOUNT that remains to be amortized in future years. It is shown as a contra account to bonds payable (bond investment) to arrive at the net liability (asset). (It should be noted that an alternative treatment is to show the bond investment account net of the discount.) When the unamortized bond discount is amortized, interest expense is charged. *See also* UNAMORTIZED BOND PREMIUM.

UNAMORTIZED BOND PREMIUM part of the BOND PREMIUM that is to be amortized in later years. It is shown as an addition (deduction) to the maturity value of the bonds payable (bond investment) to arrive at the net balance. The future periodic amortization of unamortized bond premium is credited to interest expense. *See also* UNAMORTIZED BOND DISCOUNT.

UNAPPROPRIATED RETAINED EARNINGS part of retained earnings that is "free" or available for dividends. *See also* APPROPRIATED RETAINED EARNINGS.

UNAUDITED STATEMENT one in which the auditor prepares or aids in preparing but does not examine in accordance with GENERALLY ACCEPTED AUDITING STANDARDS (GAAS). In effect, the auditor is undertaking an accounting service of accumulating and preparing financial information, but is *not* applying audit procedures as a basis to form an audit opinion. An unaudited statement must be identified as such, and the auditor must issue a disclaimer opinion in which he states that he is not rendering an opinion on it.

UNAVOIDABLE COSTS costs to be incurred regardless of the decision to make or buy a certain part or keep or drop a certain product line; these costs cannot be recovered or saved. Much or all of fixed costs in those cases are unavoidable costs, e.g. property taxes and rent.

UNCERTAINTY state of knowledge in which one or more alternatives result in a set of possible specific outcomes, but where the probabilities of the outcomes are neither known nor meaningful. Unlike RISK, uncertainty is not objective and does not assume complete knowledge of alternatives. In most practical cases, decision makers tend not to distinguish between uncertainty and risk. *See also* DECISION-MAKING UNDER UNCERTAINTY.

UNCOLLECTIBLE ACCOUNT account receivable, note receivable, or other type of receivable that is unlikely to be paid. An example is a customer who is bankrupt or on the verge of default. *See also* ALLOWANCE FOR BAD DEBTS; ALLOWANCE METHOD; BAD DEBT; DIRECT WRITE-OFF METHOD.

UNCONSOLIDATED SUBSIDIARY subsidiary showing individual financial statements that are not presented in the CONSOLIDATED FINANCIAL STATEMENTS. The EQUITY METHOD of accounting is used for unconsolidated subsidiaries. A subsidiary is not consolidated even though more than 50% of voting common stock is owned by the parent when one of the following situations exists: (1) parent is not in actual control of subsidiary (i.e., subsidiary is in a politically unstable foreign country); (2) parent has only temporary control of the subsidiary; or (3) the nature of the subsidiary's operations are significantly different than those of the parent.

UNCONTROLLABLE COSTS *see* CONTROLLABLE COSTS.

UNDER- AND OVERAPPLIED *see* OVERAPPLIED OVERHEAD; UNDERAPPLIED OVERHEAD.

UNDERAPPLIED OVERHEAD amount by which the factory overhead added to work-in-process inventory at a predetermined overhead rate (and credited to factory overhead applied) is less than the actual overhead shown in factory overhead control. *See also* OVERAPPLIED OVERHEAD; PREDETERMINED OVERHEAD RATE.

UNDERSTANDABILITY term indicating that financial information is stated in terms that enable users to perceive its significance.

UNDERSTANDING WITH THE CLIENT SAS Number 83 provides that the auditor should have a written agreement with the client concerning the engagement services so as to avoid misinterpretation. The understanding should cover such areas as the purposes of the engagement, auditors' responsibilities, management's duties, limitations of the engagement, conditions under which access to the audit workpapers may be granted to others, arrangements involving a predecessor auditor, and use of specialists and internal auditors. The understanding should be documented in the working papers.

UNDERWRITING acceptance of risk in return for payment. In a new securities issue, the underwriter, known as the INVESTMENT BANKER and his or her syndicate, may perform an underwriting function by purchasing the securities at a fixed price from the issuer, hoping to sell them at a higher offering price and making a profit on the *spread*. Underwriting is the function of investment bankers, who usually form an underwriting group, also called a SYNDICATE, to pool the risk and assure successful distribution of the issue.

UNDETACHABLE STOCK WARRANT one issued along with a bond that requires simultaneous exercise of both to obtain stock. If the warrant is *not* detachable, the bond is, in essence, CONVERTIBLE DEBT *only*. No allocation of the proceeds should be to the conversion feature. The reason to account for the issuance only as convertible debt is the inseparability of the debt and conversion option. The excess received on the issuance attributable to the undetachable stock warrants is credited to premium on bonds payable since the issuance is accounted for solely as debt. *See also* DETACHABLE STOCK WARRANT; STOCK WARRANT.

UNDISTRIBUTED PROFIT earnings of a business entity such as a syndicate, joint venture, or partnership, preceding the allocation of profit according to the member's profit distribution agreement. *See also* EARNED SURPLUS.

UNEARNED REVENUE
   1. payment received in advance of providing a good or service. Since an obligation exists on the part of the company to provide goods or services

for which the advance payment was received, unearned revenue is a liability. An example is a retainer received by an attorney. When the services are performed, revenue is then earned.

2. in taxation, revenue obtained other than from personal services.

UNEMPLOYMENT COMPENSATION TAX *see* FEDERAL UNEMPLOYMENT TAX ACT (FUTA) and STATE UNEMPLOYMENT COMPENSATION.

UNENCUMBERED BALANCE in GOVERNMENT ACCOUNTING, balance relating to a portion or the entire amount of an appropriation that has not been encumbered or expended.

UNEXPIRED COST all costs, including inventory costs and miscellaneous prepaid or deferred costs, that are associated with the revenue of future periods. Unexpired costs are carried to future periods as assets because they represent future benefits.

UNFAVORABLE VARIANCE excess of actual costs over standard costs. Unfavorable variances typically require further investigation for possible causes. *See also* STANDARD COST SYSTEM; VARIANCE.

UNFUNDED no funds have been provided for a specified obligation or liability. Such may be the case for a pension plan where part of pension expense has not been funded (cash paid) by the employer. This will result in a deferred pension credit.

UNIFORM COMMERCIAL CODE (UCC) legal code that standardizes business law in the United States. The Code was formulated in 1952 by the National Conference of Commissioners on United States Laws. The Code was offered to the state legislatures, and all states except Louisiana adopted it. For example, the Code covers regulations on commercial paper, warranties, uncertified checks, written agency agreements, security agreements, and bankruptcy. The Uniform Commercial Code is followed by practicing lawyers.

UNIFORMITY term describing the presentation of financial statements by different companies using the *same* accounting procedures, measurement concepts, classifications, and methods of disclosure. In essence, uniform accounting treatment and disclosures by companies facilitate their comparison. However, strict uniformity is not possible in accounting because of differences in company and industry practices. For example, the same event may be handled differently by competing companies, as in the case when different inventory methods are used. *See also* COMPARABILITY.

UNIFORM PARTNERSHIP ACT proposed law prepared by the National Conference of Commissioners on Uniform State Laws to apply to partnerships. Several states have adopted it. According to the Act, a partnership is an association of two or more individuals who carry on as co-owners of a business for profit.

UNIFORM RESOURCE LOCATOR (URL) used to specify addresses on the World Wide Web. URLs have the following format: protocol://hostname. The protocol used for Web resources is HyperText Transfer Protocol (HTTP) or its secure version (HTTPS). Other protocols include FTP and MAILTO, among many others.

UNISSUED STOCK shares that have been authorized but have not been issued. Assume authorized shares of 500,000 and issued shares of 200,000. The unissued shares are 300,000.

UNIT CONTRIBUTION MARGIN excess of the unit selling price over the unit variable cost. For example, if the sales price is $30 and the unit variable cost is $18, then the unit CONTRIBUTION MARGIN (CM) is $12. This means that each unit sold contributes $12 toward the fixed cost or profit.

UNIT COST cost of producing one unit of product or service, usually based on averages. For example, if total manufacturing costs are $100,000 and the production volume for a given period is 10,000 units, the unit production cost is $10 per unit ($100,000/10,000 units). Unit costs may be stated in terms of gallons, feet, tons, individual units, and so on. Unit costs must be available for comparison of varying volumes and amount and for the purpose of establishing unit sales price of the product or service. If volume of activity increases, the variable cost per unit remains the same but the fixed cost per unit drops.

UNIT COST ANALYSIS SCHEDULE process costing statement used to accumulate all costs charged to the Work-in-Process Inventory account of each department or production process and to compute cost per equivalent unit for direct material costs and conversion costs.

UNIT LEVEL ACTIVITIES activities performed each time a unit is produced; such activities vary with the number of units produced.

UNIT OF SAMPLING item in a population that is subject to sampling by the auditor to draw a conclusion regarding the acceptability of the population. The sampling unit may be based on physical, cost, or other characteristic. An example is selecting inventory items to be examined to draw an inference as to whether the inventory account is properly stated. Another example is taking a sample of sales invoices by number to test their mathematical accuracy.

UNITED STATES SERIES I SAVINGS BOND a U.S. savings bond designed to protect the purchasing power of your principal and guarantees a real fixed rate of return above inflation for the life of the bond (10 to 30 years). The current series I savings bond, called *I-bond* for short, guarantees 3% above inflation. You can purchase up to $30,000 worth of the bonds each year, you can never lose principal, earnings are free from state and local taxes, and federal taxes are deferred until you redeem the bond. Plus, there are no fees when you buy or sell these bonds. Although you can cash an I-bond 6 months after the issue date, there is a 3-month earnings penalty if you redeem them in less than 5 years. I-bonds are sold in denominations of $50 to $10,000 at most banks and also online at www.savingsbonds.gov.

UNITS OF PRODUCTION METHOD procedure in which depreciation is allocated in proportion to the asset's use in operation. First, the depreciation per unit of production is computed by dividing the total depreciable cost by the asset's projected units-of-production capacity. To find periodic depreciation expense, multiply the depreciation per unit of production by the number of units produced during the period.

UNIX a powerful, extensively used operating system that has been implemented on a variety of platforms.

UNLIMITED LIABILITY in a SOLE PROPRIETORSHIP or a GENERAL PARTNER-SHIP, liability of owners not limited to the owner's investment. In a corporation, stockholders usually have LIMITED LIABILITY; they risk their investment in the enterprise but not their personal assets.

UNQUALIFIED OPINION
1. auditor's judgment that he or she has no reservation as to the fairness of presentation of a company's financial statements and their conformity with U.S. GENERALLY ACCEPTED ACCOUNTING PRINCIPLES (GAAP); termed an unmodified opinion in the care of nonissuer's financial statements; sometimes referred to as a clean opinion. In the auditor's opinion, the company has presented fairly its financial position, results of operations, and changes in cash flows. However, if there is inconsistency in application of GAAP, there should be disclosure in the auditor's report.
2. unqualified opinion on the effectiveness of internal control over financial reporting. It is an opinion that internal control over financial reporting is effective in all material respects as of the assessment date.

UNREALIZED LOSS, GAIN change in value of an asset that is still being held. It is distinguished from a REALIZED GAIN, LOSS on the sale of the asset. The term commonly refers to the write-down or write-up of an investment portfolio of trading or available-for-sale securities resulting from applying the market value method on an aggregate basis. On a trading securities portfolio, the unrealized loss or gain is shown on the income statement. On an available-for-sale securities portfolio, the total unrealized loss or gain is presented as a separate item under "Accumulated Other Comprehensive Income" in the stockholders' equity section of the balance sheet. Assume on 12/31/2014 a trading securities portfolio has a cost of $100,000 and a market value of $88,000. The entry is:

Unrealized loss	12,000	
Allowance		12,000

If on 12/31/2015, the trading securities portfolio in market value goes to $93,000 from $88,000, the entry is:

Allowance	5,000	
Unrealized gain		5,000

UNRESTRICTED NET ASSETS in GOVERNMENT ACCOUNTING, assets with no external restriction as to use or purpose. They can be employed for any purpose designated by the governing board, as distinguished from funds restricted externally for specific purposes.

UNSECURED LOAN borrowing that is not secured by a mortgage on a specific property. It is backed only by the borrower's credit rating. Unsecured loans are typically short term. The disadvantages of this kind of loan are that, because it is made for the short term and has no collateral, it carries a higher interest rate than a secured loan, and payment in a lump sum is required.

UNSYSTEMATIC RISK one that is unique to a specific security. It is the antithesis of market (or systematic) risk. Thus, as portfolios become more diversified, the unsystematic risk moves to zero because the risks of specific securities cancel each other out. Components of unsystematic risk include economic risk, business risk, financial risk, and accounting risk. *See also* BETA.

UPLOAD process of providing data from a microcomputer to a MAINFRAME or MINICOMPUTER or another MICROCOMPUTER. For example, an accountant can upload information from his or her computer to the client's computer system. *See also* DOWNLOAD; TELECOMMUNICATIONS.

UPPER DEVIATION RATE sometimes referred to as the *upper occurrence rate*, an auditor's estimate of the population's rate of deviation from a prescribed internal control. The upper deviation rate, which is typically determined using statistical tables, is equal to the sample deviation rate plus an allowance for sampling risk. The upper deviation rate is then compared to the tolerable deviation rate (specified by the auditor) in order to determine whether a prescribed INTERNAL CONTROL may be relied on by the auditor. In turn, reliance on an internal control results in a lower assessment of control risk.

UPPER LIMIT *see* CEILING.

UPTICK a term used to designate a price higher than that on the preceding transaction in the stock; also called *plus tick*. A stock may be sold short only on an uptick, or on a zero-plus tick. *Zero-plus tick* is a term used for a transaction at the same price as the preceding trade but higher than the preceding different price. Conversely, *down tick,* or *minus tick,* is used to designate a transaction made at a price lower than the preceding trade. A *zero-minus tick* is a transaction made at the same price as the preceding sale but lower than the preceding different price. A plus sign or a minus sign is displayed throughout the day next to the last price of each company's stock traded at each trading post on the floor of the New York Stock Exchange (NYSE).

UPTICK RULE SEC rule that prohibits short selling of securities except on an uptick. The rule provides that, subject to certain exceptions, a listed security may be sold short (1) at a price above the price at which the immediately preceding sale was effected (plus tick), or (2) at the last sale price if it is higher than the last different price (zero-plus tick). *See also* UPTICK.

URL (UNIFORM RESOURCE LOCATOR) an address system used for the Internet. The http prefix is used for the World Wide Web. For example, www.barnesandnoble.com is the full address for the Barnes & Noble online bookstore.

Some Common Addresses

http://	World Wide Web
ftp://	FTP server
Gopher://	Gopher server
mailto://	e-mail
News://	Newsgroup
wais://	Wide Area Information Server

USAGE VARIANCE *see* EFFICIENCY VARIANCE.

USEFUL LIFE typical operating service life of an asset for the purpose it was acquired. The term usually applies to fixed assets. The useful life used for DEPRECIATION ACCOUNTING does not necessarily coincide with the actual physical life or any commonly recognized ECONOMIC LIFE. *See also* DEPRECIABLE LIFE; DEPRECIATION.

UTILITY
1. economic and highly subjective term describing satisfaction of a specified want. Utility and usefulness are not necessarily synonymous terms. Artwork may be functionally useless but yet provide great utility to an art lover.
2. value of a certain outcome or payoff to someone; the pleasure or displeasure that person would derive from that outcome.

UTILITY PROGRAM software supporting the processing of a computer such as diagnostic and tracing programs.

V

VALIDATE
1. attest to the correctness and reliability of a financial item. A validity review or test is required by the ACCOUNTANT to satisfy the legitimacy of the item. An example of validation is the examination and approval of an employee's expense request form by a supervisor. Another example is the counting of petty cash to see that it conforms to the amount in the financial records.
2. make something legal or effective. An example is signing one's name to a bill of sale, which closes the deal. *See also* VALIDITY TEST.

VALIDITY TEST
audit procedure that ascertains whether a recorded financial statement item is accurately stated. Validity tests are those activities associated with satisfying oneself as to the precision, reliability, relevance, and authorization of transactions recorded in the books of a company. The methods used in the testing activity depend upon the type of transactions or amounts being tested. In testing transactions, the tester may use various methods to select the sample of the transactions and perform selected tests on the transactions. *See also* VALIDATE.

VALUATION ACCOUNT
item offset against or added to the gross amount of an account to arrive at a *net* balance. Examples are the allowance account that is subtracted from trading securities to reduce cost to market value, allowance for uncollectible accounts that is netted against accounts receivable, accumulated depreciation that is deducted from the fixed asset, or bond premium that is added to bonds payable.

VALUATION, ALLOCATION, AND ACCURACY
an assertion in an entity's financial statements made by management that account balances, transactions, and disclosure items have been recorded properly at appropriate amounts.

VALUATION ALLOWANCE *see* CONTRA ACCOUNT.

VALUE
1. highly subjective term, usually an expression of monetary worth applied to a particular asset, group of assets, business entity, or services rendered. It should not be confused with the term cost even though it is frequently measured, equated, and identified by it. Thus the term should be used with an appropriate modifying adjective.
2. amounts at which items are stated in financial records and statements. Value is expenditures or amounts deemed to benefit future periods. *See also* BOOK VALUE; MARKET VALUE.
3. represented by the amount of goods, services, or money necessary to complete an exchange for a specific commodity. In economic terms, value of goods equals price multiplied by quantity.

VALUE ADDED
difference, at each stage of production, between the cost of a product and the cost of all the materials purchased to make the product.

VALUE-ADDED ACTIVITY
activity that increases the worth of a product or service and for which the customer is willing to pay.

VALUE-ADDED NETWORK (VAN) company providing a private network allowing for "store and forward" capabilities associated with electronic data interchange. A TRADING PARTNER can send information to a VAN, which ascertains the intended recipient. The data is then stored in a mailbox until the data is retrieved (forwarded). Benefits of a VAN are improved security, less scheduling difficulties, and less problems associated with protocol and communication.

VALUE-ADDED TAX (VAT) indirect percentage tax levied on products or services at various stages of production and distribution. The actual value added to the product, including raw materials, labor, and profit, is determined at each stage or state of production and the tax is computed upon the increase in value. It is basically a tax allocated among the economic units responsible for the production and distribution of goods and services. Because collection of VAT takes place at the product's ultimate destination, VAT is not charged on export sales. VAT is charged on all domestically sold products regardless of the country of origin. Thus VAT is designed to provide an incentive to export and, of course, a disincentive to import.

VALUE-ADDING COST cost of an operating activity that increases the market value of a product or service.

VALUE ANALYSIS process of trying to reduce product costs by substituting less costly materials, redesigning nonessential parts, and the like.

VALUE CHAIN linked set of all value-creating processes or activities that convert basic input materials into products or services for the final consumer.

VALUE CHAIN COSTING ACTIVITY-BASED COST model that contains all of the activities in the VALUE-CHAIN (design, procure, produce, market, distribute/render, and post-service a product or service) of one organization.

VALUE ENGINEERING means of reaching targeted cost levels. It is a systematic approach to assessing all aspects of the value chain cost of reaching targeted cost levels and the value chain cost buildup for a product: R&D, design of products, design processes, production, marketing, distribution, and customer service. The purpose is to minimize costs without sacrificing customer satisfaction. Value engineering requires distinguishing between incurring costs and locked-in costs. Costs incurred are the actual use of resources, whereas locked-in (designed-in) costs will result in the use of resources in the future as a result of past decisions. Traditional cost accounting focuses on budget comparisons, but value engineering emphasizes controlling costs at the design stage, that is, before they are locked in.

VALUE IN USE discounted value of net cash receipts to be obtained from the corporate asset. The present value calculation includes consideration of annual cash inflows plus the disposal value.

VARIABLE ANNUITY one whose periodic payments are dependent on some undetermined or uncertain outcome such as the value of a securities portfolio. A contract between an investor and insurance company may take this form and subsequently the periodic payments would change as a function of the changes in applicable securities prices or rates of return. A variable annuity may also consist of payments that vary depending on changes in money market interest rates.

VARIABLE BUDGET *see* FLEXIBLE (VARIABLE) BUDGET.

VARIABLE COSTING method in which the costs to be *inventoried* include only the *variable* manufacturing costs. Fixed factory overhead is treated as a period cost — it is deducted along with the selling and administrative expenses in the period incurred. That is,

Direct materials	$xx
Direct labor	xx
Variable factory overhead	xx
Product cost	$xx

Fixed factory overhead is treated as a period expense.

Variable costing is used for internal management only. Its uses include: (1) inventory valuation and income determination; (2) relevant cost analysis; (3) BREAK-EVEN and COST-VOLUME-PROFIT (CVP) ANALYSES; and (4) short-term decision-making. Variable costing is, however, not acceptable for external reporting or income tax reporting. Companies that use variable costing for internal reporting must convert to ABSORPTION COSTING for external reporting.

Under absorption costing, the cost to be inventoried includes all manufacturing costs, both variable and fixed. Nonmanufacturing (operating) expenses, i.e., selling and administrative expenses, are treated as period expenses and thus are charged against the current revenue.

Direct materials	$xx
Direct labor	xx
Variable factory overhead	xx
Fixed factory overhead	xx
Product cost	$xx

Two important facts are noted: 1. Effects of the two costing methods on net income: (a) When production exceeds sales, a larger net income will be reported under absorption costing. (b) When sales exceed production, a larger net income will be reported under direct costing. (c) When sales and production are equal, net income will be the same under both methods. 2. Reconciliation of the direct and absorption costing net income figures: (a) The difference in net income can be reconciled as follows:

$$\left(\begin{array}{c} \text{Difference in} \\ \text{net income} \end{array} \right) = \left(\begin{array}{c} \text{Change in} \\ \text{inventory} \end{array} \right) \times \left(\begin{array}{c} \text{Fixed factory} \\ \text{overhead rate} \end{array} \right)$$

(b) the above formula works only if the fixed overhead rate per unit does not change between the periods.

VARIABLE COST PERCENTAGE figure that equals total variable costs divided by total sales. Labor-intensive companies have a higher variable cost ratio than capital-intensive ones. If product demand declines, it is very difficult to cut the labor and raw materials (variable costs) required to produce each unit of product. It is easier to reduce fixed costs (layoff of a foreman or personnel department employee, etc.). Variable costs per unit are usually reduced through automation (increasing fixed costs). For example, if variable costs are $150 and total sales are $600, the ratio is .25.

VARIABLE-COST-PLUS PRICING method in which the unit variable cost is defined as the cost base. Fixed costs are provided for through the markup that is added to this base. *See also* COST PLUS PRICING.

VARIABLE COST RATIO relationship showing variable costs as a percentage of sales. It is also 1 minus the CONTRIBUTION MARGIN (CM) ratio. An example follows:

	Total	**Percentage**
Sales	$37,500	100%
Less: Variable costs	15,000	40
Contribution margin	$22,500	60%

The variable cost ratio is 40% ($15,000/$37,500). It is also 1 minus the CM ratio, or $1 - .6 = .4 = 40\%$.

VARIABLE COSTS expenses that vary *in total* in direct proportion to changes in activities such as machine-hours and labor-hours within a RELEVANT RANGE. Examples are direct materials and gasoline expense based on mileage driven. Variable cost *per unit* is constant. *See also* FIXED COST.

VARIABLE (FACTORY) OVERHEAD portion of total factory overhead that varies directly with changes in volume. Examples of variable overhead are indirect materials, supplies, indirect labor, and fuel and power.

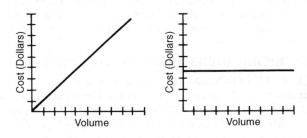

VARIABLE INTEREST ENTITY (VIE) entity whose equity investors do *not* have sufficient equity at risk such that the entity cannot finance its own activities. When a business has a controlling financial interest in a variable interest entity, the assets, liabilities, and profit of that entity must be included in consolidation. The entity that consolidates a variable interest entity is called the *primary beneficiary*. Variable interest is a contractual, ownership, or other interest in an entity that changes as the entity's net assets change. Entity is any legal structure to carry out operations or handle assets such as corporations, partnerships, limited liability companies, and trusts. There are many examples of variable interests such as guarantees, equity investments, written put options, and forward contracts. A business enterprise must consolidate a variable interest entity when that enterprise has a variable interest that will cover most of the entity's expected losses or receive most of the entity's anticipated residual return.

VARIABLE OVERHEAD EFFICIENCY VARIANCE difference in actual and budgeted variable overhead costs that results from inefficient use of indirect materials and indirect labor. Variable overhead efficiency variance = (actual labor-hours − standard labor-hours allowed for actual production) × standard variable overhead rate.

For example, assume that the standard cost of direct labor per unit of product A is 2.5 hours × $3 = $7.50. Assume further that during the month of March the company recorded 4,500 hours of direct labor time. The actual variable overhead costs were $13,750. The company produced 2,000 units of product A during the month. The variable overhead efficiency variance is (4,500 − 5,000) × $3 = $1,500, which is favorable since the actual hours used is less than the standard hours allowed. This may be the result of efficient use of labor time due to automation, use of superior production methods, or good foreman performance.

VARIABLE OVERHEAD SPENDING VARIANCE difference in actual and budgeted variable overhead costs that results from price changes in indirect materials and indirect labor and insufficient control of costs of specific overhead items. Variable overhead spending variance = actual overhead costs − (standard rate × actual hours of labor used).

For example, assume that the standard variable overhead cost per unit of product A is 2.5 hours × $3.00 = $7.50. Assume further that during the month of March the company recorded 4,500 hours of direct labor time. The total actual variable overhead cost for the month was $13,750. The company produced 2,000 units of product A during the month. The variable overhead spending variance is $13,750 − ($3.00 × 4,500 hours) = $250, which is unfavorable since actual overhead spent exceeded the budgeted amount. This may be the result of unavoidable price increases in indirect materials and indirect labor.

VARIABLE PRICING MODEL see CONTRIBUTION APPROACH TO PRICING.

VARIABLE RATE LOAN loan carrying an interest rate that may move up or down, depending on the movements of an outside standard such as the rate paid on U.S. Treasury securities; also called an *adjustable rate loan*. The lender can increase or decrease the interest rate on this type of loan at specified intervals to keep pace with changing market conditions. The frequency of the interest rate changes and the limit, if any, on the amount of change is set by the lender and must be specified in the loan document.

VARIABLES SAMPLING sampling designed to predict the value of a given variable for a population. The variables under AUDIT are typically the total population or the arithmetic mean. An example is the CPA's estimation of the cost of a group of inventory components. Initially, the accountant samples a limited number of components, computes the per-item cost, and finally statistically derives the plus or minus range of the total inventory value under examination.

VARIANCE
1. in *statistics*, measure of a dispersion of probability distribution. It is the square of the STANDARD DEVIATION. For example, if the standard deviation is 20, the variance is 400.
2. difference of revenues, costs, and profit from the planned amounts. One of the most important phases of responsibility accounting is establishing

standards in costs, revenues, and profit and establishing performance by comparing actual amounts with the standard amounts. The differences (variances) are calculated for each responsibility center, analyzed, and unfavorable variances are investigated for possible remedial action.

3. in COST ACCOUNTING, deviation between the actual cost and the standard cost. If actual cost exceeds standard cost, an unfavorable variance exists. A variance can be calculated for different cost items such as manufacturing costs (i.e., direct material, direct labor, and overhead), selling expenses, and administrative expenses. The reasons for a variance should be identified and corrective action taken. For example, actual production is 80 units. Standard cost per unit is $5 while actual cost per unit is $6. The unfavorable variance equals $80 ($400 vs $480).

VARIANCE ANALYSIS *see* ANALYSIS OF VARIANCES.

VENTURE CAPITAL financing source for new businesses or turnaround ventures that usually combine much risk with potential for high return. There are various stages of venture capital, such as beginning with seed money and then proceeding to the development stage. Sources of venture capital include wealthy individuals, small business investment companies, and limited partnerships.

VERIFIABLE confirming or substantiating an item. The term refers to the ability of accountants to ensure that accounting information is what it purports to be. The term also means that the selected method of measurement has been used without error or bias. An example of verifiability is that of two accountants looking at the same information (e.g., inventory valuation) and coming to similar conclusions.

VERIFICATION process of validating a statement, item, or account. The accountant seeks and examines evidence in support of the item. The auditor also attempts to determine accuracy in the amount of the item by conducting auditing tests and procedures. Sometimes assurance need show only that the characteristic is within a prescribed range.

VERTICAL ANALYSIS financial statement item that is used as a base value. All other accounts on the financial statement are compared to it. In the balance sheet, for example, total assets equals 100%. Each asset is stated as a percentage of total assets. Similarly, total liabilities and stockholders' equity are assigned 100% with a given liability or equity account stated as a percentage of the total liabilities and stockholders' equity. For the income statement, 100% is assigned to net sales with all revenue and expense accounts related to it. Under vertical analysis, the statements showing the percentages are referred to as COMMON SIZE FINANCIAL STATEMENTS. Common size percentages can be compared from one period to another to identify areas needing attention. An illustration follows:

Net Sales	$300,000	100%
Less: Cost of Sales	60,000	20%
Gross Profit	$240,000	80%
Less: Operating Expenses	150,000	50%
Net Income	$ 90,000	30%

See also HORIZONTAL ANALYSIS.

VERTICAL MERGER combination of a parent firm and the suppliers of its raw materials or purchasers of its finished product. Vertical merger extends the lines of distribution or production, either backward toward the source or forward toward the end-user. A firm controlling the entire production process is considered totally integrated vertically.

VESTED term indicating rights to pension benefits that are paid up and therefore not contingent upon the employee's continuing in the service of the employer. The EMPLOYEE RETIREMENT INCOME SECURITY ACT (ERISA) provides that an employee must be at least 25% vested in benefits derived from employer contributions after 5 years of covered service. By the time the employee has 15 years of covered service, vesting must have risen to 100%.

VESTED BENEFIT OBLIGATION (VBO) the actuarial present value of vested pension benefits employees have a right to receive regardless of future employment or future salary levels.

VIRAL MARKETING a marketing method used in the WEB 2.0 world in which users spread news about products and services to one another.

VIRTUAL PRIVATE NETWORK (VPN) basically a virtual version of a secure, physical network. A VPN gives an organization the ability to extend its secure network while using the INTERNET, such as by allowing its employees to remotely access a central server.

VIRUS a small software program that is designed to interfere with a computer's normal operations. A computer virus is capable of replicating itself and spreading itself from one computer to another.

VISUAL C# modern, high-level, object-oriented, general-purpose programming language for rapidly building both desktop and Web applications.

VOICE OVER INTERNET PROTOCOL (VOIP) allows voice/phone calls to be transported over an IP data network. Significant cost savings can be achieved when phone calls travel over an IP data network rather than a phone company's network.

VOLUME (PRODUCTION VOLUME) VARIANCE amount of under- or overapplied fixed factory overhead. It is the difference between budgeted fixed factory overhead and the amount applied based on a predetermined rate and the standard input allowed for actual output. It measures the use of capacity rather than specific cost outlays. *See also* FIXED OVERHEAD VOLUME (DENOMINATOR) VARIANCE; IDLE CAPACITY VARIANCE.

VOLUNTARY HEALTH AND WELFARE ORGANIZATION entity providing health-related services. It is a not-for-profit organization that follows accrual accounting. The fund groups of a voluntary health and welfare organization include current funds, plant funds, and endowment funds. *Current funds* are used for operations; they are classified as unrestricted or restricted. The restriction may relate to a specific operating objective by reason of gift, grant, etc. *Plant funds* include land, buildings and equipment, and related debt, along with assets to be used for future acquisitions and replacements. *Endowment funds* are used to account for bequests that require principal to be maintained intact.

VOLUNTARY HOSPITAL one providing patient services including surgery and testing. It follows not-for-profit accounting and has unrestricted (general) and restricted fund groups. *Unrestricted funds* include: (1) *operating funds* for routine hospital activities, including plant assets and related long-term debt; and (2) *board-designated funds,* representing resources set aside for special users. *Restricted fund* types include: (1) *specific-purpose,* applying to expenses restricted to specific operating purposes; (2) *endowment,* where principal is kept intact, and earnings may or may not be available subject to donor restrictions; and (3) *plant replacement and expansion,* applying to resources restricted for plant and equipment acquisitions.

VOUCHER form used in an internal control system to contain and verify all information about a bill to be processed or paid. Usually the original bill is then attached to the voucher. The voucher and bill are filed together until time of payment.

VOUCHER SYSTEM type of internal system used to control the cash (checks) being spent (written). The voucher system consists of vouchers, voucher files (paid and unpaid), voucher register that takes the place of the purchase journal, cash register that takes the place of the cash disbursement journal, and the general journal. This system ensures the person paying the bills that the bills are proper and should be paid. On the due date a voucher is removed from the "unpaid" voucher file and forwarded to the firm's disbursing officer for final approval of payment.

VOUCHING an audit procedure in which an auditor selects recorded items and then examines documents to support their validity. Vouching enables verification that transactions have occurred and that assets physically exist. Accordingly, vouching is a test for overstatement.

W

WAITING LINE THEORY *see* QUEUING THEORY.

WALK theory that stock prices behave in an unpredictable fashion because the stock market is efficient. The market price of a company's stock goes randomly around real (intrinsic) value. Current security prices are independent of prior prices. Thus historical prices are not a reliable predictor of future ones. According to random walk, financial information significant enough to affect future value is available to knowledgeable investors. Thus new data affecting stock price are immediately reflected in market value. At any given time, the price of a stock is the optimum estimate of its value including all available information. *See also* EFFICIENT MARKET HYPOTHESIS.

WALK-THROUGH TEST audit procedure used in evaluating the reliability of the client's accounting system. The auditor looks at the supporting documentation for a transaction from its starting point and then proceeds to examine the accounting system steps thereafter until ultimate disposition of the item. The walk-through examination is one of the COMPLIANCE TESTS that the auditor can perform.

WAREHOUSE RECEIPT document listing goods or commodities (e.g., gold) stored in a warehouse that shows retention of title to the goods. Warehouse receipts may be negotiable or non-negotiable. Negotiable receipts allow transfer without endorsement and may act as a security for a loan. Non-negotiable receipts must be endorsed upon transfer. Warehouse receipts, regulated by the Uniform Warehouse Receipts Act, allow the sale of goods without having to physically deliver them.

WARM SITE is a backup location/site from where an organization's data center can operate for the duration of a disaster. An organization may have three types of backup locations: a COLD SITE, a warm site, or a HOT SITE. A warm backup site is a compromise between a hot and a cold site. A warm site generally has all the hardware needed, though many times on a smaller scale than the original data center. Often, there is some delay in resuming data center function to full operation from a warm backup site.

WARRANT
1. *see* STOCK WARRANT.
2. guarantee of the occurrence of something, such as warranting the performance of another party.
3. in GOVERNMENT ACCOUNTING, order drawn authorizing payment to a designated payee.

WARRANTY agreement by the seller of goods or services to satisfy for a stated period of time deficiencies in the item's quality or performance. Warranty terms may be included on the buyer's receipt. The warranty usually provides for repair or replacement of the item in the case of malfunctioning or poor workmanship. Typically, there is no additional charge during the warranty period. The seller records warranty expense and related estimated liability in the year of sale. A warranty percentage is usually based on prior experience. Assume sales for 2014 are $100,000. Estimated warranty cost is 2% of sales. The entry to record warranty expense is:

12/31/2014   Warranty expense   2,000
     Estimated warranty payable   2,000

If on 1/25/2015, actual warranty services performed cost $500, the entry is:

    Estimated warranty payable   500
     Cash   500

WASH SALE

1. transaction or sale that is nullified by its reversal or offset within a short time of its initiation. Such sales are now forbidden by stock exchange rules.
2. losses on a sale of stock that, for federal income tax purposes, may not be recognized if the same stock is purchased within 30 days preceding or following the date of sale.

WASTE term used for shrinkage, evaporation, and so on. The cost of waste from these causes usually is not traced and is not recognized in the accounts. In a standard cost system an allowance for waste may be included in the determination of standard cost. Waste in excess of standard is thus revealed as a quantity or usage variance.

WASTING ASSET

1. FIXED ASSET with limited life and subject to DEPRECIATION. It therefore excludes land.
2. natural resource such as oil, coal, and timber, having a limited useful life and subject to DEPLETION. Such assets decrease in worth primarily due to the extraction of the valued commodity held by these assets. *See also* INTANGIBLE ASSET.
3. security whose value expires at a specified time in the future. An option contract (PUT or CALL) is an example of a *wasting asset.*

WATERED STOCK stock that has been issued for an amount that is below the stock's par value.

WEB BROWSER browsers for the World Wide Web (WWW) enabling one to hook up with network servers to obtain HTML documents and Web pages. It provides a linkage among pages and documents. The server may physically be on the Internet or a private network. The browser may contain "help" applications for special files.

WEBMASTER/WEBMISTRESS a person responsible for managing a Web site.

WEB PAGE a document written with HTML tags that is accessible through a Web browser. A Web page is retrieved through its URL and may contain all types of media, including text, graphics, audio/video, and hyperlinks.

WEB SEARCH ENGINE a tool designed to search for information, including accounting-related information, on the World Wide Web. The search results are usually presented in a list and are commonly referred to as hits. The accounting information may consist of accounting association Web sites, images, and other information.

WEB SERVER consists of hardware/software to manage and control a Web site. Presently, the two leading Web servers are Apache and Microsoft's Internet Information Server (IIS).

WEB SERVICE a standard way of integrating two or more Web applications over the Internet. Web services allow different applications from different sources to communicate with each other using data in EXTENSIBLE MARKUP LANGUAGE (XML) format. Web services do not have a GRAPHICAL USER INTERFACE (GUI), relying instead on a programmatic interface.

WEB SITE consists of one or more Web pages served from a single Web domain.

WEB SITE DEVELOPMENT COSTS Web site development is segregated into three stages (activities) that have an impact on the accounting treatment for costs incurred. The first stage is planning in which the costs incurred are expensed. Development is the second stage, and Web application and infrastructure as well as graphics development costs are capitalized and then amortized after the Web site is ready. However, costs to develop the content for the site may be capitalized or expensed depending on the circumstances. In the third stage of post-implementation, work is performed after the site is put into service (e.g., administration, training, security). These costs are expensed as incurred. Also in the third stage, there are expenditures for additional upgrades and features after the site is launched. The costs attributable to this are capitalized if the upgrades and enhancements provide *additional functionality*.

WEB TRUST a type of trust service that assesses an entity's Web site in terms of transaction integrity, information security, and disclosure of business practices. Web trust engagements are governed by STATEMENTS ON STANDARDS FOR ATTESTATION ENGAGEMENTS (SSAE).

WEB 2.0 a loose collection of capabilities, technologies, business models, and philosophies that characterizes the new and emerging business uses of the Internet. Software as a service is an example of Web 2.0. Web 2.0 concepts have led to the development and evolution of Web culture communities and hosted services, such as social-networking sites, video sharing sites, wikis, and blogs. The following table compares Web 2.0 with traditional processing. (For some reason, the term *Web 1.0* is not used.)

COMPARISON OF TRADITIONAL PROCESSING WITH WEB 2.0

Traditional Processing	Web 2.0 Processing
Software as product	Software as service
Infrequent, controlled releases	Frequent releases of perpetual betas
Business model relies on sale of software licenses	Business model relies on advertising or other revenue from use
Extensive advertising	Viral marketing
Product value fixed	Product value increases with use and users
Publishing	Participation
Major winners: Microsoft, Oracle, SAP	Major winners: Google, Amazon.com, eBay

WEIGHT relative importance given to an individual item included in forecasting, such as alpha in exponential smoothing. In the method of MOVING

AVERAGES all of those past values included in the moving average are given equal weight.

WEIGHTED AVERAGE average of observations having different degrees of importance or frequency. The formula for a weighted average is Weighted Average $= \Sigma wx$, where $x =$ the data values and $w =$ relative weight assigned to each observation, expressed as a percentage or relative frequency. For example, assume the XYZ Company uses three grades of labor to produce a finished product as follows:

Grade of Labor	Labor Hours Per Unit of Labor	Hourly Wages (x)
Skilled	6	$10.00
Semiskilled	3	8.00
Unskilled	1	6.00
	10	

The weighted average is computed as follows:

Weighted average $= \$10.00 \, (6/10) + \$8.00(3/10) + \$6.00(1/10)$
$= \underline{\$\ 9.00}$ per hour

Note that the weights equal the proportion of the total labor required to produce the product. A weighted average is calculated in the WEIGHTED AVERAGE INVENTORY METHOD and the COST OF CAPITAL.

WEIGHTED AVERAGE CONTRIBUTION MARGIN one in which weights are relative to sales mix. For example, assume that Company Z has two products with the following contribution margin data:

	A	B
Unit CONTRIBUTION MARGIN (CM)	$3	$5
Sales mix	60%	40%

The weighted average CM per unit is $(\$3)(0.6) + (\$5)(0.4) = \$3.80$

WEIGHTED AVERAGE COSTING procedure for computing the unit cost of a process. Beginning work-in-process inventory costs are added to the costs of the current period, then a weighted average is obtained by dividing the combined costs by equivalent units. Thus there is only one average cost for goods completed. Equivalent units under weighted average costing may be computed as follows:

Units completed $+$ (ending work-in-process $\times$ degree of completion (%)). To illustrate, the following data relate to the activities of Department A during the month of January:

	Units
Beginning work-in-process (100% complete as to materials; 2/3 complete as to conversion)	1,500
Started this period	5,000
Completed and transferred	5,500
Ending work in process (100% complete as to materials; 6/10 complete as to conversion)	1,000

Equivalent production in Department A for the month is computed, using weighted average costing, as follows:

	Materials	Conversion Costs
Units completed and transferred	5,500	5,500
Ending work in process		
Materials (100%)	1,000	
Conversion costs (60%)		600
Equivalent production		
	6,500	6,100

See also FIRST-IN, FIRST-OUT (FIFO) COSTING.

WEIGHTED AVERAGE COST OF CAPITAL weights the percentage cost of each component by the percentage of that component in the financial structure.

WEIGHTED AVERAGE INVENTORY METHOD method in calculation in which the weighted average cost per unit for the period is the cost of the goods available for sale divided by the number of units available for sale. When the perpetual inventory system is used, the weighted average method is called the MOVING AVERAGE method.

WEIGHTED COST DRIVER technique of increasing or decreasing the cost consumption intensity of an individual cost object by weighting the measured quantity of the cost driver.

WEIGHTED MEAN *see* WEIGHTED AVERAGE.

WESTLAW online database of West Publishing containing legal cases and other legal information for practicing attorneys.

W-4 FORM form known as the Employee's Withholding Allowance Certificate. It is filled out by a new employee, or an employee who wishes to change the figures in the form, to provide information needed by the employer to calculate an employee's pay net of exemptions and other tax deductions. The W-4 form does not provide information for deductions for union dues, medical insurance, pension, and so on.

WHAT-IF ANALYSIS *see* SIMULATION.

WHITE KNIGHT a company that an entity prefers to merge with, rather than going through a hostile takeover.

WHITE PAPER
1. a government report bound in white; also called a *white book*.
2. an authoritative report on a major issue, as by a team of journalists.
3. a short treatise whose purpose is to educate industry customers.

WHOLE-LIFE COST concept closely associated with LIFE-CYCLE COST. Whole-life costs equal life-cycle costs plus after-purchase costs. Attention to the reduction of all whole-life costs through analysis and management of all value-chain activities is a powerful competitive tool because of the potential for increasing customer satisfaction. Life-cycle and whole-life cost concepts are associated with target costing and target pricing. A firm may determine that market conditions require that a product sell at a given target price. Hence, a TARGET COST can be determined by subtracting the desired unit profit margin from the target price. The cost reduction objectives of life-cycle and whole-life cost management can, therefore, be determined using target costing.

WIDE AREA NETWORK (WAN) network comprising a large geographic area.

WI-FI *see* WIRELESS FIDELITY.

WIKI a knowledge base maintained by its users. It is processed on Web sites that allow users to add, remove, and edit content. The most famous wiki is Wikipedia.

WILLIE SUTTON RULE reminder to focus on the high-cost activities. The rule is named after bank robber Willie Sutton, who—when asked "why do you rob banks?"—is reputed to have replied "because that's where the money is."

WILSHIRE 5000 INDEX the broadest weighted index of all common stock issues on the NYSE, AMEX, and the most active issues on the over-the-counter market. Approximately 85% of the securities are traded on the NYSE. The index's value is in billions of dollars. It includes about 6,000 stocks (not 5,000 as its name would suggest) so it is representative of the overall market.

WINDFALL PROFITS earnings of an unexpected nature and generally not due to the efforts and expenditures of the entity that benefits. The Crude Oil Windfall Profits Tax of 1980 placed a tax on such profits on the production and sale of crude oil. The windfall profits figure is derived from complex calculations defined in the code, based on the difference between selling price less state severance taxes and a defined base price.

WINDOW portion of a computer display screen. Some programs allow the user to divide the screen into two or more windows, making it possible to work on two different tasks simultaneously.

WINDOW DRESSING making a company look better financially than it really is. Assume just before the end of the accounting year current assets are $100,000 and current liabilities are $50,000, representing a current ratio (current assets/current liabilities) of 2:1. To improve its current ratio for the annual report in order to attract prospective lenders, the company window-dresses by paying off $30,000 in current debt. This now makes current assets $70,000 and current liabilities $20,000, resulting in a misleading current ratio of 3.5:1. This current ratio is temporary and deceiving because, most likely, at the beginning of the next accounting year the firm will borrow additional short-term funds that reduce the current ratio.

WIRELESS FIDELITY (WI-FI) the popular term for a high-frequency wireless local area network. The consumer-friendly name for the 802.11b/g/n/ac engineering standard. It lets home and office users create wireless local networks, which connect two or more computers to each other and a faster Internet line. This way there is no more poking holes in walls or tripping over bulky Ethernet cables. The Wi-Fi technology is rapidly gaining acceptance as an alternative to a wired local area network (LAN).

WIRELESS TECHNOLOGY a variety of technologies to communicate without wires, namely radio transmissions.

WITHHOLDING TAX deductions by an employer from employee salaries for the payment of federal and state income taxes. It is paid in a prescribed manner to the taxing authority. Withholding tax is remitted by the employer to the IRS or deposited into the designated bank on a periodic basis as prescribed by the IRS. *See also* FEDERAL INSURANCE CONTRIBUTION ACT (FICA); FEDERAL UNEMPLOYMENT TAX ACT (FUTA).

WORD popular word processing software by Microsoft.

WORDPRESS the largest self-hosted blogging tool. While WordPress, which is used on millions of sites, started as just a blogging system, it has evolved to be used as a full content management system. Its popularity means that thousands of plug-ins, widgets, and themes are available through which it can be customized.

WORD PROCESSING method that involves the use of computerized equipment to automatically produce written letters and documents, reports, memorandums, reminder letters, audit bid proposals, contracts, confirmations, representation letters, and billings. Typically, word processing programs (e.g., WORD) allow the user to insert, delete, rearrange, search and replace, write style sheets, and move text from one document to another. A table of contents may be prepared from headings and subheadings. A glossary and index may also be furnished. Windows can display different portions of the same document or of completely independent but related documents.

WORK CELL physical or logical grouping of resources that performs a defined job or task. The work cell may contain more than one.

WORKERS' COMPENSATION program providing payments, without regard to a finding of negligence of either party, to workers involved in specific job-related injuries. These laws were enacted so that the employee would not have to go through a long and arduous lawsuit and possibly not recover due to the employer's advantageous financial standing. Payments are specifically exempt from taxation.

WORKFLOW sequence of actions accomplishing a business goal. A toolset to proactively analyze, compress, and automate information-based activities.

WORKING CAPITAL current assets less current liabilities, properly called *net working capital*. Working capital is a measure of a company's liquidity. Sources of working capital are (1) net income, (2) increase in noncurrent liabilities, (3) increase in stockholders' equity, and (4) decrease in noncurrent assets.

WORKING CAPITAL TURNOVER sales divided by average working capital. It reflects the entity's effectiveness in using working capital to obtain revenue. If sales are $100,000, beginning working capital is $20,000, and ending working capital is $30,000, the turnover rate is 4 times ($100,000/$25,000).

WORK-IN-PROCESS (WIP) partially completed inventory units at the end of the accounting period. An example is a table without legs; also called *goods-in-process*. In ABSORPTION COSTING, work-in-process is valued at the total cost to process it, including direct material, direct labor, and factory overhead (fixed and variable). In DIRECT COSTING, work-in-process is valued at only the variable costs to produce it, consisting of direct material, direct labor, and variable overhead. Ending work-in-process is shown as a current asset in the balance sheet. Beginning and ending work-in-process units are shown in the cost of goods manufactured schedule of the income statement.

WORKOUT
1. a range of prices within which a transaction or a series of transactions is likely to take place. For example, a market maker might quote a price range within which he or she would attempt to buy or sell a large order of securities.
2. the process of a debtor's meeting a loan commitment by satisfying altered repayment terms. For example, a firm in Chapter 11 bankruptcy proceedings might reach an agreement with its creditors for ways in which the firm's obligations can be worked out.

WORK MEASUREMENT determination of the length of time it should take to complete a job. Job times are vital inputs for manpower planning, estimating labor costs, scheduling, budgeting, and designing incentive systems. In addition, from the workers' standpoint, time standards provide an indication of expected output. *Time standards* used under STANDARD COST SYSTEMS reflect the amount of time it should take an average worker to do a job under typical operating conditions. The standards include expected activity time plus allowances for probable delays. The most commonly used methods of work measurement are: (1) stopwatch time study; (2) historical times; (3) predetermined data; and (4) work sampling.

WORK PAPERS documents prepared or obtained by the auditor in performing an examination of a client's financial records. The work papers may be called into court and may be subject to examination by the IRS when they relate to tax pool analysis. Included in the work papers are schedules, analyses, transcriptions, memos, and confirmation results related to balance sheet and income statement items. The work papers serve as the basis of the work performed and support the auditor's opinion. Upon review of the work papers, a reviewer can determine the quality of the work performed.

WORK SHEET document or schedule in which an accountant or auditor gathers information to substantiate an opinion concerning an account BALANCE or TEST OF TRANSACTION. Types of work sheets that may be prepared are: (1) test of transaction information showing the sample selected, attributes tested, findings for each item in the sample, and the sample as a whole; (2) BANK RECONCILIATION; (3) schedule of FIXED ASSETS; and (4) analysis of various expenses with conclusions on the findings. A group of assembled work sheets becomes the WORK PAPERS composing the documentation for the audit or review work performed by the accountant. Work sheets may include letters, minutes of meetings, and other items not prepared by the auditor.

WORK TICKET form used to charge jobs for direct labor used. This work ticket, sometimes called *time ticket* or *time card*, indicates the time spent on a specific job. An employee who is paid an hourly wage and who operates a lathe will have one *clock card* that is used as a basis for determining individual earnings; but the employee will fill out or punch several work tickets each day when starting and stopping work on particular jobs or operations. A sample form follows.

WORK TICKET

```
┌─────────────────────────────────────────────────────────┐
│                                                         │
│   Employee No. _____      Date _____    Job No. _____ │
│                                                         │
│   Operation _____      Account _____     Dept. _____ │
│                                                         │
│                                            Pieces:       │
│   Stop _____           Rate _____       Worked _____ │
│                                            Rejected _____ │
│   Start _____          Amount _____     Completed ____ │
│                                                         │
└─────────────────────────────────────────────────────────┘
```

WORLD BANK *see* INTERNATIONAL BANK FOR RECONSTRUCTION AND DEVELOPMENT (IBRD).

WORLD TRADE ORGANIZATION (WTO) an international organization that deals with the rules of trade between nations. The goal of the WTO is to assist producers of goods and services, exporters, and importers in conducting their business.

WORLD WIDE WEB (WWW) Internet system for worldwide hypertext linking of multimedia documents, making the relationship of information that is common between documents easily accessible and completely independent of physical location.

WORM a program that replicates itself and penetrates a valid computer system. It may also spread within a network.

WORTHLESS SECURITY a stock or bond that completely loses its value during the year. In general, a loss on a worthless security is treated as a capital loss.

WRITE-DOWN reduction of part of the balance of an asset by charging an expense or loss account. The reason for a write-down is that some economic event has occurred indicating that the asset's value has diminished. An example is the obsolescence of some inventory.

WRITE-OFF
1. transfer of the *entire* balance of an asset account into an expense or loss account. A full reduction in an asset indicates it is not worth anything (has no future benefit) due to some occurrence. An example is the destruction of a machine in a fire when the company has no insurance and the machine no salvage value.
2. elimination of a specific customer's account balance because of uncollectibility, as in the case of a bankruptcy.

WRITE-UP increase in the BOOK VALUE of an asset not due to a cash payment or other asset, issuance of a liability, or issuance of stock. Generally, this is *not* a permitted accounting practice. One exception is the write-up of fixed assets in a purchase method merger. Another exception is the case of a discovery of a natural resource such as oil on the land premises. In this unique situation, land can be charged for this discovery at fair market value as follows:

Land (appraisal increment)
Paid-in capital

The land (appraisal increment) account would then be subject to depletion.

WRITE-UP SOFTWARE also called *client write-up software,* accounting software structured exclusively for use by accounting professionals working in the background on a diverse array of clients.

W-2 FORM statement used for income tax purposes. Called *Wage and Tax Statement*, it is sent to an employee and shows gross earnings and deductions (such as federal, state, and local income taxes and FICA) for a calendar year. The business sends a copy of the W-2 to the Internal Revenue Service and other tax jurisdictions it covers. The employee attaches a copy of the W-2 to the employee's federal, state, and local income tax returns.

X

XBRL *see* EXTENSIBLE BUSINESS REPORTING LANGUAGE (XBRL).

XHTML (Extensible Hypertext Markup Language). *See also* HTML.

XML (EXTENSIBLE MARKUP LANGUAGE) a generic language of the World Wide Web Consortium (W3C) for creating new markup languages. Markup languages (such as HTML) are used to represent documents with a nested, treelike structure. XML is a product of W3C and a trademark of MIT.

Y

YEAR-END ADJUSTMENT process of adjusting the entry to an account at the end of the calendar or fiscal year in order to properly state it for financial statement preparation purposes. Types of required adjustments include accrual or deferral of a revenue or expense item, reclassification, adjustments to conform book figures to physical counts (i.e., inventory), and reflecting unusual transactions.

YELLOW BOOK the common name for the Generally Accepted Government Auditing Standards published by the U.S. Government Accountability Office. The Yellow Book is used by auditors of government entities and entities that receive government awards.

YIELD

1. real rate of return to the investor or effective cost to the issuer of a security for a specified time period. It differs from the NOMINAL INTEREST RATE. *See also* SIMPLE YIELD; YIELD TO MATURITY.

2. return from an asset or service provided.

3. conceding a point to another party.

YIELD TO MATURITY effective rate on a BOND; also called the EFFECTIVE INTEREST RATE. It considers the bond's FACE VALUE, market price, NOMINAL INTEREST RATE, and maturity period. If a bond was issued with a yield in excess of the nominal interest rate, it was sold at a DISCOUNT because it is costing the company more than the stated interest rate.

The yield to maturity formula equals:

$$\frac{\left(\text{Nominal Interest} + \dfrac{\text{Discount}}{\text{Years}} \right)}{\left(\dfrac{\text{Present Value} + \text{Maturity Value}}{2} \right)}$$

Note that if the bond was issued at a PREMIUM, the numerator would be:

$$\text{Nominal Interest} - \frac{\text{Premium}}{\text{Years}}$$

Assume a 10%, $100,000 bond was issued at $96,000. The life is five years. The effective rate is:

$$\frac{\left(\$10,000 + \dfrac{\$4,000}{5} \right)}{\left(\dfrac{\$96,000 + \$100,000}{2} \right)} = \frac{\$10,800}{\$98,000} = 11.02\%$$

YIELD VARIANCE effect of varying the total input of a factor of production (e.g., direct materials or labor) while holding constant the input mix (the proportions of the types of materials or labor used) and the weighted average unit price of the factor of production. *See also* PRODUCTION YIELD VARIANCE.

Z

ZERO-BASE BUDGETING planning and budgeting tool that uses COST-BENEFIT ANALYSIS of projects and functions to improve resource allocation in an organization. Traditional budgeting tends to concentrate on the incremental change from the previous year. It assumes that the previous year's activities and programs are essential and must be continued. Under zero-base budgeting, however, cost and benefit estimates are built up from scratch, from the zero level, and must be justified.

ZERO-BRACKET AMOUNT type of STANDARD (or blanket) DEDUCTION from ADJUSTED GROSS INCOME (AGI) available to taxpayers, whether or not they can itemize nonbusiness expenses in the process of calculating their taxable income. This is the term used prior to the new tax laws.

ZERO-COUPON BOND bond, sold at a deep discount, that accrues interest semiannually. Both the principal and the accumulated interest are paid at maturity. Although a fixed rate is implicit in the discount and the specific maturity, they are not fixed income securities in the traditional sense because they provide for no periodic income. Although the interest on the bond is paid at maturity, accrued interest, though not received, is taxable yearly as ordinary income.

ZERO-ONE PROGRAMMING term used in a special case of INTEGER PROGRAMMING where all the decision variables are integers and can assume values of either zero or one. The zero-one programming technique has been successfully applied to solve a project selection problem in which projects are *mutually exclusive* and/or technologically interdependent.

ZERO-SUM GAME competition in which the total gains of the winner exactly equal the total loss of the loser. For example, if two accounting firms in a small town are competing for a share of a fixed market (i.e., a fixed number of clients) and one can increase a share of the market at the other's expense, the game is *zero-sum*.

Z SCORE
1. in statistics, the standard normal variate that standardizes a normal distribution by converting an x-scale to a z-scale.
2. score produced by Altman's bankruptcy prediction model, which is as follows:

$$Z = 1.2 * X1 + 1.4 * X2 + 3.3 * X3 + 0.6 * X4 + 0.999 * X5$$

where $X1$ = working capital/total assets (%), $X2$ = retained earnings/total assets (%), $X3$ = earnings before interest and taxes/total assets (%), $X4$ = market value of equity/book value of debt (%), and $X5$ = sales/total assets (number of times). The Z score is known to be about 90% accurate in forecasting business failure one year in the future and about 80% accurate in forecasting it two years in the future.

Chapter 8
Information Technology in Accounting

This chapter discusses guidelines on the use of information technology by accountants to perform their accounting, auditing, and management advisory service functions. It also provides a list of applications of various computer software packages. More specifically, it gives a practical guide to software applications for accounting in general. The chapter contains discussions of:

- Accounting packages
- Utilization of spreadsheets
- Auditing tasks
- Spreadsheet program-assisted auditing
- Tax preparation and planning
- Using Data Base Management Systems (DBMS)
- Value Chain Manager Software
- Wireless Technology

ACCOUNTING PACKAGES

Accounting packages generally fall into one of three categories. The first category involves industry-specific applications. These applications range from automated tellers to accounting for construction projects or movie theaters. The second category deals with the management style of organization. These applications usually include budgeting, modeling, and financial reporting. The third category deals with general accounting functions. These applications are more likely to be usable by any business without extensive modification.

The accountant may acquire individual modules or an integrated package. For a small business, just a general ledger module may be sufficient; a large corporation would need several modules. Integrated accounting software links a number of modules performing related tasks; data from one module are transferred to another module. Integrated software centers around the general ledger and includes other modules for specific accounting purposes, including:

General ledger module
Accounts receivable module
Accounts payable module
Payroll module
Inventory module
Fixed assets module
Spreadsheet and word processing

Selecting Accounting Software

In selecting accounting software, consider the following:

Customization: Can the package be customized? Can it be customized enough to meet user requirements? Items to be customized include reports, forms, input screens, and source code.

Vendor reliability: Can we rely on the vendor? Do they have sufficient resources? Are they profitable and supported by sufficient, knowledgeable staff?

Reporting: Can the package produce required financial statements in a timely and accurate manner? Do the reports include the required ratios? Do they include graphical output? Do they incorporate third-party products FRx (offers reporting capabilities for the general ledger module) and Crystal Reports (extracts and reports event data from all modules) into their packages?

Database: Do the databases available with the package match the user's needs? Databases available include Btrieve, Microsoft SQL Server, Oracle, and IBM DB2. The user's number of transactions is a typical determinant of the database required.

Client/Server: Does the package come with a client/server version? This version allows the user to save the bandwidth and time on the LAN and to distribute single processes across multiple computers throughout the organization.

Account Number Structure: Does the account number structure accommodate the number of segments—for subsidiaries, divisions, accounts, subaccounts, departments, programs, and funds—and total number of characters required by the user?

Internet: Does the pack include the following Internet-related features?

- Publish Web catalogs directly from, and made links to, the software's inventory module.
- Retrieve orders directly from the Website and import them to the sales module.
- Print reports to a Web page (HTML) format.

- Allow users to access reports and accounting data across the Web.
- Support remote data entry across the Web.

International: Does the package process multiple currencies? Does the package support foreign languages?

User-Friendliness: Does the package contain user-friendly features such as graphical guidance, default-rich settings, and clear, simple, intuitive screens and labels?

Other Features: Does the package include pivot tables and hotlinking? Does the package alert users when certain conditions, such as cash on hand, gross margin, and inventory balances, reach user-defined levels?

Popular Software Packages

There are many accounting software packages on the market, with a wide range in cost, quality, features, applications, and sophistication. You have to select the one that best meets your overall needs. Some popular packages are briefly described below.

Dac-Easy

Dac-Easy by Sage (*www.sagesoftware.com*) is one of the most popular accounting packages. It contains modules for general ledger, accounts receivable, accounts payable, inventory control/purchasing, billing, and forecasting. Dac-Easy, like many other integrated accounting software packages, enables modules to share data without having to reinput the data into each module. Accountants, however, probably need a package that is a little more sophisticated. It should be noted that Dac-Easy cannot match the power or flexibility of its more expensive counterparts, but for a single, small business accounting package it is a good option.

DacEasy is available in four editions: the *Accounting* Edition, the *Payroll* Edition, the *Small Business* Edition, and the *Complete* Edition. The Accounting Edition contains tools to help a business track its activities and generate reports about business functions. The Payroll Edition automates the task of performing payroll, including calculating and paying vacation or sick time, regular and overtime, and tracking liabilities and deductions. The Small Business Edition integrates the Accounting and Payroll modules with its Business Center functions. The Complete Edition includes additional features, like tracking profitability on a job by job basis.

CYMA Accounting Software

CYMA (*www.cyma.org*) offers sophisticated accounting software solutions for medium-sized businesses and nonprofit organizations. CYMA Accounting Software is robust but easy to navigate. CYMA Payroll Software features quick-entry payroll and is the only in-house payroll software solution that supports Social Security number encryption.

CYMA Accounting Software for Business (FMS)
CYMA Payroll Software
CYMA Job Cost /Project Cost Software
CYMA Inventory Control Software
CYMA Fund Accounting Software for Nonprofit Organizations (NFP)

CYMA Accounting Software also offers a modular approach so you can add additional functionality as your organization grows. CYMA Accounting Software modules include Accounts Payable, Accounts Receivable, General Ledger, Grant Tracking, Job Costing, Inventory Control, Payroll, Project Tracking, Purchase Order, Sales Order, and Bank Reconciliation.

Web-Based Accounting Systems

Web-based software packages are transforming business. Functions such as accounting, cash-flow management, customer relationship management (CRM), inventory control, and marketing can be performed electronically anytime and anywhere in the cloud/hosted environment. For example, a small business can use ePeachtree, Intacct's eledger, or QuickBooks Online to process transactions. Not only can a business owner view and manage employee compensation via the Internet, but the outsourced services allow employees to access personal information, including earnings, income tax withholdings, retirement plans, and vacation days, without creating an added burden for the company.

Reliable and efficient access to information has become a must for business firms to stay competitive. With networking technology, staff members or users at any location can share information simultaneously.

Select and Subscribe to Software. Generally, all Web-based accounting packages listed in this section offer a free trial period. Businesses should make sure that the provider offers all the required features before subscribing to the service. A business should select a Web-based accounting package based on the company's information needs and the features offered by the software. The sidebar on the screen lists several important factors for a small business to consider when selecting Web-based accounting software.

Customize the Accounting System. Web-based accounting packages are general-purpose software, and a company needs to use and customize only the features required for its business. Working from the predefined chart of accounts, forms, and reports, a small business can set up and customize its accounting system in hours.

Prepare System Documentation. Companies need to prepare system documentation so that new staff can learn how to use the system. System documentation should provide detailed procedures, including system activation and deactivation, chart of accounts, sales cycle, purchase cycle, employee and payroll cycle, cash receipts, cash disbursements, journal entries, inventory, financial reports and queries, and error corrections. The system designer should copy the predefined forms, screens, and reports and include them within the system documentation.

Good system documentation should be easy to read, make it easy for users to find specific information (i.e., include a table of contents, page numbers, and an index), and be well organized (i.e., by cycles or accounts). The procedures should be complete, in easy-to-follow steps (e.g., showing all relevant forms, screens, and reports). The overall presentation should be professional, and the system documentation should be kept in a safe place.

Web-based accounting makes the data easily accessible to multiple remote users at one time, and of course it offers the usual benefits of Web-based software: server-side upgrades, maintenance, and backups.

Sage 300 ERP

Sage 300 ERP is a comprehensive business management solution available in an on-premise or online version. It supports multiple technologies, databases, and operating systems. It helps an organization remain compliant with government regulations such as GAAP or IFRS. Sage 300 ERP includes multicurrency capability, bank reconciliation, and tax reporting support. Sage 300 ERP Core Accounting modules include:

- General Ledger
- Accounts Payable
- Account Receivable
- Payment Processing by Sage Exchange
- System Manager-Bank Reconciliation
- Sage Active Planner-Advanced Budgeting and Allocations

- Sage Fixed Assets
- Check and Form Printing

Intacct

Intacct (*www.intacct.com*) sees itself as "an accounting utility company." The company offers a full-function package—general ledger, financial reporting, budgeting, accounts payable and receivable, invoicing, expense reporting, human resources reporting, and a payroll service. If you're a small operation looking for low cost and ease of use, you want to pick something like Intuit's Quickbooks. If you're a small or medium-size operation and you need functionality and scalability, you need something richer.

Sage One

Sage One (*www.sageone.com*) is a simple, web-based accounting solution for small businesses. It interfaces accounting, invoicing, project management, task management, and time tracking functions. Because it is web-based, there is no software to install, and it can be used on any tablet, laptop, or desktop with Internet access. Sage One allows an unlimited number of users to access the system. It contains a dedicated workspace for projects and tasks, so that activities can be tracked and reviewed. Integrated e-mail support allows reminders to be sent to keep project team members up-to-date.

Quickbooks Online

Quickbooks (*quickbooks.intuit.com*) is the market leader in small business accounting software. However, many features available in its full desktop-based products are missing.

Advice and Caveats

A recent survey published by Financial Executives International (FEI) (*www.fei.org*) revealed that outsourcing would continue to be a solution for areas where management does not believe that in-house efforts can be cost-effective. The same survey also revealed that financial executives' satisfaction levels with shared services are as high as 90%. Web-based accounting packages enable small businesses to outsource their accounting function at an affordable price, and Web-based inventory control software allows small businesses to track their inventories in real time. Web-based software has the added bonus of always being up-to-date, because providers continuously provide incremental upgrades and new features.

ACTIVITY-BASED COSTING (ABC) SOFTWARE

Activity-Based Costing (ABC) helps in determining what a product or process should cost, areas of possible cost reduction, and value-added versus nonvalue-added aspects. Numerous PC/network software packages are available for implementing ABC analysis. They are designed for ABC that cost accountants and financial officers can use to aid in accumulating cost information and perform "what-if" testing. Packages are separated into two categories: those developed by independent vendors, and those supported or developed by a Big-Four CPA firm.

PricewaterhouseCoopers' *ACTIVA* is a comprehensive ABC, profitability, and performance management software tool. Its features and capabilities include budgeting and planning, product costing and pricing, cost management and analysis, decision support, process improvement, activity-based management (ABM), and variance determination and evaluation. Lead Software's *Activity Analyzer* assigns activities to cost objects and calculates by activity costs and profitability. Profitability may be determined by product, service, customer, and territory.

Financial Planning and Budgeting Software

The following are a variety of popular computer software packages designed specifically for planning, budgeting, optimization, and simulation:

1. Budget Maestro – *www.centage.com*. Budget Maestro is cash flow forecasting software that provides managers with what-if capabilities by which to model and test alternative budgeting or financing scenarios. A limitless number of what-if scenarios can be created to gauge the impact of projected changes of operations on cash flow, balance sheets, and income statements. Rolling forecasts—monthly or several years out—can be used to predict the impact on operations and cash flow based on changing variables.
2. Business Plan Pro, Marketing Plan Pro (Palo Alto Software) – *www.paloalto.com*. This software provides projections of cash inflow and cash outflow. Data is input into seven cat-

egories: sales, cost of sales, administrative expense, long-term
debt, other cash receipts, inventory build-up/reduction, and
capital expenditures (acquisition of long-term assets, such as
equipment). The program allows changes in assumptions and
scenarios and provides a complete array of reports.

3. @RISK (Palisade Corporation) – *www.palisade.com.* How
will a new competitor affect market share? @RISK calculates
the likelihood of changes and events affecting the bottom line.
@RISK's familiar @ functions are used to define the risk in
a worksheet. The program then runs thousands of what-if
tests using Monte Carlo simulation. A clear, colorful graph
shows the likelihood of every possible bottom-line value.
The model's results can be viewed from hundreds or even
thousands of what-if scenarios. Answers are provided to such
questions as "What is the chance of a negative result?" and
"What is the chance of a result over one million?" Controllers can determine, at a glance, whether a risk is acceptable or
a contingency plan is needed.

4. What's Best! (Lindo Systems, Inc.) – *www.lindo.com.* If
resources are limited—for example, people, inventory, materials, time, or cash—What's Best! lets the controller decide
how to allocate these resources in order to maximize or minimize a given objective, such as profit or cost. What's Best!
uses proven methods—linear programming (LP), integer programming, and nonlinear programming—to solve a variety of
business problems that cut across every industry at every level
of decision making. What's Best! also has sensitivity analysis,
extensive error handling, full solution report capabilities, and
user interface via Excel or Lotus.

5. SIMUL8 (SIMUL8 Corporation) – *www.simul8.com.*
SIMUL8 is a full-feature simulation package. Fully integrated
with Excel, it uses easy-to-enter graphics to represent both
the objects in the company's system—such as machines and
workers—and the process flows that describe their interaction.
It can simulate many business processes, such as invoice and
order flow, hospital process design, and any other situations
where flows and processes can be redesigned and optimized.

6. Supply Chain Analyst—Inventory Analyst – *www.ilog.com/
products/inventory_analyst.html.* ILOG's Inventory Analyst
is a Web-based, multi-echelon inventory optimization solution that provides end-to-end functionality for manufacturers,
retailers, and distributors. Inventory Analyst handles both
inbound/outbound and distribution-focused business models
allowing companies to answer a broad range of business questions from determining the right inventory policies and stra-

tegic positioning of inventory to the ongoing setting of safety stocks and inventory levels in operational environments. LogicTools' advanced inventory optimization technology enables companies to transform supply chains into drivers of profitability, efficiency, and growth.

7. Crystal Ball (Decisioneering/Oracle) – *www.crystalball.com*. Oracle's Crystal Ball automatically calculates thousands of different "what-if" cases with Monte Carlo simulation, saving the inputs and results of each calculation as individual scenarios. It is a spreadsheet-based software unit for predictive modeling, forecasting, and optimization.

SPREADSHEETS (ELECTRONIC WORKSHEETS)

Spreadsheet programs such as EXCEL allow values (numeric data or formulas) and text (words, labels) to be entered at any location on an electronic columnar pad. Values and text are entered in cells identified by row and column locations. Spreadsheets resemble a grid. Mathematical relationships can be expressed between different areas on the worksheet. When one number is altered, every other number related to it is similarly changed. For example, an accountant can investigate how earnings change as sales change. Therefore, spreadsheets are a great tool for planning, forecasting, and modeling purposes. "What-if" scenarios are easily accessed. For all practical purposes, spreadsheets allow for applications in almost every area of accounting—audit, tax planning, financial planning, financial analysis, and management advisory service.

How Templates Can Help You Be More Productive

Many spreadsheet programs have templates or overlay programs to go with the specific spreadsheet program adopted to aid productivity. Templates are basically predefined files, including formulas and row or column labels for specific applications. In effect, they are worksheet models designed to solve specific types of problems. Since the template has the model in it, all that is needed is to input the data and obtain the outcome.

The workings of a template are as follows:

1. The spreadsheet program is run.
2. The template is loaded.
3. A problem is solved from the menu.
4. Information is input.

Templates are available for all types of accounting applications, including general ledger, financial statements, accounts payable, accounts receivable, and payroll. Templates are also available for tax planning and preparation, financial planning, and investment analysis.

Spreadsheet Applications in Accounting

The application of spreadsheets to accounting is unlimited.

General accounting applications
Preparation of various working papers (e.g., trial balances)
Any type of financial report for the client
Maintaining the ledger
Converting from cash to accrual basis and vice versa
Aging accounts receivable
Payroll preparation and analysis
Preparing financial statements
Revenue analysis by volume, price, and product-service mix
Analyzing expenses
Expense calculations and reports such as for depreciation, amortization, leases, pensions, and accrued expenses
Costs specified in terms of volume, price, and category

Planning, forecasting, and budgeting
Planning budgets and forecasts
Cash flow analysis and cash budgeting
Inventory management, planning, and control
Regression analysis for forecasting
Performing integrated business plans in which financial statements and other related schedules can be integrated into one model
Any imaginable type of what-if analysis involving alternative situations (e.g., what the client's tax liability will be assuming different tax options are taken; what the effect on the firm's market share is if price is reduced by 5%)

Financial-statement analysis
Ratio computations
Trend analysis
Vertical and horizontal schedules
Graphics

Capital budgeting analysis
   Time-value analysis
   Net present value
   Internal rate of return
   Ranking index
   Varying assumptions (e.g., interest rate) and determining the
     effect
   Lease vs. purchase

Investment and financing analysis
   Future value analysis
   Loan amortization tables
   Mergers and acquisitions
   Preparing portfolio investment transactions and balances
   Evaluating the true cost of financing
   Optimal financing mix (i.e., debt-equity)

Cost-volume-profit (CVP) analysis
   Break-even computations
   Target-income analysis
   A variety of what-if questions (e.g., pricing and advertising
     decisions)
   Graphics

Short-term decisions via contribution-margin analysis
   Make or buy
   Sales mix analysis
   Accept or reject a special order

Management of working capital
   Cash, accounts receivable, securities
   Credit-control management and analysis
   Inventory management

Income-tax-planning decisions and preparation
   Cash flow vs. profit
   Proprietorship vs. corporation
   Depreciation decisions and taxes
   Tax-loss carryforward and carryback schedules

Cost and managerial accounting
   Divisional and departmental performance evaluation
   Job and process costing
   Overhead calculations
   Variance determination (standard to actual, budget to actual)

CPA firm management
Time sheets by employee for control and billing purposes
Client statistics for evaluation and reporting purposes
Arriving at answers in seconds when meeting with the client
without the need to redo many calculations manually

AUDITING TASKS

Software potentially useful to the practitioner in audit automating
(and often practice automation in general) endeavors are:

- spreadsheet programs
- integrated programs
- file handling and database programs
- general accounting packages
- timekeeping and budgeting packages
- special-purpose applications
- customized software packages developed by the practitioner
  himself or by another CPA or CPA firm

Many of the computationally oriented aspects of the audit engagement (indeed, probably most) can be comfortably executed by spreadsheet programs that the practitioner—with a little practice—can program with confidence.

Integrated programs represent the evolution of spreadsheet programs to encompass not only electronic worksheets but also database, communications, graphics, and word processing capabilities, all of which interact in one highly useful program. EXCEL is the most widely recognized and utilized of these integrated programs. Standardized spreadsheet and integrated programs will be discussed in more detail later.

Word processing programs can be useful to the auditor when it comes time to write reports, send letters of confirmation, tabulate findings, and even prepare working papers—within limits. Report writing is made much easier with word processing capabilities, especially when first drafts are revised and updated. For confirmation letters, a standard form letter can be maintained into which particulars—name, address, etc.—can be inserted to customize it for each use. Some packages or other programs combine word processing and database or file-handling capabilities. Such a program is extremely useful in the tabulation of audit results, allowing the accountant to search, sort and/or classify based on numeric, alphabetical, or alphanumeric ranges or other criteria.

Database or file-handling software is quite useful to the practitioner. These programs are similar to audit software used on large mainframe computers in their ability to create and manipulate files and to produce reports. Appropriate data and samples can thereby be transferred to the practitioner's PCs, where the database or file-handling program can sort this information in different ways to provide reports appropriate for different applications. The practitioner is thus assisted by an orderly and efficient means of verifying pertinent data in the client's computer system, easing the task of tabulating the results of sample manipulation and recommendations based on these results. Database and file-handling programs are also ideal for keeping track of planned and completed audits, short memos, correspondence, and documentation of audit findings. Some firms have also used these types of programs to sort staff personnel by skills and areas of specialization. The software thus assists these firms in searching for the most suitable staff members for a particular audit engagement, based on the particulars of each job. This aids in more effective scheduling of staff hours and assignments.

Generalized accounting software can be useful to practitioners for the accounting administration of their own practice, as well as in performing accounting functions for clients.

Timekeeping and budgeting packages allow the practitioner to keep track of the hours for certain audit engagements; consequently, audit costs can more accurately be determined. This aids in the process of estimating costs for prospective new clients and the bidding for new audit engagements.

Comparisons can also be made between budgeting and actual staff hours in order to monitor staff efficiency and avoid problem areas. Calendar and reminder programs are available at an extremely low cost. These programs can be programmed to keep track of meetings, audits, and other scheduled engagements, and will display or print out a schedule of the activities planned for any day of the week. Such a program can assist in optimization of staff scheduling as well as in avoidance of extensions or conflicting schedules.

Audit Software Packages

Audit software aids in examining and testing client accounting data. The packages combine general accounting, spreadsheet, and word-processing programs to assist in the accounting, analysis, and reporting elements of the audit. Audit reports, footnote data, compilation and review reports, management letters, and other related auditing schedules and analyses are prepared.

Audit programs can conduct mathematical and logical operations: sampling data from a population, comparing actual data to predetermined criteria and printing out exceptions (e.g., excessive inventory balances), appraising accounting data, reading and extracting information, comparing financial data on different files for consistency, exporting data from one file to another (e.g., spreadsheet to word processing), sending out confirmations, and analytically reviewing the logic in reported figures.

Packaged ("canned") audit software often exists for a particular application. If the software cannot meet the application desired, a customized program should be written. This may require some programming knowledge. And, yet, there are many instances where DBMS packages and spreadsheet packages are all that is needed.

Products such as APG (Audit Program Generator) by the American Institute of Certified Public Accountants (AICPA) and the optional add-on modules allow the user to prepare customized audit programs.

Data extraction software, such as IDEA (Interactive Data Extraction and Analysis), also by the AICPA, allows auditors to access clients' files for audit testing. The auditor can either access the client's live data or obtain a copy of the company's data files on tape or disk. Data extraction software allows the auditor to audit "through the computer." The auditor can, for example, select a sample of accounts receivable for confirmations or perform analytical reviews and ratio analysis. Transactions may be compared to predetermined criteria. Linton Shafer's The Number—Audit Sampling software packages select random numbers and dates. It handles multiple ranges and evaluates results and performs compliance and substantive testing.

Trial Balance software, such as the AICPA's ATB (Accountant's Trial Balance) helps the auditor organize a client's general ledger balances into a working trial balance. The auditor can then perform adjustments and update account balances. The calculation of financial ratios is extremely simple with trial balance software. This type of software aids in the preparation of financial statements. While trial balance software is designed primarily for audits, it can be used instead of write-up software for compilation and review services.

PricewaterhouseCoopers' (PWC) TeamMate is an electronic working paper system that helps automate the working paper preparation, review, reporting, and storage process. It includes standard and free form schedule templates, an automatic tick-mark system, and powerful cross referencing capability. PWC's TeamMate also integrates popular spreadsheet, word processing, and imaging software. Hypertext links between documents and applications enable the auditor to jump backward through related numbers in reports or spreadsheets to the original data. The search, cross-referencing, and retrieval capabilities allow the auditor to automatically correct errors in all affected documents. The working paper review features include automatic exception reporting, a working paper navigation system, and text and voice annotation. For example, the auditor can obtain a directory of all review notes pertaining to a document. The reporting features include key audit point summarization, report drafting, audit status reports, and time summaries. Financial data are quickly accessed by the sorting and filtering tools. A standard index provides a branch and node system for all papers. A simultaneous multiuser feature enables auditors/reviewers to work with the same document set even if they are working in various locations. PWC's TeamMate improves the quality, productivity, and effectiveness of an auditor's work.

SPREADSHEET-ASSISTED AUDITING

The use of spreadsheets to assist in the audit engagement is ever increasing. They are particularly suitable for assisting in three major aspects of the audit endeavor:

- Use in fieldwork by the auditor or staff
- Preparation of financial and other audit-oriented reports
- Practice administration

Reports, tasks, and calculations that are suitable for automation on an electronic worksheet include the following:

Depreciation schedules
Workpaper schedules
Staff scheduling
Financial statement analysis
Working or audit-trial balance
Earnings-per-share computations
Line budgets
Loan amortization
Present-value calculations
Consolidations
Bad-debt-allowance calculation
Lease computations
Confirmation control
LIFO computations

Trend analysis
Allocation of partnership income
Statement of cash flows

Spreadsheets are ideally suited for everything from standard but time-consuming substantive tests to analytical review such as ratio analysis.

Current integrated spreadsheet packages contain data-file capabilities that enable them to link up with more sophisticated statistical software in order to perform more complex operations such as regression analysis. In this way, numerous different statistical analyses can be performed one after another, utilizing the same data with no need to enter data every time.

Various items can also be computed, double-checked, and/or analyzed right at the client's location, and the auditor can use these results to decide which areas should be the prime focus of the audit activities. Examples include depreciation, prepayments, and interest payable or paid.

Confirmation control is another area quite suitable for the worksheet program. On some of the new packages, random number generation within a specified range and data sorting by various criteria are features beneficial in selecting test samples for stratified sampling. These packages can also compute precision limits, point estimates, etc. The potential also exists for various tax-oriented computations, such as provisions for taxes and related deferred tax.

Once the auditor arrives at the audited trial balance on the spreadsheet, the program can be used to generate all required financial reports and supporting schedules. This is done by setting up the basic format and labeling of a given report or schedule in an unoccupied portion of the spreadsheet grid. The cells within the report that are to contain a pertinent figure are provided with a formula instructing the program where it should obtain the needed figure (from one of the cells comprising the audited trial balance). The program finds all of the appropriate figures and enters them into the report or schedule, after which it performs the needed calculations to compute the totals for that particular document. The auditor then instructs the program to print out the range of cells containing the report, and the process is complete. To increase efficiency and save time at year-end, templates can be developed during slow periods to expedite the report-production process during peak season.

Spreadsheet programs can also be very useful to the auditing practitioner in the administration of his or her practice. Earlier in the chapter, during the discussion of audit automation, some administrative aspects were mentioned. Although automation at that point was discussed in the context of utilizing specialized software, today's integrated spreadsheet packages have the capabilities to perform many of the functions. For example, many of the packages have database capabilities that can be used to improve effectiveness of staff scheduling and allocation. For example, the worksheet can be set up to track time billing and management. Also, labor rate and usage variances can be computed in order to spot potential problems. With some practice and experience, the auditor should be able to continue developing creative new ways to implement the use of spreadsheet programs in his or her practice.

TAX PREPARATION AND PLANNING

Tax return preparation and tax planning are the two main arenas of the tax practice. A key is selection of suitable computer software. Matching software capability to the requirements of an accountant's specific practice is of crucial importance. With tax-preparation software, the computer will do all the locating, organizing, calculating, checking, and rechecking necessary. The more forms and schedules the accountant has to complete along with Form 1040, the more a computer can help cut the workload. A new ruling from the IRS will make it safer than ever to rely on tax preparation software. It is advisable that the practitioner obtain a copy of *IRS Revenue-Procedure on Substitute Computer-Printed Forms and Computer-Generated Forms* (No. 1168), which provides IRS guidelines regarding these forms.

Tax software modules exist for corporations, partnerships, individuals, and estates and trusts. Much of the software is for federal and state corporate and individual returns. In addition to the spreadsheet programs that can be used for tax preparation, there are many custom software packages available. They include:

J.K. Lasser's Your Income Tax
www.jklasser.com

H&R Block At Home
H&R Block
www.hrblock.com

TurboTax
Intuit, Inc.
www.turbotax.com

Computers, with their great proficiency in rapid and accurate number crunching, can be used in income tax planning. They can be an invaluable aid in the systematic analysis of differing tax options (what-if tax options) to minimize tax liability in current and future years. Examples of tax planning applications include:

- Leasing or buying
- Investigation of writeoffs generated by a real estate investment
- Shifting income-producing assets to a child in a lower tax bracket
- Ascertaining how many years to take out funds at retirement for a Keogh plan

Tax software packages and the related tax forms are often reviewed in *The Journal of Taxation, CPA Journal,* and *PC Magazine.*

USING DATABASE MANAGEMENT SYSTEMS (DBMS)

Database programs allow practitioners to enter, manipulate, retrieve, display, extract, sort, edit, and index data. Database management systems (DBMS) packages define the structure of collected data, design screen formats for input information, handle files, and generate reports.

1. DBMS permits the creation of financial statement formats and the performance of numerical calculations.
2. DBMS allows the accountant or auditor to formulate custom programs and applications by stipulating what data must be entered into the PC and what should be done to accomplish the desired output.

Accounting Applications

Internal and external accountants may utilize DBMS for the following applications:

1. Retrieving accounting information on varied criteria. For example, you may retrieve information based on (a) the date a check was issued, (b) the payee, (c) the amount paid, or (d) the account to which an amount was posted. This type of retrieval assists in the audit-attest function.
2. Searching the accounting records for a key word or amount, such as listing accounts that are 120 days or more past due.

3. Establishing upper and lower limits for variance analysis or credit-granting decisions.
4. Making field calculations such as the footings and extensions of inventory listings.
5. Making statistical calculations such as average, variance, and maximum/minimum.
6. Asking what-if questions on financial data. This feature is most commonly found in integrated spreadsheet packages.
7. Performing audit-attest functions, such as entry-validation procedures. Also, DBMS can be used in analytical review for performing ratio analysis of selected accounts of interest to the auditor. A database showing a schedule of expenses and revenue by type and data may be made for audit analysis. Further, asset listings may be made to evaluate the adequacy of insurance coverage.
8. Keeping track of certain payroll information.
9. Monitoring inventory items by description, vendor, or price.
10. Preparing mailing lists.
11. Other applications, including preparation of general ledgers, tax preparation and planning, and investment analysis.

Database Management Systems Packages

Many of the database management packages include utility programs for interfacing with spreadsheets or other DBMS programs. This enables the accountant to analyze files of data. Such a program can merge with a word processing package to generate reports and letters. There are many good DBMS software packages on the market, notably Microsoft's Access. Reviews and buyers' guides to database products appear in periodicals such as *PC Magazine, Personal Computing,* and *InfoWorld.*

SOFTWARE SYSTEMS THAT IMPACT VALUE CHAIN MANAGEMENT

Firms employ a wide variety of software systems to process information and improve the operation of the value chain. They are Enterprise Resource Planning (ERP) systems, Supply Chain Management (SCM) systems, and Customer Relationship Management systems (CRM).

Enterprise Resource Planning Systems (ERP). Enterprise Resource Planning systems grew out of material requirements planning (MRP) systems, which have been used for more than 20 years. MRP systems computerized inventory control and production planning. Key features included an ability to prepare a master production schedule, a bill of materials, and to generate purchase orders. ERP systems update MRP systems with better integration, relational databases, and graphical user interfaces (GUI's). Features now encompass supporting accounting and finance, human resources, and various e-commerce applications, including SCM and CRM, which are explained next.

Supply Chain Management Systems (SCM). Supply chain management is the organization of activities between a company and its suppliers in an effort to provide for the profitable development, production, and delivery of goods to customers. By sharing information, production lead times and inventory holding costs have been reduced, while on-time deliveries to customers have been improved. SCM software systems support the planning of the best way to fill orders and help tracking of products and components among companies in the supply chain. Wal-Mart and Procter & Gamble (P&G) are two companies that have become well-known for their cooperation in the use of SCM. When P&G products are scanned at a Wal-Mart store, P&G receives information on the sale via satellite and thus knows when to make more product, as well as the specific Wal-Mart store(s) to which the product should be shipped. Related cost savings are passed on, at least in part, to Wal-Mart customers.

Customer Relationship Management Systems (CRM). Customer Relationship Management Systems (CRM) automate customer service and support. They also provide for customer data analysis and support e-commerce storefronts. While CRM is constantly evolving, it's already led to some remarkable changes in the way companies interact with customers. For example, Federal Express allows customers to track their packages on the Web. This service is becoming commonplace, but it didn't exist 10 years ago. Amazon.com uses CRM technology to make suggestions to customers based on their personal purchase histories. The ultimate development of CRM remains to be seen, but undoubtedly mobile communication will play a significant role. Many companies are already experimenting with systems to send messages to cell phone users offering them special discounts and buying opportunities.

WIRELESS TECHNOLOGY

Two major network technologies are: Wi-Fi (Wireless Fidelity) and Bluetooth. These two forms of wireless technology have changed the entire infrastructure of business networks. Most new hardware and software products are equipped for use with Bluetooth and Wi-Fi. The Bluetooth Special Interest Group (SIG; *www.bluetooth. com*) and the Wi-Fi Alliance (*www.weca.net*) are groups formed to help effectively develop, integrate, and implement these wireless technologies globally. These two groups have created global standards for each technology, which must be met by any company producing hardware or software to operate with Bluetooth or Wi-Fi.

BLUETOOTH

Bluetooth supports the simultaneous transmissions of information and voice data. A network of Bluetooth devices is called a piconet. Any and all devices containing Bluetooth can be potentially networked with each other. Each piconet has a master unit and slave units. The master unit synchronizes all of the slave units. The slave units are all of the other networked devices besides the master unit. Piconets may be integrated to form a scatternet by setting up a master device to synchronize several piconet master devices. Therefore, the master device of a piconet can also be a slave in a scatternet. Bluetooth technology is as secure as a wire. Furthermore, it supports data encryption.

Practical Uses

The most attractive feature of Bluetooth is that all products containing this technology work together. All manufacturers implementing Bluetooth into their products must get them tested and certified to insure interoperability.

Bluetooth's most practical usage is its ability to wirelessly synchronize devices and to serve as small networks. Its range limits its ability to serve the needs of large networks. For small businesses or sole practitioners, which require smaller networks, Bluetooth can serve this purpose. A person can coordinate each piece of his or her equipment to create a more powerful and efficient business tool. For more information about Bluetooth technology, see *www. bluetooth.com/*, or see the websites of any of the Bluetooth SIG member companies. To learn more about the Bluetooth SIG and its members, go to *www.bluetooth.com/sig/about.asp.*

WIRELESS FIDELITY (WI-FI)

Wireless Fidelity (Wi-Fi), or WLAN, has a range that is much longer than that of Bluetooth. Wi-Fi transfers data at 11 megabytes per second. Many large corporations use Wi-Fi wireless devices to extend standard wired networks to areas such as training class-rooms and large public spaces. In addition, many companies make use of Wi-Fi to provide wireless networks to their workers. These wireless networks may also be accessed remotely from workers' homes or other offices. Wi-Fi is also used to bridge the information flow between two or more offices in different buildings.

Wi-Fi networks are also found in public places such as hotels and airports. When in an area that supports Wi-Fi, a Wi-Fi certi-fied product is automatically linked to the network when the device is turned on. Wi-Fi is ideal for mid- and large-sized companies. It enables businesses to boost productivity and efficiency through constant real-time information flows, full sharing of data, and con-stant, uninterrupted communication. People are able to continue to work on projects or prepare for meetings in the airport while they are waiting to board their flight. With wireless technologies such as Wi-Fi, companies can keep their employees—whether they are in or out of the office—up-to-date at all times.

Another advantage of Wi-Fi is mobility. Having a wireless net-work gives your company many options. It is easy to add other computers to the network. Computers can just as easily be removed. Furthermore, if your business needs to move, the company will not have to abandon its network infrastructure or hire someone to rewire its new office location. All that needs to be done is simply unplug at the old office and plug in the base station to a power out-let at the new office.

What Does It All Mean for CEOs, CIOs, and Users?

CEOs

Mobile working can dramatically boost productivity and improve an organization's responsiveness and flexibility, but it also poses challenges for the chief executive. But as the trend towards mobile working gathers pace, these are issues executives cannot afford to ignore. As wired and wireless network-enabled notebook PCs, tablets, and smart phones proliferate, mobile working is becoming a reality.

This expansion has significant advantages—and risks—for corporate managements. On the positive side, mobile and remote access to corporate systems such as e-mail and enterprise portals and to applications like contact management and customer relationship management systems often provide a competitive edge for companies, while improving both customer and employee satisfaction. But, on the other hand, mobile technologies and services tend to pose security risks.

Balancing the risks and rewards of mobile working and establishing a corporate policy framework to cover, for example, remote access to corporate networks has become an important issue for chief executives—an issue that they ignore at their peril.

CIOs

One of the key challenges for CIOs in either case is to find ways to accommodate a diverse group of mobile devices while protecting the corporate IT infrastructure and minimizing the network security threat they can pose.

Given the fast pace of change in the technology industry—particularly in the mobile device sector—it is also often a challenge for a CIO to keep up with hardware, software, and service developments and to provide the level of support (often with reduced resources) that users have come to expect.

One way to minimize the support overhead is to standardize on a set of devices such as notebook PCs, tablets, mobile phones, and communicators. However, this often delays deployment and can lead to end user frustration.

One of the fastest growing areas in the mobile technology sector is security. Typically, larger companies will deploy virtual private networks to facilitate secure access for mobile and remote users such as home office workers to a corporate network.

Most CIOs have already discovered that the trend toward mobile working is like a runaway steamroller—it is not about to stop. So, while it makes sense to lay down guidelines about which mobile devices are supported and how they should be used, ultimately the CIO has to deal with the realities of mobile working.

Users

The rapid growth of mobile working and the proliferation of new hardware devices, software and services designed to enable mobile workers to do their jobs from virtually anywhere, poses both great opportunities and challenges.

For example, salespeople can use mobile technologies to update customer profiles, download price quotes, and provide their audiences with dazzling multimedia presentations. Executives can send and receive e-mail messages, peer into the corporate ERP system, or check share prices and competitors' websites while traveling using Wi-Fi or W-LAN wireless connections.

For mobile professionals in particular, as a recent study conducted by U.S. chipmaker Intel showed, technology has dramatically changed their lives—making it much easier to stay in touch while traveling and respond to colleagues and customers in a more timely fashion.

Balancing the demands of work and private life in the age of mobile technology—when the pressure for greater productivity is often unrelenting—has become one of the more interesting questions probed by sociologists.

Brief Summary

Accountants must be familiar with the features and applications of software packages in order to carry out their record-keeping, financial-reporting, audit, and tax functions optimally. Knowledge in terms of what to do and how to do it for spreadsheet, database management, graphics, local area network (LAN), statistics, financial analysis, accounting, tax, audit, and integrated packages is required. Optimal software selection and use will greatly improve productivity, efficiency, and profitability.

Chapter 9
Quantitative Methods for Accounting

A variety of quantitative models are being utilized in accounting. With the rapid development of personal computers, accountants find it increasingly easy to use them. Thus, a knowledge of mathematical and statistical methods is of great importance to accountants in their work. The Decision Support System (DSS) is in effect the embodiment of this trend.

The term quantitative models, *also known as* operations research (OR) *and* management science, *describes the sophisticated mathematical and statistical techniques used in the solution of planning and decision-making problems. There are numerous tools available under these subject headings. We will explore five of the most important of these techniques in accounting. They are:*

1. Decision making
2. Linear programming and shadow prices
3. Learning curve
4. Inventory planning
5. Program Evaluation and Review Technique (PERT)

DECISION MAKING

Decisions are made under certainty or under uncertainty. Decision making *under certainty* means that for each decision there is only one event and therefore only one outcome for each action. Decision making *under uncertainty,* which is more common, involves several events for each action with its probability of occurrence.

Decision Making Under Uncertainty

When decisions are made in a world of *uncertainty,* it is often help-ful to make computations of (1) *expected value,* (2) *standard deviation,* and (3) *coefficient of variation.*

Expected Value. For decisions involving uncertainty, the concept of *expected value ($\bar{A}$)* provides a rational means for selecting the best course of action. The expected value of an alternative is an arithmetic mean, a weighted average using the probabilities as weights. More specifically, it is found by multiplying the probability of each outcome by its payoff,

$$\bar{A} = \sum A_x P_x$$

where A_x is the outcome for the xth possible event and P_x is the probability of occurrence of that outcome.

EXAMPLE 9.1

Consider two investment proposals, A and B, with the following probability distribution of cash flows in each of the next four years:

		Cash Infows			
Probability		(.2)	(.3)	(.4)	(.1)
A		$ 50	200	300	400
B		$100	150	250	850

The expected value of the cash inflow in proposal A is $50(.2) + 200(.3) + 300(.4) + 400(.1) = $230. The expected value of the cash inflow in proposal B is: $100(.2) + 150(.3) + 250(.4) + 850(.1) = $250.

Standard Deviation. The standard deviation (σ) measures the dispersion of a probability distribution. It is the square root of the mean of the squared deviations from the expected value.

$$\sigma = \sqrt{\sum_{x=1}^{n} (A_x - \bar{A})^2 P_x}$$

The standard deviation is commonly used as an absolute measure of risk. The higher the standard deviation, the higher the risk.

EXAMPLE 9.2

In Example 9.1, the standard deviations of proposals A and B are computed as follows:

For A: $\sigma = [(\$50 - 230)^2 (0.2) + (200 - 230)^2(0.3)$
$+ (300 - 230)^2 (0.4) + (400 - 230)^2 (0.1)]^{1/2}$
$= \$107.70$

For B: $\sigma = [(\$100 - 250)^2 (0.2) + (150 - 250)^2(0.3)$
$+ (250 - 250)^2 (0.4) + (850 - 250)^2 (0.1)]^{1/2}$
$= \$208.57$

Proposal B is riskier than proposal A, because its standard deviation is greater.

Coefficient of Variation. This measure of relative dispersion or relative risk is computed by dividing the standard deviation by the expected value:

$$\sigma / \bar{A}$$

EXAMPLE 9.3

In Examples 9.1 and 9.2, the coefficient of variation for each proposal is:

For A: $\$107.70/\$230 = .47$

For B: $\$208.57/\$250 = .83$

Because the coefficient is a relative measure of risk, B is said to have a greater degree of risk.

Decision Matrix

Although statistics such as expected value and standard deviation are essential for choosing the best course of action under uncertainty, the decision problem can best be approached using *decision theory*. Decision theory is a systematic approach to making decisions, especially under uncertainty. This theory utilizes an organized approach, such as a *payoff table* (or *decision matrix*), which is characterized by:

1. The *row* representing a set of alternative *courses of action* available to the decision maker.

2. The *column* representing the *state of nature* or conditions that are likely to occur and over which the decision maker has no control.
3. The *entries* in the body of the table representing the outcome of the decision, known as *payoffs,* which may be in the form of costs, revenues, profits, or cash flows. By computing the expected value of each action, we will be able to pick the best one.

EXAMPLE 9.4

Assume the following probability distribution of daily demand for strawberries:

Daily demand	0	1	2	3
Probability	.2	.3	.3	.2

Also assume that unit cost = \$3, selling price = \$5 (i.e., profit on sold unit = \$2), and salvage value on unsold units = \$2 (i.e., loss on unsold unit = \$1). We can stock either 0, 1, 2, or 3 units. The question is, how many units should be stocked each day? Assume that units from one day cannot be sold the next day. Then the payoff table can be constructed as follows:

		State of Nature				
	Demand (probability)	0	1	2	3	Expected
Stock		(.2)	(.3)	(.3)	(.2)	Value
Actions 0		\$0	0	0	0	\$0
1		−1	2	2	2	1.40
2		−2	1*	4	4	1.90†
3		−3	0	3	6	1.50

* Profit for (stock 2, demand 1) equals (no. of units sold)(profit per unit) − (no. of units unsold)(loss per unit) = (1)(\$5 − 3) − (1)(\$3 − 2) = \$1
† Expected value for (stock 2) is: −2(.2) + 1(.3) + 4(.3) + 4(.2) = \$1.90

The optimal stock action is the one with the highest *expected monetary value,* i.e., stock two units.

Expected Value of Perfect Information

Suppose the decision maker can obtain a perfect prediction of which event (state of nature) will occur. The *expected value with perfect information* would be the total expected value of actions selected on the assumption of a perfect forecast. For example, when demand is 1, the company will stock 1. The *expected value of perfect information* can then be computed as expected value with perfect information *minus* the expected value with existing information.

EXAMPLE 9.5

From the payoff table in Example 9.4, the following analysis yields the expected value *with* perfect information:

			State of Nature			
	Demand	0	1	2	3	Expected
Stock		(.2)	(.3)	(.3)	(.2)	Value
Actions	0	$0				$0
	1		2			.60
	2			4		1.20
	3				6	1.20
						$3.00

Alternatively,

$$\$0(.2) + 2(.3) + 4(.3) + 6(.2) = \$3.00$$

With existing information, the best that the decision maker could obtain was select (stock 2) and obtain $1.90. With perfect information (forecast), the decision-maker could make as much as $3. Therefore, the expected value *of* perfect information is $3.00 – $1.90 = $1.10. This is the maximum price the decision-maker is willing to pay for additional information.

Decision Tree

Decision tree is another approach used in discussions of decision making under uncertainty. It is a pictorial representation of a decision situation. As in the case of the *decision matrix* discussed earlier, the decision tree shows decision alternatives, states of nature, probabilities attached to the state of nature, and conditional benefits and losses. The decision tree approach is most useful in a sequential decision.

EXAMPLE 9.6

Assume XYZ Corporation wishes to introduce one of two products to the market this year. The probabilities and present values (PV) of projected cash inflows are given below:

Products	Initial Investment	PV of cash inflows	Probabilities
A	$225,000		1.00
		$450,000	0.40
		200,000	0.50
		−100,000	0.10
B	80,000		1.00
		320,000	0.20
		100,000	0.60
		−150,000	0.20

A decision tree analyzing the two products is given in Figure 9–1. Based on the expected net present value in Figure 9–1, the company should choose Product A over Product B.

LINEAR PROGRAMMING AND SHADOW PRICING

Linear programming (LP) is a mathematical technique designed to determine an optimal decision (or an optimal plan) chosen from a large number of alternatives. The optimal decision is the one that meets a specified objective of a business, subject to various restrictions or constraints. It is concerned with the problem of allocating scarce resources among competing activities in an optimal manner. The optimal decision yields the highest profit, contribution margin (CM), or revenue, or the lowest cost.

A linear programming model consists of two important ingredients:

- Objective function, so that the company must define the specific objective to be achieved.
- Constraints, or restrictions on availability of resources or meeting minimum requirements.

As the name *linear programming* indicates, both the objective function and constraints must be in *linear* form.

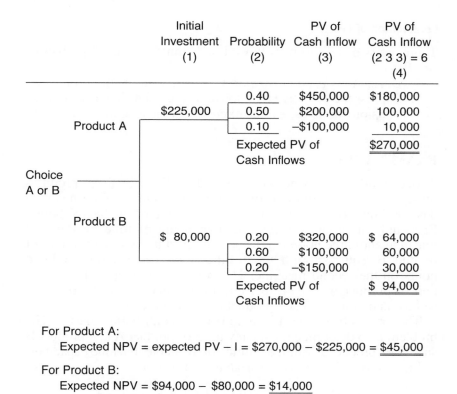

	Initial Investment (1)	Probability (2)	PV of Cash Inflow (3)	PV of Cash Inflow (2 3 3) = 6 (4)
Product A	$225,000	0.40	$450,000	$180,000
		0.50	$200,000	100,000
		0.10	–$100,000	10,000
		Expected PV of Cash Inflows		$270,000
Choice A or B				
Product B	$ 80,000	0.20	$320,000	$ 64,000
		0.60	$100,000	60,000
		0.20	–$150,000	30,000
		Expected PV of Cash Inflows		$ 94,000

For Product A:
  Expected NPV = expected PV – I = $270,000 – $225,000 = $45,000

For Product B:
  Expected NPV = $94,000 – $80,000 = $14,000

Figure 9-1. Decision tree

EXAMPLE 9.7

A firm wishes to find an optimal product mix—that is, the mix that maximizes its total CM within the allowed budget and production capacity. Or the firm may want to determine a least-cost combination of input materials while meeting production requirements, employing production capacities, and using available employees.

Applications of LP

Applications of LP are numerous. They include:

1. Developing an optimal budget
2. Determining an optimal investment portfolio
3. Scheduling jobs to machines
4. Determining a least-cost shipping pattern
5. Scheduling flights
6. Blending gasoline

Formulation of LP

There are two steps to be followed in formulating an LP problem:

1. Define the *decision variables* one is trying to solve for.
2. Express the objective function and constraints in terms of these decision variables. All the expressions must be in linear form.

EXAMPLE 9.8

A firm produces two products, A and B. Each of these products must be processed through two different machines. One machine has 100 hours of available time, the second machine has 90 hours. Each unit of product A requires two hours of time on the first machine and three hours on the second machine, while each unit of product B requires four hours of time on the first machine and two hours on the second machine. The contribution margin is $25 per unit of product A and $40 per unit of product B, and the firm can sell as many units of each product as it manufactures.

The firm's objective is to maximize total contribution margin. The problem is to determine how many units of product A and product B should be produced within the limits of available machine capacities.

First, define the decision variables as follows:

A = Number of units of product A to be produced
B = Number of units of product B to be produced

The objective function is:

$$\text{Maximize total CM} = 25A + 40B$$

The constraints are:

$$2A + 4B \leq 100 \text{ (machine 1 constraint)}$$
$$3A + 2B \leq 90 \text{ (machine 2 constraint)}$$

In addition, implicit in any LP formulation are the constraints that restrict A and B to be nonnegative, i.e.,

$$A, B \geq 0$$

The total formulation is thus:

Maximize: Total CM = 25A + 40B
Subject to: $2A + 4B \leq 100$
                 $3A + 2B \leq 90$
                 $A, B \geq 0$

Computation Methods of LP

There are several solution methods available to solve LP problems. They include the simplex method and the graphical method.

The *simplex* method is the technique most commonly used to solve LP problems. It is an algorithm, which is an iteration method of computation, moving from one solution to another until it reaches the best solution. The *graphical method* is easier to use but is limited to the LP problems involving two (or at most three) decision variables. The graphical method follows the steps:

1. Change inequalities to equalities.
2. Graph the equalities.
3. Identify the correct side for the original inequalities.
4. After all this, identify the feasible region, the area of feasible solutions. *Feasible solutions* are values of decision variables that satisfy all the restrictions simultaneously.
5. Determine the contribution margin at all of the corners in the feasible region.

EXAMPLE 9.9

In Example 9.8, after having gone through steps 1–4, we obtain the feasible region (shaded area) in Figure 9–2.

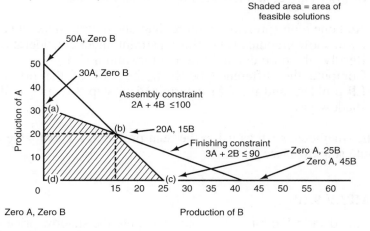

Figure 9-2. Feasible solutions

Then we evaluate all of the corner points in the feasible region in terms of their CM, as follows:

| | Corner Points | | Contribution Margin |
	A	B	$25A + $40B
(a)	30	0	$25(30) + $40(0) = $750
(b)	20	15	25(20) + 40(15) = 1,100
(c)	0	25	25(0) + 40(25) = 1,000
(d)	0	0	25(0) + 40(0) = 0

The corner, 20A, 15B produces the most profitable solution.

Shadow Prices (Opportunity Costs)

A decision maker who has solved an LP problem might wish to know whether it pays to add capacity in hours in a particular department. He or she would be interested in the monetary value to the firm of adding, say, an hour per week of assembly time. This monetary value is the additional contribution margin that could be earned. This amount is called the *shadow price* of the given resource. This price is in a way an opportunity cost, the contribution margin that would be lost by not adding an additional hour of capacity. To justify a decision in favor of a short-term capacity expansion, the decision maker must be sure that the shadow price (or opportunity cost) exceeds the actual price of that expansion. Shadow prices are computed, step by step, as follows:

1. Add one hour (preferably, more than one hour to make it easier to show graphically) to the constraint under consideration.
2. Resolve the problem and find the maximum CM.
3. Compute the difference between the CM of the original LP problem and the CM determined in step 2, which is the shadow price.

Other methods, such as using the dual problem, are available to compute shadow prices.

EXAMPLE 9.10

Using the data in Example 9, we can compute the shadow price of the assembly capacity. To make it easier to show graphically, we shall add eight hours of capacity to the assembly department, rather than one hour. The new assembly constraint is shown in Figure 9–3.

	Corner Points		Contribution Margin
	A	*B*	*$25A + $40B*
(a)	30	0	$25(30) + $40(0) = $750
(b)	18	18	25(18) + 40(18) = 1,170
(c)	0	27	25(0) + 40(27) = 1,080
(d)	0	0	25(0) + 40(0) = 0

The new optimal solution of 18A, 18B has a total CM of $1,170 per week. Therefore, the shadow price of the assembly capacity is $70($1,170 – $1,100 = $70). The firm would be willing to pay up to $70 to obtain an additional eight hours per week, or $8.75 *per hour* per week.

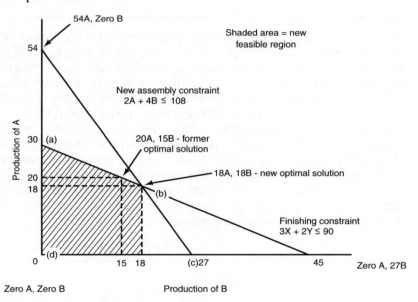

Figure 9-3. New assembly constraint

The following table shows Excel LP solution.

Excel LP Output

Adjustable Cells	*Solutions (A = 20, B = 15)*		
Name		*Final Value*	*Reduced Gradient*
Number to make: Desk		20	0
Number to make: Table		15	0

Excel LP Output (continued)

Constraints

	Final Value	Lagrange Multiplier
Assembly Used	100	8.75
Finishing Used	90	2.5

LEARNING CURVE

The *learning curve* is based on the proposition that required labor hours decrease in a definite pattern as an operation is repeated. More specifically, it is based on the statistical finding that, as the cumulative production doubles, the cumulative average time required per unit will be reduced by some constant percentage, ranging typically from 10% to 20%. By convention, learning curves are referred to by the complements of their improvement rates. For example, an 80% learning curve denotes a 20% decrease in unit time with each doubling of repetitions. As an illustration, a project is known to have an 80% learning curve. It has just taken a worker ten hours to produce the first unit. Then, each time the cumulative output doubles, the time per unit for that amount should be equal to the previous time multiplied by the learning percentage. Thus:

Unit	Unit time (hours)
1	10
2	.8(10) = 8
4	.8(8) = 6.4
8	.8(6.4) = 5.12
16	.8(5.12) = 4.096

Learning-curve theory has found useful applications in many areas, including:

1. Scheduling labor requirements
2. Setting incentive wage rates
3. Pricing new products
4. Negotiated purchasing
5. Budgeting, purchasing, and inventory planning

Example 9.11 illustrates the use of the learning-curve theory for the pricing of a contract.

EXAMPLE 9.11

Big Mac Electronics Products finds that new-product production is affected by an 80% learning effect. The company has just produced 50 units of output at 100 hours per unit. Costs were as follows:

Materials—50 units @ $20	$1,000
Labor and labor-related costs:	
Direct labor—100 hours @$8	800
Variable overhead—100 hours @$2	200
	$2,000

The company has just received a contract calling for another 50 units of production. It wants to add a 50% markup to the cost of materials, labor, and labor-related costs. To determine the price for this job, the first step is to build up the learning curve table.

Quantity	Total Time *(hours)*	Average Time *(per unit)*
50	100	2 hours
100	160	1.6 (.8 × 2 hours)

Thus, it takes a total of 60 hours to produce the new 50-unit job. The contract price is:

Materials—50 units @ $20	$1,000
Labor and labor-related costs:	
Direct labor—60 hours @$8	480
Variable overhead—60 hours @$2	120
	$1,600
50% markup	800
Contract price	$2,400

INVENTORY PLANNING

One of the most common problems that faces managerial accountants is inventory planning. This is understandable since inventory usually represents a sizable portion of a firm's total assets and, more specifically, on the average, more than 30% of total current assets in U.S. industry. Excess money tied up in inventory is a drag on profitability. The purpose of inventory planning is to develop policies that will achieve an optimal investment in inventory. This objective is achieved by determining the optimal level of inventory necessary to minimize inventory-related costs. These costs fall into three categories:

1. Ordering costs, which include all costs associated with preparing a purchase order.
2. Carrying (holding) costs, which include storage costs for inventory items plus the cost of money tied up in inventory.
3. Shortage (stockout) costs, which include those costs incurred when an item is out of stock. These include the lost contribution margin on sales plus lost customer goodwill.

There is a variety of inventory planning models available that answer the following two questions:

- How much to order?
- When to order?

They include economic order quantity (EOQ), reorder point, and determination of safety stock.

Economic Order Quantity

The economic order quantity (EOQ) determines the order quantity that results in the lowest sum of carrying and ordering costs. The EOQ is computed as:

$$EOQ = \sqrt{\frac{2\,OD}{C}}$$

where C = carrying cost per unit, O = ordering cost per order, and D = annual demand (requirements) in units.

If the carrying cost is expressed as a percentage of average inventory value (say, 12% per year), then the denominator value in the EOQ formula would be 12% times the price of an item.

EXAMPLE 9.12

Assume ABC Stone buys sets of dishes at $40 per set from an outside vendor. ABC will sell 6,400 sets evenly throughout the year. ABC desires a 16% return on investment (cost of borrowed money) on its inventory investment. In addition, rent, taxes, and other expenses changeable to each set in inventory is \$1.60. The ordering cost is \$100 per order. Then the carrying cost per dozen is 16%(\$40) + \$1.60 = \$8.00. Therefore,

$$\text{EOQ} = \sqrt{\frac{2(6,400)(\$100)}{\$8.00}}$$

$$= \sqrt{160,000} \ = \ 400 \text{ sets}$$

Total inventory costs   = Carrying cost + Ordering cost

$$= C(\text{EOQ}/2) + O(D/\text{EOQ})$$

$$= (\$8.00)(400/2) + (\$100)(6,400/400)$$

$$= \$1,600 + \$1,600 = \$3,200$$

Total number of orders   = D/EOQ = 6,400/400 = 16 orders per year

The EOQ model can easily be extended to determine the economic production-run quantity for a manufacturer. This is the quantity that results in the lowest sum of carrying and setup costs. The way it is computed is exactly the same as for the EOQ, except that the ordering cost in the EOQ formula is replaced by the setup cost—the cost incurred each time a batch is produced. This includes the engineering cost of setting up the production runs or machines, the paperwork cost of processing the work order, and the ordering cost to provide raw materials for the batch.

Reorder Point

Determining the reorder point (ROP) requires knowledge of the lead time—the interval between placing an order and receiving delivery—and lead-time sales. Reorder point (ROP) can be calculated as follows:

Reorder point = (average sales per unit of lead time
$$\times \text{ lead time}) + \text{safety stock}$$

First, multiply average daily (or weekly) sales by the lead time in days (or weeks), yielding the lead-time demand. Then add safety stock to this to provide for the variation in lead-time demand. This determines the reorder point. If average usage and lead time are both certain, no safety stock is necessary and should be dropped from the formula.

EXAMPLE 9.13

Assume in Example 9.12 that lead time is constant at one week and that there are 50 working weeks in a year. In this case the reorder point is

$$128 \text{ sets} = (6{,}400 \text{ sets}/50 \text{ weeks}) \times 1 \text{ week.}$$

Therefore, when the inventory level drops to 128 sets, the new order should be placed. Suppose, however, that the store is faced with variable usage for its dishes and requires a safety stock of 150 additional sets. Then the order point will be 128 sets plus 150 sets, or 278 sets. Figure 9–4 shows this inventory system when the order quantity is 400 sets and the reorder point is 128 sets.

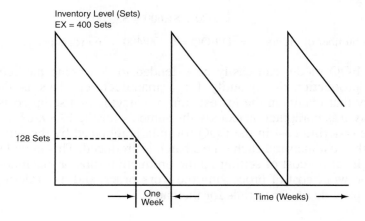

Figure 9-4. Basic inventory system with EOQ and reorder point

Assumptions and Applications

The EOQ model makes some strong assumptions. They are:

1. Demand is fixed and constant throughout the year.
2. Lead time is known with certainty.
3. No quantity discounts are allowed.
4. No shortages are permitted.

The assumptions may be unrealistic. However, the model has still proved useful in inventory planning for many firms. In fact, many situations exist where a certain assumption holds or nearly holds. For example, subcontractors who must supply parts on a regular basis to a primary contractor face a constant demand. Even where demand varies, the assumption of uniform usage is not unrealistic. Demand for automobiles, for example, varies from week to week over a season, but the weekly fluctuations tend to cancel each other out so that seasonal demand can be assumed as constant.

EOQ with Quantity Discounts

The economic order quantity (EOQ) model does not take into account quantity discounts, which is not realistic in many real-world cases. Usually, the more you order, the lower the unit price you pay. Quantity discounts are price reductions for large orders offered to buyers. If quantity discounts are offered, the buyer must weigh the potential benefits of a reduced purchase price and fewer orders that will result from buying in large quantities against the increase in carrying costs caused by higher average inventories. Hence, the buyer's goal in this case is to select the order quantity that will minimize total costs, where total cost is the sum of carrying cost, ordering cost, and product cost:

$$\text{Total cost} = \text{Carrying cost} + \text{Ordering cost} + \text{Product cost}$$

$$= C(Q/2) + O(D/Q) + PD$$

where P = unit price and Q = order quantity. A step-by-step approach in computing economic order quantity with quantity discounts is summarized below.

1. Compute the *economic order quantity (EOQ)* when price discounts are ignored and the corresponding costs use the new cost formula given above. Note EOQ = $\sqrt{2OD/C}$.
2. Compute the costs for those quantities greater than the EOQ at which price reductions occur.
3. Select the value of Q that will result in the lowest total cost.

EXAMPLE 9.14

In Example 9.12, assume that the ABC store was offered the following price discount schedule:

Order Quantity (Q)	Unit Price (P)
1 to 499	$40.00
500 to 999	39.90
1000 or more	39.80

First, the EOQ with no discounts is computed as follows:

$$\text{EOQ} = \sqrt{2(6,400)(100)/8.00}$$
$$= \sqrt{160,000} = 400 \text{ sets.}$$

$$\text{Total cost} = \$8.00(400/2) + \$100(6,400/400)$$
$$+ \$40.00(6,400)$$
$$= \$1,600 + 1,600 + 256,000 = \$259,200$$

Annual Costs with Varying Order Quantities

Order Quantity	400	500	1,000
Ordering cost			
$100 × (6,400/order quantity)	$ 1,600	$ 1,280	$ 640
Carrying cost			
$8 × (order quantity/2)	1,600	2,000	4,000
Product cost			
Unit price × 6,400	256,000	255,360	254,720
Total cost	$259,200	$258,640	$259,360

The value that minimized the sum of the carrying cost and the ordering cost but not the purchase cost was EOQ = 400 sets. Figure 9–5 shows that the further we move from the point 400, the greater will be the sum of the carrying and ordering costs. Thus, 400 is obviously the only candidate for the minimum total cost value within the first price range; Q = 500 is the only candidate within the $39.90 price range; Q = 1,000 is the only candidate within the $39.80 price bracket. These three quantities are evaluated in the table. We find that the EOQ with price discounts is 500 sets. Hence, the ABC store is justified in going to the first price break, but the extra carrying cost of going to the second price break more than outweighs the savings in ordering and in the cost of the product.

Advantages and Disadvantages of Quantity Discounts

Buying in large quantities has some favorable and some unfavorable features for a firm. The advantages are lower unit costs, lower ordering costs, fewer stockouts, and lower transportation costs. On the other hand, the disadvantages include higher inventory carrying costs, a greater capital requirement, and higher probability of obsolescence and deterioration.

Determination of Safety Stock

When lead time and demand are not certain, the firm must carry extra units of inventory, called safety stock, as protection against possible stockouts. Stockouts can be quite expensive, leading to lost sales and disgruntled customers. Idle machine time and disrupted production scheduling are examples of the internal costs of stockouts. We will illustrate the probability approach to show how the optimal stock size can be determined in the presence of stockout costs.

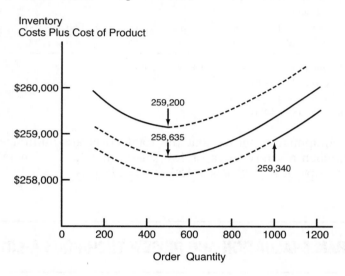

Figure 9-5. Inventory cost and quantity

EXAMPLE 9.15

In Examples 9.12 and 9.13, suppose that the total usage over a one-week period is expected to be:

Total Usage	Probability
78	.2
128	.4
178	.2
228	.1
278	.1
	$\overline{1.00}$

Suppose further that a stockout cost is estimated at $12 per set. Recall that the carrying cost is $8 per set.

Computation of Safety Stock

Safety Stock Levels in Units	Stockout and Probability	Average Stockout in Units	Average Stockout Costs	No. of Orders	Total Annual Stockout Costs	Carrying Costs	Total
0	{ 50 with .2 100 with .1 150 with .1	35*	$420†	16	$6,720‡	0	$7,140
50	{ 50 with .1 100 with .1	15	180	16	2,880	400**	3,280
100	50 with .1	5	60	16	960	800	1,760
150	0	0	0	16	0	1,200	1,200

* 50(.2) + 100(.1) + 150(.1) = 10 + 10 + 15 = 35 units
† 35 units × $12.00 = $420
‡ $420 × 16 times = $6,720
** 50 units × $8.00 = $400

The computation shows that the total costs are minimized at $1,200, when a safety stock of 150 sets is maintained. Therefore, the reorder point is: 128 sets + 150 sets = 278 sets.

PROGRAM EVALUATION AND REVIEW TECHNIQUE (PERT)

Program Evaluation and Review Technique (PERT) is a useful management tool for planning, scheduling, costing, coordinating, and controlling complex projects such as:

Formulation of a master budget
Construction of buildings
Installation of computers
Scheduling the closing of books
Assembly of a machine
Research and development activities

Questions answered by PERT include:

When will the project be finished?
What is the probability that the project will be completed by a given time?

The PERT technique involves the diagrammatic representation of the sequence of activities comprising a project as a *network*. The network (1) visualizes all the individual tasks (activities) involved in completing a given job or program; (2) points out interrelationships; and (3) consists of activities (represented by arrows) and events (represented by circles), as shown below.

1. *Arrows* represent tasks or activities, which are distinct segments of the project requiring time and resources.
2. *Nodes (circles)* symbolize events or milestone points in the project representing the completion of one or more activities and/or the initiation of one or more subsequent activities. An event is a point in time and does not consume any time in itself as does an activity.

In a real-world situation, the estimates of the completion times of activities will seldom be certain. To cope with the uncertainty in estimates of activity time, PERT proceeds by estimating *three* possible duration times for each activity. As shown in Figure 9–6, the numbers appearing on the arrows represent these three time estimates for activities needed to complete the various events. These time estimates are:

- the most optimistic time, labeled a
- the most likely time, m
- the most pessimistic time, b

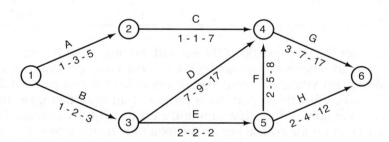

Figure 9-6. Network diagram

For example, the optimistic time for completing activity B is one day, the most likely time is two days, and the pessimistic time is three days. The next step is to calculate an expected time, which is determined as follows:

$$t_e(\text{expected time}) = (a + 4m + b)/6$$

For example, for activity B, the expected time is:

$$t_e = (1 + 4(2) + 3)/6 = 12/6 = 2 \text{ days}$$

As a measure of variation (uncertainty) about the expected time, the standard deviation is calculated as follows:

$$\sigma = (b - a)/6$$

For example, the standard deviation of completion time for activity B is:

$$\sigma = (3 - 1)/6 = 2/6 = .33 \text{ days}$$

Expected activity times and their standard deviations are computed in this manner for all the activities of the network and arranged in tabular format as shown below.

Activity	Predecessors	a	m	b	te	σ
A	None	1	3	5	3.0	.67
B	None	1	2	3	2.0	.33
C	A	1	1	7	2.0	1.00
D	B	7	9	17	10.0	1.67
E	B	2	2	2	2.0	0.00
F	E	2	5	8	5.0	.67
G	C,D,F	3	7	17	8.0	2.33
H	E	2	4	12	5.0	1.67

To answer the first question ("When will the project be finished?"), we need to determine the network's *critical path,* or sequence of connected activities. In Figure 9–6, an example of such a path would be 1-2-4-6. The critical path for a project is the path that takes the greatest amount of time. The sum of the estimated activity times for all activities on the critical path is the total time required to complete the project. These activities are "critical" because any delay in their completion will cause a delay in the project. The critical path is the minimum amount of time needed for the completion of the project. Thus, in order to speed up the project, the time alloted to the activities along this path must be shortened. Activities not on the critical path are not critical, since they will be worked on simultaneously with critical-path activities and their completion could be delayed up to a point without delaying the project as a whole.

An easy way to find the critical path involves the following two steps:

1. Identify all possible paths of a project, and calculate their completion times.
2. The critical path is the one with the longest amount of completion time.

(When the network is large and complex, we need a more systematic and efficient approach, which is reserved for an advanced management science text). In the example, we have:

Path	Completion Time
A-C-G	13 days (3 + 2 + 8)
B-D-G	20 days (2 + 10 + 8)
B-E-F-G	17 days (2 + 2 + 5 + 8)
B-E-H	9 days (2 + 2 + 5)

The critical path is B-D-G, which means it takes 20 days to complete the project.

The next important information we want to obtain is, what is the chance that the project will be completed within a contract time of, say, 21 days? To answer the question, we introduce the standard deviation of total project time around the expected time, which is determined as follows:

Standard deviation (project)

$$= \sqrt{\begin{array}{l}\text{the sum of the squares of the standard} \\ \text{deviations of all critical-path activities}\end{array}}$$

Using the standard deviation and table of areas under the normal distribution curve, as shown in the table, the probability of completing the project within any given time period can be determined.

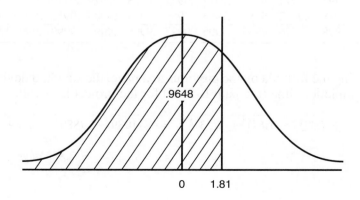

0   1.81

NORMAL DISTRIBUTION TABLE

Areas under the normal curve

Z	0	1	2	3	4	5	6	7	8	9
.0	.5000	.5040	.5080	.5120	.5160	.5199	.5239	.5279	.5319	.5359
.1	.5398	.5438	.5478	.5517	.5557	.5596	.5636	.5675	.5714	.5753
.2	.5793	.5832	.5871	.5910	.5948	.5987	.6026	.6064	.6103	.6141
.3	.6179	.6217	.6255	.6293	.6331	.6368	.6406	.6443	.6480	.6517
.4	.6554	.6591	.6628	.6664	.6700	.6736	.6772	.6808	.6844	.6879
.5	.6915	.6950	.6985	.7019	.7054	.7088	.7123	.7157	.7190	.7224
.6	.7257	.7291	.7324	.7357	.7389	.7422	.7454	.7486	.7517	.7549
.7	.7580	.7611	.7642	.7673	.7703	.7734	.7764	.7794	.7823	.7852
.8	.7881	.7910	.7939	.7967	.7995	.8023	.8051	.8078	.8106	.8133
.9	.8159	.8186	.8212	.8238	.8264	.8289	.8315	.8340	.8365	.8389
1.0	.8413	.8438	.8461	.8485	.8508	.8531	.8554	.8577	.8599	.8621
1.1	.8643	.8665	.8686	.8708	.8729	.8749	.8770	.8790	.8810	.8830
1.2	.8849	.8869	.8888	.8907	.8925	.8944	.8962	.8980	.8997	.9015
1.3	.9032	.9049	.9066	.9082	.9099	.9115	.9131	.9147	.9162	.9177
1.4	.9192	.9207	.9222	.9236	.9251	.9265	.9278	.9292	.9306	.9319
1.5	.9332	.9345	.9357	.9370	.9382	.9394	.9406	.9418	.9430	.9441
1.6	.9452	.9463	.9474	.9484	.9495	.9505	.9515	.9525	.9535	.9545
1.7	.9554	.9564	.9573	.9582	.9591	.9599	.9608	.9616	.9625	.9633
1.8	.9641	.9648	.9656	.9664	.9671	.9678	.9686	.9693	.9700	.9706
1.9	.9713	.9719	.9726	.9732	.9738	.9744	.9750	.9756	.9762	.9767
2.0	.9772	.9778	.9783	.9788	.9793	.9798	.9803	.9808	.9812	.9817
2.1	.9821	.9826	.9830	.9834	.9838	.9842	.9846	.9850	.9854	.9857
2.2	.9861	.9864	.9868	.9871	.9874	.9878	.9881	.9884	.9887	.9890
2.3	.9893	.9896	.9898	.9901	.9904	.9906	.9909	.9911	.9913	.9916
2.4	.9918	.9920	.9922	.9925	.9927	.9929	.9931	.9932	.9934	.9936
2.5	.9938	.9940	.9941	.9943	.9945	.9946	.9948	.9949	.9951	.9952
2.6	.9953	.9955	.9956	.9957	.9959	.9960	.9961	.9962	.9963	.9964
2.7	.9965	.9966	.9967	.9968	.9969	.9970	.9971	.9972	.9973	.9974
2.8	.9974	.9975	.9976	.9977	.9977	.9978	.9979	.9979	.9980	.9981
2.9	.9981	.9982	.9982	.9983	.9984	.9984	.9985	.9985	.9986	.9986
3.	.9987	.9990	.9993	.9995	.9997	.9998	.9998	.9999	.9999	1.0000

Using the formula on the previous text page, the standard deviation of completion time (the path B-D-G) for the project is as follows:

$$\sqrt{(.33)^2 + (1.67)^2 + (2.33)^2} \quad = \quad \sqrt{.1089 + 2.7889 + 5.4289}$$

$$= \quad \sqrt{8.3267} \quad = \quad 2.885 \text{ days}$$

Assume the expected delivery time is 21 days. The first step is to compute z, which is the number of standard deviations from the mean represented by our given time of 21 days. The formula for z is:

$$z = (\text{delivery time} - \text{expected time})/\text{standard deviation}$$

Therefore,

$$z = (21 \text{ days} - 20 \text{ days})/2.885 \text{ days} = .35$$

The next step is to find the probability associated with the calculated value of z by referring to the table of areas under a normal curve.

From the Normal Distribution Table, we see the probability is .6368, which means that there is close to a 64% chance that the project will be completed in less than 21 days.

To summarize what we have obtained:

1. The expected completion time of the project is 20 days.
2. There is a better than 60% chance of finishing before 21 days.
3. Activities B-D-G are on the critical path; they must be watched more closely than the others, for if they take longer than expected, the whole project falls behind.
4. If extra effort is needed to finish the project on time or before the deadline, we have to borrow resources (such as money or labor) from any activity *not* on the critical path.
5. It is possible to reduce the completion time of one or more activities. The benefit from reducing the total completion time of a project by doing so must be balanced against the extra cost of doing so. A related problem is to determine which activities must be accelerated to reduce the total completion time for the project. The critical-path method (CPM), also known as PERT/COST, is widely used to deal with this.

It should be noted that PERT is a technique for project management and control. It is *not* an optimizing decision model, however, since the decision to undertake a project has already been made. It will not evaluate an investment project according to its attractiveness or the time specifications we observe.

Brief Summary

Quantitative applications and modeling in accounting are on the rise, aided by personal computers and the wide availability of software for various quantitative decision-making tools. Accountants should take advantage of the advances in technology to analyze and solve a variety of accounting and financial problems.

Chapter 10
Auditing and Internal Control Over Financial Reporting

This chapter is directed toward accountants whose work will be audited or reviewed by external auditors. The auditee is concerned with the type of audit reports that might be rendered and what the external auditor basically does to prepare each type. The chapter also covers the compilation of financial statements as well as prospective financial statements.

The auditee can reduce the cost of an audit by preparing schedules of financial statement items including expenses, revenue, assets, liabilities, and stockholders' equity. The documentation sources for the financial statement items may be listed. By preparing schedules and analyses, the auditee can reduce the cost of the external audit because less time is required by the external auditor. This chapter details the reporting structure of Section 404 of the Sarbanes-Oxley Act.

SARBANES-OXLEY ACT AND THE PUBLIC COMPANY ACCOUNTING OVERSIGHT BOARD (PCAOB)

The Securities and Exchange Commission (SEC) has issued various regulations in compliance with the Sarbanes-Oxley Act of 2002. The Act came about because of allegations of financial reporting fraud at a number of companies such as Enron, WorldCom, and Tyco. It applies to SEC registrants and their auditors. The SEC has changed how public companies are audited. As a result, the Public Company Accounting Oversight Board (PCAOB) was formed. The PCAOB has enforcement and investigative powers over CPA firms that audit publicly traded companies. It will review audits once every three years for all audit firms and each year for audit firms having 100 or more audit clients.

The Act prohibits CPA firms who audit clients from engaging in the following additional activities:

- Designing and implementing financial information systems.
- Actuarial services.
- Expert testimony during a legal proceeding.
- Bookkeeping services.
- Internal audit outsourcing services.
- Valuation services.
- Management functions.
- Investment advisory or investment banking services.
- Human resources services.

The SEC does permit CPA firms auditing clients to conduct tax services.

The PCAOB has and will continue to set audit, independence, ethics, and quality control standards. The PCAOB is responsible for overseeing audits of SEC registrants and investigates allegations of substandard performance of auditors.

A CPA firm will be deemed to lack independence if during the audit engagement an audit partner is compensated by the client for any services other than audit, review, or attest.

Some requirements of the Sarbanes-Oxley Act are:

- CPA firms must retain audit workpapers for seven years.
- The audit report must describe the scope of the auditor's internal control testing. The auditor must include in the audit report (or in a separate report) the following:
  a. Audit results emanating from internal control testing.
  b. Overall appraisal of the company's internal control structure and procedures.
  c. Description of significant weaknesses in internal control.

Under the Act, the in-charge and concurring partners must be rotated after five years. Other audit partners are subject to a seven-year rotation. There is a one-year "cooling-off" period before an audit partner may accept certain employment with its audit client.

With respect to corporate responsibility, the chief executive officer (CEO) and chief financial officer (CFO) must certify in each annual or quarterly report filed with the SEC that:

1. He or she has reviewed the report.
2. The report does not contain any significant omissions or misleading statements.
3. The financial statements and other financial information in the report fairly present the company's financial health and operating performance.

4. The internal control system is properly designed and effective. An internal control report must be contained in each annual report.
5. Any known fraud has been disclosed.

The Act prohibits CEOs from in any way misleading the external auditor.

AUDIT REPORTS

The PCAOB adopted, as interim standards, the AICPA's Auditing Standards Board's auditing standards in effect on April 16, 2003. Accordingly, those standards specify the format of audit reports, which are applicable to audited financial statements of issuers (i.e., public entities). Under PCAOB standards, the auditor's standard report contains three paragraphs: the introductory, scope, and opinion paragraphs.

The introductory paragraph (1) identifies the financial statements audited; (2) indicates that the financial statements are the responsibility of the company's management; and (3) states that the auditor is responsible for expressing an opinion on the financial statements based on the audit.

Pursuant to PCAOB Auditing Standard No. 1, the scope paragraph indicates that the audit was conducted in accordance with Standards of the Public Company Accounting Oversight Board (United States) and describes what an audit basically involves.

The opinion paragraph includes the auditor's opinion as to whether the financial statements are presented fairly, in all material aspects, in conformity with U.S. GAAP. There should be a reference to consistency in an additional paragraph, after the opinion paragraph, *only* if generally accepted accounting principles (U.S. GAAP) have not been consistently applied. Further, an uncertainty, if existing, should be discussed in an explanatory paragraph after the opinion paragraph.

Standards of reporting require that:

1. The report shall state whether the financial statements are presented in accordance with GAAP.
2. The report shall identify those circumstances in which such principles have not been consistently observed in the current period in relation to the preceding period.
3. Informative disclosures in the financial statements are to be regarded as reasonably adequate unless otherwise stated in the report.

4. The report shall either contain an expression of an opinion regarding the financial statements, taken as a whole, or an assertion to the effect that an opinion cannot be expressed. When an overall opinion cannot be expressed, the reasons therefore should be stated. In all cases where an auditor's name is associated with the financial statements, the report shall contain a clear-cut indication of the character of the auditor's work, if any, and the degree of responsibility the auditor is taking.

Typically, the auditor's report accompanies the basic financial statements—the balance sheet, income statement, statement of retained earnings, statement of cash flows, and the notes to the statements.

An example independent auditor's standard report on comparative financial statements of an issuer appears below:

Independent Auditor's Report

We have audited the accompanying balance sheets of X Company as of December 31, 2014 and 2013 and the related statements of income, retained earnings, and cash flows for the years then ended. These financial statements are the responsibility of the Company's management. Our responsibility is to express an opinion on these financial statements based on our audits.

We conducted our audits in accordance with the Standards of the Public Company Accounting Oversight Board (United States). Those standards require that we plan and perform the audit to obtain reasonable assurance about whether the financial statements are free of material misstatement. An audit includes examining, on a test basis, evidence supporting the amounts and disclosures in the financial statements. An audit also includes assessing the accounting principles used and significant estimates made by management, as well as evaluating the overall financial statement presentation. We believe that our audits provide a reasonable basis for our opinion.

In our opinion, the financial statements referred to above present fairly, in all material aspects, the financial position of X Company as of (at) December 31, 2014 and 2013, and the results of its operations and its cash flows for the years then ended in conformity with generally accepted accounting principles.

[Signature]
[Date]
[City and State]

The audit report should be addressed to the company, the board of directors, or the stockholders.

The four types of audit reports that may be issued are:

1. *Unqualified opinion.* The auditor states that the financial statements present fairly, in all material aspects, the financial position, results of operations, and cash flows of the company in conformity with U.S. GAAP.
2. *Qualified opinion.* The auditor indicates that "except for" the matter(s) referred to, the financial statements present fairly, in all material aspects, financial position, results of operations, and cash flows in conformity with U.S. GAAP. [It should be noted that the equivalent opinion applicable to financial statements of a nonissuer (i.e., nonpublic entity) is now referred to as an "unmodified opinion."]
3. *Adverse opinion.* The auditor states that the financial statements do *not* present fairly the financial position or the results of operations or cash flows in conformity with U.S. GAAP.
4. *Disclaimer of opinion.* The auditor states that he or she does not express an opinion on the financial statements.

Let us now look more closely at each of these four types of audit reports.

Unqualified Opinion on an Issuer's Financial Statements

In expressing an unqualified opinion, the auditor is satisfied that the financial statements present fairly, in all material respects, the company's financial condition. There are instances that mandate an additional explanatory paragraph to the standard audit report, but any such addition does *not* affect the unqualified opinion. These instances follow:

- The auditor's opinion is based partly on the report of another auditor. If the principal auditor wishes to divide responsibility with another auditor, the division of responsibility must be referred to in the introductory, scope, and opinion paragraphs of the audit report. Additionally, the magnitude of the financial statements audited by the other auditor should be referred to in the introductory paragraph.
- To prevent the financial statements from being misleading owing to unusual circumstances, the financial statements contain a departure from an accounting principle formulated by a body designated by the AICPA Council.
- There exist uncertainties regarding future events for which the ultimate outcome cannot be reasonably determined at the audit report date. Uncertainties include contingencies that involve probable or reasonably possible future loss. Some uncertainties

may require a qualified opinion or disclaimer of opinion due to a scope limitation. Further, the uncertainty may dictate a qualified or adverse opinion because of a departure from GAAP.

If an explanatory paragraph is appropriate in connection with the unqualified opinion, the auditor describes the uncertainty and indicates that the outcome is not ascertainable. The separate paragraph may be shortened by referring to the appropriate footnote.

The uncertainty is not referred to in the introductory, scope, or opinion paragraphs of the audit report. An illustrative explanatory paragraph, which should be placed after the opinion paragraph, follows:

As discussed in Note X to the financial statements, the Company is a defendant in a lawsuit alleging infringement of certain patent rights and claiming royalties and punitive damages. The Company has filed a counteraction, and preliminary hearings and discovery proceedings on both actions are in progress. The ultimate outcome of the litigation cannot presently be determined. Accordingly, no provision for any liability that may result upon adjudication has been made in the accompanying financial statements.

- Substantial doubt exists regarding the company's ability to continue in business (going concern). In this circumstance, the following additional paragraph should be placed after the opinion paragraph.

The accompanying financial statements have been prepared assuming that the Company will continue as a going concern. As discussed in Note X to the financial statements, the Company has suffered recurring losses from operations and has a net capital deficiency that raises substantial doubt about its ability to continue as a going concern. Management's plans in regard to these matters are also described in Note X. The financial statements do not include any adjustments that might result from the outcome of this uncertainty.

- A change in accounting principle has been made. The explanatory paragraph, to be added after the opinion paragraph, identifies the nature of the change and makes reference to the appropriate footnote where it is discussed. An example follows:

"As discussed in Note X to the financial statements, the Company changes its method of computing depreciation in 2014."

- Certain circumstances applicable to reports on comparative financial statements exist.

- Selected quarterly financial information required under SEC Regulation S-K have been omitted or have not been reviewed.
- Required supplementary information has been omitted.
- There exists inconsistency between other information in a document containing audited financial statements and information presented in the financial statements.
- The auditor wishes to emphasize a matter regarding the financial statements. Examples are references to material transactions between related parties and significant subsequent events.

Unmodified Opinion on a Nonissuer's Financial Statements

Independent Auditor's Report

[Addressee]

We have audited the accompanying financial statements of ABC Company, which comprise the balance sheet as of December 31, 2014, and the related statements of income, changes in stockholders' equity, and cash flows for the year then ended, and the related notes to the financial statements.

Management's Responsibility for the Financial Statements

Management is responsible for the preparation and fair presentation of these financial statements in accordance with accounting principles generally accepted in the United States of America; this includes the design, implementation, and maintenance of internal control relevant to the preparation and fair presentation of financial statements that are free from material misstatement, whether due to fraud or error.

Auditor's Responsibility

Our responsibility is to express an opinion on these financial statements based on our audit. We conducted our audit in accordance with auditing standards generally accepted in the United States of America. Those standards require that we plan and perform the audit to obtain reasonable assurance about whether the financial statements are free from material misstatement.

An audit involves performing procedures to obtain audit evidence about the amounts and disclosures in the financial statements. The procedures selected depend on the auditors' judgment, including the assessment of the risks of material misstatement of the financial statements, whether due to fraud or error. In making those risk assessments, the auditor considers internal control relevant to the entity's preparation and fair presentation of the financial statements in order to design audit procedures that are appropriate in the circumstances, but not for the purpose of expressing an opinion on the effectiveness of the entity's internal control. Accordingly, we express no such opinion. An adult also includes evaluating the appropriateness of accounting policies used and the reasonableness of significant accounting estimates made by management, as well as evaluating the overall presentation of the financial statements.

We believe that the adult evidence we have obtained is sufficient and appropriate to provide a basis for our audit opinion.

Opinion

In our opinion, the financial statements referred to above present fairly, in all material respects, the financial position of ABC Company, Inc. as of December 31, 2014, and the results of its operations and its cash flows for the year then ended in accordance with accounting principles generally accepted in the United States of America.

[Auditor's signature]
[Auditor's city and state]
[Date of auditor's report]

Under certain circumstances, similar to those in the case of an audit of an issuer's financial statements, an auditor may determine that there is a need to provide additional wording in an audit report. This is accomplished by placing one or more emphasis-of-matter and/or other-matter paragraphs after the opinion paragraph.

An emphasis-of-matter paragraph is used when the matter is already disclosed in the financial statements, but the auditor feels that the matter is crucial to the user's understanding of the financial statements.

An other-matter paragraph is used when the matter is not disclosed in the financial statements, but the auditor feels that the matter is relevant to the user's understanding of the financial statements.

Qualified Opinion on an Issuer's Financial Statements

A qualified opinion states that "except for" the effects of the matter to which the qualification applies, the financial statements present fairly, in all material respects, the financial position, results of operations, and cash flows in conformity with generally accepted accounting principles. This opinion is rendered when there is insufficient competent evidential matter, when restrictions have been placed on the scope of the audit, and the auditor does not deem a disclaimer of opinion appropriate, or when the financial statements materially depart from U.S. GAAP and the auditor does not deem an adverse opinion warranted.

In a qualified opinion, the auditor discloses the reasons for the qualification in one or more separate explanatory paragraphs preceding the opinion paragraph. The opinion paragraph has the qualifying wording and a reference to the explanatory paragraph. In the qualified opinion, appropriate wording would be "except for." *Note:* The phrase "subject to" is *not* used. Further, it is *not* appropriate for the scope of the audit to be explained in a note to the financial statements.

An audit scope restriction may include the failure to observe physical inventories and confirm accounts receivable through confirmation requests. When *significant* restrictions on the scope of the audit are imposed by a company, a disclaimer of opinion may be suitable instead of a qualified opinion.

An illustrative qualified opinion relating to a scope limitation follows:

[Same first paragraph as the standard report]

Except as discussed in the following paragraph, we conducted our audits in accordance with the Standards of the Public Company Accounting Oversight Board (United States). Those standards require that we plan and perform the audit to obtain reasonable assurance about whether the financial statements are free of material misstatement. An audit includes examining, on a test basis, evidence supporting the amounts and disclosures in the financial statements. An audit also includes assessing the accounting principles used and significant estimates made by management, as well as evaluating the overall financial statement presentation. We believe that our audits provide a reasonable basis for our opinion.

We were unable to obtain audited financial statements supporting the Company's investment in a foreign affiliate stated at \$_____ and \$_____ at December 31, 2014 and 2013, respectively, or its equity in earnings of that affiliate of \$_____ and \$_____, which is included in net income for the years then ended as described in Note X to the financial statements; nor were we able to satisfy ourselves as to the carrying value of the investment in the foreign affiliate or the equity in its earnings by other auditing procedures.

In our opinion, except for the effects of such adjustments, if any, as might have been determined to be necessary had we been able to examine evidence regarding the foreign affiliate investment and earnings, the financial statements referred to in the first paragraph above present fairly, in all material respects, the financial position of X Company as of December 31, 2014 and 2013, and the results of its operations and its cash flows for the years then ended in conformity with accounting principles generally accepted in the United States of America.

The footnotes may contain *material* unaudited data (e.g., pro forma information). If the auditor is unable to apply necessary procedures to the unaudited footnote information, he or she qualifies the opinion or disclaims one owing to the scope limitation. If, however, the unaudited information is not necessary to fairly present the financial position, operating results, or cash flows, that information may be identified as "unaudited."

If the auditor is retained to report on only one financial statement (e.g., balance sheet), there is no scope limitation provided there is no restriction on the auditor's access to information underlying the basic financial statements, and the auditor performs all the procedures considered necessary. The engagement is merely a limited reporting one.

When there is a departure from U.S. GAAP materially affecting the financial statements, but the auditor has audited the financial statements in accordance with generally accepted auditing standards, a qualified or adverse opinion should be expressed, depending on the magnitude of departure (e.g., relative dollar amount). An example of a qualified opinion, when an accounting principle used is not in conformity with U.S. GAAP, follows:

[Same first and second paragraphs as the standard report]

The Company has excluded, from property and debt in the accompanying balance sheets, certain lease obligations that, in our opinion, should be capitalized in order to conform with generally accepted accounting principles. If these lease obligations were capitalized, property would be increased by $_____ and $_____, long-term debt by $_____ and $_____ , and retained earnings by $_____ and $_____ as of December 31, 2014 and 2013, respectively. Additionally, net income would be increased (decreased) by $_____ and $_____ and earnings per share would be increased (decreased) by $_____ and $_____, respectively, for the years then ended.

In our opinion, except for the effects of not capitalizing certain lease obligations as discussed in the preceding paragraph, the financial statements referred to above present fairly, in all material respects, the financial position of X Company as of December 31, 2014 and 2013, and the results of its operations and its cash flows for the years then ended in conformity with accounting principles generally accepted in the United States of America.

When the financial statements do not disclose material information in the body or footnotes, a qualified or adverse opinion should be expressed, and the information should be provided in the audit report, if practicable. An example of a report qualified due to inadequate disclosure follows:

[Same first and second paragraphs as the standard report]

The Company's financial statements do not disclose (describe the nature of the omitted disclosures). In our opinion, disclosure of this information is required by generally accepted accounting principles.

In our opinion, except for the omission of the information discussed in the preceding paragraph . . .

A qualified opinion is usually called for when the statement of cash flows is omitted from the basic financial statements. An example of a qualified opinion in this case follows:

> We have audited the balance sheets of X Company as of December 31, 2014 and 2013 and the related statements of income and retained earnings for the years then ended. These financial statements are the responsibility of the Company's management. Our responsibility is to express an opinion on these financial statements based on our audit.
>
> [Same paragraph as the standard report]
>
> The Company declined to present a statement of cash flows for the years ended December 31, 2014 and 2013. Presentation of such statement summarizing the company's operating, investing, and financing activities is required by generally accepted accounting principles.
>
> In our opinion, except that the omission of a statement of cash flows results in an incomplete presentation as explained in the preceding paragraph, the financial statements referred to above present fairly, in all material respects, the financial position of X Company as of December 31, 2014 and 2013, and the results of its operations for the years then ended in conformity with generally accepted accounting principles.

A qualified opinion should also be expressed when a newly adopted accounting principle is *not* in conformity with generally accepted accounting principles or when the company has *not* properly justified a change in principle. If the dollar impact is sufficiently material, an adverse opinion may be warranted.

Qualified Opinion on a Nonissuer's Financial Statements

In a qualified opinion, the auditor discloses the reasons for the qualification in a "Basis for Qualified Opinion" paragraph preceeding the opinion paragraph.

An illustrative qualified opinion relating to a scope limitation follows:

Independent Auditor's Report

[Addressee]

> We have audited the accompanying financial statements of ABC Company, which comprise the balance sheet as of December 31, 2014, and the related statements of income, changes in stockholders' equality, and cash flows for the year then ended, and the related notes to the financial statements.

Management's Responsibility for the Financial Statements

Management is responsible for the preparation and fair presentation of these financial statements in accordance with accounting principles generally accepted in the United States of America; this includes the design, implementation, and maintenance of internal control relevant to the preparation and fair presentation of financial statements that are free from material misstatement, whether due to fraud or error.

Auditor's Responsibility

Our responsibility is to express an opinion on these financial statements based on our audit. We conducted our audit in accordance with auditing standards generally accepted in the United States of America. Those standards require that we plan and perform the audit to obtain reasonable assurance about whether the financial statements are free from material misstatement.

An audit involves performing procedures to obtain audit evidence about the amounts and disclosures in the financial statements. The procedures selected depend on the auditor's judgment, including the assessment of the risks of material misstatement of the financial statements, whether due to fraud or error. In making those risk assessments, the auditor considers internal control relevant to the entity's preparation and fair presentation of the financial statements in order to design audit procedures that are appropriate in the circumstances, but not for the purpose of expressing an opinion on the effectiveness of the entity's internal control. Accordingly, we express no such opinion. An audit also includes evaluating the appropriateness of accounting policies used and the reasonableness of significant accounting estimates made by management, as well as evaluating the overall presentation of the financial statements.

We believe that the audit evidence we have obtained is sufficient and appropriate to provide a basis for our qualified audit opinion.

Basis for Qualified Opinion

ABC Company's investment in XYZ Company, a foreign affiliate acquired during the year and accounted for under the equity method, is carried at $XXX on the balance sheet at December 31, 2014, and ABC Company's share of XYZ Company's net income of $XXX is included in ABC Company's net income for the year then ended. We were unable to obtain sufficient appropriate audit evidence about the carrying amount of ABC Company's investment in XYZ Company as of December 31, 2014 and ABC Company's share of XYZ Company's net income for the year then ended, because we were denied access to the financial information, management, and the auditors of XYZ Company. Consequently, we were unable to determine whether any adjustments to these amounts were necessary.

Qualified Opinion

In our opinion, except for the possible effects of the matter described in the Basis for Qualified Opinion paragraph, the financial statements referred to above present fairly, in all material respects, the financial position of ABC Company as of December 31, 2014, and the results of its operations and its cash flows for the year then ended in accordance with accounting principles generally accepted in the United States of America.

[Auditor's signature]
[Auditor's city and state]
[Date of the auditor's report]

An illustrative qualified opinion, when an accounting principle used is not in conformity with U.S. GAAP follows:

Independent Auditor's Report

[Addressee]

We have auditied the accompanying financial statements of ABC company, which comprise the balance sheets as of December 31, 2014 and 2013 and the related statements of income, changes in stockholders' equity, and cash flows for the years then ended, and the related notes to the financial statements.

Management's Responsibility for the Financial Statements

Management is responsible for the preparation and fair presentation of these financial statements in accordance with accounting principles generally accepted in the United States of America; this includes the design, implementation, and maintenance of internal control relevant to the preparation and fair presentation of financial statements that are free from material misstatement, whether due to fraud or error.

Auditor's Responsibility

Our responsibility is to express an opinion on these financial statements based on our audits. We conducted our audits in accordance with auditing standards generally accepted in the United States of America. Those standards require that we plan and perform the audit to obtain reasonable assurance about whether the financial statements are free from material misstatement.

An audit involves performing procedures to obtain audit evidence about the amounts and disclosures in the financial statements. The procedures selected depend on the auditor's judgment, including the assessment of the risks of material misstatement of the financial statements, whether due to fraud or error. In making those risk assessments, the auditor considers internal control relevant to the entity's preparation and fair presentation of the financial statements in order to design audit procedures that are appropriate in the circumstances, but not for the purpose of expressing an opinion on the effectiveness of the entity's internal control. Accordingly, we express no such opinion. An audit also includes evaluating the appropriateness of accounting policies used and the reasonableness of significant accounting estimates made by management, as well as evaluating the overall presentation of the financial statements.

We believe that the audit evidence we have obtained is sufficient and appropriate to provide a basis for our qualified audit opinion.

Basis for Qualified Opinion

The company has stated inventories at cost in the accompanying balance sheets. Accounting principles generally accepted in the United States of America require inventories to be stated at the lower of cost or market. If the company stated inventories at the lower of cost or market, a write down of $XXX and $XXX would have been required as of December 31, 2014 and 2013, respectively. Accordingly, cost of sales would have been increased by $XXX and $XXX, and net income, income taxes, and stockholders' equity would have been reduced by $XXX, $XXX, and $XXX, and $XXX, $XXX, and $XXX, as of and for the years ended December 31, 2014 and 2013, respectively.

Qualified Opinion

In our opinion, except for the effects of the matter described in the Basis for Qualified Opinion paragraph, the financial statements referred to above present fairly, in all material respects, the financial position of ABC Company as of December 31, 2014 and 2013 and the results of its operations and its cash flows for the years then ended in the accordance with accounting principles generally accepted in the United States of America.

[Auditor's signature]
[Auditor's city and state]
[Date of the auditor's report]

An illustrative qualified opinion due to inadequate disclosure follows:

Independent Auditor's Report

[Addressee]

We have audited the accompanying financial statements of ABC Company, which comprise the balance sheets as of December 31, 2014 and 2013, and the related statements of income, changes in stockholders' equity, and cash flows for the years then ended, and the related notes to the financial statements.

Management's Responsibility for the Financial Statements

Management is responsible for the preparation and the fair presentation of these financial statements in accordance with accounting principles generally accepted in the United States of America; this includes the design, implementation, and maintenance of internal control relevant to the preparation and fair presentation of financial statements that are free from material misstatement, whether due to fraud or error.

Auditor's Responsibility

Our responsibility is to express an opinion on these financial statements based on our audits. We conducted our audits in accordance with auditing standards generally accepted in the United States of America. Those standards require that we plan and perform the audit to obtain reasonable assurance about whether the financial statements are free from material misstatement.

An audit involves performing procedures to obtain audit evidence about the amounts and disclosures in the financial statements. The procedures selected depend on the auditor's judgment, including the assessment of the risks of material misstatement of the financial statements, whether due to fraud or error. In making those risk assessments, the auditor considers internal control relevant to the entity's preparation and fair presentation of the financial statements in order to design audit procedures that are appropriate in the circumstances, but not for the purpose of expressing an opinion on the effectiveness of the entity's internal control. Accordingly, we express no such opinion. An audit also includes evaluating the appropriateness of accounting policies used and the reasonableness of significant accounting estimates made by management, as well as evaluating the overall presentation of the financial statements.

We believe that the audit evidence we have obtained is sufficient and appropriate to provide a basis for our qualified audit opinion.

Basis for Qualified Opinion

The Company's financial statements do not disclose [describe the nature of the omitted information that is not practicable to present in the auditor's report]. In our opinion, disclosure of this information is required by accounting principles generally accepted in the United States of America.

Qualified Opinion

In our opinion, except for the omission of the information described in the Basis for Qualified Opinion paragraph, the financial statements referred to above present fairly, in all material respects, the financial position of ABC Company as of December 31, 2014 and 2013, and the results of its operations and its cash flows for the years then ended in accordance with accounting principles generally accepted in the United States of America.

[Auditor's signature]
[Auditor's city and state]
[Date of the auditor's report]

Adverse Opinion on an Issuer's Financial Statements

In expressing an adverse opinion, the auditor indicates that the financial statements do *not* present fairly the financial position or the results of operations or cash flows in conformity with generally accepted accounting principles.

In a separate explanatory paragraph(s) preceding the opinion paragraph, the auditor provides the reasons for the adverse opinion and the major effects of the subject matter of the adverse opinion on overall financial status. If the effects cannot be determined, that is so stated. The opinion paragraph directly refers to the explanatory paragraph. An example of an adverse opinion follows:

[Same first and second paragraphs as the standard report]

As discussed in Note X to the financial statements, the Company carries its property, plant, and equipment accounts at appraisal values, and provides depreciation on the basis of such values. Further, the Company does not provide for income taxes with respect to differences between financial income and taxable income arising because of the use, for income tax purposes, of the installment method of reporting gross profit from certain types of sales. Generally accepted accounting principles require that property, plant, and equipment be stated at an amount not in excess of cost, reduced by depreciation based on such amount, and that deferred income taxes be provided.

Because of the departures from generally accepted accounting principles identified above, as of December 31, 2014 and 2015, inventories have been increased $_____ and $_____ by inclusion in manufacturing overhead of depreciation in excess of that based on cost; property, plant, and equipment, less accumulated depreciation, is carried at $_____ and $_____ in excess of an amount based on cost to the Company; and deferred income taxes of $_____ and $_____ in retained earnings and in appraisal surplus of $_____ and $_____, respectively. For the years ended December 31, 2014 and 2013, cost of goods sold has been increased $_____ and $_____, respectively, because of the effects of the depreciation accounting referred to above and deferred income taxes of $_____ and $_____ have not been provided, resulting in an increase in net income of $_____ and $_____, respectively.

In our opinion, because of the effects of the matters discussed in the preceding paragraphs, the financial statements referred to above do not present fairly, in conformity with generally accepted accounting principles, the financial position of X Company as of December 31, 2014 and 2013, or the results of its operations or its cash flows for the years then ended.

Adverse Opinion on a Nonissuer's Financial Statements

In an adverse opinion, the auditor discloses the reasons for the adverse opinion in a "Basis for Adverse Opinion" paragraph preceding the opinion paragraph.

An illustrative adverse opinion due to a material misstatement of the financial statements follows:

Independent Auditor's Report

[Addressee]

We have audited the accompanying consolidated financial statements of ABC Company and its subsidiaries, which comprise the consolidated balance sheet as of December 31, 2014, and the related consolidated statements of income, changes in stockholders' equity, and cash flows for the year then ended, and the related notes to the financial statements.

Management's Responsibility for the Financial Statements

Management is responsible for the preparation and fair presentation of these consolidated financial statements in accordance with accounting principles generally accepted in the United States of America; this includes the design, implementation, and maintenance of internal control relevant to the preparation and fair presentation of consolidated financial statements that are free from material misstatement, whether due to fraud or error.

Auditor's Responsibility

Our responsibility is to express an opinion on these consolidated financial statements based on our audit. We conducted our audit in accordance with auditing standards generally accepted in the United States of America. Those standards require that we plan and perform the audit to obtain reasonable assurance about whether the consolidated financial statements are free from material misstatement.

An audit involves performing procedures to obtain audit evidence about the amounts and disclosures in the consolidated financial statements. The procedures selected depend on the auditor's judgment, including the assessment of the risks of material misstatement of the consolidated financial statements, whether due to fraud or error. In making those risk assessments, the auditor considers internal control relevant to the entity's preparation and fair presentation of the consolidated financial statements in order to design audit procedures that are appropriate in the circumstances, but not for the purpose of expressing an opinion on the effectiveness of the entity's internal control. Accordingly, we express no such opinion. An audit also includes evaluating the appropriateness of accounting policies used and the reasonableness of significant accounting estimates made by management, as well as evaluating the overall presentation of the consolidated financial statements.

We believe that the audit evidence we have obtained is sufficient and appropriate to provide a basis for our adverse audit opinion.

Basis for Adverse Opinion

As described in Note X, the Company has not consolidated the financial statements of subsidiary XYZ Company that it acquired during 2014 because it has not yet been able to ascertain the fair values of certain of the subsidiary's material assets and liabilities at the acquisition date. This investment is therefore accounted for on a cost basis by the Company. Under accounting principles generally accepted in the United States of America, the subsidiary should have been consolidated because it is controlled by the Company. Had XYZ Company been consolidated, many elements in the accompanying consolidated financial statements would have been materially affected. The effects on the consolidated financial statements of the failure to consolidate have not been determined.

Adverse Opinion

In our opinion, because of the significance of the matter discussed in the Basis for Adverse Opinion paragraph, the consolidated financial statements referred to above do not present fairly the financial position of ABC Company and its subsidiaries as of December 31, 2014, or the results of their operations or their cash flows for the year then ended in accordance with accounting principles generally accepted in the United States of America.

[Auditor's signature]
[Auditor's city and state]
[Date of the auditor's report]

Disclaimer of Opinion on an Issuer's Financial Statements

In a disclaimer of opinion, the auditor does not express an opinion on the financial statements. A disclaimer may be issued when the auditor has not conducted an audit adequate in scope to form an opinion on the financial statements. There is an explanatory paragraph in the audit report citing the reasons why the audit did not comply with generally accepted auditing standards. The auditor indicates that the audit scope was not adequate to express an opinion. The auditor does *not* mention the procedures performed or include the scope paragraph of the audit report because such citation would take away from the thrust of the disclaimer and would also tend to confuse the reader. Further, the auditor should disclose any reservations above the fair presentation in conformity with GAAP. An illustrative disclaimer follows:

We were engaged to audit the accompanying balance sheets of X Company as of December 2014 and 2013, and the related statements of income, retained earnings, and cash flows for the years then ended. These financial statements are the responsibility of the Company's management.

[Second paragraph of standard report should be omitted]

The Company did not make a count of its physical inventory in 2014 or 2013, stated in the accompanying financial statements at $_____ as of December 31, 2014, and at $_____ as of December 31, 2013. Further, evidence supporting the cost of property and equipment acquired prior to December 31, 2013, is no longer available. The Company's records do not permit the application of other auditing procedures to inventories or property and equipment.

Since the Company did not take physical inventories and we were not able to apply other auditing procedures to satisfy ourselves as to inventory quantities and the cost of property and equipment, the scope of our work was not sufficient to enable us to express, and we do not express, an opinion on these financial statements.

Disclaimer of Opinion on a Nonissuer's Financial Statements

When disclaiming an opinion, the auditor must modify the introductory paragraph and the auditor's responsibility paragraph. In addition, the auditor discloses the basis for the disclaimer in a "Basis for Disclaimer of Opinion" paragraph preceding the "Disclaimer of Opinion" paragraph.

An illustrative disclaimer of opinion follows:

Independent Auditor's Report

[Addressee]

We were engaged to audit the accompanying financial statements of ABC Company, which comprise the balance sheet as of December 31, 2014, and the related statements of income, changes in stockholders' equity, and cash flows for the year then ended, and the related notes to the financial statements.

Management's Responsibility for the Financial Statements

Management is responsible for the preparation and fair presentation of these consolidated and financial statements in accordance with accounting principles generally accepted in the United States of America; this includes the design, implementation, and maintenance of internal control relevant to the preparation and fair presentation of consolidated financial statements that are free from material misstatement, whether due to fraud or error.

Auditor's Responsibility

Our responsibility is to express an opinion on these financial statements based on conducting the audit in accordance with auditing standards generally accepted in the United States of America. Because of the matters described in the Basis for Disclaimer of Opinion paragraph, however, we were not able to obtain sufficient appropriate audit evidence to provide a basis for an audit opinion.

Basis for Disclaimer of Opinion

We were not engaged as auditors of the Company until after December 31, 2014, and, therefore, did not observe the counting of physical inventories at the beginning or end of the year. We were unable to satisfy ourselves by other auditing procedures concerning the inventory held at December 31, 2014, which is stated in the balance sheet at $XXX. In addition, the introduction of a new computerized accounts receivable system in September 2014 resulted in numerous misstatements in accounts receivable. As of the date of our audit report, management was still in the process of rectifying the system deficiencies and correcting the misstatements. We were unable to confirm or verify by alternative means accounts receivable included in the balance sheet at a total amount of $XXX at December 31, 2014. As a result of these matters, we were unable to determine whether any adjustments might have been found necessary in respect of recorded or unrecorded inventories and accounts receivable, and the elements making up the statements of income, changes in stockholders' equity, and cash flows.

Disclaimer of Opinion

Because of the significance of the matters described in the Basis for Disclaimer of Opinion paragraph, we have not been able to obtain sufficient appropriate audit evidence to provide a basis for an audit opinion. Accordingly, we do not express an opinion on these financial statements.

[Auditor's signature]
[Auditor's city and state]
[Date of the auditor's report]

COMPILATION OF FINANCIAL STATEMENTS

A *compilation* of financial statements is essentially limited to presenting in the form of financial statements information that is the representation of management or owners. There is *no opinion* or any other form of assurance given regarding the fairness of the presentation of financial statements. The procedures conducted in a compilation are limited.

In a compilation, the accountant should do the following:

1. Obtain an engagement letter.
2. Determine the accounting principles and practices peculiar to the company's industry.
3. Comprehend the flow and nature of the company's transactions.
4. Understand the company's accounting records.
5. Evaluate the quality of the accounting department's personnel.
6. Ascertain the basis of accounting used (e.g., GAAP, cash basis).
7. Determine the need to perform the following accounting services: (a) adjusting the books, (b) consulting with appropriate personnel about accounting-related matters, and (c) performing bookkeeping services when the company's manual or automated bookkeeping does not generate financial statements as the end result.
8. Obtain satisfaction as to management's representations that seem incorrect and incomplete.
9. If the financial statements depart from the basis of accounting used, and if the company does not wish to make the needed adjustments, the accountant's report should be modified to disclose this fact.
10. Read the financial statements to determine that they are free from obvious errors, such as mathematical mistakes, omission of needed disclosures, and departures from relevant accounting principles.
11. If the accountant lacks independence, this should be stated in the compilation report. The reason(s) for the lack of independence may be disclosed.

When the compilation is completed, the report that must be prepared should include the following:

- A title.
- An addressee.
- An introductory paragraph that (1) identifies the financial statements compiled and (2) states that, because the financial statements have not been audited or reviewed, there is no opinion or any other form of assurance on them.
- A paragraph that indicates management's responsibility for the financial statements and for internal control over financial reporting.

- A paragraph that states (1) the compilation was conducted in accordance with Statements on Standards for Accounting and Review Services issued by the AICPA and (2) the objective of a compilation.
- Accountant's signature.
- Date of the report, which is the date the compilation was completed.

Each page of the financial statements must be labeled "See accountant's compilation report."

A standard compilation report appears below:

Accountant's Compilation Report

[Addressee]

I (We) have compiled the accompanying balance sheet of ABC Company, as of December 31, 2014, and the related statements of income, retained earnings, and cash flows for the year then ended. I (We) have not audited or reviewed the accompanying financial statements and, accordingly, do not express an opinion or provide any assurance about whether the financial statements are in accordance with accounting principles generally accepted in the United States of America.

Management is responsible for the preparation and fair presentation of the financial statements in accordance with accounting principles generally accepted in the United States of America and for designing, implementing, and maintaining internal control relevant to the preparation and fair presentation of the financial statements.

My (Our) responsibility is to conduct the compilation in accordance with Statements on Standards for Accounting and Review Services issued by the American Institute of Certified Public Accountants. The objective of a compilation is to assist management in presenting financial information in the form of financial statements without undertaking to obtain or provide any assurance that there are no material modifications that should be made to the financial statements.

[Signature]
[Date]

It is permissible to compile and report on only one of the financial statements typically included in the complete set.

REVIEW OF FINANCIAL STATEMENTS

A *review* is one step above a compilation, since a form of assurance on the financial statements is expressed. A review consists primarily of inquiry of company management and analytical procedures applied to management's financial data. These procedures provide the accountant with a reasonable basis to express *limited assurance* that no material modifications to the financial statements are required to make them in conformity with U.S. GAAP (or another comprehensive basis of accounting).

Because review procedures do not encompass either a study and evaluation of internal control or a gathering of audit evidence, an opinion may not be expressed. The accountant identifies matters that have a material impact on the financial statements. However, a review cannot be relied upon to uncover other significant matters that would surface in an audit.

A review engagement involves the following:

1. Obtaining an engagement letter.
2. Obtaining satisfactory knowledge of accounting principles, methods, and practices of the industry.
3. Comprehending the company's organization, operating characteristics, balance sheet and income statement items, production and distribution methods, compensation methods, products and services, operating locations, and related party transactions.
4. Conducting inquiry and analytical procedures related to the independence of company employees, basis of accounting, procedures to record and classify transactions, and presentation of disclosures. Any significant variability in financial data is noted. The minutes of the meetings of the board of directors and of the stockholders are reviewed. The financial statements are read. Changes in accounting methods and practices as well as changes in business activities are noted. Inaccurate and incomplete matters are resolved.
5. Accumulate review evidence to be able to express limited assurance.
6. Obtaining a representation letter from the client.
7. Documenting review procedures in the workpapers.
8. Preparing the review report.

When the review is completed, the report that must be prepared should include the following:

- A title.
- An addressee.
- An introductory paragraph that (1) identifies the financial statements reviewed and (2) states that a review is substantially less in scope than an audit and, accordingly, no opinion is expressed.
- A paragraph that indicates management's responsibility for the financial statements and for internal control over financial reporting.
- A paragraph that states (1) the review was conducted in accordance with Statements on Standards for Accounting and Review Services issued by the AICPA and (2) the accountant is required to perform procedures to provide limited assurance about the financial statements.
- The results of the engagement.
- Accountant's signature.
- Date of the report, which is the date on which the accountant has accumulated sufficient appropriate review evidence.

Each page of the reviewed financial statements should be labeled "See Independent Accountant's Review Report."

A standard review report appears below:

Independent Accountant's Review Report

[Adressee]

I (We) have reviewed the accompanying balance sheet of ABC Company as of December 31, 2014, and the related statements of income, retained earnings, and cash flows for the year then ended. A review includes primarily applying analytical procedures to management's (owners') financial data and making inquiries of company management (owners). A review is substantially less in scope then an audit, the objective of which is the expression of an opinion regarding the financial statements as a whole. Accordingly, I (We) do not express such an opinion.

Management (Owners) is (are) responsible for the preparation and fair presentation of the financial statements in accordance with accounting principles generally accepted in the United States of America and for designing, implementing, and maintaining internal control relevant to the preparation and fair presentation of the financial statements.

My (Our) responsibility is to conduct the review in accordance with Statements on Standards for Accounting and Review Services issued by the American Institute of Certified Public Accountants. Those standards require me (us) to perform procedures to obtain limited assurance that there are no material modifications that should be made to the financial statements. I (We) believe that the results of my (our) procedures provide a reasonable basis for our report.

Based on my (our) review, I am (we are) not aware of any material modifications that should be made to the accompanying financial statements in order for them to be in conformity with accounting principles generally accepted in the United States of America.

[Signature]
[Date]

REPORTS ON PROSPECTIVE FINANCIAL STATEMENTS

Prospective financial statements include financial forecasts and financial projections. Pro forma financial statements and partial presentations are excluded from this category.

Financial Forecasts. These prospective statements present, to the best of the responsible party's knowledge, a company's expected financial position, results of operations, and changes in cash flow. Forecasts are based on assumptions regarding conditions actually expected to exist and the course of action anticipated.

Financial Projections. These prospective statements portray a company's expected financial position, results of operations, and changes in cash flow. They are based on assumptions about conditions expected to exist and the course of action anticipated to occur, given hypothetical assumptions.

An accountant is not allowed to compile, examine, or apply agreed-upon procedures to prospective financial statements that fail to include a summary of significant assumptions.

If a company's prospective financial statements are for general use, only a financial forecast should generally be presented. ("General use" means that the statements are used by parties not negotiating directly with the company.)

Compilation procedures on prospective financial statements are not intended to provide any form of assurance on the presentation of the statements or the underlying assumptions.

An accountant is not allowed to compile forecasts and projections that fail to present a summary of significant assumptions. Further, an accountant may not compile a projection that fails to identify the hypothetical assumptions or describe the limitations on the use of the projections.

Compilation procedures related to prospective financial statements are basically the same as those applicable to historical financial statements. Additional procedures are:

- Inquiring as to the underlying assumptions.
- Compiling the underlying assumptions and taking into account the possibility of obvious omissions or inconsistencies.
- Verifying the mathematical correctness of the assumptions.
- Reading the prospective financial statements to determine if there are any departures from AICPA presentation guidelines.
- Obtaining a representation letter from the company to confirm that it acknowledges responsibility for the prospective statements including the underlying assumptions.

The accountant's report on compiled prospective financial statements includes:

- Identification of the prospective financial statements presented.
- Statement regarding the level of services provided and that the prospective statements were compiled as per AICPA standards.
- Statement noting the limited scope of a compilation.
- Warning that prospective results may not happen.
- Statement that the accountant has no responsibility to update the report for conditions taking place after the compilation report is issued.
- Date of the report, which is the completion date of the compilation.
- When a projection is involved, there should be a separate middle paragraph describing the limitations on the use of the statements.
- A separate paragraph when the statements present the expected results in the form of a range of values.
- If the accountant is not independent, that fact is stated but no reasons are given.
- A separate explanatory paragraph when the prospective financial statements depart from AICPA presentation guidelines or omit disclosures unrelated to the significant assumptions.

A standard report on compiled forecasts appears below:

I (We) have compiled the accompanying forecasted balance sheet, statements of income, retained earnings, and cash flows of ABC Corporation as of (at) December 31, 2014, and for the year then ending, in accordance with standards established by the American Institute of Certified Public Accountants.

A compilation is limited to presenting in the form of a forecast information that is the representation of management (or other responsible party) and does not include evaluation of the support for the assumptions underlying the forecast. I (we) have not examined the forecast and, accordingly, do not express an opinion or any other form of assurance on the accompanying statements or assumptions. Furthermore, there will usually be differences between the forecasted and actual results, because events and circumstances frequently do not occur as expected, and those differences may be material. We have no responsibility to update this report for events and circumstances occurring after the date of this report.

A standard report on compiled projections appears below:

I (We) have compiled the accompanying projected balance sheet, statements of income, retained earnings, and cash flow of ABC Corporation as of December 31, 2014, and for the year then ending, in accordance with standards established by the American Institute of Certified Public Accountants.

The accompanying projection, and this report, were prepared for (state special purpose, for example, "the Takeover Corporation for the purpose of negotiating a buyout of the Company,") and should not be used for any other purpose.

A compilation is limited to presenting in the form of a projection information that is the representation of management (or other responsible party) and does not include evaluation of the support for the assumptions underlying the projection. I (we) have not examined the projection and, accordingly, do not express an opinion or any other form of assurance on the accompanying statements or assumptions. Furthermore, even if (describe hypothetical assumption, for example, "the buyout is consummated") there will usually be differences between the projected and actual results, because events and circumstances frequently do not occur as expected, and those differences may be material. We have no responsibility to update this report for events and circumstances occurring after the date of this report.

Internal Control

Internal control responsibilities within the company should be specified. Internal control performance should be looked at over time. Is the internal control system properly designed and operating? Corrective action must be taken immediately when needed.

When planning an audit, the auditor must consider internal control as essential including whether controls are effective, identifying possible misstatements, and good documentation of internal control (e.g., decision tables, flowcharts, memorandums, and question-naires). Documentation must be more extensive as complexity of internal controls grow.

The cost of internal control should not be more than the antici-pated benefits expected to be derived. Limitations of internal control should also be considered by the auditor, such as poor man-agement decision making and incidence of errors.

An appraisal of internal control is necessary to determine the reli-ability of financial reporting, effectiveness and efficiency of opera-tions, and compliance to government law and regulations.

Table 10.1 shows the audit steps in appraising internal control.

Table 10.1
AUDIT STEPS IN INTERNAL CONTROL APPRAISAL

Gain an Understanding of Internal Control Structure
Evaluate Control Risk
Tests of Controls
Perform Substantive Procedures

A sound control environment must exist in that employees are competent and ethical, authority and responsibility exist, human resource policies are adequate, and meaningful organizational structure exists.

Internal control analysis must be done for the whole company, operating segments, and company business functions. Internal con-trol appraisal should be performed in context of the nature of the company's business, law and regulations, size of business, organi-zational structure, complexity of operations, diversity of activities, and methods to process and maintain financial performance.

Internal control considerations exist with various types of activi-ties. In looking at manufacturing, the auditor needs to take into account planning and control, inventory control, and cost account-ing. In examining expenditures, consideration should be given to personnel and payroll, disbursements, and purchasing. A look at revenue considers processing orders, approving credit, ship-ping, billing, accounting, and collections. With regard to security investments, consider whether securites are kept at an outside safe-deposit vault in the company's name, if there is a record of each security and certificate number, periodic inspection of certificates, authorization for buys and sells of securities, if securities written off were followed up as to possible realization, and whether dividend and interest income on securities are promptly received. In examin-ing the internal control associated with payroll, note the segregation of duties, hiring, preparing and approving payroll, distributing pay-roll, recording payroll, and payroll bank reconciliation. Authorization must exist over hiring, firing or laying off, changes in salary rates, and vacation and leave time. A change in worker status (e.g., promotion) should be external to payroll processing. Time and attendance records should be monitored. Payments should be made with prenumbered checks. If a payroll amount exceeds a specified amount, it should require two signatures. Checks should be distributed promptly. Unclaimed payroll checks should be controlled by a person divorced from the processing or distribution of payroll. The proper classification of payroll should be checked.

Duties must be segregated so that different employees are authorizing transactions, recording them, and having physical custody over the assets. If one person handles all of these functions, the potential for error or fraud exists. Assets must be safeguarded against unauthorized purchase, use, or sale.

Control activities must be examined to ascertain if management directives are being carried out. Corporate policies and procedures must be properly performed. The auditor should conduct a performance review comparing budget to actual performance as well as comparing performance over the years. A determination must be made that recorded transactions have been authorized and properly recorded. In this regard, general controls must exist over software purchase and use, computer security, and system development. Application controls relate to the accurate processing of transactions.

Audit concern is also with physical controls referring to safeguards over access to resources and records. Comparisons of actual amounts to control figures should be made.

An evaluation of internal control takes into account the company's risk in financial statement reporting such as the existence of unrecorded expenses and liabilities. In examining risk, the auditor should consider new product or service change in software, business restructuring, change in operating environment, foreign activities, new staff, and sudden and dramatic increase in growth. The internal auditor's purpose in assessing risk is to identify and manage corporate risks affecting its objectives. The outside auditor's assessment of audit risk is designed to ascertain the likelihood that significant misstatements could occur in the financial statements.

Control risk is the likelihood that a misstatement will occur in the financial statements taking into account the internal control system. In assessing control risk, the auditor looks at the effectiveness of the company's internal controls in detecting or preventing financial statement misstatements.

The lower the assessed level of control risk, the more the assurance of evidence must be that the controls pertaining to an assertion are structured and operating effectively. If control risk is below the maximum level, the auditor should document the reasons for this assessment.

The auditor must properly design substantive procedures. In order to determine an acceptable level of detection risk, the auditor should consider the vulnerability of an assertion to misstatement and the control risk. The nature, degree, and timing of substantive procedures are based on the acceptable level of detection risk. Substantive procedures are tests of details of account balances, transactions, and disclosure items, as well as substantive analytical procedures. The amount of substantive procedures is directly tied to the assessed level of control risk. If the appraisal of control risk is at the maximum amount, no reliance is given to the associated controls so the auditor will typically plan for maximum substantive procedures.

Tests of controls relate to procedures used in gauging how well the design or operation of a control is. Tests of controls applicable to the effectiveness of design are concerned if the control is able to prevent or detect misstatement in the financial statements. Tests of controls related to the operating effectiveness of a control are directed at determining the application and consistency of a control and by whom. Procedures involved when employing tests of controls include observing the use of particular controls, examining documents and records, making inquiries of client staff, and auditor's repetition of a control to establish how it is working.

Deficiencies in internal control may have to be reported to management and those charged with governance. Such conditions, for example, might be failure to correct a prior identified internal control deficiency, failure to safeguard assets, lack of segregating duties, employee theft, and failure to approve a transaction. The communication generally must be in writing.

The Public Company Accounting Oversight Board (PCAOB) issued Auditing Standard No. 5 titled, "An Audit of Internal Control Over Financial Reporting That Is Integrated With an Audit of Financial Statements." The standard requires auditors of issuers to form an opinion on the effectiveness of a company's internal control over financial reporting in addition to forming an opinion on the financial statements. The two opinions may be presented in two separate reports or in a combined report. To form an opinion on internal control, auditors must evaluate and test management's internal control process, the work performed by others (e.g., internal auditors), and the effectiveness of the controls. Among other procedures, auditors may conduct walkthroughs of transactions, from initiation of transactions through recording in the financial statements.

Auditing Standard No. 5 (AS 5):

1. Permits auditors to use, to a limited extent, the work performed by other auditors.
2. Requires auditors to use a top-down, risk-based approach, beginning with the financial statements and company-level controls, in selecting the controls to test.
3. Provides explicit and practical guidance on scaling the audit to fit the size and complexity of the company. These provisions do not create a separate standard for smaller companies. Instead, AS 5 explicitly requires the auditor to tailor the nature, extent, and timing of testing to meet the unique characteristics of smaller companies.

The auditor should comprehend how internal control over financial reporting is structured to appraise and test its workability. The auditor gains insight into this, in part, by analyzing management's process of assessing its own internal controls.

The auditor tests a client's internal control by performing procedures that include inquiries and observations of client staff who actually perform the controls, reviewing documents used in the control process, and comparing documents to the accounting records. Walkthroughs of the company's major processes represent the best way to achieve this objective.

AS 5 requires that the auditor gather evidence concerning the operating effectiveness of internal controls over financial reporting for significant accounts and disclosures.

The auditor must consider design effectiveness to ascertain whether controls are working as designed. In this regard, the auditor will make inquires of corporate personnel, observe internal controls, and appraise whether internal controls are able to prevent or detect financial statement misstatements.

AS 5 requires the auditor to evaluate the severity of identified deficiencies in internal control. Deficiencies in internal control should be communicated to the audit committee and management.

If no material weaknesses in internal control are identified, AS 5 allows the auditor to issue an unqualified opinion on internal control.

If the auditor identifies even one material weakness in internal control, he or she is required to express an adverse opinion on internal control.

If the auditor is prevented from performing all necessary procedures, and therefore encountered a restriction on the scope of the audit of internal control, he or she should withdraw from the engagement or issue a disclaimer of opinion.

Fraud in a Financial Statement Audit

Auditing standards require the auditor to evaluate the risk of significant intentional misstatement because of fraud. The major types of misstatement indicative of fraud are misstatements associated with fraudulent financial reporting and misstatements because of misappropriation of assets. Fraud may be concealed through false documentation and/or collusion. Such fraud must be detected by the auditor through his design of audit procedures. The following factors must be taken into account in appraising the risk of misstatements because of fraudulent financial reporting:

- Industry conditions such as rapid changes, competition, and instability in earnings.
- Operating characteristics and financial stability, including deficient cash flow, significant operating risk, and susceptibility to economic and political conditions.
- Management characteristics affecting the control environment, including management motivation, lack of communication over internal control, conflict between the auditor and management, past history of fraud, high turnover rate in executives, and violations of law and government regulations.

In general, the auditor is precluded from informing nonclient personnel about the fraud except when required by law (e.g., SEC reporting requirements), a prior auditor communicates with a successor auditor, or the auditor has been directed to do so by a court.

An appraisal of the risk of significant misstatement due to fraud may impact the audit in terms of needed controls, substantive testing, personnel staffing, and professional skepticism.

Risk factors associated with misappropriation of assets include vulnerability to theft (e.g., cash balance, high-value merchandise, marketable and small fixed assets), lack of controls (e.g., deficient documentation, poor safeguarding of assets, lack of segregation of duties, and lack of authorization and approval of transactions), and poor management-employee relationship.

In appraising misstatement due to fraud, the auditor should look at risk factors individually and collectively and determine if specific mitigating controls exist. The auditor must consider in risk evaluation the size, complexity, and ownership attributes of the company. Warning signs of fraud include an unusual relationship between the client and auditor, lack of evidential matter, and conflict in financial information. In an extreme case, when the client is uncooperative about taking steps to correct the fraud, the auditor should withdraw from the engagement and communicate to the audit committee the reasons for so doing.

AUDIT DOCUMENTATION

Audit documentation applicable to an issuer must be kept for a 7-year period; a 5-year retention period is applicable to a nonissuer. A specific law, however, may mandate a longer retention period. In the case of an issuer, a full set of audit documentation must be assembled not more than 45 days subsequent to the report release date. In the case of a nonissuer, the document assembly is extended to 60 days subsequent to the report release date. No audit documentation is allowed to be deleted or discarded after this date. Information may be added after the documentation completion date as long as that documentation includes the date of addition, who prepared the additional documentation, and the reason therefore.

Management Letter

A management letter is issued by the auditor at the end of an audit engagement directed to corporate management. In the letter may be included recommendations for improvements in activities, procedures, and controls. Problems may be identified and corrective action to solve them taken. Areas to be commented upon include taxes, asset management, controls, and information systems.

INTERNAL AUDITING

For many companies, it is essential to establish an internal audit function, which differs from the external audit function. While external auditors are primarily concerned with expressing an opinion as to the fairness of presentation of the entity's financial statements, internal auditors are concerned with many operational facets of the business. The concerns of the internal audit staff include:

1. Evaluating the strength of internal controls.
2. Testing compliance with entity policies and procedures.
3. Measuring effectiveness of entity performance.
4. Developing suggestions for improving operational effectiveness and efficiency.
5. Ascertaining whether or not assets are sufficiently safeguarded.

Internal auditors must understand behavioral skills. Crucial to their performance is their ability to identify human values and defense mechanisms, human needs and their effect on work performance, as well as the factors responsible for attitude change. Additionally, internal auditors must fully understand management's decision process.

The work of the internal audit function may be valuable to the external auditor who is attesting to the fairness of the financial statements. In fact, many external auditors feel it is efficient to request direct assistance from the internal auditors. In doing so, the objectivity and competency of the internal auditors must be adequately assessed. Objectivity is maintained when the internal auditors report directly to the company's chief executive officer. Competency is evidenced by a variety of factors including professional certification, i.e., the Certified Internal Auditor (CIA) certificate issued by the Institute of Internal Auditors (IIA). The types and content of the reports prepared by the internal auditors, which will vary depending upon the size, complexity, and needs of the entity, may also be useful in evaluating the competency of the internal audit function.

We now discuss the internal audit of various accounts. The audit of cash includes a reveiw of policy statements and written procedures, comparing physical cash to recorded amounts, comparing the amounts of checks and cash to recorded cash receipts, preparing bank reconciliations, and comparing invoices to cash disbursements. In auditing receivables, consideration should be given to checking incoming mail, aging customer accounts, test checking selected accounts, and reviewing files of accounts written off. The audit of inventory includes counting inventory and comparing to base amounts, checking inventory pricing, determining appropriateness of adjustments to inventory, reviewing freight bills, and verifying quantity and quality of goods returned. In auditing fixed assets, examine property records, inspect assets, ascertain locations, and determine if property acquisitions conformed to the capital budget. The audit of accounts payable includes double approval of large payments, checking supporting documents prior to payment, test checking footings of disbursement records, comparing payee's name on each instrument with the name on the supporting documents, and reviewing procedures for handling returned goods. In auditing payroll, evaluate reasons for unclaimed paychecks, verify employees, determine who approves salary changes, examine hiring practices, and personally deliver some paychecks. The audit of purchases includes examining competitive bids, approving large purchases, verifying requisition requests, reviewing method of selecting vendors, noting changes in suppliers and check reasons, comparing goods ordered to that received, and examining support for trade discounts and quantity rebates. In auditing advertising expenses, consider approval of agency billings to contract terms and space, compare budget to actual advertising expenditures, and check filing and control of agreements.

SECTION 404 OF THE SARBANES-OXLEY ACT

Section 404 of the Sarbanes-Oxley Act—"Enhanced Financial Disclosures, Management Assessment of Internal Control"—mandates sweeping changes. Section 404, in conjunction with the related SEC rules and Auditing Standard (AS) No. 5 established by the Public Company Accounting Oversight Board (PCAOB), requires management of a public company and the company's independent auditor to issue two new reports at the end of every fiscal year. These reports must be included in the company's annual report filed with the Securities and Exchange Commission (SEC).

- Management must report annually on the effectiveness of the company's internal control over financial reporting.
- In conjunction with the audit of the company's financial statements, the company's independent auditor must issue a report on internal control over financial reporting, which includes an opinion on the effectiveness of the company's internal control over financial reporting.

In the past, a company's internal controls were considered in the context of planning the audit but were not required to be reported publicly, except in response to the SEC's Form 8-K requirements when related to a change in auditor. The new audit and reporting requirements have drastically changed the situation and have brought the concept of internal control over financial reporting to the forefront for audit committees, management, auditors, and users of financial statements.

Auditing Standard No. 5 highlights the concept of a significant deficiency in internal control over financial reporting, and mandates that both management and the independent auditor must publicly report any material weaknesses in internal control over financial reporting that exist as of the fiscal year-end assessment date. Under both PCAOB Auditing Standard No. 5 and the SEC rules implementing Section 404, the existence of a single material weakness requires management and the independent auditor to conclude that internal control over financial reporting is not effective. The main features of the AS No. 5 are summarized later in this chapter.

Internal Control over Financial Reporting

Internal control over financial reporting is a process designed and maintained by management to provide reasonable assurance regarding the reliability of financial reporting and the preparation of the financial statements for external purposes in accordance with U.S. GAAP. It encompasses the processes and procedures management has established to:

- Maintain records that accurately reflect the company's transactions
- Prepare financial statements and footnote disclosures for external purposes and provide reasonable assurance that receipts and expenditures are appropriately authorized
- Prevent or promptly detect unauthorized acquisition, use, or disposition of the company's assets that could have a material effect on the financial statements

Internal control over financial reporting is defined more narrowly than the general term "internal control," which includes controls associated with the effectiveness and efficiency of operations and compliance with laws and regulations that are not directly related to the financial statements. For example, controls to improve safety or streamline manufacturing processes are not considered part of internal control over financial reporting.

An effective internal control structure involves people at all levels of the organization. It includes those who maintain accounting records, prepare and disseminate policies, monitor systems, and function in a variety of operating roles. In addition, a company's internal control over financial reporting is influenced significantly by its board of directors and the audit committee, which has ultimate responsibility for oversight of the financial reporting process.

The concept of reasonable assurance is integral to the definition of internal control over financial reporting and to management's assessment and the independent auditor's opinions.

Reasonable assurance refers to the fact that internal controls— even when they are appropriately designed and operating effectively—cannot provide absolute assurance of achieving control objectives. Inherent limitations include the potential for human error or circumvention of controls. Reasonable assurance is a high level of assurance, but it is not absolute—it recognizes that even with an effective system of internal control over financial reporting, there is a possibility that material misstatements, including misstatements due to management fraud, may occur and not be prevented or detected on a timely basis.

It should be noted that the role of internal control over financial reporting is to support the integrity and reliability of the company's external financial reporting processes. It is not intended to provide any assurances about the company's operating performance, its future results, or the quality of its business model.

Responsibilities of Management and the Independent Auditor with Respect to Internal Control over Financial Reporting

Management is responsible for designing and implementing the system of internal control over financial reporting, for evaluating the effectiveness of internal control over financial reporting, and for issuing a public report on that assessment. Management is to base its assessment on a suitable, recognized control framework, such as that established by the Committee of Sponsoring Organizations of the Treadway Commission (COSO) and support its evaluation with sufficient documented evidence.

Auditor's Role. Before the Sarbanes-Oxley Act was passed, the auditor was required to obtain an understanding of internal control sufficient to plan the audit of the financial statements. If material weaknesses were identified, they ordinarily were reported only to management and the audit committee. Section 404 now requires the auditor to perform an independent audit of internal control over financial reporting and to issue a report including an opinion on the effectiveness of internal control over financial reporting.

Audit of Internal Control over Financial Reporting

The auditor's attestation of internal control and the auditor's independent procedures to test internal control over financial reporting are collectively referred to in Auditing Standard No. 5 as the "audit of internal control over financial reporting." The objective of the audit of internal control over financial reporting is to obtain reasonable assurance about whether any material weaknesses exist as of the date of management's assessment.

Structure of the New Reporting Model

In the past, the independent auditor provided an opinion on whether the company's financial statements were presented fairly in all material respects, in accordance with U.S. GAAP. The new reporting model maintains this historical requirement for the auditor to express an opinion on the financial statements. Section 404 also institutes additional requirements for management and the independent auditor to report on the effectiveness of internal control over financial reporting, as shown in Table 10.2.

Table 10.2
HISTORICAL REPORTING VERSUS NEW REPORTING

Historical Reporting
Independent auditor's opinion on whether the financial statements are presented fairly in all material respects, in accordance with U.S. GAAP.

New Reporting
Management's report on its assessment of the effectiveness of the company's internal control over financial reporting

Independent auditor's report on internal control over financial reporting, including the auditor's opinion on the effectiveness of the company's internal control over financial reporting.

The independent auditor's opinions on the financial statements and on internal control over financial reporting may be issued in a combined report or in separate reports. Figure 10-1 identifies the various reports, and reflects the fact that management's assessment of internal control over financial reporting constitutes the starting point for the auditor's reporting.

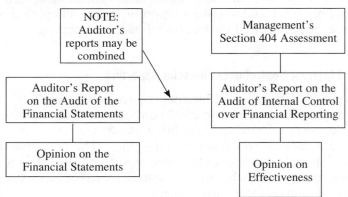

Figure 10-1. Section 404 reporting

Management's Report

Neither the SEC nor the PCAOB has issued a standard or illustrative management report on internal control over financial reporting; thus, there may be differences in the nature and extent of the information companies provide. We advise companies to consult with legal counsel on these matters. At a minimum, management's report on internal control over financial reporting should include the following information:

- Statement of management's responsibility for establishing and maintaining adequate internal control over financial reporting
- Statement identifying the framework used by management to evaluate the effectiveness of internal control over financial reporting
- Management's assessment of the effectiveness of the company's internal control over financial reporting as of the end of the company's most recent fiscal year, including an explicit statement as to whether that internal control is effective and disclosing any material weaknesses identified by management in that control
- Statement that the registered public accounting firm that audited the financial statements included in the annual report has issued a report on the effectiveness of internal control

Management's report must indicate that internal control over financial reporting is either:

- *Effective* — Internal control over financial reporting is effective (i.e., no material weaknesses in internal control over financial reporting existed as of the assessment date); or
- *Ineffective* — Internal control is not effective because one or more material weaknesses existed as of management's assessment date.

Management is required to state *whether or not* the company's internal control over financial reporting is effective. A negative assurance statement, such as "nothing has come to management's attention to suggest internal control is ineffective" is not acceptable.

If a material weakness exists as of the assessment date, management is required to conclude that internal control over financial reporting is not effective and to disclose all material weaknesses that may have been identified. The SEC chief accountant has stated publicly that he expects management's report to disclose the nature of any material weakness in sufficient detail to enable investors and other financial statement users to understand the weakness and evaluate the circumstances underlying it.

Management may not express a qualified conclusion, such as stating that internal control is effective except to the extent certain problems have been identified. If management is unable to assess certain aspects of internal control that are material to overall control effectiveness, management must conclude that internal control over financial reporting is ineffective. Although management cannot issue a report with a scope limitation, under specific conditions newly acquired businesses or certain other consolidated entities may be excluded from the assessment.

Independent Auditor's Report

Under Auditing Standard No. 5 the auditor is required to audit and express an opinion on the effectiveness of internal control over financial reporting. The content of the auditor's report on internal control over financial reporting is prescribed by Auditing Standard No. 5. Although there are many nuances to the auditor's reporting, the most common external auditor reports are likely to be:

- Unqualified opinion on the effectiveness of internal control over financial reporting as of the assessment date.
- An adverse opinion on the effectiveness of internal control over financial reporting as of the assessment date, because of one or more material weaknesses.

    When one or more material weaknesses exist as of the assessment date, the auditor *must* express an adverse opinion on the effectiveness of the company's internal control over financial reporting.

    Auditing Standard No. 5 indicates that when expressing an adverse opinion on the effectiveness of internal control over financial reporting, the auditor should provide specific information about the nature of the material weakness and its actual and potential effect on the company's financial statements. The PCAOB has also stated that it expects disclosure sufficient to allow users to understand the weakness and its actual and potential implications on the financial statements.

Disclaimer of Opinion. A disclaimer of opinion is a report stating that because of restrictions on the scope of the auditor's work, the auditor is unable to, and does not, express an opinion on the effectiveness of internal control over financial reporting.

    In a disclaimer situation, the auditor's report must also disclose any material weaknesses that have been identified.

Material Weakness

Effective internal control over financial reporting encompasses management policies and procedures to provide reasonable assurance about the reliability of a company's financial reporting and its processes for preparing financial statements in accordance with U.S. GAAP. A deficiency in internal control exists when the design or operation of a control does not allow for the prevention or detection of misstatements on a timely basis. Companies may have control deficiencies in the design of a control or in its operation.

- *Design*—A deficiency in design exists when a necessary control is missing or is not designed in a manner that enables the control objective to be met.
- *Operating Effectiveness*—A deficiency in operating effectiveness exists when a properly designed control is not operating as intended or when the person performing the control lacks the authority or qualifications to do so effectively.

The seriousness of a given deficiency or combination of deficiencies depends on both (1) the likelihood that a misstatement of an account balance or disclosure could result, and (2) the magnitude of the related potential misstatement.

Deficiencies in internal control must be evaluated to determine if they represent either material weaknesses or significant deficiencies.

- A **material weakness** is a deficiency, or a combination of deficiencies, in internal control over financial reporting, such that there is a reasonable possibility (i.e., reasonably possible or probable) that a material misstatement of the company's annual or interim financial statements will not be prevented or detected on a timely basis. Essentially, a material weakness is a deficiency that could result in a material misstatement. It does not mean that a material misstatement has occurred or that it will occur, but that it could occur.
- A **significant deficiency** is a deficiency, or a combination of deficiencies, in internal control over financial reporting that is less severe than a material weakness, yet important enough to merit attention by those responsible for oversight of the company's financial reporting.

Significant judgment goes into evaluating whether deficiencies in controls rise to the level of a material weakness. Management and the auditor must consider the following factors when evaluating control deficiencies:

- *Likelihood of a misstatement*—Including consideration of factors such as susceptibility to fraud; the cause and frequency of exceptions in the operating effectiveness of the control; the possibility of future consequences; the nature of the affected accounts and disclosures; the subjectivity, complexity, or extent of judgment required to determine the amount involved; the interaction or relationship of the control with other controls; and the interaction of deficiencies.

- *Related magnitude of a potential misstatement*—Including the financial statement amounts or total of transactions exposed to the deficiency and/or the volume of activity in the account: balance or class of transactions exposed to the deficiency in the current period or expected in future periods.

In addition, management and the auditor will consider the effect of compensating controls: that is, whether other effective controls are in place that would identify a misstatement and address the objective not being met by the deficient control.

THE SOX SECTION 302 AND SECTION 906 CONSIDERATIONS

How do the Section 302 and Section 906 certifications relate to the Section 404 reports? How do they overlap and how do they differ?

Although Section 404 is one widely known aspect of the Sarbanes-Oxley Act, two other sections of the Act—Sections 302 and 906—have significantly increased the awareness of management's responsibility for reviewing and understanding its financial reporting and internal control structure. Specifically:

- Section 302 requires the chief executive officer (CEO) and the chief financial officer (CFO) to certify to the SEC both the fairness of the financial information in each quarterly and annual report and their responsibility for maintaining adequate disclosure controls and procedures.
- Section 906 requires the CEO and CFO to certify the fairness of the financial information in the report, as well as the compliance of the report with the requirements of the Securities Exchange Act of 1934. Section 906 provides criminal penalties for knowing or willful failure to comply.

Section 302—Management Certifications

Section 302(a) of the Sarbanes-Oxley Act requires a company's CEO and CFO to certify each quarterly and annual report. They are required to certify that the financial statements and other financial information included in the report are fairly presented in all material respects. The officers must also state that the report does not contain any untrue statement of material fact or omit to state a material fact. In addition, the certifying officers must state that the company has established and maintained "disclosure controls and procedures" sufficient to ensure that the financial and nonfinancial information required to be disclosed in SEC reports is recorded, processed, summarized, and reported within the specified time periods.

As shown in Figure 10-4, disclosure controls and procedures typically include, but are broader than, internal control over financial reporting. For instance, disclosure controls extend to controls over disclosure included in SEC annual and interim reports outside the financial statements. They also encompass controls to monitor compliance with laws and regulations, other than those that directly affect the financial statements.

After the company files its first annual report pursuant to Section 404, Section 302 requires the certifying officers to state that they are responsible for establishing and maintaining internal control over financial reporting, and that such internal control is designed to provide reasonable assurance as to the reliability of financial reporting and the preparation of financial statements in accordance with GAAP. Further, they must disclose any change in the company's internal control over financial reporting during the most recent quarter that has materially affected, or is reasonably likely to materially affect, the company's internal control.

Figure 10-4.
Internal Control over Financial Reporting—
A Subset of Disclosure Controls

Disclosure Controls Procedures Section 302			Internal Controls over Financial Reporting- Section 404
• Designed to ensure that information required to be disclosed is recorded processed, summarized, and reported within prescribed time periods	Company Financial Statements Business	Notes Cash Income Statements	• Controls that relate to preparation of external financial statements, fairly presented in conformity with generally accepted accounting principles
• Includes controls and procedures to ensure that information is accumulated and communciated to executive management to allow timely decisions regarding disclosure requirements	Properties Legal Proceedings Annual Report on Form 10-K	Balance Sheet Financial Statements Safeguarding Assets	• Controls over safe-guarding of assets • Controls that address the risk of fraud

As part of the certification, the CEO and CFO must also indicate that they have disclosed to the auditors and audit committee of the company all significant deficiencies and material weaknesses in internal control and any fraud that involves management or other employees who have a significant role in internal control.

Section 906—Management Certifications (Criminal Provision)

Section 906 of the Sarbanes-Oxley Act requires the CEO and the CFO to certify each periodic report that includes financial statements. The certification, which is separate from the Section 302 certification, may state that the periodic report fully complies with the requirements of the Securities Exchange Act of 1934 and that "information contained in the periodic report fairly presents, in all material respects, the financial condition and results of operations of the issuer."

Section 906 provides for criminal penalties for an officer who provides the certification knowing it to be untrue, with harsher penalties for willful violations. Section 906 certifications may be "furnished," versus filed, as an exhibit to annual and quarterly SEC reports. As furnished information, the Section 906 certification is not subject to the civil liability provisions of Section 18 of the Securities Exchange Act of 1934, and will not be incorporated by reference into registration statements unless the company expressly specifies otherwise.

Figure 10-5 summarizes the key provisions of Section 302, Section 404, and Section 906.

Figure 10-5.
Certification Requirements of Sarbanes-Oxley

Key Requirement	Implication
302 CEO and CFO certification of periodic SEC filings (quarterly and annually)	Requires certification of the fairness of the financial statements and the operating effectiveness disclosure controls and procedures
404 Management's assessments of internal controls with auditor attestation (annual)	Requires annual assessment and reporting by both management and the auditor on the effectiveness of internal control over financing reporting
906 Financial reporting certification and criminal penalties (quarterly and annual)	In all SEC reports that include financial statements, requires the CEO and CFO to certify the fairness of the financial statements and the report's compliance with the requirements of the Securities and Exchange Act of 1934. Criminal penalties for willful violations.

A List of Questions You Need to Answer for Sarbanes-Oxley Compliance

Here is the list of questions that need to be answered in order to gauge a company's compliance with the Sarbanes-Oxley Act. Would your company have the answers?

1. How are off-balance-sheet transactions and commitments tracked and reported?
2. Are payments to the external auditing firm monitored through the transactional flags on purchase orders, check requests, or other means within the system?
3. Are rolling forecasts deployed throughout the business (business unit, product line, functional levels)?
4. How many tools are used in the forecasting process? The budgeting process?
5. Do the reporting systems trace back to the general ledgers?
6. Is cash flow from operations and U.S. GAAP cash flow automatically calculated?
7. Are key measures (drivers of financial results) delivered to the operational manager's desktop daily, weekly, monthly?
8. Are tax reporting systems integrated with the company's consolidation system?
9. Are consolidation and reporting activities performed on spreadsheets?
10. Do transactional reporting systems have agent-based alerts?
11. How are manual entries identified and approved?
12. How much time is spent compiling data and the financial statements versus analyzing the data?
13. How many top-level adjustments are made in the consolidation process?
14. Are reporting activities performed on spreadsheets?
15. How often is control documentation updated for new changes to the internal controls (transactional and financial statement)?
16. Are controls in place to ensure that any off-balance-sheet items are properly approved?
17. Do reporting systems flag reserves and other estimated accounts?
18. Have the systems been updated to identify new responsibilities under the Sarbanes-Oxley Act?
19. Are earnings forecasts tied to predictive models?
20. Do you forecast your business on cash flow drivers?
21. Are variances between the forecast and actual results reviewed and causes identified?
22. How long is the process to develop forecasts? Budgets?

23. Is there a significant difference between financial statements depending on timing, function, or system?
24. Are standard charts of accounts used across the company?
25. How long does it take the company to get the results of operations?
26. What procedures are in place by the company to detect and prevent fraud?
27. Has the company identified high-risk areas where fraud may occur and developed controls to prevent this from occurring?
28. Are the following categories of nonfinancial drivers measured: leadership, communication, brand equity, reputation, networks/alliances, technology, human capital, culture, innovation, intellectual capital, or adaptability?
29. Do sales systems flag quarter-end sales volumes over selected limits?
30. How long does it take to develop ad hoc reports?
31. Do you model the sensitivity of your off-balance-sheet commitments (swap agreements, foreign exchange risk, purchase commitments, etc.)? How often?
32. Does the company have the ability to determine the profitability by using "what-if" scenarios?
33. Have financial models been created for all high-risk operations, programs, and so on?
34. How long does it take to create the management package?
35. Does each operating unit have a financial model for the key drivers of its business?
36. Are documents backed up periodically to ensure significant reports and information are maintained?
37. Does the company have a retention policy for electronic information?
38. Are internal control reviews incorporated into all new system implementations (financial and nonfinancial)?
39. How often do you back up your data?
40. What controls are in place over record retention to avoid tampering with the data?
41. What best describes your IT capabilities related to financial transaction processing in your company?
42. How many control weakness/changes have there been to the financial statements controls (including in the authorization of transactions, safeguarding assets, maintaining records, and over the reconciliation process) in the past year?
43. How many different systems are involved in the financial statement development process?
44. Are IRS and other data retention requirements being met?
45. Is your starting point for your tax return GAAP-audited financial statements?

46. Are there flags in place to alert key resources of specific transactions taking place in the company?
47. Does the company review its transactions for unusual entries?
48. What controls are in place to detect wire/mail?

Note: Appendix B provides a practice aid set that contains self-assessment questionnaires regarding Auditor Independence and Corporate Responsibility under Title III of the Sarbanes-Oxley Act of 2002.

Brief Summary

The auditee should know that the external auditor has numerous responsibilities when engaged in auditing the financial statements. The external auditor must express the appropriate audit opinion based on the available evidence. The auditee should attempt to do as much backup work as possible to reduce the cost of the external audit. The outside accountant may also be involved with a compilation of financial statements where no opinion is rendered. In a review of financial statements, the external accountant does provide some assurance on the financial statements. With regard to prospective financial statements, the outside accountant may be involved with financial forecasts and projections.

WEBSITES

1. Institute of Internal Auditors – *www.theiia.org*
2. Association of Certified Fraud Examiners – *www.acfe.com*
3. Auditing information – *www.auditnet.org*
4. Public Company Accounting Oversight Board (PCAOB) – *www.pcaobus.org*

Selected Readings

Arens, Alvin, Randal Elder, and Mark Beasley, *Auditing and Assurance Services,* Prentice-Hall, 2013.

Beasley, Mark and Joseph Carcello, *GAAS Guide 2013,* CCH Publishers, 2012.

Boynton, William and Raymond Johnson, *Modern Auditing,* John Wiley, 2005.

Chapter 11
Personal Financial Planning

The purpose of financial planning is to help individuals reach their personal goals. Areas of personal financial planning include preparation of personal financial statements, budgeting, personal banking, debt strategy, cost savings, college education for children, career planning, investing in stocks and bonds and mutual funds, real estate investing, insurance strategy, and planning for retirement. In many planning decisions, there is a tradeoff between return and risk: the higher the return desired, the greater the risk that must be taken.

OBJECTIVES OF PERSONAL FINANCIAL PLANNING

There are many objectives to financial planning, including establishing and maintaining financial security, maximizing wealth, appraising and selecting from investment options, managing risk, using credit wisely, developing a program to satisfy financial needs, and obtaining what one really wants.

There are five key elements on which any personal financial plan must be based:

1. Age. For example, an older individual typically favors fixed-income, safe investments.
2. Marital status. For example, a married person desires sufficient life insurance to protect the family.
3. Family status. For instance, children will need a college education.
4. Risk preferences. For example, a risk-averse person will favor U.S. Government securities.
5. Investment preferences. For instance, if an individual wants growth, stocks having capital appreciation potential may be selected.

In addition, there are other factors to consider in personal financial planning:

6. Current and prospective income. For example, if future income is uncertain, only safe investments should be made.
7. Possible inheritances. For example, a person who expects to be a beneficiary to a sizable estate can take on greater risk in current investments.
8. Desired standard of living. For example, one person may accept a lower current standard of living in order to retire with adequate funds, while another person will resist postponing any gratification.
9. Health. For example, people who are in poor or declining health, or who have dependents in such a situation, must be careful to have adequate funds for medical expenses.
10. Tax status. People who are in a high tax bracket may consider investing in municipal bonds or other tax-free instruments.

Before selecting a particular investment, consideration has to be given to the amount, rate of return, risk level, security of principal and income, liquidity and marketability, diversification, tax and estate status, long-term vs. short-term potential, ability to withstand financial losses, hedging against inflation, and callability provisions.

Providing long-term health care for aging relatives is also an important issue in personal financial planning.

Personal Financial Statements

A personal balance sheet shows how much a person owns (assets) and owes (liabilities). The difference between assets and liabilities represents net worth. The balance sheet reveals financial status.

The same basis to value assets and liabilities should be used each year. For example, if the value of a family's house is based on recent area sales in one year, the same method should be used in the next year.

In preparing a personal balance sheet, assets should be listed in the order of liquidity at current market values. If assets are jointly owned, only the individual's interest as beneficial owner should be included. A listing of assets may take the following form:

| Asset | Description | Current Value | Percent of Total Assets |

Liabilities should be reported at estimated current amounts by order of maturity.

Table 11.1 shows an illustrative balance sheet:

Rule of Thumb: Debt as a percentage of total assets should typically be less than 50%. If, however, an individual's job is unstable, the debt percentage should be lower—probably no more than 25%.

Table 11.1
ILLUSTRATIVE BALANCE SHEET

Mr. Jack Smith
Balance Sheet
December 31, 20XX

ASSETS
Liquid

Cash	$ 4,000		
Money market fund	25,000		
Marketable securities	30,000		
Mutual fund	14,000		
Cash surrender value of life insurance	6,000		
Total liquid assets		$ 79,000	
Nonliquid			
Long-term investments	$ 50,000		
Real estate	150,000		
Automobile	10,000		
Personal property	25,000		
Retirement funds	40,000		
Total nonliquid assets		275,000	
Total assets			$354,000
LIABILITIES			
Short-term			
Accounts and bills due	$ 1,000		
Credit card	2,500		
Total short-term liabilities		$ 3,500	
Long-term			
Mortgage payable	$ 80,000		
Auto loan	4,000		
Bank loan	3,000		
Total long-term liabilities		87,000	
Total liabilities			$ 90,500
Net worth			$263,500

An income statement reveals total income less total expenses. It shows a person's economic health and indicates how much discretionary income there is that can be saved and invested.

An abbreviated income statement is given in Table 11.2.

Budgeting

A budget may be prepared for the different sources of income (e.g., salary, investment income, pensions) and expenses itemized by category. The preparation of a budget helps manage cash flow.

Budgeting is best done on a monthly basis to make it timely. Budgeting has many advantages:

- It helps in meeting personal goals and in planning expenditures.
- It allows planning for situations when increases in income are not going to keep up with increased expenses.
- It provides indications on how expenses can be selectively reduced.
- It points out when to pay bills.
- It helps monitor whether or not spending is within predetermined limits (e.g., credit cards).
- It establishes a timetable for major purchases (e.g., buying a house).

A financial planner should be conservative in preparing a cash inflow forecast; it is always better to underestimate. If cash flows are overestimated, the individual may overspend and thus have to go into debt.

An illustrative budget is shown in Table 11.3.

To be safe, an individual should have at least six months' income in a savings account. Realistically, however, three to six months is the best most people can do. An individual should try to put 10% of gross income each year into savings—more if income fluctuates.

Risk

Risk is the probability of a financial problem affecting a company's operational performance or financial position.

Business risk is the risk that a company will experience general business problems (e.g., changes in demand, technological obsolescence).

Liquidity risk involves the chance that it may not be possible to sell an asset for its market value on short notice. For instance, it may take months, or even years, to sell a piece of real estate.

Table 11.2
ILLUSTRATIVE INCOME STATEMENT

Mr. and Mrs. Tom Jones
Income Statement
For the Year Ending December 31, 20XX

INCOME

Salary, commission, bonus	$75,000	
Self-employment income (net)	2,000	
Interest	2,000	
Dividends	4,000	
Gain on sale of securities	4,000	
Rental, royalty, and partnership income	5,000	
Pensions, social security	10,000	
Total Income		$120,000

EXPENSES

Fixed Expenses

Insurance	$ 3,000	
Housing (mortgage, rent)	12,000	
Real estate taxes	4,000	
Utilities	2,000	
Medical	2,000	
Groceries	6,000	
Transportation (commuting)	1,000	
Repayment of debt	3,000	
Income taxes	5,000	
Contribution to pension plan	—	
Total Fixed Expenses		$38,000

Discretionary Expenses

Clothing and cleaning	$ 2,000	
Personal care	1,000	
Restaurants	5,000	
Entertainment/recreation	3,000	
Vacation/travel	4,000	
Education	3,000	
Charities and gifts	1,000	
Furniture and appliances	4,000	
Household expenses and repairs	3,000	
Total Discretionary Expenses		$26,000
Total Expenses		$ 64,000
Net Savings		$ 56,000

Table 11.3
SAMPLE CASH BUDGET

Richard and Jane Smith

Beginning Cash Balance		$15,000
CASH RECEIPTS		
Salary—husband	$40,000	
Salary—wife	20,000	
Interest income	5,000	
Dividend income	2,000	
Royalty income	3,000	
Gifts	6,000	
Tax refunds	4,000	
Sale of securities	7,000	
Sale of assets	5,000	
Total Cash Receipts		$92,000
CASH EXPENSES		
Rent	$ 4,000	
Mortgage	3,000	
Fuel bills	1,000	
Telephone	2,000	
Electricity	600	
Gas expense	400	
Water	1,000	
Loan payments	4,000	
Education expense	3,000	
Property taxes	4,000	
Income taxes	2,000	
Insurance payments	6,000	
Medical bills	8,000	
Food	10,000	
Household items	12,000	
Furniture	14,000	
Clothing	6,000	
Transportation costs	5,000	
Entertainment expense	2,000	
Gift payments	1,000	
Personal care	1,000	
Total Cash Payments		$90,000
Increase in Cash Flow		2,000
Ending Cash Balance		$17,000

Default risk involves the possibility a company will be unable to pay principal and interest payments on debt (e.g., bonds of a financially troubled company).

Market risk involves the possibility that the price of a company's stock will change to a greater extent than the change in a stock market index (e.g., Standard and Poor's). This is commonly referred to as a stock having a beta greater than 1.

Interest-rate risk applies to the fluctuations in the value of an asset as the interest rates and conditions of the money and capital markets change. Interest-rate risk relates to fixed-income securities such as bonds and real estate. For example, if interest rates rise (fall), bond prices fall (rise).

Purchasing-power risk means one may receive less purchasing power than was originally invested. Long-term debt such as bonds are the most impacted by this risk because the issuer will be paying back in cheaper dollars during or after periods of inflation.

Diversification (e.g., an investment portfolio of stocks, bonds, real estate, and savings accounts) will typically lower risk. The values of these different investments do not generally increase or decrease at the same time or in the same magnitude.

Diversification may be in terms of maturity. For example, with securities of fixed maturity dates (e.g., bonds, one-year certificates of deposit), the maturities may be spaced so the securities do not come due all at once. Hence, new principal is available to invest periodically during times of high or low interest rates.

Personal Banking

When an individual shops around for a bank, he or she should consider the following:

- *Rates and fees.* A comparison should be made of the *rates* on savings and checking accounts and *fees* (e.g., service charges).
- *Clarity of information.* The ability to comprehend bank applications and handouts.
- *Convenient hours and service.* One may inquire about direct deposit of paychecks, evening and weekend hours, automatic teller machines, and drive-in windows.
- *Quick crediting of deposits.* The bank should provide quick credit on deposits.
- *Good deal on loans.* Is there a preference on credit applications or lower loan rates to regular customers or to those with large accounts?
- *Extra free services.* Are there free notary services, no-charge money orders, etc.? Many banks provide free checking if a specific minimum monthly balance on deposits is maintained.

Debt Strategy

Credit cards are an expensive approach to borrowing money. Their average interest rate nationally is about 18%. In doing comparison shopping for a credit card, multiply the average balance by the difference in interest rates to determine increased cost. Also, consider the annual fee. What is the time period in which the bill can be paid in full without incurring an interest charge? Consider the fees charged each time a card is used for a charge purchase and/or cash advance. What are the late-payment fees?

Rule of Thumb. For most people, the best deal is a card with a low interest rate, no annual fee, and a 30-day grace period.

Watch out for credit overload. Generally, monthly credit obligations should not exceed more than 20% of the monthly take-home pay. For example, if take-home pay is $2,000 for the month, only $400 ($2000 × 20%) should go toward paying off items bought on credit. *Note:* The 20% maximum limit includes payments on credit cards and personal loans (e.g., college, auto). It does *not* include mortgage or rent payments. These obligations can account for as much as an additional 35% of total monthly expenditures. An additional benchmark is that one should be able to pay off debts within 18 to 24 months.

To determine one's debt limit, the following steps are needed:

1. Compute monthly consumer debt payments.
2. Determine monthly net income (after taxes, social security, and IRA contributions).
3. To calculate what an individual can afford each month, the monthly income should be multiplied by 20%, 15%, or 10% (depending on the personal permissible debt ratio).

Rule of Thumb: A single, middle-aged person netting $40,000 a year can probably afford 20% in debt. Reduce debt to 10% if income is not stable (e.g, based on sales commissions rather than salary). A husband and wife who are both working and taking home $50,000 can probably afford 20% in debt. If there are children, it should probably be 15%. A retired person on fixed income should have no more than a 10% level.

EXAMPLE 11.1

Byron Shelley is a single, middle-aged man who takes home $40,000 a year (or $3,333 a month). He carries an average monthly consumer debt payment of $1,000. According to the rule of thumb, the most he can afford each month would be $677 (20% × $3,333).

Since he is now well over this limit, he should cut down on existing debts and avoid additional borrowing.

There are numerous ways to manage debt properly, including:

- Avoid borrowing from the future to meet current living expenses.
- Avoid borrowing for depreciating assets (e.g., cars), and borrow only on appreciating assets (e.g., real estate).
- Use the financing alternative with the lowest interest rate.
- Avoid using a bank credit card because of the high finance charge. It is unwise to pay a credit card fee of 18% while only earning 6% on a bank deposit. Money should be withdrawn from the savings account and used to pay off the credit card balance. Otherwise, 12% is being lost annually.

EXAMPLE 11.2

Jane Austen has $100,000 in a money market account earning 8%. She owes $7,000 on her credit cards at 20% interest. In this case, her net worth is declining since the borrowing cost exceeds the return on the bank account by 12%. The $7,000 should be taken out from the bank account to pay the credit cards. The reduction in wealth on an annual basis is:

Cost of credit card $7,000 × 20%	$1,400
Return on bank account $7,000 × 8%	560
Decline in wealth	$ 840

- Avoid using borrowed funds to invest unless the interest rate is very low and there is a dependable investment return.
- Always pay off the high interest loans first.
- Establish a line of credit before it is necessary. There is usually no charge for a preapproved line until borrowing occurs.
- To reduce monthly loan payment, extend the time period for repayment.

The cost of credit may be computed in terms of dollars and/or annual percentage rate. A dollar computation follows.

EXAMPLE 11.3

A young couple named Keats wishes to take out a $100,000 mortgage for a new home. Bank A has an interest rate of 8% and points of 2%. Bank B has an interest rate of 9% with no points required. The mortgage is 20 years. The yearly payments are:

Present Value of Mortgage
Present Value of Ordinary Annuity
Bank A: $100,000/Present Value of Ordinary Annuity for $n = 20$, $i = 8\%$.
        $100,000/9.81815 = \$10,185$
Bank B: $100,000/present Value of Ordinary Annuity for $n = 20$, $i = 9\%$.
        $100,000/9.12855 = \$10,955$

The total interest and point charge for the mortgages from both banks are:

Bank A:
Interest charge

Total payments $10,185 × 20	$203,700	
Less: Principal	100,000	$103,700
Points in first year $100,000 × 2%		2,000
Total		$105,700

Bank B:
Interest charge

Total payments $10,955 × 20	$219,100	
Less: Principal	100,000	$119,100
Total		$119,100

The mortgage from Bank A should be selected because it is cheaper by $13,400.

The annual percentage rate (APR) is a simple interest rate established for the use of a given amount of money (principal) for a period of one year.

$$\text{Interest} = \text{Principal} \times \text{Rate} \times \text{Time}$$

The dollar cost of credit can be converted into APR using the following formula:

$$APR = \frac{2MC}{[P(N + 1)]}$$

where $M =$ number of payments for one year
        $C =$ dollar cost of credit
        $P =$ original proceeds from credit
and $N =$ total number of payments in the debt contract

EXAMPLE 11.4

Bank A offers a 7% loan on a household item (e.g., air conditioning system) if a customer puts 25% down. Thus, someone buying a

$4,000 used auto can finance $3,000 over a three-year period with approximate carrying charges amounting to $630 (7% × $3,000 × 3 years). There will be 36 equal monthly payments of $100.83 each.

Bank B will lend $3,500 on the household item, but here the customer must pay $90 per month for 48 months.

The APR calculations follow:

$$\text{Bank A: } 2 \times 12 \times 630/3,000 \, (36 + 1) = 13.6\%$$
$$\text{Bank B: } 2 \times 12 \times 820/3,500 \, (48 + 1) = 11.5\%$$

In the case of Bank B, it was necessary to multiply $90 × 48 months to arrive at a total time cost of $4,320. Therefore, the total credit cost is $820 ($4,320 − $3,500).

Bank B should be chosen over Bank A since it results in a lower cost.

Note: You can choose between a larger down payment/higher monthly payment/shorter payback time and a smaller down payment/lower monthly payments/longer time period. Without the APR, it would be difficult to determine the "best deal."

Many lenders will allow the borrower to pay off a loan early without penalty. The borrower has to know the interest savings before making a prepayment decision, because one may be better off investing the funds elsewhere rather than prepaying the loan. In analyzing this, one must realize that many lenders use the *rule of 78* in computing interest. This rule results in the borrower paying more interest at the beginning of a loan, when there is the use of more money, and less interest as the debt is reduced. It is thus essential to know how much interest can be saved by prepaying a loan after a certain month and how much is still owed on a loan.

Cost Savings

Ways to save on living costs must be searched out. An example is the cost of buying and operating an automobile. Some tips on reducing living costs are looking for good warranty provisions and liberal return policies on goods, emphasizing low-maintenance items, getting competitive bids for a job, using the most economical long-distance telephone company, saving on insurance by taking out high deductibles, using the same insurance company for *various* insurance needs to obtain a lower overall rate, exercising energy conservation, using a self-service gasoline station, and avoiding buying options on a new car (the dealer markup on options is typically two to three times the profit margin on the car).

Note that insurance coverage is about 20% of the overall auto expenditure for the year.

In deciding whether to buy or lease a car, the advantages and disadvantages must be considered. Advantages of leasing are that it does not require an immediate substantial cash outlay, there may be a bargain purchase option, and the lessor services the auto. The prime disadvantage of leasing is that it costs more to lease than buy in the long run because the auto rental firm has to make a profit on the operation of the car.

EXAMPLE 11.5

Stanley Steamer decides to rent a car for the day. The available options are:

1. $65 for the day with unlimited mileage
2. $29.95 for the day with 50 free miles and 25 cents per mile in excess of 50 miles

Stan plans to drive 125 miles. The cost of the options are:

1. $65
2. $29.95 + $18.75 (75 × $.25) = $48.70

He should select the second option.

There are several ways of reducing auto insurance costs, including decreasing collision coverage as the car becomes older, obtaining insurance discounts (e.g., taking an accredited driver education course), and insuring all the family cars under one policy to get a discount on the second and third cars.

The initial cost of an auto is a far more crucial factor in determining the economy of a car than miles per gallon.

EXAMPLE 11.6

Joe Ford is looking at the cost difference between buying a compact and buying a subcompact. The sales tax is 8%. He will be financing the car at 14% simple interest for one year. The difference in price of the cars is $2,000. This will cost him in total:

Basic price difference	$2,000
Tax (8% × $2,000)	160
Interest (14% × $2,160)	302
Total	$2,462

He can save 10 miles per gallon on the subcompact. If he drives 10,000 miles for the year, it translates to using 1,000 gallons

(10,000/10). If the price per gallon is $3.00, the yearly savings in gasoline cost is $3,000.

The savings in miles per gallon is only $3,000 compared to the extra cost of purchasing the car of $2,462.

Sometimes a car dealer offers a rebate or a lower finance charge to attract buyers. Typically, the lower financing cost should be selected.

EXAMPLE 11.7

General Motors is offering an $18,000 car at a rebate of $750 or financing at 1.9%. If the financing alternative is taken, a down payment of 10% is required. The financing period is one year with monthly payments. You can earn 8% on your money. Computations follow:

Savings from rebate		$750
Savings from low finance charge		
Amount subject to financing	$16,200	
Net interest earned (8.0% – 1.9%)	× 6.1%	988
Net advantage with financing the car		$238

College Education for Children

Gifts are a way to build a college fund for children while saving on taxes. The gifts earn interest taxed to the child, whose tax bracket is typically much less than the parent's. Under current tax law, a child under 18 (or over age 18, but under age 24 and a full-time student who did not "have earned income" more than half of his or her support) pays tax at the child's tax rate on the initial $2,000 of interest or dividend income from gift money. Any interest or dividend income in excess of $2,000 is taxed at the parents' tax rate.

EXAMPLE 11.8

The child earns interest and dividend income of $4,600 on gift monies. The parents' tax bracket is 28%. The tax to be paid is:

First $2,000 of income taxed at child's rate	$ 0
Balance of $2,600 of income taxed at parent's rate	728
Tax	$728

Another approach to financing a child's education is to take out a home-equity loan. Interest is deductible on a mortgage to finance the child's education.

A private university is more costly than a public institution. For example, a four-year education at a private college may range from $100,000 to $150,000, depending on the institution.

To estimate the total college cost, start with the anticipated cost for the first year. To incorporate probable inflation, add 7% to the first year's cost for the second year, 15% for the third year, and 23% for the fourth year.

EXAMPLE 11.9

Your child's estimated expenses at Tech College in the first year is $6,000. The projected costs for the remaining years are:

Year 2	$6,000 × 1.07	$6,420
Year 3	6,000 × 1.15	6,900
Year 4	6,000 × 1.23	7,380

Some ways to reduce college costs are obtaining credit by examination, thus lowering the number of credit hours the student has to earn (and therefore pay for); taking advantage of special payment plans; utilizing a cooperative education program; and attending a three-year degree program, thus reducing tuition fees and living costs by almost 25%.

You should estimate the amount needed when the child is ready for college.

EXAMPLE 11.10

The Jones family's income is $54,000. They have to save 12% of their income each year to pay for the college education of their daughter, Jennifer. This yields an annual figure of $6,480 ($54,000 × 12%). Therefore, each month they have to save $540 ($6,480/12). The Joneses expect to earn 8% on their savings. Jennifer will be going to college in 10 years. The future value of annuity table of $1 factor for $n = 10$, $i = 8\%$ is 14.48656. The Joneses will have accumulated $93,873 after 10 years, as computed below:

$$\$6,480 \times 14.48656 = \$93,873$$

A decision may have to be reached whether it pays to go for a graduate degree. Present-value analysis will be helpful.

EXAMPLE 11.11

Joe College is unsure whether to go for a graduate degree or not. It will take him two years to earn an MBA. The initial application fee is $100. The cost of tuition and books will be $4,000 in the first year and $4,800 in the second year. The salary at Joe's job will be the same while he is in school. However, after he receives the degree, his salary will be $5,000, $7,000, and $12,000 more, respectively, in years 3, 4, and 5. If he did not go to graduate school, he could earn an extra $3,000 and $4,500, respectively, in years 1 and 2. The discount rate is 10%.

The table of present value is used to obtain the appropriate factors.

TABLE OF PRESENT VALUE

	Net Present Value	Year 0	Year 1	Year 2	Year 3	Year 4	Year 5
MBA	$8,286	$–100	$–4,000	$–4,800	$+5,000	$+7,000	$+12,000
		× 1	× .90909	× .82645	× .75132	× .68301	× .62092
		$–100	$–3,636	$–3,967	$+3,757	$+4,781	$+7,451
No MBA	$6,446		$+3,000	$+4,500			
			× .90909	× .82645			
			$+2,727	$+3,719			

Investing in Common Stock

Common stock is an equity interest constituting ownership in a business. The return is in the form of dividend income and appreciation in the market price of the stock. Although equity ownership returns vary with business and financial-market cycles, stocks have shown over the years to be rewarding investments and good inflation hedges. But stock investment should only be made if there is extra disposable income over and above adequate savings in cash for unexpected emergencies, life insurance, and other necessities. Before investing, one should take into account current financial status including income, expenses, taxes, and future prospects. *General rule:* Invest about 15% of after-tax income. Before investing, total assets should be twice total liabilities.

Advantages of owning common stock include voting rights, sharing in dividends and market-price growth, hedge against inflation, preemptive right allowing present stockholders to maintain their proportionate shares of ownership in the company (e.g., if an investor owns 10% of a company's shares and there is a new issuance of 30,000 shares, she will have the right to buy 3,000 more shares).

The principal disadvantages of owning common stock are as follows: possible decline in market price; dividends may be cut back or omitted; common stockholders come last in the event of corporate bankruptcy; and stocks have greater price fluctuation than fixed-income securities.

There are six major categories of stock:

Blue Chips. Ownership in high-quality, financially strong companies involves low risk and modest, dependable return. Blue chips have a good track record in profitability and dividends. They are less vulnerable to cyclical market swings and thus are safe, long-term equity investment.

Growth Stocks. Companies having a faster growth rate than other businesses and the economy generally grows faster in the stock market, too. The stocks of high-technology companies and similar growth companies pay low or no dividends because profits are retained for future expansion. While growth stocks may rise in price faster, there is the possibility of greater price fluctuation. A growth stock may be advised if one is saving for retirement.

Income Stocks. Companies with high dividends and dividend payout ratios are advisable for those wanting high current income rather than capital appreciation. There is less risk involved. For example, public utility stocks are good for a retiree because of their stable, periodic cash dividend payments.

Cyclical Stocks. Companies that experience variability in price based on economic changes. Profits fall in recession and rise in expansion. A cyclical security may be for a young person wanting to undertake risk and who is financially secure. Airlines are cyclical stocks.

Defensive Stocks. A company not impacted by a downturn in the business cycle offers a generally safe and consistent—if often lower—return on investment. Defensive stocks may be suggested for an older individual who wants to avoid downside risk. Many consumer product companies are defensive investments.

Speculative Stocks. Companies without a track record are speculative investments. Uncertainty exists with respect to profit, though there is a chance for significant earnings. Speculative stocks are for someone desiring a very high return but willing to take high risk. An example is a biotechnology company. Particularly beware of penny stocks, which are stocks having a market price below $1 per share. Penny stocks are very risky because they are typically issued by companies with a short life or with past instability in operations. Speculative stocks have high P/E ratios and price variability.

International Stocks. Companies traded on foreign exchanges. The stocks make significant gains when the dollar is falling and foreign stock prices are rising. Examples are French, German, and Japanese companies.

Rate of Return. You can determine the return earned on your investment by computing the dollar return and yield.

The dollar return from a stock investment represents dividend income and change in market price.

EXAMPLE 11.12

Investor A bought a stock for $30 and subsequently sold it for $36. The annual dividend was $2. The return per share on the investment was:

Dividend income	$2
Gain ($36–$30)	6
Total	$8

Investor A owned 100 shares, so her total return was $800. The percentage return equals:

$$\frac{\text{(Selling price–Investment)} + \text{Dividends}}{\text{Investment}}$$

EXAMPLE 11.13

Investor B invested $80 in a stock, which he sold three months later for $90. He received a $2.50 dividend. The quarterly return is:

$$\frac{\text{(Selling price – Investment)} + \text{Dividend}}{\text{Investment}}$$

$$\frac{(\$90 - \$80) + \$2.50}{\$80} = \frac{\$12.50}{\$80} = 15.6\%$$

The equivalent annual return is $15.6\% \times 4 = \underline{62.4\%}$.

EXAMPLE 11.14

Investor C bought a stock for $60 and sold it for $100 after four years. Each year he received a dividend of $3. The annual return from the investment over the four-year period is:

$$\frac{\dfrac{\text{Selling price – Investment}}{\text{Years}} + \text{Dividend}}{\text{Average investment}}$$

$$\frac{\dfrac{\$100 - \$60}{4} + \$3}{\dfrac{\$100 - \$60}{2}} = \frac{\$13}{\$80} = 16.3\%$$

The yield on a stock is the return on common stock based on initial cost or current market price. Yield based on original investment equals:

$$\frac{\text{Dividends per share}}{\text{Investment}}$$

EXAMPLE 11.15

Investor D paid $80 for a stock currently worth $90. The dividend per share is $4. The yield on her initial investment is:

$$\frac{\$4}{\$80} = .05$$

Dividend yield based on current market price equals:

$$\frac{\text{Dividends per share}}{\text{Market price per share}}$$

EXAMPLE 11.16

Assuming the same facts as Example 11.15, the dividend yield equals:

$$\frac{\$4}{\$90} = .044$$

The price-earnings ratio equals:

$$\frac{\text{Market price per share}}{\text{Earnings per share}}$$

If market price of stock is $60 and earnings per share is $10, the price-earnings ratio (multiple) is 6.

Price-Earnings Ratio. The price-earnings ratio reveals what investors are willing to pay for a dollar's worth of earnings. The P/E multiple is how many times earnings the stock is selling for. The higher the P/E ratio, the greater the expectation of investors for future growth in the value of the stock, and vice versa. The factors bearing upon the P/E ratio include earnings growth rate, future profitability, future cash flow from operations, anticipated dividends, corporate risk, instability in operations, economic and political uncertainties, and management ability.

A high P/E multiple indicates that investors view the stock positively. A low multiple shows investors are relatively negative on the stock. *Note:* Low multiples may offer profit opportunities over the long term. Thus, a good time to buy stocks may be when multiples are below traditional levels.

If your valuation of a stock deviates from its current market price, you may decide to purchase it if it is undervalued, or sell short if it is overvalued. For instance, assume Company X's stock price is $50 and your valuation indicates it is worth $55. The investment decision would be to buy the stock.

Beta. Beta is the percentage change in the market price of a stock compared to the percentage change in a stock market index (e.g., Standard & Poor's 500). A beta greater than 1 means the company's stock price fluctuates more than the change in the stock market index pointing to a risky security. A beta less than 1 indicates less variability in price than the market index. However, it should be noted that if its beta is greater than 1, the stock offers greater stock price appreciation in a bull market but will likewise decline to a greater extent than the market index in a bear market.

Dollar-Cost Averaging. This approach may be used for a stock considered to be a sound, long-term investment. It relates to buying a constant-dollar amount of a given stock or stocks at regular intervals. In effect, it is time diversification. By investing a fixed amount each time, you purchase more shares when the price is low and fewer shares when the price is high. This program typically results in a lower average cost per share since you buy more shares with the same dollars. If stock prices drop, you lose less money than usual. If stock prices rise, you profit but less than usual. Dollar-cost averaging, however, results in greater transaction costs. *Note:* Dollar-cost averaging does not work when a stock price continually declines. Overall, dollar-cost averaging is generally a conservative means to invest since you are buying stock gradually at varying prices.

Advantages of dollar-cost averaging include the ability to buy a conservative stock with relatively little risk benefiting from long-term price appreciation, avoiding buying many shares at high prices, and having an opportunity to purchase additional shares at low prices in a bear market.

EXAMPLE 11.17

You invest $100 a month in XYZ Company and have the following transactions.

Date	Invested	Price Per Share	Shares Bought
1/15	$100	$20	5
2/15	100	15	6⅔
3/15	100	12	8⅓
4/15	100	16	6¼
5/15	100	25	4

You have bought less shares at the higher price and more shares at the lower price. The average price per share is:

$$\frac{\$88}{\$5} \; = \; \$17.60$$

However, with your $500 investment you have acquired 30¼ shares, resulting in a cost per share of $16.53. On May 15, the market price of stock of $25 exceeds your average cost of $16.53, reflecting an attractive gain.

Common Stock Valuation. The value of common stock depends on the expected growth rate in profit, dividends, and market price. The purpose of valuing common stock is to determine if the current market price is realistic, taking into account future dividends and price.

You can determine a stock's value to you by computing the present value of a stock's anticipated future cash flows, using your required rate of return as the discount rate. The value of common stock is the present value of future dividends plus the present value of the selling price. Value equals:

Present value of future dividends + Present value of selling price

This requires the use of present-value tables to arrive at the factor on the tables corresponding to the rate of return (i) and the number of years (n) in holding the stock.

Stock Volume. You should look at the trading volume in a stock. Declining volume with a strong increase in price indicates that buyers are becoming more wary. Increased volume with a decline in stock price indicates institutions may be selling the stock. It is better when volume and price move together, as in the case when a price rises on substantial volume.

It is usually best to trade in active stocks, which have better marketability and are less subject to price manipulation.

Buying Stock on Margin. If you buy stock on margin, you are buying on credit. Interest is charged on the unpaid balance. The brokerage firm usually charges 2% more than the bank charges. A brokerage firm can lend you up to 50% of the value of stocks. If the value of the portfolio declines to jeopardize the brokerage loan on the margin account, you will receive a "margin call" to put up additional money or securities, or sell some stock.

Buying on margin provides the opportunity to obtain a greater return through leverage (buying on credit). But the loss can also be magnified if the value of the security portfolio drops.

EXAMPLE 11.18

Investor A buys 50 shares of ABC Company at $40 per share, or $2,000. She pays 60% of the price, or $1,200. The remaining $800 is a loan. Assuming an interest rate of 12%, the annual interest charge is $96 ($800 × .12). The brokerage fee amounts to $50. Buying on margin can result in a greater return because the investor need make only a partial payment for stock that has appreciated in value. If the stock increases to $65 one year later, investor A can sell it for $3,250 ($65 × 50 shares). Her profit before interest and brokerage fee is $1,250 on an investment of $1,200. The return rate after the interest charge and brokerage fee is:

$$\frac{\$1,250 - \$96 - \$50}{\$1,200} = \frac{\$1,104}{\$1,200} = 92\%$$

Short Selling. Short selling is when you profit from a decline in stock price. To make a short sale, the broker borrows the stock from someone else and then sells it for you on the open market. Later, you buy back the stock. If you buy at a lower price than the broker sold the shares for, you earn a profit. You have a loss when the repurchase price is more than the original selling price.

A drawback to selling a stock short is that you must pay the dividends declared to the lender of the shares. *Tip:* Sell short a stock paying low or no dividends.

EXAMPLE 11.19

Investor B sells short 100 shares of stock having a market price of $30. The broker borrows the shares for him and sells them to someone else for $3,000. Subsequently, investor B buys the stock back at $25 a share, earning a profit per share of $5, or a total of $500 before brokerage charges.

Diversification. To reduce risk, diversify your stock holdings. Diversification may include, for example, holding blue chips, growth stocks, and income stocks. Also, you should diversify your investments over time so as to smooth out the ups and downs of the market. Investors can diversify away unsystematic risk without sacrificing returns. It should also be noted that the more brokerage fees an investor pays, the more a portfolio must perform to realize investment goals.

Stock Strategy. As interest rates drop, stock prices rise. The reason is simple: As less interest is earned on bank accounts, many investors move funds from savings accounts into stocks. Also low interest rates make it cheaper for companies to borrow, improving their earnings.

Invest in high-quality companies (financially strong leaders in their fields that have had consistently high, profitable growth). In the long run, you will profit from blue chips.

Try to buy an undervalued stock. For example, value may be found in some of the stocks that are at new 52-week lows.

One strategy is to buy stocks with relatively low P/E ratios and high dividend yields.

Investing in Options

Options provide the right to buy a security at a specified price for a stated time period. Options have their own inherent value and are traded in secondary markets. You may purchase an option to take advantage of an anticipated increase in stock price. Option prices are directly related to the prices of the common stock to which they apply. Calls and puts can be bought or sold in round lots, usually 100 shares. Calls represent the right to buy stocks while puts represent the right to sell stocks. In buying a call or put you have the opportunity to make a substantial profit from a small investment, but you also risk losing your entire investment if the stock price does not move in the right direction. Calls are in bearer negotiable form and have a life of one to nine months.

Buying a put gives you the right to sell stock at a fixed price. You might buy a put if you expect a stock price to fall.

Calls and puts are usually written for widely held and actively traded stock on organized exchanges.

EXAMPLE 11.20

XYZ stock has a market price of $35. You buy a put to sell 100 shares at $35 per share. The cost of the put is $3 per share, or $300.

At the exercise date of the put, the price of the stock goes to $15 a share. You therefore realize a profit of $20 per share, or $2,000. As the holder of the put, you simply buy on the market 100 shares at $15 each and then sell them to the writer of the put for $35 each. The net gain is $1,700 on just a $300 initial investment, or 567%.

An investment approach with calls and puts includes hedging. Hedging may involve buying a stock and later buying an option on it. For example, a holder of stock that has risen in price may buy a put to furnish downside risk protection.

EXAMPLE 11.21

You buy 100 shares of ABC Company at $26 each and a put for $200 on the 100 shares at an exercise price of $26. If the stock remains static, you will lose $200 on the put. If the price decreases, your loss on the stock will be offset by your gain on the put.

Investing in Fixed-Income Securities

Fixed-income securities typically provide current fixed income but have very limited potential for price appreciation. They are usually liquid and have low market risk. This investment does well during a stable economic environment with low inflation. Examples of fixed-income securities are corporate and municipal bonds, notes, mortgages, and preferred stocks.

Bonds. A bond is a certificate or security representing funds loaned to a company or to a government in return for fixed interest and principal repayment.

Advantages of bonds are fixed interest income paid each year and that bondholders will be paid before stockholders in the event of the Company's liquidation. Disadvantages of bonds are the failure to participate in incremental profitability and the absence of voting rights.

The various types of bonds include:

- *Mortgage bonds.* Mortgage bonds are secured by physical property.
- *Debentures.* Debentures are unsecured bonds, thus depend on the general credit of the issuing company. *Subordinated debentures* are junior issues paid after unsecured debt.
- *Convertible bonds.* Convertible bonds are convertible into stock at a later date at a specified conversion price. They are hybrid securities with characteristics of bonds and common stock and provide fixed interest income and potential of market price appreciation.

- *Income bonds.* With income bonds, interest is paid only if earned.
- *Tax-exempt bonds.* Tax-exempt bonds are usually municipal bonds, and the interest income is not subject to federal tax. Municipal bonds usually carry a lower interest rate than taxable bonds of similar quality. However, the after-tax yield from these bonds is typically more than a bond with a higher rate of taxable interest. *Note:* Municipal bonds are susceptible to interest rate and default risk.

U.S. Government Securities. Treasury bills, notes, bonds, and mortgage-backed securities like Ginnie Maes are the most common government securities. T-bills are short-term financing instruments maturing in 12 months or less; notes have a maturity of one to ten years; bonds have a maturity of 10 to 25 years and can be bought in denominations as low as $1,000. U.S. government securities are subject to federal income taxes but not to state and local income taxes. Ginnie Maes represent 25- to 30-year Federal Housing Administration (FHA) or Veterans Administration (VA) mortgages guaranteed by the Government National Mortgage Association (GNMA).

Zero-Coupon Bonds. In the case of zero-coupon bonds, principal and accumulated interest are only paid at maturity. There is no periodic interest payment. However, accrued interest, though not received, is taxable yearly as ordinary income. Zero-coupon bonds have two basic advantages relative to coupon-bearing bonds: (1) only a relatively small investment is required and (2) there is a specified yield provided throughout the investment term.

Junk Bonds. Junk bonds are speculative and have a rating of BB or lower by Moody's and Standard & Poor's. They are risky and should be avoided if you desire a conservative investment. Some junk bonds have gone into default, causing significant losses to investors, but others have maintained their payment, giving investors a high rate of return (15% or more).

In selecting a particular bond investment, consideration should be given to investment quality (bond rating), maturity period, features (e.g., conversion, call), tax status, and yield to maturity.

The bond rating reflects the probability of the bond going into default. The rating will affect the potential market behavior of the bond and its yield. *Tip:* Select a bond rated BBB or better by Standard & Poor's, even though you may have to give up 3/4 of a percentage point in yield.

The longer the maturity period of a bond, the more volatile is the price and the higher will be the yield.

If a bond has a call feature, the issuing company may redeem the bonds before the maturity date. Bonds are typically only called when their interest rates are higher than the going market rate.

There are basically two types of yield on a bond—simple yield and yield to maturity.

Simple yield equals:

$$\frac{\text{Nominal Interest}}{\text{Market Price of Bond}}$$

EXAMPLE 11.22

Assume a 12% coupon rate on a $1,000 face value bond selling for $960. The simple yield is 12.5% ($120/$960).

Yield to maturity equals:

$$\frac{\text{Nominal Interest} + \text{Discount/Years}}{\text{Average Investment}}$$

EXAMPLE 11.23

Assume that a 10-year, 8%, $1,000 face value bond is offered at a price of $877.60. The yield to maturity is:

$$\frac{\$80 + (\$1,000 - \$877.60)/10}{(\$1,000 + \$877.60)/2} = \frac{\$80 + \$12.24}{\$938.80}$$

$$= \frac{\$92.24}{\$938.80} = 9.8\%$$

Since the bond can be bought at a discount, the yield of 9.8% comes out greater than the coupon rate of 8%.

The yield to maturity is a better method to use because it takes into account not only the interest income but also the capital gain (assuming the bond is held to maturity).

Preferred Stock. Preferred stock is a hybrid security because it has the features of both common stock and a bond. It is similar to common stock in that it represents equity ownership, there is no maturity date, and it pays dividends. It is similar to a corporate bond in that it has a claim senior to common stock on earnings and assets, there is a fixed dividend rate, and there may be call and convertible features.

Because preferred stock is traded on the basis of yield offered to investors, it is considered a fixed income security.

Advantages of preferred stock are high current income, safety (preferred stock comes before common stock in corporate liquidation), and lower unit cost ($10 to $25 per share). Disadvantages are purchasing power loss during inflation, lack of substantial capital gains potential, and inferior status to bonds in the event of corporate bankruptcy.

The current yield on preferred stock equals:

$$\frac{\text{Dividends per share}}{\text{Market price per share}}$$

EXAMPLE 11.24

A preferred stock paying $4 a year in dividends and having a market price of $25 would have a current yield of 16%.

Other Fixed Income Securities. Besides bonds and preferred stock, other forms of debt instruments exist that are primarily *short-term*. They include:

Certificates of deposit (CDs) are issued by commercial banks and thrift institutions and have traditionally been in denominations of $10,000. Today, you can invest in a CD for much less (e.g., $2,000). CDs have fixed maturity periods, ranging from several months to many years, and are insured up to $250,000 by an agency of the U.S. government. *Warning:* A penalty generally will be incurred if a CD is not kept to maturity.

Commercial Paper is issued by large companies to the public. However, it typically comes in minimum denominations of $25,000. It represents an unsecured promissory note. The yield is typically higher than a small CD. The maturity period is usually 30, 60, and 90 days.

Treasury Bills have a maximum maturity of one year and common maturities of 91 and 182 days. They are traded in $10,000 denominations and are issued at a discount from face, or redemption, value. T-bills are very liquid and carry very little risk, since they are backed by the U.S. Government.

Mutual Funds

When buying shares in a mutual fund, you own a professionally managed portfolio of securities. Advantages of mutual fund investment include diversification (each share of a fund provides an interest in a cross section of stocks, bonds, and/or other investments), small minimum investment (usually $1,000), automatic reinvestment of dividends and capital gains (funds typically do not charge a sales fee on automatic reinvestments), liquidity (shares are redeemable), and ability to switch among funds in an investment company's family of funds, usually at no fee.

The value of a mutual share is measured by net asset value (NAV), which equals:

$$\frac{\text{Funds' Total Assets} - \text{Total Liabilities}}{\text{Number of Shares Outstanding in the Fund}}$$

EXAMPLE 11.25

A fund owns 100 shares each of General Motors, Xerox, and IBM. On a particular day, the market values below existed. NAV equals:

GM @ $90 per share × 100 shares	$ 9,000
Xerox @ $100 per share × 100 shares	10,000
IBM @ $180 per share × 100 shares	18,000
Total Assets	$37,000
Less: Total Liabilities	2,000
Value of the fund's net portfolio	$35,000
Number of shares outstanding in the fund	1,000
Net asset value per share	$ 35

If you own 5% of the fund's outstanding shares, or 50 shares (5% × 1,000 shares), then the value of your investment is $1,750 ($35 × 50).

Mutual funds provide returns in the form of (1) dividend income; (2) capital gains distributions; and (3) change in NAV of the fund.

Mutual funds have different organizational structure, fees schedules, methods of trading, and investment objectives. With an *open-end* fund, you buy from, and sell shares back to, the fund itself. With a *closed-end* fund, there is a fixed number of shares outstanding, and they trade among individuals in secondary markets, just as does common stock. Most such funds consistently trade at less than their net asset values. All open- and closed-end funds charge management fees. Funds charging sales commissions are called *load* funds. *No-load* funds do not charge sales commissions.

The general categories of mutual funds are:

- *Money market funds.* Money market funds only invest in debt securities maturing within one year (e.g., CDs, commercial paper). These funds are safe because the $1 price never changes.
- *Aggressive growth funds.* Aggressive growth funds stress significant capital gain rather than current dividend income. Return is potentially high and there is risk. Investment may be made in upstart, and high-technology companies. An example

of aggressive stock funds are those investing in mid-size or small capitalization companies.

- *Growth funds.* Growth funds are aimed at long-term gains by investing in established companies which are anticipated to increase in price faster than the inflation rate. They are well suited if you want steady long-term growth and have little need for current income.
- *Income funds.* Income funds are suitable when a high level of dividend income is desired. Investment is typically in high quality bonds and stocks with consistent high dividends.
- *Growth and income funds.* Growth and income funds seek both current dividend income and capital gains. The purpose is to accomplish long-term growth without much variability in share price.
- *Balanced funds.* Balanced funds combine investments in common stock, bonds, and often preferred stock. The objective is to obtain income and some capital appreciation.
- *Bonds and preferred stock funds.* These funds invest in both bonds and preferred stock concentrating on income rather than growth. The funds just investing in bonds are called *bond funds*. The two types of bond funds are those that invest in corporate bonds and those that invest in municipal bonds. When interest rates are volatile, bond funds are subject to price fluctuation.
- *Index funds.* Index funds invest in a portfolio of corporate stocks, the composition of which is based on the Standard & Poor's 500 or some other index.
- *Sector (specialized) funds.* These are funds that invest in one or two fields or industries. They are risky in that they rise and fall depending on how the particular field or industry is performing.
- *International funds.* International funds invest in corporate stocks and bonds traded on foreign exchanges. These funds provide sizable gains when foreign stock prices are rising and the value of the dollar is falling. Some international funds invest in only one region, such as Fidelity Europe or Canada Fund. Other funds invest broadly overseas such as T. Rowe Price's International Stock Fund.
- *Global funds.* Global funds diversify in corporate stocks and bonds traded on all exchanges including the United States and foreign exchanges. This achieves maximum diversification.
- *Target-date funds for retirement.* Relative newcomers to the investing scene, catching on big-time, with assets nearly tripling to $33 billion over the past 2½ years. The funds are usually available in 5- or 10-year increments from 2007 to 2050. The fund then invests your retirement money in a diversified blend of stocks, bonds, and cash that has a risk/return profile appropriate for someone your age—heavier in stocks if you're

young, heavier in bonds and cash if you're older.
- *Exchange-Traded Fund (ETF)*. A security, rather than a mutual fund, that tracks an index, a commodity, or a basket of assets like an index fund, but trades like a stock on an exchange, thus experiencing price changes throughout the day as it is bought and sold. Because it trades like a stock whose price fluctuates daily, an ETF does not have its net asset value (NAV) calculated every day like a mutual fund does.

Comparing target funds

Asset allocations, expenses and underlying investments can vary dramatically depending on which target fund you choose. As this comparison of large retail funds designed for an investor in his or her late forties to early fifties shows, Vanguard offers the most conservative mix and the lowest expenses.

Fund	Asset mix	Annual expenses	What it invests in
T. Rowe Price Retirement 2020	80% stocks 20% bonds	0.81%	10 actively managed T. Rowe Price funds and the firm's S&P 500 index fund
Fidelity Freedom 2020	72% stocks 28% bonds	0.87%[1]	18 actively managed mutual Fidelity funds
Barclays LifePath 2020	66% stocks 34% bonds	1.1%[2]	Index funds and "enhanced" index portfolios that strive to beat their benchmark
Wells Fargo Outlook 2020	66% stocks 34% bonds	1.25%[2] or 2%[3]	6 portfolios that replicate standard indexes
Vanguard Target Retirement 2025	60% stocks 40% bonds	0.23%	4 Vanguard index funds

Notes: [1]Reflects an expense waiver of 0.02%. [2]Reflects an expense waiver of 0.34%; LifePath funds in a 401(k) would have expenses of 0.85%, which also reflects a waiver of 0.34%. [3]Expenses vary depending on share class of fund and reflect a waiver of 0.02% or 0.03%; Outlook shares in a 401(k) would have expenses of 0.95%. **Source:** The funds.

Real Estate Opportunities

Types of real estate investment include:

- Undeveloped land
- Residential rental property
- Commercial property
- Real estate investment trust (REIT)

Advantages of investing in real estate are the tax deductibility of interest payments and depreciation (if commercial property), inflation hedge, equity buildup, and leverage. Leverage means you are maximizing your return with other people's money. For example, if you buy a house and make a down payment of 10% and borrow 90%, you can benefit from all the 100% appreciation even though you only put down 10% of your own money. Disadvantages of owning real estate are high transaction costs (e.g., brokerage commissions, closing fees, mortgage points), negative cash flow with little down (too much leverage), a high lump sum payment that may be due at the end of the loan (balloon payment), limited marketability, inability to meet mortgage payments resulting in forfeiture, and management headaches (e.g., unreliable tenants, high management fees).

In deciding upon a real estate investment, consideration should be given to location, method of financing, before-tax cash flow, after-tax cash flow, vacancy rate for rental property, gain or loss for tax purposes, and management problems.

Real Estate Investment Trusts (REITS). REITs are corporations that operate much like closed-end mutual funds investing in diversified real estate or mortgage portfolios. Their shares trade on the stock exchanges. By law, REITs have to distribute 95% of their net earnings to shareholders, and in turn they are exempt form corporate taxes on income or gains.

There are three kinds of REITs. Equity REITs invest mostly in income-producing properties. Mortgage REITs lend funds to developers or builders. Hybrid REITs do both. Generally, equity REITs are the safest.

Advantages of REITs are dividend income with competitive yields, potential appreciation in price, liquidity, and portfolio diversification. Disadvantages of REITs are market risk and low safety.

Valuing Income-Producing Property. There are a number of rules of thumb to determine the estimated value of income producing property including:

$$\text{Gross income multiplier} = \frac{\text{Purchase price}}{\text{Gross rental income}}$$

EXAMPLE 11.26

The purchase price of commercial real estate is $300,000 and the gross annual rental income is $30,000. Thus, the gross income multiplier is 10.

However, this approach has to be used with caution. Different properties have different operating expenses which must be taken into account in determining a property's value.

$$\text{Net income multiplier} = \frac{\text{Purchase Price}}{\text{Net operating income}}$$

Capitalization rate is the reciprocal of the net income multiplier, and is most often used. It equals:

$$\frac{\text{Net Operating Income}}{\text{Purchase Price}}$$

EXAMPLE 11.27

The Claridge Arms apartment house has a net operating income of $18,000 and a purchase price of $300,000. The capitalization rate for property is 6% ($18,000/$300,000). Whether this property is overpriced or not depends on the rate of similar property in the marketplace. Suppose the market rate is 9%. That means the fair market value of similar property is $200,000 ($18,000/.09). Thus, the Claridge is overvalued.

Using Leverage When Investing in Real Estate. Leverage increases the reward for investing but greater risk is taken. Leverage can result in big yields with small dollars. High-leveraged investing in real estate is especially powerful when inflation is in full swing. High-leverage investors may make good returns because property values increase faster than the interest charges on their borrowed money.

EXAMPLE 11.28

Investor Z pays a seller $100,000 cash for property. During the next year, the property appreciates 20%. The $20,000 gain is a 20% yield on Z's investment. But suppose Z had put down only 10% and mortgaged the balance. At an interest rate of 12% on the mortgage, the interest charge is $10,000 (12% × $90,000). Now Z's return on investment leaps to an astonishing 92%, as shown below:

$$\frac{\text{Return}}{\text{Investment}} = \frac{\$9,200}{\$10,000} = 92\%$$

There are pitfalls of high-leveraged real estate investing that have to be taken into account including:
- Property values can decline as well as increase. Some types of real estate in some part of the country have experienced sharp value declines. An example is Texas.
- Look out for negative cash flow. Income from highly leveraged property may be insufficient to cover operating expenses and debt payments.

- Watch out for deferred maintenance. You can avoid hidden costs and potential future expenditure by bargaining for a fair price and reasonable terms.

Investing in Precious Metals

Precious metals are a hedge against inflation and an opportunity to diversify holdings. However, this type of investment does not produce current income and is generally viewed as a defensive investment.

Gold and silver are highly volatile tangible assets in that price movements often run counter to events in the economy and the world. Bad news is good news (and vice versa) for precious metal investors.

Life Insurance Strategy

An integral part of a financial plan is insurance protection. The type and amount of insurance you require depends on your age, assets, income, and needs.

Life Insurance. There are two basic types of life insurance policies—term insurance and whole life insurance. All other kinds of policies are variations of them.

Term Insurance. Offers protection for your family for a stated time period. It pays a benefit only if the insured dies during the policy period. There is a level premium rate for the set period after which the policy ceases, except when renewed or changed to some other form of policy. It is the cheapest form of life insurance and has a low initial premium. The policy may be renewable and/or convertible. The premium rises with each new term. *Tip:* It is appropriate for young people who want large amounts of insurance, those who desire only death protection, and those whose insurance need will decrease over time. *Warning:* Term rates increase as the insured ages. Many people in fact discontinue needed coverage because of the increasing cost.

Whole Life Insurance. Provides insurance protection by paying a fixed premium throughout the insured's life. Besides death protection, there is a savings element called "cash value." As the policies mature, they develop cash values representing the early surplus plus investment earnings. Advantages of whole life insurance are: (1) uninsurability at a later date will not terminate the policy; (2) the policy can be cashed in; and (3) interest on cash value is tax-deferred until the policy is surrendered. Disadvantages of whole life insurance are: (1) interest rate on cash value is typically less than going market rates; and (2) there are large up-front commissions and startup expenses. Whole life policies are most appropriate for those seeking lifetime coverage and desiring a structured savings plan.

There are many variations to whole life insurance, including universal life, variable life, single-premium whole life, adjustable life, and adjustable-premium life. For example, universal life combines term insurance and a tax-deferred savings plan that pays a flexible interest (e.g., interest tied to a 90-day Treasury bill). Variable life provides lifetime protection with level premiums. The cash value is invested in a combination of stocks, bonds, or money-market funds. There is a guaranteed minimum rate, and the policyholder has the investment risk.

Single-premium whole life (SPWL) is a policy with a low-risk investment flavor. For a minimum amount of $5,000, paid once, you obtain a paid-up insurance policy. Your money is invested at a guaranteed interest rate for one year or longer. Advantages of SPWL are that the cash value earns interest, you may borrow against the interest, you may take out a loan for up to 90% of the principal at lower rates, you receive permanent life insurance coverage, there is a tax-deferred accumulation of cash values and tax-free death benefits to named beneficiaries, and withdrawals and loans are not subject to tax. Disadvantages of SPWL are the surrender charges and the fluctuating interest rate, which is typically guaranteed for only one year.

When comparing whole life policies, you should consider load charges, investment return, death benefits, net annual premiums, guaranteed cash value growth, insurance costs, policy loan rates, cost index numbers, cash surrender values and charges, and medical requirements.

There are basically two approaches to computing the amount of insurance needed. Under the *multiple-of-income* approach, multiply gross annual income by some selected number (e.g., a number typically between five and ten depending on your particular needs). For example, if gross annual income is $40,000 and the multiplier is seven, the insurance coverage should be $280,000. Under the *needs approach,* you subtract your accumulated assets from your total financial needs to determine the required life insurance.

Planning for Retirement

Two major sources of retirement income are company-sponsored and individual plans. Company-sponsored plans include qualified company retirement plans, profit-sharing plans, 401(K) salary-reduction plans, tax-sheltered annuities (TSA), employee stock ownership plans (ESOP), and simplified employee pension plans

(SEP). Individual retirement plans include IRAs, Keoghs, and annuities.

With a *qualified company retirement plan,* the IRS allows a corporate employer to make contributions to the retirement plan. *Qualified* means it meets specified criteria in order that contributions to the plan can be deducted from taxable income. The investment income of the plan accumulates untaxed.

In a *profit-sharing plan,* the company makes a contribution only when it earns a profit. The retirement benefit is highly uncertain.

A *401(K) salary reduction plan* defers a portion of an employee's salary for retirement.

A *tax-sheltered annuity (TSA)* is for an employee of a non-profit institution. It is similar to a 401(K), but the employee can withdraw funds at any age for any reason without tax penalty. Of course, ordinary taxes must be paid on all withdrawals.

An *employee stock ownership plan (ESOP)* is a stock bonus plan. Employer contributions are tax deductible.

A *simplified employee pension plan (SEP)* allows the employer to make annual contributions on the employee's behalf to an IRA set up by the employee.

Individual Retirement Plans. We now turn our attention to individually sponsored plans, comprised of individual retirement account (IRA), Keogh, and annuities.

In an *IRA,* the employees make contributions to their own established plans. The contributions not only grow tax-free but are also tax deductible, partly deductible, or not deductible, depending on your income. The amount of the contributions is adjusted annually based on inflation.

A *Keogh* plan is for a *self-employed* individual who may contribute as much as 25% of his or her net income, whichever is less. It is subject to an annual limitation, which is adjusted annually based on inflation.

An *annuity* is a savings account with an insurance company or other investment company. The individual makes either a lump-sum deposit or periodic payments to the company and at retirement will receive regular payments for a specified time period. All of the contributions build up tax free, though the money is taxed when withdrawn. The two basic types of annuities are *fixed rate* and *variable*. In a *fixed annuity,* the company guarantees the principal plus a minimum rate of interest. In a *variable annuity,* the company invests in common stock, bonds, and money market instruments. Thus, the investment value fluctuates with the performance of these investments. You bear the risk of the investment options.

Credit Card Accountability, Responsibility, and Disclosure Act of 2009

The Act, also called the Credit Card Act of 2009, is a federal law passed by the U.S. Congress and signed by President Barack Obama on May 22, 2009. It aims to protect consumers from the credit card issuers' practices of increasing rates and fees. The key provisions are:

1. The Credit Card Act of 2009 requires credit card companies to now notify a cardholder 45 days before any change such as a rate or fee increase occurs. In the past they had to give only 15 days notice.
2. The credit card companies must now mail out the credit card bill so that the cardholder receives the bill 21 days before the due date. This is an increase from the 14 days in the past and is designed to allow for postal delivery times.
3. Cardholders now have the option to opt out of a rate increase.
4. Rate increases can only be applied toward new purchases as long as the card is not past due 60 days. If the card is past due 60 days then the credit card company can go back and retroactively apply the new rate increase to purchases. If for six months the minimum payments are made on time after that, then the rate must be brought back to the original interest rate. Applicants under 21 will also have more restrictions on whether they can be approved for a credit card.

Affordable Care Act

On March 23, 2010, the Patient Protection and Affordable Care Act was signed into law. The Act, commonly referred to as the Affordable Care Act (ACA) requires individuals to obtain qualifying health care coverage beginning in 2014. Failure to obtain coverage will result in the imposition of a tax penalty.

The penalty is equal to the greater of (1) a flat dollar amount or (2) an applicable percentage of household income in excess of the federal income tax return filing threshold.

The flat dollar amount is the lesser of (1) the total of the applicable dollar amounts for all individuals for whom a taxpayer is liable or (2) 300% of the applicable dollar amount.

Tax Year	Applicable Dollar Amount	Applicable Percentage
2014	$ 95	1.0%
2015	$325	2.0%
2016	$695	2.5%

It should be noted that the penalty is prorated based on the number of months for which minimum essential coverage is not maintained.

Individuals may be exempt from the coverage requirements under certain circumstances, such as financial hardship or religious objection.

Standards in Personal Financial Planning Services

In 2014, the American Institute of Certified Public Accountants (AICPA) issued "Statement on Standards in Personal Financial Planning Services," applicable to its members.

The AICPA standards, which provide authoritative guidance, are designed to ensure that a CPA financial planner serves the best interests of clients and the public.

General Professional Responsibilities. AICPA members must comply with the requirements specified in the pronouncement, unless (1) the requirement is not relevant because it is conditional, and the condition is not present, or (2) there is reasonable justification for the departure (which is documented), and alternative procedures are performed.

If an attest engagement is performed in addition to a personal financial planning (PFP) engagement, it is important for the practitioner to maintain independence.

Responsibilities of Members in PFP Engagements. In order to perform PFP engagements, members should:

1. Comply with applicable ethical requirements.
2. Possess appropriate levels of (a) knowledge of PFP principles and theory and (b) skill.
3. Ascertain whether conflicts of interest exist that could impair objectivity, which in turn might require termination of the engagement.
4. Comply with laws and regulations.
5. Disclose in writing all compensation to be received for services to be performed or products sold.

Planning the PFP Engagement. The following should be documented and communicated to the client:

1. The scope and nature of the services to be performed, including the objectives and timing of the engagement, the responsibilities of the client and the practitioner, and any scope limitations.
2. The agreed-upon compensation.
3. Changes to the original engagement.

Obtaining and Analyzing Information. Professional judgment should be used when obtaining and analyzing information needed to make appropriate suggestions. When analyzing information, the member should evaluate the reasonableness and consistency of significant estimates and assumptions.

Developing and Communicating Recommendations. Members should:

1. Obtain a reasonable basis for recommendations.
2. Analyze and document relevant information, client goals, and client overall financial circumstances.
3. Document and communicate to the client (a) significant estimates and assumptions, (b) recommendations, and (3) limitations of the services performed.

Implementation Engagements. When assisting a client in implementing recommendations, a member should:

1. Document the understanding reached with the client as to member and client responsibilities.
2. Communicate the evaluation of product recommendations.
3. Disclose in writing compensation received for product recommendations.

Monitoring and Updating Engagements. A monitoring engagement involves tracking and communicating client progress in meeting PFP goals. An updating engagement involves making changes to an existing personal financial plan. A member should document the nature, extent, and timing of both monitoring and updating engagements.

Working with Other Service Providers. A member is allowed to refer a client to another service provider. Before doing so, the member should:

1. Determine the qualifications of the service provider.
2. Disclose, in writing, any referral fees.
3. Communicate, in writing, the extent of the member's evaluation of the work of the service provider.

Using Advice Provided by Other Service Providers. Before using the advice of another service provider, a member should comprehend the impact of advice provided. Concurrence with the service provider's advice need not be communicated to the client. A member's failure to concur with the service provider, however, should be communicated to the client in writing.

Brief Summary

Personal financial planning allows individuals to make decisions based on particular circumstances and needs in order to accomplish personal goals. One must always consider the relationship between return and risk. Key areas of personal financial planning include personal financial statements, budgeting, personal banking, debt management, cost reduction, investing in stocks and bonds, mutual funds, investing in real estate and precious metals, life insurance, and pension plans.

WEBSITES

1. Certified Financial Planning Board – *www.cfp-board.org*
2. CFA Institute – *www.cfainstitute.org*

Chapter 12

Governmental and Nonprofit Accounting

This chapter discusses governmental and nonprofit accounting and how it differs from commercial accounting. The dividing line between business and nonbusiness organizations is not always clear, depending on the incidence and relative importance of the "nonbusiness" characteristics found in an entity. Examples of "nonbusiness organizations" are governmental entities (city, county, state, and federal), colleges and universities, hospitals, and many cultural and charitable organizations that derive most of their support from grants and contributions, rather than through fees charged to users. These organizations provide many of the services our society considers essential, do not seek to make a profit, and are generally financed through taxes or donations. These funds are usually earmarked for specific purposes and must be used in accordance with laws, regulations, or contractual requirements.

CHARACTERISTICS OF NONBUSINESS ORGANIZATIONS

Nonbusiness organizations generally have no single indicator of performance such as profit or net income. Two performance indicators for nonbusiness organizations include:

1. Information about the nature and relationship between inflows and outflows of resources.
2. Information about service efforts and accomplishments.

The following are some features distinguishing a nonbusiness organization from a for-profit organization:

1. They receive significant amounts of resources from providers who do not expect to receive either repayment or economic benefits proportionate to resources provided.

---

* The authors gratefully acknowledge the assistance of Professor Dianand Terry Balkaran in reviewing and editing this chapter.

2. Their primary operating purposes are other than to provide goods or services at a profit or profit equivalent.
3. They do not have defined ownership interests that can be sold, transferred, or redeemed, or that convey entitlement to a share of a residual distribution of resources in the event of liquidation of the organization.

These features can be spelled out as follows:

1. No part of any excess of revenues over expenditures is distributed to those who contributed support through taxes or voluntary contributions.
2. There is neither a profit motive nor an expectation of earning net income, other than providing goods or services that fulfill a social need.
3. Any excess of revenues over expenditures that results from operations in the short run is ordinarily used in later years to further the purposes of the organization.
4. The performance of nonbusiness organizations is usually not subject to direct competition in markets as is that of business enterprises.

Thus, other controls such as budgets are used to ensure efficient and effective operation.

The objective of financial reporting is accountability to the public rather than investors. The accounting equation associated with nonprofit accounting is: assets = accountability.

The accounting systems for nonbusiness organizations must provide financial data to internal management for use in planning and controlling operations and to external parties, such as taxpayers and contributors, for use in determining the effectiveness of operations. Furthermore, the systems should include mechanisms (1) to ensure that management observes the restrictions imposed upon it by law, charter, or by-laws; and (2) to provide for reports—that is, financial statements—to taxpayers, members, donors, and contributors that such restrictions have been satisfied. For these reasons, a nonbusiness organization typically applies the concept of *fund accounting* in conjunction with a budget and appropriations method and *encumbrance accounting* to account for the assets and revenues received by the organization and to ensure that expenditures are made only for authorized purposes.

In this chapter, the fundamental reporting objective and principles of governmental accounting will be presented. We also summarize the accounting and reporting principles applicable to various types of nonbusiness organizations—including hospitals, colleges and universities, voluntary health and welfare organizations, and other nonprofit organizations.

GOVERNMENTAL ACCOUNTING

Features of Governmental Entities

Governmental entities differ from other nonprofit and nonbusiness organizations in many respects:

1. *Service.* Governmental entities are established to render services to a group of constituents.
2. *Taxes as source of revenue.* The principal source of revenue for governmental entities is taxes levied on their constituents.
3. *Dependence on legislative authorities and controls.* Governmental entities generally operate under very detailed and specific legal restrictions as to the sources and financial resources they may utilize, the amounts they may raise from each source, and the uses they may make of the proceeds from each source. In the absence of neither a profit motive nor an expectation of achieving surplus, they are subjected to a variety of restrictions and controls. A major restriction is on the use of resources—which led to *fund accounting*—and exercise of expenditure control through the annual budget—which led to *budgetary accounting.*
4. *Responsibility to constituents.* Governmental entities have the responsibility of demonstrating good stewardship over financial resources provided and entrusted to them by the citizenry.

Governmental Generally Accepted Accounting Principles (GAAP)

The objectives of financial reporting should be the basis for determining specific accounting principles to be used by a governmental entity. There are 11 principles of accounting and reporting applicable to municipal governments, developed by the National Council on Governmental Accounting (NCGA). These principles and concepts are summarized below as stated in NCGA Statement 1 (Governmental Accounting and Financial Reporting Principles).

Principle 1: Accounting and Reporting Capabilities. A governmental accounting system must make it possible both (a) to present fairly and with full disclosure the financial position and results of financial operations of the funds and account groups of the governmental unit in conformity with generally accepted accounting principles; and (b) to determine and demonstrate compliance with finance-related legal and contractual provisions.

Principle 2: Fund Accounting Systems. A specific governmental unit is not accounted for through a single accounting entity. Instead, the accounts of a government are divided into several funds and nonfund account groups. The NCGA defines a fund as "a fiscal and accounting entity with a self-balancing set of accounts recording cash and other financial resources, together with all related liabilities and residual equities and balances, and changes therein, which are segregated for the purpose of carrying on specific activities or attaining certain objectives in accordance with special regulations, restrictions, or limitations."

Principle 3: Types of Funds and Account Groups. NCGA recommends the following categories and types of funds and account groups:

Governmental Funds: are used to finance "general government" activities such as police and fire protection, courts, inspection, and general administration. Most of their financial resources are subsequently budgeted (appropriated) for specific "general government" uses (expenditures) by the legislative body. Governmental funds include:

(a) The General Fund, used to pay the regular operating and administrative expenses not properly accounted for in other funds.

(b) The Special Revenue Fund, used to account for the proceeds of specific revenue sources (other than expendable trusts or those for major capital projects) that are legally restricted to expenditure for specified purposes; examples of special revenue funds are those established for the purpose of financing schools, parts, or libraries.

(c) The Capital Projects Fund, used to account for financial resources earmarked for the acquisition or construction of major capital facilities and improvements (other than those financed by proprietary funds and trust funds). Resources of the fund are derived from the proceeds of various bond issues and from other aid. The total cost of a capital project is accumulated until the project is completed, at which time the fund ceases to exist.

(d) Debt Service Fund, used to account for the payment of principal and interest on long-term general-obligation bond issues and other long-term debt.

The accounting equation of most governmental funds is:

$$\text{Current assets} - \text{Current liabilities} = \text{Fund balance}$$

Thus, governmental funds are essentially "working capital" funds, and their "operations" are measured in terms of sources and uses of working capital—that is, changes in working capital. *Account Groups* are memorandum "list and offset" (self-balancing) accounts that provide a record of "general government" fixed assets and long-term debt, which are not recorded in the governmental funds. There are two types of account groups:

(a) The General Fixed Assets Account Group (GFAAG) includes property and equipment owned by the governmental entity and specifically *not* associated with and carried into another fund (e.g., proprietary fund, trust fund). These fixed assets are of significant value, with a useful life extending beyond the year of acquisition, and are usually used in the conduct of the governmental unit's activities.

(b) The General Long-Term Debt Account Group (GLTDAG) includes those items of indebtedness where the date of maturity is more than one year after issuance and which are not appropriately accounted for within other governmental funds. At maturity, the funds are transferred to the debt-service fund. The long-term debt account group has only two assets: the "amount available in debt service funds" and the "amount to be provided for retirement of general long-term debt." As assets available in debt-service funds increase, the "amount to be provided" decreases, since fewer resources must be raised in the future.

The governmental funds and account groups, taken together, account for the "general government."

Proprietary Funds are used to finance a government's self-supporting "business-type" activities (e.g., utilities). Proprietary funds include:

(a) Enterprise Funds, used to account for operations that are financed and operated in a manner similar to private business enterprises, where the intent of the governing body is that the costs (expenses, including depreciation) of providing goods or services to the general public on a continuing basis be financed or recovered primarily through user charges, or operations where the governing body has decided that periodic determination of revenues earned, expenses incurred, and/or net income is appropriate for capital maintenance, public policy, management control, accountability, or other purposes. Proprietary funds have profit-and-loss motives.

(b) Internal Service Funds, to account for the financing of goods or services provided by one department or agency to other departments or agencies of the governmental unit, or to other governmental units, on a cost-reimbursement basis.

The accounting equation of proprietary funds is identical to that of a business corporation — it includes accounts for all related assets and liabilities, not just for current assets and current liabilities — as well as for contributed capital and retained earnings. Proprietary fund "operations" are measured in terms of revenues earned, expenses incurred, and net income or loss. Examples of internal service funds are maintenance and data processing.

Fiduciary Funds are used to account for resources (and related liabilities) held by governmental entities in a trustee capacity (trust funds) or as an agent for others (agency funds). Fiduciary funds include:

(a) Nonexpendable Trust Funds
(b) Expendable Trust Funds
(c) Pension Trust Funds
(d) Agency Funds

Expendable Trust Funds are accounted for in the same way as governmental funds are accounted for, and both Nonexpendable Trust Funds and Pension Trust Funds are accounted for in the same way as proprietary funds. Agency Funds are purely custodial (assets equal liabilities).

Principle 4: Number of Funds. A government should have only one General Fund, one General Fixed Asset Account Group, and one General Long-term Debt Account Group. It may have one, none, or several of the other types of funds, depending on its activities. Every governmental unit should establish and maintain those funds that are required by law and by sound financial administration. Having too many funds makes for inflexibility, undue complexity, and unnecessary expense in the accounting system and for inefficient financial management. Only the minimum number of funds consistent with legal and operating requirements should be established.

Principle 5: The Budget and Budgetary Accounting

(a) An annual budget should be adopted by every governmental unit, whether required by law or not.
(b) The accounting system should provide budgetary control over general governmental revenues and expenditures.

(c) Budgetary comparisons should be included in the appropriate financial statements and schedules for governmental funds for which an annual budget has been adopted.

Principle 6: Valuation of Fixed Assets. Fixed assets should be accounted for at original cost, or at the estimated cost if the original cost is not available, or, in the case of gifts, at the appraised value as of the time received.

Principle 7: Depreciation of Fixed Assets

(a) Depreciation of general fixed assets should not be recorded as an expense in governmental fund accounting. It may be recorded for cost-accounting and cost-analysis purposes.
(b) Depreciation of fixed assets accounted for in a proprietary fund should be recorded in the accounts of that fund. Depreciation is also recognized as an expense in those trust funds where expenses, net income, and/or capital maintenance are measured.

Principle 8: Basis of Accounting. The modified accrual or full accrual basis of accounting, as appropriate, should be utilized in determining financial position and operating results of a governmental entity. The *modified accrual* basis is defined as follows:

Revenues should be recognized in the accounting period in which they become available and measurable. Expenditures should be recognized in the accounting period in which the fund liability is incurred, if measurable, except for unmatured interest on general long-term debt and on special-assessment indebtedness secured by interest-bearing special-assessment levies, which should be recognized when due. (*Governmental Accounting and Financial Reporting Principles,* statement 1, p. 3.)

Proprietary fund revenues and expenses should be recognized on the accrual basis. Revenue is recognized when it is earned and becomes measurable; expenses are recognized in the period incurred.

Governmental fund revenues and expenditures should be recognized on the modified accrual basis. Revenues are recorded when received in cash, except for material and/or available revenues, which should be accrued to reflect the taxes levied and the revenues earned. Expenditures (other than accrued interest on general long-term debt) are recorded at the time liabilities are incurred.

Fiduciary fund revenues and expenditures should generally be recognized on the accrual basis. Nonexpendable Trust and Pension Trust Funds should be accounted for on the accrual basis. Expendable Trust Funds and Agency Fund assets and liabilities should be accounted for on the modified accrual basis.

Principle 9: Classification of Accounts. Governmental revenues should be classified by fund and source. Expenditures should be classified by fund, function, organization unit, activity, character, and principal classes of objects in accordance with standard recognized classification.

Principle 10: Common Terminology and Classification. A common terminology and classification should be used consistently throughout the budget, the accounts, and the financial reports.

Principle 11: Financial Reporting. Financial statements and reports showing the financial position, operating results, and other pertinent information should be prepared periodically to control financial operations. At the close of each fiscal year, a comprehensive annual financial report covering all funds and financial operations of the governmental unit should be prepared and published.

Table 12.1 shows a summary of fund accounting under NCGA Statement 1.

Difference Between Basis of Accounting and Measurement Focus

One particular concept that needs elaboration is *measurement focus.* Although this concept and basis of accounting are closely related, they are distinctly different. While the basis of accounting determines *when* transactions are recognized, the measurement focus determines *what* is measured (expenditures or expenses). The NAGA's clarification of the distinction between basis of accounting and measurement focus, as shown in Table 12.1, was necessary for more widespread understanding of the different purposes of governmental and proprietary fund type accounting and financial reporting and the types of information they provide.

EXAMPLE 12.1

To illustrate the distinction, assume that Leo's Trucking purchased a truck on November 4 and paid for it on November 14. The following journal entries indicate the appropriate accounting treatments, on both a spending-measurement focus and a capital-maintenance- (or cost-of-services-) measurement focus.

	Cash Basis	*Accrual Basis*
Spending-Measurement Focus		
Nov. 4	No entry	*(Dr.)* A capital-outlay expenditure account *(Cr.)* Accounts payable
Nov. 14	*(Dr.)* A capital-outlay expenditure account *(Cr.)* Cash	*(Dr.)* Accounts payable *(Cr.)* Cash
Capital-Maintenance- Measurement Focus		
Nov. 4	No entry	*(Dr.)* A fixed-asset account *(Cr.)* Accounts payable
Nov. 14	*(Dr.)* A fixed-asset account *(Cr.)* Cash	*(Dr.)* Accounts payable *(Cr.)* Cash

Governmental Fund Account Terminology

Most governmental fund accounting systems use both budgetary accounts and regular accounts. Budgetary accounts are nominal accounts used to record approved budgetary estimates of revenues and expenditures (appropriations). Regular accounts are used to record the actual revenues expenditures, and other transactions affecting the fund. Although terminology varies, the following accounts are usually employed in governmental funds:

Estimated revenues are the amounts of revenue estimated to accrue during a given period regardless of whether or not they are all to be collected during the period. The Estimated Revenues account is debited to record the revenue budget and is closed at the end of the period.

Appropriations are authorizations granted by a legislative body to incur liabilities for purposes specified in the Appropriation account. An appropriation is usually limited in amount and as to the time when it may be expended. The Appropriations account is credited to record the budgeted expenditures and is closed at the end of the period.

Revenues are additions to assets or decreases in fund liabilities (except from "other financing sources") that increase the residual equity of the fund. Note that governmental fund "revenues" differ from the commercial concept of revenues in that they often are "levied" (e.g., taxes) rather than "earned."

Other financing sources are nonrevenue increases in fund net assets and fund balance or equity. Examples are sources from certain interfund transfers and bond issue proceeds.

Expenditures are increases in liabilities or decreases in assets (except for "other financing uses") that decrease the equity of the fund. The term designates the cost of goods delivered or services rendered, whether paid or unpaid, including expenses, provision for debt retirement not reported as a liability of the fund from which retired, and capital outlays for general fixed assets.

Other financing uses are nonrevenue decreases in assets and fund balance. Examples include uses for interfund transfers.

Fund balance is the fund equity account that is the excess of the assets of a fund over its liabilities and reserves. It is similar to the owners' equity account of a commercial business enterprise, although it does not properly show any "ownership" in a fund's assets.

Fund balance reserve is a portion of the fund equity that must be segregated for some future use (for example, reserve for encumbrance) and that is, therefore, not available for further appropriation or expenditure (for example, reserve for inventories). The Reserve account is not a liability, but a reservation of Fund Balance similar to the appropriated retained earnings of a commercial enterprise. If a portion of the fund balance is designated as reserved, the balance should be reported as unreserved fund balance, or simply fund balance.

Encumbrance accounting is a system used in most governmental funds (General, Special Revenue, Capital Projects) to prevent overexpenditure and to demonstrate compliance with legal requirements. The term "encumbrance" is unique to governmental operations and has no counterpart in commercial accounting. Encumbrances are monies that have been set aside for a specific future purpose. They are not expenditures but are treated in almost the same way as expenditures in governmental accounting. To find out whether an entity is in a surplus or deficit situation for a particular period of time, the sum of expenditures and encumbrances must be subtracted from actual revenue earned.

If an entity obligates itself to pay for something, the amount needed to pay the obligation is set aside immediately and is no longer included in the balance of money available for new obligations. This type of system keeps the government from overspending, since it is always clear as to exactly how much money is available for new commitments. The estimated amount of the planned expenditure is "encumbered" by debiting encumbrances and crediting Reserve for Encumbrances. When the invoice is received, the encumbrance entry is reversed and the expenditure is recorded along with vouchers payable. Note the following relationships:

Appropriations – Expenditures = Unexpended balance

Unexpended balance – Encumbrances = Unencumbered balance

Table 12.1

SUMMARY OF FUND ACCOUNTING UNDER NCGA STATEMENT 1

Fund Type	Fund Categories (1)	Measurement Focus (3)	Basis of Accounting (7)	Primary Means of Spending Control (9)
General	Governmental	Spending (4)	Modified Accrual	Annual Operating Budget (8)
Special Revenue	Governmental	Spending (4)	Modified Accrual	Annual Operating Budget (8)
Debt Service	Governmental	Spending (4)	Modified Accrual	Bond Indentures
Capital Projects	Governmental	Spending (4)	Modified Accrual	Bond Indentures
Special Assessment	Governmental	Spending (4)	Modified Accrual	State Laws
Enterprise	Proprietary	Capital Maintenance (6)	Accrual	Modified Marketplace
Internal Service	Proprietary	Capital Maintenance (6)	Accrual	Indirect Budgetary
Trust and Agency:	Fiduciary			
Expendable Trust		Spending (4)	Modified Accrual	State Laws
Nonexpendable Trust		Capital Maintenance (6)	Accrual	State Laws
Pension Trust		Capital Maintenance (6)	Accrual	State Laws
Agency (2)			Modified Accrual	

(1) Statement 1 further classified 1968 GAAFR's eight fund types into three broad categories—governmental, proprietary, and fiduciary—and indicated that all are accounted for as either governmental or proprietary. Expendable Trust Funds are accounted for like governmental funds, while Nonexpendable Trust and Pension Trust Funds are accounted for like proprietary funds.
(2) Under Statement 1, Agency Funds are custodial in nature (assets equal liabilities) and do not involve measurement of results of operations.

(3) Statement 1 clarified the distinction between the accounting concepts of "measurement focus" and "basis of accounting." The "measurement focus" determines *what* is being measured (expenditures or expenses), while the "basis of accounting" determines *when* it is measured.

(4) All governmental funds and Expendable Trust funds are accounted for using a spending measurement focus. This means that only current assets and current liabilities are generally included on their balance sheets. Their fund balance (net current assets) is considered a measure of "available spendable resources." (The exception to this general rule is for long-term special assessment bonds payable, which are reported on Special Assessment Fund balance sheets.) Their operating statements present increases (revenues and other financing sources) and decreases (expenditures and other financing uses) in net current assets.

(5) Fixed assets used in governmental fund operations and long-term liabilities (other than special assessment bonds) expected to be financed from governmental funds are accounted for in the General Fixed Assets Account Group and the General Long-Term Debt Account Group, respectively.

(6) All proprietary funds and Nonexpendable Trust and Pension Trust Funds are accounted for using a capital maintenance measurement focus. This means that total assets and total liabilities associated with their operations are included on their balance sheets. Their fund equity (net total assets) is segregated into contributed capital and retained earnings components. Their operating statements present increases (revenues) and decreases (expenses) in net total assets.

(7) In Statement 1, the NCGA purposely coordinated the GAAP accounting and financial reporting treatments applied to all governmental funds on the one hand and to all proprietary funds on the other. In so doing, it shifted Capital Projects, Special Assessment, and Expendable Trust Funds from the accrual to the modified accrual basis of accounting.

(8) Under Statement 1, it is *a GAAP requirement* that governmental GAAP financial reports include comparisons of approved budgeted amounts with actual results of operations *on the budgetary basis actually used to control operations.* Such comparisons are required for the General Fund and Special Revenue Funds and other governmental funds for which annual budgets are legally adopted.

(9) Different primary means of spending control are employed in the various fund types. The most common primary means are indicated above. Capital projects funds may also involve grant requirements. Most Enterprise Funds involve revenue bond indentures.

Source: Municipal Finance Officers Association, *Governmental Accounting, Auditing, and Financial Reporting* (GAAFR), 1980, p. 10.

If funds are encumbered but not yet expended at the end of the period, the usual accounting treatment is to close the encumbrances account (i.e., credit Encumbrances, debit Fund Balance).

Encumbrances must be supported by either a purchase order or contract authorizing the reservation of a portion of the present year's appropriations.

A simple illustration of a balance sheet is presented in Table 12.2 for the general fund of a typical agency, ABC School District, highlighting concepts such as *fund balance* and *encumbrance*.

The statement of revenues, expenditures, and changes in fund balance of ABC School District is shown in Table 12.3.

The *basis of accounting* used in fund accounting depends on the nature of the fund. The *accrual basis* is used in proprietary (Enterprise and Internal Service) funds, where revenues and expenses are recorded and net income (loss) is reported. The accrual basis is also used in Nonexpendable Trust and Pension Trust Funds. The *modified accrual basis* is used in the governmental funds (General, Special Revenue, Capital Projects, and Debt Service Funds), and where revenues and expenditures are recorded and in Expendable Trust and Agency Funds.

NCGA Statement 1 offers these modified accrual basis guidelines:

a. Revenues are recorded as received in cash except for (1) revenues "susceptible to accrual" and (2) revenues of a material amount that have not been received at the normal time of receipt. (1) Revenues are considered "susceptible to accrual" at the time they become both measurable and available for use. (2) "Available" means collected or collectible within the current period or early enough in the next period (e.g., within 60 days or so) to be used to pay for expenditures incurred in the current period. (3) If revenue-related assets (e.g., taxed receivable) are not "available," a Deferred Revenue account should be credited initially; when the assets become "available," the Deferred Revenue account is debited and Revenue is credited.
b. Expenditures are recorded when fund liabilities are incurred or assets are expended, except: (1) Inventory items may be recorded as expenditures either (a) at the time of purchase or (b) at the time the items are used. (2) Expenditures normally are not allocated between years by the recording of prepaids (e.g., a two-year insurance policy). (3) Interest on general long-term debt, usually accounted for in Debt Service Funds, normally should be recorded as an expenditure on its due date rather than being accrued prior to its due date.

Table 12.2

ABC SCHOOL DISTRICT
Balance Sheet
Governmental Fund
August 31, 2015

	General	Federal Programs	Capital Projects	Other Governmental Funds	Total Governmental Funds
ASSETS					
Cash and cash equivalents					$ –
Investments					
Receivables, net					
Due from other funds					
Receivables from other governments					
Inventories					
Total assets					
LIABILITIES AND FUND BALANCES					
Liabilities:					
Accounts payable					
Due to other funds					
Payable to other governments					
Deferred revenue					
Total liabilities					

Fund balances:

Reserved for:

Inventories

Encumbrances

Debt service

Other purposes

Unreserved

Unreserved, reported in nonmajor:

Special revenue funds

Capital projects funds

Total fund balances

Total liabilities and fund balances $ — $ — $ — $ —

Amounts reported for *governmental activities* in the statement of net assets (A-1) are different because:

Capital assets used in governmental activities are not financial resources and therefore are not reported in the funds.

Other long-term assets are not available to pay for current-period expenditures and therefore are deferred in the funds.

Internal service funds are used by management to charge the costs of certain activities, such as insurance, to individual funds. The assets and liabilities of certain internal service funds are included in governmental activities in the statement of net assets.

Some liabilities, including bonds payable, are not due and payable in the current period and therefore are not reported in the funds.

Net assets of governmental activities $ —

Table 12.3

ABC SCHOOL DISTRICT
Balance Sheet
Governmental Fund
August 31, 2015

	General	Federal Programs	Capital Projects	Other Governmental Funds	Total Governmental Funds
REVENUES					
5700 Local and intermediate sources					$ —
5800 State program revenues					
5900 Federal program revenues					
Total revenues					
EXPENDITURES					
Current:					
11 Instruction					
12 Instructional resources and media services					
13 Curriculum and staff development					
21 Instructional leadership					
23 School leadership					
31 Guidance, counseling, and evaluation services					
32 Social work services					
33 Health services					

34 Student transportation
36 Extracurricular activities
41 General administration
51 Plant maintenance and operations
52 Security and monitoring services
53 Data processing services
61 Community services
62 School district admin. support services
71 Principal on long-term debt
71 Interest on long-term debt
80 Capital outlay
91 Contracted instructional services between schools
92 Incremental costs related to WADA
93 Payments related to shared services arrangements
94 Payments to other school districts under the Public Education Grant Program
95 Payments to Juvenile Justice Alternative Education Programs
96 Payments to charter schools
97 Payments to Tax Increment Fund
Total expenditures
Excess (deficiency) of revenues over expenditures

Table 12.3 (continued)

ABC SCHOOL DISTRICT
Balance Sheet
Governmental Fund
August 31, 2015

	General	Federal Programs	Capital Projects	Other Governmental Funds	Total Governmental Funds
OTHER FINANCING SOURCES (USES)					
7911 Refunding bonds issued					
7911 Capital-related debt issued					
8030 Payment to bond refunding escrow agent					
7915 Transfers in					
8911 Transfers out					
Total other financing sources and uses					
SPECIAL ITEM					
7951 Proceeds from sale of land					
Net change in fund balances					
Fund balances—beginning					
Fund balances—ending	$ —	$ —	$ —	$ —	$ —

Table 12.4

ABC SCHOOL DISTRICT
Statement of Net Assets
August 31, 2015

	Primary Government			Component Unit
	Governmental Activities	Business-type Activities	Total	
ASSETS				
Cash and cash equivalents		$ —		
Investments				
Property taxes receivables (net)				
Due from other governments				
Accrued interest				
Other receivables (net)				
Internal balances				
Capital assets:				
Land				
Infrastructure, net				
Building, furniture, and equipment, net				
Construction in progress				
Total assets				

Table 12.4 (continued)

ABC SCHOOL DISTRICT
Statement of Net Assets
August 31, 2015

| | Primary Government | | | Component Unit |
	Governmental Activities	Business-type Activities	Total	
LIABILITIES				
Current liabilities:				
Accounts payable				
Due to other funds				
Compensated absences				
Claims and judgments				
Bonds, notes, and loans payable				
Noncurrent liabilities:				
Compensated absences				
Claims and judgments				
Bonds, notes, and loans payable				
Total liabilities				

Table 12.4 (continued)

ABC SCHOOL DISTRICT

Statement of Net Assets

August 31, 2015

	Primary Government			Component Unit
	Governmental Activities	Business-type Activities	Total	
NET ASSETS				
Invested in capital assets, net of related debt				
Restricted for:				
Capital projects				
Debt service				
Campus activities				
Federal and state programs				
Unrestricted	$ —	$	$	$
Total net assets	$	$ —	$	$ —

Table 12.5

ABC SCHOOL DISTRICT
Statement of Activities for the year ended August 31, 2015

		Program Revenues			Net (Expense) Revenue and Changes in Net Assets		
						Primary Government	
Expenses	Indirect Expenses Allocation	Charges for Services	Operating Grants and Contributions	Capital Grants and Contributions	Governmental Activities	Business-type Activities	Total
					$_____		$_____

General revenues:

Taxes:

Property taxes, levied for general purposes

Property taxes, levied for debt service

State aid-formula grants

Grants and contributions not restricted to specific programs

Investment earnings

Miscellaneous

Special item—gain on sale of land

Transfers

Total general revenues, special items, and transfers $ —

Change in net assets $ —

Net assets—beginning $ —

Net assets—ending $ —

Fund Structure. Governmental financial operations are built around funds and account groups, each of which is considered to be a separate accounting entity. More precisely, a fund is an independent fiscal and accounting entity in the sense that it accounts for a sum of money set aside for a particular purpose separately from the other monies of the government. Note that this definition has two key parts: a fund is an entity with a sum of money set aside for a purpose; and a fund is accounted for separately.

Each fund is self-balancing; each has its own assets, liabilities, and fund balance (equity), and the classification and recording of each financial transaction (that is, each entry to the ledger) must satisfy the accounting equation.

The basic reason for using funds is to control the handling of money to ensure that funds will be spent only for purposes intended. One example of a fund is a capital project fund. Money obtained from the sale of various bonds would be put into this fund and used only for the purpose for which the bonds were sold (acquisition or construction of capital facilities). The fund, therefore, ties the money to a particular purpose and requires that the money provided for that purpose be accounted for through a separate set of books or accounts.

GASB Statement No. 34 (Government Accounting Standards Board)

GASB Statement No. 34 sets forth the accounting and financial reporting requirements for general-purpose outside financial reporting by state and local governments, including standards for management's discussion and analysis, the basic financial statements, and supplementary information. Management's discussion and analysis introduces the basic financial statements and furnishes analytical overview of the government's financial activities. Government-wide financial statements show data concerning the reporting government as a whole except for its fiduciary affairs. These statements have separate columns for the governmental and business-type activities of the primary government and component units. Fund financial statements for the primary government's governmental, proprietary, and fiduciary funds are shown after the governmentwide financial statements. These statements present data about the major funds individually and nonmajor funds in the aggregate for governmental and enterprise funds. After the footnotes to the financial statements should be presented supplementary information including budgetary comparison information.

Management's discussion and analysis should include a brief discussion of the basic financial statements along with relationships between the statements, condensed financial information comparing the present year to the previous year, analysis of whether the financial position has gotten better or worse, and an appraisal of balances and transactions of individual funds.

Government-wide financial statements show information for the overall government without presenting individual funds or fund types. Government-wide financial statements should be based on accrual accounting.

Fund financial statements should be used to report detailed information about the primary government. Governmental fund reporting emphasizes the sources, uses, and balances of current financial resources and typically has a budgetary emphasis. Proprietary fund reporting concentrates on operating income determination, changes in net assets, financial position, and cash flows. Fiduciary fund reporting focuses on net assets and changes in net assets.

Capital assets are reported at historical cost. Donated capital assets are shown at fair market value plus ancillary charges.

A distinction should be made between fund long-term liabilities and general long-term liabilities.

In the government-wide statement of net assets, assets and liabilities may be presented in the order of liquidity. Net assets should be displayed in the following three components:

- Invested in capital assets, net of associated debt
- Restricted net assets
- Unrestricted net assets

The government-wide statement of activities presents government activities in a format reporting the net expense or revenue of its individual functions. At a minimum, the statement of activities should present government activities by function. Business-type activities should be shown at least by segment. Direct expenses should be reported by function. Three categories of program revenues should be reported in the statement of activities as follows:

- Charges for services
- Program-specific grants and contributions (operating and capital)
- Earnings on endowments or permanent fund investments

General revenues should be reported after total net expense (revenue) of the government's functions.

The focus of governmental and proprietary financial statements is on major funds. The general fund should always be reported as a major fund. Governmental fund financial statements should be presented using the current financial resources management focus and the modified accrual basis of accounting. Proprietary fund financial statements should be based on accrual accounting and include a statement of net assets or balance sheet; a statement of revenues, expenses, and change in fund net assets; and a statement of cash flows.

Governmental Accounting Standards Board Statement No. 34
Basic Financial Statements—and Management's Discussion and Analysis—for State and Local Governments (www.gasb.org)

Purpose

The primary purpose of GASB Statement No. 34, Basic Financial Statements—and Management's Discussion and Analysis—for State and Local Governments, is to establish a basic financial reporting model:

To provide more relevant information that will result in greater accountability by state and local governments, and

To enhance the understandability and usefulness of the annual financial reports to the users of these reports, to enable them to make more informed economic, social, and political decisions.

The Statement integrates the traditional focus of government fund financial statements, relating to fiscal accountability and the modified accrual basis of accounting, with new forms of reporting to meet users' needs for longer-term financial information, and to ensure that the operational accountability objective of governments is fulfilled.

Fund Financial Statements

Governmental Fund Financial Statements

Under GASB Statement No. 34, governmental fund financial statements (including financial data for the general fund and special revenue, capital projects, debt service, and permanent funds) should be prepared using the current financial resources measurement focus and the modified accrual basis of accounting. Under this measurement focus and basis of accounting, revenues should be recognized in the accounting period in which they become available and measurable and expenditures should be recognized in the accounting period in which the fund liability is incurred, if measurable, except for unmatured interest on general long-term debt, which should be recognized when due.

Proprietary Fund Financial Statements

Proprietary fund financial statements (including financial data for enterprise and internal service funds) should be prepared using the economic resources measurement focus and the accrual basis of accounting. Accordingly, revenues should be recognized in the accounting period in which they are earned and become measurable, and expenses should be recognized in the period incurred, if measurable.

Fiduciary Fund Financial Statements

Like proprietary fund financial statements, fiduciary fund financial statements (including financial data for fiduciary funds and similar component units) should be prepared using the economic resources measurement focus and the accrual basis of accounting. Revenues should be recognized in the accounting period in which they are earned and become measurable, and expenses should be recognized in the period incurred, if measurable.

Table 12.6

Measurement Focus and Basis of Accounting for Financial Statements

Financial Statements	Measurement Focus	Basis Accounting
Government-Wide Financial Statements	Economic Resources	Accrual
Governmental Funds Financial Statements	Current Financial Resources	Modified Accrual
Proprietary Funds Financial Statements	Economic Resources	Accrual
Fiduciary Funds Financial Statements	Economic Resources	Accrual

Contents

The focus of the MD&A should be on the primary government; however, information on the component units could be presented as well. GASB has stated that both the positive and negative aspects of the government's operations should be presented so that the reader can conclude whether the government is better off or worse off than in the prior year.

The following is a list of required information that should be included and addressed, at a minimum, in the MD&A as modified by TEA. MD&A is restricted to the following topics, although there is no limit to the information that may be presented about these topics.

Information and discussion on the basic financial statements presented, their relationship to one another, and the significant differences in the information they provide. The discussion could include the different methods of accounting utilized in the government-wide and fund financial statements.

Condensed financial information comparing current year to prior year. The analysis should include specific economic factors that contributed to the change from the prior year. Charts and graphs may be used to supplement information in the condensed statements but should not be used in place of them.

Objective analysis of the district's financial condition as a whole. Analysis of the government's overall financial position and results of operations should address both governmental and business-type activities separately.

An analysis of balances and transactions on a fund basis addressing the reasons for significant changes in fund balances or fund net assets. The analysis should also include information on whether restrictions, commitments, or other limitations significantly affect the availability of fund resources for future use.

Basic Financial Statements

The basic financial statements include:

- Government-wide Financial Statements
- Fund Financial Statements

Notes:
These statements replace the combined statements of the general purpose financial statements (GPFS) required by the former reporting model. Districts are required to present both the government-wide and the fund financial statements as basic financial statements. Additionally, government-wide statements should not be combined with fund financial statements.

A discussion on significant variances between the district's original budget, final budget, and actual expenditures, and the impact of these variances on the government's future liquidity.

A description of activity relating to the district's capital assets and long-term debt activity during the year. This discussion should include commitments made for capital expenditures, changes in credit ratings, and debt limitations affecting the financing of planned facilities or services.

A description of currently known facts, decisions or conditions expected to impact the district's financial position and results of operation. The term "currently known" is limited to events or decisions that have occurred, been enacted, adopted, agreed upon, or contracted as of the date of the auditor's report. The discussion should address expected effects on both governmental and business-type activities.

Information that does not address the above requirements should not be included in the MD&A but could be reported as supplementary information or could be included in the letter of transmittal.

Government-Wide Financial Statements

The purpose of government-wide financial statements is to present the financial position and the operating results of the district as a whole. The statements are expected to provide users with operational accountability information and to enable them to:

Understand the true financial position of the district, including capital and financial assets and long term as well as short term liabilities.

Determine if the district is able to continue to provide current service levels and meet liabilities as they become due.

Determine the operating results of the district, including the economic cost and the net cost of services, and assess the economy, efficiency, and effectiveness of operations.

The government-wide financial statements include:

Statement of Net Assets

Statement of Activities

NONPROFIT ORGANIZATIONS AND FINANCIAL REPORTING

Accounting and reporting standards applicable to nonprofit organizations are quite similar to the standards for governmental units. There often exists segregations of activities by fund. Table 12.7 presents a summary in terms of the basis of accounting used, related major pronouncements, and fund types of nonprofit organizations.

Table 12.7

BASIS OF ACCOUNTING, MAJOR PRONOUNCEMENT AND FUND TYPES OF NONPROFIT ORGANIZATIONS

Nonprofit Organizations	Basis of Accounting and Major Pronouncements	Fund Types
Hospitals	Primarily accrual basis American Hospital Association (AHA) AICPA Hospital Audit Guide	General Funds (Unrestricted Funds) Operating Fund Board-Designated Funds Restricted Funds Specific-Purpose Funds Endowment Funds Plant Repl. and Expansion Funds
Colleges and Universities	Accrual basis with some modifications National Association of College and University Business Officers AICPA Audits of Colleges and Univ.	Current Fund Unrestricted Restricted Loan Funds Endowment and Similar Funds Annuity and Life Income Funds Plant Funds Agency Funds
Voluntary Health and Welfare Organizations	Primarily accrual basis AICPA Audit and Accounting Guide	Operating Funds Unrestricted Restricted Endowment Funds Plant Funds

ASC 958-605; 720-25; 605-10

Nonprofit organizations record unconditional pledges as assets and revenue when made, even though the actual cash is still not received. For an unrestricted grant, advance payments must be reported in revenue as received. Reimbursement grants are recognized as revenue when reimbursements are due. Unrestricted or restricted contributions are recorded at fair market value as revenue or gains when received with the associated asset recognition or decrease in liabilities depending on the nature of the benefit received.

The pronouncement allows for a gift of a long-lived asset to be treated as unrestricted revenue in the year received.

All pledges (short-term and long-term) are time restricted until collected. Thus, time-restricted pledges are presented in the temporarily restricted class of net assets in the balance sheet. When collected, pledges are reclassified to unrestricted net assets in the balance sheet; donors use the same guidelines for expense recognition of making a gift as recipients do for the income. It is accrued at the time of the unconditional pledge.

Note: Restricted contributions are not deferred until the restriction is met.

Footnote disclosure should be made of the nature of the restriction and the amount of contribution required.

FASB Statement No. 117 (Financial Statements of Nonprofit Organizations) (ASC 958-205)

The financial statements must focus on the organization as an integrated whole. Presenting information by fund is no longer required. However, NPOs will continue fund accounting for internal purposes.

External reports issued by NPOs must conform to GAAP. For external reporting, NPOs must prepare the following financial statements:

- Statement of Financial Position (Balance Sheet)
- Statement of Activities
- Statement of Cash Flows

Presentation and reporting must be made of donor-imposed restrictions.

Unrestricted net assets may be used for any purpose because they are not restricted by donors. Temporarily restricted net assets have a donor restriction because they are to be used for a particular purpose. The restriction or condition may be satisfied through the passage of time or organizational action. Permanently restricted net assets are resources having donor restrictions providing that the resources must be maintained permanently but allowing the organization to use all or part of the income derived from the donated assets. The donor restrictions are permanent in that they never can be satisfied and never cease. Financial reports should show how resources, whether restricted or unrestricted, were used.

The Statement of Financial Position presents assets based on their nearness to cash and liabilities based on maturity dates. As an alternative, NPOs may show the balance sheet classified as current and noncurrent. It is recommended that there be a total column for assets, liabilities, and net assets (fund balance). A presentation should be made of the total change in net assets for all classes (unrestricted, restricted, and permanently restricted).

The prior practice of presenting financial statements for only certain funds has been eliminated. Fund accounting will continue to be used for internal reporting only. NPOs can continue to report financial position by fund provided the net assets are shown as either unrestricted or restricted.

Unrealized losses on noncurrent investments are to be presented in the Statement of Activities after the "excess of revenue over expenses" line.

Expenses must be reported in the unrestricted class of net assets, regardless of the financing source. Expenses cannot be presented in the temporarily or permanently restricted classes. NPOs must report expenses by functional categories (management, fund-raising, program).

A Statement of Cash Flows must be prepared. Restricted cash flows must be indicated.

If an NPO is allowed to buy goods or services at a lower price than typical, the seller is in effect giving the buyer a gift for the difference between the prevailing market value and the price charged. For example, if a charity purchases an item for $700 that sells for $950, the contribution is $250.

Tables 12.8–12.11 present the 2013 financial statements of American Red Cross.

Table 12.8

THE AMERICAN NATIONAL RED CROSS

Consolidated Statement of Financial Position

June 30, 2013
(with comparative information as of June 30, 2012)

(In thousands)

Assets		2013		2012
Current assets:				
Cash and cash equivalents	$	82,721	$	52,905
Investments (Note 8)		618,139		626,872
Trade receivables, including grants, net of allowance for				
doubtful accounts of $6,963 in 2013 and $5,657 in 2012 (Note 11)		233,089		216,517
Contributions receivable (Note 2)		80,303		70,011
Inventories, net of allowance for obsolescence of $4,714				
in 2013 and $4,105 in 2012		112,950		113,876
Other current assets		23,230		24,922
Total current assets		1,150,432		1,105,103
Investments (Note 8)		1,466,762		1,356,851
Contributions receivable (Note 2)		12,205		16,030
Land, buildings, and other property, net (Note 3)		1,018,454		1,050,793
Other assets (Note 9)		250,982		249,184
Total assets		3,898,835		3,777,961
Liabilities and Net Assets				
Current liabilities:				
Accounts payable and accrued expenses		325,810		281,012
Current portion of debt (Note 4)		18,236		14,400
Postretirement benefits (Note 10)		3,734		3,991
Other current liabilities (Note 9 and 11)		154,398		164,121
Total current liabilities		502,178		463,524
Debt (Note 4)		695,755		538,958
Pension and postretirement benefits (Note 10)		554,645		1,001,636
Other liabilities (Notes 4 and 9)		156,200		178,620
Total liabilities		1,908,778		2,182,738
Net assets (Notes 6 and 7):				
Unrestricted net assets		398,444		133,687
Temporarily restricted net assets		861,605		757,513
Permanently restricted net assets		730,008		704,023
Total net assets		1,990,057		1,595,223
Commitments and contingencies (Notes 4, 5, 8, 10, and 11)				
Total liabilities and net assets	$	3,898,835	$	3,777,961

See accompanying notes to the consolidated financial statements.

Table 12.9

THE AMERICAN NATIONAL RED CROSS

Consolidated Statement of Activities

Year ended June 30, 2013
(with summarized information for the year ended June 30, 2012)

(In thousands)

	Unrestricted	Temporarily Restricted	Permanently Restricted	Totals 2013	Totals 2012
Operating revenues and gains:					
Contributions:					
Corporate, foundation and individual giving	$ 278,866	$ 552,132	$ -	$ 830,998	$ 437,768
United Way and other federated	32,905	62,625	-	95,530	100,227
Legacies and bequests	64,022	10,191	22,011	96,224	94,629
Services and materials	16,212	38,290	-	54,502	37,424
Products and services:					
Biomedical	2,037,732	-	-	2,037,732	2,153,870
Program materials	125,153	-	-	125,153	136,876
Contracts, including federal government	73,132	-	-	73,132	82,552
Investment income (Note 8)	16,781	31,916	-	48,697	58,100
Other revenues	73,575	398	-	73,973	69,071
Net assets released from restrictions	636,997	(636,997)	-	-	-
Total operating revenues and gains	3,355,375	58,555	22,011	3,435,941	3,170,517
Operating expenses:					
Program services:					
Services to the Armed Forces	56,645	-	-	56,645	53,045
Biomedical services (Note 12)	2,164,815	-	-	2,164,815	2,239,784
Community services	57,200	-	-	57,200	77,538
Domestic disaster services	467,245	-	-	467,245	279,190
Health and safety services	216,222	-	-	216,222	195,596
International relief and development services	92,742	-	-	92,742	186,726
Total program services	3,054,869	-	-	3,054,869	3,031,879
Supporting services:					
Fund raising	189,431	-	-	189,431	172,407
Management and general	136,283	-	-	136,283	140,847
Total supporting services	325,714	-	-	325,714	313,254
Total operating expenses	3,380,583	-	-	3,380,583	3,345,133
Change in net assets from operations	(25,208)	58,555	22,011	55,358	(174,616)
Nonoperating gains (losses) (Notes 4 and 8)	42,670	45,537	3,974	92,181	(36,514)
Pension-related changes other than net periodic benefit cost (Note 10)	247,295	-	-	247,295	(385,570)
Change in net assets	264,757	104,092	25,985	394,834	(596,700)
Net assets, beginning of year	133,687	757,513	704,023	1,595,223	2,191,923
Net assets, end of year	$ 398,444	$ 861,605	$ 730,008	$ 1,990,057	$ 1,595,223

See accompanying notes to the consolidated financial statements.

Table 12.10

THE AMERICAN NATIONAL RED CROSS

Statement of Functional Expenses

Year ended June 30, 2013
(with summarized information for the year ended June 30, 2012)

(In thousands)

	Program Services						
	Services to Armed Forces	Biomedical Services	Community Services	Domestic Disaster Services	Health and Safety Services	International Relief & Development Services	Total Program Services
Salaries and wages	$ 25,439	$ 930,432	$ 20,971	$ 94,331	$ 89,853	$ 19,093	$ 1,180,119
Employee benefits	8,460	309,418	6,974	31,370	29,881	6,350	392,453
Subtotal	33,899	1,239,850	27,945	125,701	119,734	25,443	1,572,572
Travel and maintenance	2,067	34,031	877	62,112	6,496	3,580	109,163
Equipment maintenance and rental	859	69,246	2,899	21,662	1,920	1,156	97,742
Supplies and materials	1,744	483,630	3,196	6,941	12,222	494	508,227
Contractual services	10,192	298,438	10,031	67,883	69,821	7,877	464,242
Financial and material assistance	6,751	3,564	10,058	170,947	25	53,366	244,711
Depreciation and amortization	1,133	36,056	2,194	11,999	6,004	826	58,212
Total expenses	$ 56,645	$ 2,164,815	$ 57,200	$ 467,245	$ 216,222	$ 92,742	$ 3,054,869

	Supporting Services			Total Expenses	
	Fund Raising	Management and General	Total Supporting Services	2013	2012
Salaries and wages	$ 80,071	$ 73,329	$ 153,400	$ 1,333,519	$ 1,328,117
Employee benefits	26,628	24,386	51,014	443,467	400,334
Subtotal	106,699	97,715	204,414	1,776,986	1,728,451
Travel and maintenance	5,455	2,928	8,383	117,546	75,088
Equipment maintenance and rental	1,103	3,458	4,561	102,303	104,162
Supplies and materials	4,096	33	4,129	512,356	541,692
Contractual services	67,628	29,769	97,397	561,639	582,402
Financial and material assistance	1,503	334	1,837	246,548	234,413
Depreciation and amortization	2,947	2,046	4,993	63,205	78,925
Total expenses	$ 189,431	$ 136,283	$ 325,714	$ 3,380,583	$ 3,345,133

See accompanying notes to the consolidated financial statements.

Table 12.11

THE AMERICAN NATIONAL RED CROSS

Consolidated Statement of Cash Flows

Year ended June 30, 2013
(with comparative information for the year ended June 30, 2012)

(In thousands)

	2013	2012
Cash flows from operating activities:		
Change in net assets	$ 394,834	$ (596,700)
Adjustments to reconcile change in net assets to net cash used in		
operating activities:		
Depreciation and amortization	63,205	78,925
Provision for doubtful accounts receivable	1,195	2,954
Provision for obsolete inventory	610	2,930
Net gain on sales of property	(4,965)	(938)
Net investment and derivative (gain)/loss	(86,778)	24,784
Pension related changes other than net periodic benefit costs	(247,295)	385,570
Permanently restricted contributions	(22,011)	(34,748)
Changes in operating assets and liabilities:		
Receivables	(24,234)	(1,971)
Inventories	316	9,576
Other assets	(106)	(17,434)
Accounts payable and accrued expenses	44,798	(52,211)
Other liabilities	(27,943)	(35,949)
Pension and postretirement benefits	(199,953)	(52,077)
Net cash used in operating activities	(108,327)	(287,289)
Cash flows from investing activities:		
Purchases of property	(39,035)	(55,299)
Proceeds from sales of property	13,134	4,464
Purchases of investments	(320,896)	(277,416)
Proceeds from sales of investments	302,296	281,058
Net cash used in investing activities	(44,501)	(47,193)
Cash flows from financing activities:		
Permanently restricted contributions	22,011	34,748
Proceeds from borrowings	175,000	-
Repayments of debt	(14,367)	(20,023)
Net cash provided by financing activities	182,644	14,725
Net increase (decrease) in cash and cash equivalents	29,816	(319,757)
Cash and cash equivalents, beginning of year	52,905	372,662
Cash and cash equivalents, end of year	$ 82,721	$ 52,905
Supplemental disclosures of cash flow information:		
Cash paid during the year for interest	$ 17,903	$ 18,950

See accompanying notes to the consolidated financial statements.

Chapter 13

International Accounting and International Financial Reporting Standards (IFRS)

International business is a rapidly growing dimension. Advances in communication and transportation have enabled businesses to service a world market. There are numerous opportunities for companies to increase their markets by expanding overseas. Many large companies (as well as smaller ones) can now evaluate in which countries, rather than in which markets in a single country, they should conduct their business.

The basic business functions (i.e., finance/accounting, production, management, marketing) take on a new perspective when conducted in a foreign environment. There are different laws, political framework, social/cultural factors, and economic policies that all have an effect on how business is to be conducted in that foreign country. The biggest mistake a company can make is to not be aware (or to ignore) that these differences do exist, and that these differences need to be an integral part of formulating their international business plan.

This chapter will outline the issues surrounding the convergence between U.S. GAAP and International Financial Reporting Standards (IFRS). Especially, it examines IFRS differences affecting both the statement of financial position and the income statement.

INTRODUCTION: ACCOUNTING DIMENSIONS OF INTERNATIONAL BUSINESS

As we proceed further into the twenty-first century, the world economy is ever more internationalized and globalized. Advances in information technology, communications, and transportation have enabled businesses to service a world market. Many U.S. companies, both large and small, are now heavily engaged in international trade. The foreign operations of many large U.S. multinational corporations now account for a major percentage (10% to 50%) of their sales and/or net income.

The basic business functions (i.e., finance/accounting, production, management, marketing) take on a new perspective when conducted in a foreign environment. There are different laws, economic policies, political framework, and social/cultural factors that all have an effect on how business is to be conducted in that foreign country. From an accounting standpoint, global business activities are faced with three realities:

1. Accounting standards and practices differ from country to country. Accounting is a product of its own economic, legal, political, and sociocultural environment. Because this environment changes from country to country, the accounting system of each country is unique and different from all others.
2. Each country has a strong "accounting nationalism." It requires business companies operating within its borders to follow its own accounting standards and practices. Consequently, a foreign company operating within its borders must maintain its books and records and prepare its financial statements in the local language, use the local currency as a unit of measure, and be in accordance with local accounting standards and procedures. In addition, the foreign company must comply with the local tax laws and government regulations.
3. Cross-border business transactions often involve receivables and payables denominated in foreign currencies. During the year, these foreign currencies must be translated (converted) into the local currencies for recording in the books and records. At year-end, the foreign currency financial statements must be translated (restated) into the parent's reporting currency for purposes of consolidation. Both the recording of foreign currency transactions and the translation of financial statements require the knowledge of the exchange rates to be used and the accounting treatment of the resulting translation gains and losses.

The biggest mistake a company can make in international accounting is to not be aware of, or even worse, to ignore these realities. It should know that differences in accounting standards, tax laws, and government regulations do exist; and that these differences need to be an integral part of formulating their international business plan.

FOREIGN CURRENCY EXCHANGE RATES

Exchange rates are used to convert one currency into another currency. An exchange rate is the price of one currency in terms of another currency, i.e., the amount of one currency that must be given to buy one unit of another currency. Because U.S. firms have to prepare their financial statements in U.S. dollars, we shall focus on foreign currency exchange rates in terms of U.S. dollars.

Foreign currency exchange rates are quoted daily in the financial press. Two different rates are quoted for each day:

- A direct quote, which is the amount in U.S. dollars of one unit of foreign currency:

    1 British pound = U.S. $ 1.5505

- An indirect quote, which is the amount of foreign currency equivalent to 1 U.S. dollar:

    U.S. $1 = 0.6450 British pound

The above quotes are called spot rates, which are rates quoted for transactions to be settled within two business days. For some major currencies, forward rates are also quoted for future delivery (30- day, 60-day, 180-day forward) of the foreign currency.

Currencies are bought and sold like other goods. Under the current system of floating exchange rates, foreign exchange rates, like stock prices, are constantly fluctuating, depending on the forces of supply and demand. Because current exchange rates are both volatile and unpredictable, international business transactions are subject to the additional risk of exchange rate fluctuations.

Accounting for Foreign Currency Transactions

International business transactions are cross-border transactions; therefore, two national currencies are usually involved: the currency of the buyer and the currency of the seller. For example, when a U.S.

corporation sells to a corporation in Germany, the transaction can be settled in U.S. dollars (the seller's currency) or in Euros (the buyer's currency).

Transactions Denominated in U.S. Currency

When the foreign transaction is settled in U.S. dollars, no measurement problems occur for the U.S. corporation. As long as the U.S. corporation receives U.S. dollars, the transaction can be recorded in the same way as a domestic transaction.

EXAMPLE 13.1

A U.S. firm sells on account equipment worth $100,000 to a German company. If the German company will pay the U.S. firm in U.S. dollars, no foreign currency is involved and the transaction is recorded as usual:

Accounts Receivable	100,000	
Sales		100,000

To record sales to German company

Transactions Denominated in Foreign Currency

However, if the transaction above is settled in Euros, the U.S. corporation will receive foreign currency that must be translated into U.S. dollars for purposes of recording on the U.S. company's books. Thus, a foreign currency transaction exists when the transaction is settled in a currency other than the company's home currency.

A foreign currency transaction must be recorded in the books of accounts when it is begun (date of transaction), then perhaps at interim reporting dates (reporting date), and finally when it is settled (settlement date). On each of these three dates, the foreign currency transaction must be recorded in U.S. dollars, using the spot rate on that date for translation.

Accounting at Transaction Date. Before any foreign currency transaction can be recorded, it must be first translated into the domestic currency, using the spot rate on that day. For the U.S. company, this means that any receivable and payable denominated in a foreign currency must be recorded in U.S. dollars.

EXAMPLE 13.2

Assume a U.S. firm purchases merchandise on account from a French company on December 1, 2014. The cost is 50,000 euros, to be paid in 60 days. The exchange rate for euros on December 1 is $1.26. Using the exchange rate on December 1, the U.S. firm translates the €50,000 into $63,000 and records the following entry:

Dec. 1	Purchases	63,000	
	Accounts Payable		63,000

To record purchase of merchandise on account (€50,000 × $1.26 = $63,000).

Accounting at Interim Reporting Date. Foreign currency receivables and payables that are not settled at the balance sheet date are adjusted to reflect the exchange rate at that date. Such adjustments will give rise to foreign exchange gains and losses that are to be recognized in the period when exchange rates change.

EXAMPLE 13.3

Assume that on December 31, 2014, the exchange rate for the euro is $1.27. The U.S. firm will make the following adjusting entry:

Dec. 31	Foreign Exchange Loss	500	
	Accounts Payable		500

To adjust accounts payable to current exchange rate (€50,000 × $1.27 = $63,500; $63,500 − $63,000 = $500)

Accounting at Settlement Date. When the transaction is settled, if the exchange rate changes again, the domestic value of the foreign currency paid on the settlement date will be different from that recorded on the books. This difference gives rise to translation gains and losses that must be recognized in the financial statements.

EXAMPLE 13.4

To continue our example, assume that on February 1, 2014, the exchange rate for the euro is $1.265. The settlement will be recorded as follows:

Feb. 1   Accounts Payable   63,500*
             Cash   63,250
             Foreign Exchange Gain   250
          To record payment of accounts payable
          (€50,000 × $1.265 = $63,250)
          foreign exchange gain.
          *€56,000 × $1.27 = $63,500

To summarize: In recording foreign currency transactions, SFAS 52 adopted the two-transaction approach. Under this approach, the foreign currency transaction has two components: the purchase/sale of the asset and the financing of this purchase/sale. Each component will be treated separately and not netted with the other. The purchase/sale is recorded at the exchange rate on the day of the transaction and is not adjusted for subsequent changes in that rate. Subsequent fluctuations in exchange rates will give rise to foreign exchange gains and losses. They are considered as financing income or expense and are recognized separately in the income statement in the period the foreign exchange fluctuations happen. Thus, exchange gains and losses arising from foreign currency transactions have a direct effect on net income.

Translation of Foreign Currency Financial Statements

When a U.S. firm owns a controlling interest (more than 50%) in another firm in a foreign country, special consolidation problems arise. The subsidiary's financial statements are usually prepared in the language and currency of the country in which it is located and in accordance with the local accounting principles. Before these foreign currency financial statements can be consolidated with the U.S. parent's financial statements, they must first be adjusted to conform with U.S. GAAP and then translated into U.S. dollars.

Two different procedures may be used to translate foreign financial statements into U.S. dollars: (1) translation procedures and (2) remeasurement procedures. Which one of these two procedures is to be used depends on the determination of the functional currency for the subsidiary.

The Functional Currency

SFAS 52 defines the functional currency of the subsidiary as the currency of the primary economic environment in which the subsidiary operates. It is the currency in which the subsidiary realizes its cash flows and conducts its operations. To help management determine the functional currency of its subsidiary, SFAS 52 provides a list of six salient economic indicators regarding cash flows, sales price, sales market, expenses, financing, and intercompany transactions. Depending on the circumstances:

- The functional currency can be the local currency. For example, a Japanese subsidiary manufactures and sells its own products in the local market. Its cash flows, revenues, and expenses are primarily in Japanese yen. Thus, its functional currency is the local currency (Japanese yen).
- The functional currency is the U.S. dollar. For foreign subsidiaries that are operated as an extension of the parent and integrated with it, the functional currency is that of the parent. For example, if the Japanese subsidiary is set up as a sales outlet for its U.S. parent, i.e., it takes orders, bills and collects the invoice price, and remits its cash flows primarily to the parent, then its functional currency would be the U.S. dollar.

The functional currency is also the U.S. dollar for foreign subsidiaries operating in highly inflationary economies (defined as having a cumulative inflation rate of more than 100% over a three-year period). The U.S. dollar is deemed the functional currency for translation purposes because it is more stable than the local currency.

Once the functional currency is determined, the specific conversion procedures are selected as follows:

- Foreign currency is the functional currency—use translation procedures.
- U.S. dollar is the functional currency—use remeasurement procedures.

Translation Procedures

If the local currency is the functional currency, the subsidiary's financial statements are translated using the current rate method. Under this method:

- all assets and liabilities accounts are translated at the current rate (the rate in effect at the financial statement date);
- capital stock accounts are translated using the historical rate (the rate in effect at the time the stock was issued);
- the income statement is translated using the average rate for the year; and
- all translation gains and losses are reported on the balance sheet, in an account called "Cumulative Translation Adjustments" in the stockholders' equity section.

The purpose of these translation procedures is to retain, in the translated financial statements, the financial results and relationships among assets and liabilities that were created by the subsidiary's operations in its foreign environment.

EXAMPLE 13.5

To illustrate, suppose that the following trial balance, expressed in the local currency (LC) is received from a foreign subsidiary, XYZ Company. The year-end exchange rate is 1 LC = $1.50, and the average exchange rate for the year is 1 LC = $1.25. Under the current rate method, XYZ Company's trial balance would be translated as follows:

Table 13.1
TRANSLATION PROCEDURES
XYZ COMPANY
TRIAL BALANCE
12/31/2014

	Local Currency		Exchange Rate	U.S. Dollars	
	Debit	Credit		Debit	Credit
Cash	LC 5,000		(1 LC = $1.50)	$7,500	
Inventory	15,000		"	22,500	
Fixed Assets	30,00		"	45,000	
Payables		LC 40,000	"		$60,000
Capital Stock		4,000	Historical rate		5,000
Retained			to balance		
Earnings		6,000	(1 LC = $1.25)		10,000
Sales		300,000			375,000
Cost of					
Goods Sold	210,000		"	262,500	
Depreciation					
Expense	5,000		"	6,250	
Other					
Expenses	85,000		"	106,250	
	LC 350,000	LC 350,000		$450,000	$450,000

Table 13.1 shows the translation procedures applied to XYZ Company's trial balance. Note that the translation adjustment is reflected as an adjustment of stockholders' equity in U.S. dollars.

Remeasurement Procedures. If the U.S. dollar is considered to be the functional currency, the subsidiary's financial statements are then remeasured into the U.S. dollar by using the temporal method. Under this method:

- monetary accounts, such as cash, receivable, and liabilities, are remeasured at the current rate on the date of the balance sheet;
- nonmonetary accounts, such as inventory, fixed assets, and capital stock, are remeasured using the historical rates;
- revenues and expenses are remeasured using the average rate, except for cost of sales and depreciation expenses that are remeasured using the historical exchange rates for the related assets; and
- all remeasurement gains and losses are recognized immediately in the income statement.

The objective of these remeasurement procedures is to produce the same U.S. dollar financial statements as if the foreign entity's accounting records had been initially maintained in the U.S. dollar. Table 13.2 shows these remeasurement procedures applied to XYZ Company's trial balance. Note that the translation gain/loss is included in the income statement.

Table 13.2
REMEASUREMENT PROCEDURES
XYZ COMPANY
TRIAL BALANCE
12/31/2014

	Local Currency		Exchange Rate	U.S. Dollars	
	Debit	Credit		Debit	Credit
Cash	LC 5,000		(1 LC = $1.50)	$7,500	
Inventory	15,000		(1 LC = $1.30)	19,500	
Fixed Assets	30,000		(1 LC = $0.95)	28,500	
Payables		LC 40,000	(1 LC = $1.50)		$60,000
Capital Stock		4,000			5,000
Retained Earnings		6,000			7,000
Sales		300,000	(1 LC = $1.25)		375,000
Cost of Goods Sold	210,000		(1 LC = $1.30)	273,000	
Depreciation Expense	5,000		(1 LC = $0.95)	4,750	
Other Expenses	85,000		(1 LC = $1.25)	106,250	
				439,500	447,000
Translation Gain/Loss				7,500	
	LC 350,000	LC 350,000		447,000	447,000

Interpretation of Foreign Financial Statements

To evaluate a foreign corporation, we usually analyze the financial statements of the foreign corporation. However, the analysis of foreign financial statements needs special considerations:

1. We often have the tendency of looking at the foreign financial data from a home country perspective. For example, a U.S. businessman has the tendency of using U.S. Generally Accepted Accounting Principles (GAAP) to evaluate the foreign financial statements. However, U.S. GAAP are not universally recognized and many differences exist between U.S. GAAP and the accounting principles of other countries (industrialized or nonindustrialized).
2. Because of the diversity of accounting principles worldwide, we have to overcome the tendency of using our home country GAAP to evaluate foreign financial statements. Instead, we should try to become familiar with the foreign GAAP used in the preparation of these financial statements and apply them in our financial analysis.
3. Business practices are culturally based. Often they are different from country to country and have a significant impact on accounting measurement and disclosure practices. Therefore, local economic conditions and business practices should be taken into consideration to correctly analyze foreign financial statements.

Harmonization of Accounting Standards

The diversity of accounting systems is an obstacle in the development of international trade and business and the efficiency of the global capital markets. Many concerted efforts have been made to reduce this diversity through the harmonization of accounting standards. Also, as international business expands, there is a great need for international accounting standards that can help investors make decisions on an international scale. The agencies working toward the harmonization of accounting standards are as follows.

A. The International Accounting Standards Board (IASB). The International Accounting Standards Board, based in London, began operations in 2001, taking over from the former part-time IASC founded in 1973. It is funded by contributions from the major accounting firms, private financial institutions, and industrial companies throughout the world, central and development banks, and other international and professional organizations. The 14 Board members (12 of whom are full-time) reside in nine countries and have a variety of functional backgrounds. The IASB is committed to developing, in the public interest, a single set of high-quality, global accounting standards that require transparent and comparable information in general purpose financial statements. In pursuit of this objective, the IASB cooperates with national accounting standards-setters to achieve convergence in accounting standards around the world. For more information about the IASB, visit its Website at *www.iasb.org.*

B. International Financial Reporting Standards (IFRS)

IASB has a conceptual framework underlying its financial reporting standards and interpretations, the Framework for the Preparation and Presentation of Financial Statements. The Framework sets out the concepts that underlie the preparation and presentation of financial statements for external users. This involves International Financial Reporting Standards, International Accounting Standards, and Interpretations issued on or before March 31, 2004. IASB publishes its Standards in a series of pronouncements called International Financial Reporting Standards (IFRS). It has also adopted the body of Standards issued by the Board of the International Accounting Standards Committee (IASC). Those pronouncements continue to be designated "International Accounting Standards" (IAS). IASB publishes a series of Interpretations of International Accounting Standards developed by the International Financial Reporting Interpretations Committee (IFRIC) and approved by the IASB.

C. Convergence of the FASB and IASB

The Financial Accounting Standards Board (FASB) and International Accounting Standards Board (IASB) are committed to crafting one set of accounting standards. The goal of the convergence project is to unify accounting standards, which, in turn, should improve comparability of financial statements across national jurisdictions. Financial reporting in the United States is being influenced by International Financial Reporting Standards (IFRS). IFRS reporting considerations are already impacting business decisions, and not simply through non-U.S. subsidiaries. IFRS are used in many parts of the world, including the European Union, Hong Kong, Australia, Malaysia, Pakistan, Gulf Cooperation Council (GCC) countries, Russia, South Africa, Singapore, and Turkey. Many countries around the world, including all of Europe, currently require or permit IFRS reporting.

U.S. GAAP vs. IFRS

For several years, major accounting and reporting differences have existed between U.S. GAAP and international reporting standards. However, in a 2002 Memorandum of Understanding between the Financial Accounting Standards Board (FASB) and the International Accounting Standards Board (IASB), commonly known as the "Norwalk Agreement," two accounting standard-setting bodies made a firm commitment to develop high-quality accounting standards that converge. In effect, this effort has been a movement toward a globalization of accounting standards. Since the Norwalk Agreement, the FASB and IASB have issued new standards that closely converge and revised many existing ones in order to attain a near-uniform set of accounting standards. While the challenge for practitioners is to learn and eventually implement this new set of global accounting standards, the benefits of a single set of worldwide standards is expected to produce financial reporting that is more comparable, transparent, and achieves greater understandability.

U.S. companies registered with the Securities and Exchange Commission (SEC) are currently required to file financial statements in accordance with U.S. generally accepted accounting principles (GAAP). Foreign private issuers are allowed to issue financial statements in accordance with IFRS without footnote reconciliation to U.S. GAAP. On August 27, 2008, the SEC voted unanimously to adopt a "road map" for conversion of accounting standards. The SEC road map to U.S. convergence to IFRS has had many obstacles. To date, convergence is not a certainty.

In an effort to better understand how convergence will affect financial reporting in the United States if and when IFRS are fully adopted, this chapter examines some of the material differences that currently exist between U.S. GAAP and IFRS.

REQUIRED FINANCIAL STATEMENTS AND STRUCTURAL DIFFERENCES IN PRIMARY FINANCIAL REPORTING

Financial statements required under U.S. GAAP and IFRS are largely similar. IFRS require a statement of financial position similar to U.S. GAAP, an income statement, a statement of changes in equity or a statement of recognized income and expense (reported as a separate financial statement), statement of cash flows, and disclosure notes including a summary of significant accounting policies. Under U.S. GAAP, comprehensive income and changes in equity are reported as a separate financial statement (allowable under IFRS—and is reported as a statement of changes in equity) or reported in the notes to the financial statements (not allowed under IFRS). However, U.S. GAAP allows for a combined statement of income and comprehensive income, which is not allowed under IFRS.

Unlike U.S. GAAP, IFRS require comparative information on each financial statement for the preceding period only, with the option of providing additional years of comparable reporting. SEC registrants are required to present current and prior years' information on the balance sheet, while other financial statements are required to report three years of comparable results.

In addition, with regard to consolidated financial reporting, under U.S. GAAP, the parent firm must present consolidated financial statements. However, IFRS allows for exemptions if the parent is a wholly owned or partially owned subsidiary, the parent does not trade bond or equity instruments in the public market, or it did not file (or will not file) financial statements with a regulatory agency.

Financial Statement Presentation—Joint Project of the FASB and IASB

In addition to the current structure of financial reporting under U.S. GAAP and IFRS, one of the goals contained in a 2007 Memorandum of Understanding was to develop a common standard for financial statement presentation that focuses on relationships across financial statements, disaggregating information on each financial statement to allow for better efforts of predicting an operation's future cash flows, and to improve a user's ability to assess an entity's liquidity and financial strength. While two of the three phases have been completed, the proposed changes will affect financial reporting in the United States and worldwide if and when convergence of standards occurs.

Phase A of the project proposes four financial statements and requires no less than two years of comparative data to be presented in such statements. The proposed financial statements include a statement of comprehensive income, a statement of financial position, a statement of cash flows, and a statement of changes in equity. While many of the features of financial reporting will continue, the proposal recommends including a new parallel classification structure across three of the four proposed financial statements (excluding the changes in equity statement). *Phase B* of the project led the two boards to issue three proposed objectives of information that should be presented in financial statements "in a manner that":

1. Portrays a cohesive financial picture of an entity's activities, which means "that the relationship between items across financial statements is clear and that an entity's financial statements complement each other as much as possible."
2. Assists users in assessing future cash flows by "assessing the amount, timing, and uncertainty of future cash flows" by requiring that financial information be "disaggregated reasonably homogeneous groups of items"; however, should items differ economically, users may report "differently in predicting future cash flows."
3. Helps users assess an entity's liquidity and financial flexibility by providing information concerning an entity's liquidity, which will assist users in assessing an entity's ability to "meet its financial commitments as they become due . . . [and allows users to assess] an entity's ability to invest in business opportunities and respond to unexpected needs."

The statements of comprehensive income, financial position, and cash flows will each contain a business section, which will report operating activities and investing activities of the specific statement. For example, the statement of comprehensive income's business section will contain operating income and expenses as well as investing income and expenses; the statement of financial position's business section will report operating assets and liabilities and investing assets and liabilities.

In addition to the business section, in three of the four statements (excluding the changes in equity statement), a financing section is provided as well as a section on taxes and discontinued operations (net of taxes). There are many other provisions in the proposed structure of the financial statements, which is in its preliminary stage and no final outcome has been determined; the joint project (IASB and FASB) staff are currently reviewing public responses to the proposed financial statements as this book went to press. Current information on the status of the proposed financial statements and other issues regarding the joint project may be accessed at *www.fasb.org/jsp/FASB/Page/SectionPage&cid=1218220137074.*

IFRS DIFFERENCES AFFECTING THE STATEMENT OF FINANCIAL POSITION

Cash and Cash Equivalents

Cash and cash equivalents are defined similarly under IFRS and U.S. GAAP. However, U.S. GAAP does not allow bank overdraft offsets to the cash account and reports them as a liability. The only exception where offsetting is allowable is in the case where two accounts are held by the same bank; an overdrawn account may be offset against another account in the same institution. IFRS allows offsetting of overdrafts to cash as long as it is integral to the entity's cash management.

Receivables

Under U.S. GAAP, receivables are not reported at fair value. However, under IFRS they are initially reported at fair value, with subsequent adjustments accounted for using amortized cost (effective interest method). In addition, under U.S. GAAP, an estimate of bad debts impacts earnings on the income statement. When a receivable is deemed uncollectible using the allowance method for accounting for bad debts, the write-off of the specific account does not impact earnings; any recovery of a previously written-off account also does not impact earnings. Under IFRS, impairment losses previously recognized on the income statement may be reversed in subsequent years, adjusting earnings. U.S. GAAP prohibits reversals of impairment losses on bad debts.

Inventories

U.S. GAAP generally measures inventory at lower of cost or market; under IFRS, inventory is measured at lower of cost or net realizable value (estimated selling price less estimated costs of completion and sale). IFRS includes distribution and marketing costs in its cost of sales, whereas U.S. GAAP excludes marketing costs in determining cost of sale.

Inventory write-downs under GAAP are normally determined either on an item-by-item, group, or categorical basis. IFRS writes down inventory to net realizable value (floor) on an item-by-item basis, but allows write-downs to occur by groups of similar products in special circumstances. In addition, any inventory write-downs under U.S. GAAP cannot subsequently be reversed, whereas IFRS allows previous inventory write-down reversals to be recognized in the same period as the write-down.

U.S. GAAP allows for the cost of inventory to be calculated using FIFO, LIFO, or a weighted-average calculation. IFRS allows FIFO and weighted-average, but prohibits use of LIFO.

Investments

Accounting for trading, available-for-sale, and held-to-maturity instruments is similar between U.S. GAAP and IFRS. The major differences exist with unrealized gains and losses of available-for-sale securities, which are reported in comprehensive income under U.S. GAAP, whereas under IFRS such gains and losses are reported in the equity section of the balance sheet. In addition, IFRS allows for impairment reversals for only available-for-sale debt (not equity) securities and held-to-maturity securities, while U.S. GAAP does not permit impairment reversals of any investments.

Equity Method Investments

Both U.S. GAAP and IFRS account for investments where the investor possesses significant influence over the investee, holding at least 20% and up to 50% of an investee's outstanding stock, lacking control over the entity. IFRS refers to an equity investment as an investment in associates. Additionally, IFRS requires that the investee and investor firms follow the same accounting policies, whereas U.S. GAAP does not require such a practice.

Property, Plant, and Equipment

In general, U.S. GAAP and IFRS treat the accounting for property, plant, and equipment similarly, including the initial accounting for all costs necessary to bring the asset to its intended use. Additionally, there are no differences in depreciation methods used. Differences exist primarily in the treatment of capitalized interest and the subsequent revaluation of the asset's fair value.

Interest incurred is capitalized under U.S. GAAP only during construction of a qualifying asset. Under IFRS, interest costs of borrowing may either be capitalized for the acquisition, construction, or production of a qualifying asset or expensed in the period incurred. Whichever method is selected must be consistently applied.

Another difference between U.S. GAAP and IFRS is in the revaluation of property, plant, and equipment. U.S. GAAP requires that property, plant, and equipment be accounted for using the cost method. Under IFRS, property, plant, and equipment is reported on a company's books at fair value less accumulated depreciation and impairment losses (if any). The accumulated depreciation account is used to revalue plant and equipment with the permission of two treatments, which use a revaluation surplus account.

Intangible Assets and Goodwill

U.S. GAAP and IFRS are not similar in the definition of an intangible asset, as it lacks physical substance, nor is it a financial asset. In addition, U.S. GAAP and IFRS view intangibles as assets that are identifiable if they are separable or as a result of contractual or legal rights. Goodwill, in particular, is viewed similarly by both as a residual that arises from a business combination and is not amortized but is tested annually for impairment. Some significant differences exist. While U.S. GAAP bases amortization of intangibles on historical cost less any impairment, IFRS allows revaluation of the value of the intangible by crediting any upward revision to the asset to a revaluation surplus account and adjusted against equity; downward revisions to fair value reduce the revaluation surplus account (until the account declines to zero). In addition, impairment for intangibles is treated differently under U.S. GAAP and IFRS (see section on Impairment below).

With regard to research and development costs, such costs are segregated into two types: research phase costs and developmental phase costs. Under both U.S. GAAP and IFRS, research phase costs are expensed in the period incurred. Developmental phase costs are expensed in the period incurred under U.S. GAAP. Under IFRS, such costs are similarly expensed unless technological feasibility is achieved. If technical feasibility results, such development costs are capitalized only if there is an intention to complete the developed asset, if there exists an ability to either use or sell the asset, if future economic benefits are reasonably expected to result, and if the entity provides adequate resources to finish development of the asset. With regard to in-process research and development costs that are acquired as part of a business combination, U.S. GAAP and IFRS standards have converged where acquired in-process research and development costs are capitalized and treated as an indefinite-life asset, with annual testing for impairment.

Contingent Liabilities

U.S. GAAP and IFRS measure contingent liabilities similarly in that such a liability can only be recognized if the outcome is probable and can be reasonably estimated. However, IFRS contains a slight difference in estimating the contingent liability: while U.S.

GAAP uses a more conservative (low-end) estimate in recording the liability, IFRS recognizes a contingent liability at the mid-point of the estimate range.

Income Tax Deferrals

In accounting for deferred income tax differences, U.S. GAAP and IFRS both use the asset and liability approach in recognizing future tax differences arising from present transactions. There are a few differences in approaches. First, U.S. GAAP's recognition of a deferred tax asset (or liability) is based on the assumption that the underlying asset or liability will eventually be reversed (recovered or settled) in a manner consistent with its use in the business. IFRS recognizes deferred taxes based on the expected manner of settlement or recovery. Second, U.S. GAAP employs an asset valuation account to the extent that it is more likely than not that the deferred tax asset will eventually be realized (reversed) at a future date. Under IFRS, a deferred tax asset is recognized if it is probable that it will eventually be realized (reversed) in the future. Therefore, IFRS has a higher recognition threshold. Third, U.S. GAAP allows for a deferred tax asset or liability classification to be either current or noncurrent, based on the classification of the related asset or liability. IFRS instead classifies all deferred tax differences as noncurrent. Lastly, IFRS measures the deferred tax based on tax rates that are enacted or substantively enacted at the reporting date, whereas U.S. GAAP uses the enacted tax rates only at the reporting date (and ignores estimated future tax rate adjustments).

Lease Accounting

U.S. GAAP and IFRS recognize the economic substance of recording leases of both the lessor and lessee. There are some relatively significant differences in the accounting treatments. While U.S. GAAP refers to capital lease treatment, IFRS terminology refers to such leases as finance leases. First, under U.S. GAAP, leased assets consist of only property, plant, and equipment, whereas under IFRS the leased asset can consist of other types of assets, including leases to explore mineral or natural resources and other licensing agreements (e.g., motion pictures, plays, and manuscripts). Second, U.S. GAAP is more rules based. For example, four criteria are used by the lessee and lessor (plus two required additional criteria for the lessor) in determining whether a lease should be capitalized. Many of these criteria are quantitative thresholds. IFRS similarly focuses on recording a lease where it transfers substantially all of the risks and rewards of ownership from the lessor to the lessee. Unlike the specific quantitative criteria under U.S. GAAP, IFRS provides a series of indicators that are used to determine whether a lease is classified as a finance lease. This criteria determination is much more general than U.S. GAAP and is not rules based.

Another difference involves the accounting for executory costs: U.S. GAAP expenses and excludes specific costs from the calculation of minimum lease payments, including insurance, maintenance, and taxes, whereas IFRS excludes costs for services and taxes from minimum lease payments. Lastly, the present value of the minimum lease payment by the lessee is computed under U.S. GAAP as the lower of the lessor's implicit rate (if known by the lessee) or the lessee's incremental borrowing rate. IFRS uses the interest rate implicit in the lease if known by the lessee. If the lessee lacks knowledge of such rate, then the lessee uses its incremental borrowing rate.

Equity

There are several differences in the classification of items in the equity section of the Statement of Financial Position under U.S. GAAP and IFRS. First, "common stock" is referred to as "share capital" under IFRS, "additional paid-in capital" is reported as "share premium" under IFRS, and "retained earnings" are often referred to as "accumulated profit and loss" or "retained profits." Treasury stock under IFRS is reported similar to U.S. GAAP as a reduction to shareholders' equity; however, IFRS allows treasury stock amounts to be offset against specific equity accounts. Further, IFRS does not recognize gains or losses on the disposition of treasury shares and instead makes an adjustment to equity. Under U.S. GAAP, using the cost method, proceeds in excess of the purchase price are generally credited to a specific paid-in capital account from treasury stock, while subsequent losses are reduced from the paid-in capital account (to the extent of its balance) and then any residual is deducted from retained earnings.

In addition to the standard items classified in the equity section of the statement of financial position, two other common classification issues exist: the treatment of convertible bonds and the reporting of noncontrolling (minority) interest in a subsidiary. With regard to corporate bonds that are convertible into common shares, U.S. GAAP reports such financial instruments as debt. However, under IFRS, proceeds of a debt instrument that are convertible into common shares are allocated between debt (reported at fair value) and equity (reported at residual value). As for the reporting of noncontrolling interest in a subsidiary, U.S. GAAP reported minority interest in the "mezzanine section" of the balance sheet. However,

U.S. GAAP and IFRS methods recently converged and now report noncontrolling interest in a subsidiary in the equity section.

IFRS DIFFERENCES AFFECTING THE INCOME STATEMENT

Revenue Recognition

Under U.S. GAAP, revenue is generally recognized when a product has been delivered or a service performed, the sales price is fixed and determinable, and collectability is reasonably assured. Revenue recognition principles are spread over several areas of authority within the literature, particularly with the application of the concepts of realized, recognized, and earned revenues. In addition, the SEC offers specific guidance on revenue recognition for listed companies. The IASB does not receive guidance from a regulatory body like the SEC. Further, U.S. GAAP has several areas of specific industry guidance with regard to revenue recognition; IFRS has no industry guidance.

Under IFRS, revenue is generally recognized when probable economic benefits exist, the item(s) of revenue can be reliably measured, the risks and rewards of ownership are conveyed from the seller to the buyer, and the cost of sale can be measured reliably. In addition, IFRS includes gains in the definition of revenues, which are not reported separately on the income statement, whereas U.S. GAAP records gains separate from revenues and defines it as a specific element on the income statement. One additional difference in revenue recognition is in the area of long-term construction contract accounting. Under U.S. GAAP, the percentage-of-completion method is the most common method, but the completed-contract method is allowed in specific circumstances. IFRS only allows the percentage-of-completion method.

Share-Based Payment

U.S. GAAP and IFRS standards have closely converged in the accounting of share-based payment where the fair value of shares and options that are awarded to employees are recognized over their period of service (period of benefit). One significant difference that remains regarding share-based payment is that U.S. GAAP rules apply only to employee share-based payments, whereas IFRS applies to employee and nonemployee share-based payments.

Impairment

First, U.S. GAAP measures impairment as the excess of the intangible's carrying value over its fair value (expected future cash flows, undiscounted); IFRS recognizes impairment if the intangible's carrying value exceeds its recoverable amount (which is the higher of the intangible's fair value less costs to dispose of the asset and its value in use). Second, under U.S. GAAP, recorded impairment losses are not reversed in subsequent periods, as the intangible's revised basis for amortization reflects the written-down asset after impairment loss recognition. IFRS allows for recovery of impairment losses in subsequent periods if there has been a change in economic conditions or a change in the expected use of the asset. Such allowable impairment recoveries (or asset write-ups) are limited to the intangible's pre-impairment carrying value.

Earnings per Share

The calculations of basic and diluted earnings per share (EPS) are similar under U.S. GAAP and IFRS, with some minor differences. First, both require EPS to be reported on the face of the income statement if the shares are traded publicly. U.S. GAAP and IFRS each report EPS for income from continuing operations and for net income or loss; however, U.S. GAAP requires EPS for discontinued operations and extraordinary items. In addition, under U.S. GAAP, if the treasury stock method of calculating incremental shares is used, a quarterly calculation of the average stock price is used. IFRS calculates the incremental shares based on a weighted-average at the end of the accounting period, not at the end of each quarter. This topic is one that the two boards are jointly working on in order to converge accounting treatments.

Brief Summary

While the FASB and IASB are moving toward a single set of global accounting standards, there are several areas in financial reporting where differences in accounting treatment and disclosure currently exist. The purpose of this chapter was to provide insight and understanding in many of the specific areas where convergence is lacking and accounting differences exist.

IFRS are principles based and U.S. GAAP are rules based. Therefore application of IFRS will require greater professional judgment. It is extremely critical that organizations are thorough and consistent in application of the standards so financial statements will be comparable from one period to the next.

Although differences in accounting standards can create problems, complete standardization is not a conceivable alternative. This is due mainly to the inherent differences found in the environmental factors (such as the legal systems). There is, however, promise for the harmonization of accounting standards. Although we are far from complete harmonization, many agencies have made great strides toward accomplishing this goal.

Selected Readings

Choi, Frederick D. S., Carol Ann Frost, and Gary K. Meek. *International Accounting*. New Jersey: Pearson Education, 2004.
Saudagaran, Shahrokh M. *International Accounting*. Ohio: South-Western, 2003.

WEBSITES

Below are some of your best tools for exploring International Financial Reporting Standards (IFRS).

The International Accounting Standards Board. Short summaries of all IFRS standards, news, and status of projects in progress– *www.iasb.org*

IFRS Website. Developed by The American Institute of Certified Public Accountants in partnership with CPA2Biz, its marketing and technology subsidiary–*www.ifrs.com*

Ernst & Young IFRS Web page. News and downloadable documents–*www.ey.com/ GLOBAL* (search IFRS)

PricewaterhouseCoopers IFRS Web page. News and downloadable documents–*www.pwc.com* (search IFRS)

Deloitte: An Overview of International Financial Reporting Standards. Overview document–*www.iasplus.com/standard/ standard.htm*

KPMG IFRS group. News and downloadable documents– *www.kpmgifrg.com*

U.S. Securities and Exchange Commission. Proposal for First-Time Application of International Financial Reporting Standards– *www.sec.gov/rules/proposed/33-8397.htm*

Chapter 14
Forensic Accounting

Forensic accounting is a science (i.e., a department of systemized knowledge) dealing with the application of accounting facts gathered through auditing methods and procedures to resolve legal problems. Forensic accounting is much different from traditional auditing. The main purpose of a traditional audit is to examine the financial statements of an organization and express an opinion on the fairness of the financial statements. In other words, auditors give an opinion whether the financial statements have been prepared in accordance with generally accepted accounting principles. Auditors employ limited procedures and use extensive testing and sampling techniques. Audits are performed by independent accountants and are not conducted with a view to present the evidence in a judicial forum. An audit is not an investigation; its main objective is not to uncover fraud.

Forensic accounting, on the other hand, is for investigation of an allegation with the assumption that the forensic accountant will have to present the evidence in a judicial forum. A forensic accountant often employs specialists in other areas as part of a team to gather evidence. In order to present the evidence in court, there must be absolute assurance; thus, testing and sampling methods are usually not employed as part of the evidence-gathering procedures. The scope of the investigation is limited because it is determined by the client.

Forensic accounting, therefore, is a specialty requiring the integration of investigative, accounting, and auditing skills. The forensic accountant looks at documents and financial and other data in a critical manner in order to draw conclusions and to calculate values, and to identify irregular patterns and/or suspicious transactions. A forensic accountant understands the fraud risk areas and has extensive fraud knowledge. A forensic accountant does not merely look at the numbers, but rather looks *behind* the numbers.

One can extend this definition to say that forensic accounting is a discipline consisting of two areas of specialization: litigation support specialists and investigation or fraud accountants. Litigation support specialists concern themselves with business valuation, testimony as expert witnesses, future earnings' evaluation, and income and expense analysis. On the other hand, fraud accountants apply their skills to investigate areas of alleged criminal misconduct in order to support or dispel suspicion. These fields overlap — a forensic accountant may do litigation support work on one engagement and act as a fraud accountant on another. Both of these engagements could result in expert testimony by the forensic accountant. Thus, forensic accounting can be defined in a more generic way: it is a discipline where auditing, accounting, and investigative skills are used to assist in disputes involving financial issues and data, and where there is suspicion or allegation of fraud. The expertise of the forensic accountant may be used to support a plaintiff who is trying to establish a claim, or to support a defendant in order to minimize the impact of a claim against him or her. Usually such investigations involve litigation; sometimes, however, such disputes are settled by negotiation. In either case, persuasive and authoritative evidence resulting from the financial and investigative skills of the forensic accountant is imperative. Therefore, the forensic accountant must be a good businessperson and be aware of statutory law, common law, and the rules of evidence and procedure.

Usually the forensic accountant's findings are based on facts, not opinions. Facts can be investigated, and the forensic accountant can prepare a definitive report on these facts. Nevertheless, there are situations where the forensic accountant may rely on professional judgment and present findings using an opinion-type report. Needless to say, the reports based on facts usually do not present problems in court cases because they are supported by underlying documentation. Opinion reports, on the other hand, are subjective and require the forensic accountant to demonstrate competency and to provide adequate logic for the stated opinion.

Two points are often overlooked when one is involved in a case as a forensic accountant: (1) the other side usually employs a forensic accountant as well; and (2) the credibility of a forensic accountant is extremely important. Thus the forensic accountant must have high professional standards and ethics.

WHY IS FORENSIC ACCOUNTING NECESSARY?

Business and criminal activities have become so complex that lawyers and criminal investigators often do not have the expertise necessary to discharge their responsibilities. This fact, plus the marked increase in white-collar crime, marital and business disputes, and other claims, have created the need for the new industry of forensic accounting. Although this specialty is not limited to fraud issues, the reality of forensic accounting is that most of the work does involve fraud investigations. In the case of fraud, the work of a forensic accounting team is crucial, as the survival of the business may rest on the outcome. Good businesspeople must realize that fraud is a permanent risk in any and all businesses. Thus company leaders must devise ways to prevent fraud rather than trying to manage the consequences of fraud. The instances of fraud have increased because of lack of government commitment, more sophisticated criminals, inefficiency of the judicial system, more complex technology, lack of adequate penalties and deterrents, and old-fashioned greed and arrogance. Studies have suggested that fraud will continue to increase. Currently, about 75% of fraud results from employees; other sources of fraud include customers, management, suppliers, and service providers. In addition, about 55% of fraud is discovered as a result of strong internal controls. Other methods of discovery include whistleblowers, customers, internal auditors, and discovery by accident or through formal investigation.

WHEN DOES ONE EMPLOY A FORENSIC ACCOUNTANT?

Clients retain forensic accountants when they are interested in either litigation support or investigations.

Litigation Support

This is a situation where the forensic accountant is asked to give an opinion either on known facts or facts yet to be uncovered. The forensic accountant is an integral part of the legal team, helping to substantiate or disprove allegations, analyze facts, dispute claims, and develop motives. The amount of involvement and the point at which the forensic accountant gets involved varies from case to case. Sometimes the forensic accountant is called upon from the beginning of the case; other times the forensic accountant is summoned before the case is scheduled to go to court and after out-of-court settlement efforts have failed. The forensic accountant assists in obtaining documentation to support or dispel a claim, in reviewing documentation to give an assessment of the case to the legal team, and/or in identifying areas where loss occurred. Moreover, the forensic accountant may be asked to get involved during the discovery stage to help formulate questions, and may be asked to review the opposing side's expert witness report to give an evaluation of its strengths and weaknesses. During trial the forensic accountant may serve as an expert witness and help to provide questions for cross-examination; he may also assist with settlement discussions after the trial.

Investigations

Investigations most often involve fraud and are associated with criminal matters. Typically, an investigative accounting assignment would result from a client's suspicion that there is employee fraud. Other parties, such as regulatory and law enforcement agencies and attorneys, may retain a forensic accountant to investigate allegations of securities fraud, kickbacks, insurance fraud, money-laundering schemes, or to help with asset search and analysis.

WHERE IS A FORENSIC ACCOUNTANT USED?

A forensic accountant is used in a number of situations including (but not limited to) the following:

- *Business valuations:* A forensic accountant evaluates the current value of a business for various personal or legal matters.
- *Personal injury and fatal accident claims:* A forensic accountant may help to establish lost earnings (i.e., those earnings that the plaintiff would have accrued except for the actions of the defendant) by gathering and analyzing a variety of information and then issuing a report based on the outcome of the analyses.
- *Professional negligence:* A forensic accountant helps to determine if a breach of professional ethics or other standards of professional practice has occurred (e.g., failure to apply generally accepted auditing standards by a CPA when performing an audit). In addition, the forensic accountant may help to quantify the loss.
- *Insurance claims evaluations:* A forensic accountant may prepare financial analyses for an insurance company of claims, business income losses, expenses, and disability, liability, or workmen's compensation insurance losses.
- *Arbitration:* A forensic accountant is sometimes retained to assist with alternative dispute resolution (ADR) by acting as a mediator to allow individuals and businesses to resolve dis-

putes in a timely manner with a minimum of disruption.

- *Partnership and corporation disputes:* A forensic accountant may be asked to help settle disputes between partners or shareholders. Detailed analyses are often necessary of many records spanning a number of years. Most of these disputes relate to compensation and benefit issues.
- *Civil and criminal actions concerning fraud and financial irregularities:* These investigations are usually performed by the forensic accountant for law enforcement agencies. A report is prepared to assist the prosecutor's office.
- *Fraud and white-collar crime investigations:* These types of investigations can be prepared on behalf of police forces as well, or for private businesses. They usually result from such activities as purchasing/kickback schemes, computer fraud, labor fraud, and falsification of inventory. The investigation by the forensic accountant often involves fund tracing, asset identification, and recovery.

HOW DOES A FORENSIC ACCOUNTANT WORK?

Although each case is distinct and requires accounting and auditing procedures unique to the assignment, many forensic accounting assignments would include the following steps:

- *Meet with the client:* The forensic accountant should meet with the client to determine the scope of the engagement. In addition, it is advisable to obtain an engagement letter specifying the terms of the engagement.
- *Determine independence:* It is understood that a CPA should be independent when performing an audit or other attest services for clients. It is mandatory as well that the forensic accountant be independent; otherwise, the credibility of the forensic accountant will be questioned if the engagement results in a legal case.
- *Plan the engagement:* Proper advance planning is essential to any type of engagement. The plan should be similar to an audit program, detailing objectives and procedures in a form that addresses the scope of the engagement so that some type of conclusion can be reached.
- *Gather evidence and perform analyses:* The forensic accountant should match the auditing, accounting, or investigative technique employed with the type of evidence to be obtained. A specific technique may satisfy more than one objective.

When the forensic accountant, for example, performs an audit technique for a particular account, evidence for other accounts may be discovered based on the double entry system of accounting. Forensic accountants use a variety of techniques including inquiry, confirmation, physical examination, observation, inspection, reconciliation, tracing, vouching, reperformance, and analytical procedures.

- *Make a conclusion and prepare the report:* The forensic accountant should write the final report in a manner that clearly explains the nature of the assignment and the scope of the work. It should indicate the approach used for discovery of information, and detail findings and/or opinions.

FORENSIC ACCOUNTING AND FRAUD EXAMINATION

Again, forensic accounting is an accounting specialty that integrates accounting, auditing, and investigative skills in order to support or resolve allegations of fraud. Forensic accounting encompasses both litigation support (expert witness testimony, presentation of supporting documents showing fraud, etc.) and investigative accounting.

The difference between a "normal" accountant and a forensic accountant is that the latter seeks a level of evidentiary detail and analytical precision, which will be sustainable under legal scrutiny or review.

Forensic accounting focuses on both the evidence of economic transactions and reporting, and the legal framework that allows such evidence to be suitable for establishing accountability and/ or valuation. Forensic accounting engagements include transaction reconstruction, bankruptcy, family law issues, asset identification and valuation, fraud examination/detection, and many other issues.

Auditing is performed either by an employee (internal audit) or by an outside accounting firm (external audit). Internal audits examine *operational evidence* to ensure that the prescribed company operating procedures have been followed. External audits examine the assets and records of a company, leading to the expression of a professional opinion by the outside CPA, who gives credibility to the financial reports presented by the company. A key component of an audit is the review of internal control weaknesses. Fraud examination differs from auditing as shown in Table 14.1:

Table 14.1
AUDITING VS. FRAUD EXAMINATION

Issue	*Auditing*	*Fraud Examination*
Timing	**Recurring** Audits are conducted on a regular, recurring basis.	**Nonrecurring** Fraud examinations are nonrecurring. They are conducted only with sufficient predication.
Scope	**General** The scope of the audit is an examination of financial data.	**Specific** The fraud examination is conducted to resolve specific allegations.
Objective	**Opinion** An audit is generally conducted for the purpose of expressing an opinion on the financial statements or related information.	**Affix blame** The fraud examination's goal is to determine whether fraud has occurred or is occurring and to determine who is responsible.
Relationship	**Non-adversarial** The audit process is non-adversarial in nature.	**Adversarial** Fraud examinations, because they involve efforts to affix blame, are adversarial in nature.
Methodology	**Audit techniques** Audits are conducted by examining financial data and obtaining corroborating evidence.	**Fraud examination techniques** Fraud examinations are conducted by (1) document examination, (2) review of outside data such as public records, and (3) interviews.
Standard	**Professional skepticism** Auditors are required to approach audits with professional skepticism.	**Proof** Fraud examiners approach the resolution of a fraud by attempting to establish sufficient proof to support or refute a fraud allegation.

Source: Fraud Examiner's Manual, Association of Certified Fraud Examiners, 2009.

FORENSIC SPECIALISTS' INVESTIGATION PROCEDURE

In theory, the Enron scandal should never have happened. U.S. financial markets are supposed to be the best regulated in the world, with the Securities and Exchange Commission (SEC) enforcing strict rules on disclosure to protect investors, and private agencies also monitoring companies. But Enron's accounts proved impenetrable to government and private regulators alike, while its main business—energy trading—was only lightly regulated by another set of government agencies that exempted it from many reporting requirements while maintaining close ties with the company.

Beyond the congressional circus and shredded documents, the fate of the Enron case—and most investigations of suspected corporate crime—rests in the hands of computer forensic experts and forensic accountants working quietly behind the scenes. Investigators will pore through 10,000 computer backup tapes, 20 million sheets of paper, and more than 400 computers and handheld devices, according to legal papers. The electronic data is up to ten times the size of the Library of Congress.

While being equipped with many of the same skills as accountants and computer professionals, forensic detectives in all corporate investigations dig deeper. They mine computer hard drives, financial papers, and bank records for "smoking gun" evidence that is allowable in civil and criminal courts. The Justice Department and the Securities and Exchange Commission have launched criminal and civil investigations of Enron and law firms, and their private investigators hope to gather documents for their class-action lawsuits against Enron.

Here is how forensic specialists work big corporate fraud cases, and how the investigation is likely to unfold in the corporate fraud case.

- **By tracing the digital and paper trails.** Even if paper documents are trashed, investigators armed with subpoenas can scoop up duplicate papers from the auditor or law firm of the company under investigation. If critical material cannot be found in a company's computer or backup tapes, most large companies keep data in emergency backup systems off site, in case a natural disaster destroys office records. In addition, investigators with search warrants will seize records, computers, pagers, and cell phones from the homes of employees.
- **By saving and rebuilding data.** In most corporate fraud cases, investigators will squeeze every bit and byte of data from hard drives, floppy disks, computer tapes, and CD-ROMs. Investi-

gators will make copies for storage and to use for their analysis. Often, incriminating documents are deleted, or a suspect will hide records in an unmarked part of a hard drive. Regardless, special software can fish out information.

- **By financial profiling.** Some investigators will build financial profiles of suspects and their assets. They study bank documents, tax records, and corporate records to chart a suspect's pay, stock options, and 401(k) investment holdings. They will interview co-workers, family, and friends, and they also will drive by the suspect's home to see if he or she is living beyond his or her means.
- **By analyzing evidence.** Amid the mountain of records, investigators look for "hot documents"—spreadsheets, invoices, contracts, and memos—that show a pattern of suspected wrongdoing. For instance, a company's numbers and quarterly earnings statement might not jibe with accounting standards or past performance. Profit margins might suddenly rise, even though revenue is flat. Or a firm unexpectedly might write off huge amounts of inventory or unsold products.

Investigators in corporate fraud cases also look closely at auditors' work papers, called *past adjusted journal entries* (PAJEs). PAJEs are journal entries that are not posted to the financial statements and therefore do not tie to the financial statements filed with the SEC. The worksheet with the PAJEs should show a reconciliation from the financials filed with the SEC to what they would have been had the PAJEs been posted.

FORENSIC COMPUTING AND THE USE OF TECHNOLOGY

In some respects the advances in technology have enabled criminals to commit crimes more quickly and successfully. For example, by capturing database information it is easy to steal people's identity and financial data. The automation of the payroll system has enabled corrupt employees to create false identities to receive paychecks. Deleting a computer file does not necessarily remove the information. Also, data stored on one computer may exist in many locations such as on a backup tape, company Blackberry, or PDA. Such devices serve as a tape recorder, documenting and storing the evidence of a crime.

The following table lists some of the basic tools for data detective work.

Tool	Purpose
Network sniffer (hardware)	Allows user to "recreate" the crime by keeping a record of packet sessions across networks.
Portable disk duplicator and/or duplication software	Preserves the original crime scene by allowing investigators to copy hard drives in the field and the lab for later analysis.
Chain-of-custody documentation hardware	Videotapes every mouse click of the investigative process to make court testimony more credible.
Case management software	Helps link seemingly unrelated pieces of evidence.

Phone logs for office, home, fax lines, and cell phone may also prove helpful. An employee may try to use a common access phone to make calls. However, employers can also install security access cards to certain areas of the building that have sensitive files. This way an employer can track what employees are accessing.

IT AND DATA MINING USED TO DETECT CORPORATE FRAUD

IT tools such as data mining can be effectively employed by fraud auditors. This involves the analysis of data stored in an information system (e.g., a database) to identify patterns that indicate unexplained or potentially questionable transactions. The advantage of such a computer analysis technique is that large numbers of transactions can be evaluated in a relatively short period of time. Further, multiple analyses of individual data elements can be performed to provide different evaluations of potential patterns or trends. Once a pattern is identified, the auditors must further investigate specific transactions to determine whether an improper transaction actually occurred. Data mining can also be very useful in other high-risk corporate processes. Two such areas include executive travel and contract and consulting services.

A CASE IN FORENSIC ACCOUNTING

The following is an actual case involving the purchase of a business. The plaintiff alleges that the records shown to him were not accurate and that the lawyer who handled the closing for him was negligent.

MAGYAR, INC.
A Case Study in Fraud

"Since I was a little boy, I wanted to own a business. I never wanted to work for anyone else," Omar Saleem said to his wife, Sylvia.

Omar Saleem, 50, came to the United States 30 years ago and has worked for a large furniture manufacturer for 28 years. One day, he was reading the classified advertisements in the newspaper and noticed an office business for sale in the next town. He discussed the idea with his wife and she approved, so he contacted the seller and made an appointment. Three days later Omar met with Rahman Magyar, the sole owner of Magyar, Inc. Rahman was an engaging individual, very smooth and personable. Omar was very impressed with Rahman's knowledge of the business and with his self-confidence. Rahman told Omar that he was selling the business because he was bored with it. He had built the company from nothing into a very successful business and now wanted to try something else. Omar believed everything that Rahman said. Rahman said he would be glad to open his books to Omar, but would require a good-faith refundable deposit of $1,000. Omar agreed and made another appointment for the following week.

Omar met with Rahman and gave him the $1,000 good-faith deposit. Rahman in turn showed Omar his equipment and inventory and explained more about the business. Specifically, he told him that he averaged about $120,000 per year in office supplies and equipment sales, and about $30,000 in services. The latter was a mail service where he prepared and mailed packages for customers. Rahman produced a fee schedule and claimed that this end of the business had been very lucrative. After showing Omar the inventory, Rahman flashed some papers and tax returns in front of Omar to show him the growth since he opened the business in February 1994. Rahman said that the business has averaged about 20% growth each year. Omar looked at the papers, but actually didn't know what he was looking at. Furthermore, Rahman assured him that the paperwork was in order since his brother-in-law prepared them. He said his brother-in-law, Raj Kupar, was a CPA and that everything was in order. Rahman said that he would sell the business for $160,000, which was less than the normal selling price for this type of business. He said that the selling price is usually one times annual sales. He further said that "since you and I are from the same country, I will help you out. I prefer to sell to you over someone else."

He convinced Omar that he could easily make $75,000 from the business. Furthermore, he suggested that Omar move fast, as there were a number of people interested in the business. Omar said that he would have to get an attorney. He promised to get back to Rahman in a week or so. Rahman even suggested an attorney.

Omar was quite excited and couldn't wait to get home to tell his wife. His wife was very supportive. Therefore, Omar asked his good friend, Stanley, if he knew an attorney. Stanley referred him to Neil Klavin, an attorney in town. On the following Monday, Omar called the attorney and made an appointment for Friday of that week. Before the meeting, Omar called Rahman and asked if he would accept $150,000 for the business. Rahman said that he would, but wanted cash and that he would not want to finance the business. Omar said that he had $110,000 in cash, but would require a loan of $40,000. Rahman surprisingly agreed to finance $40,000, but wanted 8% interest. They verbally agreed. Omar said that he was going to see an attorney on Friday to explain the deal. Rahman said "great."

On Friday, Omar went to the attorney, Neil Klavin, with his wife. Omar and the attorney discussed the business deal at length. Klavin said that he would be happy to represent Ornar and would gladly review the contract drawn up by Rahman's attorney. Omar told the attorney that he had seen some documentation regarding income and expenses including the tax returns. Omar told Klavin that he would like him to review the documentation as well. The attorney said "fine." Omar left the office and then contacted Rahman. He gave Rahman his attorney's name and told him to have his lawyers draw up the paperwork. Omar's wife asked if he was moving a little too fast. Omar said that he had to move fast as it was a good deal and that Rahman had other interested buyers. He felt comfortable that his attorney would say it was a good deal after the attorney reviewed the numbers.

About two weeks later, Neil Klavin received the financial information from Rahman's attorney along with a contract of sale and promissory note for $40,000 at 8% interest. Neil reviewed the information and appeared to find everything in order. Although he did not understand the financials and tax returns that well, he did not suggest to Omar that anything was improper, nor did he suggest soliciting the help of an expert. For example, he did not suggest contacting a CPA to review the books, financials, and tax returns. The closing was scheduled for December 27, 1996. Rahman and Omar appeared at the closing with their wives. The contract and promissory note were signed. Omar was to start on the following Monday. Rahman agreed to stay around for a month to train both Omar and his wife. Since this was a family business (husband and wife), they only had the need for occasional casual labor. Rahman had never had a payroll.

Omar showed up on January 2, 1997, eager to learn all about the business. He met Rahman, who turned over the keys to the store. Rahman was very gracious and patient as he explained things to Omar and his wife. This went on for the whole month as agreed upon at closing. During the month, Omar and his wife discussed the relative inactivity. They even mentioned this to Rahman, who replied that January is always slow because it is after the holidays. Rahman said "don't worry, as December more than makes up for January." Omar and his wife didn't think too much about it.

Omar was now on his own. He and his wife worked diligently at the business each day. His wife prepared advertisements for the newspaper and ran a number of specials. They methodically kept track of daily revenues and expenses. It became apparent after seven months that the volume was nothing like Rahman had said. They both wondered what they were doing wrong. They were somewhat in denial and did not want to think that they may have been misled and/or tricked. They talked among themselves and decided to talk to an attorney, but not Neil Klavin. Instead they discussed the matter with one of their customers, an attorney named Ted Rich. Ted often went into the store to buy supplies and do special mailings of packages. He took a personal interest in both Omar and his wife, Sylvia. Therefore, he suggested that they make an appointment and discuss the matter further.

Omar and Sylvia talked more about the problem. Another two months went by without any appreciable increase in sales numbers. Finally they made an appointment with Ted Rich. Omar did most of the talking. He also brought copies of all the paperwork that he had, including financial information he had received from Rahman. He also included summaries of his revenues and expenses for the last nine months. They discussed alternatives. Ted asked a number of pertinent questions, including whether Omar had an accountant, preferably a CPA, to review the financial information that he received from Rahman. Omar said that he had not. He said that he gave all the information to his attorney to review. Omar made it clear to Ted that he depended on his attorney, Neil Klavin, for advice. Ted was not in the business of suing other attorneys; however, he was upset that Klavin was so sloppy with the closing. He knew that Omar and his wife were naïve. Nevertheless, that was no excuse for not following due diligence procedures. He believed that Klavin should have realized this and looked out for the welfare of his client. Not wanting to make an immediate decision, Ted told Omar that he would review the information and get back to them in a couple of weeks.

A few days later, Ted reviewed the file and decided that the best way to handle the case was to get an accountant to review the financial information including the tax returns for 1994, 1995, and 1996. Ted called Omar to ask for approval to retain an accountant. Omar agreed.

The next day Ted called George Spyros, a CPA and CFE (certified fraud examiner). George had a small forensic practice and had done work for Ted in the past. Ted and George met for about an hour the following day. George looked at the financial statements and tax returns. The first thing George did was check to see if Rahman's brother-in-law was indeed a CPA. He was not. The reason he did that first was because his cursory review of the tax returns revealed gross preparation errors. It only took George about eight hours to do a detailed review of the paperwork. George then prepared a report for Ted (Exhibit A).
Ted reviewed the report prepared by Spyros and Company. Based on the report and his discussions with George Spyros, he decided to take the case and pursue suing Neil Klavin. Over the next few months, Ted diligently worked on the case, including obtaining interrogatories from a number of individuals including Omar and his wife, Rahman Magyar, and Neil Klavin.

Ted knew that the case was not solid. Therefore, he asked for the opinion of another attorney, Richard Darius of Darius and Spivack. He also asked for a second opinion from Edward Caruso. Both of these attorneys had experience suing other attorneys. Their opinions can be found in Exhibit B and Exhibit C, respectively.

Since the two attorneys had different opinions, Ted thought that it would be in the best interest of his client to try to settle out of court.

EXHIBIT A

SPYROS AND COMPANY
CERTIFIED PUBLIC ACCOUNTANTS

447 PEARL STREET
WOODBRIDGE, NEW JERSEY 07095

Mr. Theodore R. Rich
400 Pearl Street
Woodbridge, New Jersey 07095

Dear Mr. Rich,

In accordance with your request, we have reviewed the Federal income tax returns (Form 1120) of Magyar, Inc. for the eleven months ended December 31, 1994, and the years ended December 31, 1995 and 1996. The purpose of our review was to obtain reasonable assurance about whether the tax returns are free of material misstatement. Our review included examining the propriety of the amounts presented on the returns based on analytical procedures. Specifically, we have determined that:

(1) The company employed the accrual basis of accounting (see box checked on page 2 of the 1994 return). Since the balance sheets each year do not show any accounts receivable or accounts payable, one can logically conclude that all revenues and expenses were for cash.

(2) Based on the conclusion reached in (1) above, the cash balances reflected on the balance sheets on page 4 of the 1995 and 1996 tax returns are not reasonable. This fact can be supported by the following reconciliation:

Increase (decrease) in cash—

Cash balance at inception	$ —
Issuance of stock in 1994	7,536
Loans in 1994	29,438
Equipment	(16,251)
Sales	101,792
Cost of sales	(118,326)
Expenses (excluding depreciation of $638)	(25,812)
Cash balance on December 31, 1994 should be	$ (21,623)
Cash balance on December 31, 1994 per tax return	$ 250

Comments:
It is unreasonable for cost of sales to be more than sales.
Cash is misstated by $21,873

Recalculated cash balance on January 1, 1995	$ (21,623)
Additional issuance of stock in 1995	23,960
Payoff of loans	(29,438)
Sales	141,158
Cost of sales	(139,617)
Expenses (excluding depreciation of $638)	(38,102)
Cash balance on December 31, 1995 should be	$ (63,662)
Cash balance on December 31, 1995 per tax return	$250

Comments:
It is unreasonable for cost of sales to be 99% of sales.
Cash is misstated cumulatively by $63,912

Recalculated cash balance on January 1, 1996	$ (63,662)
Sales	157,572
Cost of sales	(145,710)
Expenses (excluding depreciation of $638)	(24,417)
Cash balance on December 31, 1996 should be	$(76,217)
Cash balance on December 31, 1996 per tax return	$295

Comments:
It is unreasonable for cost of sales to be 93% of sales.
Cash is misstated cumulatively by $76,512
We also compared the tax returns to the internal financial statements prepared by Raj Kupar, who we understand is a CPA and brother-in-law of the prior owner of the business, Rahman Magyar. Please be advised that we could not find a relationship between the financial statements and the tax returns. The tax returns were materially different from the internal financial statements. Revenues on the internal financials were approximately $15,000 higher in 1994, $18,000 lower in 1995, and $30,000 higher in 1996. There appeared to be only a partial listing of expenses, such that 1994 showed a profit of $70,000, 1995 a profit of $65,000, and 1996 a profit of $74,000. The costs and expenses were substantially less than those shown on the tax returns. In addition, the tax returns reflected substantial losses each year. Finally, the internal financial statements were not prepared in accordance with generally accepted accounting principles.

You also asked us to check whether or not Mr. Kupar is a practicing CPA in New Jersey. We did check with the New Jersey State Board of Public Accountants. He is neither a licensed CPA or licensed public accountant.

Thank you for the opportunity of serving you. If you have any questions about this report, please contact us directly.

Woodbridge, New Jersey
July 24, 1998

EXHIBIT B

DARIUS AND SPIVACK

One Main Street
Hackensack, NJ 07601

March 25, 1999

Theodore R. Rich, Esq.
100 Pearl Street
Woodbridge, New Jersey 07095

Re: Saleem v. Klavin

Dear Mr. Rich:

This report relates to an action for legal malpractice brought by your clients, **Omar and Sylvia Saleem** against **Neil Klavin,** a member of the New Jersey Bar. It derives from your request for my opinion as to whether third party defendant Klavin breached any duty to his former clients, the third party plaintiffs herein, when he undertook to represent them in July, 1996, with respect to the purchase of a certain office supply and mail box business, known as Magyar, Inc., located at 189 Princeton Road, Woodbridge, New Jersey.

For purposes of this report, I have read, analyzed and relied upon multiple documents contained in all your litigation files, including the February, 9, 1998 depositions of Omar Saleem, Sylvia Saleem and Rahman Magyar; the December 27, 1996 Contract of Sale between Magyar, Inc., and Omar and Sylvia Saleem; the January 4, 1997 addendum to closing statement; the January 2, 1997 Lease between Magyar, Inc. and Marjama Company; Rahman Magyar's answers to interrogatories; the December 27, 1996 note from Omar and Sylvia Saleem to Rahman Magyar; correspondence between attorneys D'Orio (for seller) and Klavin (for buyer) dated respectively October 14, 1996 and November 2, 1996 and December 3, 1996. Kindly note that the documents listed above do not include all the materials examined by me, such as all correspondence between and among the parties, all pleadings, all discovery, and the like. Most especially did I review and analyze the July 24, 1998 expert report of Spyros and Company, Certified Public Accountants, rendered on behalf of Omar and Sylvia Saleem.

STATEMENT OF FACTS

In early 1996, Omar Saleem, a native of Syria, but living and working in the United States since 1966, expressed interest in buying a small business. He read about a business for sale in the local newspaper. He answered the advertisement and soon met one Rahman Magyar, the owner of Magyar, Inc., a company engaged in the office supply and mail service business. Later, at a meeting held in Rahman Magyar's office, Omar verbally said that he was interested in purchasing the business. About a week later Saleem called Magyar. The two agreed on a price of $150,000 including a $40,000 promissory note to Magyar. During the course of the preliminary negotiations, Magyar had assured the Saleems that the business was a very simple operation which they would have no problem understanding and that he would agree to work a month in the business free of charge to train both Omar and his wife. For whatever reason, Magyar never offered the Saleems an opportunity to examine the books and records of the Company, or to have them examined by an outside accountant. However, he did show them some tax returns and financial statements prepared by his brother-in-law, whom he alleged was a CPA. After the closing, Magyar did provide on-the-job-training, but it was hurried and did not afford the Saleems hardly any opportunity to understand the economics of the business.

The essential complaint of the Saleems is that their attorney Klavin failed to provide them with appropriate legal advice and counsel in connection with the actual purchase of the business. In this regard the Saleems contend that Klavin failed to incorporate certain conditions and contingencies in the December 27, 1997 contract which would have made the sale subject to a review of all books, records, income tax returns, and the like, by a Certified Public Accountant acting on behalf of the buyers. Thus, instead of advising the Saleems not to sign the contract and make any substantial deposit until the Saleems had all the books and records examined by their accountant; and having, alternatively, failed to incorporate such protective contingencies and conditions in the contract, Klavin put his clients on the horns of a dilemma faced, as they unfortunately were, with either losing their $1,000 deposit or purchasing the business in total ignorance of its monthly income and expenses.

CONCLUSIONS OF LAW

The matter of attorney negligence arising out of this matter, must, of course, be evaluated and judged in accordance with the standard of care applicable in legal malpractice actions. In this regard, it is settled that an attorney is obligated to exercise on behalf of his client the knowledge, skill and ability ordinarily possessed and exercised by members of the legal profession similarly situated, and to employ reasonable care and prudence in connection therewith. *McCullough v. Sullivan,* 102 N.J.L. 381, 384 (E. & A. 1926); *Sullivan v. Stoudt,* 120 N.J.L. 304, 308 (E. &A. 1938); *Taylor v. Shepard,* 136 NJ Super. 85, 90 (App. Div. 1982); *Saint Pius X House of Retreats v. Camden Diocese,* 88 N.J. 571, 588 (1982). Perhaps the most quoted statement of the rule of care applicable to attorney negligence suits is found in *Hodges v. Carter,* 239 N.C. 517, 80 S.E. 2nd 144 (1954):

> "Ordinarily when an attorney engages in the practice of the law and contracts to prosecute an action in behalf of his client, he impliedly represents that (1) he possesses the requisite degree of learning, skill and ability necessary to the practice of his profession and which others similarly situated ordinarily possess; (2) he will exercise his best judgment in the prosecution of the litigation entrusted to him and (3) he will exercise reasonable and ordinary care and diligence in the use of his skill and in the application of his knowledge to his client's cause. (Id. at 519, 80 S.E. 2nd at 145, 146)."

What constitutes a reasonable degree of care is not to be considered in a vacuum. On the contrary, it must be the facts and circumstances of each specific case, and the type of service the attorney undertakes therein. With this in mind, I now proceed to examine the conduct of the subject defendant attorney in connection with his professional duties and conduct in the management of the above matter.

The record shows an egregious failure on the part of attorney Klavin to safeguard and protect the interests of his clients when he undertook to represent them in the purchase of Magyar, Inc. This conclusion is based upon the fact that defendant Klavin made no attempt to follow the standard and elementary procedures mandated for any attorney representing a buyer in the acquisition of a corporation. Thus, if Klavin had truly represented the interests of the Saleems, he would not only have examined all Magyar Inc.'s Federal and State tax returns, he would also, as a part of that investigation, have conducted a lien search in every place that Magyar conducted its business; would have obtained from Magyar an up-to-date financial statement in order to understand the economic aspects of the deal; would have obtained an independent audit of that financial statement; would have checked the terms, acceleration clauses and restrictions on any notes or mortgages or other indebtedness of the corporation; would have examined all insurance policies to discover what unknown liabilities existed; would have examined the viability and collectability of all accounts receivable; would have made a complete physical inventory of all corporate assets, together with a current market evaluation of same; would have examined the important contracts of Magyar and its customers, which constituted the life blood of that corporation; and would have performed other common sense duties, such as talking to the main customers of Magyar, all for the overall purpose of insuring that the interests of his clients, the Saleems, were fully protected and safeguarded.

It is my opinion that if Klavin had conducted this type of basic and common sense investigation, as he was bound to do in accordance with his duties as an attorney of this state, the Saleems would not have undertaken to purchase Magyar, and would thereby have escaped all the financial damage, loss of time, mental stress, and anguish which they unfortunately suffered as a result of this purchase. Indeed, we now know that as a direct result of his negligence, Klavin caused his clients to lose at least $110,000 due to the misrepresentations made by the seller. In short, I find on the facts and the law that defendant Klavin, in his attorney-client relationship with the Saleems, fell below the standard of care and prudence exercised by ordinary members of the New Jersey Bar. Otherwise put, attorney Klavin, in his relationship with the Saleems, deviated substantially from the standard of care expected of New Jersey attorneys.

But it remains basic to the Saleems' cause of action for legal malpractice that the wrongful conduct or failures of attorney Klavin are a proximate cause of their injuries. In order to establish "causation," the burden is clearly upon the Saleems to prove that the negligence of Klavin was "more likely than not" a substantial factor in causing the unfavorable result. *Legal Malpractice, Mallen & Levit,* at pg. 502; and also see *Lieberman v. Employers Ins. of Wassau,* 85 N.J. 325, 341 (1980); *Hoppe v. Ranzini,* 58 N.J. Super. 233, 238, 239 (App. Div. 1975), *cert. denied,* 70 N.J. 144 (1976); *Lamb v. Barbour,* 188 N.J. Super. 6, 12 (App. Div. 1982); and as to the test of proximate cause see *State v. Jersey Central Power & Light Co.*, 69 N.J. 100, 102 (1976); *Ettin v. Ava Truck Leasing Inc.*, 153 N.J. 463,483 (1969). And plaintiff is obliged to carry this burden of proof by the presentation of competent, credible evidence, which proves material facts; and not conjecture, surmise, or suspicion. *Lang v. Landy*, 35 N.J. 44, 54 (1961); *Modla v. United States*, 15 F. Supp. 198, 201 (D.N.J. 1957). Otherwise stated, third party plaintiffs herein must establish a chain of causation between their damages and the negligence or other wrongful conduct on the part of defendant Klavin. *Catto v. Schnepp*, 21 N.J. supra 506, 511 (App. Div.) affld o.b. 62 N.J. 20 (1972).

Based upon the facts presented to me, and the applicable law, it is my view that the inexplicable failure of defendant Klavin to inspect or provide for the inspection of all Magyar, Inc. tax returns and corporate books and records, were the immediate factors that caused the Saleems to sustain heavy losses. It follows, therefore, that third party defendant Klavin is liable to the third party plaintiffs Saleems for legal malpractice and all causally related damages.

Very truly yours,

Richard M. Darius

EXHIBIT C

EDWARD J. CARUSO
Counselor at Law

300 Broad Street
Newark, New Jersey 07104

June 8, 1999

Theodore R. Rich, Esq.
100 Pearl Street
Woodbridge, New Jersey 07095

Re: Saleem v. Klavin
Dear Mr. Rich:

Please be advised that this opinion relates to an action for legal malpractice brought by your clients, Omar and Sylvia Saleem, against Neil Klavin, a member of the New Jersey Bar. It derives from your request for my opinion as to whether third party defendant Klavin breached any duty to his former clients, the third party plaintiffs herein, when he undertook to represent them in July, 1996, with respect to the purchase of a certain office supply and mail box business, known as Magyar, Inc., located at 189 Princeton Road, Woodbridge, New Jersey.

For purposes of this report, I have read, analyzed and relied upon the following documents contained in all your litigation files:

- February, 9, 1998 depositions of Omar Saleem, Sylvia Saleem, and Rahman Magyar;
- December 27, 1996 Contract of Sale between Magyar, Inc., and Omar and Sylvia Saleem;
- January 4, 1997 addendum to closing statement;
- January 2, 1997 Lease between Magyar, Inc. and Marjama Company;
- Rahman Magyar's answers to interrogatories;
- December 27, 1996 note from Omar and Sylvia to Rahman Magyar;
- Correspondence between attorneys D'Orio (for seller) and Klavin (for buyer) dated respectively October 14, 1996 and November 2, 1996 and December 3, 1996.
- July 24, 1998 expert report prepared by the CPA firm of Spyros and Company; and
- March 25, 1999 expert opinion of Darius and Spivack

Also please note that the documents listed above do not include all the materials examined by me, such as all correspondence between and among the parties, all pleadings, all discovery, and the like.

I have reviewed the documents referred to above in order to provide you with my opinion as to whether Neil Klavin deviated from the standard of care which would be applicable in this transaction. Based on my review of all the documents set forth above, I am of the opinion that Mr. Klavin did not deviate from the standard of care for the reasons set forth below.

The transaction that is the subject of the litigation and this report involved the purchase of a business known as Magyar, Inc. The plaintiffs, Omar and Sylvia Saleem, executed a contract to purchase the aforesaid business from Magyar, Inc. In connection with the original negotiations relative to the business, the plaintiffs received a document showing projection of income and return on equity in connection with the business. This document was reviewed by the plaintiffs prior to the execution of the contract. The document was, in fact, executed by both of the plaintiffs, namely Omar and Sylvia Saleem.

After the parties agreed on all relevant terms for the transaction, the seller's attorney, Louis D'Orio, prepared a contract of sale. Ultimately, the contract was taken to Mr. Klavin by Omar Saleem. After reviewing the contract, Klavin prepared a review letter dated November 2, 1996. The review letter set forth a number of contingencies including, but not limited to, the following:

1. Review and approval of the existing lease . . .
2. A requirement that the buyer be permitted to review the books of the seller . . . and
3. Inclusion in the contract of a more detailed listing of scheduled assets.

The response to Mr. Klavin's letter was Mr. D'Orio's letter dated December 3, 1996. In that letter Mr. D'Orio advised Mr. Klavin that a lease contingency was not necessary since the lease had already been reviewed and approved by Mr. Klavin's clients. Mr. Klavin did question his clients in connection with the aforesaid lease and ultimately was satisfied that his clients read, understood, and were willing to accept same.

The next item discussed in Mr. D'Orio's letter was Mr. Klavin's request that his clients be permitted access to the books and records of the selling corporation. Mr. D'Orio requested that the review period be limited to five days and that there be some ascertainable standard as to whether or not the review was "acceptable" or "unacceptable." In the last section of his letter, Mr. D'Orio provides Mr. Klavin with a more detailed schedule of assets.

It is obvious that the contents of Mr. D'Orio's letter were reviewed by Mr. Klavin and further reviewed by Mr. Klavin with his clients. I note that Mr. D'Orio requested that Mr. Klavin and/or his clients execute the letter so same could be incorporated as a part of the contract. I further note that Mr. Klavin, in fact, had his clients execute the letter after he reviewed same with them.

It is interesting that when Mr. Klavin forwarded the December 3, 1996 letter, which was executed by his clients, he included a cover letter in an effort to resolve the issue relative to a satisfactory review of the books and records. In that letter, Mr. Klavin indicates that his clients' review of the books would be acceptable provided the books and records indicate gross receipts in excess of $175,000. 1 believe it is unequivocally clear that Mr. Klavin was sensitive to his clients' needs to review the books and records and furthermore had a discussion with his clients in connection with same. Stated another way, Mr. Klavin had placed his clients in a position where they were able to have access to the books and records before performing the contract.

In addition, the other elements of the transaction, including lease review, etc., were all properly handled by Mr. Klavin. All of the critical issues in connection with the purchase of a business were considered and reviewed with the client and were also the subject of informed consent.

In the opinion letter of Darius and Spivak, Mr. Darius suggests that "Klavin failed to incorporate certain conditions and contingencies in the December 27, 1996 contract, which would have made the sale subject to a review of all books. . ." This obviously is inapposite to the existing fact pattern, since the letter of December 3, 1996 clearly incorporates that contingency. Mr. Darius goes on to indicate that Mr. Klavin should have advised the Saleems not to sign the contract and make a deposit until the Saleems had all the books and records examined by their accountant. This simply flies in the face of the normal business practice in connection with the sale of a business. Having conducted numerous business closings over my 31 years of practice, it is my opinion that it would be extremely unusual to be involved in a transaction where a seller would let a buyer review books on any basis unless a substantial good faith deposit was made and a contract was executed by the parties.

Finally, Mr. Darius suggests that Mr. Klavin put his clients "on the horns of a dilemma," which resulted in their being faced with either losing a deposit or purchasing a business in total ignorance of the monthly income. This dilemma was not created by Klavin. Mr. Klavin clearly gave his clients the opportunity to have the books and records reviewed. He received representations from his clients that they were reviewed and understood. If Mr. Klavin's clients had, in fact, performed their due diligence and reviewed the books and were unsatisfied with the result of their review, the contract could have been voided provided the review occurred within the contractual period. It was only at the day of the closing that the plaintiffs first indicated that *they* had not had an opportunity to review the books and records of the corporation.

At that point, Mr. Klavin properly advised his clients that in the event they refused to consummate the transaction, they faced a possible loss of their deposit, and possibly other damages for breach of contract, since they did not avail themselves of the accounting contingency within the time period set forth in the contract.

I note that Mr. Darius states in his report that "if Klavin had truly represented the interests of the Saleems, he would not only have examined all Magyar Inc's Federal and State tax returns, he would also, as part of that investigation, have conducted a lien search . . ." It appears that Mr. Darius is suggesting that Mr. Klavin should fulfill the role of an accountant and examine the books and records of the corporation. This is simply not an accurate statement, nor an accurate reflection, of the duty of a closing attorney. Insofar as the lien search is concerned, same was, in fact, conducted by Mr. Klavin, who ordered what is the normal and customary business search in connection with the proposed closing.

Mr. Darius goes on to indicate in his letter various undertakings that should have been performed by Mr. Klavin. Many of the undertakings set forth in Mr. Darius' letter do not fall within the responsibility of a lawyer's duty to his client. Many of the functions would be performed by an accountant or other professional and not within the scope of a duty owed by an attorney to his client.

In the case at bar, I believe it is clear from the deposition transcript and the correspondence referred to above that Mr. Klavin adequately performed these duties.

Very truly yours,

Edward J. Caruso

Selected Readings

Douglas R. Carmichael, "Hocus-Pocus Accounting," in *Journal of Accountancy* (October 1999), p. 59.

John B. Duncan and Dale L. Flesher, "Does Your Church Have Appropriate Internal Control for Cash Receipts?" in *The National Public Accountant* (February 2002), p. 15.

Norman Inkster, "Forensic Accounting" in *CMA – the Management Accounting Magazine* (April 1996), p. 11.

Andrew S. Lang, "Beating Embezzlement (How to Minimize Your Risk of Fraud)," in *Association Management* (December 1991), p. 27.

William M. Michaelson, "Divorce: A Game of Hide and Seek?" in *Journal of Accountancy* (March 1996), p. 67.

Daniel D. Montgomery, et al., "Auditors's New Procedures for Detecting Fraud," in *Journal of Accountancy* (May 2002), p. 63.

Lawrence Richter Quinn, "Accounting Sleuths," in *Strategic Finance* (October 2000), p. 55.

Ronald Russell, "Understanding Fraud and Embezzlement," in *The Ohio CPA Journal* (February 1995), p. 37.

Jane Schmitt, "Accountants Take a Bite Out of White Collar Crime," in *Pacific Business News* (December 8, 2000), p. 31.

Marc A. Siegel, "Recovery of Embezzled Assets Half a World Away," in *Journal of Accountancy* (August 2001), p. 45.

Joseph T. Wells, "Lapping It Up: A Skimming Method Doomed to Failure Over Time," in *Journal of Accountancy* (February 2002), p. 73.

WEBSITES

The Association of Certified Fraud Examiners – *www.acfe.com*
Forensic Accounting – *www.forensicaccounting.com*
Kessler Institute – *www.investigation.com*

---

* This chapter is contributed by Frank Grippo, Dean, School of Business, William Paterson University.

Appendix A

SUMMARY OF THE SARBANES-OXLEY ACT OF 2002

Section 3: Commission Rules and Enforcement.
A violation of Rules of the Public Company Accounting Oversight Board ("Board") is treated as a violation of the '34 Act, giving rise to the same penalties that may be imposed for violations of that Act.

Section 101: Establishment; Board Membership.
The Board will have five financially-literate members, appointed for five-year terms. Two of the members must be or have been certified public accountants, and the remaining three must not be and cannot have been CPAs. The Chair may be held by one of the CPA members, provided that he or she has not been engaged as a practicing CPA for five years.

The Board's members will serve on a full-time basis.

No member may, concurrent with service on the Board, "share in any of the profits of, or receive payments from, a public accounting firm," other than "fixed continuing payments," such as retirement payments.

Members of the Board are appointed by the Commission, "after consultation with" the Chairman of the Federal Reserve Board and the Secretary of the Treasury.

Members may be removed by the Commission "for good cause."

Section 101: Establishment; Duties of the Board.

Section 103: Auditing, Quality Control, and Independence Standards and Rules.
The Board shall:
  (1) Register public accounting firms;
  (2) Establish, or adopt, by rule, "auditing, quality control, ethics, independence, and other standards relating to the preparation of audit reports for issuers;"

(3) Conduct inspections of accounting firms;
(4) Conduct investigations and disciplinary proceedings, and impose appropriate sanctions;
(5) Perform such other duties or functions as necessary or appropriate;
(6) Enforce compliance with the act, the rules of the board, professional standards, and the securities laws relating to the preparation and issuance of audit reports and the obligations and liabilities of accountants with respect thereto;
(7) Set the budget and manage the operations of the Board and the staff of the Board.

Auditing standards. The Board would be required to "cooperate on an ongoing basis" with designated professional groups of accountants and any advisory groups convened in connection with standard-setting, and although the Board can "to the extent that it determines appropriate" adopt standards proposed by those groups, the Board will have authority to amend, modify, repeal, and reject any standards suggested by the groups. The Board must report on its standard-setting activity to the Commission on an annual basis.

The Board must require registered public accounting firms to "prepare, and maintain for a period of not less than 7 years, audit work papers, and other information related to any audit report, in sufficient detail to support the conclusions reached in such report."

The Board must require a second partner review and approval of audit reports. Registered accounting firms must adopt quality control standards.

The Board must adopt an audit standard to implement the internal control review required by section 404(b). This standard must require the auditor evaluate whether the internal control structure and procedures include records that accurately and fairly reflect the transactions of the issuer, provide reasonable assurance that the transactions are recorded in a manner that will permit the preparation of financial statements in accordance with GAAP, and a description of any material weaknesses in the internal controls.

Section 102(a): Mandatory Registration.

Section 102(f): Registration and Annual Fees.

Section 109(d): Funding; Annual Accounting Support Fee for the Board.

In order to audit a public company, a public accounting firm must register with the Board. The Board shall collect "a registration fee" and "an annual fee" from each registered public accounting firm, in amounts that are "sufficient" to recover the costs of processing and reviewing applications and annual reports.

The Board shall also establish by rule a reasonable "annual accounting support fee" as may be necessary or appropriate to maintain the Board. This fee will be assessed on issuers only.

Section 104: Inspections of Registered Public Accounting Firms.

Annual quality reviews (inspections) must be conducted for firms that audit more than 100 issues; all others must be conducted every three years. The SEC and/or the Board may order a special inspection of any firm at any time.

Section 105(b)(5): Investigation and Disciplinary Proceedings; Investigations; Use Of Documents.

Section 105(c)(2): Investigations and Disciplinary Proceedings; Disciplinary Procedures; Public Hearings.

Section 105(c)(4): Investigations and Disciplinary Proceedings; Sanctions.

Section 105(d): Investigations and Disciplinary Proceedings; Reporting of Sanctions.

All documents and information prepared or received by the Board shall be "confidential and privileged as an evidentiary matter (and shall not be subject to civil discovery or other legal process) in any proceeding in any Federal or State court or administrative agency, . . . unless and until presented in connection with a public proceeding or [otherwise] released" in connection with a disciplinary action. However, all such documents and information can be made available to the SEC, the U.S. Attorney General, and other federal and appropriate state agencies.

Disciplinary hearings will be closed unless the Board orders that they be public, for good cause, and with the consent of the parties.

Sanctions can be imposed by the Board of a firm if it fails to reasonably supervise any associated person with regard to auditing or quality control standards, or otherwise.

No sanctions report will be made available to the public unless and until stays pending appeal have been lifted.

Section 106: Foreign Public Accounting Firms.
The bill would subject foreign accounting firms who audit a U.S. company to registrations with the Board. This would include foreign firms that perform some audit work, such as in a foreign subsidiary of a U.S. company, which is relied on by the primary auditor.

Section 107(a): Commission Oversight of the Board; General Oversight Responsibility.

Section 107(b): Rules of the Board.

Section 107(d): Censure of the Board and Other Sanctions.
The SEC shall have "oversight and enforcement authority over the Board." The SEC can, by rule or order, give the Board additional responsibilities. The SEC may require the Board to keep certain records, and it has the power to inspect the Board itself, in the same manner as it can with regard to SROs such as the NASD.

The Board, in its rulemaking process, is to be treated "as if the Board were a 'registered securities association'"—that is, a self-regulatory organization. The Board is required to file proposed rules and proposed rule changes with the SEC. The SEC may approve, reject, or amend such rules.

The Board must notify the SEC of pending investigations involving potential violations of the securities laws, and coordinate its investigation with the SEC Division of Enforcement as necessary to protect an ongoing SEC investigation.

The SEC may, by order, "censure or impose limitations upon the activities, functions, and operations of the Board" if it finds that the Board has violated the Act or the securities laws, or if the Board has failed to ensure the compliance of accounting firms with applicable rules without reasonable justification.

Section 107(c): Commission Review of Disciplinary Action Taken by the Board.
The Board must notify the SEC when it imposes "any final sanction" on any accounting firm or associated person. The Board's findings and sanctions are subject to review by the SEC.

The SEC may enhance, modify, cancel, reduce, or require remission of such sanction.

Section 108: Accounting Standards.

The SEC is authorized to "recognize, as 'generally accepted'... any accounting principles" that are established by a standard-setting body that meets the bill's criteria, which include requirements that the body:

(1) Be a private entity;
(2) Be governed by a board of trustees (or equivalent body), the majority of whom are not or have not been associated persons with a public accounting firm for the past two years;
(3) Be funded in a manner similar to the board;
(4) Have adopted procedures to ensure prompt consideration of changes to accounting principles by a majority vote;
(5) Consider, when adopting standards, the need to keep them current and the extent to which international convergence of standards is necessary or appropriate.

Section 201: Services Outside the Scope of Practice of Auditors; Prohibited Activities.

It shall be "unlawful" for a registered public accounting firm to provide any non-audit service to an issuer contemporaneously with the audit, including: (1) bookkeeping or other services related to the accounting records or financial statements of the audit client; (2) financial information systems design and implementation; (3) appraisal or valuation services, fairness opinions, or contribution-in-kind reports; (4) actuarial services; (5) internal audit outsourcing services; (6) management functions or human resources; (7) broker or dealer, investment adviser, or investment banking services; (8) legal services and expert services unrelated to the audit; (9) any other service that the Board determines, by regulation, is impermissible. The Board may, on a case-by-case basis, exempt from these prohibitions any person, issuer, public accounting firm, or transaction, subject to review by the Commission.

It will not be unlawful to provide other non-audit services if they are pre-approved by the audit committee in the following manner. The bill allows an accounting firm to "engage in any non-audit service, including tax services," that is not listed above, only if the activity is pre-approved by the audit committee of the issuer. The audit committee will disclose to investors in periodic reports its decision to pre-approve non-audit services. Statutory insurance company regulatory audits are treated as an audit service, and thus do not require pre-approval.

The pre-approval requirement is waived with respect to the provision of non-audit services for an issuer if the aggregate amount of all such non-audit services provided to the issuer constitutes less than 5% of the total amount of revenues paid by the issuer to its auditor (calculated on the basis of revenues paid by the issuer during the fiscal year when the non-audit services are performed); such services were not recognized by the issuer at the time of the engagement to be non-audit services; and such services are promptly brought to the attention of the audit committee and approved prior to completion of the audit.

The authority to pre-approve services can be delegated to one or more members of the audit committee, but any decision by the delegate must be presented to the full audit committee.

Section 203: Audit Partner Rotation.
The lead audit or coordinating partner and the reviewing partner must rotate off of the audit every five years.

Section 204: Auditor Reports to Audit Committees.
The accounting firm must report to the audit committee all "critical accounting policies and practices to be used...all alternative treatments of financial information within [GAAP] that have been discussed with management...ramifications of the use of such alternative disclosures and treatments, and the treatment preferred" by the firm.

Section 206: Conflicts of Interest.
The CEO, Controller, CFO, Chief Accounting Officer or person in an equivalent position cannot have been employed by the company's audit firm during the one-year period preceding the audit.

Section 207: Study of Mandatory Rotation of Registered Public Accountants.
The GAO will do a study on the potential effects of requiring the mandatory rotation of audit firms.

Section 209: Consideration by Appropriate State Regulatory Authorities.
State regulators are directed to make an independent determination as to whether the Board's standards shall be applied to small and mid-size non-registered accounting firms.

Section 301: Public Company Audit Committees.
Each member of the audit committee shall be a member of the board of directors of the issuer, and shall otherwise be independent. "Independent" is defined as not receiving, other than for service on

the board, any consulting, advisory, or other compensatory fee from the issuer, and as not being an affiliated person of the issuer, or any subsidiary thereof.

The SEC may make exemptions for certain individuals on a case-by-case basis.

The audit committee of an issuer shall be directly responsible for the appointment, compensation, and oversight of the work of any registered public accounting firm employed by that issuer.

The audit committee shall establish procedures for the "receipt, retention, and treatment of complaints" received by the issuer regarding accounting, internal controls, and auditing.

Each audit committee shall have the authority to engage independent counsel or other advisors, as it determines necessary to carry out its duties.

Each issuer shall provide appropriate funding to the audit committee.

Section 302: Corporate Responsibility for Financial Reports.
The CEO and CFO of each issuer shall prepare a statement to accompany the audit report to certify the "appropriateness of the financial statements and disclosures contained in the periodic report, and that those financial statements and disclosures fairly present, in all material respects, the operations and financial condition of the issuer." A violation of this section must be knowing and intentional to give rise to liability.

Section 303: Improper Influence on Conduct of Audits.
It shall be unlawful for any officer or director of an issuer to take any action to fraudulently influence, coerce, manipulate, or mislead any auditor engaged in the performance of an audit for the purpose of rendering the financial statements materially misleading.

Section 304: Forfeiture of Certain Bonuses and Profits.

Section 305: Officer and Director Bars and Penalties; Equitable Relief.
If an issuer is required to prepare a restatement due to "material noncompliance" with financial reporting requirements, the chief executive officer and the chief financial officer shall "reimburse the issuer for any bonus or other incentive-based or equity-based com-

pensation received" during the 12 months following the issuance or filing of the non-compliant document and "any profits realized from the sale of securities of the issuer" during that period.

In any action brought by the SEC for violation of the securities laws, federal courts are authorized to "grant any equitable relief that may be appropriate or necessary for the benefit of investors."

Section 305: Officer and Director Bars and Penalties.
The SEC may issue an order to prohibit, conditionally or unconditionally, permanently or temporarily, any person who has violated section 10(b) of the 1934 Act from acting as an officer or director of an issuer if the SEC has found that such person's conduct "demonstrates unfitness" to serve as an officer or director of any such issuer.

Section 306: Insider Trades During Pension Fund Blackout Periods Prohibited.
Prohibits the purchase or sale of stock by officers and directors and other insiders during blackout periods. Any profits resulting from sales in violation of this section "shall inure to and be recoverable by the issuer." If the issuer fails to bring suit or prosecute diligently, a suit to recover such profit may be instituted by "the owner of any security of the issuer."

Section 401(a): Disclosures in Periodic Reports; Disclosures Required.
Each financial report that is required to be prepared in accordance with GAAP shall "reflect all material correcting adjustments . . . that have been identified by a registered accounting firm . . . ."

"Each annual and quarterly financial report . . . shall disclose all material off-balance sheet transactions" and "other relationships" with "unconsolidated entities" that may have a material current or future effect on the financial condition of the issuer.

The SEC shall issue rules providing that pro forma financial information must be presented so as not to "contain an untrue statement" or omit to state a material fact necessary in order to make the pro forma financial information not misleading.

Section 401 (c): Study and Report on Special Purpose Entities.
SEC shall study off-balance sheet disclosures to determine (a) extent of off-balance sheet transactions (including assets, liabilities, leases, losses and the use of special purpose entities); and (b)

whether generally accepted accounting rules result in financial statements of issuers reflecting the economics of such off-balance sheet transactions to investors in a transparent fashion and make a report containing recommendations to the Congress.

Section 402(a): Prohibition on Personal Loans to Executives.
Generally, it will be unlawful for an issuer to extend credit to any director or executive officer. Consumer credit companies may make home improvement and consumer credit loans and issue credit cards to its directors and executive officers if it is done in the ordinary course of business on the same terms and conditions made to the general public.

Section 403: Disclosures of Transactions Involving Management and Principal Stockholders.
Directors, officers, and 10% owner(s) must report designated transactions by the end of the second business day following the day on which the transaction was executed.

Section 404: Management Assessment of Internal Controls.
Requires each annual report of an issuer to contain an "internal control report," which shall:

(1) State the responsibility of management for establishing and maintaining an adequate internal control structure and procedures for financial reporting; and

(2) Contain an assessment, as of the end of the issuer's fiscal year, of the effectiveness of the internal control structure and procedures of the issuer for financial reporting.

Each issuer's auditor shall attest to, and report on, the assessment made by the management of the issuer. An attestation made under this section shall be in accordance with standards for attestation engagements issued or adopted by the Board. An attestation engagement shall not be the subject of a separate engagement.

The language in the report of the Committee which accompanies the bill to explain the legislative intent states, "—the Committee does not intend that the auditor's evaluation be the subject of a separate engagement or the basis for increased charges or fees."

Directs the SEC to require each issuer to disclose whether it has adopted a code of ethics for its senior financial officers and the contents of that code.

Directs the SEC to revise its regulations concerning prompt disclosure on Form 8-K to require immediate disclosure "of any change in, or waiver of," an issuer's code of ethics.

Section 407: Disclosure of Audit Committee Financial Expert.
The SEC shall issue rules to require issuers to disclose whether at least one member of its audit committee is a "financial expert."

Section 409: Real Time Disclosure.
Issuers must disclose information on material changes in the financial condition or operations of the issuer on a rapid and current basis.

Section 501: Treatment of Securities Analysts by Registered Securities Associations.
National Securities Exchanges and registered securities associations must adopt conflict of interest rules for research analysts who recommend equities in research reports.

Section 601: SEC Resources and Authority.
SEC appropriations for 2003 are increased to $776,000,000. $98 million of the funds shall be used to hire an additional 200 employees to provide enhanced oversight of auditors and audit services required by the Federal securities laws.

Section 602(a): Appearance and Practice Before the Commission.
The SEC may censure any person, or temporarily bar or deny any person the right to appear or practice before the SEC if the person does not possess the requisite qualifications to represent others, lacks character or integrity, or has willfully violated Federal securities laws.

Section 602(c): Study and Report.
SEC is to conduct a study of "securities professionals" (public accountants, public accounting firms, investment bankers, investment advisors, brokers, dealers, attorneys) who have been found to have aided and abetted a violation of Federal securities laws.

Section 602(d): Rules of Professional Responsibility for Attorneys.
The SEC shall establish rules setting minimum standards for professional conduct for attorneys practicing before it.

Section 701: GAO Study and Report Regarding Consolidation of Public Accounting Firms.
The GAO shall conduct a study regarding the consolidation of public accounting firms since 1989, including the present and future

impact of the consolidation, and the solutions to any problems discovered.

Title VIII: Corporate and Criminal Fraud Accountability Act of 2002.

It is a felony to "knowingly" destroy or create documents to "impede, obstruct or influence" any existing or contemplated federal investigation.

Auditors are required to maintain "all audit or review work papers" for five years.

The statute of limitations on securities fraud claims is extended to the earlier of five years from the fraud, or two years after the fraud was discovered, from three years and one year, respectively.

Employees of issuers and accounting firms are extended "whistleblower protection" that would prohibit the employer from taking certain actions against employees who lawfully disclose private employer information to, among others, parties in a judicial proceeding involving a fraud claim. Whistleblowers are also granted a remedy of special damages and attorney's fees.

A new crime for securities fraud that has penalties of fines and up to 10 years imprisonment.

Title IX: White Collar Crime Penalty Enhancements.

Maximum penalty for mail and wire fraud increased from 5 to 10 years.

Creates a crime for tampering with a record or otherwise impeding any official proceeding.

SEC given authority to seek court freeze of extraordinary payments to directors, officers, partners, controlling persons, agents of employees.

U.S. Sentencing Commission to review sentencing guidelines for securities and accounting fraud.

SEC may prohibit anyone convicted of securities fraud from being an officer or director of any publicly traded company.

Financial Statements filed with the SEC must be certified by the CEO and CFO. The certification must state that the financial statements and disclosures fully comply with provisions of the Securities Exchange Act and that they fairly present, in all material respects, the operations and financial condition of the issuer. Maximum penalties for willful and knowing violations of this section are a fine of not more than $5,000,000 and/or imprisonment of up to 20 years.

Section 1001: Sense of Congress Regarding Corporate Tax Returns.
It is the sense of Congress that the Federal income tax return of a corporation should be signed by the chief executive officer of such corporation.

Section 1102: Tampering with a Record or Otherwise Impeding an Official Proceeding.
Makes it a crime for any person to corruptly alter, destroy, mutilate, or conceal any document with the intent to impair the object's integrity or availability for use in an official proceeding or to otherwise obstruct, influence or impede any official proceeding; liable for up to 20 years in prison and a fine.

Section 1103: Temporary Freeze Authority.
The SEC is authorized to freeze the payment of an extraordinary payment to any director, officer, partner, controlling person, agent, or employee of a company during an investigation of possible violations of securities laws.

Section 1105: SEC Authority to Prohibit Persons from Serving as Officers or Directors.
The SEC may prohibit a person from serving as an officer or director of a public company if the person has committed securities fraud.

Appendix B

SARBANES-OXLEY COMPLIANCE PRACTICE AID

Section 201
Title II - Auditor Independence
SARBANES-OXLEY ACT OF 2002
TITLE II - AUDITOR INDEPENDENCE
SELF-ASSESSMENT QUESTIONNAIRE

This practice aid is a self-assessment questionnaire regarding Auditor Independence under Title II of the Sarbanes-Oxley Act of 2002. It may be prepared either independently by the client or with the assistance of the practitioner engaged to perform the accounting oversight compliance service. Each of the questions listed in the questionnaire is based on specific sections listed within Title II of the Sarbanes-Oxley Act covering auditor independence.

The purpose of the questionnaire is to provide the practitioner with a general guideline for developing an understanding of the scope of services being provided to the issuer by the registered public accounting firm, the necessary pre-approvals and disclosures regarding such services by the audit committee, and the information management controls and oversight activities undertaken in regard to communication between the registered public accounting firm and the audit committee.

After determining to what extent, if any, services are being provided, pre-approvals and disclosures are being made, and information is being managed and action taken, depending on the nature of the engagement, the practitioner may further develop policies and procedures, design and implement controls, and periodically test and audit the effectiveness of the controls to determine the level of conformance with the compliance requirements contained under this Act.

This questionnaire contains the following features:

- *Compliance Procedures List*—The compliance procedures listed for consideration include procedures to determine whether specific services are being provided to the issuer by the registered public accounting firm, whether necessary pre-approvals and disclosures are being made by the audit committee, and whether information is being reported and oversight activities undertaken by the audit committee regarding communication with the auditing firm.

- *Yes/No or N/A*—Each question should be responded to with either *yes*, *no*, or *not applicable*. For compliance activity procedures that have been answered with a yes *or* no, depending on the nature of the engagement, the practitioner may further develop policies and procedures, design and implement controls, and periodically test and audit the effectiveness of the controls to determine the level of conformance with the compliance requirements contained under this Act.

- *'Performed By' and 'Workpaper Index' Columns*—Each program step should be signed by the appropriate person making the inquiry about the compliance activity. Each compliance procedure that has been answered affirmatively and that *also* has a detailed description, analysis and/or test of the service, disclosure or oversight activity should be referenced to the workpapers in the workpaper index column.

Client: _____   Date: _____

Procedures for Consideration	Yes/No or N/A	Performed By	Workpaper Index
SEC. 201. SERVICES OUTSIDE THE SCOPE OF PRACTICE OF AUDITORS.			
Reference: (a) PROHIBITED ACTIVITIES.—Section 10A of the Securities Exchange Act of 1934 (15 U.S.C. 8j–1) is amended by adding at the end the following:			
(g) PROHIBITED ACTIVITIES.—Except as provided in subsection (h), it shall be unlawful for a registered public accounting firm (and any associated person of that firm, to the extent determined appropriate by the Commission) that performs for any issuer any audit required by this title or the rules of the Commission under this title or, beginning 180 days after the date of commencement of the operations of the Public Company Accounting Oversight Board established under section 101 of the Sarbanes-Oxley Act of 2002 (in this section referred to as the 'Board'), the rules of the Board, to provide to that issuer, contemporaneously with the audit, any non-audit service, including—			
(1) Are bookkeeping or other services related to the accounting records or financial statements of the audit client being provided by the registered public accounting firm?			
(2) Are financial information systems being designed and implemented by the registered public accounting firm?			
(3) Are appraisal or valuation services, fairness opinions, or contribution-in-kind reports being provided by the registered public accounting firm?			
(4) Are actuarial services being provided by the registered public accounting firm?			
(5) Are internal audit outsourcing services being provided by the registered public accounting firm?			
(6) Are management functions or human resources being provided by the registered public accounting firm?			
(7) Are broker or dealer, investment adviser, or investment banking services being provided by the registered public accounting firm?			
(8) Are legal services and expert services unrelated to the audit being provided by the registered public accounting firm?			
(9) Are any other services that the Board has determined, by regulation, as impermissible, being provided by the registered public accounting firm?			

Procedures for Consideration	Yes/No or N/A	Performed By	Workpaper Index
Reference: (h) PREAPPROVAL REQUIRED FOR NON-AUDIT SERVICES. — A registered public accounting firm may engage in any non-audit service, including tax services, that is not described in any of paragraphs (1) through (9) of subsection (g) for an audit client, only if the activity is approved in advance by the audit committee of the issuer, in accordance with subsection (i).			
(b) EXEMPTION AUTHORITY. — The Board may, on a case by case basis, exempt any person, issuer, public accounting firm, or transaction from the prohibition on the provision of services under section 10A(g) of the Securities Exchange Act of 1934 (as added by this section), to the extent that such exemption is necessary or appropriate in the public interest and is consistent with the protection of investors, and subject to review by the commission in the same manner as for rules of the Board under section 107.			
SEC. 202. PREAPPROVAL REQUIREMENTS.			
Reference: Section 10A of the Securities Exchange Act of 1934 (15 U.S.C. 78j–1), as amended by this Act, is amended by adding at the end the following:			
(i) PREAPPROVAL REQUIREMENTS. —			
(1) IN GENERAL. —			
AUDIT COMMITTEE ACTION. — Have all auditing services (which may entail providing comfort letters in connection with securities underwritings or statutory audits required for insurance companies for purposes of State law) and non-audit services, other than as provided in subparagraph (B), provided to an issuer by the auditor of the issuer been pre-approved by the audit committee of the issuer?			
(B) DE MINIMUS EXCEPTION. — The pre-approval requirement under subparagraph (A) is waived with respect to the provision of non-audit services for an issuer, if—			
(i) Does the aggregate amount of all such non-audit services provided to the issuer constitute not more than 5 percent of the total amount of revenues paid by the issuer to its auditor during the fiscal year in which the non-audit services are provided?			
(ii) Were such services not recognized by the issuer at the time of the engagement to be non-audit services?			

Procedures for Consideration	Yes/No or N/A	Performed By	Workpaper Index
(iii) Were such services promptly brought to the attention of the audit committee of the issuer and approved prior to the completion of the audit by the audit committee or by 1 or more members of the audit committee who are members of the board of directors to whom authority to grant such approvals has been delegated by the audit committee?			
(2) DISCLOSURE TO INVESTORS.— Has approval by an audit committee of an issuer under this subsection of a non-audit service to be performed by the auditor of the issuer been disclosed to investors in periodic reports required by section 13(a)?			
(3) DELEGATION AUTHORITY.—Has the audit committee of an issuer delegated to 1 or more designated members of the audit committee who are independent directors of the board of directors, the authority to grant pre-approvals required by this subsection?			
Have the decisions of any member to whom authority is delegated under this paragraph to pre-approve an activity under this subsection been presented to the full audit committee at each of its scheduled meetings?			
Reference: (4) APPROVAL OF AUDIT SERVICES FOR OTHER PURPOSES.—In carrying out its duties under subsection (m)(2), if the audit committee of an issuer approves an audit service within the scope of the engagement of the auditor, such audit service shall be deemed to have been pre-approved for purposes of this subsection.			
SEC. 203. AUDIT PARTNER ROTATION.			
Reference: Section 10A of the Securities Exchange Act of 1934 (15 U.S.C. 78j–1), as amended by this Act, is amended by adding at the end the following:			
(j) AUDIT PARTNER ROTATION.—It shall be unlawful for a registered public accounting firm to provide audit services to an issuer if:			
Has the lead (or coordinating) audit partner (having primary responsibility for the audit), or the audit partner responsible for reviewing the audit, performed audit services for that issuer in each of the 5 previous fiscal years of that issuer?			
SEC. 204. AUDITOR REPORTS TO AUDIT COMMITTEES.			
Reference: Section 10A of the Securities Exchange Act of 1934 (15 U.S.C. 78j–1), as amended by this Act, is amended by adding at the end the following:			

Procedures for Consideration	Yes/No or N/A	Performed By	Workpaper Index

(k) REPORTS TO AUDIT COMMITTEES.—Each registered public accounting firm that performs for any issuer any audit required by this title shall timely report to the audit committee of the issuer—

(1) Have all critical accounting policies and practices to be used been reported to the audit committee?

(2) Have all alternative treatments of financial information within generally accepted accounting principles that have been discussed with management officials of the issuer, ramifications of the use of such alternative disclosures and treatments, and the treatment preferred by the registered public accounting firm been reported to the audit committee?

(3) Have other material written communications between the registered public accounting firm and the management of the issuer, such as any management letter or schedule of unadjusted differences been reported to the audit committee?

SEC. 205. CONFORMING AMENDMENTS.

Reference:
(a) DEFINITIONS.—Section 3(a) of the Securities Exchange Act of 1934 (15 U.S.C. 78c(a)) is amended by adding at the end the following:

(58) AUDIT COMMITTEE.—The term 'audit committee' means—

(A) Has a committee (or equivalent body) been established by and amongst the board of directors of an issuer for the purpose of overseeing the accounting and financial reporting processes of the issuer and audits of the financial statements of the issuer?

(B) Does the issuer understand that if no such committee exists with respect to an issuer, the entire board of directors of the issuer is treated as the audit committee?

Reference:
(59) REGISTERED PUBLIC ACCOUNTING FIRM.—The term 'registered public accounting firm' has the same meaning as in section 2 of the Sarbanes-Oxley Act of 2002.

(b) AUDITOR REQUIREMENTS.—Section 10A of the Securities Exchange Act of 1934 (15 U.S.C. 78j–1) is amended—

(1) by striking ''an independent public accountant'' each place that term appears and inserting ''a registered public accounting firm'';

Procedures for Consideration	Yes/No or N/A	Performed By	Workpaper Index
(2) by striking "the independent public accountant" each place that term appears and inserting "the registered public accounting firm";			
(3) in subsection (c), by striking "No independent public accountant" and inserting "No registered public accounting firm"; and			
(4) in subsection (b)—			
(A) by striking "the accountant" each place that term appears and inserting "the firm";			
(B) by striking "such accountant" each place that term appears and inserting "such firm"; and			
(C) in paragraph (4), by striking "the accountant's report" and inserting "the report of the firm."			
(c) OTHER REFERENCES.—The Securities Exchange Act of 1934 (15 U.S.C. 78a et seq.) is amended—			
(1) in section 12(b)(1) (15 U.S.C. 78l(b)(1)), by striking 'independent public accountants" each place that term appears and inserting "a registered public accounting firm"; and (2) in subsections (e) and (i) of section 17 (15 U.S.C. 78q), by striking "an independent public accountant" each place that term appears and inserting "a registered public accounting firm."			
(d) CONFORMING AMENDMENT.—Section 10A(f) of the Securities Exchange Act of 1934 (15 U.S.C. 78k(f)) is amended—			
(1) by striking "DEFINITION" and inserting "DEFINITIONS"; and			
(2) by adding at the end the following: "As used in this section, the term 'issuer' means an issuer (as defined in section 3), the securities of which are registered under section 12, or that is required to file reports pursuant to section 15(d), or that files or has filed a registration statement that has not yet become effective under the Securities Act of 1933 (15 U.S.C. 77a et seq.), and that it has not withdrawn."			
SEC. 206. CONFLICTS OF INTEREST.			
Reference: Section 10A of the Securities Exchange Act of 1934 (15 U.S.C. 78j–1), as amended by this Act, is amended by adding at the end the following:			
(l) CONFLICTS OF INTEREST.—It shall be unlawful for a registered public accounting firm to perform for an issuer any audit service required by this title, if:			

Procedures for Consideration	Yes/No or N/A	Performed By	Workpaper Index

Has a chief executive officer, controller, chief financial officer, chief accounting officer, or any person serving in an equivalent position for the issuer, been employed by that registered independent public accounting firm and participated in any capacity in the audit of that issuer during the 1-year period preceding the date of the initiation of the audit?

SEC. 207. STUDY OF MANDATORY ROTATION OF REGISTERED PUBLIC ACCOUNTING FIRMS.

Reference:
(a) STUDY AND REVIEW REQUIRED.—The Comptroller General of the United States shall conduct a study and review of the potential effects of requiring the mandatory rotation of registered public accounting firms.

(b) REPORT REQUIRED.—Not later than 1 year after the date of enactment of this Act, the Comptroller General shall submit a report to the Committee on Banking, Housing, and Urban Affairs of Senate and the Committee on Financial Services of the House of Representatives on the results of the study and review required by this section.

(c) DEFINITION.—For purposes of this section, the term ''mandatory rotation'' refers to the imposition of a limit on the period of years in which a particular registered public accounting firm may be the auditor of record for a particular issuer.

SEC. 208. COMMISSION AUTHORITY.

Reference:
(a) COMMISSION REGULATIONS.—Not later than 180 days after the date of enactment of this Act, the Commission shall issue final regulations to carry out each of subsections (g) through (l) of section 10A of the Securities Exchange Act of 1934, as added by this title.

(b) AUDITOR INDEPENDENCE.—It shall be unlawful for any registered public accounting firm (or an associated person thereof, as applicable) to prepare or issue any audit report with respect to any issuer, if:

Has the firm or associated person engaged in any activity with respect to that issuer prohibited by any of subsections (g) through (l) of section 10A of the Securities Exchange Act of 1934, as added by this title, or any rule or regulation of the Commission or of the Board issued thereunder?

Procedures for Consideration	Yes/No or N/A	Performed By	Workpaper Index
SEC. 209. CONSIDERATIONS BY APPROPRIATE STATE REGULATORY AUTHORITIES.			
Reference: In supervising non-registered public accounting firms and their associated persons, appropriate State regulatory authorities should make an independent determination of the proper standards applicable, particularly taking into consideration the size and nature of the business of the accounting firms they supervise and the size and nature of the business of the clients of those firms. The standards applied by the Board under this Act should not be presumed to be applicable for purposes of this section for small and medium sized non-registered public accounting firms.			

Section 202
Title III - Corporate Responsibility
SARBANES-OXLEY ACT OF 2002
TITLE III - CORPORATE RESPONSIBILITY
SELF-ASSESSMENT QUESTIONNAIRE

This practice aid is a self-assessment questionnaire regarding Corporate Responsibility under Title III of the Sarbanes-Oxley Act of 2002. It may be prepared either independently by the client or with the assistance of the practitioner engaged to perform the accounting oversight compliance services. Each of the questions listed in the questionnaire is based on specific sections listed within Title III of the Sarbanes-Oxley Act covering corporate responsibility.

The purpose of the questionnaire is to provide the practitioner with a general guideline for developing an understanding of the oversight responsibilities relating to registered public accounting firms and monitoring of complaints by the audit committee, the corporate responsibility for financial reports, including certification by principal executive officers, and the prohibition of insider trading during pension fund blackout periods, along with certain bars and penalties.

After determining to what extent oversight responsibilities are being carried out, financials are being certified, and prohibitions on insider trading rules are being followed, depending on the nature of the engagement, the practitioner may further develop policies and procedures, design and implement controls, and periodically test and audit the effectiveness of the controls to determine the level of conformance with the compliance requirements contained under this Act.

This questionnaire contains the following features:

- *Compliance Procedures List*—The compliance procedures listed for consideration include procedures to determine whether oversight responsibilities relating to registered public accounting firms and monitoring of complaints by the audit committee are being carried out, whether corporate responsibility for financial reports, including certification by principal executive officers, is being made, and whether the prohibition on insider trading during pension fund blackout periods is being followed.
- *Yes/No or N/A*—Each question should be responded to with either *yes*, *no*, or *not applicable*. For compliance activity procedures that have been answered with a yes *or* no, depending on the nature of the engagement, the practitioner may further develop policies and procedures, design and implement controls, and periodically test and audit the effectiveness of the

controls to determine the level of conformance with the compliance requirements contained under this Act.

- *"Performed By" and "Workpaper Index" Columns*—Each program step should be signed by the appropriate person making the inquiry about the compliance activity. Each compliance procedure that has been answered affirmatively and that *also* has a detailed description, analysis and/or test of the oversight activity, certification or prohibition should be referenced to the workpapers in the workpaper index column.

Client: _____   Date: _____

Procedures for Consideration	Yes/No or N/A	Performed By	Workpaper Index

SEC. 301. PUBLIC COMPANY AUDIT COMMITTEES.

Reference:
Section 10A of the Securities Exchange Act of 1934 (15 U.S.C. 78f) is amended by adding at the end the following:

(m) STANDARDS RELATING TO AUDIT COMMITTEES.—

(1) COMMISSION RULES.—

(A) IN GENERAL.—Effective not later than 270 days after the date of enactment of this subsection, has the Commission, by rule, directed the national securities exchanges and national securities associations to prohibit the listing of any security of an issuer that is not in compliance with the requirements of any portion of paragraphs (2) through (6)?

(B) OPPORTUNITY TO CURE DEFECTS.—
The rules of the Commission under subparagraph (A) shall provide for appropriate procedures:

Has the issuer had an opportunity to cure any defects that would be the basis for a prohibition under subparagraph (A), before the imposition of such prohibition?

(2) RESPONSIBILITIES RELATING TO REGISTERED PUBLIC ACCOUNTING FIRMS.—Has the audit committee of each issuer, in its capacity as a committee of the board of directors, been established so that it is directly responsible for the appointment, compensation, and oversight of the work of any registered public accounting firm employed by that issuer (including resolution of disagreements between management and the auditor regarding financial reporting) for the purpose of preparing or issuing an audit report or related work, and does each such registered public accounting firm report directly to the audit committee?

(3) INDEPENDENCE.—

(A) IN GENERAL.—Is each member of the audit committee of the issuer a member of the board of directors of the issuer, and are they otherwise independent?

(B) CRITERIA.—In order to be considered to be independent for purposes of this paragraph, has a member of an audit committee of an issuer, other than in his or her capacity as a member of the audit committee, the board of directors, or any other board committee—

Procedures for Consideration	Yes/No or N/A	Performed By	Workpaper Index
(i) accepted any consulting, advisory, or other compensatory fee from the issuer?			
(ii) been an affiliated person of the issuer or any subsidiary thereof?			
Reference: (C) EXEMPTION AUTHORITY.—The Commission may exempt from the requirements of subparagraph (B) a particular relationship with respect to audit committee members, as the Commission determines appropriate in light of the circumstances.			
(4) COMPLAINTS.—Has the audit committee established procedures for—			
(A) the receipt, retention, and treatment of complaints received by the issuer regarding accounting, internal accounting controls, or auditing matters?			
(B) the confidential, anonymous submission by employees of the issuer of concerns regarding questionable accounting or auditing matters?			
(5) AUTHORITY TO ENGAGE ADVISERS.—Has the audit committee engaged an independent counsel and/or other advisers, as it determines necessary to carry out its duties?			
(6) FUNDING.—Has the provided for appropriate funding, as determined by the audit committee, in its capacity as a committee of the board of directors, for payment of compensation —			
(A) to the registered public accounting firm employed by the issuer for the purpose of rendering or issuing an audit report?			
(B) to any advisers employed by the audit committee under paragraph (5)?			
SEC. 302. CORPORATE RESPONSIBILITY FOR FINANCIAL REPORTS.			
Reference: (a) REGULATIONS REQUIRED.—The Commission shall, by rule, require, for each company filing periodic reports under section 13(a) or 15(d) of the Securities Exchange Act of 1934 (15 U.S.C. 78m, 78o(d)) that the principal executive officer or officers and the principal financial officer or officers, or persons performing similar functions, certify in each annual or quarterly report filed or submitted under either such section of such Act —			
(1) has the signing officer reviewed the report?			

Procedures for Consideration	Yes/No or N/A	Performed By	Workpaper Index
(2) based on the officer's knowledge, does the report not contain any untrue statement of a material fact or omit to state a material fact necessary in order to make the statements made, in light of the circumstances under which such statements were made, not misleading?			
(3) based on such officer's knowledge, do the financial statements, and other financial information included in the report, fairly present in all material respects the financial condition and results of operations of the issuer as of, and for, the periods presented in the report?			
(4) the signing officers—			
(A) are they responsible for establishing and maintaining internal controls?			
(B) have they designed such internal controls to ensure that material information relating to the issuer and its consolidated subsidiaries is made known to such officers by others within those entities, particularly during the period in which the periodic reports are being prepared?			
(C) have they evaluated the effectiveness of the issuer's internal controls as of a date within 90 days prior to the report?			
(D) have they presented in the report their conclusions about the effectiveness of their internal controls based on their evaluation as of that date?			
(5) have the signing officers disclosed to the issuer's auditors and the audit committee of the board of directors (or persons fulfilling the equivalent function)—			
(A) all significant deficiencies in the design or operation of internal controls which could adversely affect the issuer's ability to record, process, summarize, and report financial data and have identified for the issuer's auditors any material weaknesses in internal controls?			
(B) any fraud, whether or not material, that involves management or other employees who have had a significant role in the issuer's internal controls?			
(6) have the signing officers indicated in the report whether or not there were significant changes in internal controls or in other factors that could significantly affect internal controls subsequent to the date of their evaluation, including any corrective actions with regard to significant deficiencies and material weaknesses?			

Procedures for Consideration	Yes/No or N/A	Performed By	Workpaper Index

Reference:
(b) FOREIGN REINCORPORATIONS HAVE NO EFFECT.—Nothing in this section 302 shall be interpreted or applied in any way to allow any issuer to lessen the legal force of the statement required under this section 302, by an issuer having reincorporated or having engaged in any other transaction that resulted in the transfer of the corporate domicile or offices of the issuer from inside the United States to outside of the United States.

(c) DEADLINE.—The rules required by subsection (a) shall be effective not later than 30 days after the date of enactment of this Act.

SEC. 303. IMPROPER INFLUENCE ON CONDUCT OF AUDITS.

(a) RULES TO PROHIBIT.—It shall be unlawful, in contravention of such rules or regulations as the Commission shall prescribe as necessary and appropriate in the public interest or for the protection of investors-

Has any officer or director of an issuer, or any other person acting under the direction thereof, taken any action to fraudulently influence, coerce, manipulate, or mislead any independent public or certified accountant engaged in the performance of an audit of the financial statements of that issuer for the purpose of rendering such financial statements materially misleading?

Reference:
(b) ENFORCEMENT.—In any civil proceeding, the Commission shall have exclusive authority to enforce this section and any rule or regulation issued under this section.

(c) NO PREEMPTION OF OTHER LAW.—The provisions of subsection (a) shall be in addition to, and shall not supersede or preempt, any other provision of law or any rule or regulation issued
thereunder.

(d) DEADLINE FOR RULEMAKING.—The Commission shall—

(1) propose the rules or regulations required by this section, not later than 90 days after the date of enactment of this Act; and

(2) issue final rules or regulations required by this section, not later than 270 days after that date of enactment.

Procedures for Consideration	Yes/No or N/A	Performed By	Workpaper Index
SEC. 304. FORFEITURE OF CERTAIN BONUSES AND PROFITS.			
(a) ADDITIONAL COMPENSATION PRIOR TO NONCOMPLIANCE WITH COMMISSION FINANCIAL REPORTING REQUIREMENTS.—			
Has an issuer been required to prepare an accounting restatement due to the *material* noncompliance of the issuer, as a result of misconduct, with any financial reporting requirement under the securities laws?			
Reference: Then the chief executive officer and chief financial officer of the issuer shall reimburse the issuer for—			
(1) any bonus or other incentive-based or equity-based compensation received by that person from the issuer during the 12-month period following the first public issuance or filing with the Commission (whichever first occurs) of the financial document embodying such financial reporting requirement; and			
(2) any profits realized from the sale of securities of the issuer during that 12-month period.			
(b) COMMISSION EXEMPTION AUTHORITY.—The Commission may exempt any person from the application of subsection (a), as it deems necessary and appropriate.			
SEC. 305. OFFICER AND DIRECTOR BARS AND PENALTIES.			
Reference: (a) UNFITNESS STANDARD.—			
(1) SECURITIES EXCHANGE ACT OF 1934.—Section 21(d)(2) of the Securities Exchange Act of 1934 (15 U.S.C. 78u(d)(2)) is amended by striking ''substantial unfitness'' and inserting ''unfitness.''			
(2) SECURITIES ACT OF 1933.—Section 20(e) of the Securities Act of 1933 (15 U.S.C. 77t(e)) is amended by striking ''substantial unfitness'' and inserting ''unfitness.''			
(b) EQUITABLE RELIEF.—Section 21(d) of the Securities Exchange Act of 1934 (15 U.S.C. 78u(d)) is amended by adding at the end the following:			
(5) EQUITABLE RELIEF.—Has any action or proceeding been brought or instituted by the Commission under any provision of the securities laws, and is the Commission seeking, and any Federal court may grant, any equitable relief that may be appropriate or necessary for the benefit of investors?			

Procedures for Consideration	Yes/No or N/A	Performed By	Workpaper Index
SEC. 306. INSIDER TRADES DURING PENSION FUND BLACKOUT PERIODS.			
Reference: (a) PROHIBITION OF INSIDER TRADING DURING PENSION FUND BLACKOUT PERIODS.—			
(1) IN GENERAL.—Except to the extent otherwise provided by rule of the Commission pursuant to paragraph (3), it shall be unlawful:			
Has any director or executive officer of an issuer of any equity security (other than an exempted security), directly or indirectly, purchased, sold, or otherwise acquired or transferred any equity security of the issuer (other than an exempted security) during any blackout period with respect to such equity security if such director or officer acquired such equity security in connection with his or her service or employment as a director or executive officer?			
Reference: (2) REMEDY.—			
(A) IN GENERAL.—Any profit realized by a director or executive officer referred to in paragraph (1) from any purchase, sale, or other acquisition or transfer in violation of this subsection shall inure to and be recoverable by the issuer, irrespective of any intention on the part of such director or executive officer in entering into the transaction.			
(B) ACTIONS TO RECOVER PROFITS.—Has an action to recover profits in accordance with this subsection been instituted at law or in equity in any court of competent jurisdiction by the issuer, or by the owner of any security of the issuer in the name and in behalf of the issuer if the issuer has failed or refused to bring such action within 60 days after the date of request, or failed diligently to prosecute the action thereafter, except that no such suit shall be brought more than 2 years after the date on which such profit was realized?			
Reference: (3) RULEMAKING AUTHORIZED.—The Commission shall, in consultation with the Secretary of Labor, issue rules to clarify the application of this subsection and to prevent evasion thereof.			

Procedures for Consideration	Yes/No or N/A	Performed By	Workpaper Index

Such rules shall provide for the application of the requirements of paragraph (1) with respect to entities treated as a single employer with respect to an issuer under section 414(b), (c), (m), or (o) of the Internal Revenue Code of 1986 to the extent necessary to clarify the application of such requirements and to prevent evasion thereof. Such rules may also provide for appropriate exceptions from the requirements of this subsection, including exceptions for purchases pursuant to an automatic dividend reinvestment program or purchases or sales made pursuant to an advance election.

(4) BLACKOUT PERIOD.—For purposes of this subsection, the term "blackout period", with respect to the equity securities of any issuer—

(A) means any period of more than 3 consecutive business days during which the ability of not fewer than 50 percent of the participants or beneficiaries under all individual account plans maintained by the issuer to purchase, sell, or otherwise acquire or transfer an interest in any equity of such issuer held in such an individual account plan is temporarily suspended by the issuer or by a fiduciary of the plan; and

(B) does not include, under regulations which shall be prescribed by the Commission—

(i) a regularly scheduled period in which the participants and beneficiaries may not purchase, sell, or otherwise acquire or transfer an interest in any equity of such issuer, if such period is—

(I) incorporated into the individual account

plan; and (II) timely disclosed to employees before becoming participants under the individual account plan or as a subsequent amendment to the plan; or

(ii) any suspension described in subparagraph (A) that is imposed solely in connection with persons becoming participants or beneficiaries, or ceasing to be participants or beneficiaries, in an individual account plan by reason of a corporate merger, acquisition, divestiture, or similar transaction involving the plan or plan sponsor.

(5) INDIVIDUAL ACCOUNT PLAN.—For purposes of this subsection, the term "individual account plan" has the meaning provided in section 3(34) of the Employee Retirement Income Security Act of 1974 (29 U.S.C. 1002(34), except that such term shall not include a one-participant retirement plan (within the meaning of section 101(i)(8)(B) of such Act (29 U.S.C. 1021(i)(8)(B))).

Procedures for Consideration	Yes/No or N/A	Performed By	Workpaper Index
(6) NOTICE TO DIRECTORS, EXECUTIVE OFFICERS, AND THE COMMISSION.—In any case in which a director or executive officer is subject to the requirements of this subsection in connection with a blackout period (as defined in paragraph (4)) with respect to any equity securities-			
Has the issuer of such equity securities timely notified such directors or officers and the Securities and Exchange Commission of such blackout periods?			
(b) NOTICE REQUIREMENTS TO PARTICIPANTS AND BENEFICIARIES UNDER ERISA.—			
(1) IN GENERAL.—Section 101 of the Employee Retirement Income Security Act of 1974 (29 U.S.C. 1021) is amended by redesignating the second subsection (h) as subsection (j), and by inserting after the first subsection (h) the following new subsection:			
(i) NOTICE OF BLACKOUT PERIODS TO PARTICIPANT OR BENEFICIARY UNDER INDIVIDUAL ACCOUNT PLAN.—			
(1) DUTIES OF PLAN ADMINISTRATOR.—In advance of the commencement of any blackout period with respect to an individual account plan, has the plan administrator notified the plan participants and beneficiaries who are affected by such action in accordance with this subsection?			
(2) NOTICE REQUIREMENTS.—			
(A) IN GENERAL.—Are the notices described in paragraph (1) written in a manner calculated to be understood by the average plan participant and do they include—			
(i) the reasons for the blackout period?			
(ii) an identification of the investments and other rights affected?			
(iii) the expected beginning date and length of the blackout period?			
(iv) in the case of investments affected, a statement that the participant or beneficiary should evaluate the appropriateness of their current investment decisions in light of their inability to direct or diversify assets credited to their accounts during the blackout period?			
(v) such other matters as the Secretary may require by regulation?			

Procedures for Consideration	Yes/No or N/A	Performed By	Workpaper Index
(B) NOTICE TO PARTICIPANTS AND BENEFICIA-RIES.—Except as otherwise provided in this subsection, have the notices described in paragraph (1) been furnished to all participants and beneficiaries under the plan to whom the blackout period applies at least 30 days in advance of the blackout period?			
(C) EXCEPTION TO 30-DAY NOTICE REQUIRE-MENT.—In any case in which—			
(i) Does a deferral of the blackout period violate the requirements of subparagraph (A) or (B) of section 404(a)(1), and a fiduciary of the plan reasonably so determines in writing?			
(ii) If the inability to provide the 30-day advance notice due to events that were unforeseeable or circumstances beyond the reasonable control of the plan administrator, and a fiduciary of the plan reasonably so determines in writing, subparagraph (B) shall not apply-			
Has the notice been furnished to all participants and beneficiaries under the plan to whom the blackout period applies as soon as was reasonably possible under the circumstances unless such a notice in advance of the termination of the blackout period was impracticable?			
(D) WRITTEN NOTICE.—Was the notice required to be provided under this subsection in writing, except that such notice may be in electronic or other form to the extent that such form is reasonably accessible to the recipient?			
(E) NOTICE TO ISSUERS OF EMPLOYER SECURI-TIES SUBJECT TO BLACKOUT PERIOD.—In the case of any blackout period in connection with an individual account plan, did the plan administrator provide timely notice of such blackout period to the issuer of any employer securities subject to such blackout period?			
Reference: (3) EXCEPTION FOR BLACKOUT PERIODS WITH LIMITED APPLICABILITY.			

Procedures for Consideration	Yes/No or N/A	Performed By	Workpaper Index
—In any case in which the blackout period applies only to 1 or more participants or beneficiaries in connection with a merger, acquisition, divestiture, or similar transaction involving the plan or plan sponsor and occurs solely in connection with becoming or ceasing to be a participant or beneficiary under the plan by reason of such merger, acquisition, divestiture, or transaction, the requirement of this subsection that the notice be provided to all participants and beneficiaries shall be treated as met if the notice required under paragraph (1) is provided to such participants or beneficiaries to whom the blackout period applies as soon as reasonably practicable.			
(4) CHANGES IN LENGTH OF BLACKOUT PERIOD.—If, following the furnishing of the notice pursuant to this subsection, there was a change in the beginning date or length of the blackout period (specified in such notice pursuant to paragraph (2)(A)(iii)), did the administrator provide affected participants and beneficiaries notice of the change as soon as reasonably practicable?			
In relation to the extended blackout period, did such notice meet the requirements of paragraph (2)(D) and did they specify any material change in the matters referred to in clauses (i) through (v) of paragraph (2)(A)?			
Reference: (5) REGULATORY EXCEPTIONS.—The Secretary may provide by regulation for additional exceptions to the requirements of this subsection which the Secretary determines are in the interests of participants and beneficiaries.			
(6) GUIDANCE AND MODEL NOTICES.—The Secretary shall issue guidance and model notices which meet the requirements of this subsection.			
(7) BLACKOUT PERIOD.—For purposes of this subsection—			
(A) IN GENERAL.—The term 'blackout period' means, in connection with an individual account plan, any period for which any ability of participants or beneficiaries under the plan, which is otherwise available under the terms of such plan, to direct or diversify assets credited to their accounts, to obtain loans from the plan, or to obtain distributions from the plan is temporarily suspended, limited, or restricted, if such suspension, limitation, or restriction is for any period of more than 3 consecutive business days.			
(B) EXCLUSIONS.—The term 'blackout period' does not include a suspension, limitation, or restriction—			

Procedures for Consideration	Yes/No or N/A	Performed By	Workpaper Index

(i) which occurs by reason of the application of the securities laws (as defined in section 3(a)(47) of the Securities Exchange Act of 1934),

(ii) which is a change to the plan which provides for a regularly scheduled suspension, limitation, or restriction which is disclosed to participants or beneficiaries through any summary of material modifications, any materials describing specific investment alternatives under the plan, or any changes thereto, or

(iii) which applies only to 1 or more individuals, each of whom is the participant, an alternate payee (as defined in section 206(d)(3)(K)), or any other beneficiary pursuant to a qualified domestic relations order (as defined in section 206(d)(3)(B)(i)).

(8) INDIVIDUAL ACCOUNT PLAN. —

(A) IN GENERAL. — For purposes of this subsection, the term 'individual account plan' shall have the meaning provided such term in section 3(34), except that such term shall not include a one-participant retirement plan.

(B) ONE-PARTICIPANT RETIREMENT PLAN. — For purposes of subparagraph (A), the term 'one-participant retirement plan' means a retirement plan that (i) on the first day of the plan year —

(I) does it cover only the employer (and the employer's spouse) and the employer owned the entire business (whether or not incorporated)?

(II) does it cover only one or more partners (and their spouses) in a business partnership (including partners in an S or C corporation (as defined in section 1361(a) of the Internal Revenue Code of 1986))?

(ii) Does it meet the minimum coverage requirements of section 410(b) of the Internal Revenue Code of 1986 (as in effect on the date of the enactment of this paragraph) without being combined with any other plan of the business that covers the employees of the business?

(iii) Does it not provide benefits to anyone except the employer (and the employer's spouse) or the partners (and their spouses)?

(iv) Does it not cover a business that is a member of an affiliated service group, a controlled group of corporations, or a group of businesses under common control?

(v) Does it not cover a business that leases employees?

Reference:
(2) ISSUANCE OF INITIAL GUIDANCE AND MODEL NOTICE. —

Procedures for Consideration	Yes/No or N/A	Performed By	Workpaper Index

The Secretary of Labor shall issue initial guidance and a model notice pursuant to section 101(i)(6) of the Employee Retirement Income Security Act of 1974 (as added by this subsection) not later than January 1, 2003. Not later than 75 days after the date of the enactment of this Act, the Secretary shall promulgate interim final rules necessary to carry out the amendments made by this subsection.

(3) CIVIL PENALTIES FOR FAILURE TO PROVIDE NOTICE.—

Section 502 of such Act (29 U.S.C. 1132) is amended—

(A) in subsection (a)(6), by striking ''(5), or (6)'' and inserting ''(5), (6), or (7)'';

(B) by redesignating paragraph (7) of subsection (c) as paragraph (8); and

(C) by inserting after paragraph (6) of subsection (c) the following new paragraph:

(7) The Secretary may assess a civil penalty against a plan administrator of up to $100 a day from the date of the plan administrator's failure or refusal to provide notice to participants and beneficiaries in accordance with section 101(i). For purposes of this paragraph, each violation with respect to any single participant or beneficiary shall be treated as a separate violation.

(3) PLAN AMENDMENTS.—If any amendment made by this subsection requires an amendment to any plan, such plan amendment shall not be required to be made before the first plan year beginning on or after the effective date of this section, if—

(A) during the period after such amendment made by this subsection takes effect and before such first plan year, did the plan operate in good faith compliance with the requirements of such amendment made by this subsection?

(B) did such plan amendment apply retroactively to the period after such amendment made by this subsection took effect and before such first plan year?

Reference:
(c) EFFECTIVE DATE.—The provisions of this section (including the amendments made thereby) shall take effect 180 days after the date of the enactment of this Act. Good faith compliance with the requirements of such provisions in advance of the issuance of applicable regulations thereunder shall be treated as compliance with such provisions.

Procedures for Consideration	Yes/No or N/A	Performed By	Workpaper Index

SEC. 307. RULES OF PROFESSIONAL RESPONSI-BILITY FOR ATTORNEYS.

Reference:
Not later than 180 days after the date of enactment of this Act, the Commission shall issue rules, in the public interest and for the protection of investors, setting forth minimum standards of professional conduct for attorneys appearing and practicing before the Commission in any way in the representation of issuers, including a rule—

(1) Has an attorney been required to report evidence of a material violation of securities law or breach of fiduciary duty or similar violation by the company or any agent thereof, to the chief legal counsel or the chief executive officer of the company (or the equivalent thereof)?

(2) if the counsel or officer does not appropriately respond to the evidence (adopting, as necessary, appropriate remedial measures or sanctions with respect to the violation), has the attorney reported the evidence to the audit committee of the board of directors of the issuer or to another committee of the board of directors comprised solely of directors not employed directly or indirectly by the issuer, or to the board of directors?

SEC. 308. FAIR FUNDS FOR INVESTORS.

Reference:
(a) CIVIL PENALTIES ADDED TO DISGORGEMENT FUNDS FOR THE

RELIEF OF VICTIMS.—If in any judicial or administrative action brought by the Commission under the securities laws (as such term is defined in section 3(a)(47) of the Securities Exchange Act of 1934 (15 U.S.C. 78c(a)(47))-

Has the Commission obtained an order requiring disgorgement against any person for a violation of such laws or the rules or regulations thereunder, or has such a person agreed in settlement of any such action to such disgorgement, and has the Commission also obtained pursuant to such laws a civil penalty against such person?

Then the amount of such civil penalty shall, on the motion or at the direction of the Commission, be added to and become part of the disgorgement fund for the benefit of the victims of such violation.

Source: *www.sarbanes-oxley.com/section.php?level=1&pub_id=SOA-Manual*

Index

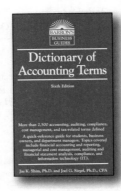
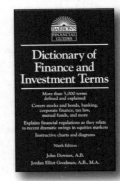